# Fodor's Road Guide USA

## Kansas
## Oklahoma
## Texas

First Edition

058961

Fodor's Travel Publications
New York  Toronto  London  Sydney  Auckland
www.fodors.com

**Fodor's Road Guide USA: Kansas, Oklahoma, Texas**

**Fodor's Travel Publications**
President: Bonnie Ammer
Publisher: Kris Kliemann
Executive Managing Editor: Denise DeGennaro
Editorial Director: Karen Cure
Director of Marketing Development: Jeanne Kramer
Associate Managing Editor: Linda Schmidt
Senior Editor: Constance Jones
Director of Production & Manufacturing: Chuck Bloodgood
Creative Director: Fabrizio La Rocca

**Contributors**
*Editor:* Amy Hegarty
*Editorial Production:* Kristin Milavec
*Additional Editing:* Nuha Ansari, Carissa Bluestone, Lisa Cole, Steve Crohn, Ensley Eikenburg, Kathryn Green, Shannon Kelly, Karen Licurse, and Emmanuelle Morgen
*Writing:* John Bigley (Texas), Diana Lambdin Meyer (Kansas), Barbara Palmer (Oklahoma), and Paris Permenter (Texas), with Hannah Fons, Karen Gibson, David Gutcheon, Kim Harwell, Janie Hayes, Satu Hummasti, Eileen LaMourie, Jessica Levenstein, Elizabeth McGuire, Sidharth Murdeshwar, Brian Rohan, and Sally Snell
*Research:* LaKeisha Light
*Black-and-White Maps:* Rebecca Baer, Robert Blake, David Lindroth, and Todd Pasini
*Production/Manufacturing:* Bob Shields
*Cover:* Michael Javorka/Stone (background photo), Bart Nagel (photo, illustration)
*Interior Photos:* Recreation Vehicle Industry Association (Kansas), Fred Marvel/Oklahoma Tourism (Oklahoma), Photodisc (Texas)

First Edition
ISBN 0–679–00501–3
ISSN 1528–1515

**Special Sales**
Fodor's Travel Publications are available at special discounts for bulk purchases for sales promotions or premiums. Special editions, including personalized covers, excerpts of existing guides, and corporate imprints, can be created in large quantities for special needs. For more information, contact your local bookseller or write to Special Markets, Fodor's Travel Publications, 280 Park Avenue, New York, NY 10017. Inquiries from Canada should be directed to your local Canadian bookseller or sent to Random House of Canada, Ltd., Marketing Department, 2775 Matheson Boulevard East, Mississauga, Ontario L4W 4P7. Inquiries from the United Kingdom should be sent to Fodor's Travel Publications, 20 Vauxhall Bridge Road, London SW1V 2SA, England.

PRINTED IN THE UNITED STATES OF AMERICA
10 9 8 7 6 5 4 3 2 1

# CONTENTS

# Great Road Trips

Of all the things that went wrong with Clark Griswold's vacation, one stands out: The theme park he had driven across the country to visit was closed when he got there. Clark, the suburban bumbler played by Chevy Chase in 1983's hilarious *National Lampoon's Vacation,* is fictional, of course. But his story is poignantly true. Although most Americans get only two precious weeks of vacation a year, many set off on their journeys with surprisingly little guidance. Many travelers find out about their destination from friends and family or wait to get travel information until they arrive in their hotel, where racks of brochures dispense the "facts," along with free city magazines. But it's hard to distinguish the truth from hype in these sources. And it makes no sense to spend priceless vacation time in a hotel room reading about a place when you could be out seeing it up close and personal.

Congratulate yourself on picking up this guide. Studying it—before you leave home—is the best possible first step toward making sure your vacation fulfills your every dream.

Inside you'll find all the tools you need to plan a perfect road trip. In the hundreds of towns we describe, you'll find thousands of places to explore. So you'll always know what's around the next bend. And with the practical information we provide, you can easily call to confirm the details that matter and study up on what you'll want to see and do, before you leave home.

By all means, when you plan your trip, allow yourself time to make a few detours. Because as wonderful as it is to visit sights you've read about, it's the serendipitous experiences that often prove the most memorable: the hole-in-the-wall diner that serves a transcendent tomato soup, the historical society gallery stuffed with dusty local curiosities of days gone by. As you whiz down the highway, use the book to find out more about the towns announced by roadside signs. Consider turning off at the next exit. And always remember: In this great country of ours, there's an adventure around every corner.

# HOW TO USE THIS BOOK

Alphabetical organization should make it a snap to navigate through this book. Still, in putting it together, we've made certain decisions and used certain terms you need to know about.

## LOCATIONS AND CATEGORIZATIONS

Color map coordinates are given for every town in the guide.

Attractions, restaurants, and lodging places are listed under the nearest town covered in the guide.

Parks and forests are sometimes listed under the main access point.

Exact street addresses are provided whenever possible; when they were not available or applicable, directions and/or cross-streets are indicated.

## CITIES

For state capitals and larger cities, attractions are alphabetized by category. Shopping sections focus on good shopping areas where you'll find a concentration of interesting shops. We include malls only if they're unusual in some way and individual stores only when they're community institutions. Restaurants and hotels are grouped by price category then arranged alphabetically.

## RESTAURANTS

All are air-conditioned unless otherwise noted, and all permit smoking unless they're identified as "no-smoking."

**Dress:** Assume that no jackets or ties are required for men unless otherwise noted.

**Family-style service:** Restaurants characterized this way serve food communally, out of serving dishes as you might at home.

**Meals and hours:** Assume that restaurants are open for lunch and dinner unless otherwise noted. We always specify days closed and meals not available.

**Prices:** The price ranges listed are for dinner entrées (or lunch entrées if no dinner is served).

**Reservations:** They are always a good idea. We don't mention them unless they're essential or are not accepted.

**Fodor's Choice:** Stars denote restaurants that are Fodor's Choices—our editors' picks of the state's very best in a given price category.

## LODGINGS

All are air-conditioned unless otherwise noted, and all permit smoking unless they're identified as "no-smoking."

**AP:** This designation means that a hostelry operates on the American Plan (AP)—-that is, rates include all meals. AP may be an option or it may be the only meal plan available; be sure to find out.

**Baths:** You'll find private bathrooms with bathtubs unless noted otherwise.

**Business services:** If we tell you they're there, you can expect a variety on the premises.

**Exercising:** We note if there's "exercise equipment" even when there's no designated area; if you want a dedicated facility, look for "gym."

**Facilities:** We list what's available but don't note charges to use them. When pricing accommodations, always ask what's included.

**Hot tub:** This term denotes hot tubs, Jacuzzis, and whirlpools.

**MAP:** Rates at these properties include two meals.

**No smoking:** Properties with this designation prohibit smoking.

**Opening and closing:** Assume that hostelries are open year-round unless otherwise noted.

**Pets:** We note whether or not they're welcome and whether there's a charge.

**Pools:** Assume they're outdoors with fresh water; indoor pools are noted.

**Prices:** The price ranges listed are for a high-season double room for two, excluding tax and service charge.

**Telephone and TV:** Assume that you'll find them unless otherwise noted.

**Fodor's Choice:** Stars denote hostelries that are Fodor's Choices—our editors' picks of the state's very best in a given price category.

## NATIONAL PARKS

National parks protect and preserve the treasures of America's heritage, and they're always worth visiting whenever you're in the area. Many are worth a long detour. If you will travel to many national parks, consider purchasing the National Parks Pass ($50), which gets you and your companions free admission to all parks for one year. (Camping and parking are extra.) A percentage of the proceeds from sales of the pass helps to fund important projects in the parks. Both the Golden Age Passport ($10), for those 62 and older, and the Golden Access Passport (free), for travelers with disabilities, entitle holders to free entry to all national parks, plus 50% off fees for the use of many park facilities and services. You must show proof of age and of U.S. citizenship or permanent residency (such as a U.S. passport, driver's license, or birth certificate) and, if requesting Golden Access, proof of your disability. You must get your Golden Access or Golden Age passport in person; the former is available at all federal recreation areas, the latter at federal recreation areas that charge fees. You may purchase the National Parks Pass by mail or through the Internet. For information, contact the National Park Service (Department of the Interior, 1849 C St. NW, Washington, DC 20240-0001, 202/208—4747, *www.nps.gov*). To buy the National Parks Pass, write to 27540 Ave. Mentry, Valencia, CA 91355, call 888/GO—PARKS, or visit www.national-parks.org.

## IMPORTANT TIP

Although all prices, opening times, and other details in this book are based on information supplied to us at press time, changes occur all the time in the travel world, and Fodor's cannot accept responsibility for facts that become outdated or for inadvertent errors or omissions. So always confirm information when it matters, especially if you're making a detour to visit a specific place.

## Let Us Hear from You

Keeping a travel guide fresh and up-to-date is a big job, and we welcome any and all comments. We'd love to have your thoughts on places we've listed, and we're interested in hearing about your own special finds, even the ones in your own back yard. Our guides are thoroughly updated for each new edition, and we're always adding new information, so your feedback is vital. Contact us via e-mail in care of roadnotes@fodors.com (specifying the name of the book on the subject line) or via snail mail in care of Road Guides at Fodor's, 280 Park Avenue, New York, NY 10017. We look forward to hearing from you. And in the meantime, have a wonderful road trip.

THE EDITORS

# Important Numbers and On-Line Info

## LODGINGS

| | | |
|---|---|---|
| Adam's Mark | 800/444—2326 | www.adamsmark.com |
| Baymont Inns | 800/428—3438 | www.baymontinns.com |
| Best Western | 800/528—1234 | www.bestwestern.com |
| | TDD 800/528—2222 | |
| Budget Host | 800/283—4678 | www.budgethost.com |
| Clarion | 800/252—7466 | www.clarioninn.com |
| Comfort | 800/228—5150 | www.comfortinn.com |
| Courtyard by Marriott | 800/321—2211 | www.courtyard.com |
| Days Inn | 800/325—2525 | www.daysinn.com |
| Doubletree | 800/222—8733 | www.doubletreehotels.com |
| Drury Inns | 800/325—8300 | www.druryinn.com |
| Econo Lodge | 800/555—2666 | www.hotelchoice.com |
| Embassy Suites | 800/362—2779 | www.embassysuites.com |
| Exel Inns of America | 800/356—8013 | www.exelinns.com |
| Fairfield Inn by Marriott | 800/228—2800 | www.fairfieldinn.com |
| Fairmont Hotels | 800/527—4727 | www.fairmont.com |
| Forte | 800/225—5843 | www.forte-hotels.com |
| Four Seasons | 800/332—3442 | www.fourseasons.com |
| Friendship Inns | 800/453—4511 | www.hotelchoice.com |
| Hampton Inn | 800/426—7866 | www.hampton-inn.com |
| Hilton | 800/445—8667 | www.hilton.com |
| | TDD 800/368—1133 | |
| Holiday Inn | 800/465—4329 | www.holiday-inn.com |
| | TDD 800/238—5544 | |
| Howard Johnson | 800/446—4656 | www.hojo.com |
| | TDD 800/654—8442 | |
| Hyatt & Resorts | 800/233—1234 | www.hyatt.com |
| Inns of America | 800/826—0778 | www.innsofamerica.com |
| Inter-Continental | 800/327—0200 | www.interconti.com |
| La Quinta | 800/531—5900 | www.laquinta.com |
| | TDD 800/426—3101 | |
| Loews | 800/235—6397 | www.loewshotels.com |
| Marriott | 800/228—9290 | www.marriott.com |
| Master Hosts Inns | 800/251—1962 | www.reservahost.com |
| Le Meridien | 800/225—5843 | www.lemeridien.com |
| Motel 6 | 800/466—8356 | www.motel6.com |
| Omni | 800/843—6664 | www.omnihotels.com |
| Quality Inn | 800/228—5151 | www.qualityinn.com |
| Radisson | 800/333—3333 | www.radisson.com |
| Ramada | 800/228—2828 | www.ramada.com |
| | TDD 800/533—6634 | |
| Red Carpet/Scottish Inns | 800/251—1962 | www.reservahost.com |
| Red Lion | 800/547—8010 | www.redlion.com |
| Red Roof Inn | 800/843—7663 | www.redroof.com |
| Renaissance | 800/468—3571 | www.renaissancehotels.com |
| Residence Inn by Marriott | 800/331—3131 | www.residenceinn.com |
| Ritz-Carlton | 800/241—3333 | www.ritzcarlton.com |
| Rodeway | 800/228—2000 | www.rodeway.com |

| Sheraton | 800/325—3535 | www.sheraton.com |
| Shilo Inn | 800/222—2244 | www.shiloinns.com |
| Signature Inns | 800/822—5252 | www.signature-inns.com |
| Sleep Inn | 800/221—2222 | www.sleepinn.com |
| Super 8 | 800/848—8888 | www.super8.com |
| Susse Chalet | 800/258—1980 | www.sussechalet.com |
| Travelodge/Viscount | 800/255—3050 | www.travelodge.com |
| Vagabond | 800/522—1555 | www.vagabondinns.com |
| Westin Hotels & Resorts | 800/937—8461 | www.westin.com |
| Wyndham Hotels & Resorts | 800/996—3426 | www.wyndham.com |

## AIRLINES

| Air Canada | 888/247—2262 | www.aircanada.ca |
| Alaska | 800/426—0333 | www.alaska-air.com |
| American | 800/433—7300 | www.aa.com |
| America West | 800/235—9292 | www.americawest.com |
| British Airways | 800/247—9297 | www.british-airways.com |
| Canadian | 800/426—7000 | www.cdnair.ca |
| Continental Airlines | 800/525—0280 | www.continental.com |
| Delta | 800/221—1212 | www.delta.com |
| Midway Airlines | 800/446—4392 | www.midwayair.com |
| Northwest | 800/225—2525 | www.nwa.com |
| SkyWest | 800/453—9417 | www.delta.com |
| Southwest | 800/435—9792 | www.southwest.com |
| TWA | 800/221—2000 | www.twa.com |
| United | 800/241—6522 | www.ual.com |
| USAir | 800/428—4322 | www.usair.com |

## BUSES AND TRAINS

| Amtrak | 800/872—7245 | www.amtrak.com |
| Greyhound | 800/231—2222 | www.greyhound.com |
| Trailways | 800/343—9999 | www.trailways.com |

## CAR RENTALS

| Advantage | 800/777—5500 | www.arac.com |
| Alamo | 800/327—9633 | www.goalamo.com |
| Allstate | 800/634—6186 | www.bnm.com/as.htm |
| Avis | 800/331—1212 | www.avis.com |
| Budget | 800/527—0700 | www.budget.com |
| Dollar | 800/800—4000 | www.dollar.com |
| Enterprise | 800/325—8007 | www.pickenterprise.com |
| Hertz | 800/654—3131 | www.hertz.com |
| National | 800/328—4567 | www.nationalcar.com |
| Payless | 800/237—2804 | www.paylesscarrental.com |
| Rent-A-Wreck | 800/535—1391 | www.rent-a-wreck.com |
| Thrifty | 800/367—2277 | www.thrifty.com |

*Note:* Area codes are changing all over the United States as this book goes to press. For the latest updates, check www.areacode-info.com.

# Fodor's Road Guide USA

## Kansas
## Oklahoma
## Texas

# Kansas

**If you are a traveler who appreciates the simplicity of wide open spaces, Native Amer-**
ican history, Wild West heritage, the enormity of the world's largest wheat harvest,
or the heroism of wagon tracks that date back to the mid-1800s, you will find much
to enjoy in Kansas.

While some of America's early white settlers saw present-day Kansas as one of those
places you must cross before reaching the fertile fields and gold of California, the people
who chose to stay and break the sod here were among the toughest breed this country has ever known, and that fortitude is reflected in the history, the towns, and the
landscape of Kansas today.

Kansans are better known as Jayhawkers, as much because of the University
mascot as the historical significance of jayhawking. "Jayhawking" is an Irish expres-
sion that refers to a mythical bird that worries its prey to death before devouring it.
Caught up in the battle over slavery more than a decade before the Civil War, the free-
staters in Kansas became known as jayhawks for their violent skirmishes into neighboring Missouri, a slave state. Over the years, the nickname has stuck and developed
a more general identity.

Kansas's Wild West past includes serving as home to legendary lawmen like Wyatt
Earp and James Butler "Wild Bill" Hickok, who, along with others, policed once rowdy
railroad and cattle towns like Abilene, Dodge City, and Ellsworth. More infamous Wild
West residents include the Dalton Gang, who fatally sought to rob two banks simultaneously in their hometown of Coffeyville.

Perhaps Kansas's greatest claim to fame, however, is serving as home to Dorothy,
Toto, and the great twister in the classic movie *The Wizard of Oz,* based on L. Frank Baum's
book *The Wonderful Wizard of Oz.* Dorothy and Toto, of course, are fictional, but their

| CAPITAL: TOPEKA | POPULATION: 2,572,000 | AREA: 82,282 SQUARE MI |
|---|---|---|
| BORDERS: MO, OK, CO, NE | TIME ZONE: CENTRAL, MOUNTAIN | POSTAL ABBREVIATION: KS |
| WEB SITE: WWW.KANSASCOMMERCE.COM | | |

story's symbolism can be found in each of the small towns, ranches, farms, and cities that makes up this "land of aaahhs."

# History

Archeological data indicate that the first humans to roam the plains now known as Kansas did so nearly 13,000 years ago, but modern history begins with the nomadic tribes of Plains Indians who followed the seasons, the rivers, and animal movement for life-supporting resources. In 1541, Francisco Vasquez de Coronado encountered these tribes as the first European or white person to explore the plains, coming up from Mexico in search of the Seven Golden Cities of Cíbola. Of course, those cities never existed, and future explorers found western Kansas so arid and desolate that it was first considered a desert.

French explorers crossed the Missouri River into the rolling, more verdant hills of eastern Kansas. Kansas was part of the Louisiana Purchase of 1803, and governed as part of the Missouri Territory until 1821, when Missouri entered the Union as a slave state. This was the first element of what developed into some of the most violent acts between pro- and anti-slavery forces in the nation's history.

When Missouri entered the Union, Congressional representation was equal between slave and free states, as the Kansas/Nebraska Act of 1854 gave people the right to choose their status. Recognizing that Kansas would eventually gain statehood, slave supporters began converging on the territory in an attempt to influence the outcome. The conflict resulted in dozens of towns being burned to the ground, massacres of entire families, and widespread threats toward others. The most famous of these raids was William Quantrill's attack on Lawrence in August 1863, when more than 200 buildings were burned and 150 people were killed. Eventually, the Free State party gained control in 1859 and the violence diminished, but these "Bleeding Kansas" days are considered by many to be as significant to the start of the Civil War as the first shots fired at Fort Sumter.

Meanwhile, the opening of the American West had begun and at least four historic trails crisscrossed Kansas, taking hundreds of thousands of pioneers on foot and by covered wagon through this region, leaving footsteps and a heritage that are still visible today. A defining moment in the history of the state was in 1874, when a group of immigrants from eastern Europe brought with them and planted a hardy winter wheat, called Turkey Red. The soil and the climate of Kansas responded perfectly to the grain's needs, forever defining the economic influence of Kansas as the breadbasket of the nation and the world.

Kansas's productive cropland, however, was almost lost in the 1930s and the great Dust Bowl of the Depression years. Years of drought combined with the loose soil of the plains resulted in several inches of top soil simply blowing away, all but devastating the agriculture industry. But Kansans bounced back by discovering oil in the southeast corner of the state, building airplanes, landing a few military bases, and raising

## KS Timeline

| 11,000 BC | 1541 | 1803 | 1855–63 |
|---|---|---|---|
| Nomadic tribes arrive in the area across the Bering Strait from Asia. | Coronado explores central Kansas. | Kansas is purchased by the United States as a part of the Louisiana Purchase. | "Bleeding Kansas" years, as acts of violence surround the question of Kansas's identity as a free or slave state. |

a president. Although Kansans will undoubtedly be rooted to the soil as firmly as the wheat crops, the state has become diversified both culturally and economically, vibrantly contributing to the face of the nation.

INTRODUCTION
HISTORY
REGIONS
WHEN TO VISIT
STATE'S GREATS
RULES OF THE ROAD
DRIVING TOURS

# Regions

## 1. FLINT HILLS

The Flint Hills region is home to one of the largest remaining native tallgrass prairies in the United States. There are hills (ever so slight in a state of great flatness) with dense rock just below the surface—thus the reason much of the grassland was never disturbed for farming or industrial purposes. The Flint Hills are a great place to explore on horseback or with an overland wagon-train ride.

*Towns listed:* Abilene, Blue Rapids, Chanute, Council Grove, El Dorado, Emporia, Eureka, Junction City, Manhattan, Marysville, Ottawa, Wichita

## 2. SMOKY HILLS

Dakota sandstone, greenhorn limestone, and chalk bluffs make up the three ranges of the Smoky Hills, which encompass an area from the Nebraska border in northeast Kansas, south through Lindsborg in central Kansas and Pawnee Rock in south central. Each range has characteristics unique to the soil and the lifestyle that developed because of it. The greenhorn limestone was easily cut for fence posts by pioneers, which later became solid red posts. The chalk beds and remaining fossils of the southern Smoky Hills are an indication of a great prehistoric sea, which covered much of Kansas.

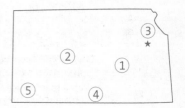

*Towns listed:* Belleville, Beloit, Concordia, Ellsworth, Hays, Hutchinson, Lindsborg, Lucas, Mankato, McPherson, Newton, Phillipsburg, Russell, Salina, Smith Center, Stockton, Victoria

## 3. BLEEDING KANSAS

A narrow strip of land north to south along the Kansas/Missouri border is representative of some of the bloodiest days of civil unrest in the United States. If you like Civil War history, you won't want to pass up visits to towns like Lawrence, Leavenworth, Osawatomie, and Fort Scott. In addition to some great history lessons, the region has some of the most colorful landscapes in Kansas, as well as opportunities for camping and fishing.

*Towns listed:* Atchison, Bonner Springs, Chetopa, Fort Scott, Kansas City, Lawrence, Leavenworth, Olathe, Osawatomie, Overland Park, Parsons, Pittsburg, Shawnee, Topeka

| 1861 | 1866 | 1867 | 1874 | 1890 |
|------|------|------|------|------|
| Kansas becomes the 34th state in the Union. | University of Kansas is founded. | Great Plains Peace Treaty is signed at Medicine Lodge. | Turkey Red wheat is introduced to Kansas. | Temperance legend Carry Nation moves to Kansas. |

### 4. GYPSUM ("GYP") HILLS

A small area of south central Kansas is nicknamed the "Gyp" Hills because of the gypsum mined here. Complete with raw wilderness and beauty, an area called "Hell's Half Acre" indicates the ruggedness of the terrain and the brilliant burning red of the sandstone and shale hills. Oil and cattle ranching are about the only way to make a living here. A few local ranchers offer trail rides or camping and backpacking on their property.

*Towns listed:* Arkansas City, Ashland, Medicine Lodge, Sedan, Winfield

### 5. HIGH PLAINS

The Kansas High Plains comprise much of the western edge of the state, where expansive fields of wheat and cattle ranches begin a slight incline toward the Colorado border and the Rocky Mountains beyond. This region is the least populated of the state, and is where the least precipitation falls. It is, however, a region of rugged beauty and hearty souls who contribute substantially to the production of food for a global population.

*Towns listed:* Colby, Dodge City, Garden City, Goodland, Great Bend, Greensburg, Larned, Liberal, Meade, Norton, Oakley, Oberlin, Pratt, Scott City, WaKeeney

## When to Visit

Because Kansas lies in the center of the continental United States, it is subject to varying weather patterns as air masses move rapidly across the state. Much of the severe weather for which Kansas is known is due to cold dry air from the Arctic coming into contact with warm moist air from the Gulf of Mexico. Despite the severity and often unpredictability of weather conditions here, the Kansas climate is partly responsible for the state's fertile soils, as well as its world-renowned agricultural industry.

Kansas weather is certainly one of extremes, and you should therefore take extreme precautions, particularly in the winter months when blizzards can drop as much as two feet of snow, closing highways and interstates. The spring months are also a time to watch the sky and pay close attention to the weather radio bands and the warnings of local residents. An average of 38 tornadoes bounce across the state each year, leaving hundreds of miles of damage to homes and businesses, and taking human life for granted. The most deadly tornado to touch down was in the town of Udall in 1955, when 80 people were killed and the town simply wiped off the map. Hail storms have dropped hailstones measuring 17 inches in diameter, weighing nearly two pounds.

The highest temperature ever recorded in Kansas was in the north central town of Alton, at 121°F on July 24, 1936. The coldest temperature on record was set nearby, in Lebanon, on February 13, 1905, with the mercury plummetting to -40°F. The most snow that fell in a 24-hour period was 20 inches, which happened in Elkhart in February 1903, and again in McPherson in February 1912. Winfield, in south central Kansas, received a state record 9.12 inches of rain in October 1973.

| 1930s | 1953 | 1954 | 1961 | 1996 |
|---|---|---|---|---|
| Dust Bowl devastates Kansas farmland and economy. | Dwight D. Eisenhower is the first Kansan elected president of the United States. | Landmark case of Brown v. Topeka Board of Education is settled, making racially segregated schools unconstitutional. | Kansas celebrates its centennial. | Kansan Bob Dole resigns as longest-serving U.S. Senate Majority Leader to run for President. |

## CLIMATE CHART
Average High/Low Temperatures (°F) and Monthly Precipitation (in inches)

INTRODUCTION
HISTORY
REGIONS
WHEN TO VISIT
STATE'S GREATS
RULES OF THE ROAD
DRIVING TOURS

| | JAN. | FEB. | MAR. | APR. | MAY | JUNE |
|---|---|---|---|---|---|---|
| COLBY | 39/12 | 44/16 | 51/24 | 63/35 | 72/45 | 83/55 |
| | .3 | .3 | 1.2 | 1.6 | 3.7 | 3.2 |
| | JULY | AUG. | SEPT. | OCT. | NOV. | DEC. |
| | 90/62 | 87/60 | 78/49 | 67/36 | 51/24 | 41/14 |
| | 3.2 | 2 | 1.7 | 1 | .6 | .4 |
| | JAN. | FEB. | MAR. | APR. | MAY | JUNE |
| TOPEKA | 37/16 | 42/21 | 55/32 | 66/42 | 75/53 | 84/62 |
| | .95 | 1.1 | 2.5 | 3.1 | 4.5 | 5.5 |
| | JULY | AUG. | SEPT. | OCT. | NOV. | DEC. |
| | 89/67 | 87/64 | 79/55 | 69/43 | 54/32 | 40/21 |
| | 3.6 | 4 | 3.8 | 3.1 | 1.9 | 1.4 |
| | JAN. | FEB. | MAR. | APR. | MAY | JUNE |
| WICHITA | 40/19 | 50/23 | 57/33 | 66/44 | 77/54 | 87/64 |
| | .8 | .9 | 2.4 | 2.4 | 3.8 | 4.3 |
| | JULY | AUG. | SEPT. | OCT. | NOV. | DEC. |
| | 93/70 | 91/48 | 91/55 | 71/46 | 55/34 | 43/23 |
| | 3.1 | 3 | 3.5 | 2.2 | 1.7 | 1.2 |

## FESTIVALS AND SEASONAL EVENTS
### WINTER

Feb.    **International Pancake Race.** Held in the small town of Liberal, this unusual event draws international attention and thousands of visitors to southwest Kansas, as women here compete simultaneously against women in England for the best time distance running with an iron skillet full of pancakes. | 316/626–0170.

### SPRING

Mar. or Apr.    **Messiah Festival.** The rural Kansas town of Lindsborg rivals the greatest concert halls with its performance of Handel's *Messiah* and Bach's *St. Matthew Passion* each Holy Season. Order tickets early. | 785/227–3311.

May    **Topeka Jazz Festival.** Nationally renowned jazz artists perform in this three-day event. | 785/234–2787.

May    **Wichita River Festival.** Concerts, sports, food, and parades are among the more than 80 events held along the riverfront. | 316/267–2817.

**1997**
Tallgrass Prairie National Preserve is added to the National Park Service.

## SUMMER

June **Corporate Woods Jazz Festival.** Local jazz artists perform at this outdoor evening event in Overland Park. | 913/451–4466.

June **Smoky Hill River Festival.** This four-day festival in Salina draws artists and musicians from around the region for one of the best folk events in the High Plains. | 785/826–7469.

## FALL

Sept. **Kansas State Fair.** This 10-day "Party on the Prairie," in Hutchinson, includes concerts, auto racing, a rodeo, free entertainment, and traditional agriculture displays. | 316/669–3600.

Sept. **Railroad Days.** A carnival and equipment displays highlight this celebration of the area's railroad heritage in Topeka. | 785/232–5533.

Sept.–Oct. **Renaissance Festival.** A 16th-century festival with music, comedy, romance, and chivalry is held for seven weekends in Bonner Springs in autumn. | 800/373–0357 | www.kcrenfest.com.

Oct. **Halloween Parade.** The nation's oldest Halloween celebration has been taking place in Hiawatha since 1914. Highlights include a children's parade and costume contest, and a queen contest. | 785/742–7136.

# State's Greats

Travelers seek out Kansas as a destination for two primary reasons: history and sports. From the Native American history of the horse culture of the Great Plains, to military history through the historic and present day forts, to the individual trials and tribulations of those who passed through Kansas in a Westward expansion, Kansas is alive with history in every small town, country road, and open field. The story of Kansas is very much the story of America.

Both indoor and outdoor sports attract people to Kansas. The University of Kansas Jayhawks are a premier athletic powerhouse that consistently receives national and international recognition. Kansas's outdoor arena offers seemingly endless opportunities for hunters, fishermen, sailors, and bikers.

## Beaches and Parks

**Pearson-Skubitz Big Hill Lake,** near Parsons, is one of the few natural-sand swimming beaches in the state. Most swimming areas come from man-made reservoirs and sand/rock beaches trucked in from other locations. Kansas has 24 state parks, most associated with recreational lakes and developed facilities for camping and swimming. Camping opportunities range from primitive to fully equipped. Horses, trail bikes, and four-wheelers are accommodated in many of these parks. **Kanopolis State Park,** just west of Salina, is the oldest in the state and is typical of what visitors expect Kansas to look like—sweeping plains, abundant wild flowers, and wildlife. More than 15,000 acres include volleyball beaches, softball diamonds, and lots of fishing and boating. **El Dorado State Park,** near Wichita, is the newest addition to the state park family, with modern swimming, 1,100 camp sites, and a large outdoor amphitheater. Bald eagles nest in the park, thereby making it a favorite with bird watchers.

## Culture, History, and the Arts

Culture in Kansas is undeniably tied to the Old West and images of cowboys and Indians, cows and wagon trains, and lawlessness and bloodshed. While Kansans are certainly proud of those roots and the agriculture economy that grew with the people who created the state in the mid-1800s, culture has continued to grow right alongside the history, the towns, and the universities.

Small yet impressive museums demonstrate the ability of Kansans to capture the natural beauty of their state on canvas and other mediums. The **Hutchinson Art Center** has the largest permanent collection in the state, housing wood engravings, sculptures, and hand-blown glass. The community of Lindsborg is filled with at least a dozen fine art galleries up and down Main Street.

Stage shows in places like Abilene and Dodge City compete with the talents of much larger metropolitan areas. The Long Branch Saloon and Variety Show in Dodge City is good family entertainment, winning awards for its originality and creativity. Overland Park offers more adult entertainment with comedy clubs and dinner theaters.

Although haute cuisine is somewhat limited to metropolitan Kansas City, chicken-fried steak and buffalo burgers never tasted any better than they do in the many roadside cafés of rural Kansas. And there are no better places for steak than in these towns, where they're cut fresh from the hoof daily.

The winding overland wagon trails (the Santa Fe, Oregon, Overland, California, Pony Express, and Chisholm) that brought pioneers and settlers to the Great American frontier crisscross throughout Kansas. The unmarked graves, the pock-marked terrain, and emotionally laden outposts are indicative of the tough breed of people who settled here. Their stories are told in the numerous museums and historical attractions in the dozens of small towns along these many trails. The **Barton County Historical Society Museum** in Great Bend is one of the better museums from which to learn about the Santa Fe Trail; some of its exhibits are especially designed to help children understand this piece of history. The **High Plains Museum** in Goodland is another family-oriented exhibitor of pioneer history, focusing on the conditions and consequences of the Dust Bowl.

## Sports

Strip pit fishing is a sport unique to southeast Kansas. Strip pits are abandoned coal mines above ground. After the mines were closed down, they were filled with water and stocked with a variety of fish. Pit fishing gives the angler a unique experience because the water is extremely clear.

Hunting, particularly for pheasant, quail, and turkey, is big business along the northern tier counties of Kansas, near the Iowa border. Fall is the ideal time to plan a rough and rugged weekend that encounters the outdoors and wildlife of Kansas. Hunting guides are available in many communities, but make sure you have reservations for lodging first; the motels, lodges, and bed-and-breakfasts fill up fast this time of year.

Sailing is not a sport most think of when envisioning the vast open plains of Kansas, but that openness is the source of great wind power, making most lakes and reservoirs ideal for wind-surfing and sailing. All 24 federal reservoirs are frequented by sailboats and sailboards from March through November. The 9,500-acre **Cheney Reservoir,** near Wichita, is known as one of the best sailing lakes in the country, and is home to several well-respected regattas. Few trees line the shores and winds are fairly constant here. Other sailing outlets in Kansas include the 7,000-acre Clinton Reservoir, which is near Lawrence and popular with college students, and **Tuttle Creek**

**Reservoir,** a 15,800-acre lake (Kansas's largest) near Manhattan. Frequent strong north/south winds demand the best from sailors.

Basketball is what comes to mind for most people when they think of sports in Kansas. The University of Kansas Jayhawks are often the focus of college sports' national spotlight. If you want to attend one of the games in Lawrence, you had better have friends in high places, or plan far in advance. Tickets are hot commodities and hard to come by, especially when the Big 12 match-up includes Missouri, Oklahoma, or Nebraska. But visit Lawrence anyway on game day; the energy and enthusiasm for the Jayhawks permeates the entire town.

## Other Points of Interest

The highest elevation in Kansas is Mount Sunflower, just south of Goodland, at 4,039 ft above sea level. It certainly isn't a mountain, but still a lot of fun for visitors to this flatland to climb.

The **World's Largest Ball of Twine** is in Cawker City, in north central Kansas along U.S. 24, near Beloit. Hundreds of thrill-seeking travelers pass through this tiny community on the shores of Lake Wakonda each year to donate twine to the ball, which presently weighs over 17,000 pounds and contains almost 7,000,000 feet of string.

Approximately 200 varieties of grass grow throughout Kansas, including the Bluestem and Indian prairie grass. Sunflowers, asters, clover, columbine, goldenrod, Sweet William, and wild morning glories bloom throughout the state. Most roadside parks and interstate rest areas will have signs describing the wildflowers of the area.

Nearly 400 species of plants and more than 200 kinds of birds can be found in **Tall-grass Prairie National Preserve.** As home to nearly 11,000 acres of protected grassland, this is the nation's largest such preserve.

# Rules of the Road

**License Requirements:** Residents of Kansas with a farm permit may drive as early as 14 years of age. However, other drivers must be at least 16 years old, have completed driver's training, and have a valid license from their state of residence.

**Right Turn on Red:** A right turn on red is allowed in Kansas after coming to a full and complete stop.

**Seatbelt and Helmet Laws:** All front seat passengers, regardless of age, must wear a seat belt. All children under the age of 4 years must be in a safety seat. Motorcycle drivers or passengers are not required, but are encouraged, to wear a helmet.

**Speed Limits:** Speed limits on the open interstate or any separated multilane highway are 70 mph, on two lane state highways 65 mph, and on county roads 55 mph.

**For More Information:** Contact the Kansas Department of Transportation at 913/296–1568.

# The Santa Fe Trail Along U.S. 56 Driving Tour

*A DRIVE FROM EDGERTON TO ELKHART*

Distance: 190 mi          Time: 3 days

Breaks: Council Grove and Dodge City both have numerous historic buildings and sites, plus unusual accommodations that will only enhance your study of this trail.

The Santa Fe Trail was opened in 1821 as a trade route between the U.S. east of the Missouri and the Mexican provinces. Hundreds of thousands of pioneers took this route, leaving wagon ruts and devastation of plant life that is still visible today. More than half of the Santa Fe Trail lies within the boundaries of Kansas, roughly following U.S. 56, starting near Edgerton, just south of metropolitan Kansas City.

**❶** U.S. 56 and 183rd Street intersect in Edgerton, about at the point where the Santa Fe Trail separated from the Oregon Trail. The trail follows U.S. 56 west through Baldwin City, home of the Ivan Boyd Prairie Preserve, a great place to study the native grasses and flowers the pioneers encountered. The preserve is one of several places where wagon ruts are still visible. About 65 mi farther west along U.S. 56, you'll come to the tiny community of Allen, founded in 1854. Here a cemetery holds 150 unmarked graves of pioneers who succumbed early on the journey. A toll bridge across 142 Creek and a mail station also operated here.

**❷** West of Allen on U.S. 56 is **Council Grove,** a former outpost for wagon freighters. Council Grove is home to 12 registered historic sites along the trail, including a jail, a tree under which peace treaties were signed, and a mission school for Native Americans. Council Grove is another spot where wagon ruts are visible. To see the ruts, take U.S. 56 (Main Street) west to the city limits sign. Drive another 5 mi west, turn left (south) on a gravel road and go a half mile. A sign indicates the ruts, a shallow trough running in a west-southwest direction. (The ruts are on private property.)

**❸** Continue following U.S. 56 through the towns of Herrington and McPherson to Lyons. The community about 30 mi west of McPherson is where the trail crosses Crow Creek. **Ralph's Ruts,** considered some of the finest examples of the trail, are seven parallel paths on a farm north of U.S. 56 and east of Chase. Watch for signs.

**❹** The trail continues along U.S. 56 and next passes through Ellinwood, where artifacts from the **Allison Fort Trading Post and Postal Relay Station** are preserved.

**❺** The trail continues along the banks of the Arkansas River to the city of **Great Bend,** where an excellent exhibit of Santa Fe Trail artifacts can be seen at the **Barton County Historical Society Museum and Village.** Great Bend is where the trail and U.S. 56 take a dramatic turn to the south, and you (just as pioneers did nearly 200 years ago) will see the Citadel of the Prairie, a huge limestone rock nearly 70 ft high, which is also called Pawnee Rock. A monument on the site tells the significance of the wagon trains' reaching this point.

**❻** Next on the route is the town of **Larned,** a must for those interested in the history of the Santa Fe Trail. Just 2 mi west of Larned on Rte. 156 is the **Santa Fe Trail Center,** the only research museum specifically designed to study the trail. **Fort Larned** was built to protect commerce along the trail, and ruts are clearly visible for miles near the old fort.

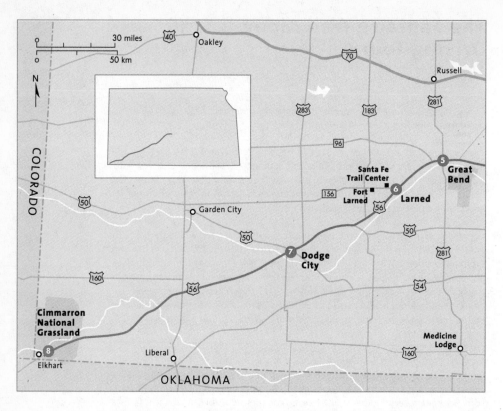

⑦ Next along the trail is **Dodge City,** another must for anyone interested in the "real" Old West. In addition to details of life in "the wickedest city of the west," Dodge City is where you will find the largest continuous stretch of clearly defined tracks along the entire route of the trail. The tracks are 9 mi west of Dodge City on U.S. 50 (watch for the "Historic Marker" signs) and are impressive, even to teenagers and others usually unimpressionable on family vacations.

⑧ The Santa Fe Trail and U.S. 56 leave Kansas, crossing into Oklahoma and New Mexico, at the **Cimarron National Grassland,** near Elkhart (approximately a two-hour drive along U.S. 56 from Dodge City). The National Forest Service offers a map for a 50-mi self-guided tour through this region, or simply continue following U.S. 56 south to continue your journey along the Santa Fe Trail.

Retracing your route on U.S. 56 is the fastest way to return to metropolitan Kansas City.

# Gypsum Hills Driving Tour
## MEDICINE LODGE LOOP DRIVE

Distance: 29 mi          Time: Depending on how much you stop for photos and to simply
                         enjoy the scenery, you could spend four or five hours on this drive.
Breaks: Every time the scenery so moves you.

Nicknamed the Southwest of the Midwest, the Gypsum Hills of south central Kansas are small in comparison to the more well-known Flint Hills to the north, but the

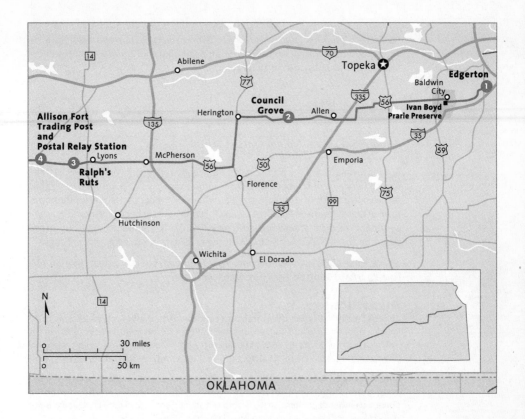

Allison Fort Trading Post and Postal Relay Station
④ ③ Lyons McPherson
**Ralph's Ruts**

300,000 acres of squatty mesas and deep ravines into the red earth are no less picturesque. Sandstone and shale stained red by nature are loaded with salt, gypsum, and oil, and are used primarily for cattle ranching purposes. This area is where the emphatic temperance crusader Carry Nation started chopping up saloons, and where the greatest of peace treaties was signed with the Five Tribes of the Great Plains.

Start at the town of **Medicine Lodge** on U.S. 160, making sure you have plenty of gas, something to drink, and lots of film for your camera. Head west out of town, past the **Carry A. Nation Home Memorial.** About 3 mi out, look for the scenic marker road signs that will send you south on an ordinary paved county road. About 2 mi later, the road bends and the scenery changes dramatically. Blood-red ragged buttes with chalk-white gypsum outcroppings jut straight up and straight down again into ravines that disappear into the red earth. For the next 4 mi, you catch glimpses, then full views, of the Twin Peaks, which are identical, conical hills standing side-by-side. Look to the northwest and you will see Flowerpot Mound, its name telling the shape of this red butte.

The road becomes gravel, then dirt, as you turn west, and it's just you, a few cows, and the untouched beauty of the hills. An occasional oil rig pumping its crude, however, will remind you that man has indeed been here. Otherwise, drive slowly or get out for a stroll through the evening primrose, prickly pear cactus, yucca, and other wildflowers. Keep an alert eye, however, for snakes, tarantulas, and porcupines, which are more common here than humans are. Armadillos, coyotes, turkey, and quail may also make an appearance.

About 11 mi after you hit the dirt road, you will turn north at a Y in the road, and 5 mi later you will be back at U.S. 160. Turn east to head back toward Medicine Lodge, but stop at the scenic overlook of the valley and hills to the south. Another mile down the road is a great spot to photograph the Twin Peaks. Paved pull-offs along the highway back into Medicine Lodge provide an additional spot for more photos of the incredible land you just traveled through.

# ABILENE

MAP 3, H5

*(Nearby towns also listed: Junction City, Salina)*

Abilene means "city of the plains," but in the late 1800s it meant wild and wicked times for the hundreds of cowboys who drove cattle along the Chisholm Trail. Things had settled down a bit by the mid-20th century when Abilene became famous as the hometown of General and later President Dwight D. Eisenhower. His home, library, and gravesite are among the many attractions in this central Kansas town. In addition to tourism and the cattle business, people also make a living in Abilene by raising greyhound dogs.

Information: **Abilene Convention and Visitors Bureau** | 201 N.W. 2nd St., Box 146, Abilene, KS 67410 | 800/569–5915 | www.abileneks.com.

## Attractions

**Abilene Smoky Valley Excursion Train.** An early diesel train takes you on a scenic 10-mi journey through farmland and wooded river valleys. | S.E. 5th at Buckeye St., I–70 Exit 275 | 785/263–1077 or 888/426–6687 | fax 785/263–4223 | www.asvrr.org | $8.50 | Memorial Day–Labor Day, Tues.–Fri. 10, 2, Sat. 10, 2, 4, Sun. 2, 4; Labor Day–Oct., Sat. 10, 2, Sun. 2, 4.

**American Indian Art Center.** All products and displays are created by Kansas Native Americans, representing more than 100 artisans from 30 tribes. Months and hours of operation are weather dependent, so it's best to call ahead. | 206 S. Buckeye St. | 785/263–0090 | Free | May–Oct., daily 9–5:30; Nov.–Apr., daily 10–5.

**Antique Doll Museum.** More than 300 dolls with hand-tailored clothes are featured in this private collection. | 1709 N. Buckeye St. | 785/263–1883 | $3 | By appointment.

**Dickinson County Historical Museum.** This museum spotlights Western heritage, and includes artifacts and research facilities. | 412 S. Campbell St. | 785/263–2681 | $2.50 | Memorial Day–Labor Day, Mon.–Sat. 10–8, Sun. 1–5; Labor Day–Memorial Day, weekdays 9–4, Sat. 10–5, Sun. 1–5.

Also here is the **Museum of Independent Telephony,** a fun place that tells the story of telephones and switchboards.

**Eisenhower Center.** The center includes a museum, library, memorial chapel, and the boyhood home of Dwight D. Eisenhower. | 200 S.E. 4th St. | 785/263–4751 | fax 785/263–4218 | www.eisenhower.utexas.edu | Free; museum $3 | Sept.–Apr., daily 9–4:45; May–Aug., daily 8–5:45.

**Greyhound Hall of Fame.** Learn about (and pet) the fastest species of dog. Displays include information from prehistoric times. | 407 S. Buckeye St. | 800/932–7881 | fax 785/263–2604 | Donations accepted | Daily 9–5.

**Lebold-Vahsholtz Mansion.** C. H. Lebold, an early Abilene entrepreneur and banker, built this 23 room Victorian mansion in 1880, and many original furnishings and antiques remain. The mansion is listed on the National Register of Historic Places. | 106 N. Vine | 785/263–4356 | $10 | By appointment.

## ON THE CALENDAR

**APR. AND OCT.:** *National Greyhound Meet.* Races and auctions of these fast animals draw enthusiasts from around the world. Venue changes each year. | 785/263–4660.

**AUG.: _Central Kansas Free Fair and PRCA Wild Bill Hickok Rodeo._** Named one of America's 10 best rodeos by the PRCA, highlights include bull riding, bucking horse roping, and steer roping. | 785/263–4570.

**OCT.: _Chisholm Trail Day._** This event celebrates the history of the Chisholm Trail (named for a cattle drive which started in Texas and ended in Abilene) with an antique tractor, farm implement show, car show, live entertainment, pioneer and farming demonstrations, and carousel rides. | 785/263–2681.

## Dining

**Brookville Hotel Restaurant.** American. Formerly in the tiny town of Brookville, this restaurant reopened in Abilene in the spring of 2000. The building is a replica of the original, which was built by the Kansas Pacific Railroad in 1870 and has been owned by the same family since 1896. The menu hasn't changed either: it still serves complete chicken dinners, which come with mashed potatoes, chicken gravy, cream-style corn, baking powder biscuits, and outstanding cole slaw. Kids' menu. | 105 E. Lafayette St. | 785/263–2244 | fax 285/263–0813 | www.brookvillehotel.com | Closed Mon. No lunch weekdays | $11 | D, MC, V.

**Kirby House.** American. The traditional Midwestern fare is nothing special, but the modestly elegant setting, in a restored Victorian mansion, makes this place worthwhile. Try the country-fried steak and the three-layer carrot cake with maple icing. Kids' menu, no smoking. | 205 N. E. 3rd St. | 785/263–7336 | $9–$19 | D, MC, V.

**Mr. K's Farmhouse.** American. Once a favorite of Dwight and Mamie Eisenhower, the "house on the hill" serves fried chicken and homemade desserts in a casual, family-friendly atmosphere. | 407 S. Van Buren | 785/263–7995 | $6–$15 | Closed Mon. No supper Sun. | D, MC, V.

## Lodging

**Best Western Abilene's Pride.** The Antique Doll Museum shares the grounds of this hotel, which is near a wooded area in the middle of town. The Eisenhower Center is approximately 2 mi away. Restaurant, bar, complimentary Continental breakfast, cable TV, pool, outdoor hot tub, exercise equipment. | 1709 N. Buckeye Ave. | 785/263–2800 or 800/701–1000 | fax 785/263–3285 | www.bestwestern.com | 80 rooms | $49–$53 | AE, D, DC, MC, V.

**Diamond.** In a calm, quiet setting, this country Victorian structure is about ½ mi from the local Abilene airport (where jets can land), about 2 mi from the Eisenhower Center, and five blocks from Eisenhower Park. Refrigerators, cable TV, some pets allowed. | 1407 N.W. 3rd St. | 785/263–2360 | fax 785/263–2186 | 30 rooms | $27–$37 | D, MC, V.

**Ehrsam Place Bed and Breakfast Inn.** This three-story, Greek Revival B&B inn along the Smoky Hill River occupies a 20-acre estate in Enterprise, 5 mi east of Abilene via First St. Grounds include nicely landscaped gardens, a gazebo, and a tire swing hanging from a walnut tree. Guest rooms have queen-size beds, antiques, and guest bathrobes. The artist-owners have an art gallery on the premises displaying the work of Kansas artists. Dining room, picnic area, complimentary breakfast, cable TV, hiking, fishing, bicycles, library, laundry facilities, no smoking. | 103 S. Grant St., Enterprise | 785/263–8747 | fax 785/263–8548 | innkeeper@ehrsamplace.com | www.ehrsamplace.com | 4 rooms | $55–$95 | AE, D, MC, V.

**Holiday Inn Express Hotel and Suites.** Opened in August 2000, this two-story hotel is right off I–70, Exit 275. A cozy fireplace can be found in the lobby. Complimentary Continental breakfast, in-room data ports, microwaves, refrigerators, cable TV, pool, hot tub, sauna, exercise equipment, laundry facilities, business services, pets allowed (fee). | 110 E. Lafayette Ave. | 785/263–4049 | fax 785/263–3201 | www.holiday-inn.com | 61 rooms, 15 suites | $69–$79, $89–$99 suites | AE, D, DC, MC, V.

**Spruce House.** This 1882 Italianate home has an eclectic decor and original art by the innkeeper, who is a founder of the Great Plains Theater Festival. The rooms are named after Jean Harlow, Doris Day, and Roy Rogers. Facilities vary in availability and pets are allowed, but you must call ahead of time. This B&B accepts long-term guests; minimum stay is two nights. | Some pets allowed, no smoking. | 604 N. Spruce | 785/263–3900 | 3 rooms | $100 (2-night minimum stay) | No credit cards.

**Super 8.** This three-story motel is on the southeast side of I–70. Rooms are no-frills and reasonably priced. Complimentary Continental breakfast, cable TV, business services, some pets allowed (fee). | 2207 N. Buckeye Ave. | 785/263–4545 | fax 785/263–7448 | www.super8.com | 62 rooms | $46 | AE, D, DC, MC, V.

# ARKANSAS CITY

MAP 3, H8

*(Nearby towns also listed: Sedan, Winfield)*

Nestled on a bluff above the junction of the Arkansas and Walnut rivers, this small border community was the site of what many historians consider the most exciting day in U.S. history. In September 1893, the federal government opened up 7 million acres for settlement and, at noon that day, more than 100,000 people raced for their share of the land. Today, people in this area primarily work in agriculture or its support industries.

Information: **Arkansas City Area Chamber of Commerce** | 106 S. Summit St. (Box 795), Arkansas City, KS 67005 | 316/442–0230 | www.arkcityks.org.

## Attractions

**Chaplin Nature Center.** This center's 230 acres along the Arkansas River are home to streams, prairies, and woodlands. | 27814 27th Dr. | 316/442–4133 | Free | Trails, open daily dawn–dusk.

**Cherokee Strip Land Rush Museum.** One of the most exciting days in U.S. history was when 100,000 settlers rushed to claim their land in Oklahoma from this spot in 1893. The museum contains approximately 21,000 artifacts, documents, and pictures. | South of Arkansas City on U.S. 77 | 316/442–6750 | www.hit.net/~cvb/ac/cstrip.html | $3.50 | Apr.–Aug., Tues.–Sat. 10–5, Sun. 1–5; Sept.–Mar., Tues.–Sat. 10–4, Sun. 1–4.

**Denton Art Center.** This headquarters for the Arkansas City Arts Council is in a former private residence, which has wonderful Arts and Crafts accents. The main floor gallery has rotating exhibits, and there are regularly scheduled tours of area bridges, barns, and other sights of architectural interest. | 525 N. Fourth St. | 316/442–5895 | dac@arkcity.com | Donation suggested | Mon.–Wed., Fri. 9–5, Thurs. 9–12, Sat. 10–2.

### ON THE CALENDAR

**JAN., FEB.: *Chapter Nature Center Eagle Watch.*** Twice yearly, guides take visitors on a walk along the Arkansas River to view bald eagles in their natural habitat. | 316/442–4133.
**JUNE: *Prairiefest.*** A juried art show, music festival, and state barbecue cook-off are part of the fun. | 316/442–0230.
**SEPT.: *Last Run Car Show.*** The largest car show put on by an individual car club in Kansas draws nearly 1,000 entries and includes a dance, craft show, and swap meet. | 316/442–0230.
**OCT.: *Arkalalah Celebration.*** Since 1928, this three-day festival whose name means "good times" has drawn more than 30,000 people annually for street games, marching band competitions, and a parade of lights. | 316/442–0230.

## Dining

**Brick's Restaurant.** American. Although you won't find anything out of the ordinary here, this popular restaurant has been serving hearty food to loyal locals for 25 years. Try the steak stuffed with Polish sausage and sauerkraut. | 301 S. Summit St. | 316/442–5390 | Closed Tues. | $5–$10 | No credit cards.

## VACATION COUNTDOWN Your checklist for a perfect journey

### Way Ahead

- ❑ Devise a trip budget.
- ❑ Write down the five things you want most from this trip. Keep this list handy before and during your trip.
- ❑ Book lodging and transportation.
- ❑ Arrange for pet care.
- ❑ Photocopy any important documentation (passport, driver's license, vehicle registration, and so on) you'll carry with you on your trip. Store the copies in a safe place at home.
- ❑ Review health and home-owners insurance policies to find out what they cover when you're away from home.

### A Month Before

- ❑ Make restaurant reservations and buy theater and concert tickets. Visit fodors.com for links to local events and news.
- ❑ Familiarize yourself with the local language or lingo.
- ❑ Schedule a tune-up for your car.

### Two Weeks Before

- ❑ Create your itinerary.
- ❑ Enjoy a book or movie set in your destination to get you in the mood.
- ❑ Prepare a packing list.
- ❑ Shop for missing essentials.
- ❑ Repair, launder, or dry-clean the clothes you will take with you.
- ❑ Replenish your supply of prescription drugs and contact lenses if necessary.

### A Week Before

- ❑ Stop newspaper and mail deliveries.
- ❑ Pay bills.
- ❑ Stock up on film and batteries.
- ❑ Label your luggage.
- ❑ Finalize your packing list—always take less than you think you need.
- ❑ Pack a toiletries kit filled with travel-size essentials.
- ❑ Check tire treads.
- ❑ Write down your insurance agent's number and any other emergency numbers and take them with you.
- ❑ Get lots of sleep. You want to be well-rested and healthy for your impending trip.

### A Day Before

- ❑ Collect passport, driver's license, insurance card, vehicle registration, and other documents.
- ❑ Check travel documents.
- ❑ Give a copy of your itinerary to a family member or friend.
- ❑ Check your car's fluids, lights, tire inflation, and wiper blades.
- ❑ Get packing!

### During Your Trip

- ❑ Keep a journal/scrapbook as a personal souvenir.
- ❑ Spend time with locals.
- ❑ Take time to explore. Don't plan too much. Let yourself get lost and use your Fodor's guide to get back on track.

**Laura's Mexican Patio.** Mexican. This pleasant restaurant in the Regency Court Inn stands out in a town heavily encroached upon by fast food places. The beribboned ceiling and view of the atrium create an airy feeling. Try the enchiladas or French dip roast beef sandwich. | 3232 N. Summit St. | 316/442–7700 ext. 400 or 800/325–9151 | No supper Sun. | $7–$15 | AE, D, MC, V.

## Lodging

**Crestview Motel.** The epitome of a place to rest your head for the night, this strip motel offers few frills, and only economical rooms. Some kitchenettes, some refrigerators, cable TV, pets allowed. | 2401 N. Summit St. | 316/442–6229 | 23 rooms | $30–$35 | AE, D, MC, V.

**Hallmark Inn.** This single story motel was built in the 1970s. A shopping center and numerous restaurants are within walking distance. Complimentary Continental breakfast, cable TV, pool, business services, pets allowed. | 1617 N. Summit St. | 316/442–1400 | fax 316/442–4729 | 47 rooms | $55 | AE, D, DC, MC, V.

**Regency Court Inn.** Floral/faunal arrangements and oil paintings by local artists are found in the atrium lobby of this moderately priced, two-story motel. Restaurant (*see* Laura's Mexican Patio), cable TV, indoor pool, outdoor hot tub, video games, business services, pets allowed (fee). | 3232 N. Summit St. | 316/442–7700 or 800/325–9151 | fax 316/442–1218 | 86 rooms | $62 | AE, D, DC, MC, V.

**Town House Inn.** This basic roadside motel is just off Rtes. 166 and 77. Simple rooms have white walls, and matching green and blue bedspreads and draperies. Some kitchenettes, some refrigerators, cable TV. | 426 S. Summit St. | 316/442–4000 | 20 rooms | $30–$47 | AE, D, MC, V.

**Victorian Inn.** Established in 1998, this inn has a bright Victorian exterior, with lacy curtains, winding stairways, and elegant furnishings inside. Complimentary Continental breakfast, cable TV, pets allowed. | 3228 N. Summit St. | 316/442–8880 | fax 316/442–8885 | 36 rooms | $57 | AE, DC, D, MC, V.

# ASHLAND

MAP 3, D8

*(Nearby town also listed: Meade)*

This seat of Clark County was named after the home of Kentucky Representative Henry Clay, known as "The Great Compromiser." Ashland is located along the historic Fort Dodge–Camp Supply Trail, and was the hometown of famed aerobatic champion Harold Krier. The cattle industry serves as the town's economic base.

**Information: Ashland Chamber of Commerce** | 430 W. Fourth, Ashland, KS 67831 | 316/635–2680.

## Attractions

**Big Basin and St. Jacob's Well.** Big Basin, approximately 1 mi wide and 100 ft deep, was formed by underground erosion 1,000 years ago. St. Jacob's Well is a spring within a smaller sinkhole along the eastern edge of the basin. Bison can often be seen grazing in the surrounding preserve. | U.S. 160 | 316/635–2680 | Free | Daily.

**Clark State Fishing Lake.** Amenities here are minimal, but the lake is stocked with crappie and largemouth bass. The drive to the lake wends through sleepy pastures and ochre canyons. | Lake Rd., 20 mi north of Ashland | 316/635–2680 | Free | Daily.

**Pioneer-Krier Museum.** Period rooms depict early pioneer life, and planes belonging to late aerobatic champion Harold Krier are on display. | 430 W. Fourth | 316/635–2227 | Donation accepted | Apr.–Dec., Mon.–Sat. 10–12, 1–5, Sun. 1–5; Jan.—Mar., Mon.-Sat. 10–12, 1–5.

## Dining

**Elmore's Pizza.** Pizza. This casual place has simple fare such as submarine sandwiches, salads, and cookies. | 316/635–4041 | Closed Mon. No lunch early Aug.–May | $4–$16 | No credit cards.

**Hardesty House.** American/Casual. High-quality American dishes are served in an old-style hotel. The prime rib is popular. | 712 Main | 316/635–4040. | Closed Mon. No lunch weekends | $7–$20 | D, MC, V.

**Ranch House Restaurant.** American. Down-home food is served with a Western flair in this brick building with large windows and wood paneling. Known for hamburgers and chicken-fried steak. Kids' menu. | U.S. 160 | 316/635–2535 | No supper on weekends | $7 | No credit cards.

## Lodging

**Red Hills Motel.** If you're looking for a place to lay your head for the night, you may want to try this small, one-level gray brick motel with very affordable rates. Cable TV. | U.S. 160 | 316/635–2239 | 8 rooms | $30 | MC, V.

**Rolling Hills Bed and Breakfast.** This two-story, yellow and white wood country home has an elegant feel. Grounds include a rock garden. Complimentary breakfast, cable TV, in-room VCRs, pool, spa. | 204 E. 4th (U.S. 160) | 316/635–2859 | waitss@ucom.net | 3 rooms | $45–$55 | No credit cards.

**Wallingford Inn Bed and Breakfast.** Built at the turn of the twentieth century, this Victorian mansion has period furnishings, and the grounds include an English garden. Complimentary breakfast, some in-room data ports, pets allowed. | 712 Main | 316/635–2129 | fax 316/635–4358 | 4 rooms (3 with shared bath) | $60–$65 | MC, V.

# ATCHISON

MAP 3, K4

*(Nearby towns also listed: Hiawatha, Leavenworth)*

Located on a bend in the Missouri River known as the Great Detour, this town of 11,000 is Kansas's easternmost city and was a major starting point for overland wagon trains heading west. It is best known as the birthplace and early home of aviator Amelia Earhart, born here in 1897. Her home is a major attraction, as is the railroad depot. Atchison was the first city in Kansas to have its own rail line, which may have contributed to the many industries that now make Atchison their home. Everything from a steel foundry to a yarn-spinning mill to grain-processing facilities benefit from their relationship with the railroad.

**Information: Atchison Area Chamber of Commerce** | 200 S. 10th St., Atchison, KS 66002 | 913/367–2427 or 800/234–1854 | www.atchison.org.

## Attractions

**Amelia Earhart Birthplace.** The simple wood-frame home is fully restored with Earhart family possessions and is owned/operated by a women pilots' organization formed by Earhart. | 223 N. Terrace | 913/367–4217 | $2 | Daily 10–4, or by appointment.

**Atchison County Historical Society Museum.** Pony Express memorabilia, Amelia Earhart's possessions, local Native American artifacts, and a 300-piece gun collection are all on display here. | 200 S. 10th St. | 913/367–6238 | $2 | Weekdays 9–4:30, Sat. 10–4, Sun. noon–4.

**Evah C. Cray Historical Home Museum.** Built in 1882, this home resembles a Scottish castle, complete with stained glass, hand-carved woodwork, and massive fireplaces. | 805 N. 5th St. | 913/367–3046 | $2 | May–Oct., daily 10–4; Oct.–Apr. by appointment.

**Independence Park.** This riverfront park commemorates the landing of Lewis and Clark on July 4, 1804. | Parallel and River Rds | 800/234–1854 | Free | Daily.

**International Forest of Friendship.** Trees from all 50 states and 30 other countries grow here, and names of famous astronauts and aviators line the paved walking paths. The forest is south of Warnock Lake. | Off Rte. 7, south of Atchison | 913/367–2427 | Donation accepted | Daily.

**Jackson Park.** This 165-acre park has one of the best views of the Missouri River from rolling hills and tree-covered slopes. | 1500 S. 6th St. | 800/234–1854 | Free | Daily.

**Muchnic Art Gallery.** Housed in an 1885 Victorian mansion, the second floor gallery has rotating exhibits of art and photography, ranging from an annual juried student event to curated shows featuring works by artists such as Picasso. The first floor, which displays much of the house's original art and artifacts, is also open to the public. | 704 N. Fourth St. | 913/367–4278 | fax 913/367–2939 | atchart@ponysexpress.net | www.atchison-art.org | $2 | Wed. 10–5, Fri., Sat. 1–5.

## ON THE CALENDAR

**MAY:** *Antique Airplane Fly-In.* The weather is a major factor in this Memorial Day weekend event, which brings as many as 100 vintage airplanes to the Amelia Earhart Airport. | 800/234–1854.

**MAY:** *Riverbend Art Fair.* This annual outdoor event is held downtown over Memorial Day weekend and affords artists from across the country the chance to display and sell their works. Food vendors, children's activities, and musical entertainment are also part of the fair. | 913/367–4278 | atchart@ponysexpress.net | www.atchison-art.org.

**JULY:** *Amelia Earhart Festival.* Atchison honors its most famous resident with a festival on her birthday, which includes a huge fireworks display. | 800/234–1854.

**AUG.:** *Atchison County Fair.* This county fair is typical of others with 4-H exhibits, carnivals, and concerts. | 913/833–5450.

**OCT.:** *Historic Homes Tour.* Eight private homes dating from the 1860s are opened to the public as a fundraiser for a private school. | 800/234–1854.

## Dining

**River House Restaurant.** Contemporary. Prior to its 1997 reincarnation as a fine restaurant, the previous lives of this turn-of-the-20th-century Victorian-style building included a railroad hotel/bordello, peanut butter factory, coffee roastery, and woodworking shop. Try the celebrated chef's popular grilled vegetable sandwich for lunch; for supper the Kansas corn chowder, filet mignon, and crème brûlée are top choices. Homemade desserts, soups. | 101 Commercial St. | 913/367–1010 | Closed Sun. | $9–$20 | AE, D, DC, MC, V.

**Time Out.** American. A very homey environment with wood-grain paneling and seasonal decorations to welcome the family. Known for hamburgers and chicken. Salad bar. Kids' menu. | 337 S. 10th St. | 913/367–3372 | $10 | MC, V.

## Lodging

**Comfort Inn.** This three-story hotel next to a mini-golf course is 2 mi from Amelia Earhart's home and 5 mi from her airport. Bar, picnic area, complimentary Continental breakfast, cable TV, pets allowed. | 509 S. 9th St. | 913/367–7666 | fax 913/367–7566 | www.comfortinn.com | 45 rooms, 10 suites | $48; $54–$64 suites | AE, D, DC, MC, V.

**St. Martin's Bed and Breakfast.** Built in 1948, this yellow, two-story B&B's individually decorated rooms have canopied beds, clawed-foot tubs, and antiques. The innkeeper's flavorful homemade scones and breads—which include banana, pumpkin, and corn—greet you in the morning. Complimentary breakfast, cable TV, in-room VCRs, library, no kids under 10, no smoking. | 324 Santa Fe St. | 913/367–4964 or 877/367–4964 | fax 877/367–496 | stmartinsbandb@aol.com | www.stmartinsbandb.com | 5 rooms | $75–$95 | D, MC, V.

# BELLEVILLE

*(Nearby towns also listed: Condordia, Mankato)*

Named after Arabelle Tutton, the wife of one of the town's founders, Belleville is very close to the geographic center of the United States. For that reason, city leaders call themselves the "Crossroads of the U.S.," in addition to "The City of Bells." A large collection of bells is on display throughout this town of 2,500, and a talented hand-bell choir travels the region promoting their city. A large feedlot on the north side of town is indicative of the community's reliance on cattle ranching as a source of income.

Information: **Belleville Chamber of Commerce** | 1819 L St., Belleville, KS 66935 | 785/527–2310 | skyways.lib.ks.us/towns/Belleville.

## Attractions

**Boyer Gallery.** Paul Boyer's animated carvings and motion displays are housed in a former ice-cream factory. | 1205 M St. | 785/527–5884 | $2 | Memorial Day–mid-Aug., Mon.–Sat. 9–6, Sun. 1–6; mid-Aug.–Dec. and mid-Mar.–Memorial Day, Sun.–Fri. 1–5, Sat. 9–5.

**Crossroads of Yesteryear Museum.** A restored school, church, and log cabin are part of the museum, as are an art gallery and special tool room. | 2726 U.S. 36 | 785/527–5971 | Donation accepted | Weekdays 1–5, Sun. 1:30–4:30, Sat. by appointment.

**Pawnee Indian Village Museum.** Take U.S. 36 west out of Belleville for approximately 10 mi, then Rte. 266 north for another 8 mi, and you will find this museum, which contains remains of earth lodge villages and other artifacts from the 16th century. | Rte. 266 | 785/361–2255 | Free | Wed.–Sat. 10–5, Sun. 1–5.

### ON THE CALENDAR

**AUG.: *North Central Kansas Free Fair.*** This has been the largest free fair in the state since the early 1900s. It is host to the annual Belleville Midget Nationals (auto racing of midget cars), an event that brings competitors from all over the world. The race is so popular that spectators swell the town's population of 2,500 to upwards of 30,000 each year. | 785/527–5554.

**SEPT.: *Pawnee Indian Village Rendezvous.*** Pioneer skills demonstration, mountain men, and authentic Native American dancing are a few of the attractions. | 785/361–2255.

**DEC.: *Christmas on the Square.*** This holiday lighting festival is held downtown in Courthouse Square the Fri. after Thanksgiving. The annual event includes carriage rides, visits with Santa, and window displays and contests sponsored by downtown businesses. | 785/527–2310.

## Dining

**Bel Villa Restaurant.** American. You can get three good, homecooked meals a day at this 1950s-era restaurant and supper club. Most of the Midwestern fare is made on the premises, and the various homemade pies and rolls are very popular. Try the filet mignon, chicken fries, baked goods. Salad bar. | 213 Rte. 36 at Rte. 81 | 785/527–2616 | Breakfast also available. Supper club closed Sun. | $7–$14 | MC, V.

## Lodging

**Best Western Bel Villa.** This single-story motel is on five acres of landscaped grounds. Restaurant, bar, in-room data ports, cable TV, pool, playground, business services, airport shuttle, some pets allowed. | 215 U.S. 36 | 785/527–2231 | fax 785/527–2572 | www.bestwestern.com | 40 rooms | $43 | AE, D, DC, MC, V.

**Plaza Motel.** This brick motel is just off Rte. 36 and K St. Rooms have white walls, matching bedspreads and draperies, and recliners and ceiling fans. Some microwaves, some refrigerators, cable TV, some in-room VCRs, pool, business services, pets allowed. | 901 28th St. | 785/527–2228 or 800/466–9605 | fax 785/527–2333 | dfranceis@mckcn.com | 22 rooms, 1 apartment | $34–$41, $45 apartment | AE, D, MC, V.

# BELOIT

MAP 3, G4

*(Nearby towns also listed: Condordia, Mankato)*

First settled by white homesteaders in 1866, Beloit had at least two names (which had been assigned to other Kansas towns) before one of the early settlers took the initiative to name the town after his hometown of Beloit, Wisconsin. Near a rushing spring in the Solomon River valley of north central Kansas, this town of approximately 4,000 is "Tree City U.S.A.," with nine heavily wooded city parks and many tree-lined streets. The North Central Kansas Technical College draws professionals to the area, while light manufacturing and agriculture provide other jobs in Beloit.

Information: **Beloit Chamber of Commerce** | 123 N. Mill (Box 582), Beloit, KS 67420 | 785/738–2717.

## Attractions

**Glen Elder State Park.** One of the best fishing lakes in Kansas is here—12 mi west of Beloit—along with the Waconda Heritage Village, an historic church moved to the park in 1994. | Junction of Rte. 128 and U.S 24, Glen Elder | 785/545–3345 | www.kdwp.state.ks.us | Free | Daily.

**World's Largest Ball of Twine.** No end is in sight for the growth of this ball, thanks to a yearly twine-a-thon, held in conjunction with the Cawker City parade and picnic. Created by a local farmer in 1953, the ball presently weighs over 17,000 pounds and contains almost 7,000,000 ft of string. | Wisconsin St. (U.S. 24), 17 mi east of Cawker City | 785/781–4713 | twinetwn@midusa.net | Free | Daily.

### ON THE CALENDAR
**JUNE:** *Kansas 8-Man All-Star Football Game.* The top high school players from across the state come together for this game, held on Trojan Field. | 785/738–2551.

## Dining
**China House.** Chinese. This small-town restaurant serves very good spicy and non-spicy Mandarin and Hunan cuisine. The dining areas have traditional furnishings, and there are supper buffets on Fri. and Sat. Try the Seven Stars Around the Moon (the top-priced meal for two, blending stir-fries, shrimp and lemon chicken dishes). | 502 Rte. 24E | 785/738–4288 | Closed Mon. | $4–$20 | D, MC, V.

## Lodging
**Super 8.** This two-story off-white stucco building opened in May 1997. Rooms are simple, but reliably clean and economical. For a small fee, you can swim at North Central Technical College across the street. Complimentary Continental breakfast, in-room data ports, some in-room hot tubs, cable TV, laundry facilities, business services, pets allowed. | 205 Rte. 24W | 785/738–4300 or 800/800–8000 | fax 785/738–2777 | 33 rooms, 7 suites | $50–$55, $65–$77 suites | AE, D, DC, MC, V.

# BLUE RAPIDS

*(Nearby town also listed: Marysville)*

White settlers from New York first arrived at the junction of the Big Blue and Little Blue rivers in 1869. The dam they built across the river to power a woolen mill created a rapid in the waters. The big event in the history of Blue Rapids came in 1913, when this little town (with a current population of approximately 1,100) hosted a world tour of the Chicago White Sox and New York Giants. Some of the original inductees into the Baseball Hall of Fame played on the field still used today for Little League teams. Gypsum, which is used in wallboard, cement, paint, and other products, is found in abundance in the Blue Rapids area. Georgia Pacific operates a huge plant near town which turns the gypsum into materials shipped worldwide.

Information: **Blue Rapids Chamber of Commerce** | 28 Public Sq, Blue Rapids, KS 66411 | 785/363–7715.

## Attractions
**Alcove Spring.** This 200-acre park was a camping stop on the Oregon Trail and remains rich with native grasses, wildflowers, trees, and wildlife. | U.S. 77, 6½ mi north of Blue Rapids | 785/363–7715 | Free | Daily.

### ON THE CALENDAR
**JULY: *Barnyard Boogie Run and Parade.*** This 10K walk/run event encourages exercise and fun in the community. | 785/363–7715.
**DEC.: *Lighted Horse Drawn Parade.*** All entries in this holiday parade must be horse drawn and decorated with Christmas lights. | 785/562–3101.

## Dining
**Blue Valley Cafe.** American. There's been a Blue Valley Cafe next to the town's library for as long as anyone here can remember, although the place has changed hands over the years. Breakfast starts at 6 AM, but you can serve yourself coffee as early as 5. Known for cheeseburgers, chicken-fried steak. Try the Mexican specials on Wed. night, sausage and gravy over biscuits on Thurs. | 16 Public Square | 785/363–7520 | Breakfast also available. Closed Sun. | $5–$10 | No credit cards.

## Lodging
**Gloria's Coffee and Quilts.** This turn-of-the-20th-century Victorian B&B is in the tiny nearby town of Barnes (14 mi east of Blue Rapids on Rte. 9). Attractive guest rooms blend contemporary and antique furnishings. The B&B's namesake is a native Kansan who is happy to help guests plan their visits. Complimentary breakfast, TV in common area, no smoking. | Rte. 9 W, Barnes | 785/363–2192 or 888/511–4569 | glorias@jbntelco.com | 3 rooms | $35–$65 | MC, V.

**Sands Motel and Restaurant.** This simple motel has been offering clean rooms and friendly service since the 1960s. Restaurant, cable TV. | E. U.S. 77 | 785/363–7707 | 12 rooms | $35 | AE, D, DC, MC, V.

# BONNER SPRINGS

MAP 3, K4

*(Nearby towns also listed: Kansas City, Lawrence, Leavenworth, Olathe, Overland Park, Shawnee, Topeka)*

This community is one of the oldest in the state and is only a few miles from Kansas City. Its roots are traced back to the early 1800s, when Francis Chouteau built a trading post along the Kaw River. Today the town is a mix of unhurried rural life and big-city entertainment. A NASCAR track is currently under construction, with an expected completion date of July 2001.

Information: **Bonner Springs Chamber of Commerce** | Box 403, Bonner Springs, KS 66012 | 913/422–5044.

## Attractions

**National Agricultural Center and Hall of Fame.** Honoring America's farmers, displays in this 172-acre museum include antique farm implements and equipment, period rooms, and the plow President Harry S. Truman used as a boy. | 630 Hall of Fame Dr. | 913/721–1075 | fax 913/721–1202 | www.aghalloffame.com | $6.50 | Mid-Mar.–Nov., Mon.–Sat. 9–5, Sun. 1–5.

**Sandstone Amphitheater.** A variety of performances, such as live music, Broadway shows, and comedy, are held in this outdoor theater. | 633 N. 130th St. | 913/721–3400 | fax 913/721–1404 | www.sfx.com | $30–$125 | Daily 10–5.

**Wyandotte County Historical Society and Museum.** Maps, artifacts, and exhibits showcase the region's history for the past 350 million years. Here you will find one of the country's few remaining Native American dugout canoes, a rare 1903 American La France Steam Fire Engine, and a monument to the people of this area who built B-25 bombers during World War II. | 631 N. 126 St. | 913/721–1078 | fax 913/721–1394 | www.kumc.edu/wcedc/museum/wcmuseum.html | Free | Tues.–Sat. 10–5.

### ON THE CALENDAR
**SEPT.–OCT.: *Renaissance Festival.*** A 16th-century festival with music, comedy, romance, and chivalry is held for seven weekends in autumn. | 800/373–0357 | www.kcrenfest.com.

## Dining

**Longhorn Bar-B-Q.** Barbecue. Housed in a building that dates back to the early 1900s, this casual restaurant has pictures throughout that highlight local history. The rib dinner and barbecue sandwiches are popular. | 228 Oak St. | 913/441–0494 | Closed Sun.–Mon. | $7–$10 | MC, V.

**Mac's Speedway Grill.** American/Casual. This affordable sports bar and grill serves fare such as steaks, burgers, and hot wings. There's live music on the weekends. | 11635 Kaw Dr. | 913/422–4764 | $5–$18 | AE, MC, V.

**Sutera's.** Italian. This place is good for casual family dining on such popular dishes as lasagna and Kansas City strip. The bar area has a large-screen TV. | 140 N. 130th St. | 913/721–5549 | Reservations not accepted | $6–$15 | AE, MC, V.

## Lodging

**Back in Thyme Guest House and Herb Garden.** Set on a 10-acre wooded lot 15 mi from downtown Kansas City, this Queen Anne building has a wrap-around veranda, two herb gardens, and a fishing pond. Complimentary evening appetizers and dessert are served on Fri. and Sat. Complimentary breakfast, cable TV, in-room VCRs, some room phones, hiking. | 1100 S. 130th St. | 913/422–5207 | 4 rooms (2 with shared bath) | $75–$110 | AE, MC, V.

**Carol's Candlelight Cottage Bed and Breakfast.** French-provincial furnishings, an enclosed sunroom, large, suite-like rooms, and elegant touches such as a fresh-cut flower on your pillow can be found at this B&B. Cable TV, hot tub. | 626 N. Nettleton | 913/441–4688 or 913/441–6646 | fax 913/422–7974 | 2 rooms | $75–$85 | MC, V.

**Holiday Inn Express.** This award-winning hotel for guest satisfaction has a large chandelier in its lobby and 15-ft ceilings done in stained wood. Fresh cookies are served each night. Complimentary Continental breakfast, cable TV, pool, hot tub. | 13031 Ridge | 913/721–5300 | fax 913/721–5445 | www.holiday-inn.com | 64 rooms | $79–$99 | AE, D, MC, V.

# CHANUTE

MAP 3, K7

*(Nearby towns also listed: Iola, Parsons, Yates Center)*

Founded by French settler and civil engineer Octave Chanute in 1873, this town of 9,500 developed along the Neosho River valley as part of the railroad line to Galveston, Texas. The town gained great popularity in the 1920s and '30s as the home to Martin and Osa Johnson, world travelers who spent a good deal of time in Africa and shot much of the footage used in the *Tarzan* movies. Their museum in town is worth a visit. The community has a rich Mexican heritage, which is reflected in numerous restaurants and festivals. Light-manufacturing plants, such as those making mobile homes, furniture, and cabinetry, also populate the edge of town.

**Information: Chanute Office of Tourism** | Box 907, Chanute, KS 66720 | 316/431–5229 or 800/735–5229 | tourism@cityofchanuteks.com | www.cityofchanuteks.com.

## Attractions
**Chanute Art Gallery.** A permanent collection of art in 25 media makes this a unique gallery for a small community. | 17 N. Lincoln Ave. | 316/431–7807 | Donation accepted | Mon.–Sat. 10–4.

**Historic Homes Driving Tour.** Get your free map from the Office of Tourism, drive along the old hand-laid brick streets in town, and view architectural styles ranging from Queen Anne and Italianate, to the Frank Lloyd Wright–influenced Prairie School of Design. | Contact: Office of Tourism, Zero East Elm | 316/431–5229 | www.cityofchanuteks.com/tourism.html | Free | Daily.

**Martin and Osa Johnson Safari Museum.** Dedicated to the adventurous couple who traveled the world from 1917 to 1936 photographing and writing about the wildlife and people they encountered. | 111 N. Lincoln Ave. | 316/431–2730 | $4 | Mon.–Sat. 10–5, Sun. 1–5.

### ON THE CALENDAR
**SEPT.: *Mexican Fiesta.*** A queen contest Friday night is followed by folk dances, ethnic foods, and live entertainment for the remainder of the weekend. | 800/735–5229.
**SEPT.: *Artist Alley and Fall Festival.*** Nearly 75 artists display their work in this juried fine arts show that fills the downtown streets. Includes live entertainment. | 800/735–5229.
**DEC.: *Christmas Parade of Lights.*** This downtown holiday parade is held each year on the Thurs. following Thanksgiving. The parade includes a notable town marshal, marching bands, and lighted floats sponsored by local organizations and businesses. | 316/431–5229 or 800/735–5229 | www.cityofchanuteks.com/tourism.html.

## Dining
**Elisa's Mexican Restaurant.** Mexican. Elisa's enchiladas are famous in Kansas; they're the cornerstone of a home cooking business that led to this restaurant and a store a few doors down that sells Mexican groceries. Try the enchiladas or the Monterey (a flat fried tortilla

with beans and meat, topped with lettuce, tomato, and cheese). | 116 W. Main St. | 316/341–4380. | Closed Sun. | $4–$6 | D, MC, V.

**Smooter's.** American. Lots of Coca-Cola memorabilia and historic newspaper clippings framed on the wall give this café a laid-back atmosphere. Known for old-fashioned hamburgers and steak sandwiches. Kids menu. | 319 S. Lincoln Ave. | 316/431–6900 | Reservations not accepted | $4–$6 | No credit cards.

## Lodging

**Holiday Park Inn 4-Less.** A massive mural of the United States in the lobby is made of featured woods from each state, attracting the interest of guests. All rooms in this L-shaped facility face the pool. Restaurant, in-room data ports, cable TV, pool. | 3030 S. Santa Fe | 316/431–0850 or 800/842–9910 | fax 316/431–6639 | 60 rooms, 4 suites | $53; $60 suites | AE, D, MC, V.

**Super 8.** Opened in Feb. 2000, this two-story motel is 1½ mi east of Chanute on Rte. 169, and across the street from Santa Fe Recreational Park, where you can fish, golf, and use exercise facilities. Complimentary Continental breakfast, in-room data ports, some microwaves, some refrigerators, some in-room hot tubs, cable TV, pool, laundry facilities, business services. | 3502 S. Santa Fe | 316/431–7788 | fax 316/431–2037 | 36 rooms, 7 suites | $49–$52, $58–$89 suites | AE, D, DC, MC, V.

# CHETOPA

MAP 3, K8

*(Nearby town also listed: Independence)*

You won't go hungry in this tiny town, founded by European pioneers in 1868 and named after an Osage Indian Chief. On the banks of the Neosho River, the town has become known as the Catfish Capital of Kansas. The area is also dotted with large pecan groves, so fall is a great time to find an abundance of whole, cracked, or shelled pecans. Fishing and outdoor activities contribute greatly to most residents' livelihood, as well as fulfill their entertainment needs.

Information: **Chetopa City Hall** | Box 203, Chetopa, KS 67336 | 316/236–7511. **Labette County Convention and Visitors Bureau** | 1715 Corning, Parsons, KS 67357 | 316/421–6500 | chamber@par1.net.

## Attractions

**Chetopa Museum.** The museum's six rooms contain artifacts depicting Chetopa's history, such as instruments that once belonged to a popular female doctor who practiced in town in the 1930s. Group tours are available by appointment. | 419 Maple St. | 316/236–7121 | Donation | Mon.–Wed., Fri. 10–4.

### ON THE CALENDAR

**MAY: *Spring Fling.*** A parade, carnival, kids games, and pony rides are held in celebration of spring. | 316/236–7371.

**DEC.: *Arts and Crafts Fair.*** Crafters from throughout the region display their goods at the high school gym. | 316/236–7511.

## Dining

**Buckboard Restaurant.** American. A sign with a wagon wheel steers you into this Western-themed restaurant, where chef/owner John Tullis serves up roast beef with homemade gravy, chicken-fried steak, and whole catfish. There's also a fresh salad bar, and Mexican dishes are served every Tues. and Fri. | 502 Maple St. | 316/236–4295 | $4–$13 | AE, MC, V.

## Lodging

**Town Motel.** True to its name, this six-unit motel right off Rtes. 59 and 166 is the only one in town. Rooms in the single-story brick building have single or double beds. Cable TV. | 115 Maple St. | 316/236–4286 | 6 rooms | $25–$40 | No credit cards.

# COFFEYVILLE

*(Nearby towns also listed: Independence, Sedan)*

This border town in southern Kansas began in the early 1800s as a trading and commercial city on the edge of Indian Territory in what is now Oklahoma. The town became famous for a moment in October 1892, as the site of the bank-robbing Dalton Gang's demise. In the early 1900s, as towns and cities paved their streets and sidewalks with bricks, the natural resources in this area were utilized, and almost a million bricks a day were made for towns all over the country. Today heavy industry still plays a major role in the town's economy; an oil refinery, foundry, and lawn-mower manufacturer employ a good number of the town's 13,000 residents. Coffeyville is also the hometown of race car driver Johnny Rutherford.

Information: **Coffeyville Area Chamber of Commerce** | 807 Walnut (Box 457), Coffeyville, KS 67337-0457 | 316/251–2550 or 800/626–3357 | www.coffeyville.com.

## Attractions

**Brown Mansion.** This four-story, 16-room mansion was built in 1906 and contains original furniture, wall, and floor coverings, and a signed Tiffany chandelier. | 2019 Walnut St. | 316/251–0431 | www.coffeyville.com | $4 | Mar., Apr., Dec., weekends 9–5; early May–mid-May, mid-Sept.–Nov., daily 1–5; mid-May–mid-Sept., daily 9–5.

**Dalton Defenders Museum.** This museum contains memorabilia from the Dalton Raid in 1892, when eight people were killed during a failed bank robbery. Memorabilia includes guns, saddles, photos, and the original First National bank doors. | 113 E. 8th St. | 316/251–5944 | www.coffeyville.com | $5 | Jun.–Aug., daily 9–7, Sept.–May, daily 9–5.

**Town Murals Walking Tour.** This self-guided walk takes visitors on a tour of murals depicting the early history of Coffeyville, all rendered by a local artist over a considerable period of time. Free maps are available at the Chamber of Commerce. | 316/251–2550 | www.coffeyville.com | Free | Daily.

### ON THE CALENDAR

**APR.: *New Beginning Festival.*** This cheese festival held in the Downtown Plaza features arts and crafts, a carnival, entertainment, dinner theater, concessions, a talent show, Shrine Parade, and many other activities. | 316/251–2550.

**JULY, AUG.: *Annual Picking and Grinning Campout.*** A local camping group sponsors this yearly event in Walter Johnson Park, celebrating folk music, companionship, and the great outdoors. | 316/251–2550 | www.coffeyville.com.

**AUG.: *Inter-State Fair and Rodeo.*** Includes two nights of music concerts, the largest demolition derby in the area, and four nights of PRCA Rodeo, livestock shows, exhibits, carnival, and concessions. | 316/251–2550.

**OCT.: *Dalton Defenders Days.*** To honor those citizens who lost their lives during the 1892 raid on two Coffeyville banks, Dalton Defenders Days has re-enactments of the raid, plus chili feed, stage coach rides, arts and crafts, and a variety of entertainment. | 316/251–2550.

## Dining

**Jack and Patty's Diner.** American. This casual diner has a mural of a general store, rendered by a local resident. The fried chicken and barbecued beef are favorites. | 111 W. Ninth St. | 316/251–8255 | Closed Sun. No supper | $3–$5 | No credit cards.

## Lodging

**Apple Tree Inn.** Native sandstone was used to construct this two-story building, which includes a 40-ft oak cathedral ceiling in the lobby. Complimentary Continental breakfast, in-room data ports, some refrigerators, in-room hot tubs (in some suites), cable TV, indoor pool, outdoor hot tub, business services, pets allowed (fee). | 820 E. 11th St. | 316/251–0002 | fax 316/251–1615 | 64 rooms, 21 suites | $57 | AE, D, DC, MC, V.

**Super 8.** This two-story budget hotel is in the middle of town and offers discounted rates for seniors and truck drivers. You can request a room with king-size or double bed. Restaurant nearby, cable TV, pool, business services, pets allowed (fee). | 104 W. 11th St. | 316/251–2250 | fax 316/215–3846 | 91 rooms | $45–$67 | AE, D, DC, MC, V.

# COLBY

MAP 3, C4

*(Nearby towns also listed: Goodland, Oakley)*

Once the home of great herds of buffalo, the arrival of white settlers from the East and the railroad in the 1880s quickly turned this portion of western Kansas into the world's breadbasket. More than 700,000 acres of wheat are harvested from Thomas County each year and processed through the great grain bins at Colby. The town has become the commercial and financial center of the region, still highly dependent on the amber waves of grain that give dimension to the landscape here.

Information: **Colby Area Chamber of Commerce** | 350 S. Range (Box 572), Colby, KS 67701 | 785/462–3401 or 800/611–8835 | chamber@colby.ixks.com | www.colbychamber.com.

## Attractions

**Northwest Research Extension Center.** Bring your camera for photos of some of the most beautiful wildflowers you'll ever see. | 105 Experiment Farm Rd. | 785/462–7575 | Free | Weekdays 8–12, 1–5.

**Prairie Museum of Art and History.** On 24 acres, a library and barn museum showcase the values, customs, and traditions of the people who settled here. Included is the Kuska collection of 28,000 artifacts of glass, dolls, silver, and furniture. | 1905 S. Franklin St. | 785/462–4590 | $4 | Weekdays 9–5, weekends 1–5; Nov.–Mar. closed Mon.

**Thomas County Courthouse.** Built in 1907, this handsome Romanesque Revival–style building with a clock tower is still a working courthouse, which visitors are welcome to explore. The courthouse is in Colby's downtown area, which still has unaltered old brick streets. | 300 N. Court St. | 785/462–4500 | Free | Weekdays 8–5.

### ON THE CALENDAR

**JUNE:** *Prairie Heritage Day.* A day-long annual event celebrating regional traditions with living history demonstrations, a Wild West shoot-out, food, kids' entertainment, and music at Fike Park, just north of City Hall. | 785/462–3401.

**JULY:** *Pickin' on the Plains Bluegrass Festival.* Blue-grass bands, folk music, children's activities, and a crafts fair fill the town. | 785/462–7643.

**JULY–AUG.:** *Thomas County Free Fair.* A PRCA Rodeo, concerts, car races, and exhibits overtake the Thomas County Fairgrounds for a week. | 785/462–7643.

## Dining

**Bourquin's Old Depot Restaurant.** American. Be sure to stop and take a table by the window in this friendly railroad depot-turned-restaurant. With wonderful food—ranging from country-style barbecued pork ribs with homemade sauce to a farmer's vegetable plate—you really can't go wrong. Here you'll find some of the best steak anywhere (in a state that provides a lot of competition). Homemade bread. Kids' menu. | 155 E. Willow/I–70 Frontage Rd. | 785/462–3300 | shirleyb@colby.ixks.com | colby.ixks.com/~bourquin | Closed Sun. and Nov.–Mar. No lunch weekdays | $6–$15 | No credit cards.

## Lodging

**Best Western Crown.** This cozy, one-story hotel is only one block from I–70. In-room data ports, cable TV, pool, business services, airport shuttle, pets allowed. | 2320 S. Range Ave. | 785/462–3943 | www.bestwestern.com | 29 rooms | $50 | AE, D, DC, MC, V.

**Desert Rose Inn.** This spacious B&B is housed in a rambling ranch-style home and has a secluded patio overlooking Villa High Park and Pond, which are within walking distance. Each room is individually decorated with a different "rose" theme, incorporating contemporary and antique pieces. Alcohol is not served on the property. 2 dining rooms, complimentary breakfast, cable TV, no room phones, hot tub, laundry facilities, business services, pets allowed, no smoking. | 1060 Villa Vista Dr. | 785/462–7189 | 4 rooms | $65–$70 | No credit cards.

**Ramada Inn.** This white stucco motel has exterior room entrances and an attractive lobby with a sitting area and a crystal chandelier. It's down the street from an outlet mall, and ½ mi from the Prairie Museum of Art and History. Restaurant, bar, in-room data ports, room service, cable TV, pool, business services. | 1950 S. Range Ave. | 785/462–3933 | fax 785/462–7255 | www.ramada.com | 117 rooms | $69–74 | AE, D, DC, MC, V.

# CONCORDIA

MAP 3, G4

*(Nearby town also listed: Belleville)*

French settlers made their home in Concordia in the 1860s and were soon followed by Easterners from all nations. One of those who eventually made his home here was Boston Corbett, the man who became a national hero by shooting John Wilkes Booth, Abraham Lincoln's assassin. In World War II, a German POW camp operated here. Today, this town of 6,000 is the seat of Cloud County, an area dominated by rich coal fields and natural resources.

Information: **Concordia Area Chamber of Commerce** | 606 Washington St., Concordia, KS 66901 | 785/243–4290 or 800/343–4290 | www.dustdevil.com.

## Attractions

**The Brown Grand Theatre.** Built in 1907, this 650-seat theater has a grand drape, which was inspired by a Horace Vernet painting, *Napoleon at Austerlitz*. | 310 W. 6th St. | 785/243–2553 | $1 | Tues.–Sat. 9–12, 1–4 or by appointment.

**Cloud County Historical Museum.** Housed in a 1908 Carnegie library building, this museum has displays and artifacts detailing the history and development of Cloud County and its inhabitants. Check out the 1940 airplane. Tours are available upon request. | 635 Broadway | 785/243–2866 | www.dustdevil.com/towns/concordia/history/museum/museum.htm | Donation ($1 suggested) | Tues.–Sat. 1–5.

**JULY:** *Cloud County Fair.* Kids' projects, such as 4-H and Future Farmers of America (FFA) displays, are the main focus, but other popular events include motorcross and mini-truck racing. | 800/343–4290.

**AUG.:** *North Central Kansas Rodeo.* A two-day attraction with seven standard rodeo events, kids' racing, and a Grandma's queen contest. | 800/343–4290.

**SEPT.:** *Clyde Watermelon Festival.* This annual Labor Day weekend event has been taking place for more than 100 years. The festival includes a theme parade with locally sponsored floats, entertainment, and, of course, all-you-can-eat watermelon. | 785/243–4290.

## Dining

**Cafe Gaston.** American/Casual. This gourmet deli is a delight from start to finish. A reading area in the back room has comfortable, overstuffed chairs where you can enjoy great coffee or Italian soda. Try the chicken salad on a croissant, Bavarian waffles, and ham salad with fresh sprouts. Open-air dining is available on the New Orleans–style patio, complete with a fish pond. | 130 W. Sixth St. | 785/243–1822 | Closed Sun. | $3–$6 | No credit cards.

## Lodging

**Best Western Thunderbird Motor Inn.** Attractions such as the sports complex and rodeo arena, as well as the public library, are only 2 mi away. Restaurant, cable TV, pool, outdoor hot tub, laundry facilities, business services, some pets allowed. | 89 N. Lincoln | 785/243–4545 | fax 785/243–4545, ext. 137 | www.bestwestern.com | 50 rooms | $65 | AE, D, DC, MC, V.

**Super 8.** An economic, two-story, tan stucco motel within walking distance of a golf course, and near restaurants, golf, a laundromat, and the Brown Grand Theatre. Complimentary Continental breakfast, in-room data ports, some microwaves, some refrigerators, cable TV, hot tub, business services, no pets. | 1320 Lincoln Ave. | 785/243–4200 | fax 785/243–1246 | 39 rooms, 5 suites | $61 rooms, $73 suites | AE, D, DC, MC, V.

# COUNCIL GROVE

MAP 3, I5

*(Nearby town also listed: Emporia)*

Kit Carson carved the name Council Grove on a buffalo hide in 1820 and nailed it to an oak tree, thus creating this little city, which is today home to 2,300. The town's name came from a huge gathering (or council) of Indian chiefs and government leaders that resulted in the sale of much of this area to the United States. Nestled in the Flint Hills, Council Grove is home to dozens of historic sites, including one of the spots where wagon ruts of the Santa Fe Trail can still be seen. Tourism, therefore, contributes quite a bit to the local economy, which is also greatly influenced by agricultural conditions.

**Information: Council Grove Convention and Visitors Bureau** | 212 W. Main, Council Grove, KS 66846 | 316/767–5882 | visitors@councilgrove.com | www.councilgrove.com.

## Attractions

**Council Grove Federal Lake.** More than 3,300 acres of water make this a top spot in Kansas for outdoors activities like fishing, boating, camping, and hunting. | Rte. 177, 1½ mi north of Council Grove | 316/767–5195 | Free | Daily.

**Council Grove Opry.** Twice a month at the Ritz Theater this show offers an evening of country and western music, with a house band and frequent appearances by music greats such as Hank Thompson or Kitty Wells. | 312 W. Main St. | 316/883–2006 | $7–$13 | Second and Fourth Sat. of each month 7:30 PM.

**Council Oak Shrine.** A sheltered stump is all that remains of a great oak tree where the U.S. government and Osage Tribe signed a peace treaty in August 1825. | 210 E. Main St. | www.councilgrove.com/cou_oak.htm | Free | Daily.

**Custer's Elm Shrine.** General George A. Custer and the 7th Cavalry camped under this tree before Custer decided to purchase 120 acres of land nearby. | Neosho St. | www.council-grove.com | Free | Daily.

**Farmers and Drovers Bank.** Built in 1892, this two-story redbrick bank is listed on the National Register of Historic Places and is still in operation. The building's striking architecture combines Romanesque arches, stained glass windows, and a Byzantine dome. Tours are available by appointment. | 201 West Main St. | 316/767–5882 | www.councilgrove.com | Free | Weekdays 9–3, Sat. 9–12.

**Kaw Mission State Historic Site.** Methodist Episcopal missionaries built this school for Kaw children in 1851, but today it showcases the heritage of the Kaw Indians, the Santa Fe Trail, and early Council Grove. | 500 N. Mission St. | 316/767–5410 | www.councilgrove.com | Free | Tues.–Sat. 10–5, Sun. 1–5.

**The Madonna of the Trail Monument.** This statue depicts a pioneer mother with two children and pays tribute to the strength of the women of this era. | Union and Main Sts. | www.councilgrove.com | Free | Daily.

**Old Calaboose.** Calaboose is an old-fashioned word for jail, and this old cowboy jail is a replica of the original home for cowboys and homesteaders who got a little out of control during their visits to town. | 502 E. Main St. | 316/767–5882 | Free | Daily.

**Post Office Oak.** Travelers along the Santa Fe Trail left messages in a hole of this tree, which served as the area's official post office. The tree is now surrounded by a local museum. | E. Main St. | 316/767–5882 | www.councilgrove.com | $1 | Sun. 1–4, and by appointment.

**ON THE CALENDAR**
JUNE: *Wah-Shun-Gah Days.* A pow-wow, parade, and carnival highlight this festival of Native American heritage. | 316/767–5413.
SEPT.: *Voices of the Wind People Pageant.* A re-enactment of the signing of the peace treaty with the Osage Indians is told in an outdoor theater setting. The event is held every other year. | 316/767–5882.

## Dining

★ **Hays House 1857.** American. The oldest continuously operating restaurant west of the Mississippi was built in 1857 by Daniel Boone's grandson and is now a National Historic Landmark. Historic pictures of the building and area line the walls, and there are a few antique church pews that serve as booths. Known for halibut and prime rib. Salad bar. Kids' menu. Sun. brunch. | 112 W. Main St. | 316/767–5911 | Closed Mon. | $8–$12 | D, MC, V.

**Station Restaurant.** American/Casual. This place serves up soup and made-to-order sandwiches with potato chips and a pickle. If you want supper, eat early, because they close at 6 PM every day except Fri. (when it's open until 12 AM). Try the Railroad Hoagie (a hero with assorted meats and vegetables), ham and bean soup, strawberry pie, pound cake. Homemade bread, desserts. | 219 W. Main St. | 316/767–5619 | $4–$6 | No credit cards.

## Lodging

**Cottage House.** Each guest room in this Prairie Victorian building is individually decorated with antiques. Complimentary Continental breakfast, in-room data ports, some refrigerators, some in-room hot tubs, cable TV, outdoor hot tub, business services, some pets allowed (fee). | 25 N. Neosho | 316/767–6828 or 800/727–7903 | fax 316/767–6414 | 40 rooms | $68 | AE, D, DC, MC, V.

**Flint Hills Bed and Breakfast.** This historic American four square house was built in 1913, and retains original yellow pine and oak woodwork and floors. Rooms are furnished with antiques. You can relax on the porch swing or chat with fellow guests in the sitting room. Complimentary breakfast, no pets, no kids under 4, no smoking. | 613 W. Main St. | 316/767–6655 | flinthills@kbba.com | 4 rooms | $50–$65 | D, MC, V.

# DODGE CITY

MAP 3, D7

*(Nearby towns also listed: Garden City, Greensburg)*

This town of 24,000 began with the establishment of a military fort here in 1865 to protect the wagon trains on the Santa Fe Trail. Buffalo hunters, railroad workers, drifters, and soldiers turned Dodge City into one of the most notorious Wild West towns; its buildings have been well preserved and the town builds commercially on its lawless legend. Dodge City is a fun place to teach children Old West history, and adults get caught up in the atmosphere as well.

**Information: Dodge City Convention and Visitors Bureau** | 400 W. Wyatt Earp Blvd., Dodge City, KS 67801 | 316/225–8186 or 800/653–9378 | www.dodgecity.org.

## Attractions

**Boot Hill Museum.** An entire block of downtown has been restored to the way it was when Bat Masterson and Wyatt Earp attempted to bring order here. The museum contains exhibits, documents, and photographs showcasing Dodge City's past, and stagecoach rides, gunfights, and dance hall shows take place all day long. | Front St. | 316/227–8188 | fax 316/227–7673 | www.boothill.org | Labor Day–Memorial Day weekend $6, Memorial Day weekend–Labor Day $7 | Memorial Day weekend–Labor Day, daily 8–8; Labor Day–Memorial Day weekend, Mon.–Sat. 9–5, Sun. 1–5.

**Dodge City Trolley.** Narrated tours spotlight sites such as the Long Branch Saloon, Fort Dodge, and the Santa Fe Trail. | 400 W. Wyatt Earp Blvd. | 316/225–8186 | $5 | Memorial Day–Labor Day, daily 8:30–6:30.

## STILL A TRAFFIC-STOPPER AFTER ALL THESE YEARS

Get your camera ready. Along Route 156, about half-way between Larned and Dodge City, is the little town of Burdett (population 277, give or take a few). Along the highway is a big metal sign that folks still stop and take pictures of nearly three-quarters of a century since it was erected. The sign reads simply: Pluto Discovered Here. It was indeed here, on a cold winter night in February 1930, that a 24-year-old farmer named Clyde Tombaugh looked up into the sky with his rinky-dink, 13-inch telescope and saw what no one else had seen before: the planet Pluto. Really. At the time, no one knew if there was a ninth planet in our solar system. Tombaugh took pictures of his discovery and sent them to the Lowell University Observatory in Arizona, where his find was confirmed.

Tombaugh went on to discover a few more things—things like a 33-day rotation of the planet Mercury, the natural vortex of Jupiter, and other things that don't make much of a difference to farmers in this part of the country. But Tombaugh, although not much of one, was indeed a local farmer, and folks here sure are proud.

© Artville

**Fort Dodge.** Several original buildings remain of the fort that supported this area from 1865–1882. | 101 Pershing Ave. | 316/227–2121 | fax 316/225–6331 | Free | Memorial Day–Labor Day, daily 10–4; Labor Day–Memorial Day, daily 1–4.

**Home of Stone.** This three-story home was built of native limestone in 1881. | 112 E. Vine St. | 316/227–6791 or 316/225–4926 | Free | Jun.–Aug., daily Mon.–Sat. 9–5, Sun. 2–4; Sept.–May, by appointment.

**Mariah Hills Golf Course.** Opened in 1975, this 18-hole golf course has great greens and huge fairways. No credit cards. | 1800 Matt Down La. | 316/225–8182 | Year-round.

★ **Santa Fe Trail Tracks.** The wide-open prairie reveals the vastness of the pioneers' undertaking as miles of wagon ruts, found 9 mi west of Dodge City, stretch to the horizon. | On U.S. 50 | 316/227–8188 | Free | Daily.

## ON THE CALENDAR

**MAY: *Cowboy Heritage Festival.*** Western-themed festivities at this weekend event include chuckwagon breakfasts, cowboy balladeers and storytellers, gunfight reenactments, and the "world's longest can-can line." | 316/225–8186 | www.dodgecity.org.

**MAY–AUG.: *Long Branch Saloon.*** A family-oriented variety show that includes dancing and comedy is offered nightly. | 316/227–8188.

**JUL.–AUG.: *Dodge City Days.*** A 10-day celebration that includes concerts, arts and crafts, barbecues, street dances, a chuckwagon breakfast, western parade, and one of the largest PRCA Rodeos in the country. | 316/227–3119 | www.dodgecitydays.com.

## Dining

**Casey's Cowtown Restaurant.** American. A brick fireplace, antiques, and local art on the walls contribute to this steak house's casual atmosphere. Known for hand-cut black angus steaks. Kids' menu. | 503 E. Trail | 316/227–5225 | $10–$15 | AE, D, MC, V.

**El Charro.** Mexican. Mexican dishes such as "enchilada delights," topped with cheese, lettuce, tomato, and sour cream, make this ranch-like restaurant with wooden tables and flowers a favorite. | 1209 W. Wyatt Earp Blvd. | 316/225–0371 | $4–$8 | Closed Sun. | AE, D, MC, V.

## Lodging

**Best Western Silver Spur Lodge.** You'll find pleasant but undistinguished rooms at this sprawling complex, just 5 minutes from Front St. and the downtown district. Restaurant, bar, cable TV, pool, business services, airport shuttle, free parking, some pets allowed (fee). | 1510 W. Wyatt Earp Blvd. | 316/227–2125 | fax 316/227–2030 | www.bestwestern.com | 120 rooms | $55–$60 | AE, D, DC, MC, V.

**Boot Hill Bed and Breakfast.** Rooms with names like the Wild West, Miss Kitty, and Annie Oakley can be found in this 1927 Dutch Colonial home. Most accommodations are spacious, and some offer such pleasing touches as cherry wood four-poster beds, fireplaces, and skylights. Complimentary breakfast, in-room data ports, cable TV, in-room VCRs, no pets, no smoking. | 603 W. Spruce St. | 316/225–7600 or 888/225–7655 | fax 316/225–6585 | boothillbb@dodgecity.net | 6 rooms | $79–$149 | AE, MC, V.

**Super 8.** Basic, economical rooms are available at this chain hotel, 2 mi west of the Boot Hill Museum. Complimentary Continental breakfast, cable TV, pool, pets allowed. | 1708 W. Wyatt Earp Blvd. | 316/225–3924 | fax 316/225–5793 | www.super8.com | 64 rooms | $48–52 | AE, D, DC, MC, V.

# EL DORADO

*(Nearby towns also listed: Newton, Wichita)*

The legend of El Dorado (which is Spanish for "The Gilded") existed among Spanish explorers of the area, and spoke of a man covered in gold dust who was sacrificed to the gods. Founded in 1871 by a party of settlers from Lawrence and spurred by the growth of the railroad, El Dorado is an oil and agriculture community with a population of 13,000. It was also the birthplace of Pulitzer Prize–winning journalist William Allen White, for whom the University of Kansas School of Journalism is named.

Information: **El Dorado Chamber of Commerce** | Box 509, El Dorado, KS 67042 | 316/321–3150 | www.eldoradokansas.com.

## Attractions

**El Dorado State Park.** About 8,000 acres of water and 4,000 acres of wilderness for public hunting and fishing make this a great outdoor destination. | 618 N.E. Bluestem Rd. | 316/321–7180 | www.kdwp.state.ks.us | Free | Daily.

**Flint Hill Overland Wagon Trips.** Authentic wagon trips across the scenic Flint Hills are offered for a weekend. | Departure points vary. Call for information | 316/321–6300 | fax 316/321–6300 | www.wagontrainkansas.com | $150 | Jun.–Sept., Sat. 9 AM–Sun. around noon.

**Kansas Oil Museum and Butler County Historical Museum.** Full-size outdoor exhibits include a drilling rig, derrick, pumping units, and railroad cars. | 383 E. Central Ave. | 316/321–9333 | $2 | Mon.–Sat. 9–5, Sun. 1–5.

**Stapleton #1 Historic Site.** This is a real ghost town from the days of the 1915 oil boom. | 5 mi north on Oil Hill Rd. | 316/321–9333 | Free | Daily.

### ON THE CALENDAR

**APR.:** *Around the World Celebration of Cultures.* Food, activities, and crafts from the various cultures that settled in Kansas are celebrated at this event, held at Butler Community College. | 316/321–2222.

**JULY:** *Prairie Port Festival.* Mud volleyball, a queen pageant, parade, and music entertainment highlight this three-day event. | 316/321–3150.

## Dining

**Silverado Restaurant and Cantina.** Tex-Mex. This place has a rustic, Old West feel, with longhorn cattle horns on the walls. Try the steak sandwiches and grilled chicken Monterey. Kids' menu. | 151 N. Main St. | 316/321–9400 | $4–$12 | AE, MC, V.

**Susie's Chili Parlor.** American. A not-to-be-missed treat that single-handedly belies any backtalk about Kansan cooking. Chili is an obvious choice, and the daily specials could include dishes such as chicken and noodles over potatoes, or ham and navy beans with corn bread. Save room for a slice of coconut cream, strawberry-rhubarb, or gooseberry pie. If you can't find a place to sit at this 14-stool diner, be sure to get takeout. Homemade baked goods. | 117 W. Second St. | 316/321–2242 | No reservations | Closed weekends | $3–$6 | No credit cards.

## Lodging

**Best Western Red Coach Inn.** Built in the mid-1970s, this brick building with red shingles is 25 blocks from downtown El Dorado, and 30 minutes from the Wichita airport. Restaurant, 1 kitchenette, room service, some in-room hot tubs, cable TV, indoor pool, hot tub, exercise equipment, video games, business services, some pets allowed. | 2525 W. Central St. | 316/321–6900 | fax 316/321–6900, ext. 208 | www.bestwestern.com | 73 rooms | $69 | AE, D, DC, MC, V.

**Sunset Inn.** This single-story inn may seem like any other basic Midwestern roadside motel, but thoughtful touches like a newspaper and thermos bottle of hot coffee at your door in the morning will make your stay that much more enjoyable. Picnic area, complimentary Continental breakfast, some microwaves, refrigerators, cable TV, laundry service, business services, pets allowed (fee). | 1901 W. Central Ave. | 316/321–9172 or 800/233–6355 | fax 316/322–7316 | 36 rooms | $46 | AE, D, MC, V.

# ELLSWORTH

MAP 3, G5

*(Nearby towns also listed: Lindsborg, Russell, Salina)*

This former cowtown once had a reputation as wild and wooly as that of Dodge City. Its preponderance as a cattle market led to the presence of gamblers, gunmen, thieves, saloons, and brothels. Proximity to Fort Harker and western expansion of the Kansas Pacific Railroad set the foundation for the town in 1867, though early floods and an outbreak of cholera in the 1860s threatened its future. Ellsworth's Old West charm is still apparent in the western shops that line its main street.

**Information: Ellsworth/Kanopolis Area Chamber of Commerce** | 114 ½ N. Douglas, Ellsworth, KS 67439 | 785/472–4071.

## Attractions

**Drover's Merchantile.** This store specializes in historically accurate cowboy shirts, pants, boots, and hats, but also sells girls' dresses, ladies clothes, and gift items such as antique metal candle holders and a cowboy or cowgirl clock. | 119 N. Douglas | 785/472–4703 or 877/DROVERS | www.droversmercantile.com | Mon.–Sat. 10–5.

**Fort Harker Guardhouse Museum Complex.** A few remaining buildings from one of the earliest forts that protected travelers along the Smokey Hill and Santa Fe Trails can be found here. Both this complex and the Hodgdon House Museum complex are operated by the Ellsworth County Historical Sociey; if you visit one, admission to the other is free. | 104 W. South Main | 785/472–3059 | $2 | May–Sept., Tues.–Sat. 9–noon, 1–5, Sun. 1–5; Apr., Oct., Tues.–Fri. 1–5, Sat. 9–noon, 1–5, Sun. 1–5; Nov.–Mar., Sat. 9–noon, 1–5, Sun. 1–5.

**Hodgdon House Museum Complex.** A collection of 1880s buildings, including the home of one of Ellsworth's early residents, offers a look at the town as it was during its cattle days. Both this complex and the Fort Harker Guardhouse Museum Complex are operated by the Ellsworth County Historical Society; if you visit one, admission to the other is free. | 104 W. South Main | 785/472–3059 | $2 | May–Sept., Tues.–Sat. 9–noon, 1–5, Sun. 1–5; Oct.–Apr., Tues.–Fri. 1–5, Sat. 9–noon, 1–5, Sun. 1–5.

## Dining

**Fabulous 50's Diner.** American/Casual. Holding true to its name, this diner will transport you back to the 1950s. Pictures of Marilyn Monroe, James Dean, Elvis, and the like line the walls, and the jukebox is full of classic '50s hits. Try the chicken-fried steak or the pork tenderloin sandwich. For dessert, have a chocolate milk shake or a slice of homemade cherry pie. | 214 Rte. 156 | 785/472–4016 | Breakfast also available. No supper Sun. | $7–$8 | No credit cards.

**Paden's Place Restaurant.** American. A little bit American, a little bit Tex-Mex, this friendly place has a casual feel, with wooden bench tables and lots of families enjoying chicken-fried steak. | 120 N. Douglas | 785/472–4013 | $6–$11 | MC, V.

## Lodging

**Best Western Garden Prairie Inn.** A single-story brick inn with exterior room access. Complimentary Continental breakfast, cable TV, pool, spa, exercise equipment. | Rtes. 156 and 140 | 785/472–3116 | fax 785/472–5703 | 37 rooms | $65 | AE, D, MC, V.

**Castle Rock Bed and Breakfast.** There's plenty of room to spread out on this 320-acre ranch. The main building is dressed with new and old Midwestern antiques and houses five of the guest rooms. The rooms in the bunk house are more spacious and have a Southwestern flair. Cable TV, hot tub. | 1086 29th Rd., Brookville | 888/225–6865 | fax 888/225–6865 | rcastle@midusa.net | www.castlerockbnb.com | 8 rooms | $70–$105.

# EMPORIA

MAP 3, J6

*(Nearby town also listed: Council Grove)*

The first white settlers here in 1857 were businesspeople from Lawrence who pounded stakes into the snow-covered, frozen earth, claiming this land as their own. Emporia was the name of a historic Greek market center on the Mediterranean Sea, and the founders had similar visions for this Emporia's future. Today, the meat packing industry, a Dolly Madison bakery, and educational facilities employ many of Emporia's 28,000 residents. Emporia is also well known for the *Emporia Gazette,* where Pulitzer Prize–winning journalist William Allen White established many of the ethical codes and guidelines for today's profession. Emporia was also the birthplace of Veterans Day, now celebrated nationwide on November 11.

Information: **Emporia Convention and Visitors Bureau** | 719 Commercial, Emporia, KS 66801 | 316/342–1803 or 800/279–3730 | www.emporia.com.

## Attractions

**All Veteran's Memorial.** A monument dedicated to all U.S. veterans, with plaques of commemoration, including one housed in a gazebo dedicated to a Medal of Honor recipient. | 99 S. Commercial St. | 316/342–1830 | Free | Daily.

**Eisenhower State Park.** This eastern Flint Hills park on the edge of 6,930-acre Melvern Reservoir has 195 electrical campsites, a 22-mi horseback trail, and a marina nearby. | 29810 South Fairlawn Rd., Osage City | 785/528–4102 | www.kdwp.state.ks.us | $4 per vehicle | Memorial Day–Labor Day, daily 8–8; Labor Day–Memorial Day, weekdays 8–4:30.

***Emporia Gazette* Building.** The *Gazette* was founded by legendary journalist William Allen White and is still operated by his family. A museum within the building tells about the journalism profession. | 517 Merchant St. | 316/342–4800 | fax 316/342–8108 | Free | Weekdays 8–7, Sat. 8–3.

**Flint Hills National Wildlife Refuge.** An abundance of ducks, geese, and deer makes its home at this 18,500-acre flood plain, created by the John Redmond Reservoir. | 530 W. Maple, Hartford | 316/392–5553 | www.r6.fws.gov | Free | Daily; some portions closed during fall waterfowl migration.

**Lyon County Historical Museum.** Artifacts relating to local farming, cowboy, and ranching history are found here, as are state and local historical records. | 118 E. 6th Ave. | 316/342–0933 | Donation accepted | Gallery open Tues.–Sat. 1–5; museum office open weekdays 8–5.

**National Teachers Hall of Fame.** The only museum that recognizes and honors K–12 teachers. | 1320 C of E Dr. | 316/341–5660 or 800/968–3224 | fax 316/341–5912 | www.nthf.org | Free | Weekdays 8–5, Sat. 9–noon.

**Peter Pan Park.** Donated to the city by the family of William Allen White, this historic park has an amphitheater, a grape arbor, and a statue of Peter Pan. | Kansas Ave. and Neosho St. | 316/342–5105 | Free | Daily.

**Prairie Passage.** Eight large limestone sculptures are engraved with symbols reflecting local history. | W. U.S. 50 at Industrial Rd. | 800/279–3730 | Free | Daily.

**Soden's Grove Park.** A former grist mill on the Cottonwood River and the Rainbow Arch footbridge dominate the setting of this park. | S. Commercial St. and Soden's Rd. | 800/279–3730 | Free | Daily.

Founded in 1934, **Emporia Zoo** (the smallest accredited zoo in the country) has just 80 species represented, but includes an exceptional botanical display. | 75 Soden Rd. | 316/342–6558 | fax 316/342–8820 | www.emporiazoo.org | Free | Labor Day–Mother's Day, daily 10–4:30; Mother's Day–Labor Day, Mon., Tues. 10–4:30, Wed., 10–8, Thurs.–Sun. 10–4:30.

**Tallgrass Prairie National Preserve.** In the middle of the Flint Hills, 20 mi west of Emporia in Cottonwood Falls, the nearly 11,000 acres of protected grassland make this the nation's largest such preserve. Nearly 400 species of plants and more than 200 kinds of birds make their home in the preserve, which is anchored by the former Z Bar/Spring Hill Ranch. The grass here can grow more than 8-ft high. | Intersection of Rte. 177 and U.S. 50 | 316/273–8494 | fax 316/273–6099 | www.nps.gov/tapr | Donation | Daily.

## ON THE CALENDAR

**JULY–AUG.:** *Lyon County Free Fair.* Activities at the Fairgrounds include a concert, mud-a-thon, demolition derby, rodeo, truck pulls, livestock shows, crafts, carnival rides, and many exhibits. | 316/342–5014.

**AUG.:** *Flint Hills Beef Festival.* You won't have to ask what's for dinner at this 3-day event, which, in addition to food, includes musical concerts and entertainment. | 316/343–4741.

**SEPT.:** *Mexican-American Fiesta.* Lots of dancing, entertainment, and food are found at the Fairgrounds. | 316/342–1803 or 800/279–3730.

**NOV.:** *All Veteran's Tribute Festival.* This week-long festival includes a Veterans Day parade, USO show and dance, concerts, barbecues, and entertainment in honor of all veterans. | 316/342–1830.

## Dining

**Bruff's Bar and Grill.** American. Everyone from out-of-town families to locals comes to this casual, split-level restaurant particularly to sample the steaks. If the 16-oz Kansas City Strip is too much for you, try the smoked ribs, burgers, or salads. | 22 E. Sixth St. | 316/342–1223 | $5–$13 | AE, MC, V.

**Oscar's Restaurant.** Mexican. Sombreros, chili peppers, and serapes are found throughout this authentic Mexican restaurant. For supper try the *Palenque* taco (flour tortilla with meat, sweet peas, and carrots topped with lettuce, tomatoes, and cheese), or the fajitas washed down with a Mexican beer or margarita. Kids' menu. | 1116 W. Sixth Ave. | 316/343–7135 | Breakfast also available | $2–$9 | AE, MC, V.

## Lodging

**Best Western Hospitality House.** The town's largest facility has a brick exterior, larger than average rooms, and a spacious, open lobby. It's 1½ mi from the National Teachers Hall of Fame, and 2 mi from Emporia State University. Restaurant, complimentary Continental breakfast, in-room data port, room service, cable TV, indoor pool, hot tub, sauna, exercise equipment, video games, laundry service, business services, pets allowed. | 3021 W. U.S. 50 | 316/342–7587 | fax 316/342–9271 | www.bestwestern.com | 143 rooms | $55 | AE, D, DC, MC, V.

**Days Inn.** This brick-facade building has medium-sized, economically priced rooms just two blocks from I–35. Complimentary Continental breakfast, in-room data ports, cable TV, indoor pool, outdoor hot tub, business services, some pets allowed. | 3032 W. U.S. 50 Business | 316/342–1787 | fax 316/342–2292 | www.daysinn.com | 39 rooms | $48 | AE, D, DC, MC, V.

**Ramada Inn.** There's nothing unique about this Ramada, but it's conveniently across the street from a mall and 2 mi from the National Teachers Hall of Fame. Restaurant, room service, cable TV, indoor-outdoor pool, hot tub, sauna, video games, laundry facilities, business services. | 2700 W. 18th Ave. | 316/343–2200 | fax 316/343–1609 | www.ramada.com | 127 rooms | $80 | AE, D, DC, MC, V.

**Seven Gables Bed and Breakfast.** Guest rooms at this handsome 1893 Queen Anne Victorian house include antiques and feather beds. One of the rooms has an adjoining greenhouse and a paved outdoor courtyard where you can relax. Both the dining room and the music room have original fireplaces, and the latter includes a grand piano and sweets. Dining room, complimentary breakfast, cable TV, no room phones, hot tub, laundry facilities, business services, no pets, no kids. | 526 Exchange St. | 316/340–0783 | fax 316/340–0854 | 7gables@valu-line.net | www.sevengables.net | 3 rooms | $75 | D, MC, V.

**White Rose Inn.** This B&B consists of Queen Anne Victorian sister houses in an older residential neighborhood just blocks from Emporia State University and the downtown area. The friendly proprietors alternate cooking duties, serving celebrated cuisine in the dining area or delivered to your room. Dining room, complimentary breakfast, in-room data ports, some microwaves, some refrigerators, some in-room hot tubs, cable TV, no pets. | 901 Merchant St. | 316/343–6336 | fax 316/342–3432 | 8 rooms | $60–$120 | AE, D, DC, MC, V.

# EUREKA

MAP 3, 17

*(Nearby town also listed: El Dorado)*

Eureka means "I found it," which is what European settlers, starving for water in 1857, shouted when they discovered the small spring nearby known as Fall River. The first settlers, predominantly Scandinavian, had first settled in Wisconsin before heading south to Kansas. Oil was discovered here in 1917 and continues to be a major economic force, although agriculture and cattle ranching dominate the livelihood of most of the 2,800 residents.

Information: **Eureka Area Chamber of Commerce** | 309 N. Oak St., Box 563, Eureka, KS 67045 | 316/583–5452.

## Attractions

**Eureka Lake.** Swim, picnic, or fish at this pleasant recreational lake, where bass, walleye, flathead, and crappie are all represented. If you're in the mood for a hike, head over to Eureka Lake Dam to see the 25-ft waterfall. | State St./Lake Rd., 5 mi north of Eureka | 316/583–5452 | Free | Daily.

**Fall River State Park.** This 900-acre state park is surrounded by more than 8,000 acres of wildlife area and 2,500 surface acres of water. | U.S. 400, 28 mi southeast of Eureka | 316/637–2213 | www.kdwp.state.ks.us | $4 per vehicle | Daily.

**Greenwood County Historical Society and Museum.** Hundreds of artifacts and exhibits demonstrate the growth of this area from the time of white settlement in the 1870s. | 120 W. 4th St. | 316/583–6682 | Free | Weekdays 9–4.

**Hawthorne Ranch Trail Rides.** Instructions on handling horses precede a three-hour trail ride on your choice of Arabian, Appaloosa, quarter horses, or Welsh ponies. Rides may be available during the winter, if the weather permits. | Main St. to 13th St., then west ½ mi and follow the country road | 316/583–5887 | $15 | Apr.–Nov., daily by appointment.

**MAY–JULY:** *Quarter Horse Racing.* Since 1872, horse lovers and race fans have come to Eureka for this event, held at Eureka Downs. | 316/583–7510 | www.eurekaherald.com/users/kqhra/quarter-horse.htm.

**JUNE:** *Mud Run.* A big mud pit west of Eureka on U.S 54 is filled with water, and you see who can get the farthest on various vehicles. Money raised goes to local charities. | 316/583–5452.

## Dining

**Copper Kettle.** American. The fare here may appear standard Kansan (mashed potatoes, fried chicken, and country-fried steak—which is just like chicken-fried steak, except it's more heavily breaded), but the quality is a cut above. Try the very fresh bread and salad bar. | 815 E. River Rd. (Rte. 54) | 316/583–5716 | Closed Mon. | $6–$10 | AE, D, MC, V.

## Lodging

**Blue Stem Lodge.** Named for the wild prairie flowers of this region, this comfortable lodge offers good service and clean rooms. In-room data ports, cable TV, pool, business services, some pets allowed. | 1314 E. River St. | 316/583–5531 | fax 316/583–6427 | 27 rooms | $41 | AE, D, DC, MC, V.

**Carriage House Motel.** This basic strip motel is sufficient for short stays, and the price is very economical. Request a room with a king-size bed, and get on the road in the morning with a cup of complimentary coffee. Some microwaves, some refrigerators, cable TV, laundry service, business services, pets allowed. | 201 S. Main St. | 316/583–5501 | 16 rooms | $33 | AE, D, MC, V.

# FORT SCOTT

MAP 3, K7

*(Nearby town also listed: Pittsburg)*

This town of 8,600 was established in 1842 as a military post to assist travelers and settlers along the Indian frontier. After the fort closed in 1855, homesteaders bought the buildings, which were frequently used as headquarters to both free-state and pro-slavery groups. Fort Scott was at the heart of "Bleeding Kansas," the period of violent social unrest prior to the start of the Civil War. In the early 1960s, community leaders began to recognize the role Fort Scott played in this nation's history; Victorian homes and buildings in the downtown area were preserved and restored, and the resulting tourism to the region has led to the creation of numerous jobs.

**Information: Fort Scott Convention and Visitors Bureau** | 231 E. Wall St., Fort Scott, KS 66701 | 316/223–3566 or 800/245–3678 | www.fortscott.com.

## Attractions

**Fort Scott Jubilee.** This country and western music show includes a house band and highlights a different entertainer every Saturday night. (T. G. Sheppard, Kitty Wells, Ferlin Husky, and Whispering Bill Anderson are past greats who have performed here.) It also sponsors group trips to spots of interest such as Nashville. | Grand Memorial Hall, Third and National Sts. | 785/883–2006 | $7–$15 | Sat. 7:30 PM.

**Fort Scott National Cemetery.** The first of the 12 original national cemeteries founded by Abraham Lincoln includes a large Civil War section. | E. National St. | 316/223–2840 | www.fortscott.com | Free | Daily 8–5.

★ **Fort Scott National Historic Site.** Eleven of this site's 20 buildings are original structures, all restored to 1840s style. A natural prairie and parade grounds are preserved. | Old Fort Blvd. | 316/223–0310 | fax 316/223–0188 | www.nps.gov | $2; special family rate | Daily 8–5.

**Gunn Park.** Ponds filled with geese and ducks are an attractive setting for the many stone bridges, pavilions, and archways built by the WPA. | 1010 Park Ave. | 316/223–0550 | www.fortscott.com | Free | Daily.

**Historic Trolley Tour.** An hour-long narrated tour showcases historic sites and Fort Scott's Victorian downtown area. | 231 E. Wall St. | 800/245–3678 | $5 | Mar.–Dec., daily 10–4.

## ON THE CALENDAR

**JUNE:** *Good Ol' Days Celebration.* A re-creation of an 1899 street fair with arts, crafts, and specialty foods from more than 200 Midwest exhibitors. Held along Main St. | 316/223–3556.
**JULY:** *Bourbon County Fair.* The Fairgrounds hosts blue ribbon 4-H and Open Class exhibits, a carnival, and Grandstand events nightly. | 316/223–5229.
**SEPT.–OCT.:** *Pioneer Harvest Fiesta.* Celebrate the past as antique gas and steam engines perform 19th-century farm chores such as threshing, grain grinding, corn shelling, and lumber sawing. Held at the Fairgrounds. | 800/245–3678.

© Artville

# HISTORIC KANSAS: FORT SCOTT AND VICINITY

Victorian mansions, military forts, and historical markers are just a few reminders of Kansas's compelling history, a history not unlike the nation's as a whole, but obviously less known. The popular vacation spot of Fort Scott and its surrounding vicinity offers visitors a local version of our nation's tumultuous past and enduring legacy.

In the early 1870s, a prominent Boston banker sent his two daughters and their new husbands to the edge of Indian territory to help establish a new bank on the frontier. He sent along enough money and floor plans for identical homes so that his daughters might live in the fashion to which they were accustomed. The mansions were built on land nearly 1 mi from the center of town, which locals considered impractical, if not insane. The twin homes are still standing in Fort Scott, on what is now National Street in a thriving residential section of town. The stately mansion of one of the banker's daughters is now a successful B&B, one of several in a town filled with historical attractions, antiques shops, and interesting architecture. Included among the town's attractions is the actual fort of Fort Scott, named for General Winfield Scott and now listed on the National Register of Historic Places.

By the late 1960s, when plans were announced to tear down Fort Scott's Old Congregation Church (built in 1873) and replace it with a fast-food restaurant, several community residents decided it was time to put a stop to the historical decay of the community. Today more than four blocks of Victorian-era shops, brick streets, and 50 restored Victorian homes provide entertainment and education to people of all ages.

The Fort Scott vicinity, just 4 mi from the state line, was a hot spot during the days of Bleeding Kansas, prior to the Civil War. Just north of the city is the Marais des Cygnes Massacre State Historic Site where pro-slavery organizers were murdered by free-state sympathizers. Numerous historical markers along U.S. 69 detail smaller, yet equally bloody, events of the time.

Twenty miles northwest of Marais des Cygnes is the city of Osawatomie, known as the Cradle of the Civil War because of the battle fought here in 1856, led by free-state organizer John Brown. A soldiers' monument, a memorial park, a statue of John Brown, and the log cabin where much of the border warfare was organized makes an interesting and leisurely afternoon of American history known to few people outside the state of Kansas.

**DEC.: *Home for the Holidays Weekend.*** An annual 2-day event held the first weekend in December, this welcome celebration includes a tour of homes and buildings of architectural interest, holiday music in Old Congregational Church, a barbecue, and a craft fair. | 316/223–3566.

## Dining
**Papa Don's.** Italian. Feast on excellent pizza and pasta, then finish up with ice cream and cookies at this charming stop on historic Main Street. | 22 N. Main St. | 316/223–4171 | $4–$6 | No supper Sun. | D, MC, V.

## Lodging
**Best Western Fort Scott Inn.** Rooms are slightly larger than usual at this motel, across the street from the Fort Scott National Historic Site. Restaurant, picnic area, complimentary Continental breakfast, cable TV, pool, hot tub, sauna, exercise equipment, laundry facilities, business services, pets allowed (fee). | 101 State St. | 316/223–0100 | fax 316/223–1746 | www.bestwestern.com | 78 rooms | $61 | AE, D, DC, MC, V.

**Chenault Mansion Bed and Breakfast.** Built in 1887, the interior includes stained and leaded glass, ash, cherry, gum, and oak woodwork, fireplaces, and antique collectibles and furnishings. Each guest room is named after one of the house's notable former residents, and decorated according to the namesake's era and personality. Complimentary breakfast, cable TV, some room phones, business services, no pets, no smoking. | 820 S. National St. | 316/223–6800 | chenault@terraworld.net | www.terraworld.net/chenault | 5 rooms | $89–$99 | AE, D, MC, V.

★ **Lyons House Victorian Mansion.** One of two identical homes built side-by-side in the 1870s for daughters of a wealthy banker, this four-story Victorian home is completely restored in rich velvets, tapestries, and detailed walnut carvings. Grounds include a koi pond and a butterfly garden. Innkeeper Pat Lyons will help coordinate biking, hiking, or other excursions across the state. Complimentary breakfast, in-room data ports, hot tub (in 1 room), cable TV, in-room VCRs, outdoor hot tub. | 742 S. National Ave. | 316/223–3644 or 800/784–8378 | fax 316/223–0062 | bedandbreakfast@lyonsmansion.com | www.lyonsmansion.com | 5 rooms | $89–$150 | AE, D, DC, MC, V.

# GARDEN CITY

MAP 3, C7

*(Nearby town also listed: Scott City)*

Many who first traveled along the Santa Fe Trail said that nothing could live in this "Great American Desert," except Native Americans and buffalo. Those folks hadn't met Mrs. William Fulton, who grew beautiful flower gardens on Main Street in the 1880s and was the inspiration for the town's name. Founded in 1878 by Mrs. Fulton's husband and brother-in-law, this town of 29,000 and the surrounding area is now in the heart of cattle country, with more than a dozen feed lots to be found here.

Information: **Garden City Chamber of Commerce** | 1511 E. Fulton Terr, Garden City, KS 67846 | 316/276–3264 or 800/879–9803 | www.garden-city.org.

## Attractions
**Agriculture/Cattle Tours.** Private companies give tours of some of largest cattle production centers in the country, highlighting what it takes to raise and feed cattle. | Reeve Cattle Co., 5665 S U.S. 83, or Brookover Cattle Co., RR 1 | 316/275–0234 (Reeve) or 316/872–2776 (Brookover) | Free | By appointment.

**Buffalo Dunes Golf Course.** Opened in 1976, this 18-hole golf course has been called the best in Kansas. | 5675 S. U.S. 83 | 316/276–1210 | www.garden-city.org | Year-round | D, MC, V.

**Finney County Historical Museum.** At the entrance to Finnup Park, this museum is dedicated to preserving and honoring the heritage of the southwest Kansas plains and the history of Finnup County. | 403 S. 4th St. | 316/272–3664 | www.gardencity.net/fico/museum | Free | Memorial Day–Labor Day, Mon.–Sat. 10–5; Labor Day–Memorial Day, Daily 1–5.

**Finney Game Refuge.** This 3,600-acre reserve is noted for its unique vegetative landscape and as home to the largest publicly owned herd of buffalo in the state. Jeep tours are available for viewing buffalo. | 785 S. U.S. 83 | 316/276–3264 or 316/276–9400 | www.gardencity.net/chamber/ctb/buffalo.html | Free | Daily.

**Finnup Park.** This 110-acre park is home to a zoo and a swimming pool about the size of a football field. | 312 E. Finnup Dr. | 316/276–1250 | fax 316/276–1259 | www.garden-city.org | Free | Daily.

More than 350 animals, including snow leopards, are in the 47-acre **Lee Richardson Zoo.** The zoo represents approximately 10 animal species. | Daily, 8–7:30 | $3 per vehicle.

## ON THE CALENDAR

**JUNE:** *Beef Empire Days.* A cattle show, PRCA rodeo, carnival, parade, cowboy poets, children's activities, sports events, Chuckwagon Breakfast, and Chuckwagons in the Park—you name it, it's all happening this weekend. | 316/275–6807 | www.beefempiredays.com.
**AUG.:** *Finney County Fair.* Five days of family fun that include carnivals, concerts, shows, and exhibits. | 316/275–8347.
**AUG.:** *Tumbleweed Festival.* Arts, music, children's activities, and more fill Finnup Park during this two-day event. | 316/275–9141 or 316/275–8621.
**SEPT.:** *Mexican Fiesta.* For more than 75 years, the Mexican heritage of this community has been celebrated with piñatas, food, dances, and more. | 316/275–7444.
**OCT.:** *Octoberfest.* This weekend event includes dance and musical entertainment, Oldies bands, a Knights of Columbus dinner dance, and a carnival. | 316/276–3264 | www.gcnet.com/chamber.

## Dining

**Hanna's Corner Restaurant.** American. It's easy to miss this little place, but the food is good, making it a popular spot with locals. Breakfast is served all day, and if you order a few pancakes, you'll get a tower as wide as your plate. People also like the smothered pork chops, chicken fries, or the 16-oz. rib eye. | 83 Mary St. | 316/276–8044 | Breakfast also available. Closed Mon. No supper Sun. | $4–$15 | No credit cards.

## Lodging

**Best Western Wheat Lands Motor Inn.** Local shopping, the business district, and the zoo are within 2–3 mi of this strip motel. Bar (with entertainment), complimentary breakfast, in-room data ports, some refrigerators, cable TV, pool, barbershop, beauty salon, exercise equipment, laundry facilities, business services, airport shuttle, pets allowed. | 1311 E. Fulton | 316/276–2387 | fax 316/276–4252 | www.bestwestern.com | 107 rooms | $68 | AE, D, DC, MC, V.

**Heritage House Bed and Breakfast.** The rooms in this late 1920s-era Cape Cod bungalow (which opened in Oct. 1999) include feather beds, family antiques, and mementos. Each guest room is named and decorated in honor of a member of the proprietors' families, and a portion of your bill is donated to charity. Dining room, complimentary breakfast, some microwaves, some refrigerators, some in-room hot tubs, cable TV, in-room VCRs, business services, no pets, no kids under 10, no smoking. | 1008 N. Main St. | 316/275–5080 | fax 316/275–6069 | hhbbinn@pld.com | 5 rooms | $55–$95 | AE, D, MC, V.

**Plaza Inn.** Exterior entrances lead to comfortable rooms with warm, soft color schemes and pleasing amenities. Restaurant, bar (with entertainment), complimentary Continental breakfast, room service, cable TV, indoor pool, hot tub, video games, business services, airport shuttle, pets allowed. | 1911 E. Kansas Ave. | 316/275–7471 or 800/875–5201 | fax 316/275–4028 | www.plazainn.com | 109 rooms | $68 | AE, D, DC, MC, V.

# GOODLAND

*(Nearby town also listed: Colby)*

It doesn't take a lot of imagination to understand how the Lutheran and Catholic settlers of this region in the mid-1880s decided upon their town's name. Fertile prairie land, abundant wildlife, and natural springs are still cherished resources to the 5,700 residents of this western Kansas community, one of the few in the mountain time zone. Golf courses, sports arenas, and modern medical facilities contribute to the town's quality of life. If you happen through this area in late June, take time to observe a few minutes of the wheat harvest in progress. It's a sight you won't forget.

Information: **Sherman County Convention and Visitors Bureau** | 104 W. 11th (Box 628), Goodland, KS 67735 | 785/899-3515 or 888/824-4222.

## Attractions

**High Plains Museum.** The country's first patented helicopter is on display here, along with Sherman County history. | 1717 Cherry St. | 785/899-4595 | Donations accepted | Weekdays 9-6, Sat. 9-4, Sun. 1-4.

**The Puppet Factory.** This small shop makes 85 kinds of hand puppets sold worldwide. | 117 E. 17th St. | 785/899-7145 | Free | Weekdays 7-4.

### ON THE CALENDAR

**JULY: *Freedomfest Celebration*.** A carnival, local musical entertainment, a picnic at the Sherman County Fairgrounds, and the "best fireworks between Kansas City and Denver" are highlights of this annual Fourth of July event. | 785/899-3515.
**AUG.: *Sunflower Festival and Free Fair*.** A street festival, yellow car parade, queen contest, and 4-H activities fill the streets downtown for a full week. | 785/899-5868.
**SEPT.: *Flatlander Fall Classic*.** An antique and hot rod car show, scruffiest dog contest, and music entertainment are on stage these three days. | 785/899-7130.

## Dining

**Anthony's Fine Dining Restaurant.** Contemporary. Housed in a restored 1904 building with brick walls, oak floors, and a pressed copper ceiling, this restaurant is a rare but welcome fine dining experience in a land of chicken-fried steak. In an open kitchen, chef-owner Anthony Spomer composes a rotating menu which could include maple-grilled rack of lamb served with sour cream-and-chive mashed potatoes and asparagus tips, and fresh vegetable-crusted salmon with rice pilaf and roasted vegetables in a curry sauce. Homemade desserts. Open-air dining in garden patio. | 1016 Main St. | 785/899-7070 | anthonys@goodland.ixks.com | www.anthonysgoodland.com | Closed Sun., Mon. No supper Tues., Wed, no lunch Sat. | $15-$20 | MC, V.

## Lodging

**Best Western Buffalo Inn.** Exterior entrances lead to simple rooms with reasonable prices. The High Plains Museum is a ½ mi from this brick motel. Restaurant, bar, cable TV, indoor pool, wading pool, hot tub, playground, laundry facilities, guest laundry, business services, airport shuttle, some pets allowed. | 830 W. U.S. 24 | 785/899-3621 or 800/436-3621 | fax 785/899-5072 | www.bestwestern.com | 93 rooms | $52 | AE, D, DC, MC, V.

**Comfort Inn.** Convenience and dependability meet at this brick and stucco hotel with green awnings, which opened in July 1997. Its location right off I-70 and Rte. 27 makes it a good choice for those passing through. A gas station and a variety of fast food choices are just down the road. Complimentary Continental breakfast, in-room data ports, some microwaves, some refrigerators, some in-room hot tubs, cable TV, pool, hot tub, video games, laundry

GOODLAND

INTRO
ATTRACTIONS
DINING
LODGING

facilities, business services, pets allowed (fee). | 2519 Enterprise Rd. | 785/899–7181 | fax 785/899–7183 | www.comfortinn.com | 49 rooms | $57–$99 | AE, D, DC, MC, V.

**Howard Johnson.** Interior halls lead to guest rooms at this chain hotel, right off I–70. A recreation dome houses pool tables, Ping-Pong, and much more. RV hookups are available for campers. Restaurant, bar, room service, cable TV, indoor pool, hot tub, miniature golf, putting green, exercise equipment, video games, playground, laundry facilities, business services, airport shuttle, pets allowed. | 2218 Commerce Rd. | 785/899–3644 | fax 785/899–3646 | www.hojo.com | 79 rooms | $64–69 | AE, D, DC, MC, V.

# GREAT BEND

MAP 3, F6

*(Nearby town also listed: Larned)*

In a big bend of the Arkansas River, this town of 15,000 was first explored by Coronado in search of the Seven Golden Cities of Cíbola in the 1500s. The opening of the Santa Fe Trail in the 1860s brought additional white settlers from across the eastern United States through the region once dominated by tribes of Pawnee, Comanche, Cheyenne, and Apache. The fertile land and abundant wildlife that attracted the Native Americans still flourish in Barton County, making fishing and hunting the top recreational and tourist activities. Cattle ranching also continues to thrive, contributing to other jobs in meat packing.

Information: **Great Bend Chamber of Commerce** | 1307 Williams St. (Box 400), Great Bend, KS 67530 | 316/792–2401 | www.greatbend.net.

## Attractions

**Allison Fort Trading Post and Postal Relay Station.** An historical marker is all that remains of this significant spot along the Santa Fe Trail. | U.S. 56, 2 mi east of Great Bend | 316/792–2401 | Free | Daily.

**Barton County Historical Society Museum and Village.** Nine buildings on a 5-acre tract of land are vivid reminders of life here nearly 100 years ago. Includes artifacts from the Santa Fe Trail. | S. Main St. | 316/793–5125 | $2 | Apr.–mid-Nov., Tues.–Sun. 1–5; mid-Nov.–Mar. by appointment.

**Brit Spaugh Park and Zoo.** More than 100 animals are sheltered in these 46 acres, including a pride of lions, bears, and hooved livestock. | N. Main St. | 316/793–4160 | Free | Daily 9–4:30.

**Cheyenne Bottoms.** This stop-over point for nearly ½ million migrating birds each year is one of the last major wetland systems in Kansas. The preserve is 5 mi north of Great Bend, off U.S. 281. | 56 N.E. 40 Rd. | 316/793–7730 | Free | Daily.

**Quilt Walk.** Seven famous quilt patterns are in-laid in the sidewalk around the Barton County Courthouse. | 1300–1400 Main St. | 316/792–2750 | Free | Daily.

**Quivira National Wildlife Refuge.** Nearly 22,000 acres of prairie grasses, salt marshes, sand dunes, and canals are home to hundreds of thousands of water fowl, reptiles, and mammals. | Rte. 484, 13 mi east from U.S. 281 | 316/486–2393 | fax 316/486–2315 | quivira.fws.gov | Free | Daily; some seasonal closings for migrations.

★ **Ralph's Ruts.** These seven parallel paths on the farm of Ralph Hathaway (considered a leading authority on the Santa Fe trail), are thought to be some of the finest examples on the trail. The ruts are north of U.S. 56 and 4 mi west of Chase. | 4222 Ave. L, Chase | 316/938–2504 | Free | By appointment.

## ON THE CALENDAR

**JUNE:** *Juneteenth.* Held in Lafayette Park, this event includes gospel singing, the sale of books and artifacts, and a ceremony honoring the Buffalo soldiers. | 316/793–6557.

**JULY:** *Barton County Fair.* This great county fair is held at the Expo Complex, 3 mi west of Great Bend, and includes 4-H exhibits, carnivals, and crafts for the whole family. | 316/797–3247 | www.ckan.com/bartoncountyfair.

**JULY:** *Greatest Fireworks Display In Kansas.* More than $20,000 worth of fireworks are exploded to music at the end of a two-day festival. | 316/793–4160.

## Dining

**Caleb's House of Fine Food and Spirits.** American. Although it specializes in steak, a huge buffet for lunch every day or supper on Fri. and Sat. allows for plenty of variety. The lounge and two dining areas have a Southwestern flair, and the enchiladas (with mild sauce brought in from New Mexico) are a favorite. Try anything with Euealle's green chili sauce, and wash down your meal with one of the 25 beers on the menu. Salad bar. | 906 McKinley St. | 316/792–9060. | $5–$20 | AE, D, MC, V.

**Tenth Street Restaurant.** Mexican. One of three Mexican restaurants owned by the same family, here the cheerful Southwestern-style interior is well-complemented by the tasty tacos, burritos, and chalupas. Order the hot made-to-order chips and the pork enchiladas, both popular with regulars. | 2210 Tenth St. | 316/793–3786 | Closed weekends | $4–$7 | No credit cards.

## Lodging

**Best Western Angus Inn.** Recreational activities are housed under the hotel's "Fun Dome," and sunshine can be enjoyed via the sundeck or open roof. Restaurant, cable TV, indoor pool, hot tub, exercise equipment, video games, business services, airport shuttle, some pets allowed. | 2920 10th St. | 316/792–3541 | fax 316/792–8621 | www.bestwestern.com | 90 rooms | $60 | AE, D, DC, MC, V.

**Holiday Inn.** This full-service hotel has a glass-domed recreation area, a lounge for relaxation, and is within a 30-minute drive of such local attractions as Fort Larned and Barton County Historical Museum. Restaurant, bar, room service, cable TV, indoor pool, hot tub, laundry facilities, business services, airport shuttle, pets allowed. | 3017 W. 10th St. | 316/792–2431 | fax 316/792–5561 | www.holiday-inn.com | 174 rooms, 1 suite | $65–$72, $75–$90 suites | AE, D, DC, MC, V.

**Lizzie's Cottage.** Two homes on adjoining property make up this delightful B&B inn. One of the homes is a 1900 Victorian; guest rooms have historic fabrics, handmade quilts, and antique linens, and a gourmet breakfast is served in the formal dining room. The other home is a turn-of-the-20th-century cleanlined Craftsman-style, with an art deco–style interior and individually decorated theme rooms. All rooms in both houses have full kitchen service, and phone service is available in the common area. Dining room, complimentary breakfast, kitchenettes, cable TV, no room phones, laundry service, no pets, no smoking. | 1315 Stone St. | 316/792–6000 | fax 316/792–1902 | 5 rooms | $65–$125 | MC, V.

# GREENSBURG

MAP 3, E7

*(Nearby town also listed: Pratt)*

This southeastern Kansas town of 1,500 was named after the flamboyant Donald Green, known as Cannonball Green because of the stagecoach line of the same name that he operated throughout the region. The coming of the railroad resulted in the creation of the world's largest hand-dug well, at 109 feet deep. Millions of years before that, however, the largest meteorite to have ever been discovered, weighing more than 1,000 pounds, landed here. Today, Greensburg's fields are loaded with corn, wheat, and soybeans; Kiowa County leads the state in corn production, which in some years exceeds wheat production in Kansas.

Information: **Greensburg Chamber of Commerce** | 315 S. Sycamore St., Greensburg, KS 67054 | 316/723–2261 or 800/207–7369 | skyways.lib.ks.us/towns/Greensburg.

## Attractions

**Big Well.** Climb a ladder to the bottom of the world's largest hand-dug well, which, at 109-ft deep, was an engineering marvel when it was built from 1887–1888. At no additional charge you can visit the onsite museum and view the world's largest pallasite meteorite, weighing in at around 1,000 lbs. | 315 S. Sycamore St. | 316/723–2261 | www.bigwell.org | $1.50 | Labor Day–Memorial Day, daily 9–5.

**Hunter Drug Store.** You'll find a 1950s-era soda fountain that's still in use in this 1917 drugstore. Pick up a few essentials and order a soda or float made with homemade syrup. | 121 S. Main St. | 316/723–2331 | Free | Weekdays 8:30–6, Sat. 8:30–1.

### ON THE CALENDAR
**MAY: *Arts and Crafts Show.*** More than 100 crafts booths are set up along Main St. in downtown Greensburg. A barbecue, live entertainment, and pony rides are part of the fun. | 800/207–7369.
**DEC.: *Candy Cane Lane.*** A local farmer decorates the Fairgrounds, where you can enjoy sleigh rides and other holiday activities. | 800/207–7369.

## Dining
**Cannonball Grill.** American. Once a drive-in movie theater, this steak-and-burger place still has the original canopy. Homemade onion rings are a favorite. | 531 E. Kansas Ave./Rte. 54 | 316/723–3388 | Closed Sun. | $3–$14 | No credit cards.

## Lodging
**Best Western J-Hawk.** This popular motel is across from the city park, and just a few blocks from the world's largest hand-dug well. Basic rooms are clean and reasonable priced. Complimentary Continental breakfast, in-room data ports, cable TV, indoor pool, hot tub. | 515 W. Kansas Ave. | 316/723–2121 or 800/528–1234 | fax 316/723–2650 | www.bestwestern.com | 30 rooms | $56–$59 | AE, D, DC, MC, V.

**Kansan Motel.** There are a handful of renovated rooms at this blond-brick-with-brown-trim strip motel. A town park with a playground and gazebo is across the street. Some in-room data ports, some microwaves, some refrigerators, cable TV, pool, laundry facilities, business services, pets allowed. | 800 E. Kansas Ave. | 316/723–2141 or 800/535–2141 | fax 316/723–2774 | 29 rooms | $42–$49 | AE, D, DC, MC, V.

# HAYS

MAP 3, E5

*(Nearby town also listed: Russell)*

First known as Fort Fletcher, Fort Hays was built as a military post along the stagecoach line from Kansas City to Denver in the 1860s. The growing town around the fort was filled with saloons, dance halls, and illegal activities. The fort was abandoned in 1889, and soon after the state designated land for an agriculture college. Fort Hays State University is now responsible for most of the cultural activities and events in this community of 20,000. The university and the cattle and wheat ranches in the surrounding countryside, heavily influence the town's economy.

Information: **Hays Convention and Visitors Bureau** | 1301 Pine, Suite B, Hays, KS 67601 | 800/569–4505. | www.haysusa.com.

## Attractions

**Buffalo Herd.** Get an up-close view of a large buffalo herd, remnant of the days when much larger herds roamed the prairie. | Across from Fort Hays Historic Site, 1472 U.S. 183 Alternate | Free | Daily.

**Ellis County Historical Society and Museum.** More than 25,000 items tell the story of early pioneer life in Ellis County. | 100 W. 7th St. | 785/628–2624 | Free | Tues.–Fri. 9–5; Jun.–Aug., also Sat. 1–5.

**Fort Hays State Historic Site.** Several original buildings remain from this fort, which was built in 1867 to protect the railroad construction. The fort is 4 mi south of Exit 157 on I–70. | 1472 U.S. 183 Alternate | 785/625–6812. | www.kshs.org | Free | Tues.–Sat. 9–5, Sun.–Mon. 1–5.

**Sternberg Museum of Natural History.** Animated life-size dinosaurs and a "fish-within-a-fish" fossil are popular attractions at this museum, named for leading researchers of North American vertebrates. | 3000 Sternberg Dr. | 785/628–4286 or 785/628–8202 | fax 785/628–4518 | www.fhsu.edu/sternberg | $5 | Tues.–Sat. 9–9, Sun.–Mon. 1–9.

**Walter Chrysler Home and Museum.** The founder of the Chrysler Motor Corporation once milked cows and playd baseball here. | 102 W. 10th St., Ellis | 785/726–3636 | $2 | May–Sept., Mon.–Sat. 9:30–4:30, Sun 12:30–4:30; Oct.–May., Mon.–Sat. 11–3, Sun. 12:30–4:30.

### ON THE CALENDAR

**JULY:** *Ellis County Fair.* A rodeo, carnival, food booths, and commercial exhibits draw crowds to this family-oriented fair. | 785/628–9410.
**JULY:** *Wild West Festival.* This celebration is held over Fourth of July weekend, and highlights include county-and-western and rock bands, a parade, arts and crafts booths, and a fireworks display in Municipal Park. | 800/569–4505.
**SEPT.:** *Pioneer Days.* This three-day event has fold art (similar to origami), crafts, scouts, soldiers, and a re-enactment of life at Fort Hays. | 785/628–8202.
**OCT.:** *Oktoberfest.* This autumn celebration of arts, crafts, and music is held in conjunction with homecoming at Fort Hays State University. | 785/628–8202.

## Dining

**Gutierrez.** Mexican. Southwestern and Wild West decorations fill this restaurant, which is popular with the college crowd. Try their famous fajitas. Kids' menu. | 1106 E. 27th | 785/625–4402 | $6–$10 | AE, D, DC, MC, V.

## Lodging

**Best Western Vagabond.** Fort Hays State Historic Site is about 3 mi from this motel, which has king- and queen-size beds and pleasing amenities at reasonable prices. Restaurant, bar, in-room data ports, cable TV, pool, hot tub, business services, pets allowed. | 2524 Vine St. | 785/625–2511 | www.bestwestern.com | 92 rooms | $54 | AE, D, DC, MC, V.

**Budget Host Villa Inn.** This two-story motel is 2½ mi from I–70 and the Sternberg Museum of Natural History. Three restaurants are within walking distance, and the downtown area is eight blocks away. Picnic area, cable TV, pool, business services, airport shuttle, some pets allowed. | 810 E. 8th St. | 785/625–2563 | fax 785/625–3967 | www.budgethost.com | 49 rooms | $45 | AE, D, DC, MC, V.

**Days Inn.** Off I–70, this chain motel offers easy access to local attractions, such as Fort Hays (2 mi) and the Sternberg Museum of Natural History (4 blocks). From late May to the beginning of Sept., twilight historical tours of the area are offered. Complimentary Continental breakfast, in-room data ports, cable TV, pool, playground, business services. | 3205 N. Vine St. | 785/628–8261 | fax 785/628–8261 | www.daysinn.com | 104 rooms | $57 | AE, D, DC, MC, V.

**Fairfield Inn.** Built in 1999, this three-story beige stucco building is just off I–70, Exit 159, and is within walking distance of restaurants. Accommodations are pleasantly decorated in pink and green tones, and "executive" rooms are more spacious. Complimentary Continental breakfast, in-room data ports, some microwaves, some refrigerators, some in-room hot tubs, cable TV, pool, hot tub, gym, business services, no pets. | 377 Mopar Dr. | 785/625–3344 | fax 785/625–3222 | 62 rooms | $60–$90 | AE, D, DC, MC, V.

**Hampton Inn.** Near I–70 at the north end of town, this motel has exterior room entrances and is 1 mi from the center of town. Complimentary Continental breakfast, in-room data ports, cable TV, business services, airport shuttle, pets allowed. | 3801 Vine St. | 785/625–8103 | fax 785/625–3006 | www.hampton-inn.com | 117 rooms | $69 | AE, D, DC, MC, V.

**Holiday Inn.** Comfortable rooms have king-size or double beds. Hays Municipal Airport is 5 mi away. Restaurant, in-room data ports, room service, cable TV, indoor pool, hot tub, business services, airport shuttle, pets allowed. | 3603 Vine St. | 785/625–7371 | fax 785/625–7250 | www.holiday-inn.com | 190 rooms | $79 | AE, D, DC, MC, V.

**Tea Rose Inn.** A handsome mixture of neo-Gothic and Queen Anne elements, this 1909 B&B has beveled glass windows and a handcrafted open staircase. Rooms include antique four-poster beds, traditional quilts, and claw-foot tubs; breakfast could include quiche, breakfast tacos, or stuffed French toast with apricot sauce. Dining room, complimentary breakfast, in-room data ports, some in-room hot tubs, no TV, TV in common area, business services, no pets, no children under 3, no smoking. | 117 W. Thirteenth St. | 785/623–4060 or 888/623–1125 | rs@tearose.net | www.tearose.net | 3 rooms (1 with shower only) | $65–$95 | AE, D, MC, V.

# HIAWATHA

MAP 3, J3

*(Nearby town also listed: Atchison)*

Officially incorporated in 1870, but named the county seat in 1858, this town of 3,600 was named after the Indian brave in Longfellow's poem "Song of Hiawatha." The first settlers of the area came from Kentucky and other eastern communities in the United States. The town is home to the nation's oldest Halloween celebration, but is best known for its reputation as the "City of Beautiful Maples," due to the hundreds of hard red trees that line its streets and turn magnificent colors in the fall. Agriculture continues to be the primary economic force in the area, although light manufacturing also contributes significantly to the economy.

Information: **Hiawatha Convention Visitors Bureau** | 602 Oregon St., Hiawatha, KS 66434 | 785/742–7136.

## Attractions

**Davis Memorial.** Mr. and Mrs. Davis, members of a local family, are remembered through more than a dozen marble or granite statues depicting the couple at different times in their lives. | Mt. Hope Cemetery, First and Main Sts. | 785/742–7136 | Free | Daily.

**Old Town Clock.** Listed on the Kansas Register, this clock is across the street from Town Square and hasn't missed a beat since it was built in 1891. | 700 Oregon St. | 785/742–7136 | Free | Daily.

### ON THE CALENDAR

**OCT.: *Maple Leaf Festival.*** The food, crafts, music, and games are all secondary to the beauty of the maple trees this time of year. | 913/742–7136.

**OCT.: *Halloween Parade.*** The nation's oldest Halloween celebration marches down Oregon St. and has been taking place here since 1914. | 913/742–7136.

## Dining

**Gus's Restaurant.** American. Here you'll find a basic country-style interior and an open kitchen area where people often chat with the cooks. Well-prepared Midwestern food is occasionally studded with a Greek specialty, courtesy of Gus. Try the hot beef sandwich, breaded pork tenderloin, Greek sandwich. Salad bar. | 604 Oregon St. | 785/742–4533 | No supper Sun. | $5–$11 | No credit cards.

**Heartland.** American. This restaurant has an airy feel, with flowers on the table and a full-glass window looking out on the pool and landscaping. Known for seafood, steak. Salad bar. Buffet. Kids' menu. | 1100 S. 1st St. | 785/742–7401 | $5–$18 | AE, D, DC, MC, V.

## Lodging

**Country Cabin.** Sit on the front porch of your log cabin and woolgather as you look across the pond at this getaway place, opened in Oct. 1999. Restaurant, complimentary Continental breakfast. Kitchenettes, microwaves, refrigerators, cable TV, in-room VCRs, no room phones, pond, fishing. | 2534 Kestral Rd. | 785/742–4320 | 4 cabins | $74 | AE, D, MC, V.

**Hiawatha Inn.** This 2-story inn was built in the early 1980s. It's 3 blocks from the convention center, and 13 mi from local casinos. The works of local artists are on display throughout. Restaurant, bar, cable TV, pool, business services. | 1100 S. 1st St. | 785/742–7401 | fax 785/742–3334 | 40 rooms | $46 | AE, D, DC, MC, V.

# HUTCHINSON

MAP 3, G6

*(Nearby towns also listed: McPherson, Newton)*

Founded in 1871 by the Reverend C. C. Hutchinson, Kansans call this mid-state city of 40,000 "Hutch"; another nickname is "Salt City," due to the vast salt deposits that lie in the earth under Reno County. The salt deposits are still mined by Cargill and Morton Salt companies, both major employers in the area. Hutchinson is the county seat and home to the Kansas State Fair, one of the best state fairs in the country. This is a progressive and modern community, although not as large as Wichita, Topeka, and other better-known Kansas towns.

Information: **Greater Hutchinson Convention/Visitors Bureau** | 117 N. Walnut, Hutchinson, KS 67501 | 316/662–3391 | info@hutchchamber.com | www.hutchchamber.com.

## Attractions

**Dillon Nature Center.** Wildflowers, perennials, and annuals provide natural beauty to walking trails, an arboretum, and wildlife sanctuary. | 3002 E. 30th St. | 316/663–7411 | www.hutchrec.com/DNC/dillon.htm | Free | Apr.–Oct., Mon.–Sat. 8–7, Sun. 1–5; Nov.–Mar., weekdays 8–5, Sat. 10–5, Sun. 1–5.

**Historic Fox Theatre.** This 1,200-seat auditorium has been fully restored to its 1931 art deco appearance and offers nightly live performances. | 18 E. 1st St. | 316/663–5861 | thefox@hutchinsonfox.com | $5–$50 | Weekdays 10–4.

**Hutchinson Art Center.** The permanent collection includes works by Sandzen, Raymer, Henry Varnum Poor, and Roualt, while rotating exhibits showcase the work of regional artists. | 405 N. Washington Ave. | 316/663–1081 | Free | Tues.–Fri. 9–5, weekends 2–4.

★ **Kansas Cosmosphere and Space Center.** One of the most comprehensive space museums in the world includes an IMAX Theater, planetarium, and laser-light shows, as well as a variety of teaching programs. | 1100 N. Plum St. | 316/662–2305 or 800/397–0330 | www.cosmo.org | $5 | Mon.–Sat. 9–9, Sun. noon–9.

**Reno County Museum.** Reno County history is interpreted through 35,000 pieces such as photographs and household items. | 100 S. Walnut St. | 316/662–1184 | fax 316/662–1184 | Donation accepted | Tues.–Sat. 9–5, Sun. 1–5.

## ON THE CALENDAR

**MAR.: *National Junior College Basketball Tournament.*** Some of the best basketball in the country is played right here during March madness. | 316/669–9846 | www.njcaa.org.

**APR.: *Mennonite Relief Sale.*** Homemade craft and food items are sold at this two-day event, established in 1978. There is also a breakfast and an auction of over 300 hand-made quilts. Proceeds from this fundraiser go to a variety of charitable organizations. | 316/662–3391.

**SEPT.: *Kansas State Fair.*** This 10-day "Party on the Prairie" includes concerts, auto racing, a rodeo, free entertainment, and traditional agriculture displays. | 316/669–3600 | www.kansasstatefair.com.

## Dining

★ **Anchor Inn.** Mexican. Dishes made with distinctive homemade flour tortillas are served in large brick-walled rooms in three older downtown buildings. Portions are generous. | 128 S. Main St. | 316/669–0311 | $2–$7 | Closed Sun. in mid-May–Oct. | AE, D, DC, MC, V.

**Carl's Bar and Deli.** American/Casual. This spot has been around since 1958, and still specializes in made-to-order deli sandwiches—although college students seem to love the nacho supreme. The Reuben sandwich is also a favorite: the meat is sliced but not grilled,

## USEFUL EXTRAS YOU MAY WANT TO PACK

- ❑ Adapters, converter
- ❑ Alarm clock
- ❑ Batteries
- ❑ Binoculars
- ❑ Blankets, pillows, sleeping bags
- ❑ Books and magazines
- ❑ Bottled water, soda
- ❑ Calculator
- ❑ Camera, lenses, film
- ❑ Can/bottle opener
- ❑ Cassette tapes, CDs, and players
- ❑ Cell phone
- ❑ Change purse with $10 in quarters, dimes, and nickels for tollbooths and parking meters
- ❑ Citronella candle
- ❑ Compass
- ❑ Earplugs
- ❑ Flashlight
- ❑ Folding chairs
- ❑ Guidebooks
- ❑ Luggage tags and locks
- ❑ Maps
- ❑ Matches
- ❑ Money belt
- ❑ Pens, pencils
- ❑ Plastic trash bags
- ❑ Portable TV
- ❑ Radio
- ❑ Self-seal plastic bags
- ❑ Snack foods
- ❑ Spare set of keys, not carried by driver
- ❑ Travel iron
- ❑ Travel journal
- ❑ Video recorder, blank tapes
- ❑ Water bottle
- ❑ Water-purification tablets

*Excerpted from Fodor's: How to Pack: Experts Share Their Secrets*
© 1997, by Fodor's Travel Publications

then served on a fresh rye bun. | 22 E. Second St. | 316/662–9875 | Reservations not accepted | Closed Sun. | $3–$4 | MC, V.

**Carriage Crossing.** Tucked away in an Amish community 8 mi south of Hutchinson at Rte. 96 and Yoder Rd., both the area and the food are worth the trip. Everything is homemade, including the cinnamon rolls and around 20 varieties of pie. Try cod filet, smoked sausage, fried chicken, sour cream raisin pie. Family-style service. | 10002 S. Yoder Rd. | 316/465–3612 | Closed Sun. | $6–$12 | D, MC, V.

**Roy's Hickory Pit BBQ.** Barbecue. This tiny restaurant seats 36 and serves barbecued pork spareribs, beef brisket, sausage, ham, and turkey. There's nothing else on the menu except beans, salad, and bread—but what more do you want? | 1018 W. 5th St. | 316/663–7421 | www.roys-bbq.com | Reservations not accepted | $6–$10 | Closed Sun., Mon. No supper | No credit cards.

## Lodging

**Astro Motel.** Clean, basic, and economical rooms are available in this centrally located, two-story, L-shaped motel. Some refrigerators, cable TV, pool, business services, pets allowed. | 15 E. Fourth St. | 316/663–1151 | fax 316/663–7169 | 30 rooms | $40.

**Comfort Inn.** Rooms are basic and reasonably priced. Both Amtrak and the Hutchinson Municipal Airport are within 2 mi of the motel. Complimentary Continental breakfast, in-room data ports, cable TV, pool, hot tub, business services, pets allowed. | 1621 Super Plaza | 316/663–7822 | fax 316/663–1055 | www.comfortinn.com | 63 rooms | $73 | AE, D, DC, MC, V.

**Hedrick's Exotic Animal Farm and Country Inn.** You can help feed giraffes, zebras, and kangaroos before bedtime in your animal-inspired room. Camel and pony rides are available. Complimentary breakfast. | 7910 N. Roy L. Smith Rd., Nickerson | 888/489–8039 | fax 316/422–3766 | www.hedricks.com | 5 rooms, 2 suites | $59–$75, $89–$100 suites | AE, D, MC, V.

**Quality Inn City Center.** This strip motel is 4 mi from the Hutchinson Municipal Airport and less than 1 mi from the Amtrak and bus depot stations. Restaurant, bar, in-room data ports, room service, cable TV, pool, business services, some pets allowed. | 15 W. 4th St. | 316/663–1211 or 800/228–5151 | fax 316/663–6636 | www.qualityinn.com | 98 rooms | $50 | AE, D, DC, MC, V.

★ **Ramada Inn Hutchinson.** Rooms in the "minidome" section of this busy convention hotel look out onto a quiet, landscaped courtyard. "Maindome" rooms open onto a recreation area with a swimming pool. Restaurant, bar, room service, in-room data ports, microwaves (in suites), refrigerators (in suites), cable TV, pool, hot tub, exercise room, laundry facilities, business services, some pets allowed (fee). | 1400 N. Lorraine St. | 316/669–9311 or 800/362–5018 | fax 316/669–9830 | www.ramada.com | 220 rooms, 6 suites | $74–$90, $100–$375 suites | AE, D, DC, MC, V.

**Wrought Iron Inn.** This three-story Prairie Victorian has oak crown molding, wainscoting, pocket doors, and large living rooms and foyer. Guest rooms are named after historic Hutchinson hotels, and are furnished with antiques such as marble-topped dressers and 1920s bedroom sets. The third floor is more casual and open, great for families or people travelling in a group. Dining room, complimentary breakfast, no room phones, no TV, TV in common area, business services, no pets, no smoking. | 1500 N. Main St. | 316/664–5975 | 5 rooms | $75–$90 | D, MC, V.

# INDEPENDENCE

MAP 3, J8

*(Nearby town also listed: Coffeyville)*

Founded in 1870 by a small group of explorers headed by R. W. Wright, Independence once had more millionaires per capita than any city in the country, thanks to the discovery of natural gas and oil in the surrounding region. Stately mansions and beautiful office buildings are testament to the wealth of those who once lived in this town of 10,000, such as Harry Sinclair of Sinclair Oil. Broadcast journalist Bill Kurtis and actress Vivian Vance of *I Love Lucy* also called Independence home. Kurtis still owns a cattle ranch in the area and often returns to visit family here.

Information: **Independence Chamber of Commerce** | 322 N. Penn St. (Box 386), Independence, KS 67301 | 316/331–1890 or 800/882–3606 | www.independencekschamber.org.

## Attractions

**DeFever-Osborn Drugs.** Owned by the town's mayor, this drugstore has many fixtures dating from the time of its opening in 1941. Don't miss having a treat at the working 1950s soda fountain, which is trimmed with old photographs of Independence. | 205 N. Penn Ave. | 316/331–4200 | Free | Weekdays 7:30–7:30, Sat. 7:30–6, Sun. 9–3.

**Elk City State Park.** This park, 5½ mi northwest of Independence off U.S. 160, is in the Osage Questas woodlands of southeastern Kansas, where thick oak-hickory woodlands meet rolling meadows of big blue stem and Indian grass. The landscape's prominent feature is a limestone bluff known as Table Mound. | 4825 Smallcreek Rd. | 316/331–6295 | www.kdwp.state.ks.us | $4 | Daily.

**Independence Museum.** Housed in the former post office, this museum has more than 20 rooms filled with antiques and art. | 8th and Myrtle Sts. | 316/331–3515 | $2 | Thurs.–Sat. 10–2.

**Independence Science and Technology Center.** An anti-gravity simulator is a fun attraction, but don't forget to have a conversation with Albert Einstein before you leave. | 125 S. Main St. | 316/331–1999 | $1.50 | Weekdays 1–5.

**Little House on the Prairie.** A reconstructed log cabin and one room school house are near the site once lived on by author Laura Ingalls Wilder and considered to be the inspiration for the famous TV series. | 13 mi southwest on U.S. 75 | 800/882–3606 | Donations accepted | Mid-May–Labor Day, Wed.–Sat. 10–5, Sun. 1–5.

**Riverside Park.** The city zoo, a miniature golf course, and a sports stadium are located in this 124-acre park. | Oak St. and Park Blvd. | 316/332–2512 | Free | Daily.

### ON THE CALENDAR

**OCT.: *"Neewollah."*** Spelled backwards, this downtown Halloween celebration lasts a full week and attracts thousands to its parades and parties. | 316/331–1890.

## Dining

**The Woods Food and Spirits.** American. Brick walls have mounted deer and elk, and the tasty food includes the popular fresh-cut steaks as well as pasta and chicken dishes. Try the twice-baked potato or chicken tortilla soups to start. | 300 N. Eighth St. | 316/331–7960. | Reservations not accepted | Closed Sun. | $8–$17 | AE, MC, V.

## Lodging

**Apple Tree Inn.** This two-story building is made with native sandstone, and its lobby includes a 40-ft oak cathedral ceiling. Complimentary Continental breakfast, in-room data ports, some refrigerators, cable TV, indoor pool, hot tub, business services, pets allowed. | 201 N. 8th St. | 316/331–5500 | fax 316/331–0641 | 64 rooms | $60 | AE, D, DC, MC, V.

**Best Western Prairie Inn.** A single-story motel, this Best Western is 5 mi from the Little House on the Prairie log cabin. Complimentary Continental breakfast, cable TV, pool, business services, some pets allowed (fee). | 3222 W. Main St. | 316/331–7300 | fax 316/331–8740 | www.best-western.com | 41 rooms | $52–$56 | AE, D, DC, MC, V.

**Microtel Inn and Suites.** This three-story hotel opened in March 2000 and is 2½ mi from Riverside Park and the city zoo. All rooms have queen-size beds and window seats, and suites have additional sofa sleepers and amenities that are useful for longer stays. Complimentary Continental breakfast, in-room data ports, some microwaves, some refrigerators, cable TV, business services, pets allowed. | 3021 W. Main St. | 316/331–0088 or 888/771–7171 | fax 316/331–5777 | www.microtel.com | 45 rooms, 22 suites | $50–$55, $61 suites | AE, D, DC, MC, V.

# IOLA

*(Nearby towns also listed: Chanute, Yates Center)*

Pro-slavery activists from the Fort Scott area founded this town in 1855 as Cofachique, in honor of an Indian chief. When Kansas became a free state, the town was renamed Iola, after the wife of the man who erected the town's first frame house. In 1871, a municipal band began hosting summer concerts in the square and has continued doing so on Thursday evenings ever since. A number of manufacturers (such as makers of rubber hoses, air brakes, and Russell Stover Candies) run their operations from this town of 6,400.

Information: **Iola Area Chamber of Commerce** | 208 W. Madison, Iola, KS 66749 | 316/365–5252 | chamber@iolaks.com | www.iolaks.com.

## Attractions

**Bowlus Fine Arts Center.** This 722-seat performing arts center hosts many activities throughout the year. | 205 E. Madison | 316/365–4765 | fax 316/365–4767 | www.bowlus-center.com | $10–$12 | Weekdays 8–4.

**Major General Frederick Funston Boyhood Home.** Built in 1860, this was the home of the child who grew up to serve John J. Pershing, Dwight D. Eisenhower, George Patton, and Douglas MacArthur. | 14 S. Washington | 316/365–3051 | Free | May–Sept., Wed.–Sat. 1:30–4:30.

**Old Jail Museum.** Built in 1869, this two-story jail housed both prisoners and the jailer's family. Graffiti from its day are still visible. | 207 N. Jefferson | 316/365–3051 | Free | May–Sept., Tues.–Sat. 1–4.

Housed in the old jail, stories of this area's legendary characters are told through photos and artifacts at the **Allen County Historical Museum Gallery.** | Donation accepted | May–Sept., Tues.–Sat. 1–4, or by appointment.

### ON THE CALENDAR

**AUG.: *Allen County Fair.*** For more than 100 years, visitors have enjoyed this fair's carnival, rodeo, music, and antique tractor pull. | 316/365–6513.
**SEPT.: *Buster Keaton Festival.*** This event is held in the Bowlus Fine Arts Center, and includes scholarly discussions of films, filmmakers, and the culture of the era when this native son was in Hollywood. | 316/365–4765 | www.bowluscenter.com.
**OCT.: *Farm City Days.*** The farmer and the cityfolk can be friends at this four-day event with a carnival, arts and crafts booths, and a parade with a "Partners in Progress" theme expressed through music, floats, and two marshals chosen from the farming and business communities. | 316/365–5252.

## Dining

**The Greenery.** American. A buffet is available for lunch and supper daily, and Sun.'s offerings include carved ham and roast beef. Try the fried chicken. Homemade pies, cinnamon rolls. Salad bar. | 1315 N. State St. | 316/365–7743 | No supper Sun. | $5–$14 | AE, D, MC, V.

## Lodging

**Best Western Inn.** This motel has basic rooms at affordable rates 5 mi from the Allen County airport, and 1½ mi from downtown. Restaurant, some refrigerators, cable TV, pool, business services. | 1315 N. State St. | 316/365–5161 | fax 316/365–6808 | www.bestwestern.com | 59 rooms | $48 | AE, D, DC, MC, V.

**Crossroads Motel.** The redbrick facade matches the fireplace bricks in an exceptionally warm and spacious lobby. Complimentary Continental breakfast, cable TV, pool, pets allowed. | 14 N. State St. | 316/365–2183 | fax 316/365–2183 | 54 rooms | $42 | AE, D, DC, MC, V.

**Hedgeapple Acres Bed and Breakfast.** Rooms at this county B&B have king-size beds and contemporary furnishings, and the grounds include more than 80 acres. Dinner is included, if you let your host know you'd like it. The B&B is 12 mi east of Iola on Rte. 54 in Moran. Complimentary breakfast, some in-room hot tubs, no room phones, no TV, TV in common area, 2 ponds, fishing, no pets, no smoking. | 4430 Rte. 54, Moran | 316/237–4646 | hedgeapple@aceks.com | www.aceks.com/hedgeapple | 4 rooms | $75–$85 | AE, D, MC, V.

# JUNCTION CITY

MAP 3, I5

*(Nearby towns also listed: Abilene, Manhattan)*

The Smoky Hill and Republican rivers intersect here, thus the town's name. Settled in 1855 by German, Scandinavian, and British pioneers, the area is dominated by the presence of Fort Riley, founded in 1852, and known then as the best cavalry training school in the country. Today, Fort Riley is home to the Big Red One, or the First Infantry Division of the U.S. Army. Approaching the city from along I-70, the base is an impressive sight, spreading as far as the eye can see. Because of its central location, this town of 17,000 is a distribution center for several major corporations.

Information: **Junction City Area Chamber of Commerce** | 425 N. Washington Ave. (Box 26), Junction City, KS 66441 | 785/762–2632 or 800/528–2489 | jccvb@flinthills.com | www.junctioncity.org.

## Attractions

**Buffalo Soldiers Memorial.** Completed in October 2000, this memorial commemorates the African-Americans of the 9th and 10th cavalry regiments posted to or near Fort Riley over an 80-year period. The horseshoe-shaped walk of honor and bronze statue stand near a 1940s-era housing area designated for the soldiers and their families during segregation, a few of whom still live there. | 18th St. and Buffalo Soldier Dr. | 785/238–2885 or 800/528–2489 | Free | Daily.

**Custer Hill Golf Course.** Opened in 1957, this 18-hole military course has good, wide, soft fairways. | 5202 Normandy Dr. | 785/239–5412 | Year-round.

**Fort Riley.** Established in 1852 to protect settlers and commerce along the Santa Fe and Oregon Trails, Fort Riley is now home to 10,500 military personnel, including a brigade of The Big Red One, America's fighting elite. | Public Affairs Officer, Building 405, Fort Riley | 785/239–6727 | fax 785/239–2592 | www.riley.army.mil | Free | By appointment.

Constructed in 1855 of native limestone, **Custer House** is the only surviving set of quarters from the fort's earliest history. | Building 24 | 785/239–6727 | Donation accepted | Memorial Day–Labor Day, Mon.–Sat. 9–4:30, Sun. noon–4:30.

Dedicated in 1992, the **1st Infantry Division Museum**'s exhibits document the division's history from 1917 to the present. | Building 207 | 785/239–6727 | Mon.–Sat. 9–4:30, Sun. noon–4:30.

The **First Territorial Capitol** was one of the casualties of the Civil War, as fraudulently elected legislators voted to move the capitol closer to Missouri, a slave state. | Building 693 | 785/784–5535 | Donation accepted | Thurs.–Sat. 10–5, Sun. 1–5.

As the first stone church in Kansas, the original **St. Mary's Chapel** was constructed by the Episcopalians in the mid-1850s. | Building 5 | 785/239–6727 | Donation accepted | By appointment.

The **U.S. Cavalry Museum** exhibits depict the colorful history of the American mounted horse soldier from the Revolutionary War through Operation Desert Storm. | Building 205 | 785/239–2743 | Donation accepted | Mon.–Sat. 9–4:30, Sun. noon–4:30.

**Geary County Historical Museum.** Rotating exhibits depicting early Native American through present day history are on display in this three-story native limestone building, which once served as the town's first high school. | Sixth and Adams Sts. | 785/238–666 | www.junctioncity.org/cvb/attract.html | Donations | Tues.–Sun. 1–4.

**Milford Lake.** With 16,000 surface acres, Milford Lake is the state's largest. The Nature Center has aquatic and terrestrial dioramas, live animal displays, nature trails, and one of the world's largest antique fishing lure collections. The lake is 4 mi northwest of Junction City via U.S. 77 and Rte. 57. | 8811 State Park Rd., Milford | 785/238–3014 | www.kdwp.state.ks.us | Free | Daily.

**Milford State Park.** The park contains more than 1,000 acres with 138 electrical hookup campsites, 17 full-service campsites, 10 boat ramp lanes, and a marina. The park is 5 mi northwest of Junction City on Rte. 57. | 8811 State Park Rd., Milford | 785/238–3014 | www.kdwp.state.ks.us | Free | Daily.

**Rolling Meadows Golf Course.** Opened in 1981, this 18-hole course is challenging but fun. | 7550 Old Milford Rd., Milford | 785/238–4303 | www.rollingmeadowsgc.com | Year-round.

### ON THE CALENDAR
**JUNE: *Music in the Park.*** Bring your lawn chairs and listen to local music every Thurs. with friends and neighbors. | 785/238–5560.
**SEPT. OR OCT.: *Apple Days.*** Enjoy 1800s crafts demonstrations, family entertainment, and everything good made from apples. | 785/239–6727.

## Dining
**Gasthaus Erika.** German. This warm and cozy restaurant has brick walls, old cabinets, and a hand-carved wooden bar, and will make you feel like you're dining in Germany. Chef Erika serves dishes such as her specialty schnitzel (breaded cutlet of veal or pork), served with sauces such as the slightly spicy *Zigeuner* (which includes red and green peppers), or the *Jager* (which incudes brown gravy and lots of mushrooms). Top it all off with a slice of Black Forest cake. | 610 N. Washington St. | 785/762–4614 | Closed Sun. | $7–$10 | D, MC, V.

**Peking Oriental.** Chinese. There are no surprises on the menu here, but as evidenced by the number of regulars, the food is respectable. Try Mongol beef (marinated in brown sauce and served over rice 'sticks'), sesame chicken. | 836 S. Washington St. | 785/238–2336. | Closed Mon. | $4–$12 | MC, V.

**Stacy's Restaurant.** American. In nearby Grandview Plaza (east of Junction City via Sixth St.), this mom-and-pop diner is popular with truckers, who stop in for the good homecooked meals. Try the fried chicken, meatloaf, or chili; for dessert, you might want the cheesecake, pudding, or applesauce. | 181 Flint Hills Blvd. | 785/238–3039 | No supper | $6–$8 | MC, V.

## Lodging
**Best Western Jayhawk.** Rooms in this modern building are comfortable and reasonably priced. The Junction City/Manhattan Airport is 12 mi away. Picnic area, complimentary Continental breakfast, some kitchenettes, some refrigerators, cable TV, pool, pets allowed. | 110 E. Flint Hills Blvd. | 785/238–5188 | fax 785/238–7585 | www.bestwestern.com | 48 rooms | $48 | AE, D, DC, MC, V.

**Days Inn.** Just off I–70, this Days Inn has the largest indoor pool of a motel in the city. Milford Lake, great for boating, fishing, and waterskiing, is 3 mi from the motel. Bar, complimentary Continental breakfast, cable TV, 2 pools (1 indoor), outdoor hot tub, video games, laundry facilities, business services, some pets allowed. | 1024 S. Washington St. | 785/762–2727 | fax 785/762–2751 | www.daysinn.com | 108 rooms | $46 | AE, D, DC, MC, V.

JUNCTION CITY

INTRO
ATTRACTIONS
DINING
LODGING

**Flagstop Resort and RV Park.** These modern cabins along Milford Lake are pleasant accommodations year-round. Single and two-bedroom cabins have carpeted bedrooms and a sofa-sleeper or futon. Ask to stay in the more secluded two-bedroom units that overlook the lake. The resort is 12 mi north of Junction City via Rte. 77, in Milford. Restaurant, picnic area, kitchenettes, some microwaves, refrigerators, cable TV, no room phones, no TV in some rooms, lake, hiking, beach, watersports, boating, fishing, playground, laundry facilities. | 8th and Whiting Sts., Milford, | 785/463–5537 or 800/293–1465 | fax 785/463–5313 | flagstop@flinthills.com | 12 cabins | $45–$85 | AE, D, MC, V.

**Golden Wheat Budget Host Inn.** Drive right up to your room at this strip motel, which has double beds and affordable rates. RV hook-ups are available. Cable TV. | 820 S. Washington St. | 785/238–5106 or 800/283–4678 | fax 785/223–6137 | www.budgethost.com | 20 rooms (6 with shower only) | $45 | AE, D, MC, V.

**Holiday Inn Express.** Built in 1997, this two-story motel is just off I–70, Exit 298. Complimentary Continental breakfast, in-room data ports, microwaves, refrigerators, cable TV, pool, hot tub, sauna, exercise equipment, laundry facilities, business services, pets allowed (fee). | 120 N. East St. | 785/762–4200 | fax 785/762–4219 | holidayinnexpress@oz-online.net | www.holiday-inn.com | 60 rooms, 5 suites | $69–$79, $89–$99 suites | AE, D, DC, MC, V.

**Super 8.** Here you'll find basic rooms 2 mi from Fort Riley and local shopping. Restaurant, bar, picnic area, complimentary Continental breakfast, in-room data ports, some refrigerators, room service, cable TV, pool, laundry facilities, business services, some pets allowed. | 1001 E. 6th St. | 785/238–8101 | fax 785/238–7470 | www.super8.com | 97 rooms | $50 | AE, D, DC, MC, V.

# KANSAS CITY

MAP 3, L4

*(Nearby towns also listed: Bonner Springs, Lawrence, Leavenworth, Overland Park, Shawnee)*

In 1869, Kansas City was founded in the bottom lands lying along the Kansas/Missouri state line. Kansas City is known locally as KCK, so as to be distinguished from its larger counterpart of the same name on the Missouri side of the river. KCK developed simultaneously with the Missouri city; although state and local governments separate the two, little more than the boundary of the Kaw River as it dumps into the Missouri separates the history and activities of the people who live in each state. Several automobile-manufacturing plants have found a productive home on the Kansas side, in an area where B-52 bombers were manufactured during World War II.

The stockyards and other agricultural influences are a little stronger on the Kansas side of the river, and the European immigrant and Native American cultures have become less diversified than in Missouri. This results in some rich pockets of heritage, ethnic food, and impressive architecture throughout the 111 square mi of KCK and Wyandotte County. Although Kansas City, Missouri, is known as the home of American jazz, legendary saxophonist Charlie Parker was born and raised in KCK. Other famous folks to call this city of 150,000 home include actors Ed Asner, Dee Wallace Stone, and Lyle Wagoner, and athlete Maurice Greene, who is considered to be the world's fastest human.

Information: **Kansas City Convention and Visitor's Bureau** | 727 Minnesota Ave. (Box 171337), Kansas City, KS 66117 | 913/321–5800 or 800/264–1563 | www.kckcvb.org.

## Attractions

**The Children's Museum of Kansas City.** This hands-on learning center is in the lower level of Indian Springs Marketplace and has more than 40 discovery-based exhibits that teach chemistry, physics, and art. | 4601 State Ave., at the intersection of I–635N and State Ave. | 913/287–8888 | www.kidmuzm.org | $3 | Tues.–Sat. 9:30–5, Sun. 1–5.

**Grinter Place State Historic Site.** This 1857 farmhouse, possibly the oldest in the state, was home to the first white settler in KCK, who established a ferry across the Kansas River. | 1420 S. 78th St. | 913/299–0373 | www.kckcvb.org | Donations accepted | Wed.–Sat. 10–5, Sun. 1–5.

**Huron Indian Cemetery.** This cemetery was established in 1843 after the forced migration of the Wyandot Nation from their homes. The dead were carried to sacred ground, a high point overlooking the meeting of two rivers. | Huron Park, Center City Plaza, between 6th and 7th Sts. | 913/321–5800 | Free | Daily.

**Strawberry Hill Cultural Museum.** This Queen Anne–style house is home to several artifacts celebrating the Eastern European immigrants who settled here. | 720 N. 4th St. | 913/371–3264 | $4 | Weekends noon–5.

**White Church Christian Church.** Built in 1832 as a white clapboard building, today this native stone building is the state's oldest church still in operation. Its stained glass windows are worth a visit. | 2200 N. 85th St. | 913/299–4056 | Free | Daily 6–6.

### ON THE CALENDAR

**MAY:** *Polski Day.* A parade and street festival in the Strawberry Hill neighborhood celebrate the Polish heritage of the area. | 913/371–4203.

**AUG.:** *Croatian Festival.* Ethnic foods, folk dances, and information booths celebrate the region's Croatian heritage. | 913/371–0627.

## Dining

**Jun's.** Japanese. Lanterns, incense, and bamboo chairs create an authentic feel. Known for sushi and teriyaki tempura. | 7660 State Line Rd., Prairie Village | 913/341–4924 | Closed Sun. | $10–$20 | AE, MC, V.

## Lodging

**Best Western Inn and Conference Center.** Built in the early 1980s, this two-story motel is 2 mi from downtown Kansas City. A handful of restaurants are within two blocks of the motel. Restaurant, bar, complimentary Continental breakfast, in-room data ports, room service, cable TV, pool, sauna, exercise equipment, laundry facilities, business services, airport shuttle. | 501 Southwest Blvd. | 913/677–3060 or 800/368–1741 | fax 913/362–0540 | www.bestwestern.com | 113 rooms | $69–$79 | AE, D, MC, V.

**Comfort Inn.** Built in 1999, this pleasant brown and beige stucco three-story hotel has attractive rooms with modern furnishings. It's conveniently located off I–70 and 78th St. (Exit 414). Complimentary Continental breakfast, in-room data ports, some microwaves, some refrigerators, some in-room hot tubs, cable TV, pool, exercise equipment, business services, no pets. | 234 N. 78th St. | 913/299–5555 | fax 913/299–5505 | vrkc@aol.com | www.comfortinn.com/hotel/ks053 | 40 rooms, 5 suites | $70–$100, $100–$150 suites | AE, D, MC, V.

**Walnut Hill Farm Bed and Breakfast.** The grounds of this 5-acre estate have wild blackberries and walnut trees. Guest rooms contain American works of fine art and antiques. Complimentary breakfast, pool, hot tub. | 10326 Richland Ave., Edwardsville | 913/422–7725 | fax 913/422–7725 | tinberg@walnuthillfarm.com | 4 rooms | $89–$125 | MC, V.

# LARNED

MAP 3, E6

*(Nearby town also listed: Great Bend)*

With the opening of the trade route from Missouri to Santa Fe in 1821, white traffic through Kansas created the need for a military post, which resulted in the construction of Fort Larned. The town of Larned is now a mecca for history buffs studying the Old West. The downtown shopping district and many Victorian homes have been preserved, making this a true step back in time along the Santa Fe Trail. Just as it did more than 100 years ago, agriculture continues to dominate the area's economy, although health care and tourism also generate a number of employment opportunities here.

Information: **Larned Area Chamber of Commerce** | 502 Broadway, Larned, KS 67550 | 316/285–6916 | fax 316/285–6917 | chamber@larned.net | www.larned.net.

## Attractions

**Fort Larned National Historic Site.** Known as the guardian of the Santa Fe Trail, many of the fort's buildings are original military structures. The fort is 6 mi west of Larned on U.S. 156. | Rte. 3 | 316/285–6911 | fax 316/285–3571 | www.nps.gov/fols | $2 | Daily 8:30–5.

★ **Santa Fe Trail Center.** See a portion of the original wagon ruts made by emigrants on this route, as well as tepees and other artifacts from the 60 years of this commerce trail. The center is 2 mi west of Larned on U.S. 156. | RR 3 | 316/285–2054 | www.larned.net/trailctr/ | $3 | Memorial Day–Labor Day, daily 9–5; Labor Day–Memorial Day, Tue.–Sun. 9–5.

**Sibley's Camp.** These bluffs were the campsite of George C. Sibley's survey team, which in 1825 commenced to oversee a survey of the Santa Fe Trail. The camp is described in Sibley's journal and diaries as "Cliffs of Soft Rock." | 502 W. Second St., at State St. | 316/285–6916 | Free | Daily.

### ON THE CALENDAR

**MAR.: *Antique Show and Sale.*** Dealers from four states sell antiques and collectibles. | 316/285–6916.

**MAY: *Santa Fe Trail Days.*** A parade, crafts show, and demonstration bring the Santa Fe Trail to life. | 800/747–6919.

## Dining

**Burgerteria.** American. This is a popular place for burgers, homemade fries, and ice cream dishes. Kids' menu. | 417 W. 14th St. | 316/285–3135 | Breakfast also available | $4–$8 | No credit cards.

**Harvest Inn.** American. Chicken, steaks, and seafood are on the menu at this family restaurant; pub grub is served in the accompanying bar, the Grain Club. | 718 Ft. Larned Ave. | 316/285–3870 | $5–$14 | MC, V.

**Papa's Family Restaurant.** American. Housed in an old historic train station, this restaurant has a full menu as well as lunch and supper buffets that include up to 20 entrées. Regulars love the barbecue, catfish, and prime rib, and rave over the sweet oatmeal pie made from a secret family recipe. Homemade desserts. Salad bar. | 320 Broadway | 316/285–0055 | $6–$12 | No credit cards.

## Lodging

**Arch River Inn Bed and Breakfast.** This contemporary lodging is housed in a geodesic dome on 150 acres of countryside 1½ mi northeast of Larned. You can hike and birdwatch, or walk to the Arkansas River for fishing or relaxation. A country breakfast is available upon request, and snacks are served in the evening. No room phones, TV in common area, hiking, fishing, no smoking. | MM 185 on Rte. 156 | 316/546–5847 | 4 rooms | $50–$75 | No credit cards.

**Best Western Townsman Inn.** Basic rooms and amenities can be found at this motel, 2 mi from the Santa Fe Trail Center and 6 mi from Ft. Larned. Complimentary Continental breakfast, in-room data ports, cable TV, pool, business services, pets allowed. | 123 E. 14th St. | 316/285–3114 | fax 316/285–7139 | www.bestwestern.com | 44 rooms | $48–$59 | AE, D, DC, MC, V.

**Country Inn.** This simple "mom and pop" motel excels in cleanliness and hospitality. Cable TV. | 135 E. 14th St. | 316/285–3216 | 16 rooms | $22–$40 | AE, D, MC, V.

# LAWRENCE

*(Nearby towns also listed: Bonner Springs, Kansas City, Leavenworth, Shawnee)*

This great university town was founded in 1854 by the New England Emigrant Aid Company and named after Amos A. Lawrence, a leading supporter of the society, which sponsored migration to Lawrence. The area became the scene of much strife between pro- and anti-slavery forces. William C. Quantrill and his band of Confederate guerrillas raided Lawrence on the morning of August 21, 1863, leaving the town in ruins. The growth of the University of Kansas has established this city of 81,000 as a leading educational, medical, and sports center for the Midwest.

Information: **Lawrence Chamber of Commerce** | 734 Vermont Ave., Suite 101, Lawrence, KS 66044 | 785/865–4411 | www.visitlawrence.com.

## Attractions

**Baker University.** This private liberal arts college, associated with the Methodist Church, has a renowned school of nursing. | 618 8th St., Baldwin City | 785/594–6451 | fax 785/594–2522 | www.bakeru.edu | Free | Daily.

**The Bottleneck.** This popular nightclub is known beyond the state's borders. It has an old hardwood floor, and pool can be played for free every night until 9; afterwards, live musical performances by mostly local bands and general good-natured pandemonium take over. A trivia show is held on Sun., and Mon. is host to an open mic. | 737 New Hampshire St. | 785/842–5483 | $3–$12 | 3 PM–2 AM.

**Clinton State Park.** This 1,500-acre park is popular with hikers, campers, and horseback riders. The 7,000-acre Clinton Reservoir, which is further surrounded by 11,000 acres of wildlife, is great for swimming, fishing, and boating. Deer, rabbit, and nesting bald eagles all make for great photographs. | 798 N. 1415 Rd. | 785/842–8562 | www.kdwp.state.ks.us | Free | Daily.

**Haskell Indian Nations University.** Drawing upon the Sacred Circle as the foundation for Native American/Alaska Native philosophy, Haskell provides higher education to federally recognized tribal members. | 155 Indian Ave. | 785/749–8404 | fax 785/749–8406 | www.haskell.edu | Free | Daily.

**Lawrence Arts Center.** Housed in the 1904 Carnegie Library building downtown, the Center is the hub of arts activities and information in Lawrence. | 200 W. 9th St. | 785/843–2787 | fax 785/843–6629 | Free | Mon.–Thurs. 9–8, Fri. 9–5, Sat. 9–3.

**University of Kansas.** This school of 30,000 students is renowned for its National Championship basketball team, the Jayhawks, as well as its schools of medicine (with facilities in metropolitan Kansas City), architecture, journalism, and law. | 230 Strong Hall | 785/864–2700 | www.ukans.edu | Free | Daily.

**Watkins Community Museum.** This 1888 three-story brick building houses exhibits and artifacts relating to the area's history. | 1047 Massachusetts St. | 785/841–4109 | wcmhist@sunflower.com | Free | Tues.–Sat. 10–4; Sun. 1:30–4.

### ON THE CALENDAR

**MAY:** *Art to Go.* Sponsored by the Lawrence Art Commission, this annual parade is for souped-up vehicles of every variety, with participants ranging from local artists to college students. The parade coincides with the yearly Art in the Park Art Fair, in South Park at 11th and Massachusetts Sts. | 785/865–4411.

**AUG.:** *Douglas County Free Fair.* Extensive 4-H exhibits, music, carnival activities, and a variety of races and contests make this fairground event fun for everyone. | 785/843–7058.

**SEPT.–OCT.:** *Indian Arts Show.* This outdoor market includes authentic Native American food, artist demonstrations, and entertainment. | 785/864–4245 | www.ukans.edu/~lias/.

## Dining

**Fifi's Nabil.** Continental. This upscale restaurant is one of this college town's best. Try the steak Diane (a 6-oz tenderloin steak grilled with brown burgundy, capers, and mushrooms), lobster fettuccine, or the fresh seafood. | 925 Iowa St. (U.S. 59) | 785/841–7226 | No lunch weekends | $16–$26 | AE, D, MC, V.

★ **Free State Brewing Co.** American. Opened in 1989, this was Kansas's first legal brew pub. There are often good specials, or you can try the fish-and-chips or black bean quesadillas. Tours of the brewery are available on Saturday by request. | 636 Massachusetts St. | 785/843–4555 | www.freestatebrewing.com | Reservations not accepted | $7–$15 | AE, D, DC, MC, V.

**La Familia.** Mexican. The atmosphere here is traditional Mexican, choices on the large menu are well executed, and you can order beer or soda to accompany your meal. After starting with good guacamole and chips, continue with chilies rellenos (cheese-stuffed peppers), the supersanchos (beef or chicken, beans, lettuce, cheese, and tomato topped with cheese sauce and sour cream), or the La Familia special (an enchilada, taco, tostada, with rice and beans). | 733 New Hampshire St. | 785/749–0105 | $4–$12 | AE, D, MC, V.

**Pachamama's New World Cuisine.** Contemporary. Known for its excellent wine list and unique dishes, this restaurant is west of downtown Lawrence, in a elegant, airy space with vaulted ceilings and lots of light. The menu rotates monthly, and includes fresh and seasonal meals beautifully presented yet unpretentious. Past dishes have included grilled filet of ostrich with Yukon Gold potatoes, rosemary, garlic, fresh peas, and pancetta; and roasted ginger-tea breast of chicken with grilled peaches and crimini mushrooms. Open-air dining is available on a patio overlooking the nearby woods and golf course. | 2161 Quail Creek Dr. | 785/841–0990 | dine@pachamamas.com | www.pachamamas.com | No lunch weekends | $15–$22 | AE, D, MC, V.

**Teller's Restaurant.** Contemporary. This downtown restaurant serves Italian-influenced cuisine in a turn-of-the-century bank building with a fun and funky interior (the rest rooms are in the vault). For starters, try the signature dish: mushroom caps filled with chicken and spinach sausage with gruyère cheese; next try the brie-stuffed filet mignon with port wine reduction sauce and shallot mashed potatoes. The restaurant also does a brisk cocktail business; the bar is open until 2 AM. | 746 Massachusetts St. | 785/843–4111 | $12–$25 | AE, D, C, MC, V.

## Lodging

**Best Western Hallmark Inn.** Just 2 mi from both downtown Lawrence and the University of Kansas, this motel is within walking distance of local restaurants and entertainment. Complimentary Continental breakfast, in-room data ports, cable TV, pool, laundry facilities, business services, some pets allowed. | 730 Iowa St. (U.S. 59) | 785/841–6500 | fax 785/841–6612 | www.bestwestern.com | 60 rooms | $95 | AE, D, DC, MC, V.

**Bismarck Inn.** Photos throughout the lobby and hallways relate local history. An outlet shopping mall is across the street. Complimentary Continental breakfast, cable TV, laundry facilities. | 1130 N. 3rd St. | 785/749–4040 or 800/665–7466 | fax 785/749–3016 | 53 rooms | $60–$64 | AE, D, MC, V.

**Circle S Guest Ranch and Country Inn.** Built in 1998, this new yet cozy country inn is on a working buffalo and cattle ranch from the late 1800s. Spend your day on a ramble through the 1,200-acre grounds, then relax on the porch with a view of the hillside, or in the spacious common areas before ordering supper at the first-rate restaurant. Rooms are decorated in a simple, slightly rustic style with accents like wrought iron furniture and fireplaces. Complimentary breakfast, in-room data ports, some in-room hot tubs, no TV, 20 ponds, hiking, fishing, bicycles. | 3325 Circle S Ln. | 785/843–4124 | fax 785/843–4474 | www.circlesranch.com | 12 rooms | $140–$195 | AE, D, DC, MC, V.

**Days Inn.** This motel is adjacent to the University of Kansas and 5 mi from the downtown area. Complimentary Continental breakfast, in-room data ports, cable TV, pool, hot tub, laundry facilities, business services, some pets allowed. | 2309 Iowa St. (U.S. 59) | 785/843–9100 | fax 785/843–1572 | www.daysinn.com | 101 rooms | $80 | AE, D, DC, MC, V.

★ **Eldridge Hotel.** Built in 1855 as a Free State hostelry for abolitionists and listed on the National Register of Historic Places, this downtown hotel's location means some traffic noise but great convenience. Guest suites are pleasantly decorated in a blithe, basic style; rooms on the top (fifth) floor have great views. Restaurant, bar, room service, refrigerators, cable TV, barbershop, beauty salon, hot tub, business services. | 701 Massachusetts St. | 785/749–5011 or 800/527–0909 | fax 785/749–4512 | www.eldridgehotel.com | 48 suites | $78–$235 | AE, D, DC, MC, V.

**Halcyon House.** This 1885 European-style Victorian inn is on the northeast edge of the University of Kansas campus and just 3 blocks from downtown. Lovely gardens and an atrium dining area are complemented by antiques-filled rooms. Complimentary breakfast, in-room data ports, no TV in some rooms, kids over 12 only. | 1000 Ohio St. | 785/841–0314 or 888/441–0314 | fax 785/843–7273 | halcyonh@aol.com | www.thehalcyonhouse.com | 8 rooms (4 with shared bath) | $47–$89 | AE, MC, V.

**Hampton Inn.** This chain hotel was built in July 1996 and is across the street from Centennial Park. Rooms are spacious, and there is an outdoor patio off the pool area where you can relax. Complimentary Continental breakfast, in-room data ports, some microwaves, some refrigerators, some in-room hot tubs, cable TV, pool, hot tub, exercise equipment, business services, no pets. | 2300 W. 6th St. | 785/841–4994 or 800/426–7866 | fax 785/841–7997 | www.hampton-inn.com | 83 rooms, 6 suites | $70–$110, $100–$125 suites | AE, D, DC, MC, V.

**Holiday Inn.** This motel has exterior entrances and is 2 mi from downtown and the University of Kansas. Restaurant, bar, room service, cable TV, pool, hot tub, exercise equipment, video games, laundry facilities, business services, pets allowed. | 200 McDonald Dr. | 785/841–7077 | fax 785/841–2799 | www.holiday-inn.com | 192 rooms, 12 suites | $90–$102 | AE, D, DC, MC, V.

**Victorian Veranda Country Inn.** On a 57-acre working farm 1 mi north of Lawrence, this 1998 Victorian-style house has plenty of common space for guests, including the signature wraparound veranda. Rooms are cozy yet roomy, with wrought iron beds. Complimentary breakfast, library, no smoking, no pets. | 1431 N. 1900 Rd. | 785/841–1265 | vvcinn@aol.com | www.vvcountryinn.com | 10 rooms | $110 | MC, V.

**Westminster Inn.** This comfortable brick and stucco inn has a warm lobby with cathedral ceilings and heavy-wood beams. Cable TV, pool, pets allowed. | 2525 W. 6th St. | 785/841–8410 or 888/937–8646 | fax 785/841–1901 | 60 rooms, 12 suites | $63, $73 suites | AE, D, DC, MC, V.

# LEAVENWORTH

MAP 3, K4

*(Nearby towns also listed: Atchison, Bonner Springs, Kansas City, Shawnee)*

Established in 1854 by the U.S. military, Leavenworth, the "First City in Kansas," is on the west banks of the Missouri River and is home to the United States Federal Penitentiary. Ft. Leavenworth is the oldest fort west of the Mississippi River in continuous service and creates a transient, military culture for much of the city. The fort has numerous attractions and interesting artifacts, as well as beautiful grounds on the banks of the Missouri River open for the public. The fort and federal prison provide many jobs for civilian and military personnel in the region. Hallmark Cards also operates a large distribution center in this town of 43,000.

**Information: Leavenworth/Lansing Convention Visitors Bureau** | 518 Shawnee St. (Box 44), Leavenworth, KS 66048 | 913/682–4113 or 800/844–4114 | lvcvb@lvnworth.com | www.lvarea.com/chamber/lv_cvb.htm.

## Attractions

**Carroll Museum.** Built in 1867, this home features elaborate handcrafted woodwork, stained-glass windows, and antiques from the Victorian Age era and the early 20th century. | 1128 5th Ave. | 913/682–7759 | $2.50 | May–Aug., Tues.–Sat. 10:30–4:30, Sun. 1–430; Sept.–Apr., Tues.–Sun. 1–4:30.

**Fort Leavenworth.** Established in 1827, this is the oldest Army fort in continuous operation west of the Mississippi River. Branches of the Oregon and Santa Fe trails traverse the fort. Some of the highlights include the National Cemetery, Command and General Staff College, Memorial Chapel, Main Post Chapel, and the Buffalo Soldiers Memorial. | 600 Thomas Ave., Unit 10 | 913/684–5604 | fax 913/684–3624 | leav-www.army.mil/ | Free | Daily 10–4.

**Fred Harvey Museum.** The home of this famous restaurateur from the 1860s includes one of the railroad dining cars he initiated. | 624 Olive St. | 913/682–1866 | $2 | Fri.–Sat. 10–4.

**Parker Carousel.** This 1913 Parker Carousel has all hand-carved animals, including two rabbits, 24 horses, three ponies, one chariot, and a lovers' cup. The carousel is presently at 743 Delaware St., but is expected to move to Choctaw and Esplanade Sts. in mid 2001. | 743 Delaware St. | 913/682–4113 | Free | Daily.

### ON THE CALENDAR

**APR.:** *Great American Yard Sale.* As military families receive orders for reassignment, others camp out at the fort's gates for days to get first dibs on great yard sale bargains. | 913/684–5604, ext. 5.
**SEPT.:** *Leavenworth River Fest.* Concerts, crafts, food, and more make a walk along the historic riverfront downtown an entertaining event. | 913/682–3924.

## Dining

**Oasis Cafe.** Mediterranean. The clean-lined and attractive dining area is dominated by leaded glass chandeliers, with pink hammered-brass plaques on the walls and wood furnishings. Open air dining is available in the garden, where Chef Mohamed gets his fresh herbs for the French-influenced Mediterranean cuisine. Begin your meal with the famous hummus, then try the Delta filet (shrimp, scallops, and crab in a cream sauce served over charbroiled tenderloin), or the rack of lamb with wine sauce, almonds, and onions. | 604 Cherokee St. | 913/772–0888 | Closed Sun., Mon. | $7–$22 | AE, D, DC, MC, V.

## Lodging

**Best Western Hallmark Inn.** Kansas City International Airport is 15 mi from this two-story motel, and Ft. Leavenworth is just 4 mi away. There are a couple of fast food joints and chain restaurants within walking distance. Complimentary Continental breakfast, in-room data ports, cable TV, pool, laundry facilities, business services. | 3211 S. 4th St. (U.S. 73) | 913/651–6000 | fax 913/651–7722 | www.bestwestern.com | 52 rooms | $62 | AE, D, DC, MC, V.

**The Prairie Queen Bed and Breakfast.** Built in 1868, this stately B&B takes its name from a Missouri River riverboat once docked at Leavenworth. All rooms have a king-size bed and private bath; two have a private porch. You may choose to eat in the dining room, or outdoors under the pergola overlooking the garden and pond. Dining room, complimentary breakfast, no room phones, no TV, TV in common area, hot tub, no pets, no smoking. | 221 Arch St. | 913/758–1959 | prairiequeen@attglobal.net | 3 rooms | $75–$110 | MC, V.

**Ramada Inn.** This motel in the heart of downtown Leavenworth has exterior entrances and is 1 mi southeast of Fort Leavenworth. Restaurant, bar, room service, cable TV, pool, business services, some pets allowed. | 101 S. 3rd St. | 913/651–5500 | fax 913/651–6981 | www.ramada.com | 97 rooms | $64 | AE, D, DC, MC, V.

# LIBERAL

MAP 3, C8

*(Nearby town also listed: Meade)*

As settlers passed through this area in the 1800s, they were frequently offered free water from a homesteader who had made his home in this uninhabitably dry region. "That's mighty liberal of you," they would respond to his gesture of kindness, and thus the town that eventually sprouted here in 1888 was named. Discovery of natural gas under the prairie in the 1920s brought an influx of residents, but cattle remain the primary inhabitants of this area. Home to 19,000 residents, this town is known worldwide for its challenging pancake race against the women of Olney, England. More importantly, however, Liberal was made the official home of Dorothy Gale from *The Wizard of Oz* in 1961, when the local attraction "Dorothy's House" was built here.

Information: **Liberal Convention and Tourism Bureau** | 1 Yellowbrick Rd., Liberal, KS 67901 | 800/542–3725 | www.liberal.net.

## Attractions

**Cimarron National Grassland.** This 108,000-acre tract is the largest area of public land in Kansas, offering outdoor experiences for campers, hikers, and hunters. Elk and antelope are often seen grazing here. | 242 U.S. 56 E, Elkhart | 316/697–4621 | fax 316/697–4340 | www.fs.fed.us/grasslands/ | Free | Daily.

**Coronado Museum.** A search for the Seven Golden Cities of Cíbola brought Spanish explorers here in the 1500s. The items on display tell the story of the pioneers who arrived and settled Seward County. | 567 E. Cedar St. | 316/624–7624 | Free | Memorial Day–Labor Day, Mon.–Sat. 10–5, Sun. 1–5; Labor Day–Memorial Day, Tues.–Sat. 10–5, Sun. 1–5.

**Dorothy's House.** A walkthrough Oz exhibit and memorabilia from *The Wizard of Oz* are on display. | 567 E. Cedar St. | 316/624–7624 | $5 | Memorial Day–Labor Day, Mon.–Sat. 10–5, Sun. 1–5; Labor Day–Memorial Day, Tues.–Sat. 10–5, Sun. 1–5.

**Mid-America Air Museum.** Includes more than 90 aircraft, as well as many hands-on exhibits and a wind tunnel. | 2000 W. 2nd St. | 316/624–5263 | www.airmuseum.net | $5 | Mon.–Sat. 10–5, Sun. 1–5.

### ON THE CALENDAR
**FEB. OR MAR.: *International Pancake Race.*** On Fat Tuesday each year, the women of Liberal race 415 yards with a pancake-filled skillet in hand, and compete against women in Olney, England, where the 500-year-old tradition was born. The race in Liberal is down Kansas Ave. | 316/626–0170 | www.pancakeday.com.
**AUG.: *Five-State Free Fair.*** Exhibitors from Oklahoma, Texas, New Mexico, Colorado, and Kansas display their products and talents. | 316/624–3743.
**SEPT.: *Mid-America Airshow.*** Highlights of this event include planes flying in formation, fast military jets, wing walkers, an evening dance, and fireworks. Special acts include the Flying Elvises—impersonators of the "King" who parachute jump for hordes of adoring fans. | 316/624–5263.
**OCT.: *Oztoberfest.*** Click your heels, fly through a tornado, and experience all of the magic of *The Wizard of Oz* in this three-day festival. | 316/624–7624.

## Dining
**King's Pit Bar-B-Q.** Barbecue. The extremely simple decor is appropriate when the food commands all your attention. Known for family-style barbecue, steak, and seafood. Family-style service. Kids' menu. | 355 E. Pancake Blvd. (U.S. 54) | 316/624–2451 | Closed Sun. | $7–$14 | AE, D, MC, V.

**Salty Dog Bar and Grill.** American. Known for steak, shrimp, and specialty sandwiches, this place has something for everyone. And don't forget its namesake: an enormous ½ pound hotdog served with your choice of sauerkraut, chili, onions, cheese, or relish. Kids' menu. | 1010 S. Kansas St. | 316/626–4444 | saltydog@swecom.com | 204.233.65.165/saltydog | Closed Sun. | $5–$17 | AE, D, MC, V.

## Lodging

**Bluebird Inn Bed and Breakfast.** This 1950s ranch-style house is surrounded by a wrought iron fence and flanked by large old elm trees. Rooms are comfortable and homey, with hanging quilts, lots of pillows, and nightstands. You can enjoy your breakfast in the formal dining room, the garden room, or on the deck. Dining room, complimentary breakfast, some in-room hot tubs, some room phones, no TV in some rooms, TV in common area, laundry facilities, no smoking. | 221 W. Sixth St. | 316/624–0720 | fax 316/626–6474 | 4 rooms | $60–$80 | AE, MC, V.

**Gateway Inn.** For a rather small town, this inn has very modern, high-tech facilities for meetings and conferences. Restaurant, bar, picnic area, in-room data ports, cable TV, pool, tennis, laundry facilities, business services, airport shuttle, some pets allowed. | 720 E. Pancake Blvd. (U.S. 54) | 316/624–0242 or 800/833–3391 | fax 316/624–1952 | 101 rooms | $46 | AE, D, DC, MC, V.

**Liberal Inn.** This two-story stone building was built in the mid 1960s and is across the street from Dorothy's House. Restaurant, picnic area, in-room data ports, room service, cable TV, pool, hot tub, laundry facilities, airport shuttle, pets allowed. | 603 E. Pancake Blvd. (U.S. 54) | 316/624–7254 or 800/458–4667 | fax 316/624–7254 | 123 rooms | $48–$53 | AE, D, DC, MC, V.

# LINDSBORG

MAP 3, G6

*(Nearby towns also listed: Ellsworth, McPherson, Salina)*

Swedish immigrants arrived in the Smoky Valley area in 1869, bent on establishing a cooperative farming community, as well as cultivating their religion and appreciation for the arts. The first church and Bethany College were constructed before many of the homes, and within the first few years a traditional performance of Handel's *Messiah* had begun during Holy Week. Many in this community of 3,000 still speak fluent Swedish, and many of the festivals are true to their Old World origins. Farming is still the predominant source of income for people in the area, although the cooperative communal approach vanished decades ago.

Information: **Lindsborg Chamber of Commerce** | 104 E. Lincoln St., Lindsborg, KS 67456 | 785/227–3706 or 888/227–2227 | www.lindsborg.org.

## Attractions

**Birger Sandzen Memorial Art Gallery.** The brilliant pastel-colored oil paintings, lithographs, and crayon drawings of the Swedish American painter fill three galleries on the south edge of Bethany College's campus. | 401 N. 1st St. | 785/227–2220 | www.sandzen.org | Free | Wed.–Sun. 1–5; Jun.–Aug, Tues.–Sun. 1–5.

**Kanopolis State Park.** Kansas's first state park has a fishing lake, 26 mi of hiking trails, and more than 5,000 acres of wildlife. The park is in Marquette, 19 mi west of Lindsborg on Rte. 4, then 7 mi north on Rte. 141. | 200 Horsethief Rd., Marquette | 785/546–2565 | www.kdwp.state.ks.us | Free | Daily.

**McPherson County Old Mill Museum and Park.** Two buildings on the National Register of Historic Places and the 1904 Swedish Pavilion from the World's Fair tell the history of this community. | 120 Mill St. | 785/227–3595 | fax 785/227–2810 | $2 | Mon.–Sat. 9–5, Sun. 1–5.

**REO Auto Museum.** A 1920s-style service station houses the first line REO cars and other vintage automobiles. | Harrison-Cole St. | 785/227–3252 | www.reoautomuseum.com | Donation accepted | Daily 1–4.

**Stenfors Mansion.** A local familiy named Stenfors still occupies this elegant, early 1900s Victorian mansion, which has original Swedish furnishings. | 119 N. 2nd St. | 785/227–4456 | $6 | Daily, by appointment.

## ON THE CALENDAR

**MAR. OR APR.: *Messiah Festival*.** A 350-voice choir perform Handel's *Messiah* and Bach's *St. Matthew Passion* to sold out performances during Holy Week. | 785/227–3311.
**JUNE: *Midsummer's Day Festival*.** This Swedish festival celebrates the longest day of the year with dancing, music, food, and crafts. | 888/227–2227.
**OCT.: *Svensk Hyllingsfest*.** This three-day tribute to the Swedish pioneers who settled the Lindsborg area is held every other year (2001). The celebration includes performances of Swedish folk music and dance, smorgasbords in three different locations, a parade, arts and crafts, and more. | 785/227–3706 or 888/227–2227 | www.lindsborg.org.
**DEC.: *Lucia Fest*.** The first Saturday of December celebrates the arrival of Santa with street dances, food, and the crowning of St. Lucia in an Old World religious ceremony. | 888/227–2227.

## Dining

**Brunswick Hotel.** Continental. Built in 1887, this Victorian hotel and restaurant serves elegant as well as casual meals in two dining rooms. Try the poached salmon with white wine and lemon. Salad bar. Kids' menu. Sun. brunch. | 202 S. Main St. | 785/227–2903 | Reservations essential weekdays | No lunch Sat. | $7–$14 | AE, D, MC, V.

**Courtyard Bakery.** American/Casual. The open dining area was created to resemble a city street in Old Stockholm, complete with brick floor. It's known for fresh deli-style sandwiches, homemade soup, and, of course, pastries and breads, which are outstanding. Try the swiss cheese broccoli soup or the *kringler* (a traditional Swedish pastry with almond paste and sliced almonds). | 125 N. Main St. | 785/227–4233 | Reservations not accepted | No supper | $4–$6 | No credit cards.

**Swedish Crown.** Scandinavian. The three dining rooms have lace curtains and pine furnishings, and a crackling fireplace can be found in the bar. Try the Swedish meatballs and Swedish ham loaf. Entertainment Fri., Sat. Kids' menu. | 121 N. Main St. | 785/227–2076 | $7–$14 | AE, D, MC, V.

## Lodging

**Rosberg House.** Rooms in this 1885 grand Queen Anne Victorian are decorated in beautiful, deep tones, and are thoughtfully furnished with four-poster beds, antique nightstands, and old linens. Dining room, complimentary breakfast, in-room data ports, some in-room hot tubs, cable TV, in-room VCRs, library, no pets, no smoking. | 103 E. State St. | 785/227–4189 or 888/215–5234 | fax 785/227–2041 | info@1885rosberghouse.com | www.1885rosberghouse.com | 5 rooms | $65–$150 | AE, D, MC, V.

**Swedish Country Inn.** Built in 1901, this inn has hand-made Swedish pine furnishings, a large fireplace in the lobby, and great-smelling goodies from its bakery. Dining room, complimentary breakfast, no smoking, sauna, bicycles. | 112 W. Lincoln St. | 785/227–2985 or 800/231–0266 | fax 785/227–2795 | www.swedishcountryinn.com | 19 rooms | $50–$80 | AE, D, MC, V.

**Viking.** If you require only simple amenities while traveling, this pleasant motel with clean rooms is right for you. RV hook-ups are available. Cable TV, pool. | 446 Harrison | 785/227–3336 | vikinghotel@kansas-usa.net | 24 rooms | $43–$56 | AE, D, DC, MC, V.

# LUCAS

MAP 3, F5

*(Nearby town also listed: Russell)*

Nestled in Kansas's Smoky Hills region, this small farming community has a population of 450. It is home to the unique Garden of Eden, which is listed on the National Register of Historic Places. In 1996, Governor Graves declared it the "Grassroots Art Capital of Kansas."

Information: **Lucas Chamber of Commerce** | Box 186, Lucas, KS 67648 | 785/525–6288 | skyways.lib.ks.us/towns/Lucas.

## Attractions

**Florence Deeble Rock Garden.** A local visionary artist re-created scenes from postcards out of colored concrete and rock. | Fairview St. | 785/525–6118 | Free | Daily.

**Garden of Eden.** Listed on the National Register of Historic Places, former school teacher and Civil War veteran S. P. Dinsmoor began building this "garden" in 1907. The site's centerpiece is the Cabin Home, built of limestone logs. The grounds contain more than 150 concrete sculptures—such as Adam and Eve, Cain and Abel, and the Devil—surrounded by a strawberry garden and a waterfall. | 305 E. Second | 785/525–6395 | Daily 10–5.

**Grassroots Arts Center.** "Grassroots" refers to artists who are self-taught and use ordinary materials to bring their work to life. Displays include a Model T and covered wagon made of carved limestone, and yard sculptures and totem poles made of scrap metal. | 213 S Main St. | 785/525–6118 | grassrootsart.home.att.net | $4 | May–Sept., Mon.–Sat. 10–5, Sun. 1–5; Oct.–Apr., Thurs.–Mon. 10–4, Sun. 1–4.

## Dining

**Bunker Hill.** Contemporary. The finest quality ingredients go into gourmet meals, found in this native limestone building in the heart of the Midwest. Try the charbroiled salmon. | 607 Elm, Bunker Hill, about 20 mi from Lucas | 785/483–6544 | Closed Sun.–Tues. No lunch | $9–$16 | No credit cards.

**K-18 Cafe.** American. You may want to linger at this casual restaurant that seems designed for conversation. Known for the homemade beef combo burger basket, and chicken-fried steak. | 5495 Rte. 18 | 785/525–6262 | Breakfast also available | $5–$7 | No credit cards.

**Linda's Cafe.** American. Antique signs decorate this small, stone, short-order restaurant that seats about 50. Known for hamburgers. | 205 S. Main St. | 785/525–7751 | Closed Sun., Mon. | $3–$7 | No credit cards.

## Lodging

**Lucas Country Inn.** This two-story inn was built in the early 1900s. Most of its guests are hunters and anglers who spend the day at Lake Wilson, which is 8 mi away. Two cafés are within walking distance. No room phones, no TV in some rooms. Pets allowed. | 229 S. Main St. | 785/525–6358 | 12 rooms | $30 | No credit cards.

**Post Rock Motel.** This theme motel has rooms paying homage to *The Wizard of Oz*, the world of sports, and more. | Junction Rtes. 14 and 18, Lincoln | 785/524–4424 | fax 785/524–5250 | 17 rooms | $40 | AE, D, MC, V.

# MANHATTAN

*(Nearby towns also listed: Blue Rapids, Junction City)*

Manhattan officially became a city on Valentine's Day in 1857. Settlers from the Ohio River valley, determined to found a city and name it "Manhattan" after the one in New York, went exploring and had their boat run aground at this spot. Residents today call their town "The Little Apple" with the same pride as residents of "The Big Apple" in New York. Kansas State University, one of the six state universities governed by the Kansas Board of Regents, was founded as a land grant college here in 1863. K-State is a member of the Big-12 sports conference and visitors would be better received by wearing purple to games or during a visit to the campus. The University is the dominant employer in this city of 60,000, followed by the Federal Government and the Kansas Farm Bureau.

**Information: Manhattan Chamber of Commerce** | 501 Poyntz Ave., Manhattan, KS 66502 | 785/776–8829 | chamber@manhattan.org | www.manhattan.org.

## Attractions

**Colbert Hills Golf Course.** Opened in May 2000, this golf center has 18-hole and 9-hole courses, a driving range, putting practice areas, lessons available, and great views of the Flint Hills, some say for 40 miles around. | 4910 Kimball Ave. | 785/776–6475 | www.colberthills.com | Free | Year-round.

**Goodnow House Museum.** The home of Isaac Goodnow, a leading educator in the state, has unique heating and cooling systems, windows, and other items from the 1860s. Goodnow's home is adjacent to Pioneer Park. | 2301 Claflin Rd. | 785/565–6490 | Free | Tues.–Fri. 8:30–5, weekends 2–5.

**Kansas State University.** This campus of 20,000 was moved to its present 664-acre site in 1875. More than 25,000 additional acres are used as teaching tools for the agriculture school. Free campus tours are offered weekdays. | 17th and Anderson Sts. | 785/532–6250 | fax 785/532–6393 | www.ksu.edu | Free | Daily.

**Riley County Historical Museum.** Displays document Flint Hills area history from 1855 to the present. | 2309 Claflin Rd. | 785/565–6490 | fax 785/565–6491 | Donation accepted | Tues.–Fri. 8:30–5, weekends 2–5.

**Sunset Zoo.** A great chimpanzee exhibit is the showcase of this 52-acre zoo, which houses hundreds of other animals, including birds and amphibians. | 2333 Oak St. | 785/587–2737 | $3 | Mar.–Nov., daily 10–5:30; Dec.–Feb., weekdays noon–3:30, weekends 10–5:30.

**Tuttle Creek State Park.** This 1,160-acre park, 5 mi north of Manhattan via U.S. 24, is on the 15,800–surface acre Tuttle Creek Reservoir. It's a great place for any type of water sport, such as windsurfing, sailing, and skiing. | 5800A River Pond Rd. | 785/539–7941 | www.kdwp.state.ks.us | tuttlecreekSP@wp.state.ks.us | Free | Daily.

### ON THE CALENDAR

**JULY:** *Kaw Valley Rodeo.* This world-class pro rodeo includes bulls, barrel racers, clowns, and skydivers. | 785/539–8585.
**SEPT.:** *Little Apple Festival.* An arts and crafts show and sale with food, entertainment, and more is held in City Park | 785/587–2757.

## Dining

**Harry's Uptown Supper Club.** American. Part of a historic hotel, the restaurant's heavy-grain woodwork and rich carpeting belie its casual, friendly atmosphere. Known for hand-cut beef, chicken, fresh seafood, and pasta. Kids' menu. | 418 Poyntz | 785/537–1300 | Closed Sun. No lunch Sat. | $12–$24 | AE, D, MC, V.

**Hibachi Hut.** Cajun/Creole. Bring your appetite to this funky Cajun spot. You can start with homemade *boudin* sausage and *habanero* sauce (a spicy sausage made with meat and rice, served with a hot chili sauce). Next try the Cajun Feast: choice of steak, fresh catfish or chicken with a cup of gumbo, jambalaya, salad, cornbread, and bread pudding with bourbon whiskey sauce. | 608 N. 12th St. | 785/539–9393 | Reservations not accepted | $6–$14 | AE, D, MC, V.

**Little Apple Brewing Company.** American. Watch your beer being brewed while enjoying Angus steak. You can also try the grilled Kansas City strip served with potatoes and steamed vegetables, or the fish-and-chips platter, with steak-cut fries and cole slaw. Salad bar. Kids' menu. | 1110 Westloop St. | 785/539–5500 | stacy@littleapplebrewery.com | www.littleapplebrewery.com | $8–$25 | AE, D, MC, V.

## Lodging

**Days Inn.** Clean, comfortable rooms are found at this strip motel. Picnic area, complimentary Continental breakfast, in-room data ports, some refrigerators, cable TV, pool, playground, laundry facilities, business services, pets allowed. | 1501 Tuttle Creek Blvd. | 785/539–5391 | fax 785/539–0847 | www.daysinn.com | 119 rooms | $62 | AE, D, DC, MC, V.

**Guest Haus Bed and Breakfast.** This contemporary, cedar-sided B&B doesn't have many rooms, but it's homey and just 2 mi from Kansas State University. Rooms are small but comfortable, with a mixture of modern and antique furnishings, such as family mementos and rattan chairs. Dining room, complimentary breakfast, no room phones, no TV, TV in common area, no pets, no smoking. | 1724 Sheffield Circle | 785/776–6543 | 2 rooms (with shared bath) | $55–$70 | No credit cards.

**Holiday Inn.** This Holidome hotel has an atrium, comfortably sized rooms, and recreational equipment. 2 restaurants, bar, in-room data ports, room service, cable TV, indoor pool, wading pool, hot tub, sauna, video games, airport shuttle, laundry facilities, business services, pets allowed. | 530 Richards Dr. | 785/539–5311 | fax 785/539–8368 | www.holiday-inn.com | 197 rooms, 5 suites | $76–$86, $169–$189 suites | AE, D, DC, MC, V.

**Morning Star Bed and Breakfast.** This 1906 three-story Queen Anne Victorian has high ceilings, a 23-columned limestone wraparound porch, and a large living room with a tile fireplace and a carved oak mantel. Guest rooms have queen-size beds and down pillows. Dining room, complimentary breakfast, in-room data ports, in-room hot tubs, no TV, TV in common area, no pets, no kids, no smoking. | 617 Houston St. | 785/587–9703 | fax 785/539–0442 | www.morningstaronthepark.com | 5 rooms | $90–$150 | MC, V.

**Prairie Flower Bed and Breakfast.** The birds are the only things that make any noise on this secluded 7-acre estate with a cedar-sided Colorado-style lodge. Complimentary breakfast, no TV in many rooms, outdoor hot tub. | 1481 Zeandale Rd. | 785/537–0986 | 3 rooms | $65 | No credit cards.

**Ramada Inn.** Across from Kansas State University, this Ramada is less than 5 min from area shopping, dining, entertainment, and attractions. Restaurant, bar, in-room data ports, refrigerators, room service, cable TV, pool, business services, airport shuttle, pets allowed. | 17th and Anderson | 785/539–7531 | fax 785/539–3909 | www.ramada.com | 115 rooms, 4 suites | $89–$149 | AE, D, DC, MC, V.

**Super 8.** This three-story motel is across the highway from a shopping mall and 2 mi from Kansas State University. A handful of restaurants are within walking distance. Complimentary Continental breakfast, in-room data ports, cable TV, business services. | 200 Tuttle Creek Blvd. (U.S. 24) | 785/537–8468 | fax 785/537–8468 | www.super8.com | 87 rooms | $69–$77 | AE, D, DC, MC, V.

# MANKATO

*(Nearby towns also listed: Belleville, Concordia, Smith Center)*

This area was home to wandering tribes of Pawnee Indians before the sodbusters and railroad arrived. This county seat was first called Jewell Center, and later changed to Mankato after a town by the same name in Minnesota, which white people who settled this area in 1872 had first called home. Mankato today is simply a pleasant small town of less than 1,000 residents on the Nebraska border, where beautiful farms dot the landscape.

Information: **Mankato Chamber of Commerce** | 703 N. West St., Mankato, KS 66956 | 785/378–3652 | slwmanks@rualtell.net.

## Attractions

**Jewell County Historical Society Museum.** A general store, school room, watch, clock, and doll collections, housewares, tools, musical instruments, and Native American artifacts provide a glimpse into local history. Off-season tours are available by appointment through the Chamber of Commerce. | 210 Commercial St. | No phone | Donation | Mid-April–mid-Oct., Thurs.–Sat. 1–5.

**Lovewell State Park.** Full-service and primitive camping are available here, and the 3,000-acre reservoir (complete with a marina) provides anglers with excellent walleye opportunities. | Rte. 14, 9 mi north of Mankato | 785/753–4971 | www.kdwp.state.ks.us | Free | Daily.

### ON THE CALENDAR

**JULY:** *Threshing Bee.* Threshing wheat, bailing hay, tractors, crafts, music, and more fill the city park. | 785/378–3652.
**JULY:** *Jewell County Fair.* 4-H, FFA, and Scout projects from kids around the county are exhibited and judged. | 785/378–3652.

## Dining

**Buffalo Roam Steak House.** American. Here the buffalo hang from the wall rather than roam on the plains. Known for buffalo and beef steak, seafood. Salad bar. Kids' menu, no smoking. | U.S. 36 E | 785/378–3971 | Closed Sun. No lunch Sat. | $7–$15 | D, MC, V.

**Sweet and Cream.** American. This white building with red trim is right off U.S. 36. Try sausage and biscuits, a hamburger, a sandwich, or salad, then end your meal with a saucer of ice cream or a malted milk shake. | 610 E. South/Rte. 36 | 785/378–3419 | Breakfast also available | $2–$6 | MC, V.

## Lodging

**Crest-Vue.** This friendly inn is renowned for its clean, spacious rooms. Picnic area, cable TV, pets allowed. | U.S. 36 E | 785/378–3515 | 12 rooms | $30–$38 | AE, D, MC, V.

**Dreamliner Motel.** An older gray strip motel in need of room renovation, there's nothing to entice you here except the price. Cable TV, pets allowed. | W. Rte 36 | 785/378–3107 | 28 rooms | $32–$48 | AE, MC, V.

# MARYSVILLE

*(Nearby towns also listed: Blue Rapids, Seneca)*

Named for the wife of Frank Marshall (the town's first white settler in 1854), Marysville became a stop on the Pony Express, as well as a large railroad center for cattle shipment. Marshall made the town a necessary stop by constructing and operating the first rope ferry across the Big Blue River. Eight trails representing America's westward movement cross through or near Marysville in northeastern Kansas, making this area rich in historic sites. This town of 3,300 is also a crew stop for the Union Pacific Railroad, a major employer in the area.

**Information: Marysville Chamber of Commerce** | 101 N. 10th St., Marysville, KS 66508 | 785/562-3101 | mcoc@mvleadvocate.com.

## Attractions

**Hollenberg Pony Express Station.** This state historic site has an exhibit gallery that draws from the Oregon/California trails and Pony Express stations throughout Kansas. | Rte. 243, near Hanover | 785/337-2635 | Free | Wed.–Sat. 10–5, Sun. 1–5.

**Koester House Museum.** Built by a German immigrant in 1876, this 11-room home is furnished with original antiques, and the grounds and flower gardens are the town's showpiece. | 919 Broadway | 785/562-2417 | $2.50; children free | Apr.–early Nov., Tues.–Sat. 10–noon and 1–4:30; and by appointment.

**Pony Express Barn Museum.** This is the only original station along the Pony Express route that remains in its original location. | 106 S. 8th St. | 785/562-3825 | $2 | Apr. or May–early Nov., Wed.–Sat. 10–4, Sun. noon–4.

**Rope Ferry.** This is a replica of the means used by pioneers, Pony Express riders, and others to cross the Big Blue River. | Center St. | 785/562-3101 | Free | Daily.

987G
8104
1156

© Artville

### BLACK SQUIRRELS IN KANSAS?

Giant black squirrels are native to the jungles of southeast Asia—certainly not the plains of Kansas—but Marysville is a town proudly infested with them. Although no one knows for sure, they think the population began in the 1920s when a traveling carnival passed through the town, staying for a few days. Someone, perhaps a child intrigued by the six pound, bushy-tailed critters, opened the cage door and a couple escaped.

Since then, the squirrels have increased their ranks by inbreeding with the more typical eastern gray squirrel, which usually weigh less than one pound. You can see the black squirrels all over town, running along the power lines, hopping from tree to tree, or just hanging out eating a nut. The best place to find the squirrels is in the city park, but many residents of Marysville have constructed large squirrel boxes on their trees, fences, and porches. According to a city ordinance, black squirrels have the freedom to trespass on all city property, to ignore any and all traffic regulations, and have the first pick of all black walnuts growing within the city limits.

The people of Marysville think the black squirrels bring them luck and have a festival each fall to celebrate their presence in the community.

**JUNE: *Germanfest.*** A car show and parade are among the activities at the heritage celebration. | 785/562–3101.

**OCT.: *Black Squirrel Night.*** Costumes, free black squirrel doughnuts, and downtown activities celebrate this town legend. | 785/562–3101.

## Dining

**Koester House Restaurant.** American. A Victorian-style home built in 1906 houses this friendly family restaurant, which serves up local staples such as fried chicken and chicken-fried steak in a setting rich with old oak trim, leaded-glass windows, and other authentic turn-of-the-20th-century details. Kids' menu. | 908 Elm St. | 785/562–1075 | $6–$12 | D, MC, V.

**Wagon Wheel Cafe.** American. Wagon-wheel light fixtures and barn-board paneling are a small part of what makes some customers drive up to 100 mi to eat steak here. Known for steaks, burgers, chicken. Kids' menu. | 703 Broadway | 785/562–3784 | Breakfast also available. Closed Sun. | $6–$13 | MC, V.

## Lodging

**Best Western Surf.** This Best Western has comfortable, affordable rooms. Complimentary Continental breakfast, refrigerators, cable TV, exercise equipment, playground, laundry facilities, business services, some pets allowed. | 2105 Center St. | 785/562–2354 | fax 785/562–2354 | www.bestwestern.com | 52 rooms | $58 | AE, D, DC, MC, V.

**Oak Tree Inn.** Built in 1999, this inn is nestled on the edge of town along the fabled Pony Express Highway. You'll find many modern conveniences, as well as an authentic 1950s-style diner with chrome toasters and hearty helpings of traditional American favorites. In-room data ports, some minibars, microwaves, refrigerators, cable TV, hot tub, gym, laundry facilities, pets allowed (fee), free parking. | 1127 Pony Express Hwy. | 785/562–1234 | fax 785/562–1100 | 104 rooms | $42 | AE, D, DC, MC, V.

**Thunderbird Motel.** Sitting high on a hill west of town, this motel is in a quiet residential area. The lobby has Pony Express memorabilia from the manager's drive along the trail in the 1960s. RV hook-ups are available. Complimentary Continental breakfast, in-room data ports, microwaves, refrigerators, cable TV, some pets allowed. | 819 Pony Express Hwy. (U.S. 36 W) | 785/562–2373 or 800/662–2373 | fax 785/562–2531 | 21 rooms | $37–$43 | AE, D, DC, MC, V.

# MCPHERSON

MAP 3, G6

*(Nearby towns also listed: Hutchison, Lindsborg, Newton)*

Named after a Union General in the Civil War, McPherson was settled by Scottish immigrants in 1872 and continues to be the dominant Scottish community in the state. It is a Main Street Kansas city, which means the downtown area is devoted to historic revitalization and authenticity. Perhaps that is one of the reasons this town of 13,000 has often been listed as one of the top 100 small towns in America. A small entrepreneurial family business has grown over the years to attract numerous plastics-related industries to this central Kansas community.

Information: **McPherson Convention and Visitors Bureau** | 306 N. Main St. (Box 616), McPherson, KS 67460 | 316/241–3340 or 800/324–8022 | www.mcphersonks.org.

## Attractions

**Maxwell Wildlife Refuge.** More than 2,200 acres of rolling prairie have been designated as a refuge, which serves as home to 200 head of bison and 50 head of elk. About 45 surface acres of water are surrounded by 260 acres of campgrounds and public use facilities.

MCPHERSON

INTRO
ATTRACTIONS
DINING
LODGING

Boat launching, fishing piers, picnic tables, and nature trails can also be found here. | 7 mi north of U.S. 56, Canton | 316/628–4455 | www.cyberkraft.com/maxwell | $7 | Daily.

**McPherson Museum.** This Victorian home has original imported wallpaper, hand-crocheted lace-edge curtains, and a separate stairway for the maid. | 1130 E. Euclid St. | 316/241–8464 | Donation accepted | Tues.–Sun. 1–5.

**McPherson Opera House.** The opera house (and its 900-seat auditorium) was one of the most elaborate and architecturally sound in the Midwest, which is why it was placed on the National Register of Historic Places. | 221 S. Main St. | 316/241–1952 | fax 316/241–8708 | www.mcphersonoperahouse.com | mohpc@mpks.net | Free | Daily, tours by appointment.

**ON THE CALENDAR**
**JUNE: *Prairie Day Celebration.*** The open prairie hosts historical re-enactments of cowboy gunfights, wildflower and bird walks, and more. | 800/324–8022.
**JULY: *McPherson County 4-H Fair.*** Youths from all over the state gather to compete in this event, 400 of them from McPherson County alone. View more than 3,000 4-H exhibits in 36 divisions, including agriculture, livestock, and geology. | 316/241–1523.
**SEPT.: *Scottish Festival and Highland Games.*** A piping competition, a caber toss, and Kirking of the Tartan services are a part of this two-day festival held in Lakeside Park. | 316/241–3340 or 800/324–8022 | www.mcphersonks.org.

## Dining

**The Pear Tree Restaurant and Peppy Partridge Club.** American. Old photos and prints in a prairie theme decorate this family restaurant specializing in robust fare such as steaks, chicken, and shrimp. Visit the adjoining Peppy Partridge Club, where adults can relax with a cocktail. | 121 W. Marlin | 316/241–1569 | $6–$15 | AE, D, MC, V.

## Lodging

**Best Western Holiday Manor.** Drive right up to your door at this two-story strip motel, 2 mi from the McPherson Museum. Restaurant, room service, cable TV, 2 pools (1 indoor), hot tub, business services, some pets allowed. | 2211 E. Kansas Ave. (U.S. 56) | 316/241–5343 | fax 316/241–8086 | www.bestwestern.com | 110 rooms | $55–$72 | AE, D, DC, MC, V.

**Red Coach Inn.** This two-story strip motel is surrounded by fast-food restaurants. Restaurant, in-room data ports, cable TV, in-room VCRs (and movies), pool, hot tub, miniature golf, playground, business services, some pets allowed. | 2111 E. Kansas Ave. (U.S. 56) | 316/241–6960, 800/362–0072 (outside KS) | fax 316/241–4340 | 88 rooms | $60–$65 | AE, D, DC, MC, V.

**Super 8 Motel.** This motel is off I–135, Exit 60. Complimentary Continental breakfast, cable TV, business services, free parking, pets allowed (fee). | 2110 E. Kansas | 316/241–8881 | fax 316/241–8853 | www.super8.com | 42 rooms | $50 | AE, D, MC, V.

# MEADE

MAP 3, D8

*(Nearby towns also listed: Ashland, Liberal)*

Founded in 1885 by an Ohio land company, this small community of 2,000 has a vivid history. Many pioneer battles with Native Americans, the elements, and each other occurred here, and, although they weren't born in Meade, the Dalton Brothers Gang lived here, at their sister's house. Meade is considered the heart of Sunflower country, where, along with corn and wheat, sunflowers are a common agricultural product. Hunting, fishing, and bird-watching are popular with locals and with visitors to the area.

Information: **Meade County Economic Development** | Box 238, Meade, KS 67874 | 316/873–8795.

## Attractions

**Dalton Gang Hideout.** This home of the Dalton brothers' sister includes an escape tunnel from the barn into the open countryside. | 502 S. Pearlette | 316/873–2731 or 800/354–2743 | $2 | Labor Day–Memorial Day, Mon.–Sat. 9–5, Sun. 1–5; Memorial Day–Labor Day, Mon.–Sat. 9–6, Sun. 1–6.

**Meade County Historical Society.** This museum chronicles pioneer life in the region. | 200 E. Carthage | 316/873–2359 | Donation accepted | Labor Day–Memorial Day, Mon.–Sat. 9–5, Sun. 1–5; Memorial Day–Labor Day, Mon.–Sat. 9–6, Sun. 1–6.

**Meade State Park.** Founded in 1927, this 800-acre park is the state's oldest and is considered one of the best places in the central United States for bird-watching. | Rte. 23, 13 mi southwest of Meade | 316/873–2572 | www.kdwp.state.ks.us | Free | Daily.

### ON THE CALENDAR

**MAY–JUNE: *Dalton Gang Hideout Festival.*** The whole town participates in this jubilant celebration of its western heritage. Festivities include a parade through town, an authentic rodeo, musicians, cowboy poets, historical recreationists in period dress, storytellers, and demonstrations of traditional crafts like blacksmithing and rope-making. The highlight of the event is the chuck-wagon barbecue cook-off, in which contestants whip up authentic cowboy grub and fairgoers award the prize. | 800/354–2743.

**MAY: *Meade Celebration.*** A Christian concert, swimming, and dancing are free to all. | 316/873–2118.

**JULY: *Meade County Fair.*** The fair includes a parade, carnival, and 4-H exhibits. | 316/873–8795.

## Dining

**Bob's Drive-In.** American/Casual. Local favorite Bob's offers classic diner fare like burgers and fries, shakes, and ice cream. Drop a nickel in the jukebox and shoot a game of pool in a relaxed, low-key environment. | 316/873–2862 | Closed Sat. | $1–$6 | No credit cards.

## Lodging

**Dalton's Bedpost.** Clean and inexpensive rooms are available in this small, unassuming, one-story motor lodge. Cable TV, pets allowed. | 519 E. Carthage Hwy. | 316/873–2131 | 12 rooms | $35 | AE, D, MC, V.

# MEDICINE LODGE

*(Nearby town also listed: Pratt)*

Before the invasion of white settlers and the town's founding in 1873, this part of southwestern Kansas was home to many Native American tribes, but was dominated by the Kiowa. The Kiowa believed the river that flows through this region, as well as the many plants and herbs along its banks, contained healing, therapeutic minerals. They erected a large timber lodge and traveled for days to bathe in the steaming, medicinal powers, thus the town's name. Medicine Lodge was the site of the Great Plains Peace Treaty of 1867, and home to temperance legend Carry Nation. As with much of Kansas, cattle ranching influences the economy of this town of 2,400, which also is home to two building products manufacturers.

**Information: Medicine Lodge Area Chamber of Commerce** | 108 West First St. (Box 274), Medicine Lodge, KS 67104 | 316/886–3417 | mlchamber@cyberlodg.com. | www.cyberlodge.com/mlchamber.

## Attractions

**Carry A. Nation Home Memorial.** The home of this international crusader against tobacco and alcohol is filled with antiques and some of her famous hatchets. | 211 W. Fowler Ave. | 316/886–3553 | $4 | Daily 10:30–5.

**Equatorial Sun Dial.** More than 2,000 pounds of Colorado granite serve as a teaching tool about the solar system. | El Dorado and Guffey Aves. | 316/886–3417 | Free | Daily.

**Medicine Lodge Stockade.** The replica of the stockade that protected settlers from attacks by Native Americans includes cabins and antiques. | 209 W. Fowler Ave. | 316/886–3553 | $4 | Daily.

**Sagebrush Gallery of Western Art.** The studio and gallery of western artist Earl Kuhn showcase his works honoring the country's ranching heritage. | 115 E. Kansas Ave. | 316/886–5163 | www.thecattle.net/sagebrush | Free | Mon.–Sat. 9–5.

### ON THE CALENDAR

**MAY: *Gyp Hills Trail Rides and Wildflower Tour.*** Identify spring flowers along this scenic horseback ride through the hills. | 316/886–5293.

**SEPT.: *Kansas Championship Ranch Rodeo.*** The best cowboys in the state compete for trophies and prizes during this event held at Pageant Rodeo Arena. | 316/886–9815.

## Dining

**Indian Grill Restaurant.** American. This truck stop on top of a hill serves filling road fare and gives a taste of community flavor. Known for daily specials such as meat loaf, pork chops, and beef stroganoff. | 301 Fowler Ave. | 316/886–3476 | $6–$8 | AE, MC, V.

## Lodging

**Copa Motel.** This strip motel with exterior entrances is just 1 mi from a fishing lake and down the hill from the Medicine Lodge Stockade. Rooms are basic and economical. Picnic area, cable TV, pool, pets allowed. | 401 W. Fowler Ave. | 316/886–5673 or 800/886–2672 | fax 316/886–5241 | 54 rooms | $40–$47 | AE, D, DC, MC, V.

**Lodge Inn.** A two-story drive-up motel, this mom-and-pop is about 1 mi from the town center. In-room data ports, some refrigerators, cable TV, laundry service, pets allowed. | U.S. 281 North | 316/886–3080 | fax 316/886–3812 | 29 rooms | $34 | AE, MC, V.

# NEWTON

MAP 3, H6

*(Nearby towns also listed: Hutchison, McPherson, Wichita)*

Named after the Massachusetts hometown of a group of Santa Fe railroad investors, this town of 17,900 was one of those lawless and bloody Wild West towns in its early days. As the railroad moved farther west, so did the element of individuals responsible for the lawlessness. In 1874 a group of Mennonites from Germany settled here, bringing with them a hard red winter wheat called Turkey Red that forever would determine the reputation of Kansas as the world's breadbasket.

Information: **Newton Area Chamber of Commerce** | 500 N. Main, Suite 101, Newton, KS 67114 | 316/283–2560 | shelley@infonewtonks.org | www.infonewtonks.org.

## Attractions

**Campus Granary.** This is the country's center for the wheat-weaving craft and crafts products. | Bethel College Campus, 300 E. 27th | 316/283–3940 | www.bethelks.edu | Free | Daily.

**Kansas Learning Center for Health.** The center includes a health museum with 25 exhibits on the human body and a see-through model of a human for exploration. | 505 Main St.,

Halstead | 316/835–2662 | fax 316/835–2755 | $2 | Feb.–Oct., weekdays 10–4, Sun. 1–5; Nov.–Jan., weekdays 8:30–5.

**Kauffman Museum.** This museum emphasizes the cultural and natural history of the Central Plains and the immigration of the Mennonites to Kansas in the 1870s. | 2701 N. Main St. | 316/283–1612 | fax 316/283–2107 | $2 | Tues.–Fri. 9:30–4:30, weekends 1:30–4:30.

**Warkentin House.** A Mennonite immigrant completed building this 16-room Victorian home in 1887. The home has 90% of its original furnishings. | 211 E. 1st St. | 316/283–7555 | $3 | Jun.–Aug., Tues.–Sun. 1–4:30; Apr.–May and Sept.–Dec., weekends 1–4:30; Jan.–Mar., by appointment.

## ON THE CALENDAR

**JULY:** *Chisholm Trail Festival.* Entertainment, food, a carnival, parade, and fireworks in Athletic Park mark the famous cattle path. | 316/283–2560.
**AUG.:** *Harvey County Free Fair.* At this authentic Midwestern county fair, you'll find traditional exhibits and displays like livestock, produce, and handicrafts, as well as parades, music, rides, a demolition derby, a rodeo, fun and games for the kids, snacks, souvenirs, and more. | 316/284–6930.
**SEPT.:** *Newton Fiesta.* This Main Street event has more than 40 food booths, manufacturing displays, and entertainment in the tradition of a Mexican fiesta, such as dancers and mariachis. | 316/283–2560.
**OCT.:** *Bethel College Fall Festival.* This distinguished event includes food, crafts, and a wide variety of entertainment. | 316/283–2500 | www.bethelks.edu/alumni/fallfest.html.

## Dining

**C&S BBQ & Mardi Gras.** Cajun/Creole. A festive New Orleans atmosphere pervades this remote outpost of authentic Southern-style cooking. Mardi Gras masks and memorabilia, as well as photographs and other mementos of Creole country, can be found throughout. Try Crawfish étouffée, Shrimp Creole, or blackened catfish. Kids' menu. | 1015 Washington Rd. | 316/283–3663 | $15 | AE, MC, V.

**Spears Restaurant.** American. This restaurant is in an old historic flour mill, and has exposed-brick walls and old photos inside. Known for steak, seafood. Kids' menu. Sun. brunch. | 310 Main | 316/283–3510 | $8–$12 | AE, D, MC, V.

## Lodging

**Best Western Red Coach Inn.** Right off Exit 31 of I–135, this two-story motel is 8 mi from the Kauffman Museum and less than 30 mi from numerous other attractions. A few restaurants are within walking distance. Restaurant, room service, cable TV, pool, outdoor hot tub, exercise equipment, video games, airport shuttle, some pets allowed. | 1301 E. 1st St. | 316/283–9120 or 800/777–9120 | fax 316/283–4105 | www.bestwestern.com | 81 rooms | $52–$109 | AE, D, DC, MC, V.

**Harrison House.** Built in the 1920s by a prominent local businessman, the Harrison House is a beautiful two-story redbrick home where friendly husband-and-wife team Ken and Neva Frey operate a cozy B&B. Each of the guest rooms is uniquely decorated with antiques and period wallpaper. Fresh cinnamon rolls are available for breakfast, and if you stay for dinner (and if you've been good), Mrs. Frey may make you her signature Special Chicken (broiled chicken in a mushroom cream sauce). Complimentary full breakfast, no smoking. | 115 South Harrison St. | 316/283–6865 | kenefrey@southwind.net | www2.southwind.net/~kenefrey/ | 3 rooms | $55 | No credit cards.

**The Old Parsonage.** In Newton's oldest neighborhood (which dates back to the turn of the 20th century), this inn served as the parsonage for the First Mennonite Church from 1946 to 1964. Complimentary breakfast, no smoking, cable TV. | 330 E. 4th | 316/283–6808 | www.kbba.com | 3 rooms (2 with shared bath) | $48 | MC, V.

# NORTON

*(Nearby towns also listed: Oberlin, Phillipsburg)*

Founded in 1871 by explorer John Fremont, but named for a captain in the Kansas Cavalry, Norton was a stagecoach stop of many of the famous names in history traveling west—Buffalo Bill Cody, Billy the Kid, and Horace Greeley. People eventually began building homes here, pleased with the productive soil and abundant wildlife. Pheasant hunting dominates the region each fall, but hunters also come for the deer, turkey, quail, and dove that flourish along the banks of the Republican River. When not hunting, many residents find employment with the state Department of Transportation and Department of Corrections, both of which have centers in this town of approximately 3,000.

**Information: Norton Area Chamber of Commerce** | Box 97, Norton, KS 67654 | 785/877–2501.

## Attractions

**Gallery of Also Rans.** First State Bank's mezzanine has a display of unsuccessful campaigns for the Presidency of the United States. | 105 W. Main St. | 785/877–3341 | Free | Weekdays 9–3, Sat. 9–11:30.

**Prairie Dog State Park.** Camping, fishing, hunting, and wildlife watching (including prairie dogs) are popular family outings at this park, which includes an 1892 adobe home. | Rte. 261, 1 mi south from U.S. 36 | 785/877–2953 | www.kdwp.state.ks.us | $4 per vehicle | Daily.

**Station 15.** This replica of a stagecoach and wagon train depot is in Wayside Park. | U.S. 36 | 785/877–2501 | Free | Daily.

### ON THE CALENDAR

**JUNE:** *Lenora Jubilee.* A celebration as old as anyone in town can remember that includes antique cars, a parade, food, and music. The event is held off Rte. 9, 20 mi southwest of Norton. | 785/567–4860.

**OCT.:** *Halloween Wiener Roast.* Before and after tricks and treats, the entire community gathers for an old-fashioned wiener roast. | 785/877–2501.

## Dining

**State Street Steakhouse.** Steak. Wood paneling and an open fireplace make this big, casual dining room a local favorite. On Fri. and Sat. nights they serve up live country and western and rock 'n' roll music along with the steak, chicken, and seafood. | 402 S. State St. | 785/877–5222 | Closed Sun. | $19 | AE, D, MC, V.

## Lodging

**Hillcrest.** This one-story motel is next to a city park. A number of fast food restaurants are a short walk away. Cable TV, pool, playground, airport shuttle. | 606 West Holme | 785/877–3343 | fax 785/877–3377 | 26 rooms | $46 | AE, D, DC, MC, V.

**The Rose of Sharon Inn.** This elegant Victorian B&B dates back to 1880. The guest rooms, fitted with regional antiques, are ideal for honeymoons, romantic getaways, or family vacations. (This region is known for its rich hunting and fishing, as well as hiking, swimming, and other outdoor pursuits). For a fee, lunch and dinner are available upon request. Complimentary full breakfast, pets allowed, no smoking. | 603 East Main St. | 785/877–3010 | 3 rooms | $65–$75 | D, MC, V.

# OAKLEY

*(Nearby town also listed: Colby)*

Oakley was one of the Wild West towns famous for shoot-outs, Indian raids, and hearty saloons. Although there is no proof, legend has it that sharpshooter Annie Oakley took her stage name from this town after a performance here. Home to 2,100 residents, Oakley is a little calmer now with three city parks, a golf course, and numerous community activities. Hunting for pheasant, turtledove, antelope, and deer are popular pastimes and draws tourists to the area during hunting season. As the seat of Logan County, much of the town's work force contributes to the functioning of county services.

**Information: Oakley Area Chamber of Commerce** | 313 Center Ave., Oakley, KS 67748 | 785/672–4862.

## Attractions

**Fick Fossil and History Museum.** Sharks' teeth, wood carvings, fossils, and pressed wildflowers are among the 11,000 items displayed here. | 700 W. 3rd St. | 785/672–4839 | Free | Memorial Day–Labor Day, Mon.–Sat. 9–5, Sun. 2–4; Labor Day–Memorial Day, Mon.–Sat. 9–5.

**Monument Rocks.** Chalk bluffs and sediment pyramids that can be seen for miles are remains of an inland sea that covered Kansas millions of years ago. | U.S. 83, 20 mi south of Oakley | 785/672–4839 | Free | Daily.

### ON THE CALENDAR

**SEPT.: *State Cow Chip Throwing Contest.*** Held in the nearby ghost town of Russell Springs, this event is not for those afraid of getting their hands dirty. | 785/672–4862.
**OCT.: *Cornhusking Contest.*** Demonstrations illustrate how corn was picked, husked, and shelled in the early 1900s, and festivities include an arts and crafts show, games, and entertainment. | 785/672–4862.

## Dining

**Colonial Steak House.** American. Many antiques and old seed sacks are found on the walls. Known for steak and fried chicken. Salad bar. Buffet. Kids' menus. | U.S. 83 | 785/672–4720 | $4–$16 | AE, D, MC, V.

**Scott's Bluff.** Steak. Here you'll find a casual, rustic atmosphere complete with antique wooden furniture, an open fireplace, and stick-to-your-ribs home cooking. Known for steak, plus chicken and seafood specialties. Kids' menu. | 210 South Freeman | 785/672–8892 | Closed Sun. | $5–$15 | No credit cards.

## Lodging

**Annie Oakley Motel.** Built in 1949, this one-story, sandy brick building is on the town's main thoroughfare, just blocks from the town center, the cinema, and the Fick Fossil and History Museum. Rooms have floral accents and queen or double beds. Some kitchenettes, cable TV, laundry facilities, pets allowed. | 428 Center St. | 785/672–3223 | 26 rooms | $40 | AE, MC, V.

**Best Western Golden Plains Motel.** Ground rooms have patios overlooking the attractive, landscaped pool area, while second floor rooms have balconies. The motel is 1 mi from the Fick Fossil and History Museum and the Oakley Municipal Airport. Picnic area, complimentary Continental breakfast, cable TV, pool. | 3506 U.S. 40 | 785/672–3254 | fax 785/672–3200 | www.bestwestern.com | 26 rooms | $48 | AE, D, DC, MC, V.

**First Interstate Inn.** Rooms have nature-themed murals on the walls in this two-story inn across the highway from a Greyhound bus depot. Cable TV, business services, pets allowed.

| 1006 U.S. 40 | 785/672–3203 or 800/462–4667 | fax 785/672–3330 | 29 rooms | $55 | AE, D, DC, MC, V.

# OBERLIN

MAP 3, C3

*(Nearby town also listed: Norton)*

First called Sappa after the creek here, the town name was changed to Oberlin to honor the Ohio hometown of one of the men who donated the land for this town. Founded in 1873 by William Montgomery of Pennsylvania, Oberlin is remembered as the site of the last Indian raid on Kansas soil, when 18 white settlers were killed in 1878 by Cheyenne, avenging a similar massacre years earlier. The Sappa Creek area is a great place for fishing and hunting, especially for pheasant. In addition to the agriculture economy and supporting industry that dominates all of rural Kansas, custom cabinets, trophies, and sculpture casting provide jobs to many of the town's 2,300 residents.

Information: **Decatur Area Chamber of Commerce** | 132 S. Penn Ave., Oberlin, KS 67749 | 785/475–3441.

## Attractions
**Decatur County Museum.** Antiques and artifacts in 12 buildings relay the area's heritage. | 258 S. Penn Ave. | 785/475–2712 | $3 | Apr.–Nov., Tues.–Sat. 10–noon and 1–5.

### ON THE CALENDAR
**AUG.:** *Decatur County Fair.* A carnival, demolition derby, games, train rides, and much more make this a fun event for everyone. | 888/722–0107.
**OCT.:** *Mini-Sappa Days.* Town history is celebrated with costumed demonstrations of antique threshing machines, as well as an antique car parade. | 888/722–0107.

## Dining
**Janey's Frontier Restaurant.** American. Wave to Janey on your way in for some frontier home cookin'. Try the Prime Rib as you relax among the old photos and Log Cabin wallpaper. Known for chicken-fried steak and hot beef. Kids' menu. The restaurant is adjacent to the Frontier Motel. | 209 E. Frontier Pkwy. | 785/475–3429 | $5–$11 | No credit cards.

## Lodging
**Frontier Motel.** A little ways out of town you'll find this one-story motel, which is adjacent to several other roadside businesses, including Janey's Frontier Restaurant. Some rooms have views of the pool and courtyard. Restaurant nearby, some refrigerators, cable TV, pool, pets allowed. | 207 E. Frontier Pkwy. | 785/475–2203 | 28 rooms | $49 | AE, D, MC, V.

**LandMark Inn.** This elegant inn is in the Historic Bank of Oberlin building, which was built in 1886. It is 1 mi from the Gateway Convention Center. Restaurant, complimentary breakfast, sauna, exercise equipment. | 189 S. Penn Ave. | 785/475–2340 or 888/639–0003 | fax 785/475–2869 | landmarkinn@juno.com | 7 suites | $79–$105 suites | AE, D, MC, V.

# OLATHE

MAP 3, K5

*(Nearby towns also listed: Atchison, Bonner Springs, Kansas City, Shawnee)*

Founded in 1857 by Virginia doctor John Barton, Shawnee Indians suggested he call the new town "Olathe" (pronounced o-LAY-tha), which means "beautiful." The town was raided by William Quantrill and his band of guerillas during the Civil War, and during World War II it became the site of an aviation training field. Today Olathe is considered one of the fastest growing cities in the Midwest. It is only 20 miles from downtown Kansas City.

Information: **Olathe Convention and Visitors Bureau** | 142 N. Cherry, Olathe, KS 66061 | 913/764–1050 | www.olathe.org.

## Attractions

**Ernie Miller Nature Center.** The first Nature Center in Johnson County, this 113-acre property contains 3 mi of trails, live animals, displays, and a gift store. Educational programs focus on the environment, history, and culture. | 909 N. Rte. 7 | 913/764–7759 | fax 913/764–0654 | www.erniemiller.com | Tues.–Sat. 9–4:30, Sun. 1–4:30.

**Mahaffie Farmstead and Stagecoach Stop.** Operating as a stagecoach stop along the Santa Fe Trail from 1863–1869, today this farmstead is a living history museum offering tours and rides, allowing you to experience stagecoach travel first-hand. | 1100 Kansas City Rd. | 913/782–6972 | fax 913/397–5114 | $3 | Daily 10–4.

**Pony Express Brewing Company.** Founded in 1995, this award-winning brewery is the largest in Kansas. All beer is made using grains from the founder's family farms in Kansas and Missouri. | 311 N. Burch | 913/782–6699 | fax 913/782–4321 | www.ponyex.com | Free | Sat. 1–3.

## Dining

**Joe's Crab Shack.** Seafood. The festive atmosphere in this place includes table-top choreographed performances by servers. The popular snow crab is served either barbecued, steamed, or with garlic. The shrimp platter is another favorite and includes fried, coconut, popcorn, and cocktail shrimp. | 11965 S. Strang Line Rd. | 913/393–2929 | www.joescrabshack.com | $5–$24 | AE, D, DC, MC, V.

**Jumpin' Catfish.** Southern. Like eating in Grandpa's fishing lodge, replete with animal mounts watching from the walls. The restaurant specializes in dishes from the Mighty Mis'. | 1861 S. Ridgeview | 913/829–FISH | www.jumpincatfish.com | Closed Mon. | $8–$13 | AE, D, MC, V.

**Kansas Machine Shed.** American. Antique farm machinery and a gift shop make this stop an attraction in its own right. The Kansas farm cooking includes corn-fed hams, huge Iowa pork chops, homemade cottage cheese, and apple dumplings the size of a dinner plate. | 12080 Strang Line Rd. | 913/780–2697 | $7–$20 | Breakfast also available | AE, D, DC, MC, V.

## Lodging

**Comfort Suites Olathe.** Windmill blades, a wooden horse statue, and deer antler chandeliers are part of the cowboy theme at this three-story tan and stucco hotel 1 mi from the Santa Fe trail. Complimentary Continental breakfast, room service, pool. | 12070 S. Strang Line Rd. | 913/397–0100 or 800/965–0502 | fax 913/397–9559 | 92 rooms | $99–$109 | AE, D, DC, MC, V.

**Holiday Inn.** Warm rooms have burgundy and green tones, soothing pictures of the outdoors, and views of the pool and courtyard area. The Great Mall of the Great Plains is across the street. Restaurant, indoor-outdoor pool, hot tub, gym. | 101 W. 151st St. | 913/829–4000 or 800/833–6632 | fax 913/829–8165 | www.holiday-inn.com | 148 rooms | $95 | AE, D, DC, MC, V.

**Sleep Inn.** Earthy colors and images of Kansas's landscape create a calm environment. Rooms have vanities and large walk-in showers. The Great Mall of the Great Plains is next door. Complimentary Continental breakfast, pool, hot tub. | 20662 W. 151st St. | 913/390–9500 | fax 913/390–6630 | 77 rooms | $85 | AE, D, DC, MC, V.

# OSAWATOMIE

MAP 3, K6

*(Nearby town also listed: Ottawa)*

This unusual name is a combination of two Native American names, Osage and Pottawatomie. Founded in 1855 by French trappers, this town was right in the middle of the bloodiest border war conflicts during the Civil War, due in great part to the presence of John Brown, an anti-slavery radical. Although rich with its own attractions and activities, this town of 4,500 is within easy driving distance of metropolitan Kansas City. A large mental health facility employs more than 600 residents, and the Union-Pacific Railroad remains a dominant influence on the area's economy.

Information: **Osawatomie Chamber of Commerce** | 526 Main (Box 338), Osawatomie, KS 66064 | 913/755–4114.

## Attractions

**John Brown Memorial Park.** This 20-acre park on the west side of town is the site of one of the first Civil War battles and includes a museum, log cabin, and statue of John Brown. | 10th and Main St. | 913/755–4384 | Free | Daily.

**Marais des Cygnes Wildlife Refuge.** Named after the river that runs through the center of it, this 12,000-acre wildlife refuge is home to wild turkey, warblers, and geese. If you look hard you might spot some deer and otter as well. | Off U.S. 69, between the towns of La Cygne and Trading Post | 913/352–6174 | Free | Daily.

### ON THE CALENDAR

**JUNE:** *John Brown Jamboree.* A parade, car show, carnival, and hobby and craft show fill the streets for four days. | 913/755–4114.
**DEC.:** *Christmas Homes Tour.* Victorian- and modern-era homes are decorated and open to the public for the holidays. | 913/755–3767.

## Dining

**Landmark Restaurant.** American. It's simple country fare at this friendly small-town eatery: burgers, steaks, and chicken. | 304 E. Gate | 913/755–2136 | Closed Sun. | $3–$11 | AE, D, MC, V.

## Lodging

**Landmark Motel.** There aren't a lot of frills at this independently owned motel/restaurant, but you're sure to receive genuine hospitality and reasonable rates. Restaurant. Cable TV, pool, pets allowed. | 304 E. Gate | 913/755–3051 | 39 rooms | $49 | AE, D, MC, V.

# OTTAWA

MAP 3, K5

*(Nearby towns also listed: Osawatamie, Overland Park)*

French explorers were the first white people to venture into this part of eastern Kansas, forcing the Ottawa Indians into Oklahoma. When this town of 11,800 was founded in 1837, settlers honored the tribe with the town's name and the Baptist university that followed. Architect George P. Washburn was born and raised here, and more than a dozen homes and office buildings he designed are on the National Register of Historic Places. Dairy farming plays a vital role in the area's economy.

Information: **Franklin County Convention Bureau** | 109 E. 2nd St. (Box 580), Ottawa, KS 66067 | 785/242–1411 | www.idir.net/~fctv.

## Attractions

**Dietrich Cabin Museum.** Built in 1859, this cabin in Ottawa City Park honors a German couple (as well as Franklin County's hundreds of other early pioneers) who endured severe hardships on the Kansas frontier. | Ottawa City Park, Main and 5th Sts. | 785/242–1250 | Donation accepted | May–Sept., weekends 1–4; Oct.–Apr., by appointment.

**Forest Park.** These 40 acres of shaded parkland in the middle of town offer something for everyone—playgrounds, picnic areas, an Olympic-size swimming pool, a kiddie pool, a horseshoe range, basketball courts, tennis courts, and softball and baseball diamonds. | Locust and Tecumseh Sts. | 785/229–3653 | Free | Daily.

**Old Depot Museum.** Built in 1888, this former office for railroad officials today houses artifacts relating to the railroad and Victorian eras. | 135 W. Tecumseh St. | 785/242–1250 | Donation accepted | Tues.–Sat. 10–4.

**Ottawa Indian Burial Grounds.** This sacred burial ground is the final resting place for nearly 100 Ottawa Indians who made their home here. | Osborne Terrace St. | 785/242–1411 | Free | Daily.

**Pomona State Park.** This 500-acre park has 47 full-service campsites, 109 electrical-only campsites, and more than 160 primitive campsites. The park also has a tepee and a marina with boat rentals. | 22900 S. Rte. 368, Vassar | 785/828–4933 | www.kdwp.state.ks.us | $4 per vehicle | Daily.

Noted for its giant flathead catfish and great crappie fishing, state record flatheads have been taken from the 4,000-acre **Pomona Reservoir.** | 785/453–2201.

**ON THE CALENDAR**

**JULY:** *Franklin County Fair.* A pro-rodeo, carnival, demolition derby, and exhibits fill the stadium for a week. | 785/229–3520.

**SEPT.:** *Ole Marais River Run.* Auto enthusiasts from around the country converge on Franklin County for this huge antique car show. There are food and drink, and prizes are awarded in different automotive categories. | 785/242–1411.

**DEC.:** *Yule Feast Weekend.* This Old English–style holiday festival has a parade, concert, nativity, and light display. | 785/242–5200 or 800/755–5200.

## Dining

**Sirloin Stockade.** American. Bigger is better seems to be this restaurant chain's simple food philosophy. Here you'll find an all-you-can-eat buffet serving massive quantities of chow, including hand-cut steaks (ribeye, sirloin, T-bone), fried chicken, chops, seafood specialties, fresh salads, homemade breads, rolls, pastries, and desserts. Fresh homemade pizza is served during lunch, and Fri. night is fried shrimp night. Kids' menu. | 2230 Princeton Circle Dr. | 785/242–4329 | fax 785/242–3342 | $6–$10 | MC, V.

## Lodging

**Best Western Hallmark Inn.** Rooms have pastel colors and pictures of country scenes at this two-story motel 3 mi from downtown Ottawa. Complimentary Continental breakfast, cable TV, pool, business services, laundry facilities, some pets allowed (fee). | 2209 S. Princeton Rd. (U.S. 59) | 785/242–7000 | fax 785/242–8572 | www.bestwestern.com | 60 rooms | $74 | AE, D, DC, MC, V.

**Village Inn Motel.** A one-story, exterior corridor motel on the edge of town, just off Exit 182B of I–35. Picnic area, some kitchenettes, some microwaves, refrigerators, cable TV, pool, volleyball, pets allowed. | 2520 S. Main | 785/242–4433 | fax 785/242–3087 | ottawamotel@usa.net | www.ottcom.org/villagemotel/ | 18 rooms | $36 | AE, D, DC, MC, V.

# OVERLAND PARK

MAP 3, L5

*(Nearby towns also listed: Bonner Springs, Kansas City, Lawrence, Leavenworth, Olathe, Ottawa, Shawnee)*

Businessman William Strang, Jr., founded Overland Park in 1905. Strang envisioned a park-like community suitable for raising families. In the first few years, the Strang Line, an interurban rail line, was developed and took passengers from southern Johnson County to Kansas City. Overland Park was officially incorporated in May 1960. With a population of 144,000, it is now the third-largest city in Kansas and a large retail center for metropolitan Kansas City. Overland Park is also the world headquarters of Sprint, the global communications corporation.

Information: **Overland Park Chamber of Commerce** | 9001 West 110th St., Overland Park, KS 66282 | 913/491–3600 | www.opkansas.org.

## Attractions

**Deanna Rose Children's Farmstead.** This 5-acre farm has picnic shelters, a nature trail, and a barnyard with buffalo, chickens, ducks, lambs, goats, pigs, and birds of prey. | 32nd St. at Main St. | 913/897–2360 | $1 | Apr.–Nov., daily 9–5.

**Overland Park Arboretum and Botanical Gardens.** This 300-acre park has 9 mi of wood-chip and sidewalk trails that wind through garden areas. | 8909 West 179th St. | 913/685–3604 | Free | Daily.

**Shawnee Methodist Mission.** The Methodist Church began this center in 1839 to teach English and trade skills to Native Americans of the region. | 3403 W. 53rd St., Fairway | 913/262–0867 | Free | Tues.–Sat. 10–5, Sun. 1–5.

### ON THE CALENDAR

**MAY: *Art In the Woods.*** Artists from seven states participate in this juried art show. | 913/491–3600.

## YOUR CAR'S FIRST-AID KIT

- ❏ Bungee cords or rope to tie down trunk if necessary
- ❏ Club soda to remove stains from upholstery
- ❏ Cooler with bottled water
- ❏ Extra coolant
- ❏ Extra windshield-washer fluid
- ❏ Flares and/or reflectors
- ❏ Flashlight and extra batteries
- ❏ Hand wipes to clean hands after roadside repair
- ❏ Hose tape
- ❏ Jack and fully inflated spare
- ❏ Jumper cables
- ❏ Lug wrench
- ❏ Owner's manual
- ❏ Plastic poncho—in case you need to do roadside repairs in the rain
- ❏ Quart of oil and quart of transmission fluid
- ❏ Spare fan belts
- ❏ Spare fuses
- ❏ Tire-pressure gauge

*Excerpted from *Fodor's: How to Pack: Experts Share Their Secrets*
© 1997, by Fodor's Travel Publications

**JUNE: *Corporate Woods Jazz Festival.*** Bring your blankets and lawn chairs and enjoy the music of local jazz artists at this evening event. | 913/451–4466.

**JUNE: *Downtown Overland Park Days.*** An arts and crafts show is a part of the festivities, as merchants roll back their prices to the time of this town's founding. | 913/491–3600.

## Dining

**Chien Dynasty.** Chinese. Chinese paintings, figurines, and vases are found in this restaurant's three dining areas. Known for Szechuan and Hunan dishes. Lunch buffet. Sun. brunch. | 9921 W. 87th St. | 913/888–3000 | $7–$26 | AE, D, DC, MC, V.

**Coyote Grill.** Southwestern. Southwestern art and an airy openness make this one of the more popular restaurants in Johnson County. Known for pastas, fresh fish, and unusual salads and dressings. Kids' menu. Sun. buffet brunch. | 4843 Johnson Dr., Mission | 913/362–3333 | $10–$23 | AE, D, DC, MC, V.

**Dick Clark's American Bandstand Grill.** American/Casual. Rock 'n' roll history comes alive in this diner, owned by America's perpetual teenager. Vintage posters, gold albums, and artists' contracts on the walls complement the varied menu. Clark and other music celebrities sometimes stop in. Try the almond chicken fingers, salmon Florentine. | 10975 Metcalf Ave. | 913/451–1600 | $6–$15 | AE, D, DC, MC, V.

**Don Chilito's.** Mexican. This is a simple Mexican restaurant with good food and friendly service. Known for burritos and chimichangas. | 7017 Johnson Dr., Mission | 913/432–3066 | Reservations not accepted | $7–$10 | D, MC, V.

**Gates Bar-B-Que.** Barbecue. This is a legendary name in Kansas City barbecue. The restaurant's dining room has a prominent mural of animals and flora. Known for barbecue ribs, beef. | 2001 W. 103rd, Leawood | 913/383–1752 | Reservations not accepted | $5–$50 | No credit cards.

**Gerts Grille.** American. Televisions and sports paraphernalia are found throughout this bar/grill. Popular menu items include the Reuben and Philly cheesesteak sandwiches, the chili, and the Wisconsin cheese soup. Live music is performed on Sat. nights. | 12018 College Blvd. | 913/469–5505 | $4–$7 | AE, D, MC, V.

★ **Hayward's Pit Bar-B-Que.** Barbecue. Locals flock to this hillside restaurant for piles of succulent smoked beef, ribs, chicken, pork, and sausage. Views of the city are available from the windows in the large dining room. | 11051 Antioch Rd. | 913/451–8080 | $6–$14 | AE, DC, MC, V.

**Hereford House.** American. Branding irons, tack, cowboy hats, and a huge stone fireplace are part of the Old West feel in this branch of the legendary Kansas City restaurant. Open-air dining is available on the patio, which overlooks City Hall. Try the whiskey steak, baseball-cut sirloin, and prime rib. Kids' menu. | 5001 Town Center Dr., Leawood | 913/327–0800 | $14–$40 | AE, MC, V.

**Houston's.** American. The second of two such restaurants in the Kansas City metro area. The eclectic decor includes a copper fireplace, an eskimo sled hanging from the ceiling, and rare Polaroids taken by a nationally renowned artist. Known for steak, fresh fish. | 7111 W. 95th St. | 913/642–0630 | $9–$26 | AE, MC, V.

**Il Trullo.** Italian. White-linen cloths and candlelight set the mood in this respected Italian restaurant. Try the *zuppa di mare* (a tomato broth with seafood) or the *orecchiette con cime di rapa* (pasta in a vegetable broth). | 9056 Metcalf Ave. | 913/341–3773 | $8–$25 | AE, D, DC, MC, V.

**India Palace.** Indian. Subdued lighting and traditional Indian artwork are found throughout. Known for Indian-style barbecue. Lunch buffet, no smoking. | 9918 W. 87th St. | 913/381–1680 | $9–$13 | AE, D, DC, MC, V.

**Italian Delight.** Italian. This is a casual restaurant that's dressed up a bit by pictures of an unnamed Italian town. Known for stromboli, eggplant parmesan, and pizza. | 6522 Martway, Mission | 913/262–7564 | Closed Sun. | $4–$7 | No credit cards.

OVERLAND PARK

INTRO
ATTRACTIONS
DINING
LODGING

**J. Gilbert's Wood-Fired Steaks.** Steak. This dark, romantic restaurant has pictures dating back to the 1930s of its namesake family throughout. Try the Louisiana skillet-seared pepper fillet and grilled barbecue salmon. Kids' menu. | 8901 Metcalf Ave. | 913/642–8070 | $12–$28 | AE, D, DC, MC, V.

**Johnny Cascone's.** Italian. One of Kansas City's longest running family-owned restaurants has set up shop in Johnson County. Known for lasagna, seafood, steak. Kids' menu. | 6863 W. 91st St. | 913/381–6837 | $10–$20 | AE, D, DC, MC, V.

**K.C. Masterpiece.** Barbecue. In a city known for barbecue, this name is one of the leaders. The restaurant has an authentic 1930s appearance, and its many awards and pictures of famous guests are on display. Known for baby back ribs, fillet of pork, turkey. Kids' menu. | 10985 Metcalf Ave. | 913/345–1199 | Reservations not accepted | $7–$23 | AE, D, DC, MC, V.

**Nikko.** Japanese. Teppanyaki table service is available at this restaurant located inside the Marriott hotel. The dining room is filled with Asian artwork, including many miniature statues. Known for swordfish and filet mignon. Kids' menu. | 10800 Metcalf Ave. | 913/451–8000 | $15–$30 | AE, D, DC, MC, V.

**Rotisserie.** Continental. A skylight, waterfall, and many plants give this tri-sectioned dining area a relaxed feel. Known for prime rib, steak, seafood. Salad bar. Kids' menu. Sun. brunch. | 10100 College Blvd. | 913/323–1978 | $14–$23 | AE, D, DC, MC, V.

**Sushi Gin.** Japanese. Japanese tapestries are on the wall and Nihongo is spoken if desired. Known for sushi boat combinations, chicken or beef sukiyaki, and tempura. Kids' menu. | 9559 Nall Ave. | 913/649–8488 | Closed Sun. | $14–$24 | AE, D, DC, MC, V.

**Tatsu's French Restaraunt.** French. This small, elegant dining room is surprisingly located in a strip mall. Try the poached salmon with a champagne sauce, the *boeuf à la bourguignonne* (a beef stew in a red wine sauce), and its popular soufflé in a Grand Marnier sauce. | 4603 W. 90th St., Prairie Village | 913/383–9801 | Closed Sun. | $17–$30 | AE, DC, MC, V.

**The Woks.** Chinese. Here you'll find dark colors, dim lighting, and a wide open bar on one side of the dining room, which are part of a simple and peaceful mood. Try the Hunan sesame chicken and honeymoon duck. Buffet Sun. Kids' menu. | 8615 Hauser Dr., Lenexa | 913/541–1777 | $6–$12 | AE, D, MC, V.

**Yiayia's Eurobistro.** Continental. This casual spot is dressed up with textured, textile walls; rock pillars; and custom-made light fixtures. Known for steak, fresh seafood, and pasta. Open-air dining is available on a cozy stone patio. Sun. brunch. | 4701 W. 119th St. | 913/345–1111 | $8–$23 | AE, D, DC, MC, V.

## Lodging

**Amerisuites.** Built in the mid 1990s, this six-story hotel is 38 mi from the airport, 17 mi from Kansas City, and within 2 mi of several restaurants. Complimentary Continental breakfast, in-room data ports, microwaves, refrigerators, cable TV, in-room VCRs (and movies), pool, exercise equipment, laundry facilities, business services, some pets allowed. | 6801 W. 112th St. | 913/451–2553 or 800/833–1516 | fax 913/451–3098 | www.amerisuites.com | 126 suites | $99–$119 | AE, D, DC, MC, V.

**Candlewood Suites.** This three-story contemporary hotel is 10 mi from downtown Kansas City. A handful of restaurants are across the street, and there are a number within the area that will deliver to the hotel. In-room data ports, kitchenettes, microwaves, refrigerators, cable TV, in-room VCRs, gym, laundry facilities, no pets. | 11001 Oakmont St. | 913/469–5557 | fax 913/469–5558 | www.candlewoodsuites.com | 122 rooms | $89 | AE, D, DC, MC, V.

**ClubHouse Inn.** This motel is less than 20 mi from downtown Kansas City and 35 mi from the Kansas City Airport. Complimentary cocktails are served in the evening. Complimentary Continental breakfast, refrigerators (in suites), cable TV, pool, outdoor hot tub, exercise equipment, laundry facilities, business services. | 10610 Marty | 913/648–5555 | fax 913/648–7130 | www.clubhouseinn.com | 143 rooms, 22 suites | $89, $99 suites | AE, D, DC, MC, V.

**Courtyard by Marriott.** This three-story hotel is 12 mi from the riverboat casinos, and within walking distance of a number of restaurants. Bar, in-room data ports, refrigerators (in suites), cable TV, pool, outdoor hot tub, exercise equipment, laundry facilities, business services. | 11301 Metcalf Ave. | 913/339–9900 | fax 913/339–6091 | www.marriott.com | 149 rooms, 12 suites | $119; $139 suites | AE, D, DC, MC, V.

**Doubletree Hotel.** This 18-story hotel is adjacent to two major highways, a business park, and a scenic public jogging trail. A bowling alley and tennis courts are less than 2 mi away, and a shopping mall is 4 mi away. Restaurants (*see* Rotisserie), bar, in-room data ports, some refrigerators, cable TV, pool, outdoor hot tub, gym, business services, airport shuttle, some pets allowed. | 10100 College Blvd. | 913/451–6100 | fax 913/451–3873 | mcidt@aol.com | www.doubletreehotels.com | 357 rooms | $139–$144 | AE, D, DC, MC, V.

**Drury Inn.** Built in the early 1980s, this four-story hotel is about 10 mi from one of the largest malls in the state and within walking distance of area restaurants. Complimentary Continental breakfast, in-room data ports, cable TV, pool, business services, some pets allowed. | 10951 Metcalf Ave. | 913/345–1500 | fax 913/345–1500 | www.drury-inn.com | 55 rooms | $83 | AE, D, DC, MC, V.

**Embassy Suites.** The Missouri border is 2 mi from this seven-story hotel. Downtown Kansas City is less than 20 mi away, and a handful of restaurants are within walking distance. Restaurant, bar, complimentary breakfast, in-room data ports, refrigerators, room service, cable TV, pool, hot tub, exercise equipment, video games, business services, business services. | 10601 Metcalf Ave. | 913/649–7060 | fax 913/649–9382 | www.embassysuites.com | 199 suites | $149–$179 suites | AE, D, DC, MC, V.

**Extended StayAmerica.** Built in 1998, well-equipped apartment-style accommodations have modern facilities, including full kitchens with full-size refrigerators. In-room data ports, kitchenettes, microwaves, refrigerators, laundry facilities. | 10750 Quivira Rd. | 913/661–9299 | fax 913/661–9774 | www.exstay.com | 119 rooms | $59 | AE, D, DC, MC, V.

**Fairfield Inn by Marriott.** This three-story hotel is within 5 mi of most area businesses, and 2 mi from golf courses. A few fast food eateries are within walking distance, and a strip of restaurants is 2 mi away. Complimentary Continental breakfast, in-room data ports, cable TV, pool, business services. | 4401 W. 107th St. | 913/381–5700 | fax 913/381–5700 | www.marriott.com | 134 rooms | $64–$75 | AE, D, DC, MC, V.

**Hampton Inn.** In a commercial part of town, this five-story hotel is about 10 mi from a few shopping malls and across the (quite busy) street from a handful of restaurants. Complimentary Continental breakfast, in-room data ports, cable TV, pool, outdoor hot tub, business services. | 10591 Metcalf Frontage Rd. | 913/341–1551 | fax 913/341–8668 | www.hampton-inn.com | 134 rooms | $89 | AE, D, DC, MC, V.

**Holiday Inn Mission-Overland Park.** Two fast food eateries are adjacent to this hotel near the interchange of U.S. 56 and 69. Downtown Kansas City is 10 mi away. Restaurant, pool, hot tub, gym, video games. | 7240 Shawnee Mission Pkwy. | 913/262–3010 or 800/795–5595 | fax 913/262–6180 | himissn@ix.netcom.com | www.holiday-inn.com | 196 rooms | $110–$120 | AE, D, DC, MC, V.

**Homestead Village.** A strip of restaurants is nine blocks from this three-story extended-stay hotel. In-room data ports, kitchenettes, microwaves, refrigerators, cable TV, laundry facilities, pets allowed (deposit). | 5401 W. 110th St. | 913/661–7111 | fax 913/661–4744 | www.stayhsd.com | 132 rooms | $59–$75 | AE, D, DC, MC, V.

**Homewood Suites KC.** Each apartment-style suite has a full kitchen in this large, attractive hotel. Numerous restaurants are within 4 mi. Complimentary Continental breakfast, room service, kitchenettes, microwaves, refrigerators, cable TV, pool, hot tub, gym, babysitting, laundry services, no pets. | 10556 Marty Ave. | 913/341–5576 | fax 913/341–5573 | www.homewood-suites.com | 92 rooms | $109 | AE, D, DC, MC, V.

**Overland Park Marriott Hotel.** This 11-story hotel is in a suburban business area. The lobby has a marble floor, and rooms on the concierge level are slightly larger than the others. Arrowhead Stadium is 15 mi away. Restaurant (*see* Nikko), bar, cable TV, indoor-outdoor pool, outdoor hot tub, gym, video games, business services, airport shuttle. | 10800 Metcalf Ave. | 913/451–8000 | fax 913/451–5914 | www.marriott.com | 397 rooms | $139–$169 | AE, D, DC, MC, V.

**Parks Lodge.** A number of restaurants are within walking distance of this modest two-story motel. Some in-room data ports, cable TV, pool, pets allowed. | 7508 Shawnee Mission Pkwy. | 913/262–9600 | 86 rooms | $39 | AE, D, DC, MC, V.

**Radisson.** Area shops and restaurants are within 5 mi of this eight-story hotel. Restaurant, bar (with entertainment), in-room data ports, room service, cable TV, indoor-outdoor pool, outdoor hot tub, exercise equipment, business services. | 8787 Reeder Rd. | 913/888–8440 | fax 913/888–3438 | www.radisson.com | 192 rooms, 46 suites | $149–$169 suites | AE, D, DC, MC, V.

**White Haven.** This motel has a white-brick facade, white wrought-iron balconies, and leaded-glass windows. Some kitchenettes, refrigerators, cable TV, pool, business services, some pets allowed. | 8039 Metcalf Ave. | 913/649–8200 or 800/752–2892 | fax 913/901–8199 | 79 rooms | $43–$85 | AE, D, DC, MC, V.

**Wyndham Garden.** Request a room with a view of the pool at this two-story hotel. A shopping mall is 3 mi away, and restaurants along Metcalf Ave. are within walking distance. Restaurant, bar, complimentary Continental breakfast, in-room data ports, some refrigerators, room service, cable TV, pool, exercise equipment, laundry facilities, business services. | 7000 W. 108th St. | 913/383–2550 | fax 913/383–2099 | www.wyndham.com | 180 rooms | $114 | AE, D, DC, MC, V.

# PARSONS

MAP 3, K8

*(Nearby town also listed: Chanute)*

Founded in 1871 by Levi Parsons, the president of the Missouri, Kansas, and Texas Railroad, this town of 12,000 has always been connected with the railroad and agriculture. Parsons boasts a lovely European-style shopping plaza with unique and interesting shops. An arboretum and flower-planting program sponsored by the city makes this a pleasant community to visit, even if you do nothing more than take a stroll while eating ice cream.

Information: **Parsons Chamber of Commerce** | Box 737, Parsons, KS 67357 | 316/421–6500 | clark@parsons.com | www.parsonsks.com.

## Attractions

**Lake Parsons.** Nearly 2,000 acres of land and water create first-class fishing, camping, swimming, and picnicking opportunities. | 32nd St. at Main St. | 316/421–7000 | $4 per vehicle | Daily.

**Marvel Park.** Numerous lighted fields make this the spot for baseball, football, and other sports. Camping and picnic facilities are also available. | E. Main St. at 10th St. | 316/421–7077 | Free | Daily.

**Neosho County State Fishing Lake.** Here you can fish, boat, camp, and picnic. | 200 S. Peacock | 316/421–7077 | fax 316/421–7079 | www.kdwp.state.ks.us | Free | Daily.

**Oakwood Cemetery.** Nearly 400 Civil War soldiers (primarily Union) are buried here. | S. Leawood | 316/421–7000 | Free | Daily.

**Parsons Arboretum.** The Union Pacific Railroad deeded approximately 19 acres of land to the City in October 1991, which became home to this lush arboretum. Here you'll find a cozy visitor center, plus a scenic gazebo, an experimental 2-acre wetlands preserve, and, of course, lots of trees. | 21st and Wilson Sts. | 316/421–5788 | Free | May–Oct., Fri.–Sun. 1:30–5 and by appointment.

**Parsons Historical Museum.** Everything from buttons to a horse-drawn hearse can be seen here. The museum doors were once those of the town's First Methodist Church. | 401 S. 18th St. | 316/421–6500 | Donation | May–Oct., Fri.–Sun. 1:30–5, or by appointment.

**Pearson-Skubitz Big Hill Lake.** One of Kansas's few natural-sand swimming beaches makes this lake a major attraction, as do the horse trails, hiking trails, and boating resources. | 19,000 Rd. | 316/336–2741 | fax 316/336–3903 | Free | Apr.–Oct., daily.

**ON THE CALENDAR**
**JUNE: *Arts and Crafts Fair.*** This-one day event brings out the best artisans in three states for a show and sale. | 316/421–6500.
**JUNE: *Flatlanders Auto Show.*** More than 200 old and new cars, trucks, and motorcycles are on display in Forest Park. | 316/421–6500.

## Dining
**The Hickory Hole.** Barbecue. This casual barbecue joint does a great job with home cooking. Known for chicken, pork, and smoked ribs. Kids' menu. | 720 E. Main St. | 316/421–9067 | Reservations not accepted | Closed Mon., Tues. | $4–$13 | D, DC, MC, V.

**Sirloin Stockade.** American. This restaurant chain serves an all-you-can-eat buffet with gigantic quantities of food, such as steaks, chops, fried chicken, seafood specialties, fresh salads, rolls, pastries, and desserts. Homemade breads. Kids' menu. | 1000 E. Main St. | 316/421–0022 | $6–$10 | MC, V.

## Lodging
**Canterbury Inn.** On the east side of town, this two-story brick motel is within 5 blocks of a few restaurants and shops. Restaurant, pool. | 400 E. Main | 316/421–5000 | 84 rooms | $42–$52 | AE, D, DC, MC, V.

**The Parsonian.** City views are available from this eight-story building built in 1954 to attract visitors to Parsons. Apartment units are rented on a monthly basis. Restaurant, bar, complimentary Continental breakfast, cable TV. | 1725 Broadway | 316/421–4400 | 55 rooms, 5 suites; 5 apartments | $38, $45 suites, $550–$750 apartments (30–day minimum stay) | AE, DC, MC, V.

**Super 8 Motel.** A number of restaurants are across the highway from this two-story motel on the east side of town. Complimentary Continental breakfast, some microwaves, refrigerators, some in-room hot tubs, cable TV, pool, laundry facilities, pets allowed (deposit). | 229 East Main | 316/421–8000 | fax 316/421–8228 | www.super8.com | 48 rooms | $55 | AE, D, DC, MC, V.

**Townsman.** Attractive, modern rooms in this white-brick motel have mirrors and pictures throughout. The lobby has a miniature house owned by the manager and decorated for all seasons. Restaurant, cable TV, business services, some pets allowed. | 1830 South U.S. 59 | 316/421–6990 or 800/552–4008 | fax 316/421–4767 | 38 rooms | $37 | AE, D, DC, MC, V.

# PHILLIPSBURG

MAP 3, E3

*(Nearby town also listed: Smith Center)*

Laid out by surveyors in 1872, this town of 2,800 became the county seat only after a fierce legal battle with Kirwin, also in Phillips County. In the early days of the county, life was so rugged here that court and church services were closed when a herd of

PHILLIPSBURG

INTRO
ATTRACTIONS
DINING
LODGING

buffalo was spotted in the area. While Buffalo-hunting is no longer the primary trade, fishing and hunting—particularly of geese—are popular activities in this northern part of Kansas. Today the area's economy relies predominantly on wheat and soybean farming.

Information: **Phillipsburg Area Chamber of Commerce** | 270 State St. (Box 326), Phillipsburg, KS 67661 | 785/543–2321 or 800/543–2321 | skyways.lib.ks.us/kansas/towns/Phillipsburg.

## Attractions

**C&R Railroad Museum.** Tucked inside a 57-ft artificial mountain range in the McDill "Huck" Boyd Center is one of the largest and most elaborate model-train environments in the country. It's the legacy of local railroad enthusiast Bill Clarke, whose labor of love now boasts 94 engines, 170 cars, 34 cabooses, 137 railroad lanterns, and more than 1,200 feet of track housed in a room with special lighting for daytime and nighttime effects. If you call and ask, Bill himself may come down and give you a guided tour. | McDill "Huck" Boyd Community Center, 860 Park St. | 785/543–5535 | www.geocities.com/crrailroad/ | Free | Weekdays 9–4 or by appointment.

**Kirwin National Wildlife Refuge.** This 11,000-acre refuge contributes to Phillips County's reputation as the Goose Capital of Kansas. | Rte. 9 | 785/543–6673 | Free | Daily.

**Old Fort Bissell.** Fort Bissell was built of cottonwood logs for the protection of white settlers from Native Americans, but never served as a military post. | City Park, U.S. 36 | 785/543–6212 | Free | Apr.–Oct., Tues.–Fri. 11–5, weekends 1–5.

### ON THE CALENDAR

**JUNE: *Riverless Festival.*** During the first weekend of June, the town of Phillipsburg accommodates a wholesome summer fair, where activities include a 5-mi run benefitting the county hospital, a radio-controlled model plane fly-in, a tractor pull, a horseshoe tournament, an arts and crafts show, food, drink, music, dance, and much more. The weekend event winds up with an evening concert, usually featuring Country and Western music. | 785/543–2321.

**JULY–AUG.: *Phillips County Fair.*** Candy apples, cotton candy, and saltwater taffy make this fair like every other, but enjoyable nonetheless. | 785/543–2722.

**AUG.: *The Phillipsburg Rodeo.*** Kansas's biggest rodeo has been drawing visitors from near and far since 1929. | 785/543–2722 | www.kansasbiggestrodeo.com.

## Dining

**Chubby Pickle.** American. You'll find simple fare such as hamburgers and deli-style sandwiches at this modest eatery. | 603 State St. | 785/543–6474 | fax 785/543–2551 | Closed Sun. | $3–$5 | No credit cards.

**Shelly Ann's Cafe.** American. Photos of Country music stars line the walls of this small, homey café. Homemade breads, pies, potatoes, and gravy as well as daily specials. | 210 State St. | 785/543–5386 | $3–$5 | No credit cards.

## Lodging

**Cottonwood Inn.** Some rooms at this modern, attractive, two-story motel have a view of the 18-hole golf course across the street. Cable TV, pool, gym, pets allowed. | Jct. E. U.S. 36 and 183 | 800/466–7332 | fax 785/543–5432 | 40 rooms | $55 | AE, D, DC, MC, V.

**Mark V.** The Italian marble statue of a Greek goddess (at the entrance of this motel) caused quite a stir when it was installed but is now the pride of the community. Rooms are large and comfortable, with paneling and painted brick walls. In-room data ports, cable TV, pool. | 320 W. State St. (U.S. 36) | 785/543–5223 or 800/219–3149 | fax 913/543–2323 | 33 rooms | $35–$46 | AE, D, MC, V.

# PITTSBURG

*(Nearby town also listed: Fort Scott)*

This part of Kansas is known as "The Little Balkans" because of the number of European immigrants who came here to work coal mines. Because of the low wages and political diversity, the area was ripe for labor union unrest and violence in the early 1900s. The railroads and the coal they transported brought growth to Pittsburg, which at one time boasted more than 50,000 residents. Founded in 1876 by lawyer Frank Playter, today Pittsburg is a comfortable town of 24,800, dominated economically and socially by the university here.

Information: **Crawford County Convention and Visitors Bureau** | Box 1115, Pittsburg, KS 66762-1115 | 316/231–1212 or 800/879–1112.

## Attractions

**Big Brutus.** You see it long before you get there. This is the second-largest electric shovel in the world, once used to strip coal from the mines of southeast Kansas. | 6 mi west of Rte. 7 and Rte. 102 junction, West Mineral | 316/827–6177 | fax 316/827–6174 | $4 | Daily 9–5.

**Crawford County Historical Museum.** Displays include vintage clothing, photos, vehicles, and coal-mining artifacts. | 651 S. U.S. 69 | 316/231–1440 | Donation accepted | Wed.–Sun. 12:30–4:30.

**Crawford State Park.** While this 500-acre park with a 150-acre lake is small in comparison to other state parks, Crawford is lush and wooded and has interpretive nature trails. | 1 Lake Rd. | 316/362–3671 | www.kdwp.state.ks.us | $4 per vehicle | Daily.

**Lincoln Park.** An 18-hole golf course, batting cages, mini-golf, tennis, a children's amusement park, swimming pools, water slides, and more can be found here. | Memorial Dr. at U.S. 69 Bypass | 316/231–8310 | Free | Daily.

### ON THE CALENDAR

**JUNE:** *Miners Day Reunion.* Primarily retired miners and their families celebrate the region's mining heritage by visiting Big Brutus and having a cook-out. | 316/827–6177.
**SEPT.:** *Little Balkans Days Folk Festival.* Polka music, bocce, horseshoes, and ethnic food are part of this celebration downtown. | 800/879–1112.

## Dining

**Trapper Jack's.** American. This hunting- and fishing-themed restaurant is the hottest place to eat in town. The interior is decorated floor-to-ceiling with taxidermy (an entire stuffed caribou can be found in the dining room; fortunately, it doesn't seem to bother the stuffed bear). Try the fried alligator or crawfish appetizers, then choose from a menu which includes fresh salmon and trout, fried chicken, steak, buffalo burgers, pasta, and soup. Known for country-fried steak, served in a hot skillet. Homemade desserts. Kids' menu. | 2912 N. Broadway | 316/231–8222 | $8–$17 | AE, D, DC, MC, V.

## Lodging

**Holiday Inn Express.** Some of the modern rooms have a view of the pool area, and each one has a work desk with a lamp. The business district is 3 mi from the hotel. Picnic area, complimentary Continental breakfast, in-room data ports, cable TV, pool, hot tub, exercise equipment, laundry facilities, business services. | 4020 Parkview Dr. (U.S. 69 N) | 316/231–8700 | fax 316/230–0154 | www.hiexpress.com/pittsburgks | 100 rooms | $51–$80 | AE, D, DC, MC, V.

**Holiday Lodge.** This two-story motor lodge built in 1998 has few frills, but there's a friendly and helpful staff, and it's adjacent to a Sizzler steakhouse. Restaurant nearby, cable TV, no pets. | 2701 N. Broadway | 316/231–1350 | fax 316/231–1350 | 22 rooms | $36 | AE, D, DC, MC, V.

# PRATT

MAP 3, F7

*(Nearby town also listed: Medicine Lodge)*

Named after a Civil War officer killed in the Battle of Wilson Creek, Pratt became the county seat in 1887, not long after its founding by European settlers in 1884. Brick-lined streets from the early 1900s remain, as do a number of Victorian mansions, some of which are on the National Register of Historic Places. As a center for agriculture, the largest livestock show and sale in the country is held each week in this town of 6,800. The sense of humor of Pratt residents is evidenced by their regionally famous twin water towers—one labeled hot, the other cold. Don't feel silly getting your picture taken before them. Everyone does.

Information: **Pratt Area Chamber of Commerce** | Box 469, Pratt, KS 67124 | 316/672–5501 | www.prattkan.com.

## Attractions

**Kansas State Fish Hatchery/Nature Center.** Channel catfish, walleye, and bluegill are the most popular of fish raised in the 87 culture ponds here. | 512 S.E. 25th Ave. | 316/672–5911 | fax 316/672–6020 | Free | Weekdays 8–5.

**Pratt County Historical Society Museum.** Displays in four galleries showcase the area's history from prehistoric times through the present. | 208 S. Ninnescah | 316/672–7874 | Free | Daily 2–4, till 5 on weekends during daylight savings.

**Pratt Livestock.** Watch as cattle are auctioned off at the largest independently owned barn in the country. | 30274 E. U.S. 54 | 316/672–5961 | Free | Thurs. 8 PM–12 AM.

### ON THE CALENDAR
**JUNE:** *Miss Kansas Pageant.* This week-long pageant and parade is held at Pratt Community College. The winner goes on to compete in the Miss America pageant. | 316/672–5501.
**JULY:** *Pratt County Fair.* This is a 4-H and Open Class fair with more than 2,500 exhibits, a carnival, and nightly entertainment. | 316/672–6121.
**SEPT.:** *Saturday Art in the Park.* This one-day event showcases the fine arts and crafts of local artists. Background musicians and food vendors are also on hand. | 316/672–5501.

## Dining

**Ricky's Restaurant.** American. This small, family-owned restaurant serves up home cookin' and homemade soup. Try the country fries, ribs, and chicken-fried steak. | 2005 W. U.S. 54 | 316/672–3681 | Breakfast also available | $3–15 | No credit cards.

**Café Bourgeois.** Cajun. You may not expect to find authentic Cajun cooking in the heart of Kansas, but you will here. Owner and proprietor Troy Bourgeois was born and raised in south Louisiana, and he's brought a taste of the bayou to prairie country. Choose from Southern seafood specialties, steaks, and chicken served in three spacious rooms with a Mardi Gras theme (which includes zydeco music in the background). Known for blackened shrimp. | 1600 East First | 316/672–2588 | Closed Mon.–Tues. | $6–$16 | MC, V.

## Lodging

**Best Western Hillcrest.** Each room has modern furnishings and pictures of country settings in this motel 1 mi from a golf course and the Pratt County Historical Society Museum. Complimentary Continental breakfast, in-room data ports, refrigerator, cable TV, pool, business services, pets allowed. | 1336 E. 1st St. | 316/672–6407 | fax 316/672–6707 | www.best-western.com | 42 rooms | $42 | AE, D, DC, MC, V.

**Evergreen Motel.** Some rooms have a view of the surrounding property with evergreen trees and bushes. RV hookups are available. Restaurant, cable TV, pool. | 2001 Rte. 54 | 316/672–6431 | fax 316/672–6431 | 16 rooms | $34 | AE, D, MC, V.

**Pratt Guest House.** Built in 1907, the Pratt Guest House is a luxurious Victorian-style B&B listed on the National Register of Historic Places. Hosts Richard and Diane Ring have five unique rooms to choose from, each neatly appointed in antiques and period furnishings. Complimentary full breakfast, cable TV, no kids under 12, no smoking. | 105 N. Luka | 316/672–1200 | fax 316/672–1080 | pghbb@socencom.net | www.prattguesthouse.com | 5 rooms | $70 | No credit cards.

# RUSSELL

*(Nearby towns also listed: Ellsworth, Hays, Lucas)*

The first white people in this part of Kansas arrived in 1871 from Germany, Russia, and Bohemia via Wisconsin. Named after a young settler who organized an infantry unit for the Civil War, this town of 4,500 is best known as the home of three-time presidential contender and retired U.S. Senate Majority Leader Bob Dole. In addition to western Kansas's wheat farms, the economy is diversified with light manufacturing that includes recreational vehicles and oil production equipment. Many people call this "post rock country" for the fence posts that remain from the earliest settlers (the lack of trees forced them to quarry red limestone and chisel it for fence posts). These posts are easily visible while driving along the interstate or more rural roads.

**Information: Russell Area Chamber of Commerce** | 610 Main St., Russell, KS 67665 | 785/483–6960 | www.russellks.org.

## Attractions

**Deines Cultural Center.** This center permanently houses the wood engravings of nationally known artist E. Hubert Deines. The work of 50 other artists as well as traveling exhibits are also featured. | 820 N. Main St. | 785/483–3742 | Donation accepted | Tues.–Sun. 1–5.

**Fossil Station Museum.** Built in 1907, this museum captures the spirit of the early settlers with historical displays from the 1860s to the present. | 331 Kansas St. | 785/483–3637 | Donation | May–Sept., weekdays 11–4, weekends 1–4; Oct.–Apr., by appointment.

**Gernon House.** When the first European settlers pushed across the plains, they were confronted with a unique obstacle: the treeless prairie provided virtually no materials with which to build homes. The settlers solved their problem by using the prairie itself. The Greenhorn Limestone, which runs in thick veins under the ground, proved to be an ideal building material; soft and malleable in the ground, it oxidizes in the air, eventually becoming hard as granite. The two-story Gernon House, built in 1872, is the oldest building made of this material (called "post rock" because it was versatile enough to roll into cylinders for fenceposts) in the town of Russell. | 818 N. Kansas | 785/483–3637 | Free | By appointment only.

**Oil Patch Museum.** Various exhibits and dioramas tell the history of Black Gold discovered in the area. | Intersection of I–70 and U.S. 281 | 785/483–6640 | Free | May–Labor Day, Wed.–Sat. 10–4, Sun. 1–4.

**Wilson Dam and Reservoir.** Lake Wilson is one of the clearest lakes in Kansas and offers boating, fishing, camping, hiking, hang gliding, and hunting facilities. | Off Rte. 232, 35 mi east of Russell | 785/658–2551 | Free | Apr.–Oct., daily.

**Wilson State Park.** Many consider this the most scenic park in the state for hiking, camping, and mountain biking. It's off Rte. 232, 8 mi north of I–70. | Rte. 232, Sylvan Grove | 785/658–2465 | www.kdwp.state.ks.us | $4 per vehicle | Daily.

ON THE CALENDAR
**JULY:** *Russell County Free Fair.* This is a 4-H and Open Class fair with more than 2,500 exhibits, a carnival, and nightly entertainment. | 785/483–3157.

**JULY–AUG.:** *NBC World Series Baseball.* Teams from across the United States compete in this baseball tournament for boys 13 years old and under. | 785/483–6960.

## Dining
**Fossil Station Mesquite Grill.** Steak. This is one of the only steakhouses in the county that serves certified Angus Beef. You can stop by the bar, watch the game, and check out the model train which chugs around the place. Or you can take a large booth under a mural in the dining room and order mesquite-grilled steaks, chicken, and chops, or perhaps grilled shrimp and pasta. | 1410 S. Fossil | 785/483–5942 | $3–$18 | AE, D, MC, V.

## Lodging
**Bonnie's Cottage Inn.** Built in 1890, this authentic Victorian home has much of its original detail intact. The proprietors live across the street, so you'll have the eight-room home to yourself. Regional antiques can be found throughout, and Main St., where you'll find antique and gift shops, a cultural center, and more, is just one block away. Complimentary full breakfast, laundry facilities, pets allowed, no smoking. | 223 W. 7th | 785/483–5837 | 3 rooms | $80 | No credit cards.

**Days Inn.** This multi-story redbrick hotel has clapboard accents and basic, affordable rooms with interior access. Complimentary Continental breakfast, cable TV, pool. | 229 S. Main | 785/525–6358 | www.daysinn.com | 49 rooms | $57–$65 | AE, D, MC, V.

**Russell's Inn.** This ranch-style inn is family-owned and has friendly service. Restaurant, bar, cable TV, pool, laundry facilities. | U.S. 281 and I–70 | 785/483–2107 or 800/736–4598 | fax 785/483–4447 | 65 rooms | $46–$54 | AE.

**Super 8.** Rooms have interior access in this two-story motel. The Fossil Station Museum and Oil Patch Museum are ½ mile away. Cable TV, business services. | 1405 S. Fossil | 785/483–2488 | fax 785/483–2488 | www.super8.com | 45 rooms | $53 | AE, D, DC, MC, V.

# SALINA

MAP 3, G5

*(Nearby towns also listed: Ellsworth, Lindsborg, McPherson)*

Before the railroad arrived in 1867, this settlement along the banks of the Smoky Hill and Saline rivers consisted of only a few families who made their living by hunting and trapping. Until the federal government opened an Air Force base here in the 1950s, the town remained relatively insignificant in its contribution to the growth of the state. When the interstate system passed through in the mid-1960s, Salina became the intersecting city between the east–west corridor of I–70 and the north–south route of I–135. This town of 47,500 is today a central distribution point for many companies, and a transportation hub for much of central Kansas.

Information: **Salina Area Chamber of Commerce** | 120 W. Ash (Box 586), Salina, KS 67402 | 785/827–9301 | www.salinakansas.org.

## Attractions
**Bicentennial Center.** On almost any given day, this convention center has something for the public, from sporting events to trade shows to concerts. | 800 The Midway | 785/826–7200 | www.bicentennial.org | Prices vary with events | Hours vary with events.

**Central Kansas Flywheels Historical Museum.** Several buildings house machinery, furniture, and shop displays of years gone by. | 1100 W. Diamond Dr. | 785/825–8473 | www.salinakansas.org/attract | $2; children free | Apr.–Sept., Tues.–Sun. 1–7.

**Salina Art Center.** Regional, national, and international exhibits are on display here. Educational programs and hands-on activities are available for both children and adults throughout the year. | 242 S. Santa Fe | 785/827–1431 or 800/284–6022 | Free | Tues.–Wed. and Fri.–Sat. noon–5, Thurs. noon–7, Sun. 1–5.

**Smoky Hill Museum.** See a rugged dug-out where early inhabitants of this region lived, as well as other artifacts of historic significance. | 211 W. Iron Ave. | 785/826–7460 | Free | Tues.–Fri. noon–5, Sat. 10–5, Sun. 1–5.

**Smoky Hill Vineyards and Winery.** More than 80 acres of grapes result in a unique wine, available for sampling. | 212 W. Golf Link Rd. | 785/825–2515 | Free | Tues.–Fri. noon–5, Sat. 10–5, Sun. 1–5.

**ON THE CALENDAR**
**JUNE: *Smoky Hill River Festival.*** Established in 1977, this 4-day event celebrates the arts and the community. | 785/826–7410.
**SEPT.: *Santa Fe Days.*** Held along Santa Fe St. in downtown Salina, this event celebrates the neighborhood's heritage with a parade, a crafts fair, and more. | 785/827–9301.
**OCT.: *Steam Engine and Antique Farm Engine Show.*** An antique tractor pull, stone post cutting, and other activities at the Central Kansas Flywheels Historical Museum make this a fun local event. | 785/825–8473.
**AUG.: *Tri-Rivers Fair and Rodeo.*** Crowds are drawn to this event's demonstrations, food, and concerts. | 785/827–4425.

## Dining
**Bayards.** American. The atmosphere is casual at Bayards, where rough wood paneling and hearty home cooking go hand-in-hand. Satisfy your cravings with chicken and apple dumplings, T-bone steaks, and homemade pies and desserts. Known for burgers. Kids' menu. | 2301 N. 9th (Jct. I–70 and U.S. 81) | 785/825–4351 | $5–$12 | MC, V.

**Gutierrez.** Mexican. Hand-painted murals with jesters and clowns in Southwestern colors create a fun atmosphere. Known for chimichangas. Kids' menu. | 1935 S. Ohio | 785/825–1649 | $9–$17 | AE, D, DC, MC, V.

**Ranger's Steak and Seafood.** Steak. Ranger's is a big, comfortable steak joint with old signs and antiques on the walls, candles on the tables, and an open fireplace in the dining room. Known for prime rib. Kids' menu. | 716 N. Twelve | 785/823–3491 | Closed Sun. | $9–$29 | AE, D, DC, MC, V.

## Lodging
**Best Western Heart of America Inn.** Rooms have contemporary furnishings in this hotel just off I–35. The family suite accommodates up to six people. 2 restaurants nearby, bar, in-room data ports, cable TV, pool, hot tub, sauna, pets allowed. | 632 Westport Blvd. | 785/827–9315 | fax 785/827–4119 | www.bestwestern.com | 100 rooms, 1 suite | $58; $100 suite | AE, D, DC, MC, V.

**Best Western Mid-America Inn.** Modern guest rooms have large couches at this motel 2 mi from the Bicentennial Center and the Smoky Hill Museum. Restaurant, bar, complimentary Continental breakfast, in-room data ports, room service, cable TV, indoor-outdoor pool, hot tub, business services, some pets allowed. | 1846 N. 9th | 785/827–0356 | fax 785/827–7688 | www.bestwestern.com | 108 rooms | $42–$64 | AE, D, DC, MC, V.

**Budget Host Vagabond II.** Bright, colorful rooms have modern furnishings and scenic pictures of mountains and landscaping on the walls. Cable TV, pool, business services, pets allowed. | 217 S. Broadway (U.S. 81 Bus.) | 785/825–7265 | fax 785/825–7003 | www.bud-gethost.com | 45 rooms | $34–$45 | AE, D, DC, MC, V.

**Candlewood Suites.** Spacious suites have full kitchens and CD players. Check out a movie at the videotape lending-library, or satisfy a craving at the 24-hour convenience store. In-room data ports, kitchenettes, microwaves, refrigerators, cable TV, in-room VCRs (and movies), gym, laundry facilities, no pets. | 2650 Planet Ave. | 785/823–6939 | fax 785/823–9679 | www.candlewoodsuites.com/salina | 69 suites | $69–$79 | AE, D, DC, MC, V.

**Comfort Inn.** Contemporary rooms have warm, pastel colors and comfortable beds and recliners. Complimentary Continental breakfast, in-room data ports, some refrigerators, cable TV, indoor pool, hot tub, business services, some pets allowed. | 1820 W. Crawford | 785/826–1711 | fax 785/827–6530 | www.comfortinn.com | 60 rooms | $59–$89 | AE, D, DC, MC, V.

**Country Inn and Suites.** This is a clean, spacious hotel with hardwood floors, elegant wallpaper, and lots of natural light. Complimentary Continental breakfast, in-room data ports, kitchenettes, gym, laundry facilities, business services, no pets. | 2760 S. Ninth | 785/827–1271 | 72 rooms | $69 | AE, D, DC, MC, V.

**Holiday Inn.** In downtown Salina, 5 mi from the Salina Regional Airport. Restaurant, bar, in-room data ports, room service, cable TV, indoor-outdoor pool, hot tub, miniature golf, exercise equipment, video games, playground, laundry facilities, business services, airport shuttle. | 1616 W. Crawford | 785/823–1739 | fax 785/823–1791 | www.holiday-inn.com | 195 rooms | $63–$125 | AE, D, DC, MC, V.

**Ramada Inn.** This two-story hotel is 6 mi from the Central Mall, where you can take care of all your shopping needs. Restaurant, bar, complimentary Continental breakfast, room service, cable TV, pool, business services, pets allowed (fee). | 1949 N. 9th St. | 785/825–8211 | fax 785/823–1048 | www.ramada.com | 103 rooms | $48–$68 | AE, D, DC, MC, V.

**Red Coach Inn.** This two-story motel is recognizable by the big red stage coach outside. A mall and a movie theater are 5 mi away. Restaurant, complimentary Continental breakfast, in-room data ports, some refrigerators, room service, cable TV, some in-room VCRs, indoor pool, hot tub, miniature golf, playground, laundry facilities, business services, some pets allowed. | 2020 W. Crawford | 785/825–2111 | fax 785/825–6973 | 114 rooms | $49–$120 | AE, D, DC, MC, V.

# SCOTT CITY

MAP 3, C6

*(Nearby town also listed: Garden City)*

Scott City and Scott County were named after General Winfield Scott, a War of 1812 hero. Considered one of Kansas's fastest growing cities in the early 1900s, the arid, dry summers and windswept, cold winters of this western Kansas town stunted its growth as harshly as they did the crops early settlers attempted to grow. Today, Scott City is a pleasant small town of 5,200, surrounded by herds of grazing cattle and hundreds of miles of open prairie.

Information: **Scott City Chamber of Commerce** | 221 W. 5th, Scott City, KS 67871 | 316/872–3525 | www.scottcity.com.

## Attractions

**Keystone Gallery.** This site is a combination of an art gallery, a fossil museum, and a souvenir shop. | 401 U.S. 83 | 316/872–2762 | www.keystonegallery.com | Free | Daily 9–6.

**Lake Scott State Park.** In the midst of a prairie, this park is an oasis of natural springs, wooded canyons, and craggy bluffs. | 520 W. Scott Lake Dr. | 316/872–2061 | www.kdwp.state.ks.us | $4 per vehicle | Daily.

**AUG.: *Beefiesta.*** This event celebrates Scott City's primary industry of cattle production with a fair and free barbecue. | 316/872–3525.
**SEPT.: *Whimmydiddle.*** More than 300 exhibitors from 11 states display original artwork, metalwork, pottery, and crafts. | 316/872–3525.

## Dining
**El Conquistador II.** Mexican. Big servings and low prices make this restaurant a local favorite. Known for giant burritos. | 109 Park Ln | 316/872–2777 | Closed Sun. | $2–$9 | D, DC, MC, V.

## Lodging
**Airliner Motel.** This one-story mom-and-pop operation is not fancy, but it's clean and comfortable, and there is a laundromat across the street. In-room data ports, some refrigerators, cable TV. | 609 E. Fifth St. | 800/239–2419 | 30 rooms | $37 | AE, D, DC, MC, V.

**Lady Di's Court Bed and Breakfast.** Innkeeper Diana Griffith has tastefully decorated guest rooms with three distinct themes (English, nautical, and safari). The family room has a big-screen TV and fireplace, and a patio is out back. Complimentary breakfast. | 1520 Court St. | 316/872–3348 | 3 rooms (with shared baths) | $40–$45 | No credit cards.

# SEDAN

MAP 3, J8

*(Nearby towns also listed: Arkansas City, Coffeyville)*

This town of 1,300 was founded in 1875 by Frenchman Thomas Scurr, who thought the area looked like his hometown of Sedan, France. The town boomed quickly because of the oil and cattle industry that flourished here, but the area was hard hit economically in the 1980s. Sedan has been re-built slowly and steadily on tourism. A road with 10,700 yellow bricks displaying the names of celebrities and common folks alike extends more than a mile around town.

**Information: Southeast Kansas Regional Tourism** | 150 E. Main St., Sedan, KS 67361 | 316/725–5797.

## Attractions
**Emmett Kelly Museum.** This is the birthplace and childhood home of one of the world's most famous clowns. | 204 E. Main St. | 316/725–3470 | Donation accepted | May–Oct., Tues.–Sun. 10–5.

**The Yellow Brick Road.** Add your name to the nearly 11,000 bricks and see where the road takes you in this tiny Kansas community. | Around town | 316/725–5797 | Free | Daily.

**APR.: *Red Bud Tour.*** The red bud trees turn the landscape pink during the second weekend of April, making a driving tour a pleasant journey. | 316/725–5797.
**MAY: *Yellow Brick Road Festival.*** Put on your ruby red slippers and follow the yellow brick road to crafts, food, and musical entertainment around town. | 316/725–5797.

## Dining
**Kim Arjo's.** American. Friendly proprietor Kim Arjo has built a self-contained tropical oasis in the middle of sleepy Sedan, Kansas. Faux palm trees and indoor waterfalls welcome visitors who come to dine on steaks, seafood, and sandwiches. Your waitress is likely to be wearing a grass skirt, and there's usually a guy in a gorilla suit making a monkey of himself for the guests' amusement. Known for fried brownies, homemade cheesecake. | 150 E. Main | 316/725–5633 | Closed Sun. | $6–$18 | D, DC, MC, V.

# SENECA

*(Nearby towns also listed: Hiawatha, Marysville)*

French and Swiss immigrants were the first white settlers to this area in the 1850s and the town is thought to be named for Seneca, Ohio, where one of the original families was from. The Pony Express came through here as it left St. Joseph, Missouri. Main Street Seneca is still paved with bricks laid in the early 1900s, and many buildings remain from that time as well. As in the days of the Pony Express, dairy and grain farming serve as the economic base for this town of 2,000. Light manufacturing plants also contribute as sources of local employment.

Information: **Glacial Hills Tourism Council** | 318 Broadway, Valley Falls, KS 66088 | 785/945–6292.

## Attractions

**Fort Markley and Indian Village.** This Old West town replica is filled with covered wagons, pioneer buildings, and places to eat buffalo burgers. | U.S. 36, ½ mi west of Seneca | 785/336–2285 | Free | Daily.

**Pony Express Museum.** This is the only original Pony Express station still standing in the United States. Inside is a collection of artifacts and memorabilia from the legendary early-American mail service. | 6th St. (jct. U.S. 36 and 77) | 785/562–3052 | $2 | May–Sept., Mon.–Sat. 10–5, Sun. 12–5.

### ON THE CALENDAR

**JUNE: *Pony Express Re-Ride.*** The sound of thundering hooves fills the streets, along with arts and crafts, music, and food. | 785/336–2294.
**JULY: *Antique and Classic Car Show.*** About 50 vintage vehicles on display draw hundreds of auto enthusiasts to the city park. | 785/336–2294.
**JULY: *Seneca County Fair.*** Traditional county fair attractions include games and rides on a midway, cotton candy, caramel apples, and livestock and produce judging. | 785/336–2294.

## Dining

**Valentino's.** Italian. This cozy, small-town Italian restaurant specializes in homemade pizza. Try the unlimited buffet for $7.25, as well as its soups and salads. Kids' menu. | 604 N. 11th | 785/336–3575 | $7–$13 | D, DC, MC, V.

**Wind Mill.** American. The windmill outside lends to the Dutch decor inside, although food is strictly American. There is a lunch buffet Tues.–Fri. and Sun. Known for prime rib, seafood, steak. Salad bar. Kids' menu. | 604 N. 4th St. | 785/336–3696 | Closed Mon. | $8–$10 | MC, V.

## Lodging

**Seneca Motel.** Clean rooms and hospitable service are what you'll find here. Some refrigerators, cable TV, some pets allowed. | 1106 North St. (U.S. 36) | 785/336–6127 | 12 rooms | $38 | AE, D, DC, MC, V.

**Starlite.** The lobby is home to the owner's doll collection, and perennials brighten the picket fence and windmill in warm weather. Cable TV, some pets allowed. | 410 North St. (U.S. 36) | 785/336–2191 | 16 rooms | $37 | AE, D, DC, MC, V.

# SHAWNEE

*(Nearby towns also listed: Bonner Springs, Kansas City, Lawrence, Leavenworth, Olathe, Overland Park)*

The Shawnee Indians inhabited this area and called it Gum Springs, due to the gum trees that lined its creek banks. In 1825, the Shawnees traded with the United States government their land in Missouri for land in eastern Kansas. In 1854, they sold back their land, keeping 200,000 acres. In 1856, Shawneetown (which later became Shawnee) was platted. The town was nearly destroyed by William Quantrill and his guerrilla band during a raid in 1862. Today the city is home to companies like Bayer and Simmons.

**Information: Shawnee Area Chamber of Commerce** | 6333 Long, Suite 350, Shawnee, KS 66216 | 913/631–6545 | www.cityofshawnee.org.

## Attractions

**Johnson County Museum of History.** Each of this museum's displays explores competing visions of the American Dream, and offers profiles of men and women who helped shape the development of the area. The permanent exhibit *Seeking the Good Life* depicts Johnson County history from 1820 through the present. The exhibit's 1950s All Electric Model House was moved from Prairie Village to Shawnee in 1994. The house was built by the Kansas City Power and Light Company for research and exhibition purposes. | 6305 Lackman Rd. | 913/631–6709 | fax 913/631–6359 | www.digitalhistory.com | Free; all-electric house $2 | Tues.–Sat. 10–4:30, Sun. 1–4:30.

**Old Shawnee Town.** More than 20 historic buildings and replicas dot the grounds of this Old West town, including the original 1843 Shawnee jail, an undertaker's shop, and a smoke house. | 11501 W. 57th St. | 913/248–2360 | fax 913/248–2363 | $1 | Feb.–late Dec., Tues.–Sat. noon–5.

**Wonderscope Children's Museum.** This former grade school had been transformed into an interactive exploration center for children of all ages. | 5705 Flint | 913/268–4176 | www.wonderscope.org | $4.50 | Mon.–Sat. 10–5, Sun. 12–5.

## Dining

**Applebee's Neighborhood Grill and Bar.** American. Sirloin steak and the Santa Fe stuffed chicken (stuffed with mild cheeses and peppers) are among the more popular dishes served here. The dining area contains sports memorabilia and photographs commemorating local school teams. | 913/962–1133 | www.applebees.com/ | Reservations not accepted | $5–$11 | AE, D, DC, MC, V.

**Leona Yarbrough's.** American. The good home-cooking that you'll find here is very popular with families. A full bakery is on site. Known for fried chicken, liver and onions and roast pork. Kids' menu. | 10310 Shawnee Mission Parkway, Shawnee | 913/248–0500 | Reservations not accepted for groups under 20 | Closed Mon. | $8–$15 | MC, V.

**Margarita's West.** Mexican. Typical but tasty Mexican dishes are served up amid sports and beer memorabilia. The most popular dish is the Margarita's special—a ground beef burrito with chili and cheese on top and rice on the side. Kid's menu. | 12200 Johnson | 913/631–5553 | $8–$9 | AE, D, DC, MC, V.

**Paulo and Bill.** Italian. Three huge vinegar vats stand on the platform dividing the bi-level dining room. Try the osso buco, lasagna *al forno* (a baked lasagna), and wood-fired pizza. Open-air dining is available on a shady patio. Kids' menu. Sun. brunch. | 16501 Midland Dr., Shawnee | 913/962–9900 | $12–$20 | AE, D, DC, MC, V.

## Lodging

**Hampton Inn.** This four-story hotel was built in 1997. A number of restaurants, fast food spots, and a movie theater are within a one block radius. Pool, spa, gym. | 16555 Midland Dr. | 913/248–1900 or 800/HAMPTON | fax 913/248–8567 | www.hampton-inn.com/ | 127 rooms, 8 suites | $79, $125 suites | AE, D, DC, MC, V.

**Hampton Inn and Suites Kansas City/Merriam.** Built in 1998, this four-story hotel is close to the spot where Shawnee, Merriam, and Overland Park meet. A park with walking and biking trails is 5 mi away. Complimentary Continental breakfast, cable TV, pool, hot tub, gym. | 7400 W. Frontage Rd., Merriam | 913/722–0800 | fax 913/722–0222 | www.hampton-inn.com | 43 rooms, 42 suites | $80, $95 suites | AE, D, DC, MC, V.

# SMITH CENTER

MAP 3, F3

*(Nearby towns also listed: Mankato, Phillipsburg)*

Smith Center (pop. 2,000) is the geographical center of the United States, and little more than a small chapel distinguishes the spot from any other place on the prairie. The Dutch settlers who came here in the 1870s made their living farming and grinding grain, much as residents do today. Take time to observe the open range here, as it was the inspiration for the American folk song "Home on the Range," adopted as the Kansas State song in 1947.

Information: **Smith Center Chamber of Commerce** | 219 S. Main, Smith Center, KS 66967 | 785/282–3895.

## Attractions

**Historical Society Museum.** Various artifacts and items from Smith County's past are on display. An original school building dates back to the early 1900s. | 1 block south Monroe St. and U.S. 36 intersection | 785/282–3895 | Free | By appointment.

**Home on the Range Cabin.** In this cabin in 1862, Dr. Brewster Higley wrote the words to "Home on the Range," which has been adopted as Kansas's official state song. | 8 mi west on U.S. 36, then 8 mi north on Rte. 8, then ¾ mi west at the sign | 785/282–6258 | Free | Daily 9–dusk.

**Old Dutch Mill.** This mill of hand-hewn logs and native limestone was built by a German immigrant in the 1870s and moved to the city park in 1938. | 3rd and Main Sts. | 785/282–3895 | Free | May–Sept., daily 8–8.

### ON THE CALENDAR

**SEPT.: *Olde Settler's Day.*** A parade, craft show, and free barbecue are just part of the fun here. | 785/282–3895.

## Dining

**Duffy's.** American. The Victorian building and furnishings add elegance to an otherwise casual menu and atmosphere. Known for steak, seafood. Kids' menu. | 233 S. Main | 785/282–3808 | $8–$15 | AE, D, MC, V.

**Lyon Den Cafe.** American/Casual. When she's not taking care of Smith County's catering needs, you'll find Debbie Lyon running her popular café on Main St. Breakfast is served all day, there are inexpensive lunch specials, and pies and other desserts are homemade. Thurs. is Mexican Night, and 99¢ burgers are served all day Tues. | 106 S. Main | 785/282–6866 | Breakfast also available. Closed Sun. | $3–$5 | No credit cards.

## Lodging

**Modern Aire.** This motel has clean rooms and has been in business since the 1950s. Cable TV, pool, airport shuttle. | 117 W. U.S. 36 | 785/282–6644 or 800/727–7332 | fax 785/282–6817 | 16 rooms | $46 | AE, D, DC, MC, V.

**Prarie Winds Motel.** This two-story motel is across the highway from a fast food restaurant and four blocks from both a café and the Old Dutch Mill. Complimentary Continental breakfast. Some kitchenettes, some microwaves, some refrigerators, cable TV. Pets allowed. | U.S. 36 E | 785/282–6608 | 17 rooms | $38 | MC, V.

**U.S. Center.** This motel with a brick and wood facade is known for its high level of service and homey atmosphere. Picnic area, cable TV, indoor pool, playground, airport shuttle. | 116 E. U.S. 36 | 785/282–6611 or 800/875–6613 | 21 rooms | $40 | AE, D, MC, V.

# STOCKTON

MAP 3, E4

*(Nearby town also listed: Hill City)*

Founded as a small farming community by the Congregational Church in 1872, Stockton missed major growth opportunities when the railroad passed it by in the 1800s. That missed opportunity, however, is now seen as an advantage for this town of 1,600 people. The area is being developed as a world-class upland hunting area, focusing on pheasant. Those who are interested in experiencing small-town and farm life might like to visit for a few days; the town pairs up residents with interested tourists for a real-life vacation experience.

Information: **City of Stockton** | 115 S. Walnut, Stockton, KS 67669 | 785/425–6703 or 785/425–6162.

## Attractions

**Log Hotel.** This replica of the first hotel in the area is often used for craft shows and special events. | Main St. | 785/425–6162 | Free | Daily; tours available Thanksgiving–Christmas.

**Nova Theatre.** This ornate 1930s theater has an art deco facade and is decorated with stained glass windows. Various performances and concerts are held year-round. | 517 Main St. | 785/425–6162 | Free; show prices $4–$12 | Daily 2–9.

**Rooks County Museum.** Area residents have donated items over the years to tell a vivid story of life in this community. | 921 S. Cedar | 785/425–7217 | Donation accepted | Mon.–Wed. 9–4; Thurs.–Sun. by appointment.

**Webster State Park.** This park 9 mi west of Stockton on U.S. 24 includes 46 utility campsites, more than 100 primitive sites, volleyball courts, horseshoe pits, and a nature trail. | 1210 Nine Rd. | 785/425–6775 | www.kdwp.state.ks.us | $4 per vehicle | Daily.

### ON THE CALENDAR
**JULY:** *Solomon Valley Threshing Bee and Craft Show.* A parade, tractor pull, antique car show, and games are part of the weekend's events. | 785/425–6162.
**OCT.:** *Stockton Art and Craft Fair.* More than 100 crafters are drawn to this event held at the St. Thomas Parish Center. | 785/425–6162.

## Dining

**Home Cookin'.** American/Casual. When in town, you may want to eat here, like the locals do. For bargain prices, munch on burgers, fries, and onion rings, or choose from daily lunch specials such as the chicken-fried steak sandwich. | 1203 Main | 785/425–6494 | $3–$5 | No credit cards.

## Lodging

**Midwest Motel.** Chuck and Linda Williams own and operate this one-story brick motel, built in 1954. In the parlor you'll find Mrs. Williams's porcelain doll collection competing for space with her husband's extensive barbed-wire collection. Complimentary Continental breakfast, cable TV, laundry facilities, pets allowed. | 1401 Main | 785/425–6706 | 13 rooms | $32 | D, MC, V.

# TOPEKA

MAP 3, J5

*(Nearby town also listed: Lawrence)*

Topeka was founded in 1854 by a group of white settlers from Pennsylvania. Its location on the banks of the Kaw River and the coming of the railroad a few years later contributed greatly to the city's growth and desirability as a business center. When Kansas gained statehood, several more developed communities on the eastern edge of the state lobbied hard to become the capital city. At the time, however, Topeka was one of the most western cities in Kansas, and legislators thought its more central location would be most suitable for the state capital.

Today, this city of 123,000 is a printing and publishing dominion, and home to the Santa Fe Railroad national headquarters. The Menninger Clinic became a groundbreaking mental therapy center in the early 1960s and continues to draw high profile clientele from around the world.

Information: **Topeka Convention and Visitors Bureau** | 1275 S.W. Topeka Blvd., Topeka, KS 66612 | 785/234–1030 or 800/235–1030 | www.topekacvb.org.

### NEIGHBORHOODS

**Oakland.** Oakland was its own town before annexation by the city in 1925. Bordered in a triangle by the Kansas River, the Municipal Airport, and the Santa Fe Rail Road tracks, Oakland has remained somewhat isolated from the larger city. The neighborhood has a small-town flavor with corner grocery stores, neighborhood churches, and small public parks.

**Potwin Place.** Like Oakland, Potwin Place was a city of its own until annexed by Topeka (this time in 1899). This neighborhood is distinctive for the hundreds of mature elm trees that line the curving streets and provide shade to gracious homes built around the beginning of the 20th century. Although most of these homes are designed in an Italianate, Victorian, or farmhouse style, Potwin Place is, however, one of the few places in the country where an airplane style was regularly used on houses. This style extends a large sleeping porch from the back of the second level, providing comfortable quarters during hot summer evenings. Potwin Place remains a residential area west of downtown Topeka in an area bounded by Grove Avenue on the north, 6th Avenue on the south, Broadmoor to the east, and Jewell on the west.

**St. Joseph's Parish.** Many city residents consider this historic German community the most appealing section of Topeka. The St. Joseph German Catholic Church, built in 1899, is the centerpiece of the community, which has a definitive Old World appeal in its architecture and community activities. Just north of downtown, St. Joseph's Parish is bounded by 4th Street to the south and 2nd Street to the north, Jackson Street to the east, and Topeka Boulevard to the west.

### TRANSPORTATION INFORMATION

**Airports: Metropolitan Topeka Airport** is better known as Forbes Field and is in the southeast section of Topeka (U.S. 75 at 77th St. | 785/862–6515).

# KODAK'S TIPS FOR TAKING GREAT PICTURES

**Get Closer**
- Fill the frame tightly for maximum impact
- Move closer physically or use a long lens
- Continually check the viewfinder for wasted space

**Choosing a Format**
- Add variety by mixing horizontal and vertical shots
- Choose the format that gives the subject greatest drama

**The Rule of Thirds**
- Mentally divide the frame into vertical and horizontal thirds
- Place important subjects at thirds' intersections
- Use thirds' divisions to place the horizon

**Lines**
- Take time to notice lines
- Let lines lead the eye to a main subject
- Use the shape of lines to establish mood

**Taking Pictures Through Frames**
- Use foreground frames to draw attention to a subject
- Look for frames that complement the subject
- Expose for the subject, and let the frame go dark

**Patterns**
- Find patterns in repeated shapes, colors, and lines
- Try close-ups or overviews
- Isolate patterns for maximum impact (use a telephoto lens)

**Textures that Touch the Eyes**
- Exploit the tangible qualities of subjects
- Use oblique lighting to heighten surface textures
- Compare a variety of textures within a shot

**Dramatic Angles**
- Try dramatic angles to make ordinary subjects exciting
- Use high angles to help organize chaos and uncover patterns, and low angles to exaggerate height

**Silhouettes**
- Silhouette bold shapes against bright backgrounds
- Meter and expose for the background illumination
- Don't let conflicting shapes converge

**Abstract Composition**
- Don't restrict yourself to realistic renderings
- Look for ideas in reflections, shapes, and colors
- Keep designs simple

**Establishing Size**
- Include objects of known size
- Use people for scale, where possible
- Experiment with false or misleading scale

**Color**
- Accentuate mood through color
- Highlight subjects or create designs through color contrasts
- Study the effects of weather and lighting

From *Kodak Guide to Shooting Great Travel Pictures* © 2000 by Fodor's Travel Publications

**Bus: Greyhound Buslines** stops in Topeka as it travels along I–70. The terminal is 2 blocks from the downtown area (200 S.E. 3rd St. | 785/233–2301).

**Intra-city Transit: Topeka Transit** is the city's public bus system, providing inexpensive service from the airport to the capitol and many points throughout downtown (735 S.W. Kansas Ave. | 785/354–9571).

### DRIVING AROUND TOWN

Generally, traffic in Topeka is not bad. It gets heavy in the morning from 7:30–8 and in the evening from 5:30–6, during rush hour. People will still be able to get around easily, as there are no particular bottlenecks here.

Major highways in and around the city include I–70, which runs through downtown Topeka, and I–35, which runs just south of the city.

There are quite a few one-way streets in Topeka, especially downtown.

On-street parking is easily available. No pass is needed.

Lots are primarily in the downtown area. The maximum cost for one day is around $4. Otherwise it is $0.75–$1.00 per half-hour.

Illegally parked cars are fined $5. Rules are strictly enforced.

The speed limit varies in Topeka and is strictly enforced. Downtown, the limit is 20 mph. Elsewhere, the limit is 30–35 mph. The highway limit is 65 mph, and the Interstate is 70 mph.

Right turns on red are permitted, as long as you stop first.

## Attractions

### ART AND ARCHITECTURE

**Columbia National Bank and Trust.** Built in 1927 and on the National Register of Historic Places, this building was the site of Topeka's first City Hall. Today it operates as a bank. | 701 Kansas Ave. | 785/233–1515 | Free | Weekdays 9–4.

**Governor's Mansion (Cedar Crest).** Built in 1928, this French mansion is on a 200-acre estate and was completely remodeled in 1999. | 1 Cedar Crest Rd. | 785/296–3636 | Free | Mon. 1–3:30.

**State Capitol.** A mural depicting John Brown and the days of Bleeding Kansas dominates the foyer of this ornate building. | 300 S.W. 10th St. | 785/296–4142 | Free | Weekdays 10–5.

### BEACHES, PARKS, AND NATURAL SIGHTS

**Gage Park.** For a very small fee, you can ride a restored 1908 carousel and enjoy a mile-long train ride through this scenic park, located in the middle of the city. | Gage Blvd., between W. 6th and W. 10th Sts. | 785/368–3700 | www.topekacvb.org | Free | Daily.

Remodeled and expanded in the early 1990s, **Topeka Zoo** has a great elephant yard and lion exhibit, as well as an impressive tropical rain forest. | 635 S.W. Gage Blvd. | 785/272–5821 | fax 785/272–2539. | $4.50 | Nov.–Mar., daily 9–4, Apr.–Oct., daily 9–6.

**Lake Shawnee.** This scenic 700-acre park has a botanical garden, arboretum, and golf course, as well as a 400-acre fishing and boating lake. | 3137 S.E. 29th St. | 785/267–1156 | Free | Daily.

**Perry State Park.** This 11,000-acre park is great for camping and fishing, and 1,100 acres of marshes are ideal for waterfowl hunting and observation. | 5441 W. Lake Rd., Ozawkie | 785/246–3449 | www.kdwp.state.ks.us/parks | Free | Daily.

**Ward-Meade Historical Home.** Three buildings and a botanical garden date to the early 1900s. The home includes an operating 1920s soda fountain. | 124 N.W. Fillmore | 785/368–3888 | fax 785/368–3890 | www.topekacvb.org | Free | Mon.–Sat. 10–4, Sun. 12–4.

### CULTURE, EDUCATION, AND HISTORY

**Brown vs. Board of Education National Historic Site.** Monroe Elementary School is where the landmark public school desegregation case of 1954 originated. The site is closed to the public until May 2003, but you can go to the second floor of the post office to watch a video and look at historic pictures in the meantime. | 424 S. Kansas Ave., Suite 220 | Weekdays 8–4 | 785/234–1030 | www.nps.gov/brvb | Free | Daily.

**Federal Building.** Built in 1933, the landmark desegregation case Brown vs. Topeka Board of Education was tried in a second-floor courtroom, which remains open to the public. Today the building is a U.S. post office. | 424 S. Kansas Ave. | 785/275–8777 or 800/ASK–USPS | Free | Weekdays 8–4.

**Washburn University of Topeka.** This four-year public university was founded in 1865 and has about 6,000 students on its urban campus. Tours are available weekdays, and are by appointment on weekends. | 1700 S.W. College Ave., at 17th St. | 785/231–1010 | fax 785/233–8495 | www.wuacc.edu | Free | Daily.

## MUSEUMS

**Combat Air Museum.** Explore two hangars of historic military aircraft and exhibits, beginning with WWI. | Forbes Field, Hangar 602, 5 mi south of Topeka on U.S. 75 | 785/862–3303 | fax 785/862–3304 | www.combatairmuseum.org | $5 | Mon.–Sat. 9–3:30, Sun. 10–3:30.

**Kansas Museum of History.** Hands-on exhibits, children's programs, and a number of galleries tell state history from pre-historic days to the present. | 6425 S.W. 6th Ave. | 785/272–8681 | fax 785/272–8682 | www.kshs.org | Donation accepted | Mon.–Sat. 9–4:30, Sun. 12:30–4:30.

## RELIGION AND SPIRITUALITY

**First Presbyterian Church.** Built in 1885, this spectacular church is a "must-see" when visiting Topeka. Floor to ceiling Tiffany windows, installed in 1911, fill the sanctuary, making this the only church of its kind west of the Mississippi. | 817 Harrison St. | 785/233–9601 | Free | Daily 9–3, or by appointment.

**St. Joseph German Catholic Church.** This church is the centerpiece of the St. Joseph's Parish community. Built in 1899, this redbrick Romanesque-style church with its twin towers is considered one of Topeka's premier landmarks. For years, sermons were conducted in German and many in the parish remain fluent in the language. | Northwest corner of 3rd and Van Buren Sts. | 785/232–2863 | Free | Daily.

## SPORTS AND RECREATION

**Heartland Park Topeka.** This is one of the country's premiere motorsports facilities and home to several NHRA events. | 1805 S.W. 71st St. | 785/862–4781 or 800/437–2237 | fax 785/862–2016 | www.hpt.com | Mar.–Nov., weekdays 8–5.

**Village Greens Golf Course.** This mom-and-pop course 30 mi northeast of Topeka has good greens and is fun to play. | 5615 Rte. 92, Meriden, | 785/876–2255 | Year-round.

## OTHER POINTS OF INTEREST

**Potwin Place.** This area of town has beautiful tree-lined streets, brick sidewalks, and Victorian homes that are decorated for the various seasons. | Between 1st and 4th Sts., on Woodlawn and Greenwood Sts. | 785/234–1030 | Free | Daily.

## ON THE CALENDAR

**MAY:** *Topeka Jazz Festival.* This three-day event features more than 30 hours of jazz performed by nationally renowned artists. | 785/234–2787.
**JUNE:** *Washburn Sunflower Music Festival.* Classical Chamber Orchestra performers from around the country convene on the Washburn University campus for a weekend of great tunes. | 785/231–1010.
**SEPT.:** *Huff 'N Puff Balloon Rally.* Balloon flights and races are held at Lake Shawnee in the early morning and late evening hours. | 785/267–1156.
**SEPT.:** *Railroad Days.* A carnival, equipment displays, and minor excursion rides highlight this celebration of the area's railroad heritage. | 785/232–5533.

## WALKING TOUR

### St. Joseph's Parish (approximately 1 hour)

Just north of the historic downtown of Topeka is St. Joseph's Parish, a predominantly German community in its origins and considered one of the most pleasant neighborhoods in Topeka today. Although 13 structures are noted, many of the homes in this tree-lined neighborhood have recently been renovated and feature detailed landscaping and a conscientious effort to maintain the Old World flavor of this community.

Begin your tour at the **St. Joseph German Catholic Church,** at the northwest corner of 3rd and Van Buren streets. Just to the right of the church, at 227 Van Buren, is the **Church Rectory,** built in 1933 in the Prairie style. The rectory resembles an early (1893) Frank Lloyd Wright residential building in River Forest, Illinois. Retrace your steps past the church to the southeast corner of Third and Van Buren to find the **St. Joseph School,** built in 1912. Pilasters with Corinthian capitals flank the round-arch openings of the north and west entrances. The building no longer serves the educational needs of parishioners, but instead houses church social agencies, including a food bank. Adjacent to the school at **306 Van Buren** is the St. Joseph Convent, built in 1917. Italian Renaissance in style, this former convent has a tripartite stained-glass window with fan light on the south side. Today, the two-story building houses Catholic Social Services.

A few steps south you'll find the Krauss Residence at **318 Van Buren.** Built in 1880, the large home was originally built for Oscar Krauss and his family, who owned a harness and hide business here. Another impressive private residence is next door at **328 Van Buren.** The home was built before the beginning of the 20th century in Folk Victorian style. Continue south on Van Buren, crossing 4th Street and turning right. At **315 W. Fourth** is the former St. John's Lutheran School, which served the German Lutheran community here from 1922 until the 1960s. The old school is now an apartment building. Across the street is the Bischoff residence at **334 Harrison Street.** Built in 1905 for Oscar Bischoff, a German Consul, this Queen Anne home remains in good condition, having been remodeled in the 1990s. Walking north on Harrison, cross 3rd Street to the northwest corner of Harrison and Third. There you will see another **private residence** built in 1900 that demonstrates the American four-square style house, complete with hipped roof and dormer windows.

A few steps north is **213 Harrison Street,** a private home built in 1895 in the Queen Anne style. In recent years, a broader porch and aluminum siding have been added. Directly across the street at **228 Harrison Street** is the Old St. Joseph's Rectory, which served the parish in that capacity from 1903 until 1934, when the new rectory was built. Originally, and once again, a private home, this house was built in 1900.

Continuing in the same northerly direction, at the corner of Second and Harrison, you will find **200 Harrison Street,** an Italianate-style home built in 1880. Decorative brackets, a low-pitched roof and tall, narrow windows are distinctive features of this home. Continue to your right, now moving east along Second Street. At the corner of Second and Van Buren, turn right. **207 Van Buren** is another private residence, built in 1910 in the Homestead style. The residence features a front-gabled roof and columned front porch. Just past the Homestead home is **St. Joseph German Catholic Church,** where your walking tour began.

## Dining

### INEXPENSIVE

**Carlos O'Kelly's.** Mexican. The hacienda atmosphere includes music, sombreros, and woven blankets. Try the enchilada de monterey (a flour tortilla with spicy chicken and monterey jack cheese topped with sour cream and chives). Lunch buffet. Kids' menu. | 3425 S. Kansas Ave. | 785/266–3457 | $5–$10 | AE, D, DC, MC, V.

## MODERATE

**Blind Tiger Brewery and Restaurant.** American. More than just Topeka's original micro-brewery, the Blind Tiger is also the largest brewery in Kansas. It's also one of the largest dining spaces in the Midwest. There is a cavernous, multi-level interior and an outdoor deck, all covered in polished cedar. Gleaming copper railings and towering brew tanks are hard to miss. Sample liberally from the extensive selection of custom microbrews, then sit down to such hearty entrées as grilled steaks and chops, hickory-smoked ribs and chicken, or homemade pizza. Known for baby-back ribs and beer. | 417 S.W. 37th St. | 785/267–BREW | Closed Oct.–Apr. | $8–$22 | AE, D, DC, MC, V.

**Kobe Steak House of Japan.** Japanese. Japanese art work and bonsai gardens accentuate this authentic menu. Known for chicken, seafood, hibachi steak. Kids' menu. | 5331 S.W. 22nd Pl. | 785/272–6633 | $12–$22 | AE, D, DC, MC, V.

**McFarland's.** American. Good home-style cooking has kept locals coming to this spot since the 1930s. Known for roast beef, pot roast, and chicken. Kids' menu. | 4133 Gage Center Dr. | 785/272–6909 | $10–$12 | MC, V.

## EXPENSIVE

**Back Porch.** Continental. This intimate, semi-formal, romantic restaurant has reliable service and a frequently changing supper menu. Three glass walls allow for views of the grounds, which include a pond, flowers, and swings. Popular dishes include the sautéed jumbo prawns served over spinach, and the lamb osso buco. | 3535 S. W. 6th Ave. | 785/233–3800 | Closed Sun., Mon. No lunch | $17–$23 | AE, D, DC, MC, V.

# Lodging

## MODERATE

**Best Western Candlelight Inn.** Some rooms overlook the attractive landscaped grounds and pool area. Restaurant, complimentary Continental breakfast, cable TV, pool, outdoor hot tub, gym, laundry facilities, free parking, no pets. | 2831 S.W. Fairlawn Rd. | 785/272–9550 | fax 785/272–8242 | www.bestwestern.com | 97 rooms | $69 | AE, D, DC, MC, V.

**Best Western Meadow Acres Motel.** Ground rooms have exterior entrances in this motel, which is comprised of a one-story and a three-story building. Complimentary Continental breakfast, some refrigerators, cable TV, pool. | 2950 S. Topeka Blvd. | 785/267–1681 | fax 785/267–1681 | www.bestwestern.com | 81 rooms in 2 buildings | $54 | AE, D, DC, MC, V.

**Days Inn.** Modern rooms have queen- or king-size beds and a large sofa. Complimentary Continental breakfast, some refrigerators, cable TV, pool, hot tub, business services, pets allowed. | 1510 S.W. Wanamaker Rd. | 785/272–8538 | fax 785/272–8538 | www.daysinn.com | 62 rooms, 6 suites | $69, $79 suites | AE, D, DC, MC, V.

★ **Heritage House.** This turn-of-the-20th-century farmhouse was once home to the world-renowned Menninger Clinic. Rooms range from dramatic to cozy, with a mix of contemporary furnishings and antiques throughout. Restaurant (*see* Back Porch), complimentary Continental breakfast, in-room data ports, cable TV, business services. | 3535 S.W. 6th St. | 785/233–3800 | fax 785/233–9793 | hhouse@inlandnet.net | 10 rooms | $65–$140 | AE, D, DC, MC, V.

**Ramada Inn.** This is the largest hotel in Kansas. Its executive tower has rooms overlooking the city. Restaurants, bar, some refrigerators, room service, cable TV, pool, barbershop, beauty salon, exercise equipment, laundry facilities, business services, airport shuttle, free parking, some pets allowed. | 420 E. 6th St. | 785/234–5400 | fax 785/233–0460 | www.ramada.com | 361 rooms, 22 suites | $68–$85; $95–$125 suites | AE, D, DC, MC, V.

**The Senate Luxury Suites.** Each suite has an arched doorway and individual touches, such as tapestries and prints by Monet, Renoir, and others. Its location next to the capitol makes it popular with business travelers. Complimentary cocktails are served in the evening. Complimentary Continental breakfast, in-room data ports, some kitchenettes, refrigerators, cable TV, outdoor hot tub, exercise equipment, laundry facilities, business services, free parking. | 900 S.W. Tyler St. | 785/233–5050 or 800/488–3188 | fax 785/233–1614 | senatesuites@earthlink.net | 52 suites | $65–$85 suites | AE, D, DC, MC, V.

### EXPENSIVE

**Brickyard Barn Inn.** Set on four secluded acres on the north edge of town, this unique 1927 redbrick barn was designed by architecture students at Kansas State University; in 1993, it was converted into a stately and romantic B&B. Each of the three bedrooms has English antiques. Complimentary full breakfast, in-room data ports, pool, no pets, no smoking. | 4020 N.W. 25th | 785/235–0057 | fax 785/234–0924 | umoo2me@cjnetworks.com | www.cjnetworks.com/~umoo2me | 3 rooms | $85 | MC, V.

**Club House Inn.** Many of the spacious rooms overlook a landscaped courtyard in this modern white and gray hotel 1 mi from the Kansas Museum of History. Complimentary breakfast, in-room data ports, kitchenettes (in suites), microwaves (in suites), refrigerators (in suites), cable TV, pool, hot tub, laundry facilities, business services, free parking. | 924 S.W. Henderson St. | 785/273–8888 | fax 785/273–5809 | www.clubhouseinn.com | 121 rooms, 17 suites | $79–$89, $115–$125 suites | AE, D, DC, MC, V.

**Hampton Inn.** Spacious rooms have modern furnishings in this two-story hotel. A number of restaurants are within 1 mi. Complimentary Continental breakfast, some microwaves, some refrigerators, cable TV, pool, hot tub, gym, no pets. | 1401 Southwest Ashworth Pl | 785/273–0003 | fax 785/273–3030 | www.hampton-inn.com | 62 rooms | $75 | AE, D, DC, MC, V.

**The Plaza Inn.** Rooms have modern furnishings in this hotel just off Topeka Blvd., the main strip where many restaurants and shops can be found. It's just 5 mi from the Expo Center and Heartland Park raceway. Restaurant, bar, dance club, cable TV, pool, business services, in-room data ports, laundry facilities, free parking, some pets allowed. | 3802 S. Topeka Blvd. (U.S. 75) | 785/266–8880 | fax 785/267–3311 | 150 rooms | $75–$80 | AE, D, DC, MC, V.

# VICTORIA

MAP 3, E5

*(Nearby towns also listed: Hays, Russell)*

Wealthy English and Scottish immigrants first settled this charming town of 1,200 in 1873. Three years later, Volga-Germans from Russia arrived in the area and were so impressed with their surroundings that they notified friends and relatives in the Old World, who arrived by the hundreds the next year. The combination of British and Russian influence created a healthy community which, on the surface, seems to have changed little in the last century and is still dominated by the agricultural riches of central Kansas.

Information: **City of Victoria** | Box 87, Victoria, KS 67671 | 785/735–2259 | www.ellisco.org/victoria.htm.

## Attractions .

**St. Fidelis Church.** Otherwise known as the Cathedral of the Plains, this Romanesque structure can be seen for miles. | 900 Cathedral | 785/735–2777 | Free | Daily.

### ON THE CALENDAR

**AUG.: *Herzogfest.*** Celebrating the coming harvest, Victoria and its neighboring community of Herzog honor their ethnic heritage with crafts, food, and dance. | 785/735–2259.

## Dining

**Hungry Haus Cafe.** American. Historic artifacts and antiques are found throughout this popular restaurant. Try the chicken strips or dumplings and beans. | 405 Main | 785/735–9726 | Breakfast also available | $5–$9 | No credit cards.

## Lodging

**Das Younger Haus.** This spacious home was built of native field stone in 1979. The full breakfast includes homemade sausage and freshly baked fruit rolls. No pets, no smoking. | 1202 Hickory | 785/735–2760 | 4 rooms | $40–$60 | MC, V.

# WAKEENEY

*(Nearby town also listed: Hays)*

Founded in 1879, WaKeeney got its unusual name from Chicago's Warren and Keeney land companies, which helped found the town. Several stage lines and historical trails passed through this area in the process of settling the American West. Located midway between Kansas City and Denver, this town of 2,200 has earned the reputation of "Christmas City of the High Plains" for its 40-foot Christmas tree adorned with handmade ornaments and more than 6,000 lights. In the heart of the Kansas breadbasket, wheat fields stretch from WaKeeney as far as the eye can see, making agriculture the town's dominant industry.

**Information: WaKeeney Chamber of Commerce** | 216 Main St., WaKeeney, KS 67672 | 785/743–2077.

## Attractions

**Cedar Bluff State Park.** The 6,000-acre lake and almost 9,000 acres of adjacent wildlife area make Cedar Bluff State Park an excellent base camp for people who like to hunt, fish, and explore year-round. | Rte. 147, Exit 135, 13 mi south of I–70 | 785/726–3212 | www.kdwp.state.ks.us | $4 per vehicle | Daily.

**Chalk Beds.** Limestone outcroppings from the primeval sea that once covered Trego County are rich with great fossils and evidence of prehistoric life here. | Throughout the Smoky Hill River Valley and Logan and Trego counties | Free | Daily.

**Elk Dreamer Art Gallery.** This Southwestern art gallery specializes in lithographs and depictions of wildlife. | 202 S. 1st St. | 800/441–5057 | Free | Mon.–Sat. 10–6 | 785/743–2408.

### ON THE CALENDAR

**AUG.:** *Trego County Free Fair.* This not-for-profit event includes 4-H displays, FFA projects, and other agricultural exhibits. | 785/743–5785.
**NOV.:** *Christmas Tree Lighting.* More than 60,000 lights illuminate the largest tree between Kansas City and Denver. | 785/743–5785.

## Dining

**Quality Cafe.** American. Pictures of local events, including the tornado of 1951 (the last to touch down in WaKeeney), decorate the walls of this casual café on the outskirts of town. Be sure to try the homemade beef stew. | I–70 and U.S. 283 | 785/743–2613 | Breakfast also available | $4–$8 | No credit cards.

## Lodging

**Best Western Wheel Motel.** This low-slung building may not look very impressive, but it has your basic amenities, as well as a suite and connecting rooms. Restaurant, cable TV, pool. | 705 2nd St. | 785/743–2118 | fax 785/743–2439 | www.bestwestern.com | 50 rooms, 1 suite | $50, $75 suite | AE, D, DC, MC, V.

**Budget Host Travel Inn.** This small, one-story motel is about 20 mi from Cedar Bluff Lake. Cable TV, pool. | I–70, Exit 128 | 785/743–2121 | fax 785/743–6704 | www.budgethost.com | 27 rooms | $55 | AE, D, MC, V.

**Cottage Garden Guest House.** Built in 1906, this quaint Country Victorian cottage has an antique oak rocking chair, hardwood floors, a sunroom, a flower and herb garden, and a picnic area. Complimentary breakfast. | 510 Warren Ave. | 785/743–2644 | 3 rooms (2 with shared bath) | $65 | MC, V.

**Thistle Hill.** Many handmade family heirlooms can be found throughout this B&B, set on a 600-acre farm with a 60-acre wildflower preserve. A covered patio/sunroom overlooks the gardens. Picnic area, complimentary breakfast. | Rte. 1 | 785/743–2644 | 3 rooms (1 with shower only) | $59–$75 | MC, V.

# WICHITA

MAP 3, H7

*(Nearby towns also listed: El Dorado, Newton, Winfield)*

With a population of 330,000, Wichita is Kansas's largest city. It was founded in 1868, when a trading post was established at the confluence of the Arkansas and Little Arkansas rivers. The city experienced impressive growth after it was incorporated in 1870, due to the cattle trade along the Chisholm Trail, which ran from Texas to Kansas. The name Wichita is a Native American word and means either "scattered lodges" or "painted faces," depending on whom you ask. Maybe because of the tough cowboy spirit that settled this land, Wichita has become home to many entrepreneurs with a national influence. Companies like Pizza Hut, Coleman (which makes camping and other outdoor recreational equipment), and Cessna and Beech (now Raytheon Aircraft Co.) are just a few of the international corporations that can trace their roots back to here.

Information: **Wichita Area Convention and Visitors Bureau** | 350 W. Douglas Ave., Wichita, KS 67202 | 316/265–2800 or 800/288–9424 | www.wichitakansas.org.

## Attractions

**Botanica, the Wichita Gardens.** Plants and flowers, both native and new to the area, thrive at Botanica. Seasonal displays and theme gardens are featured. | 701 Amidon | 316/264–9799 | $4.50 | Mon.–Sat. 9–5, Sun. 1–5; June–Sept., until 8 on Tues.

**Cheney State Park.** This 2,000-acre park is popular for fishing, swimming, and wildlife viewing. | 16000 N.E. 50th St. | 316/542–3664 | www.kdwp.state.ks.us | Free | Daily.
The 9,500-acre **Cheney Reservoir** has a reputation as one of the best sailing lakes in the country.

**Clifton Square.** This cobblestone shopping district in the historic College Hill neighborhood is home to eclectic shops, restaurants, and galleries. | 3700 E. Douglas | 316/686–2177 | Free | Daily.

**Exploration Place.** Crawl through caves, touch a 20-ft tornado, or experience a flight simulator at this modern science center, which boasts a number of unique exhibits and activities. | 300 N. McLean Blvd. | 316/263–3373 or 877/904–1444 | $7 | Tues.–Sun. 9–5.

**Frank Lloyd Wright, Allen-Lambe House Museum and Study Center.** This is the last of the Prairie-style houses designed by the famous architect in 1915. | 255 N. Roosevelt St. | 316/687–1027 | www2.southwind.net/~allenlambe | Free | By appointment.

**Indian Center Museum.** Art and artifacts showcase Native American culture and history. The sculpture "Keeper of the Plains" shows a man in full headdress with his face towards the sky and his hands uplifted and open. | 650 N. Seneca | 316/262–5221 | fax 316/262–4216 | $2 | Tues.–Sat. 10–5, Sun. 1–5.

**O.J. Watson Park.** Paddle boats, pony and train rides, and a *Wizard of Oz* playground make for a pleasant outing for all ages. | S. Lawrence Rd. at Carp St., just south of Arkansas River | 316/529–9940 | Free | Mar.–Oct., daily 8AM–10PM.

**Old Cowtown Museum.** This 17-acre living history, open-air museum re-creates life in Wichita from 1865–1880. | 1871 Sim Park Dr. | 316/264–0671 | www.old-cowtown.org | $7 | Apr.–Oct., daily 10–5; Memorial Day–Labor Day, Mon.–Wed. 10–5, Thurs. 10–8, Fri.–Sun. 10–5.

**Omnisphere and Science Center.** A hands-on science museum, dinosaurs, a flight show, and a bubble show attract the kids, as well as a presentation of "Where in the World Is Carmen Sandiego?" | 220 S. Main St. | 316/337–9174 | fax 316/268–9268 | $3; planetarium $1 | Tues.–Fri. 8–5, Sat. 9–5.

**Sedgwick County Zoo.** An open-air exhibit takes you through a simulated Australian outback at one of the country's top 25 zoos. After walking among kookaburra, view the free-flight parrots from the South American pampas. | 5555 Zoo Blvd. | 316/942–2212 | fax 316/942–5228 | www.scz.org | $7.25 | Daily 9–5; late Oct.–Mar., daily 10–5.

**Wichita Art Museum.** The famed Murdock collection of American art (including Mary Cassatt's *Mother and Child*), the M. C. Naftzger collection of Charles M. Russell works, and a sculpture deck are among the attractions. | 619 Stackman Dr. | 316/268–4921 | fax 316/268–4980 | www.wichitaartmuseum.org | Free | Tues.–Sat. 10–5, Sun. noon–5.

**Wichita Center for the Arts.** This is a regional visual and performing arts center that emphasizes unique art exhibits and theatrical performances. | 9112 E. Central | 316/634–2787 | www.wcfta.com | Price varies per show | Tues.–Sun. 1–5.

**Wichita-Sedgwick County Historical Museum.** Artifacts and displays representative of the region's early cattle and oil industry are housed in a city building from 1892. | 204 S. Main St. | 316/265–9314 | fax 315/265–9319 | $2 | Tues.–Fri. 11–4, weekends 1–5.

**Wichita State University.** This public university is home to approximately 14,000 students, and its main campus comprises 330 acres. | Bordered by 17th and 21st Sts. and Hillside and Oliver (main campus) | 316/978–3456 | www.wichita.edu/online | Free | Daily.

The **Corbin Education Center** was designed by Frank Lloyd Wright and is home to Wichita State's education program. | 1845 Fairmount, near Yale and 21st Sts. | 316/978–3300 | Free | Weekdays 8–5.

Look for the huge Miró mosaic mural on the south facade of the **Edwin A. Ulrich Museum of Art,** which houses a large private collection and traveling exhibits. | 1845 Fairmont St. | 316/978–3664 | fax 316/978–3898 | www.twsu.edu/~ulrich | Free | Weekdays 8–5.

**Lake Afton Public Observatory.** View the moon, stars, and distant galaxies, or explore the mysteries of black holes in outer space. Exhibits include a rock from space and meteorites that have landed in Kansas. | Wichita State University, 25000 W. 39th St. S (MacArthur Rd.) | 316/794–8995 | $3 | Fri.–Sat. 8:30–10.

A walking tour around the 330-acre campus takes you past the **Martin H. Bush Outdoor Sculpture Collection,** which includes numerous sculptures in a variety of mediums. | Throughout campus | 316/689–3664 | Free | Daily.

## ON THE CALENDAR

**APR.:** *Jazz Festival.* One of the oldest jazz festivals in the country, this event offers a variety of concerts, clinics, workshops, and exhibits. | 316/262–2351.

**MAY:** *Wichita River Festival.* Concerts, sports, food, and parades are among the more than 80 events held along the riverfront. | 316/267–2817.

**JULY:** *Indian Powwow.* This event has been held annually for more than 30 years and offers lots of dancing, eating, and Native American art. | 316/262–5221.

**AUG.:** *National Baseball Congress World Series.* College students and a few retired pros are the main contenders in this national amateur baseball tournament, established in 1934. About 100,000 people attend this event from around the country. | 316/267–3372.

**SEPT.: *Black Arts Festival.*** This event held on the Wichita State University campus cele-brates and showcases African-American heritage, arts, and traditional foods. | 316/691–1499.

**OCT.: *Old Sedgwick County Fair.*** Blacksmithing, weaving, soapmaking, and needle-point are reminiscent of an 1870s county fair. | 316/264–0671.

## Dining

**Brews Brothers Grill and Icehouse.** American/Casual. Friendly service and a creative menu keep patrons coming back to this eatery. Be sure to try the bourbon glazed sirloin or the fried catfish. Also look for the different dinner special each night. Kids' menu. | 3800 S. Seneca St. | 316/524–2739 | $7–$14 | AE, D, MC, V.

**The Grape.** Continental. Open-air dining is available on a wooden deck with umbrella tables at this casual restaurant on the east side of Wichita. Try the Apple Jack Chicken sautéed with brandy and sliced apples, or the Cracked Black Pepper Fettuccine Florentine (fettuc-cine tossed with red onions, shrimp, mushrooms, tomatoes, and spinach in an alfredo sauce). Entertainment Fri., Sat. | 550 N. Rock Rd. | 316/634–0113 | $9–$17 | AE, D, DC, MC, V.

**Italian Garden.** Italian. This spot serves up the best Italian cuisine in Wichita. Hanging plants, pictures of gardens and the Italian landscape, and a mural depicting the countryside are found in the dining area. The pasta is made daily on the premises and the seafood is fresh from the market. The chicken picatta and shrimp scampi are popular dishes. | 3920 W. Dou-glas Ave. | 316/943–8844 | fax 316/943–6800 | Reservations essential Fri.–Sat. | Closed Mon. No lunch Sat. | $8–$17 | AE, D, DC, MC, V.

**Larkspur Restaurant and Grill.** American. Changing exhibts that include paintings and photographs of local artists are on display in this restaurant. Specialties include the pis-tachio chicken and chili lime grilled albacore tuna. Kids' menu. | 904 E. Douglas Ave. | 316/262–5275 | No lunch Sun. | $9–$22 | AE, D, DC, MC, V.

**Olive Tree.** Continental. Lots of potted indoor trees give an atrium air to this popular café. Known for fresh salmon, lamb, and duck. An outdoor patio has many plants and umbrella tables. | 2949 N. Rock Rd. | 316/636–1100 | $9–$22 | AE, D, DC, MC, V.

**Piccadilly Grill.** Eclectic. As you step through the front doors, you can turn one way and enter the restaurant, or go the other way and purchase items from the market. Try the baked potato soup, shrimp pasta, and the hot apple dumpling or vanilla ice cream. Make sure you bring the kids on Tues., which is Family Fun Night. Kids' menu. | 7728 E. Central Ave. | 316/681–1100 | fax 316/685–3819 | $5–$17 | AE, D, DC, MC, V.

**River City Brewery.** Continental. This rustic pub lives up to its slogan: "Fresh ales, flavor-ful food, and fair prices." Fish-and-chips and handmade pizzas are regular favorites. | 150 N. Mosely St. | 316/263–2739 | Reservations not accepted | $8–$18 | AE, D, DC, MC, V.

**Scotch & Sirloin.** Continental. Hearty comfort food is served amidst red and black carpets and brass candelabras. Prime rib is the specialty, but you can opt for seafood or poultry. | 5325 Kellogg | 316/685–8701 | No lunch weekends | $15–$50 | AE, D, MC, V.

**Timberline Steakhouse and Grill.** Steak. Wood furniture and artificial pine trees through-out create a lodge-like atmosphere. A stuffed fish, fox, and deer's head hang from the wall. Try the gigantic himalayan porterhouse or the alpine pastas. On Tues. night a clown pro-vides live entertainment. Kids' menu. | 2243 N. Tyler Ave. | 316/773–3111 | fax 316/773–3211 | No lunch | $7–$20 | AE, D, DC, MC, V.

**YiaYias.** Continental. This European-style bistro with tiled floors, a high ceiling, and mirrors throughout prides itself on speedy service. Try the roasted chicken and grilled Kansas City strip. | 8115 E. 21st St. N | 316/634–1000 | Reservations essential | $7–$24 | AE, D, DC, MC, V.

## Lodging

**Best Western Red Coach Inn.** This two-story motel is across the street from a golf course. Rooms have modern furnishings. Restaurant, room service, cable TV, pool, outdoor hot tub, playground, business services. | 915 E. 53rd St. N | 316/832–9387 | fax 316/832–9443 | www.best-western.com | 152 rooms | $59–$75 | AE, D, DC, MC, V.

**Cambridge Suites.** Spacious suites have period furnishings from when they were built in the late 1920s. Complimentary Continental breakfast, in-room data ports, kitchenettes, cable TV, pool, business services. | 120 W. Orme St. | 316/263–1061 | fax 316/263–3817 | 64 suites | $94–$114 suites | AE, D, DC, MC, V.

**The Castle Inn Riverside.** Built from 1886–1888 by one of Wichita's wealthiest residents, this castle became a B&B in 1994. European antiques can be found throughout, and uniquely appointed guest rooms have names such as Mary, Queen of Scots, The Royal Court, and Scotland Yard. Guests receive a complimentary bottle of wine. Complimentary breakfast, in-room data ports, cable TV, in-room VCRs, some in-room hot tubs, no pets, no smoking. | 1155 N. River Blvd. | 316/263–9300 | fax 316/263–4998 | 1castle@gte.net | www.castleinnriverside.com | 14 rooms | $125–$295 | AE, D, MC, V.

**Clarion Hotel Airport.** As its name suggests, this hotel is close to the airport (within 5 minutes). It also has the largest outdoor swimming pool and courtyard in Wichita. Restaurant, bar (with entertainment), in-room data ports, some refrigerators, room service, cable TV, pool, video games, business services, airport shuttle, free parking. | 5805 W. Kellogg St. (U.S. 54) | 316/942–7911 | fax 316/942–0854 | 203 rooms | $85–$110 | AE, D, DC, MC, V.

**Comfort Suites.** This all-suite hotel is 1½ mi from the Wichita Mid-Continent Airport and convenient to area attractions and businesses. Bar, complimentary breakfast, refrigerators, cable TV, pool, business services, airport shuttle. | 658 Westdale Dr. | 316/945–2600 | fax 316/945–5033 | 50 suites | $79–109 suites | AE, D, DC, MC, V.

**Days Inn.** Rooms have large windows and pictures on the wall in this two-story hotel 1½ mi from the airport. A lobby done in warm earth tones has a fireplace and sitting area. Complimentary Continental breakfast, in-room data ports, refrigerators, cable TV, business services. | 550 S. Florence (U.S. 54) | 316/942–1717 or 800/329–7466 | fax 316/942–1717 | www.daysinn.com | 43 rooms | $57 | AE, D, DC, MC, V.

**Hampton Inn Wichita–East.** Spacious rooms have contemporary furnishings in this hotel 7 mi from downtown Wichita. Complimentary Continental breakfast, some microwaves, some refrigerators, cable TV, indoor pool, indoor hot tub, business services, pets allowed. | 9449 E. Corporate Hills Dr. | 316/686–3576 or 800/426–7866 | www.hampton-inn.com | 81 rooms | $59–$69 | AE, D, DC, MC, V.

**Holiday Inn Airport.** Rooms are modern and reasonably priced at this hotel 2 mi from Mid-Continent Airport. Restaurant, bar, room service, cable TV, pool, hot tub, laundry facilities, business services, airport shuttle, free parking, pets allowed (fee). | 5500 W. Kellogg St. (U.S. 54) | 316/943–2181 | fax 316/943–6587 | www.holiday-inn.com | 152 rooms | $69–$89 | AE, D, DC, MC, V.

**Hyatt Regency.** Located on the east bank of the Arkansas River, the Hyatt is connected to the Century II Convention Center, making it a convenient choice for business travelers. 2 restaurants, room service, in-room data ports, cable TV, pool, health club, laundry service, business services, airport shuttle. | 400 W. Waterman St. | 316/293–1923 or 800/233–1234 | fax 316/293–1200 | www.hyatt.com | 303 rooms | $140–$169 | AE, D, DC, MC, V.

**Inn at the Park.** Built in 1909, these suites were individually decorated by local designers, winning awards for comfort and design. Picnic area, complimentary Continental breakfast, cable TV, outdoor hot tub, business services. | 3751 E. Douglas | 316/652–0500 or 800/258–1951 | fax 316/652–0525 | 12 suites | $114–$164 suites | AE, D, MC, V.

**La Quinta Inn.** Rooms are simple, with double beds and a desk. The lobby has a Southwestern flair and a lovely mock fireplace. Complimentary Continental breakfast, in-room data ports, cable TV, pool, business services, some pets allowed. | 7700 E. Kellogg St. | 316/681–2881 | fax 316/681–0568 | www.laquinta.com | 122 rooms | $69–$90 | AE, D, DC, MC, V.

**Mark 8 Lodge.** On the eastern end of Wichita, this motel is right off U.S. 54 and adjacent to a 24-hour restaurant. Kitchenettes, cable TV, no pets. | 8136 E. Kellogg St. | 316/685–9415 | fax 316/683–8746 | mark8lodge@travelbase.com | 21 rooms | $44 | AE, MC, V.

**Marriott.** Rooms have modern furnishings at this 11-story high-rise hotel. Restaurant, bar, cable TV, indoor-outdoor pool, outdoor hot tub, exercise equipment, business services, airport shuttle. | 9100 Corporate Hills Dr. | 316/651–0333 | fax 316/651–0990 | 294 rooms, 4 suites | $139–$169; $175–$250 suites | AE, D, DC, MC, V.

**Red Barn Ostrich Farm Bed and Breakfast.** Guest rooms have antiques and collectibles in this modern country farmhouse set on an ostrich farm. Complimentary breakfast, in-room data ports, cable TV, outdoor hot tub. | 6427 N. Greenwich Rd. | 316/744–9800 | fax 316/744–7578 | 3 rooms | $75 | No credit cards.

**Residence Inn by Marriott–East.** This all-suite hotel has studios and penthouses, all with a country atmoshpere. Some suites have a view of the courtyard and pool area. Complimentary Continental breakfast, in-room data ports, kitchenettes, refrigerators, cable TV, pool, outdoor hot tub, laundry facilities, business services, pets allowed (fee). | 411 S. Webb Rd. | 316/686–7331 | fax 316/686–2345 | www.marriott.com | 64 suites | $103–$123 suites | AE, D, DC, MC, V.

**Sheraton Four Points.** Views of both the countryside and the city can be enjoyed from this ten-story high-rise hotel. Restaurant, bar, in-room data ports, cable TV, in-room VCRs available, pool, business services, airport shuttle, pets allowed (fee). | 549 S. Rock Rd. | 316/686–7131 | fax 316/686–0018 | 260 rooms, 8 suites | $59–$129; $175–$300 suites | AE, D, DC, MC, V.

**Stratford House Inn.** This two-story motel is 2 mi from the airport and 1½ mi from the mall. In-room hot tubs, cable TV, business services. | 5505 W. Kellogg St. (U.S. 54) | 316/942–0900 | fax 316/942–0900 | 40 rooms | $50 | AE, D, DC, MC, V.

**Wichita Suites.** Suites are large yet homey, and ideal for the business traveler or a family needing space. Complimentary breakfast, in-room data ports, refrigerators, cable TV, pool, outdoor hot tub, exercise equipment, laundry facilities. | 5211 E. Kellogg St. (U.S. 54) | 316/685–2233 or 800/243–5953 | fax 316/685–4152 | 90 suites | $79–$99 suites | AE, D, DC, MC, V.

**Wichita Inn West.** This basic inn has spacious rooms and is ideal for the budget-conscious traveler. Complimentary Continental breakfast. Microwaves, refrigerators, cable TV, in-room VCRs (and movies). Laundry facilities, no pets. | 6150 W. Kellogg St. | 800/272–6609 | fax 316/943–9302 | 100 rooms | $43 | AE, D, DC, MC, V.

# WINFIELD

MAP 3, H8

*(Nearby towns also listed: Arkansas City, Wichita)*

Founded in 1870, this town of 11,500 was originally named Lagonda, after the first white woman to settle here. The town was later renamed for a Baptist minister who built the first church in this area. Oil was discovered in 1910, and the area became a major training facility for the Air Force during World War II. With a number of restored Victorian and Canton homes, Winfield is consistently listed as one of the top 100 towns in America. Crops of cotton, wheat, and milo dot the landscape around the town, which is also home to a General Electric plant, RubberMaid facility, and other light manufacturing companies.

Information: **Winfield Area Chamber of Commerce** | 205 E. 9th St. (Box 640), Winfield, KS 67156 | 316/221–2420 | win@winfieldchamber.org | www.winfieldchamber.org.

## Attractions

**City Lake.** These 1,100 acres of water are a great place for boating, swimming, and fishing for catfish, bass, walleye, crappie, and northern pike. | 103 S. City Lake Rd. | 316/221–5635 | $4 per vehicle | Daily.

**Cowley County Historical Museum.** A glimpse of the county's past is offered through an old doctor's and dentist's office, as well as a classroom, library, and other artifacts. | 1011 Mansfield | 316/221–4811 | Donation accepted | Weekends 2–5; and by appointment.

**Fairgrounds and Pecan Grove.** Large pecan trees provide a picnicking and recreation area. | W. 14th and North Ave. | 316/221–9723 | Free | Daily.

**Quail Ridge Golf Course.** Opened in 1992, this beautiful 18-hole golf course provides a good balance of tough and less challenging holes. | 3805 Quail Ridge Dr. | 316/221–5645 | Year-round.

### ON THE CALENDAR

**MAR.: *Soroptimist Antique Show.*** One of the largest antique shows in the state, this event draws dealers from all over the central United States. | 316/221–1677.

**JULY: *Walnut Valley Intertribal Pow-Wow.*** More than 150 local and national tribes showcase Native American dances, arts, crafts, and foods. | 316/221–9372.

## Dining

**Western Sizzlin.** Steak. Antique plows, horse saddles, and other pieces reminiscent of Kansas's pioneer heritage can be found throughout this restaurant. The rib eye and sirloin tip steaks are popular, as is the buffet. Kid's menu. | 2010 E. 9th Ave. | 316/221–7717 | $6–$15 | AE, D, MC, V.

## Lodging

**Camelot Inn.** A white picket fence along Main Street will tell you when you've arrived at this two-story inn. A golf course is 3 mi away. Complimentary Continental breakfast, cable TV. | 1710 Main St. | 316/221–9050 | fax 316/221–7062 | 30 rooms | $45 | AE, D, DC, MC, V.

**Quail Ridge Comfort Inn.** Each room has a king-size bed in this hotel at the south end of town. Nice views are available of the adjacent 18-hole golf course. Restaurant nearby, complimentary Continental breakfast, in-room data ports, some in-room safes, some microwaves, some refrigerators, cable TV, pool, gym, laundry facilities, pets allowed. | U.S. 77 at Quail Ridge | 316/221–7529 | fax 316/221–0821 | www.comfortinn.com | 51 rooms | $64 | AE, D, DC, MC, V.

**Town House Motel.** Built in 1993, this clean, comfortable, and affordable motel is the oldest in Winfield. | 601 W. 9th St. | 316/221–2110 | 5 rooms | $30–$42 | MC, V.

# YATES CENTER

MAP 3, J7

*(Nearby towns also listed: Iola, Chanute)*

Abner Yates, a land speculator from Illinois who settled in this area in 1874, was thrilled when, in the late 1800s, five railroad lines crossed through the county and the town named in his honor became the county seat. After the county seat was moved elsewhere, however, this town of 1,900 failed to develop much. The 41 buildings of the courthouse square have been placed on the National Register of Historic Places, due to their architectural integrity and representation of the speculative railroad towns of that period. Agriculture and oil production continue to dominate the livelihood of most residents of Woodson County.

© Artville

# TOP TIPS FOR TRAVELERS

## Smart Sightseeings

**Don't plan your visit in your hotel room.** Don't wait until you pull into town to decide how to spend your days. It's inevitable that there will be much more to see and do than you'll have time for: choose sights in advance.

**Organize your touring.** Note the places that most interest you on a map, and visit places that are near each other during the same morning or afternoon.

**Start the day well equipped.** Leave your hotel in the morning with everything you need for the day—maps, medicines, extra film, your guidebook, rain gear, and another layer of clothing in case the weather turns cooler.

**Tour museums early.** If you're there when the doors open you'll have an intimate experience of the collection.

**Easy does it.** See museums in the mornings, when you're fresh, and visit sit-down attractions later on. Take breaks before you need them.

**Strike up a conversation.** Only curmudgeons don't respond to a smile and a polite request for information. Most people appreciate your interest in their home town. And your conversations may end up being your most vivid memories.

**Get lost.** When you do, you never know what you'll find—but you can count on it being memorable. Use your guidebook to help you get back on track. Build wandering-around time into every day.

**Quit before you're tired.** There's no point in seeing that one extra sight if you're too exhausted to enjoy it.

**Take your mother's advice.** Go to the bathroom when you have the chance. You never know what lies ahead.

## Hotel How-Tos

**How to get a deal.** After you've chosen a likely candidate or two, phone them directly and price a room for your travel dates. Then call the hotel's toll-free number and ask the same questions. Also try consolidators and hotel-room discounters. You won't hear the same rates twice. On the spot, make a reservation as soon as you are quoted a price you want to pay.

**Promises, promises.** If you have special requests, make them when you reserve. Get written confirmation of any promises.

**Settle in.** Upon arriving, make sure everything works—lights and lamps, TV and radio, sink, tub, shower, and anything else that matters. Report any problems immediately. And don't wait until you need extra pillows or blankets or an ironing board to call housekeeping. Also check out the fire emergency instructions. Know where to find the fire exits, and make sure your companions do, too.

**If you need to complain.** Be polite but firm. Explain the problem to the person in charge. Suggest a course of action. If you aren't satisfied, repeat your requests to the manager. Document everything: Take pictures and keep a written record of who you've spoken with, when, and what was said. Contact your travel agent, if he made the reservations.

**Know the score.** When you go out, take your hotel's business cards (one for everyone in your party). If you have extras, you can give them out to new acquaintances who want to call you.

**Tip up front.** For special services, a tip or partial tip in advance can work wonders.

**Use all the hotel resources** A concierge can make difficult things easy. But a desk clerk, bellhop, or other hotel employee who's friendly, smart, and ambitious can often steer you straight as well. A gratuity is in order if the advice is helpful.

Information: **Woodson County Chamber of Commerce** | Box 211, Yates Center, KS 66783 | 316/625–3235.

## Attractions

**Kalida Castle Cave.** Built out of native sandstone, this aboveground cave keeps farm supplies a constant temperature all year long. | Off Kalida St., 2 mi southeast of Yates Center | 316/625–3235 | Free | Daily.

**Toronto State Park.** Swimming, boating, fishing, and primitive camping draw outdoor enthusiasts to this 1,000-acre park all year long, especially in the winter months, to view the bald eagles. | 144 Rte. 105 | 316/637–2213 | www.kdwp.state.ks.us | $4 per vehicle | Daily.

### ON THE CALENDAR

**MAY: *Yates Center Days.*** There *is* such a thing as a free lunch, and it's here during this two-day festival, which includes a car show, arts, and crafts. | 316/625–3235.
**JULY: *Woodson County Fair.*** The Woodson County Fairgrounds hosts food, concerts, 4-H displays, and more during this five day event. | 316/625–8620.

## Dining

**Frannie's Fix and Go Lunchroom.** American. Frannie herself will greet you from behind the counter. Help yourself to any of dozens of homemade pies made fresh daily. Try Taco Salad (on Friday) | 108 S. Main St. | 316/625–2325 | Closed weekends | $1 | No credit cards.

**Smokey Ben's.** Barbecue. Pictures of cowboys and Indians adorn the walls of this casual restaurant and give it a Western feel. The barbecued ribs, brisket, and ham are popular. Kid's menu. | 610 W. Mary St. | 316/625–2344 | Closed Mon. | $8–$10 | AE, DC, MC, V.

## Lodging

**Townsman Motel.** This two-story motel was built in 1963, and an additional section was added in 1980. The motel is very popular with hunters and anglers who plan on spending the day at Toronto Lake, which is 12 mi west of town. Cable TV. Business services. Some pets allowed. | 609 W. Mary St. | 316/625–2131 | fax 316/625–2133 | 32 rooms | $34–$39 | AE, D, DC, MC, V.

# Oklahoma

**America meets itself in the middle in Oklahoma, a geographic and cultural crossroads** where the green mountains of the East dissolve into the golden prairies of the West. Part Midwestern, part Southern, Oklahoma's terrain, chameleonlike, offers a new view in every direction. A great swath of tallgrass prairie sweeps down from Kansas in the north, while the foothills of the Ozarks lap over the northeastern border from Arkansas and Missouri. The pine trees of the Ouachita National Forest blanket thousands of acres in the east, while the southern plains begin their majestic westward roll in central Oklahoma. In all, a dozen different ecosystems can be found in Oklahoma, creating landscapes to suit every taste: from oak, hickory, and pine forests to Rocky Mountain foothills to shady cypress swamps, pastel mesas, craggy canyons, flower-specked plains. With 52 state parks, numerous wildlife refuges, a national forest, and a national recreation area to choose from, you'll have plenty of opportunities to sample the variety.

One of the youngest states in the Union (the 46th), Oklahoma could also claim to be the most deeply connected to America's past (more Native Americans live here than in any other state). Native Americans from across the continent converged in Oklahoma in the 19th century, and 37 tribal headquarters are found within the state's borders. Many of the country's greatest Native American statesmen and personalities have called Oklahoma home, including Will Rogers, Jim Thorpe, Sequoyah, and Cherokee chief Wilma Mankiller. A series of land runs in the late 19th century brought in hundreds of thousands of immigrants to Oklahoma, homesteaders who brought with them traditions and cultures of their own.

Oklahoma is more than just a metaphorical crossroads. After the Civil War, five cattle trails that crossed what's now Oklahoma left behind a still-vibrant Western heritage.

| | | |
|---|---|---|
| CAPITAL: OKLAHOMA CITY | POPULATION: 3,277,700 | AREA: 69,903 SQUARE MI |
| BORDERS: MO, AR, TX, NM, CO, KS | TIME ZONES: CENTRAL, MOUNTAIN | POSTAL ABBREVIATION: OK |
| WEB SITE: WWW.TRAVELOK.COM | | |

There are more horses per capita in Oklahoma than in any other state, and ranching and agriculture are top industries. For visitors, that translates into rodeos, superb facilities for trail riding, and some of the best Western art collections anywhere.

Two of America's great transcontinental highways, Interstate 40 and Interstate 35, intersect one another in Oklahoma City, carrying millions of business and pleasure travelers through the state each year. More and more, travelers who once were "just passing through" pull off the interstates to explore Oklahoma's scenic and cultural attractions (approximately 16 million trips were taken here in 1998). Thousands of visitors come each year expressly for a nostalgic spin along Route 66, once known as "America's Main Street." With more than 420 drivable miles of the vintage highway—more than in any other state—Route 66 offers numerous entrées into one of the state's chief charms, its small towns.

Lots of elbow room, clean air, and a leisurely pace are found in Oklahoma, even in its largest cities. Lately, there's been an influx of "urban refugees," looking not only to make a living but to create a new life. They have brought a sophisticated sensibility to out-of-the-way places and planted gourmet restaurants, espresso bars, and art galleries next to the saddle shops and hardware stores of Oklahoma's Main Streets.

Few visitors to Oklahoma leave without remarking on the friendliness of the people, who blend Southern hospitality with the openness found in the West. Many an out-of-state visitor driving in the western plains has been mystified by the number of total strangers who wave hello. "Oklahomans are what other people think Americans are like," Will Rogers said about his native state in the 1920s. "Oklahoma is the heart, it's the vital organ of our national existence."

# History

History books have tended to paint pre-19th-century Oklahoma as blank canvas, waiting to be filled in by the U.S. policy of Native American resettlement and pioneering homesteaders. Archaeological evidence reveals a far different story: projectile points and bones dating back 17,000 years have been found in western Oklahoma, where nomadic hunters followed first the woolly mammoth and later primordial buffalo on the plains. Between AD 900 and 1400, Spiro Mounds in present-day eastern Oklahoma was the religious and cultural center for a confederation of 60 tribes stretching from the Gulf Coast to the Great Lakes.

In 1541 Francisco Vasquez Coronado became the first recorded European visitor to what is now Oklahoma. The Spanish explorer crossed the state's Panhandle in search of the legendary Seven Golden Cities of Cíbola. Trade between Native Americans and the French began after 1719, when Bernard de La Harpe established a post among the Caddoan-speaking Wichita who lived along the Red River in eastern Oklahoma, trading guns, ammunition, tools, cloth, and paint for furs.

Oklahoma was a Spanish territory from 1763 to 1800. France gained control just three years before the Louisiana Purchase made Oklahoma a part of the United States.

## OK Timeline

| c. AD 800 | 1541 | 1719 | 1786 |
|---|---|---|---|
| Eastern Oklahoma is the religious center of the Mound Builders civilization. | Francisco Vasquez de Coronado crosses western Oklahoma looking for the Seven Golden Cities of Cíbola. | French trader Bernard de La Harpe makes trading alliances with Caddoan tribes near the Red River. | A Wichita village on the Red River is a regional trading hub dealing in furs and French and Spanish goods. |

INTRODUCTION
HISTORY
REGIONS
WHEN TO VISIT
STATE'S GREATS
RULES OF THE ROAD
DRIVING TOURS

The presence of "hostile" tribes in the western plains, including Comanches and Apaches, slowed the exploration of the new territory. Settlement was further delayed by bad press. In August 1819 Major Stephen Long traveled across the western territory and suffered scorching 100° heat. He subsequently labeled the area west of the 100th Meridian the "Great American Desert."

In 1825 Congress designated Oklahoma as "Indian Territory." Five tribes—the Choctaw, Chickasaw, Cherokee, Muskogee-Creek, and Seminole—were forced to resettle west of Arkansas in one of the most ignominious chapters of American history. A full third of the 15,000-member Cherokee Nation died along the westward journey that came to be known as "The Trail of Tears." But in spite of the circumstances of their removal, the tribes flourished in Indian Territory, establishing farms, cotton plantations, schools, and churches and creating the state's first legislatures and law enforcement agencies. Four of the tribes' 19th-century capitols are still standing, as well as numerous historic homes and schools.

Fearing raids by the nomadic Plains tribes in the western part of the territory, the Five Tribes negotiated treaties requiring the federal government to build a string of forts inside Indian Territory. These were quickly abandoned at the outbreak of the Civil War, and in response the tribes allied themselves with the Confederacy (Chickasaw statesmen even penned their own Declaration of Independence). At war's end, the federal government claimed that the tribes had voided their treaties by declaring war against the United States and stripped them of thousands of acres of land in western Oklahoma. Over the next two decades, dozens of tribes and remnants of tribes were moved from other parts of the United States to Indian Territory as westward expansion continued to create friction between settlers and Native Americans.

Ultimately, homesteaders lobbied for the opening up of land within Indian Territory as well, seizing on a 2-million-acre tract that was not assigned to any specific tribe. In 1889, President Benjamin Harrison signed a proclamation opening the "unassigned lands" to settlement, and central Oklahoma was settled in a one-day, frantic race for land. In 1890, Congress created Oklahoma Territory, and over the next decade the federal government continued to make more land available to homesteaders by breaking up tribal lands into individual farms for Native Americans.

In 1905 the residents of Indian Territory asked to join the Union as a separate Indian state that would be called "Sequoyah," a resolution Congress rejected. Instead, Indian Territory and Oklahoma Territory joined together to enter the Union as the state of Oklahoma in 1907.

From 1907 to 1928, Oklahoma was the largest oil-producing state. (By 1919, $\frac{1}{5}$ of all the oil sold in the United States came from one Oklahoma oil field.) Oil money—or money made from the industry—built numerous architectural landmarks and parks. The boom continued until the 1930s, when the price of cotton toppled and sustained drought created "dust bowl" conditions in western Oklahoma. So many Oklahomans left the state looking for work during the 1930s that the term "Okies" became synonymous with migrant families.

| 1803 | 1805 | 1824 | 1830 | 1831 |
|------|------|------|------|------|
| The Louisiana Purchase transfers ownership of Oklahoma from France to the United States. | The Kiowa move from the northern plains to Oklahoma. | Fort Gibson, the state's first military post, is established on the Arkansas River. | President Andrew Jackson signs the Indian Removal Act, creating Indian Territory. | The Choctaw Tribe begins its journey to Indian Territory. |

In the years following World War II, soil-conservation and flood-control efforts effectively "drowned" the Dust Bowl, and created more than 130 man-made lakes. In recent years, attempts have been made to diversify Oklahoma's oil- and gas-based economy. And, thanks in part to all those lakes, one of the fastest-growing economic sectors is tourism. It now ranks third, just behind agriculture and oil.

# Regions

### 1. NORTHEASTERN OKLAHOMA

Heavily wooded and liberally laced with rivers and lakes, northeastern Oklahoma lies in the foothills of the Ozark Mountains and contains nearly half of the state's 52 state parks. It is Oklahoma's most rooted region—the state's first permanent European settlements and first oil fortunes were made here, and have left behind a rich legacy of historical museums and architecture, most notably in Tulsa and Bartlesville. Tulsa, on the Arkansas River and the state's second largest city, is filled with art deco architecture, outstanding parks, art museums, and shopping, and is home to a number of acclaimed performing arts companies. Three of the Five Tribes were resettled in northeastern Oklahoma and tribal history and art collections are found at Muskogee, Tahlequah, and Okmulgee.

*Towns listed:* Bartlesville, Broken Arrow, Eufaula, Grove, Miami, Muskogee, Okmulgee, Pryor, Tahlequah, Tulsa, Wagoner, Vinita

### 2. NORTH-CENTRAL OKLAHOMA

Pastures and prairies characterize north-central Oklahoma, a land of ranches and wheat fields. The largest remaining swath of virgin tallgrass prairie is preserved near Pawhuska, and Oklahoma's early character is also preserved in places like the Pawnee Bill Buffalo Ranch Site, home to buffalo and memories of Wild West shows, and the Marland Estate, a palace on the prairie built by oilman and former governor E. W. Marland. The Osage, Ponca, and Pawnee tribes are headquartered here; their tribal dances and historic sites are among the state's most venerable.

*Towns listed:* Hominy, Pawhuska, Pawnee, Perry, Ponca City, Stillwater

### 3. SOUTHWESTERN OKLAHOMA

The 600-million-year-old granite Wichita Mountains, one of the oldest mountain ranges in the country, are the scenic stars of Oklahoma's southwestern plains and the backdrop for tiny, historic towns, a rugged wildlife refuge, and a lone resort. The southern plains, traversed by the Red River, were the setting for some of the most dramatic chapters in the conflict between the U.S. government and the Plains Indian tribes. The

| 1836 | 1842 | 1853 | 1861 | 1863 |
|---|---|---|---|---|
| The Cherokee Treaty of New Echota, which exchanges Cherokee land in Georgia for land in Indian Territory, is ratified. | The Seminoles relocate to eastern Oklahoma. | The Chickasaw build a council house in Tishomingo. | Cherokees, Choctaw, Seminoles, Muscogee (Creeks), and Chickasaw ally with the Confederacy during the Civil War. | Native Americans, African-Americans, and whites fight side by side for the first time in American history at the Civil War Battle of Honey Springs in Rentiesville. |

story is unfurled at museums and historic sites in Anadarko and Lawton and at Fort Sill, a U.S. military base since 1874.

INTRODUCTION
HISTORY
REGIONS
WHEN TO VISIT
STATE'S GREATS
RULES OF THE ROAD
DRIVING TOURS

*Towns listed:* Altus, Anadarko, Chickaha, Clinton, Elk City, Lawton, Medicine Park, Weatherford

## 4. SOUTH-CENTRAL OKLAHOMA

Midway between Oklahoma City and the Red River, wooded valleys percolate with mineral springs and waterfalls, created millions of years ago where the plains abut the 250-million-year-old Arbuckle Mountains. The waterfalls and shady glens at Turner Falls, near Davis, and the Chickasaw National Recreation Area, near Sulphur, have been favored picnic spots since well before statehood, and attract thousands of visitors each year. Five major lakes, each surrounded by thousands of acres of parks, make water sports, especially fishing and boating, the region's defining activities.

*Towns listed:* Ada, Ardmore, Atoka, Davis, Duncan, Durant, Pauls Valley, Sulphur, Waurika

## 5. OKLAHOMA CITY

Nearly one in every three Oklahomans lives in the sprawling Oklahoma City metropolitan area, built on a nearly featureless plain. Oklahoma City was born in one tumultuous day during the 1889 Land Run and nearly two decades later "stole" the capital from the more refined city of Guthrie, 20 mi to the north. Oklahoma City never quite shook its reputation as an earthy scrapper: oil wells dot the lawn of the state capitol, museums celebrate everything from the trucking industry to softball to the Western heritage, and ethnic neighborhoods account for the state's spiciest restaurant scene. The nearby towns of Norman and Edmond share Oklahoma City's land run history and are known for their restaurants and shopping, while museums in Shawnee and El Reno, established to celebrate the Potawatomi and Cheyenne-Arapaho tribes, respectively, offer unique historical perspectives.

*Towns listed:* Edmond, El Reno, Guthrie, Norman, Oklahoma City, Shawnee

## 6. THE OUACHITA MOUNTAINS

Four-lane roads are a rarity in southeastern Oklahoma, the state's most remote and rugged region. The Ouachita National Forest and the Kiamichi and San Bois mountain ranges are found here, along with numerous wilderness refuges and parks that preserve the area's forests and wildlife. Fly-fishing and hunting are popular sports, but the area is perhaps best known for its trails—there are hundreds of miles of equestrian, hiking, and mountain-biking trails open to the public, many leading through landscapes little changed for a century. High-maintenance travelers should come prepared. Big-city amenities like room service or dinner and a cocktail after 9 PM are virtually nonexistent.

*Towns listed:* Broken Bow, Hugo, Idabel, McAlester, Poteau

| **1866** | **1867** | | **1871** | **1874** |
|---|---|---|---|---|
| Reconstruction treaties cede the tribes' western lands to the federal government. | Treaty of Medicine Lodge creates reservations in western Oklahoma for the Cheyenne, Arapaho, Kiowa, and Comanche. | Longhorn cattle begin moving north along the Chisholm Trail. | The first railroad, the Missouri-Kansas-Texas (M-K-T) line, is built in Oklahoma. | Fort Sill is established in southwestern Oklahoma as a base of operations for the Indian Wars. |

## 7. THE PANHANDLE

Once labeled "No Man's Land," due to arid conditions, lack of water, and conflict between settlers and native peoples, the flat northeastern strip of Oklahoma land is now referred to as the Panhandle. The terrain is flat and weather conditions are extreme in this area—flash floods in summer and blizzard conditions in winter are not uncommon.

*Towns listed:* Boise City, Guymon

# When to Visit

Oklahoma's temperate climate means long summers, short winters, and warm autumns, making travel seasonal here during most months. Just how seasonable, however, varies considerably from year to year. "If you don't like the weather in Oklahoma," advised native son Will Rogers, "just wait a minute." The state's perch on the southern plains makes it a meeting place for dry cold air from the north and warm moist air from the Gulf of Mexico, allowing for unpredictable—and sometimes unstable—weather conditions. Spring brings thunderstorms and tornadoes every year, most often in late April, May, and June; twister-wary travelers can take comfort in the fact that Oklahoma's major television and radio stations, along with the National Severe Storms Laboratory in Norman, keep the public well informed of dangerous storm conditions.

Predictably, July, August, and even early September can be quite hot throughout the state. The average temperature in July is 82°F, but in some years temperatures nudge towards 100°F on many days. The record high temperature set in Oklahoma was 120°F; three towns hit that mark in 1936, and Tishomingo did so again in 1943. Winters, correspondingly, are often very mild. The record low temperature was −27°F, set once in 1905 and again in 1930, but the temperature stays well above freezing most winter days. Snow is relatively rare, except in the Panhandle, which suffers both winter blizzards and scorching summer heat.

Spring in Oklahoma can begin as early as mid-March; April and May offer up idyllic weather, and bathing suits and jet skis are often in use well before Memorial Day. Warm days are frequent in autumn, even into mid-October, which may bring week after week of spectacular Indian summer days.

## CLIMATE CHART

Average High/Low Temperatures (°F) and Monthly Precipitation (in inches)

|  | JAN. | FEB. | MAR. | APR. | MAY | JUNE |
|---|---|---|---|---|---|---|
| BOISE CITY | 60/19 | 64/22 | 62/28 | 71/39 | 79/47 | 88/47 |
|  | .5 | .5 | .9 | 1.2 | 2.6 | 2.8 |

|  | JULY | AUG. | SEPT. | OCT. | NOV. | DEC. |
|---|---|---|---|---|---|---|
|  | 93/62 | 90/60 | 83/60 | 73/40 | 60/29 | 50/20 |
|  | 2.7 | 2.5 | 1.8 | .8 | .7 | .3 |

| 1889 | 1890 | 1893 | 1894 | 1897 |
|---|---|---|---|---|
| Central Oklahoma is opened to non-Indian settlement with a land run. | Organic Act creates Oklahoma Territory; area becomes known, along with Indian Territory, as the Twin Territories. | The Cherokee Outlet is opened to non-Indian settlement and 100,000 people race to claim 50,000 homesteads. | Chiricahua Apache tribal members, including Geronimo, are imprisoned at Fort Sill. | First commercial oil well is drilled in Bartlesville by Frank Phillips. |

INTRODUCTION
HISTORY
REGIONS
WHEN TO VISIT
STATE'S GREATS
RULES OF THE ROAD
DRIVING TOURS

| BROKEN BOW | JAN. | FEB. | MAR. | APR. | MAY | JUNE |
|---|---|---|---|---|---|---|
| | 52/27 | 56/31 | 65/39 | 75/48 | 81/57 | 88/64 |
| | 2.6 | 3.5 | 4.9 | 4.5 | 6.3 | 4.3 |
| | JULY | AUG. | SEPT. | OCT. | NOV. | DEC. |
| | 93/68 | 93/67 | 80/61 | 76/49 | 65/40 | 55/30 |
| | 3.5 | 3 | 4.5 | 4.3 | 4.2 | 4 |

| LAWTON | JAN. | FEB. | MAR. | APR. | MAY | JUNE |
|---|---|---|---|---|---|---|
| | 49/23 | 55/28 | 64/38 | 74/49 | 81/58 | 89/66 |
| | 1 | 1.3 | 2.1 | 2.4 | 4.9 | 3.6 |
| | JULY | AUG. | SEPT. | OCT. | NOV. | DEC. |
| | 95/71 | 94/60 | 85/61 | 75/49 | 63/38 | 52/27 |
| | 1.9 | 2.2 | 3.7 | 3 | 1.8 | 1.2 |

| OKLAHOMA CITY | JAN. | FEB. | MAR. | APR. | MAY | JUNE |
|---|---|---|---|---|---|---|
| | 47/26 | 52/29 | 62/39 | 72/50 | 79/58 | 87/66 |
| | 1.1 | 1.6 | 2.7 | 3.7 | 5.2 | 4.3 |
| | JULY | AUG. | SEPT. | OCT. | NOV. | DEC. |
| | 93/70 | 92/69 | 84/62 | 74/50 | 60/31 | 49/29 |
| | 2.6 | 2.6 | 3.8 | 2.4 | 2 | 1 |

| TULSA | JAN. | FEB. | MAR. | APR. | MAY | JUNE |
|---|---|---|---|---|---|---|
| | 45/24 | 51/29 | 62/39 | 73/44 | 79/58 | 87/67 |
| | 15 | 1.9 | 3.5 | 3.7 | 4.6 | 4.4 |
| | JULY | AUG. | SEPT. | OCT. | NOV. | DEC. |
| | 93/72 | 92/70 | 86/62 | 73/60 | 60/40 | 48/28 |
| | 3 | 3.1 | 4.7 | 3.6 | 3.1 | 2.1 |

## FESTIVALS AND SEASONAL EVENTS
### WINTER

Nov.–Dec. **Territorial Christmas Celebration.** Held throughout Guthrie's 400-block historic district, this event includes a "Victorian Walk" and performances of *A Territorial Christmas Carol*. | 405/282–1947.

Jan. **International Finals Rodeo.** The nation's top 15 cowboys and cowgirls compete for world titles at the state fairgrounds in Oklahoma City. | 405/235–6540.

Feb. **Bitter Creek Frontier Daze.** Roman Nose Resort Park near Watonga hosts a living-history reenactment featuring Plains Indians, fur trappers, U.S. cavalry, outlaws, and homesteaders. | 580/623–7281.

| 1904 | 1905 | 1907 | 1910 | 1919 |
|---|---|---|---|---|
| The Red Fork oil field is discovered at the Creek settlement "Tulsey Town"—later Tulsa. | A proposal to admit Indian Territory to the Union as an all-Indian state called "Sequoyah" is rejected by Congress. | Indian Territory and Oklahoma Territory are joined to create Oklahoma, the 46th state; tribal governments are abolished. | A referendum moves the state capital from Guthrie to Oklahoma City. | Cushing Drumright oil field accounts for 3 percent of the world's total oil production. |

Feb. **Bullnanza.** Bull riders from around the country compete at the Lazy E Arena, near Guthrie. | 800/595–7433.

## SPRING

Apr. **Azalea Festival.** More than 200,000 visitors come to Honor Heights Park in Muskogee to see its millions of azalea blossoms. The three-week festival includes a parade, a bicycle tour, and a crafts fair. | 918/684–6302.

Apr. **Festival of the Arts.** One of the country's ten largest art fairs, this outdoor festival in the Myriad Botanical Gardens in downtown Oklahoma City includes food, music, and children's activities along with fine art. | 405/270–4848.

Apr. **Fur Trade Rendezvous.** A pre-1840s rendezvous with trappers, traders, and other characters is re-enacted at Fort Washita Historic Site, a restored Indian Territory fort near Durant. | 580/924–6502.

Apr. **Herbal Affair and Festival.** Downtown Sand Springs (near Tulsa) fills with street vendors selling live and dried herbs, herbal products, and gardening products. There are also food and crafts booths at this huge, sweet-smelling event. | 918/246–2567.

Apr. **Medieval Fair.** Norman's Brandt Park presents a human chess game and other medieval entertainment, a crafts fair, and living-history re-creations. | 405/288–2536.

May **Pioneer Days Celebration.** At the Texas County Fairgrounds and in downtown Guymon, one of the state's largest Professional Rodeo Cowboy's Association (PRCA) rodeos includes trail rides, chuckwagon breakfasts, and barbecue along with rodeo events. | 580/338–3376.

May **Chuckwagon Gathering and Children's Cowboy Festival.** This homage to the state's Old West heritage is held at the National Cowboy Hall of Fame in Oklahoma City. Authentic chuckwagons, which are lined in a circle, dish out old-fashioned "cowboy". There is also live music and hands-on activities for kids. | 405/478–2250.

May **Jazz Banjo Festival.** A gathering of four-string banjo strummers in downtown Guthrie celebrates ragtime and the big band era with three days of concerts and jam sessions. | 405/292–1947.

| **1923** | **1936** | **1945** | **1995** |
|---|---|---|---|
| The Osage Nation receives $27 million in payment for oil leases, becomes the richest per capita nation in the world. | Oklahoma Indian Welfare Act allows tribes to enact new constitutions. | The post–Dust Bowl population drops 16%, to 2,028,000. | Alfred P. Murrah Federal Building is bombed in Oklahoma City, killing 168 people. |

June   **Aerospace America International Airshow.** More than 100 modern military aircraft, 80 war planes, a trade show, and aeronautical acrobatics can be found at Will Rogers World Airport in Oklahoma City. | 405/685–9546.

June   **Jazz in June.** Norman hosts free concerts with local, regional, and national jazz and blues bands. | 405/325–5468.

June   **OK Mozart International Festival.** The orchestra Solisti New York takes up residence at the Bartlesville Community Center for a week of concerts showcasing the work of Mozart. Lectures, tours, and workshops entertain you between performances. | 918/336–9900.

June   **Red Earth Cultural Festival.** Held at the Myriad Convention Center in Oklahoma City, here you will find Native American dancing, an art show, a film competition, games, and storytelling. | 405/427–5228.

July   **Elks Rodeo.** The oldest rodeo in the state is held at Crystal Beach Park in Woodward, and includes a parade, a queen coronation, home-style barbecues, and nightly country music. | 580/256–3549.

Aug.   **American Indian Exposition.** The oldest Indian-run fair in the world is held in Anadarko and includes ceremonial dancing, an historical pageant, a parade, and greyhound and horse racing. | 405/247–6651.

Aug.   **Freedom Rodeo and Old Cowhand Reunion.** Freedom (pop. 254, near Alva) more than quadruples in size for the annual three-day rodeo. A local cowhand is honored every year. | 580/621–3276.

Aug.   **Grant's Bluegrass and Old-Time Music Festival.** Held at Salt Creek Park, near Hugo, this is the oldest bluegrass festival west of the Mississippi River. | 580/326–5598.

Aug.   **Jazz on Greenwood.** Jazz, blues, zydeco, and other roots music is presented on three stages in the historic Greenwood area in north Tulsa. | 918/584–3378.

FALL

Sept.   **Bluegrass and Chili Festival.** Formerly held in Tulsa, this two-day event at the Claremore Expo Center and Grounds is the most celebrated of the year, with appearances by bluegrass performers from all over the country, a lauded chili cook-off, a car show, and children's activities. | 918/341–2818.

Sept.   **Dusk 'Til Dawn Blues Festival.** National, regional, and local acts perform on two stages at the vintage Down Home Blues Club in Rentiesville. | 918/473–2411.

Sept.   **State Fair of Oklahoma.** Commercial exhibits, livestock competitions, musical performances, motor sports, a rodeo, and a circus are part of one of the country's biggest fairs, held in Oklahoma City. As many as 1.7 million people visit each year. | 405/948–6700.

Oct. **An Affair of the Heart.** Arts and crafts, antiques, and collectibles fill seven buildings and draw visitors from throughout the region to the State Fairgrounds in Oklahoma City. | 405/632–2652.

Oct. **Oklahoma International Bluegrass Festival.** Traditional bluegrass and "newgrass" stars from the United States and abroad perform in historic venues in downtown Guthrie. | 405/282–4446.

Nov. **Beavers Bend Folk Festival and Craft Show.** Turn-of-the-20th-century household arts, crafts, and music are demonstrated at the Forest Heritage Center in Beavers Bend Resort Park near Broken Bow. The event corresponds with the peak of fall foliage. | 580/494–6497.

# State's Greats

From the pristine Ouachita National Forest to the rolling Tallgrass Prairie Preserve, where buffalo really do roam, to the rugged and picturesque Wichita Mountains Wildlife Refuge in the southwest, Oklahoma gives you a variety of landscapes to choose from—and plenty of breathing space with which to enjoy them. The state is unspoiled and uncrowded, with an easygoing lifestyle that evokes a certain nostalgia, especially in the small towns found along Route 66, which attracts large numbers of Europeans. Oklahoma's landscapes can be enjoyed for themselves, to be sure, but they serve as a backdrop to a complex and uniquely American drama, the state's rich Native American and settlement history. Oklahoma's frontier period, only a couple of generations ago, is brought to life in scores of museums and historic sites across the state.

## Parks, Natural Sights, and Outdoor Activities

The oldest shortleaf pine forest in the country, the **Ouachita National Forest,** is preserved in its pristine splendor in the 26,544-acre **Winding Stair Recreation Area.** The same towering pine trees and mountain streams are found at **Beavers Bend Resort Park,** along with such amenities as a golf course, a lodge, and cabins. Rumors of Oklahoma's outlaw past can be found at **Robbers Cave State Park,** built in the San Bois Mountains around a sandstone cave reputed to be an Indian Territory hideout. The hilly northeast corner of the state is where you'll find **Grand Lake O'the Cherokees,** with dozens of parks, resorts, and marinas on its shores. The centerpiece of western Oklahoma's rugged landscape is **Roman Nose Resort Park,** site of a former Cheyenne winter camp and home to springs and red canyons. **Black Mesa State Park,** in the Panhandle high plains, takes its name from a lava-topped mesa. Urban gems include the **Myriad Botanical Gardens** and **Crystal Bridge Tropical Conservatory** in Oklahoma City, containing botanical specimens from the rain forest, and the rose gardens and walkways at **Woodward Park** in Tulsa.

## Culture, History, and the Arts

Oklahoma's unique political history has left it with intriguing—and colorful—historic and cultural sites. Art and artifacts from both the real and the imagined American West can be found at the **National Cowboy Hall of Fame and Western Heritage Center** in Oklahoma City. Tulsa's **Gilcrease Museum** contains one of the most outstanding collections of Western art in the world. The collections at the **Woolaroc Ranch, Museum, and Wildlife Preserve,** once the retreat of oilman Frank Phillips, near Bartlesville, combine Native American and Western art and historical exhibits.

Oklahoma's frontier history can be found at places such as **Fort Gibson Historic Site,** the first outpost in the Territory following the Civil War, where living-history programs

INTRODUCTION
HISTORY
REGIONS
WHEN TO VISIT
STATE'S GREATS
RULES OF THE ROAD
DRIVING TOURS

are conducted, **Fort Sill Military Reservation,** established as a military base during the Indian Wars, and the **Creek Council House Museum,** which housed the Creek legislature from 1876 until statehood. Guthrie, in central Oklahoma, was the major city in territorial days, and its 300 blocks of turn-of-the-20th-century Victorian architecture make it the largest urban district listed on the National Register of Historic Places. Oil has left a legacy of art and architecture in Oklahoma. **Philbrook Museum of Art** in Tulsa is an Italianate villa that was once the home of oilman Waite Phillips and today exhibits European, American, and Native American art.

## Sports

Oklahoma's uncrowded and diverse landscapes offer endless opportunities for outdoor sports and recreation. Of the hundreds of miles of hiking trails throughout the state, some of the most picturesque and pristine are found within the **Ouachita National Forest** and **Wichita Mountains Wildlife Refuge.** At the opposite end of the state, the trail to the top of **Black Mesa** takes you to the state's highest point. Horseback is still the transportation of choice for thousands of Oklahomans, and guided trail rides and stables are recreation staples. Oklahoma's state parks have opened trails to mountain bikers; the trails in **Roman Nose Resort Park** have been named one of the nation's top rides. Fishing brings thousands of vacationers to Oklahoma; fly-fishing for brown trout in the chilly waters of Mountain Fork River in **Beavers Bend Resort Park** is a popular pursuit. Marinas dot the shores of **Lake Eufaula,** the state's largest, and Oklahoma's famous winds have made the state a prime spot for sailing regattas.

Some of Oklahoma's 250 golf courses offer the truly unusual: rattlesnakes are a hazard at Roman Nose Resort Park and wild turkey have been spotted strolling down the fairways of Cedar Creek Golf Course at **Hochatown State Park.** Among more traditional courses are standouts **Shangri-La,** near Grove, and **Karsten Creek** in Stillwater. For a state with such a moderate climate, it's a bit of a surprise that hockey is so popular—attendance at Oklahoma City Blazers games at the Myriad Arena in Oklahoma City is the highest in the Central Hockey League. More expected is the proliferation of rodeos, a Saturday-night staple in Oklahoma's small towns. The Woodward **Elks Rodeo,** Guymon's **Pioneer Days Celebration,** and events at the Lazy E Arena near Guthrie are among the most popular. The rodeo circuit is at its busiest in July and August—there are so many events that the late summer months are known as "Cowboy Christmas."

# Rules of the Road

**License Requirements:** Home state licenses are honored for non-residents.

**Right Turn on Red:** Permitted throughout the state after a complete stop, unless otherwise posted.

**Seat Belt and Helmet Laws:** Seat belts are mandatory for drivers and front-seat passengers; child restraints are mandatory for children under four years of age. Children four and five years old must use child restraints or seat belts at all times. Safety helmets are required for motorcyclists under age 18; face shields, goggles, or windscreens are mandatory. Motorcyclists are required to use their headlights at all times, even during daylight hours.

**Speed Limits:** 70 mph on four-lane or divided highways; 75 mph on turnpikes; and 55 mph on county roads. Residential and business-district limits are set by local ordinance.

**For more information:** Contact the Oklahoma Department of Public Safety | 405/ 425–2424.

# Ouachita National Forest Driving Tour Along U.S. 59

*TRAVELS INTO THE OLD CHOCTAW NATION*

Distance: 140 mi　　　　Time: 2–3 days

Suggested breaks: Eagle Creek Guest Cottages, in Octavia, have very comfortable cabins and breathtaking views.

This tour takes you along U.S. 59 to the pine-covered heart of the old Choctaw Nation and the Ouachita Forest. ("Ouachita" is the French spelling of two Choctaw words *owa* and *chito*, for "big hunt.") The highway weaves in and out of protected wilderness areas

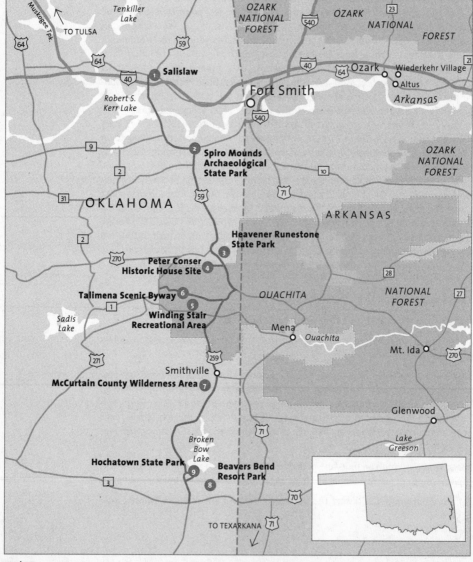

INTRODUCTION
HISTORY
REGIONS
WHEN TO VISIT
STATE'S GREATS
RULES OF THE ROAD
DRIVING TOURS

and advance planning is a must, since the few available overnight accommodations are booked months in advance. Campers have an easier time of it, since there are hundreds of both improved and unimproved campsites available. The most scenic times to travel are in the spring, when the dogwoods are in bloom, or in the fall. Southeastern Oklahoma's fall foliage is definitely the state's showiest.

❶ Begin your tour at the **Overstreet-Kerr Living History Farm,** 10 mi south of Sallisaw. Life in Indian Territory is re-created here, and period demonstrations include the making of sorghum, soap, and brooms, as well as territorial farming and gardening.

❷ **Spiro Mounds Archaeological State Park** contains eleven earthen mounds used by the Spiro Mounds people from AD 600 to 1450. The mounds have yielded burial treasure, including engraved shells, embossed copper plates, stone tools, textiles, and prehistoric lace.

❸ A purported Viking rune stone measuring 12 ft high, 10 ft wide, and 2 ft thick and carved with eight runic letters can be seen at **Heavener Runestone State Park.** The park has a visitor information center, a nature trail, and picnic tables with panoramic views.

❹ The **Peter Conser Historic House Site** is the restored 19th-century residence of a prominent politician, businessman, and member of the Choctaw Lighthorsemen, an elite tribal law-enforcement corps that patrolled the Choctaw Nation during territorial days.

❺ Bordering the Peter Conser Historic House Site is **Ouachita National Forest,** the South's oldest national forest and the largest shortleaf pine forest in the country. In addition to the pines, white and scrub oak, hickory, dogwood, and other varieties of trees blanket the blue-tinged faces of the Winding Stair Mountains. The 26,445-acre **Winding Stair Recreation Area** is home to numerous scenic lookouts and campgrounds, including **Cedar Lake Campground** and **Cedar Lake Equestrian Camp.** Cedar Lake Campground has an 84-acre lake, hiking trails, and RV and tent campsites, and is a trailhead for the 46-mi long Ouachita Trail. Cedar Lake Equestrian Camp is known as the "Cadillac of horse camps", as it provides individual corrals and hot showers for both horse and rider.

❻ The **Talimena Scenic Byway** intersects U.S. 259 15 mi south of the northern edge of Ouachita National Forest. The byway proceeds westward, scaling the peaks of the Winding Stair and Rich mountains. The road, built purely for its scenic potential, runs from Mena, Arkansas, to Talihina, Oklahoma. There are numerous scenic turnouts and picnic stops along the 56-mi-long route. The **Robert S. Kerr Nature Center Arboretum** has a visitor information center, and two 1-mi trails are designed to educate hikers about tree species.

❼ A 1-mi walking trail at the 14,000-acre **McCurtain County Wilderness Area** has markers designating prime wildlife viewing stops.

❽ The pine-studded, 3,500-acre **Beavers Bend Resort Park** is built around the Mountain Fork River and Broken Bow Lake. It's Oklahoma's most-visited park, with miles of hiking trails, canoeing on the Mountain Fork River, fly-fishing clinics, guided horseback rides, scuba diving, miniature golf, a miniature train, tennis, and more. Accommodations range from rustic cabins and a luxe 40-room lodge to RV and tent campsites. Inside the park, the **Forest Heritage Center** traces the history of the area back to prehistoric times with painted murals and artifacts. The center is built around an atrium that holds a hundred-year-old oak-log cabin moved to the park from the Kiamichi Mountains.

**9** Beavers Bend Resort Park adjoins the McCurtain County Wilderness Area as well as **Hochatown State Park.** Cedar Creek Golf Course, at the Hochatown park, was carved out of the pine woods with chainsaws and machetes; it has a winding mountain stream and a revolving cast of wildlife, including wild turkeys and bald eagles.

# Northwest Oklahoma Driving Tour

*A GEOLOGICAL TOUR OF THE PRAIRIE*

Distance: 160 mi          Length: 2–3 days
Suggested breaks: There are rustic cabins at Great Salt Plains State Park and a basic inn in Cherokee. Otherwise, overnight accommodations are more plentiful in Enid, Alva, and Woodward. Any of these towns would be an easy drive from each of the stops along this tour.

This tour, a pair of scenic detours from U.S. 412 in northwestern Oklahoma, takes you into the shortgrass plains, to land opened to homesteaders at the end of the 19th century. The tour unmasks the seemingly featureless prairies, introducing you to a number of geologically intriguing landscapes. Spring and fall are the best times to take the tour, when migratory birds are on the move. It demands a little attention to the map, since it relies on a number of state roads and highways (all well marked).

**1** Begin in **Enid,** where you'll get a grounding in regional history at the **Museum of the Cherokee Strip.** On U.S. 412, you'll find exhibits about Oklahoma's biggest and splashiest land rush, as well as historic buildings. Downtown Enid's Courthouse Square is lined

with shops and has sculptures honoring both the Plains Indians and the homesteaders. Children and parents will enjoy a stop at **Leonardo's Discovery Warehouse,** a sprawling hands-on children's science and art museum. Adjacent **Adventure Quest,** the best playground in the state, has a three-story slide.

❷ When you're finished exploring Enid, head for **Great Salt Plains State Park.** An estimated 250 species of birds can be spotted at the park and its adjacent federal wildlife refuge. Fishing, boating, and birding are the most popular activities. The park has a handful of cabins, 90 campsites, several picnic areas, a lake, and a nature trail.

❸ The **Great Salt Plains National Wildlife Refuge** (whose main entrance is 1 mi west of jct. of Rte. 38 and U.S. 64) is built around a 7-mi-long, 3-mi-wide salt-crusted plain. The more than 32,000 acres of shoreline, marshes, and salt plains draw migratory birds, and there's a visitor center, observation decks, and both hiking and automobile trails. In an area in the southwest portion of the refuge, you can dig for tea-colored selenite, a crystallized form of gypsum, from April to October.

❹ Built in 1894, the **Sod House Museum** is the last such structure on the Oklahoma prairies. Made from blocks of sod cut from a buffalo wallow, the house holds furniture and other artifacts that homesteaders would have carried into the territory on a wagon.

❺ The picturesque **Glass Mountains** are actually selenite-encrusted buttes that rise up dramatically on either side of U.S. 412. The tallest butte is 300 ft high. Information about the area geology is available at a picnic area on the south side of the highway. Camping is not permitted.

❻ **Little Sahara State Park**'s 1,500 acres of sand dunes range in height from 10 to 70 ft, and are open to dune buggies and off-road vehicles. Guided dune-buggy tours and campsites are available.

❼ The world's largest gypsum cave open to the public is thought to be at **Alabaster Caverns State Park.** Take the guided tour of the main cavern or register at the park office to explore five "wild" caves. The park has limited tent and RV campsites, a swimming pool, and a nature trail.

❽ The "boiling springs" are a bit of a letdown at **Boiling Springs State Park**; the real lure of the park is its canopy of trees, which were planted by the Civilian Conservation Corps during Dust Bowl days and create an oasis on the prairie. The grounds include hiking trails and an admirable golf course, and cabins overlook a small lake.

# ADA

MAP 4, I6

*(Nearby towns also listed: Davis, Pauls Valley, Sulphur)*

Settler Jeff Reed built a log cabin and store at a crossroads in the Chickasaw Nation in 1890; when he added a post office to his store, he named the newly formed town for his oldest daughter. This town of 17,000 is headquarters for the Chickasaw Nation, and its downtown bustles on Saturday. The town lies on the plains south of the Canadian River. Ranching, agriculture, and oil have long been its economic mainstays.

**Information: Ada Chamber of Commerce** | 300 W. Main St., Ada, OK 74820 | 580/332–2506 | adachamb@chickasaw.com | fax 580/332–3265.

## Attractions

**Chickasaw Cultural Center.** Guided tours offer insight into the workings of modern tribal government, and displays include tribal artifacts dating back to the 1500s, when the Chickasaw lived in Mississippi. | 520 E. Arlington St. | 580/436–2603 | Free | Weekdays 8:30–5, Sat. by appointment.

**East Central University.** This university was founded in 1909 as a teacher training school. One of its most intriguing buildings is the Robert S. Kerr Activities Center, a gold geodesic dome. Other campus highlights are the Art Gallery and the "Callixylon", a 5-ft fossilized tree stump that dates back 350-million years to the Devonian Period. | E. Main St. and Francis Ave. | 580/332–8000 | Free | Daily.

**McSwain Musical Theater.** This refurbished 1920s vaudeville and movie theater hosts country, gospel, and big band shows. | 130 W. Main St. | 405/332–8108 | $6 | Shows: 1st and 3rd Sat. at 7:30 PM; box office: 1st and 3rd Sat. 10AM–10PM.

### ON THE CALENDAR

**AUG.: *Western Heritage Week*.** Townspeople and windows of local businesses are dressed Western-style during this week-long celebration. A parade includes local round-ups clubs, and a rodeo has barrel riders, bull riders, and calf roping. | 580/332–2506.

## Dining

**Bandana's.** American. The Southwestern look of this restaurant includes desert-scene paintings on the walls and potted cacti throughout. The steaks, pasta, Tex-Mex dishes, and, fried peaches (for dessert) are popular. | 1600 N. Mississippi St. | 580/332–2583 | $7–$12 | AE, DC, MC, V.

**J. D.'s Cafe.** American. Home-cooked dishes are served cafeteria-style at all three meals. Plate specials include meatloaf or stewed beef with homemade noodles for lunch, and rib-eye steak and catfish for supper. Top off your meal with a slice of homemade pie; chocolate, coconut, and apple are favorites. | 911 N. Broadway | 580/332–9750 | Breakfast also available. Closed Sun., Mon. | $4–$8 | AE, D, DC, MC, V.

**Polo's Mexican Grill/Polo's Embassy.** Mexican. This pair of storefront Mexican restaurants is decorated with authentic Mexican artifacts. Known for steaks as well as Mexican dishes. Try chicken and beef fajitas, Tex-Mex platters, and chocolate chimichangas. | 219 W. Main St. | 580/332–2710 | Closed Sun. | $6–$11 | AE, D, DC, MC, V.

## Lodging

**Best Western–Raintree.** This college-town member of the Best Western chain is in down-town Ada, within walking distance of several restaurants. Restaurant, in-room data ports, cable TV, pool, business services. | 1100 N. Mississippi St. | 580/332–6262 | fax 580/436–4929 | 40 rooms | $54–$68 | AE, D, DC, MC, V.

**Economy Inn.** This centrally located light-blue roadside motel is adjacent to a restaurant, and within walking distance of a laundromat and bowling alley. Some microwaves, some refrigerators, cable TV, pool, business services, pets allowed (fee). | 1017 N. Broadway | 580/332–3883 | fax 580/332–3884 | 46 rooms | $28–$45 | AE, D, DC, MC, V.

# ALTUS

MAP 4, F6

*(Nearby town also listed: Lawton)*

Altus began as Frazier, Texas—the boundary between the two states was in dispute until 1896. In 1889 a flood forced the entire community to move, and the town was renamed Altus (Latin for "higher place"). Since 1953, this town of 27,000 has been home to Altus Air Force base.

Information: **Altus Chamber of Commerce** | 100 N. Main St., Altus, OK 73521 | 580/482–0210 | fax 580/482–0223.

## Attractions

**Museum of the Western Prairie.** Built to resemble a "half-dugout," a structure dug into the earth by homesteaders short of timber, this museum showcases the struggle to build homes and find water on the treeless plains. A working windmill is on site. | 1100 N. Hightower St. | 580/482–1044 | Free | Tues.–Fri. 9–5, Weekends 2–5.

**Quartz Mountain Resort Park.** On the western edge of the Wichita Range, this was once the domain of the Kiowa and Comanche. The park's namesake 1,800-ft granite "mountain" rises suddenly out of the surrounding plains, and rugged, rock-strewn hills surround adjacent Lake Altus-Lugert. Hiking, fishing, tennis, golfing, boating, and go-karting are popular, as are a sandy swimming beach and wildflower and bald eagle–spotting tours. Cabins and RV and tent campsites are available, and a 100-room lodge is scheduled to open in fall 2000. | Rte. 44A | 580/563–2424 | www.touroklahoma.com | Free | Daily.

**Sculptures of the West.** These larger-than-life–sized bronze statues, both rendered by H. Holden of Kremlin, OK, are emblematic of the town's heritage. *The Vision Seeker*, in East City Park, portrays a Native American chief, and *Crossing the Red*, which stands at the Jackson County Courthouse, depicts the crossing of the Red River (which runs just south of Altus) by pioneers settling the West. | Throughout town | 580/482–0210 | Free | Daily.

### ON THE CALENDAR

**AUG.: *Great Plains Stampede Rodeo.*** This PRCA rodeo includes a chili cook-off, cattle drive, and parade. | 580/477–2320.
**DEC.: *Christmas in the Park.*** This month-long celebration in East City Park is particularly geared for children, with various holiday displays, painted figures, and lighting installations. | E. Broadway between Park Ave. and Park Ln | 580/482–0210.

## Dining

**Val's It's About Time.** American. This casual bar and restaurant has a scarred wooden floor and lots of antiques and town memorabilia. Known for ribs, steaks, and hamburgers. | 800 N. Main St. | 580/482–4580 | Closed Sun. | $6–$16 | AE, D, DC, MC, V.

**Woody's Barbecue.** Barbecue. This regional barbecue chain is known for smoked ribs, beef, and chicken. Try "wood chips"—potatoes smothered in cheddar cheese. | 1100 N. Main St. | 580/477–4756 | $7–$15 | AE, D, DC, MC, V.

## Lodging

**Best Western.** Chain-hotel accommodations 2 mi west of Altus and 1 mi north of the Air Force base. Complimentary Continental breakfast, in-room data ports, some refrigerators, cable TV, in-room VCRs (and movies), indoor-outdoor pool, sauna, laundry facilities, business services, pets allowed. | 2804 N. Main St. | 580/482–9300 | fax 580/482–2245 | 100 rooms | $54 | AE, D, DC, MC, V.

**Country Charm Bed and Breakfast.** Built in 1979, this B&B has rooms with handmade quilts and convertible king-size beds for groups or families; one room has a patio that opens onto the indoor pool. Complimentary breakfast, in-room VCRs (and movies), TV in common area, pool, hot tub, no pets, no smoking. | North Shore Rd., off U.S. 283, 22 mi north of Altus | 580/846–9049 | 4 rooms | $69–$79 | MC, V.

**Days Inn.** Some rooms display the work of local artists in this motel 2 mi from downtown Altus. Complimentary Continental breakfast, cable TV, business services, pets allowed. | 3202 N. Main St. | 580/477–2300 | fax 580/477–2379 | 36 rooms | $49 | AE, D, DC, MC, V.

**Falcon Inn.** Rooms at this off-white and brick two-story motel are basic, but each is equipped with a refrigerator, the attached restaurant (and lounge) serves three meals a day, and the price speaks for itself. It's 5 m from Altus Air Force Base. Restaurant, bar, picnic area, some microwaves, refrigerators, cable TV, pool, laundry facilities, business services, pets allowed (fee). | 2213 Falcon Rd. | 580/482–0400 or 888/283–4450 | fax 580/482–1884 | 60 rooms | $27 | AE, D, MC, V.

**Ramada Inn.** This two-story hotel is ½ mi from the Air Force base. Restaurant, bar, refrigerators, room service, cable TV, pool, business services, pets allowed (fee). | 2515 E. Broadway, | 580/477–3000 | fax 580/477–0078 | 121 rooms, 12 suites | $59, $104 suites | AE, D, DC, MC, V.

# ALVA

MAP 4, G3

*(Nearby towns also listed: Enid, Woodward)*

Alva was founded as a farming community during the opening of the Cherokee Strip in 1893. Today, it is the home of Northwestern Oklahoma State University. The town's farmers provide wheat to a factory that in turn supplies dough to restaurant chains.

Information: **Alva Chamber of Commerce** | 410 College Ave., Alva, OK 73717 | 580/327–1647.

## Attractions

**Alabaster Caverns State Park.** The main cavern in what is thought to be the world's largest gypsum cave open to the public has a lighted ¾-mi trail. Wild caving is permitted in four other caves to registered visitors. There is also a hiking trail, a swimming pool, and RV and tent campsites. | Rte. 50A | 580/621–3381 | www.touroklahoma.com | $6 | May–Sept., daily 8–5; Oct.–Apr., daily 8–4.

**Cherokee Strip Museum.** More than three dozen exhibits depict local pioneer and land run history. Native American artifacts are also on display. | 901 14th St. | 580/327–2030 | Free | May–Sept., Tues.–Sun. 2–5; Apr.–Oct., weekends 2–5; group tours by appointment.

**Great Salt Plains State Park.** Adjacent to the Salt Plains National Wildlife Refuge and centered on Great Salt Plains Lake, this park has picnic areas, cabins, and RV and tent campsites. You can also fish, boat, swim, hike, and bird-watch (more than 250 species have been spotted here). | Rte. 38 | 580/626–4731 | www.touroklahoma.com | Free | Daily.

**Little Sahara State Park.** Twelve hundred acres of shifting sand dunes ranging from 7 to 70 ft in height are open to off-road vehicles. Six-passenger dune-buggy rides and RV and tent campsites are available. Quiet hours are observed 11 PM–7 AM. | U.S. 281 | 580/824–1471 | www.touroklahoma.com | $7 per vehicle | Daily, 24 hours.

**Salt Plains National Wildlife Refuge.** This 7-mi-long, 3-mi-wide swath of salt plains attracts primarily migratory birds. More than 36 species of shorebirds have been spotted in the refuge, recognized as a critical site for the survival of such shorebirds as the whooping crane. There is also an interpretive center, hiking and auto routes, observation towers, and an area set apart for digging selenite crystals. | Rte. 38, 28 mi east of Alva | 580/626–4794 | fax 580/626–4793 | Free | Apr.–mid-Oct., daily; mid-Oct.–Mar., weekdays.

**Sod House Museum.** Built in 1894, this is the only remaining example of a sod house on Oklahoma's plains. The house stands in its original location and contains some of its original furnishings. | Rte. 8, 40 mi south of Alva | 580/463–2441 | Free | Tues.–Fri. 9–5, weekends 2–5.

### ON THE CALENDAR

**JUNE: *Nescatunga Arts Festival.*** Arts and crafts exhibitors, food booths, and children's activities are part of this festival on the downtown square. | 580/327–1647.

**AUG.:** *Freedom Rodeo and Old Cowhand Reunion.* Freedom (pop. 254, near Alva) more than quadruples in size for the annual three-day rodeo. A local cowhand is honored every year. | 580/621–3276.

## Dining

**Café Bahnhof.** German. A German family runs this restaurant and biergarten, serving traditional favorites like schnitzel and red cabbage as well as American-style steaks. The German chef is renowned for his authentic bratwurst. | 131 E. Cecil St., Waynoka | 580/824–0063 | Closed Sun., Mon. No lunch | $8–$15 | AE, MC, V.

**VFW Supper Club.** Continental. In addition to the existing menu, chef Jim Clemons creates rotating weekly specials, many of which are based on suggestions made by enthusiastic diners. Each plate comes with signature half-moon skewers of assorted grilled vegetables. Choices may include chicken Oscar (breast of chicken with fresh asparagus and cheese in a white wine and cream sauce), or beef Burgundy (cubes of filet mignon with a burgundy and cream reduction sauce, served over fettucini). Homemade bread. | 1 Washington Dr. | 580/327–0867 | fax 580/327–8611 | Closed Sun.–Wed. No lunch | $8–$16 | AE, MC, V.

## Lodging

**Ranger Inn.** This one-story brick-and-siding building is ½ mi from Northwestern Oklahoma State University. Microwaves, cable TV, pets allowed. | 420 E. Oklahoma Blvd. | 580/327–1981 | fax 580/327–1981 | 41 rooms | $42–$46 | AE, D, DC, MC, V.

**Vista Motel.** Rooms are fairly spacious in this yellow brick motel (built in 1949 with a mineral shingle roof) on the far west side of town. A city pool is about 1 mi away. In-room data ports, cable TV, business services, pets allowed. | 1330 Oklahoma Blvd. | 580/327–3232 or 800/322–1821 | fax 580/327–5591 | 20 rooms | $30–$40 | AE, D, DC, MC, V.

**Western Motel.** This motel is ½ mi from Northwestern Oklahoma State University. Picnic area, in-room data ports, refrigerators, cable TV, pool, business services. | 608 E. Oklahoma Blvd. | 580/327–1363 | fax 580/327–1364 | 21 rooms | $34 | AE, D, DC, MC, V.

# ANADARKO

MAP 4, G5

*(Nearby town also listed: Chickasha)*

This town of 8,000 on the southern plains north of the Washita River was settled in 1901 in the course of a lottery that opened Native American land to settlement by non-Indians. Just north of town is the present-day site of the Bureau of Indian Affairs, an Indian agency established in the 1870s. Still home to headquarters of seven tribes, Anadarko bills itself the "Indian Capital of the World." Native American art galleries can be found downtown, where sidewalks are made of brickwork laid in a Native American motif. Jobs provided by tribal governments are augmented by farming: peanuts have been one of the area's principal crops for more than a century.

**Information: Anadarko Chamber of Commerce** | 516 W. Kentucky Ave., Anadarko, OK 73005 | 405/247–6651 | fax 405/247–6652 | www.anadarko.org.

**Visitor's Information Center** | U.S. 62 E, Box 366, Anadarko, OK 73005 | 405/247–5555.

## Attractions

**Anadarko Philomathic Museum.** Eclectic collections reflect the local mixture of various cultures, and include railroad memorabilia, pioneer artifacts, military memorabilia, vintage photos, and Native American regalia, beadwork, and dolls. | Rock Island Depot, 311 E. Main St. | 405/247–3240 | Free | May–Sept., daily 1–5; Oct.–Apr., Mon.–Sat. 1–5.

**Anadarko Post Office Murals.** Murals from the 1930s commissioned by members of the "Kiowa Five" (an internationally renowned group of local painters) depict life on the plains before the arrival of European settlers. | 120 S. 1st St. | 405/247–6461 | Free | Weekdays 8:30–5, Sat. 9–11 AM.

**Fort Cobb State Park.** This park is built around Fort Cobb Lake and was named for the nearby fort that served as a supply center for Plains Indians forced onto reservations in the 19th century. It includes a golf course, a marina, a nature center, hiking trails, tent campsites, and nine RV campgrounds with nearly 300 sites. | Rte. 146 Fort Cobb | 405/643–2249 | www.touroklahoma.com | Free | Daily.

**Indian City—U.S.A.** This outdoor museum is the only authentic Indian City in the country. It depicts the culture, religion, and daily lives of seven American Indian tribes. Indoor exhibits include artifacts, photographs, clothing, and memorabilia. Tribal dancing and lectures are presented periodically. | Rte. 8, 2½ mi south of Anadarko | 405/247–5661 | $7.50 | Daily.

**National Hall of Fame for Famous American Indians.** An outdoor sculpture garden includes bronze busts of famous Native Americans—such as Sitting Bull, Pocahontas, Black Hawk—and Oklahomans Jim Thorpe and Will Rogers. | 1101 Central Blvd. | 405/247–3331 | Free | Mon.–Sat. 9–5, Sun. 1–5.

**Southern Plains Indian Museum and Crafts Center.** Exhibits showcase the arts, traditional dress, and regalia of seven local Southern Plains tribes, and there is an Indian-owned and -operated crafts cooperative on the grounds. Tepees sprout on the lawn in summer. | 715 E. Central Blvd. | 405/247–6221 | $3; free Sun. | June–Sept., Mon.–Sat. 9–5, Sun. 1–5; Oct.–May, Tues.–Sat. 9–5, Sun. 1–4:30.

## ON THE CALENDAR

**MAY, OCT.: *Kiowa Veterans Black Leggins Ceremonial.*** This Native American ceremonial dance honors members of the Black Leggins warrior society, and is modeled after historic ceremonies honoring returning Kiowa war parties. (No video cameras allowed.) | 405/247–3987.

**AUG.: *American Indian Exposition.*** Held at the Caddo County Fairgrounds, this event dates back to the 1930s and includes ceremonial dances, an historical pageant, American Indian food, and horse racing. | 405/247–6651.

**AUG.: *Wichita Annual Dance.*** Ceremonial and social dances are held each year in Wichita Park following the American Indian Exposition. | 405/247–2425.

**SEPT.: *Caddo County Free Fair.*** This event at the Caddo County Fairgrounds includes a horse show and fair, with arts and crafts and food booths. | 405/247–6651.

## WHAT TO PACK IN THE TOY TOTE FOR KIDS

- ❏ Audiotapes
- ❏ Books
- ❏ Clipboard
- ❏ Coloring/activity books
- ❏ Doll with outfits
- ❏ Hand-held games
- ❏ Magnet games
- ❏ Notepad
- ❏ One-piece toys
- ❏ Pencils, colored pencils
- ❏ Portable stereo with earphones
- ❏ Sliding puzzles
- ❏ Travel toys

*Excerpted from *Fodor's: How to Pack: Experts Share Their Secrets*
© 1997, by Fodor's Travel Publications

## Dining

**K.I.G.Que.** Barbecue. This 1950s-style diner serves smoked kidney along with more traditional beef and pork, and side dishes including beans and potato salad. Known for smoked meats, homemade cobblers and sauces. Buffet lunch. | 115 E. Market St. | 405/247–2454 | Closed Sun., Mon. | $6–$9 | MC, V.

**Palomino Cafe.** American. This friendly, country-style café was built circa 1995 and serves home-cooked, family-style meals. Try the excellent burgers, fried chicken, chicken fries, or tacos. | 729 W. Petree Plaza | 405/247–2023 | Breakfast also available. Closed Mon. | $5–$12 | No credit cards.

**Southern Plains Restaurant.** Southern. This full-service restaurant attached to a motel serves a country breakfast all day as well as dinner specials. Try fried chicken and mashed potatoes. Homemade rolls, dessert, and ice cream. Salad bar. Buffet lunch. | 1415 E. Central | 405/247–2491 | $6–$7 | AE, D, DC, MC, V.

## Lodging

**Payless Inn.** This two-story light blue and brick motel has a Southwestern feel, with a pastel color scheme and desert-theme prints on the walls. You can get a cup of coffee or cider at the crack of dawn at the front desk, and a city park with recreational facilities, a picnic area, and playground is less than 1 mi away. Rooms can be rented by the night or by the week. Some microwaves, some refrigerators, cable TV, pool, business services, no pets. | 1602 E. Central St./U.S. 62 | 405/247–2538 | fax 405/247–5047 | 48 rooms | $43–$52 | AE, D, DC, MC, V.

**Red Carpet Inn.** Indian City is less than 4 mi from this two-story motel, and the Indian museums are all within walking distance. Restaurant, pool, video games. | 1415 E. Central Ave. | 405/247–2491 | 76 rooms | $32 | AE, D, DC, MC, V.

# ARDMORE

MAP 4, I7

*(Nearby towns also listed: Durant, Sulphur)*

Founded in 1887 in the Chickasaw Nation as a shipping center for cotton, Ardmore, halfway between the Red River and the Arbuckle Mountains, had the largest population in Indian Territory at the turn of the 20th century. Vintage sandstone and brick commercial buildings line the downtown shopping district in this town of 31,000.

**Information: Ardmore Chamber of Commerce** | 410 W. Main St., Ardmore, OK 73401-4738 | 580/223–7765 | fax 580/223–7825 | www.ardmore.org.

## Attractions

**Charles B. Goddard Center.** This center for the visual and performing arts hosts traveling exhibitions and has a permanent collection of contemporary and Native American paintings. | 401 1st. Ave SW | 580/226–0909 | Galleries free; performance prices vary | Galleries weekdays 9–4, weekends 1–4.

**Eliza Cruce Hall Doll Museum.** This collection of more than 300 vintage dolls from around the world was donated to the city by a former Oklahoma First Lady. The collection includes rare French dolls and miniature tea sets. | 320 E Street NW | 580/223–8290 | Free | Mon.–Thur. 10–8:30, Fri.–Sat. 10–4.

**Greater Southwest Historical Museum.** This sprawling museum with 150,000 objects houses exhibits depicting everyday life in turn-of-the-20th-century Ardmore, as well as military artifacts from the American Revolution to Operation Desert Storm. | 35 Sunset Dr. | 580/226–3857 | Donation accepted | Tues.–Sat. 10–5, Sun. 1–5; tours by request.

**Lake Murray State Park.** At 12,500 acres, this is Oklahoma's largest state park. It was built by Works Progress Administration and Civilian Conservation Corps workers in the 1930s and many original sandstone structures remain. Resort lodge, cabins, tent and RV campgrounds, swimming pool, golf course, tennis courts, enclosed fishing docks, horse stables, and hiking trails. | 3310 S. Lake Murray Dr. | 580/223–4044 | www.touroklahoma.com | Free | Daily.

The castle-like sandstone **Tucker Tower Nature Center** was reportedly planned as a summer retreat for Oklahoma governor "Alfalfa" Bill Murray. Construction began in the 1930s, but was not completed until 1954. Today it's used as a geological museum and nature center, with displays that include the world's fifth-largest meteorite. There's a great view from a 65-ft-high patio. | 580/223–2109 | 50¢ | Memorial Day–Labor Day, daily 9–7.

### ON THE CALENDAR

**APR.: *Ardmoredillo Chili Cook-off.*** This event includes armadillo races, live music, and area teams competing for a "best chili" title. | 580/226–6246.

**MAY: *Red River Roadkill Rally.*** Motorcycle enthusiasts and spectators from all over the Southwest partake in this event, which kicks off in the early morning with a scenic ride along Lake Murray. Participants continue with 20-, 40-, and 60-mi rides, and everyone concludes the day with food and merrymaking. | 580/223–7765.

**JUNE: *Love County Frontier Days Celebration.*** Live music, food booths, a parade, and an arts and crafts fair are part of the fun. | 580/276–3102.

**SEPT.: *Carter County Free Fair.*** Livestock, carnival rides, games, and agricultural and home arts exhibits can be found in Hardy Murphy Coliseum. | 580/223–2541.

## Dining

**Bill and Barb's.** American. This restaurant and coffee shop has been serving its customers since 1953. Try the chicken-fried steak. Salad bar. Family-style service. | 1225 N. Washington St. | 580/223–1976 | Breakfast also available. Closed Mon. | $8–$10 | AE, D, DC, MC, V.

**Cafe Alley.** American. Soups and sandwiches are the big draw here. The restaurant is in a converted downtown warehouse and is one of the most popular lunch spots in town. Try Cobb salad and buttermilk pie. | 107 E. Main St. | 580/223–6413 | Closed weekends. No dinner | $8–$12 | AE, MC, V.

**Denim's.** American. This casual family restaurant serves everything from steaks and prime rib to sandwiches and chili, and offers a full breakfast as well as evening specials. More than 20 types of cheesecakes and pies are sure to please everyone. Homemade soups, rolls and pie. Buffet. Family-style service. Kids' menu. | I–35 and Rte. 32, Marietta | 580/276–3222 | Breakfast also available. No dinner Sun. | $8–$15 | AE, D, MC, V.

**Fireside Dining.** Continental. Exposed cedar logs and a fireplace give this dining room a lodge-like feel, and an enclosed porch overlooks the gardens. Known for prime cut aged beef and fresh seafood. Kids' menu. | 3310 S. Lake Murray Dr. | 580/226–4070 | Closed Sun., Mon. No lunch | $20–$25 | AE, D, MC, V.

**The Hub.** Seafood. This restaurant is known for oysters, catfish, frogs' legs, and fried and broiled shrimp. Salad bar. There are three dining areas, each individually decorated and furnished with tables and booths. Buffet lunch and weekends. Family-style service. | 309 N. U.S. 77, Marietta | 580/276–2380 | $6–$12 | D, MC, V.

**McGehee Catfish.** Seafood. Farm-raised catfish is served in this rambling, rustic restaurant overlooking the Red River. Try the hot cherry tarts. Kids' menu. | Rte. 2, Marietta | 580/276–2751 | Closed Wed. No lunch Mon., Tues., Thurs., Fri. | $10–$15 | D, MC, V.

## Lodging

**Dorchester Inn.** Rooms are clean and quiet in this downtown motel, 1–2 blocks from the Greater Southwest Historical Museum. Restaurant, complimentary Continental breakfast, refrigerators, cable TV, pets allowed. | 2614 W. Broadway | 580/226–1761 | fax 580/223–3131 | 50 rooms | $40 | AE, D, DC, MC, V.

**Hampton Inn.** Built in 1997, this three-story hotel is the newest and nicest in the area, right off I–35 via Exit 31A. Good restaurants are within walking distance, and the Chickasaw Public Library is across the street. The customer service is first-rate, and perks like a deluxe Continental breakfast with waffles and biscuits-and-gravy are welcome. Complimentary Continental breakfast, in-room data ports, some microwaves, some refrigerators, some in-room hot tubs, cable TV, pool, hot tub, sauna, gym, laundry service, business services, no pets. | 410 Railway Express Rd. | 580/223–6394 or 800/426–7866 | fax 580/223–5898 | www.hamptoninn.com | 62 rooms | $72–$139 | AE, D, DC, MC, V.

**Holiday Inn.** This two-story hotel is 18 mi from Turner Falls and 12 mi from Lake Murray. Restaurant, in-room data ports, cable TV, pool, wading pool, gym, playground, laundry facilities, business services, pets allowed. | 2705 Holiday Dr. | 580/223–7130 | fax 580/223–7130 | 171 rooms | $69 | AE, D, DC, MC, V.

**Lake Murray.** In Lake Murray State Park, this state-owned lodge aims for the flavor of a country inn, with fluffy floral comforters and oak armoires. Bar, dining room, room service, cable TV, pool, 18-hole golf course, miniature golf, tennis, water sports, children's programs, playground, business services, airport shuttle, pets allowed. | 3310 S. Lake Murray Dr. #12A, Ardmore | 580/223–6600 or 800/654–8240 | fax 580/223–6154 | 49 rooms, 3 suites, 81 cottages | $55, $150 suites, $48 cottages | AE, D, DC, MC, V.

**St. Agnes Inn.** Built in 1897 as a Catholic boarding school for girls, antique and contemporary furnishings reflect the varied history of this B&B. Some rooms have original clawfoot tubs and pedestal sinks, and the third floor has a suite with a private kitchen and parlor. Grounds include a garden with a fish pond and waterfall. Complimentary breakfast, in-room data ports, some kitchenettes, cable TV, in-room VCRs (and movies), no room phones, outdoor hot tub, no pets, no kids under 4, no smoking. | 118 E St. SW | 580/223–5679 | fax 580/223–4668 | stagnes@ardmore.com | www.bbonline.com/ok/stagnes/index.html | 5 rooms | $75–$110 | AE, D, DC, MC, V.

# ATOKA

*(Nearby towns also listed: Ada, Durant, Hugo, McAlester)*

This Chickasaw Nation settlement was founded by a Baptist missionary in 1867 on Muddy Boggy Creek, southwest of the Jack Fork Mountains. Nearby Boggy Depot was a major Confederate supply depot in Indian Territory. Atoka has long been a trading center.

**Information: Atoka Chamber of Commerce** | P.O. Box 778, Atoka, OK 74525 | 580/889–2410.

## Attractions

**Boggy Depot State Park.** This shady 630-acre park was laid out on the site of the vanished, but once-prominent, community of Boggy Depot, a stage stop on the Butterfield Overland mail route. This park includes picnic and camping facilities, a nature trail, and historical markers. | Rte. 7, 11 mi west and 4 mi south of Atoka | 580/889–5625 | www.tourokla-homa.com | Free | Daily.

**Confederate Memorial Museum and Information Center.** On the site of the state's only Confederate cemetery, this museum celebrates the nearby Battle of the Middle Boggy, in which federal troops engaged the First Choctaw and Chickasaw Cavalry. The museum includes a re-created Civil War encampment, historical photographs, and military memorabilia. | 258 N. U.S. 69 | 580/889–7192 | Free | Mon.–Sat. 9–4.

**McGee Creek Natural Scenic Recreation Area.** This 9,000-acre reserve has 20 mi of fairly rugged hiking, biking, and equestrian trails. | 576A S. McGee Creek Dam Rd. | 580/889–5822 | Free | Daily.

**McGee Creek State Park.** Opened in 1988, this is one of the state's newest and most pristine state parks. It has fishing, camping, hiking, equestrian trails, and rustic lodging. | 576A S. McGee Creek Dam Rd. | 580/889–5822 | fax 580/889–5822 | www.touroklahoma.com | Free | Daily.

## ON THE CALENDAR

**OCT.: *Annual Quilt Show.*** Pieces and Patches, a local quilting guild, holds an annual showing of its fine needlework at the Atoka Public Library; you may even win a door prize. | 215 E. A St. | 580/889–3555.

## Dining

**Bledsoe's Diner.** American. Breakfast is served all day at this friendly homecooking restaurant just off the highway north of Atoka. A rotating daily buffet always has fried chicken, and may include beef goulash, frito chili pie, ham, fried fish, and turkey. Try one of the homemade cream pies for dessert. | 219 N. Mississippi St. (U.S. 69/75) | 580/889–5162 | Breakfast also available | $4–$10 | No credit cards.

**El Adobe.** Mexican. Piñatas hang from the ceiling beams in this popular restaurant, serving a full line of Mexican fare, from tacos and fajitas to burritos and grilled items. Known for Tex-Mex beef and chicken fajitas, gorditas, and enchiladas. | 406 S. Mississippi Ave. | 580/889–5296 | Closed Sun. | $6–$17 | V.

## Lodging

**Best Western Atoka Inn.** This motel is on the south end of Atoka off Rtes. 69 and 75. It's two mi from the Confederate Memorial Museum and Information Center and 15 mi from McGee Creek State Park. Restaurant, cable TV, pool, business services, pets allowed. | 2101 S. Mississippi Ave. | 580/889–7381 | fax 580/889–6695 | bestwest@texomaonline.com | 54 rooms | $59 | AE, D, DC, MC, V.

**Brandenburg's Motel.** This L-shaped white and blue roadside motel is right off I-75 in the middle of town, a stone's throw from restaurants, the courthouse, and police station. Nightly or weekly rates are offered, and truck parking is available. Some microwaves, some refrigerators, cable TV, pool, pets allowed (fee). | 102 S. Mississippi Ave. | 580/889–3363 | 25 rooms | $30–$35 | AE, MC, V.

# BARTLESVILLE

MAP 4, J3

*(Nearby town also listed: Pawhuska)*

Originally a Delaware trading post founded by Jake Bartles in 1887 on the Caney River east of the Osage Hills, this town was transformed by the discovery of oil in 1894. Its downtown historic district includes 48 buildings from the 1900–20 oil boom. Phillips Petroleum Company is headquartered in the city, and oil and oil-related businesses are the community's mainstays.

Information: **Bartlesville Area Convention and Visitors Bureau,** | 201 S. Keeler Ave., Bartlesville, OK 74003-2631 | 918/336–8708 or 800/364–8708 | www.bartlesville.com.

## Attractions

**Bartlesville History Museum.** Photographs and artifacts illustrate Bartlesville's ranching, oil, and Native American history. | 401 S. Johnstone Ave. | 918/337–5336 | fax 918/337–5338 | Free | Mon.–Thurs. 9–9, Fri.–Sat. 9–5:30, Sun. 1:30–5:30; closed Sun. in summer.

**Dewey Hotel Museum.** This restored 28-room, 1899 Victorian hotel has period furnishings. | 801 N. Delaware St., Dewey | 918/534–0215 | $1 | Apr.–Nov., Tues.–Sat. 10–5, Sun. 1–5; tours by appointment.

**Frank Phillips Mansion.** Built in 1909, this Greek Revival mansion is the former home of oilman and Phillips Petroleum founder Frank Phillips and his wife, Jane. | 1107 S. Cherokee Ave. | 918/336–2491 | $3 | Wed.–Sat. 10–5, Sun. 1–5.

**Johnstone Park.** Here you will find a tiny railroad station, a locomotive, an art center, a kiddie park, and the beginning of the 13-mi "Pathfinder Parkway" hiking and biking path. | 200 N. Cherokee Ave. | 918/336–8708 | Free; rides 10¢ | Daily; kiddie park Labor Day–Memorial Day, daily.

**Keepsake Candle Factory and Country Store.** This mom-and-pop candle-making company uses Depression glassware for molds. Sweet-smelling tours are available during the week, and goods are up for sale. | U.S. 60, 2 mi west of Bartlesville | 918/336–0351 | fax 918/336–0157 | Free | Weekdays 9–5:30, Sat. 10–5:30, Sun. 1–5:30.

**Nellie Johnstone No. 1 Oil Well.** Drilled on April 15, 1897, this was Oklahoma's first commercial oil well. The wooden derrick is a reproduction built after the original burned in an oil fire. | 201 S.W. Keepler | 918/336–8708 | Free | Daily.

**Prairie Song, I.T.** A re-created 1800s pioneer village with a schoolhouse, homesteader's cabin, post office, trading post, jail, covered bridge, and a cowboy line shack (shelter built on a main cattle line to house cowboys on a long drive or in bad weather). | 402621 W. 1600 Rd., Dewey | 918/534–2662 | fax 918/534–3435 | $6 | Daily 9–5; guided tours Mon., Wed., Fri. at 10 AM by appointment.

**Price Tower.** This 19-story glass and copper structure is famed architect Frank Lloyd Wright's only skyscraper. It houses the Bartlesville Art Center and Museum and original Wright-designed furniture. | 510 Dewey St. | 918/333–8558 | fax 918/336–3507 | Free; donation accepted | Tues.–Sat. 10–5, Sun. 12:30–5; tours of tower at 11 and 2.

**Tom Mix Museum.** Cowboy movie star Tom Mix once served as deputy sheriff in Dewey. The museum displays costumes, photographs, and memorabilia, and plays Mix's movies in a small theater. | 721 N. Delaware Ave., Dewey | 918/534–1555 | $1 | Tues.–Sun. 9–5.

★ **Woolaroc Ranch, Museum, and Wildlife Preserve.** The name of this former Osage Hills retreat of oilman Frank Phillips is derived from the words *wood, lake,* and *rock.* It includes a 3,600-acre refuge with bison, elk, deer, and longhorn cattle. There is also a lodge, and a museum housing a world-class collection of Native American and Western art and artifacts. | Rte. 123, 12 mi southwest of Bartlesville | 918/336–0307 | fax 918/336–0084 | www.woolaroc.org | $5 | Memorial Day–Labor Day, daily 10–5; Labor Day–Memorial Day, Tues.–Sun. 10–5.

BARTLESVILLE

INTRO
ATTRACTIONS
DINING
LODGING

## ON THE CALENDAR

**JUNE:** *OK Mozart International Festival.* An orchestra and guest artists perform the works of Mozart and other composers at the Bartlesville Community Center during this week-long celebration. | 918/336–9900.

**SEPT.:** *Indian Summer Festival.* Highlights of this event include Native American art, an intertribal powwow, and children's games. | 918/337–2787.

## Dining

**Amarillo Mesquite Grill.** American. Mesquite grilling is the big draw at this Southwestern-style restaurant, which serves smoked ribs, brisket, steak, and marinated chicken. The walls in the dining area are hung with saddles, old guns, and cattle horns, and you can take your pick of dining at a table or booth. | 3813 S.E. Frank Phillips Blvd. | 918/335–5050 | Reservations not accepted | $4–$17 | AE, D, DC, MC, V.

**Murphy's Steak House.** American. The open kitchen, service counter, and vinyl booths create a casual atmosphere in which to enjoy the "hamburger steak" (hamburger served with onions and gravy and baked potato) or the trademark "hot hamburger" (an open-face hamburger covered with fresh-cut French fries and brown gravy). Family-style service. | 1625 W. Frank Phillips Blvd. | 918/336–4789 | Closed Mon. | $8–$10 | MC, V.

**Sterling's Grille.** American. A club atmosphere is achieved with English hunting prints and dark wood. Open-air dining is available on the deck, which allow for a beautiful view of the forest. Known for steaks. Kids' menu. Sun. brunch. | 2905 E. Frank Phillips Blvd. | 918/335–0707 | $15–$30 | AE, D, DC, MC, V.

## Lodging

**Best Western Weston Inn.** This three-story hotel is 15 blocks from downtown Bartlesville, in Oklahoma Green Country. Restaurant, room service, microwaves, some refrigerators, in-room hot tubs, cable TV, pool, laundry facilities, business services, pets allowed. | 222 S.E. Washington Blvd. | 918/335–7755 or 800/336–2415 | fax 918/335–7763 | 111 rooms | $45–$80 | AE, D, DC, MC, V.

**Holiday Inn.** This full-service hotel with three banquet rooms is next to a bowling alley and one mi from the Washington Boulevard mall. Restaurant, bar, room service, in-room data ports, some kitchenettes, cable TV, pool, exercise equipment, laundry facilities, business services, pets allowed. | 1410 S.E. Washington Blvd. | 918/333–8320 | fax 918/333–8979 | www.holiday-inn.com | 104 rooms | $66 | AE, D, DC, MC, V.

**Hotel Phillips.** Rooms in this hotel are individually decorated, some in a country style. The rooftop terrace is a nice place to relax. Restaurant, bar, room service, in-room data ports, cable TV, exercise equipment, business services. | 821 Johnstone St. | 918/336–5600 or 800/331–0706 | fax 918/336–0350 | 145 rooms, 25 suites | $80, $90 suites | AE, D, DC, MC, V.

**Inn at Jarrett Farm.** This peaceful hilltop ranch house has a sophisticated country style, and rooms have king-size beds. Grounds include walking trails. Complimentary breakfast, no smoking, some in-room hot tubs, in-room VCRs (and movies), no room phones, pool, hot tub, spa, business services. | 38009 U.S. 75, Ramona | 918/371–9868 or 877/371–1200 | fax 918/371–4665 | jarrett@galstar.com | www.jarrettfarm.tulsa.net | 1 suite, 10 cottages | $145, $185–$225 cottages | AE, MC, V.

**Lundberg Inn Bed and Breakfast.** The drive up to the house is lined with old-fashioned iron street lights, a good indication of the welcome you'll find at this spacious B&B, built in 1999. Inside you'll find high cathedral ceilings, oriental rugs and many windows. The 30-acre grounds teem with wildlife, including fox, bobcat, armadillo, and wild turkey. No alcohol. Dining room, complimentary breakfast, in-room hot tubs, no TV in some rooms, TV in common area, 2 ponds, hiking, fishing, laundry facilities, business services, no pets, no smoking. | 394180 Gap Rd., Ochelata | 918/336–3351 | 4 rooms | $95–$125 | No credit cards.

**Super 8.** You can ask for a room with a recliner or sofa at this beige-and-turquoise brick hotel. It's one block or less from a handful of restaurants, and less than one mi from downtown. In-room data ports, in-room hot tubs, cable TV, pets allowed. | 211 S.E. Washington Blvd. | 918/335–1122 or 800/800–8000 | fax 918/335–1708 | 40 rooms | $45–$47 | AE, D, DC, MC, V.

# BOISE CITY

MAP 4, A3

*(Nearby town also listed: Guymon)*

Boise (pronounced to rhyme with "voice") City is practically the last stop heading west across the high plains of Oklahoma's Panhandle. The only stop light in Cimarron County is in front of its courthouse.

Information: **Cimarron County Chamber of Commerce** | 6 N.E. Sq, Boise City, OK 73933 | 580/544–3344.

## Attractions

**Black Mesa.** This 4,972-ft lava-topped mesa is Oklahoma's highest point. A 4-mi hiking trail leads to the top. It's not advised to hike it in bad weather or after dark. Maps and information are available at Black Mesa State Park. | Rte. 325, Kenton | 580/426–2222 | www.touroklahoma.com | Free | Daily.

**Black Mesa State Park.** This park is filled with intriguing Dakota sandstone formations, and has boating, fishing, and RV and tent campsites. | Off Rte. 325 | 405/426–2222 | www.touroklahoma.com | Free | Daily.

**Cimarron County Heritage Center.** Historical photographs, legends, and lore about the course of an alternate Santa Fe Trail route through Oklahoma (the infamous "Cimarron Cutoff") are on display. | 1300 N. Cimarron Ave. | 580/544–3479 | Free | Mon.–Thurs. 10–noon, 1–3:30, Fri.–Sat. 1–4.

**Kenton Mercantile.** Established in 1898, this café/gas station/general store/museum is the local gathering place for news, gossip, and hamburgers. | 101 W. Main St., Kenton | 580/261–7447 | Free | Daily.

**West End Roping, Inc.** Three-day cattle drives include chuckwagon cooking and sleeping under the stars. | HCR Box 21 | 580/426–2723 | $500 per person.

**ON THE CALENDAR**
**MAR., APR.: *Trout Derby.*** This tournament pits 40 marked fish in Lake Etling against the persistent and wily ways of local anglers: the tags can be exchanged for a $10 purchase at participating businesses, and there are two $1000, one $3000, and one grand prize $5000 fish. Kids have their own Small Fry Derby; the catcher of the biggest fish wins a bike. | 580/544–3344.
**JUNE: *Santa Fe Trail Daze Celebration.*** Visit historic sites along the Santa Fe Trail in nearby Kenton, and watch or participate in a fiddling contest or a championship post-hole digging contest. | 580/544–3344.

## Dining

**La Mesa.** Mexican. This bright, 12-table restaurant is known for enchiladas, combination plates, and *chiles rellenos* (a long, mild pepper stuffed with cheese, then deep fried and sided with beans, rice, and a garden salad). It also serves such dishes as cheeseburgers and fried shrimp. It sits just 18 mi from the Colorado border and 20 mi from the New Mexico state line. | 901 E. Main St. | 580/544–2997 | $6–$9 | D, MC, V.

**No Man's Land Beef Jerky and Deli.** American/Casual. Spurred into action by a mouthful of atrocious beef jerky, chef/owner Britt remodeled an old store into a beef jerky factory. Acclaim for the product spread, and mild and hot varieties are now sold throughout the country and abroad. The attached deli serves meals from 9 AM–7 PM, with dishes like broasted chicken, catfish, and made-to-order sandwiches. Try the Dagwood sandwich (with three meats, three cheeses, and lots of fixins), buffalo chicken bites, or potato salad. | 1016 E. Main St. | 580/544–2038 | nmlbjky@ptsi.net | Reservations not accepted | Closed Sun. | $2–$7 | MC, V.

## Lodging

**Townsman Hotel.** Black Mesa State Park and a wildlife reserve are less than 30 mi from this one-story motel. A full menu restaurant is adjacent. Cable TV. | 1205 E. Main St. | 580/544–2506 | 40 rooms | $39–$43 | AE, D, MC, V.

**Virginia's Bed and Breakfast.** Convenient to those traveling via Rtes. 3 and 287, this single-story contemporary home has a living room loft that overlooks the striking 20-ft fireplace, made with rocks selected from the proprietor's ranchland on the Santa Fe Trail. The larger of the two guestrooms has a trundle bed. You can relax outdoors on the patio in the flower garden. No alcohol. Complimentary breakfast, some in-room hot tubs, no TV in some rooms, TV in common area, no pets, no smoking. | 117 N. Freeman St. | 580/544–2834 | 2 rooms | $45–$65 | MC, V.

# BROKEN ARROW

MAP 4, J4

*(Nearby towns also listed: Tulsa, Wagoner)*

In the 19th century, Native Americans from the Southeastern United States were forced to relocate to Indian Territory, which lay in what is today Oklahoma's eastern half. The Creek Indians who settled here found many branches available for making arrows; instead of cutting them from the trees, they broke them, giving rise to this town's name. Today, Broken Arrow is a family-oriented community of 80,000 residents within minutes of metropolitan Tulsa.

Information: **Broken Arrow Visitors and Special Events** | 123 North Main, Broken Arrow, OK 74102 | 918/251–1518 | info@brokenarrow.org | www.brokenarrow.org.

## Attractions

**Persimmon Hollow Antique Village.** Forty-five antique dealers sell their goods in old-fashioned buildings made to resemble a pioneer settlement. Some buildings are sided with rough boards and have rustic porches. | 6927 S. 115th E. Ave. | 918/252–7113 | Free | Weekends 9–6.

**Indian Territory Gallery.** Oklahoma's most popular Native American artists display their drawings, paintings, and sculptures here. The non-profit gallery was instrumental in the Murals on Main project, Marion Goodwin's four large outdoor murals in the downtown area depicting the Trail of Tears. | 114 S. Main | 918/259–1772 | Free | Tues.–Fri. 10–5.

**Safari's Exotic Wildlife Sanctuary.** Animal lovers will enjoy a close-up look at exotic creatures in a natural habitat. The sanctuary includes a petting zoo. | 26881 E. 58th St. | 918/357–3386 | $5 | Mar.–Apr., Sun. 1–5; May–Sept., weekends 1–5; Oct.–Feb., call for hours.

### ON THE CALENDAR

**MAY.: *Rooster Day Festival.*** Springtime means Rooster Days in Broken Arrow. Held since 1932, this well-attended four-day festival includes a parade, entertainment, crafts, and food. | 918/251–1518.
**NOV.: *Indian Territory Festival.*** Native American history and culture are honored through storytelling, crafts, and works of nationally known artists. | 918/259–1772.

## Dining

**Brick Oven.** Italian. Fresh ingredients are key to the great pasta served here. Gourmet pizzas and homemade bread are also available. Try the shrimp linguini. | 8210 S. Elm Pl | 918/451–9707 | Reservations not accepted | Closed Sun. | $5–$15 | AE, D, MC, V.

**Peach House.** American/Casual. A working peach orchard is adjacent to this restaurant. You can buy fresh peaches and peach products at the restaurant's shop, and enjoy mouthwatering desserts such as peach ice cream and peach cobbler on the enclosed patio. For dinner, try the surf and turf. | 12500 S. 129th East Ave. | 918/455–5404 | Reservations not accepted | Breakfast also available | $12–$19 | MC, V.

**Rib Crib Barbecue.** Barbecue. Oklahomans love their barbecue, and this rustic regional chain restaurant with distressed wood throughout is often voted the best in the greater Tulsa area. Try the smoked chicken or the ever popular ribs. Kids' menu. | 121 W. Kenosha | 918/258–1557 | www.ribcrib.com | Reservations not accepted | $5–$10 | AE, D, MC, V.

## Lodging

**Best Western Kenosha Inn.** In the heart of town, this two-story motel (without an elevator) is within easy walking distance of shops, golf courses, and restaurants. In-room data ports, cable TV. | 1200 E. Lansing St. | 918/251–2795 or 800/528–1234 | fax 918/259–9500 | www.bestwestern.com/email | www.bestwestern.com | 44 rooms | $45–$60 | AE, D, DC, MC, V.

**Hampton Inn.** This four-story hotel opened in May 2000. It's right off Rte. 51. Microwave, refrigerator, cable TV, hot tub, gym. | 2300 W. Albany | 918/251–6060 or 800/426–7866 | fax 918/251–9090 | www.hampton-inn.com | 66 rooms | $79–$99 | AE, D, DC, V.

**Holiday Inn South.** Minutes from Tulsa's downtown, this branch of the Holiday Inn chain offers you convenience minus the mid-town parking hassles and noise. Restaurant, refrigerator, pool, meeting rooms. | 2600 N. Aspen | 918/258–7085 or 800/749–7085 | fax 918/251–6768 | www.holiday-inn.com | 197 rooms | $69–$89 | AE, D, DC, MC, V.

# BROKEN BOW

*(Nearby town also listed: Idabel)*

Thousands of acres of shortleaf pine forest surround Broken Bow, in the southern Ouachita Forest. They are managed for preservation and recreation, as well as for commercial logging. The town was founded in 1911 by the Dierks brothers, who built a lumber mill the next year. Timber remains the town's primary industry.

**Information: Broken Bow Chamber of Commerce** | 113 W. Martin Luther King Blvd., Broken Bow, OK 74728 | 580/584–3393 or 800/52–TREES.

## Attractions

**Beavers Bend Resort Park.** Oklahoma's most popular state park encompasses 3,500 densely forested acres. Park activities include fly-fishing in the Mountain Fork River, boating and scuba diving in Broken Bow Lake, and swimming, horseback riding, and hiking. There are also a nature center, the Forest Heritage Center, a miniature train, canoe rentals, cabins, a lakefront lodge, and RV and tent campsites. | Rte. 259A | 580/494–6300 | www.touroklahoma.com | Free | Daily.
   The **Forest Heritage Center** houses natural history exhibits, antique chainsaws, Choctaw artifacts, and a century-old cabin. (580/494–6497 | Free | Daily 8–8)

**Gardner Mansion.** This is the 1884 home of Choctaw chief Jefferson Gardner. Ruts made by wagons carrying Choctaws over the Trail of Tears can be seen on the grounds. | U.S. 70, 7 mi east of Broken Bow | 580/584–6588 | $2 | Memorial Day–Labor Day, Mon.–Sat. 8–6, Sun. 1:30–6; Labor Day–Memorial Day, Mon.–Sat. 8–5, Sun. 1:30–5.

**Hochatown State Park.** This park abuts both Beavers Bend Resort Park and the McCurtain County Wilderness Area. Its centerpiece is the 18-hole Cedar Creek Golf Course, carved out of the pine forest. Wildlife is sometimes spotted on the fairways. | U.S. 259 | 580/494–6451 | www.touroklahoma.com | Free | Daily.

**McCurtain County Wilderness Area.** Flying squirrels, bobcats, red and gray foxes, and 100 species of birds have been spotted in the 14,000-acre wilderness area. A 1-mi walking trail has markers designating prime viewing spots. | Off U.S. 259 | 800/52–TREES | Free.

### ON THE CALENDAR

**MAY: *Cool Cars Festival.*** An antique car rally and parade passes through town in the daytime, while the evening hosts a street fair with dancing and a dance contest, food and crafts vendors, entertainment, and games for children. | 580/584–3393.
**JUNE: *Kiamichi Owa Chito Festival.*** This "Festival of the Forest" held on the banks of the Mountain Fork River includes logging contests, live music, and an arts and crafts fair. | 580/494–6497.

**NOV.: *Beavers Bend Folk Festival and Craft Show.*** Turn-of-the-20th-century house-hold arts, crafts, and music are demonstrated at the Forest Heritage Center in Beavers Bend Resort Park near Broken Bow. The event corresponds with the peak of fall foliage. | 580/494–6497.

## Dining

**Beaver's Bend Restaurant.** American. Housed in a log building, this restaurant serves country breakfasts, hickory-smoked ribs, chicken-fried steak, trout, and catfish. A deck overlooks the Mountain Fork River. | Beavers Bend Resort Park, U.S. 259A | 580/494–6551 | $6–$15 | No credit cards.

**C.J.'s.** American. This full-service restaurant resembles a mountain lodge and is known for steaks as well as its country breakfasts and daily lunch specials. Salad bar. Kids' menu. | 302 N. Park Dr. | 580/584–9350 | $7–$12 | MC, V.

**El Senorial Mexican Restaurant.** Mexican. Paintings of the people and countryside of Mexico hang on the walls of this small restaurant, where the combination platters are favorites with locals. Try the popular quesadilla—a grilled flour tortilla filled with your choice of beef or cheese, served with rice, beans, and salad. | 400 N. Park Dr. | 580/584–2040 | $2–$7 | MC, V.

**Oaks Steakhouse.** Steak. Century-old oak trees surround this log building, where you can sit in a rocking chair on the porch before dining in the rustic all-wood restaurant. For lunch there are good burgers and hot open-face steak sandwiches; for supper try the delicious catfish with green tomato relish. Salad bar. | 2204 S. Park (Rte. 259N) | 580/548–5266 | Reservations not accepted | Closed Sun. | $2–$13 | AE, D, MC, V.

**Stevens Gap Restaurant.** American. Chicken-fried steak, catfish, and all-day breakfasts are favorites here. | U.S. 259 and Stevens Gap Rd. | 580/494–6350 | $6–$9 | No credit cards.

## Lodging

**Charles Wesley Motor Lodge.** Cedar-paneled walls add a warm feel to this rustic lodge. Several good canoeing rivers are nearby, including the Mountain Fork and Glover. Rooms have views of the pool. Restaurant, some kitchenettes, cable TV, pool. | 302 N. Park Dr. | 580/584–3303 | fax 580/584–3433 | 50 rooms | $46 | AE, D, DC, MC, V.

**Eagle Creek Guest Cottages.** These luxurious cabins built into the side of a mountain have private porches overlooking a stream. Kitchenettes, in-room hot tubs, cable TV, no kids allowed. | 1 mi west of U.S. 259, Octavia | 580/244–7597 | fax 580/244–7255 | www.guestcottages.com | 12 cottages | $125–$140 | AE, MC, V.

**Hochatown Resort Cabins.** Each of this resort's cabins is on an acre or two of land, amid 197,000 acres of timberland in a pristine wilderness area. There is easy access to Beavers Bend Resort Park, where you can hike, bike, canoe, and fish. Some in-room hot tubs, cable TV, in-room VCRs, some room phones, 18-hole golf course, hiking, boating, bicycles, some pets allowed (fee). | U.S. 259, 6½ mi north of Broken Bow | 580/494–6521 | 51 cabins | $125 | AE, D, MC, V.

★ **Lakeview Lodge.** Every room at this state-owned lodge has a balcony view of Broken Bow Lake. Breakfast is served in the Great Room, where a fire roars in a native stone fireplace when the weather warrants. There is no extra charge for additional guests in rooms, and each sleeps up to four. Restaurant, picnic area, cable TV, golf, hiking, dock, boating, fishing, playground, no pets, no smoking. | Rte. 259 | 580/494–6179 or 800/435–5514 | fax 580/494–6177 | information@beaversbend.com | www.beaversbend.com | 40 rooms | $80–$110 | AE, D, DC, MC, V.

**Microtel Inn.** Built in 2000, this homey, two-story hotel has rooms that are more spacious than most for this price, and breakfast is available as early as 5 AM. It's about 10 mi south of Broken Bow Lake. Complimentary Continental breakfast, in-room data ports, some kitchenettes, some microwaves, some refrigerators, cable TV, laundry facilities, business services, pets allowed (fee). | 1701 S. Park Dr. | 580/584–7708 or 888/771–7171 | fax 580/584–7709 | www.microtelinn.com | 43 rooms | $45–$78 | AE, D, DC, MC, V.

**Peckerwood Knob Cabins.** Large, secluded mountainside cabins are equipped with fireplaces, decks, and full kitchens with dishwashers. The area has good hiking, fishing, and canoeing, and a country café is less than 15 mi away. Kitchenettes, microwaves, no TV in rooms. | HC 15, Smithville | 580/494–7333 | www.cottages.org/cities/ok_smithville.htm | 2 cabins | $90–$100 | No credit cards.

**Pine Meadow Cabins.** Each of these cheery cabins, nestled in 20 acres of pine and hardwood forest, has a covered porch at its front and back, a gas grill, and a wood-burning fireplace. A pond stocked with bass, bluegill, and catfish is just a short walk away. Kitchenettes, microwaves, in-room hot tubs, cable TV, no room phones, pond, hiking, fishing, no pets, no smoking. | Off the U.S. 259A loop, 9 mi north of Broken Bow | 580/494–6521 or 800/550–6521 | pinemeadowcabin@webtv.net | www.pinemeadowcabins.com | 7 cabins | $136 | AE, D, MC, V.

**Treetop Cabins.** These elevated cabins built along the scenic Glover River 25 mi north of Broken Bow will make you feel like you're staying in a treehouse. Cabins have full kitchens, and boats are provided for all guests. Kitchenettes, no room phones, no TV in rooms. | 9 mi west of U.S. 259, Battiest | 580/241–5599 | 5 cabins | $100 | AE, D, MC, V.

**Whip-Poor-Will Resort.** Log cabins, ranging from cozy one-room models to larger family-size units, are equipped with full kitchens and fireplaces. The resort also has a fishing pond, an ice-cream parlor, and canoe rentals. Picnic area, kitchenettes, cable TV, pond, horseback riding, boating, fishing, pets allowed. | HC 75, 2 mi north of Broken Bow | 580/494–6476 | okresort.com | 17 cabins | $55–$155 | AE, D, DC, MC.

# CHICKASHA

MAP 4, G6

*(Nearby towns also listed: Anadarko, El Reno)*

Transportation has figured heavily in the history of Chickasha. A onetime watering hole for cattle on the Chisholm Trail, this town was founded as a stop along the Rock Island railroad. The first airplane built in Oklahoma was crafted in a local bicycle shop in 1911, and today the town is an antique car capital, thanks to attractions like the Chickasha Antique Automobile Club Museum of Transportation and Muscle Car Ranch.

**Information: Chickasha Chamber of Commerce** | 221 W. Chickasha Ave., Chickasha, OK 73018-2604 | 405/224–0787 | fax 405/222–3730.

## Attractions

**Chickasha Antique Automobile Club Museum of Transportation.** Prized vehicles of members of a local vintage car club are showcased. Displays range from a 1901 Stanhope White Steam Carriage (steered with a tiller), to a 1950s sports coupe. Auto memorabilia are also on display. | 18th St. and Chickasha Ave. | 405/224–4700 | Free | Weekends 2–4.

**Muscle Car Ranch.** This open-air museum on a working cattle ranch displays muscle cars, vintage motorcycles, and neon and porcelain signs. | 3609 S. 16th St. | 405/222–4910 | www.musclecarranch.com | Free | By appointment.

**Shannon Springs Park.** These historic springs once watered cattle being driven on the Chisholm Trail. The stone walkways, playground, swimming pools, and picnic areas were all built by the W.P.A. | 9th St. at Ferguson Dr. | 405/222–6079 | Free | Daily.

### ON THE CALENDAR

**MAY: *Antique Car Swap Meet*.** The Grady County Fairgrounds hosts a show and sale of pre–World War II cars and trucks, as well as tractors, bicycles, and motorcycles. | 405/224–2049.

**AUG.:** *Grady County Fair.* This fair includes a livestock show, crafts, and baked goods. | 405/224–2216.

**NOV., DEC.:** *Festival of Lights.* Preparations begin in October for this popular local event, where civic clubs, organizations, churches, and students create lighting displays for the holidays in Shanoan Springs Park. | 405/224–0787.

## Dining

**Big Daddy's Steakhouse.** Steak. Order your steak as you like it in this plain-looking, wood-walled, cafeteria-style restaurant, and enjoy it with a mashed, fried, or baked potato, a hot roll, or something from the large salad bar. For lunch, choose from chicken strips, chicken-fried steak, or a grilled sirloin burger. | 802 W. Grand St. | 405/222–2626 | $6–$12 | MC, V.

**J and W Grill.** American/Casual. Eat your meal on a stool at the long, narrow counter, or at a table. Try "onion-fried burgers" (grilled burgers with a handful of chopped onions mixed in). | 501 W. Choctaw St. | 405/224–9912 | Breakfast also available | $4–$6 | No credit cards.

**Jakes Rib.** Barbecue. This casual, wood-paneled, Western-style restaurant is so busy on the weekends that the crowd often overflows into the parking lot. Known for barbecued ribs, steak, and huge orders of French fries. Salad bar. Beer. | 100 Ponderosa St. | 405/222–2825 | No dinner Sun. | $8–$14 | MC, V.

**Ken's Steakhouse and Ribs.** Steak. Although there are no menus and no desserts here—just steak, ribs, chicken, or brisket—Ken's draws more than 500 diners on weekend nights, many of them from Oklahoma City. Salad bar. | 215 E. Main Street, Amber | 405/222–0786 | Closed Sun.–Wed. No lunch | $10–$15 | No credit cards.

## Lodging

**Best Western Inn.** This is Chickasha's only full-service hotel, and it's conveniently located at Exit 80 off I–44. Some rooms have framed prints on the wall. Restaurant, room service, refrigerators, cable TV, pool, hot tub, sauna, gym, business services, pets allowed. | 2101 S. 4th St. | 405/224–4890 | fax 405/224–3411 | www.bestwestern.com/innchickasha | 154 rooms | $60 | AE, D, DC, MC, V.

**Campbell Richison House Bed and Breakfast.** Richly colored walls, warm woodwork, and antiques decorate the rooms in this three-story 1909 Prairie-style home in a historic neighborhood. There is a formal dining room and a flower-filled wraparound porch. Dining room, complimentary breakfast, cable TV, in-room VCRs. | 1428 Kansas Ave. | 405/222–1754 | 3 rooms (2 with shared bath) | $50–$70 | MC, V.

**Days Inn.** This two-story motel is 1 mi from a golf course. Restaurant, room service, in-room data ports, some refrigerators, cable TV, pool, business services, pets allowed. | 2701 S. 4th St. | 405/222–5800 | 106 rooms | $55 | AE, D, DC, MC, V.

**Deluxe Inn.** There's nothing out of the ordinary about this turquoise-and-ivory, two-story hotel, but it's right off the highway and less than a block from a handful of restaurants. In-room data ports, some microwaves, some refrigerators, cable TV, pool, laundry facilities, pets allowed. | 728 S. Fourth St. | 405/222–3710 | 54 rooms | $37 | AE, D, DC, MC, V.

**Jordan's River Cottage.** Built in 1997, this European-style farmhouse on a hill has a wraparound porch facing pastureland and a backyard deck overlooking the River Bend Golf Course. The spacious interior includes a dining area, breakfast nook, and sun room. Rooms have mostly contemporary furnishings; one room overlooks the sixth green. Dining room, complimentary breakfast, cable TV, in-room VCRs (and movies), no room phones, hot tub, golf privileges, business services, no pets, no smoking. | Off Rte. 62, ½ mi east of downtown Chickasha | 405/222–3096 | fax 405/222–1067 | jrcbb@aol.com | www.bbonline.com/ok/jrcbb/ | 3 rooms | $75–$85 | MC, V.

# CLAREMORE

*(Nearby towns also listed: Pryor, Tulsa, Vinita)*

Claremore was named for Osage chief Clermont, but is best known as the proclaimed hometown of humorist Will Rogers. (Rogers was actually born in nearby Oologah, but said he feared no one could pronounce the name. It's OOH-la-ga.) Claremore's small-town charm and its Route 66 address make it a favorite for nostalgia buffs. Manufacturing and tourism are major economic forces.

**Information: Claremore Area Chamber of Commerce** | 419 W. Will Rogers Blvd., Claremore, OK 74017-6820 | 918/341–2818 | fax 918/341–1988 | www.claremore.org.

## Attractions

**J. M. Davis Arms and Historical Museum.** A collection of more than 20,000 vintage firearms, 70 saddles, swords, knives, and 1,200 beer steins are on display. | 333 N. Lynn Riggs Blvd. | 918/341–5707 | fax 918/341–5771 | www.state.ok.us/~jmdavis/ | Donations accepted | Mon.–Sat. 8:30–5, Sun. 1–5.

**Lynn Riggs Memorial Museum.** This museum honors the Claremore native and playwright whose work, *Green Grow the Lilacs,* was adapted as the musical *Oklahoma!* It contains photographs and artifacts, including the original "surrey with the fringe on top" used in the screen version of Riggs's play. | 121 N. Weenonah Dr. | 918/627–2716 | Free | Weekdays 9–noon, 1–4.

**Totem Pole Park.** This roadside park 10 mi north of Claremore is filled with painted stone and cement totem poles created by folk artist Ed Galloway in the 1930s and 1940s. | Rte. 28A, Foyil | 918/342–9149 | Free | Daily, dawn to dusk.

**Will Rogers Birthplace.** The great humorist's childhood home, built in 1875 on the shores of Oologah Lake, is a two-story log-and-clapboard structure containing period furnishings. Longhorn cattle and barnyard animals roam the grounds of the working ranch. | 2 mi east of Oologah, near Rte. 88 and U.S. 169 lake | 918/341–0719 or 800/828–9643 | www.will-rogers.com/birthplace/birthpla.html | Donation | Daily 8–5.

**Will Rogers Memorial.** A children's museum and eight galleries filled with memorabilia, photographs, and artifacts pay tribute to Will Rogers. A theater runs movies from Rogers's Hollywood days. He is buried at the memorial beneath an epitaph of his own choosing: "I never met a man I didn't like." | 1720 W. Will Rogers Blvd. | 800/324–WILL | www.willrogers.com | Donations accepted | Daily 8–5.

### ON THE CALENDAR

**JUNE:** *Will Rogers PRCA Rodeo.* Juried events in this award-winning rodeo include bronco-busting, bulldogging calves, roping, and riding. Winners walk away with cash prizes and local titles. | 918/341–8699.

**SEPT.:** *Bluegrass and Chili Festival.* Formerly held in Tulsa, this two-day event at the Claremore Expo Center and Grounds is the most celebrated of the year, with appearances by bluegrass performers from all over the country, a lauded chili cook-off, a car show, and children's activities. | 918/341–2818.

**NOV.:** *Will Rogers Birthday Celebration.* Birthday cake is served at Dog Iron Ranch, Will Rogers's boyhood home. | 918/443–2790.

**NOV., DEC.:** *Holiday Festivities.* Merriments include "Dickens on the Boulevard," when locals dress in period garb and stroll through town, "Christmas at the Belvedere," a month-long Christmas craft sale at a Victorian mansion, holiday home tours, and decorations throughout the historic downtown area. | 918/341–2818.

CLAREMORE

INTRO
ATTRACTIONS
DINING
LODGING

## Dining

**Hammett House.** American. This family-style restaurant was established in the 1960s and serves country-style dishes. It's known for its chicken (which is seasoned according to an old, secret family recipe) and its homemade rolls and pies. Kids' menu. | 1616 W. Will Rogers Blvd. | 918/341-7333 | www.hammetthouse.com | Closed Mon. | $6–$18 | AE, D, DC, MC, V.

**Pink House.** American. This tea room is in a pink Victorian house with period furnishings. Known for hearty stuffed pork chops and chicken enchiladas, soups, and sandwiches. A dozen desserts are offered daily. Kids' menu. | 210 W. 4th St. | 918/342-2544 | No dinner | $5–$10 | AE, D, MC, V.

**Salad Alley.** American. You'll find "good food on the quick" at this refreshing garden-themed spot dressed with vegetable wallpaper and plants. The enormous namesake salad bar has 70 items, and daily soup possibilities include German potato, Italian chicken pasta, or Mexican corn chowder. Try the baked lasagna, homemade honey wheat bread, carrot raisin muffins. | 441 S. Brady St. (Rte. 20) | 918/342-4922 | No supper Sun. | $4–$7 | MC, V.

## Lodging

**Best Western Will Rogers Inn.** Rooms are spacious in this motel four mi from the Will Rogers Museum and two mi from the Expo Center, where most rodeos are held. Bar, microwaves, refrigerators, cable TV, pool, laundry facilities, pets allowed. | 940 S. Lynn Riggs Blvd. | 918/341-4410 or 800/644-WILL (reservations) | fax 918/341-6045 | 52 rooms | $59–$75 | AE, D, DC, MC, V.

**Days Inn.** Opened in 1995, this two-story motel has a Southwestern feel, with a terra-cotta–colored stucco exterior and tile floors in the lobby and breakfast area. Health club privileges are available at a club about three blocks from the motel. Complimentary Continental breakfast, in-room data ports, some refrigerators, cable TV, pool, laundry service, business services, pets allowed. | 1720 S. Lynn Riggs Blvd. | 918/343-3297 or 877/343-3297 | fax 918/343-9434 | daysinnc@swbell.net | www.daysinn.com | 58 rooms | $48–$75 | AE, D, DC, MC, V.

# CLINTON

MAP 4, F5

*(Nearby towns also listed: Elk City, Weatherford)*

Originally called Washita Junction, Clinton was built in 1903 along a railroad line that ran through the Cheyenne-Arapaho reservations. Ranching and Native American influences are strong in this town of 10,000, as is that of Route 66, which passes through downtown.

Information: **Clinton Chamber of Commerce** | 600 Avant Blvd., Clinton, OK 73601-3916 | 580/323-2222 | fax 580/323-2223.

## Attractions

**Foss Lake State Park.** This state park has a campground, swimming beach, covered fishing dock, equestrian and hiking trails, and a marina on Foss Lake. | Rte. 44 | 580/592-4433 | www.touroklahoma.com | Free | Daily.

**McLain Rogers Park.** Built by the W.P.A. in the 1930s, this park has sandstone arches, an outdoor amphitheatre, a swimming pool, walking paths, playgrounds, and sand volleyball courts. | 10th St. and Opal Ave. | 580/323-0217 | Free | Daily.

**Mohawk Lodge Trading Post.** Established in 1892 to sell Cheyenne-Arapaho beadwork, this trading post moved to its location on Route 66 in 1942. Museum-quality vintage beadwork is on display, and pottery, hides, dance shawls, and moccasins are for sale. | Old Rte. 66, 1 mi east of Clinton | 580/323-2360 | Free | Mon.–Sat. 9–5.

★ **Oklahoma Route 66 Museum.** Decade-by-decade illustration of the evolution of Route 66 in Oklahoma—from its construction in 1920 until it was bypassed in the 1970s—are on display. | 2229 W. Gary Blvd. | 580/323–7866 | $3 | Feb.–Apr. and Sept.–Nov., Mon.–Sat. 9–5, Sun. 1–5; Dec.–Jan., Tues.–Sat. 9–5; May–Aug., Mon.–Sat. 9–7, Sun. 1–6.

## ON THE CALENDAR

**SEPT.: *Red Buck Outlaw Days.*** Named after a Clinton bad guy (buried in a nearby cemetery), this event includes demonstrations of beadworking, basketweaving, and tanning, as well as a powwow and a re-enactment of a hanging. | 580/323–2222.

**NOV., DEC.: *Festival of Lights Parade.*** Local downtown businesses light their buildings and window displays, and a parade through town has lit floats sponsored by area businesses, and a horse-drawn buggy with illuminated saddles. The parade ends in Englemann Park, where there are more lighted attractions. | 580/323–2222.

## Dining

**Adelina's Mexican Restaurant.** Mexican. The dining room is carpeted and has sombreros and serapes on the walls. Try the tacos with beans and rice, or a fajita, which mixes spiced and grilled beef and chicken, and is served with flour tortillas, sour cream, guacamole, and cheese. | 2014 W. Gary Blvd. | 580/323–6937 | Closed Sun. | $6–$15 | MC, V.

**Cafe Downtown Clinton.** American/Casual. The menu says you can't have any dessert unless you eat your lunch, so order soup and a tasty sandwich (like the mixed veggie or chicken salad), then be sure to sample the house specialty: homemade pie. The lemon chiffon or millionaire (chocolate cream in a graham cracker crust topped with whipped cream, shaved chocolate, and ground nuts) are fabulous. | 500 Frisco St. | 580/323–2289 | Closed Sun. No supper | $4–$5 | AE, D, MC, V.

**Wong's Chinese Restaurant.** Chinese. Fare such as chop suey, moo goo gai pan, and chow mein are served at this popular lunch and dinner spot. | 712 Opal St. | 580/323–4588 | $6—$10 | MC, V.

## MOHAWK LODGE

The only tip-off that there's something special inside the redbrick Mohawk Lodge Trading Post, is a canvas Plains-style tepee out front. The dimly lit interior of Oklahoma's oldest Indian goods store is a feast for the senses. Rows of brightly colored, appliquéd dance shawls glow like jewel-toned rainbows and the store's old glass cases are filled with a jumble of handmade moccasins, Pendleton blankets, and strings of glass beads. Decades-old buckskin dresses and beaded Cheyenne pouches hang on the walls next to studio portraits of Cheyenne chiefs and sepia-tinted photographs of tribal gatherings. The trading post was originally founded in 1892 in Colony, a Cheyenne-Arapaho model community established in 1886 by Indian agent John Seger. Though the trading post was moved to Route 66, just east of Clinton, in 1942, Cheyenne women in Colony continued to supply leather goods and beadwork—and owners kept some of the best work for themselves, resulting in the museum-quality collection that hangs on the wall. The heirloom beadwork is pricey, but browsers are welcome. For those on the trail of old Route 66, it's practically a mandatory stop: the combination of history and shopping make it the quintessential roadside attraction.

© Artville

## Lodging

**Best Western Tradewinds.** This one-story motel on legendary Route 66 was a stopover for Elvis Presley when he traveled from Memphis to Las Vegas. Restaurant, cable TV, pool, hot tub, pets allowed (fee). | 2128 Gary Blvd. | 580/323–2610 | 81 rooms | $58 | AE, D, DC, MC, V.

**Red Roof Inn.** Opened in 1999, this two-story tan stucco hotel off I–40, Exit 65, is built around a grassy exterior courtyard and is within walking distance of the Route 66 Museum, shopping, restaurants, and public tennis courts. Restaurant, bar, complimentary breakfast, room service, in-room data ports, some microwaves, some refrigerators, cable TV, pool, exercise equipment, video games, laundry facilities, business services, pets allowed (fee). | 2140 Gary Blvd. | 580/323–2010 or 800/734–7663 | fax 580/323–7552 | i0561@redroof.com | www.redroof.com | 100 rooms | $50–$54 | AE, D, DC, MC, V.

**TraveLodge.** The Oklahoma Route 66 Museum is only 1½ blocks from this one-story motel. Complimentary Continental breakfast, cable TV, pool, pets allowed (fee). | 2247 Gary Blvd. | 580/323–6840 | 71 rooms | $43–$47 | AE, D, DC, MC, V.

# DAVIS

MAP 4, I6

*(Nearby towns also listed: Pauls Valley, Sulphur)*

Just north of the Arbuckle Mountains, the Davis area has been populated since the 1830s, when the Chickasaw Nation were removed to Indian Territory. The town was founded in 1887 when the Santa Fe Railroad was built through the region. Today its economic base is mostly cattle ranching and tourism.

Information: **Davis Chamber of Commerce** | 300 E. Main St., Davis, OK 73030-1906 | 580/369–2402 | fax 580/369–3719 | www.brightok.net/davis.

## Attractions

**Arbuckle Historical Museum.** Housed in the former Santa Fe Depot, this museum displays photographs and artifacts relating to Chickasaw and pioneer history, including relics from now-vanished Fort Arbuckle, established in 1851 west of present-day Davis to protect the Chickasaws from the Plains tribes. | 1 S. Main St. | 580/369–2518 | Free | Tues.–Sat. 10–4, Sun. 1–4.

**Arbuckle Wilderness.** Wild and exotic animals inhabit this 400-acre drive-through theme park, which also has a zoo, a lake with paddleboats, camel rides, go-karts, and an arcade. | I–35, Exit 51, ¼ mi south | 580/369–3383 | shopoklahoma.net/arbuckle | $14.99 | Daily.

**Turner Falls Park.** In use as a recreational area since 1868, this 720-acre park is Oklahoma's oldest. A 77-ft waterfall splashes into a natural swimming pool along Honey Creek, and the park includes a rock castle, picnic areas, caves, and campsites. | I–35 and U.S. 77 | 580/369–2917 | www.brightok.net/davis/turner.html | $6 | Daily.

## ON THE CALENDAR

**MAY: *Davis Music Festival.*** This three-day country-and-western and gospel music celebration includes a talent show, craftspeople, a carnival with food vendors, and more. | 580/369–2402.

## Dining

**Dougherty Diner of Davis.** American. Formerly in the tiny town of Dougherty, this family-owned and -operated restaurant has blue-and-pink booths for dining, and serves generous portions of favorites such as catfish filets, hand-breaded chicken fries, and hamburgers. For dessert, try the chocolate or coconut pie. | 207 N. Third St. | 580/369–5119 | Reservations not accepted | Closed weekends | $3–$9 | No credit cards.

## Lodging

**Arbuckle Mountain Motel.** Rooms are clean and homey and the staff are friendly in this attractive two-story motel at the foot of the Arbuckle Mountains. It's less than 1 mi from Arbuckle Wilderness and 2 mi from Turner Falls Park. Some kitchenettes, some refrigerators, cable TV, hot tub, pets allowed (fee). | U.S. 77, 3 mi south of Davis | 580/369–3347 | 32 rooms | $52–$65 | AE, D, DC, MC, V.

# DUNCAN

MAP 4, H6

*(Nearby town also listed: Waurika)*

In 1892, William Duncan built a store along the Chisholm Trail when he learned the Rock Island Railroad planned to extend its line through the area. Today, antiques and gift stores line the downtown business district in this town of 23,000.

**Information: Duncan Convention and Tourism Bureau** | 911 W. Walnut Ave., Duncan, OK 73533-4664 | 580/255–3644 | fax 580/255–6482 | www.duncanok.com.

## Attractions

**Chisholm Trail Statue and Museum.** A 35-ft-long bronze statue depicts a chuckwagon and cowboys on horseback herding longhorn cattle along the Chisolm Trail. A small museum includes an animated likeness of Jesse Chisholm, the Cherokee trader and guide for whom the trail was named. | 1000 N. 29th St. | fax 580/252–6567 | www.onthechisholmtrail.com | Free | Daily.

**Simmons Center.** A convention center, 750-seat theater, and numerous recreational facilities (including a pool, walking and jogging track, weight room, and more) hosts association and corporate meetings, as well as private events. | 800 N. 29th St. | 580/252–2900 | www.simmonscenter.com | $7 | Weekdays 6 AM–10 PM, Sat. 8–8, Sun. 1–6.

**Stephens County Historical Museum.** Established in a vintage sandstone building that formerly served as a National Guard armory, the museum has exhibits ranging from a replica of an early oil well to Plains Indian artifacts to antique farm machinery. Vignettes illustrate various aspects of 19th- and early 20th-century local history. | Fuqua Park, U.S. 81 and Beech Ave. | 580/252–0717 | Free | Tues. 1–5, Thurs.–Sat. 1–5.

### ON THE CALENDAR

**NOV., DEC.:** *Lighting the Trail.* Drive or walk through the painted, illuminated, and animated holiday displays in Memorial and Fuqua Parks. | 580/255–3644.

## Dining

**Cedar Street Grill.** American. Vintage photographs and aluminum and enamel signs are on the walls in this small restaurant housed in a downtown building that was a neighborhood grocery in the 1930s. Known for pizza, hamburgers, barbecue, and pie. | 1001 Cedar St. | 580/252–6540 | Closed Sun. | $6–$10 | MC, V.

**Eduardo's Mexican Restaurant.** Mexican. A steady stream of customers visits this restaurant 1 mi north of downtown Davis. Try the fajitas, quesadillas, or the chicken salad (made with grilled chicken, lettuce, olives, cheese, sour cream, and guacamole). If you've got room for dessert, try the *cinnful sopapillas* (fried bread, ice cream, and honey, topped with a dollop of whipped cream and sprinkled with cinnamon). | 1304 U.S. 81N | 580/255–0781 | $5–$9 | AE, D, DC, MC, V.

## Lodging

**Chisholm Suite Hotel.** This four-story all-suites hotel is right off the highway, in the middle of town. It's the tallest building in sight, and the nicest place to stay in Duncan. Each room has ample space, and living areas include couches that pull out to an additional queen-size bed. Complimentary Continental breakfast, in-room data ports, microwaves, refrigerators, some in-room hot tubs, cable TV, in-room VCRs, pool, exercise equipment, business services, pets allowed (fee). | 1204 U.S. 81N | 580/255–0551 | fax 580/255–9132 | 60 suites | $67–$108 | AE, D, MC, V.

**Duncan Inn.** Rooms are spacious in this one-story motel 3 mi from downtown. Restaurant, cable TV, pool, laundry facilities, pets allowed. | 3402 N. U.S. 81 | 580/252–5210, ext. 336 | fax 580/252–5210 | 92 rooms | $30–$34 | AE, D, DC, MC, V.

**Holiday Inn.** A small mall is across the highway from this motel built in the 1960s. The Chisolm Trail Museum is 2 mi away. Restaurant, bar, picnic area, room service, in-room data ports, cable TV, pool, wading pool, business services, pets allowed. | 1015 N. U.S. 81 | 580/252–1500 | fax 580/255–1851 | ducokhi@starcom.net | www.holiday-inn.com | 138 rooms | $65 | AE, D, DC, MC, V.

# DURANT

MAP 4, J7

*(Nearby towns also listed: Atoka, Hugo)*

Built between the Washita and Red rivers, this town of 14,000 was an early agricultural center for cotton and peanuts. It has been the headquarters for the Choctaw Nation since 1951.

**Information: Durant Chamber of Commerce** | 215 N. 4th St., Durant, OK 74701-4354 | 580/924–0848. **Lake Texoma Association** | 1001 Texoma Park Rd., Durant, OK 73439 | 580/564–2334.

## Attractions

**Choctaw Nation Bingo Palace.** Payouts for game winners are in the thousands, even millions, of dollars, as there is no limit to the amount of prize money awarded at bingo halls built on sovereign Indian land. | 3735 Choctaw Rd. | 800/788–BINGO | Free | Daily.

**Fort Washita Historic Site.** Established in 1842 to protect the Chickasaw and Choctaw tribes from Plains tribes, this was the base for the Choctaw-Chickasaw Mounted Rifles during the Civil War. Of the 100 buildings that once stood on the site, some reconstructed barracks, a former Indian agent's cabin, and scattered foundations remain. A hiking trail identifies medicinal plants used by garrisoned soldiers. | Jct. Rtes. 78 and 199 | 580/924–6502 | Free | Mon.–Sat. 9–5, Sun. 1–5.

**Lake Texoma Resort Park.** Lake Texoma, Oklahoma's second-largest lake, can be accessed from this 1,882-acre park. You will also find an 18-hole golf course, a nature center, a swimming beach and pool, a stable, bike rentals, miniature golf, striper fishing guide services, a marina, an airstrip, hiking trails, rustic cabins, cottages, and a lodge. | U.S. 70, 13 mi east of Durant | 580/564–2311 | www.touroklahoma.com | Free | Daily.

**Three Valley Museum.** Named for the Blue, Red, and Washita river valleys, this museum is in the basement of the former Oklahoma Presbyterian College for Girls, established in 1909, and displays local and Choctaw history and artifacts. | 16th and Locust Sts. | 580/920–1907 | Free | Weekdays 1:30–4:30 or by appointment.

## ON THE CALENDAR

**APR.: *Fur Trade Rendezvous.*** An 1840s fur traders' rendezvous is re-enacted at Fort Washita Historic Site. | 580/924–6502.
**JUNE–JULY: *Oklahoma Shakespearean Festival.*** This summer theater festival held at Southeastern Oklahoma State University presents the works of Shakespeare, as well as musicals and dinner theatre. | 580/924–0121.

# Dining

**Linda's Kajun Kitchen.** Cajun/Creole. The walls of this small, casual restaurant are plastered with Mardi Gras and Louisiana State University memorabilia. The chef spent more than 20 years in Louisiana, and it shows in dishes featuring blackened chicken, fried shrimp, catfish, alligator, crawfish, frogs' legs, gumbo, red beans, and rice. | 1115 N. 6th Street | 580/931–9987 | Closed weekends | $5–$11 | No credit cards.

**Salitas.** Mexican. This casual Mexican restaurant is decorated with sombreros and patterned blankets. Outdoor dining is available on a wraparound patio. Known for tacos and fajitas. | 102 W. Main St. | 580/924–2945 | Closed Sun. No supper | $10–$15 | AE, D, DC, MC, V.

**Sanford's Steakhouse.** Steak. Rough cedar walls are softened by antiques and memorabilia, such as old signs and framed posters, in this restaurant known for top-quality, hand-cut charbroiled steaks. You can watch as your steak is cooked on the open grill. Homemade garlic croutons. | U.S. 70 | 580/564–3764 | Closed Sun., Mon. No lunch | $20–$25 | AE, D, DC, MC, V.

**Upper Crust.** American. Housed in a 1929 two-story redbrick building, the elegant interior includes leaded glass, yellow upholstered chairs, inlaid wood tables, an antique teapot collection, and fresh plants. Tasty choices include coconut shrimp (Gulf shrimp coated in a coconut batter and lightly fried), Santa Fe chicken (chicken spiced Southwestern-style with grilled red, yellow, and green bell peppers and onions), the best-selling pasta and fruit salad (chicken, pasta, red grapes, mandarin oranges, and celery in a creamy dressing), and buttermilk pie (a rich custardy treat made from an old Southern recipe). | 113 S. Fourth Ave. | 580/920–0052 | Closed Mon. | $9–$15 | AE, D, MC, V.

# Lodging

**Best Western Markita Inn.** This two-story motel is 16 mi from Lake Texoma. Restaurant, picnic area, room service, some refrigerators, cable TV, pool, business services, some pets allowed. | 2401 W. Main St. | 580/924–7676 | fax 580/924–3060 | 62 rooms | $55–$65 | AE, D, DC, MC, V.

**Comfort Inn and Suites.** On the west end of town just off U.S. 69/I–75, this hotel is a convenient choice for those passing through. The Continental breakfast is better than most. Complimentary Continental breakfast, in-room data ports, some microwaves, some refrigerators, some in-room hot tubs, cable TV, pool, putting green, laundry facilities, business services, pets allowed (fee). | 2112 W. Main St. | 580/924–8881 or 800/228–5150 | fax 580/924–0955 | 62 rooms | $69–$89 | AE, D, DC, MC, V.

**Diamond H Suites.** There's something for everyone at this sprawling property set on 9½ acres of hilly grassland and woods. Choose from motel-like units, rock cabins surrounded by hardwood and pine trees overlooking Lake Texoma, or independent houses complete with yards; some have conference rooms to accommodate groups. Restaurant, bar, picnic area, room service, kitchenettes, microwaves, refrigerators, cable TV, in-room VCRs, pool, wading pool, outdoor hot tub, basketball, hiking, volleyball, laundry facilities, business services, no pets. | U.S. 70W, Mead | 580/920–0994 or 877/610–3100 | fax 580/920–2170 | eastwood@redriverok.com | 8 rooms, 15 cabins, 7 houses | $78–$88, $88–108 cabins, $125–$295 houses | AE, D, MC, V.

**Holiday Inn.** This two-story hotel is 15 mi from Lake Texoma. Restaurant, room service, cable TV, in-room VCRs (and movies), pool, business services. | 2121 W. Main St. | 580/924–5432 | fax 580/924–9721 | 81 rooms | $69–$74 | AE, D, DC, MC, V.

**Lake Texoma Resort.** This lodge in Lake Texoma State Park is often filled with golfers and anglers. You'll have access to the park's vast facilities, including a sports director and fishing guides. Dining room, snack bar, some refrigerators, no TV in some rooms, pool, wading pool, 2 18-hole golf courses, miniature golf, putting green, exercise equipment, volleyball, marina, boating, video games, children's programs (ages 2–15), playground, laundry facilities, business services. | U.S. 70, 12 mi west of Durant | 580/564–2311 or 800/654–8240 | fax 580/564–9322 | www.oklahomaresorts.com | 120 rooms in 2 buildings (20 with shared bath, 6 with shower only), 67 cottages | $60–$75, $65 cottages | AE, D, DC, MC, V.

# EDMOND

*(Nearby towns also listed: Guthrie, Norman, Oklahoma City)*

In 1832, Washington Irving visited what would one day become the town of Edmond, and wrote about it in *A Tour on the Prairies*. At the time, Edmond was west of Indian Territory and popular with ranchers and cowboys traveling the Chisholm Trail; later it became an important stop on the Santa Fe Railroad line. Today, this town of 70,000 is a growing residential community north of Oklahoma City.

Information: **Edmond Convention and Visitors Bureau** | 825 E. Second St., Edmond, OK 73034 | 405/341–4344 | cwwhite@visitedmondok.com | www.visitedmondok.com.

## Attractions

**Ackley Park.** This 4-acre park has a miniature golf course, a miniature train with a track that winds past a pond, tunnel, and bridge, a carousel with 40 hand-carved horses, children's activities, a playground, and recreational facilities. In the winter, you can see the Christmas in the Park lighting display. | W. Third St. (U.S. 66) and Pioneer Rd. | 580/225–3250 | Free | Daily.

**Angel House.** The Angel family lived in this Queen Anne Cottage for 64 years, beginning in 1902. Today, it houses an art gallery, a gift shop, and the working studio of artist C. Butler Pendley. Inside you'll find angel etchings, pottery, and stained glass; grounds include a water pond and Victorian herb gardens. | 203 E. Main | 405/330–9278 or 800/597–9789 | fax 405/330–9274 | www.angelhouse.net | Free | Weekdays 10–6, Sat. 10–5.

**Arcadia Lake.** If you're in need of a nature fix, try hiking and biking through wooded grounds next to the 1,820-acre Arcadia Lake, also popular for boating, fishing, and swimming. | 9000 E. 2nd St. | 405/359–4570 | Mon.–Thurs. $6 per vehicle, Fri.–Sun., holidays, $7 per vehicle | Daily.

**Edmond Historical Society Museum.** Regular and traveling exhibits document the Land Run that settled Edmond and other central Oklahoma towns in a single day. Housed in a 1936 armory, this museum is on the National Register of Historic Places. | 431 S. Boulevard | 405/340–0078 | Donations accepted | Tues.–Fri. 10–4, Sat. 1–4.

### ON THE CALENDAR

**APR.:** *Southwest Farm and Home Expo.* Spanning the length of the ample Civic Center Complex, this fair displays commercial products for farming, landscaping, and the home, recreational items for boating and watersports, and hosts a new car exhibit. | 1016 Airport Industrial Rd. | 580/225–0207.

**MAY:** *Canterbury Arts Festival.* Since 1970, Edmond businesses and churches have sponsored this art and entertainment festival on the campus of the University of Central Oklahoma. A 10K race on Sat. kicks things off; musical acts follow, and lots of food is available throughout. | 405/848–1014.

**JULY, AUG.:** *Shakespeare in the Park.* The works of the bard are performed each year under the stars in Hafer Park. | 405/340–1222.

## Dining

**Around the Corner.** American. This place serves home-cooking in the heart of downtown Edmond. There are many good, filling meals to choose from, and the biscuits are light and tasty. Try the chicken-fried steak. | 11 S. Broadway | 405/341–5414 | Reservations not accepted | Breakfast also available. No dinner | $5–$7 | D, MC, V.

**Boulevard Steak House.** Steak. This is an upscale, award-winning establishment sporting white tablecloths and crystal, and serving only USDA Prime beef. It stocks over 900 varieties of wine. | 505 S. Blvd. | 405/715–2333 | No lunch | $19–$29 | AE, D, DC, MC, V.

**Cafe 501.** American/Casual. An extensive menu and delectable bakery items to choose from make this place one of Edmond's busiest destinations. Try the grilled salmon burritos and the Santa Fe tenderloin. | 501 S. Boulevard | 405/359–1501 | Reservations not accepted | Breakfast also available. No supper Sun. | $9–$15 | AE, D, DC, MC, V.

**Logan's Roadhouse.** Steak. Stop by this steak house if you're looking for a little regional flavor. The crunching noises you hear when you enter are the unlimited peanuts, served while you wait. | 3830 S. Broadway | 405/844–0909 | Reservations not accepted | $6–$12 | AE, D, MC, V.

**Simon's Catch.** American. You never know what will wander over to the pond as you look out of the west window in this lodge-style restaurant specializing in fresh seafood and steak. The grounds were once part of a wildlife safari, so you might see an elk or zebra as you enjoy your meal. Try the grilled filet mignon, lightly battered fried shrimp, or the all-you-can-eat cornmeal-crusted catfish. If you dare, top it all off with the brownie pie, served with ice cream, hot fudge sauce, whipped cream, and, yes, a cherry. | I–40S Exit 34, 1½ mi south, follow signs | 580/225–8400 | Closed Mon., Tues. No lunch | $9–$15 | AE, D, MC, V.

## Lodging

**Arcadian Inn Historic Bed and Breakfast.** Each room is individually decorated with antiques in this charming B&B. Some rooms have a fireplace and a stereo. Breakfast can be enjoyed in your private quarters, or in the dining room, whose ceiling has paintings of angels and Christ done by a local artist. Welcome extras include complimentary bath salts, robes, and chocolates. The personal service you receive is exceptional. Complimentary breakfast, in-room hot tubs, cable TV, in-room VCRs (and movies), no pets, no kids under 18. No smoking. | 328 E. First St. | 405/348–6347 or 800/299–6347 | fax 405/348–8100 | arcadianinn@juno.com | www.bbonline.com/ok/arcadian | 8 rooms | $109–$179 | AE, D, MC, V.

**Broadway Suites.** Stay for a night, week, or month in a suite containing four furnished rooms. The bedroom has a queen-size bed and ceiling fan, the kitchen is full-size and fully equipped, the living room has two recliners and a sleeper sofa, and the dining room allows you to comfortably enjoy your meal. Kitchenettes, microwaves, cable TV, laundry facilities. | 1305 S. Broadway | 405/341–6068 or 800/200–3486 | fax 405/359–7426 | www.broadwaysuites.com | 22 suites | $75 | D, MC, V.

**Howard Johnson Inn.** Rooms surround a plant-filled atrium and open onto a pool and dining area in this two-story hotel. Expect excellent rates and amenities, larger-than-average rooms, and many areas for business meetings or conferences. Restaurant, bar, complimentary breakfast, room service, in-room data ports, some microwaves, some refrigerators, cable TV, pool, hot tub, sauna, driving range, exercise equipment, laundry facilities, laundry service, business services, pets allowed. | 2606 Rte. 66E | 580/225–3111 or 800/446–4656 | fax 580/225–1531 | 72 rooms | $35–$90 | AE, D, DC, MC, V.

**Ramada Plaza Hotel.** This elegant, full-service, eight-story hotel has a soothing atrium next to a waterfall, and is just minutes from downtown Oklahoma City. It's across the street from the University of Central Oklahoma. Restaurant, bar (with entertainment), complimentary breakfast, room service, in-room data ports, microwaves, cable TV, pool, hot tub, gym, business services, exercise equipment. | 930 E. 2nd | 405/341–3577 or 800/322–4686 | fax 405/341–9279 | www.ramada.com | 145 rooms | $69–$99 | AE, D, DC, MC, V.

**TraveLodge.** Twelve-ft-wide parking spaces and clean, reasonably priced rooms can be found in this single-story motel. Kids may enjoy the "Sleepy Bear Room", where furnishings are embellished with the familiar TraveLodge mascot. Picnic area, in-room data ports, some microwaves, some refrigerators, cable TV, driving range, miniature golf, laundry service, business services, pets allowed. | 301 Sleepy Hollow Ct | 580/243–0150 or 877/243–0150 | fax 580/243–0152 | fhunt@itlnet.net | www.travelodge.com | 44 rooms | $32–$65 | AE, D, DC, MC, V.

# ELK CITY

MAP 4, E5

*(Nearby towns also listed: Clinton, Weatherford)*

This town of 11,000 has long been an agricultural center, and oil and gas were discovered nearby in 1947. It is situated along I-40 and old Route 66.

**Information: Elk City Chamber of Commerce** | 1016 E. Airport Blvd., Elk City, OK 73644 | 580/225-0207 | www.elkcitychamber.com | elkcitychamber@itl.net.

## Attractions

**Old Town Museum Complex.** Buildings housing a pioneer museum, the Farm and Ranch Museum, and the National Route 66 Museum are joined by a livery stable and working gristmill in shady Ackley Park. | Pioneer Rd. and U.S. 66 | 580/225-2207 | $5 | Mon.–Sat. 9–5, Sun. 2–5.

### ON THE CALENDAR

**SEPT.: *Fall Festival of the Arts.*** Exhibitors from all over the Southwest converge on this arts and crafts festival, which has food booths, a children's fair, and live music. | 580/225-0207.

**SEPT.: *Rodeo of Champions.*** This event sanctioned by the Professional Rodeo Cowboys Association includes bareback and saddle bronc riding, calf roping, steer wrestling, barrel racing, bull riding, and wrangler bull fights. | 580/243-2424.

## Dining

**Country Dove.** American. This flower-filled tea room is set inside a Victorian house that has been converted into a gift and antiques store. Sandwiches and daily specials are complemented by delicious desserts such as French silk pie (pecan crust with a light chocolate middle and real whipped cream and shaved chocolate) or almond pound cake with lemon curd. | 610 W. 3rd. St. | 580/225-7028 | Closed Sun. No dinner | $6–$10 | D, MC, V.

**Lupe's.** Mexican. Standard Mexican cuisine is the attraction here; enchiladas, chiles rellenos, and chalupas (open-shell tacos) are some of the favorites. Kids' menu. | 905 N. Main St. | 580/225-7109 | Closed Sun. No lunch Sat. | $6–$13 | AE, D, MC, V.

## Lodging

**Days Inn.** Local shopping is just a few miles away from this two-story stucco motel. Complimentary Continental breakfast, kitchenettes (in suites), some refrigerators, cable TV, pool, business services, pets allowed. | 1100 Rte. 34 | 580/225-9210 | fax 580/225-1278 | 132 rooms, 4 suites | $40–$50, $55–$95 suites | AE, D, DC, MC, V.

**Holiday Inn.** A full-service hotel, this is a highly ranked hotel in the state and the nation for customer satisfaction. The Holidome has entertainment and fitness opportunities, and a waterfall, gazebo, and karaoke bar are on site. Restaurant, bar, complimentary breakfast, room service, in-room data ports, cable TV, pool, hot tub, sauna, miniature golf, exercise equipment, video games, business services, some pets allowed. | 101 Meadow Ridge | 580/225-6637 | holidayinnelk@itlnet.net | 147 rooms, 4 suites | $65, $80–$120 suites | AE, D, DC, MC, V.

**Quality Inn.** This motel is within walking distance of a number of restaurants. Complimentary Continental breakfast, cable TV, pool, hot tub, business services, pets allowed. | 102 Hughes Access Rd. | 580/225-8140 | fax 580/225-8233 | 50 rooms | $45 | AE, D, DC, MC, V.

# EL RENO

*(Nearby towns also listed: Chickasha, Oklahoma City)*

The "Reno" in El Reno refers to Fort Reno; the community was first named Reno City and built around an 1870s frontier fort established to protect a Cheyenne Indian school. When a railroad line was built south of the fort in 1889, Reno City's buildings were put on skids, moved south to a new site, and it was eventually renamed El Reno. El Reno encompassed the western boundary of the lands opened in the 1889 Land Run. This town of 18,000 has a downtown with an old-fashioned flavor enhanced by the restored turn-of-the-20th-century buildings and locally famous "onion-fried burger" grills.

**Information: El Reno Chamber of Commerce** | 206 N. Bickford Ave., El Reno, OK 73036-2715 | 405/262–1188.

**Fort Reno Visitors Center** | 7107 W. Cheyenne St., El Reno, OK 73036-2153 | 405/262–3987 | fax 405/422–4917 | www.3ctn.co.canadian.ok.us/fortreno.

## Attractions

**Canadian County Historical Museum.** This museum is housed in an old Rock Island Railroad passenger depot and contains artifacts and photographs relating to area history, such as land runs, African-American "buffalo" soldiers, the Cheyenne-Arapaho reservation period, and Route 66. Grounds also include the restored Possum Hollow School, a barn filled with vintage machinery, and a restored two-story hotel. | 300 S. Grand St. | 405/262–5121 | Free | Wed.–Sat. 10–5, Sun. 1–5.

**Fort Reno.** This military post was built in 1874, after the Battle of Little Big Horn and the removal of Cheyenne and Arapaho tribes to west-central Indian Territory. Today it is an agricultural research station where remains of old buildings and the post cemetery can be seen. | 7207 W. Cheyenne St. | 405/262–5291 | Free | Weekdays 8–4:30.

### ON THE CALENDAR

**APR.: *'89ers Day.*** Held every year on the Sat. closest to Apr. 22 (the date of the Oklahoma Land Run of 1889), this event at the Rock Island Railroad Depot remembers the run with re-enactors, a pioneer fashion show, mock shoot-outs, arts and crafts, and food vendors—some of whom serve victuals cooked within authentic chuck wagons. | 300 S. Grand St. | 405/262–5121.
**MAY: *Onion-Fried Burger Day Festival.*** This event includes a classic car show, live music, children's activities, and the world's largest onion-fried burger. | 405/262–8888.
**SEPT.: *Tombstone Tales.*** Cavalry, Indian scout, and pioneer re-enactors share life stories in an historic cemetery. | 405/262–1188.

## Dining

**Robert's Grill.** American/Casual. Eat your meal at a long counter facing the grill in El Reno's oldest and most authentic onion-fried burger joint. Known for burgers, french fries, and hot dogs topped with tangy slaw. | 300 S. Bickford St. | 405/262–1262 | $5–$7 | No credit cards.

**The Wilds.** Southern. Cedar booths and chandeliers made from old wagon wheels are found throughout this restaurant, housed in a hand-cut log building whose grounds include hiking trails and fishing ponds. The buffet includes barbecue, catfish, and buffalo steaks. | On Britton Rd. 7½ mi W. of Hwy. 4 | 405/262–7275 | Closed Mon.–Wed. No lunch Thurs.–Sat. | $12 | AE, D, DC, MC, V.

## Lodging

**Best Western Hensley's.** This hotel is on 8 acres of landscaped grounds, and an RV park and gas station are on the property. It's within 3 mi of Lake El Reno, the historic downtown area, and a golf course. Restaurant, complimentary Continental breakfast, cable TV, pool, business services, pets allowed. | 2701 S. Country Club Rd. | 405/262–6490 | fax 405/262–7642 | bestwestern.com | 60 rooms | $53 | AE, D, DC, MC, V.

**Comfort Inn.** A handful of restaurants is less than a block away, and a golf course and Lake El Reno are both less than 1 mi from this three-story motel. Complimentary Continental breakfast, in-room data ports, some microwaves, some refrigerators, some in-room hot tubs, cable TV, some in-room VCRs, pool, hot tub, sauna, exercise equipment, business services, pets allowed. | 1707 S.W. 27th St. | 405/262–3050 or 800/228–5150 | fax 405/262–5303 | 30 rooms, 31 suites | $46–$55, $58–$81 suites | AE, D, DC, MC, V.

**Garrett House.** The handsome covered porch of this 1914 three-story B&B leads into an eclectic home, with individually styled theme rooms. Breakfast is served in the dining room, and lunch and supper are available by arrangement. Dining room, complimentary breakfast, some in-room hot tubs, no room phones, no TV, business services, no pets, no kids, no smoking. | 619 S. Hoff St. | 405/262–4422 | fax 405/262–2828 | okbnb@flashnet.com | www.bbonline.com/ok/garretthouse | 4 rooms (1 with shower only) | $85–$110 | MC, V.

# ENID

MAP 4, H3

*(Nearby towns also listed: Alva, Perry)*

Enid, founded the day of the largest Oklahoma land run—the opening of the Cherokee Strip on September 16, 1893—is northwestern Oklahoma's largest town.

Information: **Enid Chamber of Commerce** | 210 Kenwood Blvd., Enid, OK 73701-3805 | 580/237–2494 | chamber@enid.com.

**Enid Visitors Center** | 602 S. Van Buren, Enid, OK 73703 | 580/233–5914.

## Attractions

**Leonardo's Discovery Warehouse.** This hands-on children's science and art museum has a computer lab, fish tank, carpentry shop, and "Castle Courtyard" stocked with thrones,

## KODAK'S TIPS FOR PHOTOGRAPHING WEATHER

**Rainbows**
- Find rainbows by facing away from the sun after a storm
- Use your auto-exposure mode
- With a SLR, use a polarizing filter to deepen colors

**Fog and Mist**
- Use bold shapes as focal points
- Add extra exposure manually or use exposure compensation
- Choose long lenses to heighten fog and mist effects

**In the Rain**
- Look for abstract designs in puddles and wet pavement
- Control rain-streaking with shutter speed
- Protect cameras with plastic bags or waterproof housings

**Lightning**
- Photograph from a safe location
- In daylight, expose for existing light
- At night, leave the shutter open during several flashes

From *Kodak Guide to Shooting Great Travel Pictures* © 2000 by Fodor's Travel Publications

scepters, and crowns. "Adventure Quest" playground next door has a three-story slide. | 200 E. Maple St. | 580/233–2787 | fax 580/237–7574 | $5 | Tues.–Sat. 9:30–5:30, Sun. 2–5.

**Midgley Museum.** The former home of rock hounds Dan and Libbie Midgley holds collections of fossils, rocks, crystals, and petrified wood, plus eclectic personal collections. The museum's facade is covered in a mosaic of Texas horn crystal. | 1001 Sequoyah Dr. | 580/237–2494 | Free | Sept.–May, Wed.–Sat. 1–5; June–Aug., Tues.–Fri. 10–5, weekends 2–5.

**Museum of the Cherokee Strip.** Exhibits convey the story of the 1893 Cherokee Strip land run, and the adjacent Humphrey Heritage Village (part of the museum compound) has a restored 1890s schoolhouse, a church, a Victorian home, and an original U.S. Land Office where homesteaders registered their claims. | 507 S. 4th St. | 580/237–1907 | Free | Tues.–Fri. 9–5, weekends 2–5.

**MAR.: *Cherokee Strip Stampede P.R.C.A. Rodeo.*** This three-day event held indoors at the Chisholm Trail Expo Center includes bull riders, rodeo queens, bronco busting, mutton busting (where kids ride around on sheep), food concessions, and a rodeo dance. | 580/237–2494.

**MAY: *Tri-State Music Festival.*** Choruses, orchestras, marching and jazz bands, and other musical groups (mostly school-affiliated) compete for state honors. | 580/237–4964.

**SEPT.: *Cherokee Strip Days Celebration.*** A parade, an arts and crafts fair, food booths, and entertainment mark the anniversary of the opening of the Cherokee Strip in 1893. | 580/237–2494.

## Dining

**Pastimes.** American. In downtown's original retail area, this restored building has original hardwood floors, high ceilings, and old photographs of Enid on its exposed brick walls. Favorites on the steak, pasta, and chicken menu include chicken enchiladas and the barbecued brisket sandwich served with sides such as garlic mashed potatoes, seasoned red beans, and steamed or grilled vegetables. Round off your meal with cherry or apple strudel à la mode. | 223 N. Grand St. | 580/233–1865 | Reservations not accepted | Closed Sun. | $4–$18 | AE, MC, V.

**Port Lugano.** Eclectic. A European-influenced menu includes made-from-scratch baked goods such as Irish oatmeal bread, and baklava. Try the chicken salad sandwich on a croissant, or the marinated pasta salad. Cappuccino and cheese cake or tiramisu make for a nice ending to your meal. | 813 S. Van Buren St. | 580/233–6012 | Reservations not accepted | Breakfast also available. No supper weekdays | $6–$12 | No credit cards.

**Sage Room.** American. Linen tablecloths, candlelight, and an antique clock collection create an unhurried, elegant atmosphere. Known for steak, seafood, lamb, and frogs' legs. Kids' menu. | 1927 S. Van Buren Ave. | 580/233–1212 | Closed Sun. No lunch | $15–$20 | D, DC, MC, V.

## Lodging

**AmeriHost Inn.** This two-story redbrick hotel on the west side of town may appear to be nothing special, but the in-room facilities are gratifying. Some rooms have a king-size bed. Complimentary Continental breakfast, in-room data ports, in-room safes, some microwaves, some refrigerators, some in-room hot tubs, cable TV, pool, sauna, exercise equipment, business services, no pets. | 3614 W. Garriott Rd. | 580/234–6800 or 800/434–5800 | fax 580/234–7900 | 194@amerihost.com | www.amerihostinn.com | 60 rooms | $59–$125 | AE, D, DC, MC, V.

**Best Western Inn.** Muted, desert colors and high ceilings in the lobby lend a Southwestern feel to this two-story hotel. It's within 5 mi of the Oakwood shopping mall, antiques shops, and Leonardo's Discovery Warehouse. Restaurant, bar, in-room data ports, microwaves, cable TV, pool, video games. | 2818 S. Van Buren Ave. | 580/242–7110 | fax 580/242–6202 | www.bestwestern.com | 100 rooms | $53 | AE, D, DC, MC, V.

**Holiday Inn.** Rooms are modern in this chain hotel, and the courtyard is filled with trees and foliage. Restaurant, bar, room service, cable TV, pool, exercise equipment, business services, pets allowed. | 2901 S. Van Buren Ave. | 580/237–6000, ext. 177 | fax 580/237–6000 | www.holiday-inn.com | 100 rooms | $59 | AE, D, DC, MC, V.

★ **Island Guest Ranch.** This 3,000-acre working cattle ranch on the Cimarron River has a lodge with memorabilia from the Civil War to the present day, including guns, Native American paintings and blankets, and trophy animal heads. Low adobe-style rooms have red-tile roofs, and are right off the pool. Entertainment includes square dances and Native American powwows; you can also help out with some (optional) ranch chores. Complimentary breakfast, no room phones, no TV in rooms, TV in lodge, pool, hiking, horseback riding, fishing. | Rte. 1, Ames | 580/753–4574 or 800/928–4574. | rickksimpson@prodigy.net | www.simpsonswildwest.com | 10 rooms | $200 | Closed Labor Day–Apr. | AP | MC, V.

**Ramada Inn.** This two-story hotel is in the center of town, about 1 mi from the Museum of the Cherokee Strip. The indoor pool is surrounded by lush greenery and flowers. Restaurant, bar, room service, microwaves, cable TV, 2 pools, hot tub, sauna, gym, laundry facilities, pets allowed (fee). | 3005 W. Owen K. Garriott Rd. | 580/234–0440 | fax 580/233–1402 | 125 rooms | $45–$69 | AE, D, DC, MC, V.

**Worthington House.** Built in 1906, this Colonial Revival home has a large front porch with swings and a goldfish pond in its backyard. Rooms are simple but elegantly decorated with antiques. Complimentary breakfast, in-room VCRs, hot tub, library. | 1224 W. Maine St. | 580/237–9202 or 888/242–5009 | bbonline.com | 3 rooms | $75 | AE, D, MC, V.

# EUFAULA

MAP 4, K5

*(Nearby towns also listed: McAlester, Muskogee, Okmulgee)*

Eufaula, in eastern Oklahoma, was a small Creek Indian crossroads on the Canadian River at the turn of the 20th century; the construction of Eufaula Reservoir in 1964 turned it into a lake town. Restored downtown buildings create a tiny, charming shopping district.

Information: **Eufaula Chamber of Commerce** | P.O. Box 738, Eufaula, OK 74432 | 918/689–2791.

## Attractions

**Arrowhead State Park.** This wooded 2,200-acre state park off U.S. 69 on Lake Eufaula has an 18-hole golf course, tent and RV campsites, hiking trails, a children's playground, and a lakefront swimming beach. | St. Park Rd., 10 mi south of Eufaula | 918/339–2204 | www.touroklahoma.com | Free | Daily.

**Fountainhead State Park.** Built on the shores of Lake Eufaula on land that was once an Osage hunting ground, this park has an airstrip, an 18-hole golf course, an enclosed fishing dock, boat docks, tent and RV campsites, hiking trails, and a picnic area. Its nature center has award-winning natural history programs. | U.S. 69 N to Rte. 150 | 918/689–5311 | www.touroklahoma.com | Free | Daily.

**Lake Eufaula.** Oklahoma's largest lake, with 102,200 surface acres and 600 mi of shoreline, is nicknamed "The Gentle Giant." Fishing, boating, camping, and water sports are popular activities here. | 701 S. Main | 918/689–7751 | www.lakeeufaula.com | Free | Daily.

## Dining

**Gator's Wharf Restaurant and Lounge.** American. This waterfront restaurant's dining room is paneled in cedar and decorated with antiques. Open-air dining is available on the deck, which has a sweeping view of Lake Eufaula. Known for seafood, steaks, sandwiches, and salads. | 412 E. Lakeshore Dr. | 918/689–7900 | $8–$20 | AE, D, MC, V.

**Jim's Restaurant.** American. Built in 1955, this downtown restaurant with a loyal following serves full breakfasts and daily blue-plate specials. Friday and Saturday nights are seafood nights. Try coconut cream and pecan pies. | 115 Selmon Rd. | 918/689–9474 | Closed Sun. | $6–$13 | AE, D, MC, V.

**Trapper's Onion Burger.** American/Casual. Housed in a former Eufaula Bank building downtown and filled with Coca Cola memorabilia, the menu includes chicken, steak, and burgers. The latter are served with fixings such as mushrooms, jalapenos, bacon, cheese, and chili; the signature burger includes hand-patted beef, to which fresh-cut onions are added during grilling. | 207 N. Main St. | 918/689–7878 | Closed Sun. | $4–$7 | No credit cards.

## Lodging

**Cedar Creek Bed and Breakfast.** This country getaway 9 mi west of Eufaula is on 40 acres that teem with trees and wilderness. It has rocking chairs on its porch, and walking trails and fishing ponds on its grounds. You can stay in one of the rooms in the B&B proper, or in the small cabin off the main building. Both buildings are cedar-sided, and have rustic exteriors that complement the modern amenities within. Complimentary full breakfast. In-room hot tubs. Fishing, bicycles. | Box 471 | 918/689–3009 | bbonline.com | 2 rooms, 1 cabin | $80; $120 cabin | No credit cards.

**Days Inn of Eufaula.** This single-story redbrick motel is less than 1 mi from Eufaula Lake, and a couple of restaurants are adjacent. Complimentary Continental breakfast, in-room data ports, cable TV, business services, pets allowed (fee). | U.S. 69, 5 mi north of Eufaula | 918/689–3999 | fax 918/689–5800 | 40 rooms | $56–$62 | AE, D, DC, MC, V.

**Fountainhead.** This spacious resort on Lake Eufaula has rough wood paneling and game trophies on its walls. Restaurant, bar, dining room, picnic area, room service, some refrigerators, cable TV, 2 pools, wading pool, driving range, 18-hole golf course, putting green, tennis court, hiking, beach, playground, laundry facilities. | Off I–40 and Rte. 150, 10 mi north of Eufala | 918/689–9173 or 800/345–6343 | fax 918/689–9493 | 188 rooms | $75–$85 | AE, D, DC, MC, V.

**Lake Eufaula Inn.** This single-story hotel is ½ mi from Eufaula Lake and 2½ mi from Fountainhead State Park, where you'll find horse stables, a golf course, and a marina. Complimentary Continental breakfast, cable TV, pool, laundry facilities, business services. | I–40 and Rte. 150, Exit 259, 12 mi south of Eufaula | 918/473–2376 | fax 918/473–5774 | 48 rooms | $54 | AE, D, DC, MC, V.

**Lakeview Landing and RV Park.** Rooms have pastel hues and modern furnishings in this pink brick motel, built in 2000. Some rooms have a view of Eufaula Lake, and two have two queen-size beds and an adjoining kitchenette. Some kitchenettes, some microwaves, some refrigerators, cable TV, lake, hiking, boating, fishing, pets allowed (fee). | Junction of Rtes. 9 and 9A, 3 mi east of Eufaula | 918/452–2736 | 12 rooms | $44–$78 | AE, D, MC, V.

# GROVE

MAP 4, L3

*(Nearby towns also listed: Miami, Vinita)*

Built on the lush eastern shore of Grand Lake, Grove was a struggling agricultural trading center until the 1940s, when the lake was created. Today this town of 6,000 serves as the center for lake resort development.

**Information: Grove Area Chamber of Commerce** | 104 W. 3rd St., Grove, OK 74344-3201 | 918/786–9079 | fax 918/786–2909.

## Attractions

***Cherokee Queen I and II.*** Built to resemble the paddlewheel riverboats that cruised the Mississippi, these two boats offer daytime, dinner, and moonlight cruises on Grand Lake. | Sailboat Bridge on U.S. 59 | 918/786–4272 | $9–$25.

**Grand Grove Opry.** Grand Ole Opry–style country-and-western music show, featuring guest artists and a resident troupe of cloggers, singers, and comedians. | U.S. 59 N at Sailboat Bridge | 918/787–4111 | www.grandgroveopry.com | $10 | Mon.–Sat. 10–5.

**Grand Lake O' the Cherokees.** Built in 1940 by damming the Grand (or Neosho) River, this 42,000-acre reservoir is Oklahoma's third-largest lake and northeastern Oklahoma's preeminent recreation area. The lake's 1,300-mi shoreline winds through the wooded Ozark foothills and is dotted with dozens of private resorts and marinas. | 10100 U.S. 59N | 918/786–2289 | Free | Daily.

**Har-Ber Village.** This reconstructed turn-of-the-20th-century frontier town has more than 100 historic cabins and buildings, including a chapel, a newspaper office, a law office, and a jail—all filled with pioneer artifacts. | 4404 W. 20th St. | 918/786–6446 | Free | Mar.–Nov., Mon.–Sat. 9–6, Sun. 11–6.

**Honey Creek State Park.** Picnic areas, RV and tent campsites, a playground, a swimming pool, and a boat ramp and rentals can be found at this 30-acre lakeside park. | 901 State Park Rd. | 918/786–9447 | www.touroklahoma.com | Free | Daily.

**Lendonwood Gardens.** This 3-acre botanical garden has Japanese-style cascading pools, an English terrace garden, a bonsai collection, and rare flowers and trees. | 1308 W. 13th St. | 918/786–2938 | $5 | Daily.

**Shangri-La Golf Courses.** Part of the Shangri-La Resort, two courses are yours to choose from; both are challenging and have views of Grand Lake O' the Cherokees. Non-guests of the resort should make reservations two weeks in advance. | 57401 E. Rte. 125 | 918/257–4204 | Year-round.

### ON THE CALENDAR

**JUNE–AUG.:** *Picture in Scripture Amphitheater.* An outdoor, waterfront theater hosts a dramatic retelling of the story of Jonah and the Whale and other biblical favorites. | 918/435–8207.

**SEPT.:** *Pelican Festival.* An arts and crafts festival, entertainment, and boat tours coincide with the southward migration of thousands of pelicans. | 918/786–2289.

© Artville

## GRAND LAKE O' THE CHEROKEES

Sprawling across three counties in northeastern Oklahoma, Grand Lake covers enough ground to have produced a full range of vacation spots, each with its own rhythm and personality. Grove and its environs, for example, appeal to lake lovers who also seek entertainment—more specialty shops, antiques stores, marinas, restaurants, musical venues, and festivals are found here than anywhere else on the lake's shores. Monkey Island, across Sailboat Bridge, is upscale, offering luxe rental condominiums, a championship golf course, and two small airstrips continually abuzz with private planes. And with five small state parks on its shores, the South Grand Lake area near Disney appeals to visitors in search of the lake in its most natural, least developed state.

*Towns listed:* Grove, Miami, Vinita.

## Dining

**Bubba's Smokehouse.** Barbecue. This no-frills diner serves traditional Southern barbecue, including ribs, brisket, chicken, and pork, along with side salads and onion rings. Fri. and Sat. nights are all-you-can-eat ribs nights. | 2230 S. Main St. | 918/786–9599 | $8–$9 | D, MC, V.

**Rheingarten Restaurant.** German. A converted Victorian house holds this cozy restaurant with polished wooden floors and forest green and burgundy accents. Try Rheingarten Schnitzel, breaded pork loin topped with asparagus and Hollandaise sauce. Wine and beer. | 911 S. Main St. | 918/786–8737 | Closed Sun.–Tues. No lunch Wed., Thurs. | $15–$18 | D, MC, V.

**Stone Point Supper Club.** Continental. This upscale waterfront restaurant serves lobster, prime rib, steaks, and great chicken dishes. | 11350 U.S. 59 N | 918/786–6221 | Reservations essential Fri., Sat. | Closed Sun., Mon. No lunch Sat. | $15–$30 | MC, V.

## Lodging

**Candlewyck Bed and Breakfast Cottages.** Rustic, cedar-sided cottages and terraces overlook a lake cove. Dining room, complimentary breakfast, dock, boating, fishing, no kids under 13. | 59600 E. 307 Ln | 918/786–3636 | 13 cottages | $99–$249 | AE, D, MC, V.

**Hickory Inn Motel.** This buff brick U-shaped motel with white and brass trim has clean rooms, most with one king- or two queen-size beds. It's less than 1 mi from Grand Lake O' the Cherokees, and 1½ mi south of downtown Grove via U.S. 59. Some microwaves, some refrigerators, cable TV, pool, lake, boating, fishing, laundry facilities, pets allowed (fee). | 2320 S. Main St. | 918/786–9157 | fax 918/786–6192 | gse@greencis.net | 37 rooms | $40–$50 | MC, V.

**Honey Creek Resort and Motel.** Rooms at this strip motel have two queen-size beds with private back porches overlooking the Honey Creek arm of Grand Lake. Wood-and-siding fishermen's cabins front the lake and have tiled floors and paneled walls. For groups, the cabin with two rooms (each with two double beds) joined by a central kitchen is a great deal. Some kitchenettes, some refrigerators, cable TV, some room phones, lake, dock, boating, fishing, playground, business services, no smoking. | 2511 S. Main St. | 918/786–6113 | fax 918/786–6909 | 24 rooms, 18 cabins | $38–$70, $40–$125 cabins | AE, MC, V.

**Kristyl Inn.** This lovely white-brick building with a blue metal roof is right on Grand Lake. There's a restaurant across the street, and flea-market shopping is within a 10 minute drive. Complimentary Continental breakfast, cable TV, pool. | 10400 U.S. 59 | 918/786–9799 | 68 rooms | $60 | AE, D, DC, MC, V.

**Shangri-La.** This 650-acre resort along Grand Lake O' the Cherokees is an ideal getaway. There are beautiful panoramic views of the lake, and it's just a short drive from Tulsa. Bar, dining rooms, picnic area, cable TV, 2 pools, beauty salon, hot tub, spa, driving range, 2 18-hole golf courses, putting green, tennis, bowling, exercise equipment, beach, boating, bicycles, children's programs (ages 5–10), playground, business services. | 57401 E. Rte. 125, Afton | 918/257–4204 or 800/331–4060 | fax 918/257–5619 | info@galstar.com | 322 rooms, 66 suites | $134, $174–$595 suites | AE, D, DC, MC, V.

# GUTHRIE

*(Nearby towns also listed: Edmond, Oklahoma City, Perry, Stillwater)*

Founded during the 1889 Land Run in central Oklahoma, Guthrie was the territorial capital and Oklahoma's first state capital. After a referendum moved the capital to Oklahoma City in 1910, Guthrie seemed to move into a time warp. Today the town's 400-block historic district, the largest urban district listed on the National Register of Historic Places, is filled with more than 2,000 restored late 19th-century buildings and Victorian homes, many serving as antiques and gift stores or bed-and-breakfast inns. Guthrie has a population of 10,500.

Information: **Guthrie Chamber of Commerce** | 212 W. Oklahoma Ave., Guthrie, OK 73044-3132 | 405/282–1947 | fax 405/282–0061.

## Attractions

**First Capital Trolley.** Tour historic downtown Guthrie, the largest urban area listed on the National Register of Historic Places. The area's more than 400 city blocks include turn-of-the-20th-century commercial and residential buildings, many of which still have their original stained-glass windows and stamped-tin ceilings. Tours board hourly, on the hour. | Board at the corner of Second St. and Harrison Ave. | 405/282–6000 | fax 405/282–1081 | $2 | Oct.–Feb., Mon.–Sat. 9–4, Sun. 1–4; Mar.–Sept., Mon.–Thurs., 9–4, Fri., Sat. 9–6, Sun. 9–4.

**National Lighter Museum.** A storefront museum houses a collection of nearly 15,000 cigarette lighters. Foot-tall lighters that once sat on frontier bars are displayed, as are 3,000 Zippos. The oldest lighter is from the 1400s. | 107 S. 2nd St. | 405/282–3025 | www.natlitr-mus.com | $1 | Mon.–Sun. 10–6.

**Oklahoma Frontier Drugstore Museum.** Oklahoma Territory's first drugstore has been re-created, right down to its soda fountain and turn-of-the-20th-century apothecary jars. | 214 W. Oklahoma Ave. | 405/282–1895 | $2 | Tues.–Sat. 10–5, Sun. 1–4.

**Oklahoma Territorial Museum.** Exhibits showcase the 1889 Land Run into central Oklahoma and the social and political history of the territorial era. The museum adjoins a restored 1902 Carnegie library building; Oklahoma's first governor was inaugurated on the library steps. | 406 E. Oklahoma Ave. | 405/282–1889 | Free | Tues.–Fri. 9–5, Sat. 10–4, Sun. 1–4.

**Scottish Rite Masonic Temple.** An architectural tour de force, this huge marble-and-stone temple was built in the 1920s to reflect the great periods in history, including ancient Egypt, Renaissance Italy, Georgian England, and Gothic France. | 900 E. Oklahoma Ave. | 405/282–1281 | $5 | Tours weekdays at 10 and 2, Sat. at 10.

**State Capital Publishing Museum.** The former offices of Oklahoma's leading territorial newspaper, *The State Capital,* are now a museum offering a slice of political and civic life in turn-of-the-20th-century Guthrie. The original printing presses still stand in the basement. | 301 W. Harrison Ave. | 405/282–4123 | $1 | Tues.–Fri. 9–5, Sat. 10–4, Sun. 1–4.

### ON THE CALENDAR

**FEB.: *Bullnanza.*** Top bull riders of the Pro Bull Riders Association compete for cash prizes and regional titles. | 405/282–3004.
**MAR.: *Timed Event Championship of the World.*** The top 20 timed-event cowboys in the world compete for $40,000 at the Lazy E Arena. | 405/282–3004.
**APR.: *Eighty-niner Celebration.*** A week-long celebration of the 1889 Land Run includes a parade, a carnival, a rodeo, a chuckwagon feed, and other activities. | 405/282–1947.
**MAY: *Jazz Banjo Festival.*** This gathering of four-string banjo strummers celebrates ragtime and the big band era with three days of concerts and jam sessions. | 405/282–1947.
**OCT.: *Oklahoma International Bluegrass Festival.*** Bluegrass performers from around the world perform in multiple venues around Guthrie. Nightly jam sessions are held at the campground just south of town. | 405/282–4446.
**NOV.–DEC.: *Territorial Christmas Celebration.*** This old-fashioned Christmas celebration includes a Victorian walk, Christmas parade, home tours, and performances of *A Territorial Christmas Carol,* a re-interpretation of the Dickens classic. | 405/282–1947.

## Dining

**Blue Belle Saloon.** American. This is the oldest operating saloon in Oklahoma (it's been open continuously since territorial days). Cowboy movie star Tom Mix tended bar here. The menu is limited, but, according to some, they've got the best steak in town. | 224 W. Harrison Ave. | 405/260–2355 | Closed Sun., Mon. | $8–$15 | AE, D, MC, V.

**Cafe Desarts.** Continental. This downtown restaurant is housed in an 1890s building, and the walls are hung with works by local and international artists. For lunch, try the potato or brie soups, then the combination salad (fresh fruit, chicken salad, and Mandarin orange–spinach salad). For supper, the rotating menu may include chateaubriand with cognac mustard sauce, pecan-encrusted chicken with hazelnut liqueur cream sauce, or pork tenderloin with apricots. Finish off your meal with Swiss custard plum pie (made with fresh plums, cooked and added to an almond crust pastry and egg custard, and served with cream). | 112 E. Oklahoma St. | 405/282–6400 | Closed Mon.–Wed., Sun. | $13–$17 | AE, DC, MC, V.

**Granny Had One.** American. Hearty sandwiches served on the signature dill bread, salads, chicken, steaks, and homemade baked goods are available in this storefront, antiques-filled restaurant. | 113 W. Harrison Ave. | 405/282–4482 | No dinner Sun.–Wed. | $10–$15 | AE, D, MC, V.

**Stables Café.** American. Housed in a rustic building that served as a livery stable in the 1890s, this restaurant is packed with vintage photographs and advertising memorabilia. Signature dishes include rib and chicken dinners. Salad bar. Kids' menu. | 223 N. Division St. | 405/282–0893 | $6–$12 | AE, D, DC, MC, V.

## Lodging

**Best Western Territorial Inn.** This hotel is backed by a wooded area and has oak furniture throughout. It's 30 minutes north of Oklahoma City, and 4–5 mi from museums, antique shops, malls, and restaurants. Restaurant, bar, complimentary Continental breakfast, cable TV, pool, pets allowed. | 2323 Territorial Dr. | 405/282–8831 | www.bestwestern.com | 84 rooms | $57–$65 | AE, D, DC, MC, V.

**Byrd House Bed and Breakfast.** This small, charming, 1905 Dutch Colonial B&B has china pieces and vintage hats (on walls, tables, and decorative hat-racks) throughout. Complimentary breakfast, cable TV, in-room VCRs, hot tub, massage. | 315 N. Maple St. | 405/282–7211 | bbonline.com/ok/byrdhouse | 2 rooms | $89–$95 | AE, D, DC, MC, V.

**Gold Penny Inn.** This handsome, two-story, white "Williamsburg"-style home feels more like an inn than a B&B. Breakfast is served in the adjoining Cowboy Tearoom, and includes hearty bacon-and-eggs, biscuits-and-gravy, and blueberry pancakes (the chef-owner can also accommodate certain dietary needs). Two of the three guest rooms are more romantic, but the "Cowboy Room", hung with branding irons, chaps, and "Wanted" posters, and furnished with an iron-canopy bed, is the most popular. Restaurant, cable TV, no room phones, outdoor hot tub, no pets, no kids under 10, no smoking. | 1421 W. Noble St. | 405/282–0678 or 877/837–4667 | greppond@mmcable.com | www.goldpennyinn.com | 3 rooms | $90–$150 | D, MC, V.

**Harrison House.** Rooms are filled with antiques in this downtown inn adjacent to the Pollard Theatre. Restaurant, complimentary Continental breakfast, TV in common area, business services. | 124 W. Harrison Ave. | 800/375–1001 or 405/282–1000 | fax 405/282–7091 | 30 rooms | $90 | AE, D, DC, MC, V.

**Heilman House.** Built from 1891–1895, this imposing cut-stone and brick Gothic Victorian home has distinctive architectural details, such as walnut and ash wood flooring, "keyhole" windows with stained glass, and transoms with hand-turned spindles. Each cozy guest room is furnished with Victorian antiques. The oak bed in the Heilman Suite is from the estate of General Douglas McArthur's wife's grandmother. Dining room, complimentary breakfast, no TV in some rooms, TV in common area, library, no pets, no smoking. | 401 E. Cleveland St. | 405/282–8431 or 888/900–1251 | fax 405/282–1509 | heilmnbb@swbell.net | home.swbell.net/heilmnbb/bed_and_breakfast.htm | 2 rooms, 1 suite | $85, $135 suite | D, MC, V.

**Railroad House.** Some rooms in this lovely two-story 1904 brick home have antique armoires and dressers, four-poster beds, and hooked rugs. Complimentary breakfast, some in-room VCRs. | 316 W. Vilas Ave. | 405/282–1827 | rhousebb@qwestinternet.net | 9 rooms in 2 buildings | $79–$119 | AE, D, MC, V.

**Sleep Inn.** Rooms are off of an interior corridor in this three-story hotel. Complimentary Continental breakfast, in-room data ports, some microwaves, some refrigerators, some in-room hot tubs, cable TV, pool, hot tub, laundry facilities, no pets. | 414 Heather St. | 450/260–1400 or 800/753–3746 | fax 450/260–1000 | www.sleepinn.com | 78 rooms | $60–$91 | AE, D, DC, MC, V.

**Victorian Garden Inn.** Built in 1908, this Colonial Revival home is surrounded by a white picket fence, has a wraparound porch, a garden retreat with a swing, and antiques throughout. One guest room has a fireplace. Complimentary breakfast, some in-room hot tubs, cable TV. | 324 S. Broad St. | 405/282–8211 or 888/792–1092 | victoriangardenbb.com | 4 rooms | $79–$119 | AE, D, DC, MC, V.

**Victorian Rose Bed and Breakfast.** This two-story, Queen Anne–style 1894 home has original gas-light fixtures, stained-glass windows and lamps, a wraparound porch, and a garden. Guest rooms are done in an opulent Victorian-style, with antique furniture and wall coverings. Complimentary breakfast. | 415 E. Cleveland Ave. | 405/282–3928 | 3 rooms | $69–$88 | D, MC, V.

# GUYMON

MAP 4, C3

*(Nearby town also listed: Boise City)*

James K. Hitch built a sod house in the area in the 1880s, beginning what was to become a ranching empire. Guymon itself was established when a railroad line was extended south from Kansas (E. T. Guymon, a Kansan, sold townsites). Ranching, oil and gas, cattle-feed lots, and recent (and controversial) hog farms fuel the local economy. With 10,000 residents, Guymon is by far the largest town in the Panhandle and holds the region's only concentration of motels and restaurants. Be sure to call well in advance for overnight accommodations.

Information: **Guymon Chamber of Commerce** | Rte. 5, Box 120, Guymon, OK 73942-4708 | 580/338–3376 | fax 580/338–0014.

## Attractions

**Hitchin' Post Ranch.** You can visit this cattle ranch for the day, or stay overnight in the limited accommodations. Ride horseback or on a stagecoach, or take a three-day cattle drive and camp out in the open and eat off chuck wagons. The canyonland near Black Mesa (the highest point of land in Oklahoma at 4,973 ft, and just 3 mi from the ranch) is perhaps the most beautiful part of the state. | Rte. 325, Kenton, 100 mi west of Guymon | 580/261–7424 | cowboy@ptsi.net | Guided horseback riding: $10 per hour; 3-day cattle drives: $600 per person | Ranch: daily dawn to dusk. Cattle drives: by appointment.

**No Man's Land Museum.** Panhandle history—from prehistoric times through Dust Bowl days—is chronicled via an eclectic collection, which includes alabaster carvings and a stuffed two-headed calf. | Panhandle State University, 207 W. Sewell St. | 580/349–2670 | Free | Tues.–Sat. 9–5.

**Sunset Lake.** This 32-acre lake is surrounded by a park that has a fishing dock, a miniature train, picnic areas, paddleboats, and playgrounds. | Thompson Park, off 5th St. | 580/338–2178 | Free | Daily.

### ON THE CALENDAR
**MAY: *Pioneer Days Celebration*.** A celebration honoring Panhandle pioneers, including the largest Professional Rodeo Cowboys Association–sanctioned rodeo in the state, a parade, cookouts, an arts and crafts fair, and a chuckwagon breakfast. | 580/338–5838.
**JULY: *Fourth of July Celebration*.** Fireworks and games for the kids are held at Sunset Lake. | 580/338–2178.

Carnival, food booths, horseshoe tournament, and an antique tractor pull, plus commercial booths and livestock shows. | Texas County Fairgrounds, 5th and Sunset Sts. | 580/338–5446.

## Dining

**Eddie's Steakhouse.** Steak. This old-fashioned bar and restaurant has decades-old red-and-black decor and serves hand-cut steaks. | Village Shopping Center | 580/338–5330 | Closed Sun. No lunch | $16–$21 | AE, D, DC, MC, V.

**Leann's.** American. This popular restaurant has been in operation for three decades. Home-style lunch and dinner specials are served in the large dining room or three large party rooms. Known for cube steak and barbecue beef on a bun. | 205 S.E. 2nd St. | 580/338–8025 | $7–$8 | No credit cards.

**Pancake House.** American. Diners can choose from a full range of waffles and pancakes at this popular breakfast joint. Try the "Dutch Baby," a custardlike pancake dusted with powdered sugar and lemon. | 4th St. and U.S. 54 | 580/338–2747 | Breakfast also available. No supper Fri.–Wed. | $5–$6 | D, DC, MC, V.

**Sunset Restaurant.** American. White tablecloths and a banquet room add to the elegance of this relaxing restaurant on the perimeter of Sunset Park. Known for seafood, beef, chicken. | 6000 Sunset Dr. | 580/338–4574 | Closed Mon. | $12–$17 | AE, D, MC, V.

**Yesterday's Diner.** American/Casual. This diner revels in 1950s memorabilia and music (the jukebox is free). Known for hamburgers. | 1901 U.S. 64 | 580/338–5813 | $5–$10 | No credit cards.

## Lodging

**Ambassador Inn.** This motel was built in 1978 and sits in a quiet neighborhood at the end of town, across from a movie theater and 1 mi from a golf course. Restaurant, bar with dancing, cable TV, pool, business services, pets allowed. | U.S. 64N at 21st St. | 580/338–5555 | fax 580/338–1784 | 70 rooms | $53 | AE, D, DC, MC, V.

**Econo Lodge.** Affordable accommodations near area restaurants and golf. Cable TV, business services, pets allowed. | 923 U.S. 54 E | 580/338–5431 | fax 580/338–0554 | 40 rooms | $42 | AE, D, DC, MC, V.

**Super 8.** The larger, executive rooms have recliners and more amenities in this two-story motel on the northeast end of town. The large parking lot has truck parking. Complimentary Continental breakfast, in-room data ports, some microwaves, some refrigerators, cable TV, some in-room hot tubs, laundry facilities, business services, pets allowed. | 1201 Rte. 54E | 580/338–0507 or 800/800–8000 | 59 rooms | $40–$88 | AE, D, DC, MC, V.

**Willows Inn Bed and Breakfast.** This B&B is a nice find in a town with limited accommodations. The ranch-style home has both ground-level and second floor rooms, a gazebo, a large covered patio, and a sun patio. Dining room, complimentary breakfast, cable TV, laundry facilities, laundry service, business services, no smoking. | E. Rte. 3, 1/4 mi east of MM 32 | 580/338–1303 | dkidwell@guymon.net | 3 rooms (2 with shared bath) | $65–$95 | AE, D, MC, V.

# HENRYETTA

*(See Okmulgee)*

# HOMINY

MAP 4, J3

*(Nearby towns also listed: Pawhuska, Pawnee, Tulsa)*

One of three towns originally settled by Osage clans, Hominy is now distinguished by the more than two dozen large murals painted on its vintage redbrick buildings by local artist Cha Tullis, most with Native American themes. The murals have brought tourists to Hominy, supplementing its ranching- and oil-based economy.

Information: **Hominy Chamber of Commerce** | 300 W. Main St., Hominy, OK 74035-1036 | 918/885–4939.

## Attractions

**Drummond Home.** The family of a former mayor and leading merchant donated this 1905 three-story Victorian home filled with original furnishings to the Oklahoma Historical Society. Displays of turn-of-the-20th-century household records and personal items such as hair pomades make the home unusually evocative of the era. | 305 N. Price St. | 918/885–2374 | Free; donations accepted | Fri.–Sat. 9–5, Sun. 1–5.

### ON THE CALENDAR

**JUNE:** *I-Lon-Shka Dances.* Annual ceremonial dances bring Osage dancers from all over the country. No photographs. | 918/287–2495.

## Dining

**Hominy Diner.** American. This downtown diner has the customary neon signs and dishes such as biscuits and eggs and Little Adam burgers (named after the owner's son) are popular. | 111 W. Main St. | 918/885–2315 | Breakfast also available. Closed Mon. No supper | $3–$7 | MC, V.

**Silver Dollar Cafe.** Steak. Located in what was formerly a railroad passenger depot, this café is decorated with country accents and antiques. The space is shared with the local Chamber of Commerce. Known for its generous portions, including huge cinnamon rolls. | 300 W. Main St. | 918/885–4668 | $8–$15 | MC, V.

## Lodging

**Budget Z Motel.** The largest of this motel's modest rooms has two queen-size beds, a pull-out, full-size futon, and a separate living area. There's plenty of parking space, a restaurant is across the street, and a movie theater, roller rink, and Keystone Lake are each less than 2 mi away. Picnic area, some microwaves, some refrigerators, cable TV, playground, business services, pets allowed. | 1209 W. Caddo St., Cleveland | 918/358–3591 | fax 918/358–2441 | 20 rooms | $37–$50 | AE, D, DC, MC, V.

# HUGO

MAP 4, K7

*(Nearby towns also listed: Atoka, Durant, Idabel)*

Southeastern Oklahoma's logging industry helped make this town of 6,000 a railroad center in the early part of the 20th century, and the area's mild climate and good transportation in turn made it a popular winter quarters for traveling circuses. From the 1940s through the 1960s, five circuses made their home in Hugo.

Information: **Hugo Chamber of Commerce** | 200 S. Broadway St., Hugo, OK 74743-4626 | 580/326–7511.

## Attractions

**Frisco Depot Museum.** The two-story brick depot holds an eclectic collection of local artifacts—a scale model of a local five-ring traveling circus, a moonshine still—along with railroad memorabilia and an original Harvey House restaurant. The depot is home to the Hugo Heritage Railroad, an excursion train that operates from spring through fall. | 309 North B St. | 580/326–6630 | Museum free; fees for excursion train | Apr.– Dec., Mon.–Sat. 9–3.

**Hugo Lake.** Sand bass, crappie, and catfish fill 13,500-acre Hugo Lake; fishing docks, a marina, and camping and picnic grounds are found on its wooded shores. | U.S. 70, 8 mi east of Hugo | 580/326–3345 | Free | Daily.

**Mt. Olivet Cemetery.** Members of local circuses are buried in a special section marked "Under God's Big Top." Some monuments are shaped like circus tents and engraved with dancing elephants or unusual epitaphs such as "There's Nothing Left But Empty Popcorn Sacks and Wagon Tracks. The Circus is Gone." | Trice and S. 8th Sts. | 580/326–7511 | Free | Daily.

**Raymond Gary State Park.** On the shores of Lake Raymond Gary, this tranquil park has a limited number of RV campsites, dozens of primitive campsites, picnic areas, a fishing dock, and a swimming beach. | U.S. 70, 7 mi west of Hugo | 580/873–2307 | www.tourokla-homa.com | Free | Daily.

### ON THE CALENDAR

**AUG.: *Grant's Bluegrass and Old-Time Music Festival.*** The oldest bluegrass festival west of the Mississippi draws bands and fans from all over the country for shows and jam sessions. | 580/326–5598.

**APR.–DEC.: *Hugo Heritage Railroad.*** Excursion train departs from the historic downtown depot on Saturdays. | 580/326–6630.

## Dining

**Cedar Shed.** Barbecue. Cedar Shed barbecue is the signature dish here, but there are great steaks and hush puppies, too. Known for beef, pork, and chicken barbecue, plus traditional side dishes of potato salad, coleslaw, and baked beans, as well as iced tea, homemade pie, and cobbler. Kids' menu. | U.S. 271 S | 580/326–7282 | Closed Sun. | $7–$13 | AE, D, DC, MC, V.

**Harvey House.** American. Restored 1940s-era trains depart from the adjacent working rail platform every Sat., bound for Antlers, Fort Towson, or Paris, TX. The restaurant's two dining areas (one was the station's luggage area, the other the cash room for a Wells-Fargo bank in town) have huge, sliding-panel doors, redbrick walls, wooden floors, and high ceilings. Try the chicken-fried steak made with Angus beef and served with homemade mashed potatoes; grilled pork chops with vegetables; or chicken pasta alfredo (grilled chicken served over fettucini with alfredo sauce, topped with broccoli spears and tomato). | 300 W. B St. | 580/326–6630 | No supper Sun. | $5–$14 | AE, D, MC, V.

## Lodging

**Hugo Inn.** This homey roadside motel is for extended stays. It's on the east side of town and within walking distance of downtown. Each room has two full beds and spacious tile baths. Microwaves, refrigerators, cable TV. | 1006 E. Jackson St. | 580/326–4846 | fax 580/326–2670 | 16 rooms | $225 (7–day minimum stay) | AE, D, DC, MC, V.

**Old Johnson House.** This two-story white frame house on a shady street has cabbage-rose fabrics and wallpaper and antiques, many original to the 1910 house. Complimentary breakfast, no smoking, no room phones, no TV in rooms, TV in common area, kids over 12 only. | 1101 E. Kirt St. | 580/326–8111 | 6 rooms, 1 cottage | $60–65, $60 cottage | AE, D, MC, V.

**Village Inn.** This one–story motel was built in 1961. It's 1 mi from Mt. Olivet Cemetery and 25 mi from Fort Towson. Restaurant, cable TV, pool, business services. | 610 W. Jackson St. | 580/326–3333 | villageinn@1starnet.com | 50 rooms | $44–$47 | AE, D, MC, V.

# IDABEL

*(Nearby town also listed: Broken Bow)*

This town of 8,000 was founded in 1903 with the arrival of the Choctaw and Arkansas Railroad, and named for a railroad executive's two daughters, Ida and Belle. The area had been settled since the 1830s by members of the Choctaw Nation. Today the logging industry provides many of the area's jobs.

Information: **Idabel Chamber of Commerce** | 13 N. Central Ave., Idabel, OK 74745-4647 | 580/286–3305 | fax 580/286–6708 | www.real-estates.com/idabel.

## Attractions

**Barnes-Stevenson House.** The county's first judge following statehood built this two-story Victorian home in 1912. Furnishings are a mixture of French, Spanish, and locally crafted antiques. Call to arrange a tour. | 310 S.E. Adams St. | 580/286–6314 | Donation | By appointment.

**Museum of the Red River.** Local prehistory and early Native American history are showcased in this excellent small museum, which holds examples of Caddoan pottery dating back to AD 700. More recent Choctaw history is illustrated with a re-creation of an Indian Territory–era cabin. The museum also includes Native American pottery, baskets, and fabrics collected in North and South America. | 812 E. Lincoln Rd. | 580/286–3616 | Free | Tues.–Sat. 10–5.

### ON THE CALENDAR

**APR.:** *Dogwood Days.* Arts, crafts, and food booths fill an eight-block area downtown for this annual spring festival. Other events include a soap-box derby, a bicycle race, a chili cook-off, and children's games. | 580/286–3305.

**OCT.:** *Fall Fest.* This one-day celebration of autumn includes live entertainment, a chili cook-off, arts and crafts vendors, and a children's art zone (a special tent with a variety of crafts for kids). | 580/286–3305.

## Dining

**Avenue A.** Cafés. This tiny coffee shop with a black-and-white tile floor offers plenty of homemade soups and sandwiches as well as a nice selection of gourmet coffees and flavored teas. Known for espresso, lattes, and other coffees, along with a daily soup, sandwich, and salad lunch special. | 101 S.E. Avenue A | 580/286–5546 | Closed Sat.–Mon. No dinner | $5–$7 | No credit cards.

**Cedar Shed II.** Barbecue. Most regulars come to this country-and-western–style spot for the best-selling chicken-fried steak, beer-battered fries, or Indian tacos (meat, beans, cheese, lettuce, and tomatoes served open-faced on homemade fry bread). Save room for the popular homemade cream pies, or take a slice to go. Salad bar. | 2015 S.E. Washington St. | 580/286–7334 | Closed Sun. | $2–$13 | AE, D, DC, MC, V.

## Lodging

**Holiday Inn.** This two-story hotel is within 25 mi of several lakes and Beavers Bend Resort Park. Restaurant, bar (with entertainment), room service, in-room data ports, cable TV, in-room VCRs, pool, business services. | Box 1498 | 580/286–6501 | fax 580/286–7482 | www.holiday-inn.com | 99 rooms | $74 | AE, D, DC, MC, V.

**Spaulding-Olive House Bed and Breakfast.** Listed on the National Register of Historic Places, this B&B served as home to a federal judge from 1912–1917, a former mayor from 1917–1946, and a prominent landowner from 1946–1974. The 1912 Southern Colonial clapboard home has a pillared dual-level porch in front, and a second-story veranda overlooking mature oaks in the back. A shade garden includes a fishpond and stone patio, and the snug private cottage is nicely outfitted for longer stays. Dining room, picnic area, complimentary breakfast, some kitchenettes, some microwaves, some refrigerators, cable TV, no room phones, TV in common area, library, no kids under 16, no smoking. | 601 S.E. Adams St. | 580/208-2144 | bedandb@yahoo.com | 3 rooms, 1 cottage | $45-$75, $75 cottage | D, MC, V.

# LAWTON

*(Nearby towns also listed: Duncan, Medicine Park)*

Lawton, Oklahoma's fourth-largest city, was founded on August 6, 1901, when the Kiowa-Comanche reservation was opened for settlement by drawing lots. The townsite was surveyed just south of Fort Sill, which was established in 1869 by Major Philip Sheridan as a strategic base for "controlling" the Plains Indians. Many of Lawton's residents are in the armed forces. The town is also home to Cameron University.

**Information: Lawton/Fort Sill Chamber of Commerce and Industry** | 607 C Ave., Lawton, OK 73501-4301 | 580/355-3541 | fax 580/357-3642.

## Attractions

**Fort Sill Military Reservation.** The site for Fort Sill was selected by Randolph Scott, an army captain and explorer who called the spot "the most beautiful and romantic valley I've ever seen." The fort stands on the bluffs above Medicine Creek and holds a number of restored historic buildings. | U.S. 277, Fort Sill, 5 mi east of downtown Lawton | 580/442-8111 | Free | Daily.

**Chief's Knoll at Post Cemetery.** This small cemetery holds the grave of Geronimo, as well as those of Comanche chief Quanah Parker and Kiowa chiefs Santana and Satank. | McComb Rd. | 580/442-5123 | Free | Daily.

**Old Post Headquarters and Visitors Center.** The fort's original headquarters now serves as a museum office and resource library; next door is an 1875 stone building erected first as a supply warehouse and later used as a barracks. Exhibits trace the history of the fort from its years as a base of operations for the Indian Wars through World War I. Southern Plains tribal history is also featured, and there is a children's area as well. A display of heavy artillery dating from 1600 to the present can be seen along the **Cannon Walk.**

The **Old Guardhouse,** also known as "Geronimo's Guardhouse," is an 1873 stone structure that held Geronimo, the Chiricahua-Apache medicine man, on several occasions after the Apache band was brought to Fort Sill. The main floor and basement cells hold exhibits on the Comanche, Kiowa, and Apache tribes, as well as on 19th-century cavalry and foot soldiers. (Bldg. 336, Randolph Rd. | 580/442-6570 | Free | Daily)

Since 1875, services have been conducted continuously at the **Old Post Chapel.** Over the years, the structure has been used as both a church and a school. (Bldg. 425, Chickasha Rd. | 580/442-6570)

**Mattie Beal Home.** Mattie Beal was a 22-yr-old telephone operator from Kansas when she drew the No. 2 ticket in the Kiowa-Comanche lottery, securing for herself the right to prime real estate. Beal and her husband built this Greek Revival home in 1910 and filled it with such details as stained-glass windows depicting the nearby Wichita Mountains. | 1006 S.W. 5th St. | 580/353-6884 | $2 | Afternoon of 2nd Sun. each month.

**Museum of the Great Plains.** Dedicated to the culture and natural history of the Great Plains, the museum's exhibits range from a mammoth skull unearthed in a nearby county, to farm tools and pioneer artifacts and the contents of an Indian-owned store that operated in Anadarko for nearly a century. | Elmer Thomas Park, 601 Ferris Blvd. | 580/581-3460 | www.sirnet.net/~mgp | $2 | Daily.

**Percussive Arts Society Museum.** Marimbas, bells, chimes, xylophones, vibraphones, and drums collected from around the world are on display at this museum. The hands-on section is fun for all ages. | Elmer Thomas Park, 701 N.W. Ferris Blvd. | 580/353–1455 | www.pas.org | $1 | Weekdays 8–5; weekends and holidays 1–4.

### ON THE CALENDAR

**MAR.–APR.: *Easter Sunday Pageant.*** The nation's longest-running Passion play is set in the 110-acre "Holy City of the Wichitas," a stage built by the W.P.A. from locally quarried granite. | 580/429–3361.

**MAY: *Art For All Festival.*** Fine artists and craftspeople present their work in Shepler Plaza in a juried show and sale during this three-day event. Amateur groups and professional headliners provide musical, dance, and other entertainment, and local artists teach hands-on workshops to children aged 5–10, showing them how to make pottery, baskets, or sculptures. Proceeds from the event help support local arts groups of all disciplines. | 580/248–5384.

**AUG.: *International Festival.*** The cultural diversity brought to Lawton by nearby Fort Sill Military Reservation is celebrated with ethnic entertainment, food, and an international bazaar. | 580/581–3470.

## Dining

**Fishermen's Cove.** Cajun/Creole. Established in 1971, this restaurant at the foot of the Wichita Mountains serves Cajun-style cuisine. Hand-cut Black Angus steak and complimentary hors d'oeuvres on Wed. and Thurs. are favorite eats. Kids' menu. | Rte. 49, 2 mi west of I–44 | 580/529–2672 | Closed Mon., Tues. No lunch Wed.–Sat. | $8–$12 | AE, D, MC, V.

**Martin's.** Seafood. The lounge has mahogany walls and furnishings, and the dining room's walls have either mirrors, wood, or wallpaper. A pianist plays three nights a week. Choose from a wide range of seafood dishes, from shrimp scampi and salmon steak, to lobster and raw oysters. Steak is another mainstay on the menu. Kids' menu. | 2107 N.W. Cache Rd. | 580/353–5286 | Closed Sun., Mon. No lunch | $13–$19 | AE, D, DC, MC, V.

**Meers Store.** American. This eatery and a federal seismographic station by the register are all that's left of a boomtown that grew up during a brief gold rush in 1901. The restaurant's claim to fame is not gold but the Meersburger—a 7-inch burger made of 100 percent longhorn beef. | Rte. 115, Meers | 580/429–8051 | Breakfast also available | $4–$12 | No credit cards.

**Salas.** Mexican. Founded in 1952, this was Lawton's first Mexican restaurant. It's casual look includes an open kitchen, booths, and a long bar with stools. | 111 W. Lee Blvd. | 580/357–1600 | Closed Mon., Tues. | $6–$10 | AE, D, DC, MC, V.

## Lodging

**Days Inn.** This two–story motel is about ¼ mi from shops and restaurants. Complimentary Continental breakfast, some refrigerators, cable TV, 2 pools, hot tub, business services, airport shuttle, pets allowed. | 3110 N.W. Cache Rd. | 580/353–3104 or 800/241–3952 | fax 580/353–0992 | 96 rooms | $48 | AE, D, DC, MC, V.

**Howard Johnson Hotel and Convention Center.** The public areas of this low-rise stucco hotel just off I–44 include diverse ornaments like Victorian-style frosted glass and a rustic chandelier of antlers. Restaurant, bar (with entertainment), room service, in-room data ports, some microwaves, some refrigerators, some in-room hot tubs, cable TV, 2 pools, sauna, tennis, exercise equipment, laundry service, business services. | 1125 E. Gore Blvd. | 580/353–0200 or 800/539–0020 | fax 580/353–6801 | hojolawt@sirinet.net | www.hojo.com | 145 rooms | $53–$140 | AE, D, DC, MC, V.

**Ramada Inn.** This chain hotel has a lovely courtyard, pool, and patio. A huge park with a new bike track is across the street and shopping is within 5 to 10 minutes. Restaurant, bar, room service, cable TV, pool, business services, pets allowed. | 601 N. 2nd St. | 580/355–7155 | fax 580/353–6162 | 98 rooms | $44–$54 | AE, D, DC, MC, V.

**SpringHill Suites.** This all-suites property is good for extended stays. Rooms have well-lit desks and swivel chairs. It's a few blocks from downtown and a restaurant and lounge are

next door. Complimentary Continental breakfast, in-room data ports, microwaves, refrigerators, cable TV, pool, hot tub, exercise equipment, laundry facilities, laundry service,
business services, no pets. | 3 S.E. Interstate Dr. | 580/248–8500 or 888/287–9400 | fax 580/
248–3256 | www.springhillsuites.com/lawsh/ | 80 suites | $65–$85 | AE, D, DC, MC, V.

# MARIETTA
*(See Ardmore)*

# MCALESTER

*(Nearby towns also listed: Atoka, Eufaula)*

Started as a tent store in 1870 and operated by James J. McAlester at the intersection
of the California Trail and the Texas Road Cattle Trail, McAlester became an established
town in 1899, after coal was discovered in the area a few years earlier. The land
belonged to the Choctaw Nation but was leased to mine owners who imported much
of their labor force from Italy. The mines closed in the 1930s; however, the area's Italian heritage has endured. McAlester has a population of 20,000.

Information: **McAlester Chamber of Commerce** | 10 S. 3rd St., McAlester, OK 74501-5319
| 918/423–2550 | fax 918/423–1345.

## Attractions
**McAlester Building Foundation.** Local artifacts and memorabilia, including pieces relat-
ing to the coal-mining industry, Native American history, and regional artists, are in the
old McAlester High School. | 220 E. Adams Ave. | 918/423–2932 | Free | Weekdays 8–2.

**Robbers Cave State Park.** Built around 100-ft sandstone cliffs in the San Bois Mountains,
this park has four lakes, equestrian trails, RV, tent, and equestrian campgrounds, stables,
a lodge, cabins, a swimming pool, a nature center, and hiking trails. The park's namesake
cave is rumored to have been a hideout for outlaws after the Civil War. | Rte. 2, 35 mi east
of McAlester | 918/465–2562 | www.touroklahoma.com | Free | Daily.

### ON THE CALENDAR
**MAY: *Italian Festival.*** Italian food, arts and crafts, and games draw a fun-loving crowd.
| 918/426–2055.
**JUNE: *Sanders Family Bluegrass Festival.*** Amateur and professional country and
bluegrass acts come from across the nation to participate in this lively festival. | 918/
423–4891.

## Dining
**Isle of Capri.** Italian. This cozy restaurant was built in 1950 to resemble a private home.
Walls are painted a warm tan color and the roof is brown shingled. Try the toasted ravi-
oli with olives, peppers, and olive oil. Kids' menu. | 150 S.W. 7th St., Krebs | 918/423–3062 |
Closed Sun. No lunch | $7–$18 | AE, D, MC, V.

**Janalynn's Tea Room.** American. This antiques-filled spot is housed in a 1920s bakery near
the center of town. Staples as well as rotating specials are on the menu, and the blue plate
is usually a casserole and salad, such as chicken spaghetti with spinach salad (made with
fresh spinach, mushrooms, hard-boiled eggs, bacon, and the house vinaigrette). Other choices
may include the corn bread salad (with bell peppers, onions, tomatoes, and celery in a creamy
dressing) or soups such as baked potato or spinach cheese. Save room for homemade pies

such as strawberry, chocolate icebox, or lemon sour cream. | 324 E. Carl Albert Pkwy. (U.S. 270) | 918/423–4183 | Closed weekends. No supper | $2–$6 | No credit cards.

★ **Pete's Place.** Italian. This restaurant serves a now-legal variation of the once illicit "Choc beer," (a wheat brew that was allegedly introduced to Italian settlers in the nearby town of Krebs by local Choctaw Indians) and family-style portions of traditional Italian fare such as lasagna, pasta, and gnocchi. Kids' menu. | 120 S.W. 8th St., Krebs | 918/423–2042 | No lunch Mon.–Sat. | $9–$17 | AE, D, DC, MC, V.

**Trolley's.** Cajun/Creole. Several small dining rooms are decked out with vintage movie posters from such classics as *Gone with the Wind*. Autographed shots of stars abound, and the carpet is actually from an old movie theater. Known for prime rib and seafood, especially its all-you-can-eat catfish dinner. Kids' menu. | 21 E. Monroe St. | 918/423–2446 | Closed Sun., Mon. | $6–$22 | AE, D, DC, MC, V.

## Lodging

**Belle Starr View Lodge.** Rooms have sliding glass doors that afford a spectacular view of a valley in Robbers Cave State Park. Breakfast (not included in the rates) requires a bit of a hike (¾ mi) to the park restaurant. Restaurant, no room phones, lake, miniature golf, horseback riding, boating, playground, no pets. | Rte. 2, 32 mi east of McAlester | 918/465–2562 or 800/654–8240 | fax 928/465–5763 | 20 rooms | $78 | AE, D, DC, MC, V.

**Best Western Inn of McAlester.** You can curl up in comfortable wing-back chairs or spread out your work on large desks at this hotel. For relaxation, you can swim in the Olympic-size swimming pool. Restaurant, complimentary Continental breakfast, some refrigerators, cable TV, pool, business services, pets allowed. | 1215 George Nigh Expressway | 918/426–0115 | fax 918/426–3634 | 61 rooms | $52 | AE, D, DC, MC, V.

**Days Inn.** Try a room facing the indoor pool at this motel 5 mi north of the Municipal Airport. Restaurant, bar, room service, some refrigerators, cable TV, in-room VCRs (and movies), pool, hot tub, business services, pets allowed. | 1217 George Nigh Expressway | 918/426–5050 | 100 rooms | $54–$69 | AE, D, DC, MC, V.

**Holiday Inn Express Hotel and Suites.** Built in 1999, this all-suites hotel is a welcome addition in a town that hasn't had a new hotel since the 1960s. Rooms have two data ports, and some have special filtration systems that rid the air of allergens. Restaurant, complimentary Continental breakfast, in-room data ports, microwaves, refrigerators, some in-room hot tubs, cable TV, pool, hot tub, exercise equipment, laundry facilities, business services, pets allowed (fee). | 650 S. George Nigh Expressway | 918/302–0001 | fax 918/302–0002 | express@gxmi.com | 80 suites | $79–$129 suites | AE, D, DC, MC, V.

**Hotel Stuart.** This 1899 hotel has an attic suite (where Pretty Boy Floyd allegedly hid out in the 1930s), and a soda fountain on the first floor. Guest rooms are furnished with antiques and named after significant people in Oklahoma history. Restaurant, complimentary breakfast, some in-room hot tubs, no room phones, no TV in rooms, TV in common area, no smoking. | U.S. 270 at Roosevelt St., Stuart | 918/546–2591 or 918/546–2142 | 9 rooms (8 with shared bath) | $50–$70 | AE, V.

**Ramada Inn.** The indoor recreation dome has something for everyone—from fitness buffs to those looking for personal pampering. Extensive renovations conducted in 1997–98 added more in-room amenities. Restaurant, bar, room service, in-room data ports, refrigerators, cable TV, pool, hot tub, sauna, miniature golf, gym, video games, laundry facilities, business services, pets allowed. | 1500 George Nigh Expressway | 918/423–7766 | fax 918/426–0068 | 161 rooms | $48–$65 | AE, D, DC, MC, V.

**Windsong Inn.** Individually decorated rooms have various antique pieces in this 1907 three-story house. There is a stunning view of the Winding Stair Mountains, and three additional rooms will overlook a dramatic cliff upon completion, which is expected in spring 2001. Restaurant (weekends only), complimentary breakfast, no room phones, no TV in room, TV in common area. | 100 W. Cedar St., Wilburton | 918/465–5174 | 3 rooms | $60–$80 | No credit cards.

# MEDICINE PARK

*(Nearby towns also listed: Altus, Duncan, Lawton)*

Medicine Park began as a resort community in the 1920s, and structures in this tiny, historic town are built from native grapefruit-size granite cobblestone quarried in the nearby Wichita Mountains. It foundered after World War II, but has recently been making a comeback. Although there are as yet only a handful of shops and restaurants, the town's beautiful setting makes it a popular stop for area visitors.

**Information: Medicine Park Town Hall** | Eastlake Dr., Medicine Park 73557 | 580/529–2825.

## Attractions

**Cobblestone Village.** Downtown Medicine Park booms with art galleries, craft stores, a coffee shop, an ice cream parlor, and more. | Main St., downtown | 580/529–2825 | Free | Tues.–Sun.

**Medicine Park Music Hall.** This restored 1920s music hall hosts Western, swing, and bluegrass bands. You can pay a little extra to have a heap of barbecued beef or chicken before the show starts. | 343 E. Lake Dr. | 580/529–2511 | fax 580/529–2511 | www.medicinepark.com | $10 | Wed.–Sun. 11:30–9.

★ **Wichita Mountains Wildlife Refuge.** This 60,000-acre national refuge is the second-most-visited wildlife refuge in the United States. It straddles 600-million-year-old granite mountains, the oldest in North America. Highlights include bison, deer, elk, longhorn cattle, hiking trails, mountain biking paths, a nature center and programs, fishing lakes, campgrounds, and backcountry camping by permit. | Rtes. 49 and 115 | 580/429–3222 | Free | Daily; Visitor Center Wed.–Mon. 10–5:30.

### ON THE CALENDAR

**FEB.: *Polar Bear Plunge.*** Winter is celebrated with a dive into the frigid waters of Medicine Creek. | 580/529–2825.

## Dining

**Katie Rose.** Contemporary. This restaurant is on an 80-acre estate of hills and trees, and celebrates local tastes and interests; Native American arts and crafts surround the perimeter of the dining room, and locally grown produce is featured on the eclectic menu. Favorites include Black Angus T-bone steak served with new potatoes and broccoli with white wine, butter, and dill sauce, and the Mediterranean chicken salad (mixed greens, black olives, feta cheese, tomatoes, cucumbers, and grilled chicken breast in a balsamic vinaigrette). Dessert-lovers may want to try the Oklahoma mud pie (coffee ice cream with hot fudge in an Oreo cookie crust). | Rte. 49 | 580/529–3322 | Closed Wed. | $8–$15 | MC, V.

**Plantation Restaurant.** American. Once a landmark hotel, this restaurant is filled with decades worth of memorabilia. The owners claim that Bonnie and Clyde and Pretty Boy Floyd were once customers. Known for hamburgers, steaks, and chicken-fried steak. | Eastlake Dr. | 580/529–9641 | Closed Mon. | $8–$10 | No credit cards.

**Riverside Café.** American. A deck overlooks Medicine Creek, and Maxfield Parrish–style murals are found throughout. Known for catfish, grilled chicken, salmon, shrimp pasta, espresso, and cappuccino. | 100 Eastlake Dr. | 580/529–2626 | Closed Mon., Tues. | $8–$18 | AE, D, DC, MC, V.

## Lodging

**Wild Goose Cottages.** These simple gems in a somewhat secluded area on Gondola Lake are ideal if you're exploring Wichita Mountain Wildlife Refuge, which is practically in the backyard. The cottages resemble small homes and include ceiling fans, queen-size beds, pullout queen sofas, hand-carved cedar tables that seat four, and working desks. Picnic area, some kitchenettes, some microwaves, some refrigerators, cable TV, in-room VCRs (and movies), lake, dock, boating, fishing, no pets, no smoking. | Northlake Dr. | 580/529–2182 | lhibbetts@lawtonnet.net | 3 cottages | $80–$100 | No credit cards.

# MIAMI

MAP 4, K2

*(Nearby towns also listed: Grove, Vinita)*

Built along the old Ozark Trail between the Spring and Neosho rivers that form the Grand Lake O' the Cherokees, Miami was named for the small Native American tribe that lived in the area in the 19th century. The Ozark Trail evolved into Route 66; many modern travelers looking to follow the historic highway start the Oklahoma portion of their trip in Miami. The town's slow pace of life and scenic setting have made it one of the fastest-growing retirement communities in the nation. Miami has a population of 14,000.

Information: **Miami Chamber of Commerce** | 111 N. Main St., Miami, OK 74354-6324 | 918/542–4481 | fax 918/542–4482.

## Attractions

**Coleman Theatre Beautiful.** This Spanish Mission–style vaudeville and movie theater was designed by the Boller Brothers and built in 1929 by George Coleman, a local mining tycoon. Its fanciful exterior is embellished with terra-cotta gargoyles; highlights of the restored red-and-gold Louis XV interior include stained-glass windows, carpets woven with a miner's pick and ax, and a Wurlitzer organ. | 103 N. Main St. | 918/540–2425, ext. 454 | Movies $5 | Tues.–Sat. 10–4, and by appointment.

**Dobson Museum.** Operated by the Ottawa County Historical Society, this museum contains Native American artifacts, pioneer artifacts, a mining display, and locally curated exhibits that change monthly. | 110 A St. SW | 918/542–5388 | Free | Wed., Fri., Sun. 1–4.

**Grand Lake O' the Cherokees.** (*See* Grove.) Miami was built between the Spring and Neosho rivers, which flow into Grand Lake. The less developed north end of the lake is in the foothills of the Ozark Mountains and is serenely scenic. | Rte. 125 follows the eastern shore, Rte. 10 the western shore. | 918/542–4481 | Free | Daily.

**Riverview Park.** This park on the banks of the Neosho River has picnic areas, walking paths, and a pool; the Ottawa County Fairgrounds adjoin the park's south end. | S. Main St. | 918/541–2288 | Free | Daily.

**Twin Bridges State Park.** The Neosho and Spring rivers converge in this quiet park, popular for fishing and bald eagle–watching. You'll also find rustic lake huts, an enclosed fishing dock, and tent and RV camping. | 14801 S. Rte. 137, Fairland | 918/540–2545 | www.touroklahoma.com | Free | Daily.

### ON THE CALENDAR

**JULY:** *Quapaw Powwow.* This powwow includes competitive and social dancing, arts and crafts booths, traditional food concessions, and more. | 918/542–1853.

## Dining

**Clubhouse at the Stables.** Continental. The Stables is an entertainment center with off-track betting, electronic gaming, and a bingo hall seating 500; the handsome, horse-themed Clubhouse restaurant is casual and roomy, and separated from the facility by an etched-glass partition. The rotating menu may include chicken radicchio, pan-seared red snapper, or Kansas City strip steak. Kids' menu. Sun. brunch. | 530 H St. SE | 918/542–7884 or 877/774–7884 | www.the-stables.com | Closed Mon. No supper Sun. | $8–$16 | D, MC, V.

**Montana Mike's.** Steak. Huge portions and a lodge atmosphere mark this member of the popular steak-house chain. Known for heaps of mashed potatoes, mountains of French fries, and 22-oz steaks. Family-style service. | 840 N. Main St. | 918/542–8808 | Closed Mon. | $8–$12 | MC, V.

**Townsman Restaurant.** American. This coffee shop and restaurant attached to a motel was built in the 1940s. Known for burgers, salads, fried chicken, steaks, pork chops, roast beef, ham, liver and onions, and all-day breakfasts. Homemade pies. | 910 Steve Owens St. | 918/542–5733 | Breakfast also available. No supper Sun. | $5–$9 | No credit cards.

## Lodging

**Best Western Inn of Miami.** This one-story stucco motel is surrounded by lush landscaped grounds. Restaurant, bar, room service, refrigerators, cable TV, pool, airport shuttle, pets allowed. | 2225 E. Steve Owens St. | 918/542–6681 | fax 918/542–3777 | www.bestwestern.com | 80 rooms | $59–$69 | AE, D, DC, MC, V.

**Townsman Motel.** This simple redbrick two-story motel is 2 mi west of the I–44 Turnpike gate. The Miami Golf and Country Club is 3 mi away, and adjacent Taylor Park has a playground. Restaurant, bar, room service, cable TV, laundry facilities, laundry service, pets allowed. | 900 E. Steve Owens Blvd. | 918/542–6631 | 72 rooms | $32–$46 | AE, D, MC, V.

# MUSKOGEE

MAP 4, K4

*(Nearby towns also listed: Eufaula, Tahlequah, Wagoner)*

The site of the 1874 "Union Agency," built to consolidate government services to the Five Civilized Tribes relocated to Oklahoma, Muskogee is eastern Oklahoma's second-largest city and a center for Native American history and culture. A paper plant, light manufacturing, Bacone College, and a river port fuel the economy of this town of 40,000.

Information: **Muskogee Convention and Tourism Bureau** | 425 Boston St., Muskogee, OK 74401-7516 | 918/684–6363 | tourism@azaleanet.com.

**Muskogee Tourist Information Center** | 2424 N. 32nd St., Muskogee, OK | 918/682–6751.

**Greater Muskogee Area Chamber of Commerce** | 2626 W. Okmulgee St., Muskogee, OK 74401-5152 | 918/682–2401 | fax 918/682–2403.

## Attractions

**Ataloa Art Lodge.** Built for (and by) Native American students at Bacone Indian College, this stone lodge is now a small museum displaying Native American art and artifacts, such as paintings, carvings, pottery, blankets, rugs, and kachina dolls. | 2299 Old Bacone Rd. | 918/683–4581 | $2 | Weekdays 8–4:30, weekends by appointment.

**Five Civilized Tribes Museum.** Housed in an imposing sandstone building that once held the Union Agency for the Five Civilized Tribes, this museum traces the history of the five tribes relocated to Indian Territory in the early 19th century. Its art collection features more than 800 paintings, sculptures, and other items, including the works of Jerome Tiger and Willard Stone. | 1101 Honor Heights Dr. | 918/683–1701 | fax 918/683–3070 | www.fivetribes.com | $2 | Mon.–Sat. 10–5, Sun. 1–5.

**Fort Gibson Historic Site.** The first frontier fort in Indian Territory, Fort Gibson was built in advance of the arrival of the Cherokee Nation in the 1830s and launched dozens of expeditions into what was then unmapped territory. Most fort buildings where living-history programs are held are reproductions, but the original brick bread ovens are fired up annually for Public Bake Day. | 907 N. Gibson | 918/478–4088 | fax 918/478–4908 | www.fortgibson.com | Free | Daily.

**Greenleaf Lake State Park.** This peaceful park in the Cookson Hills has a 1,000-acre lake, from which waterskiers and jet skis are banned. There are also an 18-mi-long hiking trail, tent and RV camping, a floating restaurant, a swimming pool, a nature center, cabins, and an enclosed and heated fishing dock. | Rte. 10, 3 mi south of Muskogee | 918/487–5196 | fax 918/487–5406 | www.touroklahoma.com | Free | Daily.

**Honor Heights Park.** A 122-acre park with stone walkways and 40 acres of gardens featuring roses, tulips, and especially azaleas, planted by the thousands. Also available are a gazebo, picnic pavilions, waterfalls, and the municipal swimming pool. | 641 Park Dr. | 918/684–6302 | Free | Daily.

**Lake Tenkiller State Park.** (*See* Tahlequah.) Limestone-lined Lake Tenkiller is a popular destination for scuba diving, boating, fishing, hiking, and camping. | Rte. 82 | 918/489–5641 | www.touroklahoma.com.

**U.S.S. Batfish.** This World War II submarine is docked in the Arkansas River; tours include the torpedo room and crew cabins. An artillery display and picnic area are just a few feet away. | 3500 Batfish Rd. | 918/682–6294.

### ON THE CALENDAR

**MAR.:** *Public Bake Day and 19th Century Dance Workshop.* Fort Gibson's original 19th-century brick ovens are fired up annually, and you're encouraged to cook your own dishes here. Nineteenth-century-dance lessons are offered while you wait for your meal. | 918/478–4088.

**APR.:** *Azalea Festival.* The bloom of millions of azalea blossoms is celebrated over the course of three weeks with a bicycle tour, a parade, and an arts and crafts fair. | 918/684–6302.

**SEPT.:** *Dusk 'Til Dawn Blues Festival.* National, regional, and local acts perform on two stages at a vintage festival in Rentiesville. | 918/473–2411.

## Dining

**Jasper's.** Continental. The exterior of this 1920s former grocery store retains its authentic appearance, but the inside has been updated with textured burgundy walls and an open ceiling with original wood beams. Jasper's specializes in steaks and seafood; try the signature pepper steak (beef tenderloin with peppercorn and mushroom gravy), shrimp scampi, (shrimp sautéed in garlic, butter, and white wine), or the Pier 39 salad (diced chicken breast, greens, avocado, hard-boiled egg, blue cheese, olives, and tomatoes with a choice of dressing). For dessert, try the Magnificent 7 (a seven-tier chocolate cake). | 1702 W. Okmulgee Ave. | 918/682–7867 | Closed Sun. | $9–$18 | AE, D, DC, MC, V.

**Miss Addie's Tea Room.** American. During lunch, hearty sandwiches, soups, and rich desserts are served in a tea room decorated with floral tablecloths and fresh floral arrangements. For supper, the mood changes, as you dine amid linen tablecloths and candlelight. The beef and pork tenderloins are popular, as are its fresh fish specials and savory sauces. Additional dining space and a small Irish pub were constructed in 2000. Brunch is served on Sat. and Sun. | 821 W. Broadway | 918/682–1506 | No supper Sun., Mon. | $10–$25 | AE, D, MC, V.

**Okie's.** American. This restaurant is furnished with antiques and is known for its prime rib and seafood. Family-style service. Kids' menu. | 219 S. 32nd St. | 918/683–1056 | Closed Sun. | $12–$20 | AE, D, DC, MC, V.

**Slick's.** Barbecue. A true Southern-style barbecue joint, with battered booths, linoleum floors, and hickory-smoked barbecue served on butcher paper. | 2329 W. Shawnee Ave. | 918/687–9215 | Closed Sun., Mon. | $5–$10 | No credit cards.

## Lodging

**Budget Inn.** Rooms have double or queen-size beds in this brick motel north of downtown, at the intersection of U.S. 62 and 69. Restaurants, Honor Heights Park, and a just-opened water park are within 5 mi of the motel. In–room data ports, some microwaves, some refrigerators, cable TV, business services. | 2604 W. Shawnee Bypass | 918/683–3393 | fax 918/686–8243 | 30 rooms | $33–$42 | AE, D, MC, V.

**Days Inn.** Cherokee Nation bingo, golf courses, shopping, and restaurants—from fast food to fine dining—are up the road from this one-story motel. Complimentary Continental breakfast, microwaves, some refrigerators, cable TV, in-room VCRs, pool, business services. | 900 S. 32nd St. | 918/683–3911 | fax 918/683–5744 | 43 rooms | $40–$64 | AE, D, DC, MC, V.

**Graham-Carroll House.** Once the home of an oil-company executive and his family, this Victorian Gothic mansion has a formal dining room, English gardens, and a conservatory. Suites are individually decorated with antique furniture and luxurious bed linens. Bar, dining room, complimentary breakfast, some in-room hot tubs, cable TV, no kids under 14. | 501 N. 16th St. | 918/683–0100 | www.bbonline.com/ok/grahamcarroll/ | 6 suites | $80–$110 | AE, D, DC, MC, V.

**Holiday Inn Express.** This two-story hotel is right off U.S. 69; it's within walking distance of Honor Heights Park and is less than 2 mi from Muskogee's restaurant row. Complimentary Continental breakfast, in-room data ports, some microwaves, some refrigerators, some in-room hot tubs, cable TV, pool, exercise equipment, laundry facilities, business services, no pets. | 3133 Azalea Park Dr. | 918/687–4224 | fax 918/683–4474 | 54 rooms | $69–$99 | AE, D, DC, MC, V.

**Ramada Inn.** This hotel's atrium has a pool, exercise equipment, and games. A golf course is five mi away. Restaurant, bar (with entertainment), microwaves, room service, cable TV, in-room VCRs, pool, hot tub, sauna, exercise equipment, video games, business services, pets allowed. | 800 S. 32nd St. | 918/682–4341 | fax 918/682–7400 | 135 rooms, 7 suites | $59, $95–$135 suites | AE, D, DC, MC, V.

**TraveLodge.** This motel is 1 mi west of Muskogee. Bar, in-room data ports, cable TV, pool, business services, pets allowed. | 534 S. 32nd St. | 918/683–2951 | 104 rooms | $50–$85 | AE, D, DC, MC, V.

# NORMAN

MAP 4, H5

*(Nearby towns also listed: Edmond, Oklahoma City, Pauls Valley)*

Oklahoma's third-largest city was settled during the 1889 Land Run. It is south of Oklahoma City, in the central part of the state. Today this city of 93,000 is home to the state's largest university, as well as a variety of museums, art galleries, restaurants, and other attractions.

**Information: Norman Convention and Visitors Bureau** | 224 W. Gray St., Suite 104, Norman, OK 73069-7109 | 800/767–7260 or 405/366–8095 | fax 405/366–8095 | ncvb@ncvb.org | www.ncvb.org.

## Attractions

**Cleveland County Historical Museum.** Located in the Moore-Lindsay House, an 1899 Queen Anne–style residence, this museum is filled with period furniture and illustrates upper-middle class life in Oklahoma Territory. | 508 N. Peters Ave. | 405/321–0156 | Free | Weekdays 1–4, and by appointment.

**Fred Jones Jr. Museum of Art.** This museum's permanent collection includes post-1945 American paintings, photography, graphic arts, ceramics, and Native American art. Traveling exhibits are also scheduled throughout the year. | 410 W. Boyd St. | 405/325–3272 | Free | Mid-Aug.–mid-May, Tues., Wed., Fri. 10–4:30, Thurs. 10–9, weekends noon–4:30; mid-May–mid-Aug., Tues.–Sun. noon–4:30.

**Jacobson House and Cultural Center.** The former home of University of Oklahoma professor Oscar Jacobson showcases contemporary Native American art, including paintings, sculpture, film, and photography. | 609 Chautauqua Ave. | 405/366–1667 | Free | Tues.–Fri. 10–5; weekends 1–5.

**Lake Thunderbird State Park.** Seven thousand acres of rolling hills and water include RV and tent campsites, rustic lake huts, two marinas, hiking and bicycle trails, riding stables, a swimming beach, and a nature center. | Rte. 9, 12 mi east of Norman | 405/360–3572 | www.touroklahoma.com | Free | Daily.

The 25-acre **Little River Zoo** with its learning center features non-native and indigenous species, and has a hands-on barnyard zoo with domesticated farm animals. | 3405 S.E. 120th Ave. | 405/366–7229 | www.littleriverzoo.com | $3 | Daily 10–5.

**Oklahoma Museum of Natural History.** Oklahoma's native plant and animal life is exhibited in this 5-million-item collection. Displays include dinosaur fossils and artifacts from the Spiro Mounds. | 2401 Chautauqua Ave. | 405/325–4712 | Free | Mon.–Sat. 10–5, Sun. 1–5.

**Sooner Theatre.** Concerts, ballets, plays, and other performances are held in this restored 1929 Spanish Gothic theater. | 101 E. Main St. | 405/321–9600 | $5–$25 | Weekdays 9–5.

**University of Oklahoma.** Oklahoma's largest university was established in 1890, 17 years before Oklahoma's statehood. Highlights include the architecturally intriguing Bizzell Library, described by architect Frank Lloyd Wright as "Cherokee Gothic," the History of Science Collection, and the Western History Collection. With more than 50,000 books and thousands of manuscripts, photographs, maps, and oral histories, the latter is one of the largest collections of Western materials in existence. | Between Elm and Jenkins Sts., and Boyd and Lindsey Sts. | 800/234–6868 or 405/325–1188 | Free | Daily.

## ON THE CALENDAR

**FEB.:** *Chocolate Festival.* This event held at the Firehouse Art Center includes a chocolate dessert competition, an auction, and live entertainment. | 405/329–4523.
**APR:** *Medieval Fair.* A human chess game, an arts and crafts fair, and entertainment on two stages are part of the fun at this event held on the University of Oklahoma Campus. | 405/288–2536.
**JUNE:** *Jazz in June.* Local, regional, and national jazz, blues, and big bands perform throughout the city. | 405/325–5468.

## Dining

**Café Plaid.** American. Terra-cotta tile floors, dark wood, and, yes, lots of plaid, adorn this stylish restaurant. Known for pasta, chicken, pizza, salads, and sandwiches. Sun. brunch. | 333 W. Boyd St. | 405/364–6469 | Breakfast also available. No dinner | $6–$8 | AE, MC, V.

**Charleston's.** Continental. You may have to wait for up to an hour for a table on Fri. and Sat. nights, but the good food and service at this popular spot make it worthwhile. The menu ranges from ribs and fresh fish to pasta and specialty salads. Try the favored pepper steak (an 11-oz strip steak rolled in cracked black pepper and topped with sautéed bell peppers, red onions, and mushrooms with garlic mashed potatoes and Caesar salad on the side). | 300 Ed Noble Pkwy. | 405/360–0900 | Reservations not accepted Fri., Sat. | $6–$20 | AE, D, DC, MC, V.

**Legend's Restaurant.** Continental. A casual yet elegant place with chandeliers and antiques throughout. Known for its fresh seafood specials. Salad bar. Sun. brunch. | 1313 W. Lindsey St. | 405/329–8888 | $11–$30 | AE, D, DC, MC, V.

**Misal of India.** Indian. A feast for the senses awaits you at this tiny Indian restaurant, where chefs work in a glass-enclosed kitchen and embroidered fabrics cover the walls and tables.

Known for tandoori cooking and lamb. Try the mango shakes. | 584 Buchanan St. | 405/360–5888 | Closed weekends. No dinner | $5–$7 | AE, MC, V.

**Oskie's Roadhouse.** American/Casual. This popular (and noisy) dining spot originally served as a trolley depot in downtown Norman. The microbrews, hamburgers, and baby back ribs are favorite menu items. Beer muffins are served with all entrées and salads. Try the honey-pepper-bacon burger (they cure their own bacon). Open-air dining is available on the patio, which has lots of plants and trees. Kids' menu. | 105 W. Main St. | 405/364–7942 | $5–$15 | AE, D, DC, MC, V.

**Vista Sports Grill.** Tex-Mex. Sports memorabilia and multiple television sets adorn this restaurant. Known for sandwiches, salads, burgers. Kids' menu. | 111 N. Peters St. | 405/447–0909 | $5–$10 | AE, D, DC, MC, V.

## Lodging

**Days Inn.** This motel is between two car lots on the interstate service road. It's ½ mi from shopping and dining, and just 3½ mi from the University of Oklahoma. Some refrigerators, cable TV, pool, business services, pets allowed. | 609 N. Interstate Dr. | 405/360–4380 | fax 405/321–5767 | 72 rooms | $45–$60 | AE, D, DC, MC, V.

**Fairfield Inn.** This distinctive salmon-pink stucco hotel is just off I-35, west of downtown and among a row of restaurants. The "executive rooms" have a king-size bed and a sitting area. Complimentary Continental breakfast, in-room data ports, some microwaves, some refrigerators, cable TV, pool, hot tub, laundry service, business services, no pets. | 301 Norman Center Ct. | 405/447–1661 or 800/228–2800 | 76 rooms | $64–$85 | AE, D, DC, MC, V.

**Guest Inn.** This west side lodging just 3 mi from the University of Oklahoma has motel-style rooms you can drive up to, as well as a main building with hotel rooms. It's within walking distance of shopping and dining, and a courtyard has grills for your personal use. Restaurant, picnic area, room service, microwaves, refrigerators, cable TV, in-room VCRs, pool, video games, laundry facilities, business services, pets allowed. | 2543 W. Main St. | 405/360–1234 or 800/460–4619 | www.telepath.com/weblynx/norman | 110 rooms | $52 | AE, D, DC, MC, V.

**Holiday Inn.** This six-story hotel is north of downtown Norman, off I-35. Golf and tennis are available at a club less than 1 mi away. Restaurant, bar, room service, in-room data ports, some microwaves, some refrigerators, cable TV, indoor-outdoor pool, hot tub, exercise equipment, video games, laundry facilities, laundry service, business services, no pets. | 1000 N. Interstate Dr. | 405/364–2882 or 800/465–4329 | fax 405/321–5624 | www.holiday-inn.com | 149 rooms | $89–$149 | AE, D, DC, MC, V.

**Holmberg House.** Built in 1914 by Prof. Fredrick Holmberg, one of the University of Oklahoma's first deans, this B&B is a large two-story, wood and stone Craftsman-style home listed on the National Register of Historic Places. It's in the DeBarr Historic District, a residential neighborhood across from the university. Campus Corner, with its many shops and dining options, is just next door. All guest rooms have queen-size beds. Complimentary breakfast, some in-room hot tubs, no room phones, cable TV, no smoking. | 766 DeBarr St. | 405/321–6221 or 800/646–6221 | fax 405/321–0400 | holmberg@telepath.com | www.bbonline.com | 4 rooms | $95–$120 | MC, V.

**La Quinta.** Rooms are cheerful and soundproof in this chain hotel just off I-35. It's on the south end of town, 3 mi from the University of Oklahoma. Complimentary Continental breakfast, in-room data ports, some microwaves, some refrigerators, cable TV, pool, hot tub, exercise equipment, laundry facilities, laundry service, business services, pets allowed. | 930 Ed Noble Pkwy. | 405/579–4000 or 800/687–6667 | fax 405/579–4001 | 117 rooms | $89–$129 | AE, D, DC, MC, V.

★ **Montford Inn.** Set in the heart of Norman's historic district, this Prairie-style turn-of-the-20th-century inn is filled with antiques and Native American art. Picnic area, complimentary breakfast, in-room data ports, some in-room hot tubs, cable TV, in-room VCRs (and movies), business services, no smoking. | 322 W. Tonhawa St. | 405/321–2200 or 800/321–

8969 | fax 405/321–8347 | www.montfordinn.com | 10 rooms, 6 cottages | $90–$155, $180–
$200 cottages | AE, D, MC, V.

**Norman Travelodge.** Formerly the Stratford House Inn, this Travelodge has retained the
English Tudor style from its previous incarnation. It's directly across the interstate from a
shopping mall and within 10 min of the University of Oklahoma. Rooms have loveseats
and either two queen- or one king-size bed. Complimentary Continental breakfast, cable
TV. | 225 N. Interstate Dr. | 405/329–7194, ext. 123 | fax 405/329–7194 | www.travelodge.com
| 40 rooms | $56–$66 | AE, D, DC, MC, V.

**Ramada Inn.** At the Lindsay St. exit off I–35 and next to the University of Oklahoma, this
Ramada Inn is 1 mi from a golf course, within walking distance of restaurants, and 3 mi
from parks and area shopping. Restaurant, bar, room service, in-room data ports, cable TV,
pool, exercise equipment, video games, laundry facilities, business services. | 1200 24th Ave.
SW | 405/321–0110 | fax 405/360–5629 | 146 rooms | $62–$82 | AE, D, DC, MC, V.

**Residence Inn by Marriott.** The University of Oklahoma is only 3 mi from this Marriott,
designed for extended-stay visitors. At least three golf courses are within 5 mi of the
property and major restaurants are within 1 mi. Complimentary Continental breakfast,
in-room data ports, microwaves, cable TV, pool, hot tub, tennis, laundry facilities, business
services, some pets allowed. | 2681 Jefferson St. | 405/366–0900 | fax 405/360–6552 | 126
suites | $89–$109 suites | AE, D, DC, MC, V.

# OKLAHOMA CITY

MAP 4, H5

*(Nearby towns also listed: Edmond, Guthrie, Norman, Shawnee)*

Oklahoma's capital is the 28th-largest city in the United States. It is more suburban
than urban in character, sprawling into a full five counties. The Metropolitan area has
a population of just over 1,000,000, with slightly more than 472,000 living within the
city limits.

Oklahoma City was "born grown" on April 22, 1889, the date of the first Oklahoma
Land Run. The rush began at noon, and by nightfall 10,000 tents were pitched near
where the railroad crossed the Canadian River. The town's access to rail freight service
helped it build meat packing and other industries, but growth was relatively slow and
steady until 1928, when oil was discovered beneath the city's eastern half. Oil derricks
blossomed all over town—even on the lawn of the state capitol—and a period of rapid
expansion began.

An ambitious—and in hindsight, regrettable—urban renewal program destroyed
much of the city's old building stock in the 1960s. That, combined with an underground
concourse that moved many downtown shops and restaurants below street level
and the destruction caused by the 1995 bombing of the Alfred P. Murrah Federal Building give the downtown district a curiously deserted feeling. A large portion of the city's
commercial life now takes place away from the center, although the city has embarked
on numerous building projects designed to enhance the downtown district.

To visitors with a car, Oklahoma City offers a number of intriguing Western and
Native American attractions, as well as numerous family-oriented destinations.

Information: **Oklahoma City Convention and Visitors Bureau** | 189 W. Sheridan, Okla-
homa City, OK 73102 | 405/297–8912 | fax 405/297–8888 | www.okccvb.org.

## NEIGHBORHOODS

Turn-of-the-20th-century warehouses and manufacturing plants were some of the
few old downtown buildings to escape the wrecking ball in the 1970s, and they now
serve as a thriving entertainment district called **Bricktown.** With a brewery, ballpark,

antique shops, musical venues, and numerous restaurants and festivals, the district bustles year round.

Oklahoma City's early civic leaders built grand homes in a neighborhood just north of downtown now known as **Heritage Hills.** The shady streets of the neighborhood, bounded roughly by Shartel and Broadway avenues and 13th and 23rd streets, hold many architectural gems. Two of them, the Overholser Mansion and a home now operated as the Oklahoma Heritage Center, are open to the public.

The **Paseo Arts District** is on a tiny curving street angling south from N.W. 30th Street near Dewey Ave. Built in the 1920s in Spanish Mission–style architecture, the storefronts have been converted to artists' studios, with a handful of specialty shops and restaurants in the mix.

Listed on the National Register of Historic Places, **Stockyards City** is home to the Oklahoma National Stockyards, the world's largest live cattle auction, and numerous old-fashioned Western shops. You can order a handmade hat or boots, or even a cattle chute, browse a Western art gallery, or dine with cowboys sporting spurs at the Cattlemen's Steakhouse.

## TRANSPORTATION

**Airports: Will Rogers World Airport.** Eleven commercial carriers fly into the Will Rogers World Airport in southwestern Oklahoma City. | S. Meridian, 2 mi south of Airport Rd. | 405/680–3200.

**Rail:** Daily **Amtrak** service from Oklahoma City to Fort Worth, TX, with stops in Norman, Purcell, Pauls Valley, and Ardmore. There are currently no passenger service terminals

## KODAK'S TIPS FOR PHOTOGRAPHING PEOPLE

**Friends' Faces**
· Pose subjects informally to keep the mood relaxed
· Try to work in shady areas to avoid squints
· Let kids pick their own poses

**Strangers' Faces**
· In crowds, work from a distance with a telephoto lens
· Try posing cooperative subjects
· Stick with gentle lighting—it's most flattering to faces

**Group Portraits**
· Keep the mood informal
· Use soft, diffuse lighting
· Try using a panoramic camera

**People at Work**
· Capture destination-specific occupations
· Use tools for props
· Avoid flash if possible

**Sports**
· Fill the frame with action
· Include identifying background
· Use fast shutter speeds to stop action

**Silly Pictures**
· Look for or create light-hearted situations
· Don't be inhibited
· Try a funny prop

**Parades and Ceremonies**
· Stake out a shooting spot early
· Show distinctive costumes
· Isolate crowd reactions
· Be flexible: content first, technique second

*From Kodak Guide to Shooting Great Travel Pictures* © 2000 by Fodor's Travel Publications

in Oklahoma; reservations and ticketing are handled by telephone at | 800/872–7245.
**Bus: Greyhound Bus Lines** offers service to and from Oklahoma City from the Union
Bus Station downtown. | 427 W. Sheridan | 405/235–6426.
**Intra-City Transportation: Metro Transit Bus and Trolley System.** Oklahoma City grew
up with the automobile, and public transportation hasn't always served visitors well.
Public buses are available Monday through Saturday. "Oklahoma Spirit" trolleys run
from Meridian Avenue on the city's west side near the airport to downtown every 30
minutes, Monday through Saturday from 9:30 AM to 11 PM, and on Sundays from 10:30
AM to 6 PM. Downtown trolleys, which run every 10 minutes, operate from 7 AM to 11 PM
daily. | Terminal: 200 N. Shartel Ave. | 405/235–7433.
**For More Information: Oklahoma Department of Transportation** | 405/522–8000.

## Driving Around Town

Driving is by far the most common mode of transportation in Oklahoma City. In
general, traffic runs smoothly; rush-hour is roughly from 7:30–8:30 AM and 4:45–7:45
PM. There are no HOV lanes.

Congestion may be caused by several ongoing construction projects affecting the
major interstate arteries that connect the suburbs with downtown. The projects are
expected to continue until fall of 2003. Work crews are most active during non-rush-
hour periods, particularly midday and in the late evening.

A new interchange at the junction of I–35 and I–40 just south of downtown is being
constructed. The ongoing work affects exit and merge ramps as well as lanes; traffic
can become particularly congested during rush-hour. Keep an eye out for signs alert-
ing you to the most current area under construction.

Although most interstates in Oklahoma City are three lanes wide, I–35 running south
towards I–240 has only two lanes. Construction widening the freeway to three lanes
is ongoing and will eventually extend as far south as Norman. Presently, lanes are diverted,
sometimes with a makeshift service road on either side of the wide center median.

The Broadway Extension (U.S. 77 just north of Oklahoma City towards Edmond) is
being widened from its present two lanes to six. Traffic is routed to one side or another.

Within Oklahoma City, the speed limit on interstate highways is 60–65 mph;
outside the city limits it's 70 mph and 75 mph on Oklahoma turnpikes. Most of the
downtown area has speed limits of 25–30 mph, increasing to 55 mph as you get
farther away from the center of town.

Parking is fairly easy to find in Oklahoma City. For short stops, there are many metered
on-street parking spaces. A city ordinance stipulates, however, that you may only park
at a metered parking space for one cycle of time, i.e., no meter feeding. Cycles can
vary anywhere from 15 minutes to 5 hours. A standard ticket for an expired or over-
time meter is $10.

For longer stays, there are many parking lots and garages available. Rates for
several hours or all day are $2–$5 barring city-wide special events, during which some
facilities raise their rates.

Tow-away zones are not prevalent within the city limits, except in Bricktown and
in and around government buildings, where you should watch for signs.

The area bounded by N.W. 23rd St. to the north, I–275 to the east, I–40 to the south,
and Classen Blvd. to the west has the greatest concentration of one-way streets.

## Attractions

### ART AND ARCHITECTURE

**Governor's Mansion.** This three-story, 12-room Dutch Colonial home was built in 1928 and
completely restored in 1995. Highlights include a rug woven with the image of the state seal
and the names of Native American tribes, artwork on loan from the National Cowboy Hall
of Fame and other Oklahoma museums, a carved mahogany bed that once belonged to Emperor

Maximilian of Mexico, and an Oklahoma-shaped swimming pool (the Panhandle is a hot tub). | 820 N.E. 23rd St. | 405/523–4245 | www.state.ok.us/~governor | Free | Wed. 1–3.

**Oklahoma Heritage Center.** The former family residence of Judge Robert A. Hefner, a state Supreme Court justice, this 1917 mansion holds photographs, memorabilia, paintings, and bronze busts of Oklahomans inducted into the Oklahoma Hall of Fame. The adjacent Shepherd Oklahoma Heritage Library holds more than 10,000 books and periodicals related to Oklahoma history. | 201 N.W. 14th St. | 405/235–4458 | $3 | Daily.

**Overholser Mansion.** This three-story French Chateau–style mansion was built in 1904 by builder Henry Overholser, who came to Oklahoma Territory during the 1889 Land Run and became one of Oklahoma City's early civic leaders. The restored mansion has early 20th-century furnishings and stained-glass windows. | 405 N.W. 15th St. | 405/528–8485 | $3 | Tours on the hour Tues.–Sat. 10–4, Sun. 2–4.

**State Capitol.** The granite capitol building is distinguished as the only state capitol with a pumping oil well on its lawn. (In truth, the pump is now just for show; the well was capped a few years ago.) Interior highlights include murals in the fourth-floor rotunda depicting four eras of Oklahoma history. Murals also honor Oklahoma's Native American ballerinas and the oil industry. Two large statues near the capitol's front steps pay tribute to the state's dual Western and Native American heritage: one depicts a Native American woman and the other is of a cowboy on a rearing horse. Oklahoma's unique history is evident in the number of flags at the capitol; 13 of the 14 flags that flew over Oklahoma can be seen out front, and a flag plaza on the lawn behind the capitol displays the flags of the 37 Native American nations that are headquartered in the state. | 2300 N. Lincoln | 405/521–3356 | Free | Daily 8–6; tours every hour on the half hour weekdays 9–3.

OKLAHOMA CITY

INTRO
ATTRACTIONS
DINING
LODGING

Permanent exhibits at the granite and marble **State Museum of History** showcase Native American history and art, the territorial era, and events in Oklahoma history since statehood; the museum staff also curates numerous topical exhibits. A research library and Indian archives, which hold enrollment records for the Five Civilized Tribes, are open to the public. | 2100 N. Lincoln Blvd. | 405/521–2491 | www.ok-history.mus.ok.us | Free | Mon.–Sat. 9–4:45.

## PARKS, NATURAL SIGHTS, AND OUTDOOR ACTIVITIES

**Bricktown Ballpark.** In the Bricktown entertainment district, this ballpark is home to the AAA minor league Oklahoma Red Hawks (formerly the Oklahoma '89ers) and farm team to the Texas Rangers. | 2 S. Mickey Mantle Dr. | 405/218–1000 | $4–$13 | Apr.–Sept., Thurs.–Sun. 8:30–5.

**Frontier City.** More than 50 rides, including four roller coasters, are in this Western-style amusement park. A petting zoo and Paul Bunyan's Tiny Timber Town appeal to the youngest visitors. There are also restaurants, Western-themed shops, and a picnic area. | 11501 N.E. Expressway | 405/478–2412 | $27 | June–Aug., weekdays 10:30 AM–10 PM, weekends 11–10; Apr., May, Sept., Oct., weekends 11–10.

**Martin Park Nature Center.** This 140-acre protected wildlife area has hiking trails, a prairie dog village, wildlife-watching blinds, and a nature center with a library and hands-on activities for children. Guided hikes and special programs are available on weekends for a small fee. | 5000 W. Memorial Rd. | 405/755–0676 | Free | Mar.–Nov., Tues.–Sun. 9–6; Dec.–Feb., Wed.–Sun. 9–6.

**Myriad Botanical Gardens and Crystal Bridge Tropical Conservatory.** In the heart of downtown Oklahoma City lies this 17-acre park with landscaped walkways, goldfish ponds, and specialty gardens. The conservatory, a 224-ft-long acrylic and steel cylinder, contains a 35-ft waterfall, a rain forest, and equatorial plants. | 301 W. Reno | 405/297–3995 | $4 | Mon.–Sat. 9–6, Sun. noon–6.

**White Water Bay.** A 25-acre water park with slides, chutes, giant wave machines, a winding "lazy river," and a splash pool for toddlers. | 3908 W. Reno Ave. | 405/943–9687 | $30 | June–Aug., Mon.–Thurs. 10:30–8, Fri., Sat., 10:30–9; May, Sept., weekends 10:30–9.

**Will Rogers Park.** This 130-acre park has rose gardens, landscaped fresh-water ponds, an impressive cactus collection, a 600-tree arboretum, and an exhibition building where flower and plant shows are held regularly. There are also tennis courts, picnic and playground areas, a frisbee golf course, a swimming pool, and a sandstone outdoor amphitheater. | 3400 N.W. 36th St. | 405/946–2739 | Free | Daily.

## CULTURE, EDUCATION, AND HISTORY

**Oklahoma City National Memorial.** This 3-acre outdoor memorial with a 400-ft reflecting pool and 168 empty glass based chairs remembers the victims of the 1995 Alfred P. Murrah Federal Building bombing, which killed 168 people and wounded hundreds more. | 5th St. at Robinson St. | 888/542–HOPE | Free | Daily.

## MUSEUMS

**Enterprise Square, U.S.A.** This hands-on museum on the campus of the Oklahoma Christian University of Science and Arts illustrates principles of capitalism and market economies with video game–style tools. A Hall of Giants pays tribute to American entrepreneurs, while a "Venture" exhibit gives you a virtual look at what it's like to manage various businesses. | 2501 E. Memorial Rd. | 405/425–5030 | www.esusa.org | $4 | Wed.–Sat. 9–5.

**45th Infantry Division Museum.** The museum honors the 45th Infantry, a National Guard unit that distinguished itself in the European theater during World War II. Of special interest are items seized from Hitler's Berlin apartment and 200 original "Willie and Joe" cartoons—cartoonist Bill Mauldin was from the 45th. Along with more recent memorabilia, the collection includes military artifacts dating back to 1541. An outdoor park holds more than 50 military vehicles, aircraft, and heavy artillery. | 2145 N.E. 36th St. | 405/424–5313 | Free | Weekdays 9–4:15, Sat. 10–4:15, Sun. 1–4:15.

**Harn Homestead and 1889er Museum.** An original farmhouse built on a homestead claimed in the 1889 Land Run has been joined by a town house, two barns, a one-room school, and demonstration fields and gardens to illustrate daily life in territorial Oklahoma. Shady picnic areas and an old-fashioned swing are found on the grounds. | 313 N.E. 16th St. | 405/235–4058 | $3 | Sept.–July, Tues.–Sat. 10–4.

**International Gymnastics Hall of Fame.** Olympic medalists Nadia Comaneci and Bart Conner, who live in nearby Norman, and Oklahoman Shannon Miller have donated many items to this museum. A small library contains books, periodicals, and videos. | First National Center, 120 N. Robinson | 405/235–5600 | Free | Weekdays 10–3.

**National Cowboy Hall of Fame and Western Heritage Center.** History and art of the American West are showcased in this 220,000-square-ft museum featuring contemporary works as well as paintings and sculptures by Charles Russell, Frederic Remington, Albert Bierstadt, and Thomas Moran. A Rodeo Hall of Fame, children's exhibits, displays of Western artifacts, and traveling exhibits can also be found here. | 1700 N.E. 63rd St. | 405/478–2250 | www.cowboyhalloffame.com | $8.50 | Daily.

**National Softball Hall of Fame and Museum.** The history of softball and the game's greatest players are featured at this small museum, housed in the Amateur Softball Association/U.S.A Softball and International Softball Federation headquarters. | 2801 N.E. 50th St. | 405/424–5266 | $2 | Nov.–Apr., weekdays 8:30–4:30; May.–Oct., weekdays 8:30–4:30, Sat. 10–4, Sun. 1–4.

**Oklahoma City Art Museum.** Eclectic permanent collections include maps, works of 20th-century American painters, photography and paintings by Works Progress Administration (WPA) artists, and works by German abstract expressionists. There are also an on-going film series and traveling exhibits. | 3113 Pershing Blvd. | 405/946–4477 | $3.50 | Tues.–Sat. 10–5, Sun. 1–5.

**Oklahoma Firefighters Museum.** This firefighter-owned and -operated museum holds 30 restored fire trucks and a re-creation of Oklahoma's first fire station. Guides are retired or active firefighters who volunteer their time and love to answer questions. | 2716 N.E. 50th St. | 405/424–3440 | $3 | Daily 10–4:30.

**Omniplex.** This complex is four museums in one. Single exhibit and combination tickets are available. | 2100 N.E. 52nd St. | 405/427–5461 | www.omniplex.org | $6.50 and up | Daily.

Antique cameras and film-processing equipment, vintage and contemporary photographs, and the "World's Largest Photo-Mural" (of the Grand Canyon) are displayed at the **International Photography Hall of Fame and Museum,** along with tributes to photography pioneers Louis Daguerre, Ansel Adams, Edward Weston, and others. The museum's extensive archives are open to the public. | 405/424–4055.

The **Kirkpatrick Science and Air Space Museum** is an outstanding children's science museum that houses more than 300 hands-on exhibits. Highlights include a weather station, virtual tours to the center of the earth, and a giant molecule. "Kidspace" is for the tiniest visitors—ages 2–5. Exhibits at the Air Space Museum range from the earliest flights and aviation pioneers to the latest shuttle missions, and include the contributions to aviation made by Oklahomans from Wiley Post and Will Rogers to shuttle astronaut Shannon Lucid. | 405/602–3770.

At the **Red Earth Indian Center,** kid-friendly exhibits—a stuffed bison, scale models of Indian dwellings, and a full-size tepee—focus on the nation's Native American heritage. | 405/427–5228.

## SHOPPING

**Crossroads.** This two-level mall at the intersection of I–240 and I–35 houses department stores such as Dillard's, Foley's, and JCPenney. It has lots of plants, open spaces, and skylights. | 7000 Crossroads Blvd. | 405/631–4421 | www.shopcrossroadsmall.com | Free | Mon.–Sat. 10–9, Sun. noon–6.

**Penn Square.** This residential mall 5 mi north of downtown has department stores, 140 specialty shops, and some family-friendly restaurants. | 1901 N.W. Expressway | 405/842–4424 | Free | Mon.–Sat. 10–9, Sun. noon–6.

**Quail Springs.** This three-level mall northwest of downtown has some larger department stores, a 24-screen movie theater, a 1950s-style food court, and a carpeted playground with soft foam toys. | 2501 W. Memorial Rd. | 405/755–6530 | www.mallibu.com | Free | Mon.–Sat. 19–9, Sun. noon–6.

**Route 66.** This funky folk gallery and gift shop sells jewelry and work by regional artists, such as picture frames made of recycled vintage auto parts (like side mirrors and radiators). | 5000 N. Pennsylvania Ave. | 405/848–6166 | Free | Weekdays 10–7, Sat. 10–6, Sun. 1–5.

**Western Avenue.** Antiques, vintage and specialty clothing, collectibles, and other eclectic shops line north of 36th Street for 4 mi to Wilshire Blvd. Also known as "Restaurant Row," the street is home to Oklahoma City's trendiest restaurants. Some shops and restaurants are open daily; others close on Sun. and/or Mon.

## OTHER POINTS OF INTEREST

**Oklahoma City Zoo.** A perennial on "best zoo" lists. The Island Life exhibit features Galapagos tortoises, parrots, and other equatorial species; silverback gorillas, chimps, and orangutans romp in the trees and grassy slopes in the Great EscApe exhibit; and the Cat Forest/Lion Overlook is a 4-acre reserve for snow leopards, Sumatran tigers, and African lions. A train and an overhead Sky Safari offer quick ways to get around the 110-acre zoo. Aquaticus, the zoo's aquarium, houses displays of marine life including both fresh- and saltwater specimens; one exhibit offers an underwater look at the sea lions and dolphin shows. | 2101 N.E. 50th St. | 405/424–3344 | www.okczoo.com | $6; dolphin show $2 | Daily.

**Oklahoma National Stockyards.** The country's largest livestock auction offers a glimpse at high-volume, old-fashioned cattle sales. Stock can be viewed from elevated walkways leading to the brick auction barn, and you can sit in on the fast-paced bidding. | 2501 Exchange Ave. | 405/235–8675 | Free | Mon.–Tues., sales start at 8 AM.

**Remington Park.** Thoroughbred and quarter-horse races, as well as off-track betting, take place at this shiny racetrack outfitted with casual and more formal restaurants, a picnic area, and a children's playground. The Thoroughbred season runs from mid-August through December; quarter-horse races are held April through June. | 1 Remington Pl | 405/424–1000 | $3.50 | Feb.–July, Sept.–Dec., Thurs.–Sun. 11:30–10.

## ON THE CALENDAR

**JAN.: *International Finals Rodeo.*** The nation's top 15 cowboys and cowgirls compete for world titles at the state fairgrounds in Oklahoma City. | 405/235–6540.

**APR.: *Festival of the Arts.*** One of the country's top arts fairs, this festival combines music, food, children's activities, and entertainment with fine art. | 405/270–4848.

**MAY: *Chuckwagon Gathering and Children's Cowboy Festival.*** Meals are prepared and served from authentic 1900s chuckwagons by chefs from across the West. Live music is performed at the National Cowboy Hall of Fame, and there are a number of hands-on activities for the kids. | 405/478–2250.

**MAY: *Paseo Arts Festival.*** Community artists display their work in tents along Paseo St. in the tree-lined, Spanish-style Paseo district of Oklahoma City during this three-day event. There is also music and live entertainment, and kids can visit the children's tent for arts and crafts activities. | 405/525–2688.

**JUNE: *Aerospace America International Airshow.*** Historic aircraft, aerobatics, and more are part of one of the nation's top air shows. | 405/685–9546.

**JUNE–AUG.: *Lyric Theatre.*** This professional musical theater troupe presents five shows a season at the Kirkpatrick Fine Arts Auditorium. | 405/524–7111.

**JUNE: *Red Earth Cultural Festival.*** The world's largest Native American event includes competitive dancing, a juried art show, and a Native American film festival. | 405/427–5228.

**SEPT.–MAY: *Oklahoma City Philharmonic Orchestra.*** This symphony orchestra gives classical and pops concerts featuring a variety of guest artists. | 405/842–5387.

**SEPT.–OCT.: *State Fair of Oklahoma.*** Commercial exhibits, a carnival midway, livestock competitions, a rodeo, a circus, and musical performances are part of this fair. | 405/948–6700.

**OCT: *An Affair of the Heart.*** This three-day show and sale at the State Fairgrounds is Oklahoma's largest exhibition of arts, crafts, and antiques. Expect to see jewelry, fiber art, stained glass, folk art, and seasonal items among the many offerings. | 405/632–2652 or 405/793–9304.

**OCT.–APR.: *Ballet Oklahoma.*** The professional ballet company performs in the Kirkpatrick Fine Arts Auditorium on the Oklahoma City University campus while Civic Center Hall is under renovation until fall 2001. | 405/843–9898.

**NOV.: *World Championship Quarter Horse Show.*** Three thousand horses and 7,000 exhibitors and owners gather for this two-week show held at Fair Park. | 405/949–6800.

## WALKING TOUR

### Oklahoma City Walking Tour
### (approximately 5 hours)

Begin at the corner of EK Gaylord and Reno Ave. Walk along the south side of the Myriad Convention Center to the **Myriad Botanical Gardens and Crystal Bridge Tropical Conservatory** at Reno and Robinson. The focal point of the 17-acre landscaped park is the 224-ft-long cylinder conservatory featuring a cascading waterfall surrounded by tropical foliage. Follow Robinson north for 2 blocks to the corner of Main St., where you'll find the **International Gymnastics Hall of Fame.** Here you'll see personal items belonging to area gymnasts Shannon Miller, Bart Conner, and his wife, Nadia Comaneci. Continue north on Robinson for 5 blocks until you reach the **Oklahoma City National Memorial** at NW 5th. This outdoor memorial honors victims of the Alfred P. Murrah Federal Building bombing and pays tribute to survivors and rescuers. Continue on Robinson for 9 blocks and turn left at NW 14th. Here you can enter Heritage Hills, a 10 block residential area made up of Oklahoma City's earliest mansions. Stop by the **Oklahoma**

**Heritage Center,** a 1917 mansion operated by the Oklahoma Historical Society, at NW 14th and Harvey. On NW 14th, take the next right on Hudson and walk for 1 block. Make a left on NW 15th and look for Oklahoma City's oldest mansion, the 1902 **Overholser Mansion,** which is open for tours. Walk 3 blocks east to Robinson. Turn right on Robinson, walk 2 blocks, then turn left on NW 13th. Walk 3 blocks and turn left on Stiles to enter another historic residential area. Walk 3 blocks to NW 16th and you'll see **Harn Homestead,** an original farmhouse built after the 1889 Land Run that settled Oklahoma City in a single day. Turn left on NW 16th and walk 2 blocks to Lincoln Blvd. Turn left on Lincoln and you'll see oil wells as you approach the Capitol complex. Walk 5 more blocks to the **State Museum of History,** at NE 21st and Lincoln, where the state's earliest history is documented. Two blocks north on Phillips and NE 23rd is the Dutch Colonial–style **Governor's Mansion,** open Wed. A tunnel near the mansion parking lot takes you to the **State Capitol** building, where artwork pays tribute to Oklahoma's Native American, cowboy, and oil industry heritage. Exit the Capitol building in front onto Lincoln and walk for 10 blocks. Turn right on NW 13th, walk 4 blocks, and turn left on Broadway. For 15 blocks you can walk along sidewalks of a rejuvenated commercial area and past streetlights and brick roads. At NW 4th the street curves to the left and turns into EK Gaylord. Turn left on Sheridan and enter **Bricktown,** a renovated warehouse district where you'll find a number of entertainment venues. On your right, you'll notice water shooting up from the sidewalk; if you follow this sidewalk along the canal you will come to the **Bricktown Ballpark,** home of the Oklahoma RedHawks. Turn right on Micky Mantle Ave., which is across from the ballpark. Walk to the corner and turn right on Reno. Walk 2 blocks and you'll be back on Reno and EK Gaylord.

## Dining

### INEXPENSIVE

**Bricktown Brewery.** American. At 30,000 square ft, Bricktown is one of the largest brew pubs in the country. It has photo murals of the Oklahoma Land Run throughout, and live music draws singles crowds on weekends. A triple-A ballpark and canal are across the street, and billiards and interactive games are inside. Try the homemade chicken pot pie, smoked fire wings, or grilled buffalo sandwiches. Kids' menu. | 1 N. Oklahoma Ave. | 405/232–2739 | $9–$15 | AE, D, DC, MC, V.

★ **Cattlemen's Steakhouse.** Steak. This century-old favorite serves full country breakfasts and hand-cut steaks. The café side has a long counter, and the red vinyl–swathed dining room has a photo mural of a herd of steers. Try the T-bone steak or lemon sole. Buffet (weekend breakfast). | 1309 S. Agnew St. | 405/236–0416 | $8–$23 | AE, D, MC, V.

**Chelino's.** Mexican. Strolling musicians will serenade you while you eat in this cantina-style restaurant in a renovated warehouse. (This is the downtown location of the Oklahoma City chain.) Outdoor dining is available on multiple patios, which overlook a canal. Known for fajitas, meat stew, and margaritas. Kids' menu. | 15 E. California St. | 405/235–3533 | $6–$10 | AE, D, MC, V.

**Classen Grill.** Contemporary. This 20-yr-old city landmark is locally famous for breakfast—it's reputed to serve "the best eggs Benedict in town." The walls are studded with works by local artists. Known for chicken-fried steak, liver and onions, fresh seafood, imaginative salads. Homemade bread and croutons. Kids' menu. Sun. brunch. | 5124 N. Classen Blvd. | 405/842–0428 | Breakfast also available. Closed Mon. No supper Sun. | $6–$12 | D, DC, MC, V.

**County Line.** Barbecue. Its art deco design distinguishes this former 1930s roadhouse. Known for pork, beef, and chicken barbecue, as well as loaves of fresh-baked bread. Kids' menu. | 1226 N.E. 63rd St. | 405/478–4955 | $8–$20 | AE, D, DC, MC, V.

**Eddy's Steakhouse Restaurant.** Steak. Gift cases display a variety of figurines and crystal and china pieces in this homey restaurant illuminated with soft candlelight. Known for prime rib and seafood. Kids' menu. | 4227 N. Meridian Ave. | 405/787–2944 | Closed Sun. No lunch | $10–$50 | AE, D, DC, MC, V.

**Jimmy's Egg.** American. This no-frills diner is known for its breakfast fare: sourdough and cinnamon-raisin toast, biscuits, and dozens of omelette variations. There are several Jimmy's around Oklahoma City, but this is the original location. | 1616 N. May | 405/942–8710 | Breakfast also available. No supper | $3–$5 | No credit cards.

**Kamp's.** American/Casual. Wooden floors and a pickle barrel give character to this combination deli/coffee and pastry bar inside one of the city's most venerable grocery stores. Known for all-day lattes and espressos. | 1310 N.W. 25th St. | 405/524–2251 | No supper | $5–$8 | AE, D, MC, V.

**More than Muffins.** Brazilian. Saturday lunch, with a featured Brazilian dish, is an event at this popular restaurant. Known for dozens of different kinds of breakfast muffins, plus soups, salads, and sandwiches. Try Brazilian pie, made with spinach, mozzarella cheese, and shaved ham, or *feijoada* (black beans cooked with pork and rice, collard greens, yucca flour, and orange slices). Live jazz is performed on Sat. | 1903 N. Classen St. | 405/525–9779 | Closed Sun. | $6–$10 | D, MC, V.

**Sleepy Hollow.** American. This rambling 50-yr-old restaurant is an Oklahoma City institution. The dining room overlooks a shady glen. Try the fried chicken, steak, or family-style catfish. | 1101 N.E. 50th St. | 405/424–1614 | No lunch Sat. | $11–$22 | AE, D, MC, V.

**TerraLuna Grille.** Contemporary. Known for its California-inspired decor and fusion food, dishes like the southwest black bean lasagna and chile-encrusted sirloin have made this a popular place. | 7408 N. Western St. | 405/879–0009 | Closed Sun., Mon. | $8–$25 | AE, D, DC, MC, V.

## MODERATE

**Applewoods.** American. Endless baskets of apple dumplings are brought to your table at this popular, airy restaurant. Known for pork chops, steak, and cheese soup. Kids' menu. | 4301 S.W. 3rd St. | 405/947–8484 | No lunch Mon.–Sat. | $12–$19 | AE, D, MC, V.

**Jamil's.** Steak. Antiques from the frontier period, including Tiffany-style lamps and etched-glass doors, are found throughout. Steak is its signature dish, but you might try the ribs or grilled swordfish and salmon. Kids' menu. | 4910 N. Lincoln Blvd. | 405/525–8352 | Closed Sun. | $13–$53 | AE, D, MC, V.

**Kona Ranch Steakhouse.** Hawaiian. A little bit of Hawaii (Western style) in downtown, as bamboo fixtures meet leather saddles. Try the terriyaki chicken, fried coconut shrimp, or smoked prime rib. Kids' menu. | 2037 S. Meridian Ave. | 405/681–1000 | $9–$30 | AE, D, DC, MC, V.

**La Baguette Bistro.** French. The cozy bar, with dark painted walls, soft lighting, and small dining tables, is an intimate place for light meals. Known for pastries, sandwiches, and salads. Sun. brunch. | 7408 N. May Ave. | 405/840–3047 | No supper Sun. | $9–$20 | AE, D, DC, MC, V.

**Santa Fe.** Steak. Patrons toss the shells of complimentary peanuts on the floor in this wannabe roadhouse with murals and neon lights. Known for steak and homemade yeast rolls, fried green tomatoes, blackened chicken, and roadhouse tea (gin, rum, triple sec, pure grain alcohol, sour mix, and cola served in a mason jar). Kids' menu. | 1100 S. Meridian Ave. | 405/942–1360 | $8–$18 | AE, D, DC, MC, V.

**Shorty Small's.** American. Wild West memorabilia decorates this bustling eatery. Known for St. Louis–style ribs, barbecued brisket, chicken-fried steak, and cheese biscuits. Kids' menu. | 4500 W. Reno St. | 405/947–0779 | $6–$20 | AE, D, DC, MC, V.

**The Waterford.** Continental. Housed in the Waterford Marriott hotel, this restaurant seats 75. Flowers and candles adorn the tables. | 6300 Waterford Blvd. | 405/848–4782 | Closed Sun. No lunch | $16–$25 | AE, D, DC, MC, V.

## EXPENSIVE

**Bellini's.** Italian. In the basement of an office building, some tables have a view of a park, sculpture, and fountain, and the duck- and swan-dotted pond across the street at the Waterford Hotel. The wisteria-covered patio is a lovely place to enjoy your meal. Known for pasta, salad, steak, and a diverse selection of hamburgers and sandwiches. Sun. brunch. | 63rd St. and Pennsylvania Ave. | 405/848–1065 | $8–$21 | AE, D, DC, MC, V.

★ **Coach House.** French. Dark woods and hunting prints are part of this restaurant's clubby, upscale feel. The menu includes Oklahoma-grown vegetables, herbs, and game. | 6437 Avondale Dr. | 405/842–1000 | Closed Sun. No lunch Sat. | $24–$37 | AE, D, DC, MC, V.

**Nikz at the Top.** Continental. This rotating landmark Oklahoma City restaurant is a favorite for romantic dinners. (A full rotation takes 60 minutes.) Panoramic views of the city are breathtaking from its 20th-floor perch. There are a cigar lounge, a club lounge, and a dance floor with a D.J. Try the filet mignon in a demi-glaze red wine sauce or the lobster thermidor in white wine. | United Founders Tower, 5900 Mosteller Dr. | 405/843–7875 | No lunch | $20–$75 | AE, D, MC, V.

## Lodging

### INEXPENSIVE

**Ambrosia Rose Inn.** This handsome, three-story farmhouse was built in 1893; in 1996, it was moved from the countryside to its present location in a quiet, tree-lined neighborhood. Rooms are brightly colored and on the small side. Two parlors and an upstairs sitting room are equipped with refreshments. The outdoor patio, surrounded by flower and herb gardens, is a nice place to relax. Dining rooms, complimentary breakfast, TV in common room, no pets, no smoking. | 2718 N.W. 14th St. | 405/942–7319 | fax 405/942–7319 | arosebb@aol.com | www.bbonline.com/ok/ambrosia/index.html | 2 rooms | $40 | No credit cards.

**Howard Johnson Express Inn.** These chain accommodations are within 5 minutes of downtown, the Will Rogers World Airport, and area attractions. There are plenty of restaurants within walking distance as well. Complimentary Continental breakfast, microwaves, refrigerators, cable TV, pool, gym, laundry facilities, business services, pets allowed, free parking. | 400 S. Meridian Ave. | 405/943–9841 | fax 405/942–1869 | 96 rooms | $49–$65 | AE, D, DC, MC, V.

**Motel 6 Oklahoma City Airport.** Rooms are basic and inexpensive, and you can usually park in front of your door in this two-story, tan brick motel. It's 3½ mi north of the airport, within walking distance of many restaurants, and around the corner from recreational facilities and White Water Bay water park. In-room data ports, cable TV, pool, laundry facilities, business services, pets allowed. | 820 S. Meridian St. | 405/946–6662 | fax 405/946–4058 | www.motel6.com | 128 rooms | $46 | AE, D, DC, MC, V.

**Red Roof Inn.** This chain hotel is in the heart of Oklahoma City's hotel district, 2½ mi north of the airport. All rooms have either a single king- or two queen-size beds; more expensive rooms have two recliners. Many restaurants are within a block of the hotel. In-room data ports, some microwaves, some refrigerators, cable TV, laundry facilities, laundry service, business services, no pets. | 309 S. Meridian St. | 405/947–8777 or 800/733–7663 | fax 405/947–8777 | io503@redroof.com | www.redroof.com | 91 rooms | $45–$55 | AE, D, DC, MC, V.

**Travelers Inn.** This two-story motel is 5 mi south of Will Rogers World Airport, and within walking distance of a fun park with rides and games. Complimentary Continental breakfast, in-room data ports, cable TV, pool, laundry facilities, business services, free parking. | 504 S. Meridian Ave. | 405/942–8294 | fax 405/947–3529 | 136 rooms | $44 | AE, D, DC, MC, V.

### MODERATE

**AmeriSuites Quail Springs.** Accommodations at this all-suites property have unpartitioned sleeping and living areas. It's in northwest Oklahoma City, ½ mi west of the Quail Springs Mall. Complimentary Continental breakfast, some in-room data ports, microwaves, minibars, refrigerators, cable TV, in-room VCRs, pool, exercise equipment, laundry facilities, laundry service, business services. | 3201 W. Memorial Rd. | 405/749–1595 or 800/833–1516 | fax 405/749–1573 | amerisuites.com | 128 suites | $74–$104 suites | AE, D, DC, MC, V.

**Best Western–Saddleback Inn.** This full-service hotel is on the west side of the city, 5 mi north of the Will Rogers World Airport and within walking distance of many restaurants. Its banquet room holds over 400 people. Restaurant, room service, in-room data ports, cable TV, in-room VCRs, pool, hot tub, exercise equipment, laundry facilities, business services, airport shuttle, free parking. | 4300 S.W. 3rd St. | 405/947–7000 | fax 405/948–7636 | www.bestwestern.com | 220 rooms | $77 | AE, D, DC, MC, V.

**Best Western Santa Fe Inn.** This full-service hotel is within 2 mi of the Oklahoma City Zoo, the National Cowboy Hall of Fame, Remington Park Racetrack, and two malls. As a guest of this hotel, you may enjoy use of the premier Santa Fe Health Club, which is just a short walk from the hotel. Restaurant, bar, complimentary breakfast, room service, in-room data ports, some refrigerators, cable TV, pool, hot tub, business services, free parking. | 6101 N. Santa Fe Blvd. | 405/848–1919 | fax 405/840–1581 | www.bestwestern.com/santafeoklahomacity | 96 rooms | $74 | AE, D, DC, MC, V.

**The Biltmore.** Built in the early 1980s, this hotel is the largest in the state. It's on the west side of the city, 5 mi north of the Will Rogers World Airport, about 4½ mi from downtown, and within walking distance of many restaurants. Each of the three buildings in the complex has a tree- and flower-filled courtyard. 2 restaurants, 3 bars (with entertainment), room service, in-room data ports, microwaves, some in-room hot tubs, cable TV, in-room VCRs, 4 pools, barber shop, hot tub, tennis, exercise equipment, business services, airport shuttle, pets allowed, free parking. | 401 S. Meridian Ave. | 405/947–7681 | fax 405/947–4253 | 509 rooms | $59–$69 | AE, D, DC, MC, V.

**Courtyard by Marriott–Airport.** Two three-story building wings are connected by a lobby, and a courtyard, gazebo and pool are out back. The state fairgrounds and White Water Bay are both less than 2 mi from this popular hotel in the southeast part of the city. Restaurant, bar, in-room data ports, some refrigerators, cable TV, in-room VCRs (movies), pool, hot tub, exercise equipment, laundry facilities, business services, airport shuttle, free parking. | 4301 Highline Blvd. | 405/946–6500 | fax 405/946–7638 | 149 rooms, 12 suites | $59–$99, $89–$119 suites | AE, D, DC, MC, V.

**Days Inn–Northwest.** As the name implies, this two-story motel is in the northwest part of the city. It's within walking distance of fast-food restaurants. Restaurant, bar, room service, some refrigerators, some in-room hot tubs, cable TV, pool, laundry facilities, airport shuttle, free parking, pets allowed. | 2801 N.W. 39th St. | 405/946–0741 | fax 405/942–0181 | gertysocks@msn.com | www.daysinn.com | 117 rooms | $56–$156 | AE, D, DC, MC, V.

**Fifth Seasons Hotel.** Oversized rooms and a lovely atrium area with pool, restaurant, and fountain make this a popular choice for business and leisure travelers. Restaurant, bar, complimentary breakfast, minibars, refrigerators, cable TV, pool, laundry facilities, business services, airport shuttle, pets allowed, free parking. | 6200 N. Robinson Ave. | 405/843–5558 or 800/682–0049 (excluding OK) or 800/522–9458 (OK) | fax 405/840–3410 | 202 rooms, 27 suites | $65–$105, $85–$150 suites | AE, D, DC, MC, V.

**Hawthorne Suites.** This all-suites hotel is in the middle of downtown. It's two blocks from Penn Square shopping mall, and 2½ mi from the Oklahoma City Zoo, Firefighters Museum, National Softball Hall of Fame, and the National Cowboy Hall of Fame. All of the suites have spacious living and sleeping areas and are appointed with polished wood furniture. Restaurant, bar (with entertainment), complimentary Continental breakfast, room service, in-room data ports, microwaves, refrigerators, cable TV, pool, business services, airport shuttle, pets allowed, free parking. | 1600 Richmond Sq | 405/840–1440 or 800/843–1440 | fax 405/843–4272 | 51 suites | $74 suites | AE, D, DC, MC, V.

**Hilton–Northwest.** In the business district in the northwest part of town, this nine-story hotel is adorned with lots of marble fixtures throughout. Restaurant, bar, room service, in-room data ports, refrigerator, cable TV, in-room VCRs, pool, hot tub, exercise equipment, business services, airport shuttle, free parking. | 2945 Northwest Expressway | 405/848–4811 | fax 405/843–4829 | www.hilton.com | 218 rooms | $69–$114 | AE, D, DC, MC, V.

**Howard Johnson.** This two-story hotel is 3 mi from the state fairgrounds and 7 mi from downtown. Complimentary Continental breakfast, some kitchenettes, microwaves, some refrigerators, cable TV, pool, laundry facilities, business services, free parking, pets allowed. | 4017 N.W. 39th Expressway | 405/947–0038 | fax 405/946–7450 | www.hojo.com | 105 rooms | $55 | AE, D, DC, MC, V.

**La Quinta Oklahoma City Airport.** A beautiful courtyard with a gazebo, pool, and land-scaping is the centerpiece of this hotel 4 mi from the state fairgrounds and 20 minutes from the Myriad Convention Center. Restaurant, bar, complimentary Continental break-fast, room service, in-room data ports, microwaves, refrigerators, cable TV, in-room VCRs, pool, wading pool, business services, airport shuttle, pets allowed, free parking. | 800 S. Meridian Ave. | 405/942–0040 | fax 405/942–0638 | 168 rooms | $69 | AE, D, DC, MC, V.

**Lexington Hotel Suites.** Located ¼ mi south of I-40, this all-suites hotel is 5 minutes from downtown, and within walking distance of most major restaurants and clubs. All suites have a living room, full kitchen, and a separate bedroom area. Breakfast is served in the atrium, which has a view of the outdoor pool. Complimentary Continental breakfast, room service, in-room data ports, microwaves, refrigerators, cable TV, in-room VCRs, pool, laundry facilities, business services, airport shuttle, free parking. | 1200 S. Meridian Ave. | 405/943–7800 | fax 405/943–8346 | 145 suites | $59–$79 suites | AE, D, DC, MC, V.

**Westin Oklahoma City.** This 15-story hotel is considered by some to be the city's premier business and meeting center. Spacious rooms and a downtown location 12 mi from the Will Rogers World Airport add to the convenience for busy executives. Restaurant, bar, room service, in-room data ports, cable TV, in-room VCRs, pool, business services, parking (fee). | 1 N. Broadway | 405/235–2780 or 800/285–2780 | fax 405/272–0369 | www.westin.com | 395 rooms | $59–189 | AE, D, DC, MC, V.

**Willow Way Bed and Breakfast.** All guest rooms in this English Tudor country house have period antiques. One room is actually a converted greenhouse. Grounds include two fish ponds and a walking path. Complimentary breakfast, no TV in rooms, TV in common area, some pets allowed. | 27 Oakwood Dr. | 405/427–2133 | 3 rooms | $70–$175 | MC, V.

### EXPENSIVE

**Embassy Suites.** This hotel is 10 mi from downtown and 2 mi from the Will Rogers World Airport. The two-room suites have a living area with a couch and a wet bar. Restaurant, bar, complimentary breakfast, room service, in-room data ports, microwaves, refrigerators, cable TV, pool, hot tub, exercise equipment, business services, airport shuttle, pets allowed, free parking. | 1815 S. Meridian Ave. | 405/682–6000 | fax 405/682–9835 | www.embassy.com | 236 suites | $99–139 suites | AE, D, DC, MC, V.

**Grandison at Maney Park.** A downtown mansion has been converted into this Victorian style B&B inn. Theme rooms include the "Hunter and Hound" room (which has stained cherry woodwork and plaid patterns), and the romantic "Florence" and "Divine Provi-dence" rooms—each with a canopy bed, antiques, and scented candles. Complimentary breakfast, some in-room hot tubs. | 1200 N. Shartel Ave. | 405/232–8778 | www.bbonline.com/ok/grandison | 9 rooms | $75–$135 | AE, D, MC, V.

**Holiday Inn Airport.** Rooms surround an atrium with recreational facilities in this two-story hotel 2½ mi north of the airport. Some rooms open onto an interior corridor. Restau-rant, bar, room service, in-room data ports, some microwaves, cable TV, pool, hot tub, sauna, exercise equipment, video games, laundry facilities, laundry service, business ser-vices, pets allowed (fee). | 2101 S. Meridian St. | 405/681–1674 or 800/622–7666 | fax 405/681–1674 | holokc@ionet.net | www.holiday-inn.com/okc-airport | 236 rooms, 10 suites | $87, $135 suites | AE, D, DC, MC, V.

**Rosewood Inn Bed and Breakfast.** This charming B&B was created out of parts from old, Victorian homes in Oklahoma, Texas, Missouri, Louisiana, and Arkansas. Modern appliances meet recycled cabinets, doors, stained glass windows, and more. Wraparound porches are found on the first two stories, and the spacious guest rooms are decorated with antiques. Dining room, complimentary breakfast, some in-room hot tubs, cable TV, in-room VCRs (and movies), no pets, no smoking. | 7000 N.W. 39th St., Bethany | 405/787–3057 or 888/786–3057 | fax 405/787–7641 | innkeeper@rosewoodinnbb.com | www.rosewoodinnbb.com | 4 rooms | $89–$149 | AE, D, DC, MC, V.

### VERY EXPENSIVE

**Marriott.** This elegant, 16-story hotel 5 mi from downtown is lit with chandeliers and has lots of plants in the foyer. Restaurants and shopping are less than 1 mi away. Restaurant, bar (with entertainment), room service, in-room data ports, cable TV, pool, exercise equipment, laundry facilities, business services, pets allowed, free parking. | 3233 NW Expwy (Rte. 3) | 405/842–6633 | fax 405/840–5338 | www.marriott.com | 354 rooms | $129–$139 | AE, D, DC, MC, V.

**Residence Inn by Marriott.** This complex consists of 17 two-story buildings. It's 5 mi from downtown and within 1 mi of the Oklahoma City Zoo and White Water Bay. Picnic area, complimentary Continental breakfast, in-room data ports, microwaves, refrigerators, cable TV, in-room VCRs (and movies), pool, hot tub, laundry facilities, business services, airport shuttle, free parking, pets allowed. | 4361 W. Reno Ave. | 405/942–4500 | fax 405/942–7777 | www.residenceinn.com | 135 suites | $105–$135 suites | AE, D, DC, MC, V.

**Waterford Marriott.** This top-rated, 9-story redbrick hotel is on landscaped grounds just 15 minutes from downtown and the Will Rogers World Airport. Marble bathrooms add to the hotel's luxurious feel. Restaurant, bar (with entertainment), room service, in-room data ports, cable TV, in-room VCRs, pool, barbershop, hot tub, massage, gym, squash, business services, free parking. | 6300 Waterford Blvd. | 405/848–4782 or 800/992–2009 | fax 405/843–9161 | www.marriott.com | 197 rooms | $139 | AE, D, DC, MC, V.

# OKMULGEE

MAP 4, J4

*(Nearby town also listed: Henryetta)*

Okmulgee is a Creek word meaning "bubbling springs," and this town of 13,800 has been headquarters for the Creek Nation since 1868. More than 200 structures have been restored in Okmulgee's 20-block downtown historic district. Some residents of the community commute to work in Tulsa, 38 mi to the north. Local industries include a glass plant and biotech companies.

Information: **Okmulgee Chamber of Commerce Tourism Development Program** | 112 N. Morton Ave., Okmulgee, OK 74447-7317 | 918/756–6172 | fax 918/756–6441 | www.okmulgeechamber@ocevnet.org.

## Attractions

**Creek Council House Museum.** The Creek legislature met in this handsome sandstone building from 1878 until Oklahoma statehood in 1907. The building has been impeccably restored and displays Creek artifacts, including a 1765 treaty made between a Creek chief and a British agent, and a piece of 16th-century Spanish chain mail carried over the Creek Trail of Tears. | 6th St. between Grand and Morton Aves | 918/756–2324 | Free | Tues.–Sat. 10–4:30.

**Okmulgee State Park and Dripping Springs Lake Recreation Area.** Okmulgee Lake is popular for both fishing and waterskiing; Dripping Springs Lake, off-limits to water-skiers and jet skiers, regularly yields trophy bass. Grounds include a nature center and hiking trails,

RV and tent campsites, boat ramps, and fishing docks. | 16830 Dripping Springs Lake Rd. | 918/756–5971 | www.touroklahoma.com | Free | Daily.

ON THE CALENDAR
**JUNE:** *Creek Nation Rodeo and Festival.* This event includes horse and bull riding, arts and crafts, and live entertainment. | 918/756–8700.
**JUNE:** *Pecan Festival.* Food contests involving the use of pecans and the baking of a 10-ft pie are part of the fun, as are an arts and crafts fair, a carnival, and live music. | 918/756–6172.
**AUG.:** *Okmulgee Invitational Rodeo.* Hundreds of cowboys and thousands of fans are drawn to this rodeo, one of the oldest and largest African-American sporting events in the country. | 918/756–6172.

## Dining

**Coleman's Restaurant.** American. This family-owned and -operated restaurant was founded in 1955 and claims to serve "more hamburgers than anyone else in town." The noisy, family-oriented diner is also known for pot roast, hand-cut French fries, and onion rings. | 1015 Wood Dr. | 918/756–8983 | Closed Sun., Mon. | $2–$7 | No credit cards.

**McDonald's.** American/Casual. This burger franchise is worth special mention in Troy Aikman's hometown: photographs of the Dallas Cowboy and highlights of his high school career line the walls. There's an indoor playroom that will keep the kids happy, and a display case holds an exhibit of all the happy meals from the past 3 years. | 500 E. Main St., Henryetta | 918/652–7757 | $3–$6 | No credit cards.

## Lodging

**Best Western.** Built in 1999, this strip motel is 2 mi north of town. Restaurant, bar (with entertainment), in-room data ports, refrigerators, cable TV, pool, gym, business services, pets allowed. | 3499 N. Wood Dr. | 918/756–9200 | www.bestwestern.com | 50 rooms, 6 suites | $49–$55 | AE, D, DC, MC, V.

**Days Inn.** This two-story motel with exterior entrances was built in the early 1980s. It's 2 mi from downtown, and within 3 mi of golf, shopping, fishing, swimming, and water-skiing. Complimentary Continental breakfast, cable TV, pool, no pets. | 1221 S. Wood Dr. | 918/758–0660 | fax 918/758–0660 (ext. 301) | www.daysinn.com | 62 rooms | $45 | AE, D, DC, MC, V.

**Henryetta Inn and Dome.** Built in 1987, this domed, skylit hotel 11 mi south of Okmulgee is 3 blocks from Henryetta's Main St. A movie theater is ½ mi away. Restaurant, bar, room service, cable TV, pool, gym, racquetball, laundry facilities, business services, pets allowed. | 810 E. Trudgeon, Henryetta | 918/652–2581 | 84 rooms | $67–$78 | AE, D, DC, MC, V.

# PAULS VALLEY

MAP 4, I6

*(Nearby towns also listed: Ada, Davis, Sulphur)*

This town of 6,200 residents was founded by Smith Paul, a North Carolina native who first spotted the site on wagon-train trips to California and later lived among the Chickasaw tribe in northwestern Mississippi. Paul moved with the Chickasaw to Indian Territory in 1837, and settled in the Washita River valley a decade later. Today, Pauls Valley is a sleepy agricultural community that claims to have more brick streets than any other town in the United States—17,986 square yards of them.

**Information:** **Pauls Valley Chamber of Commerce** | 112 E. Paul Ave., Pauls Valley, OK 73075-3419 | 405/238–6491.

## Attractions

**Murray-Lindsay Mansion.** Irish immigrant Frank Murray and his wife, Alzira Murray, a member of the Choctaw Nation, lived in this three-story home. The Murrays' 20,000-acre ranch so dominated the area at one time that circuit judges held court on their front lawn. The 1907 home has been restored and holds family photos and artifacts, including a 187-piece teapot collection. | From Lindsay: 1¾ mi south on Rte. 76, then ¼ mi west on marked rd. | 405/756–2121 | Tues.–Sun. 1–5.

**Pauls Valley City Lake.** This small lake has boat ramps and a fishing dock, and the surrounding shoreline has picnic tables and tent and RV campsites. | City Lake Rd., 1 mi south of Rte. 19 | 405/238–5134 or 405/238–5531 | Daily.

**Santa Fe Depot.** The wooden building that housed the Pauls Valley stop on the Santa Fe Line is today part of a railway museum. The museum sits among elegant lawns and sprays of flowers in a public garden; it contains antique railroad memorabilia and an authentic 1901 Santa Fe Line locomotive engine and caboose. | 204 S. Santa Fe | 405/238–2244 | Free | Tues.–Sat. 10–4, Sun. 1:30–4.

**Washita Valley Museum.** Displays include photographs and artifacts depicting local history, as well as fossils and other archaeological finds from the Washita River area. | 1100 N. Ash St. | 405/238–3048 | Free | Wed.–Sun., 2:30–4:30.

### ON THE CALENDAR

**MAY:** *Brickfest.* A street dance, old-time crafts, live music, and a carnival are part of this town block party. | 405/238–2555.
**JUNE:** *Pauls Valley Heritage Days Rodeo.* This international Professional Rodeo Association–sanctioned rodeo has seven events. | 405/238–2378.
**SEPT.:** *Garvin County Fair.* Here you'll see livestock and produce judging, as well as displays of home crafts such as crocheting, needlepoint, and sewing. | 405/238–6491.

## Dining

**Bob's Pig Shop.** Barbecue. Vintage photos of local rodeo queens, old advertising signs, and antique tools are part of this landmark barbecue stop's eclectic look. Try the "pig sandwich"—barbecued pork roast topped with a tangy relish and barbecue sauce. | 829 N. Ash St. | 405/238–2332 | Closed Sun. No supper Sat. | $4–$9 | AE, D, DC, MC, V.

**Punkin's Bar-B-Que & Catfish.** Barbecue. Heaps of wood-grilled barbeque and catfish are dished up in a rustic venue lined with barnwood. Try the combo platter, piled high with ribs, chicken, beef, and pork. | 3006 W. Grant | 405/238–2320 | Closed Mon. | $7–$9 | AE, MC, V.

**Tio's.** Tex-Mex. Meals are served in a spacious, pre-fab building with tiled floors and murals on the wall. The restaurant claims to have the best rice and beans you've ever had, and that people drive from Dallas to eat here. Known for fajitas and enchiladas. | Rte. 19 and Meridian Rd., off I–35 | 405/238–3535 | Closed Sun. No lunch Sat. | $6–$12 | MC, V.

## Lodging

**Days Inn.** Built in 1985, this two-story motel is 2 mi out of town, at I–35 and Rte. 19. Complimentary Continental breakfast, cable TV, pets allowed. | 3203 W. Grant Ave. | 405/238–7548 | fax 405/238–1262 | 54 rooms | $70 | AE, D, DC, MC, V.

**Sands Inn.** This single-story motel less than 1 mi from town has a barbeque joint right in the lobby. 2 restaurants, some kitchenettes, cable TV, pool, laundry facilities, pets allowed (fee). | 3006 W. Grant | 405/238–6415 | fax 405/238–7213 | 54 rooms | $38 | AE, D, DC, MC, V.

# PAWHUSKA

*(Nearby town also listed: Bartlesville)*

Pawhuska was named for the Osage chief Paw-Hu-Scah, or White Hair. The Osage tribe purchased land from the Cherokees in 1872 and moved to Indian Territory from Kansas. The tribe discovered oil under the prairie in the 1920s and became the richest per capita nation in the world. Home to one of the largest remaining swaths of tallgrass prairie, the area has been a ranching center for more than a century.

**Information: Pawhuska Chamber of Commerce and Visitor Information** | 222 W. Main St., Pawhuska, OK 74056-4115 | 918/287–1208 | fax 918/287–3159.

## Attractions

**Bivin Garden.** Ornamental rock gardens and cultivated English gardens are in a prairie setting. | Rte. 11, 30 mi west of Pawhuska | 918/793–4011 | $2 | May–Sept., Fri.–Sun. 10–dusk.

**"Cathedral of the Osage"/Immaculate Conception Catholic Church.** Nicknamed "Cathedral of the Osage", this church has stained-glass windows from Germany, including one depicting Columbus greeting Native Americans, that were commissioned by wealthy Osage parishioners in the 1920s. | 1314 N. Lynn Ave. | 918/287–1414 | Donations accepted | Daily. Tours by appointment.

**Osage County Historical Society Museum.** Local Osage, pioneer, and ranching history is showcased in a former Santa Fe depot. A monument commemorates the first Boy Scout troop in the United States, founded in Pawhuska in 1909. | 700 N. Lynn Ave. | 918/287–9924 | Free | Weekdays 9–5, weekends 1–5.

**Osage Hills State Park.** This quiet, beautiful park with nearly 1,200 acres of rolling hills has hiking trails, tennis courts, a swimming pool, a small lake, RV and tent campsites, picnic areas, and eight native stone cabins built by the Civilian Conservation Corps in the 1930s. | U.S. 60, 13 mi east of Pawhuska | 918/336–4141 | www.touroklahoma.com | Free | Daily.

**Osage Tribal Museum.** The oldest continuously operated tribal museum in the United States preserves Osage culture with photographs, Osage ribbonwork and other regalia, and an exhibit about Osage cosmology. It's housed in the old Osage Agency, now the Osage Nation headquarters. | 819 Grandview Ave. | 918/287–4622 | Free | Tues.–Sat. 9–5.

**Tallgrass Prairie Preserve.** This 30,000-acre swath of virgin tallgrass prairie is one of the largest remnants of the prairie that once covered 152 million acres of the Midwest. It's home to bison herds and other wildlife, as well as diverse grass and plant life. The preserve has short hiking trails and a driving route called "Bison Loop." | Rte. 99, 16 mi north of Pawhuska | 918/287–4803 or 287–3623 | www.tnc.org/oklahoma/tallgrass.html | Free | Daily 24 hours.

### ON THE CALENDAR
**JUNE:** *Ben Johnson Memorial Steer-Roping Contest.* Old-fashioned steer roping is held in the heart of the Osage Hills ranch country. | 918/287–1581.
**JULY:** *International Roundup Clubs Cavalcade.* Billed as the "World's Largest Amateur Rodeo," this annual event brings together area roundup clubs at the Osage County Fairgrounds for a parade and rodeo. | 918/287–1208.
**SEPT.:** *Former Bob Will Texas Playboys Reunion.* Members of Bob Will's Texas Playboys western swing band perform for two dances and a concert. | 918/287–3316.

## Dining
**Bad Brad's Barbecue.** Barbecue. This little house converted into a restaurant has a cozy, homey feel. The rustic wood walls have photos of country-and-western and rodeo stars.

PAWHUSKA

INTRO
ATTRACTIONS
DINING
LODGING

Try the beef and pork smoked with blackjack oak and pecan wood. | 1215 W. Main St. | 918/287–1212 | Closed Sun. | $3–$8 | MC, V.

**Bluestem Restaurant.** American. This Main Street country diner serves blue-plate lunch and dinner specials. Known for biscuits and gravy, brown beans, cornbread, and desserts. | 114 E. Main St. | 918/287–2308 | Breakfast also available | $6–$12 | MC, V.

**Sally's Sandwich Shop.** American. You need to get to this place before 2 PM, as Sally rises early to roast pork and bake ham from scratch for her devoted customers. Try the sliced pork sandwich, Sally's specialty. | 614 Kihekah St. | 918/287–9919 | Closed Sun. No supper | $2–$4 | No credit cards.

## Lodging

**Black Gold Motel.** This two-story motel in the middle of town was built in 1972. Rooms have a king-size bed or two double beds. Cable TV, no pets. | 544 Matthews Ave. | 918/287–3303 | 19 rooms | $35 | AE, D, DC, MC, V.

**Inn at Woodyard Farms.** Rooms are rustic but pretty in this 1988 B&B, housed in a buttercup-yellow farmhouse on the edge of the Tallgrass Prairie. The breakfast, however, is what gets star billing; choose from eggs Benedict, chicken with mushrooms in a sour cream sauce, lemon pancakes, or blueberry waffles. Complimentary breakfast, no TV in rooms, TV in common area, ponds, fishing. | Lynn St. (Rte. 2), 3 mi north of the only stoplight in town | 918/287–2699 | 4 rooms | $65 | MC, V.

# PAWNEE

MAP 4, I3

*(Nearby towns also listed: Hominy, Stillwater)*

Former site of the Pawnee Agency and headquarters of the modern Pawnee tribe, Pawnee's tiny downtown has a handful of Native American galleries and antiques and gift shops. Chester Gould, creator of the cartoon strip "Dick Tracy," was from Pawnee; a colorful mural honors him on Harrison Street. Many of the locals are employed by the Pawnee tribe; agriculture and oil are also major economic factors in this town of 2,200.

© Artville

## THE BUFFALO ROAD

Two centuries ago, buffalo were as much a part of the western Oklahoma landscape as sky and grass. In 1819, Edwin James, who explored Oklahoma's plains with the Long Expedition, wrote in his journal: "The bison paths in this country are as frequent and almost as conspicuous as the roads in the most populous parts of the United States." Less than a century later, thanks to a killing campaign carried out by army and commercial hunters, the bison had all but disappeared—fewer than 1,000 buffalo remained in North America. Conservation efforts in Oklahoma began in 1907, when 15 bison were shipped by rail from a New York zoo to the Wichita Mountains Wildlife Refuge, and today bison once again graze on Oklahoma's prairies. The herd at the wildlife refuge is maintained at about 500 head, and 300 more roam at the Tallgrass Prairie Preserve near Pawhuska. A small number are found at the Chickasaw National Recreation Area and the Pawnee Bill Buffalo Ranch Site at Pawnee. At the 32,000-acre Tallgrass Prairie Preserve, formerly a cattle ranch, the return of the buffalo created a colorful bonus. Since buffalo graze much more selectively than cattle, the number of wildflowers has grown luxuriantly.

Information: **Pawnee Chamber of Commerce** | 608 Harrison St., Pawnee, OK 74058-2521 | 918/762–2108.

## Attractions

**Lake Pawnee Park.** This quiet, wooded park built around a small lake has an ornate sandstone bathhouse with water gardens, fishing docks, tent and RV campsites, a 9-hole golf course, and a swimming beach. | 510 Illinois St. | 918/762–2658 | Free | Daily.

**Pawnee Bill Buffalo Ranch Site.** The former home and ranch of Gordon "Pawnee Bill" Lillie, who operated a Pawnee trading post and founded Pawnee Bill's Wild West Show (reminiscent of Buffalo Bill's famous act), is part museum, part refuge (buffalo graze in the pasture), and part entertainment venue. Reenactments of the original show are held regularly in summer. | U.S. 64, ½ mi west of Pawnee | 918/762–2513 | Free | Tues.–Sat. 10–5, Sun., Mon. 1–4.

### ON THE CALENDAR

**MAY: *Steam Show and Threshing Bee.*** This event includes demonstrations of antique steam-powered farm equipment and working exhibits of a vintage machine shop and saw mill. | 918/762–2108.

**JUNE: *Pawnee Bill Wild West Show.*** Historically accurate reenactment of the Pawnee Bill Wild West Show, featuring cowboys, mock stage hold-ups, and Native American dancing. | 918/762–2108.

**JULY: *Pawnee Indian Powwow.*** Competitive ceremonial and social dances, as well as a parade and softball tournament, are part of this event. | 918/762–2654.

## Dining

**Chick's Steakhouse.** Steak. Locals flock here for large servings of beef, chicken, and fish, plus homemade pies and cobblers. The rustic look includes unfinished wood and a tin ceiling. | 409 Harrison St. | 918/762–2231 | Closed Tues., Wed. | $10–$16 | D, DC, MC, V.

## Lodging

**Pecan Grove Motel.** Built in 1995, this motel has rooms with king-size or double beds. It's two blocks from the town square and courthouse, and within walking distance of shops and restaurants. Cable TV, laundry facilities, pets allowed (fee). | 609 4th St. | 918/762–3061 | 16 rooms | $38 | AE, D, MC, V.

# PERRY

MAP 4, H3

*(Nearby towns also listed: Pawnee, Stillwater)*

The three-story granite Noble County courthouse sits on a shady shop-lined square in the heart of this slow-paced small town—complete with a bronze statue on the courthouse lawn of a pioneer couple making the Cherokee Strip Run. The town site was in the southern edge of the Cherokee Strip, in grasslands once owned by the Cherokee Nation, and was settled during the September 16, 1893 Land Run that opened the region to white settlement. (Perry had 25,000 residents by the evening of the run.) Today this town of 5,500 is home to the Charles Machine Works, which makes earthmoving equipment.

Information: **Perry Chamber of Commerce** | 300 N. 6th St., Perry, OK 73077-6607 | 580/336–4684 | fax 580/336–6622.

## Attractions

**Cherokee Strip Museum.** This museum traces the history of the Cherokee Outlet from prehistoric times to its sale to the federal government by the Cherokee Nation and its opening to settlers in a 1893 land run. Living-history programs for schoolchildren in an 1895 one-room schoolhouse. | 2617 W. Fir | 580/336–2405 | Free | Tues.–Fri. 9–5, Sat. 10–4.

**Perry CCC Park.** Built by the Civilian Conservation Corps in the 1930s, this wooded 150-acre park has a picnic area, a small lake, an outdoor chapel, and a hiking trail. | 1520 S. 4th St. | 580/336–9977 | Free | Daily dawn to dusk.

### ON THE CALENDAR

**MAY:** *Rural Heritage Festival.* Reenactors, living arts demonstrations, one-room school sessions, May Pole dances, food, and old-time music re-create the area's rural past. | 580/336–2405.

**SEPT.:** *Cherokee Strip Celebration.* A citywide celebration of the 1893 opening of the Cherokee Strip includes a parade, the Noble County Fair, a rodeo, and a carnival with food and crafts booths on the town square. | 580/336–2405.

## Dining

**Kumback Lunch.** American. This diner on the courthouse square claims to be the oldest restaurant in Oklahoma (it's been in the same place since 1926) and is still a local favorite. Known for hamburgers and salads. | 625 Delaware Ave. | 580/336–4646 | Breakfast also available | $5–$10 | MC, V.

**La Macarena.** Mexican. Built in 1998, Perry's newest hot spot is this bustling Mexican restaurant, known for enchiladas, fajitas. Mexican artwork and contemporary paintings decorate the dining room. | 600 S. Cedar St. | 580/336–6000 | Closed Sun. | $7–$9 | MC, V.

**Shady Lady Tea Room.** Steak. Regulars here order dessert first; they know that the pie is so popular their favorites may not last. The restaurant is housed in a large, three-story, wood and brick building built in 1894; in past lives it has served as a trading post, a boarding house, and a dry-cleaning establishment. Known for salads, sandwiches, and pies. | 502 5th St. | 580/336–5003 | Closed Sun. No supper | $4–$10 | MC, V.

## Lodging

**Best Western Cherokee Strip Motel.** Built in 1963, this single-story motel is right off I–35, just 2 mi west of Perry. Restaurant, bar, cable TV, in-room VCRs, pool, pets allowed. | 2819 U.S. 77 W | 580/336–2218 | fax 580/336–9753 | www.bestwestern.com | 90 rooms | $48 | AE, D, DC, MC, V.

**Perry Days Inn.** A restaurant, convenience store, and gas station are across the street from this motel right off I–35, Exit 186. The parking lot can accommodate anything from big rig trucks to motorcycles. Complimentary Continental breakfast, cable TV, laundry services, pets allowed. | Jct. I–35 and Fir Ave. | 580/336–2277 | fax 580/336–2086 | www.daysinn.com | 40 rooms | $48 | AE, D, DC, MC, V.

# PONCA CITY

MAP 4, I3

*(Nearby towns also listed: Pawhuska, Pawnee, Perry, Stillwater)*

Opened to settlement in the 1893 Cherokee Strip Land Run, Ponca City blends a ranching culture heritage, the influences of five nearby Native American tribes, and a legacy of art and architecture built with oil money. The tallgrass and shortgrass prairies fold into one another in north-central Oklahoma near Ponca City, creating a mix of wheat farming and ranching. The town has a population of 26,000.

Information: **Ponca City Visitor Information Center** | 1000 E. Grand Ave., Ponca City, OK 74601-5607 | 800/475–4400 or 580/763–8067 | www.poncacitynews.com/tourism.

# Attractions

**Cultural Center and Museums.** Originally home to E. W. Marland, an oil man and former governor, this stucco mansion holds an outstanding collection of memorabilia from the 101 Ranch, a more than 100,000-acre ranch where the Miller Brothers 101 Ranch Wild West Show originated in the 1880s. Additional collections include Native American artifacts, as well as the studio of sculptor Bryant Baker, who created the *Pioneer Woman* statue displayed in Ponca City. | 1000 E. Grand Ave. | 580/767–0427 | www.poncacitynews.com/tourism | $3 | Mon.–Sat. 10–5, Sun. 1–5.

**Kaw Lake.** This 17,000-acre lake holds crappie, walleye, and striped bass. Surrounding grounds have hiking and equestrian trails. | 9400 Lake Rd. | 580/762–5611 | www.poncacitynews.com/tourism | Free | Daily.

**Marland Estate.** The 55-room mansion and estate of oil baron and former Oklahoma governor E. W. Marland was built in the 1920s and modeled after the Davanzati Palace in Florence. It's filled with Waterford crystal chandeliers and gilt ceilings. | 901 Monument Rd. | 800/422–8340 | www.marlandmansion.com | $5 | Mon.–Sat. 10–5, Sun. 1–5; tours weekdays at 1:30 and at 3:30.

**Pioneer Woman Statue and Museum.** The plight of 19th-century pioneer women is honored with a 17-ft bronze statue. The adjacent museum pays tribute to the accomplishments of female homesteaders as well as Oklahoma women who were pioneers in law, medicine, and the U.S. space program. | 701 Monument Rd. | 580/765–6108 | www.poncacitynews.com/tourism | $3 | Tues.–Fri. 9–5, Sat. 10–4, Sun. 1–4.

**Standing Bear Park.** This 200-acre park has a small lake and a 22-ft bronze statue of Ponca chief Standing Bear. After the Ponca were removed to Indian Territory, Chief Standing Bear made history as the successful plaintiff in a suit arguing that Native Americans were citizens of the United States and therefore entitled to due process. | U.S. 60 and 77 | 405/762–5611 | www.poncacitynews.com/tourism | Free | Daily 6 AM–11 PM; tours by appointment.

**North Central Oklahoma Wild West Tours.** Custom-made tours of nearby communities may highlight historic homes, prairie preserve areas, and gardens. | Call to arrange starting point | 800/700–3928 | Prices depend on custom-made tour.

## ON THE CALENDAR

**MAY:** *Iris Festival.* This citywide festival includes a craft show, a chocolate fest, a street dance, garden shows, and trolley rides. | 580/763–8082.
**AUG.:** *101 Wild West PRCA Rodeo.* In addition to a rodeo, this event includes a parade and a country-and-western dance. | 580/765–2798.
**OCT.:** *Octoberfest.* This fall festival has arts and crafts, polka bands, and children's activities on the lawn of the Marland Estate. | 580/767–0420.

# Dining

**Rusty Barrell Supper Club.** Steak. This casual spot doesn't offer much in the way of decor, but the food is great. Specially seasoned steaks are cooked on an open grill. Filet mignon is the most popular. | 2005 N. 15th St. | 580/765–6689 | Closed Sun. No lunch Sat. | $13–$20 | AE, D, MC, V.

# Lodging

**Days Inn.** This 1975 motel is on the north side of town, within walking distance of some restaurants and stores. Complimentary Continental breakfast, microwaves, cable TV, pets allowed. | 1415 E. Bradley St. | 580/767–1406 | fax 580/762–9589 | 59 rooms | $54 | AE, D, DC, MC, V.

**Econo Lodge.** This two-story motel is on the south side of town, across the street from several restaurants. Complimentary Continental breakfast, some in-room data ports, cable TV, pool, no pets. | 212 S. 14th St. | 580/762–3401 | fax 580/762–4550 | www.econolodge.com | 88 rooms | $45 | AE, D, DC, MC, V.

**Holiday Inn.** Built circa 1990, this two-story motel is 2 mi from Standing Bear Park and 4 mi from a golf course. Restaurant, bar, room service, in-room data ports, cable TV, pool. | 2215 N. 14 St. | 580/762–8311 | fax 580/765–0014 | hipncok@fullnet.net | www.holiday-inn.com/poncacityok | 139 rooms | $66–$69 | AE, D, DC, MC, V.

**Rose Stone Bed and Breakfast Inn.** Built in 1950, this B&B is housed in a former commercial building. Complimentary breakfast, in-room data ports, some microwaves, some refrigerators, no smoking, cable TV, in-room VCRs (and movies), laundry service, business services, pets allowed. | 120 S. 3rd St. | 580/765–5699 or 800/763–9922 | 25 rooms, 3 suites | $49–$59 | AE, D, DC, MC, V.

**Super 8 Ponca City.** This modest, single-story motel has few amenities, but it's clean and centrally located. If you're in the region for golf or fishing, save money by staying here; weekly rates are available upon request. Complimentary Continental breakfast, cable TV, hot tub, pets allowed (no fee). | 301 S. 14th St. | 580/762–1616 | fax 580/762–8777 | www.super8.com | 40 rooms | $38 | AE, D, DC, MC, V.

# POTEAU

MAP 4, L5

*(Nearby town also listed: Sallisaw)*

Built in a river valley, Poteau was founded in 1887 and named for a nearby river. Coal, lumber, and, more recently, light manufacturing have been the economic mainstays of this town of 10,000. Robert S. Kerr, a former governor and U.S Senator and one of Oklahoma's most beloved statesmen, made his home here after he retired from politics.

Information: **Poteau Chamber of Commerce** | 201 S. Broadway St., Poteau, OK 74953-3319 | 918/647–9178 | fax 918/647–4099.

## Attractions

**Cedar Lake Campground.** This 200-acre campground is built around an 84-acre lake, with swimming areas, hiking trails, and RV and tent campsites. | Holson Valley Rd., 3 mi west of U.S. 59 S | 918/653–2991 | Free | Daily.

**Cedar Lake Equestrian Camp.** Tent and RV campsites are equipped with individual corrals for horses and hot and cold showers for both horses and humans. | Holson Valley Rd., 3 mi west of U.S. 59 S | 918/653–2991.

**Heavener Runestone State Park.** A 12-ft by 10-ft granite slab bearing carved markings that some claim to have been left behind by Viking explorers in AD 900 is the centerpiece of this state park. Grounds include a hiking trail, a picnic area, a playground, and a gift shop. | U.S. 259, 12 mi east of Poteau | 918/653–2241 | www.touroklahoma.com | Free | Daily.

**Kerr Museum.** Housed in the former home of Oklahoma governor and U.S. Senator Robert S. Kerr, exhibits depict the development of eastern Oklahoma from prehistoric times, including the Spiro Mounds culture, the Choctaw Indians, and 19th-century pioneers. | 1507 S. McKenna Rd. | 918/647–8221 | $1 | Weekdays 9–5, weekends 1–5.

**Lake Wister State Park.** Set in the Ouachita Mountains, this park has cabins, RV and tent campsites, hiking, mountain biking and nature trails, a nature center, a fishing dock, swimming beach, pool, a guided lake tour, and paddleboat rentals. | U.S. 270, 10 mi southwest of Poteau | 918/655–7756 | www.touroklahoma.com | Daily.

**Ouachita National Forest.** More than 200,000 acres of the nation's largest shortleaf pine forest have been set aside for recreation. Camping, hiking, mountain biking, horseback riding, hunting, and fishing. | Between U.S. 59 and Rte. 63 | 918/653–2991 (weekdays) or 918/567–2046 (weekends) | Free | Daily.

The **Robert S. Kerr Nature Center Arboretum** is in the forest and includes two 1-mi-long marked trails and a visitor center that provides information about tree species, soil conditions, and Native American traditions. | Rte. 1 and U.S. 259 | 918/653–2991.

The **Winding Stair Recreation Area** includes a 20-acre primitive campground (no showers) at scenic Emerald Vista and opportunities for camping, picnicking, and hiking. | Rte. 1, 2 mi west of the U.S. 259 junction.

**Peter Conser Historic House Site.** This is the restored 1894 home of Peter Conser, who served as a captain of the Choctaw Lighthorseman, an elite law enforcement corps that patrolled Indian Territory in the 19th century. | Conser Rd., 3 mi west of U.S. 59 | 918/653–2493 | Free | Wed.–Sat. 10–5, Sun. 1–5.

**Spiro Mounds Archaeological State Park.** This site was used by the Mound Builder civilization from AD 600 to 1450, and contains a dozen earthen mounds that have yielded enormous numbers of artifacts and ceremonial items, including jewelry, pottery, sculpture, and prehistoric lace. The mounds were plundered in the 1930s (prompting the Oklahoma Legislature to write antiquities legislation) and few artifacts remain on site. A resident archaeologist gives guided tours. | Intersection of Rtes. 13 and 12, 25 mi north of Poteau | 918/962–2062 | www.touroklahoma.com | Free | Wed.–Sat. 9–5, Sun. 12–5.

**Talimena Scenic Byway.** This 54-mi road links Talihina, Oklahoma, in the west to Mena, Arkansas, in the east. It's most popular when the fall foliage is at its peak, and in spring when the dogwood trees are in bloom. There are a number of scenic turnouts and picnic areas. | Starts in Talimena where it intersects with Rte. 1 | 918/567–3434 | Free | Daily.

**ON THE CALENDAR**

**OCT.:** *Cavanal Fall Festival.* This festival includes an arts and crafts fair, a chili cook-off, a car show, children's activities, and live entertainment. | 918/756–2324.

## Dining

**Chan's.** Chinese. The menu has Chinese as well as American dishes. Known for egg rolls, sweet and sour pork, chow mein, lemon chicken. | 1008 N. Broadway St. | 918/647–2065 | No dinner Sun., Mon. | $4–$10 | No credit cards.

**Warehouse Willie's.** American. Housed in a converted warehouse, this restaurant has music playing in the background, and a toy train that runs around the second-floor dining room. Known for hamburgers, sandwiches, shrimp, and steaks. | 300 Dewey Ave. | 918/649–3400 | Closed Sun., Mon. | $7–$15 | MC, V.

## Lodging

**Best Western Traders Inn.** This two-story mottled brick motel is within walking distance of restaurants and shops. Rooms have king-size or double beds. Complimentary Continental breakfast, in-room data ports, cable TV, pool, hot tub, no pets. | 3111 North Broadway | 918/647–4001 | fax 918/647–9555 | www.bestwestern.com | 56 rooms | $56 | AE, D, DC, MC, V.

**Kerr Country Mansion Inn.** The former home of Oklahoma statesman Robert S. Kerr has spectacular views of the river valley, a tiny museum, and a K-shape swimming pool. Complimentary breakfast, cable TV, pool. | 1507 S. McKenna | 918/647–8221 | 20 rooms | $63–$73 | MC, V.

# PRYOR

MAP 4, K3

*(Nearby towns also also listed: Claremore, Miami, Vinita)*

Coo-Y-Yah, or "mulberry grove," was the Cherokee name for the Pryor area before white settlement. Founded in 1887 as Pryor Creek, near the Neosho River and eastern Oklahoma's first non-Indian settlement, Pryor was named to honor Nathaniel Pryor, a scout with the Lewis and Clark Expedition who later became an Osage agent in Indian Territory. Today the town has a population of 9,300 and is home to a number of light manufacturing plants.

Information: **Pryor Chamber of Commerce** | 100 E. Graham Ave., Pryor, OK 74362 | 918/825–0157 | fax 918/825–0158.

## Attractions

**Coo-Y-Yah Country Museum.** Displays Cherokee and other Native American art and cultural items, along with local historical artifacts. | 8th St. at U.S. 69 S | 918/825–2222 | Apr.–Dec., Wed.–Fri., Sun. 1–4; Jan.–Mar. by appointment.

**Snowdale State Park.** This small state park on Lake Hudson has limited RV camping sites, tent campsites, picnic areas, a boat ramp, and a swimming beach. | Rte. 20, 7 mi east of Pryor | 918/435–8066 | www.touroklahoma.com | Free | Daily.

ON THE CALENDAR
**OCT.: *Early 1800s Fur Trade Living History.*** Reenactors depict the French fur trade industry in Oklahoma's first permanent European settlement. | 800/652–6552.

## Dining

**Dutch Pantry Restaurant and Bakery.** American. This small, Mennonite-owned restaurant with wooden tables serves breakfast, lunch, and a dinner buffet with home-style meats, vegetables, and extensive desserts. Baked goods and jams are for sale. | 10 W. Main St. | 918/476–6441 | Breakfast also available | $6–$7 | AE, D, MC, V.

**Rockers.** American. All manner of chairs, particularly rocking chairs signed by soap opera and sports stars such as Charles Barkley, Michael Jordan, David Robinson, and Henryetta native Troy Aikman, are found throughout this popular restaurant. Known for burgers, grilled pork chops, chicken, steaks, pot roast, brisket. Try "chicken-in-the-garden" salad (a large house salad with chicken). | 101 Cobblestone Dr. | 918/824–7625 | $6–$13 | AE, D, MC, V.

## Lodging

**Days Inn.** Green County is known for fishing. Anglers staying at this bungalow-style hotel set among sweeping lawns have their pick of three bountiful lakes; Ft. Gibson, Grand, and Hudson are all within a 20 minute drive. Restaurant, some microwaves, refrigerators, cable TV, pool, laundry services, pets allowed. | Jct. U.S. 69S and Rte. 69A | 918/825–7600 | www.daysinn.com | 55 rooms | $52 | AE, D, DC, MC, V.

**Pryor House Motor Inn.** This 1990s brick motel is in the center of town, within walking distance of a few shops and restaurants. Complimentary Continental breakfast, cable TV, pool, pets allowed. | 123 S. Mill St. | 918/825–6677 | 35 rooms | $46 | AE, DC, MC, V.

# SALLISAW

MAP 4, L5

*(Nearby town also listed: Poteau)*

Sallisaw began as a trading post along the military road linking Fort Gibson to Fort Smith in Arkansas Territory. French traders first called the area "Salliseau" in reference to a hunting party that killed a number of bison and salted them at the site. The town is a shipping point on the Arkansas River Navigation system and home to a race track.

Information: **Sallisaw Chamber of Commerce** | 111 N. Elm St., Sallisaw, OK 74955-4631 | 918/775–2558 | fax 918/775–9550.

## Attractions

**Blue Ribbon Downs.** Pari-mutuel racing with Thoroughbred, quarter horses, Appaloosa, and paint horses. The facility has covered seating and a restaurant. | 3700 W. Cherokee, Sallisaw | 918/775–7771 | $2 | Feb.–Dec., Thur.–Sun. 11:30 AM–11 PM.

**Overstreet-Kerr Living History Farm.** Once the residence of Indian Territory settlers, the grounds include a restored 1895 home and historic strains of grains, vegetables, and livestock that would have been used by the Choctaws in the late 19th century. | U.S. 59, Keota, 10 mi south of Sallisaw | 918/966–3396 | okhfarm@brightok.net | $3 | Fri.–Sat. 10–4.

**Robert S. Kerr Lake.** This 42,000-acre lake has boating, fishing, sailing, campsites, and a sandy swimming beach. Boat rentals are available at the marina. | U.S. 59, 15 mi west of Sallisaw | 918/489–5541; marina 918/775–4522 | Free | Daily.

**Sallisaw State Park at Brushy Lake.** Tent and RV campsites, picnic areas, a playground, a fishing dock, and a boat ramp can be found at this park surrounding the tranquil 300-acre lake. | Old Hwy. 17, 1 mi west of U.S. 59 | 918/775–6507 | www.touroklahoma.com | Free | Daily.

**Sequoyah's Home.** The one-room cabin built by Cherokee linguist Sequoyah after he moved to Indian Territory from Tennessee in 1829 holds exhibits about the Cherokee alphabet he invented, as well as Cherokee culture in general. | Rte. 101, 10 mi northeast of Sallisaw | 918/775–2413 | Free | Tues.–Sun.

**Sequoyah National Wildlife Refuge.** Migratory geese, ducks, and other waterfowl flock to this 28,000-acre reserve at the confluence of the Canadian and Arkansas rivers. Refuge facilities include a photo blind, hiking trails, and observation towers; fishing, hunting, and boating are permitted. | Rte. 1, 10 mi west of Sallisaw | 918/773–5251 | Free | Daily.

### ON THE CALENDAR

**OCT.:** *Grapes of Wrath Festival.* A parade, a costume contest, a chili cook-off, and a car show and cruise recall Dust Bowl days. | 918/775–2558.

**OCT.:** *Historical Farm Fest.* Tours of a re-created Indian Territory farmhouse, gardens, and outbuildings and demonstrations of living arts such as basket weaving, woodworking, and sorghum-making are part of this event, held on the Overstreet-Kerr Living History Farm. | 918/966–3396.

## Dining

**Lessley's Cafe.** American. Founded in 1947, this downtown café is the oldest place to eat in Sallisaw. Known for its huge cinnamon rolls, hamburgers, pies, and blue-plate specials. | 220 E. Cherokee St. | 918/775–4788 | Breakfast also available | $5–$10 | MC, V.

**Wild Horse Mountain Barbecue.** Barbecue. Helicopters sometimes land near this no-frills, rustic barbecue joint to pick up a slab of ribs for out-of-state fans. (Really.) | U.S. 59, 3 mi south of I–40 | 918/775–9960 | Closed Mon. | $4–$7 | No credit cards.

## Lodging

**Best Western Blue Ribbon Motor Inn.** This 1970s motel is in the center of town, 3 mi from golf and 18 mi from fishing at Lake Tenkiller. Restaurant, some refrigerators, cable TV, 2 pools, hot tub, exercise equipment, laundry facilities, pets allowed. | 706 S. Kerr Blvd. | 918/775–6294 | www.bestwestern.com | 81 rooms | $54 | AE, D, DC, MC, V.

**Days Inn.** This motel is on the south side of town. It's within 2 mi of restaurants, and 10 mi from a golf course. Some kitchenettes, some refrigerators, cable TV, pets allowed. | 1700 W. Cherokee St. | 918/775–4406 | fax 918/775–4406 | 33 rooms | $45–$65 | AE, D, DC, MC, V.

**Econo Lodge.** This modestly priced, no-frills motor inn is 1 mi from the golf course, 2 mi from the cinema, and 8 mi from boating and fishing. Complimentary Continental breakfast, cable TV, laundry facilities, pets allowed (fee). | 2403 E. Cherokee | 918/775–7981 | fax 918/775–7981 | www.econolodge.com | 40 rooms | $36 | AE, D, DC, MC, V.

**Golden Spur Motel.** Clean, modern rooms are available at this motel, just a couple of miles from the area racetrack and the Cherokee Indian Museum. Fishing at Kerr and Tenkiller lakes is a popular pastime with guests. Cable TV, pool, pets allowed. | 601 S. Kerr Blvd. | 918/775–4443 | 29 rooms | $32 | AE, D, DC, MC, V.

**McKnight.** This motel is on 3 grassy acres just off I–40 Exit 308. Shopping and dining are within walking distance. Cable TV, in-room VCRs (and movies), pool, laundry facilities. | 1611 W. Ruth St. | 918/775–9126 or 800/842–9442 | fax 918/775–9127 | 39 rooms | $32 | AE, D, MC, V.

**Sallisaw Super 8 Motel.** Horse-racing enthusiasts can visit Blue Ribbon Downs, just 2 mi from this duplex motel, while others may choose to take advantage of the fishing, hiking, scuba diving, and more at Tenkiller Lake, "Oklahoma's Clearwater Wonderland," which is 12 mi from the motel. Complimentary Continental breakfast, cable TV, pool, pets allowed. | 924 Kerr Blvd. | 918/775–8900 | fax 918/775–8901 | www.super8.com | 97 rooms | $40 | AE, D, DC, MC, V.

# SHAWNEE

MAP 4, I5

*(Nearby towns also listed: Norman, Oklahoma City)*

East of Oklahoma City in the central part of the state, Shawnee began in 1872 as a trading post along the West Shawnee cattle trail and was first known as "Old Shawneetown." Lands formerly owned by the Shawnee Indians were opened to settlement in 1892 and the town blossomed in the 1920s when the Seminole Oil Field was discovered nearby. This town of 28,000 claims two famous natives: actor Brad Pitt and astronaut Gordon Cooper.

Information: **Greater Shawnee Area Chamber of Commerce and Convention and Visitors Bureau** | 131 N. Bell Ave., Shawnee, OK 74801-6901 | 405/275–9780 | fax 405/275–9851.

## Attractions

**Mabee-Gerrer Museum of Art.** Founded in 1915 by a Benedictine monk, this varied art collection includes works by Rembrandt, Whistler, and Raphael, Native American art, Egyptian mummies, and medieval armor. | St. Gregory's College, 1900 W. MacArthur Dr. | 405/878–5300 | $3 | Tues.–Sat. 10–4, Sun. 1–4.

**Potawatomi Tribal Museum.** Artifacts and cultural items relate to the Potawati tribe, which came to Indian Territory in the 1870s. Also displayed are baskets and beadwork, along with photographs and artifacts from the Sacred Heart mission school. | 1901 S. Gordon Cooper Dr. | 405/257–5580 | Free | Weekdays 8–5, Sat. 9–4.

**Santa Fe Depot Museum.** This 1903 passenger depot built of Bedford stone in the Romanesque Revival style is now filled with an eclectic collection of Native American and pioneer artifacts, including antique medical instruments, ceremonial pipes, vintage railroad equipment, and a pump organ. | 614 E. Main St. | 405/275–8412 | Free | Tues.–Fri. 10–4, Sat. 2–4.

**Seminole Nation Museum.** Exhibits chronicle the history of the Seminole Nation, beginning with the tribe's removal from Florida and extending to the present. Local pioneer and oil-boom history is chronicled as well. The gift shop sells Seminole art, including the intricate patchwork for which the tribe is known. | 524 S. Wewoka Ave, Wewoka | 405/257–5580 | Donations accepted | Tues.–Sun.

## ON THE CALENDAR

**JUNE:** *Heritage Fest.* This festival includes vintage farm-machinery demonstrations, tractor games, blacksmithing demonstrations, and a parade. | 405/386–2862.

## Dining

**Cafe Pepperoni and Company.** Pizza. Preface your pizza with 'a trip to the tub'—the unlimited salad bar held in an antique claw-foot bathtub, that is. Build your own pie, or try specialties of the house such as Baked Pepperoni Cavitini (baked pasta with pepperoni, mixed veggies, and melted cheese), Veggie Lasagna, or taco pizza. | 2613 N. Kickapoo Ave. | 405/878–9998 | $4–$15 | AE, MC, V.

**Jay's Classic Steakhouse.** Steak. Rustic furniture and wood paneling give this restaurant a lodge-like feel. Made-in-Oklahoma crafts are displayed throughout. Known for steaks, fried chicken, lamb fries. | 37808 Old U.S 270 | 405/275–6867 | Closed Sun., Mon. | $10–$16 | AE, D, MC, V.

**Van's Pig Stand/Charcoal Room.** Barbecue. Downstairs, the Charcoal Room serves steak, seafood, and chicken dishes in an art deco, tropical setting, with palm trees and a floral mural; upstairs is the Pig Stand, where you can eat smoked ribs and brisket in a casual setting, with wood paneling, wood tables, and booths. | 717 E. Highland St. | 405/273–8704 | $5–$9 | MC, V.

## Lodging

**Best Western Cinderella.** About 30 mi from Oklahoma City and the Will Rogers World Airport, this hotel is 1 mi from the Oklahoma Exposition Center and the Mabee-Gerrer Museum of Art, and 3 mi from the Shawnee Mall. Restaurant, bar, room service, cable TV, pool, hot tub, laundry facilities, business services, pets allowed. | 623 Kickapoo Spur | 405/273–7010 | www.bestwestern.com | 92 rooms | $57–$68 | AE, D, DC, MC, V.

**Hampton Inn Shawnee.** Built in 1996, this three-story motor lodge is right off I-40 Exit 185. Complimentary Continental breakfast, some kitchenettes, some refrigerators, cable TV, hot tub, pool, pets allowed (fee). | 4851 N. Kickapoo | 405/275–1540 | 64 rooms | $56 | AE, D, DC, MC, V.

**Ramada Inn.** This two-story hotel just off I-40 is in a commercial area on the north end of town. It's adjacent to both Oklahoma Baptist University and St. Gregory's University, and it's ¼ mi from a shopping mall. Restaurant, bar (with entertainment), room service, in-room data ports, minibars, cable TV, pool, video games, laundry facilities, business services, pets allowed. | 4900 N. Harrison St. | 405/275–4404 | fax 405/275–4998 | 106 rooms | $60–$75 | AE, D, DC, MC, V.

# STILLWATER

MAP 4, I4

*(Nearby towns also listed: Pawnee, Perry)*

"Boomers," settlers who traveled illegally into federal lands in Oklahoma Territory to push for the opening of central Oklahoma to homesteaders, first gave Stillwater its name. The boomers were repeatedly evicted, and this town of 40,000 was (legally) founded during the 1889 Land Run. Oklahoma State University, one of the state's two largest universities, is a major economic force for the town.

Information: **Stillwater Convention and Visitors Bureau** | 409 S. Main St., Stillwater, OK 74074-3524 | 800/991–6717 or 405/743–3697 | fax 405/372–0765 | www.come2stillwater.com.

## Attractions

**Boomer Lake.** Fishing docks, picnic tables with grills, a frisbee golf course, and a jogging trail make this city lake a favorite warm-weather destination. | 177 Boomer St. | 405/743–3697 | Free | Daily.

**Karsten Creek Golf Course.** This challenging course opened in 1994 and is considered one of the state's best. | 1800 S. Memorial Dr. | 405/743–1658 | fax 405/743–8436 | Year-round.

**Lake Carl Blackwell.** Fishing, swimming, boating, sailing, camping, and picnicking are possible at this 3,500-acre lake and 800-acre recreation area. Cabins can be rented in the summer. | Rte. 51, 8 mi west of Stillwater | 405/372–5157 | Free | Daily.

**National Wrestling Hall of Fame.** Oklahoma State University's outstanding wrestling history is showcased here. Exhibits focus on both college and Olympic wrestling. | 405 W. Hall of Fame Ave. | 405/377–5243 | fax 405/377–5444 | Free | Weekdays 9–4; tours by appointment.

**Oklahoma State University.** The university was founded in 1890 and is known for its beautifully landscaped campus and Georgian architecture. Campus highlights include the Gardiner Art Gallery, featuring 20th-century American art, and the Oklahoma Botanical Garden and Arboretum. | Washington St. at University Ave. | 405/744–9341 | www.okstate.edu | Free | Daily.

**Oklahoma Museum of Higher Education,** or "Old Central," is the university's oldest building; it has been restored to its 1894 appearance and contains historic material (such as photographs and recreated rooms) from a variety of state higher education institutions. | Between Hester St. and Knoblock Ave., on the OSU campus | 405/744–2828 | Free | Tues.–Fri. 9–5, Sat. 10–4.

**Sheerar Museum.** Eclectic collections, including 4,000 buttons (some dating back to the 18th century), can be found in this small but outstanding local history museum. | W. 7th Ave. | 405/377–0359 | Free | Tues.–Fri. 11–4, weekends 1–4.

**Washington Irving Trail Museum.** This small museum traces the route writer Washington Irving took through the area in 1832. There are also exhibits of local Civil War and outlaw history. | 3918 S. Mehan Rd. | 405/624–9130 | www.cowboy.net/nonprofit/irving | Free | Apr.–Oct., Wed.–Sat. 10–5, Sun. 1–5; Nov.–Mar., Thurs.–Sat. 10–5, Sun. 1–5, and by appointment.

## ON THE CALENDAR

**APR.: *Run for the Arts.*** A juried fine-arts show is accompanied by jazz concerts at this outdoor festival held on the courthouse lawn. | 405/747–8084.

**JULY: *Boomer Blast.*** Boomer Lake Park plays host to this community fireworks display. There's also food and drink, and games for the kids. | 405/747–8070.

**OCT.: *Taylorsville Country Fair.*** This fair includes live music, arts and crafts, games, food, and pioneer living demonstrations. | 405/547–2420.

## Dining

**Eskimo Joe's.** American. This small beer bar established in 1975 has grown into a landmark restaurant and bar with five dining areas. Its domed ceiling lets in a lot of light. Known for burgers and cheese fries, salads, chicken, and sandwiches. | 501 W. Elm St. | 405/372–8896 | $5–12 | AE, D, MC, V.

**The Hideaway.** Pizza. Oklahoma's most popular pizzeria, decorated with colorful collages and kites hanging from the ceilings, has spawned satellite restaurants in Oklahoma City and Tulsa. Try the "Around the World"—pizza with the works. | 230 S. Knoblock St. | 405/372–4777 | $3–$10 | AE, D, MC, V.

**Stillwater Bay.** American. There are several dining rooms and a clubby upstairs bar in this restaurant, housed in a renovated 1919 downtown building. Known for Cajun spiced prime rib, pasta, and seafood. Kids' menu. Sun. brunch. | 623½ S. Husband St. | 405/743–2780 | $7–$16 | AE, D, MC, V.

## Lodging

**Best Western.** Oklahoma State University is just ¼ mi from this three-story hotel. The modern-style building has a glass facade. Restaurant, bar, room service, in-room data ports, some refrigerators, cable TV, pool, video games, laundry facilities, business services, some pets allowed. | 600 E. McElroy St. | 405/377–7010 | fax 405/743–1686 | 122 rooms | $65 | AE, D, DC, MC, V.

**Days Inn Stillwater.** This roomy, three-story hotel caters primarily to folks visiting the Oklahoma State University campus 2½ mi away. Complimentary Continental breakfast, cable TV, pool, no pets. | 5010 W. 6th St. | 405/743–2570 | www.daysinn.com | 78 rooms | AE, D, DC, MC, V.

**Fairfield Inn Stillwater.** This three-story hotel is ½ mi from both the Oklahoma State University and the National Wrestling Hall of Fame. Some rooms have pull-out couches. Complimentary Continental breakfast, cable TV, pool, hot tub, laundry services. | 418 E. Hall of Fame St. | 405/372–6300 | fax 405/372–6300 | 64 rooms | $64 | AE, D, DC, MC, V.

**Friend House Bed and Breakfast.** This former sorority house is just 2 blocks from the Oklahoma State University campus. Some rooms are Victorian-style and are filled with oak furniture and antiques; others are a more traditional American-style and have walnut furniture. Complimentary breakfast, cable TV. | 405/372–1982 | 4 rooms (2 with shared bath) | $65 | D, MC, V.

**Holiday Inn.** Oklahoma State University is less than 10 minutes away from this two–story hotel in the southwest corner of town. Restaurant, bar, room service, cable TV, pool, hot tub, exercise equipment, video games, laundry facilities, pets allowed. | 2515 W. 6th St. | 405/372–0800 | fax 405/377–8212 | www.holiday-inn.com | 141 rooms | $74–$87 | AE, D, DC, MC, V.

# SULPHUR

MAP 4, I6

*(Nearby towns also listed: Davis, Pauls Valley)*

Built near mineral springs on land that once belonged to the Chickasaw Nation, Sulphur was first a trading post and spa built near the largest of the springs north of the Arbuckle Mountains. It later flourished as a resort town in the 1920s, when the mineral water and mud was thought to have medicinal powers. A decades-long slide towards picturesque decay has recently been reversed with the restoration and reopening of historic bath houses. Today, the town's economy is helped along by tourism and businesses operated by the Chickasaw Nation.

**Information: Sulphur Chamber of Commerce** | 717 W. Broadway Ave., Sulphur, OK 73086-4609 | 580/622–2824 | fax 580/622–4217 | www.arbuckles.com.

## Attractions
**Cedarvale Botanic Garden.** Since 1976, this modest flower park has soothed visitors with secluded trails, shaded gardens, and romantic views. You can also feed the wild ducks that congregate here in season. Call before you go, as its hours are relative to the weather. | I–35, Exit 51 | 580/369–3224 | $3. | Apr.–Oct., Thurs.–Sun. 11–8:30.

**Chickasaw National Recreation Area.** The heavily wooded area once known as Platt National Park has many springs and small waterfalls, 75 mi of hiking and mountain biking trails, two lakes, a bison herd, camping and picnicking areas, and a nature center. | U.S. 177 and U.S. 77 | 580/622–3165 | www.nps.gov/chic | Free | Daily.

### ON THE CALENDAR
**JUNE:** *Sulphur Days Spring Water Festival.* This festival includes trolley tours of the town's historic district, an arts and crafts festival, a carnival, and live music. | 580/622–2824.

**SEPT.:** *Murray County Fair.* Sulphur hosts a traditional county fair the first weekend following Labor Day. The event includes produce and livestock displays, 4-H exhibits, souvenirs, and food and drinks. | 580/622–3016.

## Dining

**The Bricks.** American. Vintage advertising art, photographs, and whimsical antiques decorate the dining room. Try the fried catfish and barbecue ribs. Kids' menu. | 2112 W. Broadway | 580/622–3125 | $6–$11 | AE, MC, V.

**Cedarvale Gardens Restaurant.** American. This creekside restaurant is on acres of manicured gardens that include a swinging bridge and a nature trail. Try the trout. | U.S. 77 | 580/369–3224 | Closed Mon. and Nov.–Mar. | $6–$18 | AE, D, MC, V.

## Lodging

**Chicasaw Lodge and Restaurant.** This two-story lodge, on the original site of the old Artesian Hotel, is owned and operated by Chicasaw Nation and is within two blocks of the Chickasaw National Recreation Area. The modern, plant-filled lobby has an atrium, and a gaming center, where kids can play video games and adults can try their luck at bingo. Restaurant, cable TV, pool, wading pool, video games. | W. 1st St. | 580/622–2156 | fax 580/622–3094 | 69 rooms | $44 | AE, DC, MC, V.

**Sulphur Springs Inn.** Built in 1925, this cheery B&B was once the Caylor Bathhouse, an exclusive spa facility nestled on the edge of the Chickasaw National Recreation Area and its famous natural mineral springs. (The springs were rumored to cure everything from rheumatism to gout.) Here you'll have private access to the springs, as well as to expansive Platt National Park, with its ample camping, boating, fishing, swimming, hiking, and hunting. The guest rooms are elegantly appointed with American and European antiques. Dining room, complimentary Continental breakfast. No room phones, no TV. Massage. No pets. No kids under 18. No smoking. | 1101 W. Lindsay | 580/622–5930 | innkeeper@sulphur-springsinn.com | www.sulphurspringsinn.com | 7 rooms | $89 | AE, MC, V.

# TAHLEQUAH

MAP 4, K4

*(Nearby towns also listed: Muskogee, Stillwell)*

The Cherokee Nation established its national capital here on the banks of the Illinois River in 1839. Tahlequah's Cherokee history is one of its defining features—major street names downtown appear in both English and Cherokee. Today, Northeastern State University and tourism supply jobs to residents.

**Information: Tahlequah Area Chamber of Commerce** | 123 E. Delaware St., Tahlequah, OK 74464-2817 | 800/456–4860 or 918/456–3742 | www.tahlequah.com/chamber.

## Attractions

**Cherokee Capitol Building.** The historic square in downtown Tahlequah has been a meeting place for the Cherokee tribe since its arrival in Indian Territory; the redbrick capitol was built in 1870 and houses the judicial branch of the modern Cherokee Nation. | 101 S. Muskogee Ave. | 918/456–0671 | Free | Weekdays 9–5, when court is in session.

**Cherokee Heritage Center.** This 44-acre wooded site, includes the Cherokee National Museum, which showcases tribal history and historic and contemporary art; *Tsa-La-Gi* Ancient Village, a living-history installation illustrating Cherokee life before European contact; and Adams Corner Rural Village, which demonstrates Cherokee life in Indian Territory. A walking trail around the Heritage Center grounds identifies trees and plants used in traditional Cherokee medicine. | Willis Rd., 3 mi south of U.S. 62 | 918/456–6007 | www.powersource.com/heritage | $6 | Mon.–Sun. 10–4:30.

**Elephant Rock Nature Park.** Secluded campsites with nature trails and tepees can be found in this 120-acre wooded park overlooking the Illinois River. | Rte. 10, 2 mi north of Tahlequah | 918/456–4215 | www.elephantrock.bigstep.com | Free | May–late Aug., Mon.–Sat.

**Float trips on the Illinois River.** A dozen or more canoe and kayak livery services rent equipment for floating the Illinois, a Class II river with rapids and waves up to a foot high. The stream is protected as a Wild and Scenic River; there are nine public access areas, some with campsites and numerous commercial campgrounds. | 123 E. Delaware St. | 918/456–3742 | fax 918/456–3751 | www.netsites.net/chamber/illinois.htm | Rates vary.

**Lake Tenkiller State Park.** Surrounded by limestone bluffs and oak and hickory trees, Lake Tenkiller is one of the state's most scenic. Cabins, tent and RV campsites, trails, a marina, a swimming pool, fishing docks, a nature center, and hiking trails. | Rte. 100, 3 mi south of Rte. 82 | 918/489–5641 | www.touroklahoma.com | Free | Daily.

**Murrell Home.** This is the antebellum home of Minerva Murell, the niece of Cherokee principal chief John Ross. It was the only one of the family homes to escape destruction by troops led by Confederate general Stand Watie, a Cherokee and enemy of Ross who sided with the Union forces. A self-guided 1-mi nature trail leads through a bird sanctuary behind the mansion. | 19479 E. Murrell Home Rd., Park Hill | 918/456–2751 | Free | Wed.–Sat. 10–5, Sun. 1–5.

**Northeastern State University.** Built on a hill overlooking the very spot said to be the end of the Cherokee Trail of Tears, this state college evolved from the Cherokee seminaries established by the Cherokee Nation soon after its arrival in Indian Territory. When established, the Cherokee Female Seminary was the first institution for higher learning for women west of the Mississippi River. An 1889 seminary building has been fully restored. | 600 N. Grand Ave. | 918/456–5111 | www.netsites.net/chamber/attractions.htm | Free | Daily.

**Sequoyah State Park.** (*See* Wagoner.) Named for one of the most famous members of the Cherokee Tribe, this state park preserves more than 2,000 acres of the oak and hickory woodlands the tribe has called home since the early 19th century. One of the state's most scenic parks, here you will find boating, hiking, horseback riding, and nature center programs. | 17847 Park Ten, Hulbert | 918/772–2046 | www.touroklahoma.com.

## ON THE CALENDAR

**AUG.:** *Illinois River BalloonFest.* Hot air balloonists come from around the country to participate in this gravity-defying fun fair, which includes balloon races and rides, Cherokee arts and crafts, carnival rides for the children, and live music and entertainment. Stay until dark to see the Balloon Glow, when dozens of tethered balloons illuminated with electric lights hover in the night sky. | 800/456–4860 or 918/453–9958.
**SEPT.:** *Cherokee National Holiday.* The annual gathering of the Cherokee Nation includes a rodeo, powwow, gospel singing, Cherokee language and culture workshops, children's activities, and Cherokee craft booths with demonstrations. | 918/456–0671.

# Dining

**B&J Restaurant.** American. Dine at a table, in a booth, or at the counter. Known for daily lunch specials, steak, shrimp, soup, and sandwiches. | 2501 S. Muskogee | 918/456–6069 | Open 24 hours | $3–$12 | AE, MC, V.

**Iguana Café.** American/Casual. Mission-style tables, adobe walls, and a pot-bellied stove are found in this narrow, snug restaurant and coffee house. Known for daily soup, sandwich, and salad specials, pizza, coffee, and imported beer. | 500A N. Muskogee Ave. | 918/458–0044 | Closed Sun. | $5–$9 | AE, MC, V.

**Jasper's.** Steak. This restaurant is on a hillside perch overlooking town. Known for steak, lobster, chicken breast, and its "Dock 39" salad (a large chef salad with chicken and bacon). Kids' menu. | 2600 S. Muskogee Ave. | 918/456–0100 | Closed Sun. | $8–$26 | AE, D, MC, V.

# Lodging

**Fin and Feather.** Family-owned and -operated since 1960, this resort 1 mi from Lake Tenkiller specializes in family reunions and retreats. The grounds are littered with lush greenery and rolling hills. Dining rooms, picnic area, some kitchenettes, refrigerators, cable TV, in-room VCRs (and movies), pool, pond, wading pool, hot tub, miniature golf, tennis, basketball, volleyball, playground, laundry facilities, business services, some pets allowed. | Rte. 10 off Rte. 100 | 918/487–5148 | fax 918/487–5025 | www.finandfeatherresort.com | 82 rooms | $67–$74 | Closed Oct.–Easter | AE, D, MC, V.

**Holiday Inn Express.** This duplex hotel has a "KidSuite", which resembles a tropical aquarium and has bunk beds and video games. The heated pool is in an enclosed courtyard. In-room data ports, some refrigerators, microwaves, cable TV, pool, video games, laundry services, no pets. | One Holiday Dr. | 918/456–7800 | fax 918/456–7806 | www.holidayinnexpress.com | 62 rooms | $74 | AE, D, DC, MC, V.

**MarVal Resort.** Tent campsites and fully equipped cabins are available on this 105-acre property in the foothills of the Oklahoma Ozarks. Cable TV (in cabins), no room phones, pool, pond, miniature golf, basketball, volleyball, fishing, children's programs (ages 2–17). Pets allowed (fee). | Rte. 100, 40 mi north of Tahlequah | 918/489–2295 | www.marvalresort.com | 17 cabins | $47 cabins | D, MC, V.

**Tahlequah Motor Lodge.** Simple, contemporary rooms have double, queen-, or king-sized beds in this motor lodge 1½ mi from the center of town. The pool is enclosed in a heated glass atrium, and its banquet and conference facilities accommodate from 10 to 30 people. Restaurant, complimentary breakfast, microwaves, refrigerators, cable TV, pool, laundry facilities. | 2501 S. Muskogee Ave. | 918/456–2350 or 800/480–8705 | fax 918/456–4580 | tlodge@fullnet.net | www.tahlequah.com/tlodge | 53 rooms | $54 | AE, D, DC, MC, V.

**Tenkiller Lodge.** This luxurious lodge 4 mi out of town is the premiere destination for sportsmen and families coming to enjoy the namesake lake. Spacious guest rooms have handmade log furniture and modern amenities. Just past the heated pool and pavilion is the magnificent lake—"Oklahoma's Clearwater Wonderland"—with all the fishing, swimming, hiking, and recreation you could ask for. In-room data ports, cable TV, pool, pets allowed. | Jct. Rte. 82 S. and Indian Rd. | 918/453–9000 | 25 rooms | $70 | AE, D, DC, MC, V.

# TULSA

MAP 4, J4

*(Nearby towns also listed: Broken Arrow, Claremore, Muskogee, Pryor, Wagoner)*

At the turn of the 20th century, Oklahoma's second-largest city (pop. 390,500), built in the northeast on the banks of the Arkansas River, was a Creek crossroads known as "Tulsey," a variation on the Creek word "tallasi," for "town." The discovery of oil in the nearby Red Fork field in 1901 would soon transform Tulsa into the "Oil Capital of the World." There was so much oil beneath the city that workers once accidentally struck oil at a petroleum exposition at the fairgrounds while demonstrating a new piece of equipment. Until the 1960s, there were more oil companies and oil-related businesses in Tulsa than in any other city of its size in the world. Oil money built and endowed many of Tulsa's treasures, including two art museums, and created Tulsa's art deco–flavored skyline, as the height of the 1920s oil boom coincided with the popularity of the architectural style.

Around the city's center, old neighborhoods are becoming new again. Cherry Street, an eclectic mix of restaurants, bars, and specialty shops, is thriving between Peoria and Utica Avenues, and Tulsa's old warehouse district, north of downtown, is a nascent arts community.

**Information: Metro Tulsa Chamber of Commerce** | 616 S. Boston Ave., Suite 100, Tulsa, OK 74119-1298 | 918/585–1201 or 800/558–3311. | www.tulsachamber.com.

## Attractions

**Allen Ranch.** This working cattle ranch south of Tulsa offers guided trail rides and hayrides, chuckwagon breakfast rides, and overnight horseback campouts. Chuckwagon suppers, com-

# 6 "I'm thirsty"'s, 9 "Are we there yet"'s, 3 "I don't feel good"'s,
# 1 car class upgrade.
## At least something's going your way.

Hertz rents Fords and other fine cars. ® REG. U.S. PAT. OFF. © HERTZ SYSTEM INC., 2000/005-00

### Make your next road trip more comfortable with a free one-class upgrade from Hertz.

Let's face it, a long road trip isn't always sunshine and roses. But with Hertz, you get a free one car class upgrade to make things a little more bearable. You'll also choose from a variety of vehicles with child seats, Optional Protection Plans, 24-Hour Emergency Roadside Assistance, and the convenience of NeverLost,® the in-car navigation system that provides visual and audio prompts to give you turn-by-turn guidance to your destination. In a word: it's everything you need for your next road trip. Call your travel agent or Hertz at **1-800-654-2210** and mention PC# **906404** or check us out at **hertz.com** or AOL Keyword: **hertz**. Peace of mind. Another reason nobody does it exactly like Hertz.

## Hertz
### exactly.®

plete with cowboy music, are held on Friday and Saturday nights. | 9600 S. Memorial Dr., Bixby | 918/366–3010 | 1-hr trail rides $10; chuckwagon supper $12.50 | Daily by appointment.

**Bell's Amusement Park.** Opened in 1951, old-fashioned thrills include the Tilt-A-Whirl, a ferris wheel and carousel, motorized cars and airplanes, and a wooden roller coaster. Two miniature golf courses, arcades, and concessions are also found in this park next to the Tulsa Fairgrounds. | 3901 E. 21 St. | 918/744–1991 | $1; ride prices vary | Weekends.

**Big Splash Water Park.** A water roller coaster, a giant wave pool, and three water flumes are among this large water park's attractions, which range from relaxing to exhilarating (visitors have been clocked at 65 mph while zipping down a seven-story slide). | 4707 E. 21st St. | 918/749–7385 | $16 | May–Labor Day, daily 10–8.

**Boston Avenue United Methodist Church.** One of the most outstanding examples of Tulsa's art deco legacy, this copper and limestone church soars with a 225-ft pleated tower emblazoned with terra-cotta sculptures, including figures of circuit riders, the first traveling ministers on the frontier. | 1301 S. Boston Ave. | 918/583–5181 | Free | Daily.

**Creek Council Oak Tree.** The Creek Council met at this 300-yr-old oak tree from 1836, when they arrived in the area from Alabama, until 1898. Along with elections and tribal business, ceremonial dances were held on the square. | 18th St. and Cheyenne Ave. | Free | Daily.

**Frankoma Pottery.** The Frank family began making pottery from Oklahoma clay in the 1930s, creating Western-themed dishes and other items. Pottery production continues at the plant, and vintage pieces have become hot collectibles. | 2400 Frankoma Rd., Sapulpa | 918/224–5511 | Free | Mon.–Sat. 1–5, Sun. 1–5; factory tours weekdays 9:30–2.

**Gershon and Rebecca Fenster Museum of Jewish Art.** Torah scrolls, oil lamps from the time of the Jewish exodus, personal items from victims of the Holocaust, paintings by contemporary Israeli artists, and ceremonial art are among the pieces in the museum's wide-ranging collection of Judaica, the largest in the Southwest. Docent-led tours are available with two weeks' notice. | Mingle Valley Trade Center, 61st and Mingle Sts. | 918/294–1366 | www.jewishmuseum.net | Free | Weekdays 10–4, tours by appointment.

**Gilcrease Museum.** Oil discovered beneath the allotment granted to Thomas Gilcrease, who was part Creek, made him a millionaire by the age of 21. The collection of Western and Native American art and Americana he collected and bequeathed to the city is one

## KODAK'S TIPS FOR NIGHT PHOTOGRAPHY

**Lights at Night**
· Move in close on neon signs
· Capture lights from unusual vantage points

**Fireworks**
· Shoot individual bursts using a handheld camera
· Capture several explosions with a time exposure
· Include an interesting foreground

**Fill-In Flash**
· Set the fill-in light a stop darker than the ambient light

**Around the Campfire**
· Keep flames out of the frame when reading the meter
· For portraits, take spot readings of faces
· Use a tripod, or rest your camera on something solid

**Using Flash**
· Stay within the recommended distance range
· Buy a flash with the red-eye reduction mode

From *Kodak Guide to Shooting Great Travel Pictures* © 2000 by Fodor's Travel Publications

of the largest in existence. The 10,000 paintings, drawings, prints, and sculptures, 250,000 Native American artifacts, and 90,000 manuscripts, documents, and maps include an original signed copy of the Declaration of Independence and 18 of Frederic Remington's 22 original bronzes, as well as work by George Catlin, Charles Russell, Alfred Bierstadt, and Thomas Moran. The 440-acre museum site includes 23 acres of landscaped gardens. | 1400 Gilcrease Museum Rd. | 918/596–2700 | www.gilcrease.org | Donations accepted | Memorial Day–Labor Day, Mon.–Sat. 9–5, Sun. 11–5; Labor Day–Memorial Day, Tues.–Sat. 9–5, Sun. 11–5.

Local millionaire Thomas Gilcrease's former home, a 1914 two-story sandstone structure with a wraparound porch and formal gardens, today holds the **Tulsa Historical Society Museum.** The museum contains historic photographs depicting the growth and development of Tulsa. | 1400 Gilcrease Museum Rd. | 918/596–1350 | Free | Tues.–Thurs., Sat. 11–4, Sun. 1–4.

**Harmon Science Center.** This 25,000-square-ft science and math museum uses interactive exhibits to teach kids mechanical principles, electricity, weather patterns, and even the city's infrastructure. There's a crawl-through scale model of subterranean Tulsa. | 5705 E. 41st St. | 918/622–5000 | www.sciencecenter.org | $5 | Fri. 3:30–6, Sat. 10–6, Sun. 1–5.

**Lake Keystone State Park.** This 714-acre park on the shore of 26,000-acre Lake Keystone is popular for fishing (striper, walleye, bass, and catfish), boating, and water sports. There are 22 cabins, tent and RV campsites, picnic areas, fishing docks, bicycle rentals, hiking trails, a marina, and a restaurant. | Rte. 151 N, 20 mi west of downtown Tulsa | 918/865–4991 | www.touroklahoma.com | Free | Daily.

**Mohawk Park.** This sprawling 2,800-acre park in north Tulsa has two golf courses, a zoo, a nature center and preserve, a polo field, hiking and equestrian trails, a playground, and a picnic area. Seven nature trails introduce you to the region's native mammals, birds, insects, and plants. | E. 36th St. N | 918/669–6272 | Free | Daily.

Mohawk Park's **Oxley Nature Center** has interpretive exhibits and dispenses printed trail guides. | 5701 E. 36th St. N | 918/669–6644 | Free | Daily.

A renovated (1994) polar-bear habitat and a relatively new tropical rain-forest exhibit (1997) are two popular additions to Mohawk Park's 70-acre **Tulsa Zoo,** which is home to more than 1,400 animals. The adjacent Robert J. LaFortune North American Living Museum takes you into four regions of the United States and combines live animals and plants with cultural information. | 6421 E. 36th St. | 918/669–6200 | www.tulsazoo.org | $5 | Daily 10–5.

**Philbrook Museum of Art.** A 1927 Italianate villa donated to Tulsa by oilman Waite Phillips is filled with an 8,500-piece collection of Italian Renaissance paintings, African, Asian, and Native American art, and 19th- and 20th-century European and American paintings and photographs. The 23-acre grounds include French- and English-style gardens. | 2727 S. Rockford Rd. | 800/324–7941 or 918/749–7941 | www.philbrook.org | $5 | Tues., Wed., Fri., Sat. 10–5, Thurs. 10–8, Sun. 11–5.

**Redbud Valley Nature Preserve.** River-bottom, limestone-bluff, and Western-prairie ecosystems are represented in this 220-acre preserve; a 1-mi hiking trail takes you into all three. A small visitor center has maps. | 161st East Ave. | 918/669–6460 | Free | Wed.–Sun. 8–5; visitor center Wed.–Sun. 11–3.

**River Parks.** Built along both banks of the Arkansas River, Tulsa's River Parks offer visitors approximately 10 mi of walking, jogging, and biking trails. Other amenities include an old railroad bridge converted for pedestrian use (at 31 St. and Peoria Ave.), the Old West Playground on the west side of the river between 11th and 31st streets, featuring a stagecoach and other Western artifacts, and a floating stage. | On the east bank the park runs from 11th St. south to 81st St.; on the west bank, from 11th St. south to 31st St. | Free | Daily.

**Tulsa Garden Center.** Rooms in a 1919 Italian Renaissance home on 13 acres hold flower shows and other special events, but the real draws are a Victorian glass conservatory, a sunken garden, an arboretum, and an adjacent rose garden first planted in 1935. | 2435 S. Peoria Ave. | 918/746–5125 | fax 918/746–5128 | Free | Weekdays 9–4.

**Woodland Hills Mall.** With more than 150 stores, this mall has everything from toys to apparel to exercise machines. A food court is on the top level. | 7021 S. Memorial Dr. | 918/252–7511 | www.woodlandhillsmall.com | Free | Mon.–Sat. 10–9, Sun. noon–7.

**Woodward Park.** This 45-acre wooded park near downtown Tulsa is landscaped with 17,000 azaleas, formal rose gardens, a rock garden, fountains, pools, an English-style herb garden, and shady sandstone walkways. The park is adjacent to the Tulsa Garden Center. | 2324 S. Rockford Ave. | 918/596–7877 | Free | Daily 6 AM–11 PM.

## ON THE CALENDAR

**APR.: *Herbal Affair and Festival.*** Downtown Sand Springs fills with street vendors selling live and dried herbs, herbal products, and gardening products. There are also food and crafts booths at this huge, sweet-smelling event. | 918/245–3221.

**MAY: *International Mayfest.*** An annual spring celebration of art, food, and music with afternoon and evening performances, plus children's activities. | 918/582–6435.

**JUNE–AUG.: *Discoveryland! Outdoor Theater.*** Outdoor performances of the Broadway musical *Oklahoma!* are prefaced by a Native American dancing exhibition. | 918/245–6552.

**JUNE: *Longhorn World Championship Rodeo.*** More than 500 top North American cowboys and cowgirls compete in seven rodeo events. | 580/585–1201.

**AUG.: *Jazz on Greenwood.*** Jazz, blues, zydeco, and other roots music are presented on three stages in the historic Greenwood area in north Tulsa. | 918/584–3378.

**AUG.: *Tulsa Powwow.*** Members of more than 50 tribes compete in evening dance competitions. Native American art, crafts, and foods are also featured. | 918/744–1113.

**SEPT.–OCT.: *Tulsa State Fair.*** Ranked one of the top-ten state fairs nationwide, Oklahoma's features a livestock show, two carnival midways, and regional and national entertainment. | Tulsa Fairgrounds | 918/744–1113.

TULSA

INTRO
ATTRACTIONS
DINING
LODGING

# Dining

**Atlantic Sea Grill.** Seafood. This is one of Tulsa's most enduringly popular restaurants. A candlelit terrace is open for dining in warm weather. The shrimp skewers and tuna steaks are popular. | 8321-A E. 61st St. | 918/252–7966 | No lunch weekends | $15–$20 | AE, D, DC, MC, V.

**Bodean Seafood.** Seafood. This restaurant has been serving fresh fish from around the world since 1968. The fish combined with innovative sauces and good wine make for an elegant dining experience. | 3323 E. 51st St. | 918/743–3861 | No lunch Sat., Sun. | $25–$35 | AE, D, DC, MC, V.

**Brookside by Day.** American. Pancakes, egg dishes, French toast, and omelettes are the stars at this diner in Brookside, a trendy stretch of shops and restaurants. | 3313 S. Peoria Ave. | 918/745–9989 | Breakfast also available. No supper | $5–$10 | AE, D, MC, V.

**Camarelli's.** Italian. Italian landscape paintings hang on the walls of this traditional Italian restaurant lit with candles at night. Known for seafood alfredo, pizzas, calamari, and homemade soup. | 1536 E. 15th St. | 918/582–8900 | No lunch Sat., Sun. | $13–$18 | AE, D, DC, MC, V.

**Casa Bonita.** Mexican. Reminiscent of a Mexican village, this popular restaurant has waterfalls, caves, strolling musicians, and lots of hearty food. Try the chiles rellenos or chalupas. There is a game room with video games on site. Kids' menu. | 2120 S. Sheridan Rd. | 918/836–6464 | $9–$14 | AE, D, DC, MC, V.

**Fountains.** American. This fine dining restaurant was established in 1973. Known for steak, pasta, duck, fresh seafood, and chicken dishes. Salad bar. Kids' menu. Sun. brunch. | 6540 S. Lewis Ave. | 918/749–9916 | No lunch Sat. No supper Sun. | $13–$30 | AE, D, DC, MC, V.

**French Hen.** Continental. The small, intimate tables are reminiscent of a European café. Try the homemade ravioli, breast of pheasant, or garlic shrimp. | 7143 S. Yale St. | 918/492–2596 | Closed Sun. No lunch Sat. | $17–$40 | AE, D, DC, MC, V.

**Grady's American Grill.** American. Established in Knoxville, Tennessee in 1919, this is one of the 36 Grady's branches that can be found across the country. The restaurant has a relaxed but upscale atmosphere. Lots of carpeting, plants, and warm wood accents can be found throughout. Known for prime rib, steak, and fresh seafood. | 7007 S. Memorial Dr. | 918/254–7733 | $20–$30 | AE, D, DC, MC, V.

**Jamil's.** Middle Eastern. This rambling restaurant has four candlelit dining rooms and serves complimentary appetizers of hummus dip and cabbage rolls. Try the tabouli or savory steaks and seafood dishes. Kids' menu. | 2833 E. 51st St. | 918/742–9097 | No lunch | $13–$30 | AE, D, DC, MC, V.

**Metro Diner.** American/Casual. The faux-1950s diner design relies on lots of chrome and neon. Known for chicken-fried steak. Kids' menu. | 3001 E. 11th St. | 918/592–2616 | Breakfast also available | $10–$11 | AE, D, MC, V.

★ **Nelson's Buffeteria.** American. This cafeteria-style restaurant has been a popular downtown fixture since it opened in 1951. (The line moves lightning fast at lunchtime.) Known for chicken-fried steak and meat loaf. | 514 S. Boston | 918/584–9969 | Breakfast also available. Closed Sat., Sun. No supper | $7–$9 | MC, V.

**Polo Grill.** Contemporary. Located in Tulsa's most exclusive shopping center, at Utica Square, this restaurant has a continually changing menu. Elegant, dark-wood furnishings lend the dining area the refined feel of a traditional social club. Open-air dining is available on a patio with umbrellas for shade, and a pianist performs in the evenings. Known for fresh seafood and roast pork tenderloin sided with sweet corn relish. Its award-winning wine cellar is the largest in Oklahoma. | 2038 Utica Sq | 918/744–4280 | Closed Sun. | $18–$30 | AE, DC, MC, V.

**Richardo's.** Mexican. This popular place has been a great family-style restaurant since it first opened in 1975. Known for chiles rellenos and buritto lota (a large tortilla filled with beans and beef, smothered in cheese and guacamole). | 5629 E. 41st St. | 918/622–2668 | Closed Sun. | $5–$10 | AE, D, DC, MC, V.

**Romano's Macaroni Grill.** Italian. Stone walls, arched doorways, gladiolus plants, a fireplace, and opera music in the background create an authentic Italian-country feel. Try the penne rustico (penne pasta and prosciutto in a rich, garlicky cream sauce) or the pollo portobello sandwich (a marinated chicken breast and portobello mushroom cap topped with mozzarella and demi-glaze). Kids' menu. | 8112 E. 66th St. | 918/254–7800 | $9–$17 | AE, D, DC, MC, V.

**Rosie's Rib Joint.** Steak. A gazebo that seats up to six people is smack in the middle of the casual dining area. Known for hickory-smoked ribs, fish, steak, and chicken. Salad bar. | 8125 E. 49th St. | 918/663–2610 | No lunch Sat. | $15–$20 | AE, D, DC, MC, V.

**Warren Duck Club.** Continental. Tables are adorned with crystals and white linen in this elegant restaurant, which overlooks a tranquil greenbelt in south Tulsa. Try the blackened beef tenderloin, tiger prawns, Long Island duck, swordfish, salmon, or buffalo. Pianist Fri., Sat. Kids' menu. | Doubletree Hotel at Warren Place, 6110 S. Yale Ave. | 918/495–1000 | Closed Sun. | $25–$60 | AE, D, DC, MC, V.

## Lodging

**Adams Mark Tulsa, at Williams Center.** Over 35,000 square ft of meeting space and a downtown location make this a popular business and convention facility. Comfortable rooms and well-appointed baths are a welcome respite at the end of the day. Restaurants, bar, room service, in-room data ports, minibars, refrigerators, cable TV, in-room VCRs, pool, exercise equipment, business services, airport shuttle. | 100 E. 2nd St. | 918/582–9000 | fax 918/560–2232 | www.adamsmark.com | 462 rooms | $100 | AE, D, DC, MC, V.

**AmeriSuites.** All suites in this six–story hotel have a desk with multiple phone lines, and a large living area. A handful of restaurants are within walking distance. Complimentary breakfast, in-room data ports, kitchenettes, microwaves, refrigerators, cable TV, pool, gym, laundry service, business services. | 7037 S. Zurich Ave. | 918/491–4010 | fax 918/497–2053 | 128 rooms | $94 | AE, D, DC, MC, V.

**Baymont Inns and Suites.** This chain hotel's advantageous location puts it within walking distance of Celebration Station Amusement Park, 5 mi from Oral Roberts University, and 15 mi from Tulsa World Airport. Complimentary Continental breakfast, some microwaves, some refrigerators, cable TV, pool, business services. | 4530 E. Skelly Dr. | 918/488–8777 | fax 918/488–0220 | www.baymontinns.com | 89 rooms, 12 suites | $65, $74–$100 suites | AE, D, DC, MC, V.

**Best Western Airport.** This two-story motel is less than 1 mi from the airport and on a strip with plenty of dining options. Restaurant, bar, complimentary Continental breakfast, room service, microwaves, cable TV, pool, business services, airport shuttle. | 222 N. Garnett St. | 918/438–0780 | fax 918/438–9296 | www.bestwestern.com | 118 rooms | $55 | AE, D, DC, MC, V.

**Best Western Glenpool.** This one-story motel is less than 2 mi from downtown Tulsa and the airport, as well as many area attractions. Complimentary Continental breakfast, in-room data ports, microwaves, refrigerators, cable TV, pool, laundry facilities, business services, pets allowed. | 14831 S. Casper, Glenpool | 918/322–5201 | fax 918/322–9604 | www.bestwestern.com | 64 rooms | $70 | AE, D, DC, MC, V.

**Best Western Trade Winds Central Inn.** Most rooms have exterior entrances in this two-story motel off I-44. It's 15 minutes from downtown Tulsa and within 1 mi of two golf courses. Restaurant, bar (with entertainment), complimentary Continental breakfast, room service, in-room data ports, in-room hot tubs, cable TV, in-room VCRs (and movies), pool, laundry facilities, business services, airport shuttle, some pets accepted. | 3141 E. Skelly Dr. | 918/749–5561 | fax 918/749–6312 | www.bestwestern.com | 167 rooms | $69 | AE, D, DC, MC, V.

**Comfort Suites.** Rooms are arranged around an indoor garden atrium with a tropical fountain in this all-suites hotel. Complimentary popcorn and a beverage of your choice are served each evening in a private lounge. The hotel is less than 1 mi from Woodland Hills Mall, the largest mall in the area, and more than 80 restaurants. Restaurant, complimentary breakfast, room service, in-room data ports, microwaves, refrigerators, cable TV, in-room VCRs, pool, business services. | 8338 E. 61st St. S | 918/254–0088 | fax 918/254–6820 | 49 suites | $69–$89 suites | AE, D, DC, MC, V.

**Courtyard Tulsa Central.** This three-story hotel is part of the chain designed by business travelers. There are lots of amenities, and five 18-hole golf courses are within 12 mi of the facility. Restaurant, in-room data ports, in-room safes, cable TV, pool, hot tub, gym, laundry facilities, laundry services. | 3340 S. 79th East Ave. | 918/660–0646 | fax 918/660–0731 | www.courtyard.com | 122 rooms | $84 | AE, D, DC, MC, V.

**Days Inn.** This duplex hotel has a large banquet space, and free ice cream and popcorn are available in the lobby at night. Complimentary Continental breakfast, cable TV, pool, no pets. | 8201 E. Skelly Dr. | 918/665–6800 | fax 918/665–7653 | www.daysinn.com | 94 rooms | $48 | AE, D, DC, MC, V.

**Doubletree Downtown.** Right in the middle of downtown Tulsa's business district, this hotel is within sight of a number of malls, boutiques, and art galleries. Well-appointed guest rooms have spacious work areas. Restaurant, bar (with entertainment), in-room data ports, microwaves, cable TV, in-room VCRs, pool, hot tub, exercise equipment, business services, airport shuttle, pets allowed (fee). | 616 W. 7th St. | 918/587–8000 | fax 918/587–1642 | www.doubletreehotels.com | 417 rooms | $119 | AE, D, DC, MC, V.

**Doubletree Hotel at Warren Place.** Public areas are furnished with classic period pieces, and rooms have tranquil, sandy color schemes and textured wall treatments. 2 restaurants (*see* Warren Duck Club), bar, room service, in-room data ports, refrigerator, cable TV, in-room VCRs, pool, hot tub, exercise equipment, business services, airport shuttle, pets allowed. | 6110 S. Yale Ave. | 918/495–1000 | fax 918/495–1944 | www.doubletreehotels.com | 370 rooms | $119 | AE, D, DC, MC, V.

**Embassy Suites.** Spacious suites have balconies overlooking the atrium, which is a long, arched vault supported by massive marble pillars, filled with ferns and potted greenery. The hotel is 15 mi from the airport and 3 mi from the mall. Restaurant, bar, complimentary breakfast, in-room data ports, kitchenettes, microwaves, refrigerators, cable TV, pool, hot tub, exercise equipment, laundry facilities, business services, airport shuttle. | 3332 S. 79th E. Ave. | 918/622–4000 | fax 918/665–2347 | www.embassysuites.com | 240 suites | $119–$129 suites | AE, D, DC, MC, V.

**Fairfield Inn.** This modestly priced three-story hotel is 11 mi south of the Tulsa airport. Complimentary Continental breakfast, in-room data ports, cable TV, pool, hot tub, laundry services, no pets. | 9020 E. 71st St. | 918/252–7754 | fax 918/252–7754 | www.fairfieldinn.com | 64 rooms | $67 | AE, D, DC, MC, V.

**Guest House Suites Plus.** Bi-level suites have a living room on the first level, and a loft bedroom on the second. All kitchens are fully equipped. Picnic area, complimentary Continental breakfast, in-room data ports, kitchenettes, microwaves, cable TV, in-room VCRs, pool, hot tubs, laundry facilities, business services, airport shuttle, some pets allowed. | 8181 E. 41st St. | 918/664–7241 | fax 918/622–0314 | 135 suites | $75–$109 | AE, D, DC, MC, V.

**Hampton Inn.** Rooms range from the "Single" to the "King Deluxe", which is more spacious than other rooms, has a king-size bed, and an expanded bathroom. Complimentary Continental breakfast, in-room data ports, microwaves, refrigerators, cable TV, pool, business services. | 3209 S. 79th E. Ave. | 918/663–1000 | fax 918/663–0587 | www.hampton-inn.com | 132 rooms, 16 suites | $76–$79, $99 suites | AE, D, DC, MC, V.

**Hawthorn Suites.** All suites have two large rooms, a fireplace, and well-lit desks. The hotel is a stone's throw away from two highways (I–44 and Rte. 51), and the Woodland Hills Mall is just 3 mi away. Complimentary breakfast, some kitchenettes, microwaves, cable TV, pool, hot tub, laundry facilities, business services, airport shuttle, some pets allowed. | 3509 S. 79th E. Ave. | 918/663–3900 | fax 918/663–0548 | www.hawthorn.com | 131 suites | $99–189 suites | AE, D, DC, MC, V.

**Heritage Inn.** More than 25 restaurants and the Southroads Shopping Center are less than 1 mi from this four–story hotel. Complimentary Continental breakfast, microwaves, some in-room hot tubs, cable TV, in-room VCRs, pool, business services. | 6030 E. Skelly Dr. | 918/665–2630 | 129 rooms, 1 suite | $39, $139 suite | AE, D, DC, MC, V.

**Holiday Inn–East/Airport.** The courtyard has a recreation center and grills in this hotel 15 minutes from the downtown Tulsa area. Restaurant, bar, room service, in-room data ports, microwaves, cable TV, pool, video games, playground, business services, airport shuttle, pets allowed. | 1010 N. Garnett Rd. | 918/437–7660 | fax 918/438–7538 | www.holiday-inn.com | 158 rooms | $84 | AE, D, DC, MC, V.

**Holiday Inn Select.** Rooms are spacious at this hotel less than 5 mi from a water park, a horse-racing track, and the Tulsa Drillers Stadium. Restaurant, bar, room service, cable TV, pool, exercise equipment, laundry facilities, business services, airport shuttle, pets allowed (fee). | 5000 E. Skelly Dr. | 918/622–7000 | fax 918/664–9353 | hiseltulsa@aol.com | 294 rooms, 13 suites | $99, $159–$225 suites | AE, D, DC, MC, V.

**La Quinta Inn.** This hotel is far enough from the city's main commercial strip to be quiet and relaxing, but close enough (10 minutes or less) to the zoo, the convention center, and the downtown area to still make you feel a part of the action. Complimentary Continental breakfast, in-room data ports, cable TV, pool, business services, airport shuttle, some pets allowed. | 35 N. Sheridan Rd. | 918/836–3931 | fax 918/836–5428 | 93 rooms, 8 suites | $62, $75–$85 suites | AE, D, DC, MC, V.

**Marriott Southern Hills.** This 11-story hotel has spacious rooms and a large banquet room. It's less than 1 mi from the Woodland Hills Mall. Restaurant, bar, room service, in-room data ports, cable TV, in-room VCRs, pool, exercise equipment, business services, airport shuttle. | 1902 E. 71st St. | 918/493–7000 or 800/228–9290 | fax 918/523–0950 | 383 rooms | $69–$134 | AE, D, DC, MC, V.

**McBirney Mansion.** This 12,000-square-ft Tudor-style mansion was built in 1927 and is listed on the National Register of Historic Places. The huge stone structure overlooks the Arkansas

River and sits on 3 acres of pristine, painstakingly landscaped grounds. It is adjacent to Tulsa's wooded River Parks area, which has approximately 10 mi of trails. Stone-paved paths wind through the property, leading to freshwater spring-fed ponds. Guest rooms are individually decorated; yours may have a king-size bed, a queen-size iron canopy bed, antiques, leaded windows, a fireplace, or views of the river and parkland. The separate Carriage House has a four-room suite for those wishing total privacy and quietude. Dining rooms, complimentary breakfast, cable TV, no kids under 8. | 1414 S. Galveston Ave. | 918/585–3234 | www.mcbirneymansion.com | 6 rooms, 2 suites in two buildings | $119–$159, $195–225 suites | AE, D, MC, V.

**Radisson Inn–Tulsa Airport.** Located at the airport entrance, shopping, restaurants, the zoo, and parks are within 10 mi of this two-story hotel. Rooms are softly lit and have plenty of work space for business travelers. Restaurants, bar, room service, in-room data ports, cable TV, pool, exercise equipment, business services, airport shuttle. | 2201 N. 77th E. Ave. | 918/835–9911 | fax 918/838–2452 | www.radisson.com | 172 rooms, 2 suites | $119, $150 suites | AE, D, DC, MC, V.

**Sheraton.** Built in 1983, rooms in this 11–story hotel have wooden furniture and framed art-prints on the wall. Three major shopping malls are within 5 mi. Restaurant, bar, room service, in-room data ports, cable TV, in-room VCRs (and movies), indoor-outdoor pool, hot tub, sauna, laundry facilities, business center, exercise equipment, airport shuttle, some pets allowed. | 10918 E. 41st St. | 918/627–5000 | fax 918/627–4003 | www.sheraton.com/tulsa | 325 rooms, 5 suites | $74–$129, $450–$500 suites | AE, D, DC, MC, V.

**Sleep Inn and Suites.** Opened in 1999, this centrally located, three-story hotel is within walking distance of numerous restaurants. Complimentary Continental breakfast, in-room data ports, microwaves, some refrigerators, cable TV, pool, hot tub, sauna, spa, gym, laundry services, no pets. | 8021 E. 33rd St. S | 918/663-2777 | fax 918/858–4445 | 61 rooms, 5 suites | $61–$75, $79–$99 suites | AE, D, DC, MC, V.

**Tulsa Downtown East Super 8.** This two-story motel is within 1 mi of a number of restaurants and a few shops. Cable TV, pool, hot tub, gym, laundry services. | 3211 S. 79th E. Ave. | 918/660–8080 | fax 918/664–9652 | www.super8.com | 62 rooms | $50 | AE, D, DC, MC, V.

# VINITA

MAP 4, K3

*(Nearby towns also listed: Grove, Miami)*

Vinita was founded in 1871 where the Frisco and Missouri-Kansas-Texas railroads crossed. A town founder, Col. Elias Boudinot, named Vinita for an (unrequited) love, artist Vinnie Ream, who created the sculpture of Abraham Lincoln in the Capitol in Washington, D.C. Today this town of 6,500 is a nostalgic stop along Route 66. Wilson Avenue, Vinita's main thoroughfare, follows the path of the old road through downtown.

Information: **Vinita Chamber of Commerce** | 125 S. Scraper St., Vinita, OK 74301-3723 | 918/256–7133 | fax 918/256–8261.

## Attractions
**Eastern Trails Museum.** This small historical museum has photographs and artifacts relating to railroads, pioneer settlement, and the Civil War Battle of Cabin Creek, which took place in a field near the area's stagecoach station. The museum provides maps for a self-guided walking tour of 38 historic buildings and homes. | 215 W. Illinois Ave. | 918/256–2115 | Free | Mon.–Sat. 1–4.

**AUG.: *Will Rogers Memorial Rodeo and Parade.*** This rodeo, first staged in 1936, a year after Rogers's death in a plane crash, attracts 300 to 400 cowboys annually. The Main Street route of the Saturday parade follows old Route 66. | 918/256–7133.

**SEPT.: *Calf Fry Festival.*** A cooking contest and tasting fair are accompanied by cowboy games, such as horseshoes and team roping. | 918/256–7133.

## Dining

**Clanton's Cafe.** American. This classic Route 66 diner has red vinyl booths and stools and photos of prize-winning steers throughout. Known for blue-plate specials and steaks. | 319 E. Illinois Ave. | 918/256–9053 | $2–$7 | No credit cards | Breakfast also available.

## Lodging

**Holiday Motel.** This two-story strip motel in the center of town was built in the 1970s. Cable TV, pool, pets allowed. | 519 S. Wilson St. | 918/256–6429 | 25 rooms | $40 | AE, D, MC, V.

# WAGONER

MAP 4, K4

*(Nearby towns also listed: Broken Arrow, Muskogee, Pryor, Tahlequah, Tulsa)*

Wagoner was settled in Indian Territory in 1868, at the point where the Arkansas Valley and Kansas Railroad met the M-K-T (Missouri-Kansas-Texas) line. Around the turn of the 20th century this town of 7,000 was a major shipping point for cattle, and area ranchers built showplace homes that current residents are busy restoring. Wagoner businesses cater to people visiting two nearby state parks— Sequoyah and Sequoyah Bay. The town also has a plant that makes shopping carts—an Oklahoma invention.

Information: **Wagoner Chamber of Commerce** | 301 S. Grant Ave., Wagoner, OK 74467-4908 | 918/485–3414 | fax 918/485–2523 | www.wagoner.net.

## Attractions

**Sequoyah Bay State Park.** This unspoiled state park on the shores of Fort Gibson Reservoir has five cabins, RV and tent campsites, a picnic area, a swimming beach, a marina, lighted boat ramps, and a heated fishing dock. | Rte. 16, 4 mi south of Wagoner | 918/683–0878 | www.touroklahoma.com | Free | Daily.

**Sequoyah State Park.** Built on a peninsula extending out into Fort Gibson Reservoir, this park has secluded campsites, cottages with full kitchens, and a "guest ranch" (more motel than ranch) with a restaurant, bar, swimming pool, and recreation center. There are also stables, a golf course, a marina, a nature center, hiking and mountain biking trails, a grocery, and a laundromat. | Rte. 51, 8 mi east of Wagoner | 918/772–2545 | www.touroklahoma.com | Free | Daily.

**Wagoner City Historical Museum.** A collection of historic clothing dating back to the Civil War can be found in this small city museum. Local photographs and artifacts, including a horse-drawn taxi, are also on display. | 122 S. Main St. | 918/485–9111 | Free | Jun.–Oct., Tues.–Sat. 9–4; Nov.–May, Tues.–Sat. 10–3.

**MAR.: *Trout Derby.*** Anglers spend three days fishing for tagged trout in the hopes of winning prizes at Lake Watonga in Roman Nose Resort Park. There are divisions for both adults and children. | 580/228–2081.

**OCT.: *Cheese Festival.*** One of the last remaining small dairies and cheese factories in the state is the centerpiece of a huge arts and crafts show with entertainment, historical reenactments, and, of course, cheese tasting. | 580/623–5452.

## Dining

**Main Street Cafe.** American. Start your day with a whopping, old-style breakfast. The café opens at 5:30 AM and serves eggs, bacon, sausage, ham, hash browns, and biscuits and gravy. Classic luncheon-counter fare includes its signature piece—the Missile Burger (double meat, double cheese burger served with fries). | 112 S. Main | 918/485–3668 | Closed Sun. No supper | $3–$7 | No credit cards.

**Steakout Sports Grill.** American. Sports and hunting memorabilia, such as framed football jerseys and stuffed trophy heads, adorn the walls. Try the steak or fajitas. | 308 S. Hayes St. | 918/485–3810 | Closed Mon. | $7–$15 | AE, D, MC, V.

**Whitehorn Cove Floating Restaurant.** American. This marina and restaurant on Fort Gibson Lake is a popular lunch spot for burgers and sandwiches. Known for pasta, steak, shrimp, and catfish platters for dinner. | Whitehorn Cove Park, U.S. 69 | 918/462–7411 | Breakfast also available | $10–$15 | AE, MC.

## Lodging

**Days Inn of Wagoner.** This duplex inn is adjacent to fast-food restaurants, and is 7 mi from the magnificent Sequoyah State Park, where you can golf, camp, play tennis, and boat and fish on Ft. Gibson Lake. Complimentary Continental breakfast, in-room data ports, some in-room hot tubs, cable TV. | 1404 W. Rte. 51 | 918/485–4593 | fax 918/485–4593 | www.daysinn.com | 43 rooms | $50 | AE, D, DC, MC, V.

**Indian Lodge.** The redbrick buildings of Indian Lodge are on shaded grounds, just 2 mi from Fort Gibson Reservoir. The buildings are still holding on to their 1950s-era furnishings. Picnic area, some kitchenettes, cable TV, pool, pond, basketball, volleyball, fishing, playground. | Rte. 51 E, 5½ mi east of Wagoner | 918/485–3184 | 22 rooms, 3 suites | $45–$60, $105–$155 suites | Closed Nov.–Apr. | AE, D, MC, V.

**Western Hills Guest Ranch.** Lakeside or poolside rooms are available at this sprawling, state-owned and -operated ranch on Fort Gibson Reservoir in Sequoyah State Park. The rustic buildings have varying degrees of modern amenities. Bar, dining room, picnic area, room service (in lodge), in-room VCRs (and movies), pool, wading pool, miniature golf, putting green, tennis, boating, children's programs (6–17), playground, business services, airport shuttle. | Box 509 | 918/772–2545 or 800/654–8240 | fax 918/772–2030 | 98 rooms, 44 cabins | $70–$75, $60–$110 cabins | AE, D, DC, MC, V.

# WATONGA

MAP 4, G4

*(Nearby towns also listed: El Reno, Enid, Weatherford)*

Founded in 1892 on the Canadian River, this town of 4,500 is named for the Arapaho chief Black Coyote (which was his translated name). The canyons north of town were used as a Cheyenne winter camp in the 19th century. The historic downtown district is small but charming, with such attractions as a W.P.A.-era mural in the post office and the Noble House, once a rooming house that has been restored and is operated as a restaurant by a group of local shareholders. A local cheese factory offers tours.

**Information: Watonga Chamber of Commerce** | U.S. 270 S, Watonga, OK 73772 | 580/623–5452 | fax 580/623–5444 | watonga.com.

## Attractions

**T. B. Ferguson Home.** This restored three-story house belonged to Thomas Benton Ferguson, territorial newspaper editor and publisher, and the sixth territorial governor. Ferguson and his wife, Elva, were the models for the protagonists in Edna Ferber's novel *Cimarron*; Ferber spent months at their house researching and writing the manuscript. An 1870 cavalry remount station and the old Watonga city jail stand in the home's backyard. | 519 N. Weigel St. | 580/623–5069 | Free | Tues.–Fri. 9–5, weekends 1–5.

**Roman Nose Resort Park.** Named for Henry Caruthers Roman Nose, a Southern Cheyenne Chief, members of the Cheyenne tribe once used the natural springs and canyons of this park for a winter camp. Here you will find a spring-fed swimming pool, a fishing lake, a lodge with recreation programs, cabins, RV and tent camping areas, hiking and mountain bike trails, an 18-hole golf course, and guided horseback rides led by cavalry reenactors. | Rte. 1, 6 mi northwest of Watonga | 580/963–2111; marina 580/963–3531 | www.tourokla-homa.com | Free | Daily.

## ON THE CALENDAR
**FEB.:** *Bitter Creek Frontier Daze.* Roman Nose Resort Park near Watonga hosts a living-history reenactment featuring Plains Indians, fur trappers, U.S. cavalry, outlaws, and homesteaders. | 580/623–7281.

**OCT.:** *Watonga Cheese Festival.* Held on both Main St. and the fairgrounds, this festival presents historical reenactments of early western settler life, with an emphasis on the town's cheese production. There are more than 300 crafts and antiques booths, as well as live entertainment on Main St. and a cheese dish competition. | 580/623–5452 | www.watonga.com.

# Dining
**General Store on the Lake.** American. This log-cabin restaurant, modeled after an 1890 general store, was built in 1994 and serves as a grocery store and diner. Known for barbecued beef and pork, catfish, and hamburgers. | Roman Nose Resort Park, Rte. 1, 6 mi northwest of Watonga | 580/623–4309 | Breakfast also available | $4–$11 | MC, V.

**Noble House Restaurant.** American. Housed in a historical building that dates back to 1912, this casual spot is decorated with authentic tapestries. Steaks, fried catfish, and cheese soup are among the dishes served. Kid's menu. | 112 N. Noble Ave. | 580/623–2559 | No lunch Mon., Wed., Sat; no supper Sun.–Wed. | $6–$16 | AE, D, MC, V.

# Lodging
**Red Bud Manor.** Built in 1930 from stone and "klinker" bricks (bricks that have bubbled and cracked like lava), this unique B&B resembles a low-slung faux-French castle. The living room boasts an original carved granite fireplace, a 1917 grand piano, a Gothic chandelier and wall sconces, oak floors, and French doors leading to the terrace and gardens. Guest rooms contain an assortment of antiques, and a two-story turret houses a breakfast nook. Complimentary breakfast, cable TV, pool, laundry facilities. | 900 N. Burford | 580/623–8587 | 2 rooms | $65 | No credit cards.

**Roman Nose Lodge.** This state-owned lodge is on a bluff overlooking Lake Boecher. It's surrounded by towering cedar trees and blue sage plants. All Roman Nose Resort Park facilities are available for your use. Restaurant, some kitchenettes, cable TV, pool. 9-hole golf course, putting green, boating, children's programs (3–17), playground, business services. | Rte. 8, 6 mi north of Watonga | 580/623–7281 or 800/892–8690 | fax 580/623–2538 | 47 rooms, 10 cottages | $63 rooms, $73 cottages | AE, D, DC, MC, V.

# WAURIKA

MAP 4, G7

*(Nearby town also listed: Duncan)*

Waurika, 20 mi north of the Red River, was a stopping place in the late 1800s for herds of cattle being driven up the Chisholm Trail; later it became a rail center. The local economy is still based on ranching.

Information: **Waurika Chamber of Commerce** | 120 W. Broadway Ave., Waurika, OK 73573-2212 | 580/228–2081.

## Attractions

**Chisholm Trail Historical Museum.** Artifacts and photographs depict the history of the Chisholm Trail, which carried millions of head of cattle through Indian Territory in the decades following the Civil War. Exhibits include information about Delaware trader Jesse Chisholm, who popularized the trail, and the daily life of cattle drovers. | U.S. 70 and U.S. 81 | 580/228–2166 | Free | Sat. 10–4, Sun. 1–4, or by appointment.

**Waurika Lake.** This 10,000-acre lake is known for its striper and crappie and has been described as a "fisherman's paradise." Quiet and spacious, the park near the lake has RV and tent campsites, boat ramps, fishing docks, and a marina. The 13-mi Walker Creek Equestrian and Hiking Trail begins 5½ mi north of the dam. | Rte. 5, 6 mi north of Waurika | 580/963–2111; marina 580/963–3531 | Free | Daily.

**ON THE CALENDAR**

**JUNE: *Chisholm Trail Celebration.*** Outdoor living-history exhibits relating to life along the Chisholm Trail, Native American dances, storytelling, a beef brisket dinner, an outdoor melodrama, and Western music are part of this event held at the Chisholm Trail Museum. | 580/228–2166.

**JUNE: *Rattlesnake Hunt.*** This fundraiser for the local volunteer fire department includes snake hunting, snake handling demonstrations, and other entertainment. | 580/228–2081.

## Dining

**Moneka Haunted Tea Room.** American. Set in a former railroad rooming house, this gift and antiques store and tea room serves up ghost stories along with its daily specials. (The owners say that the spirits of two former occupants have been spotted on the premises.) Known for sandwiches, salads and hearty fare, including pot roast and chicken and dumplings. | U.S. 70 | 580/228–2575 | Closed Sat.–Tues. | $3–$7 | No credit cards.

## Lodging

**A-OK Motel.** This modest, single-story motel is the only place in town to rest your head. Cable TV, pets allowed. | Jct. U.S. 81 and U.S. 70 | 580/228–2337 | 32 rooms | $35 | AE, D, MC, V.

# WEATHERFORD

MAP 4, G5

*(Nearby towns also listed: Clinton, El Reno, Watonga)*

This town of 11,000 formed in 1898 when the Rock Island Railroad passed through the area. It was later on the path of historic Route 66. The presence of Southwestern State University gives the town more restaurants and shops than others of its size.

Information: **Weatherford Area Chamber of Commerce** | 522 W. Rainey Ave., Weatherford, OK 73096-4704 | 580/772–7744 | fax 580/772–7751 | www.weatherford.net.

## Attractions

**Red Rock Canyon State Park.** The red-walled canyons found in this state park were once used as a winter camp by the Cheyenne, Comanche, and Kickapoo. The park is popular today with rappellers, who scale the 100-ft walls, and with mountain bikers, hikers, and picnickers. Park amenities include tent and RV campsites, picnic areas, and a swimming pool. | U.S. 281, 20 mi southeast of Weatherford | 405/542–6344 | www.touroklahoma.com | Free | Daily.

**Thomas P. Stafford Museum.** Housed in the Weatherford airport, this museum chronicles the life and career of Weatherford native Gen. Thomas P. Stafford, who commanded Apollo 10. Stafford's space suit is on display, along with a Titan second-stage rocket engine and such personal items as his fourth-grade schoolwork. | 3000 Logan Rd., Stafford Field | 580/772–6143 | Free | Daily.

**Southwestern Antique Mall.** This facility is home to more than 60 vendors that deal in antiques, collectibles, glassware, toys, furniture, and much more. | 1225 E. Main St. | 580/772–1535 | Free | Mon.–Sat. 10–6, Sun. 1–5.

**Southwestern Oklahoma State University.** This public university has a student body close to 5,000 and is spread out over 25 acres on the north side of Weatherford. Undergraduate and masters programs are offered. | 100 Campus Dr. | 580/772–6611 | fax 580/774–3795 | www.swosu.edu | Free | Daily.

### ON THE CALENDAR

**FEB.: *World Championship Hog Calling Contest.*** Along with the main event, which features live hogs, there are kids' contests—such as old fashioned sack races—pork barbecue stands, and arts and crafts booths. | 580/772–0310.

**SEPT.: *Southwest Festival of the Arts.*** This juried fine arts and crafts show includes children's activities. | 580/772–7744.

## Dining

**T-Bone Steak House.** Steak. One side of this restaurant is a sports bar, the other has a quieter dining room. A fireplace provides a warm mood throughout. Known for smoked prime rib, steak, seafood, pasta, and sandwiches. Kids' menu. Sun. brunch. | 1805 E. Main St. | 580/772–6329 | No lunch | $10–$15 | AE, D, MC, V.

## Lodging

**Best Western Mark Motor Hotel.** This two–story motel is four blocks from a city park, 12 blocks from Southwestern Oklahoma State University, and 15 mi from the Oklahoma Route 66 Museum. Complimentary Continental breakfast, in-room data ports, refrigerators, cable TV, in-room VCRs, pool, business services, pets allowed. | 525 E. Main St. | 580/772–3325 | fax 580/772–8950 | www.bestwestern.com | 63 rooms | $59 | AE, D, DC, MC, V.

**Days Inn.** This duplex motel was built in the late 1970s. It's just off I–40, Exit 82, across the street from the Southwestern Antique Mall, and just a brief stroll to many restaurants and fast-food places. Complimentary Continental breakfast, cable TV, pool. | 1019 E. Main St. | 580/772–5592 | fax 405/774–2551 | www.daysinn.com | 60 rooms | $44 | AE, D, DC, MC, V.

# WOODWARD

MAP 4, F3

*(Nearby town also listed: Alva)*

Established during the Cherokee Strip Land Run in 1893, Woodward still has an old-fashioned downtown with many antiques and gift shops. Situated near Fort Supply, an early cavalry outpost, and on the Western cattle trail, Woodward has a very palpable Western heritage. Oil and agriculture have long been traditional sources of income; today those industries are supplemented by newer operations such as a claims processing center for a large insurance company.

Information: **Woodward Chamber of Commerce** | 1006 Oklahoma Ave., Woodward, OK 73801-4662 | 580/256–7411 | fax 580/254–5633.

## Attractions

**Boiling Springs State Park.** This wooded park surrounding a 7-acre lake is an oasis in the plains. It has picnic areas, RV and tent campsites, cabins, a swimming pool, hiking trails, fishing docks, and an 18-hole golf course. | Rte. 34C, 5 mi east of Woodward | 580/256–7664 | www.touroklahoma.com | Free | Daily.

**Glass Mountains.** The surfaces of this series of dramatic red buttes are covered with millions of sparkling selenite crystals. Picnic areas and information centers are scattered along the south side of Rte. 15. | Rte. 15 | 580/227–2527 | Free | Daily.

**Historic Fort Supply.** First built in 1868 as a supply camp for military operations against the Plains Indians, the fort now consists of five original buildings and a reconstructed stockade. The 1892 guardhouse holds a small museum. | U.S. 270 | 580/766–3767 | Free | Tues.–Sat. 9–4.

**Plains Indians and Pioneers Museum.** Exhibits illustrating both Native American and pioneer history are found at this small but well-regarded museum. Artifacts ranging from Cheyenne beadwork to pioneer household items are displayed along with excerpts from old journals and vintage newspaper clippings. | 2009 Williams Ave. | 580/256–6136 | Free | Tues.–Sat. 10–5, Sun. 1–4.

**ON THE CALENDAR**

**FEB., MAY** *Boiling Springs Bluegrass Festival.* Regional and state bluegrass bands perform in concerts and jam sessions under the shade trees. | 580/256–7411.
**JULY:** *Elks Rodeo.* This rodeo dates back to 1929 and includes a free hamburger feed, an old-fashioned rodeo parade, and four nights of rodeo events. | 580/256–7411.

## Dining

**Waggs Bar-B-Q.** Barbecue. Housed in a former machine shop, this place has vintage advertising art and red-and-white-checked tablecloths. Known for beef, pork, and chicken barbecue, steaks, hamburgers, and a pickle bar. | 7th St. and Oklahoma Ave. | 580/256–6721 | Closed Sun. | $6–$15 | AE, D, MC, V.

## Lodging

**Anna Augusta Inn.** This 1904 two-story house was moved from downtown to directly across from a city park and golf course and has antiques, Victorian florals, and clawfoot bathtubs. The dining room is open to nonguests for lunch and dinner. Restaurant, bar, complimentary breakfast, some in-room hot tubs, cable TV. | 2612 Lake View Dr. | 580/254–5400 | 3 rooms, 1 suite | $65–$85, $105 suite | AE, MC, V.

**Northwest Inn.** This is the only lodging in town with a swimming pool. Rooms have cherrywood furniture, and golf, parks, and museums are within 1–2 mi. Restaurant, bar (with entertainment), room service, some in-room data ports, some refrigerators, cable TV, pool, laundry facilities, exercise equipment, video games, business services, pets allowed. | U.S. 270 and 1st St. | 580/256–7600 or 800/727–7606 | fax 580/254–2274 | www.shinc.com | 124 rooms | $57–$64 | AE, D, DC, MC, V.

**Super 8.** The rooms at this 2-story motel have plenty of space, but are otherwise unremarkable. Boiling Springs State Park is a 15 minute drive away. Complimentary Continental breakfast, picnic area, cable TV, pool, business services, pets allowed (fee). | 4120 Williams Ave. | 580/254–2964 | fax 580/254–2964 | 60 rooms | $42 | AE, D, MC, V.

# Texas

**Mention Texas, and some travelers might picture the Texas of the movies: miles of rugged,** uncivilized land where outlines of cattle and lonely windmills stretch above the horizon. For others, the land near the Louisiana border might come to mind: a region of tall pine forests and bountiful lakes. Some might see the high-tech cities bustling with world-class attractions, shop-'til-you-drop opportunities, and a pulsating nightlife.

And they'd all be right. For years, Texas has promoted itself as the "land of contrasts." Rolling hills, rugged deserts, verdant forests, and sandy beaches are all found within its borders. For city slickers, everything from the culture of Dallas to the cowboy fun of Fort Worth, from the south-of-the-border style of El Paso to the youthful exuberance of Austin, awaits. For all its increasing urban growth, the state still clings to its small town roots, however, and through much of the state a good time still means a Friday night high school football game, a weekend rodeo, or jumping in the ubiquitous pick-up truck to an evening barbecue.

Because of its vast size, Texas distances are often measured in hours rather than miles. The major population centers lie hours apart and each heads a different region of the state. East Texas, with its oil fields and verdant pine forests, is home to the state's densest population—thanks to the metropolis of Houston, the largest city in the state and a veritable crockpot of cultures from around the globe. The northern plains are headed by the Dallas-Fort Worth region, the mega-city where boundaries have blurred—resulting in a combination of these two major cities and dozens of other communities. The Panhandle, consisting of miles of prairie little changed from its cattle driving days, is led by the community of Amarillo. Big Bend Country, that far west region where Texas melds with New Mexico and Mexico, looks to El Paso, a bilingual city perched on the edge of the Franklin Mountains. The Hill Country, the rolling territory in the central

| CAPITAL: AUSTIN | POPULATION: 18,378,185 | AREA: 266,807 SQUARE MI |
|---|---|---|
| BORDERS: LA, AR, OK, NM, MEXICO | TIME ZONE: CENTRAL | POSTAL ABBREVIATION: TX |
| WEB SITE: WWW.TRAVELTEX.COM | | |

part of the state, is led by both Austin and San Antonio, cities with two different atmospheres but a common sense of fun.

Texas has a strong rural heritage; the economic forces that founded the state include cattle ranching, farming, and oil production. Texas has also managed to move up the high-tech ladder. In Austin, home to a booming microchip industry, sixty-five percent of the manufacturing work force is employed by the high-tech industry, followed by state government jobs. In Dallas, finance carries the economic baton, while in Houston, the petrochemical industry still looms large. Throughout Texas, tourism plays an increasingly large role; it's now the third largest industry in the state.

Leaders from those industries as well as from the political world play a vital role in Texas life, from Austin's computer guru Michael Dell to father-son politicos former president George Bush and current president George W. Bush. Historic figures are revered throughout the state as well—the names Houston, Austin, Crockett, and Bowie identify schools and streets statewide. Not to be forgotten, former president Lyndon B. Johnson is remembered in Texas as simply LBJ, and his ranch and boyhood home are now public attractions.

# History

The history of Texas begins more than 12,000 years ago when prehistoric peoples of the High Plains first inhabited the area. Europeans first came to the region in 1519, eventually introducing ranching as well as horses to the area. The Spanish flew the first of six flags that marked this area once known as Tejas; the subsequent entities to hoist flags over the region were France, Mexico, the Republic of Texas, the Confederacy, and the U.S.

In the late 1600s the Spanish began establishing a system of missions in the eastern woodlands, gradually advancing westward, and eventually reaching the central plains when San Antonio de Valero (later known as the Alamo) was founded at San Pedro Springs in 1718. The mission system was intended to convert the Native Americans to Christianity and to have a "civilizing" influence on "hostile" tribes. In order to encourage European migration into the area, the Spanish granted land to prospective colonizers. In 1821 Spain lost control of Mexico; Mexico, busy with other affairs, exerted a loose hold on the area and land-hungry Anglo-American settlers from neighboring states trickled over the borders into present-day Texas.

The American and British settlers favored Anglo-American jurisprudence, Protestantism, decentralism, and slavery—all against the laws of the existing Mexican government. As immigration grew, tensions between the groups increased, culminating in the Texas Revolution (1835–36). After a short skirmish, the Mexicans withdrew, but early in 1836, a large Mexican army under General Santa Anna marched toward San Antonio. The siege and destruction of the Alamo followed as the superior numbers of Mexican troops prevailed. On March 6, 1836, the Alamo fell; all its defenders were killed, including Davy Crockett, James Bowie, and commander William B. Travis. However, the victory was costly for Santa Anna as nearly one-third of his army suffered casual-

## Timeline

| 1519 | 1541 | 1681 | 1685 |
|---|---|---|---|
| Alonzo Alvarez de Pineda is the first European to reach Texas. | Francisco Vazquez de Coronado of Spain explores the plains of West Texas. | Mission Nuestra Señora del Carmen, the oldest mission in TX, is founded for Tigua Indians. | French explorer Robert Cavalier, Sieur de la Salle, arrives in Matagorda Bay and establishes Fort St. Louis. |

INTRODUCTION
HISTORY
REGIONS
WHEN TO VISIT
STATE'S GREATS
RULES OF THE ROAD
DRIVING TOURS

ties. Little more than a month later, Santa Anna was defeated by Sam Houston and his men at the San Jacinto River, assuring Texas's freedom from Mexican rule. Houston was elected first president of the Republic of Texas and was inaugurated on October 22, 1836. Texas remained an independent nation from 1836 to 1845, when the U.S. government agreed to allow another slave-holding state into the Union.

In 1860 Texas seceded from the Union, but remained relatively untouched by the ravages of the Civil War. The last battle of the Civil War was fought in Brownsville, TX, by Texas troops who were unaware that the Confederacy had already fallen.

Almost immediately after the war ended, ranchers began driving their cattle east to markets in Kansas and Missouri and the period of the American cowboy was born. Railroads, backed by money from the East, soon moved into the area and assumed the role of transporting goods across the state. In 1901, oil was discovered in Texas and dominated the state's economy for the next 80 years. When the wells began to dry up and oil fields were discovered in other parts of the world, Texas entered a period of de-industrialization. Today, Texas enjoys a broad-based economy, which still includes ranching and oil-related industries, but also includes high-tech manufacturing and service-industry interests.

# Regions

## 1. Panhandle Plains

More than 400 years ago, when explorer Francisco Coronado arrived in the Panhandle (the northernmost region of Texas that's shaped like a handle), he found a terrain devoid of landmarks. The Spaniards consequently drove stakes in the soil to blaze a path across the region they called *Llano Estacado*, or staked plain. Today, interstates carve the vast, high plains of West Texas into manageable chunks and connect the widely scattered cities. This is the Texas that many picture with a mention of "the Lone Star State," a land of leathery-faced cowboys, rolling tumbleweeds, lonesome windmills, and pumping oil derricks. Roads stretch straight to the horizon, and distances are measured not in miles but in hours. Locals consider an 80-mi haul "right around the corner."

Country singer Mac Davis once sang "happiness is Lubbock, Texas, in my rearview mirror," but for many this plains community is an oasis. Lubbock is home to Texas Tech University and its more than 20,000 students. It's also the heart of Texas's burgeoning wine business.

About 120 miles north of Lubbock is Amarillo, the cultural and commercial capital of the Texas Panhandle. The town grew to become a center for cattle ranching, wheat and cotton farming, and oil production. It's also the gateway to the nation's second largest canyon: Palo Duro.

| 1691 | 1718 | 1731 | 1749 | |
|---|---|---|---|---|
| Texas becomes Spanish province. | Mission San Antonio de Valero (the Alamo) is founded. | Canary Islanders arrive in San Antonio de Bexar to establish first civilian municipality. | Spain builds a mission and a fort, establishing the state's third oldest town of Goliad. "Remember Goliad" will become a battle cry of the Texas Revolution, after Col. James W. Fannin, Jr., | and his men are massacred here in 1836. |

*Towns listed:* Abilene, Amarillo, Big Spring, Canyon, Childress, Clarendon, Dalhart, Dumas, Eastland, Fritch, Hereford, Lubbock, Pampa, Plainview, Quanah, Shamrock, Snyder, Sweetwater, Vernon, Wichita Falls

## 2. Prairies and Lakes

This region includes prairie lands termed the Post Oak Belt, the Blackland Belt, the Grand Prairie, and the East and West Cross Timbers. It also includes the shiny, sharply angled skyscrapers of Dallas.

Dallas is defined by the progress of "bidness"—the forward march of bankers, high-techsters, and oilmen—and the tearing down of the old and building of the new. Critics say Dallas is a city obsessed with appearances. And indeed, this metropolis offers a beautiful skyline, a thriving nightlife inhabited by bright young émigrés from parts north, a Super Bowl champion football team, and a splashy, $157-million symphony hall.

About 30 mi west of Dallas, the city of Fort Worth manages to retain the flavor of its Wild West past while burgeoning as a modern city. The former rip-roaring cowboy town, known for its gunfights and cattle drives, has preserved its roots by maintaining its historic Stockyards. But Fort Worth is no backwater; its cultural establishment is the envy of many larger cities, including Dallas. Some may sneeringly dismiss it as "Cowtown," but in many respects the city provides the best of what both tradition and progress have to offer.

*Towns listed:* Arlington-Grand Prairie, Bastrop, Bonham, Brenham, Canton, Cleburne, Corsicana, Dallas, Denison, Denton, Dublin, Ennis, Fort Worth, Gainesville, Glen Rose, Graham, Granbury, Grapevine, Greenville, Groesbeck, Hico, Hillsboro, Irving, La Grange, Lewisville, McKinney, Mineral Wells, Paris, Plano, Richardson, Sherman, Smithville, Stephenville, Sulphur Springs, Waco, Waxahachie, Weatherford

## 3. Hill Country

The heart of Texas is a place of hills and valleys, of small towns and the major metropolitan areas of San Antonio and Austin. All in all, San Antonio, Austin, and the Hill Country form Texas's most intriguing triangle, in terms of the area's geography and its diverse mix of cultures and attractions. German settlers left a thick accent on Comfort, Fredericksburg, and New Braunfels, where the würstfests are as common as the pink granite hills, blanketed with cedars and live oaks. Native American, Mexican, and Polish cultures have melded in Bandera, the state's dude ranch capital. A politician who started out along the Pedernales River and ended up in the White House left a mark on the Hill Country, too—in the town of Johnson City.

*Towns listed:* Austin, Bandera, Boerne, Burnet, Castroville, Comanche, Comfort, Fredericksburg, Georgetown, Gruene, Johnson City, Kerrville, Killeen, Lockhart, Marble Falls, Mason, New Braunfels, Ozona, Salado, San Antonio, San Marcos, Sonora, Temple, Uvalde, Wimberley

| 1819 | 1820 | 1821 | 1830 | 1832 |
|---|---|---|---|---|
| Florida Purchase Treaty is signed, relinquishing U.S. claim to Texas. | Moses Austin receives permission from the Spanish government to bring 300 colonists to Texas. | Texas is under Mexican rule, after Spain loses control of Mexico. | Mexico passes a law to slow immigration of English-speaking settlers into Texas. | Texans and Mexicans fight at Velasco; Texans convene to discuss the political separation of Texas from Mexico. |

INTRODUCTION
HISTORY
REGIONS
WHEN TO VISIT
STATE'S GREATS
RULES OF THE ROAD
DRIVING TOURS

## 4. East Texas

Bordered on the north by Texarkana; on the east by Caddo Lake (Texas's only natural lake); to the west by onetime rollicking Fort Worth; and to the south by the first rumblings of the Hill Country, East Texas is a land of piney woods, antiques shops, hallowed century-old neighborhoods, and traditional stone-faced Baptists proud of their roots and their property.

If you're travelling west from Shreveport, Louisiana, to Dallas on I–20, detour to Jefferson, Gladewater, Pittsburg, and Mount Pleasant; you'll discover that the woods lining the highway drape an antiques shopper's paradise. Marshall, where potters have been mining clay from East Texas's rolling hills for more than a century, turns out more than a million pots each year. In Rusk, ancient steamers of the Texas State Railroad Historical Park take visitors on a 19th-century train ride.

*Towns listed:* Athens, Baytown, Beaumont, Bryan/College Station, Crockett, Fairfield, Henderson, Huntsville, Jacksonville, Jasper, Jefferson, Kilgore, La Porte, Longview, Lufkin, Marshall, Mount Pleasant, Nacogdoches, Orange, Palestine, Port Arthur, Rusk, Texarkana, Texas City, Tyler

## 5. Coastal Plains

Stretching from south of San Antonio to the Rio Grande Valley, this area is dotted with historical sites—from missions to the ranches that first settled this area. This region encompasses the Gulf Coast, which stretches from the Sabine River at the Louisiana border to the Lower Rio Grande Valley and the U.S.–Mexico border, containing more than 600 miles of beach and numerous coastal communities. The communities in this region vary from small fishing villages to modern cities; any number of them may be enlivened with the sounds of everything from zydeco to conjunto, and spiced with dishes from gumbo to gazpacho.

On the northern reaches lies the city of Houston, filled with cultural events, family attractions, and sports events. A short drive from Houston, Galveston is a resort community located on an island and connected to the mainland by bridges.

Midway down the Texas coast lies Corpus Christi and its neighboring communities: Port Aransas, Rockport, Kingsville, and more. This region is a favorite with birdwatchers from around the world as well as windsurfers, who come to the area for its near constant breezes and protected sea conditions thanks to the barrier island, Padre.

Padre Island hugs the Texas coast for more than 100 miles before giving way to Texas's southernmost coastal destination: South Padre. This lively community has a semi-tropical climate and is popular with Winter Texans looking for relief from the season's chill, shoppers looking for bargains in nearby Mexico, and beach lovers who come to enjoy sun and surf.

*Towns listed:* Alice, Angleton, Aransas Pass, Brazosport, Brownsville, Corpus Christi, Eagle Lake, Edinburg, Galveston, Goliad, Gonzales, Harlingen, Houston, Kingsville,

| 1835 | 1836 | 1837 | 1839 | 1845 |
|---|---|---|---|---|
| Texas gains independence from Mexico in Texas Revolution. | Declaration of Texas's independence from Mexico is signed at Washington-on-the-Brazos; Sam Houston is elected first President of Texas Republic. | U.S. recognizes Texas as an independent country. | Austin becomes the capital of Republic of Texas. | Texas becomes the 28th state. |

Laredo, McAllen, Mission, Padre Island, Port Aransas, Port Isabel, Port Lavaca, Rockport, Seguin, South Padre Island, Three Rivers, Victoria

## 6. Big Bend Country

The Big Bend Country is the Texas of movies: miles of rugged countryside, little changed from its Wild West days. This area stretches from the Edwards Plateau to the east all the way west to El Paso and the Mexico and New Mexico borders. Here you'll find the only true mountains in Texas: the Guadalupe Range—an eastern portion of the Rockies that includes Texas's tallest peak, Guadalupe Peak, at 8,749 ft. South of the Guadalupe Range lie the Davis Mountains, which are a popular getaway for those headed to rugged Big Bend National Park. The park lies farther south, tucked in the region formed by a southward dip in the Rio Grande. Here the Chisos Mountains rise to 7,825 ft.

On the westernmost end of Big Bend lies El Paso, the largest city on the U.S.–Mexico border.

*Towns listed:* Alpine, Big Bend National Park, Brackettville, Del Rio, Eagle Pass, El Paso, Fort Stockton, Guadalupe Mountains National Park, Marfa, Midland, Monahans, Odessa, Pecos, San Angelo, Terlingua, Van Horn

# When to Visit

With its sprawling size and varying terrain, weather is a broad topic in the Lone Star State. In the Panhandle and North Texas, winters are cold with a Midwestern chill and more than occasional snows. Amarillo receives more than 15 inches of snow most years. The Dallas-Fort Worth metropolitan region is far more temperate; it receives just under three inches of snow annually, but both cities are known to top the 100° mark during summer days. In the far West the mountains bring snows to sunny El Paso, which receives 5½ inches of powder annually. Into Central and South Texas, temperatures warm up and winter snows are rare, with just an occasional dusting or perhaps a winter ice storm. Spring brings rains to central and south Texas, often in the form of heavy rain that can result in flash flooding in the Hill Country. (Drivers are cautioned never to drive across running water in this area.) Spring and early summer also bring the threat of tornadoes to the Hill Country, as well as to North Texas. The Panhandle can be plagued by dust storms in the spring and summer. South Texas enjoys a semi-tropical climate, with temperatures rarely reaching the freezing mark. The fertile citrus groves of this region are a testimony to the warm days and nights enjoyed year-round by these southern reaches of the state.

October and April are the prime months for a comfortable visit—a fact reflected in the high number of local festivals enjoyed during this period. You may wish to avoid the chilly cold fronts (known locally as "blue northers") that sometimes bring winter weather to Texas, as well as the heat that bakes the state from June through September.

| 1853 | 1861 | 1866 | 1870 | 1898 |
|---|---|---|---|---|
| First State Capitol built in Austin. | Texas secedes from the Union. | First Texas cattle drive. | Texas readmitted to the Union. | Theodore Roosevelt trains "Rough Riders" in San Antonio. |

INTRODUCTION
HISTORY
REGIONS
**WHEN TO VISIT**
STATE'S GREATS
RULES OF THE ROAD
DRIVING TOURS

The Texas coast reaches its peak visitation during the summer months, thanks to nearly ideal beach conditions during this time. Spring is also a busy time along the coast thanks to Spring Break, which draws college students from as far as Canada to enjoy a week of warm weather.

The winter months draw many Northerners, especially to places in far South Texas. The Rio Grande valley is home to many Winter Texans who arrive in October and remain until March or April. The area celebrates with numerous special events targeted toward these temporary residents.

Peak months for bird watching coincide not with the best weather, but with the best birding conditions. World-class birding can be enjoyed in South Texas during the fall and spring migrations, as well in winter, when many species make Texas their temporary home. The whooping cranes are just one of the species that winter along the Texas coast.

## CLIMATE CHART
Average High/Low Temperatures (°F) and Monthly Precipitation (in inches)

| | JAN. | FEB. | MAR. | APR. | MAY | JUNE |
|---|---|---|---|---|---|---|
| AMARILLO | 49/21 | 53/26 | 62/33 | 72/42 | 79/52 | 88/61 |
| | .5 | .6 | 1 | 1 | 2.5 | 3.7 |
| | JULY | AUG. | SEPT. | OCT. | NOV. | DEC. |
| | 92/66 | 89/64 | 82/56 | 73/45 | 60/32 | 50/24 |
| | 2.6 | 3.2 | 2 | 1.8 | .7 | .4 |
| | JAN. | FEB. | MAR. | APR. | MAY | JUNE |
| AUSTIN | 59/39 | 63/42 | 72/51 | 79/60 | 85/67 | 91/72 |
| | 1.7 | 2.2 | 1.9 | 2.6 | 4.8 | 3.7 |
| | JULY | AUG. | SEPT. | OCT. | NOV. | DEC. |
| | 95/74 | 96/74 | 91/70 | 82/60 | 72/50 | 62/41 |
| | 2.6 | 2 | 3.3 | 3.4 | 2.4 | .4 |
| | JAN. | FEB. | MAR. | APR. | MAY | JUNE |
| DFW | 54/33 | 59/37 | 68/46 | 76/55 | 83/63 | 92/70 |
| | 1.8 | 2.2 | 2.8 | 3.5 | 4.9 | 3 |
| | JULY | AUG. | SEPT. | OCT. | NOV. | DEC. |
| | 97/74 | 96/74 | 88/67 | 79/56 | 67/45 | 58/36 |
| | 2.3 | 2.2 | 3.3 | 3.4 | 2.3 | 1.8 |
| | JAN. | FEB. | MAR. | APR. | MAY | JUNE |
| EL PASO | 56/29 | 61/40 | 62/34 | 70/40 | 79/48 | 87/57 |
| | .4 | 3.3 | .4 | .3 | .2 | .3 |
| | JULY | AUG. | SEPT. | OCT. | NOV. | DEC. |
| | 97/64 | 96/68 | 94/67 | 87/62 | 78/50 | 66/38 |
| | .7 | 1.5 | 1.6 | 1.7 | .8 | .4 |

**1900**
Galveston is hit by a hurricane, which kills 6,000 residents.

**1901**
Oil is discovered at Spindletop.

**1923**
Miriam Ferguson becomes the state's first female governor.

**1930**
Oil discovered in East Texas.

**1961**
Texan Lyndon B. Johnson becomes U.S. vice-president.

| | JAN. | FEB. | MAR. | APR. | MAY | JUNE |
|---|---|---|---|---|---|---|
| HOUSTON | 58/31 | 65/43 | 71/50 | 78/58 | 85/64 | 91/71 |
| | .6 | 3 | 2.9 | 3.2 | 5.2 | 5 |

| | JULY | AUG. | SEPT. | OCT. | NOV. | DEC. |
|---|---|---|---|---|---|---|
| | 93/72 | 93/72 | 88/68 | 82/58 | 72/50 | 65/42 |
| | 3.6 | 3.5 | 4.9 | 4.3 | 3.8 | 3.5 |

## FESTIVALS AND SEASONAL EVENTS
### WINTER

Jan. **Dallas's Southwestern Bell Cotton Bowl Classic.** Pits a Big 12 football conference team against a Southeastern Conference team in an annual game. | 214/634–7525.

Feb. **Mardi Gras.** This Galveston event includes parades, masked balls, arts and crafts, sports, and live music along the Strand on the two weekends before Fat Tuesday. | 888/425–4753.

Feb. **Houston Livestock Show and Rodeo.** One of the Southwest's largest livestock shows and the world's largest rodeo. | 713/791–9000.

Mar. **Texas Dogwood Trails Festival.** Held in Palestine, this festival includes rides, a parade, a car show, a cook-off, and dogwood blooms. | 903/723–3014 or 800/659–3484.

Mar. **South Padre Island during Spring Break.** Students from throughout North America party during a month-long celebration with concerts, athletic events, and more. | 956/761–6433 or 800/SO–PADRE.

Mar., Apr. **Azalea Trail Tour.** Get a self-guided look at spring blossoms along a 7-mi trail in Tyler. The trail also leads you past a number of noteworthy historic homes. | 903/592–1661 or 800/235–5712.

### SPRING

Apr. **Dallas Blooms.** The largest flower show in the Southwest is held at the Dallas Arboretum and Botanical Garden in North Texas. | 214/327–4901.

Apr. **Houston International Festival.** Twenty downtown blocks are filled with arts and crafts, food, and live entertainment representing cultures from around the world. | 713/654–8808.

Apr. **Fiesta San Antonio.** San Antonio's largest festival includes carnivals, live music, parades, food booths, and concerts. | 210/227–5191 or 800/447–3372.

**1963** President John F. Kennedy is assassinated in Dallas; LBJ becomes the nation's 36th president.

**1968** San Antonio hosts the World's Fair.

**1988** Houstonian George Bush is elected the 41st president of the United States.

**2000** Texas governor George W. Bush is elected the 43rd president of the United States in one of the closest elections in U.S. history.

INTRODUCTION
HISTORY
REGIONS
WHEN TO VISIT
STATE'S GREATS
RULES OF THE ROAD
DRIVING TOURS

May **Buccaneer Days.** Corpus Christi celebrates the region's buccaneer history with fireworks, a carnival, parade, rodeo, sailing regatta, and sports tournaments. | 361/882–3242.

May **Texas State Arts and Crafts Fair.** This Kerrville event includes arts and crafts, demonstrations, wine tastings, entertainment, and food booths. | 830/896–5711.

June **Kerrville Folk Festival.** This 18-day spectacle of song is held 9 mi south of Kerrville at the Quiet Valley Ranch. | 830/257–3600.

## SUMMER

July **Freedom Fiesta/July Fourth Parade.** Held in Seguin, this is one of Texas's longest-running celebrations of Independence Day. It includes food booths, a parade, kids' rides, games, and a street dance. | 830/379–6382.

Aug. **Texas Folklife Festival.** More than 40 cultures and their statewide contributions are honored through music, food, dance, and folktales at the Institute of Texan Cultures in HemisFair Park in San Antonio. | 210/458–2300.

Sept. **Grapefest.** Local and statewide vineyards are recognized in the Grapevine event. There's a wine tasting, antique car show, children's carnival, auction, arts and crafts, and tours. | 800/457–6338.

Sept. **Hummer/Bird Celebration.** Held along the coast in Rockport, this celebration offers information on the migration of hummingbirds and other species on their way through the Coastal Bend to Mexico and Central America. Other activities include birding tours, seminars, and an art show. | 361/729–6445 or 800/242–0071.

## FALL

Oct. **Texas Rose Festival.** You'll find a Rose Museum show, Palette of Roses Art Show, Rose Queen coronation, arts and crafts show, and a parade at this Tyler event. | 903/592–1661 or 800/235–5712.

Oct. **State Fair of Texas.** The largest state fair in the nation is held in Dallas's Fair Park. It includes North America's largest Ferris wheel, a livestock show, an auto show, free concerts, and fireworks. | 214/565–9931.

Nov. **Texas Renaissance Festival.** Enjoy a re-creation of 16th-century England, with jesters, knights, food, and entertainment at the state's largest Renaissance festival, held near Houston. | 800/656–2244.

Dec. **Dickens on the Strand.** This Galveston event includes parades, costumed characters, crafts, and food. | 979/765–7834.

Dec. **Wonderland of Lights.** One of the state's largest lighting displays can be see in Marshall. | 903/935–7868.

Dec. **Las Posadas.** Held in San Antonio, this is a re-enactment of Mary and Joseph's search for an inn, beginning at the River Walk and ending at the Arneson River Theatre. | 210/224–6163.

# State's Greats

Texas is often described as being "like a whole other country"—and indeed, the state's great size and geographical and cultural diversity make it seem like a nation unto itself. From the lonely vistas of West Texas to the sprawl of Dallas and Houston to its distinctly southern eastern and Gulf Coast, Texas has enough to keep any traveler occupied.

Those who harbor dreams of the Old West and long to try their hand at mending a fence or ropin' a dogie may gravitate toward desolate West Texas where the rock outcroppings are sunbaked and cacti spike the landscape, but the real cowboy action is in the northern portion of the state, where the High Plains abut the Oklahoma prairie. Here, 10-gallon hats, dusty chaps, and boots with spurs are a dime a dozen at rodeos all over the region.

City lovers find all the shopping, dining, and nightlife they can handle in Dallas and Fort Worth on the north-central flatlands and in Houston in the southeast. Towering skyscrapers, multilane highways, and glitzy boutiques mark these modern metropolises as centers for finance, trade, and of course, the oil industry. The state's capital, Austin, calls itself the "Live Music Capital of the World"; festivals, competitions, and clubs showcase the best in country, bluegrass, rock, and blues music. Austin is also an up-and-coming tech center, rivaling California's Silicon Valley. The influx of money from the oil and computer industries has made a lot of people a lot of money here, and economic prosperity has translated into cultural wealth and vibrance.

Texas has always had strong ties to Mexico, to the south. To see how close they are, you have only to visit San Antonio and the southern Gulf Coast. The heritage comes to life at colorful festivals, in the spicy Tex-Mex cooking found everywhere from roadside tortilla stands to fancy restaurants, and at historic sites such as the Alamo.

## Beaches, Forests, and Parks

The remarkable geographical and ecological diversity of Texas is beautifully illustrated in the state's parks and wilderness areas—perhaps nowhere better than in **Big Bend National Park.** Big Bend is the largest public park in the state, covering 801,163 acres of arid desert, lush floodplains, and much in between. The park is home to more than 1,000 plant species and 500 kinds of birds and mammals. The park maintains hundreds of campsites, both primitive and modern, in addition to a very popular lodge.

On the high plains just outside the town of Amarillo is the **Palo Duro Canyon State Park,** site of the last great battle between the native Commanche on the one hand and soldiers and settlers on the other. Photographers are drawn to the park's otherworldly rock formations. Also famous for outstanding geological features is **Enchanted Rock State Natural Area** just north of Fredricksburg in the central Hill Country. The second-largest exposed underground rock formation in the country is here; it is also said to be the site of ancient human sacrifices. **Guadalupe Mountains National Park** is home to the highest point in Texas, 8,749-ft Guadalupe Peak, lording it over an arid expanse of sagebrush, sand, and bare rock. Sand dunes and prehistoric pictographs characterize West Texas' **Monohans Sandhills State Park** and for a dose of undulating, unspoiled beachfront, the **Padre Island National Seashore** in the southern Gulf Coast reaches of the state can't be beat.

## Culture and the Arts

Texas cities are home to concert halls, museums, and art collections. Houston's **Museum of Fine Arts** houses an enormous collection of Renaissance and 18th-century pieces, as well as Impressionist and post-Impressionist works. The remarkable **Menil Collection,** also in Houston, ranges in discipline from African tribal sculptures to paintings by Andy Warhol.

The **Dallas Art Museum**'s permanent collection includes striking contemporary sculpture and beautiful impressionist paintings. In Fort Worth, the **Amon Carter Museum** displays 19th and 20th century American art and photography, and the **Kimball Art Museum** houses a diverse range of work in the last building designed by acclaimed architect Louis Kann.

Conspiracy theorists and other history buffs flock to Dallas to see the Texas School Book Depository, where, some say, Lee Harvey Oswald took aim at President John F. Kennedy in 1963; for those who think the truth is still out there, there's the **Conspiracy Museum,** whose exhibits track the "true" motives and culprits behind presidential assassinations since 1835. **Deep Ellum,** a historic district east of downtown, is the epicenter of the Dallas arts and nightlife scene.

In nearby Fort Worth, the natural world reigns supreme at the **Fort Worth Water Gardens Park** and the **Botanic Gardens,** where brilliantly blooming plants, modern sculpture, and dramatic waterfalls create a pastoral haven. A huge hit with kids is the **Fort Worth Zoo,** which is home to more than 5,000 exotic and native animals. For architectural splendor, few in the city can match the **Kimball Art Museum,** the last building designed by architect Louis Kahn.

To the south, off the beach of Corpus Christi, floats the decommissioned naval aircraft carrier the *U.S.S Lexington.* The looming hulk is now a museum, and guided tours explore the innards of the great ship.

## Spectator Sports

Like almost everything else in Texas, team sports are big. Dallas is home to the champion **Dallas Cowboys,** whose blue-and-silver trimmed jerseys have graced the backs of such luminaries as Troy Aikman and Emmitt Smith. Dallas also claims the NBA's **Dallas Mavericks,** though somewhat begrudgingly, considering the team's record. The **Texas Rangers,** Dallas' hometown pro baseball team, swing their bats in suburban Arlington. Houston's Astrodome used to be base camp for the **Houston Oilers,** before the team packed up and defected to Nashville, but the 'Dome, as the arena is often called by locals, still keeps the rain off the National League's **Houston Astros.** San Antonio is home to the NBA's **San Antonio Spurs** and star center David Robinson.

Texas-sized fandom is not strictly reserved for pro teams. The long-standing, sometimes bitter rivalry between **Texas A&M's Aggies** and the **University of Texas Longhorns** is a hot topic of discussion among college football enthusiasts far beyond College Station and Austin, and often beyond state lines as well.

Of course, no mention of spectator events in Texas would be complete without at least a nod to grand tradition of rodeo. Annual events in at least a third of Texan towns, rodeos come closer than anything else to capturing the spirit of the Old West. Thousands turn out to see bronco busting, calf roping, steer bulldogging—and, of course, the event everybody loves to gasp and squirm over—bull riding. Some of the most noteworthy events are Fort Worth's **Southwestern Exposition and Livestock Show and Rodeo,** held each winter in January, Dallas' **Mesquite Championship Rodeo** in April, and in February, Brownsville's **Charro Days,** which feature rodeo in the original Mexican sense, with period costumes and pageantry.

## Parks, Natural Sights, and Outdoor Activities

The Texas coastline extends from the Louisiana state line to the Mexican border, spanning a region that ranges from swampy marshland to semi-tropical dunes. The northernmost point on the Texas coastline is **Sea Rim State Park,** best known for its wildlife. Further south, two-legged visitors are most popular at Galveston Beach, located an hour's drive from Houston.

INTRODUCTION
HISTORY
REGIONS
WHEN TO VISIT
STATE'S GREATS
RULES OF THE ROAD
DRIVING TOURS

Travelers from around the world set their sights on beach areas located farther south: **Rockport** is considered a bird-watching paradise, and nearby **Port Aransas** is best known for its Spring Break population with more than 150,000 revelers in March and April. Not far from these fishing villages is **Corpus Christi,** gateway to America's longest national seashore—**Padre Island National Seashore.**

Padre Island hugs the Texas coast for more than 100 miles before giving way to Texas's southernmost coastal destination: **South Padre Island.** Separated from the northern portion by the Port Mansfield Gulf Channel, South Padre is the capital of tourism in this tropical tip of Texas.

If you're interested in camping and picnicking, you have many options for forest getaways. Both state and national forests are found throughout Texas, with most located in the east. This area, known as the Piney Woods, is home to **Angelina, Davy Crockett, Sabine,** and **Sam Houston** National Forests.

Texas is home to an extensive state park system; the parks represent their diverse geographic, cultural, and ecological base. In East Texas, the piney woods offer fishing at swampy **Caddo Lake,** historic lore at **Mission Tejas State Historical Park,** and the lure of the iron horse aboard the **Texas State Railroad.** Along the Gulf Coast, you can tour the restored Battleship **USS *Texas,*** romp the surf at Mustang Island, or have a look at Victorian elegance at **Fulton Mansion State Historic Structure.** In the state's western reaches, **Seminole Canyon State Historical Park** preserves ancient pictographs and, in the Panhandle, **Palo Duro Canyon State Park** challenges photographers to capture its scenic beauty.

Texas is also home to several sites within the national park system, from the dense forests of the **Big Thicket National Preserve** to the restored military post at **Fort Davis Historic Site** to the 80 miles of beaches at **Padre Island National Seashore.** The state also boasts two national parks: **Big Bend** and **Guadalupe Mountains,** both in West Texas.

## History

Historic sites that recall the settlement of the frontier are scattered throughout Texas. Some East Texas towns such as Jefferson are filled with Victorian architecture and memories of steamboat travel. Other sites, such as San Antonio's famous **Alamo** and nearby missions, recall an earlier time when Spanish missionaries sought to bring Catholicism to the region.

The fight for independence following settlement is recalled at many historic attractions. San Antonio, La Grange, Goliad, and Houston are home to some of the largest sites, with museums and displays explaining the conflicts with Mexico.

The cowboy culture and history of the 19th century is remembered throughout the state but nowhere as vividly as the **Fort Worth Stockyards National Historic District,** where restored buildings commemorate the days of cattle drives. More recent history is kept alive at sites such as Corpus Christi's **USS *Lexington* Museum on the Bay,** a museum housed on a WWII aircraft carrier.

## Sports

Texas is an outdoor enthusiast's dream. Hikers, climbers, white-water buffs, bicyclists, scuba divers, and equestrians will find plenty of challenges. The state's varying topography, from flat plains to rolling hills to steep mountains, provides a variety of grades for any fitness level.

Miles of marked hiking trails can be found from the shady forests of East Texas to the Hill Country's rolling terrain. Climbers test their skills at Fredericksburg's **Enchanted**

**Rock State Natural Area** (home of the second largest stone formation in the nation) and West Texas's **Guadalupe Mountains National Park.**

Fishing records have been set in many of the state's lakes and rivers. Top bass fishing is possible at **Caddo Lake.** Saltwater fishing along the Gulf Coast includes jetty fishing, shorecasting, pier fishing, and deep-sea fishing. Here scuba divers find many sites in the offshore coral gardens.

Boating, both on lakes and offshore, is a favorite warm weather activity at places like **Amistad National Recreation Area,** North Texas's **Possum Kingdom State Park,** and Central Texas's **Lake Travis.**

Birding continues to grow as a popular Texas pastime, drawing enthusiasts from around the globe. The Great Texas Coastal Birding Trail, co-sponsored by the Texas Parks and Wildlife Department and the Texas Department of Transportation, encompasses some of the top birding sites along the Gulf coast. Major birding areas include Rockport's **Aransas National Wildlife Refuge,** the prime wintering ground for hundreds of bird species including the endangered whooping crane; South Texas's **Laguna Atascosa National Wildlife Refuge,** the southernmost waterfowl refuge in the nation; and McAllen's **Santa Ana National Wildlife Refuge,** popular for viewing green jays and other species indigenous to nearby Mexico.

# Rules of the Road

**License requirements:** To drive in Texas you must be at least 16 years old and have a valid driver's license. Residents of most other countries may drive as long as they have valid licenses from their home countries.

**Right Turn on Red:** You may make a right turn on red after a full stop anywhere in the sate, unless a sign is posted prohibiting you from doing so.

**Seat Belts and Helmet Laws:** All drivers and front-seat passengers must wear seat belts. Children under age four must wear a seat belt at all times, whether seated in the front or back. Children under age two must only ride in a federally approved child safety seat. Motorcyclists under age 21 must wear a helmet at all times; motorcyclists age 21 and over are not required to wear helmets if they have proof of insurance valued over $10,000 or have proof of completion of a motorcycle operations course.

**Speed limits:** In 1995, Texas raised the speed limit from 55 mph to 70 mph. In heavily traveled corridors, though, the limit remains 55. Be sure to check speed limit signs carefully.

**For More Information:** Contact the Texas Department of Transportation at 800/687–7846.

# Bandera to New Braunfels Driving Tour
*A GERMAN HERITAGE TOUR*

Distance: 110 miles        Time: 3 days
Breaks: Try stopping overnight in Fredericksburg, home to more than 200 bed and breakfast establishments, some located in German "Sunday houses" built by farmers a century ago. Austin, with its thriving nightlife along bustling Sixth Street and rich history in the downtown area, also makes an excellent overnight stop.

This tour will take you to the Hill Country, a scenic area tucked north of San Antonio and west of I–35. Created by an earthquake more than 30 million years ago, this region spans 23 counties and is filled with small towns, popular lakes, several caves,

INTRODUCTION
HISTORY
REGIONS
WHEN TO VISIT
STATE'S GREATS
RULES OF THE ROAD
DRIVING TOURS

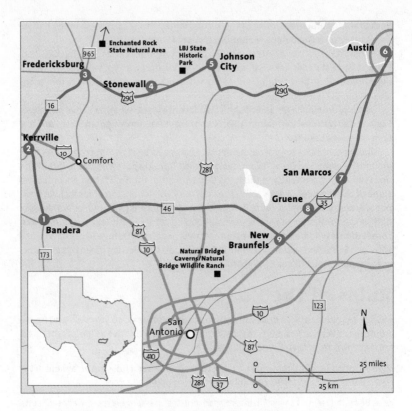

and historic attractions. Be wary of this tour during heavy rains; many roads have low water crossings that can be prone to flash flooding.

❶ Begin your tour in **Bandera.** This community is known as the "Cowboy Capital of the World," both a reminder of its Wild West history and a symbol of its present-day western theme-inspired tourism. The town is surrounded by numerous dude ranches that offer you a chance to take to the saddle for a few days of cowboy fun. Rodeos, country and western music, and horse racing are also found in the area.

❷ From Bandera, head north on Rte. 173 for approximately 25 mi to **Kerrville.** Attractions in the area include the **Y.O. Ranch,** one of the most famous in the nation. At one time the ranch covered 80 miles; today it offers guided tours as well as hunting. **The Cowboy Artists of America Museum** exhibits Western-theme paintings and sculpture.

❸ Leaving Kerrville, proceed north on Rte. 16 for approximately 25 mi into **Fredericksburg.** This quaint German community is a longtime favorite with shoppers and bed-and-breakfast lovers. Downtown, the **Admiral Nimitz Museum and State Historical Center** honors Fredericksburg native Admiral Chester Nimitz, World War II Commander-in-Chief of the Pacific. Hikers enjoy **Enchanted Rock State Natural Area.** This park contains the largest stone formation in the West; both easy and challenging climbs are available. In summer, climbers should start the hike early to avoid midday heat.

❹ When you've finished exploring Kerrville, head east on U.S. 290 for about 10 mi to Stonewall, the birth and burial place of Lyndon B. Johnson. Visit the **Lyndon B. John-**

INTRODUCTION
HISTORY
REGIONS
WHEN TO VISIT
STATE'S GREATS
RULES OF THE ROAD
DRIVING TOURS

son State Historical Park, where you can catch a guided tour of the LBJ Ranch. You can also visit the **Sauer-Beckmann Farmstead,** an historic farm with docents in period dress reminiscent of the early 1900s. During the spring months, this portion of the drive is lined with blooming peach trees, the top crop in this area.

**⑤** Approximately 10 mi east of Stonewall on U.S. 290 is **Johnson City.** Named for LBJ's grandfather, the then future president moved here from Stonewall when he was 5 years old. Headquarters for the **Lyndon B. Johnson National Historic Park** are here, as is the simply titled **Boyhood Home** of LBJ.

**⑥** From Johnson City, head east on U.S. 290 for about 40 mi, then north on I–35 into **Austin.** The centerpiece of the city as well as the state government is the **State Capitol.** Guided tours of the building that stands taller than the national capital are offered daily. Just south of the Capitol stands the **Governor's Mansion,** filled with historic reminders of the many governors of the Lone Star State. You're taken past the main staircase, through the formal parlor, and finally into the dining room. On the north side of the Capitol lies the **University of Texas at Austin,** the largest university in the nation. On its campus, the **Lyndon Baines Johnson Library and Museum** traces the history of Johnson's presidency through exhibits and films. On the eighth floor you can tour a model of the Oval Office as it looked during LBJ's administration.

**⑦** Approximately 40 mi south of Austin at Exit 206 off I–35 is **San Marcos,** a favorite with shoppers from around the state who come to browse its two massive outlet malls. Summer visitors find recreation along the banks of the San Marcos River, popular with snorkelers for its clear waters. The waters form the focal point for **Aquarena Center for Continuing Education,** an historic park that dates back to 1928 when A. B. Rogers purchased 125 acres at the headwaters of the San Marcos River to create a grand hotel. Rogers added glass-bottomed boats to cruise Spring Lake, fed by more than 200 springs that produce 150 million gallons daily. This 98 percent pure water is home to many fish (including some white albino catfish) and various types of plant life.

**⑧** When you've finished shopping, head to **Gruene** (pronounced Green), a former town and now actually a neighborhood in New Braunfels. From its founding in the 1870s, Gruene was a happening place with a swinging dance hall and busy cotton gin. But when the boll weevil arrived in Texas with the Great Depression right on its heels, Gruene became a ghost town. Today that former ghost town is alive with small shops and restaurants as well as Texas's oldest dance hall. **Gruene Hall** is as lively today as it was in the late 1800s. Burlap bags draped from the ceiling dampen the sound, 1930s advertisements decorate the walls, and a U.S. flag with 46 stars still hangs over the dance floor.

**⑨** From Gruene, reach **New Braunfels** by returning to I–35 and continuing south, or by traveling south on Gruene Rd. The self-proclaimed "Antique Capital of Texas" is home to numerous antiques shops, most in the downtown region. New Braunfels recalls its German heritage with many German festivals and even the name of its waterpark, **Schlitterbahn** (the largest in the state). Summer visitors will have the chance to canoe, raft, or inner tube down the city's Guadalupe and Comal rivers. Outside of New Braunfels, you'll find cool conditions year around in **Natural Bridge Caverns**; families also enjoy visiting adjacent **Natural Bridge Wildlife Ranch.**
From New Braunfels, take Rte. 46 W for about 50 mi back to Bandera.

# Kingsville to Aransas National Wildlife Refuge Driving Tour

*SOUTH TEXAS TOUR*

Distance: 117 mi        Time: 2 days

Breaks: Try stopping overnight at Corpus Christi, a good central point on the tour that offers a variety of accommodations and attractions.

This tour will take you to the Coastal Bend, a region spanning Rockport, Aransas Pass, Port Aransas, Corpus Christi, and Kingsville. Once a magnet for travelers in the days of buccaneers and Spanish conquistadors, the region today is one of the top ecotourism destinations in the nation. Besides drawing visitors for its relaxed atmosphere and coastal beauty, the area attracts bird-watchers from around the globe who come for a chance to view more than 400 species. The area is dotted with birding and hiking trails, guided tour boats, great photo opportunities, and more.

❶ Begin your tour at **King Ranch.** Most guests make their first stop at the visitors center for a guided tour of the expansive ranch, which was founded in 1853 by Capt. Richard King. The King Ranch ranks as one of the largest spreads in the world, spanning 825,000 acres, larger than the state of Rhode Island. Today it's home to more than 60,000 cattle and 300 quarter horses and welcomes visitors from around the world.

❷ Next, stop in **Kingsville,** at the intersection of Rte. 141 and I–77. The town named for the nearby ranch also offers several ranching attractions. The **King Ranch Museum** offers a look at the history of the ranch, including a photographic essay on life on the King Ranch in the 1940s. A collection of saddles, antique carriages, and antique cars rounds out the exhibits. Nearby, the **King Ranch Saddle Shop,** started following the Civil War to keep the ranch in saddles, today produces fine purses, belts, and, of course, saddles. It's located in downtown Kingsville's John B. Ragland Mercantile Company Building, which is included in the National Register of Historic Places.

❸ From Kingsville, head north on I–77 for about 25 mi, then east on Rte. 44 for about 10 mi into **Corpus Christi.** One of America's 10 busiest ports, Corpus Christi has a bustling waterfront filled with tour boats, shrimp boats, and deep sea fishing charters. **Corpus Christi Museum of Science and History** holds some of the state's top exhibits, including life-size replicas of the Niña, Pinta, and Santa Maria. Across the Harbor Bridge, the **Texas State Aquarium** showcases the aquatic animals and habitats indigenous to the Gulf of Mexico. Next door, the **USS *Lexington* Museum on the Bay** is set in the most decorated aircraft carrier in U.S. Naval history.

❹ Visitors to Corpus Christi shouldn't miss a stop at **Padre Island National Seashore,** open year-round for beachcombing, fishing, and swimming. Its visitors center contains exhibits on the region. Surfers will find wave action created by a surf pier at the **J.P. Luby Surf Park** on Rte. 361, while campers can enjoy covered picnic areas and overnight hookups at **Padre Balli Park** on Park Road 22.

❺ When you've finished exploring Padre Island, head north on Rte. 22, then right on Rte. 53 into **Mustang Island State Park.** This park is a great place for a fall campout. The park offers a mile and a half of beach camping, and horseback riding is popular along the island's beaches.

INTRODUCTION
HISTORY
REGIONS
WHEN TO VISIT
STATE'S GREATS
RULES OF THE ROAD
DRIVING TOURS

**6** When you've finished exploring the park, head north on Rte. 53/361 out of Mustang Island and into **Port Aransas**. Port Aransas, or just "Port A" to most Texans, is perched on the northern tip of Mustang Island. Spend an afternoon out in the Gulf aboard a deep sea fishing cruise. Large group trips, taking as many as 100 passengers, provide bait and tackle. Serious anglers looking for big game fish such as marlin and shark should book charter excursions for personalized service. For a chance to see dolphins, stop by the Roberts Point Park on Rte. 361. Dolphins often chase the ferries as they make their way across the ship channel. If you'd like to learn more about marine life, stop by the small aquarium at the **University of Texas Marine Science Institute.**

**❼** Rte. 53 becomes Rte. 361 beyond Port Aransas. Stay on Rte. 361 to **Aransas Pass.** Aransas Pass is more a genuine fishing village and less a tourist destination than many other coastal communities. (Most of its 7,000 residents are employed in the fishing industry.) The **Seamen's Memorial Tower,** a monument to the fishermen lost at sea, marks the entrance to the working harbor.

**❽** Ten mi north of Aransas Pass on Rte. 35L is **Rockport.** The town is considered a bird-watching paradise, with more than 500 species on record. Rockport's position on a major bird flyway (the Central Flyway) has made it an international birding destination. It's particularly known for migrating passerines, shorebirds, waterfowl, birds of prey, and hummingbirds. History buffs will also find plenty of activities in Rockport/Fulton. The **Fulton Mansion State Historic Structure,** completely refurbished by the Texas Parks and Wildlife Department, was somewhat of a futuristic home when first built in 1876. For an even older look at coastal history, stop by the **Texas Maritime Museum,** which traces maritime history from the Spanish shipwrecks off the Gulf coast to the offshore oil industry.

**❾** **Aransas National Wildlife Refuge** is the winter nesting ground of the endangered whooping crane, a statuesque bird with a 7-ft wingspan. A self-guided drive allows you the opportunity to spot several species of birds and mammals (as well as alligators); a visitors center explains more about the delicate ecology of the region.

To return to Kingsville, take Rte. 35N from the Aransas National Wildlife Refuge to Rte. 239W and proceed for about 10 mi to U.S. 77. Proceed south on U.S. 77 for about 90 mi into Kingsville.

# ABILENE

MAP 8, G3

*(Nearby towns also listed: Comanche, Eastland, San Angelo, Sweetwater)*

Founded in 1881 by cattlemen as a railroad shipping point, this city of 107,000 was named for Abilene, Kansas. Although Abilene has a long history as a cattle-producing area, the cattle industry yielded a bit to oil, which was discovered here in the early 1900s, and today both form the backbone of the economy. The city is home to Abilene Christian, Hardin-Simmons, and McMurry universities. A historic downtown district, which includes several renovated turn-of-the-century buildings and one of the original Paramount Theaters, is home to several arts organizations, galleries, and museums.

**Information:** **Abilene Convention and Visitors Bureau** | 1101 North 1st St., Abilene, TX, 79601 | 915/676–2556 or 800/727–7704 | fax 915/676–1630 | visitors@abilene.com | www.abilene.com/visitors.

## Attractions

**Abilene State Park.** This 621-acre park includes camping, picnic sites, a swimming pool, fishing, and hiking. The park is set in a large grove of pecan trees and once was a campground for Native Americans. | Rte. 89, 15 mi southwest of Abilene | 915/572–3204 | fax 915/572–3008 | www.tpwd.state.tx.us | $3 | Daily 8 AM–10 PM.

**Abilene Zoological Gardens.** Especially noted for its Discovery Center, this 13-acre zoo in Nelson Park is filled with more than 800 animals, including fish, birds, and small mammals from the Southwestern United States and from Africa. | Nelson Park, Rte. 36 | 915/676–6085 | fax 915/696–6084 | $3 | Daily 9–5.

**Buffalo Gap Historic Village.** This historic village contains 20 buildings from the region's frontier days, including the Old Taylor County Courthouse, a country store, a blacksmith shop, and a bank. A short video introduces you to some area history. | 133 N. William St., Buffalo Gap | 915/572–5211 | fax 915/698–7910 | $4 | Mon.–Sat. 10–6, Sun. 12–6.

**Center for Contemporary Arts.** Comprised of a group of working artists with studios that are open to the public, this arts venue displays rotating monthly exhibits, in mediums ranging from sculpture and painting to photography. | 220 Cypress St. | 915/677–8389 | www.abilene.com/art/cca | cca@abilene.com | Free | Tues.–Sat. 11–5.

**Dyess Air Force Base.** Home of the 7th Bomber Wing, this air force base includes Linear Air Park, which holds historic World War II aircraft. | Arnold Blvd. and Military Dr. | 915/696–5609 | fax 915/696–2866 | Free | Daily dawn–dusk.

**Fort Phantom Hill and Lake.** Fort Phantom was constructed in 1851 to ward off attacks by Native Americans but was abandoned by the Army in 1854, and burned shortly thereafter. (Today only ruins remain.) Camping, picnicking, watersports, and fishing are available at the neighboring lake. | www.fortphantom.org | FM 600 | 915/677–1309 | Free | Daily dawn–dusk.

**Grace Museum.** Across the street from the Convention and Visitors Bureau, the former Grace Hotel (built in 1909) now houses a fine arts museum, a historical museum for the town of Abilene, and a children's museum. | 102 Cypress St. | 915/673–4587 | fax 915/675–5993 | moa@abilene.com | www.abilene.com/grace | $3 | Tues., Wed. 10–5, Thurs. 10–8:30, Fri., Sat. 10–5, Sun. 1–5.

**Oscar Rose Park.** This local park is a favorite with families and picnickers. It has a tennis center, as well as a senior recreation center. | 7th and Mockingbird Sts. | 915/676–6217 | Free | Daily 5:30 AM–midnight.

## ON THE CALENDAR
**APR.: *Celebrate Abilene.*** Food booths, an art festival, and kids' activities round out this downtown event. | 915/676–2556.
**MAY: *Western Heritage Classic.*** This lively festival includes ranch rodeos, dances, chuck wagon cook-offs, "cowboy" poetry, music, and an art show. | 915/677–4376.
**SEPT.: *West Texas Fair and Rodeo.*** A parade, livestock shows, carnival rides, and rodeo displays are part of the fun. | 915/677–4376.

## Dining
**Joe Allen's.** Barbecue. A legendary family-run spot with a very casual and laid-back feel, there's nothing about the decor to distract you, so concentrate on the excellent barbecue and steaks. Everyone raves about the ribs, or tries the huge 2-inch-thick rib eye (weighing close to 2 pounds). The potato salad, homemade bread, vegetable buffet, and peach cobbler are also popular. Expect to wait for a table on Fri. and Sat. nights. | 1233 S. Treadaway St. | 915/672–6082 | Reservations not accepted | $6–$25 | AE, D, DC, MC, V.

**Olive Garden.** Italian. A favorite with families, this chain serves a number of specialties from pastas to grilled seafood. Try fettuccine chicken florentine. Kids' menu. | 3210 S. Clack St. | 915/691–0388 | No lunch | $12–$28 | AE, D, DC, MC, V.

**Perini Ranch Steakhouse.** Steak. This rustic restaurant 13 mi south of Abilene is partly built of old wooden railroad ties, with painted wood and brick floors and lots of windows overlooking oak trees and rolling hills. Try the signature beef tenderloin, rubbed in spices and cooked to order over mesquite served with a horseradish sauce. You may also want to try the fried chicken or catfish, or the bread pudding or jalapeño cheesecake. | 3002 FM 89, Buffalo Gap | 915/572–3339 | Reservations essential Fri., Sat. | Closed Mon., Tues. No lunch Wed., Thurs. | $9–$25 | AE, D, MC, V.

## Lodging
**Abilene Travelodge.** Most rooms are ground level at this hotel. Families or groups may want to rent the suite, which has a living room and two separate bedrooms. It's 5 mi east of downtown Abilene, and 5 mi from the Taylor Center Coliseum. Restaurant, bar, complimentary

Continental breakfast, room service, in-room data ports, some microwaves, some refrigerators, cable TV, pool, laundry facilities, laundry service, business services. | 840 U.S. 80E | 915/677–8100 or 800/880–7666 | fax 915/672–8147 | 104 rooms, 1 suite | $52–$58, $99 suite | AE, D, DC, MC, V.

**Best Inn.** This two-story, mid-size hotel has a garden courtyard on its grounds. A restaurant is behind the property. Cable TV, pool, laundry facilities, business services, airport shuttle, some pets allowed (fee). | 1625 Rte. 351 | 915/673–5271 | fax 915/673–8240 | 163 rooms | $49–$59 | AE, DC, MC, V.

**B. J.'s Bed and Breakfast.** Built in 1902, this B&B is nestled in an old residential section of town, part of the parcel of land that was the original Abilene town site in 1881. Each guest room has antique beds and dressers; one room has a 6-ft claw foot tub, and another was home to Clint Eastwood for six weeks. (It has a king-size bed, of course.) The Continental breakfast is generous, with eggs, a hot apple or peach dumpling, and fruit compote. Dining room, complimentary Continental breakfast, some in-room VCRs, no room phones, no TV in some rooms, TV in common area, business services, no pets, no kids under 12, no smoking. | 508 Mulberry St. | 915/675–5855 or 800/673–5855 | fax 915/677–4694 | bfender@earthlink.net | 4 rooms (2 with shared bath) | $65–$75 | AE, D, MC, V.

**Budget Host.** The airport and two universities are 10 miles from this motel. Restaurant, room service, cable TV, pool, wading pool, business services, some pets allowed. | 3210 Pine St. | 915/677–2683 | fax 915/677–8211 or 888/672–5293 | 100 rooms | $35–$55 | AE, D, DC, MC, V.

**Clarion Hotel and Conference Center.** This three-story hotel has a variety of meeting rooms in which business travelers can hold court. A number of fast food restaurants are four blocks away. Restaurant, bar, room service, some microwaves, cable TV, 2 pools, wading pool, hot tub, sauna, laundry facilities, business services, some pets allowed. | 5403 S. 1st St. | 915/695–2150 | fax 915/698–6742 | 176 rooms, 5 suites | $44–$64, $60–$69 suites | AE, D, DC, MC, V.

**Embassy Suites.** A shopping mall is across the street from this full-service, all-suites hotel. A hot, made-to-order breakfast is available daily, and an open bar is scheduled nightly. Restaurant, bar, complimentary breakfast, room service, in-room data ports, microwaves, refrigerators, cable TV, pool, hot tub, sauna, steam room, laundry facilities, laundry service, business services, pets allowed. | 4250 Ridgemont Dr. | 915/698–1234 or 800/362–2779 | fax 915/698–2771 | mburke@embassyabilene.com | www.embassyabilene.com | 176 suites | $86–$150 | AE, D, DC, MC, V.

**La Quinta.** This two-story hotel is 8 mi from the airport. Complimentary Continental breakfast, cable TV, pool, some pets allowed. | 3501 W. Lake Rd. | 915/676–1676 | fax 915/672–8323 | www.laquinta.com | 106 rooms | $49–$90 | AE, D, DC, MC, V.

**Quality Inn.** The civic center is across the street from this two-story motel, and the airport is 15 mi away. Restaurant, bar, complimentary breakfast, room service, cable TV, pool, business services, airport shuttle, some pets allowed. | 505 Pine St. | 915/676–0222 or 800/221–0222 | fax 915/676–0513 | 118 rooms | $49–$65 | AE, D, DC, MC, V.

**Ramada Inn.** Restaurants, shopping, and Abilene's historic downtown area are within walking distance of this two-story hotel. The airport is 12 mi away. Restaurant, bar (with entertainment), room service, cable TV, pool, laundry facilities, business services. | 3450 S. Clack St. | 915/695–7700 | fax 915/698–0546 | www.ramada.com | 146 rooms, 2 suites | $39–$66, $125 suites | AE, D, DC, MC, V.

**Royal Inn.** This single-story motel was built in the 1940s. It's less than 1 mi from Dyess Air Force Base. Restaurant, bar, room service, cable TV, pool, business services, some pets allowed (fee). | 5695 S. 1st St. | 915/692–3022 or 800/588–4386 | fax 915/692–3137 | 150 rooms | $25–$48 | AE, D, DC, MC, V.

# ALICE

*(Nearby town also listed: Kingsville)*

Named for the daughter of the founder of King Ranch (a legendary, 1.2-million-acre ranch built by a wildly successful Irish immigrant named Richard King), this South Texas community of 21,000 was once the world's largest cattle-shipping point. Today the town is also active in the petroleum business and is a favorite destination for hunters searching for javelina, white-tailed deer, wild turkey, and dove. Alice's southern location allows for tall palm trees to grow alongside deciduous trees.

Information: **Alice Chamber of Commerce** | 612 E. Main St., Alice, TX 78333 | 361/664–3454 | www.alicetx.org.

## Attractions

**Lake Corpus Christi State Park.** This 14,000-acre lake offers visitors campsites, showers, and screened shelters. Activities available include fishing, swimming, and boating. From Alice, take Rte. 359 about 30 mi to Park Rd. 25. | Park Rd. 25 | 361/547–2635 | fax 361/547–7084 | www.tpwd.state.tx.us | $3 | Daily.

**South Texas Museum.** The history and traditions of the Jim Wells County region are showcased in this museum, based architecturally on the Alamo and built in 1911. Exhibits trace human habitation from Native American settlements through the present day; farm, ranch, railroad, and oil artifacts are on display. | 66 S. Wright St. | 361/668–8891 | Donation | Weekdays 10–12, 1–5, Sat. 9–1.

### ON THE CALENDAR

**MAY: *Fiesta Bandana.*** Eat, enjoy carnival rides, and listen to a local band play during this fair's weeklong festivities. Held in Plaza Park, scheduled events include booths with crafts and food vendors, a beauty pageant and talent contest, and live entertainment. | 361/664–3454.

**OCT.: *Jim Wells County Fair.*** The County Fairgrounds hosts this four-day event, which includes viewing prize rabbits, turkeys, lambs, and steers, talent and beauty contests in various age categories, 4-H displays, the judging of baked goods, bands, a carnival, dancing, and more. | 361/664–7595.

## Dining

**Chente's.** Mexican. This restaurant doesn't offer much in the way of decor, but the food is great. Try the *pollos à la Mexicana* (spicy grilled chicken with tomatoes and onions, served with rice, beans, and avocado salad) and cheese enchiladas flavored with green chiles. There are a few American items on the menu, like the popular catfish-and-shrimp platter. Kids' menu. | 107 Cecilia St. | 361/668–9781 | Closed Sun. | $4–$15 | AE, D, DC, MC, V.

## Lodging

**Days Inn.** Built in the mid 1970s, this two-story motel is within 5 mi of two golfing facilities. Restaurant, complimentary Continental breakfast, room service, in-room data ports, cable TV, pool, golf, laundry service, business services, pets allowed. | 555 N. Johnson St. | 361/664–6616 or 800/544–8313 | fax 361/664–8016 | www.daysinn.com | 97 rooms | $40–$50 | AE, D, DC, MC, V.

# ALPINE

*(Nearby town also listed: Big Bend National Park)*

The seat of the largest county in Texas (larger than the state of Connecticut), this town of 8,000 is perched at an elevation of 4,485 ft, lofty by Texas standards. The mountainous climate makes the town a popular vacation spot; you can enjoy mountain climbing, horseback riding, rock hunting, and more. Alpine is the home of Sul Ross State University.

Information: **Alpine Chamber of Commerce** | 106 N. 3rd St., Alpine, TX 79830 | 915/837–2326 | chamber@alpinetexas.com | www.alpinetexas.com.

## Attractions

**McDonald Astronomical Observatory.** You'll find this spot 6,791 ft above sea level on the rounded peak of Mount Locke in the Davis Mountains. The Visitors' Information Center is at the base of the mountain, and on Tues., Fri., and Sat. nights, you can join them for "Star Parties"—constellation tours, viewings through telescopes, and a video. The observatory is 43 mi north of Alpine via Rte. 118. | Rte. 118N off Spur 78, Ft. Davis | 915/426–3640 or 877/984–STAR | vc.as.utexas.edu | Free; tours $4 | Daily 9–5, tours at 11 AM and 2 PM.

**Museum of the Big Bend.** Encompassing the contributions of the many groups that once called Big Bend home—Native Americans, Spanish, Mexicans, and Anglo-Americans—this museum is a good starting point for an overview of the region's cultural and natural history. Children will enjoy the Discovery Center with hands-on ways to learn about the area. Be sure to see the Chihuahuan Desert Cactus Garden. (*See also* Big Bend National Park.) | Sul Ross State University, off U.S. 90 | 915/837–8143 | fax 915/837–8381 | Free | Tues.–Sat. 9–5, Sun. 1–5.

**Sul Ross State University.** Cowboy poetry meets, its agricultural program (specializing in ranching), and its rodeo team are popular with the school's 2,500 students. | U.S. 90 | 915/837–8011 or 888/722–7778 | fax 915/837–8431 | www.sulross.edu | Free | Daily.

**Woodward Agate Ranch.** Hunt, gather, and collect famed Texas agates and other semiprecious stones on the grounds of this 3,000-acre rock-hunter's paradise. If you're less inspired, you may purchase sample rocks already weighed and cleaned. | Rte. 118, 18 mi south of Alpine, | 915/459–2361 | $5 per vehicle | Apr.–Nov., daily 11-4.

### ON THE CALENDAR

**MAR.:** *Annual Texas Cowboy Poetry Gathering.* Poetry, storytelling, live music, dancing, chuck wagon meals, and western artwork and crafts are part of this event. | 915/837–1071.

## Dining

**Cueva de León Cafe.** Mexican. Named "cave of the lion" by a local high school student after the nearby Sleeping Lion Mountain, this popular restaurant has been making quality Mexican food since 1976. Try the chiles rellenos (long green chiles roasted and peeled in-house, stuffed with jack cheese, lightly battered, and deep-fried) and beef fajitas, or sample a little of everything at the Sat. supper buffet. For dessert, there's the fried apple burrito with sugar and cinnamon. Outdoor dining is available on the patio. | 100 W. Second St., Ft. Davis | 915/426–3801 | Closed Sun. | $2–$9 | AE, D, MC, V.

**Reata Restaurant.** American. This popular restaurant is in an 1896 adobe house; the wisteria-covered patio is complete with pecan and pine trees. The "West Texas cowboy cuisine" draws from a variety of regional influences, and includes chicken-fried steak, wild game such as buffalo, a fish-of-the-day, Mexican food, and popular onion rings. Try the beef or pork tenderloin, smoked shrimp enchiladas, or jalapeño and cilantro soup. | 203 N. Fifth St. | 915/837–9232 | Reservations essential Fri., Sat. | Closed Sun. | $13–$27 | AE, MC, V.

## Lodging

**Hotel Limpia.** Built in 1912 and styled in 1944 art deco, this hotel in the town square is constructed of locally mined pink limestone. It boasts the only bar in the county. Dining room, bar, some kitchenettes, some microwaves, some in-room hot tubs, cable TV, no TV in some rooms, business services, no smoking. | Main St., Fort Davis | 915/426–3237 or 800/662–5517 | www.hotellimpia.com | 36 rooms, 2 guesthouses, 1 cottage | $79–190 rooms, $99–$169 guesthouses, $110–$130 cottage | AE, D, MC, V.

# AMARILLO

*(Nearby towns also listed: Canyon, Childress, Clarendon, Dalhart, Dumas, Fritch, Hereford, Lubbock, Pampa, Plainview)*

Historic Route 66 runs through the heart of this Panhandle city, the cultural and commercial capital of the Texas Panhandle. From a humble beginning as a staging area for the Fort Worth and Denver City Railroad in the 1880s, this city of 158,000 became a center for cattle ranching, wheat and cotton farming, and oil production.

Amarillo is the gateway to the nation's second largest canyon, Palo Duro Canyon State Park, where you can get a taste of the Old West. Truly a Texas-sized wonder, this natural chasm stretches 120 mi wide.

## TEX-MEX FOOD

"Tex-Mex" refers to the particular style of Mexican food found in the Lone Star State. Unlike New Mexico's Mexican food (which might include blue corn tortillas), or California Mexican food (which relies on avocados and black olives), Tex-Mex depends heavily on ground beef, cheese, and chili sauce.

A Tex-Mex favorite, often known affectionately as "Combination Plate No. 1," is an order of beef enchiladas, a taco, refried beans, and Spanish rice. If you're lucky, *leche quemada*, a sugary pecan praline, will be brought out with your check.

As you venture farther south into Texas, you'll find a larger variety of Tex-Mex dishes, including some that are sold primarily in Hispanic neighborhoods. One of these dishes is *cabrito*, tender young goat usually cooked over an open flame on a spit. Cabrito is a common dish in border towns, where you can often see it hanging on spits in market windows. Another Tex-Mex specialty is *barbacoa*, a spicy barbecue that's usually served in tacos. It's one of those dishes that tastes great until you discover what in fact it is that you're eating. Barbacoa starts as a head of beef (with eyes, brain and tongue intact) that's buttered, then wrapped in cheesecloth, then a burlap bag. The traditional way to prepare barbacoa begins by digging a pit or pozo and filling it about one-third full of hot coals covered with pads of the prickly pear cactus (to add moisture). Traditionally these spicy dishes are washed down with cold cerveza (beer).

If you have one too many cervezas, the Tex-Mex cure the next morning is a bowl of *menudo*. This spicy soup, made from tripe, is a popular hangover remedy. It's sold in restaurants and canned versions are found in grocery stores in South and West Texas.

© Artville

**Information: Amarillo Convention and Visitor Council** | 1000 S. Polk St., Amarillo, TX 79101 | 800/692–1338 or 806/374–1497 | www.amarillo-cvb.org.

## Attractions

**Amarillo Cattle Auction.** Every Tues. morning, spruced-up ranchers come to buy and sell cattle at auction. You're welcome to watch, and since this is serious business, no one will pay you any mind. Afterwards, you can grab a meal at the adjacent café. | 100 S. Manhattan St. | 800/692–1338 | Free | Daily.

**Amarillo Museum of Art.** Designed by the architect of Washington, D.C.'s Kennedy Center, this museum on the campus of Amarillo College showcases fine arts as well as the performing arts. | 2200 S. Van Buren | 806/371–5050 | fax 806/373–9235 | www.amarilloart.org | Free | Tues.–Fri. 10–5, weekends 1–5.

**Amarillo Zoo.** This small zoo contains herds of bison on a 20-acre range as well as more exotic species like cougars, spider monkeys, and brown bears. | Thompson Park, off U.S. 287 | 806/381–7911 | www.amarillo-cvb.org/zoo.html | Free | Tues.–Sun. 9:30–5:30.

**American Quarter Horse Heritage Center and Museum.** Devoted to the quarter horse, this expansive museum contains the world's largest equine registry, as well as numerous exhibits, hands-on displays, and videos. | 2601 I–40 E | 806/376–5181 | fax 806/376–1005 | $4 | Mon.–Sat. 9–5, Sun. 12–5.

**Cadillac Ranch.** An eccentric Amarillo businessman buried 10 new Cadillacs nose down in the middle of a large pasture in the 1960s. The elements, grazing cattle, and graffiti artists have had their way with them over the years, and it's up to you to decide if the ranch is art or an eyesore. It's 4 mi west of Amarillo via I–40 to Arnot Rd. Exit. Make a U-turn to cross the freeway, then continue east on the access road 1 mi. | I–40, 4 mi west of Amarillo | 800/692–1338 | Free | Daily.

**Carson County Square House Museum.** Recounting the history of the Panhandle, this local history museum houses exhibits on the region's agriculture, cattle, and oil. | Rte. 207 and 5th St., 25 mi northeast of Amarillo | 806/537–3524 | fax 806/537–5628 | Free | Mon.–Sat. 9–5, Sun. 1–5.

**Don Harrington Discovery Center.** This hands-on science museum off I–40 is filled with interactive exhibits with subjects ranging from exotic fish to outer space. A planetarium offers star shows and 360-degree films. In front of the Discovery Center stands the Helium Monument, which contains time capsules to be opened in 25, 50, 100, and 1,000 years. The monument recognizes Amarillo's role as "The Helium Capital of the World." | 1200 Streit Dr. | 806/355–9547 | fax 806/355–5703 | www.dhdc.org | $3 | Tues.–Sat. 10–5, Sun. 1–5.

★ **Palo Duro Canyon State Park.** This 14,103-acre park was carved by a branch of the Red River and is the second largest canyon in the nation. Hiking, horseback riding (including many guided rides with cowboy breakfasts), swimming, and camping are available. The park is also home to an amphitheater where performances of *Texas*, an outdoor drama about the founding of the region, are performed during summer months. The Sad Monkey Railroad, a miniature train, takes travelers to the recesses of the canyon. | Rte. 217 | 806/488–2227 | www.tpwd.state.tx.us | $3 | Daily 8 AM–10 PM.

**Wonderland Amusement Park.** Home of the Texas Tornado double loop rollercoaster, this amusement park has 21 rides as well as miniature golf, bumper cars, and water slides. | 2601 Dumas Dr. | 806/383–4712 | fax 806/383–8737 | $15 | Apr.–Labor Day, weekdays 7 PM–10 PM, weekends 1 PM–10 PM.

### ON THE CALENDAR

**MAY:** *Funfest.* Music, food, games, and live entertainment are all on hand for this festival, held over Memorial Day weekend in Thompson Park. | 806/374–0802.

**MAY–SEPT.:** *Cowboy Morning Breakfast.* This popular festival includes a cowboy-style breakfast, cooked and enjoyed outdoors. The event is held at the Figure 3 Ranch (where the final scenes of *Indiana Jones and the Last Crusade* were filmed), reached following a 20-minute ride on mule-drawn wagons. Following breakfast, cowboys show off their skills with some roping, riding, and branding. Evening steak dinners are also available. | 800/658–2613.

**JUNE:** *Cowboy and World Championship Chuckwagon Roundup.* Competitions are held on the Tri-State Fairgrounds between cowboys as well as chuckwagon cooks from the region. | 806/376–7767.

**SEPT.:** *Tri-State Fair.* The Tri-State Fairgrounds hosts a carnival, rodeo, food booths, live music, and dancing. | 806/376–7767.

**DEC.:** *Amarillo Nights of Light.* A mile and a half of holiday light decorations in John Stiff Memorial Park sparkles for the entire month of Dec. | 806/378–9337.

## Dining

**Beans 'n' Things.** Barbecue. A small building houses an even smaller dining room where meals include barbecued meats, an array of side vegetables from green beans to corn-on-the-cob, and treats like Cajun rice and macaroni-and-cheese. The all-you-can-eat special is $10. | 1700 Amarillo Blvd. E | 806/373–7383 | Closed Sun. | $6–$10 | AE, D, MC, V.

**Big Texan Steak Ranch.** Steak. Amarillo's most famous restaurant serves a free 72-ounce steak for anyone who can eat it in one hour. Along with good ol' Texas beef, there's also rattlesnake and buffalo. Kids' menu. | 7701 I–40E, | 806/372–5000 | $15–$23 | AE, D, DC, MC, V.

**Olive Garden.** Italian. Try the linguine with marinara sauce at this family-oriented chain restaurant. Kids' menu. | 4121 I–40W | 806/355–9973 | No lunch | $8–$12 | AE, D, DC, MC, V.

**Outback Steakhouse.** Steak. This chain restaurant seeks to serve excellent steaks in a fun, relaxed setting. There's a busy bar and casual booths. Try the 14-ounce Rockhampton Rib-Eye or the fresh fish. Kids' menu. | 7101 I–40W | 806/352–4032 | $10–$22 | AE, D, DC, MC, V.

**Stockyard Cafe.** Steak. Eat like the pioneers did (and local cowfolk still do) at this restaurant, housed in the same building as the Amarillo Cattle Auction. The steak and chicken fries are the top sellers here, served with a baked potato or fries and a salad. If you have room, don't neglect the fruit cobblers—raspberry, cherry, or peach. | 100 S. Manhattan St. | 806/374–6024 | Breakfast also available. Closed Sun. No supper Mon.–Thurs. | $3–$11 | AE, D, MC, V.

## Lodging

**Best Western Amarillo Inn.** A two-story hotel with brown brick and cream trim, you can park in front of your door on the first floor, and second floor rooms are accessed from an interior corridor via staircase. Rooms are neutrally colored, with some Southwestern-style art on the walls. Medi Park is within walking distance, with two small lakes and a walking trail. Restaurant, complimentary breakfast, room service, in-room data ports, some microwaves, some refrigerators, cable TV, pool, laundry facilities, laundry service, business services, pets allowed (fee). | 1610 Coulter St. | 806/358–7861 or 800/528–1234 | fax 352–7287 | 103 rooms | $69–$89 | AE, D, DC, MC, V.

**Days Inn/South.** This motel is just 9 mi from the Cadillac Ranch. Complimentary Continental breakfast, cable TV, pool, hot tub, exercise equipment, business services, airport shuttle. | 8601 Canyon Dr. | 806/468–7100 or 800/329–7466 | fax 806/468–7365 | 63 rooms | $79 | AE, D, DC, MC, V.

**Galbraith House.** A Prairie-style home built in 1912 by a lumber baron who liked to show off—the solarium has a parquet floor rendered in 17 different woods—this B&B has high ceilings and a shaded front porch. You can sit and relax out back in the flower and herb gardens before your morning meal of "Brunch Eggs": a baked version of eggs Benedict with ham and Swiss and Parmesan cheeses. Although it's just off I–40, blocks from downtown, it's in a quiet residential neighborhood. Dining room, complimentary breakfast, in-room data ports, some in-room hot tubs, some in-room VCRs, no TV in some rooms, TV in common area, hot tub, no pets, no kids under 12, no smoking. | 1710 S. Polk St. | 806/374–0237 | panpit@arn.net | www.galbraith-house.com | 5 rooms | $100–$195 | AE, D, MC, V.

**Hampton Inn.** This two-story hotel is 3 mi south of historic Route 66. The Amarillo Zoo is 10 mi to the north and the Amarillo Museum of Art is only 5 mi away. Complimentary Continental breakfast, cable TV, pool, business services, pets allowed. | 1700 I–40E, | 806/372–1425 | fax 806/379–8807 | www.hamptoninn.com | 116 rooms | $59–$89 | AE, D, DC, MC, V.

**Holiday Inn–Amarillo.** Restaurants and a mall are four mi from this four-story hotel, and an airport is just 10 mi away. Restaurants, bar, in-room data ports, room service, cable TV, indoor pool, wading pool, exercise equipment, video games, laundry facilities, business services, airport shuttle. | 1911 I–40E | 806/372–8741 | fax 806/372–2913 | www.holidayinn.com | 247 rooms | $89–$99 | AE, D, DC, MC, V.

**Holiday Inn Express.** This two-story hotel is 3 mi from a shopping mall, 6 mi from Wonderland Amusement Park, and 40 mi from the American Quarter Horse Heritage Center and Museum. Restaurants are within walking distance. Complimentary Continental breakfast, cable TV, pool, exercise equipment, business services. | 34111 I–40W | 806/356–6800 | fax 806/356–0401 | www.holidayinn.com | 97 rooms | $89–$99 | AE, D, DC, MC, V.

**Homegate Suites.** Spacious living and sleeping areas are available in this all-suites hotel. A shopping mall is 1/4 mi away. Picnic area, complimentary Continental breakfast, in-room data ports, kitchenettes, refrigerators, cable TV, pool, hot tub, business services. | 6800 I–40W | 806/358–7943 | fax 806/358–8475 | 125 suites | $79 suites | AE, D, DC, MC, V.

**Parkview House.** This 1908 home (formerly Amarillo's Waldorf Astoria, later a railroad hotel) is filled from floor to ceiling with marvelous finds from vintage stores. Room styles vary from colonial to eclectic, with furnishings like beaded lamps, Middle Eastern rugs, Moroccan photographs, and Indian brass. Dining room, complimentary Continental breakfast, some in-room VCRs, some room phones, no TV in some rooms, TV in common area, hot tub, bicycles, no smoking, no pets. | 1311 S. Jefferson St. | 806/373–9464 | fax 806/373–3166 | parkviewbb@aol.com | hometown.aol.com/parkviewbb/index | 5 rooms (1 with shared bath), 1 cottage | $65–$85, $135 cottage | AE, MC, V.

**Radisson Inn–Airport.** This two-story hotel is 3 miles from the airport. Restaurant, bar (with entertainment), room service, in-room data ports, minibars, cable TV, pool, exercise equipment, video games, business services, airport shuttle. | 7909 I–40E | 806/373–3303 | fax 806/373–3353 | www.radisson.com | 207 rooms, 3 suites | $99–$109, $135–$150 suites | AE, D, DC, MC, V.

**Ramada Inn West.** Guest rooms are in either a three-story atrium or a two-story wing. Rooms off the enclosed atrium are close to the pool and airy restaurant. The hotel is about 4 mi west of downtown. Restaurant, complimentary breakfast, in-room data ports, some minibars, some microwaves, some in-room hot tubs, cable TV, pool, hot tub, spa, laundry facilities, laundry service, business services, pets allowed (fee). | 6801 I–40W | 806/358–7881 or 800/858–2223 | fax 806/358–1726 | 148 rooms, 32 suites | $69–$109, $89–$109 suites | AE, D, DC, MC, V.

**Travelodge West.** Several restaurants are within 5 miles of this two-story motel, and the airport is 20 minutes away. In-room data ports, cable TV, pool, business services. | 2035 Paramount Blvd. | 806/353–3541 | fax 806/353–0201 | 100 rooms | $54 | AE, D, DC, MC, V.

# ANGLETON

MAP 8, J6

*(Nearby town also listed: Houston)*

Located on the mouth of the Brazos River, this community of 19,900 is a favorite with those looking for fresh- or saltwater fishing and other water activities such as swimming, surfing, or crabbing.

**Information: Angleton Chamber of Commerce** | 445 East Mulberry, Angleton, TX 77515 | 979/849–6443.

## Attractions

**Varner-Hogg Plantation State Historical Park.** This 67-acre park was built around the 1830s Varner-Hogg Plantation, the former home of Governor James S. Hogg. Grounds include a picnic area, and guided tours of the home are available. | 1702 North 13th St. | 979/345–4656 | fax 979/345–4412 | $4 | Daily.

**ON THE CALENDAR**
**AUG.: *Heart of Angleton Festival.*** The courthouse lawn is the site of this one-day festival, held at the end of Aug. Musicians play throughout the day in the gazebo, and there's a car show, a Li'l Miss and Mister Heart-of-Angleton Contest (for 4–6-year-olds), a diaper derby (for babies still on the crawl), a cow patty bingo, a fajita cook-off, sports like volleyball and basketball, a carnival, and a 5K fun run through town. | 979/849–6062.
**OCT.: *Brazoria County Fair.*** Held in Angleton, this annual fair includes arts and crafts, plenty of homecooked food, local music, kids' rides, livestock, and more. | 979/849–6416.

## Dining

**Smithhart's County Seat Grill.** American. Hardwood floors and walls chock full of antiques from the farm and ranch create a casual feel. The club salad, with lettuce, bacon, hard-boiled egg, cheese, tomatoes, and hand-breaded chicken nuggets with house ranch dressing, is a hit; or try the Cajun chicken (chicken breast nuggets in a spicy secret sauce), or fresh fish—tuna steak, snapper, catfish, and shrimp. | 2440 N. Velasco St. | 979/848–1320 | $6–$17 | AE, D, MC, V.

## Lodging

**Country Hearth Inn.** A brick fireplace and brick floors in the lobby create a homey, country feel. A handful of restaurants are 1 block away. Complimentary Continental breakfast, cable TV, pool, business services. | 1235 N. Velasco | 979/849–2465 | fax 979/848–1947 | 40 rooms | $57–$70 | AE, D, DC, MC, V.

**Days Inn.** This two-story stucco motel was built in 1996. Cable TV, pool. | 1809 N. Velasco | 979/849–2173 | fax 979/849–5822 | 45 rooms | $40–$100 | AE, D, DC, MC, V.

**Ramada Inn.** This two-story mid-1970s redbrick hotel is in nearby Lake Jackson, 15 mi south of Angleton via U.S. 288 to U.S. 332. Conveniences include a complimentary lunch buffet and five meeting rooms. Restaurant, bar, complimentary Continental breakfast, room service, some microwaves, some refrigerators, cable TV, pool, exercise equipment, laundry service, business services, pets allowed (fee). | 925 U.S. 332W, Lake Jackson | 979/297–1161 or 800/544–2119 | fax 979/297–1249 | www.ramadainnlakejacksontx.com | 144 rooms | $90–$155 | AE, D, DC, MC, V.

# ARANSAS PASS

MAP 8, I7

*(Nearby towns also listed: Corpus Christi, Port Aransas, Rockport)*

This community of 8,500 on the Texas Gulf Coast is named for the pass between Mustang and St. Joseph Islands. Primarily a fishing community, it serves as a gateway to Port Aransas and Mustang Island, accessible by ferry or causeway from the city.

**Information: Aransas Pass Chamber of Commerce** | 130 W. Goodnight, Aransas Pass, TX 78336 | 361/758–2750 or 800/633–3028 | info@aransaspass.org.

## Attractions

**Conn Brown Harbor.** The nexus of Aransas Pass, this harbor is home to fish-packing houses and the site of commercial shrimp boats docking and departing. Rent a boat to visit the coastal islands of Mustang and St. Joseph, picnic, or visit the memorial to lost seamen.

ARANSAS PASS

INTRO
ATTRACTIONS
DINING
LODGING

From downtown, take Business 35N to Stapp Ave., turn right and continue to the water. | 361/758–2750 | Free | Daily.

## ON THE CALENDAR
**SEPT.: *Shrimporee.*** In addition to shrimp dishes, this three-day cook-off includes live entertainment and arts and crafts. | 800/633–3028.

**NOV.–JULY: *Market Days.*** On the third Sat. of each month (excluding Aug. and Sept.), local arts-and-crafts people and downtown businesses come together at the visitors center of this small town, selling wares and providing an alternative to big-city shopping. | 361/758–2750.

## Dining
**Nopalitos Restaurant.** Mexican. The brightly painted dining area of this local favorite is festooned with sombreros, serapes, and neon signs (one in the shape of Mexico). Try the grilled beef fajitas, the beef shank–and–vegetable soup, or the popular menudo (beef tripe seasoned with secret spices, chiles, and oregano), served with hominy. Homemade tortillas come with every dish. | 306 E. Goodnight St. | 361/758–1080 | $2–$8 | AE, D, DC, MC, V.

## Lodging
**Dunes Condominiums.** The furnished units at this high-rise beachfront complex are a good choice for families or other groups. Kitchenettes, refrigerators, cable TV, pool, hot tub, tennis, exercise equipment, beach, no pets. | 1000 Lantana Dr. | 361/749–5155 or 800/288–DUNE | fax 512/749–5930 | 48 1- to 3-bedroom apartments | $157–$228 apartments | AE, DC, MC, V.

**Super 8.** This downtown motel was built in 1997. Each suite has a king-size bed, a couch, a table and chairs, and a large TV. A number of restaurants are within 2 blocks. Complimentary Continental breakfast, in-room data ports, refrigerators, some in-room hot tubs, cable TV, pool, business services, no pets. | 500 E. Goodnight St. | 361/758–7888 or 800/800–8000 | 49 rooms, 3 suites | $52–$57, $66 suites | AE, D, DC, MC, V.

# ARLINGTON–GRAND PRAIRIE
MAP 8, I3

*(Nearby towns also listed: Cleburne, Dallas, Denton, Fort Worth, Grapevine, Irving, Lewisville, Waxahachie)*

Located in the heart of the "metroplex," these neighboring cities have a combined population of 425,000 and are easily accessible by interstate highway from either Dallas or Fort Worth. Both offer a range of family vacation activities as well as plenty of family accommodations and restaurants.

Information: **Arlington Convention and Visitors Bureau** | 1905 E. Randol Mill Rd., Arlington, TX 76011 | 817/265–7721 or 800/433–5374 | www.arlington.org.

## Attractions
**Air Combat.** A favorite with teens and active travelers, this attraction features flight simulation (participants wear flight gear and control a virtual plane). | 921 Six Flags Dr. | 817/640–1886 | $40 | Daily by appointment only | www.aircombatschool.com.

**The Ballpark in Arlington.** This stadium is home to the Texas Rangers baseball team and houses the Legends of the Game Baseball Museum, focusing on the Rangers' history and that of baseball in general. There is also the Children's Learning Center, where baseball concepts are used to illustrate history, physics, and mathematics. | Rte. 360 and I–30 | 817/273–5100 or 817/748–1808 | $4–$25 | Call for game times.

**Lone Star Park.** This facility with indoor and outdoor seating has horse racing with parimutuel wagering. Grounds include a restaurant. | 2200 N. Belt Line Rd., Grand Prairie | 972/

263–7223 | $3 | Mid-Apr.–late July, Wed.–Fri. first race at 6:35 PM, weekends first race at 1:35 PM; closing time varies with races.

**Johnny High's Country Music Revue.** This popular country music show is aimed at a family audience. The stage show includes 20 singers, dancers, and musicians, and features both name acts and new stars. | 224 N. Center St. | 800/540–5127 | $13 | Fri., Sat. 7:30 PM.

**The Palace of Wax/Ripley's Believe It or Not! Museum.** These two attractions are located under the same roof. Wax replicas of Hollywood stars and historical and fantastical figures fill the Palace of Wax, while exhibits in the Ripley's museum explore things like 200 mph tornados. | 601 E. Safari Pkwy., Grand Prairie | 972/263–2391 | fax 972/262–2049 | www.tourtexas.com/ripleys | $11; $15 (both) | Weekdays 10–5, weekends 10–6.

**Six Flags Over Texas.** This 200-acre theme park is home to the state's tallest and fastest roller coaster, as well as the Texas Giant, which the park cites as the world's top wooden roller coaster. | I–30 and Rte. 360 | 817/640–8900 | www.sixflags.com | $43 | June–Aug., daily 10–10; Sept.–May, weekends 10–8.

**ON THE CALENDAR**

**JUNE:** *Texas Scottish Festival and Highland Games.* This festival includes fireworks, athletic competitions, genealogy seminars, traditional foods, and live music. | 817/654–2293 | www.texasscottishfestival.com.

**NOV.:** *Holiday Magic.* Vendors set up shop in the Arlington Convention Center and give you a headstart on holiday shopping. You'll be able to find everything from clothing to gourmet foods. | 817/277–9561.

## Dining

**Cacharel.** French. This restaurant is on the ninth floor of an office building. Its windows provide a wonderful view of the city. Try the grilled ostrich steak or wild game. No smoking. | 2221 E. Lamar Blvd., Arlington | 817/640–9981 | Closed Sun. No lunch Sat. | $22–$40 | AE, D, DC, MC, V.

**Ken's Backyard Barbecue.** Barbecue. A family-style, down-home spot that seats 40 people, this restaurant has simple red-and-white checked tablecloths and food that leaves no question as to why it's so popular. All the meats are home-smoked with pecan wood for at least 12 hours, giving offerings like the signature item, baby back pork ribs, its distinctive dense flavor. Side dishes include wedge fries, potato and macaroni salads, barbecued beans, green beans, fried okra, onion rings, and corn-on-the-cob. | 3401 E. Division St., Arlington | 817/695–1514 | Reservations not accepted | $6–$10 | AE, D, MC, V.

**Piccolo Mondo.** Italian. A piano bar is in the center of the dining room, and a pianist performs Tues.–Sat. Popular dishes include the eggplant parmesan and lasagne *alla bolognese* (lasagne in a special veal meat sauce). | 829 Lamar Blvd. E. Arlington | 817/265–9174 | No lunch Sat., Sun. | $10–$20 | AE, D, DC, MC, V.

**Portofino Ristorante.** Italian. White tablecloths, rich earth tones, and a large dining area dominated by a crystal chandelier create a warm and somewhat formal feel. A smaller, slightly elevated dining area is separated from the main one by a brass rail. Try the signature pasta, linguini *portofino* (clams, calamari, shrimp, and scallops in a classic tomato sauce), or the *filetto al pepe* (tenderloin in a peppercorn sauce served with steamed vegetables and red potatoes). The tableside dessert service offers crêpes Suzette, baked Alaska, and homemade soufflés. Pianist. | 226 Lincoln Square Shopping Center, Arlington | 817/861–8300 | Closed Sun. | $9–$20 | AE, D, DC, MC, V.

**Trail Dust Steakhouse.** Steak. A big ol' restaurant that's the epitome of lively (it's quieter at lunch), diners arriving after 5 PM are forbidden to wear ties, and many past patrons have actually cut them off and pinned them on the walls, along with their business cards. Two floors are linked by a slide, and tables are set around a dance floor where country-and-western bands play every evening (LeAnn Rimes once appeared here). Although you can order ribs or a shrimp dinner, most people go for the steaks, the king of which is the "Bull-

ARLINGTON–
GRAND PRAIRIE

INTRO
ATTRACTIONS
DINING
LODGING

shipper": a 50-oz. Porterhouse T-bone, served with salad, bread, and country-style beans. | 2300 E. Lamar Blvd., Arlington | 817/640–6411 | $11–$25 | AE, D, DC, MC, V.

## Lodging

**Amerisuites.** This six-story hotel is 11 mi from the airport and 1 mi from the Ballpark in Arlington and Six Flags Over Texas amusement park. Complimentary Continental breakfast, microwaves, cable TV, pool, exercise equipment, laundry facilities, business services. | 2380 East Rd. | 817/649–7676 | fax 817/649–7753 | 128 suites | $69–$139 suites | AE, D, DC, MC, V.

**Courtyard by Marriott.** This three-story hotel is down the block from several restaurants and 15 minutes from the Dallas–Fort Worth airport. Restaurant, bar, some refrigerators, cable TV, pool, hot tub, exercise equipment, video games, laundry facilities, business services. | 1500 Nolan Ryan Expressway | 817/277–2774 | fax 817/277–3103 | www.marriotthotels.com | 147 rooms, 14 suites | $94–$109 | AE, D, DC, MC, V.

**Fairfield Inn by Marriott.** The airport, restaurants, and shops are 15 mi from this three-story hotel. Complimentary Continental breakfast, in-room data ports, cable TV, pool, business services. | 2500 E. Lamar Blvd. | 817/649–5800 | fax 817/649–5800 | www.marriotthotels.com | 109 rooms | $69–$91 | AE, D, DC, MC, V.

**Hampton Inn.** This four-story hotel is 7 mi from the airport and 3 mi from the Six Flags amusement park. A 24-hour restaurant is adjacent. Complimentary Continental breakfast, in-room data ports, cable TV, pool, exercise equipment, laundry facilities, business services, airport shuttle. | 2050 Rte. 360N, Grand Prairie | 972/988–8989 | fax 972/623–0004 | www.hampton-inn.com | 140 rooms | $69–$79 | AE, D, DC, MC, V.

**Hawthorn Suites.** All rooms have either a private patio or balcony. Some kitchenettes, microwaves, cable TV, pool, exercise equipment, laundry facilities, business services, some pets allowed (fee). | 2401 Brookhollow Plaza Dr. | 817/640–1188 or 800/527–1133 | fax 817/649–4720 | www.hawthorn.com | 26 rooms, 130 suites | $75–$79, $149 suites | AE, D, DC, MC, V.

**Hilton.** This sixteen-story hotel is 10 mi from the airport. The Palace of Wax and Ripley's Believe It or Not! Museum are 15 mi away. Restaurant, bar, in-room data ports, cable TV, pool, hot tub, exercise equipment, laundry facilities, business services, airport shuttle. | 2401 E. Lamar Blvd. | 817/640–3322 | fax 817/633–1430 | www.hilton.com | 310 rooms | $79–$215 | AE, D, DC, MC, V.

**Holiday Inn.** Popular attractions such as Six Flags Over Texas amusement park and the Ballpark in Arlington are 8 mi from this hotel, as is the airport. Restaurant, bar, room service, in-room data ports, some refrigerators, cable TV, pool, wading pool, hot tub, exercise equipment, laundry facilities, business services, airport shuttle. | 1507 N. Watson Rd. | 817/640–7712 | fax 817/640–3174 | www.holidayinn.com | 236 rooms | $99 | AE, D, DC, MC, V.

**La Quinta Inn/Dallas Six Flags.** You can practically hear the screams of joy from Six Flags (which is less than 2 mi away) at this two-story motel. A 24-hour restaurant is adjacent to the motel. Complimentary Continental breakfast, cable TV, pool. | 1410 NW 19th St., Grand Prairie | 972/641–3021 or 800/687–6667 | fax 972/660–3041 | www.laquinta.com | 122 rooms | $59–$129 | AE, D, DC, MC, V.

**Radisson Suite Hotel.** Six Flags Over Texas and the Ballpark in Arlington are less than 1 mi from this seven-story hotel. The suites have living rooms and canopy beds. Restaurant, bar, complimentary breakfast, refrigerators, cable TV, pool, hot tub, video games, business services. | 700 Avenue H East | 817/640–0440 | fax 817/649–2480 | www.radisson.com | 203 rooms, 184 suites | $99–$159, $139 suites | AE, D, DC, MC, V.

**Ramada Inn.** Turn off I–30 2 mi north of downtown and you're right at this two-story hotel. All rooms have king-size beds, and the outdoor pool is Olympic-size. Complimentary Continental breakfast, in-room data ports, some refrigerators, cable TV, pool, business services, no pets. | 402 E. Safari Pkwy., Grand Prairie | 972/263–4421 or 800/228–2828 | fax 972/264–4763 | 130 rooms | $55–$65 | AE, D, DC, MC, V.

**Residence Inn by Marriott.** All rooms have separate living areas, making it a fine choice for extended stays or families. Complimentary Continental breakfast, in-room data ports, refrigerators, kitchenettes, cable TV, hot tub, exercise equipment, pool, tennis, laundry facilities, laundry service, business services, pets allowed. | 1050 Brookhollow Plaza Dr., Arlington | 817/649–7300 or 800/331–3131 | fax 817/649–7600 | residenceinn.com/DALAR | 114 suites | $85–$160 suites | AE, D, DC, MC, V.

**Sanford House.** Built to resemble a 19th-century French country home, this B&B is set on attractively landscaped grounds with gazebos and a garden and includes a detached "carriage house." The guest rooms are named for major composers; the quietest (the Bach and Strauss rooms) have balconies overlooking the lawn and gardens. Complimentary breakfast, no TV in some rooms, pool, massage, no smoking, no pets, no kids. | 506 North Center St., Arlington | 817/861–2129 or 877/205–4914 | fax 817/861–2030 | info@thesanfordhouse.com | www.thesanfordhouse.com | 7 rooms, 4 cottages | $125–$150 rooms, $200 cottages | MC, V.

**Wyndham Arlington.** Directly across the street from Six Flags Over Texas, the Ballpark in Arlington, and the Arlington Convention Center, this 19-story full-service hotel often hosts both summer vacationers and business travelers (players at the Ballpark usually stay here). Restaurant, bar, room service, in-room data ports, cable TV, pool, spa, health club, laundry facilities, laundry service. | 1500 Convention Center Dr. | 817/261–8200 or 800/442–7275 | fax 817/548–2873 | www.wyndham.com | 310 rooms, 18 suites | $139–$159, $189–$269 suites | AE, D, DC, MC, V.

# ATHENS

MAP 8, J3

*(Nearby towns also listed: Jefferson, Tyler)*

Established in 1850, Athens is known as the home of the hamburger, first created downtown at a small café in the late 19th century. Today this town of 13,000 celebrates that invention with an annual hamburger cook-off. Athens is also known for its black-eyed pea production and is a favorite with antiques shoppers.

**Information: Athens Convention and Visitors Bureau** | 1206 S. Palestine, Athens, TX 75751 | 903/675–5181 or 800/755–7878 | www.athenscc.org.

## Attractions
**Purtis Creek State Park.** In the historic region that was once home to Wichita and Caddo Indians, this park is home to many petroglyphs left by these early residents. Activities include camping, fishing, boating, hiking, and picnicking as well as paddle boats. | 14225 FM 316 | 903/425–2332 | www.tpwd.state.tx.us tk | $2 | Daily 7 AM–10 PM.

### ON THE CALENDAR
**APR.: *Henderson County P.R.C.A. Stampede Rodeo.*** A popular event with a professional seal of approval, this three-day event presents top rodeo performers and cowboys, a carnival, food vendors, and mechanical bull rides. It's held at the Henderson County Fair Park, east of downtown on Rte. 31. | 903/675–5181 or 800/755–7878.
**MAY: *Texas Fiddlers' Contest and Reunion.*** This gathering of top fiddle players has taken place in Athens since the 1930s. It includes music and a street dance. | 903/675–2325.
**MAY: *Uncle Fletch's Hamburger Cookoff and American Music Festival.*** This cook-off held the second Sat. in May honors Fletcher Davis, who reportedly made the world's first hamburger. Other activities include exhibits, kids' activities, arts and crafts, and an antique car show. | 903/675–5181.

**OCT.:** *Black-Eyed Pea Fall Harvest.* Cook-offs featuring black-eyed peas, as well as arts and crafts, gospel music, watermelon-eating contests, a carnival, a bass tournament, and a pet show, are part of the fun. | 800/755–7878.

## Dining

**Jubilee House.** Cajun. Housed in a late 1880s building, this restaurant has brick walls, murals of Bourbon St., French Quarter scenes, and sights in town rendered by a local artist. Try the catch-of-the-day (salmon, tuna, and swordfish make regular appearances), broccoli-and-cheese casserole, or grilled catfish. Save room for the pecan bread pudding with rum sauce. Homemade baked goods, desserts, and soups. Sun. brunch. | 114 Corsicana St. | 903/675–1795 | Breakfast also available weekends | $6–$17 | AE, D, MC, V.

**Pappatillo's.** Tex-Mex. Authentic Mexican vases hang from the walls of this restaurant in the Spanish Trace Inn. The chicken quesadillas and the enchiladas with rice are popular. Kids' menu. | 716 E. Tyler St. | 903/677–8794 | $6–$12 | AE, D, DC, MC, V.

## Lodging

**Avonlea Bed and Breakfast.** This 1890 Victorian home 1½ blocks from the town square has the antiques you'd expect, from armoires to dressers. The homestyle breakfast will most likely consist of scrambled eggs, ham, toast, and homemade blueberry, pear-apple-cinnamon, or peach jam. Dining room, complimentary breakfast. No room phones, TV in common area, no pets, no smoking. | 410 E. Corsicana St. | 903/675–5770 or 888/821–5267 | 5 rooms (4 with shared bath) | $85–$105 | AE, D, MC, V.

**Best Western Inn and Suites.** This two-story hotel is 1 mi from the Henderson County Fairgrounds. The only restaurant within walking distance is a steakhouse, which is less than ½ mi away. Restaurant, bar (with entertainment), room service, cable TV, pool, business services. | 2050 Rte. 31 | 903/675–9214 | fax 903/675–5963 | www.lodgingsus.com | 110 rooms | $50–$150 | AE, D, DC, MC, V.

**Motel 6.** Rooms have exterior corridor entrances in this two-story motel 2 miles north of downtown. Ground-floor rooms have front parking spaces. A popular fish hatchery with picnic facilities is 5 mi away. In-room data ports, cable TV, pool, business services, pets allowed. | 205 Dallas Hwy. 175 | 903/675–7511 | fax 903/675–8833 | 70 rooms | $37–$56 | AE, D, DC, MC, V.

**Spanish Trace Inn.** This two-story inn is ½ mi from downtown. Restaurant *(see* Pappatillo's), room service, cable TV, pool, business services. | 716 E. Tyler St. | 903/675–5173 | fax 903/677–1529 | 80 rooms | $47–$95 | AE, D, DC, MC, V.

**Victorian Inn.** Rooms are spacious in this Victorian-style inn, built in 1985. Restaurants and stores are less than 1 mi away. Microwaves, refrigerators, cable TV. | 1803 Rte. 31E | 903/677–1470 | fax 903/675–9293 | 39 rooms, 1 suite | $38, $50 suites | AE, D, MC, V.

# AUSTIN

MAP 8, H5

*(Nearby towns also listed: Bastrop, Georgetown, La Grange, Lockhart, San Marcos)*

When Mirabeau B. Lamar, president-elect of the Texas Republic, set out to hunt buffalo in the fall of 1838, he returned with a much greater catch: a home for the new state capital. Lamar fell in love with a tiny settlement surrounded by rolling hills and fed by cool springs. Within the coming year, the government arrived and construction on the capitol building was begun. In 1883 the University of Texas opened its doors and Austin became home to the country's largest single-campus institution in the United States.

Today, Austin is a city on the move. Hollywood has discovered this big city with a small-town atmosphere, and it's not uncommon these days to see film crews blocking off an oak-lined street. High-tech industries have also migrated to this area, making this Texas's answer to Silicon Valley. But, for all the modern offerings of this capital city, Austin is still very much a town whose identity is linked to its past—a past the city is proud to preserve and show off to visitors.

Downtown, the Colorado River slices through the heart of the city. Once an unpredictable waterway, the Colorado has been tamed into a series of lakes, including two that flow within the Austin city limits. The 22-mi-long Lake Austin, which begins at the foot of the Hill Country and meanders through the western part of the city, flows into Town Lake, a narrow stretch of water that rambles for 5 miles through the center of downtown Austin. In the late afternoon hours, locals grab their sneakers and head to Zilker Park or Town Lake's shores for a jog or a leisurely walk. On summer evenings, the lake's Congress Avenue Bridge is home to the country's largest urban colony of Mexican free-tailed bats. The bats make their exodus after sunset to feed on insects in the Hill Country.

After a day of touring this city of 567,600, check out the heart of Austin's nightlife on Sixth Street, an historic seven-block area that is compared to New Orleans's Bourbon Street.

Information: **Austin Convention and Visitors Bureau** | 201 E. 2nd St., 78701 | 512/474–5171 or 800/926–2282 | www.austintexas.org.

## NEIGHBORHOODS

**Clarksville.** Just east of the Mopac Highway, Clarksville is a historic neighborhood that began as an enclave for freed slaves after the Civil War. Unfortunately, when the highway was built it divided the neighborhood and residents were displaced. Today you'll find a number of fine restaurants in Clarksville.

**Congress Avenue and Sixth Street.** Listed in the National Register of Historic Places, Congress Avenue has been Austin's main drag since the 1800s; together with Sixth Street (formerly the bawdy Old Pecan Street), this area is a still-hopping downtown. There are many restored 19th- and 20th-century buildings, and self-guided walking tours are available through the Austin Convention and Visitors Bureau.

**Hyde Park.** Austin's oldest residential suburb is north of the University of Texas and bounded by 38th and 45th sts. on the south and north, respectively. Established in the late 1800s, Hyde Park has a number of Victorian homes and charming shops.

**Travis Heights.** Bounded by I–35, Congress Ave., Town Lake, and Oltorf, this neighborhood with elegant residential streets is becoming popular with tourists who come to check out the shops, restaurants, and clubs after taking in the sights of Austin's downtown area.

## DRIVING AROUND TOWN

With 14 million annual visitors, more than 50,000 university students, and a large commuter population, it's easy to see why Austin has more roads per capita than the other major cities in Texas. Although driving can be irksome during peak tourist seasons, Austin is generally navigable and car-friendly, with wide, open boulevards, ample parking, well-marked signs, and good road conditions.

The major entryway into Austin is I–35, which links the city with Dallas/Fort Worth to the north, and San Antonio to the south. Loop 1 (also known to locals as MOPAC) joins with I–35 on the northern and southern outskirts of Austin, dispersing traffic to the west side of the city. U.S. 183 runs at a slight north-south diagonal through Austin. Although it doesn't serve any major cities, U.S. 183 does serve as a major thoroughfare through town, eventually meandering northward to western Oklahoma and southward towards the Gulf. East–west highways 71 and 290 connect Austin and Houston.

Although the highways are clearly marked, many of them have been granted other names as they pass through Austin. Keep in mind that U.S.183 becomes Research Boulevard at one point and Anderson Boulevard at another, and Route 71 is also known as Ben White Boulevard.Congress Avenue serves as the major north-south thoroughfare in the downtown area, and convenes at the State Capitol building, Austin's heart and soul. The rest of the area is laid out in a conventional grid of numerical streets. The majority of these are one-way streets: even-numbered streets generally run one way to the west, and odd-numbered streets generally run one way to the east. Because many of Austin's businesses and attractions lie in and around the downtown area, rush hour traffic (from about 7AM–9AM and 4:30PM–6PM) is heavy here.

West of downtown, the Hill Country is more reminicent of San Francisco than the Texas plains. You may want to aquire a map before venturing onto the smaller, winding roads of this area.

Both street and garage parking are plentiful in Austin's downtown and commercial areas. Metered parking will cost around 75 cents an hour, and parking garages will charge anywhere from $5–$20 a day (prices increase during special events). For visitors to the State Capitol, there is a free two-hour parking lot adjacent to the building. Parking regulations are strictly enforced in Austin, and a ticket will run from $15–$25.

Speeding limits are also strictly enforced; tickets can run from $115—$250, and can be doubled if not paid in ten days. Speed limits range from 20–25 mph in residential and downtown areas, 30–45 mph on larger streets and boulevards, and 55–65 mph on local highways.

Seat belts are mandatory in Austin (and throughout Texas) and right turns are permitted on red lights after a full stop.

## WALKING TOUR

### Texas History and Culture
### (approximately 3½ hours)

Begin at Congress Avenue and 8th Street at the **Paramount Theatre.** This restored neoclassical city landmark has hosted performances by Katherine Hepburn, Sarah Bernhardt, and Helen Hayes. Continue north on Congress to 10th Street. Turn left and walk up the hill one block. At 10th and Colorado is the Greek Revival-style **Governor's Mansion,** home to every Texas governor since 1856. The mansion offers guided tours every weekday morning. Walk north one block on Colorado to 11th Street. Texas's **State Capitol** building, the largest in the country, will be in front of you. Go inside to see the giant dome that reaches nearly 300 ft, as well as the terrazzo floor commemorating the centennial of Texas's independence from Mexico. To get to the **Capitol Visitors Center,** continue down 11th Street to the end of the block. The center is on your left, inside the Capitol gates, in the General Land Office Building. (This is the oldest remaining Texas state office building.) After your visit, walk from the north side of the building 100 yards to the **Lorenzo de ZavalaState Archives and Library Building.** Inside, the giant mural, "Texas Moves Toward Statehood," depicts 400 years of tumultuous Texas history. From the north side of the building turn right on 12th Street and walk two blocks to Trinity. Turn left on Trinity and continue six blocks to Martin Luther King Boulevard. You are now at the southern boundary of the **University of Texas,** the country's largest university. Cross Martin Luther King Boulevard and continue through campus on what becomes San Jacinto Boulevard. Notice the Texas Aquatic Center and Memorial Stadium, both on your right. Just past the stadium, take a right on 23rd Street and walk up the hill towards the large grassy area. This lawn is flanked on the left by the **Lyndon Baines Johnson Library and Museum.** Have a look inside this vast memorial to one of the country's most colorful leaders, then walk back down 23rd Street. On your right is **Bass Concert Hall,** the largest and most impressive venue of the UT Performing Arts Center. At Trinity, take a right. The **Texas Memorial Museum,** where you can view extensive geological and archeological collections, is the second building on your left. Walk back down 23rd Street to the bottom of the hill. On your right is the **Jack S. Blanton Art Gallery.** This museum, one of Austin's best, displays permanent and rotating exhibits by national and international artists. Walk south on San Jacinto and turn right onto 11th Street. Walk two blocks and the State Capitol building will be on your right. At Congress, take a left and walk 3 blocks back to the **Paramount Theatre.**

## TRANSPORTATION

**Airports: Austin-Bergstrom International Airport.** This airport about 10 mi from downtown Austin on Rte. 71 opened in 1999 on the site of the former Bergstrom Air Force Base. | 3600 Presidential Blvd. | 512/369–6600.

**Airport Transportation: SuperShuttle.** Services the Austin-Bergstrom International Airport. | 512/258–3826 (in Austin) or 800/258–3826 (outside of Austin) | www.super-shuttle.com. | 482–0000. Additionally, there is **Capital Metro Bus** | 512/474–1200. The full roster of rental car companies is available at the airport.

**Rail:** Austin is on Amtrak's Sunset Limited route with westbound service to San Antonio, El Paso, Tucson, and Los Angeles, and eastbound service to New Orleans and Orlando. | 250 N. Lamar | 512/476–5684 or 800/872–7245 for reservations.

**Bus: Greyhound Bus Lines.** Has routes to major cities in Texas, across the United States, and Canada. | 916 E. Koenig Ln | 512/458–4463 | 1201 I–35 | 512/473–8344.

**Intra-city Transit: Capital Metro Bus.** Provides transit service for the greater Austin area. | 512/474–1200.

Taxi services in the Austin area include **American Yellow Checker Cab Company** (512/452–9999), **Austin Cab** (512/478–2222), and **Roy's Taxi** (512/482–0000).

## ELISABET NEY

One of Austin's most colorful characters graced the city in the late 1800s. Elisabet Ney, Texas's acclaimed sculptor, worked in a small stone studio hidden in a thick grove of trees; here she entertained guests such as Enrico Caruso and William Jennings Bryan.

Born in Germany in 1833, Ney studied in Berlin and Munich, and at an early age became one of the world's first prominent sculptresses, molding the likenesses of King Ludwig II (the "Mad King of Bavaria," who later became her friend), writer Joseph Grimm, composer Richard Wagner, and Prussian Chancellor Otto von Bismark.

Ney's career continued to soar, and at the age of 42 she married Dr. Edmund Montgomery; she continued to call herself "Miss Ney," would not wear a wedding ring, and always referred to her husband as "my best friend." This unconventional behavior led to rumor and scandal that began in Europe and followed the couple when they immigrated to America in 1871.

The couple settled in Hempstead, near Houston. Their mansion, named "Liedo," was home for Ney, Montgomery, and their two sons—Arthur and Lorne. At one time, the community was rife with rumors that Ney had burned the body of son Arthur in the parlor fireplace after he died of diphtheria. (He was actually cremated on the plantation to prevent an epidemic.)

For many years, Elisabet continued to live at Liedo. She stopped sculpting when she came to America, but her career began anew at age 59, when she was commissioned to sculpt Sam Houston and Stephen F. Austin for the World's Fair Colombian Exhibit in Chicago. The plaster models for both of these sculptures can be seen at the Elisabet Ney Museum in Austin.

© Artville

## Attractions

### ART AND ARCHITECTURE

**Austin Museum of Art at Laguna Gloria.** This museum is set on 12 acres once owned by Stephen F. Austin, who purchased the land in 1832 but died before he could build on it. The museum has become nationally known for its art exhibits, sculpture gardens, and educational programs. | 3809 W. 35th St. | 512/458–8191 | $2 | Tues., Wed., Fri, Sat. 10–5, Thurs. 10–8, Sun. 12–5.

**Governor's Mansion.** For more than 130 years, Texas governors have resided in this grand, modified Greek Revival home. The mansion has an impressive collection of 19th century American antiques and furnishings. Tours (scheduled every 20 minutes) are conducted weekdays from 10 AM to 12 PM. Call to check the status of tours; the home is sometimes closed because of incoming dignitaries. | 1010 Colorado St. | 512/463–5516 | Free | Weekdays 10–5.

**Neill-Cochran House.** Abner Cook, the builder of the Governor's Mansion, designed this Greek Revival home in the mid-1800s. | 2310 San Gabriel | 512/478–2335 | $2 | Wed.–Sun. 2–5.

**State Capitol.** Pink granite quarried from Granite Mountain, near the town of Marble Falls, was used to construct the state capitol building (the nation's largest), which houses the governor's office, the Texas legislature, and several other executive state agencies. From 1892 to 1898, hundreds of stonecutters from Scotland along with gangs of Texas convicts performed the backbreaking work of cutting the stone. | 11th St. and Congress Ave. | 512/463–0063 | Free | Weekdays 8:30–4:30, Sat. 9:30–4:30, Sun. 9:30–4:30.

Located on the east side of the State Capitol is the **Lorenzo de Zavala State Archives and Library Building,** which contains archives of the Texas State Library. A genealogical collection is housed on the first floor. | 1201 Brazos St. | 512/463–5480 | Free | Library: Weekdays 8–5; Archives: Tues.–Sat. 8–5.

### CULTURE, EDUCATION, AND HISTORY

**O. Henry Home and Museum.** From 1893 to 1895 this small home was the residence of William Sidney Porter, better known as short-story writer O. Henry. The home contains the writer's personal belongings. | 409 E. 5th St. | 512/472–1903 | Donation accepted | Wed.–Sun. 12–5.

**Paramount.** This restored downtown movie theater is home to classic film showings in summer, and musical or comedy acts and touring theater companies the rest of the year. | 713 Congress Ave. | 512/472–5470 | www.theparamount.org | $6 movies, $13–$55 other entertainment | Box office: Mon.–Sat. 12–5:30.

**State Cemetery.** In car-crazy Texas, walking, outside of malls and commercial districts, is positively quaint. Most people who simply like to stroll end up at this 22-acre cemetery, and those who do usually return. It's close to downtown, and safe: between Seventh and Eleventh Sts., one block east of I–35. | E. Seventh and Comal Sts. | 512/463–0605 | www.cemetery.state.tx.us | Free | Daily 8–5.

**University of Texas at Austin.** Founded in 1883, UT–Austin is home to the largest member of the University of Texas system. Its student population is approximately 48,000. | Guadalupe between 22nd and 23rd Sts. | www.utexas.edu | 512/471–3434.

The **Texas Memorial Museum** displays a mixture of state and natural history exhibits, which include antique firearms, wildlife dioramas, Native American artifacts, rare gems and minerals, and the original Goddess of Liberty statue removed from the capitol dome during restoration. | 2400 Trinity St. | 512/471–1604 | Free | Weekdays 9–5, Sat. 10–5, Sun. 1–5.

The **Harry Ransom Humanities Research Center** contains one of only 48 copies of the Gutenburg Bible in existence. The center also holds more than 9,000 works from Australia, Europe, Latin America, and the United States that range from ancient to contemporary. | Guadalupe and 21st Sts. | 512/471–8944 | Free | Mon.–Wed., Fri. 9–5, Thurs. 9–9, Sat., Sun. 1–5.

Considered one of the top 10 university art galleries in the country, the **Jack S. Blanton Art Gallery** is housed in two separate facilities on the university campus—including the Harry Ransom Humanities Research Center. The galleries contain 20th-century artwork as well as popular culture items from the late 19th and early 20th centuries. Works from Mexican artists are also on display. | 23rd and San Jacinto Sts. | 512/471–7324 | Free | Mon.–Wed., Fri. 9–5, Thurs. 9–9, weekends 1–5.

The largest presidential library in the nation, the **Lyndon Baines Johnson Library and Museum** is housed in an eight-story building made of travertine marble. The building is the repository for all 35 million documents produced during the LBJ administration and contains many exhibits on Johnson's life, family, and presidential years. | 2313 Red River | 512/916–5136 | Free | Daily 9–5.

**Performing Arts Center and Bass Concert Hall.** Austin's Lyric Opera, the Austin Symphony, and Ballet Austin all perform at this venue on the University of Texas at Austin campus, adjacent to the Huntingdon Art Gallery. | 23rd St. and E. Campus Dr. | 512/471–7744 | www.utpac.org | Box office: weekdays 9–6, Sat. 9–3.

**Zachary Scott Theatre.** Local theater flourishes at this center named for the 1930s film star and Austin native son. In addition to regularly scheduled performances, there are drama classes for children and adults. | 1510 Toomey Rd. | 512/476–0594 | $16–$31 | Box office: Mon.–Sat. 12–7.

## MUSEUMS

**Austin Nature and Science Center.** Adjacent to the Zilker Botanical Gardens, this complex has an 80-acre preserve trail, interactive exhibits in the Discovery Lab that teach about the ecology of the Austin area, and animal exhibits focusing on subjects such as bees and birds of prey. | 301 Nature Center Dr. | 512/327–8180 | www.ci.austin.tx.us/nature-science | Donation | Mon.–Sat. 9–5, Sun. 12–5.

**Elisabet Ney Museum.** Acclaimed European-born sculptress Elisabet Ney molded the likenesses of many distinguished people. Later in her career, in 1892, she received commissions to model Sam Houston and Stephen F. Austin for the Colombian Exposition in Chicago. Today these marbles are in the capitol, but the plaster models are in this museum. | 304 E. 44th St. | 512/458–2255 | Free | Wed.–Sat. 10–5, Sun. 12–5.

**French Legation Museum.** Austin's oldest standing building, this 1841 home was built by Alphonse Dubois de Saligny, named chargé d'affaires to the Republic of Texas when Louis Philippe of France recognized the republic in 1839. The legation's kitchen is the only authentic reproduction of an early Creole kitchen in the United States. | 802 San Marcos St. | 512/472–8180 | $3 | Tues.–Sat. 1–5.

## PARKS, NATURAL SIGHTS, AND OUTDOOR ACTIVITIES

**Barton Creek Greenbelt.** This park follows the contour of Barton Creek and the canyon it created west along a 7-mi area. It has a trail for hiking and biking, plus swimming holes when the creek is full (very rain-dependent, it's usually in spring and fall). | 512/499–6700 or 512/472–1267 | Free | 5 AM–10 PM.

**Lady Bird Johnson Wildflower Center.** This 43-acre complex founded in the early 1980s has extensive plantings of wildflowers that bloom all year round. The grounds include a visitors center, nature trail, observation tower, elaborate stone terraces, and flower-filled meadows. | 4801 LaCrosse Ave. | 512/292–4100 | www.wildflower.org | $4 | Tues.–Sun. 9–5:30.

**McKinney Falls State Park.** This 643-acre state park is just 13 mi southeast of the capitol. A 4½-mi nature trail is used for hiking and biking; fishing, picnicking, camping, and wildlife viewing are other popular activities. Wildlife sightings include white-tailed deer, raccoons, squirrels, and armadillos. | 5808 McKinney Falls Pkwy, off U.S. 183 | 512/243–1643 | www.tpwd.state.tx.us | $2 | Daily.

**Mount Bonnell.** Rising to a height of 785 ft, Mount Bonnell offers the best views of Austin. Stop by during the day for a glimpse of the sweeping panorama of rolling hills and the Colorado River. Turn right on Mount Bonnell Rd., just before E. 35th St. dead-ends. | Mount Bonnell Rd. | 817/265–7721 or 800/433–5374 | Free | Daily.

**Wild Basin Wilderness Preserve.** Stunning contrasting views of the hill country and the Austin skyline make it worth the trip to this outlying area. You can wander along 227 acres of walking trails; guided tours are offered on weekends. | 805 N. Capitol of Texas Hwy. | 512/327–7622 | Donation | Daily dawn—dusk; tours: Sat. 10–2, Sun. 1–3; office: daily 9–4.

**Zilker Park.** The former site of temporary Franciscan missions in 1730 and a former Native American gathering place is now a popular park. The 351-acre site along the shores of Lake Austin includes Barton Springs Pool, whose clear springs produce from 12 million to 90 million gallons in any 24-hour period; the swimming pool is more than 300 yards long, and the water varies from 66° to 70°. The park also includes numerous gardens, a meditation trail, and a Swedish log cabin dating from the 1840s. Plays are held in the park's theater during the summer. | 2201 Barton Springs Rd. | 512/397–1463; 512/476–9044 (pool) | Free; parking $2 per vehicle | Daily.

## SIGHTSEEING TOURS/TOUR COMPANIES

**Capitol Visitors Center.** Stop in here for free tours of the capitol and the adjacent governor's mansion, as well as a host of information on other attractions in Austin or elsewhere in Texas. | 112 E. 11th St. | 512/305–8400 | www.tspb.state.tx.us/tspb/spbg/visitor/ccvc.htm | Free | Daily 9–5.

## OTHER POINTS OF INTEREST

**Austin Zoo.** This privately owned zoo near Oak Hill has train rides, a petting zoo, and plenty of exotic creatures. Children can purchase animal food, which they can then hand-feed to many of the zoo's residents. | 10807 Rawhide Trail | 512/288–1490 | $6 | Daily 10–6.

**Broken Spoke.** Grab your favorite two-step dancing partner and head on over to this country-and-western spot, where live music is performed five days a week. | 3201 S. Lamar Blvd. | 512/442–6189 | $4–$10 | Tues. 10 AM–11 PM, Wed., Thurs. 10 AM–midnight, Fri., Sat. 10 AM–1:30 AM.

**Continental Club.** This popular club has a cover-free happy hour Tues.–Fri. 4–7; entertainment ranges from country-and-western to rockabilly. | 1315 S. Congress Ave. | 512/441–2444 | $3–$20 | Tues.–Fri. 4 PM–2 AM, Sat.–Mon. 9 AM–2 AM.

**Guadalupe Street.** Also known as "the Drag," this thoroughfare bordering the west side of the University of Texas campus is lined with restaurants and trendy boutiques. | 512/474–5171 | Free | Daily.

## ON THE CALENDAR

**APR.:** *Capitol 10,000 Road Race.* One of the top races in the nation, this event sends thousands of runners through Austin's streets. | 512/445–3596.

**APR.:** *Old Pecan Street Arts Festival.* This festival includes arts and crafts, live outdoor music, and food. | 512/474–5171.

**MAY:** *Museum of Art Fiesta Laguna Gloria.* This art festival also includes crafts, food, and entertainment. | 512/323–6280.

**SEPT.:** *Zilker Park Jazz Festival.* A variety of local artists are spotlighted at this outdoor jazz festival. | 512/442–2263.

# Dining

## INEXPENSIVE

**Bitter End.** Contemporary. A polished, slightly industrial interior sets the stage for the cool crowd at this sleek brew pub. The semolina-fried calamari, wood-fired jerk chicken pizza, and a revolving Mediterranean menu are all heightened by standout home-brewed ales. | 311 Colorado St. | 512/478–2337 | No lunch weekends | $8–$23 | AE, D, DC, MC, V.

**Castle Hill Cafe.** Contemporary. This boisterous, fun, and wildly popular two-story café is fancifully decorated with Oaxacan animal sculptures, and ochre- and eggplant-colored walls. Try the delicious spicy duck and sausage gumbo, imaginative salads, and eclectic entrées such as black pepper fried shrimp with crabmeat creole and savory grits. | 1101 W. 5th Ave. | 512/476–0728 | www.castlehillcafe.com | Closed Sun. No lunch Sat. | $11–$20 | AE, D, MC, V.

**County Line on the Hill.** Barbecue. This spot overlooks 20 mi of land belonging to the Barton Creek Country Club. You can dine outdoors on a semi-covered patio. Known for barbecued meats, especially the baby back ribs, and the grilled salmon filet. Kids' menu. | 6500 W. Bee Cave Rd. | 512/327–1742 | No lunch | $8–$18 | AE, D, DC, MC, V.

**Güeros.** Tex-Mex. This former feed store is now a spacious and popular restaurant with high ceilings, a rustic bar, a worn wood floor, tall windows, and live music. After President Clinton ordered the Numero Dos (a Mexican plate including one tamale, one marinated chicken taco, one beef taco, guacamole, beans, and rice) during a visit to Austin, the dish was renamed El Presidente. The little *tacos al pastor* (marinated rotisserie-roasted pork with pineapple, cilantro, and onions) are stellar, and the fresh-lime margaritas justly famous. | 1412 S. Congress Ave. | 512/447–7688 | Reservations not accepted | Breakfast also available weekends | $7–$14 | AE, D, DC, MC, V.

**Irons Works Barbecue.** Barbecue. Housed in a tin shed that once served as an iron mill, today this restaurant is roomy and rustic. Outdoor dining is available on a deck or porches. Try the pork and beef ribs, pork loin, or homemade sausage. | 100 Red River St. | 512/478–4855 | ironworksbbq.com | Closed Sun. | $7–$15 | AE, D, DC, MC, V.

**Jean-Pierre's Upstairs.** Continental. Dine on beef tenderloin, veal chops, bacon-wrapped salmon, or the popular souflée at this restaurant on the terrace of a commercial building. | 3500 Jefferson St. | 512/454–4811 | Closed Sun. | $11–$22 | AE, D, DC, MC, V.

**Las Manitas Avenue Café.** Tex-Mex. Downtown office workers and Mexican-breakfast fanatics fill this place, usually ordering the scrambled eggs with crispy tortillas, cheese, black beans, and rancheros sauce, served with soft flour tortillas. | 211 Congress St. | 512/472–9357 | Breakfast also available. No supper | $4–$6 | AE, D, DC, MC, V.

**Magnolia Cafe.** American/Casual. A neighborhood café with a puckish feel (half funky trailer-style diner, half airy garden restaurant). Try the gingerbread pancakes, "love veggies" (spinach, broccoli, zucchini, yellow squash, bell peppers, onions, and mushrooms sautéed in a garlic butter with serrano peppers and served over rice) or one of the 12 omelettes. Anything with one of the house sauces is not to be missed. | 2304 Lake Austin Blvd. | 512/478–8645 | Reservations not accepted | Open 24 hours. Breakfast also available. | $6–$13 | AE, DC, MC, V.

**Matt's El Rancho.** Tex-Mex. A longtime Austin favorite, this restaurant was established by the present owner's grandfather in 1925. Known for chiles rellenos and shrimp à la Matt (grilled jumbo shrimp served with flautas and guacamole salad). Open-air dining is available on the patio, which has a waterfall and a garden. Kids' menu. | 2613 S. Lamar Blvd. | 512/462–9333 | www.mattselrancho.com | Closed Tues. | $9–$19 | AE, D, DC, MC, V.

**Oasis-Lake Travis.** Tex-Mex. Scenic view makes this place especially popular for sunset dinners. Request a table that overlooks Lake Travis. Known for shrimp, fajitas, and margaritas. Open-air dining is available on an enormous, partially covered patio. | 6550 Comanche Tr. | 512/266–2442 | $8–$33 | AE, D, MC, V.

**Ruta Maya Coffeehouse.** American/Casual. Sit outside this fun joint on the raised sidewalk and watch the Texas thunderclouds roll by; inside, the place is chock-full of local paintings, works by nearby schoolchildren, and Mayan folk art from Chiapas (where the managers also get coffee beans). Try the garlicky pizza with lamb, tomatoes, cheese, and olives, the gooey cinnamon rolls, or the chocolate cake. | 218 W. Fourth St. | 512/472–9637 | $3–$5 | MC, V.

**Scholz Garten.** American. Established in 1866, this beer garden and dining room is a venerable local favorite. In addition to standard American fare, the menu includes Tex-Mex barbecue and some German dishes like bratwurst. Sides could include German potato salad, red cabbage sauerkraut, creamed corn, and green beans. | 1607 San Jacinto Blvd. | 512/474–1958 | Closed Sun. | $3–$9 | AE, D, DC, MC, V.

**Shady Grove.** American/Casual. Sit outside under the shade of a huge pecan tree and dine on anything from an all-American burger to a vegan dish. Try the award-winning spicy Texas-style chili or the popular catfish rolled in tortillas, served with tasty cheese sauce and fresh salsa. | 1624 Barton Springs Rd. | 512/474–9991 | Reservations not accepted | $4–$10 | AE, D, DC, MC, V.

**Southside Market.** Barbecue. This former butcher shops serves traditional barbecue fare like brisket, beef, pork or mutton ribs, steaks, and whole chickens; the house special is hot sausage. Service is cafeteria style. | 1212 U.S. 290E, Elgin | 512/285–3407 | www.sausage.cc | Reservations not accepted | $5–$9 | D, MC, V.

**Threadgill's.** Southern. Janis Joplin was drawn to this local legend for its massive chicken-fried steak. The homemade cobbler, free seconds on its extensive vegetable side orders (butter beans, okra and tomatoes, black-eyed peas, and squash casserole are but a few), and live music should not be overlooked. | 6416 N. Lamar Blvd. | 512/451–5440 | Reservations not accepted | $6–$18 | MC, V.

**West Lynn Cafe.** Vegetarian. The tasty food that even non-vegetarians might love includes Caribbean stir fry, mushroom stroganoff, and spinach enchiladas. | 1110 W. Lynn St. | 512/482–0950 | berp@flash.net | $7–$11 | AE, D, DC, MC, V.

## MODERATE

**Basil's.** Italian. Basil's has several dining rooms and a menu that includes pesto pasta, lobster tail and scallops, osso buco, and more. | 900 W. 10th St. | 512/477–5576 | No lunch | $13–$26 | AE, D, DC, MC, V.

**Cafe at the Four Seasons.** Continental. Every table at this restaurant overlooking Town Lake is outfitted with roses and candles. Try the snapper with crawfish sauce. Open-air dining is available on the brick patio area. Kids' menu. | 98 San Jacinto Blvd. | 512/478–4500 | $17–$34 | AE, D, DC, MC, V.

**Chez Nous.** French. This small café, just off bustling Sixth St., has a mural of Montmartre and French posters throughout. Try the veal scaloppinese, rack of lamb, and confit. | 510 Neches St. | 512/473–2413 | Closed Mon. No lunch Sat., Sun. | $16–$25 | AE, DC, MC, V.

**Fonda San Miguel.** Mexican. Known for traditional fare from the Yucatan, Veracruz, and Oaxaca regions of Mexico, this elegant restaurant is decked with handmade tiles and artifacts from Old Mexico. Try the shrimp Veracruz (broiled shrimp covered in chopped onions, green olives, capers, and tomatoes). Kids' menu. Sun. brunch. | 2330 W. North Loop Blvd. | 512/459–4121 | No lunch | $13–$19 | AE, D, DC, MC, V.

**Louie's 106.** Mediterranean. Although best known for its tapas, this downtown eatery also serves up such meals as duck confit and pork chops with its large wine selection. Kids' menu. | 106 E. 6th St. | 512/476–1997 | No lunch Sat., Sun. | $14–$22 | AE, D, DC, MC, V.

**Old San Francisco Steak House.** Steak. Red velvet accents, an 1890s-costumed waitstaff, and an antique bar lend an old-fashioned feel to this restaurant. Known for prime rib and lobster. Kids' menu. | 8709 I–35 N | 512/835–9200 | No lunch | $12–$43 | AE, D, DC, MC, V.

**The Belgian Restaurant.** French. Candles and lace tablecloths set the mood at this romantic spot that serves Country French cuisine. Try the Belgian surf and turf (a combination lobster and Angus beef tenderloin dish), or the Dover sole cardinal (a flat Belgian fish that is stuffed with spinach and topped with lobster). No smoking. | 3520 Bee Caves Rd. | 512/328–0580 | No lunch Fri.–Sun. | $15–$35 | AE, D, DC, MC, V.

**Trattoria Grande.** Italian. Northern Italian specialties are served in a small candlelit dining area with pretty views of the verdant Texas hill country. Known for fish and pastas. | 9721 Arboretum Blvd., Renaissance Arboretum | 512/343–2626 | No lunch | $15–$25 | AE, D, DC, MC, V.

**U. R. Cooks.** Steak. You can grill steaks and seafood at this cook-your-own meal restaurant, with a salad and side dish bar. Kids' menu. | 9012 Research Blvd. | 512/453–8350 | No lunch weekdays | $12–$25 | AE, D, DC, MC, V.

**Z'Tejas Grill.** Contemporary. The menu includes tasty blends of German, French, and Mexican cuisine; specials could include such things as herb-grilled chicken with artichoke hearts, sautéed spinach and wild mushrooms, or chiles rellenos stuffed with smoked chicken, dried apricots, walnuts, and cheese. Sun. brunch. | 1110 W. Sixth St. | 512/478–5355 | $12–$19 | AE, D, DC, MC, V.

## EXPENSIVE

**Brio Vista.** Contemporary. This Tuscan-inspired restaurant has outdoor dining on a terrace overlooking the hill country. The kitchen creates inventive dishes, often mixing fresh produce and seafood with Provençal ingredients and techniques—the rotating menu could include seared rare tuna with spring vegetable risotto and sweet pea mint sauce or a roasted veal chop with rhubarb–celery heart sautée. Worthy wine suggestions are paired with each entrée, appetizer, and dessert. The El Rey chocolate cake (with a unique Venezuelan chocolate) is wickedly good. | 9400 B. Arboretum Blvd. | 512/342–2642 | briovista.citysearch.com | Reservations essential | $18–$30 | AE, D, DC, MC, V.

**Green Pastures.** Continental. Southern flavored Continental cuisine is served in this restaurant set in a late 1800s mansion. Try the Duck Texana, a stuffed duck breast wrapped in bacon and grilled. Sun. brunch. | 811 W. Live Oak St. | 512/444–4747 | $22–$32 | AE, D, DC, MC, V.

**Jeffrey's.** Contemporary. Exquisite artwork graces the interior of Jeffrey's, one of Austin's most lauded restaurants. Although its menu changes daily, its game and fresh seafood are popular. | 1204 W. Lynn St. | 512/477–5584 | No lunch | $22–$33 | AE, D, DC, MC, V.

**Pappadeaux.** Cajun/Creole. You may have to wait awhile before being seated for dinner at this popular, casual family place. Known for excellent seafood. Kids' menu. No smoking. | 6319 I–35N | 512/452–9363 | $18–$29 | AE, MC, V.

**Ruth's Chris Steak House.** Steak. Steak is king at this elegant, candlelit chain restaurant. You can relax in the plush lounge area in the front of the restaurant. | 107 W. 6th | 512/477–7884 | No lunch | $22–$58 | AE, DC, MC, V.

**Shoreline Grill.** Seafood. Right on the shoreline of Town Lake, this spot is popular for power lunches, as well as romantic dinners. Floor-to-ceiling windows provide wonderful views of the lake, and candlelight and hardwood floors add to the elegant feel. Known for prime rib, crème brûlée, and shark. Open-air dining is available on an enclosed patio with a view of the lake. Kids' menu. | 98 San Jacinto Blvd. | 512/477–3300 | No lunch Sat., Sun. | $18–$35 | AE, D, DC, MC, V.

**Zoot.** Contemporary. Four intimate dining areas are tucked inside a former residence built in the 1920s. Try the pork tenderloin or fresh fish. Sun. brunch. No smoking. | 509 Hearn St. | 512/477–6535 | No lunch | $18–$28 | AE, D, DC, MC, V.

## VERY EXPENSIVE

**Hudson's on the Bend.** Continental. This place outside of town and near Lake Travis is known for its great wine list. The interior dining area is candlelit and displays paintings by the owner's wife. Try the hot and crunchy trout, grilled pheasant, and venison stuffed with smoked lobster. Open-air dining is available under a covered patio, or out in the yard under oak trees. | 3509 Ranch Rd. (Rte. 620 N) | 512/266–1369 | No lunch | $25–$32 | AE, DC, MC, V.

## Lodging

### INEXPENSIVE

**AmeriSuites.** This all-suites hotel was built with the extended-stay executive in mind, with large desks and a well-equipped 24-hour business center. Complimentary Continental breakfast, in-room data ports, microwaves, refrigerators, cable TV, in-room VCRs, pool, exercise room, laundry facilities, laundry service, business services, free parking. | 3612 Tudor Blvd. | 512/231–8491 or 800/833–1516 | fax 512/231–9437 | amerisuites.com | 128 suites | $89–$179 suites | AE, D, DC, MC, V.

**Austin Motel.** Although built in 1938, this motel has a 1950s-style kidney-shape pool and quirky, individually decorated rooms—which range from small and budget-friendly to bigger suites with marble tubs. It's within 1 mi of the downtown entertainment district, and the neighborhood around the motel is full of art galleries and antiques shops. Restaurant, some microwaves, some minibars, some refrigerators, some in-room hot tubs, cable TV, pool, laundry facilities, business services, free parking. | 1220 S. Congress Ave. | 512/441–1157 | www.austinmotel.com | 39 rooms, 2 suites | $50–$80, $107 suites | AE, D, DC, MC, V.

**Austin's Inn at Pearl Street.** Built in the early 1900s, this Greek Revival mansion is on a ½-acre estate with live oak and pecan trees. Guest rooms are individually decorated, and there's ample space for you to relax on the porches or huge covered deck. The inn is two blocks from Guadalupe Street and five blocks from the University of Texas. Dining room, complimentary Continental breakfast weekdays, complimentary breakfast weekends, cable TV, in-room VCRs, library, business services, free parking, no smoking, no pets, no kids under 12. | 809 W. Martin Luther King Jr. Blvd. | 512/477–2233 or 800/494–2261 | fax 512/478–0033 | lodging@sprintmail.com | www.innpearl.com | 6 rooms | $100–$200 | AE, D, MC, V.

**Carrington's Bluff.** Set on wooded grounds, this 1877 Texas farmhouse has an English country feel. The large porch overlooks a 500-year-old oak tree. Complimentary breakfast, cable TV, business services, no smoking, free parking. | 1900 David St. | 512/479–0638 or 800/871–8908 | fax 512/476–4769 | $80–$120 | AE, D, MC, V.

**Courtyard by Marriott.** A mall and a movie theater are less than 1 mi from this hotel, and the University of Texas is 5 mi away. Restaurant, bar, in-room data ports, cable TV, pool, hot tub, exercise equipment, business services. | 5660 I–35N | 512/458–2340 | fax 512/458–8525 | www.marriotthotels.com | 198 rooms | $69–$139 | AE, D, DC, MC, V.

**Days Inn North.** This three-story motel is 2 mi from a mall, 3 mi from Austin's downtown area, and 5 mi from the University of Texas. Complimentary Continental breakfast, some refrigerators, cable TV, pool. | 820 E. Anderson Ln. | 512/835–4311 or 800/725–ROOM | fax 512/835–1740 | 147 rooms | $79–$89 | AE, D, DC, MC, V.

**Days Inn University/Downtown.** Its downtown location puts this two-story motel just blocks from the University of Texas. Complimentary Continental breakfast, microwaves, refrigerators, cable TV, pool, pets allowed. | 3105 I–35N | 512/478–1631 or 800/725–7666 | fax 512/236–0058 | 61 rooms | $64–$89 | AE, D, DC, MC, V.

**Doubletree.** This six-story hotel is 5 mi from Austin's downtown area and the University of Texas. Restaurant, bar, room service, in-room data ports, microwaves, cable TV, pool, hot tub, business services. | 6505 I–35N | 512/454–3737 | fax 512/454–6915 | www.doubletreehotels.com | 350 rooms | $89–$129 | AE, D, DC, MC, V.

**Doubletree Guest Suites.** The State Capitol building, which is just across the street, is visible from many rooms in this all-suites hotel. The University of Texas is just 2 mi away. Restaurant, bar, room service, in-room data ports, microwaves, refrigerators, cable TV, pool, sauna, exercise equipment, laundry facilities, laundry service, business services, parking (fee), pets allowed (fee). | 303 W. 15th St. | 512/478–7000 or 800/424–2900 | fax 512/478–5103 | www.doubletree.com | 189 suites | $125–$250 suites | AE, D, DC, MC, V.

**Drury Inn.** A mall and a restaurant are across the street from this four-story hotel. Austin's downtown area is 5 mi away, and the airport is 12 mi away. Complimentary Continental breakfast, in-room data ports, some microwaves, cable TV, pool, exercise equipment, laundry facilities, business services, free parking, some pets allowed. | 6711 I–35N | 512/467–9500 | fax 512/467–9500 | 224 rooms | $73–$85 | AE, D, DC, MC, V.

**Exel Inn.** This three-story hotel is three mi from Austin's downtown and 5 mi from the Governor's mansion. Complimentary Continental breakfast, cable TV, pool, video games, laundry facilities, some pets allowed. | 2711 I–35S | 512/462–9201 | fax 512/462–9371 | 89 rooms | $59–$79 | AE, D, DC, MC, V.

**Hampton Inn.** This four-story hotel is surrounded by restaurants. It's 3 blocks from a mall and about 15 mi from Austin's downtown area. Complimentary Continental breakfast, in-room data ports, cable TV, pool, exercise equipment, business services. | 7619 I–35N | 512/452–3300 | fax 512/452–3124 | www.hamptoninn.com | 121 rooms | $79–$89 | AE, D, DC, MC, V.

**Hawthorn Suites–Northwest.** A number of shops are 3 mi away from this limited service three-story hotel in the northwest part of Austin. Complimentary breakfast, in-room data ports, many kitchenettes, microwaves, refrigerators, cable TV, pool, hot tub, laundry facilities, business services, free parking. | 8888 Tallwood Dr. | 512/343–0008 | fax 512/343–6532 | www.hawthorn.com | 14 rooms, 91 suites | $89–$99, $99–$169 suites | AE, D, DC, MC, V.

**Hilton–North.** Austin's downtown area, a mall, and a theater are within 4 mi of this nine-story hotel. Restaurant, bar, room service, in-room data ports, cable TV, pool, exercise equipment, business services, free parking, some pets allowed (fee). | 6000 Middle Fiskville Rd. | 512/451–5757 | fax 512/467–7644 | 7416162@compuserv.com | 189 rooms | $79–$199 | AE, D, DC, MC, V.

**Holiday Inn Express.** Attractions within less than 5 mi from this four-story hotel include an arboretum, a mall, and the State Capitol building. Complimentary Continental breakfast, in-room data ports, some refrigerators, cable TV, pool, business services, airport shuttle, free parking. | 7622 I–35N | 512/467–1701 | fax 512/451–0966 | www.holiday-inn.com | 125 rooms | $79 | AE, D, DC, MC, V.

**Holiday Inn–South.** This five-story hotel is just 5 mi from downtown Austin and the State Capitol Building. Be sure to reserve in advance if you want a poolside suite. Restaurant, bar, room service, in-room data ports, refrigerators, cable TV, pool, hot tub, exercise equipment, laundry facilities, business services, airport shuttle, pets allowed. | 3401 I–35S | 512/448–2444 | fax 512/448–4999 | www.holiday-inn.com | 190 rooms, 20 suites | $84, $114 suites | AE, D, DC, MC, V.

**Holiday Inn–Town Lake.** Picturesque views are available from this hotel on the shores of Town Lake. A hiking and biking trail are behind the hotel, and the airport is just 7 mi away. Restaurant, bar, room service, in-room data ports, cable TV, pool, hot tub, exercise equipment, laundry facilities, airport shuttle, free parking. | 20 I–35N | 512/472–8211 | fax 512/472–4636 | www.holiday-inn.com | 320 rooms | $109–$140 | AE, D, DC, MC, V.

**La Quinta–Capitol.** Restaurants and the State Capitol building are two blocks from this four-story hotel. In-room data ports, cable TV, pool, business services, pets allowed, parking (fee). | 300 E. 11th St. | 512/476–1166 or 800/687–6667 | fax 512/476–6044 | www.laquinta.com | 145 rooms | $69–$109 | AE, D, DC, MC, V.

**La Quinta–North.** This two-story motel is less than 1 mi from a mall and restaurants. In-room data ports, cable TV, pool, business services, some pets allowed. | 7100 I–35N | 512/452–9401 | fax 512/452–0856 | www.laquinta.com | 115 rooms | $69–$125 | AE, D, DC, MC, V.

**La Quinta/Round Rock.** The downtown area is about 12 mi from this three-story motel. A 24-hour restaurant is 2 blocks away. Complimentary Continental breakfast, in-room data ports, some microwaves, cable TV, pool, hot tub, exercise equipment, some pets allowed. | 2004 I–35N, Round Rock | 512/255–6666 | fax 512/388–3635 | www.laquinta.com | 116 rooms | $77–$84 | AE, DC, MC, V.

**Lakeway Inn Conference Resort.** This resort is on Lake Travis, about 20 mi from downtown Austin. Some rooms have elegant chandeliers and fireplaces. Restaurant, bar (with entertainment), room service, in-room data ports, some kitchenettes, some refrigerators, cable TV, 2 pools, hot tub, driving ranges, golf courses, putting greens, tennis court, exercise equipment, marina, water sports, boating, playground, business services, airport shuttle. | 101 Lakeway Dr. | 512/261–6600 or 800/525–3929 | fax 512/261–7311 | www.dolce.com | 271 rooms | $125–$270 | AE, D, DC, MC, V.

**Motel 6–Austin North.** Truck parking is available at this two-story motel in northern Austin. A bowling alley is within walking distance. Cable TV, pool, free parking, pets allowed. | 9420 I–35N | 512/339–6161 | fax 512/339–7852 | 158 rooms | $49 | AE, D, DC, MC, V.

**Motel 6–North Central.** Several restaurants are less than 2 mi from this two-story motel. Cable TV, pool, pets allowed. | 8010 I–35N | 512/837–9890 | fax 512/339–3045 | 111 rooms | $49 | AE, D, DC, MC, V.

**Omni-Southpark.** This 14-story hotel is 5 mi from a mall, Austin's downtown area, and the airport. A movie theater is 1 mi away. Restaurant, bar, room service, in-room data ports, cable TV, pool, hot tub, basketball, exercise equipment, business services, airport shuttle, free parking. | 4140 Governor's Row | 512/448–2222 | fax 512/442–8028 | www.omni.com | 313 rooms | $99–$159 | AE, D, DC, MC, V.

**Quality Inn–Airport.** The airport is 15 mi from this motel. Sixth Street, where there are numerous bars and restaurants, is just 2 mi away. Complimentary Continental breakfast, cable TV, pool, free parking, pets allowed (fee). | 909 E. Koenig La. | 512/452–4200 | fax 512/374–0652 | 91 rooms | $59–$69 | AE, D, DC, MC, V.

**Red Lion.** A mall and shopping plaza are 2 mi from this seven-story hotel. A number of restaurants are within two–blocks. Restaurant, bar, room service, in-room data ports, some refrigerators, cable TV, pool, hot tub, exercise equipment, laundry facilities, business services, free parking, pets allowed. | 6121 I–35N | 512/323–5466 | fax 512/453–1945 | 300 rooms | $99 | AE, D, DC, MC, V.

**Red Roof Inn.** This four-story motel is 1½ mi from a shopping mall. Pool, free parking, pets allowed. | 8210 I–35N | 512/835–2200 | fax 512/339–9043 | info@redroof.com | www.citysearch.com/aus/redroof | 143 rooms | $46–$56 | AE, D, DC, MC, V.

**Sheraton.** This eighteen-story hotel is at the intersection of I–35 and Sixth St. Restaurant, bar, room service, cable TV, pool, hot tub, exercise equipment, business services, parking (fee). | 500 I–35N | 512/480–8181 | fax 512/457–7990 | www.sheraton.com | 254 rooms | $89–$199 | AE, D, DC, MC, V.

**Super 8.** The downtown area and the State Capitol building are 10 mi away from this four-story motel. Complimentary Continental breakfast, some refrigerators, cable TV, pool, hot tub, business services, free parking. | 8128 I–35N | 512/339–1300 | fax 512/339–0820 | 123 rooms | $62–$77 | AE, D, DC, MC, V.

**Woodburn House.** Built in 1909, the rooms inside Hyde Park's only B&B are simply and functionally decorated, with rocking chairs and firm mattresses. The proprietor can provide a brochure detailing a walking tour of Austin's historic Hyde Park area. Dining room, complimentary breakfast, some in-room hot tubs, no TV in some rooms, TV in common area, library, free parking, no pets, no kids under 12, no smoking. | 4401 Ave. D | 512/458–4335 or 888/690–9763 | fax 512/458–4339 | woodburnhouse@hotmail.com | www.woodburnhouse.com | 5 rooms | $98–$138 | AE, MC, V.

## MODERATE

**Driskill.** Built in 1888, the lobby of this downtown hotel has a stained-glass dome and 30-ft high ceilings. Restaurant, bar (with entertainment), room service, cable TV, business services. Parking (fee). | 604 Brazos St. | 512/474–5911 | fax 512/474–2214 | information@driskillhotel.com | 188 rooms | $165–$225 | AE, D, DC, MC, V.

**Embassy Suites.** Shopping and entertainment are four blocks from this nine-story hotel in the heart of downtown. Restaurant, bar, complimentary breakfast, in-room data ports, microwaves, refrigerators, cable TV, pool, hot tub, exercise equipment, laundry facilities, business services, free parking. | 300 S. Congress St. | 512/469–9000 | fax 512/480–9164 | www.embassysuites.com | 262 suites | $150–$199 suites | AE, D, DC, MC, V.

**Hawthorn Suites–South.** Numerous restaurants are less than 1 mi from this two-story hotel, 4 mi south of downtown Austin. Picnic area, complimentary Continental breakfast, kitchenettes, microwaves, cable TV, pool, hot tub, laundry facilities, business services, free parking, pets allowed (fee). | 4020 I–35S | 512/440–7722 | fax 512/440–4815 | www.hawthorn.com | 120 suites | $149–$179 suites | AE, D, DC, MC, V.

**Intercontinental Stephen F. Austin Hotel.** This hotel built in 1924 is in the heart of downtown, one block from Sixth Street, four blocks from the capitol, and next door to the historic Paramount Theatre. 2 restaurants, bar, room service, in-room data ports, minibars, cable TV, pool, massage, steam room, exercise equipment, laundry service, business services, parking (fee), no pets. | 701 Congress Ave. | 512/457–8800 or 800/327–0200 | fax 512/457–8896 | www.interconti.com | 189 rooms, 16 suites | $169–$325, $325–$675 suites | AE, D, DC, MC, V.

**Marriott at the Capitol.** Some of the rooms on the upper floors of this sixteen-story hotel have nice views of the State Capitol building and downtown Austin. Restaurant, bar, in-room data ports, some refrigerators, room service, cable TV, pool, hot tub, exercise equipment, video games, parking (fee). | 701 E. 11th St. | 512/478–1111 | fax 512/478–3700 | www.marriotthotels.com | 365 rooms, 4 suites | $179–$184, $225–$325 suites | AE, D, DC, MC, V.

**Omni.** The State Capitol building is four blocks from this nineteen-story hotel in the downtown area. Restaurant, bar (with entertainment), room service, in-room data ports, some refrigerators, cable TV, pool, hot tub, massage, exercise equipment, business services, parking (fee). | 700 San Jacinto St. | 512/476–3700 | fax 512/397–4888 | www.omni.com | 350 rooms | $139–$189 | AE, D, DC, MC, V.

**Radisson.** New tower suites, built in 1998, overlook Town Lake in this downtown hotel. It's thirteen blocks from the State Capitol building and five blocks from historic Sixth Street. Restaurant, bar, room service, in-room data ports, cable TV, pool, exercise equipment, business services, parking (fee). | 111 E. Cesar Chavez St. | 512/478–9611 | fax 512/473–8399 | www.radisson.com | 413 rooms | $135–$249 | AE, D, DC, MC, V.

**Renaissance.** An imposing atrium lobby is filled with plants, birds, statues, and tiki bells. Restaurant, bar (with entertainment), in-room data ports, some microwaves, cable TV, 2 pools, hot tub, exercise equipment, business services, some pets allowed, free parking. | 9721 Arboretum Blvd. | 512/343–2626 | fax 512/346–7953 | www.renaissancehotels.com | 478 rooms, 16 suites | $189, $240–$325 suites | AE, D, DC, MC, V.

## EXPENSIVE

**Barton Creek Resort.** This conference resort is on 4,000 acres of manicured grounds in beautiful Texas Hill Country. Restaurant, bar, room service, in-room data ports, minibars, refrigerators, cable TV, 2 pools, barbershop, beauty salon, hot tub, massage, driving range, golf courses, putting green, tennis court, gym, video games, business services, airport shuttle, free parking. | 8212 Barton Club Dr. | 800/336–6158 | fax 512/329–4597 | www.bartoncreek.com | 300 rooms, 3 suites | $250, $395 suites | AE, DC, MC, V.

**Four Seasons.** Built along the shoreline, this luxury hotel has views of beautiful sunsets over Town Lake. Restaurant, bar, room service, in-room data ports, some microwaves, cable TV, pool, hot tub, massage, gym, business services, parking (fee), some pets allowed. | 98 San Jacinto Blvd. | 512/478–4500 | fax 512/478–3117 | www.fourseasons.com | 291 rooms | $235–$350 | AE, DC, MC, V.

**Hyatt Regency.** A marble lobby and sunlit atrium greet you upon entry of this 17-story hotel on Town Lake. Restaurant, bar (with entertainment), room service, in-room data ports, cable

TV, pool, lake, hot tub, exercise equipment, playground, business services, parking (fee). | 208 Barton Springs Rd. | 512/477–1234 | fax 512/480–2069 | www.hyatt.com | 446 rooms | $220–$300 | AE, D, DC, MC, V.

# BANDERA

MAP 8, G6

*(Nearby towns also listed: Castroville, Kerrville)*

"The Cowboy Capital of the World" is well known for its plentiful dude ranches, country-and-western music, rodeos, and horse racing. This town of 1,000 is also one of the nation's oldest Polish communities (dating from 1855) and the site of an 1854 Mormon colony.

Bandera Pass, located 12 mi north of town on Rte. 173, was the site of many battles between Spanish conquistadors and both Apache and Comanche Indians. Legend has it that, following a battle with the Apaches in 1732, a flag (or *bandera* in Spanish) was hung at the pass to mark the boundary between the two opposing forces.

Information: **Bandera Convention and Visitors Bureau** | 606 Rte. 16S, Bandera, TX 78003-0171 | 830/796–3045 or 800/364–3833.

## Attractions

**Bandera County Historic Tours.** A walking or driving tour of the county can bring you to the original town jail and county courthouse, historic 11th St., present-day blacksmiths and saddle makers, and a working ranch. Information on self-guided tours is available at the Bandera Convention and Visitors Bureau. | 606 Rte. 16S | 830/796–3045 or 800/364–3833 | Free | Daily.

**Frontier Times Museum.** Cowboy paraphernalia, Indian arrowheads, Western show posters, Buffalo Bill memorabilia, and prehistoric artifacts are on display in this museum, established in 1927. | 506 13th St. | 830/796–3864 | $2 | Mon.–Sat. 10–4:30, Sun. 1–4:30.

### ON THE CALENDAR

**MAY:** *Cowboy Capital Rodeo.* Mansfield Park Rodeo Arena hosts this three-day pro rodeo event, which includes bull riding, barrel racing, bareback riding, steer wrestling, a calf scramble, and team roping. | 830/796–3045.

**JULY:** *Texas International Apple Festival.* On a single Sat. each year, the tiny town of Medina (pop. 250) swells to 20,000 as visitors descend upon a local pecan grove. The family-oriented celebration has historical reenactments, arts, crafts, and food vendors, four stages with entertainment (one is devoted entirely to children), and anything that you can think of made with apples. | 830/796–3045 or 800/364–3833.

## Dining

**Busbee's Barbecue.** Barbecue. Right on the town's main drag, this popular spot serves traditional chicken, brisket, and ribs. As a variation on the usual ultra-heavy barbecue meal, the chef will slice your grilled chicken or beef and toss it onto a bed of fresh greens. | 319 Main St. | 830/796–3153 | $6–$15 | No credit cards.

**Cabaret Cafe and Dance Hall.** Continental. The dance hall of this all-wood ranch-style restaurant is the second-oldest in Texas, ca. 1936. The wait on weekends is worth it for the mesquite-grilled prime rib or mahi-mahi, embellished with such sauces as lemon wine salsa or garlic shrimp cream. There's only one dessert on the menu, but when it's a big brownie with ice cream, what's not to like? | 801 Main St. | 830/796–8166 | Reservations not accepted | Closed Mon. | $8–$16 | AE, MC, V.

**O.S.T. Restaurant.** American. An institution for over 75 years, the acronym stands for Old Spanish Trail, which once passed through Bandera. Expect down-home country-style American food such as chicken-fried steak with cream gravy, and Mexican dishes such as enchiladas. Come early before the homemade biscuits run out, or if you're there for lunch, try the all-you-can-eat buffet. Breakfast is served all day. | 305 Main St. | 830/796–3836 | Breakfast also available | $5–$12 | D, DC, MC, V.

## Lodging

**Bandera Lodge.** This two-story motel is within walking distance of the Medina River. Restaurant, bar, cable TV, pool, laundry facilities. | 700 Rte. 16S | 830/796–3093 | fax 830/796–3191 | 44 rooms | $69 | AE, D, DC, MC, V.

**Dixie Dude Ranch.** This working stock ranch has been run by the same family since 1901. Follow the numerous hiking trails if you want to explore the property's 725 acres. Restaurant, pool, wading pool, horseback riding, playground, laundry facilities, business services. | 1077 Ranch Rd. | 830/796–4481 or 800/375–9255 | fax 830/796–4481 | www.dixieduderanch.com | 18 rooms, 4 cottages | $95, $105 cottages; per person | AE, D, MC, V. AP.

**Flying L.** This Western-style guest ranch is on 500 acres. All accommodations have wrought iron beds and views of the grounds. Restaurant, bar (with entertainment), microwaves, some in-room hot tubs, cable TV, pool, driving range, 18-hole golf course, putting green, horseback riding, children's programs (ages 3–12), playground, laundry facilities, business services. | 566 Flying L Dr. | 830/460–3001 or 800/292–5134 | fax 830/796–8455 | www.flyingl.com | 44 cottages | $90–$118 cottages | AE, D, MC, V.

**Hackberry Lodge Bed and Breakfast.** All but one of the guest rooms in this turn-of-the-20th-century home are two-bedroom suites. Help yourself to whatever you crave from the summer kitchen, then relax on one of the porches or the hammock. Breakfast is served in the garden, and you can request a five-course dinner in the dining room. Dining room, complimentary breakfast, microwaves, cable TV, no room phones, library, business services, pets allowed, no kids, no smoking. | 1005 Hackberry St. | 830/460–7134 | fax 830/460–7500 | www.hackberrylodge.com | 7 suites | $95–$155 suites | MC, V.

**Mayan Dude Ranch.** Picturesque trails cover 340 acres on this ranch, which has been family-owned since 1949. A social director is on-site from June–Sept. Tubing on the Medina River can be arranged. Restaurant, bar, picnic area, snack bar, TV in all rooms, pool, tennis, video games, children's programs (7–12), playground, laundry facilities, business services. | 350 Schmidtke Rd. | 830/796–3312 | fax 830/796–8205 | www.mayanranch.com | 38 rooms, 30 cottages | $240 rooms, $240 cottages | AE, D, DC, MC, V.

**Muller's Ark Ranch.** A private fishing lake is stocked with bass and catfish at this 110-acre working sheep ranch right on the Medina River. Other residents include peacocks, deer, and wild turkeys. You can sleep in a converted railroad caboose on the lake, a two-bedroom home with a Mexican tile floor, or a two-bedroom cottage on a bluff overlooking the river. The ranch is 5 mi northwest of Bandera via Rte. 16. | 714 Peaceful Valley Rd. | 830/796–3420 | fax 830/460–3420 | 1 apartment, 1 cottage, 4 homes | $60 apartment, $80 cottage, $90–$100 home (2–day minimum stay) | No credit cards.

# BASTROP

MAP 8, I5

*(Nearby towns also listed: Austin, Smithville)*

Bastrop is best known for its unique vegetation. Unlike the juniper-dotted hills to the west or the rolling farmland to the east, the Bastrop area is surrounded by the Lost Pines region, which is the westernmost stand of loblolly pines in the United States. It is believed that these trees were once part of the forests of East Texas, but were separated by climatic changes over the past 10,000 years.

The community of 5,000 also holds the honor of being one of the oldest settlements in the state: It was built in 1829 along the El Camino Real (or "King's Highway"), a road also known as Old San Antonio Road. This was the western edge of the "Little Colony" established by Stephen F. Austin. Settlers came by the wagonload from around the country to claim a share of fertile land and establish a home in the dangerous territory.

Today the verdant community is favored by outdoors lovers due to the presence of two state parks and the Colorado River, which winds through the heart of downtown. Canoe rentals and guided trips along the river are available. Shoppers enjoy the quiet country atmosphere still found in the downtown area.

Information: **Bastrop Chamber of Commerce** | 927 Main St., 78602-3809 | 512/321–2419 | www.bastropchamber.com.

## Attractions

**Bastrop Opera House.** This not-for-profit opera house was built in 1889. In 1979 it was rescued by local citizens from its condemned status and restored to the glory it knew in its early days. Today the building presents various performances, including children's theater, as well as special events. | 711 Spring St. | 512/321–6283 | $5–$17 | Tues.–Sat. 10–5.

**Bastrop State Park.** Tucked in the piney woods for which Bastrop is known, this popular state park has camping, swimming, picnicking, hiking, a nine-hole golf course, a nature study, trailer sites, and cabins. | Rte. 21, 1 mi east of Bastrop | 512/321–2101 | fax 512/321–3300 | www.tpwd.state.tx.us | $3 | Daily 8 AM–10 PM.

**Buescher State Park.** Just a short distance from Bastrop State Park, this park is accessible either through Bastrop or nearby Smithville. Buescher (pronounced bisher) offers camping, fishing, a playground, a 7.7-mi hiking trail, and screened shelters. | Off FM 153 | 512/237–2241 | fax 512/237–2580 | www.tpwd.state.tx.us | $3 | Daily 8 AM–10 PM.

### ON THE CALENDAR

**APR.: *Yesterfest.*** This frontier festival on the banks of the Colorado River includes arts and crafts, historical reenactments, live music, and food. | 512/303–6283.

**OCT.: *Cajunfest.*** Cajun culture is celebrated in Riverbend Park with drinks, music, Cajun cuisine, and a live auction. | 512/303–3548.

**DEC.: *Christmas in the Park.*** This holiday celebration includes the lighting of a Christmas tree, Christmas caroling, and crafts. | 512/584–2214.

## Dining

**Guadalahara Restaurant.** Mexican. Mexican sombreros and serapes adorn the walls of this restaurant. Chicken or cheese enchiladas, tacos, and rice and beans are popular menu items. | 494 Rte. 71W, Suite #180 | 512/321–3002 | $3–$9 | D, MC, V.

## Lodging

**Comfort Inn.** This two-story cream stucco hotel was built in 1999. Shopping, restaurants, and a dry cleaner are within walking distance, and The Colovista and Pine Forest golf courses are each about 7 mi away; guests play at a reduced rate. Complimentary Continental breakfast, some refrigerators, some microwaves, cable TV, pool, spa, business services, no pets. | 106 Hasler Blvd. | 512/321–3303 or 800/228–5150 | fax 512/321–3004 | www.comfortinn.com | 41 rooms | $67–$80 | AE, D, DC, MC, V.

# BAYTOWN

*(Nearby towns also listed: Houston, La Porte)*

Located on the mouth of the San Jacinto River, this community of 70,000 began as a store and a sawmill. In 1822 the Lynchburg Ferry was established to convey passengers and goods across the waterway. Today the town is active in the petrochemical and oil refining industries and offers plenty of watersports, from sportfishing to sailing.

**Information: Baytown Chamber of Commerce** | 4721 Garth Rd., Suite C, Baytown, TX 77521 | 281/422–8359 | bccl@gte.net | www.baytownchamber.com.

## Attractions

**Anahuac National Wildlife Refuge.** A favorite with birders, this coastal refuge of over 30,000 acres is filled with waterfowl, migrant birds, alligators, and more. Take Rte. 61 to Rte. 562 to Rte. 1985 | Rte. 1985 | 409/267–3337 | fax 409/267–4314 | southwest.fws.gov/refuges/texas/anahuac.html | Free | Daily.

**Baytown Historical Museum.** This small museum houses exhibits of local history. | 220 W. Defee St. | 281/427–8768 | fax 281/420–9029 | Free | Tues.–Sat. 10–2.

**Evergreen Point Golf Club.** This 18-hole course 20 mi southeast of Houston opened in 1996. It's very scenic and wooded and has a fine driving range. | 1530 Evergreen Rd. | 281/837–9000 | Year-round.

**Lynchburg Ferry.** When Sam Houston defeated Santa Anna's army in 1836, the Lynchburg Ferry carried wounded soldiers back across the San Jacinto River into Lynchburg. | 1001 Lynchburg Rd. | 281/424–3521 | fax 281/424–7867 | Free | Daily.

### ON THE CALENDAR

**JULY: *July 4th Celebration.*** This all-day event starts with a parade in the morning, and includes food vendor and arts-and-crafts booths, various contests for kids and adults, a disc jockey during the afternoon, and country-and-western and pop performances in the evening. | 281/420–6590.

## Dining

**Luna's.** Mexican. Beef and chicken fajitas in a distinctive marinade with peppers and spices are the most popular dishes at this restaurant right on Baytown's main drag. Try the specially prepared *cabrito* (goat meat served with grilled onions and flour tortillas). | 4539 Garth Rd. | 281/422–9090 | $5–$13 | AE, D, DC, MC, V.

**Outback Steakhouse.** Steak. From the busy bar (packed with diners watching sporting events) to the casual booths, this restaurant has a fun atmosphere aimed at giving diners excellent steaks served in a relaxed setting. Known for steak and seafood. Kids' menu. | 5218 I–10E | 281/421–9001 | No lunch | $12–$23 | AE, D, DC, MC, V.

## Lodging

**Holiday Inn Express.** The Houston airport is one hour from this three-story motel, and a shopping mall and steak house are across the Interstate. Cable TV, pool, pets allowed. | 5222 I–10E, | 281/421–7200 | fax 281/421–7209 | www.holidayinn.com | 62 rooms | $49–$75 | AE, D, DC, MC, V.

**La Quinta.** Right off I–10, this two-story hotel is across the highway from the San Jacinto Mall. You can request a free pass for use at a gym 2 mi away. Complimentary Continental breakfast, some microwaves, some refrigerators, cable TV, pool, laundry service, business services, pets allowed. | 4911 I–10E | 281/421–5566 or 800/687–6667 | fax 281/421–4009 | 130 rooms | $60–$75 | AE, D, DC, MC, V.

BAYTOWN

INTRO
ATTRACTIONS
DINING
LODGING

**Motel 6.** This two-story motel is within walking distance of several restaurants and is 4 mi from a shopping mall. Cable TV, pool, pets allowed. | 8911 Rte. 146 | 281/576–5777 | fax 281/576–2351 | 124 rooms | $35–$40 | AE, D, DC, MC, V.

# BEAUMONT

MAP 8, K5

*(Nearby towns also listed: Jasper, Orange, Port Arthur)*

Established as a trading post, this city of 114,000 boomed in 1901 with the discovery of oil at Spindletop (a gusher). Today this is a port city, home to Lamar University, and the gateway to Big Thicket National Preserve.

Information: **Beaumont Convention and Visitors Bureau** | 801 Main St., Beaumont, TX 77701 | 409/880–3749 800/392–4401. | www.beaumontcvb.com.

## Attractions

**Art Museum of Southeast Texas.** A variety of media including paintings, sculpture, folk art, and more, are showcased at this museum. Traveling exhibits are on display periodically. | 500 Main St. | 409/832–3432 | fax 409/832–8508 | www.amset.org | Free | Weekdays 9–5, Sat. 10–5, Sun. 12–5.

**Babe Didrikson Zaharias Memorial Museum.** The awesome athletic accomplishments of Mildred "Babe" Didrikson Zaharias (1914–1956), Olympian and championship golfer, are chronicled at this museum. The Beaumont Convention and Visitors Bureau operates a visitors center in the museum as well. | 1750 I–10E, Exit 854 | 409/833–4622 | fax 409/880–3750 | Free | Daily 9–5.

**Big Thicket National Preserve.** The park has several entrance points but most visitors stop by the Turkey Creek Unit (30 mi north of Beaumont off Rte. 420) for the Visitors Information Station. Hiking is the most popular activity in Big Thicket, and you'll find nine trails from which to choose. Before you head off on the trails, make a stop at the Big Thicket Information Center, where you'll find a helpful ranger, displays on Big Thicket wildlife and plants, information on upcoming programs, videotapes and books, and restrooms. It's important to note that Big Thicket and its environs can flood easily in a heavy rain, and that you should never cross a trail that's under water. | Headquarters: 3785 Milam St. | 409/246–2337 | Free | Daily 9–5; Headquarters: 8–4:30.

**Cattail Marsh.** A favorite with bird watchers, this wetlands is a favorable habitat for many species of both birds and plants. | I–10 to Walden Rd. to Tyrell Park | 409/842–0458 | fax 409/842–1076 | Free | Daily dawn–dusk.

**Doguet's Rice Milling Company.** Learn how rice is grown and see it prepared for distribution at this working mill. | 795 S. Major Dr. | 409/866–2297 | Free | Weekdays 8–5.

**Edison Plaza Museum.** The largest collection of Thomas A. Edison artifacts west of the Mississippi River is housed in this museum. Displays include personal objects and the inventor's notes. | 350 Pine St. | 409/839–3089 | Free | Tues.–Fri. 1–3:30, or by appointment.

**Jefferson Theater.** This theater hosts plays, musical performances, and variety shows. | 345 Fannin St. | 409/832–6649 | fax 409/838–4318 | Prices vary with shows | Weekdays 9–12, call for performance schedules.

**John Jay French Museum (Historic House).** Built in 1845, this is the oldest house in Beaumont. One-hour guided tours of the interior furnished with period furniture are available. | 2995 French Rd. | 409/898–3267 | $3 | Tues.–Sat. 10–4.

**Lamar University.** This univerisy was founded as South Park Junior College in 1923. Today it hosts a student body of almost 9000. | 4400 Martin Luther King Pkwy. | 409/880–7011 | www.lamar.edu | Free | Daily.

Spindletop, the gusher that brought oil wealth to the state, is reconstructed at the **Spindletop/Gladys City Boomtown Museum,** as is a boomtown. The town includes a blacksmith shop, photo studio, post office, and wooden oil derricks. Also on view is the Lucas Gusher Monument, which commemorates Anthony F. Lucas, who drilled the Spindletop gusher in 1901. | Lamar Universiy, University Dr. at U.S. 69 | 409/835–0823 | fax 409/838–9107 | $3 | Tues.–Sun. 1–5.

**McFaddin-Ward House.** This colonial mansion is decorated in the lavish style favored by its owners in the early 20th century. | 1906 McFaddin Ave. | 409/832–2134 | $3 | Tues.–Sat. 8–4, Sun. 1–4.

**Texas Energy Museum.** Exhibits at this museum explore the formation of petroleum and its uses. | 600 Main St. | 409/833–5100 | fax 409/833–4282 | $2 | Tues.–Sat. 9–5, Sun. 1–5.

**Tyrrell Historical Library.** Listed on the National Register of Historic Places, this former church built in 1903 is filled with exhibits on Texas and Beaumont history. | 695 Pearl St. | 409/833–2759 | fax 409/833–5828 | Free | Tues. 8:30–8, Wed.–Sat. 8:30–5:30.

## ON THE CALENDAR

**APR.:** *Neches River Festival.* This festival includes fishing tournaments, boat races, waterskiing shows, a parade, and an art show. | 409/835–2546.

**APR.:** *Tracy Byrd Homecoming.* Joining the ranks of well-known local greats like Mark Chestnut and George Jones, this popular country-and-western singer and hometown son has an annual three-day event held in his honor. There are golf tournaments and bass-fishing, and the grand finale is a concert performance given by Byrd himself. | 409/880–3749 or 800/392–4401.

**OCT.:** *South Texas State Fair.* Livestock, poultry, and rice contests, food booths, live entertainment, and kids' activities are part of the fun at this state fair. | 409/832–9991.

## Dining

**Chula Vista.** Mexican. The dining area of this casual family restaurant has Mexican artwork painted on the walls. The menu includes Mexican standards, including tasty fajitas and enchiladas. Open-air dining is available on a patio with umbrellaed tables. Kids' menu. | 1135 N. 11th St. | 409/898–8855 | $5–$15 | AE, D, DC, MC, V.

**Hoffbrau Steaks.** Steak. The walls are adorned with animal heads, license plates, and school flags from area universities at this casual meat-lovers' haven. You can dine on a rustic brick patio with a fireplace year-round. Try the spicy grilled shrimp with peppers or the tender filet mignon. Live music is performed Mon.–Sat. Kids' menu. | 2310 N. 11th St. | 409/892–6911 | No lunch Sat. or Sun. | $9–$17 | AE, D, DC, MC, V.

**Olive Garden.** Italian. Preferred by families, the Olive Garden chain offers Italian food at a reasonable price. Try veal parmigiana and shrimp primavera. Kids' menu. | 585 I–10N | 409/832–9058 | No lunch | $8–$15 | AE, D, DC, MC, V.

**Outback Steakhouse.** Steak. Part of a large chain, Outback Steakhouse is known for top of the line beef served in a friendly, family-style atmosphere. Try the Rockhampton Rib-Eye, New York Strip and Porterhouse. Kids' menu. | 2060 I–10S | 409/842–6699 | No lunch | $10–$20 | AE, D, DC, MC, V.

**Sartin's.** Seafood. Formerly a 1940s-era pharmacy, today this nothing-fancy building houses a popular restaurant. The interior contains unpainted concrete floor covered with red carpeting and rows and rows of tables filled every night of the week. Most people come for the legendary all-you-can-eat barbecued crab platters, served family-style with catfish and fried shrimp, crabmeat-stuffed jalapeños, cold crab claws, hush puppies, French fries, and salads. Try the homemade coleslaw. Salad bar. | 6725 Eastex Fwy. | 409/892–6771 | $10–$18 | AE, D, MC, V.

## Lodging

**Best Western–Beaumont Inn.** The airport is 20 mi from this two-story motel, and a shopping mall is within walking distance. Several restaurants are within three blocks. Complimentary Continental breakfast, in-room data ports, some refrigerators, cable TV, pool, laundry facilities, business services, some pets allowed. | 2155 N. 11th St. | 409/898–8150 | fax 979/898–0078 | 152 rooms | $54–$72 | AE, D, DC, MC, V.

**Best Western–Jefferson Inn.** Several restaurants are within walking distance of this two-story motel, and a shopping mall is 3 mi away. Complimentary Continental breakfast, in-room data ports, some kitchenettes, some refrigerators, cable TV, pool, laundry facilities, business services, some pets allowed. | 1610 I–10S | 409/842–0037 or 800/528–1234 | fax 979/842–0057 | 120 rooms | $67 | AE, D, DC, MC, V.

**Courtyard by Marriott.** This low-rise cream stucco hotel has three floors accessible by elevator. Being a smaller hotel it lacks the full business center found in most Courtyards (although there is a meeting room). Many restaurants are 1 mi away, along I–10. In-room data ports, some microwaves, some refrigerators, cable TV, pool, hot tub, exercise equipment, laundry facilities, laundry service, business services, no pets. | 2275 I–10S | 409/840–5750 or 800/321–2211 | fax 409/842–6364 | cybmt@pineappleinc.com | courtyard.com/BPTCY | 78 rooms | $79–$129 | AE, D, DC, MC, V.

**Fairfield Inn.** Some rooms have king-size bed and a pullout sleeper sofa in this three-story hotel. The Port of Beaumont is 2 mi away. Complimentary Continental breakfast, in-room data ports, some microwaves, some refrigerators, cable TV, pool, hot tub, exercise equipment, laundry service, business services, no pets. | 2265 I–10S | 409/840–5751 or 800/228–2800 | fairfieldinn.com | 79 rooms | $55–$72 | AE, D, DC, MC, V.

**Hampton Inn.** This five-story hotel is 5 mi southwest of downtown Beaumont via I–10. Restaurants and a movie theater are within walking distance, and a country club and golf course are less than 1 mile away. In-room data ports, some microwaves, some refrigerators, cable TV, pool, outdoor hot tub, exercise equipment, laundry facilities, laundry service, business services, no pets. | 3795 I–10S | 409/840–9922 or 800/426–7866 | fax 409/840–9929 | www.hampton-inn.com | 122 rooms | $73–$84 | AE, D, DC, MC, V.

**Hilton.** Some rooms overlook the pool in this nine-story hotel. It's about 10 mi from the airport and 7 mi from a shopping mall and several restaurants. Restaurant, bar, room service, in-room data ports, cable TV, pool, exercise equipment, business services, airport shuttle. | 2355 I–10S | 409/842–3600 | fax 409/842–1355 | 284 rooms | $80–$149 | AE, D, DC, MC, V.

**Holiday Inn–Beaumont Plaza.** A three-story waterfall is in the lobby of this eight-story hotel. The convention center is next door. Restaurant, bar, in-room data ports, some refrigerators, cable TV, pool, hot tub, exercise equipment, business services, airport shuttle, pets allowed (fee). | 3950 I–10S | 409/842–5995 | fax 409/842–0315 | www.holidayinn.com | 253 rooms, 80 suites | $90, $113 suites | AE, D, DC, MC, V.

**Holiday Inn–Midtown.** This six-story hotel is 2 mi from Beaumont's downtown area and a shopping mall. Restaurant, bar, room service, in-room data ports, cable TV, pool, laundry facilities, business services, airport shuttle, some pets allowed. | 2095 N. 11th St. | 409/892–2222 | fax 409/892–2231 | hi-beaumont@bristolhotels.com | www.holiday-inn.com | 190 rooms | $69–$99 | AE, D, DC, MC, V.

**La Quinta.** This motel is within walking distance of several restaurants, 2 mi from a shopping mall, and 8 mi from the airport. Complimentary Continental breakfast, in-room data ports, cable TV, pool, business services, some pets allowed. | 220 I–10N | 409/838–9991 | fax 405/832–1266 | www.laquinta.com | 122 rooms | $57–$63 | AE, D, DC, MC, V.

**Scottish Inns.** This two-story motel is 2 mi from a shopping mall and across the Interstate from a number of chain restaurants. Cable TV, pool, some pets allowed. | 2640 I–10E | 409/899–3152 | fax 409/895–0228 | 118 rooms | $35 | AE, D, MC, V.

# BIG BEND NATIONAL PARK

*(Nearby towns also listed: Alpine, Terlingua)*

★ This remote, little-visited national park is a place to get away from it all and enjoy nature along the banks of the Rio Grande. That massive river, which forms part of the border between Texas and Mexico, marks the location of Big Bend. (Picture a map of the western side of Texas where the river—and thus the state's boundary—makes a big bend . . . well, you figured it out.) A strategic crossroad for thousands of years, the park has witnessed a parade of Comanche, Apache, Spanish conquistadores, U.S. soldiers, Mexican revolutionaries, and many others. Big Bend National Park spans more than 800,000 acres and offers a backdrop of canyons, desert, the Chisos Mountains, more than a thousand plants, and a wide range of animal and bird life.

Hiking is definitely the number one activity in this park; you can choose from all grades of trails that span over 150 mi of the park. Guided nature walks led by naturalists are offered year-round (several a day in the peak months from Nov.–Apr.). Check with the visitors centers for current offerings. The park also has wildlife viewing and bird watching trips.

**Information: Big Bend National Park** | Box 129, Big Bend National Park, TX 79834 | 915/477–2251 | www.nps.gov/bibe/.

## Attractions

**Visitors Center.** Brochures, maps, and exhibits on area wildlife and natural history can be found here. Rangers are on hand to provide additional information. There are stations is

BIG BEND
NATIONAL PARK

INTRO
ATTRACTIONS
DINING
LODGING

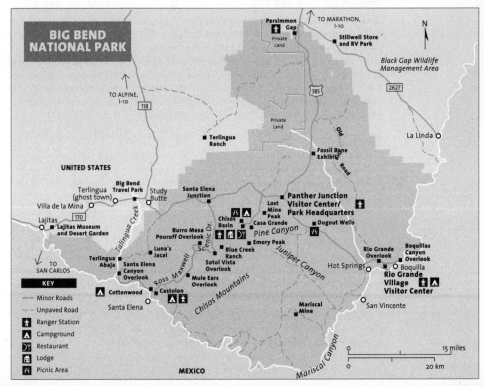

Chisos Basin, Persimmon Gap, and Rio Grande Village. | Off I–10 | 915/477–2251 | fax 915/477–2357 | Free | Daily 8–6.

**Fort Davis.** The community of Fort Davis is one of the gateways to the Big Bend region. It began as a U.S. Army post in the mid-1800s, located at the intersection of two important mail routes. Fort Davis is located in the Davis Mountains, which provide a respite from the heat of the surrounding Chihuahuan Desert. | Fort Davis Chamber of Commerce, Box 378, Fort Davis, TX | 915/426–3015 or 800/524–3015 | ftdavis@overland.net | www.fortdavis.com.

**Hallie's Hall of Fame Museum.** Hallie Stillwell was a local pioneer, teacher, and rancher. Her namesake museum is located next to a general store and RV park. To enter the museum go next door to the store and obtain the key. | Rte. 2627, 6 mi east of Big Bend National Park | 915/376–2244 | Donation accepted | Daily 7AM–8:30PM.

### ON THE CALENDAR
**OCT.: *International Good Neighbor Fiesta*.** Held each year on the third Sat. in Oct., this celebration aims to strengthen relations between the cultures along the Texas/Mexico border. There are performances by schoolchildren from nearby towns in Mexico and Texas, local talent acts, and a headliner. You'll also find arts-and-crafts and food vendors. | 915/477–1108.

## Dining
**The Badlands.** American. Cow skulls and old pictures portraying the history of the Lajitas region and Old Mexico adorn the walls of this restaurant serving standard American fare (such as grilled ham-and-cheese sandwiches and lemon chicken) as well as Mexican dishes. Try the Pancho Villa special, with beef and cheese enchiladas, a taco, and rice and beans. The restaurant is in the Lajitas Resort, in Lajitas, 20 mi southeast of the Alpine/Study Butte entrance to Big Bend National Park via Rte. 170. | Lajitas Resort, Lajitas | 915/424–3471 | Reservations not accepted | Breakfast also available | $3–$9 | AE, D, MC, V.

**La Kiva Restaurant and Bar.** Southwestern. Open the big wooden door at the entrance and descend into this unusual underground restaurant, with native limestone and sandstone walls, a 300-year-old buffalo skull, and a slab of redwood from California's Russian River serving as the bar, which has over 60 different tequilas. Lighter fare is offered in summer, but the rest of the year the kitchen specializes in mesquite-grilled barbecue, cooked outside in a big barbecue pit. Outdoor dining is available on the large outdoor patio overlooking Terlingua Creek. | 3½ mi southwest of the Alpine/Study Butte entrance of Big Bend National Park on Rte. 170 | 915/371–2250 | No lunch | $6–$17 | No credit cards.

## Lodging
**Chisos Mining Co. Motel.** This mom-and-pop motel's bright colors and rustic decor make it stand out from its desert setting. Cable TV, some pets allowed. | Box 228, Terlingua | 915/371–2254 | fax 915/371–2430 | 20 rooms, 10 cabins | $56 room, $56 cabin | AE, D, MC, V.

**Chisos Mountains Lodge.** Though Big Bend National Park has hundreds of campsites, this is the only hotel; it's therefore often booked months in advance. Although it isn't fancy, most rooms have private balconies and spectacular views of the mountains and the desert floor. Dining room, no air-conditioning in some rooms, no room phones, no TV, pets allowed. | From the Alpine/Study Butte entrance, follow Basin Rd. 22 mi east to its end | 915/477–2291 | fax 915/477–2352 | www.chisosmountainslodge.com | 72 rooms (6 with shower only) | $70–$81 | AE, D, DC, MC, V.

**Indian Lodge.** Four mi west of Fort Davis National Historic Site, this pueblo-style lodge on a hillside has rustic decor and is state-owned and -operated. All park facilities are available for use. Restaurant, picnic area, cable TV, pool. | Park Rd. 3, Fort Davis | 915/426–3254 | fax 915/426–2022 | 39 rooms | $55–$85 | Closed mid–late Jan. | D, MC, V.

# BIG SPRING

*(Nearby towns also listed: Midland, San Angelo, Snyder)*

The "big spring" from which this town of 25,000 got its name first attracted settlers in 1849; today those clear waters beautify City Park. Big Spring is proud of its frontier heritage and its location along the Overland Trail to California and the Chisholm Trail that stretched between El Paso and Arkansas. Today this town 88 mi north of San Angelo is an agricultural center for many of the outlying communities located in the Permian Basin.

Information: **Big Spring Area Chamber of Commerce** | 215 W. 3rd St., Big Spring, TX 79720 | 915/263–7641. | tdavis@crcom.net | www.bigspringtx.com.

## Attractions

**Big Spring State Park.** This day-use park has a prairie dog town, a playground, and nature trails. | 1 Scenic Dr. | 915/263–4931 | www.tpwd.state.tx.us | $2 | Daily 8 AM–10 PM.

**Comanche Trail Amphitheater.** Built by the Civilian Conservation Corps in the mid-1930's from limestone quarried at Big Spring State Park, this outdoor theater seats nearly 7,000 and hosts concerts, theatrical productions, and the annual July 4th Pops in the Park celebration. Take Gregg St. south to the city limits, U.S. 87 1 mi to Comanche Trail Park, follow signs. | 800 Comanche Park Rd. | 915/263–7641 | Free | Daily 6AM–10PM.

**Heritage Museum.** This museum holds the distinction of having the largest collection of horns from the Texas longhorn cattle anywhere. It also has a collection of railroad memorabilia. | 510 Scurry St. | 915/267–8255 | $2 | Tues.–Fri. 9–5, Sat. 10–5.

**Lake Colorado City State Park.** Swimming, boating, and fishing are possible activities here, and you can stay overnight in a cottage or at a camp site. Take I–20 east to Rte. 2836, then drive south for 6 mi. | Rte. 2836 | 915/728–3931 | fax 915/728–3420 | www.tpwd.state.tx.us | $3 | Daily 8 AM–10 PM.

**Potton House.** Antique furnishings fill this restored 1901 home. | 200 Gregg St. (U.S. 87) | 915/263–0511 | Tues.–Sat. 1–5.

### ON THE CALENDAR

**MAR.:** *Gem and Mineral Show.* Exhibits and the sale of gems and minerals from around the world are the focus of this event. | 915/263–7641.

**MAR.:** *Rattlesnake Roundup.* This event includes rattlesnake exhibits and daredevil displays with rattlesnakes, as well as food booths and live entertainment. | 915/263–7641.

**MAY:** *Big Spring Square Dance and Round Dance Festival.* In addition to various dances, this festival includes competitions and live entertainment. | 915/263–7641.

**JUNE:** *Nature Walks and Sunset Tales.* Every Sat. evening in June, Big Spring State Park offers a guided ½-mi hike to a woodland pavilion where you can listen to Texas legends and historical stories and watch the sun go down. | 915/263–4931.

**AUG.–SEPT.:** *Howard County Fair.* The Howard County Fairgrounds hosts live entertainment, dancing, food booths, and the "battle of the cheerleaders." | 915/263–7641 or 800/734–7641.

## Dining

**Red Mesa Grill.** Tex-Mex. The Southwestern-style decor includes Mexican tile floors and cacti and longhorn cattle skulls throughout. Menu options include soft tacos and fajitas, mesquite-grilled steak, and huge salads like the Fandango (grilled chicken with mixed greens, black olives, avocado, cheddar cheese, bell peppers, and tomatoes, served with hot sauce or honey-mustard dressing). The homemade guacamole, green and red chili sauces, and salsa are all intensely popular. | 2401 S. Gregg St. | 915/263–2205 | Closed Sun. | $6–$17 | AE, D, DC, MC, V.

## Lodging

**Best Western Mid-Continent Inn.** This motel is 4 mi from a mall and is 3 mi from a scenic mountain park. There is a restaurant next door at the truck stop. Complimentary Continental breakfast, room service, cable TV, pool. | 700 I–20W | 915/267–1601 | fax 915/267–6916 | 155 rooms | $48–$64 | AE, D, DC, MC, V.

**Econolodge.** Rooms have exterior access in this two-story motel 1 mi north of downtown Big Spring via Rte. 87. Complimentary Continental breakfast, in-room data ports, some microwaves, some refrigerators, cable TV, pool, exercise equipment, business services, pets allowed. | 804 I–20W | 915/263–5200 | fax 915/263–5457 | 50 rooms | $55–$65 | AE, D, DC, MC, V.

# BOERNE

MAP 8, G5

*(Nearby towns also listed: Castroville, Comfort, San Antonio)*

Boerne (pronounced "Bernie") was founded in 1847 by German immigrants, members of the same group who settled nearby New Braunfels. They named the town for author Ludwig Börne, whose writings inspired many people to leave Germany for the New World.

During the 1880s, Boerne became known as a health spot, and vacationers came by railroad to soak in mineral water spas and enjoy the clean country air. Although no mineral spas remain today, this town of 6,100 is a popular weekend getaway for its Hill Country atmosphere and numerous antiques shops.

Information: **Boerne Chamber of Commerce** | One Main Plaza, Boerne, TX 78006 | 830/249–8000 or 888/842–8080 | boerne@boerne.org | www.boerne.org.

## Attractions

**Agricultural Heritage Center.** Historic farm equipment typical of that used in central and south Texas is on display. | Rte. 46 at City Park Rd. | 830/249–9373 | Free | Sun. 1:30–4:30, Wed. 1:30–4:30.

**Cascade Caverns.** These formation-filled caverns include a small lake. A 105-acre park surrounding the cave has picnic grounds. Take I–10 east to the Cascade Cavern Rd. exit. | 226 Cascade Caverns Rd. | 830/755–8080 | $9 | June–Aug., daily 9–6; Sept.–May, weekdays 10–4, weekends 9–5.

**Cave Without a Name.** Six major rooms are filled with cave formations and a subterranean river. | 325 Kreutzberg Rd. | 830/537–4212 | $8 | June–Aug., daily 9–6; Sept.–May, daily 10–4:30.

**Cibolo Wilderness Trail and Nature Center.** This protected area includes grasslands, marshlands, and woodlands, as well as a nature center with exhibits. The surrounding Wildscape Garden contains local plants that attract hummingbirds and butterflies. | Rte. 46 in Boerne City Park | 830/249–4616 | Free | Daily.

**Kuhlmann-King House Museum.** Built in the late 1880s, this home has a separate kitchen filled with period furnishings. | 420 E. Blanco | 830/249–2030 | Free | Sun. 1–4.

### ON THE CALENDAR

**MAR.:** *Hill Country Optimist Antique Show.* This large antiques show attracts dealers from around the state. | 830/995–3750 or 800/995–3670.

**JUNE:** *Boerne Berges Fest.* German music is provided by the Boerne Village Band (the oldest continuously active German band in the country and the oldest in the world outside of Munich), but there are also country-and-western entertainment, crafts, food, horseshoe pitching, an egg toss, canoe races, and parades. | 830/249–8000 or 888/842–8080.

## Dining

**Boerne Bistro.** Continental. A two-story wall with bookshelves holding vases, pictures, and other curios dominates this restaurant's dining area. The menu includes grilled salmon with spinach cream sauce and blackened filet mignon served with garlic–mashed potatoes and a vegetable medley. Dessert-lovers can dig into the seven-layer chocolate cake or hot bread pudding with caramel-pecan sauce. | 911 S. Main St. | 830/249–9563 or 888/282–7722 | $7–$15 | AE, D, DC, MC, V.

**Family Korner.** Southern. Fried chicken and roast beef are popular at this casual family restaurant adorned with antiques. Kids' menu. | 1234 Main St. | 830/249–3054 | No lunch | $6–$11 | D, MC, V.

**Peach Tree Kountry Kitchen.** Southern. This family restaurant, housed in an 1896 Victorian home, serves up meatloaf, soups, burgers, and chicken-fried steak, as well as pecan chicken and peach cobbler. | 448 S. Main St. | 830/249–8583 | Closed Sun., Mon. No supper | $7–$10 | AE, D, DC, MC, V.

## Lodging

**Guadalupe River Ranch.** Built in the 1920s, this ranch was once home to actress Olivia de Havilland. The inviting sitting rooms, rock fireplaces, solarium, and stone Mayan-style grotto add to its old-fashioned Texas-style glamour. The 360 acres surrounding the ranch are home to longhorn cattle and horses, as well as deer, armadillos, turkeys, and Corsican sheep. Most rooms have views of the cypress-lined Guadalupe River or the canyon; others have a shared courtyard, many with screened-in porches. Restaurant, complimentary breakfast, in-room data ports, some minibars, some refrigerators, 2 pools, hot tub, massage, sauna, spa, tennis, exercise equipment, hiking, horseback riding, fishing, bicycles, business services, no pets. | 605 FM 474 | 830/537–4837 or 800/460–2005 | fax 830/537–5249 | grranch@gvtc.com | www.guadaluperiverranch.com | 46 rooms | $239–$309 | MAP | AE, D, DC, MC, V.

**Ye Kendall Inn.** The center section of this historic, two-story downtown hotel was built in 1859. Over the years, guests of the hotel have included Robert E. Lee and Dwight D. Eisenhower. Restaurant, bar, cable TV. | 128 W. Blanco St. | 800/364–2138 | fax 830/249–2138 | 17 rooms | $85–$160 | AE, D, DC, MC, V.

# BONHAM

MAP 8, J2

*(Nearby towns also listed: Dallas, Paris, Sherman)*

This North Texas community of 10,000 just south of the Red River is set in fertile Blackland Prairie. Bonham is best known as the home of the late Sam Rayburn, former Speaker of the U.S. House of Representatives. The hometown hero is remembered with the Sam Rayburn House (his former dwelling) and the Sam Rayburn Library and Museum, which includes a replica of his office in Washington, DC.

Information: **Bonham Chamber of Commerce** | 110 E. 1st St., Bonham, TX 75418 | 903/583–4811.

## Attractions

**Bonham State Park.** Camping, fishing, swimming, and boating are all available here. The park also has miniature golf, a playground, and pedal boat rentals. Take Rte. 78 1½ mi southeast of Bonham to Rte. 271, then drive 2 mi southeast. | Enter at Park Rd. 24 | 903/583–5022 | www.tpwd.state.tx.us | $2 | Daily 8 AM–10 PM.

**Fannin County Museum of History.** A restored railroad depot ca. 1900 serves as home to this area museum, showcasing the development of the county through the mid-20th century. Highlights include Native American artifacts, Sulphur River fossils, and antique clothing and toys. The building also houses the Red River Art Gallery, which contains the work of area artists and special traveling exhibits. | 1 Main St. | 903/583–8042 | Donation | Apr.–Labor Day, Tues.–Sat. 10–4; Labor Day–Mar., Tues.–Sat. 12–4.

**Fort Inglish Village.** This village contains a replica of a stockade that surrounded Fort Inglish, built in 1837. The village also has an authentic 1849 cabin. | Bonham City Park, Chinner St. and Rte. 56 | 903/640–2228 | Free | Apr.–Aug., Tues.–Fri. 10–4, Sat. 1–4.

**Sam Rayburn House.** Home of the former speaker of the U.S. House of Representatives, this 1916 home is filled with original furniture. | U.S. 82, 2 mi west of Bonham | 903/583–5558 | fax 903/640–0800 | Free | Tues.–Fri. 8–5, Sat. 1–5, Sun. 2–5.

**Sam Rayburn Library and Museum.** This library includes a replica of Rayburn's office in the U.S. Capitol building, and memorabilia from his long term in office—which was the longest of any Speaker of the House in history. | 800 W. Sam Rayburn Dr. | 903/583–2455 | fax 903/583–7394 | Free | Weekdays 9–5, Sat. 1–5, Sun. 2–5.

### ON THE CALENDAR
**OCT.:** *Autumn in Bonham Bike Rally.* An 11–68 mi ride through Fannin county kicks of the festivities, and church group and youth organization activities on the town square follow. An evening goat roast at the Homestead Winery wraps things up. | 903/583–4811.
**OCT.:** *Fannin County Fair.* Fort Inglish Park hosts a carnival, junior livestock show, rides, games, food booths, live entertainment, and children's activities. | 903/583–7453.

## Dining
**Hickory Barbecue.** Barbecue. Get your dinner by the plate or pound at this pared-down family-style restaurant with wooden images of Texas and Oklahoma festooned with barbed wire on the walls. Enthusiastic regulars line up in the bi-level dining area for cafeteria-style servings of barbecued ham, turkey, chopped or sliced beef, sausage, hot links, and ribs. Homemade desserts include banana pudding, cherry crunch, and peach cobbler. | 208 E. San Rayburn Dr. | 903/583–3081 | Reservations not accepted | Closed Sun., Mon. | $4–$9 | No credit cards.

## Lodging
**Granny Lou's Bed and Breakfast.** Named for the proprietor's mother, this three-story turn-of-the-20th-century Victorian B&B has somewhat formal accommodations. Guest rooms may include a queen-size rosewood Victorian bed, a queen-size Louis XV–style bed in a turret, a claw-foot tub, and a small private balcony. The backyard deck overlooks an expansive lawn. Dining room, complimentary breakfast, in-room data ports, some in-room hot tubs, cable TV, library, no pets, no kids under 12. | 317 West Sam Rayburn Dr. | 903/583–7912 or 800/997–7912 | bmoore@grannylou.com | www.grannylou.com | 4 rooms, 1 cottage | $75–$105, $125 cottage | AE, D, MC, V.

# BRACKETTVILLE

MAP 8, F6

*(Nearby town also listed: Del Rio)*

Brackettville began as the home of Fort Clark, built by the U.S. Cavalry in 1852 to protect the frontier from Indian attacks and later serving as a German POW camp during World War II. Through the years this town of 3,200 was home to many famous military personalities, including Gen. George S. Patton.

Even if you've never visited the region, you just might recognize the Brackettville area thanks to the movies. The town is home to Alamo Village, a family amusement park and frequently used movie set. The village is built around a replica of the Alamo that was constructed for the John Wayne movie of the same name.

Information: **Kinney County Chamber of Commerce** | Box 386, Brackettville, TX 78832 | 830/563–2466 | www.brackettville.com.

## Attractions

**Alamo Village.** Built for the movie *The Alamo*, starring John Wayne, this park is now used by many movie and television production companies as a Wild West set. You can tour the sets, have lunch in a Western cantina, and see a Wild West show. | Rte. 674, 7 mi north of Brackettville | 830/563–9226 | fax 830/563–2580 | $6 | Daily 9–5 | www.alamovillage.com | alamovillage@email.com.

**Kinney County Heritage Museum.** Built in 1884 by Giovanni B. Filippone and once a general store, today this two-story museum contains an assortment of historical photographs, religious iconography, tools and household implements, and other artifacts. | El Paso St. at James St. | 830/563–2466 | Donation | 2nd and 4th Sat. of each month, 1–4.

### ON THE CALENDAR

**SEPT.:** *Seminole Indian Celebration.* This two-day event commemorates the lives and achievements of Native American Seminole scouts who worked for the U.S. Cavalry stationed at Fort Clark during the 19th century. (Some of the scouts were honored with a Medal of Honor for their bravery.) There are historical displays to view, as well as food and art-and-crafts for sale. | 830/563–2466.

## Dining

**Las Moras Restaurant.** Continental. Part of historic Fort Clark, this restaurant is the former officer's club, and retains a resemblance to its rustic Colonial past. You can visit the cavalry room and dine amid photographs of the officers and other notables hanging on the walls while fires crackle in the working fireplaces. The menu includes prime rib, platters of catfish and shrimp, bowls of cheese or brothy seafood soup, and daily specials such as meatloaf with green beans and mashed potatoes. The restaurant is 1 mi east of downtown Bracketville. | U.S. 90 | 830/563–2290 | Breakfast also available. No supper Sun. | $5–$12 | AE, D, MC, V.

## Lodging

**Fort Clark Springs.** This two-story motel is on the former site of Fort Clark. Restaurant, bar, cable TV, pool. | Off U.S. 90W | 830/563–2493 | fax 915/263–2790 | 38 rooms | $48–$58 | AE, D, MC, V.

# BRAZOSPORT

MAP 8, J6

*(Nearby towns also listed: Galveston, Houston)*

Located in south Texas at the mouth of the Brazos and San Bernard rivers, this multi-community approximately 50 miles south of Houston comprises nine cities: Brazoria, Clute, Freeport, Jones Creek, Lake Jackson, Oyster Creek, Quintana, Richwood, and Surfside Beach. Brazosport is best known for its fishing—both saltwater and freshwater. Its 44 mi of sandy beaches, green forests, and coastal plains make this a popular tourist area.

Information: **Brazosport Convention and Visitors Council** | 420 Rte. 332 W, Brazosport, TX 77531 | 979/265–2505.

## Attractions

**Brazoria National Wildlife Refuge.** Over 42,000 acres on the Gulf Intercoastal Waterway constitutes this bird-watcher's dream, a nesting area for mottled ducks, wintering grounds for snow geese, and home to nearly 250 species of birds. Drive or hike through, or enter

BRAZOSPORT

INTRO
ATTRACTIONS
DINING
LODGING

by boat (fishing, crabbing, and oystering are allowed in public areas). Call ahead for information and additional open hours by appointment. | Off Rte. 227, Freeport | 979/849–6062 | fax 979/849–5118 | Free | Sept.–May, weekdays 8–4.

**Brazosport Museum of Natural Science.** Exhibits on local natural history, the Brazos river, and the freshwater and saltwater regions that surround Brazosport are the focus of this museum. | 400 College Dr., Clute | 979/265–7831 | Free | Tues.–Sat. 10–5, Sun. 2–5.

**City Docks.** You can view cargo ships from around the globe at these docks. This bustling area is the heart of Brazosport's economy. | 1001 Navigation Blvd., Freeport | 979/233–2667 | fax 979/233–5625 | Free | Daily.

## ON THE CALENDAR
**APR.: *Annual Bird Migration*.** Visit the Brazoria National Wildlife Refuge and see up to 30 warbler species as the prairieland is transformed into a wildflower paradise. Although also occurring in Mar. and May, the highest concentration of migrating shorebirds is during Apr. | 979/849–6062.
**JULY: *Great Mosquito Festival*.** Live entertainment, food booths, and arts and crafts are part of this event. | 979/265–2505.

## Dining
**Dido's.** Seafood. Right on the San Bernard River, boaters pull up to the dock and order the good-size burger or seafood platter. Landlubbers can sit on the screened-in porch cooled by ceiling fans, or at a table indoors and choose one of the fish dinners. Try the grilled shrimp, pickled shrimp, or fried calamari, and save room for the piña colada cake. Salad bar. Kids' menu. | Rte. 519, Brazoria | 979/964–3167 | Closed Mon.–Wed. No lunch Thurs., Fri. | $4–$16 | AE, D, MC, V.

**Small Town Cafe.** American. Big breakfasts, po' boy sandwiches, burgers, steaks, seafood, and large salads are what you'll find here. With such starters as stuffed jalapeño peppers and crab "ringoons" (crabmeat blended with cream cheese, wrapped in phyllo dough and baked) and specials such as the all-you-can-eat catfish and shrimp dinner with seafood gumbo or bisque, hush puppies, and seasoned fries, who cares that they don't have any dessert? Kids' menu. | 511 S. Brooks St., Brazoria | 979/798–7055 | Reservations not accepted | Breakfast also available | $4–$14 | No credit cards.

## Lodging
**Country Hearth Inn.** This two-story motel is adjacent to a seafood restaurant and only five mi to the beach. Cable TV, pool. | 1015 W. Second St., Freeport | 979/239–1602 or 800/848–5767 | fax 979/239–2326 | 40 rooms | $52–$70 | AE, D, MC, V.

**Days Inn.** Basic rooms have two double beds and exterior corridors. The motel is 7 mi from Newport Beach. Complimentary Continental breakfast, some refrigerators, cable TV, pool, exercise equipment, laundry facilities, business services, no pets. | 805 Rte. 332, Clute | 979/265–3301 or 800/544–8313 | fax 409/265–3301 | www.daysinn.com | 98 rooms | $39–$59 | AE, D, DC, MC, V.

**Holiday Inn Express.** Several restaurants and a shopping mall are just blocks from this two-story motel. The beach is 8 mi away. Complimentary Continental breakfast, in-room data ports, some microwaves, refrigerators, cable TV, pool, hot tub, business services. | 809 Rte. 332W, Clute | 979/265–5252 | fax 979/265–8185 | www.holidayinn.com | 60 rooms | $69–$84 | AE, D, DC, MC, V.

**La Quinta.** This two-story motel is less than 1 mi from several restaurants, and 2 mi from a mall and a theater. Complimentary Continental breakfast, in-room data ports, cable TV, pool, exercise equipment, some pets allowed. | 1126 Rte. 332W, Clute | 979/265–7461 | fax 979/265–3804 | www.laquinta.com | 135 rooms | $49–$65 | AE, D, DC, MC, V.

**Ramada Inn.** The waters of the Gulf are about 10 mi from this two-story hotel. It's within walking distance of several restaurants and 2 mi from a mall. Restaurant, bar, room service, cable TV, pool, some pets allowed. | 925 Rte. 332W, Lake Jackson | 979/297–1161 | fax 979/297–1249 | ramadainn@computron.net | www.ramada.com | 144 rooms | $117 | AE, D, DC, MC, V.

**Roses and the River Bed and Breakfast.** Green lawns slope towards the shore of the San Bernard River, and the long verandas, rose gardens, and rocking chairs may beckon you to while away an afternoon reading or woolgathering. Attractive, sun-filled rooms in the black-shuttered, Texas farmhouse–style B&B overlook the gardens or the river. Breakfast fare could be grapefruit baked Alaska, lemon pancakes, and apple enchiladas. Dining room, complimentary breakfast, some in-room hot tubs, cable TV, in-room VCRs (and movies), dock, no pets, no kids under 12, no smoking. | 7074 Rte. 506, Brazoria | 979/798–1070 or 800/610–1070 | hosack@roses-and-the-river.com | www.roses-and-the-river.com | 3 rooms | $125 | AE, D, MC, V.

# BRENHAM

*(Nearby town also listed: Bryan/College Station)*

Founded by German settlers in 1844, this community of 14,000 is the gateway to Washington-on-the-Brazos State Historical Park, which includes historical buildings and a museum devoted to Texas history. The city is also home to the state's biggest independent manufacturer of ice cream (you might want to tour the plant).

**Information: Brenham/Washington County Convention and Visitors Bureau** | 314 S. Austin St., Brenham, TX 77833 | 979/836–3695 | brenham@brenhamtx.org | www.brenhamtexas.com.

## Attractions

**Antique Rose Emporium.** Specializing in antique varieties of roses, this nursery also has extensive displays. It's on Rte. 50, 12 mi northeast of Brenham. | 10,000 Rte. 50 | 979/836–5548 | fax 979/836–7236 | www.antiqueroseemporium.com | Free | Mon.–Sat. 9–6, Sun. 11–5:30.

**Blue Bell Creamery.** This factory produces Texas's best-selling ice cream. Tours end with a taste of the local product. Hours are subject to change, so call in advance. | Rte. 577, 2½ mi north of U.S. 290 | 979/830–2197 or 800/327–8135 | fax 979/830–2177 | www.bluebell.com | $2 | Weekdays, 10–2.

**Chappell Hill Historic District.** On the National Register of Historic Places, here you will find antebellum homes, antiques stores, restaurants, and craft shops. Stop at the Chappell Hill Bank, still in operation since 1907. For more information, contact the Chappell Hill Historical Society. | U.S. 290, 8 mi east of Brenham | 979/836–6033 | Free. | Daily.

**Historical Markers Trail.** Pick up a Washington County Historical Markers Guide—available for free at the Brenham Visitor Center—and proceed on a self-guided tour with over 120 possibilities. Visit the site of the signing of the Texas Declaration of Independence, the place where Sam Houston was baptized, an 1800s cotton gin, and the resting places of Texas heroes. | 314 S. Austin St. | 409/836–3695 | Free | Daily.

**Lake Somerville State Park and Trailway.** Lake Somerville has a full menu of water activities in two areas, Birch Creek and the Nails Creek. Over 14 mi of trails are available for horseback riding, as well as mountain biking and hiking. Campgrounds can be used by backpackers and equestrians. | Birch Creek: off Rte. 36 on Park Rd. 57; Nails Creek: off U.S. 290 on Rte. 180 | 979/535–7763 | fax 979/289–2251 | www.tpwd.state.tx.us | $2 | Daily 8 AM–10 PM.

**Monastery of St. Clare Miniature Horse Ranch.** This monastery is occupied by a group of Catholic nuns who raise miniature horses to support themselves. The tiny horses, some less than 34 inches tall, sell for anywhere from $3,000 to $30,000. On self-guided tours you see the barn and grooming facilities (with miniature carriages and harnesses) and the Mini Mansion where the horses are reared. The Art Barn brims with thousands of ceramics made by the nuns, including tiny reproductions of the horses. | 9300 Rte. 105 | 979/836–9652 | Free | Daily 2–4.

**Stephen F. Austin State Historical Park.** In addition to golfing, camping, bird watching, and fishing, you can take a historic guided nature hike or a historic tour of the former township of San Felipe. | Rte. 1458 to Park Rd. 38 in San Felipe | 979/885–3613 | fax 979/885–3383 | www.tpwd.state.tx.us | $3 | Daily 8 AM–10 PM.

**Texas Baptist Historical Center.** The church attended by Sam Houston is the oldest active Baptist church in Texas. Baylor University began here. | 10405 Rte. 50, Independence | 979/836–5117 | Free | Tues.–Sat. 9–4.

**Washington-on-the-Brazos State Historical Park.** This park includes a new 10,000-square-ft visitors center that traces the history of the area through interactive displays. You can learn more about the 59 men who gathered here on a cold March day in 1836 when Texas signed its own Declaration of Independence. To reach the park from Brenham, drive 14 mi northeast on Rte. 105, then 5 mi northeast on Rte. 912. | 23200 Park Rd. 12 | 979/878–2214 | www.starmuseum.org | Free for grounds; $6 for combination ticket for attractions | Daily.

**Barrington Farm,** the homestead of Anson Jones, the fourth and last president of the Republic of Texas, includes a two-story home that was relocated from behind the museum to the farm. An orchard, carriage shed, corn crib, kitchen, slave quarters, and demonstration crop acreage are found here. | Wed.–Sun. 9:30–4:30.

**Independence Hall** is a replica of the original building where the signing of the Texas Declaration of Independence took place. A new interpretive trail winds from Independence Hall to the historic Washington townsite. | 979/878–2214 | $4 for guided tour | Daily 10–5.

The **Star of the Republic Museum,** built in the shape of a star, highlights the history of the Republic of Texas with exhibits and special collections. Exhibits also cover all aspects of commerce during the 19th century, including displays on the general store, blacksmithing, steamboats, and carpentry. | 979/878–2461 | fax 979/878–2462 | $4 | Daily 10–5 | www.txpd.state.tx.us.

## ON THE CALENDAR

**MAR.:** *Texas Independence Day Celebration.* This event is held over the weekend of Texas Independence Day in Washington-on-the-Brazos State Historical Park, the "Birthplace of Texas." Activities include historical reenactments, musical performances, and tours of the historic park. | 979/878–2461.

**MAR.–APR.:** *Bluebonnet Trails/Wildflowers Tours.* Take a self-guided tour of blooming local bluebonnet fields, or partake in an arts and crafts fair held along Main St. | 888–BRENHAM.

**SEPT.:** *Washington County Fair.* This fair includes a livestock show and rodeo, arts and crafts, food, a carnival, and a greased pig contest. | 979/836–4112.

**DEC.:** *Downtown Christmas Stroll.* The Christmas holiday is celebrated with dancers, shopping, food, drinks, hayrides, and Christmas lights. | 979/836–3695.

## Dining

**K and G Restaurant.** Continental. This place has been in operation since the 1960s. The well-prepared standard fare includes steak and chicken dishes and seafood. There's a daily lunch buffet, and a Fri. night all-you-can-eat seafood buffet that includes frog's legs, crispy shrimp, and homemade onion rings. Salad bar. | 2209 South Market St. | 979/836–7950 | Breakfast also available | $4–$16 | AE, D, MC, V.

**Volare Italian Restaurant.** Italian. You might want to start off your meal at this popular place just off the courthouse square with mushrooms stuffed with crabmeat, spinach, and Parmesan. Popular entrées include the chicken cooked with mushrooms and Marsala wine, and the salmon with glazed onions and artichokes in a creamy lemon dill sauce. Homemade bread, desserts. | 205 S. Baylor St. | 979/836–1514 | Closed Mon., Tues. | $7–$19 | AE, D, MC, V.

## Lodging

**Ant Street Inn.** Antiques and turn-of-the-20th-century pieces can be found in this 1899 property. Complimentary breakfast, in-room data ports, cable TV, business services, no kids under 12, no smoking. | 107 W. Commerce St. | 979/836–7393 or 800/481–1951 | fax 979/836–7595 | www.antstreetinn.com | 14 rooms (5 with shower only) | $95–$235 | AE, D, MC, V.

**Heart of My Heart Ranch.** This log, lakeside home was built in 1828. Six of the guest rooms have fireplaces. Picnic area, complimentary breakfast, some kitchenettes, microwaves, refrigerators, in-room VCRs (and movies), pool, hot tubs, massage, driving range, playground, business services, no smoking. | 403 Florida Chapel Rd., Round Top | 979/249–3171 or 800/327–1242 | fax 979/249–3193 | www.heartofmyheartranch.com | 13 rooms (1 with shower only), 4 suites, in 4 buildings | $135–$195, $175–$255 suites | AE, D, MC, V.

**Holiday Inn Express.** At the junction of U.S. 290W and I–36, this two-story hotel is well-situated for those passing through town. The Blue Bell Creamery is about 5 mi away. Complimentary Continental breakfast, in-room data ports, some microwaves, some refrigerators, some in-room hot tubs, cable TV, pool, outdoor hot tub, laundry facilities, laundry service, business services, no pets. | 555 U.S. 290W | 979/836–4590 or 800/465–4329 | fax 979/836–4330 | 57 rooms | $60–$84 | AE, D, DC, MC, V.

# BROWNSVILLE

MAP 8, H9

*(Nearby towns also listed: Mission, South Padre Island)*

The southernmost city in Texas, Brownsville evolved from Fort Brown, which was strategically placed along the Rio Grande to defend the area as a U.S. boundary line when Texas became a state. The establishment of the fort started the Mexican–American War.

Today this city of 150,000 is the largest community in the Rio Grande Valley, and serves as a gateway into Mexico. The area is a favorite with birders who come to have a look at the more than 370 species that have been identified in the region.

Information: **Brownsville Convention and Visitors Bureau** | Box 4697, Brownsville, TX 78523 | 956/546–3972 or 800/626–2639 | visinfo@brownsville.org | www.brownsville.org.

## Attractions

**Gladys Porter Zoo.** This 31-acre zoo is home to 1,900 animals, most contained by waterways rather than fences. | 500 Ringgold St. | 956/546–2177 | fax 956/541–4940 | www.gpz.org | $6.50 | Daily 9–5.

**Matamoros, Tamaulipas, Mexico.** This border town across U.S. 281 has a variety of stores, restaurants, and evening entertainment venues. You can walk across the international bridge, then take a taxi to the mercado. The tourist office is a few blocks from the border bridge at Tamaulipas and Obregón (Daily 8–6); there you can pick up various leaflets and maps of Matamoros. | Mercado Juárez: Calles 9 and 10.

**Palo Alto Battlefield National Historic Site.** The Battle of Palo Alto, the first major battle of the Mexican–American War, was held at this site in 1846. | Rte. 1847, near Rte. 511 | 956/541–2785 | fax 956/541–6356 | www.nps.gov/paal | Free | Weekdays 8:30–4:30.

**Port of Brownsville.** You can watch ships as they bring in cargo from around the world at this bustling port in the south end of town. | Foust Rd. | 956/831–4592 | Free | Daily.

**Stillman House Museum.** This 19th-century house was the residence of Charles Stillman, the founder of Brownsville. The rooms include many period furnishings. | 1305 E. Washington St. | 956/542–3929 | $2 | Weekdays 10–12, 2–5, Sun. 3–5.

### SIGHTSEEING TOURS/TOUR COMPANIES

**Surftran.** Guided bus tours include "Christmas Tours," "Border City Tours," and "One Day Tours." | 956/761–4343 or 800/321–8720 | www.gosurftran.com | $17–$45 | Daily.

### ON THE CALENDAR

**FEB.: *Charro Days.*** Held in Brownsville and Matamoros, Mexico, this festival includes carnivals, parades, and dancing. | 956/542–4245.

**MAR.: *Confederate Air Force Air Fiesta.*** The Brownsville/South Padre Island International Airport hosts WWII-era aircraft and displays of acrobatic stunt flying. | 956/541–8585.

## Dining

**Los Comparos.** Mexican. This casual spot has flowers and pictures of Mexico throughout. Known for chicken and steak. Entertainment Fri.-Sat. Kids' menu. | 1442 International Blvd. | 956/546–8172 | $9–$16 | AE, D, DC, MC, V.

**Mi Pueblito.** Mexican. Try the fajitas, ribs, or filet mignon while dining under a gigantic palapa (dried palm) roof at this restaurant within walking distance of the U.S./Mexico border. The spicy salsa and margaritas are popular. From downtown Brownsville, take the new bridge to Mexico, follow the road about ½ mi, and it's on the left hand side. | 011/52–88–16–05–86 | $6–$16 | AE, D, MC, V.

**Resaca Club.** Continental. Dine or drink an old-fashioned cocktail at a table right on the dance floor at this fun nightclub/restaurant in the Holiday Inn. If you're feeling daring, consider ordering one of the flaming entrées or desserts. The variety club–style entertainment could include singers, a choreographed floorshow, or a comedy act. | 1900 E. Elizabeth St. | 956/546–2201 | Reservations essential Fri., Sat. | No lunch | $7–$24.

**Valley Inn.** American. This casual restaurant has a view of a golf course. Try the red snapper or prime rib. Salad bar. | Ruben Torres Blvd. | 956/546–5331 | No supper Mon.–Wed., Sun. | $18–$23 | AE, D, DC, MC, V.

## Lodging

**Best Western Rose Garden.** The Gladys Porter Zoo and the U.S. border are both 10 mi from this two-story motel. Two shopping malls are 5 mi away. Complimentary Continental breakfast, some refrigerators, cable TV, pool, laundry facilities. | 845 Rte. 77N | 956/546–5501 | fax 956/546–6474 | 121 rooms | $42–$99 | AE, D, DC, MC, V.

**Comfort Inn.** Most rooms in this two-story motel have a single king-size bed or two queen-size beds; one bi-level room has 3 king-size beds and a full kitchen. It's 5 mi from the Brownsville/South Padre Island International Airport, and about the same distance to the bridge linking Brownsville to Matamoros, Mexico. Complimentary Continental breakfast, some kitchenettes, some microwaves, some refrigerators, cable TV, pool, business services, no pets. | 825 N. Expressway/U.S. 77/83 | 956/504–3331 | fax 956/546–0379 | www.comfortinn.com | 52 rooms | $55–$175 | AE, D, DC, MC, V.

**Days Inn.** This two-story motel is across the street from several 24-hour restaurants. The Brownsville/South Padre Island International Airport is 10 mi away. Restaurant, bar, some refrigerators, cable TV, pool, laundry facilities. | 715 Frontage Rd. | 956/541–2201 | fax 956/541–6011 | 124 rooms | $49–$54 | AE, D, DC, MC, V.

**Four Points by Sheraton.** Both the Gladys Porter Zoo and a 10-screen movie theater are within 5 mi of this two-story hotel. The Brownsville/South Padre Island International Airport is 7 mi away. Restaurant, bar (with entertainment), room service, in-room data ports, hot tub (in suites), refrigerators, cable TV, 2 pools, hot tub, business services, some pets allowed. | 3777 N. Expressway | 956/547–1500 | fax 956/350–4153 | www.sheraton.com | 141 rooms | $99–$109 | AE, D, DC, MC, V.

**Hawthorn Suites.** This three-story, all-suites hotel has an inviting lobby and one- to two-bedroom suites whose decor ranges from country-style plaids to handsome jewel tones.

The smaller suites are studios with an unpartitioned bedroom and living area; larger spaces have queen-size beds in individual bedrooms, a pullout couch, and a separate kitchen. Picnic area, complimentary Continental breakfast, in-room data ports, microwaves, refrigerators, cable TV, in-room VCRs (and movies), pool, exercise equipment, laundry facilities, laundry service, business services. | 3759 N. Expressway (U.S. 77/83) | 956/574–6900 or 800/527–1133 | fax 956/574–6910 | www.hawthorn.com | 86 suites | $89–$169 | AE, D, DC, MC, V.

**Holiday Inn.** This full-service hotel is on 12 acres of land filled with tropical plants and surrounded by a lagoon. Business travelers may appreciate the 5,000 square ft of meeting space. The hotel is two blocks from downtown Brownsville and the border with Matamoros, Mexico. A golf course is ½ mi away. 2 restaurants, bar with entertainment, room service, in-room data ports, cable TV, 2 pools, exercise equipment, baby-sitting, laundry facilities, laundry service, business services, no pets. | 1900 E. Elizabeth St. | 956/546–2201 | fax 956/546–0756 | www.holiday-inn.com | 154 rooms, 14 suites | $87–$137, $129–$200 suites | AE, D, DC, MC, V.

**Holiday Inn Fort Brown.** This two-story hotel is two blocks from the International Gateway Bridge. Restaurant, bar (with entertainment), room service, in-room data ports, cable TV, pool, business services, some pets allowed. | 1900 E. Elizabeth St. | 956/546–2201 | fax 956/546–0756 | www.holidayinn.com | 168 rooms | $72–$95 | AE, D, DC, MC, V.

**Motel 6.** Several restaurants and a mall are within walking distance of this motel. Cable TV, pool, pets allowed. | 2255 N. Expressway Feeder Rd. | 956/546–4699 | fax 956/546–8982 | www.motel6.com | 190 rooms | $36–$47 | AE, D, DC, MC, V.

**Rancho Viejo.** Rooms have clay pottery and lots of turquoise and green pieces throughout. The resort is 5 mi from several gourmet restaurants, shopping, and golf, and it's 12 mi from the Mexican border. Restaurant, bar (with entertainment), some kitchenettes, refrigerators (in suites), cable TV, pool, wading pool, barbershop, beauty salon, driving range, golf courses, putting green, tennis, business services. | 1 Rancho Viejo Dr., Rancho Viejo | 956/350–4000 or 800/531–7400 | fax 956/350–9681 | 55 rooms, 10 suites | $125–$150, $175–$325 suites | AE, D, DC, MC, V.

**Red Roof Inn.** A shopping mall and a 10-screen movie theater are across the street from this motel. Some refrigerators, cable TV, pool, hot tub, laundry facilities. | 2377 Rte. 83 N | 956/504–2300 or 800/843–7663 | fax 956/504–2303 | www.redroof.com | 124 rooms, 3 suites | $49–$58, $82 suites | AE, D, DC, MC, V.

BRYAN/
COLLEGE STATION

INTRO
ATTRACTIONS
DINING
LODGING

# BRYAN/COLLEGE STATION

MAP 8, I5

*(Nearby towns also listed: Brenham, Huntsville)*

These combined communities hold more than 126,000 residents and several attractions; the area is best known as home to Texas A&M University (the state's first public institution of higher education). The school is well-known for its agricultural, veterinary, and engineering programs as well as its military Cadet Corps.

Information: **Bryan-College Station Convention and Visitors Bureau** | 715 University Dr. E. 77840 | 979/260–9898 or 800/777–8292 | www.b-cs.com.

## Attractions

**Brazos Valley Museum of Natural History.** Founded in 1961, this museum devoted to natural history has a various permanent exhibits, such as "Cotton in the Brazos Valley" and "Ice Age Fossils." | 3232 Briarcrest Dr., Bryan | 979/776–2195 | bvmuseum.myriad.net | $6 | Mon.–Sat. 10–5.

**Children's Museum of the Brazos Valley.** This hands-on museum has exhibits for young children ranging from tabletop science to "Our Town Farmhouse." | 202 S. Bryan Ave., Bryan | 979/779–KIDS | fax 979/775–4908 | www.mymuseum.com | $3 | Tues.–Sat. 10–5.

**George Bush Presidential Library and Museum.** Dedicated in 1997, this library details the life and career of the nation's 41st president. | 1000 George Bush Dr. West, College Station | 979/260–9552 | www.csdl.tamu.edu/bushlib | $3 | Mon.–Sat. 9:30–5, Sun. 12–5.

**Messina Hof Wine Cellars.** Opened in 1983, this winery includes 45 acres of vineyards and demonstrates the wine-making skills of the Messina, Italy, and Hof, Germany, regions. Its restaurant serves lunch daily, and supper Wed.–Sat. | 4545 Old Reliance Road, Bryan | 979/778–9463 or 800/736–9463 | fax 979/778–1729 | www.messinahof.com | free | Weekdays 8:30–5:30, Sat. 10–5, Sun. 12–4.

**Texas A&M University.** The state's first public university, this institution is still one of Texas's best-known schools. Popular programs are agriculture, engineering, architecture, geoscience, medicine, and veterinary medicine. Tours of the campus are available with notice. | University Drive at Wellborn Rd. | 979/845–5851 | www.tamu.edu | Free | Daily.

## ON THE CALENDAR

**APR.: *Wine and Roses Festival.*** Along with a grape stomp, this festival includes food booths, crafts vendors, live music, and hay rides. | 979/778–9463.
**JULY, AUG.: *Harvest.*** Messina Hof Wine Cellars hosts grape picking, stomping, wine tastings, and wine seminars. | 979/778–9463.
**DEC.: *Holiday on the Brazos.*** The Christmas holiday is celebrated with crafts, live music, sports, and illuminated decorations. | 979/764–3773.

# Dining

**Cafe Eccell.** Contemporary. Fresh seafood, mesquite-grilled steaks, homemade desserts, and more are served in the former city hall building built in 1947. Have a drink at the bar and watch the chef cook your barbecued chicken pizza in the open wood-fired oven; or dine on one of the breezy outdoor patios, perhaps while enjoying the field green salad with walnuts, Gorgonzola, and poached pear vinaigrette. | 101 Church St., College Station | 979/846–7908 | www.cafeeccell.com | $6–$19 | AE, D, DC, MC, V.

**Cenare.** Italian. Stained glass windows, pictures of the Tuscan countryside, and candlelit tables dressed with white linen make this a favorite for both romantic dinners and quiet family gatherings. Try the veal Marsala, salmon Vesuvio (salmon broiled with jalapeño, garlic, and mushrooms), or fettucine. Homemade pasta. | 404 University Dr., College Station | 979/696–7311 | $8–$16 | AE, D, DC, MC, V.

**Christopher's World Grille.** Contemporary. Built in 1910, this former ranch house has individually decorated dining rooms. Black and white tile floors and a copper pot chandelier furnish the "galley"; the "living room" has matching monkey chandeliers and wall sconces; and the "dining room" features original stained-glass windows and a wooden buffet table. The Casablanca-style bar was hand-carved by Honduran artisans. Menu offerings include blackened oyster, spinach-stuffed filet mignon, snapper with lump crabmeat, and various chicken and pasta dishes. | 5001 Boonville Rd., Bryan | 979/776–2181 | Reservations essential weekends | Closed Mon. No lunch. No supper Sun.

**Jose's.** Tex-Mex. This casual, family-friendly restaurant has bright Mexican paintings, large tables, and a bustling waitstaff. Try the Pollo à la Parrilla (grilled chicken breast served with Spanish rice and guacamole salad), or the popular fajitas. Kids' menu. | 3824 Texas Ave. S., Bryan | 979/268–0036 | Closed Mon. | $15–$25 | AE, D, MC, V.

# Lodging

**Angelsgate Bed & Breakfast.** The leaded glass doors of this handsome, pale-blue American Foursquare home built in 1909 leads you into a spacious B&B, where your room may have a fireplace, sitting area, or claw-foot tub. The gazebo, sun porch, and parlor are nice places to relax. Dining room, complimentary breakfast, some kitchenettes, some refrigerators, cable TV, library, no pets, no kids under 12, no smoking. | 615 E. 29th St., Bryan | 979/779–1231 or 888/779–1231 | fax 409/775–7024 | www.angelsgate.com | 3 rooms | $100–$120 | AE, MC, V.

**Best Western Inn at Chimney Hill.** Easterwood Airport and a shopping mall are 5 mi from this two-story motel. Texas A&M University is 1½ mi away. Bar, complimentary Continental breakfast, cable TV, pool, laundry facilities. | 901 University St. E. | 979/260–9150 | fax 979/846–0467 | 98 rooms | $62–$69 | AE, D, DC, MC, V.

**Comfort Inn.** A number of chain restaurants are within a two-block radius, and Easterwood Airport is 3 mi away from this three-story hotel. Picnic area, complimentary Continental breakfast, cable TV, pool, hot tub, laundry facilities, airport shuttle. | 104 Texas Ave. S | 979/846–7333 | fax 979/846–5479 | 116 rooms | $69–$130 | AE, D, DC, MC, V.

**Fairfield Inn by Marriott.** Built in 1994, this three-story hotel is a few blocks from Texas A&M University and 3 mi from a mall. Complimentary Continental breakfast, some microwaves, cable TV, indoor pool, hot tub, video games. | 4613 Texas Ave. S | 979/268–1552 | fax 979/268–1552 | www.marriotthotels.com | 62 rooms | $65–$80 | AE, D, DC, MC, V.

**Hampton Inn.** Easterwood Airport is 3 mi from this four-story hotel, and several restaurants are within short walking distance. Complimentary Continental breakfast, in-room data ports, cable TV, pool, business services, airport shuttle, free parking. | 320 Texas Ave. S | 979/846–0184 | fax 979/268–5807 | www.hampton-inn.com | 135 rooms | $68–$78 | AE, D, DC, MC, V.

**Hilton.** This 11-story hotel is the only full-service accommodation in the Bryan/College Station area. As with most hotels in the area, it's close to Texas A&M University—about 1½ mi west via University Dr. E. Restaurant, bar, complimentary Continental breakfast, in-room data ports, some microwaves, some refrigerators, some in-room hot tubs, some in-room VCRs, pool, outdoor hot tub, exercise equipment, laundry service, business services, pets allowed. | 801 University Dr. E, College Station | 979/693–7500 or 800/445–86 | fax 979/260–6720 | www.hiltoncs.com | 250 rooms, 53 suites | $89–$185, $109–$260 suites | AE, D, DC, MC, V.

**La Quinta.** This two-story motel is across the street from Texas A&M University and 5 mi from Easterwood Airport. Picnic area, complimentary Continental breakfast, in-room data ports, cable TV, pool, airport shuttle, pets allowed. | 607 Texas Ave. S | 979/696–7777 | fax 979/696–0531 | www.laquinta.com | 176 rooms | $69–$79 | AE, D, DC, MC, V.

**Manor House.** All rooms have exterior access in this two-story motel 6 mi from Easterwood Airport. Complimentary Continental breakfast, in-room data ports, refrigerators, cable TV, pool, airport shuttle, pets allowed (fee). | 2504 Texas Ave. S, College Station | 979/764–9540 or 800/231–4100 | fax 979/693–2430 | 115 rooms | $51–$79 | AE, D, DC, MC, V.

**7 F Lodge Bed and Breakfast.** You can stroll through woods and pastures, meditate in a little chapel, then return to your private cottage amid live oaks and yaupon thickets. Breakfast comes in a basket delivered to your room, and could contain fresh whole fruit, pain au chocolat, breakfast quiche, and coffee. Complimentary breakfast, microwaves, refrigerators, some in-room hot tubs, no room phones, no TV, pond, no pets, no kids, no smoking. | 16611 Royder Rd., College Station | 979/690–0073 | fax 979/690–7377 | 7flodge@txcyber.com | 3 cottages | $150 | AE, D, MC, V.

BRYAN/
COLLEGE STATION

INTRO
ATTRACTIONS
DINING
LODGING

# BURNET

*(Nearby towns also listed: Georgetown, Johnson City, Marble Falls)*

This town of 5,000 was founded in 1849 as Hamilton. It grew up around Fort Croghan and was re-named in 1858 after David G. Burnet, the provisional president of the Republic of Texas. Its proximity to Lake Buchanan makes it a good place to stop for picnic supplies and sunscreen products during summer visits (be warned: there are few facilities once you leave the city limits). Outdoor activities, including spelunking and bird-watching, are popular throughout the year.

Information: **Burnet Chamber of Commerce** | 703 Buchanan Dr., 78611 | 512/756–4297 | bchamber@tstar.net | www.burnetchamber.org.

## Attractions

**Fall Creek Vineyards.** On the northwestern shores of Lake Buchanan between graceful ranges of limestone and granite in Llano county, this Texas hill country location provides an excellent climate for growing wine grapes, and a nice setting for a leisurely tour of the vineyards and Fall Creek Ranch. | 1820 Rte. 222, Tow | 915/379–5361 | www.fcv.com | Free | Weekdays 11–4, Sat. 12–5, Sun. 12–4.

**Fort Croghan Museum.** Constructed in the 1840s, this was one of eight forts built from the Rio Grande to the Trinity Rivers to protect the region from Indian attacks. Exhibits include household items used by residents in the 19th century. Walking tours cover the fort, the blacksmith shop, the powder house, and a two-room cabin. | 703 Buchanan Dr. (entrance on Rte. 29) | 512/756–8281 | Free | Apr.–Sept., Thur.–Sat. 10–5.

**Inks Lake State Park.** This 2,000-acre park offers golfing, camping, lakeside picnicking, and swimming. | Rte. 29 to Park Rd. 4 | 512/793–2223 or 512/389–8900 | fax 512/793–2065 | www.tpwd.state.tx.us | $4 | Daily.

**Lake Buchanan.** Contained by one of the largest multiple-arch dams in the world, this lake covers 23,000 acres and spans more than 30 mi. For a good look at the dam, walk out on the observation site—a concrete walkway built over part of the dam. You can also stop by the Chamber office for brochures and maps. Spend a few minutes in the museum across from the Chamber; it showcases life in this area in the early 1900s, the construction of the dam, and wildlife in the lake region. | Rte. 29, 11 mi northwest of Barnett, towards Llano | 512/793–2803 | Free | Weekdays 9–5.

**Longhorn Cavern State Park.** This dry cavern has few formations, but it does have an interesting history including a Comanche kidnapping of a young woman and her rescue by a Texas Ranger she later married. The guided tour is nonstrenuous, with wide, well-lit trails through the huge limestone rooms. | From Burnet: 6 mi on U.S. 281, then 5 mi west on Park Rd. 4 | 830/598–CAVE | www.tpwd.state.tx.us | $8 | Weekdays 10–4, weekends 10–5.

**Vanishing Texas River Cruise.** Cold-weather cruises offer a look at American bald eagles that nest along the upper reaches of Lake Buchanan, while in the summer you'll see perhaps deer, feral hogs, and wild turkey as they come from the hills to drink at the river's edge. | Office: 433 Waterway Ln | 512/756–6986 or 800/728–8735 | fax 512/756–4249 | $15 | Daily, by appointment.

## ON THE CALENDAR

**MAR., APR.: *Bluebonnet Festival.*** Self-guided look at annual blooms; crafts shows, art shows, food booths. Bus tours available. | Burnet, Buchanan Dam, Kingsland, Lampasas, Llano, Marble Falls | 512/793–2803.
**JUNE: *Burnet County Fair and Rodeo.*** | There are lots of kid-centered events during this three-day extravaganza, including the show of steers and heifers raised by chil-

dren. For adults, the rodeo portion includes bronco busting, bull riding, steer wrestling, and calf roping, with dances in the evening. Other highlights include a carnival, a flea market, Western crafts, and plenty of food vendors | 512/756–2359.

## Dining

**Burnet Country BBQ.** Barbecue. This casual family restaurant is reminiscent of a rustic log cabin. It serves authentic, pit-cooked barbecue that includes smoked meats, sausage, brisket, and ribs. | 616 Buchanan Dr. | 512/756–6468 | Closed Mon., Tues. | $6–$9 | No credit cards.

**Gude's Bakery and Deli.** Delicatessens. People come to this popular spot as early as 5:30 AM for homemade donuts or kolaches (Czechoslovakian pastries with a sweet dough, filled with cream cheese, fruit, or savory sausage). For lunch, sandwiches reign supreme, from the hot roast beef with Swiss cheese that's baked in the oven to the "everything," with ham, beef, turkey, salami, several cheeses, and spicy mustard on homemade bread. | 307 W. Polk St. | 512/715–9903 | Reservations not accepted | Breakfast also available. Closed Sun. No supper | $4–$6 | No credit cards.

**Riverwalk Cafe.** American. A Holstein cow statuette guards the door at this homestyle café filled with an eclectic mix of rodeo, airplane, motorcycle, and railroad memorabilia. Try the barbecue or teriyaki chicken, one of the many steak dishes, or the chicken and seafood croquettes. Salad bar. | 635 Rte. 29 W | 512/756–4100 | Breakfast also available. Closed Mon. No supper Sun. | $3–$12 | No credit cards.

## Lodging

**Canyon of the Eagles Lodge.** On Lake Buchanan in a 940-acre nature park, this out-of-the-way place has 2 mi of trails, a 5-mi beach, a general store, and an astronomical observatory. Bird-watchers might spot a bald eagle, black-capped vireo, and golden-cheeked warbler. Guest rooms have porches, most of which are equipped with rocking chairs. Restaurant, bar, in-room data ports, some microwaves, some refrigerators, pool, hiking, beach, boating, fishing, business services, pets allowed (fee). | 16942 Ranch Rd. 2341 | 512/756–8787 or 800/977–0081 | fax 512/715–9819 | www.canyonoftheeagles.com | 64 rooms | $87–$127 | AE, MC, V.

# CANTON

MAP 8, J3

*(Nearby town also listed: Dallas)*

Once known primarily for its thriving farming and livestock market, Canton is now widely recognized for its "First Monday Trade Days," an enormous flea market that runs for four days every month. Canton serves as the seat of Van Zandt County and has a population of 3,000.

**Information: Canton Chamber of Commerce** | 315 First Monday Ln., Canton, TX 75103 | 903/567–2991 | cantoncc@vzinet.com | www.cantontx.com.

## Attractions

**First Monday Trade Days.** Every month 6,000 dealers descend on Canton and fill the town with antiques and arts and crafts, creating a large and very popular flea market. The first day (Thurs.) is just for vendors to set up. | Throughout town | 903/567–2991 | Free; parking $3 | Thurs.–Sun. prior to first Mon. of each month 8–5:30.

**Blackwell House Museum.** One of Canton's most popular museums resides in the oldest house in town. The residence was built in 1886 for Henry F. Blackwell II and his wife Nannie Jane Blackwell, who were early Canton merchants. It's filled with antiques and furnishings that date back to the early 1900s and belonged to the Blackwell family. | 315 First Monday Ln | 903–567–2991 | Free | Weekdays 8–5:30.

**Backward S Ranch.** When visiting this working ranch northeast of Canton you can view the beautiful Tennessee Walking Horses that live on the grounds. | 6480 RM 2339, Murchison, TX | 903/469–3383 | Free | Daily 8–5.

## Dining

**Old Mill Creek Cafe.** American. The eclectic look of this restaurant includes antiques, old movie photos, hub caps, and cowboy hats hanging from the walls. Try the double-dipped catfish and enormous onion rings. It's closed on Sun., except during First Monday Trade Days. | 501 E. Dallas | 903/567–6241 | Closed Sun. No supper Tues.–Thurs. | $3–$10 | No credit cards.

**Tea Room on the Square.** American. Every dish is homemade at this friendly lunchtime café, where specialties include quiche, roast beef croissant sandwiches, and cheesecake. On First Monday Trade Days weekends, it opens Sat. and Sun. for lunch. | 131 Buffalo | 903/567–6221 | Closed weekends. No supper | $3–$7 | No credit cards.

**Two Senoritas.** Mexican. Located on the service road of the highway, this Mexican restaurant serves up hot and spicy fare for lunch and dinner. Popular menu items include fajitas, chicken or steak *tampico* (grilled meat topped with a ranchero sauce over a cheese enchilada), and fruit flautas (deep-fried tortillas stuffed with cherry or apple compote). | 107 S. I–20 | 903/567–6520 | Closed Mon. | $5–$12 | AE, D, MC, V.

## Lodging

**Best Western Canton Inn and Good Sam RV Park.** An RV park with full hookups is on site at this two-story chain hotel. Restaurant, picnic area, complimentary Continental breakfast, cable TV, pool, laundry facilities, some pets allowed. | 2521 N. Trade Days Blvd. | 903/567–6591 or 800/528–1234 | 82 rooms | $59–$89 | AE, D, MC, V.

**Canton Square Bed and Breakfast.** Each of the five guest rooms is furnished with antiques and queen-size beds in this 1893 Victorian home. It's on the town square and within walking distance of First Monday Trade Days. Complimentary breakfast, no pets, no kids under 10, no smoking. | 133 S. Buffalo St. | 903/567–6195 or 800/704–8769 | kimored@flash.net | www.cantonsquarebnb.com | 5 rooms | $145 | MC, V.

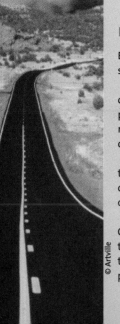

© Artville

## FIRST MONDAYS TRADE DAYS

Every month, the East Texas hamlet of Canton (pop. 3,000) swells with 150,000 shoppers and 5,000 vendors during First Mondays Trade Days.

Trade Days is the town's largest industry, spilling $2 million annually into the city coffers. The atmosphere at Trade Days is part garage sale, part flea market, and part carnival. Merchandise varies from antique marbles to leather gloves to restored furniture. Shoppers spend the day scanning table after table for bargains or hard-to-find items.

First Mondays dates back to 1873, when court was held on the first Monday of the month. To pass the time while waiting for the judge, the townspeople began to do some trading, swapping a goat for a quilt, or a pair of wagon wheels for a load of hay. After a while, trade days became a regular event on the courthouse square.

For nearly a century, the practice continued and grew. Finally, in 1965, the City of Canton decided to relocate the monthly swap meet to grounds two blocks north of the courthouse. With more room as well as promotion by the city, the popularity of the event soared; today both buyers and sellers come from all over the country to partake in some way.

**Ramada Limited Suites.** This small, two-story, all-suites hotel opened in 1997. It's at the junction of Rte. 19 and I–20. Restaurant, complimentary Continental breakfast, cable TV, pool, hot tub, pets allowed. | 3001 N. Trade Days Blvd. | 903/567–0455 | www.ramada.com | 40 rooms | $110–$125 | AE, D, MC, V.

# CANYON

MAP 8, J9

*(Nearby towns also listed: Amarillo, Hereford)*

This Panhandle town of 12,000 is known as the gateway to Palo Duro Canyon State Park, and the home of West Texas A&M University and the Buffalo Lake National Wildlife Refuge.

Information: **Canyon Chamber of Commerce** | 1518 5th Ave., Canyon, TX 79015 | 806/655–1183 | cocadmin@tcac.com.

## Attractions

**Buffalo Lake National Wildlife Refuge.** This grass prairie is home to migrant birds, deer, raptors, and waterbirds. In addition to an auto tour road, the park has a unique walking trail and a Cottonwood Canyon birding trail. | Rte. 168 S | 806/499–3382 | $2 per vehicle | Mar.–Sept., daily 8–8; Oct.–Feb., daily 8–6.

**West Texas A&M University.** Founded in 1909, WTAMU offers more than 50 undergraduate and 30 graduate degree programs. The campus is located in a quiet, rural community, and is spread out over 125 acres. Average annual enrollment is close to 7,000. | 2501 W. 4th Ave., Canyon | 800/99–WTAMU | www.wtamu.edu | Free | Daily.

The **Panhandle-Plains Historical Museum** on the Texas A&M University campus has paleontology, transportation, art, and West Texas history displays, including some on the oil industry. | 2401 4th Ave. | 806/656–2244 | fax 806/651–2250 | www.wtamu.edu | $4 | Mon.–Sat. 9–5, Sun. 1–6.

## Dining

**Ranchhouse Cafe.** American. Chicken-fried steak, rib-eye, and some Mexican favorites are what you'll find on the menu of this casual family restaurant with Western art, wooden tables and chairs, and a few antiques throughout. The owner/chef makes a traditional New Mexican–style chunky green chili sauce that diners put on everything from enchiladas to cheeseburgers. For dessert, try the homemade coconut cream or pecan pie. | 1810 23rd St. | 806/655–8785 | Closed Sun. | $4–$12 | AE, MC, V.

## Lodging

**Buffalo Inn.** Downtown restaurants are within walking distance of this single-story, U-shape redbrick motel. A city pool is 1 mile away, and a state park is 10 mi away. Microwaves, refrigerators, cable TV, business services, no pets. | U.S. 87 | 806/655–2124 or 800/526–9968 | fax 806/655–5844 | 21 rooms | $40–$50 | AE, D, MC, V.

**Country Inn.** This small property, furnished with antiques, has the feel of a country home. Complimentary breakfast, no room phones. | 806/655–7636 or 800/664–7636 | 2 rooms (2 with shared bath) | $85–$95 | AE, D, MC, V.

CANYON

INTRO
ATTRACTIONS
DINING
LODGING

# CASTROVILLE

*(Nearby towns also listed: Bandera, Boerne, New Braunfels, San Antonio, Uvalde)*

This small town west of San Antonio is known as the "Little Alsace of Texas." The town's deep French roots began with founder Henri Castro, who first came to Texas in 1842. Every August the town celebrates the St. Louis Day Church Festival, which began in the mid-1800s in honor of the feast day of St. Louis IX of France.

Information: **Castroville Chamber of Commerce** | 802 London, Box 572, Castroville, TX 78009 | 830/538–3142 or 800/778–6775 | www.castroville.com.

## Attractions

**Moye Center.** The Sisters of Divine Providence were the first residents of this 1873 convent. Later it was used as a school. The tiny original St. Louis Catholic Church stands on the grounds. | U.S. 90W | 830/931–2233 | Free | Tues.–Fri. 8:30–5.

**Medina Lake.** More than 5,500 acres of water welcomes boaters and swimmers. Take Route 471 north about 15 mi to Route 1283; head west to Park Rd. 37, then southwest to lake. | Park Rd. 37 | Free | Daily.

**St. Louis Catholic Church.** You can hear a recorded account of the history of this 1868 Gothic-style church. | Houston Sq. | 830/538–3142 | Free | Daily 9–5.

### ON THE CALENDAR

**AUG.: *St. Louis Day Church Festival.*** This event began in the mid-1800s in honor of the feast day of St. Louis IX of France. Today it is a popular event that draws guests from across the state, country, and world. The day begins with a Mass in St. Louis Catholic Church, and includes a picnic, silent auction, barbecued beef and Alsation-style sausage dinner, rides and games, performances by popular bands and dance groups, and more. | 830/931–2826.

## Dining

**The Alsatian.** French. Housed in a chalet built in the mid-1800s, this place is perhaps best known for its Alsatian sausage. | 1403 Angelo St. | 830/931–3260 | No supper Mon.–Wed. | $5–$15 | AE, D, MC, V.

**La Normandie Restaurant.** French. This unassuming restaurant has drawn rave reviews from food critics. Try the *escalope à la Normandie* (tender veal flambé with mushrooms). | 1302 Fiorella St. | 830/538–3070 or 800/261–1731 | Closed Mon. No supper Tues.–Wed. | Reservations essential | $10–$18 | No credit cards.

**Sammy's Restaurant.** American. Established in 1948 and expanded over the years, this restaurant has long been a local favorite. Texas-size portions of homestyle cooking are served up daily for breakfast and lunch. Try the handbreaded fried catfish, open roast beef sandwich, or homemade dumplings and chicken. | 202 U.S. 90E | 830/538–2204 | Breakfast also available. No supper | $5–$15 | D, MC, V.

## Lodging

**Alsatian Inn.** This two-story motel overlooks town. Cable TV, pool, some pets allowed. | 1650 U.S. 90 W | 830/538–2262 or 800/446–8528 | 40 rooms | $45–$60.

**Ihnken Inn.** Formerly an 1860 carriage house, today this building is a roomy B&B just a few blocks from Castroville's historic district. The guest cottage, which sleeps 4–5 people, is filled with French and Alsatian antiques, and has a view of the surrounding fields. Special rates are available for extended stays. Complimentary breakfast. Cabl TV, no room phones. No pets. | 1202 Gentilz St. | 830/931–9276 | 1 cottage | $110 | No credit cards.

**Landmark Inn State Historic Site.** A former stagecoach stop, this historic building became a hotel in 1863. Today, the site includes an interpretive center and an old gristmill. No room phones, no TV. | 402 Florence | 830/931–2133 | 8 rooms | $55–$65 | D, MC, V.

# CHILDRESS

*(Nearby towns also listed: Amarillo, Lubbock, Quanah, Shamrock, Wichita Falls)*

Named for the author of the Texas Declaration of Independence, this small town of 6,000 was established in 1876. It's primarily an agricultural center known for its production of cotton, wheat, peanuts, and cattle.

Information: **Childress Chamber of Commerce** | 237 Commerce St., 79201 | 940/937–2567 | fax 940/937–8836.

## Attractions

**Caprock Canyons State Park.** Named after the local term for "high plains," this park in the Panhandle is distinguished by eye-catching geologic formations, canyons, and an abundance of wildlife, including antelope, African aoudad, golden eagles, and mule deer. It's also home to a bison herd. | Rte. 1065, Quitaque | 806/455–1492 | www.tpwd.state.tx.us/expltx/eft/bison | $2 | Daily 6 AM–10 PM.

**Childress County Heritage Museum.** Exhibits in this former post office cover local industries such as cotton, cattle, and railroading. There are some Native American artifacts as well. | 210 3rd St. NW | 940/937–2261 | Free | Weekdays 9–5, or by appointment.

**ON THE CALENDAR**
**MAY:** *Rolling Plains Heritage Festival.* Native American exhibits, a parade, music, arts and crafts, and an inter-tribal powwow are part of this festival. | 940/937–2567.
**JULY:** *Old Settlers Rodeo and Reunion.* Held annually since the late 1800s, this two-day event includes a parade, a rodeo, and dancing. | 940/937–2567.

## Dining

**K-BOB's Steakhouse.** Steak. Although part of a small franchise that operates in Colorado, New Mexico, and Oklahoma, the down-home cooking and friendly atmosphere make it feel one-of-a-kind. Wagon wheels and hitching posts adorn the outside of the restaurant, and bare wooden planks give the interior a rustic charm. Try the premium cuts of beef and dessert cobblers. | 1805 Ave. F NW | 940/937–6184 | $6–$16 | AE, D, MC, V.

## Lodging

**Econolodge.** This two-story motel is within walking distance of stores and restaurants. Restaurant, cable TV, pool, business services, pets allowed. | 1612 Avenue F NW | 940/937–3695 or 800/542–4229 | fax 940/937–6956 | 28 rooms | $38–$49 | AE, D, DC, MC, V.

**Holiday Inn Express.** This two-story hotel has a semi-circular drive covered by a large, looming carport. Both the carport and main building are topped with squarish cupolas that are easily seen from the road. In-room data ports, safes, refrigerators, cable TV, pool and hot tub, exercise equipment, laundry, business services, pets allowed. | 2008 Ave. F NW | 940/937–3434 | fax 940/937–2270 | 52 | $55–$70 | AE, D, DC, MC, V.

# CLARENDON

MAP 8, K9

*(Nearby town also listed: Amarillo)*

Considered the oldest thriving community in the Panhandle, this town of 2,000 was established as a "sobriety society" and an alternative to the wild boomtowns nearby. Nicknamed "Saints Roost" by cowboys, today the history of the community is recalled at a local museum.

Information: **Clarendon Chamber of Commerce** | Box 730, Clarendon, TX 79226 | 806/874–2421 | www.clarendonedc.org.

## Attractions
**Greenbelt Lake.** Located in the Red River Basin, this lake is a summer favorite with families, boaters, anglers, and swimmers. | Rte. 70 | 806/874–2746 | Daily.

**Saints Roost Museum.** The Saints Roost Museum, in a former hospital, is devoted to local history and ranching life in the past century. | U.S. 287 to Rte. 70 | 806/874–2746 | ptmc.webtex.com/saints | Free | Thurs.–Sun. 1–5.

**Taylor Lakes Wildlife Refuge.** Fauna—such as white-tailed deer, Rio Grande turkeys, quail, and muskrat—and flora—such as mesquite, red berry juniper, cottonwood, hackberry, and willow—make a visit to this nature-lover's dream worthwhile. You'll need a point-of-sale public access permit prior to your arrival; the permit is good for over a year and available in Clarendon wherever hunting and fishing licenses are sold. Call ahead from Oct.–Mar., as the refuge is sometimes closed to visitors during hunting season. Although the refuge is managed, it's not maintained daily by a staff. | 5½ mi southeast of Clarendon via U.S. 287 just east of Lelia Lake | 806/492–3405 | Free with public access permit | Daily.

### ON THE CALENDAR
**SEPT.:** *Colonel Charles Goodnight Chuckwagon Cook-off.* Cooks great and small are expected to whip up a tasty meal of steak, sourdough bread, side dishes, and fruit cobbler in this two-day competitive event. On Fri. evening, participants in full period attire set up their chuckwagons and build fires of mesquite wood. You can rank the chuckwagons for authenticity, buy some award-winning food for supper, listen to a cowboy poet and strolling guitar players, and dance to the music of a live band. | 806/874–2421.

## Dining
**Sam Hill's Pit BBQ.** Barbecue. Eat at the red-and-white check covered tables from plates filled with brisket, ham, sausage, ribs, potato salad, coleslaw, and peach and apple cobbler. | 614 W. Second St. | 806/874–3358 | Closed Thurs. | $4–$9 | AE, D, MC, V.

## Lodging
**Bar H Dude Ranch.** Guests at this all-inclusive 1,500-acre working ranch sleep in bunk houses—five bunks to a room—ride horses, and help with ranch chores daily. Restaurant, no room phones, no TV, TV in common area, pool, hiking, horseback riding, volleyball, laundry facilities, pets allowed. | Rte. 3257 and Rte. N | 806/874–2634 or 800/627–9871 | fax 806/874–3679 | 17 rooms (with shared bath) | $130 | AP | AE, D, MC, V.

**Western Skies.** Greenbelt Lake is 3 mi from this motel built in the mid-1950s. Cable TV, pool, playground, business services, some pets allowed. | 800 W. 2nd St. | 806/874–3501 | fax 806/874–5303 | 23 rooms | $35–$45 | AE, D, MC, V.

# CLEBURNE

*(Nearby towns also listed: Arlington-Grand Prairie, Fort Worth, Whitney)*

Named for a Confederate general, this town of 26,500 is a center for the region's agricultural industry. Groups and individual shoppers come from big cities like Dallas to tour the Layland Museum, then try their hands at treasure-hunting in one of the many malls and stores in and around the historic downtown area.

**Information: Cleburne Chamber of Commerce** | 1511 W. Henderson, Cleburne, TX 76033 | 817/645–2455 | nell@digitex.net | www.cleburnetexas.net.

## Attractions
**Cleburne State Park.** Activities at this park include camping, fishing, picnicking, swimming, boating, and hiking. The park is also home to a wildlife refuge and a lake. | 5800 Park Rd 21 | 817/645–4215 | fax 817/641–6013 | www.tpwd.state.tx.us | $3 | Daily 8 AM–10 PM.

**Layland Museum.** This museum includes exhibits on the numerous groups that settled this region: Native Americans, Euro-Americans, African-Americans, and Hispanics. One of the museum's prized artifacts is a rare Confederate uniform. | 201 N. Caddo St. | 817/645–0940 | fax 817/641–4161 | Free | Weekdays 9–5, second and fourth Sat. of each month 10–4.

### ON THE CALENDAR
**APR.:** *Springfest.* This downtown festival includes a barbecue contest, arts and crafts, an antique car show, and live music. | 817/645–2455.
**JUNE:** *Sheriff's Posse PRCA Rodeo.* Barrel racing, rodeo clowns, roping, and precision riding. | 817/645–2455.
**DEC.:** *Christmas Candle Walk.* Christmas is celebrated with a tour of historic homes, holiday festivities, and a candlelit walk of downtown. | 817/645–2455.

## Dining
**Susannah's Homestyle Cooking.** American. Booths line the walls, which are adorned with antiques and crafts, and tables are situated in the center. The cornbread and warm crusty rolls are popular; dinner fare can include chicken-fried steak, squash, black-eyed peas, and a five-vegetable plate. For dessert, try the fruit cobbler: apple, blackberry, or peach. | 1514 W. Henderson Rd. | 817/641–3848 | $6–$11 | AE, D, MC, V.

## Lodging
**Comfort Inn.** Built in July 2000, this is the newest hotel in town. Complimentary Continental breakfast, in-room data ports, microwaves, refrigerators, some in-room hot tubs, cable TV, pool, exercise equipment, laundry facilities, laundry service, business services, pets allowed (fee). | 2117 N. Main St. | 817/641–4702 or 800/228–5150 | fax 817/641–4336 | www.comfortinn.com | 36 rooms, 18 suites | $69–$89, $89–$120 suites | AE, D, DC, MC, V.

**Days Inn.** This motel is within walking distance of restaurants and just 2 mi from the Cleburne airport. It's comprised of one two-story building, and two one-story buildings. Cable TV, pool, pets allowed. | 101 N. Ridgeway Dr. (Rte. 67 Business) | 817/645–8836 | fax 817/645–4813 | 45 rooms | $45–$69 | AE, D, MC, V.

CLEBURNE

INTRO
ATTRACTIONS
DINING
LODGING

# COMANCHE

MAP 8, H3

*(Nearby towns also listed: Abilene, Eastland, Stephenville)*

This community of 4,600 was formed in the mid-1800s and named for the Comanche Indians. Comanche is near Lake Proctor and favored for its camping, fishing, and boating. The town is also home to the oldest courthouse in Texas. Nearby Brownwood contains Howard Payne University and the personal effects of Gen. Douglas MacArthur.

Information: **Comanche Chamber of Commerce** | 100 Indian Creek Dr., Comanche, TX 76442 | 915/356–3233 | chamber.edc@itexas.net | www.comanchetx.org.

## Attractions

**Comanche County Historical Museum.** Many local history exhibits, including artifacts on Native American life in the region, can be found in this museum located in a historic barn. | 402 Moorman Rd. | 915/356–3233 | Sat., Sun. 2–4 or by appointment | Free.

**Douglas MacArthur Academy of Freedom.** The personal effects of Gen. Douglas MacArthur are on display in a musem at the Academy, an academic building at Howard Payne University. The exterior of the striking building has a three-story glass center, massive stone walls, and pointed spires. | 1320 Austin Ave., Brownwood | 915/649–8700 | fax 915/649–8923 | www.hputx.edu | Free | Tours: daily 1, 2, and 3.

**Lake Brownwood State Park.** This 538-acre park offers boating, hiking, and swimming. Cabins and shelters are available, as are opportunities for nature study. Take Rte. 279 to Rte. 15, then drive east for 7 mi. | Rte. 15 | 915/784–5223 | fax 915/784–6203 | www.tpwd.state.tx.us | $2 | Daily.

**Lake Proctor.** Activities on this lake's 38 mi of shoreline include boating, camping, fishing, and swimming. Each of its four parks spans 250 acres. Take Rte. 377 N to Rte. 2861 W. | Rte. 2861 W | 254/879–2424 | fax 254/879–2341 | $1 | Daily 6 AM–10 PM.

**Old Cora.** Built in 1856, this is the oldest existing original Texas courthouse. It's of special interest to architects for its classic courthouse style. | On town square | Free | Daily.

### ON THE CALENDAR

**SEPT.:** *County Powwow.* The City Park hosts art shows, antique tractor and car shows, crafts, and food booths. | 915/356–3233.

## Dining

**Golden Arrow.** American. The two separate dining areas are full of greenery and potted plants in this family-style restaurant. Food is served cafeteria-style during lunch. You can eat at one of the large tables, or in a more intimate booth. Brisket and chicken-fried steak are popular. | 901 W. Central St. | 915/356–3217 | $6–$10 | No credit cards.

## Lodging

**Days Inn.** This two-story motel is within walking distance of a mall and restaurants. In-room data ports, cable TV, pool, hot tub, exercise equipment, laundry facilities, business services, pets allowed (fee). | 515 E. Commerce St., Brownwood | 915/646–2551 | fax 915/643–6064 | 140 rooms | $50–$75 | AE, D, DC, MC, V.

**Guest House at Heritage Hill.** This 1930s ranch house with a full kitchen is on a 120-acre working cattle and goat ranch just outside of town. See armadillos, turkeys, and white-tail deer, and observe the panoramic sweep of stars in the night sky from your private porch. The single-story home has antique furnishings from the 1920s and 1930s, with a few Victorian-style details thrown in—like the claw-foot tubs in two of the three bathrooms. Microwave, refrigerator, cable TV, in-room VCR, pond, hiking, fishing, business services, pets allowed. | Rte. 36, 2½ mi east of Comanche | 915/356–3397 | fax 915/356–2308 | perkin-shhp@itexas.net | 4 rooms | $100 | No credit cards.

# COMFORT

*(Nearby towns also listed: Boerne, Kerreville, San Antonio)*

This community northwest of San Antonio on I–10 has strong German roots. (Settlers first planned to name the town "Gemuetlichkeit," meaning peace, serenity, comfort, and happiness.) Today the streets here are as busy as they were a century ago, when customers would come into the local establishments for kerosene, oil, and washboards. Many historic buildings (the downtown area boasts 120) today house antiques shops, restaurants, and bed-and-breakfast inns, instead of feed, dry goods, and grocery stores.

**Information: Comfort Chamber of Commerce** | 7th and High Sts., Comfort, TX 78013 | 830/995–3131 | fax 830/995–5252.

## Attractions

**Cowgirl Corral.** If you're dying to get your hands on some curios or that one-of-a-kind antique, check out this vintage store specializing in pieces from the 1920s. Furniture, memorabilia, and Western items from periods other than the 1920 are also for sale. The store is housed in the former #9 railroad depot right near the chamber of commerce. | 508 Rte. 27 | 830/995–2175 | Free | Daily 10–5.

**Ingenhuett Store.** Built in 1880 by Peter J. Ingenhuett, this general store is now operated by fourth- and fifth-generation family members. One of the oldest continuously operated general stores in Texas, the store includes the Ingenhuett history display, complete with photos of the Ingenhuett ancestors and Comfort's early days. | 834 High St. | 830/995–2149 | Free | Weekdays 8–5:30, Sat. 8–4:30.

**"Treue der Union" (True to the Union) Monument.** During the Civil War, German residents of Comfort who did not approve of slavery were burned out of their farms. Several German farmers decided to defect to Mexico but were caught by Confederate soldiers and killed on the banks of the Nueces River, their bodies left unburied. Finally retrieved in 1865, the remains were returned to Comfort and buried in a mass grave. A white obelisk, the oldest monument in Texas and the only monument to the Union located south of the Mason-Dixon line, was dedicated here in 1866. One of only six such sites in the country, the shrine received congressional approval to continually fly the flag at half-mast. The flag that waves here has 36 stars, the same number it had when the marker was dedicated in 1866. | High St. | Free | Daily.

### ON THE CALENDAR

**NOV.:** *Christmas in Comfort.* Four square blocks are sectioned off each year to make way for this one-day event. You'll find live musical performances, arts-and-crafts, concession stands, and performers dressed in Wild West garb reenacting shootouts. | 830/995–3131.

## Dining

**Cypress Creek Inn.** American. This unfussy, casual family restaurant is styled to look like a ranch. Known for steak, pork chops, seafood, and sandwiches. | 408 Rte. 27 W | 830/995–3977 | No supper Sun.–Tues. | $6–$12 | AE, D, DC, MC, V.

**Mimi's Cafe.** Contemporary. A former 1910 post office houses this restaurant. You can dine indoors in an airy space with tin ceilings, or outdoors under a covered patio surrounded by a New Orleans–style garden. Menu options might include chicken and asparagus pasta with lemon cream sauce, or green chili and chicken spaghetti. For dessert, try the bread pudding with Bourbon sauce, or the French silk chocolate pie. | 814 High St. | 830/995–3470 | Closed Sun., Mon. No supper Tues.–Thurs. | $5–$17 | AE, D, MC, V.

## Lodging
**Comfort Common.** Built in 1880, today the single-story inn has several antiques shops on site and is within walking distance of all downtown shops. Complimentary breakfast. | 717 High St. | 830/995–3030 | fax 830/995–3455 | 10 rooms | $70–$125 | AE, D, MC, V.

**Meyer Bed and Breakfast.** Four buildings from the late 1860s through 1920 sit on 2½ acres on the banks of clear Cypress Creek. Rooms are simple and filled with antiques. Dining room, complimentary breakfast, cable TV, no room phones, pool, fishing, business services, no pets. | 845 High St. | 830/995–2304 or 800/364–2138 | 9 rooms | $69–$85 | AE, D, MC, V.

# CORPUS CHRISTI
MAP 8, I7

*(Nearby towns also listed: Aransas Pass, Kingsville, Padre Island, Port Aransas, Rockport)*

This city was charted in 1519 by Spanish explorer Alonzo Alvarez de Pineda, who named the bay Body of Christ, or *Corpus Christi*. For several years, the coastal area was of interest mainly to pirates, men who used its bay and islands as hideouts. Today the port is much friendlier, welcoming ships from around the globe and holding the title as the sixth largest port in the nation. There are many attractions in town, and both bus and boat tours are available. Its population is just over 285,000.

Information: **Greater Corpus Christi Convention and Visitors Bureau** | 1201 N. Shoreline, Corpus Christi, TX 78401 | 361/881–1888 or 800/678–6232 | www.corpuschristi-tx-cvb.org.

## Attractions
**Asian Cultures Museum and Educational Center.** Asian art ranging from dolls to pagodas can be seen here. | 1809 N. Chaparral | 361/882–2641 | fax 361/882–5718 | Free | Tues.–Sat. 10–5.

**Bob Hall Pier.** This fishing pier extends beyond the third sand bar into the Gulf of Mexico. Rod, reel, and bait can be bought or rented. | 15820 Park Rd. 22, Corpus Christi | 361/949–8121 | $1 | 24 hours.

**Corpus Christi Museum of Science and History.** Exhibits at this museum cover everything from dinosaurs to Spanish shipwrecks. Don't miss the "Seeds of Change" exhibit, designed by the Smithsonian's National Museum of Natural History for the 500th anniversary of the European discovery of America. See for yourself what it was like to make the Atlantic crossing aboard the Niña, Pinta, and Santa Maria; life-size replicas of these Spanish ships are in a shipyard repair facility adjacent to the museum. | 1900 N. Chaparral St. | 361/883–2862 | $5 | Daily.

**Heritage Park.** Here you can see nine historic homes dating from 1851. Each has been restored and is used occasionally by civic groups for concerts and performances. | 1581 N. Chaparral | 361/883–0639 | Free | Mon.–Sat. 10–2; tours: Wed.–Thurs. 10:30, Fri.–Sat 10:30, 12:45.

**International Kite Museum.** Two thousand years of kite history—from Imperial China to modern-day scientific and military applications—are charted here. Colorful displays and engaging videos make this an excellent destination for families with children. The museums is housed inside a local beach resort complex. | 3200 Surfside Dr. | 361/883–7456 | Free | Daily 10–6.

**South Texas Institute for the Arts.** Traditional and contemporary work by artists associated with Texas is displayed here. | 1902 N. Shoreline Blvd. | 361/980–3500 | Free | Tues., Wed., Fri, Sat. 10–5, Thurs. 10–9, Sun. 1–5.

**Texas State Aquarium.** Aquatic animals and habitats indigenous to the Gulf of Mexico are showcased through exhibits and outdoor touch tanks. The Flower Gardens Coral Reef exhibit focuses on the beautiful coral gardens found 115 mi off the coast, which attract marine animals such as moray eels, tarpon, and rays. In the Octopus's Garden, a 20-ft tall purple octopus invites young visitors to enjoy a marine-inspired playground. The interpretive center is entered from beneath a cascading waterfall. | 2710 N. Shoreline Dr. | 361/881–1200 or 800/477–GULF | fax 361/881–1257 | $9 | Mon.–Sat. 9–5, Sun. 10–5.

**USS *Lexington* Museum on the Bay.** Housed in the most decorated aircraft carrier in U.S. Naval history, this museum offers five self-guided tour routes that give you a close look at the ship termed "The Blue Ghost." | 2914 N. Shoreline Blvd. | 361/888–4873 or 800/LADY–LEX | fax 361/883–8361 | www.usslexington.com | $9 | Daily 9–5.

## SIGHTSEEING TOURS/TOUR COMPANIES

**Flagship Cruises.** One-hour narrated cruises tour the port of Corpus Christi. | Slip 49, Peoples St. T-Head, on Shoreline Dr. | 361/884–1693 or 361/884–8306 | $8 | Wed.–Mon. 3 PM.

**FunTime bus tours.** These bus tours take you to area casinos. | 5875 Agnes St. | 361/289–7113 | $10–$25 | Weekdays 8:30–4:30.

## ON THE CALENDAR

**APR.: *Artfest.*** Artists from around the state and neighboring states display their work and offer demonstrations. | 361/884–6406.

**APR.: *Buccaneer Days.*** Fireworks, a carnival, parade, rodeo, sailing regatta, and sports tournaments celebrate Corpus Christi's buccaneer history. | 361/882–3242.

**MAY–SEPT.: *Summer Bayfront Concerts.*** Live entertainment is performed outdoors on selected evenings. | 361/881–1888 or 800/678–6232.

**JULY: *Fourth of July: Celebration/Big Band Weekend.*** Festivities include a picnic, barbecue, seed-spitting contest, an orchestra performance, and fireworks. | 361/880–3100.

**SEPT.: *Bayfest.*** This festival by the water includes boat races, fireworks, arts and crafts, and live entertainment on six stages. | 361/887–0868.

# Dining

**The Astor.** American. Known far and wide for its savory mesquite-grilled steaks and fresh seafood, the Astor has been a Corpus Christi institution since 1957. Banquet rooms are available. | 5533 Leopard St. | 361/289–0101 | Breakfast also available | $6–$25 | AE, D, DC, MC, V.

**Blackbeard's on the Beach.** American. This very laid-back place meant to appeal to beach-combing vacationers is popular for its mounds of fried shrimp and fierce margaritas. It's right down the beach from the USS *Lexington* Museum on the Bay and the Texas State Aquarium. | 3117 Surfside Blvd. | 361/884–1030. | $5–$17 | AE, D, DC, MC, V.

**Black-Eyed Pea.** American. If you're craving an old-fashioned, home-style chicken-fried steak, this chain restaurant is the place for you. Soups and salads are served, but locals favor the pot roast. Kids' menu. | 4801 S. Padre Island Dr. | 361/993–4588 | $6–$10 | AE, D, DC, MC, V.

**City Diner.** Seafood. Try the thin crisp onion rings, amberjack, and other fish off the mesquite grill in this diner that looks straight out of the 1950s. Kids' menu. | 622 N. Water St. | 361/883–1643 | Breakfast also available | $8–$18 | AE, D, DC, MC, V.

**Crawdaddy's.** Cajun/Creole. Specializing in tear-inducing Cajun fare, Crawdaddy's makes up for its roadhouse amenities with some of the best swamp food in the downtown area. The restaurant's claim to fame is its "Cajun Boil," a dish of shrimp, crawdad, crab claws, sausage, corn on the cob, and new potatoes, all boiled together in a powerfully spicy broth. For the less adventuresome, there's the relatively tame red beans and rice dish. | 414 Starr St. | 361/883–5432 | $10–$12 | AE, D, MC, V.

**Czech-Mex Bakery and Cafe.** Czech. Specializing in Czechoslovakian pastries and Mexican snacks, this somewhat nondescript bakery is open early on weekday mornings and serves

CORPUS CHRISTI

INTRO
ATTRACTIONS
DINING
LODGING

a novel array of quick, tasty food at very reasonable prices. Try the pigs-in-a-blanket, fruit *kolaches* (sweet rolls), and muffins. | 150 American Bank Plaza | 361/883–2253 | Closed Sat., Sun. No supper | $2–$5 | No credit cards.

**Harvey's Barn Door.** American. This smallish, down-home place attracts an eclectic crowd of musicians, local regulars, and adventuresome tourists. Try baby-back ribs, locally caught redfish steak, or fried oysters. | 4135 Alameda Dr. | 361/854–2656 | Open 24 hours | $6–$10 | MC, V.

**Island Italian Restaurant.** Italian. Recommended dishes at this casual family-owned spot include the lasagna and anything with Alfredo sauce. There is live musical entertainment Thurs.–Sat. nights. Kids' menu. | 15370 South Padre Island Dr., Corpus Christi | 361/949–7737 | $10–$20 | AE, D, DC, MC, V.

**La Bahia.** Mexican. Here you'll find a satisfying blend of authentic Mexican and Tex-Mex fare. The hip, stylish interior has exposed brick, high ceilings, arched doors and windows, and richly textured wall treatments. The flour and corn tortillas are homemade, the breakfast taquitos are available all day, and the full bar is open late. | 224 S. Mesquite | 361/888–6555 | No supper Sun. | $6–$10 | AE, D, DC, MC, V.

**Landry's Seafood House.** Seafood. This restaurant is set in a former army housing barge anchored along the T-Head, one of the major docks in downtown Corpus Christi. Open-air dining is available on the covered deck, and you can enjoy views of the bay and the yacht mooring area. Try the Mellissa fish (white fish topped with sautéed mushrooms, blackened shrimp, scallops, and crabmeat). Kids' menu. | 600 N. Shoreline Blvd. | 361/882–6666 | $13–$26 | AE, D, DC, MC, V.

**Lighthouse.** Seafood. Enjoy a spectacular view of the bay and downtown Corpus Christi from this restaurant built in the shape of a lighthouse. Dine inside or out on a menu that features fresh Gulf fare. Steak, chicken, and pasta specialties are popular. Kids' menu. | 444 N. Shoreline Blvd. | 361/883–3982 | $19–$25 | AE, D, DC, MC, V.

**Mao Tai.** Chinese. The dining area is adorned with carved wood, ornate wall-hangings, lanterns, and life-sized Buddhas. The menu's 80 dishes represent the Hunan, Szechuan, and Cantonese cooking styles. The eggrolls, General Tso's Chicken, Hunan-style shrimp, and sesame chicken are popular. | 4601 S. Padre Island Dr. | 361/852–8877 | $8–$10 | AE, D, MC, V.

**Snoopy's Pier.** Seafood. Seafood and scenery are the main attractions here. Arrive early on summer weekends for a spot at one of the outdoor tables and order from the huge menu hanging from the ceiling. | 13313 S. Padre Island Dr. | 361/949–8815 | $6–$8 | No credit cards.

**Water Street Oyster Bar and Seafood Company.** Seafood. This casual yet elegant restaurant has ceilings, oak furniture, and a patio. Try the large local Gulf oysters. Raw bar. Kids' menu. | 309 N. Water St. | 361/881–9448 | $10–$15 | AE, D, MC, V.

## Lodging

**Days Inn Corpus Christi Beach.** This three-story motel is one block from the beach and within walking distance of the Texas State Aquarium and the USS *Lexington* Museum on the Bay. Complimentary Continental breakfast, cable TV, in-room VCRs (and movies), business services. | 4302 Surfside Blvd. | 361/882–3297 | fax 361/882–6865 | www.daysinn.com | 56 rooms | $39–$90 | AE, D, DC, MC, V.

**Drury Inn.** The Corpus Christi International Airport is 3 mi from this motel, and popular attractions such as the Texas State Aquarium and the USS *Lexington* Museum on the Bay are just 5 mi away. Complimentary Continental breakfast, in-room data ports, refrigerators (in suites), cable TV, pool, business services, airport shuttle, pets allowed. | 2021 N. Padre Island Dr. | 361/289–8200 | www.drury-inn.com | fax 361/289–8200 | 105 rooms | $64–$80 | AE, D, DC, MC, V.

**Embassy Suites.** Both downtown Corpus Christi and the international airport are within 11 mi of this hotel, and five restaurants are within 1 mi. Restaurant, complimentary breakfast, in-room data ports, kitchenettes, refrigerators, cable TV, indoor pool, hot tub, exercise equipment, video games, laundry facilities, business services, airport shuttle. | 4337 S. Padre Island Dr. | 361/853–7899 | fax 361/851–1310 | www.embassysuites.com | 150 suites | $129–$139 suites | AE, D, DC, MC, V.

**Fortuna Bay.** This stunning, Spanish Mission–style B&B sits at the intersection of five canals on North Padre Island, facing the Gulf of Mexico. Whitewashed walls and terra-cotta tiles provide a distinct Caribbean flavor. You can fish right off the back deck, or head over to the nearby country club for golf, tennis, or fine dining. Corpus Christi's shopping district is 20 minutes away, as is a gorgeous white sand beach. Kids are allowed with prior arrangement only. In-room data ports, kitchenettes, cable TV, golf privileges, beach, dock, fishing, some pets allowed, no smoking. | 15405 Fortuna Bay Dr. | 361/949–7554 | 5 suites | $110 | No credit cards.

**George Blucher House.** Just a block from downtown Corpus, this quiet B&B occupies a 1904 Victorian house. Guest rooms are sunny and have antique furniture. Bird-watchers might want to visit Blucher Park across the street; it's a stopping point on a major flyway between Canada and South America. Complimentary breakfast, in-room data ports, cable TV, VCRs, laundry service, no pets, no kids under 12, no smoking. | 211 N. Carrizo St. | 361/884–4884 | fax 361/884–4885 | www.georgeblucherhouse.com | 6 rooms, 1 suite | $100–$125, $150 suite | AE, D, MC, V.

**Gulfstream.** This condominium complex on the island's undeveloped north side offers modern apartments for rental and access to a sparsely populated, pristine beach. Kitchenettes, microwaves, refrigerators, in-room data ports, cable TV, pool, hot tub, golf privileges, beach, video games, laundry facilities, business services, no pets. | 14810 Windward Dr. | 361/949–8061 or 800/542–7368 | fax 361/949–1497 | www.condominium-rental.com | 132 2-bedroom apartments | $150–$200 | AE, D, MC, V.

**Holiday Inn–Emerald Beach.** This downtown hotel is on the bay and overlooks Emerald Beach. It's comprised of one seven-story building and one five-story building. Restaurant, bar, room service, in-room data ports, cable TV, pool, wading pool, hot tub, exercise equipment, beach, playground, business services, pets allowed, airport shuttle. | 1102 S. Shoreline Blvd. | 361/883–5731 | fax 361/883–9079 | www.holiday-inn.com | 368 rooms | $125–$149 | AE, D, DC, MC, V.

**Knolle Farm Bed and Breakfast.** This B&B is on a working cattle ranch. Anglers can capture their own dinner in the fully stocked tank, and hunters can participate in a guided dove, goose, duck, or pheasant hunt. You can also bird-watch, go horseback riding, or enjoy a full picnic served on the banks of the Nueces River, which flows through the property. Picnic areas, some kitchenettes, cable TV, pond, horseback riding, fishing, laundry service, some pets allowed, no smoking. | 13016 Rte. 70, Mathis | 361/547–2546 | fax 361/547–3934 | knollefarm@thei.net | 6 rooms, 1 suite | $75–$100, $150–$250 suites | AE, D, MC, V.

**La Quinta North.** The Corpus Christi International Airport is within 6 miles of this two-story motel, and the downtown area is 4 mi away. Restaurant, complimentary Continental breakfast, in-room data ports, cable TV, pool, business services, pets allowed. | 5155 I–37N | 361/888–5721 | fax 361/888–5401 | www.laquinta.com | 121 rooms | $65–$76 | AE, D, DC, MC, V.

**Marina Grand Hotel.** Rooms are mid-size in this 11-story hotel on the bayfront, situated between downtown Corpus Christi and the marina. The hotel's Grandview Restaurant has a fabulous, panoramic view of the downtown area. Kids under 17 stay free. Restaurant, in-room data ports, microwaves, refrigerators, cable TV, pool, exercise equipment, laundry facilities, no pets. | 300 N. Shoreline Blvd. | 361/883–5111 | fax 361/883–7702 | 172 rooms | $99 | AE, D, DC, MC, V.

**Monterrey Motel.** This is the closest motel to the Padre Island National Seashore and it is across the street from the Bob Hall Pier. There are a few restaurants less than 2 mi away. Some kitchenettes, some refrigerators, cable TV, some pets. | 15705 South Padre Island Dr., Corpus Christi | 361/949–8137 | fax 361/949–8137 | 24 rooms | $35–$75 | AE, D, MC, V.

**Motel 6–Corpus Christi East.** This two-story motel is 3 mi from a shopping mall and 10 mi from the beach. Cable TV, pool, laundry facilities, pets allowed. | 8202 S. Padre Island Dr. | 361/991–8858 | fax 361/991–1698 | 126 rooms | $38–$50 | AE, D, DC, MC, V.

**Motel 6–Corpus Christi Northwest.** This two-story motel is 5 mi from the Texas State Aquarium and 24 mi from the beach. Cable TV, pool, laundry facilities, pets allowed. | 845 Lantana St. | 361/289–9397 | fax 361/289–0280 | 124 rooms | $35–$40 | AE, D, DC, MC, V.

**Omni Corpus Christi Hotel–Bayfront and Marina Towers.** This hotel has two towers, each with bayfront views. It's 12 mi from the Corpus Christi International Airport and five blocks from several restaurants. Restaurant, bar, room service, in-room data ports, some refrigerators, cable TV, pool, barbershop, beauty salon, hot tub, exercise equipment, business services, airport shuttle. | 900 N. Shoreline Blvd., | 361/887–1600 | fax 361/887–6715 | www.omnihotels.com | 820 rooms, 19 suites | $125–$250, $225–$300 suites | AE, D, DC, MC, V.

**Puente Vista Condominiums.** Apartments are available on a daily or monthly basis. Downtown Corpus Christi is 15 minutes away. Kitchenettes, microwaves, refrigerators, cable TV, pool, laundry facilities, no pets, no smoking. | 14300 Aloha St. | 361/949–7849 or 800/234–0117 | 2 apartments | $110–$120 | MC, V.

**Ramada Hotel Bayfront.** This ten-story hotel is in the downtown business district, one block from the bay and marina. Restaurant, bar, room service, in-room data ports, cable TV, pool, exercise equipment, laundry facilities, business services, airport shuttle. | 601 N. Water St. | 361/882–8100 | fax 512/888–6540 | www.ramada.com | 200 rooms | $69–$99; $109–$250 suites | AE, D, DC, MC, V.

**Sandy Shores Beach Hotel.** This two-story hotel is on the beach, across the bridge from downtown Corpus Christi. Restaurant, bar, room service, in-room data ports, cable TV, pool, wading pool, hot tub, beach, laundry facilities, business services. | 3200 Surfside Ave. | 361/883–7456 | fax 361/883–1437 | www.bestwestern.com | 271 rooms | $69–$210 | AE, D, DC, MC, V.

**Sea Shell Inn.** All rooms have balconies and ocean views in this motel 10 minutes from the downtown area. Some kitchenettes, cable TV, pool, beach, laundry facilities. | 202 Kleberg Pl. | 361/888–5391 | fax 361/888–5391 | 26 rooms | $69–$85 | AE, D, DC, MC, V.

**Villa del Sol.** Perched on the Gulf's edge, this condominium hotel has breathtaking views of the bay. Each unit has a full kitchen, a living room, and a private balcony. It's a three-minute walk to downtown Corpus Christi, and the USS *Lexington* Museum on the Bay is ½ mi away. Kitchenettes, cable TV. 2 pools. Hot tub. No pets. | 3938 Surfside Blvd. | 800/242–3291 | 238 apartments | $115–$135 | AE, D, DC, MC, V.

**Western Isles Motel.** This one-story motel is 13 mi from Padre Island National Seashore, and a 20-minute drive from downtown Corpus Christi. Some kitchenettes, some refrigerators, some microwaves, cable TV, pets allowed. | 15378 South Padre Island Dr., Corpus Christi | 361/949–8111 | fax 361/949–1768 | 22 rooms | $49–$69 | AE, D, MC, V.

# CORSICANA

MAP 8, I3

*(Nearby town also listed: Ennis)*

Established in 1849, Corsicana's population boomed with the discovery of oil here near the turn of the 20th century. Today this town of 24,000 primarily serves as a retail hub for the surrounding farmland. Statewide, the town is known for its fruitcake.

**Information: Corsicana Area Chamber of Commerce** | 120 N. 12th St., Corsicana, TX 75110 | 903/874–4731 | corsicana.tx.chamber@airmail.net | www.corsicana.org.

## Attractions

**Collin Street Bakery.** Corsicana is best known in Texas as the home of fruitcake, baked at this operation since 1896. | 401 W. 7th Ave. | 800/248–3366 | Free | Mon.–Sat. 8–5, Sun. noon–5.

**Lefty Frizzell Country Music Museum.** Local musician Lefty Frizzell is honored at this museum filled with country music memorabilia. | 912 W. Park Ave. | 903/654–4846 | $2 | Mon.–Sat. 9–5, Sun. 1–5.

**Navarro Mills Lake.** Operated by the U.S. Army Corps of Engineers, this lake has public beaches and facilities for year-round recreation, such as camping, picnicking, fishing, swimming. | 1174 Rte. 667 | 800/284–2267 | Free | Daily.

**Pioneer Village.** Structures from the 19th century—including a blacksmith shop, a stagecoach, and a doctor's office—are on display. | 912 W. Park Ave. | 903/654–4846 | $2 | Mon.–Sat. 9–5, Sun. 1–5.

**Robert S. Reading Indian Artifact Collection.** The more than 48,000 artifacts are part of what's considered one of the finest Native American museums in the Southwest. | Navarro College Library, U.S. 31 (7th Ave.) | 903/874–6501 | www.nav.cc.tx.us | Free | Mon.–Thurs. 8AM–9PM, Fri. 8–5, Sun. 5PM–8PM.

### ON THE CALENDAR

**APR.: *Derrick Days.*** The home of the first commercial oil well drilled west of the Mississippi celebrates its heritage with a two-day festival. Arts and crafts vendors are on hand, and there are a chili cook-off, a parade, a rodeo, live music, and the Derrick Derby (a combination obstacle course and relay race involving everyone from toddlers to seniors on tricycles, bicycles, roller-skates, and some years, even a canoe). | 903/874–4731.

## Dining

**Old Mexican Inn and Cantina.** Mexican. This restaurant has been a town favorite since it opened in 1941. Try the Mexican Inn Platter (one cheese enchilada, one tamale, one beef taco, beans, rice, and queso dip). | 2407 W. 7th Ave. | 903/874–9061 | Reservations essential Tues. | Closed Mon. | $3–$9 | AE, D, MC, V.

## Lodging

**Wicklow Inn.** Named after the Irish ancestral province of the O'Toole clan (bearers of the name own the inn), this Victorian B&B was built in 1890. It's constructed of California redwood and has a French walnut staircase and leaded glass windows. The spacious front porch has an inviting swing and rocking chairs. Kids aren't allowed in the main house, but families with children are welcome to stay in the adjoining carriage house. Dining room, complimentary breakfast, in-room data ports, no room phones, no TV, TV in common room, business services, no pets, no smoking. | 220 N. Fourteenth St. | 903/872–7311 | fax 903/872–4173 | www.wicklowinn.com | 6 rooms (2 with shared bath) | $60–$125 | MC, V.

# CROCKETT

MAP 8, J4

*(Nearby towns also listed: Huntsville, Lufkin, Palestine)*

This historic town of 7,500 was named for Davy Crockett, who supposedly camped at some local springs on his way to the fateful battle at the Alamo. The agricultural-based community is the seat of Houston County, which became the first county with the founding of the Republic of Texas.

**Information: Crockett Chamber of Commerce** | 1100 Edmiston Dr., Crockett, TX 75835 | 936/544–2359 | crockett.org.

## Attractions

**Crockett Museum and Visitors Center.** Local history exhibits and displays focusing on the Republic of Texas are found at this museum, housed in an old railroad depot. | 629 N. 4th St. | 936/544–9520 | Free | Wed. 2–4.

**Davy Crockett Memorial Park.** This city park named for the frontier hero who died defending the Alamo has tennis courts, playgrounds, and areas for picnicking. | S. 5th St. at Anson Jones Blvd. S | 936/544–2359 | Free | Daily.

**Davy Crockett Spring.** Legend has it that Davy Crockett camped at this site on his way to the battle of the Alamo. It's near the town square and identified by an historical marker. | E. Houston | 936/544–2359 | Free | Daily.

**Mission Tejas State Historical Park.** This park between the towns of Crockett and Alton recalls the first Spanish mission built in East Texas in 1690. Today it offers camping, picnicking, and hiking. | Rte. 21 to Rte. 44 | 936/687–2394 | fax 936/687–3623 | www.tpwd.state.tx.us | $2 | Daily 8 AM–10 PM.

### ON THE CALENDAR

**SEPT.: *Davy Crockett Pioneer Festival.*** This event includes live music, arts and crafts, and food. | 936/544–2359.
**NOV.: *Christmas in Crockett.*** This one-day holiday festival is held outdoors on the courthouse square. It's so popular that the town's population reached 20,000 for the day. Arts and crafts vendors sell their goods, and there are food and entertainment as well. | 936/544–2359.

## Dining

**Camp Street Cafe and Store.** American. Built in 1936, this restaurant once served as a taxi stand, barber shop, and an illegal gambling venue. The rustic interior includes wood floors and handmade tables and benches; country-and-western music plays in the background. Menu choices and daily specials could include chicken and dumplings, hand-battered fried shrimp, chicken-and-sausage gumbo, and German chocolate cake. Everything from the cornbread to the hamburger buns is homemade. Entertainment Sat. | 115 S. Third St. | 936/544–8656 | Closed Sun. | $7–$13 | MC, V.

## Lodging

**Warfield House.** Built in 1897, this B&B was made of rough-cut pine and has a handsome wraparound porch, high ceilings, and elaborate moldings. The colorful rooms have four-poster beds and Victorian-style furnishings, and once housed the Kingston Trio. Breakfast is served in the dining room on a maple table dating back to the mid 1800s. The B&B is in downtown Crockett, and within walking distance of just about all local attractions. Dining room, complimentary breakfast, no room phones, no TV, TV in common area, pool, hot tub, no pets, no kids under 12, no smoking. | 712 E. Houston Ave. | 936/544–4037 or 888/988–8800 | fax 936/544–4037 | jcostler@sat.net | 4 rooms | $75–$100 | AE, D, MC, V.

# DALHART

MAP 8, J7

*(Nearby towns also listed: Amarillo, Dumas)*

Once a part of the massive XIT Ranch of long ago (which is remembered through a museum in town), this Panhandle community of 7,500 has long been a railroad shipping point for area cattle. Today the plains city is visited by birders because of its location on the southern flyway.

Information: **Dalhart Area Chamber of Commerce** | 102 E. 7th St., Dalhart, TX 79022 | 806/249–5646 | chamber@dahlhart.org | www.dalhart.org.

## Attractions

**Empty Saddle Monument.** This statue of an empty saddle remembers fallen cowboys. | U.S. 385 and U.S. 87 | 806/249–5646 | Free | Daily.

**XIT Museum.** Once the world's largest ranch, the XIT is remembered at this museum. Items on display include frontier artifacts, cowboy memorabilia, and turn-of-the-20th-century farm equipment. | 108 E. 5th St. | 806/244–5390 | Donation accepted | Tues.–Sat. 9–5.

### ON THE CALENDAR

**JULY:** *July Fourth Celebration.* Rita Blanca Lake Park hosts food booths, games, fireworks, and a tribute to the town's veterans. | 806/249–5646.
**AUG.:** *XIT Rodeo and Reunion.* Rodeo events, food booths, barrel racing, roping, performers, parade, and a fiddlers' contest are part of the festivities. | 806/249–5646.

## Dining

**Bar H Steakhouse.** Steak. This is a basic American steak house serving food such as burgers and chicken-fried steak. The filet mignon and vast salad bar are popular. | 1010 Hwy. 54E | 806/244–3813 | Closed Sun. | $7–$17 | AE, D, MC, V.

**Sonic Drive-in.** American/Casual. Stop into this place quick before the "carhop service" restaurant is a thing of the past. The attraction is less for the food, which is basic burger joint fare, than for the fine *American Graffiti*–style ambience. Aside from burgers, try the breaded chicken strips and shakes. | 401 Rte. 87S | 806/249–8488 | Breakfast also available | $3–$5 | No credit cards.

## Lodging

**Best Western Nursanickel.** This two-story motel is 4 mi from the municipal airport and less than 1 mi from restaurants. Restaurant, some refrigerators, cable TV, pool. | 102 Scott St. | 806/249–5637 | fax 806/249–5803 | 55 rooms | $49–$67 | AE, D, DC, MC, V.

**Comfort Inn.** This one-story motel is adjacent to a restaurant. Complimentary Continental breakfast, some refrigerators, cable TV, pool, business services. | Rte. 54 E | 806/249–8585 | fax 806/249–2827 | 36 rooms | $45–$65 | AE, D, DC, MC, V.

**Dalhart Days Inn.** The Dalhart airport is 6 mi from this two-story motel. Complimentary Continental breakfast, cable TV, pool, hot tub, business services, some pets allowed. | 701 Liberal St. | 806/244–5246 | fax 806/249–0805 | 40 rooms | $52–$99 | AE, D, DC, MC, V.

**Dalhart Super 8.** This motel is six blocks east of the town's major intersection at U.S. 54 and U.S. 87. The largest room right over the lobby has a pullout couch, a king-size bed, and a recliner. A steakhouse is within walking distance. Complimentary Continental breakfast, in-room data ports, cable TV, hot tub, sauna, pets allowed (fee). | Box 1325, Denver St./Rte. 54E | 806/249–8526 or 800/800–8000 | fax 806/249–5119 | 45 rooms | $52–$62 | AE, D, DC, MC, V.

**Western Skies Motor Inn.** Motor in with your car or camper and park directly in front of your room. Restaurant, complimentary breakfast, cable TV, pool, hot tub, sauna, steam room, exercise equipment, laundry facilities. | 623 Denver St. (Rte. 54W) | 806/249–4538 | 56 rooms | $34–$38 | AE, D, DC, MC, V.

# DALLAS

MAP 8, I3

*(Suburbs also listed: Arlington-Grand Prairie, Bonham, Canton, Ennis, Ft. Worth, Grapevine, Irving, Lewisville, McKinney, Plano, Waxahachie)*

From J. R. to the Dallas Cowboys, for many visitors this is the land of icons that are endlessly associated with Texas.

This city of almost 1,100,000 is rich with culture, offering a cornucopia of more than 160 museums, galleries, and artistic attractions. Many of these attractions are found in the Dallas Arts District, 60 acres on the north edge of downtown and the largest urban arts district in the country.

Shopping galore can be enjoyed in the north part of town, and the West End, a former warehouse district, has lots of restaurants. (With more than 5,000 eateries, Dallas boasts more restaurants per capita than New York City.) Near West End, you'll find Deep Ellum, the lively center of the city's alternative arts and music scene.

Dallas is also the site of a painful episode in American history—the assassination of President John F. Kennedy. That fateful event is remembered at the Sixth Floor Museum, housed in the former Texas School Book Depository where it is alleged that assassin Lee Harvey Oswald was located at the time of the shooting.

Information: **Dallas Convention and Visitors Bureau** | 1201 Elm St., Suite 2000, Dallas, TX 75270 | 214/571–1000 or 800/232–5527 | www.dallascvb.com.

## NEIGHBORHOODS

**Dallas Arts District.** Sixty acres on the north edge of downtown make up the largest urban arts district in the United States. The area's numerous attractions include the Dallas Museum of Art and the Morton H. Meyerson Symphony Center. Key thoroughfares include Harwood and Flora Sts.

**Deep Ellum.** In the early 20th century this neighborhood was a focal point of African-American culture; it was one of the more prolific producers of blues artists and music in the United States. Today, it is filled with numerous art galleries, bars, clubs, and restaurants. The heart of this district is on Commerce, Main, and Elm Sts.

**Greenville Ave.** This lively, bustling neighborhood stretches from the downtown area to northeast Dallas. It's kept buzzing by the many young professionals who live here and frequent the restaurants (where outdoor dining is popular) and shopping outlets from Mockingbird Lane northward. From Ross Ave. to Mockingbird Lane,

## CAR RENTAL TIPS

❏ Review auto insurance policy to find out what it covers when you're away from home.

❏ Know the local traffic laws.

❏ Jot down make, model, color, and license plate number of rental car and carry the information with you.

❏ Locate gas tank—make sure gas cap is on and can be opened.

❏ Check trunk for spare and jack.

❏ Test the ignition—make sure you know how to remove the key.

❏ Test the horn, headlights, blinkers, and windshield wipers.

*Excerpted from *Fodor's: How to Pack: Experts Share Their Secrets*
© 1997, by Fodor's Travel Publications

Greenville Ave. is largely a residential neighborhood with a sprinkling of shops, clubs, and pubs.

**Highland Park.** Lavish homes line the tree-shaded streets of this affluent neighborhood just minutes north of downtown Dallas. (Highland Park was designed by landscape architect Wilbur David Cook, the same man who laid out Beverly Hills.) The luxurious homes, serene Turtle Creek, and lovely flower displays make this a neighborhood worth visiting. Another point of interest is Highland Park Village, a shopping center known for its trendy shops and striking architecture.

**Knox-Henderson.** This area is named after two streets that cross Central Expressway north of downtown. Knox St. is home to a number of eateries, as well as furniture shops and antiques galleries. Henderson St., in addition to a smaller selection of antiques shops, is also home to a number of restaurants and clubs.

**McKinney Ave.** Accessible from the downtown area via trolley, this redbrick avenue is lined with restaurants, boutiques, and galleries, many of which are housed in historic homes. The trolley runs daily and is historic in itself.

**Swiss Avenue.** This neighborhood in East Dallas is rich with representations of early 20th-century architecture; you'll see more than 200 homes built in a dozen different architectural styles, ranging from prairie to Tudor to Art Deco.

**West End Historic District.** Dallas's busiest entertainment district has lots of converted brick warehouses that now house eight trendy nightclubs, many restaurants, and the Artisans' Gallery, which is filled with one-of-a-kind shops. You'll also find a 10-screen movie theater, Planet Hollywood, and a game arcade.

## WALKING TOUR
**Downtown Dallas**
**(approximately four hours)**

Begin at the corner of Elm and Houston streets at **The Sixth Floor** museum, the former Texas School Book Depository and the spot from where it is believed that Lee Harvey Oswald fired upon President John F. Kennedy. Turn right on Houston and walk past Dealey Plaza and its infamous triple underpass (the site of President Kennedy's assassination) to the intersection of Main and Houston streets. Here you will find the **Old Red Courthouse,** a Romanesque-revival building that now houses a visitors' center on its first floor. Behind the former courthouse, on Main Street at Market, is the stark, white **John F. Kennedy Memorial,** a Philip Johnson–designed cenotaph. Cross Market and stop into the **Conspiracy Museum,** where you can explore theories on the assassinations of President Kennedy, Robert F. Kennedy, and Martin Luther King, Jr. Walk back down Market toward Main, then cross the street to the Dallas County Historical Plaza and its **John Neely Bryan Cabin,** which provides insight into how early Dallas settlers lived. Upon exiting the plaza, turn left on Market and walk four blocks to the **West End MarketPlace.** This five-story building, once a cracker factory, now houses retail shops and eateries, as well as **Dallas Alley,** where partiers can pay one cover charge for admittance to a variety of nightclubs. Walk back down Market Street two blocks to Ross Avenue, then turn left and continue approximately two blocks to Griffin. Turn left to visit **Dallas World Aquarium,** an indoor re-creation of a tropical rain forest. After exiting the museum, turn right on Griffin and walk two blocks to Pacific. Turn left and walk two blocks to **Thanks-Giving Square,** at the corner of Bryan and Pacific. After exploring this site's tranquil chapel and park, exit on Ervay Street, turn right, and walk two blocks to Main Street, where you'll find the flagship of luxe retailer **Neiman Marcus.** Walk four blocks down Ervay to Young Street. Turn right on Young and walk past the I. M. Pei–designed City Hall, with its Henry Moore sculpture in front. Continue on Young past Akard and Field streets and enter Pioneer Park on your left. The park is notable for its cemetery, which contains the remains of some of Dallas's first residents. At the corner of Young and Griffin you'll see Pioneer Plaza and its massive **Robert Summer Sculpture,** which is a bronze rendering of a herd of longhorn cattle. Cross Griffin and continue down Young for five blocks to Houston. Enter Union Station train depot and take its underground tunnel to **Reunion Tower,** which has a revolving restaurant and cocktail lounge, as well as a 50-story observation deck with a 360° view of the city. Return to Union Station, exit, and turn left on Houston to head back to **The Sixth Floor Museum.**

## DRIVING AROUND TOWN

As the eighth-largest city in the nation, in a huge state known for wide-open spaces, it comes as no surprise that Dallas/Fort Worth is a car town. Thousands of people commute every day from outlying suburbs of the Dallas/Ft. Worth Metroplex, streaming into the city via the area's interstate and highway arteries.

The main approaches to Dallas proper include I–35 from Oklahoma in the north and Waco to the south. I–35 actually forks near Denton, with I–35E going into Dallas and I–35W heading for Fort Worth. I–30 serves the area from Arkansas, I–20 from Louisiana and New Mexico, and I–45 from Houston. Dallas and Fort Worth themselves are linked by I–20, but the more useful route for travelers wishing to see the city's most notable points of interest is I–30, which better connects the northern parts of town.

The Dallas area has two tollways: the Dallas North Tollway (running from I–35E north of downtown Dallas into Collin County), and the Mountain Creek Bridge (which serves southwestern Dallas County). The I–30, I–35, and I–635 expressways all have High Occupancy Vehicle (HOV) lanes for autos carrying two or more people.

While almost all thoroughfares in the Dallas/Fort Worth Metroplex are well signed and clearly marked, they often go by unlisted local names, which can be confusing for out-of-towners. For example, U.S. 75 is marked as such on the map, but is known locally as the Central Expressway. Be sure to check for such discrepancies when asking for directions.

Downtown Dallas and the areas surrounding it contain many of the city's tourist attractions; as a result, traffic can often be a force to contend with. Weekday morning rush hour congests the downtown area and main roads leading into it from about 7:30 AM until 9 AM and again in the evening from 4:30 PM until around 8 PM. Most of the streets in the downtown business district are one-way. Expect the occasional delay if you plan to head into or out of the downtown area during these times.

Once you arrive in the downtown area, you'll be pleased to find no shortage of safe, affordable parking spaces. Dallas has 75,873 off-street parking spots, split equally between guarded lots and ramps. Daytime parking in surface lots averages about $2.50 per day. Ramp rates average about $7 per day.

Dallas contains over 2 miles of underground pedestrian walkways, and a mile of elevated skywalks providing access to over 250 restaurants and shops.

Because tow-away zones are common in the downtown area, you're advised to make sure you're not attempting to park in a government lot or in a reserved private space. Fines for minor violations range from $5 to $100, depending on the infraction. You should also note that anyone caught littering from a vehicle in Texas may be fined up to $500 under the "Don't Mess With Texas" program.

Speed limits in the downtown area vary from neighborhood to neighborhood—the most common limits being between 20–25 mph. Traffic sometimes moves more slowly, especially in the entertainment districts on weekend nights when pedestrian traffic is heavy. Outside the city limits, speed limits are 70 mph on interstates and 65 mph on rural highways. Speed limits are more strictly enforced within city limits than on the open road, though speeders with out-of-state plates would be well-advised to mind the speedometer.

Right turns on red are permitted after a full stop throughout Texas, including Dallas/Fort Worth.

## TRANSPORTATION

**Airports:** Most of the major airlines fly into the **Dallas/Fort Worth International Airport** (3200 E. Airfield Dr. | 972/574–8888 | www.dfwairport.com) and the **Dallas Love Field Airport** (214/670–6073).

**Rail:** Amtrak's service to Los Angeles, Chicago, and San Antonio is available from Dallas. | 400 S. Houston St. | 800/872–7245.

**Bus:** **Greyhound Bus Lines** connects Dallas to Fort Worth, San Antonio, Houston, and beyond. | 205 S. Lamar | 800/231–2222.

**Intra-city Transit. Dallas Area Rapid Transit (DART)** is a light rail and city bus system which serves the greater Dallas urban area (214/979–1111).

Taxi companies that operate in the area include **Allied Taxi Service** (214/654–4440), **Cowboy Cab Company** (214/428–0202), and **Kelley Cab** (972/235–7777).

## Attractions

### ART AND ARCHITECTURE

**Bank of America Tower.** Formerly the Nations Bank Tower, this 72-story office building is outlined in bright green lights at night and is visible for miles around. | 901 Main St. | Free | Daily.

**Dallas City Hall.** Designed by renowned architect I. M. Pei, City Hall is distinguished by a massive, bronze Henry Moore sculpture on the plaza outside. | 1500 Marilla St. | 214/670–3322 | Free | Daily.

### DEEP ELLUM

New Orleans may have Bourbon Street, and Memphis has Beale Street, but Dallas has Deep Ellum.

Deep Ellum is the hottest spot in Dallas, the cutting edge of the city's music and art, but the neighborhood, now stretching to Commerce and Main Streets, began on Elm Street as a railroad crossing in the 1860s. The area was the home of many blue collar laborers who, with their Southern drawl, pronounced Elm Street as "Ellum." Gradually, businesses developed, but the district remained on the fringe of society, a place rife with prostitution, pawn shops, and a general seediness that earned it the nickname "the Bowery of the South."

Deep Ellum's days as a music capital date back to the 1920s. Blues clubs thrived and recording scouts began prowling the streets looking for talent. Blind Lemon Jefferson, a regular performer in Deep Ellum's brothels, saloons and streets, was reportedly discovered—with a tin cup in his hand—by a Paramount scout here.

After Blind Lemon's day, Deep Ellum's popularity waned. The Central Expressway (I–75) was completed in the 1940s and further separated the neighborhood from the downtown area. Little by little, the district fell into decline. Since the early 1990s however, artists have begun moving back to the neighborhood, attracted by spacious lofts and inexpensive rent. The area became revitalized as creative residents took warehouses and converted them into storefronts, studios, and modern-day music clubs.

Today, Deep Ellum is a thriving community with both residential and commercial areas.

© Artville

**Dallas Museum of Art.** Established in 1903, this extensive museum was the first to survey the art of the western hemisphere. Exhibits trace the lost civilizations of the Americas through sculpture, ceramics, and sacred objects; the collection also looks at American artists including O'Keeffe and Wyeth. The Reves Collection, one of the museum's largest, showcases works by Renoir, van Gogh, Pissaro, Cézanne, Redon, and others. The Contemporary Art exhibit is considered one of the largest collections of post-1945 artwork in the Southwest. Ancient American, African, and Indonesian art are on display as well. | 1717 N. Harwood St. | 214/922–1200 | fax 214/922–1825 | www.dm-art.org | Free | Tues.–Sun. 11–5, Thurs. 11–9.

**De Musica.** Gracing the front of the Morton H. Meyerson Symphony Center, this solid-iron monument was created by the great Basque sculptor, Eduardo Chillida. | Free | Daily.

**Meadows School of the Arts.** Considered one of the top collections of Spanish art found outside Spain, exhibits include works from the 10th through the 20th centuries. Works by Miró, Goya, Picasso, Velazquez, and others are featured. | 6101 Bishop Blvd. | 214/768–ARTS | Free | Aug.–May, daily 12–5.

**Old City Park.** This is a collection of historic homes and structures that reflects the appearance of Dallas from 1840–1910. The 1860s Living Farmstead has costumed docents who reenact farm chores. | 1717 Gano St. | 214/421–5141 | www.oldcitypark.org | $6, free on Mon. | Tues.–Sat. 10–4, Sun. 12–4.

**Old Red Courthouse.** This 1892 Romanesque building of red sandstone is one of the city's oldest surviving structures. Inside, you'll find the Dallas Visitor Information Center, with videos, touch-screen tourist information, and Internet access. A full staff is available to answer your questions. | 600 Commerce St. | 214/571–1300 | Free | Weekdays 8–5.

**Reunion Tower.** The observation deck on the 50th story gives you an unparalleled 360° view of downtown Dallas. If the view's not enough, there's also a revolving rooftop restaurant and bar. | 300 Reunion Blvd. | 214/651–1234 | Observation deck: $2 | Sun.–Thurs. 10–10, Fri., Sat. 10 AM–midnight.

**Robert Summer Sculpture.** Said to be the largest bronze sculpture in the world, this piece represents life on the old Shawnee Trail. | Pioneer Plaza | Free | Daily.

## CULTURE, EDUCATION, AND HISTORY

**Arts District Theater.** Dallas Theater Center productions are held in this 1985 building, which resembles a metal barn. Buy tickets at the Center's other performance venue, the Kalita Humphreys Theatre. | 2401 Flora St. | 214/522–8499 | fax 214/922–0430 | www.dallastheatercenter.org | $17–$55 | Box office: Sept.–May, weekdays 10–8, weekends noon–8; Oct.–Apr., weekdays 9–6, closed weekends.

**Coca-Cola Starplex.** When big-name entertainment comes through town, the show usually happens at this venue, also called the Smirnoff Music Centre. The business office extends its hours on showdates. | 1818 1st Ave., Fair Park | 214/421–1111 | fax 214/428–8365 | www.hob.com/business/corporate/hobconcerts/starplex/ | $12–$67 | May–Nov., weekdays 9:30–5:30.

**Kalita Humphreys Theatre.** This theater was designed by Frank Lloyd Wright and serves as home of the Dallas Theater Center. | 3636 Turtle Creek Blvd. | 214/522–8499 | fax 214/922–0430 | www.dallastheatercenter.org | $17–$55 | Box office: Sept.–May, weekdays 10–8, weekends noon–8; Oct.–Apr., weekdays 9–6, closed weekends.

**John F. Kennedy Memorial.** Architect Philip Johnson, a personal friend of John F. Kennedy, designed this stark monument to symbolize an open, empty tomb. The cenotaph is a short walk away from Dealey Plaza, at Main and Market streets. | Dallas County Historic Plaza | Free | Daily.

**John Neely Bryan Cabin.** This replica of the first home built in Dallas, by settler John Bryan, now resides adjacent to the Old Red Courthouse in Founder's Plaza, a quarter-mile from the original cabin, which was destroyed in a flood and restored in 1935. | Dallas County Historic Plaza | No phone | Free | Daily.

**Majestic Theatre.** A beautifully restored 1920s vaudeville house and movie palace, the Majestic hosts Dallas Summer Musicals, touring Broadway performances, the Dallas Black Dance Theater, the Dallas Classical Guitar Society, and Ballet Dallas. | 1925 Elm St. | 214/880–0137 | fax 214/880–0097 | $6–$80 | Box office: 1 hr before showtime.

**Music Hall at Fair Park.** Home to the State Fair of Texas musical events, this Spanish Baroque–style structure has six massive stair towers, five 40-ft arcaded porches, and enough seating for 3,420 music fans. | 909 First Ave. | 214/565–1116 or 214/443–5678 | fax 214/565–0071 | $9–$70 | Weekdays 9–5.

**Morton H. Meyerson Symphony Center.** Designed by I. M. Pei, this structure boasts sweeping, dramatic curves, ever-changing vanishing points, and surprising views. It's home to both the Lay Family Organ, a hand-built and installed Fisk organ with 4,535 pipes, and the Dallas Symphony Orchestra, and hosts volunteer programs, community events, children's activities, and, of course, concerts. Tours are available. | 2301 Flora St. | 214/670–3600 or 214/670–3721 | www.dallassymphony.com | $35–$100 | Box office: weekdays 8:30–5:30.

## MUSEUMS

**Conspiracy Museum.** If you don't buy the lone-gunman theory, or if a trip to the grassy knoll just wasn't enough, pay a visit to the Conspiracy Museum, where the history of presidential assassinations and cover-ups from 1835 to the present is meticulously examined by the staff "assassinologist." | 110 S. Market St. | 214/741–3040 | fax 241/741–9339 | www.conspiracymuseum.com | $7 | Daily 10–6.

**Fair Park Dallas.** The largest state fair in the nation is held here each Oct. Year-round you can visit many museums here, most of which were built for the 1936 Texas Centennial and sport an art deco style. | 3601 Martin Luther King Blvd. | 214/670–8400 | Free | Daily.

★ The **African American Museum** is housed in a two-story building with a rotunda and 60-ft dome at its center. It's the only major facility in the Southwest devoted to African-American history, art, and culture. Permanent exhibits include the Billy R. Allen Folk Art Collection, with works by Clementine Hunter, David Butler, and Johnny Banks. Folk art and historic artifacts from the Negro Baseball League can be viewed. | 3536 Grand Ave. | 214/565–9026 | Donation accepted | Tues.–Fri. 12–5, Sat. 10–5, Sun. 1–5.

★ The **Age of Steam Railroad Museum** recalls the grand days of rail travel with Pullman cars, large locomotives, and a 1905 depot. | 1105 Washington Ave. | 214/428–0101 | www.startext.net/homes/railroad | $4 | Wed.–Sun. 10–5.

Built in the shape of an inverted T, the **Hall of State** documents Texas history and has statues of Texas heroes. | 3939 Grand Fair Park | 214/421–4500 | www.hallofstate.com | Free | Tues.–Sat. 9–5, Sun. 1–5.

The **Dallas Museum of Natural History** opened in 1936. Today it has many dioramas of animals found in Texas, as well as the first mounted Texas dinosaur. | 3535 Grand Ave. | 214/421–3466 | www.dallasdino.org | $5 | Daily 10–5.

Home to 5,000 aquatic animals in fresh and saltwater displays, the **Dallas Aquarium at Fair Park** is active in conservation efforts for Texas species such as the Texas blind salamander. Shark or piranha feedings are held every afternoon excluding Mon. | 1462 1st Ave. | 214/670–8443 | www.dallas-zoo.org/aquarium | $3 | Daily 9–4:30.

The **Science Place** seeks to make scientific principles accessible to both children and adults, and thus employs a hands-on approach to its exhibits. Highlights include an IMAX theater with a 79-ft domed screen, and Kids Place. The latter makes good use of math skills in the "Numbers Forest," while the ideal playhouse can be constructed in "Building Things." | 1318 2nd Ave. | 214/428–5555 | www.scienceplace.org | $6 | Daily 9:30–8.

Decorative and native Texas plants are housed in the **Dallas Horticulture Center.** The William Douglas Blanchly Conservatory, the first conservatory built in the Southwest, contains African plants. | 2nd Ave. and Martin Luther King Jr. Blvd. | 214/428–7476 | Free | Tues.–Sat. 10–5, Sun. 1–5.

**Mary Kay Museum.** This museum enshrines beauty-secret memorabilia in honor of Dallas native Mary Kay Ash, who founded a humble cosmetics company in 1963, and watched it grow into an empire. The 3,000-square-ft exhibit hall contains the household checkbook with which the company was founded, advertising memorabilia, and plenty of pink. Call to schedule guided tours. | 16251 N. Dallas Pkwy. | 972/687–6300 | Free | Weekdays 8:30–5.

**McKinney Avenue Contemporary.** The MAC, dedicated to "the presentation of art from all disciplines," is an 18,000-square-ft building housing two art galleries, a black-box theater, a small cinema, coffee shop, bookstore, and cyber-cafe. | 3120 McKinney Ave. | 214/953–1212 | fax 214/953–1873 | www.the-mac.org | Free | Wed.–Sat. 11–10, Sun. 1–5.

★ **The Sixth Floor Museum at Dealey Plaza.** Housed in the former Texas School Book Depository, this museum is devoted to the life, career, and assassination of President John F. Kennedy. | 411 Elm St. | 214/747–6660 | www.jfk.org | $9 | Daily 9–6.

## PARKS, NATURAL SIGHTS, AND OUTDOOR ACTIVITIES

**Dallas Burn.** See Dallas's hometown soccer club go up against rivals from as far away as New Zealand. From March to July, before every weekend home game, Gate 2 of the Cotton Bowl is given over to Soccer Celebration, a festival for all ages, complete with soccer celebrities, friendly competition, and instructional clinics. | Cotton Bowl, Fair Park | 214/979–0303 or 214/373–8000 | www.burnsoccer.com | $6–$60.

**White Rock Lake Park.** Sailing, fishing, hiking, biking, horseback riding, picnicking, and bird watching are possible here. | 8200 Garland Rd. | 214/670–8281 or 214/670–4100 | Free | Daily.

## RELIGION AND SPIRITUALITY

**Biblical Arts Center.** Housed in a building with a limestone entrance modeled after Paul's Gate in Damascus, this gallery contains a variety of biblical art. Among the items are a reproduction of a site in Jerusalem many believe to be the garden tomb of Christ. The "Miracle at Pentecost" mural is 124-ft long and includes more than 200 biblical characters. The mural is unveiled with a 30-minute sound and light presentation several times daily. | 7500 Park Ln. | 214/691–4661 | www.biblicalarts.org | Free; mural $7 | Tues.–Sat. 10–5, Sun. 1–5.

## SHOPPING

**Crescent.** This plaza is home to retailers, offices, and a hotel with some *very* ritzy shops. | 500 Crescent Ct., off McKinney Ave. | 214/871–3200 or 800/654–6541 | Free | Daily.

**Dallas Farmer's Market.** One of the largest—and last—of its kind, this market brings over 1,000 area producers together to sell their wares. Not just about tomatoes and melons, many vendors display baked goods, plants, flowers, and seasonal crafts. | 1010 S. Pearl St. | 214/939–2808 | Free | Daily, dawn–dusk.

**Galleria.** Boasting more than 200 retailers and anchor stores, such as Macy's, Nordstrom, Saks Fifth Avenue, and Marshall Field, this is one of Dallas's most luxurious malls. | LBJ Freeway at the Dallas North Tollway | 972/702–7100 | Free | Mon.–Sat. 10–9, Sun. noon–6.

**Highland Park Village.** Well known for its collection of exclusive luxury retailers, this mall was one the first planned shopping centers in America. | Mockingbird La. at Preston Rd. | 214/559–2740 | www.hpvillage.com | Free | Mon.–Sat. 10–6, Thurs. 10–8, Sun. 12–5.

**Neiman Marcus.** See where a deluxe shopping dynasty began; the original Neiman Marcus resides in downtown Dallas. | 1618 Main St. | 214/741–6911 | Free | Mon.–Sat. 10–5:30.

**NorthPark Center.** Developed by art collector Ray Nasher as one of the country's first indoor shopping centers, you'll find rotating exhibits of world-class art in this mall. | Central Expressway at Northwest Hwy. | 214/361–6345 or 214/363–7441 | Free | Mon.–Sat. 10–9, Sun. 12–6.

**West End MarketPlace.** Once a candy-and-cracker factory, this West End Historic District fixture is now a lively, five-story shopping and dining center. | 603 Munger Ave. | 214/748–4801 | Free | Mon.–Thurs. 11–10, Fri.–Sat. 11–midnight, Sun. noon–6.

## SPECTATOR SPORTS

**Professional sports.** Nearly every major professional sport is covered in Dallas.

The **Dallas Cowboys** make their home at Texas Stadium | 2401 E. Airport Fwy., Irving | 214/972/785–5000 | $36–$58.

For a ferocious game of indoor soccer, watch the **Dallas Sidekicks** play at Reunion Arena. | 777 Sports St. | 972/988–3865 | www.dallassidekicks.com | $8–$25 | July–Dec.

The **NBA Dallas Mavericks** basketball team shoots for the hoop at Reunion Arena. | 777 Sports St. | 214/800–3089 | $8–$70.

Those interested in hockey can root for the **NHL Dallas Stars** at Reunion Arena. | 777 Sports St. | 214/GO–STARS | $22–$275.

The **Texas Rangers** American League baseball team plays at The Ballpark at Arlington, at the junction of Rte. 360 and I–30. | 1000 Ballpark Way | 817/273–5100 or 817/748–1808 | $5–$50.

## SIGHTSEEING TOURS/TOUR COMPANIES

**Gray Line Bus Tours.** Narrated bus tours highlighting Dallas's top attractions leave from several hotels in the city. | 972/263–0294 or 800/256–4723 | fax 972/262–2761 | www.grayline.com | $22–$63.

**McKinney Ave. Trolley Line.** Trolley service brings you to Dallas's top sights. | 214/855–0006 | fax 214/855–5250 | $2 | Weekends 10–10.

## OTHER POINTS OF INTEREST

**Club Clearview.** This complex is housed in a Deep Ellum warehouse and attracts both national and local music acts. Actually four distinct clubs, the Clearview is united by a 6,000-square-ft mural adorning its facade and the famous "blacklight room" which connects the four clubs within. | 2803 Main St. | 214/939–0077 | fax 214/744–0293 | www.clubclearview.com | $6–$10 | Thurs.–Sat. 9 PM–2 AM.

**Club Dada.** You can catch live music here five nights a week. Club Dada has three stages: two inside and one outside on the club's huge, landscaped patio. The scene is often young; there are a Beatles night and a Grateful Dead night once a week. | 2720 Elm St. | 214/744–3232 | www.clubdada.com | $6–$10 | Wed.–Thurs. 6 PM–2 AM, Fri.–Sat. 5 PM–2 AM.

The **Cotton Bowl Stadium** is the home of the Cotton Bowl as well as the University of Texas vs. University of Oklahoma football game every Oct. | 214/670–8400 or 214/638–2695 (ticket office).

**Country 2000.** To call this a big club would be a grave understatement. Country 2000 is a 40,000-square-ft nightlife mecca with two massive dance floors connected by an elevator, three full bars, in-house dance instructors (lessons are free), and enough room for over 3,000 revelers. On concert nights, opening hours are extended and ticket charges apply. | 10580 N. Stemmons Freeway | 214/654–9595 | fax 214/654–0549 | www.country2000.com | $4–$10 | Wed.–Fri. 6 PM–2 AM, Sat. 7 PM–2 AM, Sun. 4 PM–2 AM.

**Dallas Alley.** A one-stop destination for West End revelers of all ages; one cover charge provides admission to several clubs. | 2019 N. Lamar St. | 214/880–7420 | fax 214/720–7268 | www.dallasalleydallastexas.com | $5–$10 | Daily 6 PM–2 AM.

**Dallas Arboretum and Botanical Garden.** This expansive arboretum is alive with flowers year-round. It's especially known for its annual "Dallas Blooms" show in the spring. | 8525

Garland Rd. | 214/327–8263 | fax 214/324–9801 | $6, $3 parking | Mar.–Oct., daily 10–6, Nov.–Feb., daily 10–5.

**Dallas World Aquarium.** You'll find a South American rainforest, the world's largest freshwater aquarium filled with giant catfish, and a 22,000-gallon walk-through tunnel here. Two restaurants are also on site. | 1801 N. Griffin St. | 214/720–2224 | fax 214/720–2242 | www.dwazoo.com | $11 | Daily 10–5.

**Dallas Zoo.** Founded in 1888, the Dallas Zoo includes the modern "Wilds of Africa" section, which you can visit by hopping on the narrated Monorail Safari tour. The Bird and Reptile Building is home to 130 reptile and amphibian species. | 650 R. L. Thornton Freeway | 214/670–5656 | www.dallas-zoo.org | $6 | Daily 9–5.

**Dubliner.** Come to this rowdy Irish pub to hoist a few pints or throw a game of darts. | 2818 Greenville Ave. | 214/818–0911 | Free | Weekdays 4 PM–2 AM, weekends 2 PM–2 AM.

**Lounge at the Inwood.** Connected to Dallas's premier art-house movie theater, this suave bar is decorated like the set of a sophisticated film. With 40s-era murals on the ceiling and a soothing "water wall," the lounge creates an ideal setting for one of its perfect martinis. | 5458 W. Lovers Ln | 214/350–7834 | Free | Mon., Fri., Sat. 5 PM–2 AM, Sun., Tue.–Thurs. 5 PM–1 AM.

**Mick's.** Most of the Dallas nightlife swirls around lower and upper Greenville Avenue, north of downtown, and Mick's is a low-key spot to sip a well-mixed beverage and watch the activity. | 2825 Greenville Ave. | 214/827–0039 | Free | Daily 5 PM–2 AM.

**Poor David's Pub.** This cozy, coffeehouse setting is a good place to chat with friends, and maybe catch a big-name folk music act for an impromptu performance. Cover charges depend on who's playing. | 1924 Greenville Ave. | 214/821–9891 | www.poordavidspub.com | $8–$20 | Tue.–Sat. 7 PM–2 AM.

**Red Jacket.** From house music on Wednesdays to swing on Thursdays to disco and funk on Fridays, the Red Jacket aims to satisfy all music tastes. When you're tired of dancing, relax in the club's "Ruby Room", a tongue-in-cheek homage to the man who gunned down JFK's assassin. Valet parking is available. | 3606 Greenville Ave. | 214/823–8333 | $6–$8 | Wed.–Thurs. 10 PM–2 AM, Fri.–Sun. 9 PM–2 AM.

**Scarborough Faire Renaissance Village.** This 35-acre Renaissance theme village 30 mi south of Dallas has food, music, magic shows, jesters, and falconry displays. | I–35E, Exit 399A | $16 | Apr.–June, weekends and Memorial Day 10–7 PM | 972/938–3247.

**Thanks-Giving Square.** This small, triangular plaza was designed by Philip Johnson to include quiet gardens and a chapel with stained-glass windows by Gabriel Loire. | Pacific Ave. and Ervay St. | 214/969–1977 or 888/305–1205 | fax 214/754–0152 | www.thanksgiving.org | Free | Office: Weekdays 9–5.

**Trees.** Set in a dark, cavernous warehouse, this is the place to see up-and-coming local acts, traveling shows, and the occasional big-name performer. The drinking, like the music, is hard. | 2707 Elm St. | 214/748–5009 | $6–$12 | Wed.–Thurs. 8:30 PM–1 AM, Fri.–Sat. 9 PM–2 AM.

**Village Station.** Mere steps from a half-dozen other vibrant nightspots, the Station caters to a predominantly gay and lesbian crowd. The multi-leveled club sports an outdoor patio, plenty of seating and mingling areas, and the Rose Room, a small lounge upstairs featuring drag. "Trash Disco" on Sundays is not to be missed. | 3911 Cedar Springs Rd., Oaklawn | 214/526–7171 | $5–$10 | Wed.–Sun. 9 PM–4 AM.

## ON THE CALENDAR

**JAN.:** *Southwestern Bell Cotton Bowl Classic.* This annual game pits the champions of the NCAA's Big 12 and the Southeastern Conference in an exciting matchup on New Year's Day. | 214/634–7525.

**JAN., FEB., JULY:** *Boat Show.* One of the largest boat shows in the nation. | 972/714–0177.

**MAR.:** *North Texas Irish Festival.* Held in Fair Park, the largest music festival in Texas celebrates Celtic heritage with live entertainment on seven stages, craft demonstrations, music and dance exhibitions, traditional food and drink, and more. | 214/821–4174 | www.ntif.org.

**MAR., APR.:** *Dallas Blooms.* The largest flower show in the Southwest is held at the Dallas Arboretum and Botanical Garden. | 214/327–4901.

**APR.–OCT.:** *Mesquite Championship Rodeo.* This event includes barrel racing, roping, and rodeo clowns. | 972/285–8777.

**MAY:** *Byron Nelson Golf Classic.* Some of the top names in the golf world attend this tournament. | 972/717–1200.

**OCT.:** *State Fair of Texas.* Fair Park hosts the nation's largest state fair, which includes North America's largest Ferris wheel, a livestock show, an auto show, free concerts, and fireworks. | 214/565–9931.

## Dining

### INEXPENSIVE

**Arc-en-Ciel.** Vietnamese. Although this is a very large restaurant, you can have an intimate dining experience in a private, curtained area. Try the charcoal-broiled pork, lobster, or shrimp baked with cheese. Sun. brunch. | 3555 W. Walnut St., Garland | 972/272–2188 | $8–$20 | AE, D, DC, MC, V.

**Athenee Cafe.** Mediterranean. Popular dishes include the rack of lamb, stuffed cabbage, and snapper. | 5365 Spring Valley Rd. #150 | 972/239–8060 | Reservations essential Fri., Sat. | No lunch Sat. | $11–$15 | AE, D, DC, MC, V.

**Aw Shucks.** American. A casual place specializing in all things tasty and aquatic, Aw Shucks serves a huge, whole catfish lightly fried in cornmeal batter, and many other catch-of-the-day specials. Paper towels are used for napkins here, you can mix your own sauces to taste, and everybody pays on the honor system. | 3601 Greenville Ave. | 214/821–9449 | $6–$10 | AE, DC, MC, V.

**Blue Mesa Grill.** Southwestern. This informal restaurant has a tree-filled covered patio for outdoor dining. Try the tequila-roasted duck or smoked chicken enchiladas. Kids' menu. Sun. brunch. | 5100 Belt Line Rd. | 972/934–0165 | $8–$14 | AE, DC, MC, V.

**Bread Winners Cafe and Bakery.** Contemporary. This café has an in-house bakery which makes fresh breads and pastries. Try the New York Strip steak. For dessert, the cheesecake is popular. Sun. brunch. | 3301 McKinney Ave. | 214/754–4940 | No supper Mon.–Tues. | $10–$15 | AE, D, DC, MC, V.

**Campisi's Egyptian.** Italian. This family-friendly restaurant is home to renowned pizzas and pasta dishes. Add low lighting and quick, congenial service to Campisi's tasty, inexpensive food, and you've got a lively setting and sometimes lines out the door. | 5610 E. Mockingbird Ln. | 214/827–0355 | $6–$10 | AE, D, MC, V.

**Celebration.** American. Dine outdoors on the covered patio, which has a fireplace. Known for pot roast. Kids' menu. | 4503 W. Lovers Ln. | 214/351–5681 | $9–$16 | AE, D, DC, MC, V.

**Dream Cafe.** Contemporary. This festive restaurant blends Mediterranean-style cuisine with flavors from the American Southwest for a healthful, organic menu. Try the crunchy coconut shrimp appetizer, or stop into the bakery for a quick bite to go. Dream Cafe is especially known for its fabulous breakfasts. Ask for seating on the spacious back patio. | 2800 Routh St. | 214/954–0486 | Reservations recommended for brunch | $9 | AE, D, DC, MC, V.

**French Corner.** French. This restaurant only seats 11 inside and a few more outside, but the close quarters do not hamper the kitchen's enthusiasm. Specializing in crêpes of all descriptions, French Corner is best known for its delicate Florentine crêpe: a mixture of chicken, spinach, and a subtle sauce. You'll also find varied quiches, salads, and soup dishes. | 2221 Greenville Ave. | 214/828–8783 | $6–$10 | No credit cards.

**Gloria's.** Latin. The food here is Mexican and Salvadoran, with plentiful servings and intriguing desserts; you must try the chocolate flan. Gloria's also has a wider variety of margaritas than you might have thought possible. The restaurant's interior is typical Tex-Mex, and it's known to get loud at peak times. The outside dining is good for people-watching. | 3715 Greenville Ave. | 214/874-0088 | $8–$14 | AE, D, MC, V.

**La Calle Doce.** Mexican. The most mouthwatering *mariscos* (seafood) in Dallas, particularly the fish soup, keep local customers coming back to this relatively undiscovered restaurant in the little, blue house in Oak Hill. | 415 W. 12th St. | 214/941-4304 | $5–$15 | AE, D, DC, MC, V.

**Lombardi's.** Italian. In addition to Dallas, this Italian restaurant chain has franchises in Miami, Ft. Lauderdale, Captiva Island, Atlanta, and Phoenix. Dine outdoors on one of the 15 sidewalk tables with umbrellas and tablecloths. Try the crab soufflé. | 311 N. Market St. | 214/747-0322 | $10–$28 | AE, DC, MC, V.

**Mama's Daughter's Diner.** American. Favored by bikers and long-haul truckers, this diner serves up super hearty portions of classic American comfort food: potatoes 'n' gravy, chicken-fried steak, and meatloaf. | 2014 Irving Blvd. | 214/742-8646 | $5–$10 | AE, D, MC, V.

**Matt's Rancho Martinez.** Mexican. Part of an extensive, much-loved network of Martinez-family establishments, Matt's does Tex-Mex with flair—minus the usual Dallas overload of sombrero-and-cactus kitsch. Topping the list of reasonably priced, well-prepared dishes is Bob Armstrong Dip, named for a local official devoted to its consumption. Essentially a big bowl of queso loaded with chunks of beef, sour cream, and guacamole, and sided with a pile of tortilla chips, the dip is more like a meal. | 6332 La Vista Dr. | 214/823-5517 | Closed Sun. | $8–$10 | AE, D, DC, MC, V.

**Mi Piace.** Italian. A moon-roof that opens to the sky, huge windows that overlook a patio with a garden and duck pond, and cream-colored archways lend a Tuscan charm to this restaurant. Risottos and homemade pastas are made daily on the premises, and fish and seafood dishes like calamari and Dover sole are delicately prepared with flavorful southern Italian sauces. | 14854 Montfort Dr. | 972/934-8424 | $10–$30 | AE, D, DC, MC, V.

**Patrizio.** Italian. Try the angel-hair artichoke pasta or crab claws at this local eatery that specializes in New York-style Italian cuisine. Open-air dining is available on a shady patio with a view of a shopping village. | 25 Highland Park Village | 214/522-7878 | $10–$25 | AE, D, DC, MC, V.

**Rodeo Steakhouse.** Steak. This moderately priced, downtown restaurant serves "the best darn steaks in town." You'll find it mere steps from three major hotels and just down from Sundance Square. | 1309 Calhoun St. | 817/332-1288 | fax 817/332-4723 | No lunch | $10–$30 | AE, D, MC, V.

**Sonny Bryan's.** Barbecue. Wooden benches and tables are part of this restaurant's rustic look. The outdoor dining area has wrought iron, umbrellaed tables. Try the ribs, beef brisket, or smoked turkey; popular side dishes include green bean casserole, homemade macaroni and cheese, and fried okra. Kids' menu. | 302 N. Market St. | 214/744-1610 | $8–$15 | AE, D, DC, MC, V.

**Thai Taste.** Thai. This longtime local favorite with raised cielings, huge windows, and subtle paintings on the wall moved here from the Highland Park area in 1995. Popular dishes include eggplant with green curry and basil, garlic prawns with broccoli, and Phad Thai (rice noodles with shrimp and peanuts). | 3101 N. Fitzhugh Ave. | 214/521-3513 | No lunch Sun.–Tues. | $9–$11 | AE, D, DC, MC, V.

**Ziziki's.** Mediterranean. Open-air dining is available on a patio. Try the paella. | 4514 Travis St., Suite 122 | 214/521-2233 | $10–$23 | AE, DC, MC, V.

## MODERATE

**Addison Café.** French. This small restaurant is know for its Gallic dishes, bistro setting, and extensive wine list. The rabbit and duck dishes are popular. | 5290 Belt Line Rd. #108, Addison | 972/991-8824 | $13–$22 | AE, D, DC, MC, V.

**Adelmo's.** Mediterranean. Tablecloths, candles, fresh flowers, and mauve walls create a cozy and romantic feel inside this 25-table, two-story restaurant. Head upstairs for a little more space and privacy. Try the lobster, duck with strawberry brandy sauce, or the 20-oz. veal chop. | 4537 Cole Ave. | 214/559-0325 | Closed Sun. No lunch Sat. | $14–$29 | AE, D, DC, MC, V.

**Cafe Cipriani.** Italian. Romantic lighting, lots of warm, dark wood and snow-white linens enhance a menu of made-from-scratch north Italy specialties. Try the chef's lasagna, the canelloni filled with fresh shrimp, scallops, and crabmeat, or the rolled chicken breast stuffed with wild mushrooms. The restaurant is always packed, particularly on weekends when there's live piano music. | 220 E. Colinas Blvd. | 972/869-0713 | fax 214/869-2281 | Closed Sun. | $17 | AE, D, DC, MC, V.

**Chez Gerard.** French. Gallic dishes are served in a classic bistro setting, with fabric walls, hardwood floors and fresh flowers throughout. Outdoor dining is possible on a covered patio. Try the chateaubriand. | 4444 McKinney Ave. | 214/522-6865 | Closed Sun. No lunch Sat. | $16–$30 | AE, D, DC, MC, V.

**Dakota's.** American. Marble tables, dark wood accents, French doors, and an Italian marble floor create a sleek look. The granite outdoor patio has a five-tier waterfall. Try the swordfish. | 600 N. Akard St. | 214/740-4001 | No lunch Sat., Sun. | $12–$20 | AE, D, DC, MC, V.

**Ferrari's Italian Villa.** Italian. Tables surround a masonry oven that stands in the dining area. Try linguini *pescatore* or veal *piccata al limone* (veal served in a white wine lemon sauce with capers). Homemade pasta. | 14831 Midway Rd., Addison | 972/980-9898 | Closed Sun. No lunch Sat. | $15–$30 | AE, D, DC, MC, V.

**Gershwin's.** American. The dining room is adorned with wood, brass, wrought-iron, and white linen. Try the red snapper for supper and, for a truly special dessert, indulge in the chocolate sack (Godiva chocolate melted into the shape of a delicate sack and stuffed with pound cake, strawberries, kiwis, and Grand Marnier). Pianist. Kids' menu. | 8442 Walnut Hill Ln | 214/373-7171 | Closed Sun. No lunch Sat. | $16–$30 | AE, D, DC, MC, V.

**Javier's.** Mexican. Exposed brick walls, antiques, and dim lighting give this restaurant a burnished glow. Specials include the *filete cantinflas* (beef tenderloin stuffed with Chihuahua cheese and seasoned butter, topped with a mild Chile mulato sauce and sliced avocado served with black beans and rice). | 4912 Cole Ave. | 214/521-4211 | www.javiersrestaurant.com | No lunch | $15–$20 | AE, D, DC, MC, V.

**Jennivine.** Continental. This popular restaurant resembles a country cottage. Known for rack of lamb, beef tenderloin, and duck. Open-air dining is available on a patio with umbrellaed tables, surrounded by a garden. Sun. brunch. | 3605 McKinney Ave. | 214/528-6010 | $14–$25 | AE, D, DC, MC, V.

**L'Ancestral.** French. Dine outdoors on the stone terrace at this French bistro, which has long been a favorite in the Highland Park area. Try the pepper steak. | 4514 Travis St. #124 | 214/528-1081 | Closed Sun. | $15–$30 | AE, D, DC, MC, V.

**La Trattoria Lombardi.** Italian. Antique furnishings and exposed brick walls hung with pictures and tapestries are found throughout. The southern Italian menu includes specials like fettucine pescatore (scallops, shrimp, and mussels in a white wine sauce over fettucine) and veal chop served with portobello mushrooms. Open-air dining is available on a patio with 12 umbrellaed tables. | 2916 N. Hall St. | 214/954-0803 | No lunch Sat., Sun. | $12–$25 | AE, DC, MC, V.

**The Landmark.** Contemporary. This restaurant is in the Melrose hotel. Try the pumpkin seed-crusted beef filet. Sun. brunch. | 3015 Oaklawn Ave. | 214/521-5151 | Breakfast also available Mon.–Sat. | $16–$40 | AE, D, DC, MC, V.

**Lavendou.** French. Outdoor dining is possible on the covered terrace with a fountain and greenery. Try the cassoulet or *daube de boeuf.* No smoking. | 19009 Preston Rd. #200 | 972/248-1911 | Closed Sun. No lunch Sat. | $15–$23 | AE, D, DC, MC, V.

DALLAS

INTRO
ATTRACTIONS
DINING
LODGING

**Mediterraneo.** Continental. Specializing in southern French and northern Italian seafood dishes, this restaurant serves inspired meals like horseradish–encrusted halibut and polenta-coated north Atlantic salmon. The elegant dining room has linen tablecloths, chandeliers, and fine art on the walls. An outdoor patio has spiraled juniper trees, fountains, imported Indian tile inlays, and a delicate wrought-iron fence. Live entertainment Fri.–Sat. | 18111 Preston Rd., Suite 120 | 972/447–0066 | No lunch Sat., Sun. | $17–$27 | AE, DC, MC, V.

**Newport's Seafood.** Seafood. Housed in a former brewery, a 55-ft-deep, 30-ft-wide artesian well that fed the brewery stands in the middle of this restaurant's dining room. Try the almond-crusted filet of sole. | 703 McKinney Ave. | 214/954–0220 | www.newport-srestaurant.com | No lunch Sat., Sun. | $16–$34 | AE, D, DC, MC, V.

**Ruggeri's.** Italian. A favorite for "power lunches" as well as romantic dinners, this restaurant is known for Northern Italian fare. Muted lighting lends an intimate feel. Known for veal dishes. | 2911 Routh St. | 214/871–7377 | No lunch Sat., Sun. | $12–$23 | AE, D, DC, MC, V.

**Seventeen Seventeen.** Continental. Housed in the Dallas Museum of Art, this restaurant's patio lies outside of windows designed by Frank Lloyd Wright. Sun. brunch. | 1717 N. Harwood St. | 214/880–0158 | Closed Mon., Sat. | $12–$23 | AE, D, MC, V.

**Sushi.** Japanese. This sushi bar is in a lobby area of the elegant Stoneleigh hotel. No smoking. | 2927 Maple Ave. | 214/871–7111 | Closed Sun. | $12–$30 | AE, D, DC, MC, V.

**Toscana.** Italian. Dine outdoors on a covered patio and enjoy live jazz Tues.–Thurs. nights. Try the risotto or a sampling from the extensive wine list. Kids' menu. | 4900 McKinney Ave. | 214/521–2244 | $12–$31 | AE, DC, MC, V.

**Uncle Tai's.** Chinese. There's a formal dining section as well as a casual patio area that overlooks the ice rink of the Galleria mall. Popular dishes include General Tso's chicken and sweet and sour pork. No smoking. | 13350 Dallas Pkwy. | 972/934–9998 | $15–$25 | AE, DC, MC, V.

## EXPENSIVE

**AquaKnox.** Contemporary. Celebrity chef Stephan Pyles creates delicious, memorable seafood dishes in this sleek and trendy venue. From the primarily seafood menu, you can order elegant presentations of rock shrimp dumplings and cinnamon-scented, oak-roasted lobster. | 3214 Knox St. | 214/219–2782 | Reservations essential | No lunch | $24–$38 | AE, D, DC, MC, V.

**Cafe Pacific.** Seafood. Dine outdoors on the partly covered terrace. Try the almond crusted sole or pepper steak. | 24 Highland Park Village | 214/526–1170 | Closed Sun. No lunch Sat. | $20–$40 | AE, D, DC, MC, V.

**Chamberlain's Steak and Chop House.** Steak. The dining room has lots of cloth-covered tables and brass accents. Known for lamb, aged prime beef, and wild game. Kids' menu. | 5330 Belt Line Rd., Addison | 972/934–2467 | No lunch | $25–$30 | AE, D, DC, MC, V.

**The Enclave.** Continental. Curtained booths, tuxedoed wait-staff, and candlelit tables with fresh roses create a romantic setting. Popular dishes include the chateaubriand and rack of lamb. Live entertainment. | 8325 Walnut Hill Ln | 214/363–7487 | Reservations accepted | Closed Sun. No lunch Sat. | $20–$32 | AE, DC, MC, V.

**Kobe Steaks.** Japanese. The interior of this deluxe teppan-style steakhouse was designed by a noted Japanese architect and is an excellent setting in which to enjoy traditional cuisine prepared before your eyes. Separate rooms for larger groups are available. | 5000 Belt Line Rd. | 972/934–8150 | fax 972/404–9238 | No lunch | $13–$32 | AE, D, MC, V.

**Lawry's The Prime Rib.** Steak. Choose your meat from a silver cart for later tableside preparation. Known for prime rib and lobster tails. Kids' menu. | 14655 Dallas Pkwy. | 972/503–6686 | No lunch Sat. | $20–$40 | AE, D, DC, MC, V.

**Morton's of Chicago.** Steak. Meals are cooked on an open grill at this intimate restaurant in the basement of a historic building. Try the filet mignon or seafood. | 501 Elm St. | 214/741–2277 | No lunch | $20–$40 | AE, D, DC, MC, V.

**Old Warsaw.** French. Try the lobster thermidor or chateaubriand in this restaurant established in the mid-1900s. Live music is provided by a violinist or pianist. | 2610 Maple Ave. | 214/528–0032 | Reservations essential | Jacket required | No lunch | $21–$32 | AE, D, DC, MC, V.

**Palm.** Steak. This West End restaurant, with its clubby mahogany and caricatures of Dallas's rich and famous, is popular with the downtown business crowd. Known for surf and turf. | 701 Ross Ave. | 214/698–0470 | No lunch Sat., Sun. | $15–$60 | AE, DC, MC, V.

**Pyramid Grill.** American. An extended wine list, live piano music, and elegant furniture, gas lamps, linens, and silverware make this restaurant in The Fairmont Hotel a popular place. Try the Angus beef. | 1717 N. Akard St. | 214/720–5249 | $19–$40 | AE, D, DC, MC, V.

**Rooster.** Contemporary. This relaxed eatery's menu changes frequently. Try the baby lamb chops. Sun. brunch. | 3521 Oak Grove Ave. | 214/521–1234 | $18–$25 | AE, D, DC, MC, V.

**Royal Tokyo.** Japanese. Dine amid knife-wielding chefs in the Hibachi Steak Room or kimono-clad servers in one of the Tatami Rooms. The restaurant's sushi bar is the largest in Texas. The grounds include a pond surrounded by bonsai trees and an authentic Japanese garden. Try the *Wagyu* beef (tender meat from cattle bred in Japan), or any of the carefully prepared sashimi or sushi combinations. Kids' menu. | 7525 Greenville Ave. | 214/368–3304 | www.royaltokyo.com | $20–$36 | AE, D, DC, MC, V.

**Ruth's Chris Steak House.** Steak. This branch of the chain steakhouse has a country club feel, with dark paneled walls, heavy wood chairs, and prominently placed sports memorabilia. Popular dishes include live lobster, roasted chicken, and buffalo steaks. | 5922 Cedar Springs Rd. | 214/902–8080 | No lunch | $20–$34 | AE, D, DC, MC, V.

**York Street.** French. This small, intimate restaurant has just 12 tables. The menu is varied and there is an extensive wine list. Try the roast rack of lamb or the Cajun sea bass stuffed with crab. No smoking. | 6047 Lewis St. | 214/826–0968 | Closed Sun., Mon. No lunch | $16–$34 | MC, V.

## VERY EXPENSIVE

**Del Frisco's Double Eagle Steakhouse.** Steak. Eat an outrageously good steak in this country-club setting; you'll also find excellent veal and seafood, but the legendary beef is really the point here. | 5251 Spring Valley Rd. | 972/490–9000 | Reservations recommended | Closed Sun. No lunch | $45–$65 | AE, DC, MC, V.

**Enigma.** Contemporary. True to its name, this restaurant's seemingly themeless style is hard to define. No two tables are the same shape, no two place settings alike. There are even 26 different menus. Enigma's big claim to fame—outside of world-class cuisine—is the fact that it lacks a freezer, thus requiring that all dishes be made absolutely fresh. Look for unusual delicacies such as Scottish partridge and rack of kangaroo. | 3005 Routh St. | 214/999–0666 | fax 214/999–0667 | Reservations essential | Closed Sun. No lunch | $35–$60 | AE, DC, MC, V.

**French Room.** Contemporary. Housed in the 1912 beaux arts Aldolphus Hotel, Dallas's finest old hotel, this elegant restaurant serves such classics as roasted duck breast in port sauce. | 1321 Commerce St. | 214/742–8200 | Jacket required | Closed Sun. and Mon. No lunch | $52–$70 | AE, D, DC, MC, V.

**Hotel St. Germain.** Continental. This may be the most formal, most elegant restaurant in Dallas. Food is served on fine antique china and silver. White-gloved waiters move silently about, refilling water goblets and replenishing baskets of fragrant bread. You must call or fax in orders from the Hotel's seven-course dinner menu at least 24 hours in advance. The overall mood is quiet, discrete, and refined. | 2516 Maple Ave. at Cedar Springs Rd. | 214/

871–2516 | fax 214/871–0740 | Reservations essential | Jacket required | No lunch. Closed Sun./Mon. | $75 prix fixe | AE, D, DC, MC, V.

**Laurel's.** Contemporary. Its location at the top of the Westin Park Central Hotel allows for great panoramic views. Try the marinated Chicago lamb rack with goat cheese and potatoes. | Westin Park Central Hotel, 12720 Merit Dr. | 972/851–2021 | Closed Sun., Mon. No lunch | $28–$40 | AE, D, DC, MC, V.

**Lola.** New American. The small dining rooms in this century-old, ivy-covered cottage have dark wood and rich wall treatments. Lola's chef makes creative and celebrated appetizers: the signature Stilton cheese and chive soufflé; venison and wild mushrooms wrapped in phyllo and cut like spring rolls; and seared sea scallops with crisp, fried carrot and chilled cucumber slaw. Try a lamb entrée or the mahi-mahi, and finish off with the sweet "strawberry martini." | 2917 Fairmount St. | 214/855–0700 | Reservations recommended | Closed Sun./Mon. | $32–$47 prix fixe | AE, D, DC, MC, V.

★ **Mansion on Turtle Creek.** Southwestern. Housed in one of the top hotels in the Southwest, the legendary food of Chef Dean Fearing helped pioneer Southwestern cuisine. Not surprisingly, the rich and the beautiful flock here for the tortilla soup, halibut with cashews in basil sauce, and warm lobster tacos. Other menu items include grilled antelope with tequila/apple chutney, and pan-roasted ostrich with red bean mousse. Sun. brunch. | 2821 Turtle Creek Blvd. | 214/559–2100 | Reservations essential Fri., Sat. | Jacket required | $26–$50 | AE, D, DC, MC, V.

**Nana Grill.** Contemporary. High atop the Wyndham Anatole Hotel, this restaurant is the popular choice for a romantic dinner. Known for ostrich, rack of lamb, and buffalo. Entertainment Wed.–Sat. nights. Sun. brunch. | 2201 Stemmons Freeway | 214/761–7479 | $30–$46 | AE, D, DC, MC, V.

**Riviera.** French. One of Dallas's best known restaurants, this crowded spot is a favorite for business lunches. Try the Dover sole and bouillabaisse. | 7709 Inwood Rd. | 214/351–0094 | Jacket required | No lunch | $47–$59 | AE, DC, MC, V.

★ **Star Canyon.** Southwestern. Housed on the main floor of a skyscraper, this top restaurant has huge windows that overlook a courtyard atrium, creating an open feel. You may choose to dine in the atrium, next to a small fountain. Try the cowboy rib-eye (a 16 oz steak served with wild mushroom and bean ragout). | 3102 Oak Lawn Ave. | 214/520–7827 | Reservations essential | No lunch Sat., Sun. | $35–$41 | AE, D, DC, MC, V.

## Lodging

### INEXPENSIVE

**Best Western Dallas North.** The Dallas/Fort Worth International Airport is 12 mi from this hotel, and attractions within 5–10 minutes include the Galleria mall, West End Historic District, and the Dallas Arboretum. Restaurant, bar, room service, in-room data ports, cable TV, pool, hot tub, laundry facilities, business services, airport shuttle, free parking, some pets allowed. | 13333 N. Stemmons Fwy. | 972/241–8521 | fax 972/243–4103 | www.bestwestern.com | 185 rooms | $59–$69 | AE, D, DC, MC, V.

**Best Western Park Suites Hotel.** This hotel aims to offer luxurious, spacious rooms for extended-stay travelers, business travelers, or large families. The Dallas/Ft. Worth International Airport is 35 mi away. Bar, complimentary Continental breakfast, in-room data ports, microwaves, refrigerators, some in-room hot tubs, cable TV, pool, hot tub, exercise equipment, laundry facilities, business services, free parking, some pets allowed (fee). | 640 E. Park Blvd., Plano | 972/578–2243 | fax 972/578–0563 | www.bestwestern.com | 84 suites | $55–$95 suites | AE, D, DC, MC, V.

**Clarion Suites.** Several restaurants are within walking distance of this all-suites hotel. Complimentary Continental breakfast, in-room data ports, microwaves, refrigerators, cable TV, pool, hot tub, exercise equipment, laundry facilities, business services, airport shuttle, free parking. | 2363 Stemmons Trail | 214/350–2300 | fax 214/350–5144 | 96 suites | $104–$114 suites | AE, D, DC, MC, V.

**Comfort Inn.** Two shopping malls, several restaurants, and the Dallas/Ft. Worth International Airport are within 10 mi of this two-story motel. Complimentary Continental breakfast, in-room data ports, cable TV, pool, hot tub, laundry facilities, business services, free parking. | 14040 Stemmons Fwy., Farmers Branch | 972/406–3030 | fax 972/406–2929 | 50 rooms | $65 | AE, D, DC, MC, V.

**Dallas Grand.** Built in 1956, this two-story hotel in the downtown area is within walking distance of several restaurants and a theater. Restaurant, bar, in-room data ports, some microwaves, cable TV, exercise equipment, laundry facilities, business services, parking (fee). | 1914 Commerce St. | 214/747–7000 or 800/421–0011 | fax 214/747–1342 | 710 rooms | $79–$89 | AE, D, DC, MC, V.

**Drury Inn–North.** Five restaurants are within blocks of this four-story motel. It's 10 mi from downtown Dallas and 12 mi from the Dallas/Ft. Worth International Airport. Complimentary Continental breakfast, in-room data ports, some microwaves, some refrigerators, cable TV, pool, business services, free parking. | 2421 Walnut Hill | 972/484–3330 | fax 972/484–3330 | 130 rooms | $79–$99 | AE, D, DC, MC, V.

**Executive Inn–Garland.** In a suburb 15 mi from the center of Dallas, this motel is a 15-minute drive to the Galleria mall and less than 1 mi from several restaurants. Complimentary Continental breakfast, in-room data ports, cable TV, pool, business services, free parking. | 12670 E. Northwest Hwy., Garland | 972/613–5000 | fax 972/613–4535 | 125 rooms | $49–$69 | AE, D, DC, MC, V.

**Fairfield Inn by Marriott.** This three-story hotel is 3 mi from downtown Dallas and the convention center. Complimentary Continental breakfast, cable TV, pool, hot tub, free parking. | 2110 Market Center Blvd. | 214/760–8800 | fax 214/760–1659 | www.marriotthotels.com | 117 rooms | $99–$104 | AE, D, DC, MC, V.

**Hampton Inn–Southwest.** Downtown Dallas and the convention center are 8 mi from this hotel. Dallas/Ft. Worth International Airport is 25 mi away. Complimentary Continental breakfast, in-room data ports, cable TV, pool, laundry facilities, business services, free parking. | 4154 Preferred Pl. | 972/298–4747 | fax 972/283–1305 | www.hampton-inn.com | 119 rooms | $49–$69 | AE, D, DC, MC, V.

**Hampton Inn–West End.** This downtown hotel is connected to the Underground Tunnel, where you'll find numerous shops and restaurants. The tunnel also connects the buildings of downtown Dallas. The Dallas/Ft. Worth International Airport is 18 mi away. Complimentary Continental breakfast, in-room data ports, cable TV, pool, barbershop, exercise equipment, laundry facilities, business services, parking (fee), pets allowed (fee). | 1015 Elm St. | 214/742–5678 | fax 214/744–6167 | www.hamptoninn.com | 311 rooms | $70–$119 | AE, D, DC, MC, V.

**Harvey Hotel–Dallas.** Dallas's downtown area is just 15 minutes away from this three-story hotel. Restaurant, bar, in-room data ports, room service, cable TV, pool, business services, free parking, pets allowed (fee). | 7815 L.B.J. Fwy. | 972/960–7000 or 800/922–9222 | fax 972/788–4227 | 313 rooms | $89–$109 | AE, D, DC, MC, V.

**Harvey Hotel–Plano.** This three-story hotel is across the street from a shopping mall and within walking distance of several restaurants. Restaurants, bar, room service, in-room data ports, some refrigerators, cable TV, pool, hot tub, exercise equipment, laundry facilities, business services, free parking, pets allowed (fee). | 1600 N. Central Expressway, Plano | 972/578–8555 | fax 972/578–9720 | 279 rooms | $110–$120 | AE, D, DC, MC, V.

**Hawthorn Suites at Market Center.** This all-suites hotel is 3 mi from Love Field airport, 10 mi from downtown Dallas, and 12 mi from Dallas/Ft. Worth International Airport. Complimentary breakfast, in-room data ports, kitchenettes, cable TV, pool, laundry facilities, business services, airport shuttle, free parking, some pets allowed (fee). | 7900 Brookriver

Dr. | 214/688–1010 or 800/527–1133 | fax 214/638–5215 | www.hawthorn.com | 97 suites | $80–$115 suites | AE, D, DC, MC, V.

**Holiday Inn Select–L.B.J. Northeast.** You can relax in the shaded poolside area of this three-story hotel 8 mi from downtown Dallas. Restaurant, bar (with entertainment), room service, in-room data ports, cable TV, pool, exercise equipment, laundry facilities, business services, free parking. | 11350 L.B.J. Fwy. | 214/341–5400 | fax 214/553–9349 | www.holiday-inn.com | 244 rooms | $59–$109 | AE, D, DC, MC, V.

**Holiday Inn Select–North.** Love Field airport is 13 mi from this six-story hotel, and both the Dallas/Ft. Worth International Airport and downtown Dallas are 12 mi away. Restaurants, bar (with entertainment), in-room data ports, some refrigerators, cable TV, indoor-outdoor pool, hot tub, exercise equipment, free parking. | 2645 L.B.J. Fwy. | 972/243–3363 | fax 972/243–6682 | www.holidayinn.com | 378 rooms, 3 suites | $89–$149 rooms, $159 suites | AE, D, DC, MC, V.

**Howard Johnson Express Inn.** Seven miles from downtown Dallas, this modestly priced, two-story property can fulfill your traveling requirements, from truck parking to rooms especially arranged for families. Complimentary Continental breakfast, some in-room hot tubs, cable TV, pool, business services, free parking. | 4610 South R. L. Thorton Freeway (I–35, Loop 12) | 214/371–6800 or 800/406–1411 | fax 214/372–6108 | www.hojo.com | 85 rooms | $40–$79 | AE, D, MC, V.

**La Quinta Inn–East.** This limited-service hotel is about 5 mi from a mall and many restaurants. Complimentary Continental breakfast, in-room data ports, cable TV, pool, business services, free parking, some pets allowed. | 8303 E. R. L. Thornton Freeway (I–30) | 214/324–3731 | fax 214/324–1652 | www.laquinta.com | 102 rooms | $49–$99 | AE, D, DC, MC, V.

**La Quinta Northwest–Farmers Branch.** This two-story hotel is 10 mi from Love Field airport and 5 mi from the Galleria mall. Complimentary Continental breakfast, in-room data ports, some microwaves, cable TV, pool, business services, airport shuttle, free parking, some pets allowed. | 13235 Stemmons Freeway N | 972/620–7333 | fax 972/484–6533 | www.laquinta.com | 121 rooms | $52–$57 | AE, D, DC, MC, V.

**Motel 6–Dallas Addison.** This two-story motel is less than 1 mi from several restaurants, a movie theater, and shopping. Cable TV, pool, laundry facilities, free parking, pets allowed. | 4325 Beltline Rd. | 972/386–4577 | fax 972/386–4579 | 161 rooms | $44–$50 | AE, D, DC, MC, V.

**Motel 6–Dallas Forest Plains North.** Downtown Dallas is 7 mi from this motel, and Six Flags Over Texas (in Arlington) is 24 mi away. Cable TV, pool, laundry facilities, free parking, pets allowed. | 2753 Forest Ln. | 972/620–2828 | fax 972/620–9061 | 100 rooms | $40–$46 | AE, D, DC, MC, V.

**Motel 6–Dallas Forest Plains South.** This motel is 3 mi from the Galleria mall, 8 mi from the Love Field airport, and 12 mi from Dallas/Ft. Worth International Airport. Cable TV, pool, laundry facilities, free parking, pets allowed. | 2660 Forest Ln. | 972/484–9111 | fax 972/484–0214 | 117 rooms | $40–$46 | AE, D, DC, MC, V.

**Motel 6–Dallas Southwest.** The Ballpark in Arlington is 13 mi away, and downtown Dallas is 10 mi away. Cable TV, pool, laundry facilities, free parking, pets allowed. | 4220 Independence Dr. | 972/296–3331 | fax 972/709–9438 | 129 rooms | $35–$50 | AE, D, DC, MC, V.

**Radisson Central.** This nine-story hotel is 3 mi from downtown Dallas. Love Field airport is 5 mi away, and Dallas/Ft. Worth International Airport is 23 mi away. Restaurant, bar, some microwaves, cable TV, pool, hot tub, sauna, business services, airport shuttle, free parking. | 6060 N. Central Expressway | 214/750–6060 | fax 214/750–5959 | www.radisson.com | 293 rooms | $99–$108 | AE, D, DC, MC, V.

**Ramada Plaza Hotel Downtown Convention Center.** This twelve-story hotel, within walking distance of the Convention Center, is also the closest to Fair Park, and provides free van transportation within 5 mi of the hotel. All rooms have private balconies, and the restaurant and bar have a great view of the downtown skyline. Restaurant, bar, room service, in-room data ports, cable TV, pool, barbershop, beauty salon, spa, golf, tennis, gym, laundry facilities, laundry service, shops, business services, baby-sitting, pets allowed, free parking. | 1011 S. Akard St. | 214/421–1083 or 888/298–2054 | fax 214/428–6827 | www.ramada.com | 238 rooms | $79–$150 | AE, D, DC, MC, V.

**Ramada Texas Stadium/Love Field.** A 12-story, full-service high-rise hotel on Rte. 183, Texas Stadium is 1 mi away, and Love Field airport is 7 mi away. Restaurant, bar, some refrigerators, cable TV, pool, tennis, exercise equipment, video games, business services, airport shuttle, free parking, some pets allowed. | 1055 Regal Row | 214/634–8550 | fax 214/634–8418 | www.ramada.com | 322 rooms | $69–$85 | AE, D, DC, MC, V.

**Sleep Inn.** Several restaurants and three shopping malls are less than 2 mi from this motel. Complimentary Continental breakfast, in-room data ports, cable TV, pool, business services, free parking, pets allowed. | 4801 W. Plano Pkwy., Plano | 972/867–1111 | fax 972/612–6753 | 104 rooms | $49–$89 | AE, D, DC, MC, V.

**Stoneleigh.** This old, elegant, brick hotel has long been favored by celebrities—Oliver Stone stayed here while working on the film, *JFK*. In the posh Turtle Creek neighborhood north of downtown, the hotel is blocks away from the McKinney Avenue shopping and restaurant district. Try a meal at the sushi bar on site. 2 restaurants (*see* Sushi), pool, exercise equipment. | 2927 Maple Ave. | 214/871–7111 or 800/255–9299 | fax 214/871–9379 | www.netpp.com/stoneleigh | 143 rooms | $129 | AE, D, DC, MC, V.

**Super 8.** This motel is 5 mi from downtown Dallas, and eight mi from Dallas/Ft. Worth International Airport. Complimentary Continental breakfast, in-room data ports, some microwaves, cable TV, pool, exercise equipment, laundry facilities, business services, airport shuttle, free parking. | 9229 Carpenter Fwy. | 214/631–6633 | fax 214/631–6616 | 135 rooms | $60 | AE, D, DC, MC, V.

## MODERATE

**AmeriSuites Dallas West End.** This all-suites hotel is blocks away from the Dallas Convention Center and the Kennedy Memorial, and just a mile from Deep Ellum. Complimentary Continental breakfast, in-room data ports, microwaves, minibars, refrigerators, cable TV, pool, exercise equipment, laundry facilities, laundry service, business services. | 1907 N. Lamar St. | 214/999–0500 or 800/833–1516 | fax 214/999–0501 | www.amerisuites.com | 149 suites | $105–$179 | AE, D, DC, MC, V.

**Aristocrat Hotel.** Conrad Hilton built this hotel in 1925. Today this member of the Holiday Inn chain is a National Historic Landmark in the center of downtown Dallas's business district. Restaurant, bar, in-room data ports, minibars, refrigerators, cable TV, exercise equipment, business services. | 1933 Main St. | 214/741–7700 | fax 214/939–3639 | www.hotel-dallas.com | 172 rooms | $109–$229 | AE, D, DC, MC, V.

**Crowne Plaza Dallas Market Center.** This 22-story hotel is 13 mi from the Dallas/Ft. Worth International Airport and 6 mi from downtown Dallas. Restaurant, bar, in-room data ports, cable TV, pool, hot tub, exercise equipment, laundry facilities, business services, free parking. | 7050 N. Stemmons Fwy. | 214/630–8500 | fax 214/630–9486 | www.bristolhotels.com | 354 rooms | $99–$149 | AE, D, DC, MC, V.

**Crown Plaza–North Dallas/Addison.** This four-story hotel is 15 mi from downtown Dallas and 17 mi from Dallas/Ft. Worth International Airport. 2 restaurants, room service, in-room data ports, some microwaves, refrigerators, cable TV, pool, hot tub, exercise equipment, laundry facilities, business service, airport shuttle, free parking, some pets allowed (fee). | 14315 Midway Rd. | 972/980–8877 | fax 972/788–2758 | www.bristolhotels.com | 429 rooms | $69–$159 | AE, D, DC, MC, V.

**Crowne Plaza Suites Dallas.** This 10-story all-suites hotel with 14 meeting rooms is a good choice for business travelers. It's 18 mi from the Dallas/Ft. Worth International Airport, 15 mi from downtown Dallas, and 15 mi from the convention center. Restaurant, bar, room service, in-room data ports, microwaves, refrigerators, cable TV, 2 pools, hot tub, exercise equipment, laundry facilities, business services, free parking, pets allowed (fee). | 7800 Alpha Rd. | 972/233–7600 | fax 972/701–8618 | www.bristolhotels.com | 295 rooms | $79–$159 | AE, D, DC, MC, V.

**Doubletree Dallas Lincoln Center.** You'll find this 20-story hotel in North Dallas, near Valley View and across the street from the Galleria. 3 restaurants, 2 bars, in-room data ports, cable TV, pool, exercise equipment, business services, parking (fee). | 5410 L.B.J. Freeway | 972/934–8400 or 800/222–8733 | fax 972/701–5244 | www.doubletree.com | 484 rooms, 18 suites | $179–$200 | AE, D, DC, MC, V.

**Embassy Suites–Love Field.** Love Field airport and several restaurants are 5 mi from this hotel. Restaurant, bar, complimentary breakfast, in-room data ports, refrigerators, cable TV, indoor pool, wading pool, hot tub, exercise equipment, business services, airport shuttle. | 3880 W. Northwest Hwy. | 214/357–4500 | fax 214/357–0683 | www.embassysuites.com | 248 suites | $99–$209 suites | AE, D, DC, MC, V.

**Le Meridien.** This modern 25-story high-rise has everything you may need, from dining and entertainment, outlets, to a gym. Restaurant, 2 bars, room service, cable TV, beauty salon, hot tub, sauna, tennis, exercise equipment, racquetball, parking (fee). | 650 N. Pearl St. | 214/979–9000 or 800/225–5843 | fax 214/953–1931 | www.lemeridien-hotels.com | 143 rooms | $99–$300 | AE, MC, V.

**Market Center Courtyard by Marriott.** The convention center and downtown Dallas are within 3 mi of this hotel. The Dallas/Ft. Worth International Airport is about 18 mi away. Restaurant, bar, in-room data ports, cable TV, pool, hot tub, exercise equipment, laundry facilities, business services, free parking. | 2150 Market Center Blvd. | 214/653–1166 | fax 214/653–1892 | www.marriotthotels.com | 184 rooms | $89–$179 | AE, D, DC, MC, V.

**Omni Dallas Hotel Park West.** Rooms are spacious and modern in this hotel 4 mi from Texas Stadium and the Galleria mall. The landscaped grounds include a 12½-acre lake surrounded by a 10-km trail. Restaurant, bar, cable TV, in-room VCR (and movies), pool, hot tub, massage, exercise equipment, business services, free parking. | 1590 L.B.J. Fwy. | 972/869–4300 | fax 972/869–3295 | www.omnihotels.com | 354 rooms | $89–$189 | AE, D, DC, MC, V.

**Radisson Hotel and Suites.** Most of the suites are poolside in this eight-story hotel. Love Field airport is 6 mi from this hotel, and Dallas/Ft. Worth International Airport is 14 mi away. Restaurant, bar, in-room data ports, cable TV, some kitchenettes, some microwaves, some refrigerators, pool, hot tub, exercise equipment, laundry facilities, business services, airport shuttle, free parking, some pets allowed (fee). | 2330 W. Northwest Hwy. | 214/351–4477 | fax 214/351–2364 | www.radisson.com | 145 rooms, 36 suites | $109 rooms, $119–$139 suites | AE, D, DC, MC, V.

**Renaissance–Dallas.** A breathtaking chandelier graces the lobby of this hotel 15 mi from the Dallas/Ft. Worth International Airport. Restaurant, bar (with entertainment), in-room data ports, some refrigerators, cable TV, pool, hot tub, exercise equipment, business services. | 2222 Stemmons Fwy. | 214/631–2222 | fax 214/905–3814 | www.renaissancehotel.com | 540 rooms | $149–$180 | AE, D, DC, MC, V.

**Renaissance Dallas North.** This atrium hotel is 11 mi from downtown. Restaurant, bar, in-room data ports, cable TV, pool, massage, gym, business services. | 4099 Valley View Ln. | 972/385–9000 | fax 972/458–8260 | 300 rooms | $75–$189 | AE, D, DC, MC, V.

**Residence Inn by Marriott–Market Center.** This all-suites hotel is 3 mi from Love Field airport and 15 minutes from numerous restaurants. Picnic area, complimentary Continental breakfast, kitchenettes, cable TV, pool, hot tub, exercise equipment, laundry facilities, business services, free parking, pets allowed (fee). | 6950 N. Stemmons St. | 214/631–2472 | fax 214/634–9645 | www.marriotthotels.com | 142 suites | $119–$149 suites | AE, D, DC, MC, V.

**Residence Inn by Marriott–North Central.** This all-suites hotel off I–75 is within 1 block of several restaurants and a movie theater, and 4 mi from the Galleria mall. Complimentary Continental breakfast, in-room data ports, kitchenettes, microwaves, refrigerators, cable

TV, pool, hot tub, laundry facilities, business services, free parking, some pets allowed (fee). | 13636 Goldmark Dr. | 972/669–0478 | fax 972/644–2632 | 70 suites | $99–$179 suites | AE, D, DC, MC, V.

**Sheraton Suites–Market Center.** Each suite has a living room and bedroom separated by French doors and connected with a marble bathroom in this downtown hotel. Restaurant, bar, in-room data ports, refrigerators, cable TV, pool, hot tub, exercise equipment, business services. | 2101 Stemmons Fwy. | 214/747–3000 | fax 214/742–5713 | www.sheraton.com | 251 suites | $99–$205 suites | AE, D, DC, MC, V.

**Westin Park Central.** This fine hotel is 15 minutes from Deep Ellum, an arts district with all kinds of music, dance clubs, restaurants, and more. Restaurant, room service, in-room data ports, cable TV, pool, tennis, exercise equipment, business services. | 12720 Merit Dr. | 972/385–3000 | fax 972/991–4557 | www.sheraton.com | 540 rooms | $149–$190 | AE, D, DC, MC, V.

**Wyndham Anatole.** A 27-story tower is the centerpiece of this luxury hotel 6 mi from downtown Dallas. The landscaped grounds include fountains, statues, and palm trees. Deluxe rooms are spacious and ultra-modern. Restaurants, bar (with entertainment), room service, in-room data ports, minibars, refrigerators, cable TV, 3 pools, barbershop, beauty salon, hot tub, gym, shops, business services, free parking. | 2201 Stemmons Fwy. | 214/748–1200 | fax 214/761–7520 | www.wyndham.com | 1,620 rooms | $189 | AE, D, DC, MC, V.

**Wyndham Garden.** In the heart of Dallas, this 11-story hotel has comfortable lounges with cushy sofas, and spacious rooms with desks, armoires, and reclining chairs. Restaurant, in-room data ports, cable TV, pool, exercise equipment, library, laundry facilities. | 2015 Market Center Blvd. | 214/741–7481 | fax 214/747–6191 | 228 rooms | $129–$139 | AE, D, DC, MC, V.

## EXPENSIVE

**Fairmont Hotel.** This 24-story hotel is in the middle of downtown Dallas and at the heart of the city's arts district. The massive lobby has columns, chandeliers, and tapestries. Restaurant (see Pyramid Grill), bar (with entertainment), room service, in-room data ports, cable TV, pool, wading pool, shops, business services. | 1717 N. Akard St. | 214/720–2020 | fax 214/871–0673 | fdallas1@aol.com | 550 rooms | $250–$350 | AE, D, DC, MC, V.

**Inter-Continental.** This 15-story hotel is close to shops and attractions. 2 restaurants, bars, in-room data ports, some refrigerators, barbershop, beauty salon, gym, shops, business services, free parking. | 15201 Dallas Pkwy. | 972/386–6000 or 800/426–3135 | fax 972/991–6937 | 529 rooms | $149–$205, $259–$325 suites | AE, D, DC, MC, V.

**Hotel Adolphus.** Beer Baron Adolphus Busch built this beaux arts building in 1912. It's home to the celebrated French Room restaurant. Restaurants, bar, room service, in-room data ports, minibars, refrigerators, cable TV, barbershop, beauty salon, massage, exercise equipment, business services. | 1321 Commerce St. | 214/742–8200 or 800/221–9083 | fax 214/651–3588 | www.adolphus.com | 435 rooms | $199–$295 | AE, D, DC, MC, V.

**Hyatt Regency.** The 50-story Reunion Tower is adjacent to this 18-story hotel. Dallas/Ft. Worth International Airport is 23 mi away. Restaurant, bar, in-room data ports, minibars, some refrigerators, cable TV, pool, hot tub, exercise equipment, business services, airport shuttle. Parking (fee). | 300 Reunion Blvd. | 214/651–1234 | fax 214/742–8126 | www.hyatt.com | 943 rooms | $214–$245 | AE, D, DC, MC, V.

**Melrose.** Love Field airport is just 3 mi from this eight-story luxury hotel. Individually decorated rooms have marble baths, dark wood furniture, and deep rich colors; some rooms have four-poster beds. Restaurant (see The Landmark), bar (with entertainment), room service, in-room data ports, some microwaves, cable TV, library, business services, airport shuttle. Parking (fee). | 3015 Oak Lawn Ave. | 214/521–5151 or 800/635–7673 | fax 214/521–2470 | www.melrosehotel.com | 184 rooms | $245–$295 | AE, D, DC, MC, V.

**Westin Galleria Hotel.** This 20-story hotel has direct access to the dazzling Galleria mall, which boasts an ice-skating rink, a movie theater, and over 200 shops. Subdued pastel-colored rooms offer respite from the bustling location. Restaurants, bar, room service,

refrigerators, cable TV, pool, barbershop, beauty salon, gym, business services, free parking. | 13340 Dallas Pkwy. | 972/934–9494 | fax 972/851–2869 | www.westin.com | 431 rooms | $269 | AE, D, DC, MC, V.

### VERY EXPENSIVE

**Hotel Crescent Court.** The centerpiece of the Crescent Complex (which includes office buildings, shops, and galleries), this hotel is on the edge of Dallas's central business district and uptown art scene. Each room has French doors, a vanity, and down-feather love seat. Suites are either one- or two-story, and may have spiral staircases and hardwood floors. Restaurant, bar, room service, in-room data ports, refrigerators, cable TV, pool, hot tub, gym, shops, business services, airport shuttle. Parking (fee), some pets allowed (fee). | 400 Crescent Ct. | 214/871–3200 or 800/654–6541 | fax 214/871–3272 | www.rosewood-hotels.com | 178 rooms, 40 suites | $360–$490 rooms, $445–$2,000 suites | AE, D, DC, MC, V.

★ **Hotel St. Germain.** Housed in a restored, Victorian-style mansion, this all-suites hotel is decorated with French antiques and has a fireplace and chandelier in each room. Restaurant, complimentary breakfast, room service, minibar, cable TV, in-room VCRs (and movies), business services, free parking. | 2516 Maple Ave. | 214/871–2516 or 800/683–2516 | fax 214/871–0740 | 7 suites | $290–$650 suites | Closed first week in Aug. | AE, MC, V.

★ **Mansion on Turtle Creek.** Guest rooms are decorated with antiques, fine fabrics, and original artwork in this remarkable hotel that many think is the best in the Southwest. Each guest room covers at least 450 square ft, and includes a living area, bath, and vanity. The various suites may include a king-size canopy bed, a private terrace, and a decorative fireplace. Chef Dean Fearing in the hotel's legendary restaurant helped pioneer Southwestern cuisine. Restaurants, bar (with entertainment), room service in-room data ports, minibars, cable TV, in-room VCRs, pool, beauty salon, massage, gym, business services, airport shuttle. Parking (fee). | 2821 Turtle Creek Blvd. | 214/559–2100 or 800/527–5432 (outside TX) or 800/442–3408 (TX) | fax 214/528–4187 | www.rosewood-hotels.com | 126 rooms, 15 suites | $440–$530, $675–$2,400 | AE, D, DC, MC, V.

# DEL RIO

MAP 8, F6

*(Nearby towns also listed: Brackettville, Eagle Pass, Uvalde)*

Del Rio calls itself "the best of the border," and with a quick look around town it's easy to see why. With opportunities for shopping, swimming, hiking, and hunting, Del Rio's got a lot to offer. Perched at the edge of the Chihuahuan Desert, the town of 37,000 is an oasis lush with vegetation, thanks to the San Felipe Springs (artesian wells that gush more than 90 million gallons of water through the town daily).

Almost every Del Rio visitor takes at least a short trip to Ciudad Acuña, Mexico, located directly across the border. Del Rio and Ciudad Acuña are separated by the Rio Grande, one of three rivers that form Lake Amistad.

Northwest of Del Rio about 9 mi past the town of Comstock lies a must-see attraction: Seminole Canyon State Historical Park. The park has some quiet sites with spectacular views of the Chihuahuan Desert, dotted with cacti and populated with numerous bird species.

Information: **Del Rio Chamber of Commerce** | 1915 Ave. F, Del Rio, TX 78440 | 830/775–3551 or 800/889–8149 | www.drchamber.com.

## Attractions

**Ciudad Acuña, Mexico.** Located across the border in Mexico, this town is a popular shopping destination with many restaurants. | U.S. 90 to the International Bridge | 830/775–3551 or 800/889–8149.

**The Firehouse.** This gallery features the work of both local and non-local artists in permanent and travelling exhibits. Art classes are available. | 120 E. Garfield | 830/775–0888 | fax 830/774–0803 | Free | Weekdays 8:30–5:30, Sat. 12–5.

**Judge Roy Bean Visitor Center.** This visitors center has information about attractions throughout the state, as well as displays recounting the wild stories of Judge Roy Bean, one of the most famous characters of the Wild West era. Next door is the Jersey Lilly, Judge Bean's courtroom and saloon, where he dispensed frontier justice in the 1880s. | U.S. 90, Langtry | 915/291–3340 | fax 915/291–3366 | Free | Daily 8–5.

**Amistad National Recreation Area.** The construction of Lake Amistad (derived from the Spanish word for "friendship") was a cooperative project between the United States and Mexico. Completed in 1969, the 67,000-acre lake was built as a way to control flooding, provide irrigation for South Texas farms and ranches, and offer water recreation. Head south on I–35 and take the Marsalis Exit. | 650 E. S.R.L. Thorton Fwy | 830/775–7491 | www.nps.gov/amis | Free.

**Laughlin Air Force Base.** The largest pilot training installation in the country, this base has more operational aircraft than any other in the Air Force. Tours last 2½ hours and leave from the Del Rio Chamber of Commerce on the 2nd and 4th Wed. of every month. | 561 Liberty Dr., Suite 6 | 830/298–5201 | www.laughlin.af.mil | Free | Tours 2nd and 3rd Wed. of every month.

**San Felipe Springs.** The town of Del Rio grew around these springs, which today supply 90,000 gallons of water daily to the community. | U.S. 90 | 830/775–3551.

**Seminole Canyon State Historical Park.** This park was occupied by prehistoric man about 8,500 years ago. Today you can see pictographs as part of a 90-minute guided tour (a somewhat strenuous 1-mi hike; bring water, as there are no drinking facilities in the canyon). Camping is possible in the park. | U.S. 90 | 915/292–4464 | fax 915/292–4596 | www.tpwd.state.tx.us | $2 | Daily 8–5.

**Val Verde Winery.** Established by Italian immigrant Frank Qualia in 1883, this is the oldest winery in Texas. Tours and tastings are available. | 100 Qualia Dr. | 830/775–9714 | fax 830/775–5394 | Free | Mon.–Sat. 10–5.

**Whitehead Memorial Museum.** This complex is home to a replica of the Jersey Lilly, Judge Roy Bean's saloon and courtroom. (Judge Roy Bean was one of the most colorful characters to ever leave his mark on the American West.) Other structures include an 1870s store, a windmill, a log cabin, a caboose, and the Cadena Nativity, a cultural folk art exhibit. | 1308 S. Main St. | 830/774–7568 | www.whitehead-museum.com | $3 | Tues.–Sat. 9–4:30, Sun. 1–5.

## ON THE CALENDAR

**APR.:** *George Paul Memorial Bull Riding Event.* Top riders from all over the country come to the Val Verde City Fairgrounds to compete in this bull-only rodeo. | Main St. and 17th St. | 830/775–3551.

**MAY:** *Cinco de Mayo Celebration.* This celebration includes live entertainment, food booths, and more. | 830/775–3551 or 800/889–8149.

**SEPT.:** *Diez y Seis de Septiembre.* Brown Plaza hosts live entertainment, games, and music. | 830/775–3551 or 800/889–8149.

**OCT.:** *Fiesta de Amistad Arts and Crafts Show.* This large arts and crafts show has sales, displays, and demonstrations. | 830/775–3551 or 800/889–8149.

# Dining

**Crosby's.** Mexican. Known to boarder-crossers as a good dinner spot, this American outpost serves up Mexican as well as Continental fare. Try the quail dish or the *tortillas portuguesas* (sliced, fried tortillas, covered with cheese sauce). | 195 Hidalgo, Ciudad Acuña, Mexico | 011–52–877/2–2020 | $5–$16 | V, MC.

**Memo's.** Tex-Mex. Near the San Felipe Creek, this enduring hangout has Saltillo tile floors and a piano bar. Since 1936, it's been serving up dishes from both sides of the border, though the enchiladas always sell the best. Piano jams take place every Tues. and Thurs. night, with occasional appearances by country stars. | 804 E. Losoya | 830/774–8104 | fax 830/775–3600 | Closed Sun. | $5–$12 | AE, D, MC, V.

## Lodging

**Best Western Inn.** This two-story motel is within walking distance of restaurants, and offers extra perks like cherry wood furniture in the rooms, and complimentary cocktails every evening. Complimentary breakfast, in-room data ports, cable TV, pool, hot tub, laundry facilities, business services, pets allowed (fee). | 810 Ave. F | 830/775–7511 | fax 830/774–2194 | 62 rooms | $69 | AE, D, DC, MC, V.

**Holiday Inn Express.** Boat hook-ups are available in the parking lot for those on their way to or from Lake Amistad. Complimentary Continental breakfast, pool, pets allowed. | 3616 Ave. F | 830/775–2933 or 888/775–2933 | fax 830/775–2466 | www.holiday-inn.com | $48–$65 | AE, D, DC, MC, V.

**La Quinta.** This two-story motel is one block from several restaurants and ½ mi from a shopping mall. Complimentary Continental breakfast, in-room data ports, cable TV, pool, laundry facilities, pets allowed. | 2005 Ave. F | 830/775–7591 | fax 830/774–0809 | www.laquinta.com | 101 rooms | $55–$70 | AE, D, DC, MC, V.

**Laguna Diablo Resort.** Erected as a dude ranch in 1944, this rustic resort is built of native stone and rough-sawn wood. All apartments have a covered porch and are within 100 ft of the water. Units are available on a daily or monthly basis. Kitchenettes, microwaves, refrigerators, laundry facilities. | 1 Sanders Point Rd. | 830/774–2422 | www.delrio.com/~ldresort/ | 10 apartments | $69–$79 | D, DC, MC, V.

**Ramada Inn.** Numerous fast food places are within walking distance of this two-story hotel. A mall is two blocks away. Restaurant, bar, room service, refrigerators, cable TV, in-room VCRs (and movies), pool, hot tub, sauna, exercise equipment, laundry facilities, business services, some pets allowed. | 2101 Ave. F | 830/775–1511 | fax 830/775–1476 | www.ramada.com | 155 rooms | $66–$137 | AE, D, DC, MC, V.

# DENISON

MAP 8, I2

*(Nearby towns also listed: Paris, Sherman)*

This community of 25,000 has undergone an extensive historic restoration thanks to the Texas Main Street program. Along with the town's historic structures, Denison is also the gateway to two state parks.

Information: **Denison Area Chamber of Commerce** | Box 325, Denison, TX 75021 | 903/465–1551. **Visitor Center** | 313 W. Woodard St. | 903/465–1551 | www.denisontx.com.

## Attractions

**Denison Dam.** This dam contains the waters of Lake Texoma. An interpretive center houses fossils found during construction. | Rte. 91, 3 mi north of Denison | 903/465–4990 | fax 903/465–6571 | Free | Daily 7:30–5.

**Eisenhower Birthplace State Historical Park.** Operated by the Texas Parks and Wildlife Department, this frame house has been restored to its appearance at the time of the former president's birth in 1890. | 208 E. Day St. | 903/465–8908 | fax 903/465–8988 | www.eisenhowerbirthplace.org | $2 | Mon.–Sat. 10–4, Sun. 1–5.

**Eisenhower State Park.** This park offers swimming, fishing, and camping on Lake Texoma. | 50 Park Rd. 20 | 903/465–1956 | fax 903/465–3317 | www.tpwd.state.tx.us | $1 | Daily 8–5.

**Grayson County Frontier Village.** The collection of historic structures here dates from 1840 to 1900. You can have a look at a log schoolhouse, a jail, and period homes with typical furnishings. | From Rte. 75, take Loy Lake Rd. exit | 903/463–2487 | Free | Wed.–Sun. 1–4.

**Hagerman National Wildlife Refuge.** This waterfowl refuge located on Lake Texoma is a favorite spot with birders who come to identify some of the 300 species that have been spotted here. The visitors center has interpretive displays and bird lists, and self-guided driving tours are possible. | Rte. 1417 | 903/786–2826 | Free | Weekdays 7:30 AM–4 PM, Sat. 9–1, Sun. 11–3.

## ON THE CALENDAR

**APR.: *Texoma Lakefest Regatta.*** One of the top charity races in the United States, this regatta also includes a silent auction, a dance, a dinner, and live entertainment. | 903/465–1551.

**OCT.: *Main Street Fall Festival.*** This festival includes arts and crafts, food, games, a car show, and a pet show. | 903/464–4452.

# Dining

**O'Brien's Main Street Cafe.** Tex-Mex. Despite the weather, this place serves up soups and stews year-round. It's decorated with local newspapers and memorabilia dating back to 1887. Try the chicken salad and frito chili pie (a Texas staple). No alcohol. | 409 W. Main | 903/465–8222 | Closed Sun. No supper | $3–$6 | No credit cards.

# Lodging

**Molly Cherry.** Built in 1890, this three-story Victorian home on seven acres was once owned by J. J. Fairbanks, a local real estate tycoon. Allegedly, it was once used to host gambling nights (there's a look-out widow's walk still attached to the attic). Guest rooms are in both the main house and individual cottages. All rooms are decorated with period antiques and fixtures. The wooded walking paths are a favorite for bird-wathchers. Complimentary breakfast, some in-room hot tubs, TV in common area, pool. | 200 Molly Cherry Lane; 1 mi south of downtown Denison | 903/465–0575 | fax 903/465–1904 | www.molly-cherry.com | 6 rooms | $79–$89 rooms; $89–$179 rooms in cottages | AE, D, DC, MC, V.

# DENTON

MAP 8, I2

*(Nearby towns also listed: Arlington-Grand Prairie, Fort Worth, Gainesville, Grapevine, Irving)*

Located 35 mi north of the Dallas/Ft. Worth "Metroplex," Denton still offers much of the atmosphere of a small Texas town, complete with a limestone courthouse. Downtown, you'll find several restored historic buildings thanks to the city's participation in the Main Street program. This town of 79,250 is home to the University of North Texas and the Texas Women's University, noted as the nation's largest university designed primarily for women.

**Information: Denton Convention and Visitors Bureau** | 414 West Pkwy., Denton, TX 76201 | 940/382–7895 or 888/381–1818 | cvb@iglobal.net | www.denton-chamber.org.

# Attractions

**Denton County Courthouse Museum.** Exhibits range from early 20th century pottery and blue glass to local historical photos. There's also a genealogy and family research center. | Courthouse on the Square, 110 W. Hickory | 940/565–5667 | Weekdays 10:30–4:30, Sat. 1–4:30.

**Ray Roberts Lake State Park.** You can picnic, camp, and hike at this 35,000-acre state park. | Rte. 455 | 940/686–2148 or 940/334–2150 | fax 940/686–2898 | www.tpwd.state.tx.us | $3 | Daily 8 AM–10 PM.

**Texas Motor Speedway.** A wide variety of races (including NASCAR) are held here. Peak racing season is Mar.–June, though the complex is open for tours throughout the year. The speedway is in Justin, 15 mi south of Denton on I–35W. | 3601 Rte. 114, Justin | 817/215–8500 | fax 817/491–3749 | www.texasmotorspeedway.com | Tours $6; races $16–$96 | Tours: weekdays 9–4, Sat. 10–4, Sun. 1–4.

**Texas Women's University.** Founded in 1901, this is the largest university in the country designed primarily for women. Its student population is approximately 9,000. | University Dr. and Bell Ave. | 940/898–3644 | Free | Daily.

The campus's **Little-Chapel-in-the-Woods** has many stained-glass windows designed by students and is a popular site for weddings. | (940/898–3601).

## ON THE CALENDAR
**AUG.:** *North Texas State Fair.* The North Texas Fairgrounds hosts cook-offs, contests, live music, carnival rides, and a rodeo. | 940/387–2632.

## Dining
**Outback Steakhouse.** Steak. From the busy bar (replete with diners watching sporting events) to the casual booths, this chain restaurant has a fun atmosphere and is known for top of the line beef. Try the 14-ounce New York Strip. Kids' menu. | 300 I–35S | 940/320–5373 | $9–$24 | AE, D, DC, MC, V.

**Ruby's Diner.** American. This family-style diner, decorated with local memorabilia, is lauded for its homestyle meals, pie, and chicken-fried steak. It's also known for its wild game "safari" menu. | 111 N. Elm | 940/387–7706 | No supper Sun.–Tues. | $5–$12 | AE, D, DC, MC, V.

**Trail Dust Steakhouse.** Steak. Western decorations adorn the walls, and meals are served by costumed waitstaff. Try the Cowboy or Stud steak. Kids' menu. | 26351 U.S. 380, Aubrey | 940/440–3878 | No lunch Mon.–Sat. | $8–$24 | AE, D, DC, MC, V.

## Lodging
**Clayton House Motel.** This 15-floor motel is located 1 mi from both the town and from the Texas Women's University campus. Cable TV, pool, laundry facilities. | 111 W. University Dr. | 940/382–9626 | 52 rooms | $36–$42 | AE, MC, V.

**Holiday Inn.** A grassy poolside courtyard rests at the center of the three two-story buildings at this comfortable motor inn. Rooms are decorated in dark greens and maroons, and some have sofas and desks. Restaurants are within 1 mi of this 2-story motel, and Texas Women's University is 2 mi away. Restaurant, bar (with entertainment), room service, in-room data ports, exercise room, cable TV, pool, laundry facilities, business services. | 1500 Dallas Dr. | 940/387–3511 | fax 940/387–7917 | www.holiday-inn.com | 144 rooms | $69 | AE, D, DC, MC, V.

**La Quinta.** Families will feel at home at this comfortable, basic, two-story chain hotel, which 1 mi from University of North Texas and 7 mi from Texas Women's University. Complimentary Continental breakfast, in-room data ports, cable TV, pool, business services, pets allowed. | 700 Fort Worth Dr. | 940/387–5840 | fax 940/387–2493 | www.laquinta.com | 99 rooms | $65 | AE, D, DC, MC, V.

**Radisson.** This upscale hotel is country-western in style and is an ideal place to stay for sports enthusiasts, especially Monday Night Football watchers. Restaurant, bar, room service, cable TV, pool, driving range, 18-hole golf course, putting green, exercise equipment, business services, some pets allowed. | 2211 I–35E, North | 940/565–8499 | fax 940/387–4729 | www.radisson.com | 150 rooms | $99–$189 | AE, D, DC, MC, V.

**Roadrunner Farms Bed and Breakfast.** This Texas limestone house is on 32 rolling acres in Horse Country. It's 3 mi from Denton and 30 mi to the Dallas/Fort Worth area. Riding lessons are available on the property at the equestrian facility. Complimentary breakfast, cable TV, pool, hot tub, horseback riding. | 10501 Fincher Rd., Argyle, TX | 940/241–3089 | www.roadrunnerfarms.com | 2 | $100 | AE, MC, V.

# DUBLIN

MAP 8, H3

*(Nearby towns also listed: Glen Rose, Hico, Stephenville)*

The original spelling of this town was "Doublin," though historians are undecided on its exact origins. One theory is that the town was named from the practice of "doubling" wagons to avoid Indian raids; a second is that it was named for the city in Ireland. Today the town prospers on its peanut and dairy farming, but is best known as the home of the first Dr Pepper franchise.

**Information: Dublin Chamber of Commerce** | 218 E. Blackjack, Dublin, TX 76446 | 254/445–3422 or 800/938–2546 | www.dublintexas.com.

## Attractions

**Dr Pepper Bottling Co.** Opened in 1891, the world's oldest Dr Pepper bottling plant still uses pure cane sugar instead of artificial sweeteners. Bottling takes place on Tues. A memorabilia-filled museum and soda shop are on site. | 221 S. Patrick | 254/445-3466 | www.dublindrpepper.com | $1.50 | Weekdays 9–6, Sat. 10–5, Sun. 1–5.

**Dublin Historical Museum.** The history of Dublin and its surrounding area (such as tales of local war heroes) is told at this museum. | 116 W. Blackjack | 254/445–4550 | Free | Daily 1–5.

**The Art Gallery in Dublin.** More than 200 pieces of oil and acrylic artwork are on display, and for sale, at this downtown gallery. | 112½ N. Patrick St. | 254/445-3434 | www.theartgalleryindublin.com | Free | Mon.–Sat. 10–6, Sun. 1–6.

## Dining

**Burgers and Beans.** American. The name does the talking for the menu at this friendly joint. | 231 S. Patrick | 254/445–4439 | Closed Sun. No lunch Thurs., Fri. | $2–$5 | No credit cards.

**Sunset Cafe.** American. Homemade spaghetti sauce is just one of the specialties at this neighborhood café. Hearty fare such as catfish and steaks is also available. | 906 N. Patrick | 254/445–3392 | No supper on Monday | $5–$12 | D, MC, V.

**Woody's Place.** American. This food will stick to your ribs: chicken-fried steak, BBQ, and ribeye steak, served up for lunch and dinner. | U.S. 377 | 254/445–3737 | $4.75–$17.95 | AE, D, MC, V.

## Lodging

**Central Inn.** This small, one-floor hotel is in the heart of town. Cable TV, pool. | 723 N. Patrick | 254/445–2138 | 21 rooms | $35–$40 | AE, D, MC, V.

# DUMAS

MAP 8, K8

*(Nearby towns also listed: Amarillo, Dalhart, Fritch)*

This Panhandle community of 14,000 is rich in many natural resources. It's located in one of the world's largest natural gas fields, allowing it to produce two-thirds of the nation's helium; it's located on oil fields, which brought the community to boomtown status in the 1920s; and it's located amid the nation's largest grain sorghum area. Beyond the city boundaries lie canyons and Lake Meredith, popular for fishing and swimming.

Information: **Moore County Chamber of Commerce** | 523 Porter, Dumas, TX 79029 | 806/935–2123 | www.dumaschamber.com.

## Attractions

**Moore County Historical Museum.** A variety of household and agricultural items depicting the early days of Moore County are on display. | 800 Dumas Ave. | 806/935–3113 | Free | May–Aug., Mon.–Sat. 10–5; Sept.–Apr., weekdays 1–5.

### ON THE CALENDAR
**JULY: *Julyfest.*** This July 4th weekend event in McDade Park has arts, crafts, food, games, and live entertainment for the whole family. | 806/935–2123.

## Dining

**Albert's Manor House.** American. This restaurant serves a fish buffet on Friday nights and a daily lunch buffet. Try the chicken-fried steak or one of the many sandwiches. | 1817 S. Dumas Ave. | 806/935–5507 | $3–$10 | D, DC, MC, V.

**D.K. Branding Iron.** Steak. This country-western joint next to a golf course occasionally hosts the Outdoor Country Music Classic. Besides the beef, try the Philly cheesesteak sandwiches, salads, or buffalo wings. | FM 2203 and Rte. 119 (Schuman Rd.) | 806/935–6988 | Closed Sun., Mon. | $10–$20 | AE, D, MC, V.

## Lodging

**Best Western Windsor Inn.** This two-story motel is within blocks of numerous fast food restaurants, and 1 mi from the Moore County Historical Museum. The Amarillo International Airport is 45 minutes away. Complimentary Continental breakfast, some refrigerators, cable TV, pool, hot tub, laundry facilities, exercise equipment, some pets allowed (fee). | 1701 S. Dumas Ave. | 806/935–9644 | fax 806/935–9730 | 57 rooms | $69–$79 | AE, D, DC, MC, V.

**Comfort Inn.** This two-story motel is only 7 blocks from Dumas's town center; restaurants and shopping are all within walking distance. Truck parking and RV hook-ups are available. Complimentary Continental breakfast, cable TV, some in-room hot tubs, indoor pool. | 1620 S. Dumas Ave. | 806/935–6988 | www.comfortinn.com | 50 rooms | $60–$90 | AE, D, DC, MC, V.

**Konakai Dumas Inn.** This hotel has a tropical-theme atrium and is 3 blocks from a shopping center. Restaurant, room service, in-room data ports, cable TV, pool, hot tub, exercise equipment, video games, business services, pets allowed. | 1712 S. Dumas Ave. | 806/935–6441 | fax 806/935–9331 | 102 rooms | $55–$75 | AE, D, DC, MC, V.

**Serendipity House.** Set back from the highway behind a pasture, this two-story Victorian-style home has a great view of a local canyon. Individual cottage suites are also available. Complimentary breakfast, some room phones. | Hwy 287, 1 mi South of Dumas | 806/935–0339 | fax 806/935–2742 | www.wwirr.com/serendipity | 6 rooms, 2 suites | $89–$150 | AE, D, DC, MC, V.

**Super 8.** This motor inn allows truck parking and is within walking distance of shopping and restaurants. Complimentary Continental breakfast, refrigerators, cable TV, business services, some pets allowed (fee). | 119 W. 17th St. | 806/935–6222 | fax 806/935–6222 | 30 rooms | $60 | AE, D, DC, MC, V.

# EAGLE LAKE

*(Nearby town also listed: Houston)*

This rice-producing community is well known by birders and bird hunters. The area is a stop for ducks and geese during fall and spring migrations. The region is also home to the Attwater Prairie Chicken National Wildlife Refuge, which protects a coastal prairie chicken whose numbers have dwindled to near-extinction.

**Information: Eagle Lake Chamber of Commerce** | 121 N. McCarty, Eagle Lake, TX 77434-2534 | 979/234–2780 | www.elc.net/chamber.

## Attractions

**Attwater Prairie Chicken National Wildlife Refuge.** This refuge is dedicated to the conservation of the endangered prairie chicken, whose numbers were once in the thousands. Tours can be arranged. | 6½ mi northeast of Eagle Lake off Rte. 36 | 979/234–3021 | Daily dawn–dusk.

**Eagle Lake Town Park.** A tower overlooks the water in this small park next to Eagle Lake. Tennis, golf, a pool, walking trails, and picnic areas are available. | U.S. 90A, 1 mi southwest of town | 409/234–2640 | Free | Dawn–dusk.

**Prairie Edge Museum.** The natural and cultural history of the Eagle Lake area is showcased in this museum. Some exhibits focus on prehistoric mammoths that once roamed the area. | 408 E. Main | 979/234–2780 | Free | Weekends 2–5, and by appointment.

### ON THE CALENDAR
**APR.: *Eagle Lake Prairie Chicken Festival.*** Dances, crafts, food booths, and a parade are part of this festival, which is dedicated to the endangered Prairie Chicken. Buses leave from town to go chicken-watching. | 409/234–2780 | www.elc.net/festival.

## Lodging
**Eagle Hill Inn and Retreat.** The largest hotel in town, this four-building complex specializes in corporate events and religious retreats. Outdoor basketball court, laundry, complimentary breakfast, cable TV, TV in common area, outdoor pool, tennis cable tv, tennis, basketball, business services. | 307 E. State St. | 800/324–3551 or 979/234–3551 | 15 | $95–$150 | MC, V.

# EAGLE PASS

*(Nearby town also listed: Del Rio)*

This town of 28,000 residents was founded after the Texas Revolution, when Mexico prohibited all trade with Texas. Smugglers began a new route to the north and the Texas militia set up an observation camp at a crossing called Paso del Aguila (Eagle Pass). In 1849 the U.S. Infantry built Fort Duncan to defend the new territory from Indian attack. The fort later was used during the Civil War and manned by Confederate soldiers.

Like other border towns, Eagle Pass is bilingual. Many Mexican citizens cross the border to shop at the large Mall de las Aguilas and in the downtown dress and specialty shops. For Americans, much of Eagle Pass's appeal lies in its proximity to Mexico; many visitors spend the cooler hours shopping in Piedras Negras, then return to Eagle Pass.

**Information: Eagle Pass Chamber of Commerce** | 400 Garrison, Eagle Pass, TX 78852 | 830/773–3224 | www.eaglepasstexas.com.

## Attractions

**Fort Duncan Park.** Established as a frontier post in 1849, this fort was later occupied by Confederate soldiers. The historic buildings are now in use as museums. | 480 S. Adams St. | 830/773–4343 | Free | Mon.–Fri. 8–noon, 1–5 PM.

**Kickapoo Lucky Eagle Casino.** Owned by the Kickapoo Tribe, this casino has state-of-the-art equipment, a bingo hall, a restaurant, and sports bar. | Rosita Valley Rd., off FM 1021 (El Indio Hwy.) | 888/255–8259 | Mon.–Thurs. noon–2 AM, Fri. noon–Mon. 4 AM.

### ON THE CALENDAR

**MAR.:** *International Friendship Festival.* This festival includes a parade, a carnival, food booths, and children's activities. | Shelby Park | 888/355–3224.

## Dining

**Club Moderno.** Mexican. The American hang-out in Piedras, this place claims to be where *tortillas portuguesas* and nachos were invented. | Zaragoza and Allende, in Piedra Negras | 011–52–878–2–0098 | $6–$14 | AE, D, DC, MC, V.

## Lodging

**Best Western.** Eat and shop in the area, or drive 3 mi to the Mexican border. In-room data ports, microwaves, refrigerators, cable TV, pool, business services, some pets allowed. | 1923 Loop 431 | 830/758–1234 | fax 830/758–1235 | 40 rooms, 14 suites | $77–$83, $83 suites | AE, D, DC, MC, V.

**Holly Inn.** This motel is within walking distance of restaurants and shopping, and it's 7 mi from Kickapoo Lucky Eagle Casino. Complimentary Continental breakfast, cable TV, outdoor pool, microwaves, refrigerators, laundry facilities, pets allowed. | 2423 E. Main | 830/773–9261 | fax 830/773–1619 | 70 rooms | $40–$48 | AE, D, DC, MC, V.

**La Quinta.** A shopping mall is 1½ mi away, and the Mexican border is 2½ mi away. Complimentary Continental breakfast, in-room data ports, microwaves, cable TV, pool, pets allowed. | 2525 Main St. | 830/773–7000 | fax 830/773–8852 | www.laquinta.com | 130 rooms | $65–$80 | AE, D, DC, MC, V.

# EASTLAND

MAP 8, G3

*(Nearby towns also listed: Abilene, Comanche)*

Founded in 1891, this community of 4,100 was named for a hero of the battle of San Jacinto. The small town boomed in 1917 with the discovery of oil. Today Eastland is known for its Lake Leon, a favorite with anglers.

Information: **Eastland Chamber of Commerce** | 102 S. Seaman St., Eastland, TX 76448 | 254/629–2332 | ecofc@eastland.net | www.eastland.net.

## Attractions

**Kendrick Religious Museum.** Thirty dioramas with special lighting and sound effects highlight scenes from the Bible. | Rte. 6, 4 mi west of Eastland | 254/629–8672 | $3 | Daily 10–4.

**Post Office Mural.** This mural is made of 12,000 postage stamps. | 411 W. Main | 254/629–2383 | Free | Mon.–Fri. 8 AM–4:30 PM.

## Dining

**Rip's Diner.** American. This modular 1950s-style diner has a soda fountain counter and serves home-cooked blue plate specials. | 3200 E. Interstate 20 | 254/629–3392 | fax 254/629–0978 | $6–$12 | AE, D, DC, MC, V.

## Lodging

**Super 8.** This motel is within walking distance of many restaurants and shopping, including an antiques market. Complimentary Continental breakfast, in-room data ports, some microwaves, some refrigerators, some in-room hot tubs, cable TV, pool, pets allowed. | 3900 I–20E | 254/629–3336 | fax 254/629–3338 | 30 rooms | $49–$69 | AE, D, DC, MC, V.

# EDINBURG

*(Nearby towns also listed: Harlingen, McAllen, Mission)*

This Rio Grande valley community of 47,000 is best known for its citrus industry. It's home to many "Winter Texans" who enjoy the season in Edinburg's semi-tropical climate.

**Information: Edinburg Chamber of Commerce** | 602 W. University Dr., Edinburg, TX 78539 | 956/383–4974 or 800/800–7214 | fax 956/380–3621 | chamber@edinburg.com | www.edinburg.com.

## Attractions

**Hidalgo County Historical Museum.** Local history exhibits begin with the earliest Native Americans in the region and move through Spanish exploration and colonization, the Mexican War, the Rio Grande steamboat trade, the Civil War, bandit wars, and more. | 121 E. McIntyre | 956/383–6911 | fax 956/381–8518 | www.hiline.net/~hchm | $2 | Tues.–Fri. 9–5, Sat. 10–5, Sun. 1–5.

**Southern Pacific Railroad Depot.** Built in 1927, this former depot now houses both the visitors center and a small museum, where signals, lamps, and railroad equipment are on display. | 602 W. University Dr. | 956/383–4974 | Free | Weekdays 8:30–5.

### ON THE CALENDAR

**FEB.:** *Fiesta Edinburg.* This three-day event begins with a parade down Closner St. and ends up at the Supersplash waterpark, which fills up with live concerts, food booths, and talent displays. | 956/383–4974 | www.edinburg.com.

## Dining

**La Jaiba.** Seafood. This little house near the university has many photos of big catches brought in by guests. Traditional fried fish is served along with gourmet Mexican dishes. Try the Sailor, which is two filets broiled in a white wine mushroom sauce. | 524 W. University Dr. | 956/316–3474 | $6–$14 | AE, D, MC, V.

## Lodging

**Best Western Edinburg Inn and Suites.** Completed in 1999, this property has both motel-style rooms and suites. It's 1 mi from the Hidalgo County Historical Museum, and four blocks from a golf course. Complimentary Continental breakfast, microwaves, refrigerators, some in-room hot tubs, cable TV, pool, exercise equipment, laundry, business services. | 2708 S. U.S. 281 Business | 956/318–0442 | fax 956/318–0702 | 34 rooms, 22 suites | $69–$79, $89–99 suites | AE, D, DC, MC, V.

**Echo Hotel and Conference Center.** Set on 16 immaculately landscaped acres, this four-story hotel is surrounded by palm and mesquite trees and is within walking distance of golfing. Restaurant, room service, pool, exercise equipment, playground, laundry, business services, airport shuttle, pets allowed. | 1903 S. Closner | 956/383–3823 | fax 956/381–5913 | echohotel@aol.com | 122 rooms | $60–$92 | AE, D, DC, MC, V.

**Edinburg Executive Inn.** This motel is 15 minutes from the airport and 2 mi from a waterpark. Cable TV, pool. | 2006 S. Closner Blvd. | 956/380–6201 | fax 956/381–0807 | 30 rooms | $50 | AE, D, MC, V.

**Holiday Inn Express.** This hotel is 3 mi from a waterpark. Cable TV, pool. | 1806 S. Closner | 956/383–8800 | fax 956/383–1540 | 48 rooms | $65 | AE, D, MC, V.

**University Inn.** Texas Pan-American University is across the street from this hotel. A multiplex and golf course are within 3 miles. Cable TV, pool. | 1400 University Dr. | 956/381–5400 | fax 956/381–6709 | 70 rooms | $58 | AE, D, DC, MC, V.

# EL PASO

MAP 8, B3

*(Nearby town also listed: Guadalupe Mountains National Park)*

Dramatically situated a few miles between the southern end of the Rockies and the northern terminus of Mexico's Sierra Madre range, El Paso, established by the Spanish in 1598, was a major stopping point on the way to the west during the California gold rush. With its 600,000 residents, El Paso is the anchor of the Trans-Pecos and the largest American city on the U.S.-Mexico border. Filled with stucco-facade homes and mock pueblo architecture, the city looks like a tourism poster for modern Mexico. It overflows with south-of-the-border charm, big city excitement, and historic attractions, including the oldest Spanish mission in Texas. No visit to El Paso would be complete without a visit to its sister city just across the Mexican border, Ciudad Juárez, where the shopping is often sensational. The city is also just a few miles from the state of New Mexico, so it's easy to visit sights such as Carlsbad Caverns, White Sands, and Ruidoso, all within a two- to three-hour drive.

Information: **Greater El Paso Civic, Convention, and Tourism Department** | One Civic Center Plaza, El Paso, TX 79901 | 915/534–0600 or 800/351–6024 | www.elpasocvb.com | info@elpasocvb.com.

## Attractions

**Border Patrol Museum.** The history of the U.S. Border Patrol from the Old West to the present is portrayed in this museum in a Spanish Colonial Revival building. Uniforms, weapons, surveillance equipment, and interesting confiscated items are on display, and the memorial room commemorates agents killed on duty. | 4315 Transmountain Rd. | 915/759–6060 | www.borderpatrolmuseum.org | Free | Tues.–Sun. 9–5.

**Chamizal National Memorial.** This memorial celebrates the resolution of century-long boundary disputes between Mexico and the United States. Both sides converted their lands into national parks. El Paso's side houses a border history museum, a theater, and a graphic arts gallery. The Mexican side has been developed into acres of botanical gardens and includes an interesting archaeological museum. | 800 S. San Marcial St. | 915/532–7273 | fax 915/532–7240 | www.nps.gov/cham | Free | Daily 8–5.

**Ciudad Juárez, Mexico.** Across the Rio Grande from El Paso, this city of 1.5 million is the largest Mexican city on the U.S.-Mexico border. You'll find great shops, restaurants, and historic sites here, as well as bullfights, festivals, and lively markets. One of the easiest ways to enter Mexico and enjoy El Paso's neighbor is aboard the El Paso-Juárez Trolley. Red-and-green trains depart hourly from the El Paso Convention Center and many points throughout the city, then travel across the border, stopping at key sites in Ciudad Juárez, including the Central Market. | Trolley Company: 915/544–0062 or 800/259–6284 | $12 | Daily.

**Concordia Cemetery.** This cemetery just north of I–10 is the final resting place of many Chinese laborers who helped build the railroad westward in the nineteenth century. Also among the graves, which were once segregated by ethnicity, religion, and status, is the burial site of John Wesley Hardin, a Texas outlaw who claimed to have killed 40 people. | Gateway North and U.S. 54 | Free | Daily.

**El Paso Mission Trail.** Passing through El Paso's oldest Mexican and Indian districts—neighborhoods filled with notable restaurants, craft shops, and antique stores—this famed trail leads to three active missions and several other historical sites. | Off I–10, 12 mi from downtown | 915/534–0677 | www.missiontrail.com | Free | Daily dawn to dusk.

The formal name of oldest Spanish mission in the Southwest, **Mission Ysleta,** is Nuestra Señora del Carmen. The original mission was established here in 1681 for the Tigua Indians, after they were expelled in the Pueblo Rebellion. Flood waters destroyed the original structure and several subsequent structures. The building that stands today was built in 1851; its familiar silver dome was added in the 1880s. | 100 Old Pueblo Rd. | 915/858–2588.

The **Tigua Indian Reservation** is adjacent to Mission Ysleta. Stop by to purchase native pottery, taste homemade bread baked in adobe ovens, or try your luck at the Speaking Rock Casino. | 119 S. Old Pueblo Rd. | 915/859–7913, casino: 915–860–7777.

**Mission Socorro** was established in 1682. The present building was constructed in 1843 and is known for its fine *vigas* (carved ceiling beams) and bell tower. | 328 S. Nevaraz | 915/534–0677 or 800/351–6024.

The **San Elizario Presidio** was built to protect the missions. Its chapel is still in use. | 1556 San Elizario Rd. | 915/534–0630 or 800/351–6024.

**El Paso Museum of Art.** The museum's diverse collections include classic European sculptures, Mexican folk art, local photography, and contemporary installations. A portrait of George Washington is a highlight. | One Arts Festival Plaza | 915/532–1707 | fax 915/532–1010 | www.elpasoartmuseum.org | $1 | Tues.–Sat. 9–5, Sun. noon–5.

**El Paso Museum of History.** Life-size dioramas depict the people of El Paso, past and present: Indians, Spanish explorers, cowboys, and cavalrymen. | 12901 Gateway W | 915/858–1928 | Free | Tues.–Sat. 9–4:50, Sun. 1–4:50.

**El Paso Zoo.** Eighteen acres house 175 animal species, including the rare Santa Cruz sheep and the endangered Malayan tapir. | 4001 E. Paisano St. | 915/544–1928 | www.elpaso-zoo.org | $4 | Daily 9:30–4.

**Fort Bliss.** Established as an outpost to guard against Indian attack in 1848, the facility was later used by Confederate soldiers. Today the base is the site of the largest air-defense establishment in the nation and headquarters for the U.S. Army Air Defense. | corner of Pershing Rd. and Pleasonton Rd. | 915/568–3137 | open from 9–4:30 daily | free admission.

The **Fort Bliss Replica Museum** is a reconstruction of the original fort as it stood from 1848 to 1948. | Building 5051, Pershing and Pleasanton Rds | 915/568–4518 | Free | Daily 9–4:30.

The unique **U.S. Army Air Defense Artillery Museum** displays anti-aircraft weapons in the country's only collection of Army air defense memorabilia. | Building 5000, Pleasanton Rd. | 915/568–5412 | Free | Daily 9–4:30.

**Underwood Golf Complex.** Fort Bliss's 36-hole complex has both a desert course with generous fairways and a parkland course with trees and grass. | 3200 Coe Ave. | 915/562–2066 | Greens fees: $15–$18 | Daily dawn to dusk.

**Guadalupe Mountains National Park.** This gorgeous park is home to Guadalupe Peak, the highest patch of land in Texas at 8,749 ft, and El Capitan, a massive limestone formation rising 8,085 ft. In winter people visit the park to see snow, in fall to see the colorful foliage, and in spring and summer to glimpse the smooth red bark of the madrone tree, which grows wild nowhere else in the state. Camping is permitted, but overnight facilities in the park are very scant. Bring water—this is desert country with limited amenities. | U.S. 62/180, Pine Springs, 40 mi from El Paso | 915/828–3251 | www.nps.gov/gumo | Free | Daily dawn to dusk; Visitor Center 8–4:30.

**Hueco Tanks State Historical Park.** The natural rock formations in this 860-acre park served as rain-water reservoirs for native settlers some 10,000 years ago. Today it's a haunt for rock-climbers, and a good site for a hike or a picnic. Among other attractions are some 2,000

Indian pictographs (guided tours are available), 190 bird species, and 10 varieties of wild-flowers. Advance reservations essential. | 6900 Hueco Tanks Rd., off U.S. 62/80, 32 mi north-east of El Paso | 915/857–1135 | fax 915/857–3628 | www.tpwd.state.tx.us/park/hueco/hueco.htm | $4 | Daily dawn to dusk.

**Magoffin Home State Historic Site.** Completed in 1875 by Joseph Magoffin, this hacienda is filled with ornate Victorian furnishings and adobe walls scored to look like stone. Mogof-fin was the son of James Wiley Mogoffin, for whom Magoffinsville (now El Paso) was named. | 1120 Magoffin Ave. | 915/533–5147 | fax 915/544–4398 | $2 | Daily 9–4.

**Painted Dunes Desert Golf Course.** This 27-hole desert course is considered one of the finest public courses in the state. | 12000 McCombs | 915/821–2122 | www.painted-dunes.com | Year-round.

© Artville

## TEXAS ARCHITECTURE

Early pioneers came to Texas with few belongings, but they did bring the architec-tural influences of their homelands—influences that are still evident throughout the state today.

Nowhere in Texas is French heritage more evident than in the community of Castroville, west of San Antonio. Here settlers from the Alsace-Lorraine region of France re-created the architectural flourishes of their homeland—houses with three chimneys, ventilation windows (or sometimes doors) near the roofline, and a steeply pitched roof that was distinctly asymmetrical, falling sharply in the back. Some settlers even made sure they added a traditional Alsatian good luck symbol: a stone stork on the rooftop.

German settlers also introduced a distinct architectural style, still evident in communities such as Comfort, New Braunfels, and Fredericksburg. The latter swells with pride for its historic homes, some of which now serve as bed-and-breakfasts. Among the town's most charming are the 19th-century "Sunday houses." Today the old Sunday houses scattered throughout Fredericksburg are easy to identify by their small size; most also have half-story exterior staircases.

In addition to heritage, local conditions (such as weather) influenced Texas's early architecture. Out on the open range of West Texas, the first settlers were most concerned with surviving sometimes harsh conditions. Pioneers used native materials to make the simplest of structures (crude dugouts were built using the earth itself as part of the dwelling) and Native Americans and Hispanic settlers built homes of picket and sotol. Examples of these early houses can still be seen on the Panhandle plains at the National Ranching Heritage Center in Lubbock.

Adobe made a more permanent structure, and soon settlers were borrowing this Spanish architectural style. Adobe bricks made of mud, grass, and often goat manure were baked in the sun, later to be stacked and finally covered with adobe plaster. Today, many of these early structures can be seen throughout West Texas in towns such as Alpine, Socorro, San Elizario, Sierra Blanca (home of the state's largest adobe courthouse), and Ysleta.

**Scenic Drive.** Drive north on Mesa Street, then head right on Rim Road for panoramic views of El Paso and Ciudad Juárez. On clear days, you can see New Mexico. | Free | Daily.

**Transmountain Road.** This road, just off I–10 west of town, takes you through Smuggler's Gap, a dramatic cut across the Franklin Mountains. | Free | Daily.

**University of Texas at El Paso.** The campus opened in 1914 as the Texas School of Mining and Metallurgy; 17,000 students now attend. The annual Sun Bowl is played here. | University Ave. | 915/747–5000 | www.utep.edu | Free | Daily.

**El Paso Centennial Museum.** Opened during the Texas Centennial in 1936, this museum focuses on the region's human and natural history. Exhibits include dinosaur remains, stone tools, shell jewelry, and native plants. | University of Texas at El Paso, University Ave. and Wiggins Rd. | 915/747–5565 | www.utep.edu/museum | Free | Tues.–Sat. 10–5.

**Wilderness Park Museum.** This 17-acre, indoor-outdoor museum traces the evolution of the region's climate and recreates Pueblo Indian life. | 4301 Transmountain Rd. | 915/755–4332 | fax 915/759–6824 | $1 | Tues.–Sun. 9–4:45.

## ON THE CALENDAR

**FEB.: *Southwestern International Livestock Show and PRCA Rodeo.*** The El Paso Coliseum hosts a livestock show and rodeo with barrel racing, bull riding, and roping. | 915/532–1401.

**MAR.: *Siglo de Oro Drama Festival.*** Daily performances of Spanish dramatic arts are part of this week-long celebration at the Chamizal National Memorial Theater. | 915/532–7273.

**JUNE: *Tigua St. Anthony's Day.*** The feast day of St. Anthony, the patron saint of the Tigua tribe, is celebrated with dances, feasts, and ceremonies. | 915/859–5287.

**JUNE–AUG.: *Viva El Paso!*** This lavish musical pageant chronicles 400 years of El Paso history. Performances are held Thurs.–Sat. at the McKelligon Canyon Amphitheater. | 915/565–6900.

**AUG.: *Fiesta de San Lorenzo.*** Live music and entertainment are highlights of this festival held at San Lorenzo Catholic Church in Clint, 10 mi outside El Paso. | 915/851–2255.

**SEPT.: *Fiesta de las Flores.*** A month-long celebration of Hispanic culture is held at the El Paso Coliseum. | 915/542–3464 | www.fiestadelasflores.org.

**DEC.: *Wells Fargo Sun Bowl.*** The annual college football classic is held the last weekend of each year. | 915/533–4416 | www.sunbowl.org.

# Dining

**Avila's.** Mexican. This family-run favorite first opened in 1956 and has been serving hearty Mexican fare ever since. The lively dining room showcases works by local artists. Try the chili con queso or carnitas. | 6232 N. Mesa | 915/584–3621 | fax 915/845–5578 | www.avilas.com | $5–$9 | AE, D, DC, MC, V.

**Bella Napoli.** Italian. A piano player serenades the crowd on weekends at this romantic, dimly lit spot. Known for classic Italian specialties such as chicken Marsala and osso buco. Beer and wine only. | 6331 N. Mesa St. | 915/584–3321 | Closed Mon., Tues. | $7–$20 | AE, D, MC, V.

**Bill Park's Bar-B-Que.** Barbecue. Aquariums fill the rustic dining room at this family-friendly joint. Try the all-you-can-eat ribs. Kids' menu. Beer and wine only. | 3130 Gateway E | 915/542–0960 | Closed Sun. | $10–$18 | AE, D, DC, MC, V.

**Casa Jurado.** Mexican. Owned and operated by the Jurado family since 1968, Casa Jurado is known for its innovative menu, which features six kinds of enchiladas and several steak dishes. | 4772 Doniphan Dr. | 915/833–1151 | Closed Mon. | $5–$14 | AE, D, DC, MC, V.

**Cattleman's Steak House.** Steak. Readers of the *El Paso Times* have named Cattleman's the area's #1 steak house for five years running. The large, family-style restaurant is on the grounds of the working Indian Cliffs Ranch, approximately 30 mi from downtown El Paso. Enjoy a tour of the ranch and zoo or take a hay ride before or after your meal. Known for great steaks, mesquite-smoked barbecue, and fresh seafood. Kids' menu. Sun. brunch. | I–10, exit 49 | 915/544–3200 | $15–$26 | AE, DC, MC, V.

**Great American.** American. This is one of five western-themed Great American restaurants that dot the city's landscape. Large dining rooms, huge portions, and expansive menus make this a good choice for groups. Try the seasoned steak burger, grilled chicken, or beer-battered shrimp. Kids' menu. | 2200 N. Yarborough | 915/566–2300 | fax 915/595–0202 | www.grtamerican.com/rest/ | $5–$18 | AE, D, MC, V.

**Grigg's.** Mexican. There's an antique piano bar in this adobe-style restaurant, which has been serving up classic Mexican and New Mexican dishes since 1939. Try the red and green enchiladas or Grigg's Grinder plate, a mix of chopped sirloin, chili con queso, and grilled vegetables. | 9007 Montana Ave. | 915/598–3451 | $3–$11 | MC, V.

**Jaxon's.** Southwestern. More than 500 archival photos and a mural depicting El Paso history crowd the walls of this busy food emporium, which serves home-brewed beer. Favorite dishes include tortilla soup, Santa Barbara beef, and Jaxon's rib-eye (served with sauteed onions and green chile strips). There's another Jaxon's about ½ mi from the airport. Kids' menu. | 4799 N. Mesa St. | 915/544–1188 | www.jaxons.com | $6–$15 | AE, D, DC, MC, V.

**La Hacienda.** Mexican. The oldest continually operating restaurant in El Paso serves Mexican and New Mexican cuisine. Try steak Tampiquena or the "Old El Paso Combo," an assortment of tacos and enchiladas. Lighter fare, including salads and fish dishes, are available on the covered patio out back. | 1720 W. Paisano Dr. | 915/533–1919 | fax 915/533–3636 | $6–$15 | AE, D, MC, V.

**La Nortena y Cafe Deluxe.** Mexican. Dine in a former jailhouse at this good spot for border-style Mexican cuisine, with tasty choices such as *salpicon* (spicy minced meat salad), quesadillas, *chilorio* (venison sausage), chili-roasted corn, and more. | 212 W. Overland | 915/533–0533 | $4–$15 | DC, MC, V.

**State Line.** Barbecue. Enjoy the outdoor patio as you wait for your table in the nostalgic dining room. Fred Astaire and Ginger Rodgers grace the walls and music of a time gone by fills the classic jukebox. Don't miss the beef and pork ribs and the homemade desserts. Kids' menu. | 1222 Sunland Park Dr. | 915/581–3371 | $11–$29 | AE, D, DC, MC, V.

**Wyng's.** Mexican. This casual spot is on the Tigua Indian Reservation, adjacent to the Speaking Rock Casino. Have a drink in the Spirit Garden bar, then try the fajitas and the famous Tigua bread, which is baked on the reservation in adobe ovens. | 122 S. Pueblo | 915/859–3916 | $5–$26 | AE, D, MC, V.

## Lodging

**Baymont Inn and Suites–El Paso West.** This chain is 7 miles from downtown, right on the Mexico border. Complimentary Continental breakfast, in-room data ports, pool, video games, laundry facilities, free parking, pets allowed. | 7620 Mesa St. | 915/585–2999 | fax 915/585–1667 | www.baymontinn.com | 102 rooms, 4 suites | $49–$96 | AE, D, DC, MC, V.

**Camino Real.** Built in 1912, this elegant, brick downtown hotel with commanding views of the city is listed on the National Register of Historic Places. The jewel of lobby is the dark-wood circular Dome Bar, which sits under a superb Tiffany skylight. 3 restaurants, bar (with entertainment), in-room data ports, room service, cable TV, pool, exercise equipment, business services, free parking, airport shuttle, some pets allowed (fee). | 101 S. El Paso St. | 915/534–3000 or 800/769–4300 | fax 915/534–3024 | www.caminoreal.com | 395 rooms | $135–$150 | AE, D, DC, MC, V.

**Chase Suite Hotel by Woodin.** This all-suites property is at El Paso International Airport. Complimentary Continental breakfast, in-room data ports, microwaves, refrigerators, cable TV, 2 pools, hot tubs, laundry facilities, business services, airport shuttle, free parking. | 6791 Montana Ave. | 915/772–8000 | www.woodfinsuitehotels.com | fax 915/779–2330 | 200 rooms | $90–$110 | AE, D, DC, MC, V.

**Cliff Inn.** Italian Renaissance art and antique furniture adorn this unique hotel set on a cliff in a quiet neighborhood. The views of downtown are extraordinary. Bar, complimentary Continental breakfast, in-room data ports, some kitchenettes, cable TV, outdoor pool, laundry facilities, free parking, no pets. | 1600 Cliff Dr. | 915/533–6700 or 800/333–2543 | fax 915/544–2127 | 76 rooms | $60–$100 | AE, D, DC, MC, V.

**Comfort Inn.** All rooms in this three-story hotel open onto the street. It's 12 mi from downtown, 5 mi from the airport, and as a guest, you'll have free access to a nearby Gold's Gym. Complimentary Continental breakfast, in-room data ports, some microwaves, some refrigerators, cable TV, pool, hot tub, laundry facilities, airport shuttle, free parking, pets allowed (fee). | 900 N. Yarbrough Dr. | 915/594–9111 | fax 915/590–4364 | www.comfortinn.com | 195 rooms, 5 suites | $59–$74 | AE, D, DC, MC, V.

**Embassy Suites.** Three mi from the Mexican border and 2.5 mi from the airport. Complimentary breakfast, room service, in-room data ports, microwaves, refrigerators, cable TV, pool, hot tub, golf privileges, tennis, health club, video games, baby-sitting, laundry facilities, business services, airport shuttle, free parking, some pets allowed (fee). | 6100 Gateway E | 915/779–6222 | fax 915/779–8846 | www.embassysuites.com | 185 suites | $79–$114 | AE, D, DC, MC, V.

**Hawthorne Suites.** Fifteen mi from downtown El Paso, this hotel is within walking distance of restaurants and shopping. Complimentary Continental breakfast, in-room data ports, pool, laundry facilities, airport shuttle, free parking, some pets allowed. | 6789 Boeing | 915/778–6789 | fax 915/778–2288 | www.hawthorn.com | 191 suites | $95–$129 | AE, D, DC, MC, V.

**Hilton–Airport.** This chain property has a convenient walkway that connects to the airport. Restaurant, bar, complimentary Continental breakfast, room service, in-room data ports, cable TV, pool, barbershop, beauty salon, hot tub, gym, business services, airport shuttle, free parking, pets allowed. | 2027 Airway Blvd. | 915/778–4241 | fax 915/772–6871 | www.hilton.com | 272 rooms | $75–$147 | AE, D, DC, MC, V.

**Holiday Inn–Sunland Park.** Located at the foothills of the Franklin Mountains, 5 mi from downtown. Restaurant, bar, room service, some microwaves, room service, cable TV, pool, wading pool, hot tub, gym, business services, airport shuttle, free parking, some pets allowed. | 900 Sunland Park Dr. | 915/833–2900 | fax 915/833–6338 | www.holiday-inn.com | 178 rooms | $69–$98 | AE, D, DC, MC, V.

**Howard Johnson.** Three mi from the airport, 8 mi from downtown. There's a 24-hour International House of Pancakes on site and a shopping mall across the street. In-room data ports, some refrigerators, cable TV, pool, wading pool, gym, laundry facilities, business services, airport shuttle, free parking, pets allowed. | 8887 Gateway W | 915/591–9471 | fax 915/591–5602 | www.hojoelpaso.com | 140 rooms | $57–$69 | AE, D, DC, MC, V.

**La Quinta–Airport.** This chain motel is 2 mi from the airport. In-room data ports, cable TV, pool, business services, airport shuttle, free parking, pets allowed. | 6140 Gateway E | 915/778–9321 | fax 915/778–9321 | www.laquinta.com | 121 rooms | $49–$70 | AE, D, DC, MC, V.

**Marriott.** Convenient to the airport. Restaurant, bar, room service, in-room data ports, cable TV, pool, hot tub, exercise equipment, laundry facilities, shops, business services, airport shuttle, free parking, pets allowed. | 1600 Airway Blvd. | 915/779–3300 | fax 915/772–0915 | www.marriott.com | 296 rooms | $89–$149 | AE, D, DC, MC, V.

**Quality Inn.** For those who want to visit Ciudad Juárez, this is a good choice. The El Paso–Juárez Trolley stops right out front. Restaurant, bar (with entertainment), room service, in-room data ports, cable TV, pool, wading pool, business services, airport shuttle, free parking, pets allowed. | 6201 Gateway W | 915/778–6611 | fax 915/779–2270 | www.qualityinn.com.com | 307 rooms | $48–$52 | AE, D, DC, MC, V.

**Ramada Inn.** All rooms have either a courtyard or mountain view at this two-story motel 1 mi from the University of Texas at El Paso. Restaurant, bar, complimentary Continental breakfast, room service, in-room data ports, some refrigerators, cable TV, pool, hot tub, laundry facilities, business services, free parking, pets allowed (fee). | 500 Executive Ctr | 915/532–8981 | fax 915/577–9997 | www.ramada.com | 99 rooms | $69–124 | AE, D, MC, V.

**Sunset Heights.** A three-story 1905 home with beveled glass accents and oak floors, Sunset Heights Bed and Breakfast is in a historic district just a half mile from downtown. Breakfast is an affair to remember with five- to eight-course masterpieces, and the yard is a nice spot to relax. Picnic area, complimentary breakfast, cable TV, pool, hot tub, business services, airport shuttle, no smoking, free parking, no pets allowed, no children under 16. | 717 W. Yandell Ave. | 915/544–1743 | fax 915/544–5119 | 3 rooms (with bath) | $85–$150 | AE, D, MC, V.

# ENNIS

MAP 8, I3

*(Nearby towns also listed: Corsicana, Dallas, Waxahachie)*

Named for Cornelius Ennis, a railroad official, this town boomed in the early 20th century as a shipping point for Texas cotton. Today, this town of 24,000 is a quiet getaway from Dallas. You can fish and sail on Lake Bardwell.

Information: **Ennis Convention and Visitors Bureau** | 100 East Ennis Ave., Ennis, TX 75120 | 888/366–4748 | www.visitennis.org.

## Attractions
**Lake Bardwell.** You can go camping, fishing, boating, and water skiing at this lake, which covers over 3,500 acres. Visit the Buffalo Creek Wetlands, which includes an outdoor classroom and nature trail designed to showcase Texas wildlife. | Rte. 34, 3 mi west off of U.S. 287 | 972/875–5711 | fax 972/875–9711 | Free | Daily 6 AM–10 PM.

**Texas Motorplex.** You can catch one of the two annual National Hot Rod Association (NHRA) national competitions as well as more than 70 other drag racing events held at this strip, which is home to a number of national records. | 7500 W. U.S. 287 | 972/878–2641 | www.texasmotorplex.com | $15–$59 | Call for race times, office hours are 8-5.

### ON THE CALENDAR
**APR.:** *Bluebonnet Trails.* A self-guided drive through more than 40 mi of marked trails to view bluebonnets, a rite of spring in Texas. | 888/366–4748.
**MAY:** *National Polka Festival.* Live polka bands, dancing, and Czech food are part of the fun at this long-running festival held Memorial Day weekend. | 972/878–4748 or 888/366–4748.
**DEC.:** *Texas Christmas Celebration.* Held on the first weekend of December, this arts and crafts festival has live music, a baking contest, and a parade of lights. | 972/878–2625.

## Dining
**Chez Willy's.** Cajun. This restaurant, in an 1890s bank, specializes in Creole seafood, and is filled with Louisiana street signs and old bank documents. Try the shrimp creole, jambalaya, gumbo, or the crawfish étouffée, which consists of crawfish tails in a cream sauce over rice. | 110 W. Ennis Ave. | 972/875–3080 | Closed Sundays | $7–$15 | AE, D, DC, MC, V.

## Lodging
**Quality Inn.** This hotel is within walking distance of Ennis's antiques and clothing shops. It is only 2 mi to the Bluebonnet Trails, 3 mi to Lake Bardwell, and 30 mi to Dallas. | I–45SW at Hwy. 34. Restaurant, bar, complimentary Continental breakfast, in-room data ports, cable TV, outdoor pool, outdoor hot tub, golf privileges, laundry services, business services. | 107 Chamber of Commerce Dr. | 972/875–9641 or 800/228–5151 | fax 972/875–4026 | 69 rooms | $59–$69 | AE, D, DC, MC, V.

# FAIRFIELD

*(Nearby town also listed: Palestine)*

The Texas Historical Commission selected Fairfield as an official Texas Main Street city for its many preservation activities. After indulging your interest in local history, you can take part in Fairfield's many outdoor activities, which range from sighting bald eagles to deer hunting and fishing.

Information: **Fairfield Chamber of Commerce** | 900 W. Commerce St., Fairfield, TX 75840 | 903/389–5792 | chamber@pflash.com | www.fairfieldtx.com.

## Attractions

**Burlington-Rock Island Railroad Museum.** This museum displays railroad engines and equipment. Part of the museum is a real log cabin with period furnishings. | 208 S. Third St., Teague | 254/739–2061 | www.therailroadmuseum.com | $1 | Weekends 1–5.

**Fairfield Lake State Recreation Park.** You can swim, boat, fish, camp, and hike a 4½-mi trail at this 1,450-acre park. | 6 mi NE from Fairfield on Rte. 3285 | 903/389–4514 | www.tpwd.state.tx.us | $2 | Daily.

**Freestone County Historical Museum.** This museum, in a former jail, contains local history exhibits. | 302 E. Main St. | 903/389–3738 | Donations accepted | Wed.–Fri. 9 AM–9:30 PM.

**Moody-Bradley House.** The birthplace of W. L. Moody, a philanthropist and founder of the Moody Foundation of Galveston, this 1860 house is filled with furniture and antiques from its long history. | 318 Moody St. | 903/389–7008 or 903/389–2945 | www.fairfieldtex.com | Free | By appointment only.

### ON THE CALENDAR
**JULY: *Peach Festival.*** This July 4th weekend festival has games for adults and kids, including a peach pit spitting contest, arts and crafts, food, live music, and a fireworks display. | 903/389–5792.

## Dining
**Something Different.** American. Styled like a diner with booths and a countertop full of homemade pies, cakes, and brownies, this restaurant serves hot sandwiches and burgers as well as their famous specialty salads. | I–45 and U.S. 84E | 903/389–3022 | $6–$9 | AE, MC, V.

## Lodging
**Sam's Motel.** Across the street from a popular restaurant which bears the same name, this motel is less than a mile from town and shopping. Microwaves, refrigerators, cable TV, outdoor pool. | I–45 and Hwy. 84 | 903/389–2172 | fax 903/389–7005 | 72 rooms | $44–$53 | AE, D, MC, V.

# FORT STOCKTON

*(Nearby towns also listed: Monahans, Pecos)*

This West Texas community lies in the heart of the Chihuahuan Desert and is a popular stop on the road to or from El Paso. Fort Stockton is a designated Texas Main Street city and has refurbished many storefronts to their original appearance. Buildings such as the 1884 jail and the Grey Mule Saloon recall the days when this town was a frontier army post.

Information: **Fort Stockton Chamber of Commerce** | 100 Railroad Ave., Fort Stockton, TX 79735 | 915/336–2264 or 800/336–2166 | chamber@fortstocktontx.com | www.fort-stocktontx.com. **Visitor Center** | 116 W. Second St., Fort Stockton, TX 79735 | 800/334–8525 | www.tourtexas.com/fortstockton.

## Attractions

**Annie Riggs Memorial Museum.** Built in 1899 as a hotel, today this museum is filled with local history exhibits and memorabilia from Camp Stockton. | 301 S. Main St. | 915/336–2167 | $2 | Daily 10–5.

**Big Bend National Park.** The Rio Grande, the border between Texas and Mexico, marks the location of Big Bend. Truly Texas-size, this little-visited park spans over 800,000 acres, giving you a place to get away from the crowds. | Rte. 118, Study Butte | 915/477–2251 | www.big.bend.national-park.com | Free | Daily.

**Historic Fort Stockton.** The original and reconstructed buildings from the 1858 fort include officers' quarters, a guardhouse, and a jail. Off of U.S. 290. | 300 East 3rd St. | 915/336–2400 | $2 | Mon.–Sat. 10–1, 2–5.

**Paisano Pete.** This 22-ft fiberglass bird is allegedly the largest roadrunner statue in the world. | Dickenson St. and Main St. | 800/334–8525 | Free | Daily.

### ON THE CALENDAR

**JAN.:** *Pecos County Livestock Show.* This show highlights prize livestock in several categories. | 915/336–2264.

**JULY:** *Water Carnival.* This three-night festival has a different theme each year. Expect to see synchronized swimming, dancing, and musical numbers staged by a cast of locals, as well as several pageants, including the Miss Fort Stockton Pageant. | 800/334–8525.

## Dining

**Comanche Springs Restaurant.** American. Local history and cowboy art cover the walls and booths of this restaurant, which serves a Mexican-American buffet daily. Eat the "Sitting Bull," a 5-lb burger, in under an hour and it's free. | 2501 W. I–10 | 915/336–9731 | fax 915/336–6945 | Open 24 hours | $3–$19 | AE, D, MC, V.

## Lodging

**Atrium Inn.** Just a half mile from town, this hotel has the only heated pool in the area. Tropical plants and a rock fountain in the lobby give the inn its name. Bar, complimentary Continental breakfast, some microwaves, some refrigerators, cable TV, indoor pool, exercise equipment, business services, pets allowed. | 1305 N. Hwy. 285 | 915/336–6666 | fax 915/336–5777 | 85 rooms | $69–$119 | AE, D, DC, MC, V.

**Best Western Swiss Clock Inn.** This motel is within walking distance of shopping and restaurants. Lounge in the garden under the shade of mulberry trees. Restaurant, room service, cable TV, pool, business services, pets allowed. | 3201 W. Dickinson St. | 915/336–8521 | fax 915/336–6513 | 112 rooms | $45–$60 | AE, D, DC, MC, V.

**La Quinta.** This motel is right on the highway and has truck parking available. Complimentary Continental breakfast, cable TV, pool, business services, some pets allowed. | 2601 I–10W | 915/336–9781 | fax 915/336–3634 | 97 rooms | www.laquinta.com | $52–$69 | AE, D, DC, MC, V.

# FORT WORTH

*(Nearby towns also listed: Arlington-Grand Prairie, Cleburne, Denton, Glenrose, Grapevine, Irving, Lewisville, Mineral Wells, Weatherford)*

If you're looking for a chance to dress like a cowboy, do a little line dancing, or ride the mechanical bull, then Fort Worth, the "place where the West begins," is your city.

Fort Worth was founded in 1849 and was the last major stop along the Chisholm Trail. Soldiers, settlers, cattle herders, and even outlaws (such as the Sundance Kid) spent quality time here. When the railroad arrived in the late 1800s, Fort Worth became a major livestock shipping center.

Nowhere is the city's heritage more evident than at the Fort Worth Stockyards National Historic District. This area is still home to cowboys on horseback, as well as historic hotels and the city's top nightlife (it's where you'll find Billy Bob's Texas, the world's largest honky-tonk). South of the Stockyards lies another historic site, Sundance Square. Also a cowboy hangout, this 20-block, redbrick-paved area has been transformed into an upscale dining, shopping, and entertainment district.

Fort Worth may be proud of its western heritage, but this city of a half-million residents also has a cultural bent. Here you'll find the small Kimbell Art Museum, which showcases varied art from around the world, the Fort Worth Museum of Science and History, and the Amon Carter Museum, with its world-class collection of Western art.

FORT WORTH

INTRO
ATTRACTIONS
DINING
LODGING

**Information: Fort Worth Convention and Visitors Bureau** | 415 Throckmorton St., Fort Worth, TX 76102 | 817/336–8791 or 800/433–5747 | www.fortworth.com.

## NEIGHBORHOODS

**Downtown.** Bounded by Houston, Commerce, Weatherford, and 9th Sts., downtown Fort Worth is home to modern glass-and-steel skyscrapers that stand alongside restored century-old Victorian buildings.

**Fort Worth Cultural District.** Just minutes west of downtown on W. 7th St., most of the Cultural District can be found between University Dr. on the east, White Settlement Rd. on the north and I–30 on the bottom; some attractions, however, can be found south of I–30. The district spans a 2-mi area and contains numerous noteworthy shops, restaurants, theaters, museums, and galleries. Highlights include the Kimbell Art Museum, Will Rogers Memorial Center, and the Fort Worth Zoo.

**Fort Worth Stockyards National Historic District.** Cattle once filled Exchange Ave. and were traded at the Livestock Exchange. Today this area is one of the state's most visited tourist attractions. You can watch a rodeo at the Cowtown Coliseum, learn about the cattle auctions of the past, and catch a ride aboard a historic locomotive to Grapevine.

**Sundance Square.** Within the downtown area is the 20-block Sundance Square, which is bounded by Houston, Commerce, 2nd, and 3rd Sts. Named after the Sundance Kid, who was known to have hidden in the area in the late 1890s, Sundance Square is an extremely popular entertainment and shopping district whose brick-lined streets boast a variety of restaurants, art galleries, boutiques, theaters, and night spots.

## DRIVING AROUND TOWN

The roads in Fort Worth are not too busy and rarely ever the site of bumper-to-bumper traffic. There is sufficient signage and warning to help avoid bottlenecking.

Interstate 30 runs on the southern border of the city; I–35, which runs north–south, is on the eastern border. No major highways run through Fort Worth. The downtown area has numerous one-way streets, so be sure to keep an eye out for them.

Rush hours are 8 AM–9 AM and 5 PM–6 PM. There are no particular bottlenecks, but try to steer clear of the big parking garages downtown around 5 PM, as numerous cars will be exiting, thereby causing delays. The area near the intersection of I–30 and I–35 gets congested during rush hour.

Fort Worth has meter-parking but, like any major city, available spaces are not always easy to find. Meter parking is free after 5 PM. You'll find plenty of parking garages downtown. Fees for a three-hour stay range from $6–$7.50; eight hours will cost you from $8–$10. Parking regulations are strictly enforced everywhere by police in patrol cars and on bicycles. Violations can result in a ticket ranging from $11–$17.

Speed limits in Fort Worth vary, but are usually set between 20 mph and 30 mph. Speed limits on rural highways are 65 mph, and those on interstates are 70 mph. Regulations are fairly strict. A right turn on red is permitted in Fort Worth, unless otherwise noted.

## WALKING TOUR

### Stockyards (approximately two hours)

Begin at the eastern end of Exchange Avenue at **Stockyards Station,** a marketplace of restaurants and tourist-friendly shops housed in former livestock barns. After exiting the complex, turn left, cross the railroad tracks, and walk past the Stockyards Visitors Center. Cross the street to the Fort Worth Livestock Exchange Building. Now an office complex, the building also houses the **Stockyards Museum,** a homey repository for such decidedly Western relics as collections of barbed wire, arrowheads, and Native American artifacts. Upon exiting the museum, turn right and cross the driveway to the **Cowtown Coliseum,** where rodeos are held every Friday and Saturday night. Cross Rodeo Plaza to **Fincher's,** a purveyor of Western wear since 1902. The smell of leather hits you as soon as you enter, and a bar in the back serves beer and sarsaparilla. Cross the street and head to the legendary **White Elephant Saloon.** Even if you're not ready to down a Lone Star beer, duck into this celebrated bar, where the ceiling is covered in cowboy hats and one wall is taken up by an extensive collection of—what else?—white elephants. If you're hungry, turn left, go to the corner of Exchange and Main, turn left on Main, and walk approximately four blocks to 22nd Street. Turn left on 22nd and walk one block to **Joe T. Garcia's,** home to some of the region's best Tex-Mex food and most potent margaritas. Retrace your steps back to the corner of Main and Exchange and you will find **M. L. Leddy's Boot and Saddlery,** a more spacious, more upscale Western-wear shop than Fincher's. Cross Main Street and stop into the **Stockyards Hotel.** Built in 1907, the area's first brick building played host to Clyde Barrow (of Bonnie and Clyde fame) during a 1932 trip to Fort Worth. In the hotel's Booger Red Saloon, bar stools are topped with saddles. Return to the corner of Main and Exchange, turn right, and walk two blocks up Main Street. Cross Stockyards Boulevard to see the "Texas Gold" bronze statue of longhorns and cattlemen. Cross Stockyards Boulevard again and **Billy Bob's Texas** will be on your left. The "world's largest honky-tonk" has live country music, bull riding on Friday and Saturday nights, and a family entertainment area. Walk through Rodeo Plaza for about one block, then turn left on Exchange and head back to Stockyards Station where, depending on the day and time, you may be able to see (or take a ride on) the **Tarantula Train,** a historic locomotive that runs between Fort Worth and nearby Grapevine. You might want to time your visit so that you can see the twice-daily (11:30AM and 4PM) cattle drives that take place on Exchange Avenue in front of **Stockyards Station.**

## TRANSPORTATION

**Airports:** Most of the major airlines fly into the **Dallas/Fort Worth International Airport** (3200 E. Airfield Dr. | 972/574–8888 | www.dfwairport.com).

**Airport Transportation:** The cheapest way from Fort Worth to DFW International Airport is by **The Airporter Bus** operated by The T, Fort Worth's public bus system. Fare is $8 one way and departs a downtown terminal at 1000 E. Weatherford Street, Fort Worth. (817/215–8600)

**Super Shuttle** is the shared-ride van service that picks you up at your home or business and takes you to the airport terminal of your choice. Fares are $25–$50, one-way. Taxi rides cost about $30 from downtown to DFW. (817/329–2000)

**Rail: Amtrak's** service to Los Angeles, Chicago, and San Antonio is available from Fort Worth. (1501 Jones St. | 800/872–7245)

**Bus: Greyhound Bus Lines** connects Fort Worth, San Antonio, Houston, and beyond. (901 Commerce St. | 800/231–2222)

**Intra-city Transit. The T,** Fort Worth's city bus line, operates from 5 AM to midnight weekdays and from 6 AM to midnight Saturday. Sunday service is available on eight routes from 7 AM to 7 PM. Regular city bus service is available on routes in Fort Worth, Lake Worth, and Richland Hills. Eight Express routes allow virtually non-stop travel weekdays from designated park-and-ride lots to downtown Fort Worth and downtown Dallas. The T provides park-and-ride locations, a convenient meeting point for carpools and vanpools, and free all-day parking. In downtown Fort Worth, a Downtown Free Zone provides free transportation to restaurants, shopping, and offices within the area bounded by Henderson, Jones, Belknap, and Lancaster streets. Basic bus fares are 50¢ for children and seniors and $1 for adults; Park and Ride is $2, and Dallas Express is $3. (817/215–8600)

The only Fort Worth **subway** is the train that takes you from a free parking lot along the Trinity River, near the county courthouse, to the Tandy Center. This is most often used by downtown workers and residents on jury duty.

Taxi companies that operate in the area include **Checker Cab Co.** (817/332–1919) and **Yellow Checker Cab** (817/534–5555).

## Attractions

### ART AND ARCHITECTURE

**Flatiron Building.** This gargoyle-crowned Renaissance Revival building was built in 1907 and patterned after similar structures in New York and Philadelphia. It is presently being renovated into office space and retail stores. | 1000 Houston St. | 817/336–8791 | Free | Daily.

**Knights of Pythias Hall.** Built in 1901 as the world's first Pythian temple, this medieval-style building is the oldest in Sundance Square. | 317 Main St. | 817/336–8791 | Free | Daily.

**Thistle Hill.** Tours are available of this 1910 restored cattle baron's mansion, known for its Georgian Revival architecture. The mansion is filled with period pieces from the late 19th century and early 20th century. | 1509 Pennsylvania Ave. | 817/336–1212 | $4 | Weekdays 11–2, Sun. 1–3.

### CULTURE, EDUCATION, AND HISTORY

**Allied Theatre Guild.** Various classical and contemporary plays are performed in this 1920s Art Deco theater. | 3055 S. University Dr. | 817/784–9378 | fax 817/926–8650 | www.alliedtheatregroup.org | $10–$20 | Call for showtimes, Box office: daily, 10-6.

**Caravan of Dreams.** Jazz and blues greats are often featured performers at this world class, downtown music venue. Be sure to check out the rooftop cactus garden. | 312 Houston St. | 817/877–3000 | www.caravanofdreams.com | call for info, usually $10-60, depending on the show | Box office: Mon.-Wed. 10-6, Th,Fri 10-8, Sat.12-8.

**Casa Mañana Theater.** This geodesic dome was Texas's first performance theater-in-the-round and one of Buckminster Fuller's first projects. Today it hosts the city's summer series of musicals. | 3101 W. Lancaster Ave. | 817/332–9319 | fax 817/332–5711 | www.casamanana.org | $33–$78 | Box office: daily, 9-5.

**Circle Theatre.** National touring companies perform here. | 230 W. 4th St. | 817/877–3040 | fax 817/877–3536 | www.circletheater.com | $15–$20 | Call for showtimes, Box office: Tue.–Fri. 1–5.

**Jubilee Theatre.** Local performers put on dramas, comedies, and musicals. | 506 Main St. | 817/338–4411 | www.jubileetheater.org | $12–$16 | Box office: Tue.–Fri. 2–6.

**Nancy Lee and Perry R. Bass Performance Hall.** This majestic space in Sundance Square is home to the Fort Worth-Dallas Ballet, the Fort Worth Opera, and the Fort Worth Symphony Orchestra. | 555 Commerce St. | 817/212–4300 | fax 817/810–9294 | www.basshall.com | $18–80 | Call for showtimes, Box Office: Tue.–Fri. 10–6, Sat. 10–4.

**Southwestern Baptist Theological Seminary.** Southern Baptists are the largest Protestant denomination in Texas, and most of the state's preachers are schooled here. Newsman Bill Moyers is perhaps its most famous non-clerical graduate. Be sure to visit the Tandy Archeological Museum in the Roberts Library. | 2001 West Seminary Dr. | 817/923–1921 ext. 4000 | Free | Mon. 8AM–11PM, Tues. & Thurs. 7:30AM–11PM, Wed. 7:30AM–5PM, 9PM–11PM, Fri. 7:30AM–10PM, Sat. 10AM–6PM.

## MUSEUMS

**Amon Carter Museum.** This museum began with the private collection of Amon Carter and his 391 Frederic Remington and Charles M. Russell paintings and sculptures. Today it showcases over 358,000 objects and is considered one of the nation's best centers for the study of American art. | 3501 Camp Bowie Blvd. | 817/738–1933 | www.cartermuseum.org | Free | Tues.–Sat. 10–5, Sun. 12–5.

**Cattle Raiser's Museum.** The history of Texas's cattle industry is showcased through audiovisual displays, historic artifacts, and photographs. Ranching pioneers and black cowboys who joined the industry after the Civil War are also honored. | 1301 W. Seventh St. | 817/332–8551 | fax 817/332–8749 | $3 | Daily 9–5.

**Fire Station Museum.** Built in 1907, this was the city's first firehouse. Today, the building is a museum highlighting 150 years of city history. Displays include streetside building fronts which cattle headed for the Chisholm Trail used to pass. | 215 Commerce St. | 817/732–1631 | Free | Daily 9–6.

**Fort Worth Museum of Science and History.** This hands-on museum includes DinoDig, an outdoor sand pit where dinosaur "artifacts" can be uncovered by young archaeologists. | 1501 Montgomery St. | 817/732–1631 | www.fwmuseum.org | $5 | Mon.–Wed. 9–5, Thurs.–Sat. 9–9, Sun. 12–9.

At the museum's **Noble Planetarium,** visitors can view informative shows on the solar system and the many constellations in our sky all day. | 817/255–9300 | $3 | Wed.–Fri. 2:30–4:30, Sat. 11–4:30, Sun. 12:30–4:30.

The **Omni Theater** shows history and natural history films on a 360° screen. | $6 | Daily, call 817/255-9300 for showtimes.

★ **Kimbell Art Museum.** Often cited as one of the top public modern art-gallery facilities in the world, this museum's collection includes works by Matisse, El Greco, Caravaggio, Rembrandt, Picasso, and Miró. It's also home to one of the largest collections of Asian art in the Southwest. | 3333 Camp Bowie Blvd. | 817/332–8451 | fax 817/877–1264 | www.kimbellart.org | Free | Tues.–Thurs. 10–5, Fri. 12–8, Sat. 10–5, Sun. 12–5.

**Modern Art Museum of Fort Worth.** Founded in 1892, this museum holds the distinction as the oldest art museum in Texas. Today it houses works by Picasso, Pollock, Lichtenstein, and others. It also has many pieces of outdoor sculpture. | 1309 Montgomery St. | 817/738–9215 | fax 817/735-1161 | www.mamfw.org | Free | Tues. 10–5, Wed.–Fri. 10–5, Sat. 11–5, Sun. 12–5.

**Sid Richardson Collection of Western Art.** Located in the heart of downtown in the Sundance Square, this museum includes a collection of Russell and Remington artwork as well as works by other Western artists. | 309 Main St. | 817/332–6554 | fax 817/332–8671 | www.sidr-museum.org | Free | Tues.–Wed. 10–5, Thurs., Fri. 10–8, Sat. 11–8, Sun. 1–5.

## PARKS, NATURAL SIGHTS, AND OUTDOOR ACTIVITIES

**Benbrook Lake.** Camping, boating, and swimming are popular on the 3,770-acre lake. | Off U.S. 377. | 817/292–2400 | fax 817/346–0021 | Free; fee for some activities | Daily 6 AM–9 PM.

**Botanic Gardens.** Extensive gardens in Trinity Park include a conservatory and Japanese gardens. | 3220 Botanic Garden Blvd. | 817/871–7686 or 817/871–7689 | fax 817/871–7638 | Free, $1 for conservatory, $2 for Japanese gardens | Daily 10 AM–dusk.

**Fort Worth Nature Center and Refuge.** Bison and white-tailed deer are among the residents of this 3,500-acre refuge. | 9601 Fossil Ridge Rd., Lake Worth . | 817/237–1111 | Free | Daily 9–5.

★ **Fort Worth Water Gardens Park.** These cascading water gardens and fountains are adjacent to the convention center. | Behind Fort Worth/Tarrant County Convention Center | Free | Daily.

**Lake Worth.** You can boat, fish, swim, and picnic here. | Hwy. 199 exit off 820 loop | 817/237–0060 | Free | Daily.

★ **Fort Worth Zoo.** This is one of Texas's best known zoos and it's noted for its animal-friendly habitats and its efforts to protect Texas species. The zoo recently opened an exhibit of American plains animals and another featuring native Texas species. | 1989 Colonial Pkwy. (in Forest Park) | 817/871–7050 | www.fortworthzoo.com | $7 | Daily 10–5.

**Sugartree Golf Club.** This demanding 18-hole golf course is tree-lined with lots of wildlife. It's approximately 35 mi west of Fort Worth via I–20. | Rte. 1189, Dennis | 817/596–4991 | Year-round.

## SHOPPING

**Barber's Book Store.** Founded in 1925, this is the oldest bookstore in Texas. It specializes in Texana and rare and fine books. | 215 W. 8th St. | 817/335–5469 | Free | Mon.–Sat., 11–5.

**Fincher's.** This western outfitter has been around since 1902. Half of the store is in a former bank building; you can walk into the old vaults. | 115 E. Exchange Ave. | 817/624–7302 | fax 817/624–1992 | Free | Mon.–Sat. 9–6; Sun. 1–5.

**Fort Worth Outlet Square.** Attached to Sundance Square, this large, modern indoor mall has its own privately operated subway. It contains over 25 retail store outlets and 12 restaurants. Also home to "The Ice," an indoor skating rink. | 150 Throckmorton St. | 800/414–2817 | Free | Mon.–Thurs. 10–6, Fri.–Sat. 10–7:30, Sun. 12–6.

**M. L. Leddy's Boot and Saddlery.** Run by the Leddy family since it opened in 1921, this store is a great place for boots and other leather products. | 2455 N. Main St. | 817/624–3149 | fax 817/625–2725 | Free | Mon.–Sat. 10–6.

**Old Ellis Pecan Company.** A sad reminder of American History, the building that houses this company was once the 1920s Ku Klux Klan Building. Since then, the original building was destroyed, and the Ellis Pecan Co. has moved. | 1012 N. Main St. | 817/336–8791 | Free.

**Stockyards Station.** This area is a fast-growing marketplace of shops and restaurants, all housed in former sheep and hog pens. There are also several good western wear and furniture outlets here. | 130 E. Exchange Ave. | 817/625–9715 | fax 817/625–9744.

## SPECTATOR SPORTS

**Cowtown Coliseum.** This stadium was constructed in 1908 to house what became the Southwestern Exposition and Fat Stock Show; today it is the site of Fri. and Sat. night rodeos. | 121 E. Exchange Ave. | 817/625–1025 or 888/269–8696 | $8–$12 | Box office: daily 9-5, Fri.–Sat. nights during the rodeos.

**Fort Worth Brahmas.** Hockey at the Fort Worth Convention Center. | 1111 Houston St. | 817/884–2222 or 817/336–4423 | $10–$15 | Season Oct.–Mar.

**Texas Motor Speedway.** A wide variety of races (including NASCAR) are held here. Peak racing season is Mar.–June, though the complex is open for tours year-round. | 3601 Rte. 114, Justin | 817/215–8500 | fax 817/491–3749 | www.texasmotorspeedway.com | Tours $6, races $16–$96 | Tours weekdays 9–4, Sat. 10–4, Sun. 1–4.

**Will Rogers Memorial Center.** One of the country's top equestrian facilities, this facility is also the site of the annual Fort Worth Southwestern Exposition and Livestock Show. | 3401 W. Lancaster St. | 817/871–8150 | Prices vary with shows, $7–$20 | Weekdays 8–5.

## OTHER POINTS OF INTEREST

**Billy Bob's Texas.** Big-name country music artists perform at this bar, which is Fort Worth's most famous honky-tonk. It's housed in an old cattle pen building. | 2520 Rodeo Plaza | 817/624–7117 or 817/589–1711 | fax 817/626–2340 | www.billybobstexas.com | Weekdays $1 before 8PM, $3 after; weekends more depending on the musical act | Mon.-Sat. 11–2AM, Sun. 12–2AM.

**Fort Worth Stockyards National Historic District.** In the mid-1800s, Ft. Worth earned its reputation as "Cowtown." It was in the middle of the Chisholm Trail, and many cattlemen herding through the area made frequent stops here. Cattle once filled Exchange Ave. and were traded like stock in the Livestock Exchange, formerly called the Wall Street of the West. The Stockyards were also known as the biggest hog and sheep marketing center in the Southwest. In 1976, the area was designated as a National Historic Landmark. Today it is one of the state's most visited tourist attractions. | Between Main St. and Exchange | 817/624–4741 | Free | Daily.

Home of the world's first indoor rodeo, the historic **Cowtown Coliseum** still hosts weekly rodeos as well as a traditional Wild West show. | 121 E. Exchange Ave. | 817/625–1025 or 888/269–8696 | Prices vary with shows | Daily.

Exhibits documenting the history of local auctions can be found in the **Stockyards Museum.** The museum is in two rooms of a building that houses cattle auction companies. | 131 E. Exchange Ave., Suite 111–114 | 817–625–5087 | Free | Mon.–Sat. 10–5.

**Tarantula Train** offers a nostalgic ride aboard historic locomotives through historic Fort Worth to the community of Grapevine. Open-air cars are popular in the spring and fall. The train's unusual moniker is a reference to an 1873 railroad map that had Ft. Worth in its center, and proposed rail lines stemming out in all directions like spider legs. | 140 E. Exchange Ave. | 817/625–RAIL or 888/952–5717 | www.tarantulatrain.com | $10–$20 | Sat., Sun. only, trains leave Sat. 10–2, Sun. 1–5.

**Log Cabin Village.** Volunteer interpreters and crafts people bring pioneer heritage to life at this living history museum. Grounds include six log cabins from local parts of Texas that were moved here and restored in the mid-1950s. | 2100 Log Cabin Village Ln | 817/926–5881 | www.sed.tcu.edu/sed/logcabin/lcv.html | $2 | Tues.–Fri. 9–4:30, Sat. 10–4:30, Sun. 1–4:30.

## ON THE CALENDAR

**JAN., FEB.: *Southwestern Exposition and Livestock Show.*** More than 200,000 head of livestock compete in this annual event. You can watch the bidding on donkeys, horses, cattle, pigeons, rabbits, goats, and sheep. There's also a rodeo with a calf scramble and chuck wagon races. | 817/877–2400.

**APR.: *Main Street Fort Worth Arts Festival.*** Artists from around the state participate in this festival that includes demonstrations, arts and crafts, food booths, children's activities, an art show, and more than 400 entertainers. | 817/336–ARTS.

**MAY: *Mayfest.*** Held beside the Trinity River in Trinity Park, this family event now in its third decade includes food, arts and crafts, sports, and entertainment. | 817/332–1055.

**JUNE: *Chisholm Trail Round-Up.*** This lively festival includes armadillo races, chuck-wagon cooking contests, chili cook-offs, barbecue cook-offs, gunfight re-enactments, fiddlers' contests, live music, and children's activities. | 817/625–7005 | www.chisholmtrail.org.

**JUNE, JULY: *Shakespeare in the Park.*** This summer festival is held Tues.–Sun. Two plays are performed, and each runs three weeks. | 817/923–6698.

**SEPT.: *Pioneer Days.*** Pioneers who settled on the Trinity River are honored with live music, food booths, and children's activities. | 800/433–5747.

## Dining

### INEXPENSIVE

**Angelo's Barbecue.** Barbecue. Besides a great brisket, this restaurant is famous for its succulent smoked ribs, so tender that the meat falls off the bone. Arrive early, as the ribs have been known to disappear well before closing. | 2533 White Settlement Rd. | 817/332–0357 | Reservations not accepted | $7–$18 | No credit cards.

**Paris Coffee Shop.** American. Enthusiastic diners claim that this breakfast spot, oddly enough, has the best chicken-fried steak in Texas. Try the chicken-and-dumplings. | 700 W. Magnolia | 817/335–2041 | Breakfast also available. Closed Sun. No supper | $6–$8 | AE, D, MC, V.

**Possum Lodge.** Barbecue. On the north side of town on the grounds of a gas station, this pit barbecue restaurant draws crowds from miles away for its ribs, burgers, and catfish. | 9120 Boat Club Rd. | 817/236–4499 | $6–$10 | AE, MC, V.

**Pour House Sports Grill.** Continental. Lunch and dinner, happy hour, and big screen TVs are the norm at this sports bar, and cover bands perform live music on Fri. and Sat. nights. There are plenty of good burgers and sandwiches, as well as more eclectic dishes such as blackened chicken étouffée and catfish pecan chicken sandwich. A covered patio on the second floor overlooks 4th St. The restaurant is closed Sun., excluding football season. | 209 W. 5th St. | 817/335–2575 | fax 817/335–2577 | Closed Sun. | $5–$9 | AE, D, DC, MC, V.

**Railhead Smokehouse.** Barbecue. Most people come to this casual place with cafeteria-style dining for the tender smoked ribs. The beer and wine are inexpensive, and the brisket is also tasty. | 2900 Montgomery St. | 817/738–9808 | Closed Sun. | $4–$7 | V, MC.

**Wan Fu.** Chinese. Serves Szechuan specialties. | 6399 Camp Bowie Blvd. | 817/731–2388 | $5–$16 | AE, MC, V.

### MODERATE

**Bistro Louise.** Contemporary. People drive 30 mi from Dallas to dine on pecan-fried chicken, macadamia-crusted shrimp, rosemary-crusted chicken with lump crab meat and shiitake mushrooms, and the like. Decor includes wood-beam ceilings and flowered tablecloths. | 2900 S. Hulen St. | 817/922–9244 | fax 817/922–8148 | Closed Sun. | $12–$30 | AE, D, DC MC, V.

**Cattlemen's Steak House.** Steak. Steaks are charcoal-grilled at the front of the room, and you can pick out your own cut of meat. The seafood is also popular. | 2458 N. Main St. | 817/624–3945 | $11–$32 | AE, D, DC, MC, V | www.cattlemenssteakhouse.com.

**Edelweiss.** German, American. Alpine decor. Specializing in schnitzel and roulade. Entertainment Tues.–Sat. | 3801-A Southwest Blvd. | 817/738–5934 | Closed Sun., Mon. | $12–$34 | AE, D, DC, MC, V.

★ **Joe T. Garcia's.** Mexican. This restaurant has family-style service and is extremely popular on weekends, when a mariachi band performs. Known for fajitas and enchiladas. Kids' menu. | 2201 N. Commerce St. | 817/626–8571 | $10–$12 | No credit cards.

**Lucile's.** American. There's been a restaurant of some sort in this building since the 1930s; the original pressed-tin ceiling is still in place. Known for pasta and wood-roasted entrées. Open-air dining is available on a patio with seven umbrellaed tables. | 4700 Camp Bowie St. | 817/738–4761 | Breakfast also available weekends | $9–$19 | AE, D, DC, MC, V.

## EXPENSIVE

**Angeluna.** Contemporary. High ceilings painted to look like clouds and a soft marble bar adorn this stylish restaurant, known for its see-and-be seen crowd. Chef Clark McDaniel serves eclectic winners such seared ahi tuna with jasmine rice and black vinegar butter sauce. The hickory-grilled ribeye steak is also popular. | 215 E. 4th St. | 817/334–0080 | fax 817/334–0903 | $13–29 | AE, MC, V.

**Balcony.** Continental. This is a longtime favorite with diners looking for a quiet, relaxed place to eat. Semi-formal wear is the order of the day, with business casual suits and dresses being popular. Pianist weekends. Try pan-seared rack of lamb or lamb mozzarella. | 6100 Camp Bowie Blvd. | 817/731–3719 | Closed Sun. No lunch Sat. | $21–$32 | AE, D, DC, MC, V.

**Cafe Aspen.** American. This cozy eatery is frequented by romantic diners and is known for its fresh fish. The beef tenderloin and rib-eye steak are also popular. Entertainment Fri., Sat. | 6103 Camp Bowie Blvd. | 817/738–0838 | Closed Sun. | $15–$24 | AE, DC, MC, V.

**Michaels.** Southwestern. The Southwestern or "contemporary ranch" cuisine is what you'll find here, with an emphasis on fruits and chiles. The decor is rustic and comfortable. Try the pecan-crusted goat cheese chicken, or southwestern crab cakes. | 3413 W. Seventh | 817/877–3413 | fax 817/877–3430 | $14–$28 | AE, D, DC, MC, V.

**Reata.** Contemporary. Cowhide seats, murals, and a view of the Ft. Worth skyline can be enjoyed in this hot spot on the 35th floor of the Bank One Tower. Try the excellent steaks, bock beer–batter quail, pan-seared pecan-crusted beef tenderloin, or the tamales. You may also want to sample something from the vodka and tequila bars. | 500 Throckmorton St. | 817/336–1009 | fax 817/336–0267 | $13–$30 | AE, MC, V.

**Riscky's Sirloin Inn.** Steak. If you've been hanging out in the vicinity of the Stockyards, this western-theme steakhouse is a good place to grab a meal. Try the Stockyard Special—a 10-oz NY strip with red-wine mushroom gravy. | 120 E. Exchange | 817/624–4800 | fax 817/624–7444 | $13–$25 | AE, D, DC, MC, V.

★ **Saint-Emilion.** French. Near the museum district, this French café is a favorite with romantically minded diners and for those in search of an excellent Gallic meal. The roasted duck, beef tenderloin, rack of lamb, and fresh fish are all popular. | 3617 W. 7th St., | 817/737–2781 | Closed Sun., Mon. No lunch | $22–$35 | AE, D, DC, MC, V.

## Lodging

### INEXPENSIVE

**La Quinta–West.** This motel is 10 mi west of downtown Fort Worth. Complimentary Continental breakfast, in-room data ports, cable TV, pool, some pets allowed. | 7888 I–30W | 817/246–5511 | fax 817/246–8870 | www.laquinta.com | 106 rooms | $49–$60 | AE, D, DC, MC, V.

**Motel 6–Forth Worth East.** Shops and fast-food restaurants are within walking distance of this motel. Cable TV, pool, some pets allowed. | 1236 Oakland Blvd. | 817/834–7361 | fax 817/834–1573 | 244 rooms | $36–$48 | AE, D, DC, MC, V.

**Motel 6–Fort Worth South.** This motel is 3 mi from a shopping mall and restaurants. Cable TV, pool, some pets allowed. | 6600 S. Fwy. | 817/293–8595 | fax 817/293–8577 | 279 rooms | $46 | AE, D, DC, MC, V.

### MODERATE

**American Inn.** Just an exit away from the mall and restaurants. Complimentary Continental breakfast, in-room data ports, some microwaves, cable TV, pool, laundry facilities, business services, some pets allowed. | 7301 W. Fwy. | 817/244–7444 | fax 817/244–7902 | 118 rooms | $59–$99 | AE, D, DC, MC, V.

**Courtyard by Marriott.** Two large shopping malls are within 6 mi of this hotel. Bar, in-room data ports, some refrigerators, cable TV, pool, hot tub, exercise equipment, laundry facilities, free parking. | 2201 Airport Fwy., Bedford | 817/545–2202 | fax 817/545–2319 | www.marriotthotels.com | 145 rooms, 14 suites | $69–$99, $121 suites | AE, D, DC, MC, V.

**Fort Worth Inn Suites Hotel.** Three mi from the Fort Worth and Sundance Square Mall. Restaurant, bar, in-room data ports, room service, cable TV, pool, hot tub. Tennis, exercise equipment, business services. | 2000 Beach St. | 817/534–4801 | fax 817/534–3761 | www.holiday-inn.com | 103 rooms | $60–$129 | AE, D, DC, MC, V.

**Hampton Inn.** This Hampton Inn is near a movie theater, shopping, and several restaurants. Complimentary Continental breakfast, in-room data ports, cable TV, pool, laundry facilities, business services. | 4681 Gemini Place | 817/625–5327 | fax 817/625–7727 | www.hampton-inn.com | 66 rooms | $69–$79 | AE, D, DC, MC, V.

**Holiday Inn–North.** This hotel is near downtown Fort Worth and is 25 mi from the Dallas/Ft. Worth International Airport. Restaurant, bar (with entertainment), room service, in-room data ports, some in-room hot tubs, cable TV, pool, hot tub, exercise equipment, laundry facilities, business services. | 2540 Meacham Blvd. | 817/625–9911 | fax 817/625–5132 | www.holidayinn.com | 247 rooms | $69–$85, $109–$189 suites | AE, D, DC, MC, V.

## EXPENSIVE

**Azalea Plantation.** On the north end of town, this plantation-style Colonial home sits on 1½ landscaped acres with oak trees, a fountain, and a gazebo. Rooms are large and furnished with colonial antiques. The complimentary breakfast is full during the week, and Continental on the weekends. Dining room, complimentary breakfast, some microwaves, some refrigerators, some in-room hot tubs, business services, no smoking. | 1400 Robinwood Dr. | 817/838–5882 or 800/687–3529 | fax 817/838–5882 | 4 rooms | $98–$149 | AE, D, MC, V.

**Comfort Inn.** Shops and restaurants are within 3 mi of this motel. Complimentary Continental breakfast, cable TV, pool. | 4850 N. Fwy. | 817/834–8001 | fax 817/834–3159 | 60 rooms | $55–$65 | AE, D, DC, MC, V.

**Green Oaks Park Hotel.** This two-story hotel is next to the Naval Air Station, Carswell Joint Reserve Base, and several restaurants. Restaurant, bar (with entertainment), room service, in-room data ports, cable TV, 2 pools, 18-hole golf course, exercise equipment, business services, pets allowed (fee). | 6901 W. Fwy. | 817/738–7311 or 800/433–2174 (outside TX) or 800/772–2341 (TX) | fax 817/377–1308 | greenoak@onramp.net | 284 rooms in 5 buildings | $79–$150 | AE, D, DC, MC, V.

**Miss Molly's.** In past lives this B&B above the Star Cafe in the Stockyards was a prim boarding house, then a raucous bordello. Each guest room has lace curtains, shutters, antique quilts, an iron bed, and oak furniture. Complimentary breakfast. | 109½ W. Exchange Ave. | 817/626–1522 or 800/996–6559 | fax 817/625–2723 | www.missmollys.com | 8 rooms (7 with shared bath) | $95–$170 | AE, D, DC, MC, V.

**Radisson Plaza.** This top-notch hotel is in the heart of downtown Fort Worth. Restaurant, bar, cable TV, pool, barbershop, beauty salon, exercise equipment. | 815 Main St. | 817/870–2100 | fax 817/882–1300 | radstw@startext.com | www.radisson.com | 517 rooms | $99–$199 | AE, D, DC, MC, V.

## VERY EXPENSIVE

**Etta's Place.** This three-story B&B is named for Etta Place, the girlfriend of the Sundance Kid. It originally served as living quarters for traveling artists who performed at the Caravan of Dreams (which is just around the corner) during the 1980s. A handsome music room has a baby grand Steinway. Complimentary breakfast, some kitchenettes, some microwaves, some refrigerators, massage, library, laundry service, business services. No smoking. No pets. | 200 W. Third St. | 817/654–0267 | fax 817/878–2560 | www.caravanofdreams.com | 10 rooms | $125–$165. AE, D, DC, MC, V

**Lockheart Gables.** As a guest here you'll stay in one of two stone cottages, formerly the carriage houses of the main 1893 brick home. Romantic touches include a heart-shaped jetted tub for two and a remote-control fireplace (although there's also a pullout couch in the living room for kids). Breakfast is delivered to your room, and includes cinnamon rolls, the house specialty. Complimentary breakfast, hot tub, no pets, no smoking. | 5220 Locke Ave. | 817/738–5969 or 888/224–3278 | www.lockheartgables.com | 2 cottages | $160–$175 | AE, D, DC, MC, V.

★ **Renaissance Worthington Hotel.** This modern, geometric-shaped downtown hotel is in historic Sundance Square. It's 19 mi from the Dallas/Ft. Worth International Airport and within walking distance of many local attractions, restaurants, entertainment venues, and shops. 3 restaurants, bar, room service, in-room data ports, some refrigerators, cable TV, pool, hot tub, massage, golf privileges, tennis, gym, shops, business services. | 200 Main St. | 817/870–1000 or 800/433–5677 | fax 817/388–9176 | www.renaissancehotels.com/dfwdt | 504 rooms | $159–$189 | AE, D, DC, MC, V.

**Residence Inn by Marriott.** This hotel is 1 mi south of I–30, and just 3 mi from downtown Fort Worth. Picnic area, complimentary breakfast, in-room data ports, kitchenettes, microwaves, refrigerators, cable TV, pool, hot tub, laundry facilities, business services, free parking, pets allowed (fee). | 1701 S. University Dr. | 817/870–1011 | fax 817/877–5500 | www.marriotthotels.com | 120 suites | $105–$175 suites | AE, D, DC, MC, V.

**Stockyards Hotel.** Built in 1907, this hotel is on the State Register of Historic Places. The spacious lobby has antiques and objets d'art reminiscent of the Old West. Carpeting in the common areas has images of Texas longhorn woven into the design. All guest rooms are decorated to reflect one of four themes: "Victorian," "Mountain Man," "Cowboy," or "Native American." It's 4 mi north of downtown Ft. Worth and within walking distance of many shops, restaurants, and saloons. Restaurant, bar, in-room data ports, cable TV, business services. | 109 E. Exchange Ave. | 817/625–6427 or 800/423–8471 (outside TX) | fax 817/624–2571 | www.stockyardshotel.com | 42 rooms, 10 suites | $119, $150–$260 suites | AE, D, DC, MC, V.

# FREDERICKSBURG

MAP 8, G5

*(Nearby towns also listed: Johnson City, Kerrville, Mason)*

Once the edge of the frontier and home to German pioneers, Fredericksburg, population 8,000, is now a favorite weekend getaway from San Antonio. During the week, the streets of this charming town are quiet, but from Friday through Sunday they bustle with shoppers looking for antiques bargains, history buffs exploring the town's many attractions, and fans of good German food. The community is home to more B&Bs than any other part of Texas. The city is also the gateway to Enchanted Rock State Natural Area, home of a giant stone monolith.

**Information: Fredericksburg Convention and Visitors Bureau** | 106 N. Adams, Fredericksburg, TX 78624 | 830/997–6523 | www.fredericksburg-texas.com.

## Attractions

**Admiral Nimitz Museum and State Historical Center.** This site honors Fredericksburg's most famous resident: Adm. Chester Nimitz, World War II Commander-in-Chief of the Pacific. Today the former hotel, built by Nimitz's grandfather, houses a three-story museum honoring Admiral Nimitz as well as Fredericksburg's early residents. Many exhibits are devoted to World War II, including several that illustrate the Pacific campaign. Several hotel rooms, the hotel kitchen, and the bathhouse have been restored. Behind the museum lies the Garden of Peace, a gift from the people of Japan. | 340 E. Main St. | 830/997–4379 | fax 830/997–8220 | www.nimitz-museum.org | $5 | Daily 10–5.

**Enchanted Rock State Natural Area.** This park features the largest stone formation in the West. Nationally this 640-acre granite outcropping takes second place only to Georgia's Stone

Mountain. Travelers can enjoy a climb up Enchanted Rock. Experienced climbers can scale the smaller formations located next to the main dome. Picnic facilities and a 60-site primitive campground at the base of the rock round out the offerings here. No vehicular camping is permitted. Entry into the park is limited during busy weekends. | Off Rte. 965, 18 mi north of Fredricksburg | 915/247–3903 | www.tpwd.state.tx.us/park/enchantd/enchantd.html | $5 | Daily 8 AM–10 PM.

**Lady Bird Johnson Municipal Golf Course.** This highly scenic, water-intensive course is part of Lady Bird Johnson Municipal Park. Some regulars tout the 18-hole course as fun and others want to keep it their favorite secret. All agree that the greens fees are very reasonable. | 126 Main St. | 830/997–4010 or 800/950–8147 | $26–$33 | Year-round; Tues.–Sun. 6:30 AM– 7 PM, Mon. 12–7.

**Luckenbach.** The classic country song "Luckenbach, Texas" made this tiny town (pop. 25) famous. A little east of Fredericksburg on Rte. 1376, Luckenbach was founded in 1850 and remains largely unchanged, with one unpainted general store and tavern, a rural dance hall, and a blacksmith's shop. Try to stop by on Sunday afternoon, when informal groups of fiddlers, guitarists, and banjo pickers gather under the live oaks.

**Pioneer Museum.** This collection of historic buildings includes an 1849 pioneer log home and store, an old First Methodist Church, and a smokehouse. Also on the premises stands a typical 19th-century "Sunday house." Sunday houses catered to farmers and their families who traveled long distances to attend church services and had to stay the night. With the advent of the automobile, such accommodations became obsolete. | 309 W. Main St. | 830/997–2835 | www.pioneermuseum.com | $3 | Mon.–Sat. 10–5, Sun. 1–5.

## EASTER FIRES

Fredericksburg has a unique Easter Bunny story, dating back to 1847. John Mueseback and other men from a small settlement rode out to make a peace treaty with the Comanches. (Mueseback was the leader of the German immigrant families who had settled in the Pedernales Valley the year before.) The final points of the treaty were being drawn up on Easter eve, and the Comanches kept watch over the town, wary that the settlers might trick them in some way. At night, the Indians's campfires dotted the horizon.

A pioneer mother tried to calm her frightened children, and answer their questions about the ominous campfires. The fires, she explained, were those of the Easter Bunny. His huge pots were filled with a special dye made from colorful wildflowers, and he was busily dying eggs for Easter day. If the children went to sleep, they would find a nest of eggs the next morning.

The men returned from their successful negotiations and heard the new Easter Bunny story. Every year since, the fires have been re-created in honor of both Easter and the peace treaty.

The Fredericksburg Easter Fires pageant, which re-creates the treaty, the fires, and the story-telling, has grown into a major event. Residents spend weeks gathering wood for the campfires, and about 800 townspeople participate in some way. The pageant is often a sell-out, so it's wise to buy tickets ahead of time.

© Artville

**Vereins Kirche Museum.** This eight-sided church was Fredericksburg's first public building. Today it contains local history displays. | Main St. in Market Square | 830/997–2835 | www.pioneermuseum.com/ourmuseums.htm | Free | Mon.–Sat. 10–4, Sun. 1–4.

## ON THE CALENDAR

**MAR., APR.: *Easter Fires Pageant.*** This very popular event is held the Sat. before Easter. Hundreds of local citizens pitch in to produce this play that is a retelling of the Easter Fires story. | 830/997–2359.

**JUNE: *Peach Jamboree and Rodeo.*** Peach-related foods, a rodeo, dancing, fiddlers' contest, and live entertainment converge on Peach St. in Stonewall, 9 mi east of Fredericksburg. | 830/644–2735.

**JULY: *Night in Old Fredericksburg.*** Arts and crafts, dancing, games, and festivities are featured from a different culture each night in Market Sq. | 830/997–6523.

**AUG.: *Gillespie County Fair.*** This long-running county fair has the traditional carnival rides, games, food booths, and exhibits. | 830/997–6523.

**SEPT.: *Texas Hunters' Opening Day.*** Live music, arts and crafts, and hunting displays celebrate the first day of the hunting season on the Marketplatz at North Adams and West Austin St. | 830/990–1294.

**OCT.: *Oktoberfest.*** German culture is celebrated with polka music, German food, dancing, arts and crafts, and children's activities in Market Sq. | 830/997–4810.

## Dining

**Altdorf German Biergarten and Dining Room.** German. It's hard to escape Texas's rich ethnic heritage at this casual restaurant, where schnitzels and bratwurst mix with enchiladas on the menu. Dine inside in a historic settler's home or outside in the graveled biergarten. | 301 W. Main St. | 830/997–7865 | Closed Tues. No dinner Sun. | $10–$14 | D, DC, MC, V.

**Friedhelm's Bavarian Inn.** German. This often lauded eatery serves Bavarian specialties in a family-friendly atmosphere. Don't miss the home baked breads. Kids' menu. | 905 W. Main St. | 830/997–6300 | Closed Mon. | $7–$25 | AE, D, MC, V.

**George's Old German Bakery and Cafe.** German. This casual storefront cafe has solid German fare like schnitzels and rouladen on the menu. Locals swear by the rye wheat bread and rich strudels. | 225 W. Main St. | 830/997–9084 | Breakfast and lunch only | $5–$10 | No credit cards.

**Mamacita's.** Tex-Mex. With traditional Mexican tile, old-style adobe decor, and a menu full of Tex-Mex favorites, Mamacita's provides a satisfying alternative to Fredericksburg's many German restaurants. Kids' menu. | 506 E. Main St. | 830/997–9546 | $6–$13 | AE, D, DC, MC, V.

## Lodging

**Austin Street Retreat.** Only a block from Main Street and within walking distance of Fredericksburg's shopping district, this B&B consists of a main house and two small cottages. The accommodations are luxurious, with piles of pillows and linens, private courtyards, fireplaces, and authentic furnishings. In-room hot tubs, some phones, some TVs, no smoking, no pets. | 408 W. Austin | 830/997–5612 | 5 rooms | $125 | AE, D, MC, V.

**Best Western Sunday House.** Farmers coming into town during the last century used to spend the night in their "Sunday house" before returning to the outlying communities. Today, this Best Western has its own log cabin Sunday house on the premises—it's now used as the lobby and fireplace area. Restaurant, in-room data ports, cable TV, pool, business services, some pets allowed. | 501 E. Main St. | 830/997–4484 | fax 830/997–5607 | 124 rooms | $65–$130 | AE, D, DC, MC, V.

**Comfort Inn.** This standard motel is 9 blocks from downtown, within walking distance of shopping and restaurants. Picnic area, complimentary Continental breakfast, cable TV, pool, tennis, some pets allowed. | 908 S. Adams | 830/997–9811 | fax 830/997–2068 | 46 rooms | $64–$69 | AE, D, DC, MC, V.

**Das Kleine Nest.** This small limestone cottage was built in 1875 by a young man for his betrothed—just before their nuptials were called off. Despite that fact, the place is often used as a honeymoon retreat. The house mixes antiques and contemporary furnishings and has two enclosed patios. Kitchenette, microwave, refrigerator, cable TV, no smoking, no pets, no kids. | 208 East San Antonio | 830/997–5612 | fax 830/997–8282 | 1 room | $75 | AE, D, MC, V.

**Delforge Place.** This B&B is housed in an 1898 Victorian "Sunday house", and features several different period theme rooms, such as Victorian, colonial, nautical, and German settler. Breakfast usually includes the proprietor's famous German sour cream twists, tasty homemade crêpes, and a cold fruit soup. Complimentary breakfast, refrigerator, cable TV. | 710 Ettie St. | 830/997–7190 | www.delforgeplace.com | 4 rooms | $99–$115 | AE, D, MC, V.

**Dietzel Motel.** Only 1 mi from downtown and next to Friedrich's Bavarian Restaurant, weary truckers and business travelers tend to put up at this privately owned motel. Picnic area, cable TV, pool, some pets allowed ($5 fee). | 1141 West U.S. Hwy. 290 | 830/997–3330 | fax 830/997–3330 | 20 rooms | $42–$62 | AE, D, MC, V.

**Fredericksburg Bed and Brew.** The second "B" of this unusual B&B stands for beer, not breakfast: Included in the room rate is a sampler of the Fredericksburg Brewing Co.'s four current beers. Each room is decorated by a different store in town, and everything is for sale. It's right on Main St., convenient to shopping and local sightseeing. No smoking, no pets, no kids. | 245 E. Main St. | 830/997–1646 | fax 830/997–8026 | www.yourbrewery.com | 12 rooms | $89 | MC, V.

**Fredericksburg Inn and Suites.** This family-owned motel was built around a mid-19th-century Sunday House. The original building serves as the breakfast room, with authentic wood floor and hand-cut limestone walls. The rest of the motel is loaded with modern conveniences. Complimentary Continental breakfast, microwaves (in suites), refrigerators, cable TV, phones, in-room data ports, pool, hot tub, business services, free parking, playground. | 201 S. Washington St. | 830/997–0202 or 800/446–0202 | fax 830/997–5740 | www.fredericksburg-inn.com | 106 rooms, 6 suites | $79–$99, $99 suites | AE, D, MC, V.

**Fredericksburg Lodge.** This convenient motel is one block east of the Nimitz Museum and within walking distance of shopping and restaurants. Cable TV, pool, phones, in-room data ports, free parking, no pets. | 514 E. Main St. | 830/997–6568 | fax 830/997–7897 | 60 rooms | $63–$90 | AE, D, DC, MC, V.

**Frontier Inn Motel.** This independent motel has friendly service, and it's only ¼ mi from Main St. It also has an RV park. Cable TV, some kitchenettes, some microwaves, some refrigerators, laundry facilities, pets allowed ($5 fee). | 1704 U.S. 290 W | 830/997–4389 | fax 830/997–1500 | 13 rooms | $36–$58 | AE, D, DC, MC, V.

**Herb House.** This 1940s frame guest house is on the Fredericksburg Herb Farm, a four-acre plot of organic herb and flower gardens just six blocks off Main St. Guests can sample the farm's homemade herb breads, spiced butter, and fresh fruit at breakfast. Restaurant, complimentary breakfast, kitchenette, cable TV, no smoking, no pets, no kids. | 402 Whitney St. | 830/997–8615 or 800/259–4372 | fax 830/997–5069 | herbfarm@ktc.com | www.fredericksburgherbfarm.com | 1 two-bedroom guest house | $105 | AE, D, MC, V.

**Magnolia House.** This stately B&B promises a luxurious stay—from the full southern breakfast on antique china right down to the monogrammed bathrobes in the rooms. Built in 1923 by Edward Stein, the architect responsible for Gillespie County Courthouse, the inn features historic touches such as antique glass cabinets, a working cistern in the butler's pantry, and antique built-in iceboxes with wooden doors in the kitchen. Complimentary breakfast, refrigerator (in suite), no smoking, cable TV, kids over 6 only (kids over 12 on weekends). | 101 E. Hackberry St. | 830/997–0306 or 800/880–4374 | fax 830/997–0766 | magnolia@hctc.net | www.magnolia-house.com | 5 rooms (2 with shared bath), 2 suites | $95–$140 | AE, D, MC, V.

**Nagel House.** One of the prettier Victorian guest homes in Fredericksburg, the smooth pastels and lace curtains in this 1907 two-story house lend a soft touch to its antiques and period light fixtures. Complimentary Continental breakfast, cable TV, microwave, refrigerator, cable TV, no kids under 10, no smoking. | 106 W. Creek St. | 830/997–5612 | fax 830/997–8282 | www.fbglodging.com | 1 3-bedroom cottage | $95–$105 | AE, D, MC, V.

**Peach Tree Inn.** This motel is prettily situated around a grassy courtyard with a waterfall fountain and large pecan trees and is within walking distance of the Nimitz museum, restaurants, and shopping. Picnic area, complimentary Continental breakfast, some microwaves, refrigerators, cable TV, pool, business services, playground, some pets allowed. | 401 S. Washington U.S. 87S | 830/997–2117 or 800/843–4666 | fax 830/997–0827 | www.thepeachtreeinn.com | 34 rooms, 10 suites | $30–$98 | AE, D, MC, V.

**Schmidt Barn.** One of the first guest houses in Fredericksburg, this B&B is a restored century-old barn behind the 1860s Schmidt farmhouse. The sunken brick tub and wood burning stove provide a truly authentic setting. The house's refrigerator contains fixings for a German-style breakfast of meats, cheeses, and pastries. Complimentary breakfast, microwave, refrigerator, no smoking. | 231 W. Main St. | 830/997–5612 | fax 830/997–8282 | www.fbglodging.com | 1 1-bedroom guest house | $90 | AE, D, MC, V.

**Settlers Crossing.** This top-notch B&B contains a series of reconstructed homes and log cabins from around the country now resting on 35 acres of rolling countryside. From the robin's-egg-blue stenciled ceiling in the Pioneer Homestead to the collection of 19th-century folk art in the Von Heinrich Home, each of these guest houses offers something uniquely beguiling. Complimentary breakfast, some kitchenettes, some in-room hot tubs, in-room VCRs, no smoking. | Settlers Crossing Rd., Box 315, Rte. 1 | 830/997–2722 or 800/874–1020 | fax 830/997–3372 | www.settlerscrossing.com | 5 2-bedroom guest houses, 1 3-bedroom guest house, 1 1-bedroom guest house | $135–$185 | AE, D, MC, V.

# FRITCH

MAP 8, K9

*(Nearby towns also listed: Amarillo, Dumas, Pampa)*

This small town (pop. 2,700) makes a good stop on the way to Amarillo. The community is noted for its Alibates Flint, and it's one of the few places where this material is found. In fact, flint has been sought since the first inhabitants came to the region.

**Information: Lake Meredith Aquatic and Wildlife Museum** | 103 N. Robey St., Box 758, Fritch, TX 79036 | 806/857–2458.

## Attractions

**Hutchinson County Historical Museum.** Take a walk down memory lane with these exhibits of domestic and agricultural implements from Hutchinson County's early days. | 618 N. Main St., in nearby Borger | 806/273–0130 | Free | Weekdays 9–5, Sat. 11–4:30.

**Lake Meredith Aquatic and Wildlife Museum.** This museum contains aquariums filled with fish and other marine life found in Lake Meredith. | 104 N. Robey | 806/857–2458 | Donations accepted | Mon.–Sat. 10–5, Sun. 2–5.

**Lake Meredith National Recreation Area.** This 16,500-acre lake showcases the bluffs of the Canadian River valley. Camping, picnicking, boating, and fishing are available as well as ranger-led tours (by appointment only) of the **Alibates Flint Quarries National Monument,** which contains quarries used by prehistoric man to obtain flint. | Off Rte. 136, 7 mi south of Fritch | 806/857–3151 | fax 806/857–2319 | www.nps.gov | Free | Daily.

**McBride House.** Built into side of a hill, this old ranch was owned by the McBride family, who were prosperous ranchers. At this time, you can only take a look at the outside of this unusual house; the interior has not been restored. | McBride Canyon Rd., 6 mi. south of Fritch off of Hwy. 136.

**ON THE CALENDAR**
**OCT.: *Howdy Neighbor Day.*** Food booths, carnival games, and rides make up this fair in City Park on Hwy. 136. There are also races and a talent contest, as well as barbecue. | 806/857–2458.

## Dining
**Caroline's Restaurant.** American. Get a great home-cooked meal in this family establishment, which is filled with paintings of deer. The menu offers a good range with entrées such as hamburger steak, broiled catfish, enchiladas, and tacos. | 804 W. Broadway | 806/857–2055 | $4–$7 | No credit cards.

## Lodging
**Lake Town Inn.** This motel is within walking distance of a grocery, 1 mi from the Lake Meredith Center, and 15 miles from the Huchinson County Historical Museum and Alibates Flint Quarries. Truck parking available. Cash only. Cable TV, pets allowed. | 205 East Broadway | 806/857–3191 | 20 rooms | $40 | No credit cards.

# GAINESVILLE

MAP 8, I2

*(Nearby towns also listed: Denton, Sherman)*

GAINESVILLE

INTRO
ATTRACTIONS
DINING
LODGING

Just south of the Texas-Oklahoma border, Gainesville, pop. 15,000, is often noted for its Victorian architecture, a reminder of the cattle and cotton fortunes made here in the mid-1800s. The town is also home to Lake Texoma, which offers camping, picnicking, and fishing.

Information: **Gainesville Area Chamber of Commerce** | 101 S. Culberson, Gainesville, TX 76241 | 940/665–2831 | gainsvllechamber@ntin.net | www.gainesville.tx.us.

## Attractions
**Lake Texoma.** This huge lake is a weekend mecca for outdoorsy Metroplexers. It offers every kind of watersport imaginable, plus there's loads to do on dry land with 2 wildlife refuges, 2 state parks, and hundreds of campgrounds. Bald eagle watching is a popular autumnal activity. | U.S. 82 to U.S. 377 or U.S. 69 | Free | 580/564–2334 | www.laketexomaonline.com | Daily.

**Leonard Park.** Picnicking and play areas are available at this 30-acre park. | 1000 W. California | 940–668–4551 | Free | Daily.
Within Leonard park is **Frank Buck Zoo** which features exotic species. | 940/668–4530 | Free | Daily 10–5, summers until 7:30.

**Morton Museum of Cooke County.** This local history museum in a restored firehouse has exhibits ranging from frontier homestead items to agricultural tools used during the early days of Morton County. Special exhibits focus on pioneer days, Native Americans, and geology of the region. | 210 S. Dixon St. | 940/668–8900 | Free | Tues. –Fri. 10–5, Sat. 12–5.

**Moss Lake.** This lake is popular with anglers, but there are no picnic facilities. | Moss Lake Rd. | 940/665–2831 | U.S. 82 west to Moss Lake Rd./FM 1201.

**Ray Roberts Lake State Park, Johnson Unit.** Fishing, camping, boating, swimming, and more are available at this state park, located just east of I-35. | FM 3002 | 940/686–2148 | 8 AM–10 PM.

## ON THE CALENDAR

**JULY:** *Gainesville Area Annual Rodeo.* Roping, riding, and kids, events can be found at this event, held at the Gainesville Riding Club Arena. | 940/665–2831.

## Dining

**California St. Tea Room.** American. Atop the Miss Pitty Pat's antiques store, this lunch spot was once the women's apparel department of a 1920's J. C. Penney. Ivy and plants hang from the original tin-lined ceiling of this small restaurant, which also has some antiques. Try the soup and sandwich specials, as well as the homemade quiche. | 111 W. California | 940/665–6540 | closes at at 2 PM daily, closed Sunday | $5–$6 | No credit cards.

**Fried Pie Company.** American. Breakfast and lunch are served at this famous pie stop, which also does take-out. Although deep-fried apricot sells the best, coconut cream is the owner's favorite. | 202 W. Main | 940/665–7641 | Closes weekdays at 4:30 PM, closed Sunday | $4–$6 | AE, D, MC, V.

## Lodging

**Alexander B&B.** On 65 acres of woods and meadows, this three-story Queen Anne home has a several walking trails and a working farm, complete with animals. Complimentary breakfast, some room phones, TV in common area, outdoor pool, outdoor hot tub, laundry facilities. | 3692 County Rd. 201 | www.bbhost.com/alexanderbbacres | 8 rooms | $60–$125 | AE, D, MC, V.

**Best Western Southwinds.** This convenient chain accommodation is 1 mi from outlet malls and within walking distance of restaurants. Continental breakfast, cable TV, pool. | 2103 I–35N | 940/665–7737 | fax 940/668–2561 | 35 rooms | $54–$60 | AE, D, DC, MC, V.

**Gainesville Bed & Bath.** The cheapest overnight stay in Gainesville, the small, affordable rooms available in this motel are only 2 mi from the town center, restaurants, and shopping. Cable TV, laundry facilities, pets allowed. | 2000 I–35N | 940/665–5555 | fax 940/612–3003 | 22 rooms | $37 | AE, D, MC, V.

**Holiday Inn.** This convenient accommodation is a block from California St., the main drag loaded with shopping and restaurants. Restaurant, bar, room service, cable TV, phones, pool, laundry facilities, business services, no pets allowed. | 600 Fair Park Blvd. | 940/665–8800 | fax 940/665–8709 | www.holidayinn.com | 116 rooms | $57–$65 | AE, D, DC, MC, V.

**Ramada Inn.** This standard chain motel is 6 mi from the center of town. Complimentary Continental breakfast, cable TV, phone, pool, shuttle services. | 1936 I–35N, | 940/665–5599 | fax 940/665–4266 | 60 rooms | $48–$58 | AE, D, DC, MC, V.

# GALVESTON

MAP 8, K6

*(Nearby towns also listed: Brazosport, Houston, Texas City)*

Galveston Island is a marriage of the best of both worlds: city culture and seaside resort. Besides historical and cultural attractions, it offers opportunities for swimming and sunbathing.

Galveston and its 60,000 inhabitants have weathered more than one hurricane, but the 1900 hurricane was by far the most devastating. More than 6,000 residents were killed by the storm, and many structures were demolished. The hurricane prompted city officials to raise the island and add a seawall, making Galveston today a safe place to visit. The historical district of the city, the Strand, is filled with specialty shops and outdoor dining.

After the 1900 hurricane and the opening of the Houston Ship channel, Galveston lost its position as Texas's busiest seaport and The Strand was no longer a bustling center of commerce. Now, a century later, The Strand is one of the largest collections of historic buildings in the country.

Information: **Galveston Island Convention and Visitors Bureau** | 2428 Seawall Blvd., Galveston, TX 77550 | 409/763–4311 or 800/351–4236 | cvb@phoenix.net | www.galvestoncvb.com.

## Attractions

**1839 Williams Home.** A historic home with Republic of Texas–era furnishings. | 3601 Ave. P | 409/762–3933 | www.galvestonhistory.org | $3 | Weekends 12–4.

**Ashton Villa.** One of Galveston's most historic homes, this Italianate mansion was the first of Galveston's grand residences constructed on Broadway. Built by James Moreau Brown, a wealthy Texas businessman, it's now filled with family heirlooms and original art. | 2328 Broadway | 409/762–3933 | fax 409/762–1904 | $4 | Weekdays 10–4.

**The Bishop's Palace.** This Victorian 1886 palace is considered one of the top 100 U.S. outstanding buildings by the American Institute of Architecture, comparable only to North Carolina's Biltmore House. | 1402 Broadway | 409/762–2475 | fax 409/762–1801 | $5 | June–early Sept. 12–4, mid-Sept.–May 10–4:45.

**East End District.** Comprised mostly of the area from 10th St. to 19th St. between Broadway and Mechanic St., this 40-block district is listed on the National Register of Historic Places and is home to several of the grandest houses on the island. Most of the mansions were built between 1875 and 1905, when the neighborhood was home to the city's elite. Self-guided walking or driving tours are available at the Strand Visitor's Center. | 409/763–5928.

**Factory Stores of America.** Shop for designer clothing, shoes, luggage, leather items, and more at this extensive collection of factory outlet stores. | 11001 Delany Rd. | I–45 Exit 13, in La Marque | 409/938–3333 | Mon.–Sat. 10–8, Sun. 12–6.

**Gallery Row.** This revitalized arts area is home to galleries, antiques stores, and the Grand 1894 Opera House. | Post Office Rd. between 21st and 23rd Sts.

**Galveston County Historical Museum.** Housed in a 1906 bank building, this local history museum has exhibits on the Karankawa Indians, notorious pirates, and the hurricane of 1900. | 2219 Market St. | 409/766–2340 | $2 | Mon.–Sat. 10–4, Sun. 12–4.

**Galveston Island State Park.** Camping and picnicking are available at this park, as well as bird watching and fishing. The park also has a nature trail. | 14901 Farm Market Rd./FM 3005 | 409/737–1222 | fax 409/737–5496 | $3 | Daily 8 AM–10 PM.

**Galveston Island Trolley.** Galveston has island bus service, but this trolley tour is far more interesting, passing through the Strand area as well as the "silk stocking" historic homes district. | 2100 Seawall Blvd. or 2016 Strand St. | 409/797–3900 | www.islandtransit.net | 60¢.

**Galveston-Port Bolivar Ferry.** This 15-minute ferry ride will take you across Galveston Bay, providing transportation to and from Port Bolivar. | Ferry Rd. (Rte. 87) | 409/763–2386 | fax 409/762–6039 | Free | Daily.

**Gatherings.** Shop for upper-end gifts and home decor at this store, located in the historic Tremont House. | 2300 Ships Mechanic Row | 409/763–1770 or 409/763–7177.

**Grand 1894 Opera House.** This historic opera house has been restored to its turn-of-the-20th-century style. It's open for daily tours. | 2020 Post Office St. | 800/821–1894 | fax 409/762–6039 | Free | Mon.–Sat. 9–5; Sun. 12–5.

★ **Moody Gardens.** These extensive gardens offer myriad attractions. The Rain Forest Pyramid is a ten-story glass pyramid that houses thousands of plants, fish, butterflies, birds, and fish native to the rainforests of Africa, Asia, and S. America. The pyramid also has a bat cave and butterfly hatching hut. The IMAX theater shows regular and 3D IMAX movies; the IMAX Ridefilm Theater is a motion-based ride with 180 degree, wraparound screens.

GALVESTON

INTRO
ATTRACTIONS
DINING
LODGING

The Discovery museum has more than 30 interactive exhibits with a focus on what it might be like to live, work, and explore outer space. There is the full service Moody Gardens Hotel, Colonel Paddlewheel Boat, and Aquarium. | 1 Hope Blvd. | 409/744–4673 or 800/582–4673 | www.moodygardens.com | $7.50 | Daily 10–8, except Palm Beach, which is open on a seasonal basis only.

The **Aquarium** showcases marine life from the oceans of the world. | $11.

Guided tours of Galveston Bay and the port are available on the **Colonel Paddle-wheeler Boat.** | Daily tours at 12, 2, and 4. The glass **Discovery Pyramid** houses an interactive museum and three IMAX theaters with moving seats that simulate space travel. The Discovery Pyramid was developed in conjunction with NASA's Johnson Space Center.

**Palm Beach** is a white-sand beach with paddleboats, a playground, and swimming areas. The **Rainforest Pyramid** is filled with exhibits on the rain forests of the world.

**Moody Mansion and Museum.** Completed in 1895 by English architect William H. Tyndall, this mansion served as home to generations of one of Texas's most powerful families. Its interior of exotic woods and gilded trim is filled with family heirlooms and personal effects. | 2618 Broadway | 409/762–7668 | $6 | Daily 10–4, Sun. 12–3:30.

**Ocean Star Offshore Drilling Rig and Museum.** For a complete education on the offshore oil business, begin with the 15-minute film, then view exhibits such as an aquarium with a model of a pumpjack. You can also cross a catwalk to an actual rig. | Harborside Dr. at Pier 20 | 409/766–7827 | $5 | June–Aug., daily 10–5, Sept.–May, daily 10–4.

**Old Strand Emporium.** This charming deli and grocery store is reminiscent of an old-fashioned ice-cream parlor and sandwich shop, with candy bins, packaged nuts, and more. Seascape paintings and local art are also sold here. | 2112 Strand | 409/763–9445 | weekdays 10–6, Sat. 10–7, Sun. 11–6.

**Railroad Museum at the Center for Transportation and Commerce.** The museum traces the history of railroading throughout the region, with model trains and exhibits. Two trains are available for touring. | 123 Rosenberg | 409/765–5700 | $5 | Daily 10–4.

**Rosenberg Library.** The first free public museum in the state, this library contains many historic documents and papers of Texas leaders such as Sam Houston and Stephen F. Austin. | 2310 Sealy Ave. | 409/763–8854 | Free | Aug.–May, Mon.–Thurs. 9–9, Fri., Sat. 9–6, Sun. 1–5; June, July, Mon.–Sat. 9–9.

**Seawall Boulevard.** Beginning at the island's eastern edge and stretching 10 mi west, this area was originally built to protect the island from hurricanes. Today it's a hot beachfront property, although below the seawall the beach is undesirable for swimmers. | 409/763–4311.

**Seawolf Park.** Tour a submarine, a Navy jet, and check out other military naval equipment. | Pelican Island | 409/744–5738 | fax 409/762–8911 | $4 | Daily dawn to dusk.

**Stewart Beach Park.** A bit of Coney Island on the Gulf, this park has a bathhouse, amusement park, bumper boats, miniature golf course, and a water coaster. | 6th St. and Seawall Blvd. | 409/765–5023 | $5 vehicle entry fee ($10 for oversize vehicle such as buses) which is charged every time that a vehicle enters | March 1st-end of Sept., 9am-6pm.

**The Strand National Historic Landmark District.** Once called "The Wall Street of the Southwest," this historic district contains numerous ironfront buildings that now house restaurants, pubs, and shops. The Strand is on the opposite side of the island from the Gulf, a block away from the once-busy seaport. This is where shippers unloaded merchandise from around the world. | From 20th to 25th Sts. | 888/425–4753 or 409/765–7834 | www.galvestontourism.com | Daily.

**Strand Street Theater.** This 200-seat, year-round repertory theater also hosts children's and college performances. | 2317 Ships Mechanic Row | 409/763–4591 | fax 409/763–4879 | www.galveston.com/strandtheatre | $15 | Fri., Sat. 8 PM, Sun. 2:30.

**Texas Seaport Museum.** Thousands of immigrants made their way through this port, earning it the name "little Ellis Island." In fact, it's second only to Ellis Island as an immigration station. The museum surveys Galveston's shipping history and there's a database containing the names of over 133,000 immigrants who entered the United States here. You can take a self-guided tour of the *Elissa*, an 1877 square-rigged ship that now serves as a maritime museum. | No. 8, Pier 21 | 409/763–1877 | $6 | Daily.

**Treasure Island Tour Train.** Take a 17½-mi tour of the island aboard a train-shaped bus. The bus departs regularly from outside the Galveston Island Convention and Visitors Bureau on Seawall Blvd. | 2106 Seawall Blvd. | 409/765–9564 | $5 | Tour daily at 11 and 1, weather permitting.

## ON THE CALENDAR

**FEB.: *Mardi Gras.*** Parades, masked balls, arts and crafts, sports, and live music enliven the Strand two weeks before Fat Tuesday. | 888/425–4753.

**MAR.: *Spring Art Walk.*** Galleries throughout historic downtown are filled with artwork in a variety of media. | 409/763–2403.

**APR.: *Grand Kids Festival.*** This children's festival held in the Grand 1894 Opera House includes theatrical performances, arts and crafts, food booths, and puppet shows. | 409/765–1894.

**MAY: *Historic Homes Tour.*** Guided tours of Galveston's numerous historic homes and mansions. | 409/765–7834.

**DEC.: *Dickens on the Strand.*** Operated by the Galveston Historical Foundation and held in the Strand Historic Landmark District, this festival includes parades, costumed characters from Dickens's novels, crafts, and food. | 409/765–7834.

# Dining

**Clary's.** Seafood. Sit in a glassed-in garden room overlooking the bay and order the specialty of the house, a rich dish of white lump crab meat mixed with bacon and green onions and topped with cheese. The menu also features seasoned baked shrimp and grilled oysters. | 8509 Teichman Rd. | 409/740–0771 | Closed Mon. No supper Sat. | $12–$23 | AE, D, DC, MC, V.

**DiBella's Italian.** Italian. Lots of veal and seafood dishes are served here, and the Alfredo sauce has quite a reputation. Try the tuscano shrimp. | 1902 31st St. | 409/763–9036 | $8–$20 | No credit cards.

**Fisherman's Wharf.** Seafood. Although new restaurants have cropped up over the years, fresh seafood keeps locals coming back to this harborside institution on the renovated piers that front the Strand. Start off the with a cold combo—boiled shrimp and grilled rare tuna—then pick from the wide variety of local catches. | 3901 Ave. O | 409/765–5708 | $15–$24 | AE, D, DC, MC, V.

**Gaido's Restaurant.** Seafood. Sine 1911, this landmark restaurant with sweeping Gulf views has been serving up hand-prepared seafood. In the spring and summer, you can expect a wait of one to two hours for a table, so be sure to arrive early. Try the lump crab meat with Parmesan cheese or the iron skillet garlic snapper. Kids' menu. | 3900 Seawall Blvd. | 409/762–9625 | $13–$21 | AE, D, DC, MC, V.

**The Garden.** American. Part of the Moody Gardens entertainment complex, the restaurant serves burgers, salads and other casual fare and has views of the bay. Open-air dining. Entertainment. Kids' menu. | 1 Hope Blvd. | off 81st St. | 409/744–4673, ext. 238 | Summer hours vary | $12–$27 | AE, D, MC, V.

**Landry's.** Seafood. Started 14 years ago in Louisiana, this casual, family restaurant is decorated with paintings and music pieces from jazz artists. Signature dishes include jumbo lump crab meat, red snapper, lobster and salmon. Enjoy warm breezes from the patio overlooking the Gulf of Mexico. Kids' menu. | 5310 Seawall Blvd. | 409/744–1010 | $10–$25 | AE, D, DC, MC, V.

**Luigi's Ristorante Italiano.** Italian. Built in 1895 in the Strand district, Luigi's is an informal 3-star restaurant with historic charm. Specialties include grilled snapper with lump crab meat, chicken with fresh roasted garlic, and baby lamb chops. Kids' menu. | 2328 Strand | 409/763–6500 | $12–$38 | AE, D, DC, MC, V.

**Mario's Ristorante.** Italian. There's a full Italian menu and many seafood dishes (such as red snapper and seafood fettuccine), but islanders rave about this restaurant's hand-tossed pizza. | 2202 61st St. | 409/744–2975 | fax 409/744–1188 | $8–$17 | AE, D, DC, MC, V.

**Merchant Prince.** Continental. In the Tremont House, this eatery reflects the Victorian elegance of that accommodation. But the Merchant Prince isn't only about atmosphere: locals love the sophisticated menu with loads of seafood specialties. Open-air dining in atrium. Sun. brunch. | 2300 Ship's Mechanic Row | 409/763–0300 ext. 607 | Breakfast also available Mon.–Sat. | $14–$23 | AE, DC, MC, V.

**The Phoenix.** American/Casual. From New Orleans beignets to country-style bacon and eggs, this place serves the best breakfast in town. Assorted pastries, scones, and strudel beignets go great with the fresh-brewed java and espresso. For lunch, try the soup and salad combo with the popular chicken salad. | 221 Tremont St. | 409/763–4611 | Breakfast also available. No supper | $4–$7 | AE, D, DC, MC, V.

**The Spot.** American. The beef is ground on the premises of this burger joint, which consists of several bright beach cottages connected by walkways. Try the po'boy sandwiches or the Spot burger (a homemade ½ lb or ⅓ lb hamburger pattie served on a homemade bun) with the works. | 3204 Seawall Blvd. | 409/621–5237 | fax 409/621–5419 | $9–$12 | AE, D, DC, MC, V.

**Strand Brewery.** American. The four microbrews and hand-tossed pizzas cooked in a wood-fired brick oven are popular. Also try the po'boy shrimp sandwich. | 23rd St. at Harborside Dr. | 409/763–4500 | $7–$12 | AE, DC, MC, V.

**Yaga's.** American. Although the food is American, this restaurant's look is reminiscent of the Caribbean, with a bamboo bar and murals depicting island scenes. On weekends, the dance floor opens up for reggae and R&B nights. Try the burgers or peppered shrimp. | 2314 Strand | 409/762–6676 | fax 409/762–7415 | $6–$11 | AE, MC, V.

## Lodging

**Casa del Mar.** This hotel on the beach is within walking distance of restaurants, shopping, and historic areas. In-room data ports, kitchenettes, microwaves, refrigerators, 2 pools, laundry facilities, business services. | 6102 Seawall Blvd. | 409/740–2431 | www.casadelmartx.com | 276 rooms | $69–$189 | AE, D, DC, MC, V.

**Harbor House.** In the historic Strand area, this hotel is decorated like an old cotton plantation. In-room data ports, cable TV, marina, shops, business services. | No. 28, Pier 21 | 409/763–3321 or 800/874–3721 | fax 409/765–6421 | 42 rooms | $135–$195 | AE, DC, MC, V.

**Hilton Resort.** In walking distance of shopping, restaurants, and the beach, this newly renovated resort is beautifully landscaped with tropical plants. Some rooms have partial views of the Gulf while others have balconies with full views. Restaurant, bar, in-room data ports, cable TV, pool, hot tub, exercise equipment, business services. | 5400 Seawall Blvd. | 409/744–5000 | fax 409/740–2209 | www.galvestonhotel.com | 153 rooms | $95–$229 | AE, D, DC, MC, V.

**Holiday Inn on the Beach.** A cheerful Hawaiian atmosphere enlivens the rooms, which also have views of the Gulf of Mexico. The beach is just across the street or you can go 3 mi to Stewart Beach. Moody Gardens is 3 mi away. Restaurant, bar (with entertainment), cable TV, pool, wading pool, exercise equipment, laundry facilities. | 5002 Seawall Blvd. | 409/740–3581 | fax 409/744–6677 | www.holidayinn.com | 178 rooms | $89–$179 | AE, D, DC, MC, V.

**Hotel Galvez.** With a view of the Gulf, this turn-of-the-20th-century Spanish-style villa is decorated with 1930s furnishings. Once called the "Queen of the Gulf," the Hotel Galvez has a rich history of hosting families, celebrities, and Galvestonians for vacations and special celebrations. Restaurant, bar (with entertainment), in-room data ports, refrigerators (in suites), cable TV, pool, wading pool, hot tubs, business services, pets allowed. | 2024 Seawall Blvd. | 409/765–7721 or 800/392–4285 | fax 409/765–5780 | www.wyndham.com | 228 rooms | $139–$239 | AE, DC, MC, V.

**La Quinta.** This La Quinta is just five blocks away from Stewart Beach, 7 mi from the State Park, and 4 mi from Moody Gardens. Complimentary Continental breakfast, in-room data ports, cable TV, pool, business services, some pets allowed. | 1402 Seawall Blvd. | 409/763–1224 | fax 409/763–1224 | www.laquinta.com | 117 rooms | $62–$139 | AE, D, DC, MC, V.

**Moody Gardens Hotel.** On the grounds of the popular Moody Gardens complex, this contemporary nine-story hotel is surrounded by lush gardens, waterfalls, and pyramids housing various natural habitats. It's 1 mi from the beach and within walking distance of all area attractions. 2 restaurants, complimentary Continental breakfast, 2 pools, exercise equipment. | 7 Hope Blvd. | 409/741–8484 or 800/582–4673 ext. 215 | fax 409/744–1631 | www.moodygardens.com | 303 rooms | $175–$190 | AE, D, DC, MC, V.

**Tremont House.** Dating from 1879, the Tremont House was once a busy dry-goods warehouse. The four-story atrium lobby, with ironwork balconies and full-size palm trees, showcases an 1872 hand-carved rosewood bar. The rooftop terrace is a great place to watch the sunset and harbor activity. Restaurant, bar (with entertainment), room service, cable TV, massage, shops, business services. | 2300 Ship's Mechanic Row | 409/763–0300 or 800/874–2300 | fax 409/763–1539 | tremont@phoenix.net | 117 rooms | $125–$225 | AE, DC, MC, V.

**The Victorian.** This beachfront condominium property is within walking distance of restaurants and shopping. Most rooms have a view of the beach, and all have fully equipped kitchens. Restaurant, kitchenettes, pool, exercise equipment, tennis. | 6300 Seawall Blvd. | 409/740–3555 or 800/231–6363 | fax 409/744–3801 | 250 apartments | $109–$159 | AE, D, DC, MC, V.

# GEORGETOWN

MAP 8, I5

*(Nearby towns also listed: Austin, Burnet, Salado)*

With a population of 26,500 and serving as the seat for the second fastest growing county in the nation, Georgetown continues to hang on to its cozy charm. The town is home to Southwestern University, one of the oldest colleges in Texas. Georgetown also boasts rich Victorian architecture; it won a Great American Main Street Award, which recognizes success in preserving historic buildings.

## POPPIES

Georgetown holds the title of the "Red Poppy Capital of Texas," with both native and cultivated varieties growing throughout the town.

Although the concerted effort of citizens to make Georgetown a poppy showplace is fairly recent, the town's landscape has been brightened by this flower since the first half of the 20th century. Henry Purl "Okra" Compton collected seeds in Europe while serving in World War II. Upon his return to the United States, he planted them in his mother's lawn in Georgetown.

Today the poppies brighten yards and highway right-of-ways from late March through May. As you travel through town, look for white signs indicating a "Poppy Zone"; poppies can be found brightening yards and fields from late March–May.

© Artville

Information: **Georgetown Convention and Visitors Bureau** | Box 409, Georgetown, TX 78627 | 512/930–3545 or 800/436–8696. **Visitor Center** | 609 Main St., Georgetown, TX 78626 | www.georgetown.org.

## Attractions

**The Candle Factory.** More than 80 percent of the various candles made here are crafted by hand. Demonstrations are available for groups of 10 or more, by appointment. | 4411 S. I–35 | www.thecandlefactory.com | 512/863–6025 | Free | Daily 9–5:30.

**Inner Space Cavern.** Discovered during the construction of the interstate, this cave was once a hideaway for animals. A skull of a peccary (a pig-like hoofed mammal) estimated to be a million years old has been found here, along with bones of a giant sloth and a mammoth. Tours include cave formations, a small lake, and evidence of those prehistoric visitors. | Off I–35, exit 259 | 512/931–2283 (cave) | fax 512/863–4276 | www.innerspace.com | $9 | Late May–early Sept., daily 9–6; Sept.–May, daily 10–5.

**Lake Georgetown.** Built on the north fork of the San Gabriel River, this lake offers swimming, fishing, boating, camping, and hiking. The 17-mile Good Water Trail follows the upper end of the lake. | Off of I–35; if coming from north, exit 266; if coming from south, exit 261A | 512/930–5253 | www.swf.usace.army.mil | Free | Daily.

**San Gabriel Park.** At the intersection of the North and South San Gabriel Rivers, this park offers playgrounds and areas for picnicking. | Off of I–35, exit 261 | 512/930–3595 | Free | Daily.

**Southwestern University.** This private liberal arts college is known as one of Texas's first institutions of higher learning. | 1001 E. University Ave. | 512/863–6511 | www.southwestern.edu | Free | Daily.

### ON THE CALENDAR

**FEB.:** *Williamson County Gem and Mineral Show.* Displays and sales of gems and minerals from around the globe at the Georgetown Community Center. | 512/930–3545 or 800/436–8696.

**MAR.:** *Quilt and Stitchery Show.* Demonstrations and sales of quilts and handmade stitched pieces take place at the Georgetown Community Center. | 512/869–2955.

**JUNE:** *Sheriff's Posse Rodeo.* This festival includes a rodeo, parade, and dance at the Williamson County Show Barn. | 512/869–2648.

**SEPT.:** *Fiesta San Jose.* Mexican Independence Day is celebrated with dancing, food, and kids' activities in San Gabriel Park. | 512/863–6302.

## Dining

**Chuckwagon.** Tex-Mex. Photos of local homes adorn the walls surrounding the dining area and bar. Besides a large lunch menu, specialties include farm-raised catfish and chicken-fried steak. | I–35N and Williams Drive Rd. | 512/863–8431 | $7–$10 | AE, MC, V.

**Monument Cafe.** American. Slide into a booth in this traditional black-and-white diner, filled with reminders of Georgetown's early days, including many historic photos. Try the burgers, breakfast tacos, and chicken-fried steak. | 1953 S. Austin Ave. | 512/930–9586 | Breakfast also available | $5–$15 | AE, D, DC, MC, V.

## Lodging

**Claibourne House.** This 1896 Victorian home is set on wooded property with lots of pecan trees. Abstract art and antiques fill the interior of this B&B, and large porches and a brick terrace are found outside. It's two blocks from Georgetown's Historic Square, where you'll find shops and restaurants. Complimentary Continental breakfast, cable TV, no kids under 12. | 912 Forest St. | 512/930–3934 | www.bbonline.com/tx/claibourne | 4 rooms | $85–$125 | AE, MC, V.

**Comfort Inn.** Decorated in a Southwestern style, this Comfort Inn is on the south end of town, 2 mi from historic Georgetown and 6 mi from Lake Georgetown. Complimentary

Continental breakfast, cable TV, pool, some pets allowed. | 1005 Leander Rd. | 512/863–7504 | fax 512/819–9016 | www.comfortinn.com | 55 rooms | $54–$80 | AE, D, DC, MC, V.

**Days Inn.** Standard chain accommodations close to shopping area and restaurants. Cable TV, pool, some pets allowed. | 209 I–35N, exit 262 | 512/863–5572 | fax 512/869–5301 | www.daysinn.com | 55 rooms | $44–$75 | AE, D, DC, MC, V.

**Inn on the Square.** Built in the 1890s, this Victorian building is on the National Register of Historic Places. Its large rooftop terrace overlooks the courthouse and town square. Dining, lodging, and entertainment are within walking distance. Complimentary breakfast, in-room data ports, cable TV, no smoking. | 104½ W. 8th St. | 512/868–2203 or 888/718–2221 | 4 rooms | $85–$125 | AE, D, DC, MC, V.

**La Quinta Inn.** This chain motel is 3 mi from historic Georgetown and Lake Georgetown. Restaurant, complimentary Continental breakfast, in-room data ports, room service, cable TV, pool. | 333 I–35N | 512/869–2541 | fax 512/863–7073 | www.laquinta.com | 98 rooms | $49–$109 | AE, D, DC, MC, V.

# GLEN ROSE

MAP 8, H3

*(Nearby towns also listed: Dublin, Fort Worth, Granbury, Hico, Stephenville)*

A popular day trip for Dallas-Fort Worth urbanites, this beautiful town with a population of only 6,500 and located 80 mi southwest of Dallas was once aptly known as "Glen of Roses." Along with its relaxing atmosphere, the town is a favorite as a gateway to Dinosaur Valley State Park, one of the state's best sites for viewing evidence of dinosaur habitation.

**Information: Glen Rose/Sovervell Chamber of Commerce** | Box 605, Glen Rose, TX 76043 | 254/897–2286 | grsccc@itexas.net | www.itexas.net/glenrose/chamber.

## Attractions

**Creation Evidences Museum.** This museum is a must if you haven't yet seen such prehistoric evidence as Acrocathosaurus bones, dinosaur footprint casts, and other artifacts and fossil displays. Don't miss the impressive biosphere exhibit. | 3105 Rte. 205 | 254/897–3200 | fax 254/897–3100 | www.creationevidence.org | $2 | Tues.–Sat., 10–4.

**Dinosaur Valley State Park.** Five mi west of Glen Rose, this park showcases several dinosaur tracks in the riverbed of the Paluxy River. | U.S. 67 to Rte. 205 | 254/897–4588 | fax 254/897–3409 | www.tpwd.state.tx.us | $5 | Daily 8 AM–10 PM.

**Fossil Rim Wildlife Center.** Three mi southwest of Glen Rose, this drive-through wildlife ranch is filled with exotic species. It's noted for its conservation efforts made for many species, including the cheetah. | Off U.S. 67 on Rte. 1 | 254/897–2960 | fax 254/897–3785 | www.fossilrim.com | $15 | Daily 9–6, except Thanksgiving day and Christmas day.

**Squaw Valley Golf Course.** This beautiful 18-hole course opened in 1992, and it has since expanded and improved to be one of Texas's best. Enormous native trees dot the challenging back nine. | U.S. 67 | 254/897–7956 or 800/831–8259 | Year-round, weekdays 8–dusk, weekends 7–dusk.

## ON THE CALENDAR

**MAR.:** *Bluegrass Jamboree.* The best professional and amateur bluegrass bands from all over come to play in this four-day festival in Oakdale Park. Fiddlers and banjo pickers play into the night, while a huge outdoor supper is served. | 254/897–2286 or 254/897–2321.

## Dining

**M K Corral Restaurant.** American. Old metal post office and traffic signs cover the walls of this casual eatery. Fried catfish and chicken-fried steak are the most popular dishes. Kids' menu. | 902 NE Big Bend Tr | 254/897–2761 | Breakfast also available | $6–$16 | AE, D, MC, V.

## Lodging

**Inn on the River.** All rooms in this Texas Historical Landmark inn are individually decorated with antiques and the comfortable beds are decked out in fine European linens, feather beds, and down comforters. Three- and four-course gourmet dinners are available. Complimentary breakfast, no TV, no smoking, pool, kids over 16 only. | 205 S.W. Barnard St. | 800/575–2101 | fax 972/424–7119 | 22 rooms | $115–$195 | AE, D, DC, MC, V.

**Lilly House.** This Victorian B&B in the heart of historic Glen Rose is renowned for its gracious hospitality. Each room has a theme: the Big Sky Room has a juniper stick bed, a natural rock shower, and a screened porch. Choose Mr. Buck's Room or the Blue Room for a fireplace, or the Treetop Room for a whirlpool bath. Complimentary breakfast, no TV, library, no pets, no kids, no smoking. | 107 Lilly St. | 254/897–9747 or 800/884–1759 | fax 254/897–3270 | lilly@hcnews.com | www.lillyhouse.com | 5 rooms | $110–$120 | No credit cards.

# GOLIAD

MAP 8, 16

*(Nearby towns also listed: Gonzales, Port Lavaca, Three Rivers, Victoria)*

Founded by the Spanish, Goliad is the third oldest city in Texas. To protect their passage to the Gulf, the Spaniards moved their Espiritu Santo mission and its royal protector, Presidio La Bahia (Fort of the Bay), here in 1749. Years later, the town was named Goliad (an anagram for "Hidalgo"—the "h" is silent). Hidalgo was a priest who became a hero during the Mexican war for independence from Spain.

In 1835 Texas colonists made a bid for independence by taking over the Presidio. The next year these Texans surrendered at the Battle of Coleto about 9 mi east of town. After being imprisoned at the Presidio for about a week, 342 Texans were killed by the Mexicans. "Remember Goliad" soon became a cry alongside "Remember the Alamo."

Today the Presidio and the Mission Espiritu Santo are restored and open to the public. Visitors can also see the resting place for the Texas soldiers.

**Information: Goliad County Chamber of Commerce** | Box 606, Goliad, TX 77963 | 361/645–3563 | www.goliad.org.

## Attractions

**Goliad County Courthouse.** This historic courthouse was built in 1894 and is still operational. The infamous Hanging Tree, where death sentences were carried out from 1846 to 1870, is also on the premises. | Historic Courthouse Sq. between Commercial St. and Market St. | 361/645–3337 | Free | Weekdays 8–5.

**Goliad State Historical Park.** This park offers swimming, a nature trail, and camping. Screened shelters are available. Within the park, the restored Mission Espiritu Santo de Zuniga features spinning, weaving, and pottery-making demonstrations, primarily on weekends. | Off of U.S. 183 | 361/645–3405 | fax 361/645–8538 | www.tpwd.state.tx.us | $2 | Daily.

**Market House Museum.** This museum contains exhibits on local history. It also houses the Goliad Chamber of Commerce. | 25 S. Market at Franklin St. | 361/645–3563 | www.goliad.org | Free | Weekdays 9–5, Sat. 10–4.

**Presidio La Bahia.** On Oct. 9, 1836, Texas colonists made a move in their battle for independence by taking over the old Spanish presidio and raising the "Bloody Arm Flag," picturing a severed arm holding a sword. The next year the Texans, led by Col. James Fannin, surrendered at the Battle of Coleto about 9 mi east of town. Approximately 390 soldiers were marched back to the presidio and, after a week of imprisonment, 342 were killed in front of a firing squad. Today the fully-restored presidio is the oldest fort in the West. | U.S. 183 | 361/645–3563 | $3 | Weekdays 9–5, Sat. 10–4.

### ON THE CALENDAR

**MAR.:** *Goliad County Fair and Rodeo.* Precision riding and rodeo activities such as barrel racing, calf roping, rodeo clowns, and live entertainment take place at the Fairgrounds. | 361/645–3563.

**MAR.:** *Goliad Massacre Re-enactment.* Events surrounding the occupation of Fort Defiance by Colonel Fannin are re-created. | 361/645–3752.

**OCT.:** *Annual Missions Tour de Goliad.* On the third Saturday of the month, bike riders can select from four tours of 10 to 100 miles. | 800/848–8674.

**DEC.:** *Christmas in Goliad.* Enjoy yuletide arts and crafts, booths, food, Pony Express stamp cancellation for Christmas cards and mail, and the Las Posadas procession. | 361/645–3563.

## Dining

**Empresario Restaurant.** Mexican. You'll find this casual eatery in an historic building from 1903. Hungry people go for the zaragosa plate, composed of chalupas, tacos, enchiladas, and rice. Whatever your entrée, the homemade pies, which are famous in Goliad, are worth saving room for. | 141 S. Courthouse Sq., Goliad | 361/645–2347 | Breakfast also available | $4–$13 | AE, D, DC, MC, V.

### LODGING

**Budget Inn.** This motel has reasonable prices and is easy to find, at the intersection of U.S. 77A and U.S. 59. Microwaves, refrigerators, cable TV, pets allowed (fee). | 124 S. Jefferson St. | 361/645–3251 | fax 361/645–2714 | www.budgetinns.com | 17 rooms | $35–$38 | AE, D, DC, MC, V.

# GONZALES

MAP 8, I6

*(Nearby towns also listed: Goliad, La Grange)*

Established in 1825, Gonzales lies on Kerr Creek, 2 miles east of the confluence of the San Marcos and Guadalupe Rivers. It was here on October 2, 1835, that the first shot in the Texas Revolution was fired. It was also here that Gen. Sam Houston heard about the fall of the Alamo. Upon learning of the defeat, the general gathered troops and defeated Santa Anna at San Jacinto.

Today Gonzales is know as a top producer of egg, turkey, and chickens.

Information: **Gonzales Chamber of Commerce and Agriculture** | 414 St. Lawrence St., Gonzales, TX 78629 | 830/672–6532 | www.gonzalestexas.com.

## Attractions

**Gonzales County Jail Museum.** This 1887 jail includes a dungeon. The Chamber of Commerce office is housed here. | 414 St. Lawrence | 830/672–6532 | Free | Weekdays 8–5, Sat. 9–4, Sun. 1–4.

**Gonzales Memorial Museum.** This museum honors soldiers of the first battle of the Texas Revolution, fought here in 1835. The battle was triggered by attempts by Mexican soldiers (after Texan/Mexican relations soured) to retrieve a small brass cannon that the Mexcian government had given to Gonzales residents in 1831, so that they may be protected from Indian attacks. Highlights include the cannon that fired the first shot for Texas independence and the original constitution of Gonzales that was printed in 1841. | 414 Smith St. | 830/672–6350 | Free | Tues.–Sat. 10–12, 1–5, Sun. 1–5.

**Gonzales Pioneer Village.** Eleven buildings, including a church, a broom factory, and a smoke-house, date from the 19th century. | 183 Business | 830/672–2157 | $3 | Sept.–May, Sat. 10–5, Sun. 1–5; June–Aug., Fri. 10–4, Sat. 10–5, Sun. 1–5.

**J. B. Wells House.** Built in 1885, this 10-room, two-story house provides a glimpse into life at the turn of the 20th century. The wallpaper and most of the furniture is original and in excellent condition. | 823 Mitchell St. | 830/672–6532 | $2.50 | Sat. 10–12, 2–4 or by appointment.

**Palmetto State Park.** The marshy swamp at this park is estimated to be 18,000 years old. It's filled with palmettos as well as moss-draped trees, 4-ft-tall irises, and many bird species. The park also has nature trails, camping, and picnicking. Drive 10 mi northwest of Gonzales on U.S. 183 to Rte. 1586, then drive 2 mi west on Rte. 1586 to Ottine, then drive south on Park Rd. 11. | Park Rd. 11 | 830/672–3266 | www.tpwd.state.tx.us | $2 | Daily 8 AM–10 PM.

**ON THE CALENDAR**
**APR., MAY, JULY, DEC.:** *Courthouse Trade Days.* Held four times a year in Courthouse Square, this outdoor festival includes live music and showcases the artwork of local and regional artists. | 830/672–6532.
**OCT.:** *Come and Take It Days Celebration.* This re-enactment of the "Come and Take It" skirmish that started the Texas Revolution is fueled by games, street dancing, a carnival, and a biergarten. | 830/672–6532.

## Dining
**Cafe on the Square.** American. This unique place doubles as a restaurant and antique shop. There's a varied, hot buffet for lunch; for supper try a succulent T-bone or rib-eye steak. Kids' menu. | 511 N. Saint Joseph St. | 830/672–2253 | No supper weekends | $4–$11 | No credit cards.

## Lodging
**Houston House.** This late Queen Anne Victorian home has towers, turrets, wraparound porches and other unique architectural embellishments. The public rooms are lavishly decorated—the parlor ceiling and dining room walls even boast hand-painted murals. Each bedroom comes with with period antiques, floral arrangements, and a fireplace. Complimentary breakfast, cable TV, VCR, no smoking, no kids under 13. | 621 E. St. George St. | 830/672–6940 or 888/477–0760 | fax 830/672–6940 | www.houstonhouse.com | 5 rooms (2 with shared bath) | $100–$150 | AE, D, DC, MC, V.

**St. James Inn.** This historic inn has a cheerful mix of contemporary and period furnishings. The spacious bedrooms—each with its own fireplace—are individually decorated to reflect aspects of the house's rich history. Complimentary breakfast, no smoking, cable TV, no room phones, kids over 12 only, business services. | 723 St. James St. | 830/672–7066 | fax 830/672–4821 | www.stjamesinn.com | 5 rooms, 1 suite | $65–$95 | AE, MC, V.

**Texas Lexington.** This three-story motel is on U.S. 90, and has very affordable rates. Cable TV, some pets. | U.S. 90A E | 830/672–2807 | fax 830/672–7941 | 30 rooms | $45 | AE, MC, V.

# GRAHAM
MAP 8, H2

*(Nearby towns also listed: Mineral Wells, Wichita Falls)*

This north central Texas community is well known for its outdoor activities: canoeing, fishing, hunting, swimming, and more. Graham claims to have the largest town square in the United States.

Information: **Graham Chamber of Commerce** | Box 299, Graham, TX 76450 | 800/256–4844 | grahamcc@ws.net.

## Attractions

**Confederate Air Force Museum.** A restored bomber plane is among the World War II memorabilia you'll find here. Most of the items were donated by former military men and their families. | Grand Municipal Airport | 940/549–3355 | Free | Thurs. 1–5 or by appointment.

**Fort Richardson State Historical Park.** Thirty mi east of Graham, Fort Richardson was established after the Civil War to protect against Indian attack. The park features several stone buildings, as well as camping, nature trails, fishing, and interpretive center. | On U.S. 281 in Jacksboro | 940/567–3506 | fax 940/567–5488 | www.tpwd.state.tx.us | $2 | Mon.–Thurs. 8–7, Fri., Sat. 8–9, Sun. 8–8. In winter, hours vary.

**Possum Kingdom State Park.** One of Texas's largest lakes, Possum Kingdom offers boating, boat rentals, and fishing. Visitors can also camp and picnic. Longhorn cattle can be seen at the park. | Park Rd. 33, Hwy. 180 | 940/549–1803 | www.tpwd.state.tx.us | $3 | Daily.

## Dining

**Marlene's at the Big Chill.** American. Enjoy an old-fashioned milkshake at the antique granite soda bar, or sit in the old wooden dining booths for a 1950s-style lunch. The sandwich platters and the baked potatoes, served for both lunch and supper, are tasty and filling. For dessert, try the hot cobbler. Kids' menu. | 518 Oak St. | 940/549–4772 | No supper Mon. | $3–$8 | No credit cards.

## Lodging

**Austin Road Guest House.** Relax on the front patio or in almost any of the sunlight-flooded rooms of this warm, brick, one-story house. Kitchenette, cable TV, VCR, no pets, no kids under 12, no smoking. | 907 Austin Rd. | 940/549–2665 | 1 room | $80 | MC, V.

**Gateway Inn.** This well-kept motel, located southeast of downtown, was remodeled in 2000 with a southwestern decor. Restaurant, cable TV, pool, laundry facilities, airport shuttle, some pets allowed (fee). | 1401 Rte. 16S | 940/549–0222 | fax 940/549–4301 | 77 rooms | $48–$60 | AE, D, DC, MC, V.

# GRANBURY

MAP 8, H3

*(Nearby towns also listed: Glen Rose, Stephenville, Weatherford)*

Located on Lake Granbury, this community is a favorite getaway for Dallas/Fort Worth metroites. It's especially popular in the fall when the pecan crop ripens. The charm of Granbury lies in its history: the Victorian town square was the first in Texas listed in the National Register of Historic Places.

Information: **Granbury Convention and Visitors Bureau** | 100 N. Crockett St., Granbury, TX 76048 | 817/573–5548 or 800/950–2212 | www.granbury.org.

## Attractions

**Granbury Opera House.** This historic 1886 opera house has been restored. Today it is used for a variety of performances. | 133 E. Pearl St. | 817/573–9191 | $15 | Closed Mon.

**The Great Race Automotive Hall of Fame.** Let your imagination run wild as you sit behind the wheel of numerous vintage cars dating back to the early 1900s. Lots of authentic Great Race memorabilia is on display. | 114 N. Crockett St. | 817/573–5200 | www.greatrace.com | $1 | Fri.–Sun. 10–6 or by appointment.

## ON THE CALENDAR

**MAR.:** *General Granbury's Birthday Celebration.* The Courthouse Square hosts a parade, arts and crafts, and children's games. | 817/573–5548.

## Dining

**George Pit Bar-B-Q.** Barbecue. In business for 24 years, George's is the best barbecue restaurant in town. A casual environment and friendly service awaits you; specialties of the house include ribs, brisket, and turkey breast. Kids' menu. | 2441 E. Hwy. 377, Granbury | 817/573–9612 | Closed Sun. | $5–$8 | No credit cards.

**Kelly's on the Square.** American. In an historic building and decorated with antiques, this restaurant has a split personality. The first floor is casual and serves bistro fare while upstairs diners can choose from more gourmet selections. Specialties include country-fried steak, marinated rib-eye steak, and dessert crêpes. Entertainment Fri., Sat. Kids' menu. | 110 Pearl St. | 817/573–9722 | Closed Tue | $6–$22 | AE, D, DC, MC, V.

**La Fiesta Authentic Mexican.** Mexican. Renowned for its tasty and authentic fajitas and quesadillas, La Fiesta is often busy and loud even on weekdays. Green, white, and red curtains (colors corresponding to the Mexican flag) decorate the windows. | 1112 S. Morgan St. | 817/579–1275 | $5–$7 | AE, D, DC, MC, V.

## Lodging

**Classic Inn.** This is a no-frills one-story motel. Complimentary Continental breakfast, microwaves, refrigerators, cable TV, pool, some pets allowed. | 1209 N. Plaza Dr. | 817/573–8874 | fax 817/573–8874 | 42 rooms | $45–$54 | AE, D, DC, MC, V.

**Comfort Inn.** This Comfort Inn is 1.5 mi from the center of town and the Granbury Opera House. Complimentary Continental breakfast, microwaves, refrigerators, cable TV, pool, business services. | 1201 N. Plaza Dr. | 817/573–2611 | fax 817/573–2695 | 48 rooms | $50–$150 | AE, D, DC, MC, V.

**Dabney House Bed & Breakfast.** Built in 1907, this elegant, Craftsman-style B&B has its original hardwood floors and beveled and stained glass. Each guest room is spacious and elegantly decorated with antique furniture. With 48 hours' advance notice, you can order the Candlelight Romance Package, which includes a specially cooked supper for two. Complimentary breakfast, no TV in some rooms, outdoor hot tub, no pets, no kids under 10, no smoking. | 106 S. Jones St. | 817/579–1260 or 800/566–1260 | safe-dabney@flash.net | home.flash.net/~safe-dabney | 4 rooms | $70–$105 | AE, MC, V.

**Days Inn.** Standard chain accommodations last renovated in 1996. Restaurant, cable TV, pool, laundry facilities, business services, pets allowed. | 1339 N. Plaza Dr. | 800/858–8607 | fax 817/573–7662 | 67 rooms | $49–$79 | AE, D, DC, MC, V.

**Lodge of Granbury.** Set on a lake providing great views, the Lodge's condominium suites feature one or two bedrooms with living areas, complete kitchens, woodburning fireplaces, and private balconies. Picnic area, microwaves, refrigerators, cable TV, pool, hot tub, business services, pets allowed. | 401 E. Pearl St. | 817/573–2606 | fax 817/573–2077 | 48 suites | $89–$109 suites | AE, D, DC, MC, V.

**Pearl Street Inn Bed & Breakfast.** This quaint, prairie-style B&B has two porches and guest rooms with names like "English Garden Suite" and the "Pearl Room." It's only three blocks from Granbury's Historic Square. Complimentary breakfast, no room phones, TV in common area, outdoor hot tub, no pets, no smoking. | 319 W. Pearl St. | 888/732–7578 | danette@itexas.net | www2.itexas.net/~danette | 5 rooms | $79–$119 | AE, D, MC, V.

**Plantation Inn.** Overlooking Lake Granbury, this motel is 1 mi from the center of town. Complimentary Continental breakfast, in-room data ports, microwaves, cable TV, pool, wading pool, some pets allowed. | 1451 E. Pearl St. | 817/573–8846 or 800/422–2402 | fax 817/579–0917 | www.plantationinngranbury.com | 53 rooms | planinn@hcnews.com | $60–$90 | AE, D, DC, MC, V.

# GRAPEVINE

*(Nearby towns also listed: Arlington-Grand Prairie, Dallas, Denton, Fort Worth, Irving, Lewisville, Plano)*

Established in 1844, the oldest settlement in Tarrant County was named for the wild mustang grapes that grew abundantly in the area. Today, this area 5 mi north of the Dallas/Ft. Worth International Airport is home to six of Texas's 27 wineries. It also contains nearly 40 restored historic sites, as well as Grapevine Mills—a mall that serves as a staggering symbol of the idea "bigger is better."

**Information: Grapevine Convention and Visitors Bureau** | One Liberty Park Plaza, Grapevine, TX 76099 | 817/410–3185 or 800/457–6338 | gvtexas1@aol.com | www.tour-texas.com/grapevine.

## Attractions

**Downtown Grapevine.** A good place to begin exploring Grapevine is in its downtown area, filled with businesses, homes, and shops. Stop by the Grapevine Visitor Information Center for self-guided walking tours, maps, and informative suggestions. | 701 S. Main St. | 817/410–8136 | Free | Tues.–Sat. 9–5, Sun. 11–5.

**Grapevine Lake.** Located about 1 mile north of downtown, Grapevine Lake is the state's fourth busiest lake. The spot is known for its premier windsurfing, sailing, and fishing. The lake's 146 miles of shoreline include one of the best mountain biking trails in north Texas. | 110 Fairway Drive | 972/481–4541 | Fee and non-fee areas.

**Grapevine Mills.** Shopping enthusiasts shouldn't miss this mall. With more than 1½ million square ft of retail and discount space, it's one of the largest in the state. In addition to more than 200 stores, it also has theme restaurants and a 30-screen movie theater. | 3000 Grapevine Mills Pkwy. | 972/724–4900 | www.millscorp.com/grapevine | Free | Mon.–Sat. 10–9:30, Sun. 11–8.

**Grapevine Municipal Golf Course.** Golf legend Byron Nelso designed this 18-hole championship golf course, which opened in 1979. It's one of three public golf courses in the city. | 3800 Fairway Dr. | 817/481–0421 | Year-round.

### ON THE CALENDAR

**APR.: *New Vintage Wine and Art Festival.*** The Grapevine Heritage Center hosts wine seminars, a chef's brunch, an art show, live music, and more. | 800/457–6338.
**MAY: *Main Street Days.*** This event includes living history demonstrations, a carnival, food, and arts and crafts. | 800/457–6338.
**SEPT: *Grapefest.*** Street dances, live entertainment, and food booths are part of this harvest festival. | 972/252–3838.

## Dining

**Bartley's Bar-B-Que.** Barbecue. Traditional Texas barbecue is served up for lunch and dinner in a no-frills setting. | 413 E. Northwest Hwy. | 817/481–3212 | Closed Sun., Mon. | $5–$10 | AE, D, MC, V.

**Esparza's Restaurante Mexicano.** Tex-Mex. This popular restaurant is in a renovated home just off Main St. A second restaurant, Esparza's Too, is about 1 mi away on Rte. 114. Many diners come for the high-octane frozen margaritas. | 124 E. Worth St. | 817/481–4668 | Reservations not accepted | $7–$15 | AE, D, DC, MC, V.

**Meritage Grille.** Seafood. In a Hilton hotel, this new restaurant has a changing menu. Sun. brunch. Open-air dining is available on a covered patio. | 1800 Rte. 26 E | 817/481–8444 | Breakfast also available | $23–$37 | AE, D, DC, MC, V.

**Willhoite's.** Housed in a former gas station preserved since the early 1900s, crowds pour into this restaurant for its live music in the evening and its giant salad bar (Texas style, with plenty of meat). | 432 S. Main St. | 817/481–7511 | $6–$14 | AE, D, DC, MC, V.

## Lodging

**Allen's Liberty House.** Constructed around the time of the founding of the Republic of Texas, this B&B inn was built in a modified Georgian-plantation style. It includes a front porch, verandah, parlor, and a side porch with a wicker rocker. Rooms have queen-size beds. Dining room, complimentary breakfast, TV in common room, library. | 205 East College St. | 817/251–9201 or 888/281–9201 | www.allenslibertyhouse.com/ | 3 rooms, 1 suite | $90–$145.

**Embassy Suites Outdoor World.** This full-service, 12-story, all-suites hotel was built in Aug. 1999. Suites have separate living and sleeping areas, a dining table/work desk, and pull-out sofa. The corner suites on the 12th floor are pricier, but have cathedral ceilings and private, covered balconies. It's across the street from the Grapevine Mills mall. Restaurant, bar, complimentary breakfast, room service, in-room data ports, minibars, microwaves, refrigerators, some in-room data ports, cable TV, pool, sauna, exercise equipment, video games, laundry facilities, laundry service, business services, airport shuttle, free parking, pets allowed. | 2401 Bass Pro Dr. | 972/724–2600 or 800/362–2779 | fax 972/724–2670 | www.embassyoutdoorworld.com | 329 suites | $109–$350 | AE, D, DC, MC, V.

**Hilton Dallas/Fort Worth Lakes Hilton Executive Conference Center.** Although set on 27 wooded, lakeside acres, this conference center is only 2½ mi north of Dallas/Ft. Worth International Airport. Restaurant, bars (with entertainment), in-room data ports, minibars, refrigerators, cable TV, 2 pools, lake, hot tub, 8 tennis courts, gym, business services, airport shuttle. | 1800 Rte. 26E | 817/481–8444 | fax 817/481–3160 | www.hilton.com | 377 rooms, 18 suites | $210 | AE, D, DC, MC, V.

**Hyatt Regency-Dallas/Fort Worth.** On the grounds of Dallas/Ft. Worth International Airport, this 12-story hotel is the largest airport hotel in the country. Its east tower connects to the American Airlines terminal. Restaurant, bar (with entertainment), room service, in-room data ports, some refrigerators, cable TV, pool, driving range, golf courses, putting green, tennis, exercise equipment, shops, business services, airport shuttle. | International Pkwy., Dallas/Fort Worth Airport | 972/453–1234 | fax 972/456–8668 | www.hyatt.com | 1369 rooms, 23 suites | $99–$199 | AE, D, DC, MC, V.

# GREENVILLE

MAP 8, J2

*(Nearby towns also listed: McKinney, Sulphur Springs)*

This North Texas community started as a trading outpost for local cotton farmers. Today the small town is home to several industries and offers outlet and antique shopping. Visitors come to Greenville to fish in Lake Tawakoni and indulge in the rich pecan fruit cakes from Mary of Puddin Hill.

**Information: Greenville Convention and Visitors Bureau** | Box 1055, Greenville, TX 75403 | 903/455–1510. **Visitor Center** | 2713 Stonewall St., Greenville, TX 75403.

## Attractions

**American Cotton Museum.** You can learn all about the cotton-making process, from planting to weaving, as well as the history of Blackland Prairie and famous local personalities. There are two working cotton gin models. | 600 Interstate 30, Greenville | 903/450–4502 or 903/454–1990 | www.cottonmuseum.com | $2 | Tues.–Sat. 10–5.

**Lake Tawakoni.** At more than 36,000 acres, this is one of the largest lakes located completely within Texas. It's a popular spot for catfish and bass fishing. | 6553 State Park Rd., Greenville | 903/662–5134 | Daily.

**Mary of Puddin Hill.** This longstanding bakery is known for its pecan fruit cakes. | I–30; exit 95 | 903/455–6931 or 800/545–8889 | Oct.–Dec., Mon.–Sat. 10–5, Sun. 1–5; Jan.–Sept., Mon.–Sat. 8–5, Sun. 1–5; tours by appointment.

## ON THE CALENDAR

**JUNE: *Audie Murphy Days.*** This three-day event, hosted by the American Cotton Museum, celebrates the life of WWII hero Audie Murphy with photography exhibits, military memorabilia, keynote speeches, and a barbecue luncheon. | 903/450–4502 | www.audiemurphy.com/celebrate.htm.

**JUNE: *Hunt County Fair.*** The fairgrounds hosts carnival rides, games, food booths, and exhibits. | 903/455–1510.

**OCT.: *Cotton Jubilee.*** This event includes arts and crafts, food booths, and children's activities. | 903/455–1510.

## Dining

**Puddin Hill Store.** American. Grab a sandwich, sip some soup, and take a dessert break while shopping at this famed fruit, candy, and gift store. Kids' menu. | I–30; exit 95 | 903/455–6931 | $6–$12 | No supper | AE, D, MC, V.

**Tony's Italian Kitchen.** Italian. This family-oriented, casual eatery is in downtown Greenville. Green, white, and red, the colors of the Italian flag, are dominant in the restaurant's decor. Try the veal Rossini or shrimp scampi. | 6106 Wesley St. | 903/455–2225 | $5–$9 | AE, D, MC, V.

## Lodging

**Best Western Inn.** This Best Western has easy access to Lake Tawakoni. Bar, complimentary Continental breakfast, cable TV, pool, laundry facilities, business services, free parking, pets allowed. | 1216 I–30 W | 903/454–1792 | fax 903/454–1792 | www.bestwestern.com | 99 rooms | $54–$70 | AE, D, DC, MC, V.

**Motel 6.** This two-story motel is 16 mi from the Texas International Speedway. Cable TV, pool, laundry facilities, some pets. | 5109 I–30 | 903/455–0515 | fax 903/455–8314 | www.motel6.com | 94 rooms | $41 | AE, D, DC, MC, V.

**Ramada Inn.** Standard chain accommodations. Cable TV, pool, hot tub, laundry facilities, business services, free parking, some pets allowed. | 1215 I–30 | 903/454–7000 | www.ramada.com | 138 rooms | $49–$69 | AE, D, DC, MC, V.

# GROESBECK

MAP 8, I4

*(Nearby town also listed: Fairfield)*

Located in north central Texas near the town of Mexia, Groesbeck (pronounced grossbeck) lies in the heart of cotton farmland. The community is best known as the hometown of Audie Murphy, the most decorated U.S. soldier in World War II. Groesbeck is also home to a state park and Lake Limestone.

**Information: Groesbeck Chamber of Commerce** | Box 326, Groesbeck, TX 76642 | 254/729–3894.

## Attractions

**Fort Parker State Park.** This state park honors Cynthia Ann Parker, a pioneer girl who was kidnapped by Native Americans and later became the mother to the great leader Quanah

Parker (Old Fort Parker State Historical Park). The state park has year-round walking trails, fishing, and camping, and swimming in summer. | U.S. 14 between Groesbeck and Mexia | 254/562–5751 | www.tpwd.state.tx.us | $2 | Daily.

**Limestone County Historical Museum.** This local history museum includes exhibits on the pioneer days of the region, including memorabilia and exhibits on Old Fort Parker and the legendary story of Cynthia Ann Parker. | 210 W. Navasota St. | 254/729–5064 | 50¢ | Mon., Thurs. 1–5., Fri. 12–5, Sat. 9–5.

**Old Fort Parker State Historical Park.** This site is where pioneer daughter Cynthia Ann Parker was kidnapped at the age of nine. She later became the mother of Quanah Parker, the Native American leader. | Off U.S. 14; Park Rd. 35 | 254/729–5253 | $2 | Daily.

### ON THE CALENDAR
**MAY:** *Southwest Fiddlers Championship.* This competition attracts participants from around the state. A barbecue in City Park kicks off the festivities. | 254/729–3293.

© Artville

## THE HILL COUNTRY LAKES TOUR

One of the most popular tourist regions in Texas traces its roots to a 3½-minute earthquake that occurred more than 30 million years ago. In less time than it takes to describe it, the ground trembled and shook, and the Hill Country was born.

But it took an act of man—and Congress—to paint the finishing touches on the landscape. As a young U.S. Senator, Hill Country native Lyndon B. Johnson delivered the Highland Lakes project to this Central Texas region in the 1930s. The program brought electricity to the once isolated area, controlled flooding on the sometimes raging Colorado River, and saw the creation of numerous lakes.

**Lake Buchanan,** which covers 23,000 acres, is contained by one of the largest multiple-arch dams in the world. (For a good look at the dam, walk out on the observation site.) One of the most popular ways to view the lake is aboard the Vanishing Texas River Cruise (see Burnet). Cold-weather cruises provide a look at American bald eagles that nest along the upper reaches of the lake; in the summer you may see deer, javelinas (feral hoep), feral hogs, and wild turkey along the shoreline.

Drive south on Rte. 1431 from Lake Buchanan to visit one of the quietest of the Hill Country lakes. Cottage-lined **Inks Lake** is only three miles long and is bordered by Inks Lake State Park.

If you continue down Rte. 1431 you'll come to **Lake LBJ.** Once named Granite Shoals, the lake was renamed to honor Johnson for his work to create these Hill Country lakes. Here you'll find cottages for rent at the confluence of the Llano and Colorado Rivers, where quiet coves afford a catch of black bass, white bass, crappie, catfish, and perch.

**Lake Marble Falls** is in the town of the same name. It's named for slick ledges over which waterfalls spill.

The rough, rocky terrain of Marble Falls diminishes somewhat by the time you reach **Lake Travis,** a large, meandering lake that winds its way from the Hill Country to Austin's front door. At 65 miles long, Travis is the longest of the Hill Country lakes; it has literally hundreds of coves and inlets along its snakelike boundaries. Much of the land on Travis's shores is controlled by the Lower Colorado River Authority and remains undeveloped, but there are several excellent public parks from which to choose.

**NOV.: *Holiday at the Fort.*** Holiday fun includes food, tours of Old Fort Parker, and docents in pre-1840 period clothing. | 254/729–3894.

## Dining
**Buffa Bubba.** American. You'll have to resist taking the cowboy boot napkin holders home from this uniquely decorated, country-western style restaurant. Try the T-bone or the chicken-fried steak. | 812 W. Yeagua St. | 254/729–8757 | Breakfast also available. No supper Sun. | $7–$12 | No credit cards.

## LODGING
**Limestone Inn.** You'll be sure to get a good night's sleep at this inn—the Limestone is located in a rural, quiet neighborhood. However, you'll still find a restaurant within walking distance. Cable TV, pets allowed. | 300 S. Ellis St. | 254/729–3017 | 75 rooms | $40 | AE, D, DC, MC, V.

# GRUENE

MAP 8, H5

*(Nearby towns also listed: New Braunfels, San Antonio, San Marcos)*

Although it has the feel of a separate community, Gruene actually sits within the northern New Braunfels city limits. The pronunciation of Gruene is one of those things that set a real Texan apart. To sound like a local, just say "Green."

In the days when cotton was king, Gruene was a roaring town. Developed in the 1870s by H. D. Gruene, it featured a swinging dance hall and a cotton gin. Prosperity reigned until the boll weevil came to Texas, with the Great Depression right on its heels. H. D.'s plans for the town withered like the cotton in the fields. Gruene became a ghost town.

One hundred years after its founding, investors began restoring Gruene's historic buildings. Now the town is favored by antiques shoppers and country music lovers. On weekdays Gruene's streets may be quiet, but expect crowds every weekend.

Information: **Gruene Tourist Information** | 1601 Hunter Rd., New Braunfels, TX 78130 | 830/629–5077 | www.gruene.net.

# GUADALUPE MOUNTAINS NATIONAL PARK

MAP 8, C3

*(Nearby town also listed: El Paso)*

The only true mountains in Texas are 110 mi east of El Paso. Guadalupe's peaks rise up out of the desert to a height of 8,749 ft (nosebleed heights in Texas). The pinnacle of the park is Guadalupe Peak, Texas's highest point, but other notable spots include the El Capitan limestone formation and McKittrick Canyon, where you'll find some of the best fall color in the Lone Star State thanks to bigtooth maple, walnut, ash, oak, and the Texas madrone. Several trails with varying degrees of difficulty are available for hikers, who are rewarded with plenty of color, serenity, and the chance to enjoy natural beauty, unaccompanied by crowds. Be sure to bring in supplies; there are no fuel or food facilities in the park.

Information: **Guadalupe Mountains National Park Visitors Center** | On U.S. 62/180 | 915/828–3251 | fax 915/828–3269 | gumo_superintendent@nps.gov | www.nps.gov/gumo/index.html.

GUADALUPE
MOUNTAINS
NATIONAL PARK

INTRO
ATTRACTIONS
DINING
LODGING

## Attractions

**Frijole Ranch Museum.** This museum, in a ranch house built in the late 1800s, chronicles the history of Guadalupe National Park park with informative displays and photographs. There are hiking trails adjacent to the museum. | U.S. 62/280, 1 mi from the park visitors center | 915/828–3251 | Free. | Call for hours.

## Dining

**Nickel Creek Cafe.** American. This is the only restaurant within 30 mi of the park. It serves up standard American fare and some Tex-Mex dishes, such as burritos and fajitas. | U.S. 62/180, 30 mi east of the park | 915/828–3295 | Breakfast also available. No supper | $4–$7 | No credit cards.

## Lodging

**Best Western Cavern Inn.** Thirty-five miles northeast of Guadalupe National Park, this is the closest lodging facility to the park. All rooms at this single-story motel are quite spacious. 2 restaurants, cable TV, 2 pools, 2 spas, video games, pets allowed. | 17 Carlsbad Caverns Hwy., White's City, NM | 505/785–2291 | fax 505/785–2283 | www.bestwestern.com | 63 rooms | $84 | AE, D, DC, MC, V.

# HARLINGEN

MAP 8, I9

*(Nearby towns also listed: Edinburg, McAllen, Port Isabel, South Padre Island)*

Harlingen is a top destination in the Rio Grande Valley and makes a good central point from which to explore the southern tip of Texas. Within a one-hour drive are opportunities for a romp in the surf of South Padre, shopping in Mexico, and bird watching in national refuges. Like the rest of the Valley, Harlingen is a bilingual community, with Spanish spoken as often as English.

**Information: Harlingen Convention and Visitors Bureau** | Box 189, 311 E. Tyler, Harlingen, TX 78550 | 956/423–5440 or 800/531–7346 | www.harlingen.com.

## Attractions

**Iwo Jima Memorial and Museum.** Here visitors can view the original working model of the well-known sculpture, the Iwo Jima Memorial. The visitors center features exhibits on the battle, as well as a film. | 320 Iwo Jima Blvd. | 956/412–2207 | www.mma-tx.org | Free | Mon.–Sat. 10–4, Sun. 12–4.

**Laguna Atascosa National Wildlife Refuge.** This wetlands refuge is a popular stop for ecotourists interested in learning more about the habitats of South Texas, with birding trails, self-guided trails, and visitor centers. Birders come during the winter months as well as for the fall and spring migrations. | Off Rte. HM 106; 18 mi east of Rio Hondo on HM 106 | 956/748–3607 | $2 | Daily.

**Rio Grande Valley Historical Museum.** Check out local and natural history displays, video presentations, and historic buildings, including the original Harlingen Hospital. | Loop 499 at Boxwood and Raintree Sts. | 956/430–8500 | www.mma-tx.org | $2 | Wed.–Sat. 10–4, Sun. 1–4.

## ON THE CALENDAR

**APR.: *RioFest*.** Music, food booths, arts and crafts, live entertainment, and Mexican folk crafts demonstrations are at Casa de Amistad and Fair Park. | 956/425–2705.
**OCT.: *Jackson Street Jubilee*.** Kids and adults alike will enjoy the car show and musical performances held along Jackson St. in downtown Harlingen. | 956/427–8703.
**NOV.: *Rio Grande Valley Birding Festival*.** This event includes birding trips to several area wildlife refuges, as well as bird-related seminars and trade shows. | 956/423–5440.

## Dining

**Courtyard Cafe.** Continental. Steaks and burgers are the usual fare at this casual eatery, although there is a different "chef's special" every day. If you can't make it for supper, come for a weekend brunch. | 1725 W. Fillmore Ave. | 956/412–7800 | Breakfast also available. No supper Sun. | $5–$17 | AE, D, DC, MC, V.

**Olive Garden.** Italian. Well liked by families, the Olive Garden chain provides a wide range of traditional Italian choices. Try the lasagna classico, veal parmigiana, seafood Alfredo, and Mediterranean garlic shrimp. Kids' menu. | 3802 W. Lincoln St. | 956/428–7381 | $12–$23 | AE, D, DC, MC, V.

## Lodging

**Courtyard Harlingen.** This three-floor hotel is just off U.S. 77, 25 mi from the Mexican border. The Rio Grande Valley Museum, the Texas Air Museum, and the Gladys Porter Zoo are all within 30 mi of the hotel. Restaurant, in-room data ports, some microwaves, some refrigerators, cable TV, pool, exercise facilities, baby-sitting, laundry services, business services, no pets. | 1725 W. Fillmore Ave. | 956/412–7800 or 888/267–8927 | fax 956/412–7889 | www.courtyard.com | 114 rooms, 6 suites | $69–89, $115 suites | AE, D, DC, MC, V.

**Harlingen Super 8 Motel.** This three-story motel was built in 1995. Both South Padre Island and Gladys Porter Zoo are 35 mi away. Complimentary Continental breakfast, refrigerators, microwaves, cable TV, pool, laundry services, pets allowed (fee). | 1115 S. U.S. 83 | 956/412–8873 | fax 956/412–8873 | www.super8.com | 55 rooms | $55–$60 | AE, D, DC, MC, V.

**Holiday Inn Express.** This Express is within 4 mi of the center of town. Complimentary Continental breakfast, some refrigerators, cable TV, pool, laundry facilities. | 501 S. "P" St. | 956/428–9292 | fax 956/428–6152 | www.holiday-inn.com | 129 rooms | $65–$89 | AE, D, DC, MC, V.

**La Quinta.** This La Quinta is 7 mi from the Iwo Jima Memorial and Museum. Complimentary breakfast, in-room data ports, cable TV, pool, laundry facilities, business services, airport shuttle, free parking, pets allowed. | 1002 U.S. 83S | 956/428–6888 | fax 956/425–5840 | www.laquinta.com | 130 rooms | $59–$79 | AE, D, DC, MC, V.

**Regency Inn and Suites.** Standard chain accommodations 5 mi from the airport. Cable TV, pool, laundry facilities, business services. | 1901 W. Tyler St. | 956/425–1810 | fax 956/425–7227 | 70 rooms | $56–$64 | AE, D, DC, MC, V.

# HENDERSON

MAP 8, K3

*(Nearby town also listed: Kilgore)*

This East Texas community boomed with the discovery of oil in 1930. Today oil continues to be the prime attraction of this city, which also serves as a center for surrounding farms. Downtown, travelers will find many restored historic buildings thanks to the city's participation in the Main Street preservation program.

**Information: Henderson Tourist Development** | 201 N. Main St., Henderson, TX 75652 | 903/657–5528 | info@hendersontx.com | www.hendersontx.com.

## Attractions

**Depot Museum and Children's Discovery Center.** This 1901 railroad depot now contains a hands-on learning center, historic structures, and local history displays. | 514 N. High St. | 903/657–4303 | fax 903/657–2979 | www.depotmuseum.wm | $2 | Weekdays 9–5, Sat. 9–1.

**Gaston Museum.** Exhibits here chronicle the lives of the children who attended the former Gaston Independent School District, one of the largest and richest school districts of its time. Contains numerous exhibits on Henderson's long boomtown history from the late 1920s and early 1930s. | 6558 Rte. 64 W | 903/657–5493 | Free | Fri., Sat. 9–4:30.

**Howard Dickinson House.** This 1855 house was one of the first brick homes in Rusk County and was often visited by Sam Houston. It's open for guided group tours. | 501 S. Main St. | 903/657–6925 | $5 | Call for appointment.

## ON THE CALENDAR

**SEPT.: *Rusk County Rodeo.*** This PRCA event, held in the Expo Center, is a full rodeo, complete with bull riding and calf roping. | 903/657–2161.

**NOV.: *Heritage Syrup Festival.*** The old tradition of making ribbon cane syrup is cele-brated on the second Sat. of the month. The festival also includes the largest folk art show in East Texas. | 903/657–5528.

## Dining

**Bob's BAR-B-QUE.** Barbecue. There's take-out service only for good barbecue, beef, chicken, and sausage. | 1205 Pope St. | 903/657–8301 | Closed Sun., Mon. | $2–$8 | AE, D, DC, MC, V.

**Cotton Patch Cafe.** American. Daily specials include home-style dishes made from scratch. Casual family atmosphere. Burgers, chicken-fried steak, and homemade rolls. | 420 S. Rte. 79 | 903/657–1414 | $9–$13 | AE, D, DC, MC, V.

**Smokehouse Restaurant.** American/Casual. This casual spot has tables and booths, and antique plates are found throughout. Known for chicken-fried steak. | 207 U.S. 79 N | 903/657–7524 | Closed Sun. | $4–$7 | AE, MC, V.

## Lodging

**Best Western of Henderson.** This two-story motel is 3 mi from the Depot Museum and Chil-dren's Discovery Center, and 19 mi from Gregg County Airport. Cable TV, pool, laundry facilities, pets allowed. | 1500 Rte. 259S | 903/657–9561 | fax 903/657–9183 | 130 rooms | $50–$60 | AE, D, DC, MC, V.

**Lazy Staehs Bed and Breakfast.** In the Piney Woods, this large, two-story B&B is perfect for a quiet, tranquil getaway. All of the rooms are oversized and have plush, new furnish-ings. For fun you can play croquet, badminton, backgammon, or chess, or simply kick back on the balcony. Complimentary breakfast, TV in common area, pool, library, no pets, no kids under 12, no smoking. | 1816 Millville Dr. | 903/655–6680 or 877/655–5299 | fax 903/655–6483 | www.lazystaehs.com | 3 rooms | $89–$100 | AE, D, DC, MC, V.

# HEREFORD

MAP 8, J9

*(Nearby towns also listed: Amarillo, Canyon)*

This Panhandle town was named for the many Hereford cattle that once grazed here. Today cattle remain an important part of the city's economy: an estimated three million head of cattle are moved through here every year. Although you won't find many attractions in the city, it makes a good stopping point as you drive through the region.

**Information: Deaf Smith County/Hereford Chamber of Commerce** | Box 192, Hereford, TX 79045 | 806/364–3333 | www.herefordtx.com.

## Attractions

**Deaf Smith County Historical Museum.** This local history museum traces pioneer life in Deaf Smith County. One of its most interesting exhibits is a handcarved wooden circus model made in the 1930s. | 400 Sampson St. | 806/364–4338 | Free | Mon.–Sat. 10–5.

**JUNE: *Town and Country Jubilee.*** A quilt show, parade, and fireworks display are some of the highlights of this celebration. The events take place all over the town of Hereford, so call the chamber of commerce for a schedule. | 806/364–3333.

## Dining
**Taqueria Jalisco.** Mexican. This lively spot serves authentic Mexican food and is popular with locals. Try the *carne asada* (steak served with rice, beans, and guacamole) or the spicy shrimp cocktail. | 628 W. 1st St. | 806/364–4211 | $3–$6 | AE, D, DC, MC, V.

## Lodging
**Best Western Red Carpet Inn.** This two-story motel is 7 mi from Hereford Airport, 30 mi from West Texas A&M University, and 42 mi from Palo Duro Canyon State Park. Some refrigerators, cable TV, pool. | 830 W. First St. | 806/364–0540 | fax 806/364–0818 | 90 rooms | $55–$65 | AE, D, DC, MC, V.

**Relax Inn.** This motel is just a few minutes from the town's center and a number of restaurants. Refrigerators, cable TV, no pets. | 520 W. 1st St. | 806/364–0800 | 25 rooms | $23–$30 | AE, D, DC, MC, V.

# HICO

MAP 8, H3

*(Nearby towns also listed: Dublin, Glen Rose, Stephenville)*

Settled in 1856 on Honey Creek, Hico (pronounced "HIGH-ko") relocated three miles away on the Bosque River when the railroad was built in 1880. Local legend says that Billy the Kid was never killed in New Mexico, but instead lived in Hico until he was 92.

Information: **Hico Chamber of Commerce** | Box 533, Hico, TX 76457 | 800/361–4426 | hicotexas@htcomp.net | www.hico-tx.com.

## Attractions
**Billy the Kid Museum.** Convincing stories and so-called evidence tell how Bill Roberts (aka Billy the Kid) lived among the Hico locals until he was 92, while Billy Barlowe was buried in the outlaw's grave. | 111 Pecan St. | 254/796–4004 | $2 | Mon.–Sat. 10–5, Sun. 1–5.

**Wisemanhouse Chocolates.** You'll have trouble resisting the European chocolates, specialty truffles, and rich toffee sold at this antiques-filled chocolatier. Gift baskets are available. | U.S. 281 and Rte. 6 | 254/796–2565 | Free | Mon.–Sat. 10–6, Sun. 1–5.

**Texas Cowboy Art and Hall of Fame.** This museum honors Texas cowboys and cowgirls who have excelled in their careers. More than 30 pieces of memorabilia are displayed concerning each inductee. | Hico | 254/796–2462.

## Dining
**Koffee Kup.** American. Burgers and homemade pies are the specialties of this casual restaurant. | Rte. 6 and U.S. 281 | 254/796–4839 | Breakfast also available | $8–$9 | No credit cards.

**Lilly's Restaurant.** Mexican. Downstairs, standard Mexican fare such as fajitas and quesadillas are served in a casual setting in which desert scenes are painted on the walls. On the upper level, feel free to dine on the two outdoor decks. The menu is southwestern, with coulibiac salmon and barbecue ribs. | 128 N. Pecan St. | 254/796–0999 | $5–$19 | AE, D, MC, V.

**Our Daily Bread.** American. This café is in the Two Sisters Mercantile shop serves coffee drinks, milkshakes, and sandwiches. Its Reuben sandwich is its most popular item. | 102 S. Pecan | Closed Sun. | $3–$4 | D, MC, V.

## Lodging

**Hico Hills Inn.** Only blocks from downtown and near the town's main intersection, this inn is within walking distance of the community center, restaurants, and a park. | U.S. 281 and Railroad St. | 254/796–4217 | 17 rooms | $35–$50 | AE, D, MC, V.

**Railroad St. Bed and Bath.** Located downtown in an historic building, this one-room building is adjacent to an antiques store. | 110 Railroad St. | 254/796–4334 | 1 room | $65 | D, MC, V.

# HILLSBORO

MAP 8, I3

*(Nearby town also listed: Waco)*

Hillsboro, located between Waco and the Dallas-Fort Worth region, is a popular shopping stop for I–35 travelers. Along with a large factory outlet mall, the community has many antiques stores, tearooms, and historic attractions.

**Information: Hillsboro Convention and Visitors Bureau** | Box 358, Hillsboro, TX 76645 | 254/582–2481 or 800/HILLSBORO | chamber@hillsboro.net | www.hillsboro.net/chamber.

## Attractions

**Confederate Research Center and Audie Murphy Memorial Gun Museum and Weaponry Library.** This museum features research materials on local Confederate history. It also holds an extensive collection of historic guns and weapons collected by Audie Murphy, the most decorated soldier in WWII. | 112 Lamar Dr. | In Library Building of Hill College | 254/582–2555 | Free | Mon.–Thurs. 8–4:30, Fri. 8–4.

**Prime Outlets.** Outlet stores abound including Gap, Liz Claiborne, Levi's, Van Heusen, Bass, Guess, Nike, and more. | 104 NE I–35; exit 368A | 254/582–9205 | Mon.–Sat. 10–8, Sun. 11–6.

### ON THE CALENDAR

**MAR.:** *Hill County Fair.* This fair includes a carnival, rides, games, food booths, and exhibits. | 254/582–2481.
**SEPT.:** *Go Texas-Cotton Pickin' Fair.* Food booths, arts and crafts, games, rides, children's activities, and live entertainment are part of the fun. | 254/582–2481.

## Dining

**Grandy's Restaurant.** American. Serving country cooking for a following of faithful customers since 1973, this old-fashioned restaurant has expanded to more than 140 chains. Come for homestyle chicken-fried steak, chicken nuggets, or fried catfish and be sure to sit in one of the worn leather booths. | 1509 E. Rte. 22 | 254/582–0839 | Breakfast also available | $4–$7 | AE, D, DC, MC, V.

## Lodging

**Ramada Inn.** Standard chain accommodations. Cable TV, pool, business services, some pets allowed. | 254/582–3493 | fax 254/582–2755 | www.ramada.com | 94 rooms | $45–$50 | AE, D, DC, MC, V.

**Tarlton House of 1895.** This three-story Queen Anne Victorian home has seven coal fireplaces, pinewood floors, and five original stained-glass windows. Rooms are large and plush, with queen-size beds. Complimentary breakfast, no TV, no pets, no kids under 12, no smoking. | 211 N. Pleasant St. | 254/582–7216 or 800/823–7216 | tarlton@hotmail.com | www.triab.com/tarlton | 8 rooms | $85–$118 | AE, D, DC, MC, V.

# HOUSTON

*(Nearby towns also listed: Angleton, Baytown, Brazosport, Eagle Lake, Galveston, Texas City)*

Now the nation's fourth largest city, Houston is a thriving city bustling with activities, shopping, and nightlife. Linked by the Houston Ship Channel to the Gulf of Mexico, 50 mi away, the city is a giant in the world of international shipping as well as oil, aerospace, and finance.

Truly Texas-size, the city sprawls across 617 square mi of bayou country while the metropolitan area takes in close to 9,000 square mi, all connected by one of the nation's most extensive highway systems. Dozens of languages are heard in the ethnically diverse community whose residents have relocated here from around the globe.

The city of Houston was founded by two brothers from New York: Augustus and John Allen. In 1836, the brothers followed Buffalo Bayou from the coast, searching for investment opportunities. After founding a town named for General Sam Houston, the hero of the nearby Battle of San Jacinto, the Allens offered building sites to the new Republic of Texas government which was located here for a short time. However, it was the rich farmland in the area rather than the government which guaranteed Houston's early success. As local cotton production increased, Houston's position as a trade center grew accordingly. Steamships from the nearby port of Galveston navigated the Buffalo Bayou until the early 1900s when the Houston Ship Channel was constructed. Commerce was enhanced further with the arrival of the railroads. By the time of the Civil War, Houston was the undisputed commercial center of southeast Texas.

The second chapter in Houston's rise to prominence began in 1901 with the discovery of petroleum at Spindletop oilfield in East Texas. The Houston Ship Channel area was a logical location for oil refineries and, by 1930, some forty petroleum companies had located their headquarters here. It was partly Houston's reputation as a commercial energy center which led to its selection in 1961 as the location for NASA's Lyndon B. Johnson Space Center.

Houston has emerged as a cultural center as well as a commercial center. The city ranks second to New York in total number of theater seats and has over 30 museums. It also has permanent companies in opera, symphony, ballet, and theater, a distinction shared by few other U.S. cities. Star cultural attractions include the Houston Grand Opera and the Houston Ballet, both performing at the Wortham Theater Center, the Houston Symphony at Jones Hall, and theatrical productions at the Alley Theater.

There are over 500 parks in Houston, including Hermann Park, home to the Houston Zoological Gardens and adjacent to the Museum District, and Six Flags Astroworld theme park, which draws thousands of visitors annually. Several professional sports teams are based here, including the Rockets of the National Basketball Association and Major League Baseball's Houston Astros. In 2000, the Astros retired their longtime home, the Houston Astrodome, for a new stadium near downtown, Enron Field. The Astrodome will continue as a venue for other events.

**Information: Houston Convention and Visitors Bureau** | 901 Bagby Ave., Houston, TX 77002 | 713/227–3100 or 800/365–7575 | houstongde@aol.com | www.houston-guide.com.

## NEIGHBORHOODS

Like most every city that came into its own in the later part of the 20th century, Houston consists of one neighborhood built on top of another stretching south towards the coast to Clear Lake and NASA and to the north to the planned community of the Woodlands. The 610 Loop is the great divider in Houston. Inside the Loop you'll find

HOUSTON

INTRO
ATTRACTIONS
DINING
LODGING

the older neighborhoods—and most of the attractions on every visitor's list. Outside the Loop you'll find more of everything—more shopping centers, more restaurants, more movie theaters, and, of course, more cars.

**The Galleria.** Just west of the 610 Loop is the mighty Galleria, the swank indoor shopping mall that created the shopping experience as we know it today. The neighborhood that has grown up around it has become Houston's second downtown, with its many businesses, hotels, and restaurants.

**Downtown.** Philip Johnson skyscrapers gracefully preside over Houston's main business pulse point and are responsible for its knockout skyline. Here in the center of the 610 Loop you'll find the George R. Brown Convention Center, Enron Field, Sam Houston Park, Bayou Place, and the vibrant theater district, which includes the Wortham Theatre Center, Jones Hall, and the prestigious Alley Theater.

**Montrose.** Houston's hippest, most eclectic neighborhood is between River Oaks and the Museum District. Come here for cool nightlife, cutting-edge restaurants, colorful shops—and some of the best people-watching west of the Mississippi.

## KODAK'S TIPS FOR PHOTOGRAPHING THE CITY

### Streets
- Take a bus or walking tour to get acclimated
- Explore markets, streets, and parks
- Travel light so you can shoot quickly

### City Vistas
- Find high vantage points to reveal city views
- Shoot early or late in the day, for best light
- At twilight, use fast films and bracket exposures

### Formal Gardens
- Exploit high angles to show garden design
- Use wide-angle lenses to exaggerate depth and distance
- Arrive early to beat crowds

### Landmarks and Monuments
- Review postcard racks for traditional views
- Seek out distant or unusual views
- Look for interesting vignettes or details

### Museums
- Call in advance regarding photo restrictions
- Match film to light source when color is critical
- Bring several lenses or a zoom

### Houses of Worship
- Shoot exteriors from nearby with a wide-angle lens
- Move away and include surroundings
- Switch to a very fast film indoors

### Stained-Glass Windows
- Bright indirect sunlight yields saturated colors
- Expose for the glass not the surroundings
- Switch off flash to avoid glare

### Architectural Details
- Move close to isolate details
- For distant vignettes, use a telephoto lens
- Use side light to accent form and texture

### In the Marketplace
- Get up early to catch peak activity
- Search out colorful displays and colorful characters
- Don't scrimp on film

### Stage Shows and Events
- Never use flash
- Shoot with fast (ISO 400 to 1000) film
- Use telephoto lenses
- Focus manually if necessary

From *Kodak Guide to Shooting Great Travel Pictures* © 2000 by Fodor's Travel Publications

**Museum District.** With its ancient oaks, graceful fountains, and public sculpture this elegant neighborhood may remind you more of Paris than the Lone Star State. Clustered around the acres of green space afforded by Herman Park are the Houston Zoological Gardens, the Houston Museum of Natural Science, the Holocaust Museum, the Museum of Fine Arts, and the Contemporary Arts Museum. Nearby, on its self-contained campus, the Menil Collection and its satellites beckon with grassy lawns and picture-perfect, color-coordinated buildings.

**River Oaks.** Beautiful old homes fill Houston's most prestigious neighborhood, next to downtown. You can tour them along the Azalea Trail in March and drive through to ogle them from the outside the rest of the year. Some of Houston's ritziest restaurants and shopping are in the River Oaks Shopping Center and Highland Village.

## DRIVING AROUND TOWN

Downtown Houston is quite busy, but outside and within the greater Houston area the roads are good and not too congested. Interstate 10 runs East–West through the city, Interstate 45 and Route 59 run North–South, and Loop 610 and Beltway 8 run around Houston. Almost all of the one-way streets are downtown. There are no narrow streets. Signs are very clear and easy to see.

Houston's busiest rush hours are from 6:45–8 AM, and 5–6 PM. Traffic is the most congested in the downtown area during these times. Additionally, there is a lot of construction right now, affecting about 40 percent of Houston's roads.

Meter-parking is available downtown, but sometimes it can be hard to find. Parking garages and lots are plentiful, especially in the downtown area. One hour in a lot usually costs $1–$2. The maximum for a day is usually from $6–$10. Parking regulations are strictly enforced everywhere. The penalty for illegal parking varies depending on where you park; usually the fee is $20.

Right turns are permitted on red lights in Houston, except where signs explicitly state otherwise. Houston highways have lanes for multi-occupant vehicles (MOVs). During rush hour, the occupancy requirement for an MOV is 3 people; during non-rush-hour times and on weekends, the requirement is two people.

## TRANSPORTATION

**Airport: George Bush Intercontinental Airport.** Roughly 9 mi from downtown. | 281/233–3000.

**William P. Hobby Airport.** About 15 mi from downtown. | 713/640–3000.

**Rail:** Amtrak's daily *Sunset Limited* has service to San Antonio, El Paso, Tucson, Los Angeles, New Orleans, and Orlando. No local rail service is available. | 902 Washington Avenue | 800/872–7245.

**Bus:** Greyhound Bus Lines connects Houston to Dallas, Fort Worth, San Antonio, and beyond. | 2121 Main Street | 800/231–2222.

**Intra-city Transit:** METRO bus system has citywide service with express routes to downtown, the medical center, and major shopping and business areas. METRO also has free trolleys around the downtown areas. Cash, tokens, or vendor cards are accepted. | 713/635–4000.

A number of taxicab companies serve Houston: **Yellow Cab Company** | 713/236–1111. **United Cab Company** | 713/699–0000. **Square Deal Cab Company** | 713/659–5105. **Liberty Cab Company** | 713/695–6700. **Fiesta Cab Company** | 713/236–9400. Typical cab fares from George Bush Intercontinental Airport to downtown: $32; to the Texas Medical Center: $38. From William P. Hobby Airport to downtown: $17; to the Medical Center: $20.

# Attractions

## ART AND ARCHITECTURE

**Byzantine Fresco Chapel Museum.** Frescoes from a 13th-century votive chapel are preserved here. The dome and apse were rescued from thieves and restored under a unique arrangement with the Greek Orthodox Church and the Republic of Cyprus. | 4011 Yupon St. | A block from the Rothko Chapel | 713/521–3990 | Free | Wed.–Sun. 11–6.

**Chase Tower.** Designed by I. M. Pei, this 75-story granite building is the masterpiece of Houston's numerous downtown skyscrapers. Climb to the observatory on the 60th floor for awesome views of Houston. | 600 Travis St. | 713/223–0441 | Free | Weekdays 6–6.

**Contemporary Arts Museum.** Housed in a striking metal building, this downtown museum focuses on modern art created within the last 40 years. The museum doesn't have a permanent collection but has hosted works by Alexander Calder, Max Ernst, Robert Rauschenberg, William Wegman, and Texas artists. | 5216 Montrose Blvd. | 713/284–8250 | fax 713/284–8275 | www.camh.org | Free | Tues.–Sat. 10–5, Sun. 12–5, Thurs. 10–9.

**The Cullen Sculpture Garden.** Designed by Isamu Noguchi, this elegant garden is filled with 19th- and 20th-century sculptures by Rodin, Matisse, Giacometti, and Stella. | 1001 Bissonet | 713/639–7300 | Free | Daily 9–9.

**Lawndale Art Center.** Known for avant-garde events such as the Hair Ball and the 20th Century Modern Market, Lawndale Art Center displays contemporary works by more than 500 artists each year. | 4912 Main Street | 713/528–5858 | Free | Weekdays 10–5, Sat. 12–5.

★ **The Menil Collection.** This contemporary art museum is one of the city's premier cultural treasures. Houstonians John and Dominique de Menil collected the eclectic art, which ranges from tribal African sculptures to Andy Warhol's paintings of Campbell's soup cans. A separate gallery across the street houses the paintings of artist Cy Twombly. | 1515 Sul Ross | 713/525–9400 | Free | Wed.–Sun. 11–7.

**Museum of Fine Arts.** By opening the Audrey Jones Beck Building, the museum is now ranked the sixth largest in exhibition space in the country. The collection itself is also quite large. Renaissance, 18th-century, Impressionist, and post-Impressionist works are particularly well represented. | 1001 Bissonnet | 713/639–7300 | $3, free Thurs. | Tue., Wed., Sat. 10–7, Thur., Fri. 10–9, Sat. 10–7, Sun. 12:15–7.

**Rothko Chapel.** In this octagonal sanctuary designed by Philip Johnson, 14 Mark Rothko paintings panel the walls. At first the paintings look like black canvases. It's only when you come close that you can see the subtle coloring. Outside is Barnett Newman's sculpture *Broken Obelisk*, which symbolizes the life and assassination of Martin Luther King, Jr. | 3900 Yupon St. | At Sul Ross St., next to the Menil Collection | 713/524–9839 | Free | Daily, 10–6.

**Williams Tower.** Houstonians recognize this 64-story structure by its former name, the Transco Tower. It was designed by Phillip Johnson and there is a monumental 20-ft. water fountain adjacent to the building. The observation deck on the 51st floor provides a wonderful view of the west side of Houston. | 2800 Post Oak Blvd. | 713/966–7799 | Free | Weekdays 8–6.

## CULTURE, EDUCATION, AND HISTORY

**Alley Theatre.** One of the oldest resident theater companies in the world, the Alley began in a literal alley in 1947. Today it presents plays by contemporary dramatists. | 615 Texas Ave. | 713/228–8421.

**Bayou Place.** Formerly a convention center, Bayou Place was renovated by the city into a multi-level plaza of entertainment options. Several restaurants and bars with both indoor and outdoor seating; a movie theater; and a huge concert hall, the Aerial Theater, now keep traffic bustling around the area. | 500 Texas Ave. | 713/221–8883 | Free | Daily.

**Jones Hall for the Performing Arts.** This elegant, colonnaded hall is home to the Houston Symphony Orchestra and the Society for the Performing Arts. | 615 Louisiana St. | 713/227–ARTS or 800/828–2787.

**Rice University.** With an elite student enrollment of 4,000, Rice is sometimes called the "Harvard of the South." It is named after business pioneer William Marsh Rice, whose estate provided the money for opening the school in 1912. Stroll through 285 green acres and view the Mediterranean-style architecture. | 6100 Main St. | 713/348–0000 | www.rice.edu | Free | Daily.

Behind the hedges of one of the country's leading universities lies the cultural find of **Rice University Art Gallery.** Here you will find new exhibitions by contemporary artists, with an emphasis on installation art. | Sewall Hall | 713/348–6069 | Free | Tues.–Sat. 11–5, Thurs. 11–8, Sun. 12–5, closed during summer.

**University of Houston.** This large university enrolls almost 50,000 students through its various branches. In recent years it has been especially known for its creative writing program, whose faculty has included Rosellen Brown and Daniel Stern. Visit UH downtown or at its Clear Lake location, midway between Houston and Galveston, adjacent to NASA's Johnson Space Center and the Armand Bayou Nature Center. | 4800 Calhoun Rd. | 713/743–2255 | www.uh.edu | Free | Daily.

Within the university lies the **Blaffer Gallery.** Since 1973, Blaffer has been the most prestigious public university museum and gallery in Houston, exhibiting art that pertains to the community and is "intellectually stimulating." | Fine Arts Bldg., entrance #16 off Cullen Blvd. | 713/743–9530 | fax 713/743–9525 | Free | Tues.–Fri. 10–5; weekends 1–5.

**Wortham Theater Center.** Since it was opened in 1987, this center has entertained audiences totaling more than 3 million people. It is home to some of the most accomplished performers and is a mecca for entertainment in Houston. | 510 Preston St. | 713/237–1439 | fax 713/237–1439 | $12–$52 | Daily, 9–6. The center is home to the **Houston Grand Opera,** which is one of the five largest opera companies in the United States. | 713/227–ARTS, 800/828–ARTS or 713/546–0200.

Also headquartered at the Wortham is the **Houston Ballet.** The ballet company has toured around the world since its first performance in 1969. | 713/523–6300 or 800/828–2787.

## MUSEUMS

**Byzantine Fresco Chapel.** Two 13th-century frescoes belonging to the Church of Cyprus are housed in this functioning chapel. They were stolen from the island of Cyprus in the 1980s, but rescued by the Menil Foundation in Houston and are kept in the Chapel Museum with permission from the Church of Cyprus. They are the only intact Byzantine frescoes in the Western Hemisphere. | 4011 Yupon St. | 713/525–9400 | Free | Wed.–Sun. 11–6.

**Children's Museum of Houston.** This hands-on museum has nine galleries for children to explore everything from the environment to art to science. | 1500 Binz, at La Branch | 713/522–1138 | $5 | Tues.–Sat. 9–5, Sun. 12–5, Closed Mon.

**Holocaust Museum Houston.** This large museum remembers the victims of the Holocaust through permanent exhibits and a sculpture garden. The museum also screens a film about local survivors. | 5401 Caroline St. | 713/942–8000 | Free | Weekdays 9–5, weekends 12–5.

**Houston Museum of Natural Science.** The Houston Museum of Natural Science is the most visited science center in the nation. The permanent collection covers much ground from dinosaurs to gems and minerals. It includes a butterfly house, a tropical rainforest, and more. | One Hermann Circle Dr. | 713/639–4600 | $4 for permanent exhibits, $4 for Butterfly Center | Mon.–Sat 9–6, Sun. 11–6.

**Burke Baker Planetarium** offers star shows and laser-rock shows. | 713/639–4600 | $4 | Shows: weekdays 12, 1, 2, 3; weekends 12, 1, 2, 2:30, 3, 4, 4:30.

Houston Museum of Natural Science has an **IMAX Theater.** | 713/639–4629 | $6 | Daily.

**The Houston Zoological Gardens.** The zoological gardens features exhibits on primates, giraffes, and pygmy hippos. There are also sea lion training exhibitions and vampire bat feedings. | 1513 North MacGregor Way | Near Texas Medical Center | 713/523–5588 | $3 | Daily 10–6.

**The Museum of Health and Medical Science.** This museum is devoted to the human body. Visitors can walk through a model human to learn more about the body's vital systems. | 1515 Hermann Dr. | Near Texas Medical Center | 713/521–1515 | $4, free from 4-7 on Thurs. | Tues., Wed., Fri., Sat. 9–5, Thurs. 9–7, Sun. 12–5.

**National Museum of Funeral History.** This museum contains the country's largest collection funerary items, which range from Civil War caskets to a funeral sleigh. | 415 Barren Springs Dr. | 281/876–3063 | $5 | Weekdays 10–4, weekends 12–4.

**The Orange Show.** Jeff McKissack constructed this folk-art complex with a colorful collage of metal, cement, tile, and other cast-off material. The result of two decades of work, McKissack's ambition was recognized by numerous organizations who donated funds to begin the Orange Show Foundation, which serves the community with workshops and other participatory activities. | 2402 Munger St. | 713/926–6368 | www.orangeshow.org | $1, special rates for children | Wed.–Fri. 9–1; weekends 12–5.

## PARKS, NATURAL SIGHTS, AND OUTDOOR ACTIVITIES

**Hermann Park.** Here you will find the Japanese Garden, the Miller Outdoor Theatre, an extensive playground, and many picnic spots. The park is adjacent to the Museum District, where many of the city's best museums are located. | 6001 Fannin St., Wayside, TX | 713/845–1000 | Free.

**Houston Arboretum and Nature Center.** Native plants of Houston are showcased here, and there is a wildlife refuge on site. | 4501 Woodway | 713/681–8433 | Free | Daily 8–6.

**Memorial Park.** Bordering the Buffalo Bayou, this park welcomes joggers, picnickers, bikers, and skaters. The park's natural flora includes sycamore, ash, and palmetto. The Houston Arboretum and Nature Center is adjacent. | I–10 at Loop 610 W | 713/802–1662 | Free | Daily.

**Sam Houston Park.** This unique park is in the heart of downtown Houston, amidst towering skyscrapers. On the grounds, you'll find eight of the city's oldest buildings, restored and containing original period furnishings. | 1100 Bagby St. | 713/655–1912 | www.heritagesociety.org | Free | Mon.–Sat. 10–4; Sun 1–4.

**San Jacinto Battleground State Historic Park.** Located in LaPorte, 20 mi east of downtown Houston, this is the site where Texas won its independence from Mexico in 1836. The park is home to the 570-ft San Jacinto monument, which is made of Texas limestone. At the base of the monument stands the San Jacinto Museum of Texas History, offering exhibits on the state. | 3527 Battleground Rd. | On U.S. 134 | 281/479–2421 | Free | Daily 9–6.

Also at the park is the **Battleship USS *Texas*.** This ship fought in both World Wars and was renovated by money raised by the schoolchildren of Texas. It is considered the world's last remaining dreadnought battleship. Tours take visitors through crew quarters, engine rooms, and the navigation bridge. (281/479–2411 | $5 | Daily 10–5)

## RELIGION AND SPIRITUALITY

**Rothko Chapel.** This octagonal, non-denominational chapel houses 14 works by the Abstract Expressionist painter Mark Rothko. The chapel has a large meditation space and welcomes thousands of visitors every year. | 3900 Yupon St. | 713/524–9839 | Free | Daily 10–6.

## SHOPPING

**Galleria.** Modeled after a famous shopping plaza in Milan, Italy, the Galleria hosts many top retailers. There are also two hotels and an ice-skating rink within the complex. | 5085 Westheimer | 713/622–0663 | Free | Mon.–Sat. 9–10, Sun. 12–6.

**Pavilion on Post Oak.** Some of the most high-end stores in town can be found here, including Hermes. | 1800 Post Oak Blvd. | 713/850–3100 | Mon.–Sat. 10–6, Thurs. 10–8.

## SPECTATOR SPORTS

**Professional Sports.** Houston is not for want of professional sports teams.
NBA basketball is represented by the **Houston Rockets,** and the NWBA is represented by the reigning **Houston Comets.** Both teams dribble at the Summit. | 10 Greenway Plaza | 713/627–3865.
The National League baseball team, the **Houston Astros,** batter-up at the newly built Enron Field, located downtown and adjacent to Union Station. | Crawford and Travis Aves | 713/627–8767.
It may be hot outside but that doesn't stop the local hockey team, the **Houston Aeros,** from tearing up the ice. The team plays at the Compaq Center. | 713/974–7825. Place your bet on your favorite horse at the **Sam Houston Race Track** | 7575 Sam Houston Pkwy. W | 800–807–RACE or 281–807–7223.

## SIGHTSEEING TOURS/TOUR COMPANIES

**Gray Line Bus Tours.** Guided, narrated tours of the city's top attractions. | 713/670–3254 or 800/334–4441 | Prices vary with tours | Mon.–Sat.

## OTHER POINTS OF INTEREST

**Allen's Landing Park.** This park and walkway commemorates the spot on Buffalo Bayou where the Allen brothers first explored the region and established a trading post. | Main St. and Buffalo Bayou, Downtown | No phone | Free | Daily.

**Armand Bayou Nature Center.** This private wildlife refuge protects 2500 acres of wetlands, riparian hardwood forests, and a coastal tall grass prairie. It's one of the last bayous in the Houston area not canalized. | 8500 Bay Area Blvd. | 281/474–2551 | Tue.–Sat. 9–5, Sun. 12–5.

**Astrodome USA.** The 260-acre Astrodome USA includes the Astrohall Convention Center, Expo Centers and Arena, and the Astrodome. | S. Loop 610 and Kirby Dr. | 713/799–9544 or 800/776–4995.
Also within the complex is the **Six Flags AstroWorld** theme park, which is home to more coasters than any other theme park in Texas. | 713/799–1234 | $36 | July–Sept., daily; Apr.–June, Sept.–Nov., weekends; opens at 10; closing hours vary.
Adjacent to the theme park, **Six Flags WaterWorld** is a water park with a man-made beach and water rides. | 713/799–1234 | $18 | May, weekends 10–6; June–Aug., daily 10–6.

**Bayou Bend Collection.** Part of the Museum of Fine Arts, this collection houses the museum's American decorative arts from the 17th century to the present. The museum is the former home of Ima Hogg, daughter of a Texas governor, and includes nearly 5000 objects ranging from silver to paper to glassware. Behind the home, you can tour the 14-acre garden. | 1 Westcott St. | 713/639–7750 | $10 | Tues.–Sun. 10–12:30 PM.

**Rienzi.** This River Oaks home, which once belonged to philanthropists Carroll Sterling Masterson and her husband, Harris Masterson III, houses a collection of European art and antiques. Rienzi was designed by John Staub in 1954 and expanded in 1972 with the aid of architect Jugo Neuhaus. | 1406 Kirby Dr. | 713/639–7800 | $6 | Mon., Thurs.–Sat. 10–3; Sun. 1–5. Closed Aug.

**Space Center Houston.** This interactive $70 million complex brings the technology of space travel to a level that any visitor can enjoy. Starting with a mock-up of the space shuttle, the center is filled with hands-on displays. Kids Space Place offers 17 interactive areas where children can ride across the moon's surface in a Lunar Rover or command a space shuttle. At Mission Status Center, guests can eavesdrop on conversations with the crew of the space shuttle. The Feel of Space hands-on area offers computer simulators that permit guests to land the space shuttle or retrieve a satellite. After a view of flying at the IMAX theater, participants can take a NASA tram tour for a behind-the-scenes look at the John-

son Space Center to view the weightless environment training facility, the control center complex, and an outdoor park with retired flight hardware. | 1601 NASA Rd. 1, Houston, TX | Off I–45S; exit 25 | 281/244–2100 | $14 | Sept.–May, weekdays 10–5, weekends 10–7; Jun.–Aug., daily 9–7.

**The Port of Houston.** This is one of the three busiest ports in the United States. Free 90-min tours are available, but be sure to call ahead. | 713/670–2400 and 713/670–2576 for tours | Off of 6-10; exit 29 | Free | Port open daily 9–5; tours Tues.–Sun. except holidays and month of Sept.

## ON THE CALENDAR

**FEB.–MAR.:** *Houston Livestock Show and Rodeo.* This weeks-long event at the Astrodome is one of the southwest's largest livestock shows and the world's biggest rodeo. Performances are given by music superstars. | 713/791–9000.

**MAR., OCT:** *Bayou City Art Festival.* This art show also includes children's activities, food booths, and live entertainment. The Mar. show is held in Memorial Park and the October show is held downtown. | 713/521–0133.

**MAR.:** *River Oaks Garden Club's Azalea Trail.* This trail takes in several private gardens as well as 14 acres at Bayou Bend. | 713/523–2483.

**APR.:** *Houston International Festival.* Twenty blocks of downtown become an open-air market filled with arts and crafts, food, and live entertainment representing cultures from around the world. | 713/654–8808.

**MAY:** *Cinco de Mayo.* Houston celebrates Mexico's triumph over French invaders with mariachi performances, food, arts and crafts, and dances at Miller Outdoor Theater in Hermann Park. | 713/227–3100.

**OCT.:** *Greek Festival.* Music, dance, and food celebrating the culture of Greece at the Greek Orthodox Cathedral. | 713/526–5377.

**NOV.:** *Texas Renaissance Festival.* The state's largest Renaissance festival is held in Plantersville and includes a re-creation of 16th-century England, replete with jesters, knights, food, and entertainment in Plantersville. | 800/458–3435.

# Dining

## INEXPENSIVE

**Baba Yega Restaurant.** American. An excellent choice for vegetarian cuisine, this eclectic bungalow in the Montrose District will serve you an avocado- and cheese-topped veggie burger plate popular since 1974. The grilled salmon is also delicious. Dine on an outdoor covered patio before a waterfall and herb garden. | 2607 Grant St. | 713/522–0042 | Reservations not accepted | $5–$13 | AE, D, DC, MC, V.

**Berryhill Hot Tamales.** Mexican. This casual diner is a local favorite. Though tamales are the title dish and quite tasty (especially the chicken verde), the real treat here is Baja tacos with spicy grilled catfish. | 2639 Revere St. | 713/526–8080 | Reservations not accepted | Breakfast available on weekends | $6–$13 | AE, D, MC, V.

**Butera's Fine Foods.** Delicatessen. Diners can select from tables and booths to enjoy casually served good food. Known for its sandwiches, of course. Open-air dining on the patio with umbrellas for shade. | 4621 Montrose Blvd. | 713/523–0722 | $8–$12 | AE, D, DC, MC, V.

**Cafe Noche.** Mexican. Plenty of outdoor dining is the main draw here, but primo Mexican cuisine keeps crowds coming back for more. The menu presents Tex-Mex favorites and authentic regional options. In particular, ceviche made with big chunks of salmon, snapper, and shrimp in a zesty marinade gets high marks. Sunday brunch is a $12 bargain. One peculiarity here is the mandatory 18% tip for weekend reservations. | 2409 Montrose Blvd. | 713/529–2409 | $7–$11 | www.cafenoche.com | AE, DC, MC, V.

**Chuy's Comida Deluxe.** Tex-Mex. Every night is a party at Chuy's, where Elvis is the patron saint and eclectic is the norm. The mission here is to feed you well and keep you happy.

Try the "big as yo face" burritos, the Elvis Special (a Tex-Mex sampler platter), or the 9-1-1 Hot Plate (with hunka burnin' green chile sauce), and most likely, you'll join the groupies. | 2706 Westheimer Rd. | 713/524–1700 | 6328 Richmond Ave. | 713/974–2322 | $8–$10 | AE, D, DC, MC, V.

**Doneraki.** Tex-Mex. Festive and authentic, Doneraki is a great choice for a Tex-Mex fix at any of its three locations, though locals claim the best experience is at the original on Fulton. Kids' menu. | 7705 Westheimer Rd. | 713/975–9815 | 2836 Fulton | 713/224–2509 | 5505 FM 160 W | 713/893–1400 | $8–$12 | AE, D, MC, V.

**Empire Cafe.** Café. This casual café attracts a variety of diners, from professionals to punk rockers. Italian coffees and light fare are served; try the roasted or grilled chicken. Or come just for dessert—you'll find a wide selection of desserts and pastries. | 1732 Westheimer Rd. | 713/528–5282 | Breakfast also available | $6–$11 | AE, D, DC, MC, V.

**Fox Diner.** Eclectic. This casual spot is a popular local hangout and attracts an artsy crowd. Dishes on the menu are creative; try the chef-recommended shrimp and grits, the fried chicken with garlic mashed potatoes and cream gravy, or the spice-rubbed rib-eye steak. | 905 Taft St. | 713/523–5369 | No lunch Sat. No supper Sun. | $9–$18 | AE, D, DC, MC, V.

**Gugenheim's.** Delicatessen. Nostalgic fifties decor will take you back in this traditional New York–style deli and full-service restaurant. Try the corned beef or pastrami sandwich—the meat is flown in from Chicago. | 1708 Post Oak Blvd. | 713/622–2773 | Breakfast also available | $10–$12 | AE, D, DC, MC, V.

**Kim Son.** Vietnamese. This informal restaurant boasts an extensive menu with more than 100 options. Particularly popular are the spring rolls, beef fajitas Vietnamese style, and black pepper crab. | 2001 Jefferson St. | 713/222–2461 | 300 Milam | 713/222–2790 | 7531 Westheimer | 713/783–0054 | $8–$12 | AE, D, DC, MC, V.

**Otto's Barbecue.** Barbecue. Some Houstonians will tell you this is the best barbecue in town. Famous for its bush plate which includes beef, links, and ribs. Open-air dining. Kids' menu. | 5502 Memorial Dr. | 713/864–2573 | Closed Sun. | $9–$15 | AE, D, MC, V.

**Pico's Mexican Restaurant.** Mexican. Families, couples, Bellaire area neighbors, and cross-town devotees come here for authentic traditional and contemporary Mexican cuisine. Be sure to try the *camarones adobados* (poblano-stuffed, bacon-wrapped shrimp) and have one of Pico's famous goldfish bowl–size margaritas. | 5941 Bellaire Blvd. | 713/662–8383 | Reservations not accepted | $8–$21 | AE, D, DC, MC, V.

**Solero.** Spanish. Housed in a restored 1882 building in the historic district of downtown Houston, with high ceilings and upholstered booths, this chic spot serves up Spanish and South American tapas that keep the crowds coming in. Try the exceptional paella and bouillabaisse, made with fresh gulf coast seafood, or the vegetarian paella; then cross over for a drink at the Swank Lounge next door. | 910 Prairie St. | 713/227–2665 | Reservations not accepted | Closed Sun. | $6–$19 | AE, D, MC, V.

## MODERATE

**Arcodoro.** Italian. With executive chefs hailing from Sardinia, Italy, Arcodoro is the place to go for authentic cuisine. The various pasta dishes, such as artichoke-filled ravioli and gnochetti with wild boars are very popular as are the chicken and osso buco (veal) dishes. Arcodoro also boasts a succulent rib-eye steak. | 5000 Westheimer Rd. | 713/621–6888 | $9–$27 | AE, D, DC, MC, V.

**Backstreet Cafe.** American. This homey restaurant is located in an old two-story house and serves innovative dishes such as coffee-crusted beef tenderloin and jalapeño fettuccine. For a real urban retreat, ask to eat outside on the brick patio plentiful with plants and trees. | 1103 S. Shepherd Dr. | 713/521–2239 | Sun. brunch also available | $13–$19 | AE, MC, V.

**Birraporetti's.** Italian. This family-friendly mini-chain serves pizza and other standard fare. The Louisiana branch near the Alley Theater is a favorite with theater-goers. The

West Gray branch turns into a hopping bar scene after hours. Kids' menu. | 500 Louisiana St. | 713/224–9494 | 1997 West Gray | 713/529–9191 | $8–$15 | AE, D, DC, MC, V.

**Bistro Vino.** French. It's hard to decide where to sit in this romantic neighborhood restaurant. Should you choose inside–in the remodeled historic two-story mansion? Or, perhaps, outside in the lush garden near the fountain? Either way you're sure to be able to hear the live piano music as you tuck into something nice like the veal Milanese, osso buco, or filet au poivre. | 819 W. Alabama St. | 713/526–5500 | Closed Sun. | $12–$25 | AE, DC, MC, V.

**Boulevard Bistro.** Continental. Named one of the 10 best chefs by *Food and Wine*, owner Monica Pope whips up globally inspired dishes using local organic produce. Open-air dining. Vegetarian menu. Kids' menu. Sun. brunch. | 4319 Montrose Blvd. | 713/524–6922 | Closed Mon. No supper Sun. | $12–$20 | AE, D, DC, MC, V.

**Cafe Japon.** Japanese. Don't be fooled by the ritzy decor: This mini-chain is not as expensive as it looks. Dig into the fresh sushi or sample some of the creative appetizers without worrying about sticker shock. | 3915 Kirby Dr. | 713/529–1668 | 11312 Westheimer | 281/531–9100 | $12–$18 | AE, D, DC, MC, V.

**Canyon Cafe.** Southwestern. Southwestern fare gets an update in this popular Dallas-import. If the chicken-fried tuna with jalapeño cream gravy is too adventurous for you, you can opt for the more classic dishes such as the crab cakes and the King Ranch chicken casserole. Both adventurers and traditionalists alike will enjoy sitting under the ceiling fans on the balcony. Kids' menu. | 5000 Westheimer | 713/629–5565 | $8–$20 | AE, D, DC, MC, V.

**Carrabba's.** Italian. Once a place where 45-minute waits were considered short, Carrabba's maintains a thriving, but more tolerable level of business. The name has been franchised (there are a total of seven locations), but both Kirby and Voss locations remain with the original owner, Johnny Carrabba. The wood-burning oven churns out stellar pizzas and focaccia. Pastas are varied from simple picchi pacchu (tomato and basil) to sublime rigatoni campagnolo (Italian sausage, peppers, and caprino cheese in a pomodoro sauce). | 3115 Kirby Dr. | 713/522–3131 | 1399 S. Voss Rd. | 713/468–0868 | $10–$26 | AE, DC, MC, V.

**Chianti.** Italian. Perfectly acceptable rustic Tuscan food is served here, but it's the setting in the renovated manor house complete with garden that makes dining here a treat—not to mention the hip martini bar. | 1515 S. Post Oak Ln | 713/840–0303 | Closed Sun. No lunch Sat. | $12–$20 | AE, DC, MC, V.

**Daily Review Cafe.** Contemporary. Named one of the 20 best restaurants in the country by *Esquire* magazine, this casual Fourth Ward eatery proves that comfort food and urbanity can coexist. The menu's appeal is as broad as the crowd is diverse—from buzz cut hip-young-things to Downtown blue-suits. Entrées are imaginative twists on traditional favorites, such as the chicken pot pie perked up with shaved fennel and carrots in cream sauce. The penne with tender spicy meatballs is a knock-out. Go early to avoid a wait. Open-air dining on a covered patio. | 3412 W. Lamar St. | 713/520–9217 | Lunch only Mon. and Sun. | $12–$18 | AE, DC, MC, V.

**Damian's.** Italian. High-set windows, romantic lighting, and walls crowded with framed photos, posters, and artwork, give a cozy feel to Damian's. The slightly formal atmosphere is nonetheless welcoming, and the waitstaff well informed and competent. From the kitchen you can expect the very best: try the spaghetti alla carbonara (rich with bacon and garlic) or linguine with seafood. Veal dishes shine, also, as do the seafood entrées. | 3011 Smith St. | 713/522–0439 | Closed Sun. No lunch Sat. | $14–$27 | AE, DC, MC, V.

**Dong Ting.** Chinese. One of the most elegant places to eat Chinese in Houston, this is a great place for special occasions and to indulge in its many traditional Shanghai and Hunan specialties. Be sure to try the Lion's Head, a Chinese meatball. | 611 Stuart St. | 713/527–0005 | Closed Sun. No lunch on Sat. | $12–$18 | AE, D, DC, MC, V.

**Empress of China.** Chinese. Tucked in a corner of an expansive maze-like shopping center in this country club area, Empress holds court with white glove service, a gracious dining room and an eclectic semi-Chinese menu with Asian and European influences. Try the shrimp-and-avocado salad, or mixed seafood in white wine and lemon sauce, or the boneless chicken tenderloin with ginger and fennel. | 5419 FM 1960 W | 281/583–8021 | Closed Sun. | $10–$28 | AE, D, MC, V.

**Flying Dutchman.** Seafood. The outdoor dining is especially popular since this restaurant is perched right above Galveston Bay. Downstairs, there's a casual atmosphere with rustic decor, and upstairs, it's more elegant with linen tablecloths and great views. Be sure to check out the ultimate seafood platter piled high with stuffed shrimp and crab, oyster, snapper, gulf shrimp, and soft shell crab. Open-air dining on lower and upper deck areas. Kids' menu. | #9 Boardwalk, Kemah | 281/334–7575 | $9–$20 downstairs; $17–$22 upstairs | AE, D, DC, MC, V.

**Golden Room.** Thai. Set on the north edge of the Montrose district, this cozy restaurant is welcoming, with banquettes lining one wall, and deep green walls accented with gold touches. Try the fresh spring rolls, chockablock with grilled chicken and vegetables. A zesty garlic sauce tops off the notable ginger chicken and, for the calorie counters, consider steamed snapper done up with chopped ginger, carrots, and jalapeños. | 1209 Montrose Blvd. | 713/524–9614 | Closed Sun. No lunch Sat., no smoking | $12–$19 | AE, D, DC, MC, V.

**Goode Co. Texas BAR-B-Q.** Barbecue. Known far and wide for its barbecue and pecan pie, this where Houstonians take out-of-towners for a Texas fix. A friendly down-home feeling prevails in this spot, which is constructed like a Texas barn. A covered patio with park benches seats about 100. | 5109 Kirby Dr. | 713/522–2530 | $14–$22 | AE, D, DC, MC, V.

**Goode Co. Texas Seafood.** Seafood. This old railroad car packs in the passengers. The draw? Tasty, plentiful, and cheap seafood. For starters, *campechana de mariscos* (shrimp, crab, and avocado with spicy red sauce) served in a soda fountain glass with tortilla chips is a standout. Impeccably cooked entrées include mesquite-grilled flounder, smoky shrimp verde, and trout amandine. | 2621 Westpark Ave. | 713/523–7154 | Reservations not accepted | $11–$23 | AE, D, DC, MC, V.

**Great Caruso.** Continental. Get a decent meal and lively entertainment at Houston's only dinner theater featuring Broadway and light operetta performances as well as singing waiters. | 10001 Westheimer Rd. | 713/780–4900 | Closed Mon., Tues. No lunch | $32 for 3 courses and show Wed., Thurs., Sun.; $37 for 3 courses and show Fri.–Sat. | AE, D, DC, MC, V.

**Grotto.** Italian. The crowd is the junior beautiful set, and no wonder—these are Tony Vallone's less formal New Italian eateries. Ribald murals set the mood for feasting and frivolity, but these meals would be great in a dark closet. Take, for instance, plump oysters mimmo (infant) crisply encased in Italian breading as your appetizer. Move on to seafood ravioli topped with shrimp and crab claws or chicken francese (prepared with artichoke hearts and mushrooms). | 3920 Westheimer Rd. | 713/622–3663 | 6401 Woodway | 713/782–3663 | $13–$23 | AE, D, DC, MC, V.

**Guadalajara.** Tex-Mex. People come here to enjoy all the usual Mexican standards in south-of-the-border surroundings. Open-air dining on the patio. Kids' menu. | 2925 Southwest Fwy. | 713/461–5300 | $10–$17 | AE, D, MC, V.

**Hunan Paradise.** Chinese. Tired of indistinguishable Column-A and Column-B Chinese restaurants? The menu at this nouvelle-Pacific place is blessedly limited, yet imaginative. Appetizers of finger-sized seafood egg rolls or grilled oysters with ginger sparkle, but the real stars are entrêes—scallops in a creamy sake and caviar sauce, Peking duck crepes with plum sauce, grilled salmon topped with pungent onions, and shrimp garnished with honeyed walnuts. | 2649 Richmond Ave. | 713/526–1688 | $11–$15 | No lunch Sun. | AE, D, MC, V.

**JAGS.** Contemporary. This trendy restaurant in the dramatic, high-ceilinged atrium of the Decorative Center is where the well-turned-out and their decorators come for special ambiance and service, as well as for caterer Jackson Hicks's food. No credentials are checked at the door, however; anyone can enjoy his crab blinis, salmon with cucumber salad, and health-conscious salads and sandwiches—presented, of course, with proper panache. | 5120 Woodway Dr. | 713/621–4766 | Lunch only. Closed Sat.–Sun. | $12–$16 | AE, MC, V.

**Jalapeños.** Mexican. This popular River Oaks eatery is known for its decadent Sunday brunch and spinach enchiladas, but you can also find more unusual offerings such as crawfish enchiladas and grilled calamaris. Open-air dining. Kids' menu. | 2702 Kirby Dr. | 713/524–1668 | $12–$19 | AE, MC, V.

**Joyce's Oyster Resort.** Seafood. How do you like dem oysters? This casual seafaring eatery has them any way you want them: raw, fried, baked, or in a spicy gumbo. Kids' menu. | 6415 San Felipe St. | 713/975–9902 | Closed Sun. No lunch Sat. | $8–$23 | AE, D, MC, V.

**Khyber.** Indian. Plain decor belies tasty fare at this neighborhood favorite. Convenient lunch buffet between 11–2. Open-air dining. | 2510 Richmond Ave. | 713/942–9424 | $12–$17 | AE, D, DC, MC, V.

**La Griglia.** Italian. Dramatic decor, open kitchen, imaginative and dependable food, and fair prices make this River Oaks favorite a touchstone among Houston's many fine affordable restaurants. This place fills by 7 PM, so arrive early or prepare to enjoy the scenery for a while. Try seafood cheesecake, maybe the richest appetizer in town, and worth every calorie, or smooth, silky shrimp bisque. Soft-shell crabs and filet of red snapper are excellent entrées. Open-air dining. | 2002 W. Gray St. | 713/526–4700 | No lunch Sat., Sun. | $13–$28 | AE, D, DC, MC, V.

**La Mora.** Italian. Before you're even seated you will have choices to make: seating in the snug, romantic front room, or back in the sometimes noisy atrium with its soaring, glass topped roof. The menu offers much more difficult choices, though. For starters, try the smoked mozzarella with sweet peppers and mushrooms or the hearty pasta and bean soup. You can't go wrong with the roasted pork loin with rosemary pancetta or veal scaloppini in a lemon butter sauce. | 912 Lovett Blvd. | 713/522–7412 | Closed Sun. | $12–$26 | AE, D, DC, MC, V.

**Las Alamedas.** Mexican. You could forget you're in the city at the grand hacienda of Las Alamedas, which overlooks a peaceful wooded ravine. The menu is upscale Mexican cuisine, and the kitchen is sometimes uneven, but generally very good. Two splendid entrées are *tacos de cochinita pibil* (chunks of pork simmered in achiote sauce) and *huachinango à la azteca* (red snapper stuffed with corn mushrooms in poblano sauce). Kids' menu. Sun. brunch. | 8615 Katy Fwy. | 713/461–1503 | No lunch Sat. | $12–$18 | AE, D, DC, MC, V.

**La Strada.** Italian. This large, trendy restaurant is a place to see and to be seen. The interior is brightened by large windows, yet subdued with dark wood tables and chairs. An enormous single lantern suspends from a high ceiling, across from a mezzanine and balcony. Contemporary paintings are scattered about. Try the handmade tortellini stuffed with Italian sausage and spinach, the oak-roasted chicken, or the black Angus beef filet. Don't miss the chocolate mousse pie for dessert. | 322 Westheimer Rd. | 713/523–1014 | $9–$22 | AE, D, DC, MC, V.

**Mesa Grill.** Southwestern. Decorated attractively in Santa Fe style, Mesa features food that reflects New Mexico as clearly as it does Mexico. The complimentary sweet potato chips, served with both a typical salsa and an outstanding smoky-flavored one, may fill you before you can sample the trendy enchiladas or adobe pie casserole. Open-air sitting. Sun. brunch. Kids' menu. | 1971 W. Gray St. | 713/520–8900 | $9–$18 | AE, D, DC, MC, V.

**Nino's.** Italian. This granddaddy of Houston restaurants was one of the first to bring fine, reasonably priced Italian cooking to the city. Nino's appetizers and entrées can go head on with the trendier and tonier places in town. Owner Vincent Mandola keeps updating the menu but retains the classics that put him on the map. Start with antipasto misto (marinated and roasted vegetables), then enjoy wood-fired rotisserie lemon-garlic chicken with mashed potatoes for inspired comfort food. | 2817 W. Dallas St. | 713/522–5120 | Closed Sun. No lunch Sat. | $9–$17 | AE, DC, MC, V.

**Nit Noi.** Thai. Voted "Best Thai Restaurant" by the Houston Press, this minichain serves fresh, flavorful fare, no smoking. | 2426 Bolsover | 713/524–8114 | 6395 Woodway Dr. | 713/789–1711 | $12–$22 | AE, D, DC, MC, V.

**Ouisie's Table.** Southwestern. Whether you want to lunch with the ladies, partake with your parents, or feast with your friends, Ouisie's gracious, country-lodge setting on the edge of River Oaks is hard to beat. So is her food. A huge chalkboard posts daily specials and a list of food and wine pairings. If you're really in a comfort food mode, try macaroni and cheese, with penne pasta and not even a dab of Velveeta. Also satisfying are crab cakes and fried oysters with jalapeño tartar sauce. Open-air dining. | 3939 San Felipe St. | 713/528–2264 | Closed Sun., Mon. | $12–$18 | AE, D, DC, MC, V.

**Pappadeaux.** Cajun/Creole. Another Pappas gold mine, this Cajun kitchen puts out consistently good food to consistently satisfied crowds at seven locations citywide. Bring the kids; bring the folks; bring the whole gang because there is plenty of seating in these cavernous spots. While you wait (and you will) enjoy beverages on the pretty patios reminiscent of French Quarter courtyards, but twice the size. | 6015 Westheimer Rd. | 713/782–6310 | 10499 I–10W | 713/722–0221 | $14–$20 | AE, MC, V.

**Pappasito's Cantina.** Tex-Mex. Ask Houstonians their favorite place for Mexican food and Pappasitos will claim the majority vote, by far. What's so great about it? Monstrous servings of reliably good Tex-Mex with family budget tabs may be the leading cause of affection for this 10-location chain. | 6445 Richmond Ave. | 713/784–5253 | 2515 Southwest Loop 610 | 713/668–5756 | $7–$19 | AE, MC, V.

**Post Oak Grill.** American. This Houstonian standby dishes up reliable meals of salads, pastas, seafood, and chops and the handily adjacent Slide Bar serves up live jazz Mon. through Sat. nights. | 1415 S. Post Oak Ln | 713/993–9966 | No lunch Sun. | $13–$32 | AE, D, DC, MC, V.

**Prego.** Italian. With the spiffy interior as backdrop, the imaginative fare really shines here. The grilled portobello mushroom salad and a good bread basket start you off well. Add rich, spicy poblano-and-red-pepper soup, and you have a good meal indeed. The rotisserie turns out attractive meat dishes such as mustard-crusted lamb chops. The pasta is also enticing, from the jalapeño fettuccine with grilled chicken to sophisticated ravioli with veal in Marsala wine sauce. Kids' menu. | 2520 Amherst St. | 713/529–2420 | $8–$23 | AE, MC, V.

**Rio Ranch.** Southwestern. This rambling sister outpost to Café Annie offers relaxed dining in a Texas setting. Knife-and-fork burgers and chile-crusted quail share the menu with city-slicker-pleasing salads and grilled red snapper. The inexpensive Sunday brunch buffet features border-style breakfast plus all your favorites: waffles, omelettes, meats, and sweets. Most appealing, the Ranch has the perfect front porch on which to sip smooth margaritas next to the pretty man-made Rio. Kids' menu. | 9999 Westheimer Rd. | 713/952–5000 | Breakfast also available Mon.–Sat. | $12–$21 | www.rioranch.com | AE, D, DC, MC, V.

**Ruggles Grill.** Southwestern. Why do crowds repeatedly return to Ruggles' loud, packed dining room? For the food! The New Southwestern menu compensates for the notorious waits with wild mushroom soup with thyme and barbecued chicken quesadillas. Indulge in the red snapper with shrimp and avocado or the pecan-crusted salmon filet with crab, corn, and horseradish sauce. It's possible to escape the customary boisterous crowd by coming at lunch time. Sun. brunch. | 903 Westheimer Rd. | 713/524–3839 | Reservations essential | Closed Mon. | $9–$22 | AE, DC, MC, V.

**Sausalito Seafood and Pasta.** American. If you're in the neighborhood, this casual, California-style eatery is a reliable choice. The menu of salads and pasta is spiced up by the Peruvian ceviche. | 3215 Westheimer Rd. | 713/529–6959 | No lunch Sat. | $12–$18 | AE, D, DC, MC, V.

**Shanghai River.** Chinese. One of Houston's sleepers, Shanghai River serves up delicious, carefully prepared Chinese favorites in elegant surroundings. Don't miss the vegetable dumplings and the spicy jalapeño jumbo shrimp. | 2407 Westheimer Rd. | 713/528–5528 | $8–$24 | AE, DC, MC, V.

**Sierra.** Southwestern. Reminiscent of Taos, New Mexico, the dining room and the menu combine influences from southwest and Native American cuisine with Texas twists. Interesting and tasty starters such as blue-cornmeal oysters, bisque of sweet corn, and smoke-

HOUSTON

INTRO
ATTRACTIONS
DINING
LODGING

roasted salmon will have you wishing for more. Touted for wondrous seafood, the kitchen also turns outs noteworthy meats such as pork chops with jalapeño mint and grilled chicken with goat cheese and chipotle sauce. | 4704 Montrose Blvd. | 713/942–7757 | Reservations essential | No lunch | $14–$40 | AE, D, DC, MC, V.

**Tony Mandola's Blue Oyster Bar.** Seafood. A Texan Italian seafood restaurant is not as strange a concept as you might think. And one look at the menu with delectables such as blackened snapper with lump crabmeat and stick-to-your-ribs roast beef po' boys and this bustling, festive restaurant will make you wonder why no one ever thought of it before. Kids' menu. | 7947 Katy Fwy. | 713/680–3333 | No lunch Sat. | $8–$25 | AE, DC, MC, V.

**Tony Mandola's Gulf Coast Kitchen.** Seafood. This more upscale sister restaurant to Tony Mandola's Blue Oyster Bar proves that the concept of a Texas Italian seafood restaurant is here to stay with loads of tastebud-popping menu choices. Open-air dining. Kids' menu. | 1962 W. Gray St. | 713/528–3474 | No lunch Sun. | $14–$26 | AE, DC, MC, V.

## EXPENSIVE

**Americas.** Latin. Dramatic South American rain forest decor may make you think you're in Peru while you dine on gulf snapper, roasted pork tenderloin, and, of course, plantains. Kids' menu. | 1800 S. Post Oak Blvd. | 713/961–1492 | Closed Sun. No lunch Sat. | $22–$65 | AE, D, DC, MC, V.

**Anthony's.** Continental. One of Houston's top restaurants, Anthony's is a creation of well-known restaurateur Tony Vallone, who also works his magic at Tony's. With the menu changing daily, every visit can be a new experience, from snapper stuffed with shrimp to ravioli of duck to warm chocolate midnight cake. | 4007 Westheimer Rd. | 713/961–0552 | Closed Sun., no lunch on Sat., reservations recommended on Sat. | $24–$38 | AE, D, DC, MC, V.

**Baroque.** Continental. One of Houston's most romantic restaurants is decked out in old-fashioned frills from the fresh roses to the lacy linen to the crystal chandeliers. Try the pecan-encrusted swordfish or the beef tenderloin in brandy peppercorn sauce. | 1700 Sunset Blvd. | 713/523–8881 | No lunch weekends | $20–$38 | AE, MC, V.

**benjy's in the village.** Contemporary. You can easily pretend you're in New York in this sleek, modern loft space, but once you take a bite you'll be transported to the West Coast with California fusion dishes such as black and white sesame ahi tuna and wild mushroom enchiladas. | 2424 Dunstan | 713/522–7602 | Closed Mon. No lunch on Sat. | $18–$34 | AE, DC, MC, V.

**Bistro Lancaster.** American. Breakfast and lunch can be had at this small restaurant in the Lancaster Hotel downtown, but dinner is the ticket at this classy spot, especially for the pre-theater crowd. Try the crab cakes and bread pudding. | 701 Texas Ave. | 713/228–9502 | Reservations accepted | $18–$29 | AE, D, MC, V.

★ **Cafe Annie.** Southwestern. Even after winning slews of awards and being subjected to much hype over the years, Cafe Annie is still one Houston's most popular restaurants. And why not? Its elegant decor and fresh innovative dishes such as the coffee-roasted filet, gulf crab meat tostada, and mussel soup continue to be a winning combination. | 1728 Post Oak Blvd. | 713/840–1111 | Jacket required | Closed Sun. No lunch Sat. | $19–$35 | AE, D, DC, MC, V.

**Chez Nous.** French. If you're willing to leave town, you will be duly rewarded at this cozy French country inn with such classic Gallic goodies as foie gras with caramelized apples and berries, garlicky escargot, and hearty steak in wine sauce. | 217 S. Ave. G, Humble | 281/446–6717 | Closed Sun. No lunch | $16–$30 | AE, DC, MC, V.

**Churrascos.** South American. The house is always packed at these South American hotspots (Churrascos and America's (above) have the same ownership). Amid the beams and stucco walls, you will feel like guests in the dining room of a busy hacienda. If service is sometimes sketchy, gratis plantain chips and tender entrées are well-nigh perfect. Surrender to the Churrascos practiced Latin way with its signature dish—tenderloin sautéed with lime, roasted peppers, and scallions. | 2055 Westheimer Rd. | 713/527–8300 | 9705 Westheimer Rd. | 713/952–1988 | Closed Sun. No lunch Sat. | $14–$25 | AE, D, DC, MC, V.

**Clive's.** Eclectic. A standing favorite of theater-goers who appreciate the friendly, efficient service, this clubby haunt allows you to explore your inner chef. Choose your meat—from beef tenderloin, to rack of lamb, to Gulf snapper—and select a sauce such as wild mushroom, rosemary garlic, or béarnaise. Your entrée is cooked to your liking: chargrilled, pan-seared, or oven-roasted. | 517 Louisiana St. | 713/224–4438 | Closed Sun. No lunch Sat. | $18–$34 | AE, DC, MC, V.

**Confederate House.** Southern. Once the province of blue-hairs and old-timers, this Houston institution has a new chef and a more laid-back atmosphere. It still has a formal air of gentility cultivated in the finest of Southern homes, but jackets are no longer required and the menu has been updated to include more modern ingredients, although the signature Confederate country-fried steak can't be beat. | 2925 Weslayan St. | 713/622–1936 | Closed Sun. No lunch Sat. | $15–$25 | AE, D, DC, MC, V.

**River Oaks Grill.** Steak, seafood. It's just a neighborhood restaurant, but the neighborhood happens to be the well-to-do River Oaks. The paneled dining room with brass accents and a piano bar has a clubby feel and so does the menu. To begin, try the velvety lobster bisque, oysters Rockefeller, or lump crab meat. And then move on to filet of beef stuffed with Roquefort or rack of pork loin with mustard sauce. Or if you prefer something lighter, there's veal piccata with capers and a roasted vegetable napoleon with mozzarella. | 2630 Westheimer Rd. | 713/520–1738 | Reservations essential weekends | Closed Sun. No lunch | $19–$35 | AE, D, DC, MC, V.

**Rotisserie for Beef and Bird.** Continental. The chef-owner Joe Mannke keeps the home fires lit at this elegant and welcoming colonial-style restaurant. Expectations are quickly raised with gratis salmon pâté and unusually good rolls, then sustained by entrées of wild game, prime beef, and fresh seafood. Treat yourself to one of the special dinners, such as the annual fall Harvest Dinner featuring the "agricultural bounty of the Lone Star State" from wines to produce, to fish and game. | 2200 Wilcrest Dr. | 713/977–9524 | Reservations essential | Closed Sun. No lunch Sat. | $24–$28 | AE, D, DC, MC, V.

**Taste of Texas.** Steak. With Texana to the max, this expansive place is as much about pride as prime beef. The entry looks like a sprawling ranch house and the lobby evokes longings for evenings on the front porch, complete with rockers. So relax, you will wait a while for your table. Famous for its steaks, the kitchen also offers chicken, lobster, and shrimp grilled "just the way you like it"—guaranteed. | 10505 Katy Fwy. | 713/932–6901 | Reservations not accepted | No lunch weekends | $12–$32 | AE, D, DC, MC, V.

## VERY EXPENSIVE

**Brennan's.** Cajun/Creole. This New Orleans–imported institution's longevity (founded 1967) attests to its quality. The elegant setting with a lovely courtyard and gracious service are equally fine for a romantic dinner or special occasion. Visit the classics like the 3-3-3 soups—gumbo, turtle, and mushroom soups served in three small bowls. Crawfish enchiladas, warm spinach salad, and peppercorn-crusted steak with generous sides are all dependably delicious. Sun. brunch. | 3300 Smith St. | 713/522–9711 | Reservations accepted | Jacket required | $24–$34 | AE, D, DC, MC, V.

**Brownstone.** Continental. With its dramatic rooms stuffed to the gills with antiques, the Brownstone takes you back to a time when a more ornate aesthetic reigned. In keeping with the rich decor, the menu offers satisfying, old-fashioned delights such as crab cakes topped with lemon beurre-blanc, individual beef Wellingtons, and crème brûlée. | 2736 Virginia St. | 713/520–5666 | Closed Sun. | $24–$29 | AE, D, DC, MC, V.

**DeVille.** Contemporary. From maître d' to server, attention to your enjoyment is given unobtrusively in this hushed, but friendly, dining room located in the Four Seasons. The upscale atmosphere is perfect for an important business lunch, a special family occasion, or when you simply want to have a conversation (without shouting) during a meal. Smoked yellow pepper gazpacho with salmon ceviche is a good way to start the meal. Pan-seared Chilean sea bass shows off the exceptional skills of the chef and the desserts can be memorable.

Kids' menu. Sun. brunch. | 1300 Lamar St. | 713/652–6250 | Breakfast also available Mon.–Sun. No lunch Sat. No dinner Sun. | $25–$35 | AE, D, DC, MC, V.

**La Colombe D'Or.** French. This charming, sophisticated restaurant occupies the first floor of a turn-of-the-20th-century mansion whose upper floors have been converted into a small luxury hotel by longtime owner Steve Zimmerman. Forget about budgets and calories and succumb to classic preparations of lobster, lamb, prime cuts of beef, and vegetables. Expect the elaborate desserts to be—what else?—rich. | 3410 Montrose | 713/524–7999 | Reservations essential | No lunch weekends | $25–$35 | AE, DC, MC, V.

**La Reserve.** Continental. The definition of fine dining, this restaurant in the Omni Hotel covers all the bases–elegant atmosphere, well-trained staff, lovingly presented dishes, and high price tag. The menu changes daily, but some favorites include charred citrus-pepper tuna, grilled double lamb chops, and porcini-crusted monkfish. | 4 Riverway | 713/871–8181 | Jacket required (dinner) | Closed Sun. and Mon. No lunch | $25–$35 | AE, D, DC, MC, V.

**La Tour D'Argent.** French. This artfully rustic log cabin, overlooking White Oak Bayou, is now a series of intimate dining rooms, making this one of the most romantic dining spots in town. But the raves don't stop at the setting: La Tour d'Argent was recently named one of Houston's top 20 restaurants by *Gourmet* magazine. | 2011 Ella Blvd. | 713/864–9864 | Reservations essential weekends | Jacket required (dinner) | Closed Sun. | $16–$37 | AE, D, DC, MC, V.

**Maxim's.** Continental. Picture a grand special-occasion/expense-account dining room, and you've captured this Houston landmark, owned and personally managed for 50 years by the Bermann family. Bending only slightly to trends, Maxim's continues to please its pampered regulars with oysters Rockefeller and Mornay, generous Gulf shrimp cocktails, and grilled or sautéed trout and snapper, often daubed with a butter or cream sauce. | 3755 Richmond Ave. | 713/877–8899 | Jacket required | Closed Sun. No lunch Sat. | $20–$46 | AE, D, DC, MC, V.

**Morton's of Chicago.** Steak. This national chain is a popular choice for Houstonians who come here for the excellent steaks, extensive wine list, and attentive service. The presentation carts piled with raw cuts of meat and fish add an earthy touch to the clubby brass and mahogany decor. | 5000 Westheimer Rd. | 713/629–1946 | No lunch | $25–$46 | AE, DC, MC, V.

**Pappas Bros Steakhouse.** Steak. "Prime" is the operative word at this popular steakhouse—prime beef, a prime setting, and a clientele primed for coddling, conversation, and cholesterol. The Steakhouse, poshest of the Pappas restaurant dynasty, gains a clubby look from dark wood, cushy booths, and phones at the tables. Thumbs up to a tomato-and-mozzarella salad (big enough to share) and to fork-tender New York strip steak with peppercorn sauce. Creamy mashed potatoes and giant fried onion rings provide delicious accompaniments to filets. Expect a wait, even with reservations. | 5839 Westheimer Rd. | 713/780–7352 | Jacket preferred | Reservations essential | Closed Sun. No lunch | $25–$75 | AE, D, MC, V.

**Rivoli.** Continental. A good bet for expense-account dining, this old Houston standby reliably serves simple chops, seafood, and dietbusting dessert soufflés. On most nights, you can dine to the tinkling of the piano. | 5636 Richmond Ave. | 713/789–1900 | Jacket required | Closed Sun. No lunch Sat. | $32–$44 | AE, D, DC, MC, V.

**Ruth's Chris Steak House.** Steak. This New Orleans remoulades–orginating chain combines luxurious steaks and traditional side dishes along with creole favorites such as gumbo and shrimp remoulade. | 6213 Richmond Ave. | 713/789–2333 | No lunch | $28–$39 | AE, D, DC, MC, V.

★ **Tony's.** Continental. Houston's toniest spot, Tony's is refined and priced to the sky, but not stuffy. Servers and diners alike seem to enjoy themselves. From the plush setting to the complimentary treats (pâté to start; cookies and chocolates to end), you'll feel privileged indeed. Velvety lobster bisque and the Ashley salad of spinach, pears, Gorgonzola, and blueberries are favorite starters. For entrées, consider these inspirations: halibut bouillabaisse with mushrooms, asparagus, and crab; pan-seared snapper with lobster medallions; and cheese-filled caramelli pasta in truffle sauce. | 1801 Post Oak Blvd. | 713/622–6778 | Closed Sun. No lunch | $25–$45 | AE, D, DC, MC, V.

## When it Comes to Getting Cash at an ATM, Same Thing.

**Whether you're in Yosemite or Yemen, using your Visa® card or ATM card with the PLUS symbol is the easiest and most convenient way to get cash.** Even if your bank is in Minneapolis and you're in Miami, Visa/PLUS ATMs make getting cash so easy, you'll feel right at home. After all, Visa/PLUS ATMs are open 24 hours a day, 7 days a week, rain or shine. And if you need help finding one of Visa's 627,000 ATMs in 127 countries worldwide, visit **visa.com/pd/atm**. We'll make finding an ATM as easy as finding the Eiffel Tower, the Pyramids or even the Grand Canyon.

It's Everywhere You Want To Be.®

# Find America *with a Compass*

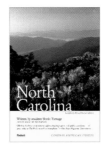
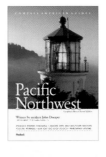

Written by local authors and illustrated throughout with images from regional photographers, Compass American Guides reveal the character and culture of America's most spectacular destinations. Covering more than 35 states and regions across the country, Compass guides are perfect for residents who want to explore their own backyards, and for visitors seeking an insider's perspective on all there is to see and do.

**Fodor's** Compass American Guides

*At bookstores everywhere.*

**Vargo's International Cuisine.** Continental. Old-fashioned romance is the name of the game at this lovely restaurant that sits on 8 acres of gardens, which includes a private lake with swans, ducks, and peacocks. The standard fare—mostly steaks and lobster—gets ho-hum marks—but food is not the reason you're coming here anyway. Sun. brunch. | 2401 Fondren Rd. | 713/782–3888 | Jacket preferred | Closed Mon., no lunch Sat., no dinner Sun. | $22–$42 | AE, D, DC, MC, V.

## Lodging

### INEXPENSIVE

**Allen Park Inn.** The Allen Park Inn is a motel near downtown Houston and the museum and theater districts. Restaurant, bar, in-room data ports, some microwaves, room service, cable TV, pool, barbershop, beauty salon, exercise equipment, laundry facilities, business services. | 2121 Allen Pkwy. | 713/521–9321 or 800/231–6310 | fax 713/521–9321 | 249 rooms | $79–$89 | AE, D, DC, MC, V.

**Angel Arbor Bed and Breakfast.** This stately, Gregorian-style residence was built in 1923. The house boasts an antique-filled parlor, reading room, and a formal dining room. Rooms are frilly and luxurious, with four-poster or canopied beds and gilt-framed 18th- and 19th-century-style paintings. Complimentary breakfast, cable TV, in-room VCR, some in-room hot tubs, no pets, no kids, no smoking. | 848 Heights Blvd. | 713/868–4654 or 800/722–8788 | fax 713/861–3189 | www.angelarbor.com | 5 rooms | $95–$125 | AE, D, DC, MC, V.

**Best Western NASA–Space Center.** This chain hotel is near NASA and the Johnson Space Center, Baybrook Mall, and Clear Lake Area Marinas. Complimentary Continental breakfast, microwaves, refrigerators, cable TV, pool, business services. | 889 W. Bay Area Blvd., Webster | 281/338–6000 | fax 281/338–2834 | www.bestwestern.com | 80 rooms | $54–$59 | AE, D, DC, MC, V.

**Courtyard by Marriott.** This Marriott is 5 mi from the the Galleria and 3 mi from Memorial Park. Restaurant, bar, complimentary Continental breakfast, in-room data ports, some refrigerators, cable TV, pool, hot tub, exercise equipment, laundry facilities, business services, valet parking, free parking. | 2504 North Loop W | 713/688–7711 | fax 713/688–3561 | $59–$105 | www.courtyard.com | 191 rooms | AE, D, DC, MC, V.

**Days Inn West.** This two-story motel is near Bush Intercontinental Airport and Hobby Airport. Many restaurants and shops are within 1 mile. There is a tennis facility and fitness center less that 5 mi away. Restaurant, complimentary Continental breakfast, in-room data ports, some refrigerators, some microwaves, some in-room hot tubs, cable TV, pool, business services, pets allowed (fee). | 9535 Katy Fwy | 713/467–4411 | fax 713/467–3647 | www.daysinn.com | 160 rooms, 4 suites | $39–$54, $99 suites | AE, D, DC, MC, V.

**Doubletree at Allen Center.** This hotel is right in the middle of downtown and is within walking distance of the Theater District, Bayou Place, Enron Field, and the George R. Brown Convention Center. Guest rooms offer views of the Sam Houston Park and Memorial Park greenbelt, the downtown skyline, or the Allen Center Courtyard. Restaurants, bar (with entertainment), in-room data ports, cable TV, exercise equipment, business services, some pets allowed. | 400 Dallas St. | 713/759–0202 | fax 713/752–2734 | www.doubletree.com | 341 rooms | $89–$215 | AE, D, DC, MC, V.

**Doubletree–Post Oak.** This Doubletree is in the heart of Houston's uptown business district, 2 mi from the Galleria and within 7 mi of downtown. Restaurant, bar, in-room data ports, some refrigerators, room service, cable TV, pool, barbershop, beauty salon, exercise equipment, business services. | 2001 Post Oak Blvd. | 713/961–9300 | fax 713/623–6685 | www.doubletree.com | 449 rooms | $72–$240 | AE, D, DC, MC, V.

**Drury Inn and Suites–Houston West.** Located throughout mid-America, this motel chain is into free stuff. Look for free breakfast, free evening beverages and snacks, free HBO, and free local calls. This motel is far from downtown (12 mi) but convenient to the Energy Corridor. Complimentary Continental breakfast, in-room data ports, some microwaves, cable TV, indoor pool, hot tub, pets allowed, free parking. | 1000 Rte. 6N | 281/558–7007 | fax 281/558–7007 | www.drury-inn.com | 120 rooms | $59–$89 | AE, D, DC, MC, V.

**Drury Inn and Suites–Near the Galleria.** Adjacent to the Galleria, this Drury is 6 mi from downtown and 8 mi from the Medical Center. Complimentary Continental breakfast, in-room data ports, some microwaves, cable TV, pool, hot tub, business services, pets allowed, free parking. | 1615 W. Loop 610S | 713/963–0700 | fax 713/963–0700 | www.drury-inn.com | 134 rooms | $87–$107 | AE, D, DC, MC, V.

**Embassy Suites.** Suites include living rooms with a foldout sofa, kitchenettes, and private bedrooms. This hotel is 1 mi from Southwest Memorial Hospital and 1.5 mi from the Sharpstown Mall. Complimentary breakfast, in-room data ports, microwaves, refrigerators, cable TV, indoor pool, hot tub, exercise equipment, business services. | 9090 Southwest Fwy. | 713/995–0123 | fax 713/779–0703 | www.embassysuites.com | 243 suites | $119 | AE, D, DC, MC, V.

**Fairfield Inn by Marriott.** This motel is 8 mi from downtown. Bar, picnic area, complimentary Continental breakfast, in-room data ports, cable TV, pool, wading pool, laundry facilities, business services, valet parking, free parking. | 10155 I–10E | 713/675–2711 | fax 713/674–6853 | www.marriott.com | 160 rooms | $55–$70 | AE, D, DC, MC, V.

**Fairfield Inn by Marriott at the Galleria.** Mere feet from the Galleria, this Fairfield Inn is 6 mi from the Medical Center and 6 mi from downtown. Bar; complimentary Continental breakfast, in-room data ports, room service, cable TV, pool, wading pool, hot tub, exercise equipment, laundry facilities, business services, pets allowed. | 3131 West Loop S | 713/961–1690 | fax 713/627–8434 | 107 rooms | $59–$84 | AE, D, DC, MC, V.

**Hampton Inn–Bush Intercontinental Airport.** This property is 5 mi from the airport with easy access to I–45, I–59, and the Hardy Toll Road. The area immediate to the hotel is known as Greenspoint with a mall and a number of family and fast-food restaurants. Complimentary Continental breakfast, cable TV, pool, hot tub, exercise equipment, laundry facilities, business services, airport shuttle. | 502 N. Sam Houston | 281/820–2101 | fax 281/820–9652 | www.hamptoninn.com | 157 rooms | $69–$77 | AE, D, DC, MC, V.

**Hampton Inn–I–10 East.** On the east side of the loop, this Hampton Inn is convenient to Jacinto City, Channelview, and the Port of Houston and is 8 mi from downtown. Complimentary Continental breakfast, in-room data ports, some refrigerators, cable TV, pool, laundry facilities, business services, valet parking, free parking, pets allowed. | 828 Mercury Dr. | 713/673–4200 | fax 713/674–6913 | www.hamptoninn.com | 90 rooms | $69–$77 | AE, D, DC, MC, V.

**Hampton Inn–I–10 West.** Located on the West side of Houston towards San Antonio, this Hampton Inn is within 2 mi of the Energy Corridor and 14 mi from downtown. Complimentary Continental breakfast, in-room data ports, cable TV, pool, exercise equipment, business services. | 11333 Katy Fwy. | 713/935–0022 | fax 713/935–0989 | www.hamptoninn.com | 120 rooms | $73–$77 | AE, D, DC, MC, V.

**Hilton Nassau Bay & Marina.** On the shores of Clear Lake, guests can enjoy a number of water sports and easy access to NASA, which is across the street. Restaurant, bar, in-room data ports, cable TV, pool, beauty salon, hot tub, exercise equipment, watersports, boating, business services. | 3000 NASA Rd. 1 | 281/333–9300 | fax 281/333–3750 | www.hilton.com | 243 rooms | $79–$144 | AE, D, DC, MC, V.

**Hilton–Westchase.** In the Westchase 1,300-acre office and shopping development in the heart of suburban West Houston, this hotel is just a few miles from the Energy Corridor and 20 mi from downtown. Restaurant, bar, minibars, room service, cable TV, pool, barbershop, beauty salon, hot tub, exercise equipment, business services. | 9999 Westheimer Rd. | 713/974–1000 | fax 713/974–2108 | www.hilton.com | 300 rooms | $69–$169 | AE, D, DC, MC, V.

**Holiday Inn–Astrodome.** In southwest Houston, this Holiday Inn is next to the Astrodome, 3 mi from the Medical Center, and 8 mi from downtown. Restaurant, bar, in-room data ports, refrigerators, room service, cable TV, pool, hot tub, exercise equipment, business services, valet parking, free parking. | 8111 Kirby Dr. | 713/790–1900 | fax 713/799–8574 | www.holiday-inn.com | 235 rooms | $79–$185 | AE, D, DC, MC, V.

**Holiday Inn Hotel and Suites.** In the Medical Center, this property is 2 mi from the Astrodome and 3 mi from downtown. Restaurant, bar, in-room data ports, many kitchenettes, room service, cable TV, pool, beauty salon, exercise equipment, game room, laundry facilities, business services, valet parking, free parking. | 6800 South Main St. | 713/528–7744 | fax 713/528–6983 | www.holiday-inn.com | 285 rooms, 134 suites | $79–$130 | AE, D, DC, MC, V.

**Holiday Inn–International Airport.** This Holiday Inn is 1 mi south of the International Airport and 18 mi from downtown. Restaurant, bar, in-room data ports, some microwaves, room service, cable TV, pool, wading pool, tennis, exercise equipment, laundry facilities, business services, airport shuttle, valet parking, free parking, pets allowed (fee). | 15222 J.F.K. Blvd. | 281/449–2311 | fax 281/449–6726 | www.holiday-inn.com | 402 rooms | $79–$149 | AE, D, DC, MC, V.

**Holiday Inn Select–I-10 West.** Holiday Inn Selects are a cut above the typical roadside motels. This one is located on the west side of town and is convenient to the Energy Corridor and is 17 mi from downtown. Restaurant, bar, in-room data ports, room service, cable TV, indoor pool, hot tub, exercise equipment, business services. | 14703 Park Row | 281/558–5580 | fax 281/496–4150 | www.holiday-inn.com | 349 rooms | $59–$139 | AE, D, DC, MC, V.

**Hotel Sofitel.** This French-style hotel near the Greenspoint Mall and Bush Intercontinental Airport is cheerfully decorated with pastels and murals. Restaurant, bar (with entertainment), in-room data ports, room service, cable TV, pool, massage, exercise equipment, business services, airport shuttle. | 425 Sam Houston Pkwy. E | 281/445–9000 | fax 281/445–9826 | 334 rooms | $79–$179 | AE, DC, MC, V.

**Hyatt Regency–Houston Airport.** Set in a wooded complex known as the World Houston Business Development, this hotel is 1 mi from Houston's Bush Intercontinental Airport. Restaurant, bar, in-room data ports, cable TV, pool, hot tub, exercise equipment, business services, airport shuttle, pets allowed (fee). | 15747 J.F.K. Blvd. | 281/987–1234 | fax 281/590–8461 | www.hyatt.com | 314 rooms | $69–$195 | AE, D, DC, MC, V.

**La Quinta–Greenway Plaza.** Greenway Plaza's La Quinta is close to the Compaq Center and the Galleria. Complimentary Continental breakfast, cable TV, pool, laundry facilities, some pets allowed. | 4015 Southwest Fwy. | 713/623–4750 | fax 713/963–0599 | www.laquinta.com | 131 rooms | $75–$95 | AE, D, DC, MC, V.

**La Quinta–Wilcrest.** This La Quinta is in western Houston and is within 5 mi of the Energy Corridor and 17 mi from downtown. Complimentary Continental breakfast, in-room data ports, cable TV, pool, laundry facilities, pets allowed. | 11113 Katy Fwy. | 713/932–0808 | fax 713/973–2352 | www.laquinta.com | 176 rooms | $55–$65 | AE, D, DC, MC, V.

**Lovett Inn.** Once the home of Houston mayor and Federal Court Judge Joseph C. Hutcheson, this historic home is in the heart of the Montrose-Museum District. Each room has a distinct aesthetic quality: Room 5 is flowery and romantic, while Room 10 is Art Deco and modern. Most of the rooms overlook the inn's finely landscaped grounds and pool. Complimentary Continental breakfast, some refrigerators, some microwaves, some in-room hot tubs, cable TV, pool, spa, some pets, no smoking. | 501 Lovett Blvd. | 713/522–5224 or 800/779–5224 | fax 713/528–6708 | www.lovettinn.com | 4 rooms, 2 suites, 2 cottages | $75–$85, $115–$150 suites/cottages | AE, D, DC, MC, V.

**Marriott Airport.** The hotel is on the grounds of Bush Intercontinental Airport and offers complimentary underground train service to the airport. Restaurant, bar, in-room data ports, refrigerators, cable TV, pool, exercise equipment, business services. | 18700 J.F.K. Blvd. | 281/443–2310 | fax 281/443–5294 | www.marriott.com | 566 rooms | $79–$169 | AE, D, DC, MC, V.

**Marriott North at Greenspoint.** This Marriott, in northwest Houston, is adjacent to the Greenspoint Mall and is 15 minutes from Bush Intercontinental Airport. Restaurant, bar, in-room data ports, refrigerators, cable TV, pool, hot tub, exercise equipment, laundry facilities, business services, airport shuttle. | 255 N. Sam Houston Pkwy. E | 281/875–4000 | fax 281/875–6208 | www.marriott.com | 391 rooms | $75–$179 | AE, D, DC, MC, V.

**Marriott–Westside.** This property is convenient to the Energy Corridor and is within 3 mi of the Memorial City and Town & Country malls. Restaurant, bar (with entertainment), in-room data ports, cable TV, pool, hot tub, tennis, exercise equipment, business services, pets allowed (fee). | 13210 Katy Fwy. | 281/558–8338 | fax 281/558–4028 | www.marriott.com | 400 rooms | $75–$169 | AE, D, DC, MC, V.

**Patrician Bed and Breakfast Inn.** This B&B is housed in a three-story, Colonial-style mansion in the heart of Houston's Museum District. Enjoy your breakfast in the large dining room or solarium. All of the rooms are uniquely decorated according to different themes: the Ivy Room, for example, is covered with ivy, from wallpaper to bedspread; the Kathleen Room is flowered, with oak furniture and Tiffany lamps. Complimentary breakfast, cable TV, in-room VCR's, no pets, no kids, no smoking. | 1200 Southmore Blvd. | 713/523–1114 or 800/553–5797 | fax 713/523–0790 | www.texasbnb.com | 4 rooms | $95–$130 | AE, D, DC, MC, V.

**Radisson Hotel and Conference Center.** Only 1 mi from Hobby Airport, this 10-story atrium hotel has one of the largest conference facilities in South Houston. Complimentary transportation is available for the Almeda Mall and a golf course, both 3 mi away. Restaurant, bar (with entertainment), in-room data ports, cable TV, indoor pool, hot tub, exercise equipment, business services, airport shuttle, some pets allowed. | 9100 Gulf Fwy. | 713/943–7979 | fax 713/943–2160 | www.radisson.com | 288 rooms | $119–$129 | AE, D, DC, MC, V.

**Ramada Limited International Airport South.** This Ramada is near the Greenspoint Mall and Bush Intercontinental Airport and is 6 mi from the Sam Houston Race Track. Complimentary Continental breakfast, cable TV, pool, hot tub, exercise equipment, business services, airport shuttle. | 15350 J.F.K. Blvd. | 281/442–1830 | fax 281/987–8023 | www.ramada.com | 126 rooms | $58–$65 | AE, D, DC, MC, V.

**Red Lion.** Owned by Hilton, Red Lion hotels are mostly found in the western United States. This outpost is adjacent to the Galleria and 8 mi from downtown. Restaurant, bar, in-room data ports, cable TV, pool, hot tub, exercise equipment, business services, pets allowed (fee), airport shuttle. | 2525 West Loop S | 713/961–3000 | fax 713/961–1490 | www.redlion.com | 319 rooms | $89–$140 | AE, D, DC, MC, V.

**Red Roof Inn.** In western Houston, this motel is 20 mi from downtown and 15 mi from the Galleria. In-room data ports, cable TV, business services, pets allowed. | 15701 Park Ten Pl. | 281/579–7200 | fax 281/579–0732 | 123 rooms | $32–$50 | AE, D, DC, MC, V.

**Residence Inn by Marriott–Astrodome.** Designed for people on longer stays, this motel is close to the Medical Center and 1.5 mi from the Astrodome. Bar, picnic area, complimentary Continental breakfast, in-room data ports, kitchenettes, cable TV, pool, hot tub, business services, valet parking, free parking, pets allowed (fee). | 7710 S. Main St. | 713/660–7993 | fax 713/660–8019 | 285 suites | $89–$199 suites | AE, D, DC, MC, V.

**Residence Inn by Marriott–Clear Lake.** With larger than average rooms, the Residence Inn chain is designed for longer-staying guests. This motel is located 2 mi from Clear Lake and 3 mi from the Space Center. Complimentary Continental breakfast, in-room data ports, kitchenettes, microwaves, cable TV, pool, exercise equipment, laundry facilities, business services, pets allowed (fee). | 525 Bay Area Blvd. | 281/486–2424 | fax 281/488–8179 | 110 rooms | $124–$145 | AE, D, DC, MC, V.

**Robin's Nest Bed and Breakfast.** This 1898 Victorian home is one-and-a-half miles south of downtown Houston. Most of the artwork and the furnishings in the house come from the various foreign countries that owner Robin Smith visited during her work with the U.S. Foreign Service. Antiques and hardwood floors decorate the rooms. Complimentary breakfast, cable TV, library, some pets, no smoking. | 4104 Greeley St. | 713/528–5821 | fax 713/521–2154 | www.therobin.com | 4 rooms | $110–$120 | AE, D, MC, V.

**Sara's Bed and Breakfast.** This Queen Anne mansion, complete with wraparound porch and rocking chairs, is in the historic Heights neighborhood and is 4 mi from downtown. Each room has its own theme and is decked out with antiques and floral-patterned linens. Complimentary Continental breakfast, no smoking, cable TV, in-room VCRs (movies), business services. | 941 Heights Blvd. | 713/868–1130 or 800/593–1130 | fax 713/868–3284 | www.saras.com | 13 rooms (2 with shared bath) | $70–$150 | AE, D, DC, MC, V.

**Sheraton Houston Brookhollow.** In northwest Houston, this Sheraton is within 25 mi of both Bush Intercontinental and Hobby Airports. Restaurant, bar, in-room data ports, room service, cable TV, pool, hot tub, exercise equipment, some pets allowed. | 3000 North Loop W | 713/688–0100 or 800/688–3000 | fax 713/688–9224 | www.sheraton.com | 382 rooms | $119–$139 | AE, D, DC, MC, V.

**Westin Oaks.** Rooms and suites at this 18-story hotel are oversized and elegantly decorated in cream and white. The hotel is within the Galleria in uptown Houston, near to many museums, shops, and the theater district. There is also an outdoor jogging track. 2 restaurants, bar, in-room data ports, cable TV, pool, exercise facility, laundry services, business services, pets allowed. | 5011 Westheimer | 713/960–8100 | fax 713/960–6554 | www.westin.com | 395 rooms, 11 suites | $99–$109, $205–$750 suites | AE, D, DC, MC, V.

## MODERATE

**Adam's Mark.** The showcase feature of this hotel, located in West Houston's Westchase business district, is the 10-story open-air lobby. The hive of rooms surrounding it are all efficient pods for the business traveler, but not unwelcoming. Restaurant, bars (with entertainment), some microwaves, room service, cable TV, indoor-outdoor pool, wading pool, hot tub, exercise equipment, free valet parking, business services. | 2900 Briar Park | 713/978–7400 | fax 713/735–2727 | www.adamsmark.com | 604 rooms | $155–$225 | AE, D, DC, MC, V.

**Crowne Plaza–Galleria.** In the Galleria, this Crowne Plaza is 3 mi from the Compaq Center and 8 mi from downtown and the theater district. Restaurants, bar (with entertainment), in-room data ports, some refrigerators, cable TV, indoor pool, hot tub, exercise equipment, laundry facilities, business services. | 2222 West Loop S | 713/961–7272 | fax 713/961–3327 | www.crowneplaza.com | 477 rooms | $169 | AE, D, DC, MC, V.

**Doubletree Guest Suites.** This luxury, all-suites hotel is one block west of the Galleria and within 10 minutes of downtown. Restaurant, bar, in-room data ports, kitchenettes, refrigerators, room service, cable TV, pool, hot tub, exercise equipment, business services, laundry facilities, some pets allowed. | 5353 Westheimer Rd. | 713/961–9000 | fax 713/877–8835 | www.doubletree.com | 335 suites | $155–$165 suites | AE, D, DC, MC, V.

**Four Seasons Hotel–Houston Center.** With its skyline view, impressive lobby, and huge rooms, business travelers are made very comfortable in this luxury hotel situated in the middle of downtown. You can get a gourmet meal at the Deville restaurant located on the premises and can do a little window shopping (or more) across the street at The Park Shops Downtown mall. Restaurant, bar (with entertainment), in-room data ports, minibars, some microwaves, room service, cable TV, pool, beauty salon, hot tub, massage, gym, business services, valet parking, parking (fee), pets allowed. | 1300 Lamar St. | 713/650–1300 or 800/332–3442 | fax 713/276–3393 | www.fshr.com | 426 rooms | $155–$175, $195–$215 suites | AE, DC, MC, V.

**Hilton Houston Plaza.** Adjacent to Rice University, the Hilton Plaza is also close to the Medical Center, Houston Museum of Fine Art, and the Museum of Natural Science. Restaurant, bar (with entertainment), in-room data ports, refrigerators, room service, cable TV, pool, hot tub, gym, business services. | 6633 Travis St. | 713/313–4000 | www.hilton.com | fax 713/313–4660 | 181 rooms | $140–$160 | AE, D, DC, MC, V.

**Holiday Inn Select.** The Holiday Inn Selects are a cut above the regular roadside Holiday Inns, and this one is conveniently located in Greenway Plaza, 2 mi from downtown, 2 mi from the Medical Center, and 5 mi from the Astrodome. Restaurant, bar, in-room data ports, refrigerators (in suites), cable TV, pool, hot tub, exercise equipment, laundry facilities, business services. | 2712 Southwest Fwy. | 713/523–8448 | fax 713/526–7948 | www.holiday-inn.com | 355 rooms, 36 suites | $159–$179, $190 suites | AE, D, DC, MC, V.

**J.W. Marriott–Houston.** This upscale business hotel is adjacent to the Galleria and 9 mi from downtown. Restaurant, bar, in-room data ports, refrigerators (in suites), cable TV, pool, barbershop, beauty salon, hot tub, exercise equipment, business services. | 5150 Westheimer Rd. | 713/961–1500 | fax 713/961–5045 | www.marriott.com | 508 rooms | $180–$229 | AE, D, DC, MC, V.

**Marriott–Medical Center.** This hotel is attached to the Texas Medical Center and is convenient to Hermann Park, the museum district, and Rice University. Restaurant, in-room data ports, microwaves, cable TV, indoor pool, hot tub, exercise equipment, laundry facilities, business services. | 6580 Fannin St. | 713/796–0080 | fax 713/770–8100 | www.marriott.com | 386 rooms | $159–$179 | AE, D, DC, MC, V.

**Omni Houston Hotel.** This upscale resort-style high-rise, located in the Post Oak/Galleria area, has a dramatic modern lobby and an especially large pool, as well as fountains and sculpture. Guest rooms have sitting areas, marble vanities and bathrooms, dark-wood furniture, and floor-to-ceiling windows. Restaurant, bar (with entertainment), in-room data ports, minibars, room service, cable TV, 2 pools, hot tub, massage, tennis, gym, business services. | 4 Riverway | 713/871–8181 or 800/843–6664 | fax 713/871–0719 | www.omnihotels.com | 381 rooms | $129–$389 | AE, D, DC, MC, V.

**Renaissance.** At first glance, this tower in an office complex may seem all business, but it's attached to Greenway Plaza shops, which include the Landmark Greenway Cinema. The rooms, all the way up to the top of the tower, are gracious and offer expansive views of the city. The Renaissance is close to the Compaq Center and the Galleria. Restaurant, bar, in-room data ports, some refrigerators, room service, cable TV, pool, exercise equipment, business services, valet parking, parking (fee), some pets allowed. | 6 Greenway Plaza E | 713/629–1200 | fax 713/629–4702 | www.renaissancehotels.com | 389 rooms | $144–$179 | AE, D, DC, MC, V.

**Sheraton Crown Hotel and Conference Center.** The Crown is close to the International Airport and shopping at the Greenspoint Mall. Restaurants, bars, some refrigerators, cable TV, 2 pools (1 indoor), hot tub, putting greens, exercise equipment, business services, airport shuttle. | 15700 J.F.K. Blvd. | 281/442–5100 | fax 281/987–9130 | 420 rooms | $144–$194 | AE, D, DC, MC, V.

**Warwick.** The 1929 Warwick has been through some major renovations since being celebrated on Lyle Lovett's first release. The older rooms, which were in danger of becoming dowdy, are now refitted, and the glorious marble lobby, lavish Sunday brunch, views of Hermann Park, and proximity to the Museum District and Rice University are unchanged. Restaurant, bar, in-room data ports, refrigerators, cable TV, pool, beauty salon, hot tub, exercise equipment, business services. | 5701 Main St. | 713/526–1991 | fax 713/639–4545 | 308 rooms, 46 suites | $139–$199 | AE, D, DC, MC, V.

**Woodlands Resort.** This lakefront lodge is on acres of manicured lawns, creating a quiet and lovely retreat with all the amenities anyone could ask for. The championship golf course is home to the Shell Houston Open. 3 restaurants, 2 bars, in-room data ports, microwaves, room service, cable TV, 2 pools, wading pool, beauty salon, hot tub, massage, 3 driving ranges, 36-hole golf course, 3 putting greens, tennis courts, gym, hiking, bicycles, game room with pool tables, business services, airport shuttle, valet parking, free parking. | 2301 N. Millbend St. | 281/367–1100 or 800/433–2624 (outside TX), 800/533–3052 (TX) | fax 281/364–6345 | www.weccr.com | 364 rooms | $99–$199 | AE, D, DC, MC, V.

**Wyndham Greenspoint.** In Modern Gothic architecture that rises 15 stories, the Wyndham Greenspoint is built around a 45-foot-high atrium lobby filled with landscaping and topped by glass skylights. This fine business hotel is adjacent to the Greenpoint Mall and close to Bush Intercontinental Airport. Restaurant, bar (with entertainment), in-room data ports, some refrigerators, cable TV, pool, exercise equipment, laundry facilities, business services, airport shuttle. | 12400 Greenspoint Dr. | 281/875–2222 | fax 281/875–1652 | www.wyndham.com | 472 rooms | $159–$259 | AE, D, DC, MC, V.

## EXPENSIVE

**Houstonian.** The expansive lobby has the clubby, wood-beam look of an expensive lodge. Other floors have well-appointed lounges and meeting rooms. The hotel's health club facilities have everything, including a rock-climbing wall. Although many formal exercise classes are offered, some may choose to simply stroll the 18 acres of wooded grounds. There is complimentary transportation to and from the Galleria. Restaurant, bar, in-room data ports, minibars, refrigerators, room service, cable TV, 3 pools, hot tub, massage, tennis court, gym, top-rated golf course, youth center with movie theatre, bistro, and TV area, children's programs (ages 3–16), business services, valet parking, free parking. | 111 N. Post Oak Ln. | 713/680–2626 or 800/231–2759 | fax 713/680–2992 | www.houstonian.com | 288 rooms | $249–$375 | AE, D, DC, MC, V.

**Hyatt Regency.** Located downtown, Houston's largest hotel with 66,000 square ft still manages a graceful air thanks to a recent renovation. Restaurant, bar, in-room data ports, refrigerators, cable TV, pool, beauty salon, exercise equipment, business services, airport shuttle. | 1200 Louisiana St. | 713/654–1234 | fax 713/951–0934 | www.hyatt.com | 963 rooms | $250–$350 | AE, D, DC, MC, V.

**La Colombe d'Or.** Originally the W. W. Fondren mansion, this exclusive, European-style hotel has lost some exterior charm to the addition of a banquet facility, but the rooms, lounge, and restaurant still draw the rich and famous (and discreet). Genuine antiques, usually dark woods with luxe brocades, do much to complete the Montrose hotel's successful attempt at old-world charm. The tiny, but warm, bar and a small library room are both perfect spots for a cozy drinks. Restaurant, bar, room service, cable TV, hot tub. | 3410 Montrose Blvd. | 713/524–7999 | fax 713/524–8923 | www.lacolombedorhouston.com | 6 suites | $195–$575 suites | AE, D, DC, MC, V.

**Lancaster.** The rooms are small and packed with exactly what it takes to make anyone feel pampered and secure. Overstuffed sofas and chairs, fat pillows, and thick curtains that effectively shut out both light and noise make a homey, yet elegant retreat. Although the downtown hotel is just steps from Jones Hall, the Alley Theatre, the Wortham Center, Bayou Place, and the Angelica cinema, you might elect to stay in. Town car transportation to downtown is available. Restaurant, bar, in-room data ports, minibars, refrigerators, room service, cable TV, in-room VCRs (movies), exercise equipment, business services. | 701 Texas Ave. | 713/228–9500 | fax 713/223–4528 | www.slh.com | 93 rooms | $250–$300 | AE, D, DC, MC, V.

**St. Regis.** Wealthy locals and well-heeled travelers enjoy the hotel's plush accommodations and thorough service (including butlers on some floors). Rooms have trademarked "Heavenly Beds" with duvet covers. Luxuries such as orchid plants come in each room, but thought goes into practicalities as well—such as written instructions for the CD/clock-radio. Located in River Oaks, the St. Regis is convenient to downtown and the Galleria area. Restaurants, bar (with entertainment), complimentary Continental breakfast, hot tubs (in suites), cable TV, pool, exercise equipment, business services. | 1919 Briar Oaks Ln. | 713/840–7600 or 800/241–3333 | fax 713/840–8036 | www.luxurycollections.com | 232 rooms | $295 | AE, D, DC, MC, V.

# HUNTSVILLE

MAP 8, J4

*(Nearby towns also listed: Bryan/College Station, Crockett)*

This East Texas community began as a trading post. Surrounded by tall forests, the city is a gateway to Sam Houston National Forest, named for Huntsville's most famous resident. The city is also home to the world's tallest statue of an American hero: a 77-foot remembrance of Sam Houston at the Sam Houston State University. Among Texans, Huntsville is best known as the home of the state prison system.

Information: **Huntsville Chamber of Commerce** | Box 538, Huntsville, TX 77342 | 409/295–8113 or 800/289–0389 | jcq@lcc.net | www.chamber.huntsville.tx.us.

## Attractions

**Huntsville State Park.** This park offers swimming, fishing, boating, paddleboats, and canoes. There are also hiking trails and areas for picnicking. | I–45, exit 109 at Rte 40 | 409/295–5644 | www.tpwd.state.tx.us | $3 | Daily.

**Oakwood Cemetery.** This cemetery is the burial site of Sam Houston and other famous Texans. You'll see the graves of Union and Confederate soldiers, pioneers, and some of Huntsville's first residents. The oldest marked burial site dates back to 1846. Walking tours can be arranged through the Chamber of Commerce office. | 9th St. at Ave. I | 936/295–8113 | Free | Daily.

**Sam Houston Memorial Museum Complex.** Artifacts from the Houston family, as well as two residences, are featured at this museum. There are also exhibits on the secession and annexation of Texas. The Woodland Home, Sam Houston's residence, was built by Sam Houston. The site has interpretive panels on the history of the home. Steamboat House is the home where Sam Houston died. | 1836 Sam Houston Ave. | 409/294–1832 | Free | Tues.–Sun. 9–4:30.

**Sam Houston National Forest.** This piney woods forest offers hiking trails and picnic sites 14 mi south of Huntsville. | Off I–45 at the New Waverly exit | 936/344–6205 or 713/592–6461 | Free | Daily.

**Sam Houston State University.** Founded in 1879, this university enrolls close to 12,000 students annually. Among its notable alumni is CBS news anchor Dan Rather. Walk through the campus's green lawns and trees to view the Old Main Memorial, commemorating the historic building which burned down in 1982, then see the Sam Houston Memorial Museum and Exhibit Hall. | 1803 Ave. I | 936/294–1111 | www.shsu.edu | Free | Daily.

**Texas Prison Museum.** Complete with a vintage electric chair, this historic prison exhibits a number of items. Prisoner-produced goods are also on display. | 1113 12th St. | 409/295–2155 | $2 | Tues.–Fri. 12–5, Sat. 9–5, Sun. 12–5.

### ON THE CALENDAR

**MAR.–APR.:** *Walker County Fair.* This fun-filled event includes a rodeo, livestock display, country-western dancing, and a barbecue cook-off. | 936/291–8763.

**APR.:** *General Sam Houston Folklife Festival.* A tribute to Sam Houston with people in historic dress, drama performances, dancing, live music, food, and folklore at the Sam Houston Memorial Museum Complex. | 409/294–1832 or 800/238–0389.

## Dining

**The Junction.** American. This 150-year-old plantation house was remodeled in 1976 as a restaurant. The attic is now an upstairs dining area where you can soak up the historic charm as you tuck into the prime rib, steak, chicken, catfish, or vegetable plate. Salad bar. Kids' menu. | 2641 11th St. | 936/291–2183 | $7–$16 | AE, D, DC, MC, V.

**Zach's Bar and Grill.** American/Casual. Sports memorabilia and beer advertisements cover the walls of this sports bar/grill. Try the catfish on Fri. or Zach's renowned juicy burgers anytime. | 1226 17th St. | 936/295–0938 | $3–$6 | AE, D, MC, V.

## Lodging

**Best Western Sam Houston Inn.** This quaint, two-story inn prides itself on providing a warm, small-town feel and attentive service. Most rooms have king-size beds. There are many shops and restaurants in the vicinity, as well as a cocktail lounge on the premises. Visit the Huntsville State Amusement Park or Sam Houston State University, both 2 mi away. Complimentary Continental breakfast, cable TV, pool, business services, pets allowed. | 613 I–45 | 936/295–9151 | fax 936/295–9151 | www.bestwestern.com | 72 rooms | $55 | AE, D, DC, MC, V.

**La Quinta.** This La Quinta is near the Westhills Mall, a movie theater, and plenty of restaurants. Complimentary Continental breakfast, some refrigerators, cable TV, pool, wading pool, pets allowed. | 124 I–45N | 409/295–6454 | fax 409/295–9245 | 120 rooms | $65–$75 | AE, D, DC, MC, V.

**Motel 6.** This economic motel is at the intersection of I–45 and U.S. 90, off Exit 116. Both the Sam Houston Memorial Park and the State University are 3 mi away; Huntsville State Park is 6 mi away. Cable TV, pool, laundry facilities, some pets. | 1607 I–45 | 936/291–6927 | fax 936/291–8963 | www.motel6.com | 122 rooms | $39 | AE, D, DC, MC, V.

**University Hotel.** This hotel is situated on the Sam Houston State University campus and is close to movies, shopping, and restaurants. Microwaves, no smoking, cable TV, some pets allowed. | 1610 Ave. H | 409/291–2151 | fax 409/294–1683 | 95 rooms | $37–$42 | AE, DC, MC, V.

# IRVING

MAP 8, I3

*(Nearby towns also listed: Arlington-Grand Prairie, Dallas, Fort Worth, Grapevine, Lewisville)*

Just 15 minutes from the Dallas–Fort Worth International Airport, Irving has become a corporate headquarters for many companies. The city of 160,000 residents is home to top corporations such as Exxon, GTE, and Sprint. Irving is also well known to American travelers as the home of the Dallas Cowboys football team, which is based at Texas Stadium.

Information: **Irving Convention and Visitors Bureau** | 3333 N. MacArthur Blvd., Ste. 200, Irving, TX 75062 | 972/252–7476 or 800/247–8464 | icvb@airmail.net | www.irving-texas.com.

## Attractions

**The Movie Studios of Las Colinas.** Kids or anyone interested in the entertainment industry will be star-struck by this place, about 25 minutes northwest of downtown Dallas. Tours include a visit to the soundstage facilities used in the filming of such movies as *JFK*, *Silkwood*, and *Robocop*. The tour also shows how the special effects studio creates many of the frightening scenes seen in familiar films. Movie memorabilia are also on display. Call for tour schedules. | 6301 N. O'Connor Rd. | 972/869–3456 | $12.95 | Daily at 12:30, 2:30, 4.

**Mustangs at Las Colinas.** One of most recognized statues in Texas, this is the largest equestrian sculpture in the world. The visitors center has displays on the creation of the sculpture which is located next to the West Tower of Williams Square. | Williams Sq. | 972/869–9047 | Free | Tues.–Sat. 10–6 (exhibit).

**Texas Stadium.** Tours of the home of the NFL Dallas Cowboys take you behind the scenes to the press box, dressing rooms, and Stadium Club. | 2401 E. Airport Fwy. | 972/554–1804 | www.dallascowboys.com | $5 | Mon.–Sat. 10–3.

**ON THE CALENDAR**
**JUNE:** *Heritage Festival.* This festival includes a street dance, home tours, and food booths. | 972/252–3838.
**JULY:** *July 4th Celebration.* A concert by the Irving Symphony, followed by a fireworks display, is held in Williams Sq. on the evening of July 4th. | 972/252–7476.

## Dining

**Bruno's Italian Restaurant.** Italian. Picasso reproductions deck the walls of this upscale and romantic family-owned restaurant. You'll enjoy attentive service as well as inventive and traditional recipes. Start with one of Bruno's delicious salads, then try the veal chops, Bruno's rigatoni (famous for its robust tomato sauce), or the capellini primavera, an excellent choice for vegetarians. Warm homemade bread accompanies all dishes. | 9462 N. Macarthur Blvd. | 972/556–2465 | Reservations essential | Closed Sun. No lunch Sat. | $12–$24 | AE, D, DC, MC, V.

**Cafe on the Green.** Continental. Located within the Four Seasons hotel, this café overlooks villas and a pool. Try rack of lamb with lentils, cedar-planked salmon fillet, or ravioli with scallops and shrimp. Sun. brunch. | 4150 N. McArthur | 972/717–0700 | Breakfast also available Mon.–Sun. | $23–$35 | AE, DC, MC, V.

**Emperors.** Indian. Through glass windows, you can watch how the tandoori chicken and flavorful nan are made at this busy, popular restaurant. Try a prix fixe dinner for the most variety for your money. | 3225 W. Airport Fwy. | 972/256–2127 | $7–$14 | AE, D, MC, V.

**Fred's Barbecue Restaurant.** Barbecue. In an Old West setting, you can join the locals supping on such specialties of the house as the stuffed baked potato and barbecue ham and brisket. | 808 E. Irving Blvd. | 972/579–7655 | Closed Sun.–Mon. | $5–$9 | D, MC, V.

**Golden India Restaurant.** Indian. This authentic Punjabi restaurant is a good choice for vegetarians and meat-eaters alike. The chicken tikka masala and vegetable paneer are delicious. Traditional paintings line the walls and candles light up the tables. | 2912 N. Belt Line Rd. | 972/257–8806 | $8–$14 | AE, DC, MC, V.

**I Fratelli Italian Restaurant.** Italian. Gaze at a mural of the Tuscan landscape while feasting on savory chicken Parmesan or the homemade Italian sausage and peppers. Kids' menu. | 7750 N. Macarthur Blvd. | 972/501–9700 | $7–$10 | AE, D, DC, MC, V.

**Olive Garden.** Italian. The Olive Garden chain offers a number of specialties from pastas to grilled items and seafood, in a casual family atmosphere. Try veal parmigiana, shrimp primavera, seafood Alfredo, and Mediterranean garlic shrimp. Kids' menu. | 4001 W. Airport Fwy. | 972/258–5191 | $10–$18 | AE, D, DC, MC, V.

**Outback Steakhouse.** Steak. The Outback Steakhouse chain is known for excellent beef served in a relaxed, family style atmosphere. Try the 20-oz porterhouse or rack of lamb. Kids' menu. | 3510 W. Airport Fwy. | 972/399–1477 | www.outback.com | No lunch | $10–$32 | AE, D, DC, MC, V.

**Veranda.** Greek. The live belly-dancing on Fri. and Sat. nights always draws a crowd to this otherwise quiet and relaxed Mediterranean restaurant. The traditional souvlaki and rack of lamb are winners, or try the occasional Lebanese special. | 5433 N. Macarthur Blvd. | 972/518–0939 | No lunch Sat. Closed Sun. | $10–$16 | AE, DC, MC, V.

## Lodging

**Amerisuites.** This all-suites motel is 6 mi from Texas Stadium and 1.5 miles from the Dallas/Ft. Worth International Airport. Complimentary Continental breakfast, microwaves, refrigerators, cable TV, pool, exercise equipment, laundry facilities, business services, airport shuttle. | 4235 W. Airport Fwy. | 972/659–1272 or 800/833–1516 | fax 972/570–0676 | www.amerisuites.com | 128 suites | $69–$109 suites | AE, D, DC, MC, V.

**Comfort Suites Las Colinas.** Located in the heart of the Las Colinas business district, this all-suites motel is convenient to Texas Stadium and the Dallas/Ft. Worth International Airport. Complimentary Continental breakfast. Cable TV, exercise equipment, business services, refrigerators, free parking. | 1223 Greenway Circle | 972/518–0606 | fax 972/518–0722 | www.comfortsuites.com | 54 suites | $49–$150 suites | AE, D, DC, MC, V.

**Country Suites by Carlson.** This motel is 2 mi east of Dallas/Ft. Worth International Airport and within 10 mi of Texas Stadium. Complimentary Continental breakfast, in-room data ports, kitchenettes, microwaves, cable TV, pool, wading pool, hot tub, business services, laundry facilities, airport shuttle. | 4100 W. John Carpenter Fwy. | 972/929–4008 | fax 972/929–4224 | www.countryinns.com | 18 rooms, 72 suites | $59–$139 | AE, D, DC, MC, V.

**Courtyard Las Colinas.** This four-story hotel is off of U.S. 114, about 4 mi from Hyatt Bear Creek Golf Course and 3 mi from Texas Stadium. A variety of restaurants and shops are within walking distance. Restaurant, bar, in-room data ports, cable TV, pool, exercise equipment, laundry services, laundry facilities, business services, some pets. | 1151 West Walnut Hill | 972/550–8100 | fax 972/550–0764 | www.courtyard.com | 147 rooms, 13 suites | $122, $155 suites | AE, D, DC, MC, V.

**Days Inn Texas Stadium.** Just across the street from Texas Stadium, this hotel fills up with Cowboy fans during football season. Rooms are spacious and the staff here prides itself on prompt and courteous service. Restaurant, bar, some microwaves, some refrigerators, in-room data ports, cable TV, pool, laundry services, no pets. | 2200 E. Airport Fwy. | 972/438–6666 | www.daysinn.com | 172 rooms, 6 suites | $59–$69, $75 suites | AE, D, DC, MC, V.

**Doubletree Guest Suites.** The atrium lobby of this 10-story hotel has tropical-style plants. Restaurant, bar, in-room data ports, microwaves, cable TV, pool, hot tub, sauna, laundry facilities, business services, airport shuttle. | 4650 W. Airport Fwy. | 972/790–0093 | fax 972/790–4768 | 305 suites | $99–$169 suites | AE, D, DC, MC, V.

**Drury Inn.** This chain motel is 1 mi from the Dallas/Ft. Worth International Airport, 6 mi from Texas Stadium, and 6 mi from University of Dallas at Irving. Complimentary Continental breakfast, in-room data ports, cable TV, pool, business services, airport shuttle, some pets allowed. | 4210 W. Airport Fwy. | 972/986–1200 | fax 972/986–1200 | www.druryinn.com | 129 rooms | $75–$87 | AE, D, DC, MC, V.

**Embassy Suites South.** This all-suites hotel is located 2 mi from Dallas/Ft. Worth International Airport, 5 mi from Texas Stadium, and 7 mi from the Las Colinas business district. Restaurant, bar, in-room data ports, microwaves, cable TV, indoor pool, hot tub, laundry facilities, business services, airport shuttle. | 4650 W. Airport Fwy. | 972/790–0093 | fax 972/790–4768 | www.embassysuites.com | 308 suites | $119–$169 suites | AE, D, DC, MC, V.

**Fairfield Inn by Marriott.** The Fairfield is 5 mi from Dallas/Ft. Worth International Airport, 4 mi from Texas Stadium, and 6.5 mi from the Grapevine Mills Outlet Mall. Complimentary Continental breakfast, cable TV, pool, hot tub, business services, free parking. | 630 W. John Carpenter Fwy. | 972/550–8800 | fax 972/756–9175 | www.marriott.com | 109 rooms | $49–$72 | AE, D, DC, MC, V.

★ **Four Seasons Resort and Club (Dallas at Las Colinas).** This luxury resort is set on 400 rolling acres. Rooms have balconies that overlook the Tournament Players Course golf course, where the Professional Golfers' Association's GTE Byron Nelson Classic is held. 3 restaurants, room service, in-room data ports, minibars, cable TV, 4 pools, barbershop, beauty salon, hot tub, massage, driving range, 18-hole golf course, 2 putting greens, 12 tennis courts, gym, baby-sitting, children's programs (6 months–8), business services, some pets allowed. | 4150 N. MacArthur Blvd. | 972/717–0700 | fax 972/717–2550 | www.fourseasons.com | 345 rooms, 12 suites | $305–$510, $650–$1200 suites | AE, DC, MC, V.

**Hampton Inn.** This Hampton Inn is 1 mi from Dallas/Ft. Worth International Airport, 6 mi from Texas Stadium, and 1 mi from the Irving Mall. Complimentary Continental breakfast, some microwaves, cable TV, pool, airport shuttle, free parking. | 4340 W. Airport Fwy. | 972/986–3606 | fax 972/986–6852 | www.hamptoninn.com | 81 rooms | $60–$102 | AE, D, DC, MC, V.

**Harvey Suites.** This all-suites motel is 1.5 mi from the Dallas/Ft. Worth International Airport. Restaurant, picnic area, complimentary Continental breakfast, in-room data ports, refrigerators, cable TV, pool, hot tub, exercise equipment, laundry facilities, business services, airport shuttle, free parking. | 4550 W. John Carpenter Fwy. | 972/929–4499 or 800/922–9222 | fax 972/929–0774 | www.bristolhotels.com | 164 suites | $69–$159 suites | AE, D, DC, MC, V.

**Hilton Garden Inn Las Colinas.** This five-story hotel is classically decorated in the Biedermeier Style popular in Germany and Austria in the 1800s. You'll find it near to I–635, off of Macarthur Blvd., 6 mi from DFW Airport. Restaurant, bar, room service, refrigerators, in-room data ports, cable TV, pool, exercise equipment, business services, no pets. | 7516 Las Colinas Blvd. | 972/444–8434 | fax 972/910–9246 | www.hilton.com | 130 rooms, 44 suites | $149, $169 suites. | AE, D, DC, MC, V.

**Holiday Inn Select–DFW Airport North.** Holiday Inn Selects are a cut above the typical roadside motels. This one is 2 mi from Dallas/Ft. Worth International Airport, 5 mi from Texas Stadium, and 2 mi from Grapevine Outlet Mills Mall. Restaurant, bar, in-room data ports, microwaves, room service, cable TV, pool, exercise equipment, laundry facilities, business services, airport shuttle, free parking. | 4441 Hwy 114 at Esters Blvd. | 972/929–8181 | fax 972/929–8233 | www.holiday-inn.com | 282 rooms | $79–$139 | AE, D, DC, MC, V.

**Holiday Inn Select–DFW Airport South.** This Select is 2 mi from the Dallas/Ft. Worth International Airport, 4 mi from Texas Stadium, and 4 mi from Las Colinas business district. Restaurant, bar, in-room data ports, room service, cable TV, pool, wading pool, hot tub, exercise equipment, game room with pool tables and air hockey, laundry facilities, business services, airport shuttle, free parking. | 4440 W. Airport Fwy. | 972/399–1010 | fax 972/790–8545 | www.holiday-inn.com | 409 rooms | $79–$139 | AE, D, DC, MC, V.

**Irving Howard Johnson Inn.** This family-friendly, two-story inn will provide you with a free shuttle to all Dallas Cowboy games, and give your kids a coloring book and crayons when you check in. The hotel is on U.S. 183, about 12 mi from DFW Airport. Restaurant, bar, complimentary Continental breakfast, room service, some microwaves, some refrigerators, in-room data ports, cable TV, pool, laundry services, business services. | 120 West Airport Freeway (U.S. 183) | 972/579–8911 | fax 972/721–1846 | dfwhojo@aol.com | www.hojo.com | 119 rooms, 1 suite | $50–$60, $100 suite | AE, D, DC, MC, V.

**La Quinta–Dallas/Fort Worth.** This two-story motel is in a commercial area. There is a 24-hour restaurant right next door and there are many others within a two-block radius. Complimentary Continental breakfast, in-room data ports, cable TV, pool, business services, airport shuttle, pets allowed. | 4105 W. Airport Fwy. | 972/252–6546 | fax 972/570–4225 | www.laquinta.com | 169 rooms | $59–$80 | AE, D, DC, MC, V.

**Marriott–DFW Airport.** This 20-story hotel is 1 mi from the Dallas/Ft. Worth International Airport and 3 mi from the Grapevine Mills Mall. Restaurants, bar, in-room data ports, some refrigerators, cable TV, pool, hot tub, exercise equipment, laundry facilities, business services, airport shuttle, some pets allowed. | 8440 Freeport Pkwy. | 972/929–8800 | fax 972/929–6501 | www.marriott.com | 491 rooms | $69–$179 | AE, D, DC, MC, V.

**Omni Mandalay at Las Colinas.** This upscale chain hotel is located in the heart of the Las Colinas business district and is 10 minutes from the Dallas/Ft. Worth International Airport. Restaurant, bar, in-room data ports, room service, cable TV, pool, hot tub, gym, summer children's programs (ages 8–18: swan feeding on lake next to hotel, cooking classes, flower arrangements; younger children: coloring books and games), business services. | 221 E. Las Colinas Blvd. | 972/556–0800 | fax 972/556–0729 | www.omnihotels.com | 402 rooms | $109–$219 | AE, D, DC, MC, V.

**Sheraton Grand Hotel DFW Airport.** You'll find this 10-story hotel off of U.S. 114 (the Esters Blvd. exit), just one-and-a-half miles from the Dallas airport and 15 mi from downtown Dallas. The hotel accommodates several conventions per year, and plenty of business travelers, with 23 meeting rooms, a huge conference center, and exhibit facilities; service here is very professional. Restaurant, bar, in-room data ports, cable TV, pool, indoor hot tub, sauna, exercise equipment, business services, airport shuttle, pets allowed (fee). | 4440 W. John Carpenter Fwy. | 972/929-8400 | fax 972/929-4885 | www.sheraton.com | 297 rooms, 3 suites | $82-$140, $250 suites | AE, D, DC, MC, V.

**Wilson World.** This full-service hotel with gift shop is 1 mi south of Dallas/Ft. Worth International Airport. Restaurant, bar, in-room data ports, microwaves, cable TV, indoor pool, hot tub, exercise equipment, business services, airport shuttle, some pets allowed. | 4600 W. Airport Fwy. | 972/513-0800 | fax 972/513-0106 | 200 rooms, 96 suites | $89-$119, $99-$119 suites | AE, D, DC, MC, V.

# JACKSONVILLE

*(Nearby towns also listed: Nacogdoches, Palestine, Rusk, Tyler)*

When the railroads first came to this part of East Texas in 1872, this community relocated itself from 3 mi away. The area's fertile soil yields a plentiful and "celebrated" tomato crop—an annual "Tomato Fest" is held in June. The town is also home to the Baptist Missionary Association Theological Seminary, Jacksonville College, and Lon Morris College.

Information: **Jacksonville Chamber of Commerce** | Box 1231, Jacksonville, TX 75766 | 903/586-2217 or 800/376-2217 | jacksonville.chamber@e-tex.com | www.jacksonvilletexas.com.

## Attractions
**Killough Monument.** This stone monument marks the place of one of the worst retaliations by Native Americans against settlers in 1838. Settlers were attacked by neighboring Native Americans from whom land had been taken away a few years back. | South of FM 855, 3 mi west of Mt. Selman | 903/586-2217 | Free | Daily.

**Lake Jacksonville.** Camping, picnicking, and barbecue sites are the local draw here, plus there's volleyball action if you're so inclined. | U.S. 79, to College Ave. Exit | 903/586-5977 | fax 903/586-4609 | Free | Daily 6 AM-10 PM.

**Love's Lookout Park.** There are views of the surrounding countryside at this lookout spot built by the Works Progress Administration (WPA) in the late 1950s. This spot was named for Wesley Love, a local farmer who grew peaches here. | U.S. 69, to Lookout Exit | 903/586-2217 | Free | Daily.

### ON THE CALENDAR
**JUNE: *Tomato Fest.*** In homage to the tomato—and its generous local bounty—this annual event includes various contests, cook-offs, and live music. | 903/586-2217.
**JULY: *Western Week.*** Week-long events include a parade, a chuckwagon luncheon, a street dance, and a rodeo day for the kids. | 800/376-2217.
**DEC.: *Old Fashioned Christmas.*** Tours are available of homes and a flotilla on Lake Jacksonville, all of which are decorated with holiday ornaments and lights. | 800/376-2217.

## Dining
**Stacy's Bar-B-Q.** Barbecue. Housed in an early 20th-century home, this informal, buffet-style eatery has a rustic interior done in a traditional east Texan motif. The rib plates and

chopped beef sandwiches are very popular. | 1217 S. Jackson St. | 903/586–1951 | Closed Sun. | $4–$8 | D, MC, V.

## LODGING

**Holiday Inn Express.** A shopping center with a grocery store is in the next complex, and a number of fast-food restaurants are about ½ mi away from this two-story hotel on U.S. 69S. Refrigerators, microwaves, some in-room hot tubs, in-room data ports, cable TV, pool, outdoor hot tub, laundry services, business services, no pets. | 1848 S. Jackson St. (U.S. 69 S) | 903/589–8500 | fax 903/589–0800 | www.holiday-inn.com | 44 rooms, 4 suites | $69, $89 suites | AE, D, DC, MC, V.

# JASPER

MAP 8, K4

*(Nearby town also listed: Beaumont)*

Jasper was settled by John Bevil in the early 1800s. Bevil changed the town's name from Bevilport to Jasper in honor of a Revolutionary War hero. Today, this town of 8,500 is a gateway to the region's beautiful nearby forests—Angelina National Forest and the Big Thicket National Preserve. The native pines and hardwoods of this area shade a landscape broken up by rolling hills.

Information: **Jasper Chamber of Commerce** | 246 E. Milam St., Jasper, TX 75951 | 409/384–2762 | jaspercc@jaspercoc.org | www.jaspercoc.org.

## Attractions

**Angelina National Forest.** The U.S. Forest Service administers this 153,000-acre preserve of rolling hills and pine and hardwood forest around the Sam Rayburn Reservoir. You can camp, hike, fish, or picnic in the area. | On Rte. 63 | 936/639–8620 | Free | Daily.

**B. A. Steinhagen Lake.** There are several recreation areas here, including the 27-mi Trail Between the Lakes which wends its way between Toledo Bend Reservoir and Lake Sam Rayburn. | Headquarters: U.S. 190 to Rte. 92 | 409/429–3491 | Daily dawn to dusk.

**Beaty Orton House.** This Victorian home was built by John T. Beaty, a state senator. It's made of native pine lumber and is furnished with period antiques. | 200 S. Main | 409/383–6138 | $2 | Weekdays 8–5, weekends by appointment.

**Martin Dies, Jr., State Park.** Here you'll find camping, screened shelters, boating, fishing, a playground, a nature center, and walking trails. | U.S. 190 to Rte. 48, on east shore of B. A. Steinhagen Lake | 409/384–5231 | fax 409/384–1437 | www.tpwd.state.tx.us | $2 | Daily. The **Sam Rayburn Reservoir** is used for fishing, boating, swimming, and camping. | U.S. 96 to Park Rd. 255 | 409/384–5716 | Free.

**Rayburn Country Resort.** This resort is a recreational paradise. You can go fishing, golfing, boating, jet-skiing, and bird watching along Lake Sam Rayburn and on grounds surrounded by dogwood trees and towering pines. | 1000 Windgate Blvd. | 409/698–2444 | fax 409/698–2372 | resort@mail.jas.net | www.rayburnresort.com | Green fees: $38–$49; call for additional rates | Daily 7–11.

**Toledo Bend Dam and Reservoir.** This reservoirs offers fishing, boating, camping, and swimming. | Project HQ, U.S. 96 to Rte. 255 | 409/565–2273 | Free | Daily dawn to dusk.

**Sabine National Forest.** Approximately 30 mi north of Jasper, Sabine National Forest is spread out over more than 160,000 acres. There are many recreational and wilderness areas located throughout the forest. | 201 S. Palm, off Rte. 83, Hemphill | 409/787–3870 | Free | Daily.

**MAR.:** *Azalea Festival.* A driving tour of residential areas highlights spring blooms. | 409/384–2762.
**JULY:** *Jamboree and Fireworks Display.* This July 4th event includes fireworks, live entertainment, and food. | 409/384–2762.
**OCT.:** *Fall Fest.* Cook-offs, a scarecrow contest, and soapbox derby are held in the Courthouse Square. | 409/384–2762.

## Dining

**Cotton Patch Cafe.** American. With 17 locations in Texas and New Mexico, this dinner house is a local favorite for good reason: savory home-cooked food served up with a smile. Try the grilled catfish, the hand-breaded chicken-fried steak, or one of the daily specials. Freshly made berry cobblers are also very popular. Kids' menu. | 201 W. Gibson St. | 409/384–9000 | Closed Sun. | $5–$7 | AE, D, DC, MC, V.

**Patrick's Steakhouse and Seafood Restaurant.** Steak. Choice cuts individually sliced and the freshest seafood are elegantly presented in this refined steakhouse. European paintings and photographs adorn the walls and lighting is low and pleasant. | U.S. 96N | 409/384–8861 | No lunch Sat. Closed Sun.–Mon. | $10–$20 | D, MC, V.

## Lodging

**Best Western Inn of Jasper.** This motel is on U.S. 190, three blocks west of the intersection of U.S. 190 and U.S. 96. There are shops and restaurants less than 1 mile from the motel, and the Martin Dies Park and lake is 12 mi away. Complimentary Continental breakfast, cable TV, outdoor pool, outdoor hot tub, pets allowed. | 205 W. Gibson St. | 409/384–7767 | fax 409/384–7665 | www.bestwestern.com | 59 rooms | $51–$63 | AE, D, DC, MC, V.

**Holiday Inn Express.** This two-story motel with exterior corridors is about ½ mi from a local movie theater. Complimentary Continental breakfast, cable TV, pool, exercise equipment, laundry facilities, business services. | 2100 N. Wheeler | 409/384–8600 | fax 409/384–8600 | www.holiday-inn.com | 57 rooms | $69–$86 | AE, D, DC, MC, V.

**Jasper Days Inn.** Constructed in the early 80s, this two-story inn is off U.S. 96 and just minutes from downtown. There are several restaurants within walking distance. Cable TV, pool, laundry services, some pets. | 1730 S. Wheeler St. | 409/334–6816 | fax 409/384–6085 | www.daysinn.com | 31 rooms | $38–$46 | AE, D, DC, MC, V.

**Ramada Inn.** There are plenty of restaurants and even a movie theater close by this standard Ramada facility near to airport. Restaurant, bar, in-room data ports, some refrigerators, cable TV, pool, laundry facilities, business services, pets allowed. | 239 E. Gibson St. | 409/384–9021 | fax 409/384–9021, ext. 309 | 100 rooms | $55–$58 | AE, D, DC, MC, V.

**Rayburn Country Resort.** This recreational resort along lake Sam Rayburn is just north of Jasper. Brilliant dogwoods and flowering magnolias provide the picturesque backdrop for this lakeside resort. Most of the rooms offer views of pine forests or lush fairways. Restaurant, bar, cable TV, pool, driving range, golf courses, putting green, boating, fishing, video games, playground, business services. | 100 Windgate Blvd. | 409/698–2444 or 800/882–1442 | fax 409/698–2372 | www.rayburnresort.com | 50 rooms in main building; 126 apartments | $45–$75, $75–$225 | AE, D, DC, MC, V.

# JEFFERSON

MAP 8, K3

*(Nearby towns also listed: Athens, Tyler)*

In the 1840s Jefferson was established as a port city on the Big Cypress Bayou, linking northeast Texas with Shreveport and the Red River. In time it became known as the "River

Port to the Southwest," but after Reconstruction, river traffic declined as the railroad industry grew. Although it never returned to its former status, Jefferson now enjoys a new role—that of tourist capital of East Texas. Tucked beneath tall pines and moss-draped cypress trees, Jefferson is home to many bed-and-breakfast facilities and antiques shops.

Information: **Jefferson Chamber of Commerce** | 118 N. Vale St., Jefferson, TX 75657 | 903/665-2672 | www.jefferson-texas.com.

## Attractions

**Atalanta.** This private rail car was once owned by financier Jay Gould. Its furnished dining room, kitchen, and staterooms recall another era—and tax bracket. | 210 W. Austin St. | 903/665-2513 | $2 | Daily 9:30-2:30, tours only.

**Caddo Lake State Park.** This 480-acre park offering daytime activities and services for overnight guests has been open since the 1930s. The visitors center has displays about the lake and its wildlife. | Rte. 2198 | 903/679-3351 | fax 903/679-4006 | www.tpwd.state.tx.us | $2 | Daily 8 AM–10 PM.

**Excelsior House.** This hotel has been in continuous operation since its construction in 1850 when it was built by the captain of the first steamboat to visit Jefferson. Its many famous guests include Oscar Wilde, Ulysses S. Grant, Rutherford B. Hayes, and Lady Bird Johnson. Guided tours are available. | 211 W. Austin St. | 903/665-2513 | fax 903/665-9389 | $4 for tours | Daily 8 AM–9 PM.

**Freeman Plantation.** This antebellum plantation home displays unique period furnishings. It's open for guided tours. | Rte. 49 W | 903/665-2320 | Thurs.–Mon.; tours only, 3 and 3:30.

**House of the Seasons.** Tours of this 1872 home with authentic furnishings include a look at its dome and elaborate frescoes. Three suites are available in the carriage house. | 409 S. Alley | 903/665-1218 | $5 | Tour times posted daily.

**Jefferson Historical Society Museum.** Among the four floors of local history exhibits from the age of the steamboat is a 19th-century tea set belonging to a czar of Russia. | 223 W. Austin St. | 903/665-2775 | $2 | Daily 9:30-5.

**Jefferson Riverboat Landing and Depot.** The history of steamboat traffic in Jefferson is illustrated throughout the displays here. | U.S. 59 and Cypress River Bridge | 903/665-2222 | $6.50 | Daily 10, 12, 2, and 4.

**Lake o' the Pines.** You can enjoy fishing, boating, camping, waterskiing, and swimming here. | Rte. 726 | 800/284-2267 or 903/755-2530 | Free | Daily.

**Scarlett O'Hardy's *Gone with the Wind* Museum.** This private collection focuses on the Civil War period of Southern history. In the museum is a first edition of Margaret Mitchell's book, as well as items relating to the movie. | 408 Taylor St. | 800/284-2267, 903/665-1939 | scarlettohardy.com | $3 | Wed.–Sat. 10-5, Sun. 1-4.

### ON THE CALENDAR

**MAY:** *Historical Pilgrimage.* Tours of historic homes are led by docents in period dress. | 903/665-2672.
**JUNE:** *Jefferson Jazz Festival.* This festival includes music and jam sessions, exhibits, workshops, and food. | 903/665-2672.
**DEC.:** *Christmas Candlelight Tour.* Homes are opened for public tours to view holiday decorations. | 903/665-2672.

## Dining

**The Bakery.** American. The small dining room at this casual spot is decorated with pictures of the owners on various trips they have taken over the years. Popular items include the pot roast beef and chicken salad. | 201 W. Austin St. | 903/665-2253 | Breakfast also available. No supper weekdays, Sun. | $9–$19 | AE, MC, V.

**The Galley.** Creole. This 25-year-old restaurant recently saw the restoration and redecoration of its late-1860s building. Steak, chicken, and seafood are on the menu. | 121 W. Austin St. | 903/665–3641 | Closed Mon. | $10–$25 | AE, DC, MC, V.

**Lyle's Catfish and Fried Chicken.** American. This casual eatery is pleasantly decorated with hanging plants and numerous windows. The catfish strips and fried chicken are the most popular dishes. Be sure to have an ice-cream shake or malt to finish off your meal. Kids' menu. | 106 N. Walcott St. | 903/665–8941 | Breakfast also available. Closed Sun. | $3–$6 | No credit cards.

**Stillwater Inn.** Seafood. The house was built in 1893. Dine on rack of lamb, breast of duck with blackberry sauce, salmon, trout, or beef tenderloin. Guest rooms are also available. | 203 E. Broadway | 903/665–8415 | Reservations essential | Closed Mon. No lunch | $23–$35 | AE, MC, V.

## Lodging

**Excelsior House.** The hotel was built in 1852, and is decorated in the Victorian style. Cable TV. | 211 W. Austin St. | 903/665–2513 | fax 903/665–9389 | www.excelsior@jeffersontx.com | 15 rooms | $65–$110 | AE, D, DC, MC, V.

**Falling Leaves.** This early Greek-revival mansion, built in the mid-1800s, is filled with antiques. Complimentary breakfast, cable TV, no room phones, no kids under 18 allowed. | 304 Jefferson St. | 903/665–8803 | fax 903/665–8803 | 4 rooms (with shower only) | $90–$100 | MC, V.

**Hale House Bed and Breakfast.** A beautiful sun porch surrounding the house and extending out to a gazebo encourages a stroll around this large, two-story Victorian home, also lending it a romantic air. Rooms have hardwood floors and turn-of-the-20th-century antiques and chandeliers. Complimentary breakfast, cable TV, in-room VCR's (and movies), no room phones, library, no pets, no kids under 12, no smoking, no pets. | 702 S. Line St. | 903/665–8877 | http://jeffersontx.com/halehouse | 6 rooms | $80–$100 | MC, V.

**Jefferson Hotel.** Built in 1851 as a cotton warehouse, this restored hotel is in the center of Jefferson's Riverfront District. Owners Ron and Carol Meissner aspire to make you feel as though you've stepped back in time when you enter the hotel. Victorian-era furniture and decorations greet you in every room. Restaurant, some in-room hot tubs, some room phones, no pets, no smoking. | 124 W. Austin St. | 903/665–2631 or 800/226–9026 | fax 903/665–6222 | http://jeffersontx.com/jeffersonhotel | 24 rooms, 2 suites | $85–$100; $120 suites | AE, D, MC, V.

**McKay House.** 1851 historic house. Complimentary breakfast, in-room data ports, cable TV, business services, no smoking. | 306 E. Delta St. | 903/665–7322 | fax 903/665–7322 | 8 rooms (3 with shower only), 3 suites | $139–$159 | MC, V.

**Pride House.** This two-story Victorian mansion was built in 1889 and is in a commercial area, just six blocks from downtown. Rooms are elegantly appointed with Victorian antiques. Complimentary breakfast, cable TV, no room phones, business services, no smoking. | 409 E. Broadway | 903/665–2675 or 800/894–3526 | fax 903/665–3901 | www.jeffersontexas.com | 11 rooms | $75–$200 | MC, V.

# JOHNSON CITY

MAP 8, H5

*(Nearby towns also listed: Burnet, Fredericksburg, Kerrville, Marble Falls)*

Historic Johnson City was named for Sam Johnson, grandfather of President Lyndon Baines Johnson, but it was LBJ who brought the attention of the world to his hometown, 14 mi north of Blanco on U.S. 281. The most popular stop here is Johnson's boyhood home, managed by the U.S. Park Service. LBJ was five years old in 1913 when his family moved from their country home near the Pedernales River to this simple frame house. The Visitors Center provides information on this location, nearby Johnson Settlement, and other LBJ attractions.

**Information: Johnson City Convention and Visitors Bureau** | Box 485, Johnson City, TX 78636 | 830/868–7684 | jcchamber@texanet.net.

## Attractions

**The Exotic Resort Zoo.** Take a safari through 137 acres of land designed as a sanctuary for wild animals. Over 500 animals comprising 80 different species, most of which were on endangered animal lists at some time, live on the preserve. Some of the animals will come right up to you to be touched. There is also a petting zoo with baby deer, llamas, and kangaroos that love attention, especially from kids. Drive 4 mi north of Johnson City on U.S. 281. | 235 Zoo Trail | 830/868–4357 | www.zooexotics.com | $9.95; special rates for seniors and children | Daily 9–6.

**Lyndon B. Johnson National Historical Park.** Headquarters for this park are in downtown Johnson City. The former U.S. president moved here from Stonewall, approximately 10 mi west of Johnson City, when he was 5 years old. (The Lyndon B. Johnson State Historical Park and the Sauer-Beckmann Farmstead, an historic farm with docents in period dress reminiscent of the early 1900s, are in Stonewall.) | Visitor Center, off Main St. | 830/868–7128 | Free | Daily, 8:45–5.

From 1913 to 1934 Lyndon Johnson lived in a simple white frame house. Johnson's father, Sam Ealy Johnson, Jr., was a state representative, and the **Boyhood Home** often echoed with political debate. At the same time, a future statesman was being tutored on the front porch at the knee of his mother, Rebekah Baines Johnson. | Free | Daily, by guided tour only, 9–5.

The **Johnson Settlement** consists of a restored cabin and other buildings that belonged to Sam Ealy Johnson, Sr., LBJ's grandfather and the town's namesake. Photos, farm implements, and clothing from the 1800s are displayed in a visitors center. An old cypress cistern serves as a mini-auditorium featuring recorded readings of letters written by original settlers of this rugged land. | Free | Daily, self-guided tour, 9:30–4:30.

In Stonewall, this reconstructed **Birthplace** (about 10 mi from the visitors center on U.S. 290, Rte. 49 | free, by park-led bus tour only) is best seen on a guided tour that begins at the visitor center in the state park.

**Lyndon B. Johnson State Historical Park.** This state park is in Stonewall, where Lyndon Johnson lived until he was 5 years old. It's the boarding point for the guided tours of the LBJ ranch. The park also contains interpretive exhibits about the Hill Country and the Johnson family.

A large white home sprawling under shady oaks, the LBJ Ranch hosted many national and international visitors during LBJ's presidency. For this reason it was dubbed the "Texas White House." The home is not open to the public and is seen only as a drive-by attraction on guided tours operated from the visitors center. | From Johnson City, 14 mi west on U.S. 290, enter on Rte. 52 | 830/644–2252 | Free | Daily; tours available 10–4.

Costumed docents carry on farm chores typical of the early 1900s and children can see farm animals at the **Sauer-Beckmann Farmstead** living history farm on the park grounds. | 830/644–2455 | Free | Daily 8–4:30.

**Pedernales Falls State Park.** This scenic park is noted for its waterfalls, swimming, and hiking. | On Rte. 2766; at junction FM 2766 and FM 3232 | 830/868–7304 | fax 830/868–4186 | www.tpwd.state.tx.us | $4 | Daily.

**Texas Hills Vineyard.** The rolling hills and rich soil of this Texan vineyard recall the Tuscan landscape. The vineyard prides itself on minimal chemical usage and a highly organic growing process. Currently produced wines include Pinot Grigio, Sangiovese, Moscato, and Chardonnay. Take a tour, then be sure to visit the tasting room and gift shop. | Rte. 2766, off U.S. 281 | 830/868–2321 | fax 830/868–7027 | www.texashillsvineyard.com | Free | Mon.–Sat. 10–5:30; Sun. 12–5.

## KODAK'S TIPS FOR PHOTOGRAPHING LANDSCAPES AND SCENERY

### Landscape
- Tell a story
- Isolate the essence of a place
- Exploit mood, weather, and lighting

### Panoramas
- Use panoramic cameras for sweeping vistas
- Don't restrict yourself to horizontal shots
- Keep the horizon level

### Panorama Assemblage
- Use a wide-angle or normal lens
- Let edges of pictures overlap
- Keep exposure even
- Use a tripod

### Placing the Horizon
- Use low horizon placement to accent sky or clouds
- Use high placement to emphasize distance and accent foreground elements
- Try eliminating the horizon

### Mountain Scenery: Scale
- Include objects of known size
- Frame distant peaks with nearby objects
- Compress space with long lenses

### Mountain Scenery: Lighting
- Shoot early or late; avoid midday
- Watch for dramatic color changes
- Use exposure compensation

### Tropical Beaches
- Capture expansive views
- Don't let bright sand fool your meter
- Include people

### Rocky Shorelines
- Vary shutter speeds to freeze or blur wave action
- Don't overlook sea life in tidal pools
- Protect your gear from sand and sea

### In the Desert
- Look for shapes and textures
- Try visiting during peak bloom periods
- Don't forget safety

### Canyons
- Research the natural and social history of a locale
- Focus on a theme or geologic feature
- Budget your shooting time

### Rain Forests and the Tropics
- Go for mystique with close-ups and detail shots
- Battle low light with fast films and camera supports
- Protect cameras and film from moisture and humidity

### Rivers and Waterfalls
- Use slow film and long shutter speeds to blur water
- When needed, use a neutral-density filter over the lens
- Shoot from water level to heighten drama

### Autumn Colors
- Plan trips for peak foliage periods
- Mix wide and close views for visual variety
- Use lighting that accents colors or creates moods

### Moonlit Landscapes
- Include the moon or use only its illumination
- Exaggerate the moon's relative size with long telephoto lenses
- Expose landscapes several seconds or longer

### Close-Ups
- Look for interesting details
- Use macro lenses or close-up filters
- Minimize camera shake with fast films and high shutter speeds

### Caves and Caverns
- Shoot with ISO 1000+ films
- Use existing light in tourist caves
- Paint with flash in wilderness caves

From *Kodak Guide to Shooting Great Travel Pictures* © 2000 by Fodor's Travel Publications

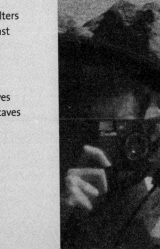

**MAR.:** *St. Francis Xavier Church Festival.* Arts and crafts are for sale, and there are also paddlewheel boats, and a chicken dinner. | 830/644–2218.

## Dining

**Uncle Kunkel's Bar-B-Q.** Barbecue. This barbecue joint has won blue ribbons at four state fairs and they have a successful mail-order business. Be sure to stop here if you're in the mood for barbecue brisket, pork, ribs, or sausage. If you want chicken, be sure to call ahead. | 210 U.S. 290/281S | 830/868–0251 or 888/814–5900 | fax 830/868–9122 | No supper. Closed Mon.–Tues. | $5–$8 | MC, V.

## Lodging

**Save Inn Motel.** There is a restaurant adjacent to this two-story motel. The Exotic Resort Zoo is just 4 mi away. Restaurant, complimentary Continental breakfast, cable TV, pool, pets allowed (fee). | 107 U.S. 281 | 830/868–4044 | fax 830/868–7888 | 53 rooms | $36–$46 | AE, D, MC, V.

**Zoo Exotic Resort B&B.** Enjoy the company of friendly wild animals roaming around this B&B in the Zoo Exotic Resort. There is a fence around the area and even along a walkway to the fishpond, so you can fish without visits from some of the larger animals. You can cook what you catch in the barbecue pit. Rooms overlook the lake and have polished wooden walls, large plants, and basic, comfortable furniture. Complimentary Continental breakfast, some kitchenettes, no room phones, no TV, pool, outdoor hot tub, fishing, pets allowed, no smoking. | 235 Zoo Trail | 830/868–4357 | www.zooexotics.com | 3 cabins | $100–$120 | AE, D, MC, V.

# KERRVILLE

MAP 8, G5

*(Nearby towns also listed: Bandera, Comfort, Fredericksburg, Johnson City, Mason)*

Texas's rolling Hill Country—streams and rivers shaded by tall cypress trees—has been an inspiration to many artists, so it's not surprising that this community is home to a fine Western art museum. Also in Kerrville is the Y. O. Ranch, open to visitors. Created by Charles Schreiner in the 1850s, the Y. O. Ranch at one point encompassed more than 600,000 acres, covering a distance of 80 mi.

**Information: Kerrville Convention and Visitors Bureau** | 1700 Sidney Baker, Suite 200, Kerrville, TX 78028 | 830/792–3535 or 800/221–7958. | kerrcvb@ktc.com | www.ktc.net/kerrcvb.

## Attractions

**Cowboy Artists of America Museum.** Filled with Western-theme paintings and sculpture, this hilltop museum features work by members of the Cowboy Artists of America. | 1550 Bandera Hwy. (Rte. 173) | 830/896–2553 | fax 830/896–2556 | $5 | Mon.–Sat. 9–5, Sun. 1–5.

**Hill Country Museum (Capt. Charles Schreiner Mansion).** This local history museum traces the town's development and the story of Charles Schreiner, whose family's name is synonymous with Kerrville. Charles Schreiner, a Texas Ranger at the age of 16, came to Kerrville as a young man in the 1850s. After the Civil War he opened a dry goods store and began acquiring land. Schreiner's company was the first business in America to recognize the value of mohair, the product of Angora goats; and before long, Kerrville became the mohair capital of the world. | 226 Earl Garrett St. | 830/896–8633 | $3 | Mon.–Sat. 10–4:30.

**Kerrville-Schreiner State Park.** There are 7 mi of hiking trails, as well as fishing and swimming in the Guadalupe River to be enjoyed here. Screened shelters and campsites are available. | 2485 Bandera Hwy. | 830/257–5392 | fax 830/896–7275 | www.tpwd.state.tx.us | $3 | Daily.

**Scott Schreiner Municipal Golf Course.** You will love the scenery surrounding this gorgeous 18-hole golf course. Green hills and clusters of trees will practically glow under the bright sunshine. Reservations are needed on the weekend. | Country Club Rd. at Sidney Baker St. | 830/257–4982 | Year-round, Tues.–Sun. 7–dusk.

**Y. O. Ranch.** This ranch once sprawled over more than 600,000 acres in Mountain Home, covering a distance of 80 mi.; today it spans 40,000 acres. Tour the ranch and view its famous Texas longhorns and many exotic animal species. | Rte. 41 W, Exit 490 (Mountain Home) | 830/640–3222 | fax 830/640–3227 | www.yoranch.com | $27 for tour | Daily, tours at 10 and 1.

### ON THE CALENDAR

**MAY:** *Texas State Arts and Crafts Fair.* One of the largest arts and crafts festivals in the state is held Memorial Day weekend on Schreiner College campus. The festival includes arts and crafts, demonstrations, wine tastings, entertainment, and food booths. | 830/896–5711.

**MAY, JUNE:** *Kerrville Folk Festival.* Beginning in 1972 with three folk musicians, this large music festival has become a driving force behind the growth of contemporary folk music. The festival includes plenty of music, as well as arts and crafts. Bring your own tents and RVs as camping out at the Quiet Valley Ranch, which is just 9 mi south of Kerrville on Hwy. 16, is part of the experience. | 830/257–3600.

**MAY–AUG.:** *Smith/Ritch Point Theatre.* Local talent is showcased in a variety of productions over the summer months. | 830/367–5122.

**SEPT.:** *Kerrville Wine and Music Festival.* Texas wine and music is celebrated with musicians, arts and crafts, and seminars. | 830/257–3600.

**OCT.:** *Kerr County Fair.* This fair includes food booths, carnival rides, and kids' activities. | 830/792–3535.

## Dining

**Alpine Lodge.** Swiss. Alpine horns and cow bells set the mood here. Try a Swiss Alpine platter or *birchermuesli* from among the many buffet items. Salad bar. Kids' menu. Sun. brunch. | 1001 Junction Hwy. | 830/257–8282 | $6–$16 | AE, D, DC, MC, V.

**Biggardi's.** American. Shiny chrome tables and movie memorabilia accent the classic American diner style. Burgers, steak, and shrimp are among the choices. Salad bar. | 843 Junction Hwy. | 830/895–1441 | $11–$18 | AE, D, MC, V.

**Bill's Barbecue.** Barbecue. This rustic dining spot has been a local fixture for over 30 years. Menu items include brisket, sausage, chicken, and ribs. | 1909 Junction Hwy. | 830/895–5733 | Closed Sun., Mon. No supper | $9–$18 | No credit cards.

**Del Norte Restaurant.** Southern. Casual dining in a family atmosphere with good down-home cookin' that includes steak, catfish, sandwiches, and some Mexican dishes. Breakfast tacos, barbecue, chicken-fried steak, and burgers round out the offerings. | 710 Junction Hwy. | 830/257–3337 | Breakfast and lunch also available. Closed Sun. No supper | $2–$9 | D, MC, V.

**Joe's Jefferson Street Cafe.** Southern. Housed in an 1890 Victorian mansion, this casual spot serves up some traditional Texas dishes like steak, Gulf shrimp, catfish, and chicken-fried steak. | 1001 Jefferson St. | 830/257–2929 | Closed Sun. | $8–$15 | MC, V.

**Kathy's on the River.** Eclectic. This spot overlooks the Guadalupe River. Outdoor seating is available under a partially covered patio. Try the teriyaki-grilled chicken breast, wontons and salsa, or the chicken-fried steak. | 417 Water St. | 830/257–7811 | Closed Mon. | $12–$19 | AE, D, MC, V.

**Mamacitas.** Tex-Mex. Stained-glass windows and a fountain enhance a Mexican courtyard where you can enjoy fajitas, enchiladas, or grilled steak. | 215 Junction Hwy. | 830/895–2441 | $12–$21 | AE, D, DC, MC, V.

**Mencius.** Chinese. Mencius has an Asian atmosphere and is a good choice for reliable Chinese fare. Known for Hunan dishes. Early bird suppers. | 208 Cully Dr. | 830/257–8868 | $11–$22 | AE, D, DC, MC, V.

**Rich's Hill Country Cafe.** American. This longtime breakfast and lunch café is popular with local residents for its down-home cooking. American breakfasts, huevos rancheros, breakfast tacos, baked chicken, and chicken-fried steak are among the choices. | 806 Main St. | 830/257–6665 | Breakfast also available. Closed Sun. No supper weekdays | $9–$14 | No credit cards.

**Sam Houston Dining Room.** Contemporary. A selection of wild game and hearty mesquite-broiled steaks await you at this restaurant tucked away in the Y. O. Ranch Resort Hotel. Try the grilled quail or fried catfish. The champagne brunch on Sunday is very popular. | 2033 Sidney Baker St. | 830/257–4440 | Breakfast also available. No supper Sun. | $7–$19 | AE, D, DC, MC, V.

## Lodging

**Best Western Sunday House Inn.** This chain hotel is near the River Hills Mall, a movie theater, and lots of restaurants. Quiet and comfortable with friendly service and great accommodations. Restaurant, bar, cable TV, pool, pets allowed (fee). | 2124 Sidney Baker St. | 830/896–1313 | fax 830/896–1336 | www.bestwestern.com | 97 rooms | $64–$84 | AE, D, DC, MC, V.

**Econolodge.** This native limestone hotel, handsomely surrounded by native plants and shrubs, sits in the middle of town, near Shriner College and several restaurants. It's two blocks off I–10, exit 508. Restaurant, bar, complimentary Continental breakfast, cable TV, pool, wading pool, laundry facilities, pets allowed (fee), free parking. | 2145 Sidney Baker St. | 830/896–1711 | fax 830/257–4375 | www.hc.net/econo | 102 rooms | $59–79 | AE, DC, MC, V.

**Holiday Inn–Y. O. Ranch Hotel and Conference Center.** This hotel has Western accents and Mexican tile floors. Restaurant, bar, room service, in-room data ports, refrigerators, cable TV, pool, wading pool, hot tub, tennis, business services, airport shuttle, pets allowed. | 2033 Sidney Baker St. | 830/257–4440 | fax 830/896–8189 | www.holidayinn.com | 200 rooms | $79–$119 | AE, D, DC, MC, V.

**Inn of the Hills.** The balconies in many of the rooms here overlook the Guadalupe River. The inn has a convenient location at the west end of town near a shopping center and restaurants. Restaurant, bar (with entertainment), room service, in-room data ports, some kitchenettes. microwaves, cable TV, 5 pools (2 indoor), wading pool, barbershop, beauty salon, hot tub, playground, laundry facilities, free parking, pets allowed. | 1001 Junction Hwy. | 830/895–5000 or 800/292–5690 | fax 830/895–6091 | www.innofthehills.com | 228 rooms | $70–$360 | AE, D, DC, MC, V.

**Lamb Creek Inn Bed and Breakfast.** This lovely inn is surrounded by over 100 acres of rolling hills. Lamb Creek runs through the property and goats, sheep, and other animals roam the fields. Rooms and cottages are all elegantly furnished with antiques and queen- or king-size beds. You'll find a library, a video and book store, and an antique shop on the grounds. Complimentary Continental breakfast, kitchenettes, microwaves, refrigerators, no room phones, no TV, some pets, no smoking. | 6121 Medina Hwy. | 830/792–5262 | www.lambcreekinn.com | 5 rooms, 2 cottages | $159 | MC, V.

**River Run Bed and Breakfast Inn.** This country home is built of native stone and decorated with antiques and Texas memorabilia. You can walk along the nearby Guadalupe River or relax on the porch. Country-style rooms are named after notable Texan rangers, writers, and a historian. Complimentary Continental breakfast, in-room hot tub, cable TV, some in-room VCR's, library, no pets, no kids, no smoking. | 120 Francisco Lemos St., Kerrville | 830/896–8353 or 800/460–7170 | www.riverrunbb.com | 4 rooms, 2 suites | $98, $134 suites | MC, V.

# KILGORE

*(Nearby towns also listed: Henderson, Longview, Tyler)*

Best known as the home of the Kilgore Rangerettes, the first precision drill team, Kilgore started life as a railroad town in 1872. But with the discovery of oil in the 1930s, the city boomed; soon 1,200 oil fields covered the landscape. Local oil derricks still pump the precious resource throughout the community.

**Information: Kilgore Chamber of Commerce** | Box 1582, Kilgore, TX 75663 | 903/984–5022 | bendelp@kilgore.net | www.ci.kilgore.tx.us/home.

## Attractions
**East Texas Oil Museum at Kilgore College.** The oil-rich boomtown era of East Texas is on display here. There are exhibits on drilling rigs and life in the oil fields, along with a simulated elevator ride down into oil formations beneath the earth. | Kilgore College, jct. U.S. 259 and Ross St. | 903/983–8295 | $4 | Tues.–Sat. 9–4, Sun. 2–5.

**Rangerette Showcase.** There's plenty of memorabilia here about Kilgore College's famous Rangerette drill team, the first team of its kind. | 1100 Broadway | 903/983–8265 | Weekdays 9–4, Sat. 10–4.

**Shakespeare Garden.** This garden is a horticultural display of flora native to William Shakespeare's England. All of the plants in the garden are referred to in one of his plays. | U.S. 259 at Brook Dr. | 903/984–5022 | Free | Daily.

### ON THE CALENDAR
**SEPT., OCT.: *KTPB Fine Arts Festival*.** Locally produced artwork, live music, and a kids' arts festival are part of the fun. | 903/983–8625.

## Dining
**Trail Riders Grill.** American. You can get basic fare such as hamburgers and chicken-fried steak at this no-frills eatery. | Hwy. 42N and Farm Road 1252, Kilgore | 903/984–4746 | No supper | $3–$6 | AE, D, MC, V.

## Lodging
**Best Western Inn of Kilgore.** This inn is conveniently located, only 2 mi from the East Texas Oil Museum and 3 mi from Kilgore College. Rooms are clean and affordable. Complimentary Continental breakfast, some in-room hot tubs, cable TV, pool, business services, no pets. | 1411 Hwy. 259 N., Kilgore | 903/986–1195 | fax 903/986–3996 | www.bestwestern.com | 43 rooms | $51–$90 | AE, D, DC, MC, V.

# KILLEEN

*(Nearby towns also listed: Salado, Temple)*

Fort Hood, one of the largest military bases in the world, makes its home here. The town is a good destination for military buffs because of its military museums. Nearby Belton Lake has parklands for picnics and camping.

**Information: Killeen Convention and Visitors Bureau** | Box 548, Killeen, TX 76540 | 254/526–9551 or 800/869–8265 | mbrenner@gkcc.com | www.gkcc.com.

## Attractions

**Belton Lake Outdoor Recreation Area (BLORA).** You can rent paddleboats and jetskis or enjoy the waterslides on this man-made lake. For land lovers, there is horseback riding and picnic areas. | Fort Hood, off N. Nolan Rd. | 254/287–8303 | $3 | Wed.–Thurs. noon–8; Fri.–Sat. 10–8; Closed Sun.–Mon.

**Fort Hood.** Fort Hood is the largest military base in the free world. Within the complex are two museums (visitors must stop at gate at U.S. 190 west of Killeen before entering). | Rte. 317 | 817/287–8506 | Free | Daily.

The **1st Cavalry Division Museum** has displays on the history of the base's first cavalry unit. | 761st Tank Destroyer Blvd. | Free | Weekdays 9–3:30, weekends noon–3:30.

With many historic vehicles, the **4th Infantry Divison Museum** offers exhibits on the history of the base's 4th Infantry Divison. | Free | Weekdays 9–3:30, weekends noon–3:30.

**Stillhouse Hollow Lake.** Damming up the Lampasas River created this 6,500-acre lake. Five public parks offer boat services, camping, and picnicking. | Rte. 1670 from U.S. 190 west | 254/526–9551 | Free | Daily.

ON THE CALENDAR
**MAY: *Festival of Flags*.** This festival brings the whole town together for a rodeo show, a carnival, an international food fair, and a parade. | 254/526–0550.

## Dining

**Divino's.** Italian. There's a feeling of the Italian countryside at this small family eatery. Try the fettuccine Alfredo or veal Marsala. Kids' menu. | 2100 S.W. S. Young Ave. | 254/680–3383 | $14–$23 | AE, D, DC, MC, V.

**Remington's Restaurant.** American. Plants and paintings of landscapes and flowers line the inside of this friendly restaurant. Be sure to try the grilled chicken Caesar salad or a succulent steak. | 1721 E. Central Texas Expressway (U.S. 190) | 254/634–1555 | No lunch Sat. No supper Sun. | $7–$13 | AE, D, DC, MC, V.

## Lodging

**Days Inn.** This Days Inn is near Killeen Mall, the Killeen Special Events Center, and Fort Hood. Its contemporary design includes Spanish deco accents. Cable TV, pool. | 810 Central Texas Expressway | 254/634–6644 | fax 254/634–2751 | 40 rooms | $50–$70 | AE, D, DC, MC, V.

**Holiday Inn Express.** This two-story motel is on U.S. 190, 3 mi from downtown Killeen, and 12 mi from Fort Hood. The Texas Roadhouse restaurant is nearby. Bar, complimentary Continental breakfast, in-room data ports, some refrigerators, some microwaves, cable TV, business services, pets allowed. | 1602 E. Central Texas Expressway (U.S. 190) | 254/554–2727 | fax 254/554–9980 | www.hiexpress.com | 68 rooms | $61–$65 | AE, D, DC, MC, V.

**La Quinta.** You can enjoy this hotel for its Mediterranean Spanish feel and beautifully landscaped grounds, all convenient to Fort Hood and the Killeen Mall. Rooms are modern and well equipped. Restaurant, complimentary Continental breakfast, in-room data ports, cable TV, pool, airport shuttle, free parking, pets allowed. | 1112 S. Hood St. | 254/526–8331 | fax 254/526–0394 | 105 rooms | $59–$72 | AE, D, DC, MC, V.

**Plaza Hotel.** The Plaza Hotel is near shopping centers, the Killeen Airport, and local restaurants. Its six-story contemporary design is punctuated by an atrium. Banquet facilities and suites are available. Restaurant, room service, in-room data ports, some refrigerators, cable TV, pool, exercise equipment, business services, airport shuttle. | 1721 Central Texas Expressway | 254/634–1555 or 800/633–8756 | fax 254/519–2945 | 146 rooms | $75–$98 | AE, D, DC, MC, V.

**Ramada Inn Fort Hood/Killeen.** You'll find this large, standard inn on manicured grounds near to U.S. 190 and U.S. 195. The entrance to the east gate of Fort Hood is less than 1 mi away, and there are several restaurants within walking distance as well as one on the premises. Restaurant, bar, room service, complimentary breakfast, in-room data ports, cable TV, pool, laundry services, business services, airport shuttle, some pets. | 1100 S. Fort Hood Rd. | 254/634–3101 | fax 254/634–8844 | www.ramada.com | 164 rooms | $43–$77 | AE, D, DC, MC, V.

# KINGSVILLE

*(Nearby towns also listed: Alice, Corpus Christi, Padre Island)*

The legacy of the world famous King Ranch, once the largest in the world, is apparent throughout this city, just a few miles from the cattle ranch. An array of downtown antiques shops and boutiques lies on Kleberg Avenue and King Street, named for the families who founded the famous ranch.

**Information: Kingsville Convention and Visitors Bureau** | 1501 N. Hwy. 77, Kingsville, TX 78363 | 361/592–8516 or 800/333–5032 | cvb@kingsvilletexas.com | www.kingsvilletexas.com.

## Attractions

**King Ranch.** Sprawling across 825,000 acres, the King Ranch traces its history to 1853 when it was founded by Capt. Richard King, a self-made man who made his fortune on Rio Grande riverboats. Visitors can enjoy a guided tour of the working ranch in air-conditioned buses. Still one of the largest in the world, the ranch developed the Santa Gertrudis and King Ranch Santa Cruz breeds of cattle as well as the first registered American quarter horse. Today it's home to 60,000 cattle and 300 quarter horses and welcomes visitors from around the world. | Santa Gertrudis Ave. or Hwy. 141, 1½ mi. west of town | 361/592–8055 or 800/333–5032 | fax 361/595–1344 | www.king-ranch.com | Free | Mon.–Sat. 9–4, Sun. noon–5.

**King Ranch Museum.** The King Ranch Museum provides visitors with a look at the history of the ranch, including a stunning photographic essay of life on King Ranch in the 1940s. A collection of saddles, antique carriages, and antique cars rounds out the exhibits. | 405 N. Sixth St. | 361/595–1881 | www.king-ranch.com | $4 | Mon.–Sat. 10–4, Sun. 1–5.

## BIRDING

Along the Texas coastline, bird lovers from around the globe cast their binoculars on approximately 400 recorded species. In fact, Texas is the number-one North American bird watching destination.

Birders are drawn to the Texas coast for the richness of species found throughout the year in its refuges, preserves, and shorelines. The Coastal Bend is located on the Central Flyway, a bird highway that brings migrators from Canada, through Montana, and over the Central states on their way to Mexico. This area also receives migrators from the Mississippi Flyway that travel the coastline instead of venturing across the open Gulf waters. Even more feathered visitors come east from the Rocky Mountain Flyway, and occasionally up from Mexico.

Numerous birding sites are scattered along the Coastal Bend and down to South Padre. The Great Texas Coastal Birding Trail, co-sponsored by the Texas Parks and Wildlife Department and the Texas Department of Transportation, identifies sites most popular with birders.

© Artville

**King Ranch Saddle Shop.** The King Ranch Saddle Shop carries on the tradition of saddle-making that began after the Civil War when Captain King started his own saddle shop. Today the King Ranch Saddle Shop produces fine purses, belts, and, of course, saddles in downtown Kingsville's John B. Ragland Mercantile Company Building. | 201 E. Kleberg | 361/595–1881 | www.king-ranch.com | Free | Mon.–Sat. 10–6.

**Texas A&M University–Kingsville.** Formerly the South Texas State Teachers College, this university has an extensive agriculture program. | Armstrong St. between Santa Gertrudis and Corral Aves | 361/595–2111 | Free | Daily.
Within the university lies the **John E. Conner Museum,** which highlights the natural and social history of South Texas. Exhibits focus on ranching, South Texas ecosystems, and the area's fossils and minerals. | 821 W. Santa Gertrudis Ave. | 361/593–2849 | Free | Mon.–Sat. 9–5.

### ON THE CALENDAR
**MAR.:** *International Young Performers Musical Competition.* The competition brings together award-winning performers from around the world, ranging from junior high school to college students. The competition focuses on classical music, including piano and stringed instruments. | 361/592–8516 or 800/333–5032.
**MAR.:** *Texas A&M National Intercollegiate Rodeo.* Rodeo riding, trick riding, and roping are featured at this festival, held at the Northway Exposition Center. | 930/592–8516 or 800/333–5032.
**OCT.:** *Fiesta de Colores.* This arts and crafts sale at the Northway Exposition Center showcases the work of many South Texas artisans selling everything from needlework to pottery. | 930/592–8516 or 800/333–5032.

## Dining
**El Tapatio.** Mexican. Tortillas are homemade in this casual local favorite. Try any of the fajita plates or chicken strips. | 630 W. Santa Gertrudis St. | 361/516–1655 | Breakfast also available. No supper | $3–$6 | AE, D, MC, V.

**King's Inn.** Seafood. Fresh Gulf seafood is served family-style at this specialty restaurant. Pick from catfish to shrimp, and everything in between; you pay by the pound. Enjoy a view of Baffin Bay while you dine. | Loyola Beach on Rt. 1 | 361/297–5265 | Closed Sun.–Mon. | $8–$22 | AE, DC, MC, V.

## Lodging
**B-Bar-B Ranch.** Originally part of the historic King Ranch, this ranch-house-turned-lodge has kept its rustic feel, down to the Old West-style rooms. You can arrange to go hunting for quail, turkey, or nilgai, or go bird watching. Complimentary breakfast, some in-room hot tubs, pool, outdoor hot tub, fishing, some pets allowed, no kids, no smoking. | 325 E. CR 2215 | 361/296–3331 | fax 361/296–3337 | bbarb@rivnet.com | www.b-bar-b.com | 15 rooms, 1 suite | $85, $125 suite | D, MC, V.

**Best Western Kingsville Inn.** For large rooms at a reasonable rate, this Best Western is the perfect choice. The King Ranch Museum and Texas A&M University are both 1 mi away. Complimentary Continental breakfast, some microwaves, some refrigerators, in-room data ports, cable TV, pool, outdoor hot tub, laundry services, business services, some pets. | 2402 East King Ave. | 361/595–5656 | fax 361/595–5000 | www.bestwestern.com | 50 rooms | $53–$59 | AE, D, DC, MC, V.

**Quality Inn.** This chain motel is close to the Southgate Mall, movie theaters, a restaurant, and local museums. Standard but comfortable chain accommodations. Complimentary Continental breakfast, refrigerators, cable TV, pool, wading pool, exercise equipment, business services, pets allowed. | 221 S. Hwy. 77 Bypass | 361/592–5251 | fax 361/592–6197 | 117 rooms | $50–$55 | AE, D, DC, MC, V.

# LA GRANGE

*(Nearby towns also listed: Austin, Gonzales, Lockhart, Smithville)*

When some folks hear "La Grange" they think of the home of "The Best Little Whore-house in Texas," a long-running Broadway musical about Chicken Ranch, once the oldest continually operating brothel in the country. Though the memory of the Chicken Ranch lives on, the brothel is long gone and, to locals, La Grange is just a quiet farm town with a classic Texas courthouse square.

Information: **La Grange Area Chamber of Commerce** | 171 S. Main St., La Grange, TX 78945-2610 | 979/968–5756 or 800/LA–GRANGE | chamber@lagrangetx.org | www.lagrangetx.org.

## Attractions

**Fayette Heritage Museum.** This museum includes a genealogy collection, census indexes and records, and a Texana book collection and art. | 855 S. Jefferson | 979/968–6418 | lagrange.fais.net/museum/ | Free | Tues.–Fri. 10–5, Sat. 10–1, Sun. 1–5.

**Fayette Power Project Lake and Parks.** You can go bass fishing at this lake, which is used as a cooling pond for the electric generating plant. | Rte. 159 at Rte. 71 | 979/249–3111 | Free | Daily.

**Hostyn Grotto.** On a hilltop with a panorama of La Grange below, several shrines and a 40-ft replica of an 1856 church take the form of a unique rock grotto. Churchgoers still drive the 5 mi south from town to attend this working church. | U.S. 77 S | 979/968–5756 or 800/524–7264 | Free | Daily, dawn to dusk.

**Monument Hill and Kreische Brewery State Historical Park.** The hill is the burial place for Texans who died in the Dawson Massacre and the Mier Expedition, two important con-flicts that occurred in 1842, six years after the fall of the Alamo. The bodies of the Texans were returned here to be buried on the hilltop in a mass grave. Nearly a century later, in 1936, the state erected a monument to honor the fallen Texans. A visitors center here details the confrontations.

The park was also the site of one of Texas's first breweries. German immigrant Hein-rich Kreische purchased the hilltop and adjoining land, including the burial ground of the Texas heroes, in 1849. Although Kreische Brewery eventually became the third largest beer producer in the state, today it is in ruins. | Off U.S. 77 on Spur 92 | 979/968–5658 | fax 979/968–5659 | www.tpwd.state.tx.us | $2 | Daily.

**Old Fayette County Jail.** You can view the old jailhouse and its artifacts, including a hang-ing rope and shackles. | 171 S. Main St., south of Courthouse Square | 979/968–5756 | Free | Weekdays 8–5, Sat. 10–4.

**Winedale Historical Center.** The 215-acre complex is home to a collection of historic struc-tures, a research center, a nature trail, and a picnic area. On the weekend, you can tour homes furnished with period antiques and stenciled ceilings, which recall the German cul-ture of the area. During the summer months, the University of Texas at Austin hosts an annual Shakespeare production here. | 3841 Rte. 2714 | 979/278–3530 | $3 | Sat. 9–5, Sun. noon–5, weekdays by appointment.

## ON THE CALENDAR

**AUG./SEPT.:** *Fayette County Country Fair.* This Labor Day weekend event includes a livestock/poultry show, arts and crafts, live music, and food booths. | 979/968–3781 or 979/968–3911.

**OCT.:** *Czhilispiel.* Savor some famous Texas chili with tastings and barbecue cook-offs. | 979/968–5756.

**DEC.: *Christmas in La Grange.*** This celebration includes Christmas shopping, carriage rides, homemade baked goods, and a parade. Santa visits in the afternoon to take pictures with the kids. | 800/524–7264.

## Dining

**Bon Ton.** German. This diner is a longtime local favorite. Try the homemade breads and pies, and German sausage dishes. | Rte. 71W | 979/968–5863 | Breakfast also available | $12–$23 | AE, D, MC, V.

**Schulze's Southern Grill.** Mexican. Various floral arrangements contribute to the friendly atmosphere in this eatery. Try the chicken flautas (chicken wrapped in a corn tortilla and then deep-fried) or the spicy enchiladas. You'll also find seafood and steak on this varied menu. | 658 S. Jefferson St. | 979/968–6612 | $6–$14 | AE, D, DC, MC, V.

## Lodging

**Oak Motel.** This small motel is within walking distance of downtown shops and restaurants. Cable TV, some pets allowed. | 227 S. Jefferson St. | 979/968–3133 | www.oakmotel.8m.com | 18 rooms | $39–$45 | AE, D, DC, MC, V.

# LA PORTE

MAP 8, K6

*(Nearby towns also listed: Baytown, Texas City)*

On the upper reaches of Galveston Bay, this port city was founded by the French in 1889. Today, it is home to many shipping and petrochemical industries.

Information: **La Porte Bayshore Chamber of Commerce** | 712 West Fairmont Parkway, La Porte, TX 77572 | 281/471–1123 | www.nwwin.com/laporte.tx/chamber.html.

## Attractions

**San Jacinto Battlefield State Historical Park.** In the community of Deer Park near Houston, this is the site of the fateful battle between the Texas patriots and the Mexican army of Gen. Antonio Lopez de Santa Anna, which won Texas its independence in 1836. A 570-ft San Jacinto Monument made of Texas limestone commemorates the battle, at the base of which is the San Jacinto Museum of Texas History with displays on the region's history and a multimedia show. | 3523 Rte. 134 | 713/479–2421 or 281/479–2431 | www.tpwd.state.tx.us/park/battlesh/battlesh.htm | Nov.–Feb., daily 8–7; Mar.–Oct., daily 8 AM–9 PM.

The **Battleship USS *Texas*,** active in both world wars, was renovated using money raised by the schoolchildren of Texas. You can tour crew quarters, engine rooms, the navigation bridge, and more, of this ship, which is considered the last remaining dreadnought battleship. | 3523 Rte. 134, La Porte, TX | 281/479–2431 | $5 | Daily, 10–5.

ON THE CALENDAR
**APR.: *Sylvan Beach Festival.*** This mid-Spring festival is held the last Sat. in Apr. and includes live music, crawfish eating contests, and a beauty pageant. | 281/471–1123.

## Dining

**Sonny's Happy Cajun Restaurant.** Cajun. This rustic-looking eatery is adorned with mounted moose and deer heads on dark brown walls. Among the more popular dishes are fish ponchatrain and BBQ shrimp. Kid's menu. | 129 N. 10th St. | 281/470–9380 | $8–$24 | AE, D, DC, MC, V.

## Lodging

**Best Western La Porte Inn.** The rooms at this motel are spacious with big windows and lots of light. NASA and the Greyhound Race Track are only 12 mi away. Complimentary Continental breakfast, in-room data ports, some kitchenettes, microwaves, refrigerators, some in-room hot tubs, cable TV, pool, laundry facilities, business services, no pets. | 705 U.S. 146S | 281/471–4040 | fax 281/470–9191 | www.bestwestern.com | 46 rooms, 3 suites | $58–$60, $80 suites | AE, D, DC, MC, V.

# LAREDO

*(Nearby town also listed: San Antonio)*

Founded by an officer of the Royal Army of Spain in 1755, Laredo sits on the banks of the Rio Grande. Following the war with Mexico, many Laredo residents headed across the border to start their own town. They named their fledgling community "Nuevo Laredo" or "New Laredo." Healthy trade between the two counties, as well as the fact that many family properties straddle both sides of the border continue to link the cities, earning them the nickname "Los Dos Laredos"—The Two Laredos. You can begin your tour in the original Laredo and easily visit its Mexican sister city by walking just a short distance across one of the international bridges that span the Rio Grande.

**Information: Laredo Convention and Visitors Bureau** | 501 San Agustin, Laredo, TX 78040 | 956/795–2200 or 800/795–2185 | www.visitlaredo.com.

## Attractions

**Lake Casa Blanca International State Park.** At this 2,021-acre park, you can hike, swim, fish, boat, mountain bike, or just relax at one of the many picnic sites. | East of Laredo, off U.S. 59, off Loop 20 | 210/725–3826 or 800/792–1112 | www.tpwd.state.tx.us/park/lakecasa/lakecasa.htm | $3 | Daily 7 AM–10 PM.

## GLASS BLOWER

When visiting Texas, save time for a trip across the border to Nuevo Laredo's El Cid, the city's only glass factory, at 3861 Avenida Reforma. You'll need to drive or catch a taxi to the property, but the shopping here makes the effort worthwhile. Romualdo Canales has owned El Cid for more than 20 years, and he still comes in seven days a week to produce the colorful glassware.

Romualdo carries on a long-time Mexican craft of glassblowing, a tradition that he sees gradually eroding. He sees traditional Mexican culture being replaced in school by new ideas and new techniques. He would prefer to be more creative, even, he says, if that means losing time and money.

Behind the showroom, six to seven men work the 1,400° ovens to produce bowls and glasses, most edged with color. Minerals such as copper and cobalt produce many of the colors: aquamarine, red, and, the most popular tint, bullet blue. Other colors reflect recycling at its best; melted beer bottles create amber-tinted rims, and whisky bottles yield green-rimmed glasses. If you're looking for more than just the traditional glasses and bowls, however, according to Romualdo, he uses his creativity to make "anything and everything."

© Corbis

**Lamar Bruni Vergara Environmental Science Center.** Great for people of all ages, this hands-on science center in Lamar Community College has live alligators on display, as well as a turtle beach, and an exhibit of live animals and plants native to the Rio Grande River. | 1 West End Washington St. | 956/764–5701 | $3 | Mon.–Thurs. 7:30–4:30, Fri. 8–1, Sat. 9–noon.

**Laredo Children's Museum.** This museum has "hands-on" exhibits dealing with science, technology and the arts. It also holds regular afternoon arts and crafts workshops for kids and their parents. | Laredo Community College, West End Washington St. | 956/725–2299 | fax 956/725–1776 | $1 | Wed.–Fri. 9–2, Sat. 9–6, Sun. 11–4.

**Republic of the Rio Grande Museum.** Six flags have flown over most of Texas, but Laredo has seen seven, thanks to the short-lived Republic of the Rio Grande, a country formed when Northern Mexico seceded in 1839. The new state existed until 1841. Housed in a one-story adobe structure that was once the capitol building of the republic, the museum contains guns, saddles, and household belongings from that brief period. | 1003 Zaragoza St. | 956/727–3480 | $1 | Tues.–Sat. 8:30–4, Sun. 1–4.

**San Agustin Church.** Founded in 1778, this church overlooks San Agustin Plaza, the site of one of the West's bloodiest shoot-outs. In 1886 the *Botas* (boots) and *Huaraches* (sandals), two rival political groups, battled here, leaving more than 80 dead when the smoke cleared. | 214 San Agustin Ave. | Free | Daily.

## ON THE CALENDAR

**FEB.: *George Washington's Birthday Celebration.*** This 10-day event honors George Washington with a carnival, parades, and more. | 956/795–2200, 956/722–0589, or 800/795–2185.

**MAR.: *Laredo International Fair and Exposition.*** You can enjoy the rides, play games, participate in an auction, watch a rodeo, or visit the petting zoo. | 800/795–2185 | $5.

**MAY: *Pow Wow Festival.*** Native American arts and crafts, food, and intertribal dances are highlights of this national festival. | 956/795–2200 or 800/795–2185.

**SEPT./MAR.: *Expomex National Fair.*** This fair includes arts and crafts, live music, folk dancing, fireworks, a rodeo, cockfights, and food from all regions of Mexico. The fair is held twice a year. | 800/361–3360.

## Dining

**El Metate Restaurant.** Mexican. Paintings of the Mexican landscape, created by the owner herself, decorate this wonderful eatery. All of the chairs inside are hand-carved and imported from Mexico. Everything here is tasty but El Metate is renowned for its ranchero steaks and enchiladas. Be sure to have some soup with your meal—try either caldo or menudo. | 319 W. Del Mar Blvd. | 956/722–9457 | Breakfast also available. No supper. Closed Sun. | $5–$8 | No credit cards.

**Favorato's Restaurant.** Italian. An upscale restaurant and popular lounge, Favorato's has both a comprehensive wine list and a delicious menu. The pasta and meat dishes are unbeatable: try the veal Parmesan. A painting of the Leaning Tower of Pisa completes the experience. Kids' menu. | 1916 San Bernardo Ave. | 956/722–1802 | Closed Sun. | $8–$28 | AE, D, DC, MC, V.

**Laredo Bar and Grill.** American. This restaurant on the north side of town caters to casual yet upscale diners. Eclectic specialties include the seafood pasta and the prime rib. You can hear live music here in the evenings. Kids' menu. | 102 Del Court Rd. | 956/717–0090 | $5–$25 | AE, D, DC, MC, V.

**Pelican's Wharf.** Seafood. You'll find some of the best seafood in town in this beach-cabin restaurant flanked by palm trees. Try the mahi-mahi or the Alaskan king crab. | 619 Chicago St. | 956/727–5070 | Reservations essential | No lunch | $7–$21 | AE, D, DC, MC, V.

**Sirloin Stockade.** Steak. You can see across the Mexican border as you dine here. You can get brisket, lasagna, and barbecue ribs in the comprehensive, all-day buffet. The sirloins are also top sellers. Kids' menu. | 5301 San Dario Ave. | 956/724–3800 | $6–$10 | AE, D, DC, MC, V.

# Lodging

**Best Western Fiesta Inn.** This motel is 3 mi from Texas A&M University. | 150 rooms. Complimentary Continental breakfast, some refrigerators, cable TV, pool, laundry facilities, business services, airport shuttle, some pets allowed. | 5240 San Bernardo | 956/723–3603 | fax 956/724–7697 | $69–$73 | AE, D, DC, MC, V.

**Courtyard by Marriott.** This five-story hotel is off I–35 and is 1 mi from the Mexican border. It has a shuttle to the mall, the airport, and the border. | 110 rooms. Restaurant, bar, some refrigerators, cable TV, pool, hot tub, exercise equipment, laundry facilities, business services, airport shuttle. | 2410 Santa Ursula Ave. | 956/725–5555 | fax 956/724–8848 | www.courtyard.com/lrdcy/ | $79–$99 | AE, D, DC, MC, V.

**Econo Lodge.** This motel is 2½ mi from the Mexican border. | 75 rooms. Complimentary Continental breakfast, some microwaves, refrigerators, cable TV, pool, laundry facilities, business services. | 2620 Santa Ursula Ave. | 956/722–6321 | fax 956/722–5502 | $35–$70 | AE, D, DC, MC, V.

**Family Gardens Inn.** This lovely complex has a number of facilities and special services to keep you and your family entertained, and its pricing encourages extended visits. There are grills available in the picnic area for outdoor cooking, and there's evening entertainment accessible both at the inn and in nearby Laredo. Picnic area, complimentary Continental breakfast, in-room data ports, some microwaves, refrigerators, cable TV, pool, spa, exercise equipment, video games, playground, laundry facilities, airport shuttle, pets allowed (fee). | 5830 San Bernardo Ave. | 956/723–5300 | www.familygardens.com | 192 rooms | $54–$61 | MAP | AE, D, DC, MC, V.

**Hampton Inn Laredo.** You'll find this hotel on the north side of the city, 5 mi from the downtown area. Many restaurants and shopping opportunities are within blocks of the hotel. Complimentary Continental breakfast, some microwaves, cable TV, pool, indoor hot tub, business services, no pets. | 7903 San Dario Ave. | 956/717–8888 | fax 956/717–8391 | www.hamptoninn.com | 120 rooms | $78–$82 | AE, D, DC, MC, V.

**Holiday Inn Civic Center.** This stunning 14-story hotel is only 2 mi from the Mexican border. There is live entertainment in the lounge Thurs., Fri., and Sat. nights. Restaurant, bar, in-room data ports, cable TV, pool, outdoor hot tub, sauna, exercise equipment, laundry services, business services, airport shuttle, pets allowed. | 800 Garden St. | 956/727–5800 | fax 956–727–0278 | www.holiday-inn.com | 200 rooms, 3 suites | $98, $170 suites | AE, D, DC, MC, V.

**La Posada.** On the Rio Grande, this two-story hotel, once a 19th-century Spanish Colonial convent, has red-tile roofs, archways, and two tropical courtyards. | 208 rooms, 57 suites. 3 restaurants, bars (with entertainment), room service, in-room data ports, some refrigerators, cable TV, 2 pools, exercise equipment, business services, airport shuttle, free parking. | 1000 Zaragoza St. | 956/722–1701 or 800/444–2099 | fax 956/722–4758 | www.laposadahotel-laredo.com | $99–$149 | AE, D, DC, MC, V.

**Motel 6–Laredo South.** A mall is across the highway from this two–story motel, and the Mexican border is 3 mi away. | 94 rooms. Cable TV, pool, pets allowed. | 5310 San Bernardo Ave. | 956/725–8187 | fax 956/725–0424 | $40–$45 | AE, D, DC, MC, V.

**Motel 6–North.** Rooms have either indoor or outdoor access. Restaurants are within walking distance. | 109 rooms. Cable TV, pool, laundry facilities, pets allowed. | 5920 San Bernardo Ave. | 956/722–8133 | fax 956/725–8212 | $39–$45 | AE, D, DC, MC, V.

**Red Roof Inn.** Rooms have interior entrances at this four-story motel close to Laredo Community College, Seven Flags over Texas, and shopping. | 150 rooms. Cable TV, pool, laundry facilities, pets allowed. | I–35 at Calton Rd. | 800/843–7663 | fax 956/712–4337 | $40–$68 | AE, D, DC, MC, V.

**Rio Grande Plaza.** Overlooking the Rio Grande River, this 15-story hotel has unique round architecture. All rooms have floor to ceiling, wall to wall views of the city or of the Rio Grande and Old Mexico. Close to shopping, museums, and restaurants. | 207 rooms. Restaurant, bar, in-room data ports, cable TV, gym, laundry facilities, business services, airport shuttle, pets allowed. | 1 S. Main Ave. | 956/722–2411 | fax 956/722–4578 | $110–$125 | AE, D, DC, MC, V.

# LEWISVILLE

MAP 8, I2

*(Nearby towns also listed: Arlington–Grand Prairie, Dallas, Ft. Worth, Grapevine, Irving, Plano, Richardson)*

Lewisville first boomed in the late 1850s, with the arrival of a mill, trading post, dry goods store, and Denton county's first cotton gin. Today, this city, 26 miles north of Dallas, is part of one of the fastest growing counties in Texas. It's popular for its lakeside recreation, as well as its proximity to the Dallas/Ft. Worth International Airport. Its seven golf courses make it the golf mecca of the Dallas/Ft. Worth area.

Information: **Lewisville Visitors Bureau** | 551 N. Valley Pkwy., Lewisville, TX 75067 | 972/436–9571 or 800/657–9571 | www.visitlewisville.com.

## Attractions

**Lake Lewisville.** This lake spans 23,000 acres, has 233 miles of shoreline, is surrounded by miles of nature trails, and has an average depth of 25 ft. It's particularly enjoyed by water-skiers, wind surfers, boaters, and anglers. The lake is east of the I–35 and Rte. 4071 junction. | N. Mill St. | 972/434–1666 | Parks $3 for entry.

**Tour 18.** Opened in 1992, this course is a recreation of the greatest 18 golf holes in the country. | 8718 Amen Corner, Flower Mound, TX | 817/430–2000 | Year-round.

**Vista Ridge Mall.** More than 160 specialty stores, four department stores, a food court, and a 12-screen movie theatre are found within this mall's more than 1 million square ft. | 2401 S. Stemmons Fwy | 972/315–0015 | Free | Mon.–Sat. 10–9, Sun. 11–7.

## Dining

**Angelina's Mexican Restaurant.** Tex-Mex. Popular Tex-Mex dishes are served in a relaxed atmosphere. | 1396 W. Main St. | 972/436–3466 | $5–$12 | AE, D, MC, V.

**Marshall's Bar-B-Q.** Barbecue. Texas barbecue is served cafeteria-style. Barbecue ribs and chicken are speciality. | 1183 S. Mill St. | 972/221–4303 | $5–$8 | AE, D, MC, V.

**Salerno Restaurant.** Italian. Traditional and new Italian fare is served in this casual restaurant and club. | 3407 Long Prairie Rd. | 972/539–9534 | $6–$19 | AE, D, DC, MC, V.

## Lodging

**Comfort Suites.** This hotel is adjacent to Vista Ridge Mall. It's 7 mi from Dallas/Ft. Worth International Airport, 16 mi from Love Field airport, and 6 mi from Lake Lewisville. Complimentary Continental breakfast, in-room data ports, cable TV, pool, hot tub. | 755 Vista Ridge Dr. | 972/315–6464 | www.comfortinn.com | 60 rooms | $80–$85 | AE, D, MC, V.

**Hampton Inn.** This hotel is on I–35. It's 8 mi from the Dallas/Ft. Worth International Airport, 2 mi from Vista Ridge Mall, and 5 mi from Grapevine Mills mall. Complimentary Continental breakfast, cable TV, pool, gym, hot tub, laundry service, no pets. | 885 S. Stemmons Fwy. (I–35) | 972/420–1318 | www.hampton-inn.com | 54 rooms | $65–$79 | AE, D, MC, V.

**Homewood Suites Hotel.** This all-suites hotel is 5 miles from the heart of Lewisville. Complimentary breakfast. Cable TV. Pool. Hot tub. Kitchen, microwaves. In-room data ports. Business Services. | 700 Hebron Pkwy. | 972/315–6123 | 97 suites | $119–$169 | AE, D, MC, V.

# LOCKHART

*(Nearby towns also listed: Austin, La Grange, San Antonio, San Marcos)*

Formerly called Plum Creek, this town was re-named for pioneer surveyor Byrd Lockhart. Today it's the self-proclaimed barbecue capital of Texas, due to the praise its restaurants have received from prominent state, national, and international newspapers and magazines.

In the 1800s, Lockhart was the southern end of the Chisholm Trail. Today it is strategically located between Austin and San Antonio and just 25 minutes from the Austin-Bergstrom International Airport.

**Information:** **Lockhart Chamber of Commerce** | 205 S. Main, Lockhart, TX 78644 | 512/398–2818 | www.lockhart-tx.org.

## Attractions

**Lockhart State Park.** One of the few state parks with a golf course, this 364-acre escape offers picnicking, fishing, camping and swimming. | Off Rte. 20 | 512/398–3479 | $2 | Daily.

**Caldwell County Museum.** County history unfolds in the cells of a former 1910 jailhouse. Pioneer furnishings, farm equipment and artifacts fill the museum. | 315 E. Market | 512/398–2828 | Donation | Weekends 1–5.

**Caldwell County Courthouse.** This elaborately designed limestone and red sandstone building looms over the town square. Built in 1894, it underwent renovations that were completed in 2000. | 110 S. Main | 512/398–2818 | Free | Mon–Fri. 9–5.

## Dining

**Kreuz Market.** Barbecue. This legendary, no-frills, barbecue joint (pronounced "krites") serves meat on brown butcher paper, with white bread, a hunk of cheese, avocado slices, tomatoes, and onions. Ask for sauce and they might show you the door. | 619 N. Colorado | 512/398–2361 | Daily | $7–$15 | AE, D, MC, V.

## Lodging

**Albion Bed and Breakfast.** Wraparound porches are found on both stories of this beautiful 1898 home. Each guest room is filled with antiques and includes a private bath. | 604 W. San Antonio | 512/376–6775 | 5 rooms | $75–$100 | AE, D, MC, V.

**Best Western Plum Creek.** This mid-size hotel is near the main highway through town. | 2007 S. Colorado | 512/398–4911 | 40 rooms | $40–$60 | AE, D, MC, V.

**Lockhart Inn.** This motel is a solid value with a full breakfast in the restaurant next door included with the price of the room. Plus, it's only 5 blocks from downtown. | 1207 S. Colorado | 512/398–5201 | 32 rooms | $30–$40 | MAP | AE, D, DC, MC, V.

# LONGVIEW

*(Nearby towns also listed: Kilgore, Jefferson, Marshall, Tyler)*

Longview was founded in 1870 by O. H. Methvin. A successful farmer, Methvin made a deal with Southern Pacific Railroad to hand over 100 acres of land for one gold dollar on the condition that the railroad build a town on the land. Longview, which was once an oil boomtown, still has many reminders of the past, like the Gregg County Courthouse and the "Hundred Acres of Heritage" in the downtown area, of which you can take self-guided tours. It is also a gateway to the Piney Woods, a region that is known for its great fishing, camping, and swimming.

Information: **Longview Convention and Visitors Bureau** | Box 472, Longview, TX 75606 | 903/753–3281 | lcvb@longviewtx.com | www.longviewtx.com.

## Attractions

**GAF Auto Museum.** You'll see over 55 American automobiles in this museum's gleaming collection, the oldest of which dates back to 1916. Among the more notable vehicles on display are a 1918 Chandler and a 1924 Buick Roadster. | 340 W. Tyler St. | 903/758–0002 | Free | Weekdays 8–5.

**Longview Museum and Arts Center.** The museum's contemporary collection of paintings, drawings, photography, and sculpture focuses on artists of the Southwest, especially Texans. | 215 E. Tyler St., Longview, TX | 903/753–8103 | Free | Tues.–Fri. 10–4, Sat. noon–4.

**R. G. LeTourneau Museum.** On the top floor of the student center, this museum contains exhibits and models of earth-moving equipment invented by local industrialist R. G. LeTourneau. | Memorial Student Center, 2100 S. Mobberly Ave. | 903/753–0231 | Free | Tues.– Sun. 8–5.

### ON THE CALENDAR

**JUNE:** *AlleyFest.* This festival, which began as a small art show held in Bank Alley, has grown tremendously to include live music on two stages, sports activities including a 10K run around the downtown area, and arts and crafts and science exhibits for the kids. | 903/753–3281 | www.alleyfest.org.

**SEPT.:** *Gregg County Fair and Expo.* In operation since 1949, this fair gives authentic cowboys the chance to strut their stuff with bull riding, calf roping, and bareback riding demonstrations. | 903/753–4478.

## Dining

**Bodacious West Bar-B-Q.** Barbecue. Known for chopped beef and ribs, this casual eatery is a Longview favorite. Inside, various pictures from the early 20th century adorn the walls. | 1402 W. Marshall St. | 903/236–3215 | Closed Sun. | $4–$8 | AE, D, MC, V.

**Johnny Cace's Seafood and Steak House.** Cajun/Creole. This family-run restaurant specializes in steak, fresh seafood, and Southern hospitality. Try one of the many catfish or lobster dishes or the famous "shrimp in shorts," a dish of breaded Gulf butterfly shrimp. Kids' menu. | 1501 E. Marshall St. | 903/753–7691 | www.johnnycaces.com | No lunch Sun., Mon. | $12–$30 | AE, D, DC, MC, V.

**Papacita's.** Tex-Mex. Sombreros, candelabras and old furniture fill this casual family restaurant, which serves the usual Tex-Mex fare: quesadillas, fajitas, enchiladas and Mexican pizzas. It also has a mesquite pit for steaks, ribs and chicken. Kids' menu. | 305 Loop 281 | 903/663–1700 | www.papacitas.com | $17–$22 | AE, D, MC, V.

## Lodging

**Best Western Inn of Longview.** A friendly staff and comfortable rooms await you at this family-owned Best Western. The inn is minutes away from three golf courses, freshwater fishing, and LeTourneau University. Restaurant, bar, complimentary Continental breakfast, room service, some microwaves, some refrigerators, in-room data ports, some in-room hot tubs, cable TV, indoor/outdoor pool, indoor hot tub, exercise equipment, game room, laundry services, business services, airport shuttle, no pets. | 3119 Estes Pkwy., Longview | 903/758–0700 | fax 903/758–8705 | www.bestwestern.com | 169 rooms, 18 suites | $69, $85 suites | AE, D, DC, MC, V.

**La Quinta Inn.** This hotel is near the convention center, mall, and LeTourneau University. | 105 rooms. Complimentary Continental breakfast, in-room data ports, cable TV, pool, business services, free parking, some pets allowed. | 502 S. Access Rd. | 903/757–3663 | fax 903/753–3780 | $55–$80 | AE, D, DC, MC, V.

**Longview Arms.** Located in the heart of historic downtown Longview, this B&B was originally constructed as a deluxe apartment complex serving oil field producers in the 1930s. Each of the five suites is roomy and luxurious. Complimentary breakfast, microwaves, refrigerators, in-room data ports, cable TV, business services, no pets, no smoking. | 110 W. Methvin St. | 903/236–3000 or 888/321–4720 | fax 903/236–0643 | inn@longviewarms.com | www.longviewarms.com | 5 suites | $95–$120 | AE, D, MC, V.

**Motel 6.** This motel is off of I–20 and about 1 mi from LeTourneau University. | 86 rooms. Cable TV, pool, laundry facilities, pets allowed. | 110 S. Access Rd. | 903/758–5256 | fax 903/758–0711 | $33–$49 | AE, D, DC, MC, V.

**Travelodge.** | 86 rooms. Restaurant, in-room data ports, cable TV, pool, laundry facilities, airport shuttle, pets allowed. | 3304 S. Eastman Rd. | 903/758–0711 | fax 903/758–0711 | $33–$49 | AE, D, DC, MC, V.

# LUBBOCK

MAP 8, E2

*(Nearby towns also listed: Amarillo, Childress, Plainview)*

Located on a plain the Spanish explorer Francisco Coronado named the Llano Estacado, Lubbock's climate and soil are ideal for growing grapes. This has led to the growth of many wineries in the community, and the use of Lubbock grapes by wine makers throughout the state. The town is also the home of Texas Tech University.

**Information: Convention and Visitors Bureau of Lubbock** | 1301 Broadway, Suite 200, 79408 | 806/747–5232 or 800/692–4035 | mmuse@lubbocklegends.com | www.lubbocklegends.com.

## Attractions

**Buddy Holly Center.** This center includes the Texas Musicians Hall of Fame and a fine arts gallery. | 1801 Ave. G, Lubbock | 806/767–2686 | fax 806/767–0732 | www.buddyhollycenter.org | $3 | Tue.–Fri. 10–6, Sat. 10–7, Closed Sun.–Mon.

**Buddy Holly Statue and Walk of Fame.** This statue of Lubbock's most famous resident is surrounded by plaques honoring other entertainment greats from West Texas, such as James Dean, Mac Davis, and Waylon Jennings. | Sixth St. and Ave. Q | 806/747–5232 | Free | Daily.

**Buffalo Springs Lake Recreational Area.** Activities available at this recreation area include camping, fishing, volleyball, jet skiing, and waterskiing. There are also nature trails, horseshoe pits, areas to hike, and volleyball. | On Rte. 835 | 806/747–3353 | fax 806/747–3714 | $2 | Daily.

**Cap Rock.** This winery can store up to 139,000 gallons of wine. Its grapes are harvested on 98 acres of vineyards that lie within the property's total 199 acres. Tours and tastings are available. | Woodrow Rd. and U.S. 87 | 806/863–2704 | www.caprockwinery.com | free | Mon.–Sat. 10–5, Sun. noon–5.

**Llano Estacado Winery.** Established in 1976 and now the largest premium winery in the state, Llano Estacado produces some of the best wine to come out of Texas. The winery makes 18 different wines, from Cabernet to Chenin Blanc. Tours are given daily, and there is a sampling room and gift shop. | Rte. 1585, 7 mi southeast of Lubbock | 806/745–2258 | www.llanowine.com | Free | Daily 9–5.

**Mackenzie Park.** This 260–acre day-use park features a prairie dog town. There's also a picnic area and a small amusement park. | Off I–27 to Broadway to Rte. 18 | 806/775–3000 | Free | Daily.

**Science Spectrum–Omnimax.** This dome-screen theater presents specially produced movies on a variety of natural history themes. The Science Spectrum is a hands-on museum illustrating the concepts of science for all ages. | 2579 S. Loop 289 | 806/745–2525 or 806/745–MAXX | fax 806/745–1115 | www.sciencespectrum.com | $5.50 for Science Spectrum, $6 for Omnimax | Weekdays 10–5:30, Sat. 10–7, Sun. 1–5:30.

**Texas Tech University.** This college has a special emphasis on petrochemical studies. | University Ave. and Broadway Ave. | 806/742–1299 | Free | Daily.

On campus you'll find the **Museum of Texas Tech University,** which offers a survey collection encompassing history, art, and science. The museum is also home to the Moody Planetarium, which features star programs. | 4th St. and Indiana Ave. | 806/742–2490 | www.ttu.edu/~museum | Free | Tues.–Wed. 10–5, Thurs. 10–8:30, Fri., Sat. 10–5, Sun. 10–5.

**Texas Water Rampage.** This water park, with its serpentine slides, wave pool, and sand volleyball, guarantees fun for the entire family. | 6600 Brownfield Hwy. | 806/796–0701 | fax 806/799–5701 | $12.75 | Mon.–Sat. noon–7, Sun. noon–6.

**Ranching Heritage Center.** The center includes 33 period buildings ranging from ranch homes to bunkhouses. These, together with the museum, explore the history of the Panhandle and its role in ranching. | 3121 4th St. | 806/742–2482 | fax 806/742–0616 | Free | Mon.–Sat. 10–5, Sun. 1–5.

**Lubbock Lake Landmark State Historic Park.** This site has been inhabited by humans since 12,000 BC. Evidence of mammoth, camels, giant bison and other prehistoric animals has been discovered here. The park includes an interpretive center with artifacts and a children's learning center. | 2202 Landmark Ln., just north of Campus Loop 289 and Landmark Dr. | 806/765–0737 | fax 806/763–1968 | www.tpwd.state.tx.us | Free | Tues.–Sat. 9–5, Sun. 1–5.

## ON THE CALENDAR
**APR.:** *Lubbock Arts Festival.* The South Plains Fairgrounds hosts this large art festival with sales, demonstrations, and food. | 806/744–2787.
**JULY:** *Fourth on Broadway Parade and Celebration.* The entire city shows up for this festive celebration, which includes live music, food booths, a basketball tournament, and a fireworks display. | 806/747–5232.
**SEPT.:** *Buddy Holly Music Festival.* The music legend is remembered in this event including live music, food, classic cars, and a street festival. | 806/749–2929 or 800/692–4035.

## Dining
**Chez Suzette.** French. Casual bistro-style dining with candlelit tables. Known for their steaks, seafood, and pastas. Kids' menu. | 4423 50th St. | 806/795–6796 | Closed Sun. | $9–$16 | AE, DC, MC, V.

**Gardski's Loft.** American. | 2009 Broadway | 806/744–2391 | $15–$19 | AE, D, DC, MC, V.

**Harrigan's.** Steak. This restaurant, in a restored old library, is dark and quiet, and a great place for dates. Try the New Orleans potatoes, prime rib, and black magic cake. Along with steaks, Harrigan's serves a selection of Tex-Mex dishes and pastas. | 3801 50th St. | 806/792–4648 | $6–$19 | AE, DC, MC, V.

**Jimenez Bakery and Restaurant.** Mexican. This restaurant is lined with authentic Mexican tiles. A mural on display depicts two Aztec Native Americans making prayer offerings. Try the tampampiquena, an 8-oz steak smothered in a special sauce. | 1217 Ave. G | Breakfast also available. No supper. Closed Sun. | $4–$7 | No credit cards.

**Santa Fe.** Mexican. A casual eatery that's a good choice for families and has a kids' menu. | 401 Avenue Q | 806/763–6114 | $15–$21 | AE, D, DC, MC, V.

# Lodging

**Barcelona Court.** This hotel is close to the South Plains Mall, Texas Tech University, and Lubbock Christian University. It has rooms that overlook the tropical atrium and fountains outside. Complimentary breakfast, in-room data ports, cable TV, pool, laundry facilities, business services, airport shuttle. | 5215 S. Loop 289 | 806/794–5353 or 800/222–1122 | fax 806/798–3630 | 161 rooms | $58–$68 | AE, D, DC, MC, V.

**Broadway Manor Bed and Breakfast.** In Lubbock's historic Overton District, this B&B was originally constructed for a wealthy banker in 1926. The four rooms are themed and quite spacious. Guests can relax in the sun room or on the garden terrace. Texas Tech University is just a few blocks away. Complimentary breakfast, some in-room hot tubs, no room phones, TV in common area, no pets, no smoking. | 1811 Broadway St., Lubbock | 806/749–4707 or 877/504–8223 | fax 806/763–0196 | fortyford@juno.com | www.broadwaymanor.net | 4 rooms | $68–$125 | D, MC, V.

**Fairfield Inn Lubbock.** This three-story inn is just 15 mi from the Lubbock Airport. There are a number of restaurants within walking distance and many of them will deliver to the hotel. Complimentary Continental breakfast, some microwaves, some refrigerators, in-room data ports, cable TV, pool, indoor hot tub, laundry services, business services, no pets. | 4007 S. U.S. 289 | 806/795–1288 | fax 806/795–1288 | www.fairfieldinn.com | 58 rooms, 6 suites | $83, $93 suites | AE, D, DC, MC, V.

**Four Points by Sheraton.** Located in downtown Lubbock, near the Civic Center, Lubbock International Airport, and Texas Tech University, this six-story hotel has rooms with views of the atrium, and a lively bar popular with students from the local colleges. Restaurant, bar (with entertainment), in-room data ports, some minibars, refrigerators, cable TV, indoor pool, business services, airport shuttle, free parking. | 505 Ave. Q | 806/747–0171 | fax 806/747–9243 | 141 rooms, 4 suites | $59–$99 | AE, D, DC, MC, V.

**Holiday Inn–Civic Center.** This Holiday Inn stands beside the Lubbock Civic Center and is close to Texas Tech University and the Lubbock International Airport. It is one of the largest hotels in Lubbock, and is within walking distance of restaurants. Restaurant, bar, some kitchenettes, cable TV, indoor pool, hot tub, exercise equipment, laundry facilities, business services, airport shuttle, pets allowed. | 801 Avenue Q | 806/763–1200 | fax 806/763–2656 | www.holidayinn.com | 295 rooms | $76–$90 | AE, D, DC, MC, V.

**Holiday Inn–Park Plaza.** This full-service hotel in southwest Lubbuck boasts a popular restaurant, a lounge in its tropical atrium, and more than 25,000 square ft of meeting space. Restaurant, bar, room service, in-room data ports, cable TV, pool, wading pool, laundry facilities, business services, airport shuttle, some pets allowed. | 3201 South Loop 289S | 806/797–3241 | fax 806/793–1203 | www.holiday-inn.com | 202 rooms | $69–$108 | AE, D, DC, MC, V.

**La Quinta Inn.** This motel is down the street from the Civic Center. Complimentary Continental breakfast, in-room data ports, cable TV, pool, business services, pets allowed. | 601 Ave. Q | 806/763–9441 | fax 806/747–9325 | 137 rooms | $62–$69 | AE, D, DC, MC, V.

**Lubbock Inn.** This three-story inn is close to Texas Tech University and the Bodyworks gym. It offers a convention area for business travelers. Restaurant, bar, room service, in-room data ports, some refrigerators, cable TV, pool, wading pool, business services, airport shuttle. | 3901 19th St. | 806/792–5181 or 800/545–8226 | fax 806/792–1319 | 119 rooms | $60–$70 | AE, D, DC, MC, V.

**Residence Inn by Marriott.** This hotel is 10 minutes from Lubbock International Airport, 6 mi from downtown, 8 mi from the Buddy Holly Center, and 4 mi from Texas Tech University. Picnic area, complimentary Continental breakfast, in-room data ports, kitchenettes, refrigerators, cable TV, pool, hot tub, tennis, laundry facilities, business services, airport shuttle, free parking, pets allowed. | 2551 S. Loop 289 | 806/745–1963 | fax 806/748–1183 | www.residenceinn.com | 80 suites | $97–$135 suites | AE, D, DC, MC, V.

LUBBOCK

INTRO
ATTRACTIONS
DINING
LODGING

**Woodrow House Bed and Breakfast.** This three-story, Colonial B&B, constructed in 1995, boasts very large rooms richly decorated according to different themes: the pink and white Victorian room, for example, is furnished with an antique cherry bedroom suite; while the furniture in the green and burgundy President's room is in solid mahogany. If you have kids, a stay in the restored Red Caboose is a must. You may get to hear hostess Dawn Fleming play a tune on the harp. Complimentary breakfast, TV in common area, library, business services, no pets, no smoking. | 2629 19th St. | 806/793–3330 | fax 806/793–7676 | www.woodrowhouse.com | 8 rooms | $85–$105 | AE, MC, V.

# LUFKIN

MAP 8, K4

*(Nearby towns also listed: Crockett, Nacogdoches)*

Surrounded by pine forests, this East Texas community is known for its lumber industry. Vacationers will find that Lufkin is a good access point to the Sam Rayburn Reservoir, the largest lake in Texas, as well as the Angelina and Davy Crockett national forests.

Information: **Lufkin Convention and Visitors Bureau** | Box 1606, Lufkin, TX 75901 | 409/634–6305 or 800/409–5659 | www.chamber.angelina.tx.us.

## Attractions

**Angelina National Forest.** The Lufkin area is home to some of the region's best forests, tall stands of trees known as the piney woods. The Angelina National Forest, 21 mi east of Lubbock, has many recreation areas including Bouton Lake, Boykin Springs, Sandy Creek, and Caney Creek. It also offers the 5½-mi Sawmill Hiking Trail. | off Hwy 63 | 936/639–8620 | www.southernregion.fs.fed.us/texas | $2 | Daily dawn to dusk.

**Davy Crockett National Forest.** The large Davy Crockett Park, 20 mi from Crockett, has several recreation areas. Among these are the 4-C's Hiking Trail with its 19 mi of marked trail, and the Big Slough Canoe Trail and Wilderness Area. | Hwy 7E | 409/655–2299 or 409/831–2246 | www.r8web.com/texas | Free | Daily 6 AM–1 PM.

**Crown Colony Golf Course.** This challenging 18-hole golf course, rated in the top five of the state each year, hosts several minor tournaments annually. | 900 Crown Colony Dr. | 936/634–4927 | www.crowncolonygolfclub.com | Year–round, Tues.–Sun. 7–Dusk, Closed Mon.

**Ellen Trout Park Zoo.** This zoo is especially known for its breeding programs for the West African crowned crane, the Louisiana pine snake and other exotic species. | Loop 287 N at Martin Luther King Dr. | 409/633–0399 | fax 409/633–0311 | $2 | June–Aug., daily 9–6; Sept.–May, daily 9–5.

**Museum of East Texas.** Housed in an historic 1905 Episcopal church, this museum features changing exhibits on art, science, and history. | 503 N. Second St. | 409/639–4434 | Free | Tues.–Fri. 10–5, weekends 1–5.

**Texas Forestry Museum.** This unique museum looks at the forestry industry of East Texas with exhibits including a sawmill town, early firefighting equipment, and logging machinery. | 1905 Atkinson Dr. | 409/632–9535 | fax 409/632–9543 | www.txforestrymuseum.org | Free | Mon.–Sat. 10–5, Sun. 1–5.

## ON THE CALENDAR

**SEPT.:** *Texas Forest Festival.* This festival includes the Southern hushpuppy Olympics (a cook-off), a fun run, and a lumberjack competition. | 409/634–6305.

## Dining

**Barnhill's Steak and Buffet.** Steak. Turn-of-the-20th-century antiques and a variety of flora help set the mood at this eatery. The T-bone steak is popular, as is the comprehensive buffet, which includes pizza, brisket, ribs and much more. | 3102 S. John Redditt Dr. | 409/634–4919 | $6–$12 | AE, D, DC, MC, V.

**Roma Italiano Ristorante.** Italian. You'll love this classy restaurant for its piano lounge, delicious food, and extensive wine collection. You can't go wrong with the rack of lamb, the Dover sole, or the chicken Genovese. | 112 S. 1st St. | 409/637–7227 | Reservations essential | No lunch Sat. Closed Sun. | $8–$20 | AE, D, DC, MC, V.

## Lodging

**Best Western Expo Inn.** This hotel is on Loop 287 and U.S. 59N, and it's only 15 minutes from any part of town. You'll find Dude's Lounge, with live entertainment, on the premises and a 24-hour restaurant next door. Fishing, golfing and a zoo are all within 10 miles. Complimentary Continental breakfast, room service, in-room data ports, cable TV, pool, laundry facilities, business services, pets allowed (fee). | 4200 N. Medford Dr. | 409/632–7300 | fax 409/632–8094 | www.bestwestern.com | 83 rooms | $67 | AE, D, DC, MC, V.

**Days Inn.** This Days Inn is near the Angelina Junior College, Angelina County Airport, Lufkin Mall, and some restaurants. Restaurant, bar, complimentary Continental breakfast, room service, some refrigerators, some in-room hot tubs, cable TV, pool, wading pool, laundry facilities, business services, some pets allowed. | 2130 S. 1st St. | 409/639–3301 | fax 409/634–4266 | 126 rooms | $38–$80 | AE, D, DC, MC, V.

**Holiday Inn.** This is a two-story hotel located near the Lufkin mall, the Angelina Junior College, United Pentecostal Campgrounds, and Crown Colony Country Club. Restaurant, bar, room service, in-room data ports, some minibars, some refrigerators, cable TV, pool, laundry facilities, business services, airport shuttle, free parking, pets allowed (fee). | 4306 S. 1st St. | 409/639–3333 | fax 409/639–3382 | www.holidayinn.com | 102 rooms | $66–$73 | AE, D, DC, MC, V.

**La Quinta Inn.** This motel is 6 mi from the Angelina County airport. Complimentary Continental breakfast, in-room data ports, cable TV, pool, business services, free parking, some pets allowed. | 2119 S. 1st St. | 409/634–3351 | fax 409/634–9475 | 106 rooms | $49–$89 | AE, D, DC, MC, V.

**Lufkin Super 8 Motel.** This light-colored, two-story motel, built in 1999, is a quarter mile from Angelina college and 2 mi from downtown Lufkin. Complimentary Continental breakfast, some microwaves, some refrigerators, cable TV, indoor pool, spa, laundry services, business services, no pets. | 2216 S. 1st St. | 409/632–8885 | www.super8.com | 42 rooms, 3 suites | $62–$67, $73 suites | AE, D, DC, MC, V.

# MARBLE FALLS

MAP 8, H5

*(Nearby towns also listed: Burnet, Johnson City)*

The waterfalls which earned this town its name are now hidden in the depths beneath Lake Marble Falls and can only be seen when the water level drops. You may not get to view the marble falls, but there's no way to miss the granite for which this town is famous. This glimmering stone is visible throughout the town.

**Information: Marble Falls Chamber of Commerce** | 801 Hwy. 281, Marble Falls, TX 78654 | 830/693–4449 or 800/759–8178 | chamber@orion.tstar.net | www.marblefalls.org.

## Attractions

**Granite Mountain.** At more than 800-ft tall, this is the largest granite quarry in the United States. Souvenirs and products can be purchased from the shop. | Off of Rte. 1431 | 830/598–6570 | Free | Weekdays 7–7, Sat. 7–4, Sun. 10–6.

## Dining

**Bluebonnet Cafe.** American. This informal, country-style cafe has long been a favorite with local residents. Pot roast, meatloaf, and sandwiches are among the selections. | 211 U.S. 281 | 830/693–2344 | Breakfast also available. No supper Sun. | $8–$12 | No credit cards.

**Dock's.** Southern. Dock's is decorated in café style with wood accents and plants. Steaks, chicken-fried steaks, and fried fish are among the menu choices. | 900 Rte. 1431 | 830/693–2245 | $8–$12 | AE, D, MC, V.

**Mark's Family Restaurant.** Southern. This is a casual restaurant, decorated with Western accents and local game. Chicken-fried steak, baked potatoes, and fajita potatoes are some of the dishes on the menu. | 1125 U.S. 281 N | 830/693–7896 | Breakfast also available | $7–$13 | AE, D, MC, V.

### ON THE CALENDAR

**NOV.–JAN.** *Walkway of Lights.* From the end of Nov. to the beginning of Jan., hundreds of lighted Christmas trees along Lake Marble Falls can be seen from miles away. | 830/693–4449.

## Dining

**Inmans Ranch House.** Barbecue. This informal eatery has been serving up turkey sausage and brisket for 36 successful years. Come dine with the locals among country Western furnishings. | 707 6th St. | 830/693–2711 | No supper on weekends. Closed Mon. | $3–$6 | No credit cards.

**Margarita's Mexican Restaurant.** Mexican. Margarita's is housed in a ramada-style stucco structure. They serve a varied menu that includes seafood and steaks, but they are best known for their fajitas. Kids' menu. | 1205 W. Rte. 1431 | 830/693–7434 | Reservations not accepted | Breakfast also available | $7–$15 | AE, D, MC, V.

**Santa Fe House.** Mexican/American. The most frequently ordered dishes at this casual eatery, a favorite among the locals, are the fajitas, enchiladas, and chicken-fried steak. | 1700 Rte. 1431 | 830/693–4144 | $3–$6 | AE, D, MC, V.

## Lodging

**Best Western Marble Falls Inn.** A good base for exploring, this two-story hotel resides on the Texas Wildflower/Bluebonnet Trail. Before you head out, enjoy breakfast before a stone fireplace in the lobby. Complimentary Continental breakfast, some microwaves, some refrigerators, in-room data ports, cable TV, pool, outdoor hot tub, exercise equipment, laundry facilities, business services, some pets. | 1403 Rte. 281N | 830/693–5122 | fax 830/693–3108 | www.bestwestern.com | 61 rooms | $65–$99 | AE, D, DC, MC, V.

**Hampton Inn Marble Falls/On the Lake.** You can choose a room that overlooks the downtown area or one that overlooks Lake Marble Falls. There are a number of restaurants within walking distance. Complimentary Continental breakfast, refrigerators, microwaves, in-room data ports, cable TV, pool, outdoor hot tub, business services, no pets. | 704 First St. | 830/798–1895 | fax 830/798–1897 | www.hamptoninn.com | 64 rooms | $89–$104 | AE, D, DC, MC, V.

**Mystic Cove Bed and Breakfast.** This B&B is is on the western shore of Lake Buchanan, just 15 mi from Marble Falls. Bird watchers are in for a special treat—over 40 different species have been spotted at Mystic Cove. It falls under the migratory pattern of birds such as the Whooping Crane and the Canadian Snow Goose. Rooms here are spacious and peaceful. Complimentary Continental breakfast, cable TV, no room phones, fishing, boating, water sports, no pets, no smoking. | 115 Cherokee Trail, Buchanan Dam | 512/793–6642 | www.touringtexas.com/mystic.htm | 3 rooms, 3 cottages | $65–$75, $95 cottages | No credit cards.

**Ramada Limited of Marble Falls.** Breathe in the fresh air of the Texas Hill Country, and relax beside one of the five lakes near to this motel. You'll find many restaurants in the vicinity. Complimentary Continental breakfast, refrigerators, in-room data ports, cable TV, pool, outdoor hot tub, business services, no pets. | 1206 Rte. 281N | 830/693–7531 | fax 830/693–7531 | www.ramada.com | 48 rooms, 1 suite | $63–89, $129 suite | AE, D, DC, MC, V.

# MARFA

*(Nearby towns also listed: Big Bend National Park, Van Horn)*

Set on a desert plateau, this west Texas town was named for a character in *The Brothers Karamazov* and thrived as a railroad stop. Today the community is often visited by those traveling to Big Bend National Park and by vacationers seeking to spot the Marfa Lights, an unexplained phenomena dating to 1883, when they were first recorded. Look for colored lights that move across the sky, disappearing and reappearing without explanation.

**Information: Marfa Chamber of Commerce** | Box 635, Marfa, TX 79843 | 915/729–4942 or 800/650–9696 | www.iglobal.net/marfacoc.

## Attractions

**Chinati Foundation.** One of the largest permanent installations of contemporary art in the world, the Chinati Foundation displays works by its founder Donald Judd and others. It has a total of 32 buildings (currently 13 are restored) on 400 acres, with numerous outdoor sculptures by a variety of artists. | One Cavalry Row | 915/729–4362 | Free | Thurs.–Sat. 1–3 by appointment.

### ON THE CALENDAR

**SEPT.: *Marfa Lights Festival.*** This festival includes live music, arts and crafts, food and drink, a 5K run, and dancing. | Vizcaino Park | Labor Day weekend | 800/650–9696.

## Dining

**Mike's Place.** American. This family-owned restaurant has been in business since 1959. There are two large, separate dining rooms for smokers and non-smokers. Specialties include chicken-fried steak and hamburger steak. | 111 S. Highland Ave., Marfa | 915/729–8146 | Breakfast also available. No dinner Sat. Closed Sun. | $3–$7 | MC, V.

## Lodging

**Arcon Inn Bed and Breakfast.** This two-story, yellow Victorian adobe home is located in the historic district. Guests can relax on the patio or on the front porch swing. Rooms are decorated with European and Latin American antiques. Complimentary breakfast, no room phones, TV in common area, pets allowed (restrictions), no smoking. | 215 N. Austin, Marfa | 915/729–4826 | fax 915/729–3391 | 3 rooms, 1 cottage | $75–$95 | AE, D, DC, MC, V.

# MARSHALL

*(Nearby towns also listed: Jefferson, Longview, Tyler)*

This East Texas town is best known for its pottery, produced by the several pottery companies in town. Marshall is especially popular during spring and fall months for its brilliant blooms and colors.

Information: **Marshall Chamber of Commerce** | Box 520, Marshall, TX 75671 | 903/935–7868 | www.marshalltxchamber.com.

## Attractions

**Caddo Lake State Park.** This 480-acre park has offered camping, hiking, swimming, picnicking, nature study, fishing, and boating opportunities for both day and overnight guests since the 1930s. The Visitors Center has displays about the lake and its wildlife. | Rte. 43 to Rte. 2198 to Rte. 2 | 903/679–3351 | fax 903/679–4006 | www.tpwd.state.tx.us | $2 | Daily 8 AM–10 PM.

**Ginocchio National Historic District.** This three-square-block historic district is in the heart of downtown Marshall. Main attractions include the 1896 Ginocchio Hotel, the T&P Depot and the Allen house. | Off Hwy. 80, N. Washington St. | 903/935–7868 | www.marshalltxchamber.com/historical/historical.htm | Free | Daily.

**Harrison County Historical Museum.** A former county courthouse, this museum of Marshall and Harrison County history displays exhibits of Caddoan artifacts, the Civil War, and pioneer history. | Old Courthouse, Peter Whetstone Sq | 903/938–2680 | Free | Tues.–Sat. 10–5.

**Marshall Pottery and Museum.** This workshop has been producing glazed pottery since 1896, making it one of the oldest such companies in the nation. The museum includes displays on the history of the business as well as how pottery is made. | 4901 Elysian Fields Rd. | 903/938–9201 | fax 903/938–8222 | Free | Mon.–Sat. 9–6, Sun. 10–6.

**Michelson Museum of Art.** This collection features the work of the late Leo Michelson, a French Impressionist whose works are well known in Europe. The museum also displays traveling exhibits. | 216 N. Bolivar | 903/935–9480 | fax 903/935–1974 | Free | Tues.–Fri. noon–5, weekends 1–4.

**T. C. Lindsey and Co.** This country store has been in business for more than 150 years. Along with antiques, it sells pottery, cookware, oil lamps, and boot scrapers. | 2293 Rte. 134, Jonesville | I–20 to Rte. 134 | 903/687–3382 | Free | Tues.–Sat. 10–4.

### ON THE CALENDAR

**MAY:** *Stagecoach Days Celebration.* Marshall's history is celebrated with arts and crafts, food, a parade, and a Wild West show. | 903/935–7868.

**JULY:** *Fourth of July Celebration.* A frog-jumping and watermelon seed spitting contest highlight this event. There is a fireworks display at night. | 903/935–7868.

**OCT.:** *Fireant Festival.* This festival includes games, food booths, live entertainment, kids' activities, and more. | 903/935–7868.

**NOV., DEC.:** *Wonderland of Lights.* One of the state's largest lighting displays. | 903/935–7868.

## Dining

**Hungri Maverick.** American. The Maverick has been around for 15 years and has become a local favorite. Pictures honoring veterans decorate the walls. The chicken-fried steak and hamburgers are popular. Breakfast is served all day. | 5902 E. End Blvd. S., Marshall | 903/934–9426 | Open 24 hours | $4–$9 | AE, D, DC, MC, V.

## Lodging

**Guest Inn.** This motel is near a mall and plenty of restaurants less than a mile away. Complimentary Continental breakfast, some refrigerators, cable TV, pool, free parking, pets allowed. | 4911 E. End Blvd. | 903/927–1718 | fax 903/927–1747 | 46 rooms | $51–$95 | AE, D, DC, MC, V.

**Heart's Hill Bed and Breakfast.** Built in 1900, each guest room in this Victorian home has antiques and a fireplace with original Italian tile. There is a semi-circular turret that overlooks the grounds. Complimentary breakfast, no room phones, some refrigerators, some microwaves, TV in common area, exercise equipment, no pets, no kids, no smoking. | 512 E. Austin St., Marshall | 888/797–7685 | heartshill@internetwork.net | www.heartshill.com | 3 rooms, 1 cottage | rooms $100–$115, cottage $100 | No credit cards.

**Motel 6.** This motel is 16 mi from Caddo State Park and 20 mi from Lake O'the Pines. Cable TV, pool, laundry facilities, pets allowed. | 300 I–20E | 903/935–4393 | fax 903/935–2380 | 121 rooms | $41 | AE, D, DC, MC, V.

# MASON

*(Nearby towns also listed: Fredericksburg, Kerrville)*

Mason was settled by cattle ranchers and German families who came from Fredericksburg. In 1851, Fort Mason was built on a hilltop to afford a better look at oncoming Comanches. (The post's best known soldier was Lieut. Col. Robert E. Lee.) In 1869 the sandstone fort was dismantled and the salvaged stone was used to build local businesses and homes.

Rock hounds come to Mason County today in search of topaz, the Texas state gem, which ranges from clear to sky blue. Most local topaz turns up near the small communities of Streeter, Grit, and Katemcy, all north and northeast of Mason.

Information: **Mason County Chamber of Commerce** | Box 156, Mason, TX 76856 | 915/347–5758 | masoscoc@hctp.net.

## Attractions

**Eckert James River Bat Cave Preserve.** This cavern is home to about six million Mexican free-tail bats. This is a "maternity cave," used during the spring and summer months by female bats to bear and rear their young. Visitors can view the evening flight out of the cave, a sight heralded by high-pitched sounds. | U.S. 87 to Ranch Road 1723 | 915/347–5970 | Free | May–Oct., Thurs.–Sun. dawn–one hour after sunset.

**Fort Mason.** These reconstructed officers' quarters are furnished with typical 1850s belongings as well as photographs from Mason's early days. | Post Hill St. | 915/347–5758 | Free | Daily.

**Fort Mason City Park.** This 125-acre park has a rodeo arena, a nine-hole golf course, and a hiking trail. You can picnic amidst the large pecan trees. | Rte. 87, 1 mi south of Fort Mason | 915/347–5758 | www.sig.net/~masoncoc/fmpark | Free | Daily.

**Rocks and Minerals.** The Mason area is rich in rocks and minerals and a favorite with rockhounds. Two private areas charge a daily fee for topaz hunting. Visitors must bring their own equipment (including water during warm summer months) and may keep whatever they find. Most rock hunting areas are open from mid-January through October, avoiding deer hunting season. For information on rock hunting, contact the Mason Chamber of Commerce (above). | 915/347–5758.

### ON THE CALENDAR

**JULY: *Roundup Weekend.*** This family-oriented event includes a rodeo, an arts and crafts fair, a parade, and a dance. | 915/347–5758.

## Dining

**Cooper's Pit Barbecue.** Barbecue. This family restaurant (with rustic decor) is known for its brisket, ribs, goat, and chicken. | U.S. 87S | 915/347–6897 | Closes at 5:30 PM | $5–$17 | DC, MC, V.

**Willow Creek Cafe.** American. A historic building houses this casual, stylish restaurant filled with antique furnishings. Choices on the menu include Mexican food, grilled chicken salad, chicken-fried steak, hamburgers, and sandwiches. | 102 Ft. McKavitt | 915/347–6124 | Breakfast also available | $8–$17 | No credit cards.

**Zavala's Cafe.** Tex-Mex. This family-oriented restaurant is decorated with a Mexican village mural. It is known for tacos, nachos, enchiladas, and chicken-fried steak. | U.S. 87N | 915/347–5365 | Breakfast also available | $9–$18 | MC, V.

## Lodging

**Hill Country Motel.** This two-story motel is in the heart of Marble Falls, with shopping and restaurants nearby. Complimentary Continental breakfast, cable TV, pool. | 1101 Hwy. 281N | 830/693–3637 | fax 830/693–6028 | 69 rooms | $49–$79 | AE, D, DC, MC, V.

**Red Door Bed and Breakfast.** Built in 1893, this B&B still has many original furnishings and an authentic pressed-tin ceiling. All of the rooms have fireplaces and comfortable Queen Anne chairs. The balcony overlooks Courthouse Square. Complimentary Continental breakfast, in-room hot tubs, no room phones, in-room VCRs (and movies), no pets, no smoking. | 226 Fort McKavitt, Mason | 915/347–6398 | 4 rooms | $75 | MC, V.

# MCALLEN

MAP 8, H9

*(Nearby towns also listed: Edinburg, Harlingen, Mission, South Padre Island)*

Home to more than 100,000 residents, McAllen is 8 mi from the Mexican city of Reynosa, a favorite with visitors looking for a chance to shop at a traditional Mexican market. Several hotels offer van service to the International Bridge or you can drive to Hidalgo and park for the day on the Texas side. McAllen is also a favorite destination for bird-watchers, with the Santa Ana National Wildlife Refuge about 16 mi southeast of the city.

Information: **McAllen Convention and Visitors Bureau** | Box 790, McAllen, TX 78505 | 956/682–2871 | chamber@mcallen.org | www.mcallenchamberusa.com.

## Attractions

**McAllen International Museum.** This museum features a variety of Mexican folk crafts and costumes. | Bicentennial Blvd. at 1900 Nolana Loop | 956/682–1564 | fax 956/686–1813 | www.mcallenmuseum.org | $2 | Tues.–Sat. 9–5, Sun. 1–5.

**McAllen Nature Center.** Trees, birds, and area wildlife are on display here, and guided tours are available for visitors. | 1000 S. Ware Rd. | On Rte. 83 Business | 956/682–1517 | fax 956/618–3382 | Free | Daily dawn to dusk.

**Mountasia.** This park is loads of fun for children and adults alike. Facilities include a miniature golf course, go-carts, and a video arcade. | West of McAllen, on U.S. 83 | 956/682–9761 | Free. Prices for activities vary | Mon.–Thurs. noon–10; Fri. noon–midnight; Sat. 11 AM–midnight; Sun. noon–10.

**Reynosa.** This border city of 500,000 residents is located 8 mi south of McAllen and has numerous shops and restaurants. Many McAllen hotels offer van shuttles to the International Bridge; parking is available on the U.S. side. | U.S. 83 to Rte. 907 to U.S. 281 | 956/787–3079 | fax 956/787–8338 | $3 | Daily dawn to dusk.

**Santa Ana National Wildlife Refuge.** Over 100,000 birders travel here every year to view green jays, rare species, and species indigenous to Mexico. About 388 species have been identified here. Interpretive tram rides are available during winter months. | U.S. 83 to Rte. 907 to U.S. 281 | 956/787–3079 | fax 956/787–8338 | $3 | Daily dawn to dusk.

### ON THE CALENDAR

**APR.:** *Texas Tropics Nature Festival.* This festival celebrates the spring migration of birds and butterflies through South Texas field trips and guest speakers. | 956/682–2871.
**DEC.:** *Candlelight Posada.* Candlelit streets, traditional Mexican dances, a parade, music, and kids' events are part of the fun. | 956/682–2871.

## Dining

**Ali Baba Middle Eastern Food.** Middle Eastern. Islamic arches and artwork contribute to the traditional atmosphere of this restaurant/grocery store. The falafel and kebabs are recommended. | 504 N. 10th St., # 11 | 956/631–8640 | Closed Sun. | $5–$13 | AE, D, MC, V.

**Dorina's Italian Cuisine and Pastries.** Italian. This informal eatery doubles as a grocery and pastry shop. All of the sauces and pasta are made from scratch. Popular dishes include the lasagna and veal piccata. | 415 W. Nolana St. | 956/668–1441 | Closed Mon. | $7–$13 | AE, DC, MC, V.

**Johnny's.** Tex-Mex. This is a casual, family-oriented restaurant. Try the enchiladas, nachos, and tacos. A kids' menu is also available. | 1010 Houston St. | 956/686–9061 | Breakfast also available | $14–$23 | AE, D, MC, V.

**La Terraza.** Spanish. This restaurant was constructed in 1918 and retains its original period style. The menu includes rack of lamb, duck, grilled wild boar, and beef tenderloin, or you can choose from the salad bar. Open-air dining is available on the patio, with umbrellas for shade and live bands and musicians for entertainment. | 101 N. Main St. | 956/631–1101 | Closed Sun. No lunch | $16–$21 | AE, D, DC, MC, V.

**Lone Star Bar-B-Q.** Barbecue. This rustic BBQ joint has on display original picks and axes that were used to clear Texas at the turn of the 20th century. All of the meat is mesquite smoked and the turkey and chicken are most popular. | 315 W. US 83 | 956/686–7113 | Closed Sun. | $6–$8 | AE, D, MC, V.

## Lodging

**Airport International Inn.** This inn is across the street from McAllen Miller International Airport and minutes away from the international bridge to Mexico. Rooms are spacious. Cable TV, some pets. | 817 Bales Rd. | 956/682–3111 | fax 956/682–3245 | 63 rooms | $35–$40 | AE, D, MC, V.

**Best Western Rose Garden Inn and Suites.** This two-story Best Western is just 5 miles from the McAllen International Museum and 7 miles from the Mexican border. There is a restaurant and lounge nearby. Complimentary breakfast, in-room data ports, some microwaves, some refrigerators, cable TV, outdoor pool, no pets. | 300 U.S. 83E | 956/630–3333 | fax 956/687–9550 | www.bestwestern.com | 71 rooms, 23 suites | $64, $74 suites | AE, D, DC, MC, V.

**Courtyard McAllen Airport.** This three-story hotel is ½ mi from a mall, 5 mi from McAllen International Museum, and 10 mi from Santa Ana National Wildlife Refuge. Restaurant, bar, in-room data ports, some refrigerators, cable TV, pool, hot tub, exercise equipment, laundry facilities, business services, airport shuttle. | 2131 S. 10th St. | 956/668–7800 | fax 956/668–7801 | 110 rooms | $69–$85 | AE, D, DC, MC, V.

**Drury Inn.** This three-story motel is a half-mile from a mall, movie theater, hospital, and Miller International Airport. Complimentary Continental breakfast, in-room data ports, some refrigerators, cable TV, pool, business services, some pets allowed. | 612 W. U.S. 83 | 956/687–5100 | fax 956/687–5100 | www.druryinn.com | 89 rooms | $75–$86 | AE, D, DC, MC, V.

**Embassy Suites.** This hotel is located 15 minutes from the Mexican border and about 15 mi from an amusement park. It provides transportation to the mall and the airport, and has a recently expanded four-level parking lot. Restaurant, bar (with entertainment), complimentary breakfast, in-room data ports, refrigerators, cable TV, indoor pool, hot tub, exercise equipment, business services, airport shuttle. | 1800 S. 2nd St. | 956/686–3000 | fax 956/631–8362 | www.embassy-mcallen.com | 224 suites | $125–$135 suites | AE, D, DC, MC, V.

**Four Point Sheraton.** All of the rooms in this five-story hotel have balconies. It is less than 1 mi from the mall and the airport. Restaurant, bar, in-room data ports, cable TV, pool, hot tub, business services, airport shuttle. | 2721 S. 10th St. | 956/984–7900 | fax 956/687–8651 | 150 rooms | $103–$185 | AE, D, DC, MC, V.

**Hampton Inn.** This inn is close to the airport and has four stories with room entrances from the inside. Complimentary Continental breakfast, in-room data ports, cable TV, pool, business services, pets allowed. | 300 W. U.S. 83 | 956/682–4900 | fax 956/682–6823 | www.hampton-inn.com | 91 rooms | $73–$77 | AE, D, DC, MC, V.

**Holiday Inn Civic Center.** Remodeled in early 2000, this two-story Holiday Inn hosts many conventions and sees a lot of business travelers. There are two malls within 1 mi and a golf course only 7 mi away. Restaurant, bar, in-room data ports, some microwaves, some refrigerators, cable TV, outdoor pool, indoor pool, indoor hot tub, sauna, exercise equipment, laundry services, business services, airport shuttle, some pets. | 200 U.S. 83W | 956/686–2471 | fax 956/682–7609 | www.holiday-inn.com | 173 rooms | $68–$85 | AE, D, DC, MC, V.

**Holiday Inn Express–Airport.** This Holiday Inn is right beside the mall and the Sante Fe Steakhouse, less than a mile from the airport, and a few miles from the night club Metropolis. Its rooms are easily accessible from the outside, and it caters to the business traveler with its business center. Continental breakfast, some refrigerators, cable TV, pool, laundry facilities, business services, airport shuttle. | 2000 S. 10th St. | 956/686–1741 | fax 956/682–7187 | www.holidayinn.com | 150 rooms | $59–$89 | AE, D, DC, MC, V.

**La Quinta Motor Inn.** Scenic South Padre Island is 30 minutes away from this inn. It is within walking distance of the Plaza mall. Bar, complimentary Continental breakfast, in-room data ports, cable TV, pool, business services, airport shuttle, pets allowed. | 1100 S. 10th St. | 956/687–1101 | fax 956/687–9265 | 120 rooms | $73–$110 | AE, D, DC, MC, V.

**Motel 6.** This motel is 3 mi from McAllen Park. Cable TV, pool, laundry facilities, pets allowed. | 700 U.S. 83W | 956/687–3700 | fax 956/630–3180 | 93 rooms | $38–$44 | AE, D, DC, MC, V.

# MCKINNEY

MAP 8, I2

*(Nearby towns also listed: Dallas, Greenville, Plano)*

Listed on the National Register of Historic Places, McKinney is one of the oldest towns in Texas, founded in 1848. If you take a self-guided walking tour of the well-preserved downtown square and adjacent areas, you will see many architectural styles, including Victorian, Gothic, and Prairie. Today McKinney has a population of 50,200.

**Information: McKinney Convention and Visitors Bureau** | Box 621, McKinney, TX 75070 | 972/542–0163 or 888/649–8499 | mckcoc@waymark.net | www.mckinneytx.org.

## Attractions

**Bolin Wildlife Exhibit.** See over 100 animals from North America, Africa, and other parts of the world that have visited the taxidermist. There is also an antique car exhibit and various turn-of-the-20th-century furnishings. | 1028 N. McDonald St., McKinney | 972/562–2639 | Free | Weekdays 9–noon, 1:30–4.

**Heard Natural Science Museum and Wildlife Sanctuary.** Here you will see many natural history displays, including some on local geology. The museum is also home to many live animals that represent native species. Picnic area. | One Nature Pl | 972/562–5566 | fax 972/548–9119 | www.heardmuseum.org | $4 | Mon.–Sat. 9–5, Sun. 1–5.

**Lavon Lake.** Formed on the east fork of the Trinity River, Lake Lavon covers 21,400 acres, offers swimming, waterskiing, and has a playground. | 3375 Skyview Dr., Wylie | 972/442–5711 | Free | Daily.

## ON THE CALENDAR

**MAY: *Mayfair Art Festival.*** This festival includes maypole dancing, storytelling, food booths, pony rides, live entertainment, a carnival, a parade, and a petting zoo. | 972/562–6880.

**OCT.: *Harvestfest.*** The fall harvest is celebrated with food booths, games, and live entertainment. | 972/542–0163 or 888/649–8499.

**NOV.: *Dickens of a Christmas.*** This Victorian extravaganza is fun for the whole family. There are live reindeer and all of the local merchants dress in Victorian costumes. | 972/562–6880.

**DEC.: *Heritage Guild's Christmas Tour of Homes.*** Take a guided tour of homes filled with Christmas decorations. | 972/542–0163 or 888/649–8499.

## Dining

**Rhineland Haus.** German. This restaurant is 100 percent German, from the live musical entertainment on Fri. and Sat. nights, to the pictures and furnishings hanging on the walls, and the beer on tap at the bar. A variety of sausages and authentic German dishes are served. For dessert try the apple strudel. Kids' menu. | 1330 N. Mcdonald St. | 972/562–0124 | $9–$23 | AE, D, MC, V.

## Lodging

**Amerihost Inn.** A sprawling ice-skating facility is adjacent to this hotel, and a 14-screen multiplex theater is behind it. Cable TV, pool, exercise equipment. | 951 S. Central Expressway | 972/547–4500 | fax 972/547–4340 | 61 rooms | $57–$62 | AE, D, DC, MC, V.

**Bingham House Bed and Breakfast.** Built in 1883 by a Civil War veteran, each room in this Georgian Italianate home is furnished with antiques and has a claw-foot tub. Complimentary breakfast, no room phones, cable TV, library, no pets, no kids under 15, no smoking. | 800 S. Chestnut St., McKinney | 972/529–1883 | fax 972/529–1883 | binghamhouse@binghamhouse.com | www.binghamhouse.com | 4 rooms | $79–$149 | No credit cards.

**Super 8.** This motel is less than 10 mi from wildlife exhibits at the Heard Natural Science Museum and Wildlife Sanctuary. Cable TV. | 951 S. Central Expressway | 972/548–8880 | fax 972/548–0486 | 61 rooms | $47–$58 | AE, D, MC, V.

# MIDLAND

MAP 8, E3

*(Suburbs also listed: Big Spring, Odessa)*

Often mentioned with its sister city, Odessa, Midland has a rich oil history. This area is the hub of the Permian Basin's oil and gas reserves and many businesses in the city are related to the industry.

Information: **Midland Chamber of Commerce** | 109 N. Main, Midland, TX 79701 | 915/683–3381 or 800/624–6435.

## Attractions

**Confederate Air Force and American Airpower Heritage Museum.** See the nation's largest collection of flyable WWII combat aircraft from around the world. | 9600 Wright Dr., at Midland International Airport | 915/563–1000 | fax 915/563–8046 | www.avdigest.com/cas/cas.html | $7 | Mon.–Sat. 9–5, Sun. noon–5.

**Midland Community Theatre.** Local theater productions are performed here; check local newspaper for latest information. | 2000 W. Wadley Ave. | 915/682–4111 | fax 915/682–6136 | www.coleorg.com | $8–$14 | Box office: weekdays 10–5:30, Sat. 10–1.

**Midland County Historical Museum.** Exhibits showcasing local history include early pictures, World Wars I and II mementoes, and Native American artifacts. | 301 W. Missouri | 915/688–8947 | Free | Mon., Wed., Fri.–Sat. 2–5.

**Museum of the Southwest Complex.** This former house, built in 1934, now contains an art collection highlighting artists of the Southwest, as well as a museum and a planetarium. | 1705 W. Missouri Ave. | 915/683–2882 | fax 915/570–7077 | www.museumsw.org | Free; $3 for planetarium shows | Tues.–Sat. 10–5, Sun. 2–5.

The **Fredda Turner Durham Children's Museum.** Enjoy this hands-on museum for children of all ages. There are a special computer area and play area.

The **Marion West Blakemore Planetarium.** This facility presents special sky shows as well as exhibits and a gallery. | $3.

**Nita Stewart Haley Memorial Library/J. Evetts Haley History Center.** You will find local history exhibits at this museum and history center, as well as an extensive collection on Billy the Kid and the Lincoln County War. The museum is also home to the original Alamo bell. | 1805 W. Indiana | 915/682–5785 | Free | Weekdays 9–5.

**The Petroleum Museum.** This museum tells of advancements in the petroleum industry with a pumping unit, rig, and other field equipment. | 1500 I–20W | 915/683–4403 | fax 915/683–4509 | $5 | Mon.–Sat. 9–5, Sun. 2–5.

### ON THE CALENDAR

**OCT.: *World War II Flying Air Show.*** Antique aircraft are on display at this air show, and food is available. | 915/683–3381 or 800/624–6435.

## Dining

**Gerardo's Casita Grill.** Mexican. This restaurant has a festive environment with lots of plants and fountains. The fajitas and quesadillas are popular. Kids' menu. | 2407 N. Big Spring Rd., Midland | 915/570–8012 | No supper Sun. | $6–$11 | AE, D, MC, V.

**Luigi's Italian.** Italian. This family restaurant has theater memorabilia throughout and has jazz music in the background. Try the pasta, pizza, or lasagna. Kids' menu. | 111 N. Big Spring St. | 915/683–6363 | Closed Sun. No lunch Sat. | $11–$18 | AE, D, DC, MC, V.

**Olive Garden.** Italian. This chain is a comfortable choice for families. Try fettuccine chicken florentine, lasagna classico, and Mediterranean garlic shrimp. Kids' menu. | 2705 W. Loop 250N | 915/687–4400 | No lunch | $12–$25 | AE, D, DC, MC, V.

**Tampico.** Mexican. Try the enchiladas, tacos, tamale, and fajitas. Kids' menu. | 2411 W. Wall | 915/682–5074 | Closed Mon. No dinner Sun. | $15–$17 | AE, DC, MC, V.

**Venezia.** Italian. You have your choice of four dining areas here. The homey, antiques-filled lower level has a fireplace. Private dinner rooms have fountains, balconies, and high-rise ceilings. Try the veal, rack of lamb, pasta, fresh seafood, or tenderloin steak. Open-air dining is available on a courtyard patio with candlelight and fans. Beer and wine only. | 2101 W. Wadley Ave. | 915/687–0900 | Closed Sun. No lunch Sat. | $6–$23 | AE, D, DC, MC, V.

**Wall St. Bar and Grill.** Seafood. Housed in an early 1900s building that used to be a saddle shop, this place has an antique bar that dates back to 1867. Try the steak or charbroiled shrimp. Kids' menu. | 115 E. Wall St., Midland | 915/684–8686 | No lunch Sat. | $7–$20 | AE, D, DC, MC, V.

## Lodging

**Best Inn and Suites.** This motel is about 10 mi from the Confederate Air Force and American Airpower Heritage Museum. Complimentary Continental breakfast, cable TV, indoor pool, hot tub, exercise equipment, business services, airport shuttle, some pets allowed. | 3100 W. Wall St. | 915/699–4144 | fax 915/699–7639 | www.bestwestern.com | 137 rooms | $49–$69 | AE, D, DC, MC, V.

**Fairfield Inn Midland.** This two-story hotel is 5 mi from two golf courses. Complimentary Continental breakfast, in-room data ports, some microwaves, some refrigerators, cable TV, indoor pool, indoor hot tub, laundry services, business services, no pets. | 2300 Faulkner Ridge Dr. | 915/570–7155 | fax 915/570–7155 | www.fairfieldinn.com | 53 rooms, 18 suites | $65, $75 suites | AE, D, DC, MC, V.

**Hampton Inn Midland.** This hotel is located in a residential neighborhood in the northwest part of Midland. The Confederate Air Force and American Airpower Heritage Museum is 10 mi away. Complimentary Continental breakfast, in-room data ports, some microwaves, some refrigerators, cable TV, outdoor pool, indoor hot tub, laundry services, business services, pets allowed. | 3904 W. Wall St. | 915/694–7774 | fax 915/694–0134 | www.hamptoninn.com | 110 rooms, 6 suites | $55, $70 suites | AE, D, DC, MC, V.

**Hilton Midland & Towers.** This 11-story hotel is in the heart of downtown Midland. It's 15 minutes from the Midland International Airport, and the Midland Convention Center is across the street. two restaurants, bar, complimentary Continental breakfast, in-room data ports, some kitchenettes, some refrigerators, some in-room hot tubs, cable TV, outdoor pool, outdoor hot tub, exercise equipment, laundry services, business services, airport shuttle, some pets. | 117 W. Wall St. | 915/683–6131 | fax 915/683–0958 | www.hilton.com | 242 rooms, 7 suites | $69–$109, $125–$145 suites | AE, D, DC, MC, V.

**Holiday Inn.** This two-story hotel is on landscaped grounds. It has over 30,000 square ft of meeting space. Restaurant, bar, room service, cable TV, indoor pool, hot tub, exercise equipment, laundry facilities, business services, airport shuttle, pets allowed. | 4300 W. Wall St. | 915/697–3181 | fax 915/694–7754 | www.holidayinn.com | 252 rooms, 31 suites | $72–$107, $79–$130 suites | AE, D, DC, MC, V.

**La Quinta.** This hotel is about 10 mi from Midland International Airport. Complimentary Continental breakfast, in-room data ports, cable TV, pool, laundry facilities, business services, pets allowed. | 4130 W. Wall St. | 915/697–9900 | fax 915/689–0617 | 146 rooms | $49–$65 | AE, D, DC, MC, V.

**Midland Days Inn.** Rooms are spacious in this three-story motel. There is a 24-hour restaurant across the street. Restaurant, complimentary Continental breakfast, kitchenettes, microwaves, refrigerators, cable TV, pool, outdoor hot tub, business services, pets allowed (fee). | 1003 South Midkiff Ave., Midland | 915/697–3155 | fax 915/699–2017 | www.daysinn.com | 177 rooms | $50–$67 | AE, D, DC, MC, V.

**Motel 6.** This motel is 6½ mi from the Confederate Air Force Museum. Pool, laundry facilities, pets allowed. | 1000 S. Midkiff Rd. | 915/697–3197 | fax 915/697–7631 | 87 rooms | $27–$31 | AE, D, DC, MC, V.

**Ramada Inn–Airport.** This three-story motel was built in 1982. It's ½–¾ mi from the airport. Restaurant, bar, in-room data ports, some microwaves, cable TV, pool, exercise equipment, laundry facilities, business services, airport shuttle. | 100 Airport Plaza Dr. | 915/561–8000 | fax 915/561–5243 | www.ramada.com | 97 rooms | $50–$70 | AE, D, DC, MC, V.

**Victorian Inn.** This hotel, with Victorian appeal, is near the highway and area restaurants. Complimentary Continental breakfast, in-room data ports, cable TV, pool, business services. | 4714 W. Rte. 80 | 915/699–7727 | fax 915/699–7813 | 90 rooms | $35–$55 | AE, D, DC, MC, V.

# MINERAL WELLS

*(Nearby towns also listed: Fort Worth, Graham, Weatherford)*

Named for mineral water that was discovered here in 1880, Mineral Wells is also surrounded by water in the form of lakes. The area is a popular getaway for swimming, boating, and fishing.

Information: **Mineral Wells Chamber of Commerce** | Box 1408, Mineral Wells, TX 76068 | 940/325-2557 or 800/252-4989 | info@mineralwellstx.com | www.mineralwellstx.com.

## Attractions

**Lake Mineral Wells State Park and Trailway.** Surrounding Lake Mineral Wells, this state park includes camping, screened shelters, boating, equestrian trails, hiking trails, fishing, and swimming. | 100 Park Rd. 71, on U.S. 180 | 940/328-1171 | www.tpwd.state.tx.us | $2 | Daily.

**Palo Pinto County Jail Museum.** This jailhouse was built in 1882. Today it contains various Palo Pinto County memorabilia and a chamber where prisoners are believed to have been hanged. | off U.S. 180 onto S. 5th Ave, 12 mi west of Mineral Wells | 940/659-9908 | Donations accepted | By appointment only.

### ON THE CALENDAR

**MAY:** *Palo Alto County Livestock Association Rodeo.* Barrel racing, rodeo clowns, cook-offs, and a dance are part of this rodeo event. | 800/252-6989.
**OCT.:** *Crazy Water Festival.* This festival celebrates the history and heritage of Mineral Wells. The petting zoo and arts and crafts fair are among the more popular draws. | 940/325-2557.

## Dining

**Shotgun's Bar-B-Q.** Barbecue. Western decor and wooden floors, booths, and tables help set the relaxed mood at Shotgun's. Try the brisket or ribs, or its popular fried catfish. Kids' menu. | 215 NE 27th Ave. | Closed Sun. | $6–$14 | AE, D, MC, V.

### LODGING

**Silk Stocking Row Bed and Breakfast.** Built in 1904 as a boarding house, this Queen Anne-style mansion was remodeled in 1996. Guests can relax in the parlor or on the wraparound verandas. Rooms are very spacious and decorated lavishly with antiques. Complimentary breakfast, no room phones, cable TV, library, no pets, no kids. | 415 NW 4th St. | 940/325-4101 | fax 940/325-4005 | silkrowbb@aol.com | 4 rooms, 1 suite | $68–$84, $85–$96 suite | D, MC, V.

# MISSION

*(Nearby towns also listed: Brownsville, Edinburg, McAllen, South Padre Island)*

This Rio Grande Valley community dates back to 1824 when citrus groves were first planted here. Today, Mission is the center of the state's grapefruit industry. The area is also home to Bentsen-Rio Grande Valley State Park, a favorite among bird-watchers.

Information: **Mission Chamber of Commerce** | 220 E. 9th St., Mission, TX 78572 | 956/585-2727 or 800/580-2700 | www.missionchamber.com.

## Attractions

**Anzalduas Park and Dam.** This picturesque park on the Rio Grande has a covered bird watching area and boat dock. There are grills available for those who wish to enjoy an outdoor cookout and picnic. | From Mission, go south on Shary Rd. | 956/585–2727 | Free | Daily, dawn to dusk.

**Bentsen-Rio Grande Valley State Park.** Bird-watchers come from around the globe for the chance to spot the 200 species often seen here. The park includes camping, picnic sites, fishing, and a group shelter. Take U.S. 83 to Loop 374 and drive west for 2½ mi; drive south on Rte. 2062 for a little more than 2½ mi and enter on Park Rd. 43. | Park Rd. 43 | 956/585–1107 | fax 956/585–3448 | www.tpwd.state.tx.us | $2 | Daily.

**La Lomita Chapel.** Built in 1865, this chapel was a nightly stop for priests on their way through the valley. The chapel is surrounded by a park with picnic sites. | U.S. 83 to Rte. 2062 to Rte. 43 | 956/580–8760 | Free | Daily dawn–dusk.

**Los Ebanos International Ferry.** Visit the only hand-operated ferry on the U.S.-Mexico border. It shuttles cars and passengers across the Rio Grande. | U.S. 83 | 956/485–2721 | Daily 8–4.

### ON THE CALENDAR

**FEB.:** *Texas Citrus Fiesta.* This festival celebrating the Rio Grande Valley's citrus crop includes food, demonstrations, exhibits, and live music. | 956/585–2727 or 800/580–2700.
**OCT.:** *Texas Butterfly Festival.* The butterfly is paid homage through art shows, nature shows and studies, tours of local gardens, and seminars for children and adults. | 800/580–2700.

## Dining

**Ferrell's Pit.** Barbecue. Food is prepared in a barbecue pit at this low-key, down-home cookin' barbecue joint. Try the barbecue rib or chicken plates. | 2204 E. U.S. 83 Business | 956/585–2381 | Closed Tues. | $9–$14 | No credit cards.

**Gracie's Restaurant.** Mexican. All of the paintings inside this restaurant are done by a local Mexican artist. The enchiladas and *botanas* (grilled and seasoned fajita strips) are very popular. Kids's menu. | 1119 E. 9th St., Mission | 956/581–1776 | Breakfast also available. Closed Sun. No supper Mon.–Thurs. Closed Sun. | $3–$9 | AE, D, DC, MC, V.

## Lodging

**Comfort Inn.** This motel was built in 1998. It's 9 mi from the Mexican border. Complimentary Continental breakfast, in-room data ports, some kitchenettes, microwaves, refrigerators, some in-room hot tubs, cable TV, pool, exercise equipment, laundry services, business services, no pets. | 203 S. Shary Rd., Mission | 956/583–0333 | fax 956/584–3755 | www.comfortinn.com | 48 rooms, 4 suites | $62–$69, $115–$135 suites | AE, D, DC, MC, V.

# MONAHANS

MAP 8, D4

*(Nearby towns also listed: Fort Stockton, Odessa, Pecos)*

This West Texas community was established as a railroad stop. Today it is the retail and business center for the surrounding oil and cattle country. The city is often visited by those wanting a glimpse at the unique sand dunes, formed from ancient sandstone. These dunes are not found elsewhere in West Texas and are ever changing with the shifting wind.

Information: **Monahans Chamber of Commerce** | 401 S. Dwight Ave., Monahans, TX 79756 | 915/943–2187.

## Attractions

**Million Barrel Museum.** This structure, built in 1928, was first an oil-storage facility. Today, the museum recalls the oil wells that made this community a boom town. You can also see a former jail and an historic home here. | 400 Museum Blvd. | 915/943–8401 | Free | Tues.–Sun. 10–6.

**Monahans Sandhills State Park.** This park contains dunes that span thousands of acres. The Sandhills Interpretive Center provides information about the dunes, including their use by Native Americans, as well as the barrier they presented to pioneers traveling through the region. | I–20 to MM 86 to Rte. 41 | 915/943–2092 | fax 915/943–2806 | www.tpwd.state.tx.us | $2 | Daily.

**Pyote Museum and Rattlesnake Bomber Base.** This historical base was the home of the 19th (B-17) Bomb Group during WWII. The museum displays base memorabilia and other local artifacts. | I–20, 15 mi west of Monahans | 915/389–5660 | Donations accepted | Sat. 9–5; Sun. 2–6.

### ON THE CALENDAR

**AUG.:** *Butterfield Overland Stagecoach and Wagon Festival.* This festival, held the first weekend of Aug., celebrates the history of the Butterfield Overland Stagecoach that ran through Monahans in the 1800s. Highlights include a kid's rodeo and bull rides. | 915/943–2187.

## Dining

**Fred's Bar-B-Q.** Barbecue. This barbecue joint has been around since 1966. You'll find various antiques inside, including a functioning early 1900s Coke machine. The brisket, ribs, and hot links combo plate is very popular. For dessert try the peach cobbler. | 305 N. Bruce Ave. | 915/943–2885 | Closed Sun.–Mon. | $4–$6 | No credit cards.

## Lodging

**Best Western Colonial Inn.** This single-story motel is 3 mi from the Million Barrel Museum and 6 mi from Monahans Sandhills State Park. Restaurant, some in-room data ports, pool, some pets allowed. | 702 W. I–20 | 915/943–4345 | fax 915/943–3627 | www.bestwestern.com | $48–$51 | AE, D, DC, MC, V.

# MOUNT PLEASANT

MAP 8, K2

*(Nearby towns also listed: Jefferson, Paris, Texarkana)*

This small community's name is a tribute to its lofty location on the northeast Texas hills. The town has access to several area lakes, making it popular with swimmers, anglers, and boaters. Mount Pleasant also draws bird-watchers, who come to spy the bluebirds, attracted to the area for its numerous birdhouses. You can contact the Chamber of Commerce about birding tours.

Information: **Mount Pleasant–Titus County Chamber of Commerce** | Box 1237, Mount Pleasant, TX 75456 | 903/572–8567 | mtplescc@1starnet.com | www.mtpleasant-tx.com.

## Attractions

**Lake Bob Sandlin State Park.** You can camp, picnic, boat, and fish at this state park. There are also screened shelters. | Rte. 21, 12 mi southwest of Mount Pleasant | 903/572–5531 | www.tpwd.state.tx.us | $2 | Daily.

**Mount Pleasant Art Center and Gallery.** These two galleries, housed in a former church, display oils, watercolors, pastels, and fine china. | Off Rte. 1402 | 903/572–2710 | Free | Mon., Tues. 10–4, Thurs. 10–noon.

**Mount Pleasant Historical Museum.** This local history museum contains exhibits on the early days of Mount Pleasant, from pioneer items to artifacts from the Caddo Indians, the first inhabitants. | 213 N. Madison | 903/572–8567 | Free | Mon. 1–6, Tues.–Fri. 9–6, Sat. 9–1.

## ON THE CALENDAR
**JUNE:** *Mount Pleasant Championship Rodeo.* This event includes rodeo performances, roping, barrel racing, and precision riding. | 903/572–8567.
**SEPT.:** *Titus County Fair.* The Titus County Fairgrounds hosts art contests, a junior livestock show, live entertainment, and cook-offs. | 903/577–8117.
**OCT.:** *Northeast Texas Travelers' Rod Run.* More than 100 pre-1949 automobiles are displayed at this fall event. There are also various games for kids and adults to participate in. | 903/572–7466.

## Dining
**Hot Link Palace.** American. This restaurant, known for its tasty hot links, is housed in a renovated 1950s gas station. The chili is also popular. | 502 N. Jefferson Ave., Mount Pleasant | 903/572–6301 | Closed Sun.–Mon. | $2–$5 | No credit cards.

## Lodging
**Best Western Mt. Pleasant Inn.** This two-story motel was renovated in 1997, and is 2 mi from the bus terminal. Complimentary Continental breakfast, in-room data ports, microwaves, refrigerators, some in-room hot tubs, cable TV, outdoor pool, outdoor hot tub, laundry facilities, business services, pets allowed (fee). | 102 E. Burton Rd. | 903/577–7377 | fax 903/577–0401 | www.bestwestern.com | 41 rooms, 15 suites | $66, $76–$109 suites | AE, D, DC, MC, V.

# NACOGDOCHES
MAP 8, K4

*(Nearby towns also listed: Jacksonville, Lufkin)*

Nacogdoches, the oldest town in Texas, began as a Native American settlement. In 1867, French explorer Robert de La Salle visited, and later, in the 1700s, a Spanish mission was established. The town grew up along El Camino Real, or the Old San Antonio Road, a highway that dates back to 1691. Today it has a population of 35,000.

**Information: Nacogdoches Convention and Visitors Bureau** | 200 E. Main St., Nacogdoches, TX 75963 | 936/564–7351 | www.visitnacogdoches.org.

## Attractions
**Millard's Crossing.** These 19th-century structures have been restored and filled with period furnishings. Open for guided tours. | 6020 North St. | 936/564–6631 | $3 | Mon.–Sat. 9–4, Sun. 1–4. ·

**Old University Building.** Built in 1858, this modified Grecian structure was once a university. Today it houses antiques and period artifacts. | Washington Square, intersection of Mound St. and Hughes St. | 936/569–7292 | Free | Tues.–Fri., Sun. 1–4, Sat. 10–4.

**Sterne-Hoya Home.** Adolphus Sterne, an early resident who was active in the founding of the Republic of Texas, built this home in 1828. Today it's open to the public for guided tours. | 211 S. Lanana St. | 936/560–5426 | Free | Mon.–Sat. 9–noon, 2–5.

**Stone Fort Museum.** The fort, built in 1779 by the Spanish as a trading post, later became the headquarters for early attempts to form the Republic of Texas. Today it is on the campus of the Stephen F. Austin State University. Changing exhibits focus on Texas history, art, and culture. | Stephen F. Austin State University, Clark and Griffith Blvds | 936/468–2408 | fax 936/468–7084 | Free | Tues.–Sat. 9–5, Sun. 1–5.

### ON THE CALENDAR
**JUNE:** *Heritage Festival.* This week-long festival includes tours of homes, arts and crafts, and a charity ball. | 936/568–3165.
**JUNE:** *Texas Blueberry Festival.* The blueberry is honored via blueberry cook-offs, arts and crafts, a car rally, and family activities. | 936/560–5533.
**SEPT.:** *Piney Woodstock.* Musicians from throughout East Texas perform at the County Expo Center. | 936/564–0849.

## Dining
**Californian.** Seafood. This hill-top restaurant has a California-rustic-meets-Victorian design. Try the filet mignon, pasta primavera, or fresh fish specials. Kids' menu. | 342 N. University Dr. | 936/560–1985 | $9–$35 | AE, D, DC, MC, V.

**La Hacienda.** Mexican. Set in a 1913 home, this restaurant serves up delicious authentic Mexican cuisine. The *pollo magnifico* (stuffed and breaded chicken breast) is recommended. Kids' menu. | 1411 North St., Nacogdoches | 936/564–6450 | $6–$16 | AE, D, DC, MC, V.

## Lodging
**Best Western Inn.** This hotel is 3 mi from downtown Nacogdoches. The state university and the Stone Fort Museum are less than 2 mi away. Cable TV, pool. | 3428 South St. | 936/560–4900 | fax 409/569–9752 | 60 rooms | $47–$95 | AE, D, DC, MC, V.

**Fredonia.** Built in the 1950s, this six–story, full-service hotel is one block from historic downtown Nacogdoches. It has a redbrick and iron exterior with New Orleans–style furnishings. Restaurant, complimentary breakfast, in-room data ports, cable TV, pool, business services, pets allowed. | 200 N. Fredonia St. | 936/564–1234 | fax 936/564–1234, ext. 240 | www.fredoniahotel.com | 113 rooms | $150–$163 | AE, D, DC, MC, V.

**Holiday Inn.** Nacogdoches may be the oldest town in Texas, but this chain hotel offers many tempting modern conveniences. Restaurant, room service, in-room data ports, cable TV, pool, hot tub, exercise equipment, laundry facilities, business services. | 3400 South St. | 936/569–8100 | fax 936/569–0332 | www.holidayinn.com | 126 rooms | $59–$69 | AE, D, DC, MC, V.

**PineCreek Lodge.** This lodge is on 140-acres. You can relax on the porch swing or tough it out on the hiking trail. The guest rooms are filled with hand-crafted pine furniture. Picnic area, complimentary breakfast, some microwaves, refrigerators, some in-room hot tubs, in-room VCRs (and movies), outdoor pool, outdoor hot tub, fishing, no pets, no smoking. | 2782 S. Alazan Rd., Nacogdoches | 936/560–6282 or 888/714–1414 | fax 936/560–1675 | info@pinecreeklodge.com | www.pinecreeklodge.com | 17 rooms | $65–$150 | AE, D, MC, V.

**Stepan Inn.** Built in 1900, today this B&B is located in historical Washington Square. Though customers tend to be couples looking for an escape, children are more than welcome. Rooms are decorated in an eclectic style, with both modern furnishings and antiques. Complimentary Continental breakfast, kitchenettes, microwaves, refrigerators, cable TV, no pets, no smoking. | 418 N. Mound St., Nacogdoches | 936/560–9511 or 888/569–2282 | fax 800/357–1320 | www.avccomm.com/inn/index.html | 5 suites | $75 | AE, D, MC, V.

# NEW BRAUNFELS

*(Nearby towns also listed: Castroville, Gruene, San Antonio, San Marcos)*

Prince Carl of Solms, Braunfels, and a group of German settlers founded the city of New Braunfels 150 years ago, naming it for their homeland. Under constant fear of Indian attack, the prince donned an iron vest, wearing it everywhere, even in the sweltering summer heat. After 11 months in Texas, Prince Solms returned to Germany to marry Sophie, a woman he had hoped would return to Texas with him. Sophie had no interest in coming to this frontierland, however, so the prince remained in Germany, leaving New Braunfels to his group of immigrants.

Today the city is a favorite because of its German festivals and food, antiques shopping, and summer water activities on the Guadalupe River and at the Schlitterbahn Water Park, the largest of its kind in Texas.

**Information: New Braunfels Convention and Visitors Bureau** | Box 311417, New Braunfels, TX 78131 | 830/625–2385 or 800/572–2626 | nbcc@nbcham.org | www.nbcham.org.

## Attractions

**Canyon Lake.** You can boat, picnic, and camp at the public parks that line this lake. It is a popular destination with anglers in search of catfish, largemouth bass, and, below the dam, rainbow and brown trout. | 601 Coe Rd.; Headquarters is on Rte. 306 | 830/964–3341 or 800/528–2104 | fax 830/964–2215 | www.swf.usace.army-mil.com | $1 | Daily 7 AM to dusk.

**The Children's Museum in New Braunfels** 5,000 square ft of interactive explorations into art, science, history, culture and music are housed in Suite 530 of the New Braunfels Marketplace—a delight for parents and children alike. | 183 I–35, New Braunfels | 830/620–0939 or 888/928–8326 | www.nbchildren.org | $3 | Mon.–Sat. 9–5, Sun. noon–5.

**Historic Outdoor Art Gallery.** Two large murals depict the history of New Braunfels and how the Germans founded the area. One of the murals also depicts the famous botanist Ferdinand Lindheimer. | Downtown, at the corner of Castell Ave. and San Antonio St. | 830/609–1369 | fax 830/620–0970 | Free | Daily.

**Museum of Texas Handmade Furniture.** Furniture hand-crafted in Texas during the 1800s is on display. There is an extensive Biedermeier collection. | 1370 Church Hill Dr. | 830/629–6504 | $5 | Tues.–Sun. 1–4. Closed Mon.

**Hummel Museum.** Sister Maria Innocentia Hummel's extensive collection is on display here, including 350 original paintings and early sketches that spawned the popular figurines, plates, and other collectibles. This is the only museum in the world to highlight her work. | 199 Main Plaza | 830/625–5636 or 800/456–4866 | www.bigmac.bullcreek.austin.tx.us/hummel/index.htm | $5 | Mon.–Sat. 10–5, Sun. noon–5.

**Landa Park.** Located on the banks of the Comal, the world's shortest river, this 300-acre park is a center for family picnics and gatherings. Enjoy a dip in the park's 1.2 million gallon swimming pool, fed with spring water, or go for a glass-bottom boat ride for a peek at the varied aquatic life. You can also play miniature golf and rent paddleboats. To reach the park, take I–35 to Seguin Ave. to downtown. | Landa St. | 830/608–2160 | Free | Daily 6 AM–midnight.

**Lindheimer Home.** This home belonged to Ferdinand Lindheimer, a botanist who lent his name to more than 30 Texas plant species. Now restored, it contains early memorabilia from Lindheimer's career as both botanist and newspaper publisher. A backyard garden is filled with examples of his native floral discoveries. | 491 Comal Ave. | 830/629–2943 | $2 | Late May–Aug., Tues.–Sun. 2–5; Sept.–late May, weekends 2–5.

**Natural Bridge Caverns.** Named for the rock arch over the entrance, this cave is one of the most spectacular in the area. Guided tours are available. | 26495 Natural Bridge Caverns | 830/651–6101 | fax 830/438–7432 | www.naturalbridgetexas.com/cavern | $9 | Late May–Aug., daily 9–6; Sept.–late May, daily 9–4.

**Natural Bridge Wildlife Park.** See zebras, gazelles, antelopes, and ostriches, and even feed them, at this drive-through wildlife ranch. There's a petting zoo with pygmy goats at the entrance. | 26515 Natural Bridge Caverns Rd. | 830/438–7400 | www.naturalbridgetexas.com/cavern | $9.50 | Daily 9–6:30.

**New Braunfels Marketplace.** WestPoint Pepperell, Casual Corner, Bass, American Tourister, Famous Footwear, and other top shops are represented in this open-air mall. | 651 Rte. 81 E | 830/620–6806 or 888/SHOP–333 | www.charter-oak.com/newbraunfels | Free | Daily.

**Schlitterbahn Water Park.** Come enjoy the largest tubing park in the world. Schlitterbahn, which means "slippery road" in German, ranks first in Texas and fourth in the United States in number of visitors. The Comal River supplies cool springwater at the rate of 24,000 gallons a minute and also provides uniquely natural river rapids. Brave the 60-ft Schlittercoaster and the mile-long Raging River tube chute or go for a dip in the 50,000-gallon hot tub with a swim-up bar. For the less adventurous there's a gentle wave pool. Picnic sites. | 305 W. Austin | 830/625–2351 | fax 830/620–4873 | www.schlitterbahn.com | $26 | Late Apr.–mid-May, weekends Sat. 10–7, Sun. 10–6; mid-May–late Aug., daily 10–8; late Aug.–late Sept., weekends 10–6.

**Sophienburg Museum and Archives.** Named for the wife of settlement leader Prince Carl of Solms, this museum displays a reproduction of an early New Braunfels home, a doctor's office complete with medical tools, a blacksmith's shop, and carriages used by early residents. | 401 W. Coll St. | 830/629–1572 | fax 830/629–3906 | www.nbtx.com/sophienburg | $2 | Mon.–Sat. 10–5, Sun. 1–5.

## ON THE CALENDAR
**APR.: *Folkfest*.** This heritage and culture festival includes historic building tours, demonstrations by craftspeople, furniture making, and food. | 830/629–2943.
**SEPT.: *Comal County Fair*.** One of the oldest and largest fairs in the state, this one includes rides, a rodeo, games, food booths, children's areas, and live entertainment. | 830/625–2385 or 800/572–2626.
**OCT.: *Clayfest*.** Clay artists from all over Texas converge upon Gruene to give demonstrations and conduct workshops. | 830/629–7975.
**OCT., NOV.: *Wurstfest*.** This is one of the largest German festivals held outside of Germany. Expect lots of German food, and enjoy polka and waltz music provided by numerous German bands. | 800/221–4369.

## Dining
**Granzin Bar-B-Q.** Barbecue. This family-owned, take-out only restaurant has been in business for 17 years. The sliced beef sandwich and ribs are popular with the locals. | 954 W. San Antonio St., New Braunfels | 830/629–6615 | Closed Sun. | $4–$7 | AE, D, MC, V.

**Grist Mill.** Southern. Eat chicken-fried steak and admire the great view of the Guadalupe River at this low-key family restaurant. The mill was built over 100 years ago and was restored and converted into a restaurant in the 1970s. The burgers and salads are also good. Open-air dining is available on the patio. Entertainment Fri., Sat. in summer. Kids' menu. No air-conditioning. | 1287 Gruene Rd. | 830/625–0684 | $5–$17 | AE, D, DC, MC, V.

**Huisache Grill.** New American. People come from near and far to visit this gorgeous restaurant, which was formerly a train station, built at the turn of the 20th century. Its parklike setting, downtown location, and recycled glass and wood interior attract the crowd, but once you try the seafood, steak, pasta, and salads you will be back for more. There are live music and jazz on the weekends. Open-air dining is available on the courtyard-style covered patio with an open-cut stone fireplace. Kids' menu. | 303 W. San Antonio | 830/620–9001 | $10–$16 | AE, D, DC, MC, V.

**New Braunfels Smokehouse.** Barbecue. There's plenty of barbecue and hickory-smoked meat to be had at this casual restaurant with indoor and outdoor dining. It seats nearly 300 and, in addition to barbecue, serves sausage, chicken and dumplings, apple dumplings, and bread pudding. The all-you-can-eat buffet is served on the wooden patio. Kids' menu. Beer and wine only. | 146 Rte. 46 E | 830/625–2416 | Breakfast also available | $15–$23 | AE, D, MC, V.

**Oma's House.** German. Authentic German cuisine is served at this family-owned restaurant. The Wiener schnitzel is a local favorite. | 541 Highway 46, New Braunfels | 830/625–3280 | fax 830/625–9681 | $8–$13 | AE, DC, D, MC, V.

**Ryan's Family Steakhouse.** American. This family restaurant is known for an excellent buffet. Individual dishes such as the sirloin steak and grilled salmon are recommended. | 485 E. Hwy. 81, New Braunfels | 830/606–0096 | $4–$11 | AE, D, DC, MC, V.

## Lodging

**Best Western Inn and Suites.** This motel is 2 mi from Schlitterbahn Water Park. It's also ½ mi from the local mall and close to area restaurants. Complimentary Continental breakfast, refrigerators, microwaves in suites, cable TV, pool, wading pool, laundry facilities, business services. | 1493 I–35N | 830/625–7337 | www.bestwestern.com | 60 rooms, 20 suites | $99–$109, $109 suites | AE, D, DC, MC, V.

**Faust Hotel.** This National Historic Landmark opened in October 1929, just 2 weeks before the stock market crash. Although it's been renovated many times over the years, the hotel still contains authentic 1930s furnishings. A micro-brewery is on site. Restaurant, bar, some refrigerators, cable TV, business services, no pets. | 240 S. Seguin Ave., New Braunfels | 830/625–7791 | fax 830/620–1530 | www.fausthotel.com | 61 rooms, 1 suite | $59–$99, $145–$175 suite | AE, D, DC, MC, V.

**Hampton Inn.** This two-story hotel is across the street from a movie theater, and within walking distance of a number of restaurants. Complimentary Continental breakfast, in-room data ports, cable TV, pool, hot tub, exercise equipment, laundry facilities, business services. | 979 I–35N | 830/608–0123 | fax 830/608–0121 | 62 rooms | $99–$110 | AE, D, DC, MC, V.

**Holiday Inn.** Business travelers and vacationing families alike feel at home in this comfortable, two-story, full-service chain hotel. Restaurant, bar, room service, in-room data ports, cable TV, pool, wading pool, exercise equipment, laundry facilities, business services, pets allowed (fee). | 1051 I–35E | 830/625–8017 | fax 830/625–3130 | www.holidayinn.com | 140 rooms | $79–$99 | AE, D, DC, MC, V.

**John Newcombe's Tennis Ranch.** If you're a tennis lover, this is the place for you. Treat yourself to a stay at this ranch established by the Australian tennis star. Bar, snack bar, pool, hot tub, 28 tennis courts, children's programs (ages 8–18), laundry facilities, business services, airport shuttle. | 325 Mission Valley Rd. | 830/625–9105 or 800/444–6204 | fax 830/625–2004 | www.lone-star.com/newks | 46 rooms in 2 buildings, 10 cottages | $60–$140, $120 cottages | AE, D, MC, V.

**Karbach Haus.** Housed in a meticulously restored, turn-of-the-20th-century brick mansion, this historic B&B is renowned for its comfort, world-class breakfasts, and personalized service. Walk less than four blocks to downtown restaurants, museums, antiques stores, and local attractions. Complimentary breakfast, some kitchenettes, microwaves, refrigerators, some in-room hot tubs, cable TV, in-room VCRs (and movies), no room phones, pool, hot tub, laundry facilities, business services, no kids under 16, no smoking. | 487 W. San Antonio St. | 830/625–2131 or 800/972–5941 | fax 830/629–1126 | khausbnb@aol.com | www.virtualcities.com | 6 rooms (2 with shower only) | $110–$200 (2–day minimum stay) | D, MC, V.

**Lamb's Rest Inn.** Located just 1 mile from Gruene, you can stroll among the gardens or enjoy riverfront views from either veranda at this B&B. The suite has a private entrance and a full kitchen. Complimentary breakfast, some kitchenettes, some in-room hot tubs, cable

TV, no room phones, outdoor pool, no pets, no kids, no smoking. | 1385 Edwards Blvd., 78132 | 830/609–3932 or 888/609–3932 | fax 830/620–0864 | lambsbb@aol.com | 4 rooms, 1 suite | $95–$150 | D, MC, V.

**New Braunfels Super 8 Motel.** Built in 1996, this two-story motel with spacious rooms is in the middle of Texas Hill Country. Shopping is a mile away, and recreational activities within 3 mi. Complimentary Continental breakfast, in-room data ports, some microwaves, some refrigerators, cable TV, pool, outdoor hot tub, spa, laundry services, some pets. | 510 S. State Hwy. 46, New Braunfels | 830/629–1155 | fax 830/629–1155 | www.super8.com | 36 rooms, 14 suites | $54–$99, $59–$119 suites | AE, D, DC, MC, V.

**Prince Solms.** Built in 1898, this is the oldest Victorian hotel in Texas. Enjoy the friendly service, antique furnishings, and a patio that's good for relaxing. Bar (with entertainment), complimentary breakfast, business services, no pets, no kids. | 295 E. San Antonio St. | 830/625–9169 or 800/625–9169 | fax 830/625–9169 (call first) | 14 rooms | $99–$165 | AE, DC, MC, V.

**Rodeway Inn.** This motel is 3 mi from Gruene and the Schlitterbahn Water Park. There are a number of fast-food and fine dining restaurants next-door. Complimentary Continental breakfast, in-room data ports, cable TV, pool, outdoor hot tub, business services, some pets. | 1209 I–35E, New Braunfels | 830/629–6991 | fax 830/629–0754 | www.choicehotels.com | 130 rooms | $69–$89 | AE, D, DC, MC, V.

**Schlitterbahn Waterpark Resort.** If you're planning a visit to the water park, this resort on the Comal River is right next door. Cable TV, pool, business services. | 305 W. Austin St. | 830/625–2351 | fax 830/620–4873 | 220 rooms | $90–$142 | AE, D, MC, V.

**Texas SunCatchers Inn.** Nestled behind a cedar fence, this contemporary house was built in 1939. Feel free to take a dip in New Braunfels' first private pool or enjoy a relaxing evening by the fireplace. The rooms are lavishly decorated with antiques. Complimentary breakfast, no room phones, TV in common area, outdoor pool, outdoor hot tub, no pets. | 1316 West Coll St. | 830/609–1062 | fax 830/609–1062 | txsuncatch@aol.com | 4 rooms | $100–$150 | AE, D, MC, V.

# ODESSA

MAP 8, E4

*(Nearby towns also listed: Midland, Monahans)*

Often mentioned with the adjacent city of Midland, Odessa is located in the mineral-rich Permian Basin. The city is home to many thriving petroleum businesses, as well a campus of the University of Texas and a number of vast ranches.

Information: **Odessa Chamber of Commerce** | 700 N. Grant, Ste. 200, Odessa, TX 79761 | 915/332–9111 or 800/780–HOST | www.odessachamber.com.

## Attractions

**Ellen Noel Art Museum of the Permian Basin.** Exhibits are constantly changing and vary from paintings to sculptures to photography. There is an excellent collection of bronzes by contemporary Italian sculptors. | University of Texas of the Permian Basin, 4909 E. University Dr., Odessa | 915/368–7222 | Free | Tue.–Sat. 10–5, Sun. 2–5. Closed Mon.

**Globe of the Great Southwest Theatre.** This 410-seat octagonal-shape theatre is an authentic replica of England's original Globe Theatre, home of William Shakespeare's acting company. Year-round productions include Shakespearean classics, community performances, and country-western revues. The Ann Hathaway Cottage next door is a re-creation of the home of Shakespeare's wife and contains an archival library and many period antiques. | Odessa College, 2308 Shakespeare Rd. | 915/332–1586 | www.globesw.org | $2 | Weekdays 10–noon, 1–4, weekends by appointment.

**Meteor Crater.** The country's second-largest crater was formed approximately 20,000 years ago by a storm of falling meteors. It's 10 mi west of Odessa via I–20. | Meteor Crater Rd. | Free | Daily.

**Presidential Museum.** Created after the death of President John F. Kennedy, this is the only museum in the country devoted exclusively to the study of the U.S. presidency. Exhibitions include the Library of the Presidents, an extraordinary assemblage of original documents and periodicals, and collections of campaign memorabilia, political cartoons, and miniature dolls of the First Ladies. | 622 N. Lee, at Seventh St. | 915/332–7123 | www.presidential-museum.org | $2 | Tues.–Sat. 10–5.

### ON THE CALENDAR
**JAN.:** *SandHills Stock Show and Rodeo.* Cowboys and cowgirls compete for top prizes in rodeo riding, roping, and precision riding competitions. | 915/366–3951.
**FEB.:** *Shakespeare Festival.* The Bard is celebrated for twelve days with special theatrical performances, trail rides, a carnival, and art exhibits. | 915/332–1586.
**SEPT.:** *Permian Basin Fair and Exposition.* This nine-day festival attracts visitors from all over the country. Highlights include a livestock show, a petting zoo, and the largest carnival in west Texas. | 915/550–3232.

## Dining
**Barn Door.** American. Housed in a railroad depot built in 1892, this casual restaurant is known for its extensive wine list and delicious porterhouse steaks. The Tex-Mex specialties and seafood platters are also popular. | 2140 N. Andrew Hwy. | 915/337–4142 | Closed Sun. | $7–$20 | AE, MC, V.

**La Bodega.** Mexican. A colorful dining room and reliable Mexican and American dishes make this a good choice for a nice meal. Try the enchiladas, fajitas, or a juicy hamburger. Kids' menu. | 1024 E. 7th St. | 915/333–4469 | $10–$14 | AE, D, MC, V.

## Lodging
**Best Western Garden Oasis.** Rooms overlook the pool and a garden atrium in this motel 3 miles from the heart of town. Restaurant, room service, cable TV, pool, hot tub, sauna, laundry facilities, business services, airport shuttle, some pets allowed. | 110 I–20W, at Grant Ave. | 915/337–3006 or 877/574–9231 | fax 915/332–1956 | www.bestwestern.com | 118 rooms | $60–$68 | AE, D, DC, MC, V.

**Holiday Inn Centre.** This is one of the largest hotels in Odessa. It's on I–20, just a few minutes from Odessa College. Restaurant, bar, room service, in-room data ports, microwaves (in suites), cable TV, 2 pools, hot tub, putting green, exercise equipment, laundry facilities, business services, airport shuttle, some pets allowed. | 6201 I–20E | 915/362–2311 | fax 915/362–9810 | www.holiday-inn.com | 245 rooms, 36 suites | $74–$83 | AE, D, DC, MC, V.

**K-Bar Ranch Lodge.** Stay at this working 44,000-acre ranch and watch the grazing cattle or examine European, Asian, and African species in the 700-acre game preserve. There is also an Apache campground for those who want to rough it. Hunting packages are available. Complimentary breakfast, some room phones, TV in common area, no pets, no smoking. | 15448-A South Jasper Ave., Odessa | 915/580–5880 | fax 915/580–3089 | 4 rooms | $150 | MAP | AE, MC, V.

**La Quinta.** Rooms with balconies and lots of light are available at this hotel 1 mi from the University of Texas, Permian Basin campus. Complimentary Continental breakfast, picnic area, cable TV, pool, business services, some pets allowed. | 5001 I–20E | 915/333–2820 | fax 915/333–4208 | www.laquinta.com | 122 rooms | $62–$69 | AE, D, DC, MC, V.

**Motel 6.** An economical option just south of town with basic amenities. | 95 rooms. Cable TV, pool, laundry facilities, some pets allowed. | 200 I–20E Service Rd. | 915/333–4025 | fax 915/333–2668 | www.motel6.com | $28–$32 | AE, D, DC, MC, V.

**Odessa Days Inn.** This three-story motel is on the outskirts of town. The Globe Theater is only 4 mi away and there are restaurants within walking distance. Complimentary Continental breakfast, in-room data ports, some microwaves, some refrigerators, cable TV, outdoor pool, business services, pets allowed. | 3075 E. Business Loop 20, Odessa | 915/335–8000 | fax 915/335–9562 | www.daysinn.com | 94 rooms, 2 suites | $46–$48, $52 suites | AE, D, DC, MC, V.

**Radisson.** This eight-story high rise has spacious rooms with Southwest decor and is a good choice for business travelers. Enjoy stand-up comedy every Saturday night at Spirits Lounge and complimentary membership at a local health club. Restaurant, 2 bars (with entertainment), room service, some microwaves, cable TV, pool, hot tub, laundry service, business services, airport shuttle, no pets. | 5200 E. University Blvd. | 915/368–5885 | fax 915/362–8958 | www.radisson.com | 194 rooms | $99–$109 | AE, D, DC, MC, V.

# ORANGE

MAP 8, L5

*(Nearby towns also listed: Beaumont, Port Arthur)*

A small community set on the Sabine River at the Texas-Louisiana border, Orange was named for a grove of wild oranges found in the area. Today the town has an active port and a unique Cajun culture. Go bird watching or freshwater fishing, or take a trip across the border (4 mi) to try your luck at Louisiana's casinos and the Delta Downs raceway.

Information: **Orange Convention and Visitors Bureau** | 1012 Green Ave., Orange, TX 77630 | 409/883–3536 or 800/528–4906 | www.org-tx.com/chamber.

## Attractions

**Frances Ann Lutcher Theater for the Performing Arts.** Broadway musical troupes, symphonies, and community theater groups take the stage at this performing-arts venue which first opened in 1980. | 707 W. Main St. | 409/886–5535 or 800/828–5535 | www.lutcher.org | Prices vary with shows | Call for performance schedules.

**Heritage House Museum.** This 1902 home is listed on the National Register of Historic Places; it now offers exhibits on life in the early 20th century as well as traveling displays and educational programs. The adjacent Heritage History Museum tells the story of Orange County with memorabilia and artifacts. | 905 W. Division St. | 409/886–5385 | www.heritage-houseoforange.org | Free | Tues.–Fri. 10–4.

**Stark Museum of Art.** Paintings by John J. Audubon, Charles Russell, and the Taos Society of Artists highlight this museum's impressive collection of 19th- and 20th-century Western American art. The museum also houses Native American artifacts and a decorative arts exhibit featuring a collection of Steuben crystal. | 712 Green Ave. | 409/883–6661 | fax 409/883–6361 | www.starkmuseumofart.org | Free | Wed.–Sat. 10–5, Sun. 1–5.

**Super Gator Tours.** Cruise through Cypress Lake and the Blue Elbow Swamp and get a glimpse of the area's pristine wilderness. You might see alligators, egrets, and innumerable other birds. | 106 E. Lutcher Dr. | 409/883–7725 | ww.pnx.com/gator | $25.50 | Mon.–Sat. 10–4, Sun. by appointment.

**W. H. Stark House.** Original period furnishings distinguish this elegant 1894 home. Open only to adults and children age 14 and over. | 610 Main St. | 409/883–0871 | $2 | Tues.–Sat. 10–3, tours available.

## ON THE CALENDAR

**MAY:** *International Gumbo Cook-off.* More than 22,000 hungry visitors pack the streets each year to share winning recipes and listen to live music. | 409/883–3536.

## Dining

**Cajun Cookery.** Cajun. For a truly nautical dining experience, come to the Cajun Cookery. Diners can examine the mounted fish and numerous fishing traps that decorate the restaurant. People come from miles away to have the deep-fried barbecue crab. The seafood gumbo is also very popular. | 2308 I–10 E., Orange | 409/886–0990 | $7–$13 | AE, D, DC, MC, V.

**Cody's Restaurant.** Seafood. You'll notice the ornate stained-glass windows when you arrive at this restaurant. Try its fried shrimp, grilled snapper, or steak. | 3130 16th St., Orange | 409/883–2267 | Closed Sun. | $9–$18 | AE, D, DC, MC, V.

## Lodging

**Best Western Inn.** This basic chain property is just a half mile from downtown. There's a casual restaurant next door. In-room data ports, some refrigerators, cable TV, pool, some pets allowed. | 2630 I–10 | 409/883–6616 | fax 409/883–3427 | www.bestwestern.com | 60 rooms | $55–$66 | AE, D, DC, MC, V.

**Days Inn Orange.** This motel is across the street from a 24-hour restaurant, and a casino is a 25-minute drive away. Complimentary Continental breakfast, cable TV, laundry services, pets allowed (restrictions). | 401 27th St., Orange | 409/883–9981 | fax 409/883–7902 | www.daysinn.com | 53 rooms | $38 | AE, D, DC, MC, V.

**Holiday Inn Express.** Off I–10, this two-story motel is within walking distance of a few fast-food restaurants. The Piney Woods Country Winery is only 2 mi away. Complimentary Continental breakfast, in-room data port, some microwaves, some refrigerators, cable TV, pool, laundry services, business services, pets allowed (fee). | 2900 I–10, Orange | 409/988–0110 | fax 409/988–0105 | www.holiday-inn.com | 97 rooms | $79 | AE, D, DC, MC, V.

**Motel 6.** Several restaurants and a tasty waffle shop are within walking distance of this basic two-story motel, 4½ mi from the center of Orange. Cable TV, pool, some pets allowed. | 4407 27th St. | 409/883–4891 | fax 409/886–5211 | www.motel6.com | 126 rooms | $27–$32 | AE, D, MC, V.

**Ramada Inn.** You'll find basic rooms and a casual restaurant at this chain hotel just off 16th St. in the heart of town. Restaurant, bar (with entertainment), in-room data ports, some microwaves, refrigerators, room service, cable TV, pool, wading pool, business services, pets allowed. | 2610 I–10 | 409/883–0231 or 800/635–5312 | fax 409/883–8839 | 125 rooms | $60–$135 | AE, D, DC, MC, V.

# OZONA

MAP 8, E5

*(Nearby towns also listed: San Angelo, Sonora)*

Located on the Edwards Plateau, Ozona is the largest unincorporated town in Texas and the only community in Crockett County. A popular hunting destination, with large populations of white-tail deer and javelina, the area is also a center for wool production and ranching.

Information: **Ozona Chamber of Commerce** | 1110 Avenue East, Ozona, TX 76943 | 915/392–3737.

## Attractions

**Crockett County Museum.** The artifacts on display here date from as early as 10,000 BC and include mammoth bones, Native American tools, and frontier antiques. | 404 11th St. | 915/392–2837 | $2 | Weekdays 10–5.

**Crockett County Memorial Fair Park.** This park on the eastern edge of town is the home of the Emerald House, a West Texas ranch built in 1926. The house retains its period furnishings. There is a picnic area for those who wish to spend a relaxing day in the sun. | Off U.S. 290 | 915/392–2837 | Free | Daily.

**Davy Crockett Monument.** This statue located on the town square honors the namesake of Crockett County who died defending the Alamo. | 163 Ave. E, in front of courthouse | Free | Daily.

**Fort Lancaster State Historic Site.** This military post was built in 1855 to protect the frontier. Abandoned in 1861, the 25-building site now houses a visitor and interpretive center with displays on 19th-century military life. | I–290, 33 mi west of Ozona | 915/836–4391 | Free | Late May–early Sept., daily 9–6; Sept.–May, Thurs.–Mon. 9–5.

### ON THE CALENDAR
**JUNE:** *World Championship Goat Roping.* This contest held the third weekend in June draws participants from all over the state of Texas. It includes a cook-off, as well as a Sat. night ball. | 915/392–2837.

## Dining
**R&L Bar-B-Q.** Barbecue. A steer head and pictures of outlaws Billy the Kid and Butch Cassidy adorn the walls of this barbecue joint. The pork ribs are popular. | 1309 Sheffield Rd. | 915/392–5191 | Closed Sun.–Mon. | $6–$9 | MC, V.

## Lodging
**Comfort Inn.** This two-story motel is less than 1 mi from the Davy Crockett Monument. In late summer the motel fills up with deer hunters. Complimentary Continental breakfast, in-room data ports, cable TV, pool, laundry services, business services, no pets. | 1307 Ave. A | 915/392–3791 | fax 915/392–5277 | www.comfortinn.com | 50 rooms | $59–$65 | AE, D, DC, MC, V.

# PADRE ISLAND

MAP 8, I8

*(Nearby towns also listed: Corpus Christi, Kingsville, South Padre Island)*

A favorite of birders, surfers, and campers, Padre Island is known for its miles of unspoiled beaches. This 110-mi-long barrier island protects much of the Texas coast from hurricanes and tropical storms. The northern and southern ends of the island are developed with parks and resorts, but the majority of the island's landmass is protected as part of the Padre Island National Seashore.

Padre Island features beaches dotted with rolling dunes, clean sand, and flocks of gulls. The surf is usually gentle and shallow enough to walk for hundreds of yards before reaching chest-deep water. Occasionally, undertow is a problem, but on most summer days the waves are gentle and rolling, and the water is warm.

Information: **Corpus Christi Convention and Visitors Bureau** | 1201 North Shoreline, Corpus Christi, TX 78401 | 361/881–1888 or 800/678–OCEAN | www.padreislandbeaches.com.

## Attractions
**Padre Balli Park.** One of the most popular areas of the island is Padre Balli Park, home of a 1,200-ft fishing pier and campgrounds. It was named for the priest who managed a ranch on the island in the early 19th century. | 15820 Park Rd. 22 | 361/949–8121 | Free | Daily dawn to dusk.

**Padre Island National Seashore.** This 70-mi stretch of unblemished seashore was first established in 1962 and is a haven for beachcombers, boaters, and swimmers. Go in spring to enjoy wildflowers, bird watching, and windsurfing; in summer to view nesting sea turtles. You can drive along parts of the island, but a four-wheel drive vehicle is required to explore most areas. Hiking trails abound and swimming is permitted on all beaches, though lifeguards are on duty only at Malaquite Beach Memorial Day–Labor Day. Camping facilities are available at Malaquite Beach and Bird Island Basin. The Malaquite Beach visitor center, open year-round, offers educational programs, brochures, a small museum, and a concession stand. | 20301 Park Rd. | 361/949–8173 | www.nps.gov/pais | $10 for seven-day pass | Daily.

## ON THE CALENDAR

**JUNE:** *C-Sculptures.* Highlights of this festive event include individual and team sand sculpting contests and a volleyball competition. There is also a "Beauty on the Beach" contest. | 361/949–7193 | www.c101.com.

## Lodging

**Holiday Inn SunSpree Resort.** The only full-service beachfront property on the north end of Padre Island, this six-story hotel has a marine motif complete with aquariums in the lobby. The rooms are spacious; many have balconies and gulf views. Restaurant, bar (with entertainment), picnic area, room service, in-room data ports, microwaves, refrigerators, cable TV, 2 pools, hot tub, sauna, golf privileges, exercise equipment, beach, bicycles, video games, playground, business services, pets allowed (fee). | 15202 Windward Dr. | 361/949–8041 | fax 361/949–9139 | www.northpadreholidayinn.com or www.holiday-inn.com | 149 rooms | $119–$209 | AE, D, DC, MC, V.

**Island House.** The apartment-style accommodations have balconies that afford great views of the gulf. Picnic area, kitchenettes, cable TV, pool, wading pool, beach, laundry facilities, business services, no pets. | 15340 Leeward Dr. | 361/949–8166 or 800/333–8806 | fax 361/949–8904 | 65 1- to 3-bedroom apartments | $105–$200 | AE, D, MC, V.

# PALESTINE

MAP 8, J4

*(Nearby towns also listed: Crockett, Fairfield, Jacksonville, Rusk, Tyler)*

Restored Victorian homes and buildings dating to the 1840s fill this quaint East Texas town, the second oldest in the state. Stop by in spring when the dogwoods and magnolias are in bloom and climb aboard the famous Texas State Railroad for a journey through pastures, pine, and hardwood forests.

Information: **Palestine Convention and Visitors Bureau** | Box 2828, Palestine, TX 75802 | 903/723–3014 or 800/659–3484 | www.visitpalestine.com.

## Attractions

**Community Forest.** Fish, swim, or boat on one of the four lakes, or pack a picnic and hike on the trails that traverse this 700-acre woodland 2½ mi northwest of Palestine. | U.S. 287 | 800/659–3484 | Free | Daily.

**Museum for East Texas Culture.** This museum is housed in a 1914 schoolhouse and features rooms devoted to railroading, home life, and education. There is a restored caboose outside the museum. | 400 Micheaux Ave., Palestine | 903/723–1914 | $1 | Mon.–Sat. 10–5, Sun. 1–4.

**National Scientific Balloon Facility.** This NASA-operated research center launches and tracks high-altitude balloons used in atmospheric studies. Tours are available. | Rte. 3224, off U.S. 287 | 903/729–0271 | By appointment only.

**Texas State Railroad.** Antique steam locomotives carry you between the towns of Rusk and Palestine through piney woods, across 30 bridges, and into depots built to recall the heyday of steam-powered travel. The 51-mi round-trip journey takes 3 hours, and you can catch a short film on the history of the railway in Rusk. Peak visitation is in late March and early April, when flowering dogwoods dot the landscape, or in November when the woods are alive with autumn's colors. Reservations recommended year-round. | Palestine Train Depot, Hwy. 84E | 903/683–2561 | fax 903/683–5634 | $15 round-trip; $10 one-way | Mar–Nov., weekends 11; reservations advised.

### ON THE CALENDAR
**MAR., APR.: *Texas Dogwood Trails Festival.*** The blooming of the dogwoods is celebrated with scenic walks, trail rides, an arts-and-crafts fair, a parade, and a cooking competition. | 903/723–3014 or 800/659–3484.
**OCT.: *Hot Pepper Festival.*** The streets of Palestine heat up with parades, a chili cook-off, hot-pepper eating contests, and the Tour de Pepper bike race. | 903/729–6066.
**DEC.: *Victorian Christmas Train Ride.*** Enjoy a scenic nighttime train ride between Palestine and Rusk on the only steam-operated train in Texas. Carolers dressed in traditional Victorian outfits parade up and down the train. | 903/723–3014 or 800/659–3484.

## Dining
**Pitt Grill.** American. The waffles and T-bone steak are very popular at this 24-hour restaurant. Kids' menu. | 1600 W. Palestine Ave., Palestine | 903/723–9120 | Open 24 hours. Breakfast also available | $5–$9 | No credit cards.

## Lodging
**Best Western Palestine Inn.** This motel is 3 mi from the center of town. Restaurant, in-room data ports, cable TV, pool, playground, business services, pets allowed. | 1601 W. Palestine Ave. | 903/723–4655 or 800/523–0121 | fax 903/723–2519 | www.bestwestern.com | 66 rooms | $44–$55 | AE, D, DC, MC, V.

**Talley Inn.** This charming two-story Victorian-style inn was built in the early 1900s. Rooms are luxuriously decorated with antiques. There is a VCR in the common area and there is a common kitchenette. Complimentary breakfast, no room phones, cable TV, laundry facilities, no pets, no smoking. | 901 N. Sycamore St., Palestine | 903/731–4252 or 800/863–5974 | mail@thetalleyinn.com | www.thetalleyinn.com | 4 rooms | $75 | MC, V.

# PAMPA
MAP 8, K8

*(Nearby towns also listed: Amarillo, Fritch, Shamrock)*

This Panhandle town, named for its surrounding plains (*las pampas* in Spanish), was founded in 1888. Today it is a thriving industrial community serving the surrounding oil fields and ranches.

Information: **Pampa Economic Development Corporation** | Box 2494, Pampa, TX 79066-2494 | 806/665–5553 or 800/766–3143 | www.pampa.com.

## Attractions
**Freedom Museum USA.** Military memorabilia including guns, swords, and uniforms are on display. | 600 N. Hobart St. | 806/669–6066 | Free | Tues.–Sat. noon–4.

**White Deer Land Museum.** The restored former headquarters of the White Deer Land Company (a prominent local land company founded in 1886) houses this museum dedicated to the history of the company and the region. | 116 S. Cuyler St. | 806/669–8041 | fax 806/669–8030 | Free | May–Sept., Tues.–Sun. 10–4; Oct.–Apr., Tues.–Sun. 1:30–4.

## ON THE CALENDAR

**JULY: *Top O'Texas Rodeo, PRCA.*** Held annually since 1946, this is one of the country's oldest Professional Rodeo Cowboys Association events. Barbecues, parades, and barrel races mark the occasion. | 806/665–5553 or 800/766–3143.

**SEPT.: *Chautauqua Festival.*** Arts and crafts displays and live musical performances are the highlights of this celebration. There is a tent devoted to country singer Woody Guthrie. | 806/669–3241.

## Dining

**Amber's Mexican Food Restaurant.** Mexican. Piñatas and plants provide the scenery at this Mexican spot. Try the chicken fajita salad or ground beef quesadillas. Kids' menu. | 2014 N. Hobart St. | 806/665–1173 | Closed Sun. | $3–$15 | AE, D, DC, MC, V.

**Dyer's Bar-B-Que.** Barbecue. This busy barbecue joint has been serving up huge portions at reasonable prices for more than 30 years. The all-you-can-eat combination platter (with pork ribs, brisket, and sausage, plus two side dishes) is a good bet. Kids' menu. Beer and wine only. | Rte. 60 W | 806/665–4401 | Closed Sun. | $6–$10 | AE, MC, V.

**Texas Rose Steakhouse.** Steak. The dining room is packed with local memorabilia and hunting souvenirs. Watch the chef work in the glass-enclosed kitchen as you dine on prime rib, Cajun shrimp, or roast chicken. Kids' menu. | 2537 Perryton Pkwy. | 806/669–1009 | Closed Sun. | $6–$15 | AE, MC, V.

## Lodging

**Best Western Northgate Inn.** This two-story motel is 3 mi from downtown and two blocks from the mall. Complimentary Continental breakfast, in-room data ports, some refrigerators, some microwaves, some in-room hot tubs, cable TV, pool, laundry facilities, business services, no pets. | 2831 Perryton Pkwy. | 806/665–0926 | fax 806/665–8027 | www.bestwestern.com | 100 rooms | $49–$59 | AE, D, DC, MC, V.

# PARIS

MAP 8, J2

*(Nearby towns also listed: Bonham, Denisson, Mount Pleasant, Sherman, Sulphur Springs, Texarkana)*

The 1983 Wim Wenders film *Paris, Texas* immortalized this northeast Texas town, which dubs itself the "second largest Paris in the world." The movie was actually filmed in the Trans-Pecos and Houston; nonetheless, Paris has a lot to offer, including a nicely restored downtown area dating from the 1920s. The town, which sits between the Red and Sulphur rivers, now serves as a hub for the area's agriculture industry and the site of Paris Junior College and a Campbell's Soup factory.

Information: **Paris Visitors and Convention Office** | 1651 Clarksville St., Paris, TX 75460 | 903/784–2501 or 800/PARIS TX | www.paristexas.com.

## Attractions

**A. M. and Welma Aikin, Jr. Regional Archives.** This library houses historical archives and documents from several area counties. There is also a replica of state senator A. M. Aiken's

PARIS

INTRO
ATTRACTIONS
DINING
LODGING

office. | Paris Junior College, 2400 Clarksville Rd. | 903/785–7661 | www.paris.cc.tx.us/archives | Free | Mon.–Thur. 8–5, Fri. 8–noon.

**Eiffel Tower.** The world's "other" Eiffel Tower stands more than 65 ft and is topped with a cowboy hat. | Jefferson Rd. and Collegiate Dr. | Free | Daily.

**Evergreen Cemetery.** This cemetery contains headstones that date back to the late 1800s. | 560 Evergreen St. | 903/784–6750 | Free | Daily.

**Sam Bell Maxey House State Historical Park.** Confederate general and U.S. Senator Sam Bell Maxey built this high Victorian Italianate–style house in 1867; his family lived here for nearly a century. Guided tours explore the furnished home and landscaped grounds. | 812 S. Church St. | 903/785–5716 | www.tpwd.state.tx.us/park/sambell/sambell.htm | $2 | Fri. and Sun. 1–5, Sat. 8–5.

### ON THE CALENDAR

**JUNE, JULY:** *Municipal Band Concerts.* Enjoy outdoor music under the summer sky the last three Fridays in June and the first three Fridays in July. Performances feature the Paris Municipal Band and culminate in the crowning of the Crape Myrtles Queen. | 903/784–2501 or 800/PARIS TX.

**JULY:** *Longhorn National Dragboat Race.* Top dragboat racers compete for cash prizes in a weekend-long event. | 903/784–2501 or 800/PARIS TX.

**AUG.:** *Paris CRCA/CRA Annual Rodeo.* This annual event includes all the usual rodeo activities—calf roping, bull riding, and barrel racing—as well as a parade and street dance. | 903/784–2501 or 800/PARIS TX.

## Dining

**Capizzi's Italian Kitchen.** Italian. With olive and grape vines hanging from the ceiling and pictures of Italian landscapes decorating the walls, you might think you are in Italy. The shrimp scampi and chicken capellini are very popular. Kids' menu. | 2525 Clarksville St., Paris | 903/785–7590 | Closed Sun. | $5–$11 | AE, MC, V.

**Fish Fry.** Seafood. With nine dining rooms, this casual spot is good for large groups. Known for good steaks and seafood specialties. Kids' menu. No smoking. | 3500 NE Loop 286 | 903/785–6144 | Closed Sun., Mon. No lunch | $11–$25 | No credit cards.

**TaMolly's.** Mexican. Lively Mexican music adds to the fun at this large local favorite. Known for nachos, fajitas, and beef dishes. Kids' menu. | 2835 NE Loop 286 | 903/784–4706 | $7–$16 | AE, MC, V.

## Lodging

**Cane River.** Built in 1880, this B&B is housed in a Queen Anne mansion with parquet floors, oak furnishings, and antiques. Enjoy a quiet evening on the porch or patio. Restaurant, complimentary breakfast, no TV in some rooms, laundry facilities, no pets, no kids under 6, no smoking. | 441 12th St. SE | 903/784–7402 | fax 903/784–3524 | caneriver@neto.com | www.neto.com/caneriver | 2 rooms, 1 suite | $85–$115, $135 suite | MC, V.

**Comfort Inn.** This reliable chain property (2½ mi from downtown) offers proximity to family restaurants and local businesses. Complimentary Continental breakfast, cable TV, pool, business services, some pets allowed. | 3505 NE Loop 286 | 903/784–7481 | fax 903/784–0231 | www.comfortinn.com | 62 rooms | $55–$65 | AE, D, DC, MC, V.

**Holiday Inn.** The on-site Denny's is open 24 hours a day. Restaurant, in-room data ports, room service, cable TV, pool, gym, laundry facilities, business services, pets allowed. | 3560 NE Loop 286 | 903/785–5545 | fax 903/785–9510 | www.holiday-inn.com | 114 rooms, 10 suites | $79 | AE, D, DC, MC, V.

# PECOS

*(Nearby towns also listed: Fort Stockton, Monahans)*

On the banks of the Pecos River in west Texas sits the town of Pecos, known for its succulent cantaloupes, and as the launching pad for wheeler-dealer Billy Sol Estes. The town was established when the Texas and Pacific Railroad put a stop here in 1881, a time when to "pecos" a man meant to kill him and throw him in the river. Pecos claims to have held the world's first rodeo, an 1883 contest held on Independence Day, and maintains that heritage with an annual rodeo that's the fourth largest in the state.

**Information: Pecos Chamber of Commerce and Convention and Visitors Bureau** | 111 South Cedar (Hwy. 285), Pecos, TX 79772 | 915/445–2406 | www.pecostx.com.

## Attractions

**Balmorhea State Park.** The highlight of this park 32 mi south of Pecos is the 77,053-square-ft spring pool fed by the chilly waters of the Solomon Springs. It is one of the largest in the world and home to a variety of aquatic life including fish and turtles. Some scuba diving is allowed. There are also a playground, lodging, and areas for camping and picnicking. | 9207 Hwy. 17S, Toyahvale | 915/375–2370 | fax 915/374–2429 | www.tpwd.state.tx.us/park/balmorhe/balmorhe.htm | $3 | Daily 8 AM–10 PM.

**Maxey Park and Zoo.** This zoo is home to bears, mountain lions, buffalo, and many other animals. There are also picnic areas and a "Kid's City" playground for children. | I–20, Exit 40 | 915/445–2406 | Free | Daily.

**West of the Pecos Museum and Park.** For a glimpse of what life was like in the 1880s, stop by this former saloon turned museum. In the courtyard out back are horse-drawn buggies and wagons, as well as the grave of gunfighter Clay Allison. | 120 E. 1st St. at Cedar St. | 915/445–5076 | $4 | Sept.–May, Tues.–Sat. 9–5; May–Aug., weekdays 9–6, Sat. 9–5, Sun. 1–4.

### ON THE CALENDAR

**JULY: *West of the Pecos PRCA Rodeo.*** This Independence Day–weekend commemoration of the world's first rodeo is a fine place to see classic rodeo events, plus special ones like the wild-cow milking contest. | 915/445–2406.

## PACKING IDEAS FOR HOT WEATHER

- ❏ Antifungal foot powder
- ❏ Bandanna
- ❏ Cooler
- ❏ Cotton clothing
- ❏ Day pack
- ❏ Film
- ❏ Hiking boots
- ❏ Insect repellent
- ❏ Rain jacket
- ❏ Sport sandals
- ❏ Sun hat
- ❏ Sunblock
- ❏ Synthetic ice
- ❏ Umbrella
- ❏ Water bottle

*Excerpted from *Fodor's: How to Pack: Experts Share Their Secrets*
© 1997, by Fodor's Travel Publications

**SEPT.: *Diez y Seis de Septiembre Festival*.** This annual fair held at Santa Rosa Catholic Church celebrates the Hispanic roots of the community with dancing, music, and food vendors. | 915/445–2406.

**OCT.: *Reeves County Fall Fair and Livestock Show*.** Carnival rides, crafts booths, and pie-eating contests are just part of the fun at Pecos's autumn festival. | 915/445–2406.

## Dining

**Old Mill BBQ and Burritos.** Barbecue. Old Mill is a very casual dining spot. The breakfast burrito and brisket and hot links combination plate are quite popular. Fish dishes are also served. | 1310 S. Eddy St. | 915/447–6106 | Breakfast also available. No supper Sat. Closed Sun. | $5–$8 | AE, D, MC, V.

**Sandra's Tejano Steakhouse.** Steak. Antique guns and other Western memorabilia give this steakhouse an authentic Old West feel. Try the Mexican-style rib-eye and T-bone. Kids' menu. | 500 S. Cedar St. | 915/445–7458 | Closed Sun. | $7–$15 | AE, D, DC, MC, V.

## Lodging

**Best Western Swiss Clock Inn.** This Swiss-theme Best Western is just off I–20, right next to Maxey Park. The attached Alpine Inn restaurant serves German and Southwest dishes. Restaurant, bar, in-room data ports, room service, cable TV, pool, business services, laundry services, some pets allowed. | 900 W. Palmer Rd. | 915/447–2215 | fax 915/447–4463 | www.bestwestern.com | 103 rooms | $56–$62 | AE, D, DC, MC, V.

**Motel 6.** This bargain motel is 2 mi south of town at the junction of I–20 and Rte. 285. Cable TV, pool, laundry facilities, some pets allowed. | 3002 S. Cedar St. | 915/445–9034 or 800/332–5255 | fax 915/445–2005 | www.motel6.com | 96 rooms | $29–$37.95 | AE, D, DC, MC, V.

**Quality Inn.** Basic accommodations are available here, 3 mi from the West of the Pecos Museum and the Buck Jackson Memorial Rodeo. Restaurant, bar, in-room data ports, room service, cable TV, pool, business services, pets allowed. | 4002 S. Cedar St. | 915/445–5404 | fax 915/445–2484 | www.qualityinn.com | 96 rooms | $45–$61 | AE, D, DC, MC, V.

**Town and Country Motel.** This one-story motel is just outside of Pecos, off Hwy. 20. Cable TV, refrigerators, pets allowed (fee). | 2128 W. Hwy. 80, Pecos | 915/445–4946 | 35 rooms | $30–$35 | AE, D, MC, V.

# PLAINVIEW

MAP 8, E1

*(Nearby towns also listed: Amarillo, Lubbock)*

Named for its views of the Panhandle Plains, Plainview is a center for thriving cotton, grain, and oil businesses. The city also has a fine downtown antiques district and the campus of Wayland Baptist University, plus there's good hunting nearby.

**Information: Plainview Chamber of Commerce** | 710 W. 5th St., Plainview, TX 79072 | 806/296–7431 | www.texasonline.net/chamber.

## Attractions

**Kidsville.** Parents and kids have a blast on the swings, slides and climbing apparatus of this state-of-the-art wooden playground facility, built in 1991. For younger children, there's a separate infant area. A paved walking track circles the playground for those who would rather watch than play. | 4th St. | 806/296–7431 | Free | Open daily until 10 PM.

**Llano Estacado Museum.** This museum and research center tracks the physical, cultural, and economic development of the region, from prehistoric times to the present. | 1900 W. 8th St., on the campus of Wayland Baptist University | 806/296–4735 | www.wbu.edu/glance/museum.htm | Free | Mar.–Nov., daily 9–5; Dec.–Apr., weekdays 9–5.

**FEB.:** *High Plains Gem and Mineral Show.* Gem dealers from around the country meet to showcase their wares and demonstrate techniques in polishing, silversmithing, and gold wirewrapping. | 806/296–9731.

**MAR.:** *Texas Plains 2-Cylinder Tractor Show.* Vintage tractors and farm machinery are on display. | 800/296–7431.

## Dining

**Cotton Patch Cafe.** American. Texas favorites keep customers coming back to this popular restaurant. First established in 1989 by two native Texans, the chain has expanded at the rate of two restaurants per year. To eat like a local, order the hand-breaded chicken-fried steak, the grilled catfish, or one of the daily specials. And try to save room for one of the sure-to-please homemade berry cobblers. | 3314 Olton Rd. (U.S. 70) | 806/293–5522 | $7–$13 | AE, D, DC, MC, V.

## Lodging

**Best Western–Conestoga.** There's a 24-hour restaurant on the premises and shopping nearby. Restaurant, bar, complimentary Continental breakfast, in-room data ports, some refrigerators, cable TV, pool, business services, some pets allowed. | 600 N. I–27 | 806/293–9454 | www.bestwestern.com | 82 rooms | $56–$100 | AE, D, DC, MC, V.

**Days Inn.** One block east of I–27, on U.S. 70, this one-story hotel is within walking distance of shopping and several restaurants, including the Cotton Patch Cafe. Complimentary Continental breakfast, cable TV, pool, laundry facilities, pets allowed (fee). | 3600 Olton Rd. (U.S. 70) | 806/293–2561 | fax 806/293–2561 | 48 rooms | $45–$65 | AE, D, DC, MC, V.

# PLANO

MAP 8, I2

*(Nearby towns also listed: Dallas, Grapevine, Lewisville, McKinney, Richardson)*

This city 20 mi north of downtown Dallas dates to 1845, when farmers from Tennessee and Kentucky settled here in search of flat land and rich soil. Several major fires in the late 1800s destroyed most of the original buildings in the business district; the area was later rebuilt and is now meticulously restored. A nice walking tour takes you through the quaint downtown, with its brick streets, and to 17 historic landmarks, including a number of restored Victorian homes. Always a thriving bedroom community for Dallas workers, Plano's population has more than doubled in the last decade. In fact, it is the fourth-fastest-growing city in the United States. The city is now a center for business in its own right, with a number of firms setting up shop here, including many high-tech start-ups.

Information: **Plano Convention and Visitors Bureau** | Box 860358, Plano, TX 75086-0358 | 214/422–0296 or 800/81–PLANO | www.planotx.org.

## Attractions

**Heritage Farmstead Museum.** Once the site of a working farm (1891), this museum offers a look at turn-of-the-20th-century rural life. | 1900 W. 15th St., at Custer Rd. | 972/881–0140 | www.heritagefarmstead.org | $3.50 | Aug.–May, Thurs.–Fri. 10–1, Sat.–Sun. 1–5; June–July., Tues.–Fri. 10-1, Sat.–Sun. 1–5.

**Southfork Ranch.** J. R. and Miss Ellie may be gone and *Dallas* may be nothing more than a syndicated rerun now, but the Ewing presence lives on at Southfork Ranch, 6 mi outside Plano, where the exterior scenes for the popular TV series were shot. The interior of the mansion is decorated in a style befitting a wealthy oil family and includes a museum with memorabilia from the show. You can see the gun that shot J. R. or catch of glimpse of Jock

Ewing's 1978 Lincoln Continental. There's also a rodeo arena, a conference center, and a restaurant on the grounds. | 3700 Hogge Rd. | 972/442–7800 | fax 972/442–5259 | www.south-forkranch.com | $7.95 | Daily 9–5.

### ON THE CALENDAR

**MAR.:** *Taste of Plano.* Sample delicacies from more than 40 of the area's best restaurants under one roof. Proceeds provide scholarships for local students. | 972/519–8014 | www.tasteofplano.com.

**SEPT.:** *Plano Balloon Festival.* More than 100 hot-air balloons fill the skies during this three-day event that attracts more than 300,000 people. Parachute jumps, fireworks, concerts, and a crafts market add to the party. | 972/867–7566 | www.planoballoonfest.org.

## Dining

**Joe's Crab Shack.** Seafood. This tasty crab chain has locations all over Texas. This one has memorabilia on the walls, newspaper lining the tables, and a nice porch out back. Try the Clutter Fest (a sampling of both Dungeness and Snow crab served barbecue style) or the broiled seafood platter with scallops, jumbo shrimp, shrimp scampi, and fish filet. | 3320 Central Expressway | 972/423–2800 | www.joescrabshack.com | $9–$24 | AE, D, DC, MC, V.

**Olive Garden.** Italian. A family-oriented chain restaurant, the Olive Garden is known for serving familiar Italian dishes at reasonable prices. Good choices include chicken scampi, shrimp primavera, or the creative pizzas. Kids' menu. | 700 N. Central Expressway | 972/578–8576 | No lunch | $8–$16 | AE, D, DC, MC, V.

**Outback Steakhouse.** Steak. Dependable service and good steaks are to be expected at this busy chain restaurant. Try the 14-oz Rockhampton Rib-Eye or the fresh catch of the day. Kids' menu. | 1509 N. Central Expressway | 972/516–4100 | No lunch | $13–24 | AE, D, DC, MC, V.

**Patrizio.** Italian. This unpretentious restaurant in the Preston Park Village serves up traditional fare to an attractive crowd. Lunching professionals enjoy the frozen champagne cocktails on a vine-covered patio. You'll find hand-tossed pizzas and inventive salads. The lasagna is made according to a family recipe. | 1900 Preston Rd., Suite 343 | 972/964–2200 | fax 972/985–7823 | $5–$10 | AE, D, DC, MC, V.

## Lodging

**Comfort Inn.** You'll find king-size beds and some connecting rooms in this hotel, which is less than a block east of U.S. 75. Complimentary Continental breakfast, cable TV, pool, laundry facilities, pets allowed (fee). | 621 Central Pkwy E | 972/424–5568 | fax 972/881–7265 | bobbiedill@yahoo.com | www.comfortinn.com/hotel/tx299 | 102 rooms | $52–$65 | AE, D, DC, MC, V.

**Courtyard by Marriott.** This hotel is a quarter mile north of the George Bush tollway and 2 mi east of the Dallas North tollway. The restaurant in the hotel is for breakfast only but you'll find more dining and shopping 1 mile north at Park and Preston Road. Outdoors, you'll find a gazebo. Restaurant, pool, hot tub, gym, laundry facilities, no pets. | 4901 W. Plano Pkwy. | 972/867–8000 | fax 972/596–4009 | www.courtyard.com | 149 rooms | $49–$114 | AE, D, DC, MC, V.

**Harvey Hotel.** A conveniently located full-service hotel. A mall and restaurants are within walking distance. Restaurant, bar, cable TV, pool, business services, pets allowed. | 1600 N. Central Expressway | 972/578–8555 | fax 972/578–9720 | 279 rooms | $110–$120 | AE, D, DC, MC, V.

**Holiday Inn.** This hotel is on the north side of town, near several restaurants and a mall. Restaurant, bar, cable TV, pool, business services, pets allowed. | 700 E. Central Pkwy. | 972/881–1881 | fax 972/422–2184 | www.holiday-inn.com | 160 rooms | $89–$109 | AE, D, DC, MC, V.

**La Quinta Inn and Suites.** In addition to its basic accommodations, La Quinta also offers special rooms for extended stays. Complimentary Continental breakfast, in-room data ports, some microwaves, some refrigerators, cable TV, pool, spa, video games, laundry facilities, business services, some pets allowed. | 4800 W. Plano Pkwy. | 972/599–0700 or 800/NU–ROOMS | www.laquinta.com | fax 972/599–1361 | 121 rooms, 8 suites | $59–$99 | AE, D, DC, MC, V.

**Motel 6.** A low-priced option right off I–75. Cable TV, pool, laundry facilities, pets allowed. | 2550 N. Central Expressway | 972/578–1626 | fax 972/423–6994 | www.motel6.com | 118 rooms | $41–$48 | AE, D, DC, MC, V.

**Red Roof Inn.** This is an economical choice located at the busy intersection of I–75 and Parker Rd. Cable TV, some pets allowed. | 301 Ruisseau Dr. | 972/881–8191 or 800/843–7663 | fax 972/881–0722 | www.redroof.com | 123 rooms | $40–$70 | AE, D, DC, MC, V.

**Sleep Inn.** This hotel is 5 mi south of a business hub, Legacy Park. Over 20 restaurants are within a 1-mi radius, and guests have free access to an off-site health club. Complimentary Continental breakfast, cable TV, pool, pets allowed (fee). | 4801 W. Plano Pkwy. | 972/867–1111 | fax 972/612–6753 | www.choicehotels.com/hotel/tx338 | 102 rooms | $65–$79 | AE, D, DC, MC, V.

**Super 8.** Drive right up to your door—this motel is right off the highway. Complimentary Continental breakfast, cable TV, business services, some pets allowed. | 1704 N. Central Expressway | 972/423–8300 or 800/800–8000 | www.super8.com | fax 972/881–7744 | 102 rooms | $52–$63 | AE, D, DC, MC, V.

# PORT ARANSAS

MAP 8, I7

*(Nearby towns also listed: Aransas Pass, Corpus Christi, Padre Island, Rockport)*

Port Aransas—or "Port A" to most Texans—is a resort town perched on the northern tip of Mustang Island, about 30 minutes from Corpus Christi. It is known for excellent fishing and bird watching. The town's population of just 2,800 swells to more than 150,000 each spring as college students fill the streets.

**Information: Port Aransas Convention and Visitors Bureau** | 421 W. Cotter St., Port Aransas, TX 78373 | 361/749–5919 or 800/452–6278 | www.portaransas.org.

## Attractions

**Mustang Island State Park.** This 3,500-acre park offers 5 mi of open beaches and such facilities as freshwater showers, picnic tables, and tent and RV camping. | Rte. 361, 14 mi south of Port Aransas | 361/749–5246 | www.tpwd.state.tx.us/park/mustang/mustang.htm | $3 | Daily.

**San Jose Island.** Pirate Jean Lafitte is said to have camped here. Large iron rings, thought to have been used to tie up his group's small boats, were discovered at the site. Even today, the island is accessible only by boat, and there are no public facilities. It is a quiet getaway for fishing, beachcombing, swimming, or shelling. Ferries leave throughout the day year-round from Woody's Sport Center. | 136 W. Cotter St. | 361/749–5252 | www.gulfcoastfishing.com/jetty.htm | $9.95 round-trip | Daily.

**University of Texas Marine Science Institute.** Students of oceanography, ecology, marine chemistry, and botany train at this branch of the University of Texas, located on 82 beachfront acres. Stop by the visitor center for a self-guided tour or to view exhibits and films on Texas Gulf life. | 750 Channel View Dr. | 361/749–5246 | www.utmsi.utexas.edu | Free | Weekdays 8–5.

ON THE CALENDAR

**MAY:** *Anglers on Wheels.* Anglers who use wheelchairs, and their friends and families, board the *Island Queen II*, a converted ferryboat, for this annual fishing trip in Redfish Bay. The boat is completely wheelchair accessible and bait and tackle are complimentary. Later, there is a free barbecue at Robert's Point Park Pavilion. Space is limited, and reservations are required. | 361/749–5252.

**JULY:** *Deep-Sea Roundup.* Anglers from across the state take part in bay and ocean competitions. | 361/749–5919 or 800/452–6278.

## Dining

**Crazy Cajun.** Cajun. Butcher paper covers the wooden tables inside this restaurant, and it's a good thing because if you order the specialty of the house, the Hungry Cajun, your waiter will dump a heap of Cajun-spiced shrimp, crawfish, crab, sausage, corn, and potato directly onto your table. On weekends, live Cajun-style music gets the joint jumping. | 303 Beach St. | 361/749–5069 | No lunch weekdays | $6–$13 | AE, D, MC, V.

**Pelican's Landing Restaurant.** Seafood. Serving island cuisine before a magnificent waterfront view of Lake Texoma, this bustling eatery specializes in locally caught fresh fish, freshcut steaks and crab-cakes. Dine inside the windowed, covered deck or on the breezy outdoor patio. A kids' menu and a seniors' menu are also available. | 337 Alister St. | 361/749–6405 | fax 361/749–6485 | $8–$18 | AE, D, DC, MC, V.

## Lodging

**Best Western Ocean Villa.** With the beach three blocks away, and a barbecue spot for guests to use, this hotel is a perfect base for fishing trips. Fishing locations around the hotel abound, but you're also within walking distance of restaurants and stores. Complimentary Continental breakfast, microwaves, refrigerators, cable TV, outdoor pool, video games and pool room, laundry facilities, no pets. | 400 East Ave. G | 361/749–3010 | fax 361/749–3150 | 48 rooms | $80–$159 | AE, D, DC, MC, V.

**Days Inn.** This basic chain property is 7 mi from Port Aransas. Complimentary Continental breakfast, in-room data ports, refrigerators, cable TV, pool, exercise equipment, business services, some pets allowed. | 410 Goodnight Ave, Aransas Pass | 361/758–7375 | fax 361/758–8175 | www.daysinn.com | 32 rooms, 18 suites | $65–$105 | AE, D, DC, MC, V.

**Plantation Suites.** This all-suites hotel, owned by fourth-generation Texans and styled after southern mansions, is 1 mile from the beach, provides a barbecue area and boat parking, and will even clean the fish you catch when you return from the beach. Complimentary Continental breakfast, microwaves, refrigerators, cable TV, pool, hot tub, laundry facilities, no pets, no smoking. | 1909 U.S. 361 | 361/749–3866 or 877/836–3866 | fax 361/749–7873 | www.plantationsuites.com | 50 rooms | $99–$139 | AE, D, DC, MC, V.

**Tarpon Inn.** The original Tarpon Inn was built in 1886 with surplus lumber from a Civil War barracks. The current location, built in 1904 after a fire destroyed the earlier version, sits two blocks from the lively fisherman's wharf and is filled with antiques. It is listed on the National Register of Historic Places. Restaurant, no room phones, no pets. | 200 E. Cotter St. | 361/749–5555 or 800/365–6784 | fax 361/749–4305 | www.texhillcntry.com/tarponinn | 24 rooms (12 with shower only) | $55–$125 | AE, MC, V.

# PORT ARTHUR

MAP 8, L5

*(Nearby towns also listed: Beaumont, Orange)*

Port Arthur sits at the southernmost point of Texas, some 20 mi off I–10, the highway that frames East Texas on the south. It is a bustling port city (population 62,000) through which millions of gallons of oil are transported annually, and a favorite of anglers and birders. Port Arthur is the hometown of the late Janis Joplin, former Dallas Cowboys coach Jimmy Johnson, and Joe Ligon, the mainstay of gospel's Mighty Clouds of Joy.

Information: **Port Arthur Convention and Visitors Bureau** | 3401 Cultural Center Dr., Port Arthur, TX 77642 | 409/985–7822 or 800/235–7822 | www.portarthurtexas.com/pavb.

## Attractions

**Museum of the Gulf Coast.** An old bank is home to displays on local history, from Native American times through the Civil War to the present. Don't miss the Southeast Texas Musical Heritage Room, which contains memorabilia of singer Janis Joplin, as well as other local music legends. | 701 4th St. | 409/982–7000 | fax 409/982–9614 | www.pa.lamar.edu/museum/gulf.html | $3.50 | Mon.–Sat. 9–5, Sun. 1–5.

**Nederland Windmill Museum.** This exact replica of a Dutch windmill was erected in Ritter Park in Nederland (5 mi north of Port Arthur) to honor the town's many Dutch immigrants. The 40-ft structure houses a museum dedicated to Tex Ritter, the late country music star, who hailed from the area. | 1500 Boston Ave., Nederland | 409/722–0279 | Free | Mar.–Labor Day, Tues.–Sun. 1–5; Labor Day–Feb., Thurs.–Sun. 1–5.

**Pleasure Island.** The Army Corps of Engineers constructed this 18-mi island in 1899. Now connected to Port Arthur by the Martin Luther King, Jr. Bridge and the Sabine Causeway, it's a great spot to try your hand at golfing, boating, fishing, horseback riding, crabbing, or other activities. | 520 Pleasure Pier Blvd. | 489/982–4675 | www.portarthur.com/island | Free | Daily.

**Pompeiian Villa.** Isaac Elwood, the "Barbed Wire King," built this copy of a Pompeii home as his winter residence in 1900. It's listed on the National Register of Historic Places. | 1953 Lakeshore Dr. | 409/983–5977 | $2 | Weekdays 10–2.

**Queen of Peace Shrine and Gardens.** Here in the Hoahbinh area of the city stands a 40-ft statue of the Virgin Mary, dedicated to the city of Port Arthur by the Vietnamese community. At Christmas, nearly one million lights illuminate the statue and Biblical scenes decorate the surrounding gardens. | 801 9th Ave. | 409/983–1037 or 409/982–1212 | Free | Daily.

**Sabine Lake.** Spanning 181,600 acres, this saltwater lake sits at the mouth of the Sabine River. | Rte. 82 | 800/235–7822 | Free | Daily.

**Sabine Pass Battleground State Historical Park.** In 1863, Confederate troops defeated the Union at this site 15 mi south of Port Arthur. It is now a day-use park, great for hiking, picnicking, camping, and fishing. | Rte. 87 | 409/971–2451 | www.tpwd.state.tx.us/park/sabine/sabine.htm | $2 | Daily dawn to dusk.

**Sea Rim State Park.** Camp, hike, or swim on this park's 5 mi of coastline, or visit its neighboring wetlands unit to view alligators, minks, nutria, raccoons, and occasionally even river otters, on a self-guided hike or canoe tour. | Rte. 87 | 409/971–2559 | fax 409/971–2917 | www.tpwd.state.tx.us/park/searim/searim.htm | $2 | Daily dawn to dusk.

**Texas Artist Museum.** Exhibits of artwork by contemporary local and regional artists are displayed here and change monthly. There are free programs and performances, such as piano or bluegrass concerts, on the second Sunday of every month. | 3501 Cultural Center Dr. | 409/983–4881 | Free | Tues.–Fri. 10–5, closed Sat.–Mon.

### ON THE CALENDAR

**JAN.: _Janis Joplin Birthday Bash._** This annual celebration of the life and music of Port Arthur's hometown rock 'n' roll legend is staged on the Saturday closest to Joplin's birthday (January 15th). Concerts and an induction into the Hall of Fame of the Museum of the Gulf Coast pay tribute to both Joplin and the varied music of the Gulf Coast area. | 409/722–3699 or 800/235–7822.

**FEB.: *Mardi Gras of Southeast Texas.*** The whole town celebrates with parades, costumes, carnival rides, and concerts. | 409/721–8717 | www.portarthur.com/mardigras.
**APR.: *Pleasure Island Music Festival.*** Logan Music Park comes alive with the sound of music at this party held each year on the last weekend of April. | 409/962–6200.
**SEPT.: *Mexican Fiesta.*** Mexican Independence Day is celebrated with music, dancing, crafts, contests, and more. | 409/722–0405.
**OCT.: *CavOILcade.*** An antique car show, parade, and flea market honor the oil industry. | 409/983–1009.

## Dining
**Esther's Cajun Seafood and Oyster Bar.** Seafood. In this rambling wooden house on the Neches River, seafood platters are piled high with fish, oysters, and stuffed crab. The flounder is also a favorite item on the menu, or try the fried crawfish tails in season. | 7237 Rainbow Ln | 409/962–6268 | No lunch Sat. | $7–$16 | AE, D, DC, MC, V.

## Lodging
**Comfort Inn.** Constructed in 1997, this sparkling Comfort Inn sits right on U.S. 69. Complimentary Continental breakfast, microwaves, refrigerators, some in-room hot tubs, cable TV, pool, outdoor hot tub, gym, pets allowed (fee). | 8040 Memorial Blvd. (U.S. 69) | 409/729–3434 | fax 409/729–3636 | 43 rooms | $65–$75 | AE, D, DC, MC, V.

**Holiday Inn Park Central.** There's a golf course next door, and rooms overlook the pool, courtyard, or dining patio. Restaurant, bar, in-room data ports, microwaves, room service, cable TV, pool, business services, airport shuttle, some pets allowed. | 2929 Jimmy Johnson Blvd. | 409/724–5000 | fax 409/724–7644 | www.holiday-inn.com | 164 rooms | $72–$84 | AE, D, DC, MC, V.

**Ramada Inn.** This basic motel is just 1 mi from the city center. Restaurant, bar, some refrigerators, room service, cable TV, pool, wading pool, tennis, business services, airport shuttle, some pets allowed. | 3801 Rte. 73 | 409/962–9858 | fax 409/962–3685 | www.ramada.com | 125 rooms | $59–$155 | AE, D, DC, MC, V.

# PORT ISABEL

MAP 8, I9

*(Nearby towns also listed: Harligen, South Padre Island)*

Port Isabel, the gateway to South Padre Island, is on the lower Laguna Madre. Gold seekers landed here in 1848 on their way to California. The casual community is now a center for shrimping and fishing, with a variety of deepwater cruises and many piers and jetties.

Information: **Port Isabel Chamber of Commerce** | 421 E. Queen Isabella Blvd., Port Isabel, TX 78578 | 956/943–2262 or 800/527–6102 | www.portisabel.org.

## Attractions
**Port Isabel Lighthouse State Historic Site.** Climb to the top of this 60-ft lighthouse (used from 1853 to 1905) for wonderful views of the coast. The adjacent cottage, which houses the visitors' center, is a replica of the lighthouse keeper's original abode. | 421 E. Queen Isabella Blvd. (Rte. 100) | 956/943–2262 or 800/527–6102 | www.tpwd.state.tx.us/park/portisab/portisab.htm | $2 | Daily.

## ON THE CALENDAR
**AUG.: *Texas International Fishing Tournament.*** The state's oldest fishing tournament attracts fishermen and women of all ages and abilities. | 956/943–8438.
**NOV.: *Annual World's Championship Shrimp Cook-Off.*** Dozens of amateur and professional chef teams compete for prizes on the first Sun. of Nov., while thousands of

spectators line up to taste the results. When you've had your fill, cross over to the annual Folk Arts Festival to check out the arts, crafts, and rides. | 956/943–2262 or 800/527–6102 | info@portisabel.org.

## Dining

**Marcello's.** Italian. Have a drink in the cigar bar or sit by the fountain as you wait to dine at this Mediterranean favorite that's right across the street from the Port Isabel Lighthouse. Favorites include veal, red snapper, homemade pastas, and gourmet pizzas. Kids' menu. | 110 N. Tarnava | 956/943–7611 | Reservations essential Fri., Sat. | No lunch Sat., Sun. | $12–$21 | AE, D, DC MC, V.

**Pirate's Landing.** Seafood. This waterfront restaurant serves fresh seafood to a crowd of all ages on Historical Lighthouse Square. Earlybirds indulge in an all-you-can-eat seafood buffet from 4 to 7 PM. A brand new addition to the restaurant with a full-size bar and outdoor deck opened in summer 2000. | 110 N. Garcia | 956/943–3663 | www.searanchtx.com/landing.html | Reservations not accepted | $8–$12 | AE, D, DC, MC, V.

**Yacht Club.** American. Dark wood and nautical artifacts don the walls at this fine restaurant, a former yacht club built in 1926. Seafood, steaks, and more than 150 wines dominate the menu. Kids' menu. | 700 Yturria St. | 956/943–1301 | Closed Wed. No lunch | $14–$19 | AE, D, MC, V.

## Lodging

**Yacht Club Hotel.** Built in 1926, this historic Mexican-style hotel was the second building in Port Isabel. It houses one of the finest restaurants in the area and a range of rooms, plus an over-sized executive suite. Restaurant, bar, cable TV, pool, no pets. | 700 N. Yturria St. | 956/943–1301 | fax 956/943–2330 | 24 rooms | $90–$140 | AE, MC, V.

# PORT LAVACA

MAP 8, I7

*(Nearby towns also listed: Goliad, Victoria)*

Spanish explorer Alonzo Alvarez de Peneda first stepped foot in Port Lavaca in 1519. The beach-filled town, which is now home to more than 12,000 year-round residents, sits on Lavaca Bay, near the center point of the Texas Gulf Coast. It is the gateway to beautiful Matagorda Island State Park, and a popular destination for fishing, birding, swimming, and boating.

**Information:** **Port Lavaca, Calhoun County Chamber of Commerce** | Box 528, Port Lavaca, TX 77979 | 361/552–2959 or 800/556–7678 | www.calhouncounty.org.

## Attractions

**Calhoun County Museum.** An 1864 jail house once housed this interesting collection of local artifacts. It's now in an annex of the county courthouse. | 301 S. Ann St. | 361/553–4689 | calhouncountymuseum.tripod.com/ | Free | Tue.–Fri. 8:30–4:30, Sat. 10–3.

**Indianola County Historic Park.** Once a bustling port city settled by German immigrants, Indianola was ravaged by massive hurricanes in 1875 and 1886, and is now a ghost town showing no evidence of its past prosperity. | Rte. 361 | 512/389–4800 or 800/792–1112 | $2 | Daily.

**Port Lavaca State Fishing Pier.** Though shortened by a fire in 1999, Lighthouse Beach's 2,000-ft, 24-hr lighted pier remains a popular spot for fishing enthusiasts. | Rte. 35 | 409/552–4402 | www.tpwd.state.tx.us | Free | Daily.

**MAY:** *Summerfest.* Live entertainment, games, and more fill Lighthouse Beach. | 361/552–2959 or 800/556–7678.
**OCT.:** *Calhoun County Fair.* Carnival rides, games, food, and local exhibits are just part of the fun. | 361/552–2959 or 800/556–7678.

## Dining
**Gordon's.** Seafood. For 35 years, this establishment has been serving tasty seafood and steaks to loyal customers. Come for dinner or a drink and soak in the dramatic view of the bay. | 2615 N. U.S. 35 | 361/552–1000 | $12–$15 | AE, D, DC, MC, V.

## Lodging
**Days Inn.** Amenities are plentiful at this choice 1 mi from Lighthouse Beach. Restaurant, bar, complimentary Continental breakfast, in-room data ports, some refrigerators, cable TV, pool, laundry facilities, business services, pets allowed. | 2100 N. Rte. 35 | 361/552–4511 | fax 361/552–4511 | www.daysinn.com | 99 rooms | $59–$63 | AE, D, DC, MC, V.

**Executive Inn.** This modern hotel, built in 1996, is 1 mile north of downtown Port Lavaca. Three rooms have hot tubs. Complimentary Continental breakfast, microwaves, refrigerators, some in-room hot tubs, cable TV, pool, laundry facilities, no pets. | 2007 N. U.S. 35N | 361/552–1050 | fax 361/552–6105 | 52 rooms | $55 | AE, D, DC, MC, V.

# QUANAH

*(Nearby towns also listed: Childress, Vernon)*

This north Texas community was, at its founding in 1881, named after Quanah Parker, the great Native American leader and son of Cynthia Ann Parker, probably the best-known woman in Texas during the latter half of the 19th century. She was captured by the Comanche from a pioneer fort and is said to have died of a broken heart at age 37 after the death of her daughter. Though Quanah never lived here, the town chose the name to connect itself to its Comanche past. Today, Quanah is an agricultural center with thriving cotton and gypsum businesses.

Information: **Quanah Chamber of Commerce** | Box 158, Quanah, TX 79252 | 940/663–2222.

## Attractions
**Copper Breaks State Park.** The Comanche Indians once roamed these grounds along the Pease River. Today, the park is alive with blue herons, mule deer, jack rabbits, and the rare horned toad. Joining them are hikers, bird-watchers, equestrians, and more. You'll find rest rooms, campsites, a fishing pier, and a visitor center. | Rte. 6, 13 mi south of Quanah | 940/839–4331 | fax 940/834–4332 | www.tpwd.state.tx.us/park/copper/copper.htm | $2 | Daily.

**Medicine Mounds.** Legends tell of the miraculous medicinal value of these four cone-shaped hills—a mixture of the mounds' earth and water is said to have cured a Comanche chief's gravely ill daughter. On private property about 10 miles east of Quanah on U.S. 287 East, the mounds rise 350 feet and are visible from the road. Turn right on Farm and Market Road for a better view. | U.S. 287 E | 940/663–2222 | Free | Daily.

**SEPT.:** *Fall Festival.* Arts and crafts, food, music, game booths, seminars, and classic car shows. | 940/663–2248.

## Dining

**Medicine Mound Depot.** Steak. In a famous depot building from 1910, this restaurant remains a favorite with locals and tourists alike. Order the chicken-fried steak and don't be alarmed when a model train emerges from the walls to circle the dining room. | 1802 U.S. 287E | 940/663–5619 or 800/484–9336 ext. 4654 | $5–$13 | AE, D, DC, MC, V.

## Lodging

**Casa Royale Inn.** This modern hotel sits 1 mi west of the center of Quanah. Spanish-style architecture and a warm brick lobby add distinction to comfort. Cable TV, pool, hot tub, playground, pets allowed. | 1500 W. 11th St. | 940/663–6341 | 40 | $47 | AE, D, DC, MC, V.

# RICHARDSON

MAP 8, I2

*(Nearby towns also listed: Dallas, Lewisville, Plano)*

The town began as a railroad stop after the Civil War (it was named for railroad contractor E. H. Richardson) and later became a thriving suburb of Dallas and home to more than 80,000 people. Today telephone lines are far more prevalent than railroad lines, with dozens of high-tech firms setting up shop here; the area dubs itself the "Telecom Corridor."

**Information: Richardson Convention and Visitors Bureau** | 411 Belle Grove, Richardson, TX 75080 | 972/234–4141 | www.cor.net.

## Attractions

**Owens Spring Creek Farm.** Mr. and Mrs. C. B. Owens started their sausage-making business here in 1928. On your free tour, you'll view turn-of-the-20th-century farm equipment, a vintage country kitchen, and a variety of farm animals, including Spanish goats and miniature horses. There's also a petting zoo. | 1401 E. Lookout Dr. | 972/235–0192 | www.owensinc.com | Free | Weekdays 9–4.

### ON THE CALENDAR

**MAY: *Cottonwood Art Festival.*** The works of more than 200 artists are on display at this annual event. | 972/669–0912.

## Dining

**Texas Land and Cattle Steakhouse.** Steak. The signature smoked sirloin of this Texas Ranch style restaurant satisfies appetites in 17 different locations. Its private dining rooms can accommodate very large parties with advance notice. | 812 S. Central Expressway | 972/705–9700 | fax 972/705–9339 | $9–$21 | AE, D, DC, MC, V.

## Lodging

**Hawthorn Suites.** Special corporate rates and a location just off I–75 accommodate the business traveler. Complimentary Continental breakfast, in-room data ports, microwaves, refrigerators, cable TV, pool, hot tub, exercise equipment, laundry service, business services, airport shuttle, pets allowed (fee). | 250 Municipal Dr. | 972/669–1000 | fax 972/437–4146 | www.hawthorn.com | 72 suites | $89–$102 suites | AE, D, DC, MC, V.

**Omni Hotel.** A high-rise luxury hotel in the heart of the Richardson Telecom Corridor, the Omni has a number of dining and entertainment options ranging from the casual Prime Bird Rotisserie and Grill to the elegant Pheasant Room, and Poulets, which has cocktails and dancing. 2 restaurants, bar, room service, cable TV, in-room movies, pool, hot tub, massage, sauna, gym, laundry service, business services, free parking. | 701 E. Campbell Rd. | 972/231–9600 | fax 972/907–2578 | www.omnirichardson.com | 342 rooms | $170–$208 | AE, D, DC, MC, V.

# ROCKPORT

*(Nearby towns also listed: Aransas Pass, Corpus Christi, Port Aransas)*

From late August through September, thousands of hummingbirds and other birds from as far away as Canada use Rockport and other nearby coastal communities as filling stations. They stop and refuel before the arduous, non-stop journey over the Gulf of Mexico on their way to warmer climates. Bird watchers should not miss it. Rockport is also a favorite spot for fishing, sailing, shopping, and boating.

Information: **Rockport-Fulton Area Chamber of Commerce** | 404 Broadway, Rockport, TX 78382 | 361/729–6445 or 800/242–0071 | www.rockport-fulton.org.

## Attractions

**Aransas National Wildlife Refuge.** The National Park Service set aside this 54,829-acre refuge as the prime wintering ground for the endangered whooping crane and 300 other bird species. A chartered boat can take you out to the birds' protected area, or you can hike or drive the paved, 15-mi loop to see some of the area's other critters, including bats, armadillos, bobcats, feral hogs, and alligators. Be sure to visit the observation tower and the Wildlife Interpretive Center. | 25 mi north of Rockport on Rte. 35, then east on Rte. 774 to Rte. 2040 | 361/286–3559 | fax 361/286–3722 | www.southwest.fws.gov/refuges/texas/aransas.html | $5 | Daily dawn to dusk.

**Connie Hagar Cottage Sanctuary.** More than 6 acres of bayside trails run through this historical sight, named after the woman who helped put Rockport on the birding map. The bay is ideal for sighting many shore bird species. Just follow signs along Broadway until you see bird watching platforms across the street from the bay. | Church and 1st. St. | 361/729–6445 or 800/242–0071 | Free | Daily.

**Copano Bay Causeway State Park.** This 5.9-acre facility has a lighted fishing pier, public boat ramp, picnic area, and bait shop. | Rte. 35, 5 mi north of Rockport | 361/729–8519 | www.tpwd.state.tx.us/park/copano/copano.htm | Free | Daily.

**Fulton Mansion State Historic Structure.** Col. George Fulton's regal 1874 home overlooks Aransas Bay. The French-Second-Empire mansion was built with surprisingly modern conveniences, including central forced-air heating, hot and cold running water, and a gas plant at the back of the house to fuel the chandeliers. | 317 Fulton Beach Rd., Fulton | 361/729–0386 | fax 361/729–6581 | www.tpwd.state.tx.us/park/fulton/fulton.htm | $4 | Daily, call for tour times.

**Goose Island State Park.** "Big Tree," considered one of the largest oak trees in the world, sits in this 314-acre park. It is said to be more than 1,000 years old, and is 35 ft in circumference and 44 ft in height. | Rte. 35 to Park Rd. 13, 12 mi north of Rockport | 361/729–2858 | fax 361/729–1041 | www.tpwd.state.tx.us | $2 | Daily 8 AM–10 PM.

**Rockport Center for the Arts** The center's galleries, classrooms, pottery studio and sculpture garden are used to exhibit local and theme-based artwork, and for art education classes. The landscaped grounds are a tranquil place to unwind. | 902 Navigation Circle | 361/729–5519 | rockart@2fords.net | Free | Tues.–Sun. 10–4, Sat. 1–4.

**Texas Maritime Museum.** Displays at this two-story complex in Rockport Harbor highlight shipbuilding, prominent seafaring Texans, shipwrecks through the ages, the development of the offshore oil industry, and much more. | 1202 Navigation Blvd. | 361/729–1271 | fax 361/729–9938 | $4 | Tues.–Sat. 10–4, Sun. 1–4.

### ON THE CALENDAR
**MAR.: *Oysterfest.*** Oyster-shucking competitions are a highlight of this community event, which also features live entertainment, crafts booths, and family activities. | 361/729–2388 or 800/826–6441.

**SEPT.:** *Fiesta en la Playa.* The festivities at Rockport's "Party on the Beach" include live Tejano bands, jalapeno-eating contests, mariachis, and more. | 361/729–6683.
**SEPT.:** *Hummer/Bird Celebration.* As bird lovers flock to see the amazing humming-bird migration each autumn, Rockport, and neighboring Fulton, celebrate with educa-tional programs, boat trips, and a nature fair. | 361/729–6445 or 800/242–0071.
**OCT.:** *Rockport Seafair.* A seaside town pays tribute to its heritage with boat races, fresh seafood, and parades. | 361/729–6445 or 800/242–0071.

## Dining
**Palopa.** Seafood. Watch the sun set over Key Allegro from this waterfront restaurant or listen to a local band at the outdoor bar on weekends. The chef will even grill whatever fish you've caught that day (if it's already cleaned and scaled) and serve it with two side dishes. | 39 Mazatlan | 361/729–2636 | fax 361/729–2022 | No lunch Sun. | $9–$25 | AE, D, DC, MC, V.

## Lodging
**Best Western Inn by the Bay.** This quiet property is just ½ mi from the the gulf and 1 mi from the Fulton Mansion. Restaurant, complimentary breakfast, some refrigerators, cable TV, pool, laundry facilities, business services, pets allowed. | 3902 N. Hwy. 35, Fulton | 361/729–8351 or 800/235–6076 | fax 361/729–0950 | www.bestwestern.com | 72 rooms | $54–$66 | AE, D, DC, MC, V.

**Holiday Inn Express.** This gleaming hotel, built in 1997, is just across U.S. 35 from the Rock-port Beach Park. Ask for one of the rooms with a water view. Complimentary Continental breakfast, cable TV, pool. | 901 U.S. 35N | 361/727–0283 | fax 361/727–0024 | 50 rooms | $77–$85 | AE, D, DC, MC, V.

# RUSK

MAP 8, J4

*(Nearby towns also listed: Jacksonville, Palestine)*

This East Texas city was named for Thomas Jefferson Rusk, one of the signers of the Texas Declaration of Independence. The community of 4,800 is a gateway to the east Texas piney woods, a stopping point on the scenic Texas State Railroad, and home to the longest footbridge in the world.

Information: **Rusk Chamber of Commerce** | 415 North Main St., Rusk, TX 75785 | 903/683–4242 | www.rusktx.com.

## Attractions
**Jim Hogg State Historical Park.** James Stephen Hogg was governor of Texas from 1891–1895. This park honors him with a replica of the cabin where he was born, and a museum and cemetery dedicated to his family. Explore the park's nature trails or enjoy a lunch in the picnic area. No camping. | Rte. 84 | 903/683–4850 | fax 903/683–4994 | www.tpwd.state.tx.us/park/jhogg/jhogg.htm | $1 | Sept.–May, Fri.–Sun. 8–5, June–Aug., Fri.–Sun. 8–8.

**Rusk Footbridge.** Possibly the nation's longest, this footbridge spans 546 feet and stands 4 feet wide. It was built in the 19th century to enable the citizens of Rusk and New Bir-mingham to cross One Eye Creek during the rainy season, when the valley was subject to extensive flooding. You'll find it 2 blocks east of the historic courthouse square. | At the end of 5th St. | 903/683–4242 or 800/933–2382 | Free | Daily.

**Rusk/Palestine State Park.** Board the popular Texas State Railroad (Palestine) at the depot inside this 100-acre park for a breathtaking ride through the dogwood-filled forest. There are also a lake, tennis courts, campsites, and a picnic area here. | Rte. 84, 3 mi west of Rusk | 903/683–5126 | www.tpwd.state.tx.us | $2 | Daily.

### ON THE CALENDAR
**OCT.: *Indian Summer Arts and Crafts Fair and Pioneer Festival.*** Since 1968, Rusk has celebrated Indian Summer with this annual festival of arts, crafts, and entertainment. Demonstrations and re-enactments illustrate the daily life of early settlers in the pioneer village at Footbridge Park. | 903/683–4242 or 800/933–2382.

## Dining
**Courthouse Cafeteria.** American. The homestyle cooking, always served up with a smile, is sure to please at this friendly, lunch-only restaurant in the center of town. Crispy chicken-fried steak and hearty meatloaf are always on the menu; there are seafood or Mexican specialties on different days during the week. | 520 North Henderson | 903/683–5510 | Closed weekends. No dinner | $3–$5 | No credit cards.

## Lodging
**Weston Inn and Suites.** This motel, opened in August 2000, is walking distance from downtown Rusk. Flexible suite configurations allow up to 12 people to sleep comfortably in a combination of rooms equipped with a full kitchen. In-room data ports, cable TV, pool, laundry facilities. | 1600 N. Dickinson (U.S. 69N) | 903/683–8383 | 43 rooms | $59 | AE, D, DC, MC, V.

# SALADO

MAP 8, I4

*(Nearby towns also listed: Georgetown, Killeen, Temple)*

Salado was once a stagecoach stop on the old Chisholm Trail, serving the line that stretched from San Antonio to Little Rock. The old stagecoach route is now Main Street, lined with antiques shops, galleries, inns, and specialty stores, many housed in historic structures listed on the National Register of Historic Places. Salado Creek, which runs through the community, provides a nice respite from a day of shopping with shady picnic areas and cool waters that fill with summertime swimmers.

Information: **Salado Business Association** | Box 1161, Salado, TX 76571 | 254/947–5040 | www.salado.com.

## Attractions
**Stillhouse Hollow Lake.** Locals retreat to the seven parks that surround Stillhouse Hollow Lake to camp, fish, boat, hike, hunt, and picnic. | Rte. 1670, 5 mi northwest of Salado | 817/939–2461 | Free | Daily.

### ON THE CALENDAR
**AUG.: *Salado Art Fair.*** Local artists displays their works on the banks of the Salado River. | 254/947–5040.
**NOV.: *Gathering of the Scottish Clans.*** Scottish descendents from all over the U.S. gather to celebrate their heritage. There's a Scottish story-telling event, a Highland dance contest, a parade of tartans and bands, genealogical seminars, and much more. | 254/947–5232 or 254/947–5040.

## Dining
**Range at the Barton House.** Continental. Applying classical French techniques, the chef prepares American food with French and Mediterranean influences in this elegant historic home. The signature dish is pan-seared salmon fillet served over warm mustard-seed potato salad. The Range is also known for its delectable crème brûlée. | 101 N. Main St. |

254/947–3828 | fax 254/947–3968 | Closed Mon.–Tues. No lunch Wed.–Fri. | $16–$24 | AE, D, DC, MC, V.

**Salado Mansion.** Mexican. Feast on the area's best Mexican food on the outdoor patio or amid antiques inside the grand, 1857 mansion. Fajitas, steaks, and pork specialties are always popular. No smoking. | 128 S. Main St. | 254/947–5157 | $5–$16 | AE, D, DC, MC, V.

**Stagecoach Inn Dining Room.** Continental. This rustic two-story clapboard building once housed stagecoach travelers passing through town. It is now home to the Stagecoach, a Salada dining institution for more than 40 years. While the owners have added an open-air atrium and new dining rooms that can accommodate up to 300 people in recent years, the traditional atmosphere remains: the veteran waitresses recite the menu—consisting of enormous steaks, fried chicken, and tasty desserts—by heart. Kids' menu. | 1 Main St. | 254/947–9400 | $16–$30 | AE, D, DC, MC, V.

## Lodging

**Inn at Salado and the Allen Hall.** Salado's first bed and breakfast, in the heart of the historical district, is styled in its original 1872 splendor. Each room is decorated with antiques and has a private bath with a claw-foot tub. Relax in a hammock on one of the inn's covered porches or explore the two acres of landscaped property. Complimentary breakfast, no TV, no pets, no smoking. | N. Main St. at Pace Park Dr. | 254/947–0027 or 800/724–0027 | fax 254/947–3144 | rooms@inn-at-salado.com | www.inn-at-salado.com | 9 rooms | $70–$160 | AE, D, DC, MC, V.

**Stagecoach Inn.** George Armstrong Custer, Robert E. Lee, and the outlaw Jesse James are just a few of the notable guests that have spent the night at this historic property right on Main Street. Established in the early 1860s as the Shady Villa Hotel, it became an important rest stop on the Chisholm Trail stagecoach line. Today guests stay in the modern motel-style addition and enjoy the landscaped grounds. The original building, where Sam Houston once delivered an anti-secession speech, is an elegant restaurant. Restaurant, coffee shop, room service, cable TV, pool, hot tub, tennis courts, shuffleboard, volleyball, playground, business services, no pets. | 1 Main St. | 254/947–5111 or 800/732–8994 | fax 254/947–0671 | www.touringtexas.com/stage | 82 rooms | $56–$63 | AE, D, DC, MC, V.

**Super 8.** This basic chain property is 2 mi from the center of town. Cable TV, pool. | 290 N. Robertson Rd. | 254/947–5000 or 800/800–8000 | fax 254/947–5000 | 42 rooms | $40–$65 | AE, D, DC, MC, V.

# SAN ANGELO

MAP 8, F4

*(Nearby towns also listed: Big Spring, Lockhart, Ozona, Sonora)*

San Angelo grew around Fort Concho, which was built in 1867 to protect settlers moving west following the end of the Civil War. Today, this city of 103,000 is the largest wool and mohair market in the country. It is home to Angelo State University.

Information: **San Angelo Convention and Visitors Bureau** | 500 Rio Concho Dr., San Angelo, TX 76903 | 915/653–1206 or 800/375–1206 | cvb@sanangelo-tx.com | www.sanangelo-tx.com.

## Attractions

**Angelo State University Planetarium.** This is the fourth largest university planetarium in the nation. It's in the Vincent Physical Science Building on Angelo State University's campus, which is home to approximately 6,300 students. Planetarium shows are open to the public on Thurs. and Sat. evenings when classes are in session. | 2601 W. Avenue End | 915/942–2136 or 915/942–2188 | $3 | Thurs. 8 PM, Sat. 2.

**Fort Concho National Historic Landmark.** This former military post is one of the best preserved forts in the state. You can tour the 23 buildings that once were part of the fort; several include exhibits about the history of the site. | 630 S. Oakes | 915/481–2646 | fax 915/657–4540 | www.fortconcho.com | $2 | Tues.–Sat. 10–5, Sun. 1–5.

**Miss Hattie's Bordello Museum.** After 50 years as a "gentleman's social center," this former bordello was shut down by the Texas Rangers in 1946. Now, after restoration, the 10 bedrooms look as they did in the property's heyday. If you eat at Miss Hattie's Cafe and Saloon you can get it for half price. | 18 E. Concho Ave. | 915/653–0570 | $5 | Saturdays or late afternoons, by appointment only.

**San Angelo State Park.** On the shores of O. C. Fisher Reservoir, this 7,577-acre park is popular for fishing, boating, hiking, camping, and bird watching. | 3900-2 Mercedes | 915/949–4757 | fax 915/947–2963 | www.tpwd.state.tx.us | $2 | Daily 8 AM–10 PM.

## ON THE CALENDAR
**MAR.:** *Stock Show and PRCA Rodeo.* Rodeo events include bullriding, roping, and barrel racing. | 915/653–7785.
**APR.:** *Texas Wine and Brew Festival.* Take a seminar or enjoy a tasting at this annual event. | 800/375–1206.

# Dining
**China Garden.** Chinese. There are five different rooms for dining and the most popular is the garden room. China Garden's more popular dishes include sushi and mooshu dishes (pork, beef, chicken, or shrimp). Kids' menu. | 4217 College Hill Blvd. | 915/949–2838 | $16–$30 | AE, D, DC, MC, V.

**John Zentner's Daughter.** Steak. Beef tenderloin and T-bone steaks are the draw. | 1901 Knickerbocker St. | 915/949–2821 | $17–$69 | AE, D, DC, MC, V.

**Mejor Que Nada.** Mexican. Brick walls and wooden tables make the dining room warm and snug in this well-liked, family restaurant. The combination platters are perfect if you can't make up your mind what to order, and if you're starved, go for the Super Mexican Plate (a stuffed pepper, two enchiladas, two chalupas, plus rice and beans) or Carla's Special Mexican Stir-Fry (with chicken, beef and shrimp). | 1911 S. Bryant | 915/655–3553 | fax 915/655–8340 | $3–$23 | AE, D, DC, MC, V.

**Taste of Italy.** Italian. This cozy family restaurant has a large selection of pasta dishes, from spaghetti to lasagna. Kids' menu. | 3520 Knickerbocker Rd. | 915/944–3290 | $17–$23 | AE, D, DC, MC, V.

# Lodging
**Best Western Inn of the West.** A local theater, which hosts a variety of plays, is 10 blocks from this two-story motel. Restaurant, room service, in-room data ports, cable TV, pool, business services, some pets allowed. | 415 W. Beauregard Ave. | 915/653–2995 | fax 915/659–4393 | www.bestwestern.com | 75 rooms | $45–$50 | AE, D, DC, MC, V.

**Dun Bar East.** An economical choice with a family-style restaurant on the premises, this hotel is 10 miles east of downtown San Angelo. The Quicksand Golf Course is across the street. Restaurant, room service, cable TV, pool, laundry facilities, no pets. | 1728 Pulliam | 915/653–3366 or 800/628–2691 | 100 rooms | $31 | AE, D, DC, MC, V.

**Holiday Inn–Convention Center.** The new San Angelo Museum of Fine Arts is only 2 blocks from this full-service hotel. Restaurant, bar, some microwaves, some refrigerators, cable TV, pool, hot tub, business services, some pets allowed. | 441 Rio Concho Dr. | 915/658–2828 | fax 915/658–8741 | www.holidayinn.com | 148 rooms | $79–$98 | AE, D, DC, MC, V.

**Inn of the Conchos.** This is the first hotel in San Antonio that you'll reach when traveling south on U.S. 87. The Crossroads Club in the lobby has entertainment on the weekends. Bar, room service, cable TV, pool, some pets allowed. | 2021 N. Bryant | 915/658–2811 | fax 915/653–7560 | www.inn-of-the-conchos.com | 125 rooms | $49–$54 | AE, D, DC, MC, V.

**La Quinta.** A seven-screen multiplex is adjacent to this two-story motel. Complimentary Continental breakfast, in-room data ports, cable TV, pool, business services, some pets allowed. | 2307 Loop 306 | 915/949–0515 | fax 915/944–1187 | www.laquinta.com | 170 rooms | $49–$89 | AE, D, DC, MC, V.

**Motel 6.** There are fast food restaurants within a block, Concho Lake is 10 mi away. | 106 rooms. Cable TV, pool, some pets allowed. | 311 N. Bryant Ave. | 915/658–8061 | fax 915/653–3102 | $28–$32 | AE, D, DC, MC, V.

**Super 8.** The unusual Spanish-style architecture of this hotel distinguishes it from other Super 8s. Food and entertainment are just outside: La Scala restaurant is in the hotel parking lot and Santa Fe Junction, a country-western nightclub, is across the street. Complimentary Continental breakfast, cable TV, pool, hot tub, pets allowed (fee). | 1601 S. Bryant Blvd. | 915/653–1323 | fax 915/658–5769 | 81 rooms | $47 | AE, D, DC, MC, V.

# SAN ANTONIO

MAP 8, H6

*(Nearby towns also listed: Boerne, Castroville, Comfort, Gruene, Laredo, New Braunfels)*

Wake up in the Alamo City with the scent of huevos rancheros in the air, the sound of mariachis, and the sight of barges winding down the San Antonio River, and you know you're someplace special.

In fact, San Antonio is the number one tourist destination in the state. The heart of the visitor area is the Paseo del Rio or the River Walk, a magical place located 20 feet below street level. Nestled behind tall buildings, away from street noise, the River Walk is the top attraction in town, with luxury hotels and plenty of specialty shops and European-style al fresco cafés.

The River Walk is just steps from Texas's most recognized landmark: the Alamo, a symbol of Texas liberty. If you'd like to learn more about the city's history, tour the San Antonio Missions National Historic Park, which winds south from downtown to several scenic missions.

San Antonio also offers the excitement of a south-of-the-border getaway: Mexican crafts, jewelry, and plenty of Tex-Mex food can be found throughout the city.

**Information: San Antonio Visitors Information Center** | 317 Alamo Plaza, San Antonio, TX 78298 | 210/207–6748 | www.sanantoniocvb.com.

## Attractions

**The Alamo.** First called "San Antonio de Valero," this former mission became a symbol for Texas independence as the site of the fateful battle. The Texan forces took cover in the mission for 12 days in 1836 against the Mexican troops led by General Santa Anna. On the 13th day of the battle, the Texans lost but the defeat inspired the later victory of the Texans in their bid for independence with the cry "Remember the Alamo." Today, it's often referred to as the "cradle of Texas liberty" and maintains a quiet atmosphere. Visitors can tour the shrine and a museum. | 300 Alamo Plaza | 210/225–1391 | fax 210/229–1343 | Free | Daily.

**Alamodome.** This 65,000-seat, $186 million dome is a busy place. Home of the San Antonio Spurs NBA basketball team, the site also hosts concerts, trade shows and conventions, as well as other sporting events. Visitors can take a tour for a behind-the-scenes look; the

Alamodome is the only place in North America with two permanent Olympic-sized ice rinks under the same roof. | Just east of HemisFair Park, across I–37 | 210/207–3652 or NBA ticket information 210/554–7700 | Prices vary with events | Mon.–Fri. 8–5.

**Arneson River Theatre.** Erected in 1939, this unique theater was designed by River Walk architect Robert Hugman and built by the WPA. Have a seat on the grass-covered steps and enjoy a look at a San Antonio institution. In this open-air format, the river, not a curtain, separates performers from the audience. Some of San Antonio's top events take place here, including Fiesta Noche del Rio, a summer show that has been in operation nearly 4 decades. | 418 La Villita | 210/207–8610 | Prices vary with shows | Mon.–Sun. 10–6.

**Brackenridge Park.** A fine place for a picnic or a stroll, but it also offers many other attractions. Families should budget at least half a day, for example, to visit the zoo. Garden lovers, too, will find a wealth of sites to explore. And the San Antonio Botanical Gardens and the Halsell Conservatory are nearby. Besides the sights listed below, other park activities include a carousel, a railroad, and a skyride. | 3910 N. Saint Mary's St. | 210/736–9534.

**Buckhorn Saloon and Museums.** In 1881 the Buckhorn Saloon opened as a Texan watering hole. Soon hunters and trappers were stopping by, and, eager for a cold brew, they traded furs and horns. Owner Albert Friedrich collected the horns, some which his father made into horn chairs. Today you can see trophies on guided tours through the Buckhorn Hall of Fins (marine trophies and fishing lures), the Buckhorn Hall of Feathers (mounted birds), and Buckhorn Hall of Horns. The Hall of Texas History Wax Museum features a recreation of the Battle of the Alamo and other important Texas events. | 318 E. Houston | 210/247–4000 | $8 | Daily 10–6.

© Corbis

## HAUNTED SAN ANTONIO

Behind a home built in the 1700s, a night watchman hears the sound of a woman's cries coming from the depths of a sealed well. A museum's former curator still roams his former place of employment. And in an art center, a photographer feels a hand on his shoulder and turns to see a dark shadow in the room with him.

These are just a few examples of the spirited encounters which have occurred in San Antonio and the nearby area. According to Docia Williams, an author and tour guide who leads groups on night excursions of the city's "occupied" buildings, San Antonio is a "very haunted city." Williams has interviewed policemen, night watchmen, and residents of private homes throughout the city and searched the library's archives. She has gathered documented material for her "Spirits of San Antonio" bus tour and for a ghostly tome, *Spirits of San Antonio and South Texas* (Wordware Press).

One of San Antonio's oldest buildings, the Alamo, is also reported to be one of the most haunted. Today's night watchmen have heard unexplained sounds in the old mission, but the hauntings date back to the days of the historic battle. Following the battle, Mexican soldiers were said to have run from the Alamo shouting "diablos" (devils). (It's debatable whether the reference was to their opponents, or to some other presence in the mission.)

Another story relates to the order that was issued to burn the Alamo following the Battle of San Jacinto. Soldiers entered the old building but soon fled, refusing to carry out their mission. When their leader came to speak to them, upon entering the building he was met by six ghosts holding swords of fire. The ghosts were rumored to be those of the Spanish priests who built the Alamo.

Utilizing a former rock quarry, the **Japanese Tea Gardens** are a quiet, serene oasis of lush flowers, climbing vines, and tall palms. The ponds, with beautiful rock bridges and walkways, are home to hundreds of koi. | Free | Daily 8–dusk.

**Fort Sam Houston Museum and National Historic Landmark.** This National Historic Landmark, an army base dating back to 1870, has nine times as many historic buildings as Colonial Williamsburg. These include the residence where Gen. John J. Pershing lived in 1917; the Chinese Camp, which was once occupied by Chinese who fled Mexico to escape Pancho Villa; and the home where Lt. and Mrs. Dwight Eisenhower lived in 1916. Visitors can stroll past the structures (most are not open to the public). The Fort Sam Houston Museum is filled with exhibits on the site's early days. | 1210 Stanly Rd., Fort Sam Houston | 210/221–1886 | fax 210/221–1311 | Free | Wed.–Sun. 10–4.

**Guadalupe Cultural Arts Center.** Founded in 1980 to preserve and develop Latino arts and culture, the GCAC stages regular dance, music, and theatrical performances. It also displays the art of emerging artists, and schedules various classes. Of the center's major annual events, the Tejano Conjunto Music Festival, with over 42 hours of live performances, is in May; the San Antonio Inter-American Bookfair and Literary Festival is in February; and the Cinefestival, five days of Latino film, is in January. | 1300 Guadalupe St. | 210/271–3151 | Free | Mon.–Fri. 10–4, Sat. 11–3 | www.guadalupeculturalarts.org.

**HemisFair Park.** This is the home of the 1968 World's Fair, HemisFair. Today most of the activity here surrounds the Tower of the Americas, the nearby water gardens, and the museums. Other buildings remain, but many are closed.

    **The Tower of the Americas.** The symbol of the 1968 World HemisFair remains a landmark for downtown San Antonio. The Tower soars 750 ft from the base to the top of the antennae, but visitors view the city from the observation deck at 579 ft. Close to three decades after its construction, this is still one of the tallest free-standing structures in the Western hemisphere, 87 ft taller than the Seattle Space Needle and 67 ft higher than the Washington Monument. | 600 Hemisfair Park | 210/207–8615 | $3 | daily 8 AM–11 PM.

    **Instituto Cultural Mexicano** is a HemisFair park attraction that features the works of contemporary Mexican artists.

**Hertzberg Circus Collection and Museum.** One of the largest circusiana collections in the world, this unusual museum contains more than 20,000 items of big top memorabilia, including antique circus posters, Tom Thumb's miniature carriage, and a scale model of a three-ring circus. | 210 W. Market St. | 210/207–7810 | $3 | Mon.–Sat. 10–5, Sun. noon–5.

**Institute of Texan Cultures.** Operated by the University of Texas, this museum explores the 30-plus ethnic cultures that settled Texas. Don't miss the dome slide show four times daily for a look at the many faces of the Lone Star State. Children especially love this place. Most days costumed docents mill about the museum, ready to educate visitors on the role of a chuck wagon cook on a cattle drive or the rigors of frontier life for women. | HemisFair Park | 210/558–2300 | www.texancultures.utsa.edu or www.utsa.edu/itc | $4 | Tues.–Sun. 9–5.

**José Antonio Navarro State Historical Site.** Former residence of a signer of the Texas Declaration of Independence. The adobe and limestone structure includes an office used by Navarro, who was a lawyer and legislator. | 228 S. Laredo St. | 210/226–4801 | www.tpwd.state.tx.us | $2 | Wed.–Sun. 10–4.

**Kiddie Park.** Established in 1925, this is America's original Kiddie Park. The Herschell-Spillman Carousel's 36 jumping horses have been revolving since 1928. A ferris wheel, a small rollercoaster and many other rides will keep your kids busy for hours. You can get popcorn, pizza and more at the snackbar. | 3015 Broadway | 210/824–4351 | 75¢ per ride or $5.95 for a day of unlimited rides | Mon.–Sat. 10–9, Sun. 11–9.

**La Villita.** This is the "little village" that was the original settlement in Old San Antonio. Here you'll find the workshops and boutiques of many of the city's artisans and jewelers and a few good restaurants. The historic structures have been well preserved; look for the outdoor theater, with shows and music, where La Villita meets the River Walk. | South Alamo St., at River Walk | 210/207–8610 | Free | Daily.

**Market Square.** This two-block area includes Farmer's Market, a former produce market now ripe with crafts, open-air boutiques, and El Mercado, the largest Mexican market in the United States. The history of Market Square dates back to the early 1800s. This was the birthplace of chili con carne, the spicy meat and bean mixture that today is generally considered the state dish of Texas. Once young girls known as "chili queens" sold the concoction from small stands in the market. | Bordered by San Saba, Santa Rosa, West Commerce and Dolorosa Sts. | 210/207–8600 | Free | Daily.

**McNay Art Museum.** This was the home of Marion Koogler McNay, an artist and heiress to an oil fortune. Built in the 1920s, the 24-room house was converted to a museum in the 1950s. Today the world's finest artists, from Gauguin to Picasso to Manet, grace the walls of this museum's numerous galleries. | 6000 N. New Braunfels | 210/824–5368 | fax 210/805–1760 | www.mcnayart.org | Free | Tues.–Sat. 10–5, Sun. noon–5.

**Majestic Theater.** The San Antonio Symphony performs at the Majestic Theater, a national historic landmark. | 228 E. Houston St. | 210/554–1010 | Prices vary with shows | Mon.–Fri. 9–5, Sat. 10–7.

**Menger Hotel.** This historic hotel was built in 1859 and has remained a popular stop ever since. Some of its most famous guests include Civil War generals Robert E. Lee and William Sherman, Mount Rushmore sculptor Gutzon Borglum (who had a studio at the hotel), playwright Oscar Wilde, and author William Sydney Porter (O. Henry), who mentioned the hotel in several of his short stories. Today the Menger has been restored to its Victorian splendor. | 204 Alamo Plaza | 210/223–4361 | Free | Daily.

**Pioneer Memorial Hall Museum** traces the role of the Texas Rangers on the frontier, with exhibits covering everything from badges to saddlebags. Western art is displayed here as well. | 3805 Broadway | 210/822–9011 | $2 | Mon.–Sat. 11–4, Sun. noon–4.

**Plaza Theater of Wax/Ripley's Believe It or Not!** The Plaza Theater of Wax museum depicts the famous, from Jesus to John Wayne. Many figures are displayed in elaborate sets featuring movie scenes. Alamo visitors will appreciate the "Heroes of the Lone Star" exhibits on the fateful battle. Ripley's displays an assortment of more than 500 oddities ranging from miniatures to freaks of nature. | 301 Alamo Plaza | 210/224–9299 | $15 for both attractions | Daily.

**Retama Park.** Thoroughbred and quarter horse racetrack with simulcast racing year-round. There are live races May through October. | 1 Retama Parkway, Selma | 210/651–7100 | $3 | Daily.

★ **River Walk.** is the heart of the tourist area. Nestled behind tall buildings, away from traffic and street noise, the River Walk is the most popular spot in town, lined with specialty shops and European-style al fresco cafes. Visitors stroll the walkways that follow the winding river. | 315 E. Commerce | No phone | Free | Daily.

**San Antonio Botanical Gardens.** Roses, herbs, a garden for the blind, flowering species, and native plants are found within the setting of these 38-acre gardens. The centerpiece here is the Halsell Conservatory, a futuristic-looking, 90,000-square-ft structure composed of seven tall glass spires. A self-guided tour of the conservatory takes visitors through the plants and flowers found in different environments around the world, from desert to tropics. The conservatory sits partially underground for a cooling effect in the hot Texas summers. | 555 Funston Pl | 210/207–3250 | $4 | Mon.–Fri. daily.

**San Antonio Missions National Historical Park.** This national park stretches for 9 mi along the San Antonio River and comprises four remaining missions (outside of the Alamo) constructed by the Franciscan friars in the 18th century. The missions are active parish churches today, and all are open to the public. Each of the four illustrates a different concept of mission life. | Park Headquarters: 2202 Roosevelt Ave. | 210/534–8833 | www.nps.gov/saan/ | Free | Daily.

**Mission Concepcion** is especially notable for its wall paintings. Geometric and religious symbols in ochre, blue, and brown decorate the ceilings and walls of several rooms. The most striking is the "Eye of the God," a face from which rays of light emanate. Displays at each of the four missions illustrate different aspects of mission life. At Concepcion, the theme is "The Mission as a Religious Center." Concepcion is the oldest unrestored Catholic church in the nation. | 807 Mission Rd. | 210/534–0749 | Free | Daily.

In its heyday, the **Mission San Jose** boasted 300 residents, a granary that held 5,000 bushels of corn, and elaborate ornamentation. Its full name is San Jose y Miguel de Aguayo, named for the Governor of Texas at that time. The theme of San Jose is "The Mission as a Social Center and a Center for Defense." Displays show that Indian residents were taught the use of guns and lances to help defend against raiding Apache and Comanche Indians. | 6539 San Jose Dr. | 210/932–1001 | Free | daily.

**Mission San Juan,** fully named San Juan Capistrano, once supplied all its own needs from cloth to crops. The park includes the San Juan Woodlands Trail. After about a third of a mile, the trail winds along the low river bottom land and provides a look at many of the indigenous plants formerly used by the mission. San Juan also has a small museum featuring items found at the site and artifacts typically used by missionaries in Texas. The theme of San Juan is "The Mission as an Economic Center," and displays show how this self-sufficient mission provided food and goods. The chapel is an active parish church. | 9101 Graf Rd. | 210/532–3914 | Free | Daily.

**Mission Espada** was named for St. Francis of Assisi, founder of the monastic order of Franciscans. The mission's full name is Mission San Francisco de la Espada. This mission's theme is "The Mission as a Vocational Education Center." This theme is reflected by displays on the education of the Indians in blacksmithing, woodworking, and other vocations. | 10040 Espada Rd. | 210/627–2021 | Free | Daily.

**San Antonio Museum of Art.** Housed in the former Lone Star Brewery, this museum is noted for its permanent display of artwork ranging from Greek antiquities and pre-Columbian sculpture to 18th-, 19th-, and 20th-century paintings by artists including John Singleton Copley and Benjamin West. The recent Rockefeller addition presented the museum with a world-class collection of Latin American art. | 200 W. Jones Ave. | 210/978–8100 | $4 | Mon, Wed–Sat. 10–5, Tues. 10–9, Sun. noon–5.

**Six Flags Fiesta Texas.** This amusement park features sections that highlight Texas's rich diversity, from Mexican and German sections to a part that celebrates the Lone Star State's rip-roarin' Western past. There are thrill rides and many musical shows. | 17000 I-10W, at jct. of Loop 410 | 210/697–5050 | $33 | Sept.–Oct., Sat. 10–10, Sun. 10 AM–8 PM; Mar.–May, 10–8; June–Oct. 10–9.

**San Fernando Cathedral.** A Spanish church was built at this site in 1738 by the city's Canary Island colonists. Later Mexican general Santa Anna raised a flag of "no quarter" here before he stormed the Alamo in 1836, signifying to the Texans that he would take no prisoners. In 1873, following a fire after the Civil War, the chapel was replaced with the present-day construction. Although a tomb holds the remains of some unknown soldiers, modern historians do not believe these were the bodies of the Alamo defenders because evidence of military uniforms, never worn by the Texans, has turned up among the remains. | 115 Main Plaza | 210/227–1297 | Free | Daily 6 AM–7 PM.

**Sea World of San Antonio.** Sprawled across 250 acres northwest of the city, this Texas-sized park offers everything from marine shows to trick water-skiing performances, all amid acres of manicured gardens. | 10500 Sea World Dr. | 210/523–3611 | www.seaworld.org | $32 | June–July, daily 10–10; Aug.–Oct., weekends; Nov.–Mar. closed; Apr.–May, weekends 10–8 (various days).

SAN ANTONIO

INTRO
ATTRACTIONS
DINING
LODGING

**Southwest Craft Center.** The Center is housed in the former Ursuline Academy, which in 1851 became the first girls' school in the city. The long halls of the once busy dormitory are now filled with photography, jewelry, fibers, paper making, painting, and the like. The Ursuline Gift Shop sells hand-crafted items, including silver Southwestern jewelry, hand-painted plates, and wooden Christmas ornaments. Grab a sandwich or salad at the Craft Center's Copper Kitchen, or some sweets at the Garden Room. | 300 Augusta | 210/224–1848 | Free | Mon.–Sat. 10–5.

**Spanish Governor's Palace.** The only remaining example in Texas of an early aristocratic Spanish home. | 105 Military Plaza | 210/224–0601 | $1 | Mon.–Sat. 9–5, Sun. 10–5.

**Splashtown.** This 18-acre park has dozens of slides, a kids' activity pool, a giant wave pool, and six sand volleyball courts. | I–35 at Exit 160 | 210/227–1100 | fax 210/225–7946 | $18 | May and Sept., weekends 11–6; June–Aug., daily 11–9.

**Steves Homestead.** This King William Historic District (a district that was once home to wealthy German merchants who set up businesses throughout town and built homes in the district near the San Antonio River) home was positioned right on the banks of the river. Besides a natatorium and a carriage house, the home also boasted has the finest furnishings and detail work of its era. Today the 25-block neighborhood still holds some of San Antonio's finest homes. Tours are available. | 509 King William St. | 210/225–5924 | fax 210/224–6168 | $3 | Daily 10–4:15.

**Sunset Station.** Four live-music stages, five dance floors, and three restaurants entertain in a turn-of-the-20th-century Southern Pacific train depot at the heart of downtown San Antonio. There's something for everyone here: the nightly music choices range from country western to merengue and the food runs the gamut from Aldaco's Mexican Cuisine to Ruth's Chris Steak House. The depot is open during the day but the bands take the stage after dark. Call ahead to see whether any nationally known acts are scheduled. | 1174 E. Commerce | 210/222–9481 | www.sunset-station.com | $0–$10 | 11 AM–2 AM.

**Vietnam Veterans Memorial.** Created by artist Austin Deuel, this sculpture in front of Municipal Auditorium represents a Marine holding a wounded soldier looking skyward as he awaits evacuation. | E. Martin and Jefferson Sts. | Free | Daily.

**The Witte Museum** is a favorite with children for its interactive exhibits, and covers all things Texan, from the area's dinosaur inhabitants to the white-tailed deer that roam the region today. | 3801 Broadway | 210/357–1900 | www.wittemuseum.org | $6 | Mon., Wed.–Sat. 10–5, Tues. 10–9, Sun. noon–5.

**The Zoological Gardens and Aquarium** is best known for its excellent collection of African antelopes, as well as other hoofed species. The Children's Zoo, a $3 million addition, features rides, a nursery, a playground, and an education center. The highlight of the Children's Zoo is the "Round-the-World Voyage of Discovery" exhibit. | 3903 N. St. Mary's St. | 210/734–7183 | fax 210/734–7291 | www.sazoo-aq.org | $6 | Late May–early Sept., daily 8–6:30; Sept.–May, daily 9–5.

## SIGHTSEEING TOURS

**Gray Line bus tours.** Guided, narrated tours of San Antonio's top visitor attractions. | 217 Alamo Plaza | 210/226–1706 | Prices vary with tours | Mon.–Fri. 7:30–5, Sat.–Sun. 7:30–4.

**VIA San Antonio Streetcar.** These motorized, open-air trolleys make stops at all the major hotels and attractions such as Market Square, the Alamo, the Southwest Craft Center, and the Spanish Governor's Palace. Trolleys follow four different routes that encompass just about all the downtown region. | 210/362–2020 | $1 | Daily.

## ON THE CALENDAR

**FEB.: *Livestock Exposition and Rodeo.*** This event at the Freeman Coliseum features country, Tejano, and rock music, along with a rodeo and livestock show. | 210/225–5851.
**MAR.: *Irish Festival.*** The San Antonio River is dyed green during this festival, which also offers live music, food, arts and crafts, and dances. | 210/344–4317.

**MAR.:** *Remembering the Alamo Weekend.* Educational exhibits about those involved with either side of the Battle of the Alamo are on display at 300 Alamo Plaza. | 210/978–8100.

**APR.:** *Fiesta San Antonio.* The largest of the city's festivals, this one features carnivals, live music, parades, food booths, and concerts. | 210/227–5191 or 800/447–3372.

**JUNE:** *Fiesta de Oaxaca.* Displays Oaxacan culture through dances, crafts, food, and music. | 210/822–2453.

**JUNE:** *Texas Folklife Festival.* More than 40 cultures exhibit their contributions to the development of Texas through music, food, dance, and folktales at the Institute of Texan Cultures in HemisFair Park. | 210/458–2300.

**NOV.–DEC.:** *Fiestas Navidenas.* Mariachi bands, visit by Pancho Claus in Market Square. | 210/207–8600.

**DEC.:** *Las Posadas.* Re-enactment of Mary and Joseph's search for an inn begins at the River Walk and ends at the Arneson River Theatre; followed by a party at Maverick Plaza. | 210/224–6163.

## Dining

**Aldaco's.** Mexican. The work of local artists is displayed on the walls throughout this pleasant restaurant. Try chili rellenos or brocheta al carbon. You can dine on the covered patio. Entertainment weekends. Kids' menu. | 1141 E. Commerce St. | 210/222–0561 | Breakfast also available. Closed Sun. | $16–$25 | AE, D, MC, V.

**Aldino Cucina Italiana.** Italian. Eclectic Californian and Italian decor with marble floors and counters and a secluded candlelit area for romantic dining. Family friendly with a view of the kitchen. Try the various pastas, pizza, salad, fresh fish or chicken. Kids' menu. | 622 N.W. Loop 410 | 210/340–0000 | $13–$24 | AE, D, MC, V.

**Aldo's Ristorante.** Italian. This restaurant is in a century-old house filled with antiques and a romantic candlelit atmosphere. Try the pasta, seafood, veal, chicken, or filet mignon. There is a beautiful lounge with a piano player on the weekends. A patio seats about 11 for a more intimate meal with a view of trees and flowers. | 8539 Fredericksburg Rd. | 210/696–2536 | No lunch Sat.–Sun. | $13–$26 | AE, D, DC, MC, V.

**Anaqua Grill.** Seafood. In the San Antonio Marriott, this oft lauded restaurant features many local dishes such as fresh fish, salmon and shrimp. The patio overlooks the courtyard with a great view of roaming exotic birds. Kids' menu. Sun. brunch. | 55 S. Alamo St. | 210/229–1000 | Jacket required | Breakfast also available Mon.–Sat. | $18–$36 | AE, D, DC, MC, V.

**Antlers Lodge.** Southwestern. You'll find upscale dining with a rustic flair at this restaurant in the Hyatt Hill Country Resort. Its centerpiece is a huge chandelier with over 500 naturally shed pairs of antlers. Known for rattlesnake fritters, buffalo shrimp and 14-oz. New York strip steak. Try the chili-dusted Ahi tuna steak. | 9800 Hyatt Resort Dr. | 210/520–4001 | Closed Mon. No lunch | $18–$30 | AE, D, DC, MC, V.

**The Bayous.** Cajun/Creole. This pleasant restaurant has water views. Enjoy semi-casual dining inside with walls decorated with prints from the New Orleans Bayou. Known for the crawfish, shrimp gumbo, rib-eye steak and oysters. Try the red snapper Valerie. You can also eat on the patio on the River Walk for a pleasant scenic view. Entertainment. Kids' menu. Sun. brunch. | 517 N. Presa St. | 210/223–6403 | $18–$23 | AE, D, DC, MC, V.

**Biga.** Eclectic. Dine in style at this converted old mansion. Known for Gulf seafood, breads, and wild game. | 203 S. St. Mary's St. | 210/225–0722 | Closed Sun. No lunch | $15–$25 | AE, D, DC, MC, V.

**Bistro Time.** Continental. This is a small, intimate fine dining restaurant that caters to an adult clientele. Known especially for crab cakes and bacon-wrapped filet mignon. Earlybird supper Mon.–Thurs. | 5137 Fredericksburg Rd. | 210/344–6626 | $20–$30 | AE, DC, MC, V.

**Boudro's, a Texas Bistro.** Southwestern. This is a semi-formal American Bistro with a rustic interior and limestone walls. Dinner cruises are available with reservations or dine out-

SAN ANTONIO

INTRO
ATTRACTIONS
DINING
LODGING

side by the patio by the river. Try the blackened prime rib, smoked shrimp, enchiladas or the cured herb and cured salmon tacos. | 421 E. Commerce St. | 210/224–8484 | $17–$32 | AE, D, DC, MC, V.

**Brazier at Los Patios.** Southwestern. Dining with an airy feeling, on Salado Creek. Known for Mexican and Continental food. Salad bar. | 2015 N.E. Loop I–410 | 210/655–9270 | Closed Mon. Closed Jan.–Feb. | $17–$28 | AE, D, DC, MC, V.

**Cappy's.** Seafood. Everything here is made from scratch. The restaurant is known for the freshness of its fish as well as the steak. There is a covered patio that seats a few for a more intimate scene. Kids' menu. Sat.–Sun. brunch. No smoking. | 5011 Broadway St. | 210/828–9669 | $15–$24 | AE, MC, V.

**Carranza Meat Market.** Steak. This informal eatery in a building which dates from 1870 is popular with local residents. It boasts high ceilings and limestone walls. Try the shrimp scampi, soft shell crab, blackened rib eye, filet mignon, veal chop, pepper steak and spaghetti. | 701 Austin St. | 210/223–0903 | Closed Sun. No lunch Sat. | $8–$29 | AE.

**Casa Rio.** Tex-Mex. This Mexican restaurant is filled with Mexican objets d'art and colorful piñatas and pictures of San Antonio fiestas. Try the green chicken or cheese enchiladas, fajitas, and tamales. There's a patio by the river with colorful umbrellas for shade. Kids' menu. | 430 E. Commerce St. | 210/225–6718 | $16–$21 | AE, D, DC, MC, V.

**Cascabel.** Southwestern. | 37 Loop 410 | 210/321–4860 | Breakfast also available | $27–$34 | AE, D, DC, MC, V.

**Crumpet's.** Continental. Dine by candlelight at this elegant restaurant which has live music on weekends. Try the charbroiled chicken, seafood or pasta salad. There's also a patio with a beautiful waterfall. | 3920 Harry Wurzbach | 210/821–5454 | $10–$25 | AE, D, DC, MC, V.

**Dick's Last Resort.** Barbecue. The wait staff here known for their funny offhand comments to customers. It's casual dining with a rustic flavor in the basement of a downtown hospital. Known for ribs, catfish and shrimp. There's a covered patio if you want to eat outside. Entertainment. | 406 Navarro St. | 210/224–0026 | $11–$26 | AE, D, DC, MC, V.

**Earl Abel's.** American. Open since 1933, this cavernous San Antonio mainstay is full of retro-sleek appeal and draws a faithful crowd of regulars. The crispy fried catfish is a winner, as is the fried chicken. You can get your fried chicken fix from the to-go stand in the parking lot, but if you take the time to sit, you can also savor one of Earl Abel's homemade pies. Try the coconut or lemon meringue. | 4210 Broadway | 210/822–3358 | $5–$18 | AE, D, MC, V.

**El Jarro de Arturo.** Tex-Mex. Classic and upscale with lots of tile, more authentic Mexican dishes. Try the Red Snapper a la Pepe (tomatoes and onions with a splash of tequilla). Music weekends. Kids' menu. | 13421 San Pedro Ave., | 210/494–5084 | $29–$33 | AE, D, DC, MC, V.

**El Mirador.** Mexican. Southwestern contemporary furnishings and colorful paintings and plates from Mexico distinguish this restaurant just 4 blocks from the River Walk. Try the fajitas, enchiladas and shrimp. There's also a covered patio set among banana plants. | 722 S. St. Mary's St. | 210/225–9444 | Breakfast also available. No supper Sun.–Tues. | $16–$25 | AE, D, DC, MC, V.

**Ernesto's.** Mexican. Crab and shrimp crepes are among the favorite dishes at this casual, charming restaurant. | 2559 Jackson Keller Rd. | 210/344–1248 | Closed Sun. | $16–$31 | AE, DC, MC, V.

**Fig Tree.** Continental. This is an elegant European-style restaurant inside a historic home, with silver flatwear and crystal on the tables. Try the fresh Maine lobster, rack of lamb, veal chop or duck. The patio overlooks the River Walk and is festooned with flowers and artifacts from France. | 515 Villita St. | 210/224–1976 | No lunch | $29–$50 | AE, D, DC, MC, V.

**5050 Diner.** American. This diner was built in the 1920 and serves the best burgers around. Kids' menu. | 5050 Broadway St. | 210/828–4386 | $15–$18 | AE, D, DC, MC, V.

**Formosa Gardens.** Chinese. This is a casual contemporary restaurant with separate rooms for private parties. Signature dishes include the shrimp and scallops and Peking duck. Early-bird suppers. | 1011 N.E. Loop 410 | 210/828–9988 | $8–$22 | AE, D, DC, MC, V.

**Gazebo at Los Patios.** Mexican. Enjoy casual eating on 18 acres of beautifully landscaped grounds. Try the shrimp salad, grilled chicken, rib eye steak or the many Mexican dishes. Eat outside on one of the many decks which surround the restaurant. | 2015 N.E. Loop I-410 | 210/655–6190 | No supper | $11–$23 | AE, D, MC, V.

**Grey Moss Inn.** Continental. This restaurant is inside a historic inn which was moved to Texas from England in the 1920s. The patio has an open grill surrounded by tables topped by umbrellas, trees, flowers and Christmas lights. Kids' menu. | 19010 Scenic Loop Rd. | 210/695–8301 | Reservations essential Fri.–Sat. | No lunch | $26–$50 | AE, D, MC, V.

**Guenther House.** Continental. This restaurant is housed in a small, 19th-century cottage. Known for its Belgian waffles and pastries. Open-air dining is available on a covered patio with a view of the city. | 205 E. Guenther St. | 210/227–1061 | Breakfast also available. No supper | $6–$11 | AE, D, MC, V.

**Jailhouse Cafe.** American. Come hungry to the Jailhouse Cafe—the hearty portions are huge enough to tide you over for the day. The famous cinnamon roll served at breakfast weighs in at three and a half sticky-sweet pounds. At lunch and dinnertime, the chicken-fried steak comes in two generous sizes: the Deputy is almost a pound of meat, and the Sheriff is a whopping pound and a half. | 1126 W. Commerce St. | 210/224–5001 | $5–$14 | AE, D, DC, MC, V.

**Jim Cullum's Landing.** Continental. Mondays through Fridays at 8:30, fans flock to this lively restaurant to hear the Jim Cullem Jazz Band play classic pre-war jazz while dining on Euro-Mexican food. At the base of the Hyatt Regency hotel, the restaurant doesn't open until 8, but the outdoor patio, with its own duet seven days a week, starts serving at 4:30. Call in advance to make sure the Jim Cullum Jazz Band is not away on tour. | 123 Losoya St. | 210/223–7266 | fax 210/227–1172 | www.landing.com | No lunch weekdays | $7–$31 | AE, D, DC, MC, V.

**Koi Kawa Japanese Restaurant and Sushi Bar.** Japanese. When you've had your fill of chicken-fried steak and enchiladas, join local sushi aficionados in this airy and unpretentious restaurant just north of the Witte Museum. The menu will satisfy your craving for ocean-fresh fish; call 24 hours in advance to order the nine-course Omakase Dinner. An all-glass dining room offers views of the San Antonio river and Brackenridge Park. | 4051 Broadway St. | 210/805–8111 | fax 210/805–0773 | Closed Sun. | $8–$70 | AE, D, DC, MC, V.

**La Calesa.** Mexican. Try pork tenderloin marinated in Mexican spices and rubbed with banana leaves and red onions. | 2103 E. Hildebrand Ave. | 210/822–4475 | Breakfast also available Sat. | $15–$30 | AE, D, MC, V.

**La Fogata.** Tex-Mex. Decorated in south-of-the-border style, this restaurant features mariachi music. Enjoy the homemade tortilllas on the covered patio with ceiling fans. Kids' menu. | 2427 Vance Jackson Rd. | 210/340–1337 | Breakfast also available Sat.–Sun. | $16–$23 | AE, D, DC, MC, V.

**La Fonda.** Mexican. This cheerful family-friendly restaurant, open since 1932, serves traditional Mexican fare, such as steak Tampiquena (grilled tenderloin strips with a green enchilada and charra beans), and a few Tex-Mex specialties as well. You'll get your money's worth with the Tex-Mex Deluxe: a 3-oz tenderloin, oak-grilled and served with an enchilada, a beef taco, refried beans, and Spanish rice. | 2415 N. Main Ave. | 210/733–0621 | No dinner Sun. | $7–$13 | AE, MC, V.

**La Margarita.** Tex-Mex. In Market Square eat surrounded by Spanish tile and light music. Try the fajitas, enchiladas and puffy tacos inside or outside on the patio under colorful umbrellas with a great view of the city. Entertainment. Kids' menu. | 120 Produce Row | 210/227–7140 | $12–$23 | AE, D, DC, MC, V.

**Las Canarias.** Seafood. A nice choice with views of the River Walk. Try the seven-spiced tuna steak or grilled swordfish filet. Entertainment. Kids' menu. Sun. brunch. | 112 College St. | 210/518–1000 | Breakfast also available Mon.–Sat. | $25–$39 | AE, D, DC, MC, V.

**Liberty Bar.** French, Mexican. Liberty Bar is one of the state's oldest saloons and it's very popular with locals. | 328 E. Josephine | 210/227–1187 | $16–$26 | AE, MC, V.

**Little Rhein Steak House.** Steak. Built in 1847, it was the first two-story structure in San Antonio and was originally used as a home and museum. Known for the filet mignon. There is also dining on the terrace. Kids' menu. | 231 S. Alamo St. | 210/225-2111 | No lunch | $29–$50 | AE, D, DC, MC, V.

**Lone Star.** Steak, American. This River Walk restaurant offers casual dining both indoors and out. Known for its old-fashioned country cooking. Try chicken-fried steaks and fried chicken. There is a great view of the River Walk, while the whole restaurant has a tree-house feeling because it is shaded by so many trees. Kids' menu. | 237 Losoya | 210/223–9374 | $16–$30 | AE, D, MC, V.

**Los Barrios.** Mexican, Tex-Mex. This family-run restaurant gets its recipes from the grandmother's place in Mexico. So the food is authentic. Eat in a relaxed casual atmosphere with lots of light. Try the fajitas, tacos and classic enchiladas. Known for its authentic gourmet Mexican dishes. Entertainment weekends. Kids' menu. | 4223 Blanco Rd. | 210/732–6017 | $13–$21 | AE, D, DC, MC, V.

**Mario's Restaurante Mexicano.** Mexican. Hector Cantu, the exacting chef at Mario's, insists on the freshest ingredients and most authentic recipes at this upscale restaurant. The specialty is meat, which is all hand-cut; the Abuja, a charcoal-grilled cut of meat taken from the prime rib, is not to be missed. Other top-sellers are the Cilantro Cream Enchiladas and the Asparagus Anissa, an appetizer named after Hector's sister. | 4841 Fredricksburg Rd. | 210/349–0188 | fax 210/349–1057 | $7–$15 | AE, D, DC, MC, V.

**Mencius' Hunan.** Chinese. This is a modern casually elegant restaurant with Asian decor in a medical center. Try the lemon chicken or the shrimp and scallop Hunan. | 7959 Fredericksburg Rd. | 210/615–1288 | $8–$25 | AE, D, DC, MC, V.

**Mi Tierra.** Tex-Mex. This restaurant is decorated for Christmas year-round. It has four rooms for eating decorated with piñatas and baskets. It's extremely popular on weekends. Next door is a Mexican bakery. Try the sizzling fajitas, tacos and enchiladas. There's a covered deck for outdoor dining. | 218 Produce Row | 210/225–1262 | Open 24 hrs | $10–$23 | AE, D, DC, MC, V.

**Michelino's.** Italian. River Walk restaurant with casual dining indoors and out. Try the fettucine verde, chicken Florentine, or pizza. Eat on either the covered or uncovered patio with a view of the river. Kids' menu. | 521 River Walk | 210/223–2939 | $17–$26 | AE, D, MC, V.

**Morton's of Chicago.** Steak. Elegant and contemporary in look. Folks come for the great steaks. | 300 Crockett St. | 210/228–0700 | No lunch | $45–$55 | AE, DC, MC, V.

**Old San Francisco Steak House.** Steak. This restaurant has an 1890s theme with red velvet accents, a costumed waitstaff, and a girl on a swing who kicks a bell on the ceiling. This family-friendly restaurant is also a popular spot for business lunches. Known for their prime rib, 6-oz bacon-wrapped petite filet and Jamaican chicken. | 10223 Sahara St. | 210/342–2321 | No lunch | $15–$32 | AE, D, DC, MC, V.

**Paesano's.** Italian. With two San Antonio locations, this popular eatery includes a downtown location (Basse Rd.) and a River Walk location, situated right on the banks of the Paseo del Rio. Both Italian and Mediterranean dishes are the specialties of the house. The River Walk location also offers barge dining. | 555 E. Basse Rd. | 210/828–5191 | $19–$32 | AE, DC, MC, V.

**Pico de Gallo.** Mexican. Just a block west of Market Square, this eatery is a favorite spot for business breakfasts and lunches as well as family dinners. Try the crispy beef tacos, nachos, enchiladas and tamales. There is a patio which seats about 40 that is partially covered by trees and boasts a fountain. Entertainment most nights. Kids' menu. | 111 S. Leona Ave. | 210/225–6060 | Breakfast also available | $10–$24 | AE, D, DC, MC, V.

**Pieca d'Italia.** Italian. Dine in the fresh air on the patio overlooking the river. Known for Chicken Romano (chicken breast with spinach and cheese) and cannelloni Florentine (pasta with veal, spinach and cheese). | 502 River Walk | 210/227–5511 | $14–$22 | AE, D, DC, MC, V.

**Polo's at the Fairmount.** Continental. An elegant restaurant with Southwestern flair often praised in the national press. Try the broiled sea bass, fillet of sole, king salmon or the imaginative pizzas. There is a patio that is available only upon request. Kids' menu. | 401 S. Alamo | 210/224–8800 | Breakfast also available. No lunch Sat. No supper Sun. | $16–$35 | AE, D, DC, MC, V.

**Razmiko's Ristorante Italiano.** Italian. Dine by candlelight at this restaurant which is a favorite place for romantic meals. | 8055 West Ave., Selma | 210/366–0416 | $8–$24 | AE, D, DC, MC, V.

**Rio Rio Cantina.** Tex-Mex. The restaurant has indoor and outdoor dining, and it serves up Southwestern favorites from quesadillas to enchiladas. The interior is decorated with colorful piñatas. The patio has tan umbrellas and a great view of the river. Vegetarian dishes are also on the menu. Kids' menu. | 421 E. Commerce St. | 210/226–8462 | $10–$23 | AE, D, DC, MC, V.

**Romano's Macaroni Grill.** Italian. A family restaurant with Italian decor. There are strolling opera singers and violin players. Try the scallapini di pollo or the penne rustica. | 24116 I–10W | 210/698–0003 | $9–$16 | AE, DC, MC, V.

**Rosario's.** Mexican. Contemporary decor enhanced by custom-made Botoro-style portraits. The authentic Mexican food includes favorites like green enchiladas and fajitas and they also serve great margaritas. Entertainment weekends. | 1014 S. Alamo St. | 210/223–1806 | Closed Sun. No supper Mon. | $7–$12 | AE, D, DC, MC, V.

**Ruth's Chris Steak House.** Steak. Part of the chain and one of the best places for delicious steaks. | 7720 Jones Maltsberger Rd. | 210/821–5051 | No lunch | $35–$48 | AE, DC, MC, V.

**Tower of the Americas.** Steak. Set in a revolving tower, this restaurant offers a bird's-eye view of the city. The elevator fee is added to bill. Try the steak, New York strip steaks, seafood, lobster and sea bass. Kids' menu. | 222 HemisFair Plaza | 210/223–3101 | No supper Sun. | $17–$32 | AE, D, DC, MC, V.

★ **Zuni Grill.** Southwestern. The cream, blue and yellow bricks lend this River Walk eatery a Southwestern flavor. Try the blue corn enchiladas, pork loin and for dessert, the crème brûlé. Eat outside on the open patio shaded by white umbrellas. Kids' menu. | 223 Lasoya | 210/227–0864 | Breakfast also available | $16–$33 | www.joesfood.com | AE, D, DC, MC, V.

## Lodging

**Adam's Mark Riverwalk.** This hotel is popular for its easy access to the River Walk scene. Soak in a view of the river from the sundeck, taste the inventive Mediterranean offerings of the hotel's Restaurante Marbella, or cheer on the Spurs in the Players Sports Bar. Restaurant, bar, room service, in-room data ports, cable TV, pool, outdoor hot tub, sauna, gym, laundry facilities, parking (fee), no pets. | 111 Pecan St. E | 210/354–2800 or 800/444–2326 | fax 210-354-2700 | www.adamsmark.com | 450 rooms | $225–$275 | AE, D, DC, MC, V.

**Beckmann Inn and Carriage House.** This 1886 Victorian with a Greek influence is filled with antiques and high-back beds. It is known for their two-course breakfast served on china with crystal. It's in the King Williams Historic District along the San Antonio River Walk. Complimentary breakfast, refrigerators, cable TV, no kids under 12, no smoking. | 222 E. Guenther St. | 210/229–1449 or 800/945–1449 | fax 210/229–1061 | www.beckmanninn.com | 5 rooms (4 with shower only), 2 suites | $99–$150 | AE, D, DC, MC, V.

**Bed and Breakfast on the River.** This 1916 Victorian house is furnished true to the period. The rooms have wraparound balconies and porches. It's 10 minutes from the River Walk and downtown area. Complimentary breakfast, in-room data ports, cable TV, business services, free parking, no smoking. | 129 Woodward Pl. | 210/225–6333 or 800/730–0019 | fax 210/271–3992 | 12 rooms (4 with shower only) | $99–$175 | AE, D, MC, V.

**Best Western Continental Inn.** This corporate hotel is near the Alamo historical site and plenty of shopping malls. Restaurant, bar, complimentary breakfast, in-room data ports, some refrigerators, room service, cable TV, pool, wading pool, hot tubs, playground, laundry facilities, business services. | 9735 I–35N | 210/655–3510 | fax 210/655–0778 | www.bestwestern.com | 161 rooms | $59–$79 | AE, D, DC, MC, V.

**Bonner Garden.** Built in 1910 for Louisiana aristocrat and artist Mary Bonner, the 4,000-square-ft, Palladian-style villa is decorated with Bonner's art and retains many of the Italianate details of the original building, such as hand-painted porcelain fireplaces and tile floors. From the roof-top patio, you can see a panoramic view of downtown San Antonio. Complimentary breakfast, cable TV, VCR, pool, no pets, no smoking. | 145 E. Agarita St. | 210/733–4222 or 800/396–4222 | fax 210/733–6129 | www.bonnergarden.com | 5 rooms | $85–$125 | AE, D, DC, MC, V.

**Brackenridge House.** Brackenridge House is in the King William Historic District (originally settled by Germans) and has a self-described "country-Victorian" decor. Complimentary breakfast, no smoking. | 230 Madison | 210/271–3442 or 800/221–1412 | fax 210/226–3139 | www.brackenridgehouse.com | 6 rooms (2 with shower only) | $95–$250 | AE, D, DC, MC, V.

**Bullis House Inn.** This three-story Victorian mansion has oriental rugs, 14-ft ceilings, hardwood floors and oak paneling. All the rooms are furnished with both antiques and reproductions as well as fireplaces. It is across the street from Fort Sam Houston which was built in 1909. Complimentary Continental breakfast, refrigerators, cable TV, some room phones, pool. | 621 Pierce St. | 210/223–9426 | fax 210/299–1479 | 7 rooms (4 with shared bath) | $59–$79 | AE, D, MC, V.

**Comfort Inn Airport.** This chain hotel is near the airport and designed to please the business traveler. There are many bars and nightclubs in the area, including the Far West Rodeo. Complimentary Continental breakfast, in-room data ports, cable TV, pool, business services, airport shuttle, pets allowed (fee). | 2635 Loop 410 | 210/653–9110 | fax 210/653–8615 | 203 rooms | $69–$79 | AE, D, DC, MC, V.

**Courtyard by Marriott.** This Marriott is 5 minutes away from the Fiesta Texas theme park and 15 minutes from the walrus and sea lion shows at Seaworld. Restaurant, bar, in-room data ports, refrigerators (in suites), cable TV, pool, hot tub, exercise equipment, laundry facilities, free parking. | 8585 Marriott Dr. | 210/614–7100 | fax 210/614–7110 | 146 rooms | $84–$99 | AE, D, DC, MC, V.

**Doubletree.** Families and corporate travelers are welcome at this hotel. It's a 10-minute drive from the airport and across the street from the North Star Mall, one of the largest malls in San Antonio. Restaurants, bar, in-room data ports, some refrigerators, cable TV, pool, hot tub, exercise equipment, business services, airport shuttle. | 37 Loop 410 | 210/366–2424 | fax 210/341–0410 | www.doubletreehotels.com | 292 rooms | $129–$149 | AE, D, DC, MC, V.

**Drury Inn and Suites.** The interior of this hotel is both modern and rustic with a large fountain in the lobby. The Henry B. Gonzales Convention Center is 6 mi away and the airport is nearby. There's also the convenience of an Applebee's restaurant next door. Complimentary Continental breakfast, in-room data ports, microwaves, refrigerators, cable TV, pool, hot tub, business services, airport shuttle, some pets allowed. | 95 NE Loop 410 | 210/366–4300 | fax 210/308–8100 | www.drury-inns.com | 289 rooms | $75–$112 | AE, D, DC, MC, V.

**Econo Lodge.** Economical, comfortable, and convenient—downtown San Antonio is at your fingertips. It is within 6 minutes of Six Flags, SeaWorld, the Freeman Coliseum, the Alamo and across from the mall. It is 1 mi from the airport. Complimentary Continental breakfast, some microwaves, refrigerators, cable TV, pool, laundry facilities, business services, free parking. | 218 S.W. White Rd. | 210/333–3346 | fax 210/333–7564 | 40 rooms | $39–$89 | AE, D, DC, MC, V.

**Embassy Suites.** Piano bars, shopping, and theaters are a 10-minute drive from this conveniently located hotel. It's also close to the airport. Restaurant, bar, complimentary breakfast, in-room data ports, microwaves, refrigerators, cable TV, indoor pool, hot tub, exercise equipment, game room, laundry facilities, business services, airport shuttle. | 10110 U.S. 281N | 210/525–9999 | fax 210/525–0626 | 261 suites | $124–$169 suites | AE, D, DC, MC, V.

**Executive Guesthouse.** This hotel strives to make its corporate guests feel at home while they're away on business. It's convenient to Fiesta Texas, the airport, and Northstar Mall and within walking distance of several restaurants. Complimentary breakfast, some in-room hot tubs, in-room data ports, microwaves, refrigerators, cable TV, indoor pool, exercise equipment, airport shuttle, valet parking, free parking, some pets allowed (fee). | 12828 U.S. 281N | 210/494–7600 or 800/362–8700 | fax 210/545–4314 | 124 rooms | $99–$109 | AE, D, DC, MC, V.

**Fairfield Inn by Marriott.** The interior of this four-story hotel was renovated in January 2000. You'll find it close to many tourist attractions and just half a mile north of the Alamo. Complimentary Continental breakfast, cable TV, pool, gym, laundry facilities, free parking, no pets. | 620 S. Santa Rosa | 210/299–1000 or 800/228–2800 | fax 210/299–1030 | www.fairfieldinn.com | 110 rooms | $89–$159 | AE, D, DC, MC, V.

**Fairmount.** This 1906 hotel made the Guinness Book of World Records for the largest building ever moved on wheels. Furnished in Victorian style it caters to corporate business guests with special rates. Restaurant, bar (with entertainment), in-room data ports, cable TV, in-room VCRs (movies), exercise equipment, business services. | 401 S. Alamo St. | 210/224–8800 or 800/642–3363 | fax 210/224–2767 | www.wyndham.com | 37 rooms, 17 suites | $195–$215, $228–$550 suites | AE, D, DC, MC, V.

**Four Points by Sheraton.** This Southwestern hotel is set on the San Antonio River. It's 20 minutes from major attractions and restaurants. Restaurant, bar, refrigerators (in suites), room service, cable TV, pool, exercise equipment, laundry facilities, business services, valet parking, parking (fee). | 110 Lexington Ave. | 210/223–9461 | fax 210/223–9267 | 324 rooms | $79–$139 | AE, D, DC, MC, V.

**Hampton Inn Downtown.** You'll appreciate the Mediterranean flavor at this hotel which has plants everywhere. The Alamo and the River Walk are only 2 blocks away from the hotel. Market Square, an open-air Mexican market, is 6 blocks away. Complimentary Continental breakfast, in-room data ports, cable TV, pool, laundry facilities, business services, valet parking, free parking. | 414 Bowie St. | 210/225–8500 | fax 210/225–8526 | 169 rooms | $89–$139 | AE, D, DC, MC, V.

**Hampton Inn Fiesta Park.** If you feel compelled to shop, just cross the expressway and browse the vast Huebner Oak shopping center. This recently modernized inn is traditionally furnished. Complimentary Continental breakfast, in-room data ports, some microwaves, cable TV, pool, business services, valet parking, free parking. | 11010 I–10W | 210/561–9058 | fax 210/690–5566 | 122 rooms | $59–$95 | AE, D, DC, MC, V.

★ **Havana Riverwalk Inn.** This hotel on the river has deluxe suites, executive queen and king suites and lofts. The rooms have 1920s furnishings, antiques, and great views. Complimentary Continental breakfast, in-room data ports, cable TV, room service, business services, valet parking, no kids under 14, no smoking. | 1015 Navarro Ave. | 210/222–2008 or 888/224–2008 | fax 210/222–2717 | www.havana-hotel.com | 37 rooms | $110–$155 | AE, D, DC, MC, V.

**Hawthorn Suites.** The Malibu Miniature Golf course nearby also has go-carts and arcade games. Farther east on I–10, Dave and Buster's lounge has music on weekends and a pool table, and across the street from the hotel there is a 24-screen multiplex and shopping center. Picnic area, complimentary breakfast, in-room data ports, kitchenettes, microwaves, cable TV, pool, hot tub, laundry facilities, business services, valet parking, free parking, some pets allowed (fee). | 4041 Bluemel Rd. | 210/561–9660 | fax 210/561–9663 | www.hawthorn.com | 128 suites | $79–$169 suites | AE, D, DC, MC, V.

SAN ANTONIO

INTRO
ATTRACTIONS
DINING
LODGING

**Hilton Palacio del Rio.** This is a towering complex with a central location downtown on the River Walk. It is the only hotel with extended balconies that overlook the river. It is across the street from the River Center Mall, the Alamo, and the Convention Center. Restaurant, bars with entertainment, in-room data ports, microwaves, cable TV, pool, hot tub, exercise equipment, business services, valet parking, parking (fee), some pets allowed. | 200 S. Alamo St. | 210/222–1400 | fax 210/270–0761 | www.hilton.com | 481 rooms | $100–$289 | AE, D, DC, MC, V.

**Holiday Inn Crockett Hotel.** Built in 1909 and listed on the National Register of Historic Places, this hotel is a relic of turn-of-the-20th-century San Antonio. You'll find traditional American food and a view of passing horse-drawn carriages in its Landmark Restaurant. Take in the city from the seventh-story sundeck or relax to nightly piano music in the central atrium. Restaurant, bar, room service, in-room data ports, cable TV, pool, outdoor hot tubs, laundry service, parking (fee), some pets allowed (fee). | 320 Bonham St. | 210/225–6500 or 800/292–1050 | fax 210/225–6251 | crockett.sales@gal-tex.com | 206 rooms | $79–$139 | AE, D, MC, V.

**Holiday Inn Express–Sea World.** A stay at this modern Holiday Inn comes with interesting neighbors: walruses, sea lions, and the many other underwater creatures at Sea World. It's within walking distance of restaurants. Complimentary Continental breakfast, in-room data ports, microwaves, cable TV, pool, laundry facilities, business services. | 7043 Culebra Rd. | 210/521–1485 | fax 210/520–5924 | www.holidayinn.com | 72 rooms | $99 | AE, D, DC, MC, V.

**Holiday Inn Market Square.** This Spanish-style hotel is two blocks away from a bustling shopping area: the Market Square. Inside the hotel, a game room will keep you entertained with pool, video games, and a full-swing golf simulator. Restaurant, bar, room service, cable TV, outdoor pool, outdoor hot tub, gym, video games, laundry facilities, free parking, pets allowed (fee). | 318 W. Durango | 210/225–3211 | fax 210/225–1125 | hi-sanantonio@bristol-hotels.com | www.holiday-inn.com | 317 rooms | $70–$140 | AE, D, DC, MC, V.

**Holiday Inn–River Walk.** This modernized hotel has views of the San Antonio River. The rooms are contemporary and elegant, although the lobby has more of a Southwestern theme. It's 1 block from the Hard Rock Café. In-room data ports, refrigerators (in suites), room service, cable TV, pool, hot tub, exercise equipment, business services, some pets allowed. | 217 N. St. Mary's St. | 210/224–2500 or 800/445–8475 | fax 210/223–1302 | www.holidayinn.com | 313 rooms | $129–$179 | AE, D, DC, MC, V.

**Homewood Suites.** Homewood Suites has contemporary decor, upgraded rooms and excellent service. It is 15 minutes from the downtown area where you can visit Ripley's Believe It Or Not Museum or watch the Alamo recreated at an IMAX theater. Complimentary Continental breakfast, in-room data ports, kitchenettes, microwaves, refrigerators, cable TV, in-room VCRs (movies), pool, exercise equipment, laundry facilities, business services, valet parking, parking (fee). | 4323 Spectrum One | 210/696–5400 | fax 210/696–8899 | www.homewood-suites.com | 123 suites | $109–$199 suites | AE, D, DC, MC, V.

**Hyatt Regency Hill Country.** This sprawling resort-hotel is a pleasant change from the city scene. It's out in the country a bit with lots of space for sports facilities and active pursuits. Restaurants, bar (with entertainment), in-room data ports, microwaves, room service, cable TV, 2 pools, beauty salon, hot tub, massage, 18-hole golf course, tennis, gym, hiking, bicycles, game room, children's programs (ages 3–12), playground, laundry facilities, business services, valet parking, free parking. | 9800 Hyatt Resort Dr. | 210/647–1234 | fax 210/681–9681 | www.hyatt.com | 454 rooms, 46 suites | $120–$300, $300–$500 suites | AE, D, DC, MC, V.

**Hyatt Regency San Antonio.** This hotel has a modern Texas style and an interesting design with the San Antonio River running through it. It's on the River Walk across from the Alamo. Within walking distance of 50 restaurants and 20 minutes from Sea World and Fiesta Texas. Restaurants, bar (with entertainment), in-room data ports, minibars, some refrigerators, cable TV, pool, hot tub, exercise equipment, business services, valet parking, parking (fee).

| 123 Losoya St. | 210/222–1234 | fax 210/227–4925 | www.hyatt.com | 631 rooms | $159–$298 | AE, D, DC, MC, V.

**Jackson House.** Built in 1894, this B&B has elegant Victorian decor. For additional pampering, guests can savor time in the conservatory, surrounded by Victorian stained glass windows, and unwind in the heated swim-spa. Complimentary breakfast, in-room data ports, some in-room hot tubs, cable TV, indoor pool, business services, valet parking, parking (fee), no kids under 14, no smoking. | 107 Madison St. | 210/225–4045 or 800/221–4045 | fax 210/227–0877 | nobleinns@aol.com | 6 rooms (1 with shower only) | $105–$175 | AE, D, MC, V.

**La Mansion del Rio.** This hotel on the river is conveniently located on River Walk, nicely furnished, and has good service and a very pleasant staff. Restaurants, bar (with entertainment), in-room data ports, minibars, room service, cable TV, pool, business services, airport shuttle, pets allowed. | 112 College St. | 210/225–2581 or 800/323–7500 | fax 210/226–0389 | www.lamansion.com | 337 rooms | $214–$324 | AE, D, DC, MC, V.

**La Quinta–Ingram Park.** This chain hotel is 20 minutes from downtown San Antonio and welcomes families as well as business travelers. Complimentary Continental breakfast, in-room data ports, microwaves (in suites), refrigerator, cable TV, pool, some pets allowed. | 7134 Loop I–410 | 210/680–8883 | fax 210/681–3877 | www.laquinta.com | 195 rooms | $85–$95 | AE, D, DC, MC, V.

**La Quinta–Market Square.** Market Square is across the street from the hotel, and the 600-ft Tower of Americas (commanding views of the area) is 1 mi away. Complimentary Continental breakfast, in-room data ports, cable TV, pool, business services, valet parking, free parking, some pets allowed. | 900 Dolorosa St. | 210/271–0001 | fax 210/228–0663 | 124 rooms. | $105–$115 | AE, D, DC, MC, V.

**Marriott Plaza.** This hotel and resort is set on 6 acres and is known for the exotic birds and peacocks which roam the grounds. It's across from the HemisFair and 1 block from the Convention Center and the River Walk. This is a full-service hotel with many amenities to please executives in town during the week or families on vacation. Restaurant, bar (with entertainment), in-room data ports, room service, cable TV, pool, hot tub, massage, tennis court, exercise equipment, bicycles, business services, some pets allowed. | 555 S. Alamo St. | 210/229–1000 | fax 210/229–1418 | www.plazasa.com | 252 rooms | $95–$219 | AE, D, DC, MC, V.

**Marriott Riverwalk.** This hotel has a Southwestern theme. Half of the rooms have balconies facing the River Walk. There are 10,000 square ft of Grand Ballroom space. Restaurant, bar (with entertainment), in-room data ports, refrigerators, room service, cable TV, pool, hot tub, exercise services, valet parking, parking (fee), pets allowed. | 711 E. River Walk | 210/224–4555 | fax 210/224–2754 | 500 rooms | $199–$244 | AE, D, DC, MC, V.

**Marriott Rivercenter.** This large hotel has over 80,000 square ft of meeting space and a 40,000-square-ft Grand Ballroom. It is 1 block from the San Antonio Zoo and 5 minutes from The Alamo, the Convention Center and 10 minutes from the airport. Restaurant, bar, in-room data ports, some refrigerators, room service, cable TV, pool, barbershop, beauty salon, hot tub, driving range, putting green, exercise equipment, business services, valet parking, parking (fee), pets allowed. | 101 Bowie St. | 210/223–1000 | fax 210/223–6239 | 1,000 rooms | $91–$219 | www.marriott.com | AE, D, DC, MC, V.

★ **Menger.** This 1859 hotel is filled with antiques and offers full amenities. It is across from the Alamo, one block from the River Walk and most downtown area attractions. Restaurant, bar (with entertainment), in-room data ports, room service, cable TV, pool, hot tub, massage, exercise equipment, business services, valet parking, parking (fee). | 204 Alamo Plaza | 210/223–4361 or 800/345–9285 | fax 210/228–0022 | www.mengerhotel.com | 350 rooms | $145–$155 | AE, D, DC, MC, V.

**Oge House.** This B & B is downtown about 10 minutes from the River Walk. There's a cozy library and breakfast is served each morning with a daily changing menu. Each room is individually decorated with both American and European furniture. Complimentary breakfast, in-room data ports, refrigerators, cable TV, business services, no kids under 16.

| 209 Washington St. | 210/223–2353 or 800/242–2770 | fax 210/226–5812 | ogeinn@swbell.net | www.ogeinn.com | 10 rooms (1 with shower only) | $110–$225 | AE, D, DC, MC, V.

**Omni.** This hotel combines luxury with Texas hospitality to create an unforgettable stay. The comfortable guest rooms feature a dazzling array of amenities along with a rooftop ballroom with a magnificent skyline view. There is dining, entertainment and attractions can all be found within 10 mi. Restaurant, bar (with entertainment), in-room data ports, some refrigerators, cable TV, 2 pools (1 indoor), hot tubs, exercise equipment, business services, airport shuttle. | 9821 Colonnade Blvd. | 210/691–8888 | fax 210/691–1128 | www.omni-hotel.com | 326 rooms | $139–$159 | AE, D, DC, MC, V.

**Pear Tree Inn.** Next to this traditionally decorated Pear Tree you'll find Jim's Restaurant, and across the freeway, Texas Land and Cattle and Red Lobster. The airport is also convenient. Complimentary Continental breakfast, in-room data ports, some microwaves, cable TV, pool, laundry facilities, business services, airport shuttle, some pets allowed. | 143 Loop 410 | 210/366–9300 | 125 rooms | $66–$76 | AE, D, DC, MC, V.

**Radisson Downtown Market Square.** This upscale, full-service hotel with a Southwestern theme is in the heart of San Antonio's commercial district. It's a few blocks from the River Walk, across from UTSA College and 2 blocks from Market Square. Restaurant, bar, refrigerators (in suites), cable TV, pool, hot tub, exercise equipment, laundry facilities, business services, pets allowed. | 502 W. Durango St. | 210/224–7155 | fax 210/224–9130 | 250 rooms | $139–$169 | AE, D, DC, MC, V.

**Ramada Emily Morgan.** Built in the 1820s, this hotel was restored in the 1980s and has recently been renovated. It has a unique triangle architecture with a neo-gothic design. It is across the street from the Alamo. Restaurant, bar, in-room data ports, cable TV, pool, hot tub, exercise equipment, business services. | 705 E. Houston St. | 210/225–8486 | fax 210/225–7227 | 177 rooms | $99–$199 | AE, D, DC, MC, V.

**Red Roof Inn.** This chain hotel is close to the airport, shopping, and restaurants. Complimentary Continental breakfast, in-room data ports, cable TV, business services, airport shuttle, pets allowed. | 333 Wolfe Rd. | 210/340–4055 | fax 210/340–4031 | 135 rooms | $68–$84 | AE, D, DC, MC, V.

**Residence Inn by Marriott.** Some of the amenities at this Marriott make it an excellent choice for families visiting the River Walk area. Complimentary Continental breakfast, in-room data ports, kitchenettes, microwaves, refrigerators, cable TV, pool, hot tub, exercise equipment, laundry facilities, business services, pets allowed (fee). | 425 Bonham Ave. | 210/212–5555 | fax 210/212–5554 | 220 suites | $159 suites | AE, D, DC, MC, V.

**Riverwalk Inn.** This charming inn provides lodging in a couple of original old buildings. Complimentary Continental breakfast, in-room data ports, refrigerators, cable TV, business services, no smoking. | 329 Old Guilbeau | 210/212–8300 or 800/254–4440 | fax 210/229–9422 | 11 rooms (with shower only) | $99–$155 | AE, D, MC, V.

**Riverwalk Plaza.** This six-story 20-year-old hotel is modern and central to the southern end of the River Walk. Restaurant, bar, in-room data ports, cable TV, pool, exercise equipment, business services. | 100 Villita St. | 210/226–2271 | fax 210/226–9453 | www.riverwalkplaza.com | 133 rooms | $119–$139 | AE, D, DC, MC, V.

**Royal Swan Guest House.** This charming B&B in the King Williams district was built in 1897. It is 2 blocks from the River Walk. Complimentary breakfast, in-room data ports, cable TV, business services, no kids under 12, no smoking. | 236 Madison St. | 210/223–3776 or 800/368–3073 | fax 210/271–0373 | theswan@onr.com | 5 rooms (1 with shower only), 1 suite | $95–$120, $130 suite | AE, D, MC, V.

**St. Anthony Wyndham.** This somewhat formal 1909 historic hotel is decorated with oil paintings, chandeliers, and a handsome central staircase. It is in the center of downtown near all the major attractions such as the Alamo, Six Flags, the River Walk, the San Antonio Zoo and area golf courses. Restaurant, bar, in-room data ports, cable TV, pool, exercise equipment, business services, valet parking, parking (fee). | 300 E. Travis St. | 210/227–4392 or 800/355–5153 | fax 210/227–0915 | stanthonyhotel@compuserve.com | www.stanthonyhotel.com | 350 rooms, 42 suites | $99–$135, $250–$575 suites | AE, D, DC, MC, V.

**Sheraton Gunter.** Black and white pictures in the rooms and lobby detail the transition of this hotel from a United States military headquarters during the Civil War to its current use. It's 1 block from the River Walk and across the street from the Majestic Theatre. Restaurant, bar, in-room data ports, refrigerators, cable TV, pool, barbershop, hot tub, exercise equipment, business services. | 205 E. Houston St. | 210/227–3241 | fax 210/227–3299 | www.camberleyhotel.com | 322 rooms | $150–$165 | AE, D, DC, MC, V.

**Sierra Royale Hotel.** This condo-style all-suites hotel is on the northwest side of San Antonio and is only 10 minutes from SeaWorld and Fiesta Texas. All the rooms have a living room, dining room, washer and dryer and a full kitchen. Bar, picnic area, complimentary Continental breakfast, kitchenettes, microwaves, cable TV, pool, hot tub, business services, valet parking, parking (fee). | 6300 Rue Marielyne | 210/647–0041 or 800/289–2444 | fax 210/647–4442 | 88 suites | $130–$160 suites | AE, D, DC, MC, V.

**Travelodge Suites.** There are shopping centers and movie theaters near this chain hotel, which is 15 minutes from downtown and 20 minutes from the Brackenridge Park and Zoo. Complimentary Continental breakfast, kitchenettes, microwaves, cable TV, pool, laundry facilities, business services, airport shuttle. | 4934 Loop 410NW | 210/680–3351 | fax 210/680–5182 | www.dcci.com/travelodge | 201 suites | $59–$79 suites | AE, D, DC, MC, V.

**Westin River Walk.** Built in 1999, this deluxe addition to the River Walk scene was named most luxurious hotel in San Antonio by the *New York Times*. Savor the river view from your own private balcony (half of the rooms face the river) and enjoy the sumptuous marble bathroom; then delight in the Nuevo Latino cuisine of the hotel restaurant, La Caliza Grille. Restaurant, bar, room service, in-room data ports, in-room safes, refrigerators, cable TV, in-room movies, pool, outdoor hot tub, gym, laundry service, parking (fee), no pets. | 420 W. Market St. | 210/224–6500 | fax 210/444–6000 | www.westin.com | 474 rooms | $189–$310 | AE, D, DC, MC, V.

**A Yellow Rose.** Built in 1878, this bed-and-breakfast is found in the leafy King William Historic District, 5 blocks from downtown. The inn is decorated in traditional English antiques and has a large front porch. Complimentary breakfast, cable TV, free parking, no pets, no kids under 12, no smoking. | 229 Madison St. | 210/229–9903 or 800/950–9903 | fax 210/229–1691 | yellowrs@express-news.net | www.yellowrose.com | 6 rooms | $114–$144 | AE, D, MC, V.

# SAN MARCOS

MAP 8, H5

*(Nearby towns also listed: Austin, Gruene, New Braunfels, Seguin)*

Located between Austin and San Antonio on Interstate 35, this city is home to the largest outlet malls in Texas and brings in devoted shoppers by the busload. The downtown area, located west of I–35, recently underwent $16 million in renovations and has been transformed into a shopping and dining area.

In summer San Marcos is a popular getaway because of the San Marcos River. The crystal-clear waters of the river flow through downtown and several companies offer float trips down the waterway; snorkeling is also popular.

**Information: San Marcos Convention and Visitors Bureau** | 202 N. C.M. Allen Parkway, San Marcos 78667 | 512/396–2495 or 888/200–5620 | www.sanmarcostexas.com.

## Attractions
**Aquarena Center for Continuing Education.** This resort dates back to 1928, when A. B. Rogers purchased 125 acres at the headwaters of the San Marcos River to create a grand hotel. He

provided glass-bottomed boats to cruise Spring Lake, fed by more than 200 springs that produce 150 million gallons daily. This 98 percent pure water is home to many fish (including some white albino catfish) and various types of plant life. Today you can still enjoy a cruise on a glass-bottomed boat and even see the site of an underwater archaeological dig. Visible is the spot that yielded the remains of Clovis Man, a hunter-gatherer who lived on the San Marcos River 13,000 years ago. The park has an educational focus with many ecotourism displays. | 921 Aquarena Springs Dr. | 512/245–7575 or 800/999–9767 | Free; $5 for glass-bottom boats | Daily 9:30–7:30.

**Calaboose African-American History Museum.** This rich collection of photographs and memorabilia documents the history and experiences of African-Americans in southwest Texas. Well-trained docents will guide you through permanent exhibits on, for example, the Tuskeegee Airmen, the Buffalo Soldiers, and the Cotton era in the San Marcos area. The museum is in the original Hays County Jail building, built in 1873. | 200 Martin Luther King Dr. | 512/393–8421 or 512/353–0124 | $3 | By appointment.

**Lockhart State Park.** This 263-acre park has a nine-hole golf course, fishing on Plum Creek, picnic areas, a swimming pool, and campsites for both tents and trailers. Many of the facilities were built by the Civilian Conservation Corps in the 1930s. | 4179 State Park Rd., Lockhart | 512/398–3479 | fax 512/396–7175 | Daily.

**Prime Outlets.** One of Texas's largest collections of outlet stores, with shops such as Gap, Calvin Klein, Guess, J. Crew, Polo, Bass, Nike attracting shoppers from around the state and Mexico. | 3939 I–35S | 512/396–2200 | Free | Daily.

**Southwestern Writers Collection and Wittliff Gallery of Southwestern and Mexican Photography.** This archival repository contains the works of writers and photographers with links to the southwest. Exhibits of photography and manuscripts, which change three times a year, have explored Texan music, Mexican women photographers, and Larry McMurtry's Lonesome Dove. | Albert B. Alkek Library, Southwest Texas State University, 601 University Blvd., 7th fl | 512/245–2313 | www.library.swt.edu/swwc/index.html | Free | Weekdays 8–5, except Tues. 8 AM–9 PM, Sat. 1–5, Sun. 2–6.

**Wonder World.** A guided tour lasting nearly two hours covers the entire park, including the 7½-acre Texas Wildlife Park, Texas's largest petting zoo. A miniature train chugs through the animal enclosure, stopping to allow riders to pet and feed white-tail deer, wild turkeys, and many exotic species. The next stop on the tour is Wonder Cave, created during the earthquake that produced the Balcones Fault, an 1,800-mi line separating the western Hill Country from the flat eastern farmland. Within the cave is the actual crack. Huge boulders are lodged in the fissure. At the end of the cave tour, an elevator takes travelers to the top of the 110-ft Tejas Tower, which offers a spectacular view of the Balcones Fault. The last stop is the Anti-Gravity House, a structure employing optical illusions and a slanted floor. | 1000 Prospect St. | 512/392–3760 | $14 | June–Aug., daily 8–8; Sept.–Oct., daily 9–6; Nov.–Feb., weekdays 9–5, weekends 9–6; March–May, weekdays 9–6, weekends 9–6.

## ON THE CALENDAR

**APR.–MAY:** *Viva! Cinco de Mayo.* Cook-off, parade, arts and crafts, food, music. | 512/396–2495 or 888/200–5620.

**MAY:** *Tours of Distinction.* Guided home tours of several of the city's historic structures. | 512/353–1258 or 512/396–2495 or 888/200–5620.

**AUG.:** *Salado Art Show.* Large art show in Pace Park on the banks of the Salado River; kids' art area. | 254/947–5040.

**SEPT.:** *Republic of Texas Chilympiad.* More than 600 chili chefs compete in cook-off at Hays County Civic Center where there are also live music, Miss Chilympiad contest, and sports tournaments. | 512/396–5400.

## Dining

**Café on the Square and Brew Pub.** Tex-Mex. Café and pub located in an historic building with a pressed-tin ceiling and southwestern artwork. Known for migas, enchiladas, fajitas, venison, and buffalo burgers. | 126 N. LBJ St. | 512/396–9999 | $6–$13 | AE, D, MC, V.

**Centerpoint Station.** American. This family restaurant is filled with antique memorabilia featuring everything from jewelry and clothes to furniture, toys and candles. Known for burgers, tacos, enchiladas and shakes. | 3946 I-35 Exit 200 | 512/392–1103 | $2–$7 | AE, D, MC, V.

**Gordo's Grill.** American. Housed in a former movie theater, the stage is still used for live entertainment. Known for burgers, chili, sandwiches, and steak. | 120 E. San Antonio St. | 512/396–1874 | $7–$19 | AE, D, DC, MC, V.

**Joe's Crab Shack.** Cajun/Creole. There is a festive atmosphere with great music and dancing. Enjoy the crab claws, fried shrimp and the gumbo along with the nautical theme. | 100 Sessums Dr. | 512/396–5255 | $9–$24 | AE, D, DC, MC, V.

**Outback Steakhouse.** Steak. This chain restaurant has a fun atmosphere aimed at giving diners excellent steaks served in a relaxed atmosphere. Specialties of the house include the 14-oz Rockhampton Rib-Eye and a 14-oz New York Strip. Try the 20-oz porterhouse. Kids' menu. | 4205 I-35S | 512/353–2500 | No lunch | $18–$32 | AE, D, DC, MC, V.

## Lodging

**Best Western.** This property was built in the late 1990s and the contemporary feeling reflects this. There is an interesting combination of things to do near this hotel: Shop for bargains at the Outlet Mall or take a tour of the caves in nearby Wonderworld. Complimentary Continental breakfast, in-room data ports, some refrigerators, microwaves, cable TV, pool, wading pool, laundry facilities, business services, some pets allowed. | 917 I-35N | 512/754–7557 | fax 512/754–7557 | www.bestwestern.com | 51 rooms | $59–$89 | AE, D, DC, MC, V.

**Blair House.** A country-style inn with art-filled rooms, fine linen, fresh flowers, and complimentary chocolates. Complimentary breakfast, many in-room hot tubs, cable TV in some rooms, no room phones, business services, no kids under 11, no smoking. | 100 Spoke Hill Rd., Wimberly | 512/847–8828 | fax 512/847–8820 | www.blairhouseinn.com | 7 rooms (3 with shower only) | $135–$165 | AE, D, MC, V.

**Comfort Inn.** This hotel, built in 1996, is near many area restaurants, including a San Marcos favorite, Joe's Crab Shack. In the early evening, join the other guests for a complimentary happy hour in the lobby. Complimentary Continental breakfast, cable TV, pool, outdoor hot tub, no pets. | 1611 I-35N | 512/396–5665 | fax 512/396–5692 | 54 rooms | $50–$100 | AE, D, DC, MC, V.

**Crystal River Inn.** The main house is an old 1889 historic Victorian mansion. This inn is one of the 12 best in Texas and has a beautiful rose garden complex. It is close to Canon Lake, San Marcos and only 5 minutes to Aquarena Springs, Austin and San Antonio. Full complimentary breakfast, some TVs and room phones, business services, kids allowed with prior arrangement. | 326 W. Hopkins St. | 512/396–3739 | fax 512/353–3248 | www.crystalriverinn.com | 12 rooms in 3 buildings, 4 suites | $80–$130 | AE, D, DC, MC, V.

**Econo Lodge Marcos.** If you are visiting Southwest Texas State University, this Econo Lodge will put you within a mile of campus. It's also 2 miles north of the San Marcos outlet malls. Complimentary Continental breakfast, some microwaves, some refrigerators, cable TV, pool, no pets. | 811 S. Guadalupe St. | 512/353–5300 | fax 512/353–8010 | 55 rooms | $80 | AE, D, DC, MC, V.

**Holiday Inn Express.** A good choice for shopaholics, this hotel is 3 miles north of the San Marcos outlet malls. Three restaurants are within walking distance of the hotel. Complimentary Continental breakfast, cable TV, pool, outdoor hot tub, gym, laundry facilities, no pets. | 108 I-35N | 512/754–6621 | fax 512/754–6946 | www.stonebridgehotels.com | 105 rooms | $109 | AE, D, DC, MC, V.

**Howard Johnson.** This two-story motel is on the expressway and close to all area attractions. Complimentary Continental breakfast, in-room data ports, cable TV, pool, business services, pets allowed. | 1635 Aquarena Springs Dr. | 512/353–8011 | fax 512/396–8062 | 100 rooms | $39–$90 | AE, D, DC, MC, V.

**Inn Above Onion Creek.** Set on 500 acres, this luxurious country inn has sitting areas, fireplaces, and a porch or balcony in every room. Many in-room hot tubs, in-room data ports, refrigerators, cable TV, in-room VCRs (and movies), pool, business services, no kids under 12, no smoking. | 4444 Rte. 150W, Kyle | 512/268–1617 or 800/579–7686 | fax 512/268–1090 | www.innaboveonioncreek.com | 9 rooms | $150–$275 | AE, MC, V.

**La Quinta.** Near this La Quinta there are movie theaters, outlet malls, and the famous glass-bottom boat at the Aqua-Marina. It is also very close to the Wonder World Cave and South West Texas State University. Complimentary Continental breakfast, in-room data ports, some refrigerators, cable TV, pool, some pets allowed. | 1619 I–35N | 512/392–8800 | fax 512/392–0324 | www.laquinta.com | 117 rooms | $79–$89 | AE, D, DC, MC, V.

# SEGUIN

MAP 8, H6

*(Nearby town also listed: San Marcos)*

Seguin was the home of a 19th-century chemist who held several of the first patents on the production of concrete. His invention was used to construct about 90 area buildings, many still seen downtown. While you're downtown, don't miss the "World's Largest Pecan," a statue located on the courthouse lawn at Court Street and a fun place for a photo.

Seguin's history is becoming well known due to a recent bestseller—*True Women* by Janice Woods Windle—that was filmed as a miniseries. Travelers interested in learning more about the sites mentioned in *True Women* can take guided tours offered by the Seguin Chamber of Commerce

Information: **Seguin-Guadalupe County Chamber of Commerce** | 427 N. Austin St., 78155 | 830/379–6382 or 800/580–7322 | segcvb@connecti.com | www.seguin.net/corp/segcvb/.

## Attractions

**Los Nogales Museum.** This small museum is housed in an adobe building constructed in 1849 by some of the area's earliest settlers. Next door, peek in the windows of the Doll House, a child-size Victorian gingerbread home built by local cabinetmaker Louis Dietz in 1909. Today the home is filled with children's toys and dolls. | E. Live Oak and S. River Sts. | Free | By appointment only.

**Sebastopol State Historic Site.** One of the best examples of the early use of concrete in the Southwest. Sebastopol, once a private home, was constructed of concrete with a plaster overlay. Today it is open for tours and contains exhibits illustrating the construction of this historic building and its 1988 restoration. | 704 Zorn St. | 830/379–4833 | www.tpwd.state.tx.us | $2 | Fri.–Sun. 9–4.

***True Women* Tour.** Just as readers of Gone with the Wind might go looking for Scarlett's home, fans of *True Women* come to Seguin looking for a peek back into the past. The book chronicles the story of author Janice Woods Windle's ancestors in Seguin. Led by local docents, the tours take a look at sites that play an important role in the historical novel: the live oak-shaded King Cemetery, the old First Methodist Church where two *True Women* characters were married, and the river bottom where horses were daringly rescued in the tale. | 427 N. Austin St. | 830/379–6382 | Free for self-guided tours | Daily for self-guided tours; guided tours by appointment.

**MAR.:** *Noche Gala Mariachi Competition.* Mariachi groups from South Texas compete at Texas Lutheran University during this annual event. | 800/580–7322.
**APR.:** *Texas Ladies' State Chili Cookoff.* Devoted to chili, this festival includes cook-offs, tastings, and entertainment. | 800/580–7322.
**JULY:** *Freedom Fiesta/July Fourth Parade.* One of Texas's oldest celebrations of Independence Day; food booths, parade, kids' rides, games, street dance. | 830/379–6382.
**OCT.:** *Guadalupe County Fair and PRCA Rodeo.* This livestock and agriculture fair on the County Fairgrounds includes live music and a carnival. | 830/379–6477.

## Dining

**Soilita's.** Mexican. The Solita Rita, a sweet, potent drink served in a fishbowl, is the standard accompaniment to the sophisticated Mexican food served in this rustic restaurant, decorated in a Spanish style. Try the Camarones al Moja de Ajo, butterfly shrimp sautéed in garlic, olive oil, and white wine, and for dessert, the Fried Ice Cream: deep-fried vanilla ice cream with a roasted coconut crust on a plate of caramel. | 1540 N. U.S. 46 | 830/401–0195 | Closed Tues. | $6–$15 | AE, D, DC, MC, V.

## Lodging

**Best Western.** A mile and a half west of the fairgrounds and less than a mile from downtown, this hotel puts you in striking distance of all of Seguin's attractions. Two restaurants are on the same lot as the hotel. Complimentary Continental breakfast, cable TV, pool, pets allowed (fee). | 1603 I–10, Highway 46 | 830/379–9631 | fax 830/379–9631 | 80 rooms | $90–$130 | AE, D, DC, MC, V.

**Holiday Inn.** This recently updated hotel is near city hall and the Heritage Museum with exhibits explaining the history of the region. It is close to San Antonio. Restaurant, bar, cable TV, pool, hot tub, exercise equipment, laundry facilities, business services. | 2950 N. 123 Bypass | 830/372–0860 | fax 830/372–3028 | www.holidayinn.com | 139 rooms | $65–$96 | AE, D, DC, MC, V.

# SHAMROCK

MAP 8, L8

*(Nearby towns also listed: Childress, Pampa)*

This Panhandle community was founded by an Irishman and today remembers that heritage with an annual St. Patrick's Day celebration. The town is also home to oil and natural gas wells.

**Information:** **Shamrock Chamber of Commerce** | 207 N. Main St., Shamrock, TX 79079 | 806/256–2501.

## Attractions

**Blarney Stone.** Another reminder of its Irish roots, the city is home to a piece of the Blarney Stone. | Elmore Park | No phone | Free | Daily.

**Pioneer West Museum.** Local history exhibits and artifacts of the Plains Indians are on hand here. The museum is housed in a former hotel. | 204 N. Madden St. | 806/256–3941 | Free | Weekdays, 10–noon, 1–4, weekends by appointment.

**MAR.:** *St. Patrick's Day Celebration.* Food, games in celebration of St. Patrick's Day. | 806/256–2501.
**OCT.:** *Crafts Festival.* For two days in October, the local community center is transformed into a crafts market, with booths of varied arts and crafts for sale to the public.

SHAMROCK

INTRO
ATTRACTIONS
DINING
LODGING

Woodworking, quilts, and Christmas ornaments abound; the emphasis is on south-western design. Facepainters keep the kids entertained. | 806/256–2501.

## Dining

**Irish Inn Restaurant.** Contemporary. This restaurant has great home cooking. It seats approximately 80 and has a conference room area for meetings of 25–30. Salad bar. Kids' menu. | 303 I–40E/Frontage Rd. | 806/256–2332 | Open 24 hrs | $13–$22 | AE, D, DC, MC, V.

**Mitchell's Family Restaurant.** American. This old-fashioned restaurant specializes in down-home cooking, with such favorites as chicken-fried steak and freshly made coconut pie. The Sunday buffet will be sure to fill you up. For seniors, small-portion meals are available at $5 a plate. | I–40 and U.S. 83 | 806/256–3424 | $3–$11 | AE, D, DC, MC, V.

## Lodging

**Best Western Irish Inn.** The name of this two-story motel honors the heritage of the post-master who founded Shamrock. There is shopping within walking distance. Restaurant, in-room data ports, cable TV, in-room VCRs (and movies), pool, hot tub, laundry facilities, business services, pets allowed. | 301 I–40E | 806/256–2106 | fax 806/256–2106 | www.best-western.com | 157 rooms | $54–$59 | AE, D, DC, MC, V.

**Econo Lodge.** One mile east of town, this motel is on historic Route 66, 2 blocks off of I–40. You can get hearty biscuits and gravy with your complimentary breakfast and free admission at a local golf course. Complimentary Continental breakfast, cable TV, pool, pets allowed (fee). | 1006 E. 12th St. | 806/256–2111 | fax 806/256–2302 | 72 rooms | $35–$80 | AE, D, DC, MC, V.

**Western Motel.** This family run motel is right off Rte. 66. The rooms are comfortably and traditionally furnished and the price is right. Restaurant, cable TV, pool, pets allowed. | 104 E. 12th St. | 806/256–3244 | fax 806/256–3244, ext. 128 | 24 rooms | $34–$38 | AE, D, DC, MC, V.

# SHERMAN

MAP 8, I2

*(Nearby towns also listed: Bonham, Denison, Gainesville)*

This community is named for Texas Republic officer Gen. Sidney Sherman who first said "Remember the Alamo!" Sherman is home to Austin College as well as many business headquarters.

Information: **Sherman Chamber of Commerce** | 307 West Washington, Suite 100, Sherman, TX 75090 | 903/893–1184 | shermanchamber@texoma.net | www.sherman-texas.com.

## Attractions

**Grayson County Frontier Village.** A complex of 19th-century houses were restored and arranged to demonstrate an early Grayson County community. In the log-cabin museum, artifacts and pictures are displayed that further illustrate the county's history. | U.S. 75 at Loy Lake Park (exit 67) | 903/463–2487 | $1 | Apr.–Sept., Wed.–Sun. 1–4. Closed Mon.–Tues.

**Hagerman National Wildlife Refuge.** This waterfowl refuge on Lake Texoma is a favorite with birders who come to identify some of the 300 species that have been spotted here. Self-guided driving tours are available. There's also a visitors center with interpretive displays and bird lists. | 6465 Refuge Rd. | 903/786–2826 | Free | Daily.

**Lake Texoma.** Offering miles of shoreline with numerous parks, this reservoir covers part of Texas and Oklahoma. There is camping, picnic sites, boating, marinas, fishing. | U.S. 75A | Free | Daily.

**Red River Historical Museum.** Local history exhibits are housed in the former Carnegie Library (1914). The building includes historic WPA murals. | 301 S. Walnut | 903/893–7623 | $2 | Tues.–Fri. 10–4:30, Sat. 2–5.

ON THE CALENDAR
**MAR.–APR.: *Texoma Junior Livestock Exposition.*** This livestock show held at Loy Lake Park features the work of local students. | 903/893–1184.
**APR.: *Sherman Preservation League Tour of Homes.*** Guided tours of historic homes in the city. | 903/893–1184.
**DEC.: *Jaycees Christmas Parade.*** Parade, marching bands and Santa Claus go through downtown. | 903/892–8576.

## Dining
**Steak Kountry.** Steak. The rib-eye steak, served with a baked potato and Texas toast, is a particular favorite at this low-key, family restaurant, but if you long for something green, the large salad bar will satisfy your craving. The dessert specialties are scrumptious bread pudding and crunchy fried apple sticks. | 1940 Grand Ave. | 903/892–1700 | $5–$13 | AE, D, DC, MC, V.

## Lodging
**Grayson House Hotel.** Lake Texoma is 17 mi from this two-story hotel, and Eisenhower's birthplace is less than 10 mi away. Restaurant, in-room data ports, cable TV, pool, hot tub, business services, airport shuttle. | 2105 Texoma Pkwy. | 903/892–2161 or 800/723–4194 | fax 903/893–3045 | www.bestwestern.com | 146 rooms | $33–$79 | AE, D, DC, MC, V.

**Holiday Inn.** The hotel is built as a square with its sides surrounding an indoor pool. It is 10 minutes from downtown and close to a Red Lobster, a steakhouse, and other restaurants. Restaurant, in-room data ports, some refrigerators, room service, cable TV, pool, wading pool, hot tub, laundry facilities, parking (fee). | 3605 Rte. 75 | 903/868–0555 | fax 903/892–9396 | hisher£trmangement.com | 142 rooms | $79–$99 | AE, D, DC, MC, V.

**La Quinta Inn and Suites.** This hotel is 2 mi north of downtown Sherman and steps away from many familiar chain restaurants. Each room features an entertainment system with pay-per-view movies and pay-per-play Nintendo games. Complimentary Continental breakfast, in-room data ports, some microwaves, some refrigerators, cable TV, pool, outdoor hot tub, gym, laundry facilities, laundry service, pets allowed. | 2912 U.S. 75N | 903/870–1122 | fax 903/870–1132 | 115 rooms | $69–$79 | AE, D, DC, MC, V.

# SMITHVILLE

MAP 8, I5

*(Nearby towns also listed: Bastrop, La Grange)*

Smithville was once a riverboat ferry stop on the Colorado River. In the 1880s, the railroad replaced the ferries as the main mode of transportation, and tracks were laid across town. Today the railroad still plays an important part in Smithville's economy.

Information: **Smithville Chamber of Commerce** | Box 716, Smithville, TX 78957 | 512/237–2313 | smithcoc@totalaccess.net | www.smithvilletx.org.

## Attractions
**Buescher State Park.** This park is 2 mi northwest of Smithville and connects with Bastrop State Park. It has piney woods and live oak stands. Camping, picnic sites, fishing, and a hiking area are available. | Hwy. 71 to FM 153 to Park Road 1 | 512/237–2241 | www.tpwd.state.tx.us | $2.

**Railroad Historical Park and Museum.** This park and playground include several historic cabooses and a museum with exhibits on the city's railroad history. Picnic sites available. The museum is adjacent to the Chamber of Commerce office. | 102 W. First St. | 512/237–2313 | Free for park | Park daily; museum weekdays 8–5.

**The Smithville Heritage Museum** This museum in a turn-of-the-20th-century, two-story house is devoted to preserving the history of Smithville. The town archives are kept here, and the museum periodically mounts exhibits pertaining to an aspect of Smithville's past. A recent exhibit highlighted the Smithville residents, both men and women, who served in the second World War. Leave a message to arrange for an appointment and a volunteer will get back to you. | 602 Main St. | 512/237–4545 | Free | Tues. 9:30–noon and 1–4, or by appointment.

### ON THE CALENDAR
**APR.: *Jamboree*.** A four-day festival of parades, picnics, music, farm animal shows, antique and vintage automobile shows, and a variety of other exhibitions is hosted by the Vernon Richards Riverbend Park on the Thursday after Easter. | 512/237–2313.

## Dining
**Caboose Cafe.** American. A country-style café, with a train motif reminding diners of Smithville's rich railroad heritage, serves breakfast, lunch, and dinner all week. Locals come for the fried catfish, chicken-fried steak and the homemade blackberry cobbler. | 1307 Loop 230 | 512/237–2222 | Breakfast also available | $2–$12 | No credit cards.

## Lodging
**Pine Point Inn.** This small motel, built in 1998, is on the highway 2 mi from Smithville and 2 blocks from the hospital. Complimentary Continental breakfast, cable TV, pool, outdoor hot tub, pets allowed (fee). | 1503 Dorothy Nichols Lane (U.S. 71) | 512/360–5576 | fax 512/360–5576 | 34 rooms | $55–$65 | AE, D, MC, V.

# SNYDER

MAP 8, F3

*(Nearby towns also listed: Big Spring, Sweetwater)*

This community began as a trading post and remained a quiet prairie community until the discovery of oil in the 1950s. Today the city is the home of the largest oil field in the world to be run by a single operator. Snyder is also the home of the Western Texas College.

Information: **Snyder Chamber of Commerce** | 2302 Ave. R, Snyder, TX 79550 | 915/573–3558 | snychcom@snydertex.com | www.snydertex.com/chamber/.

## Attractions
**Lake J. B. Thomas.** Watersports, swimming, camping, boating, and fishing are all available at Lake J. B. Thomas. | 6200 College Ave. | Free | Daily.

**Scurry County Museum.** The local history exhibits at this museum include a chuck wagon and pioneer artifacts. | Off Rte. 350 on Western Texas College campus | 915/573–6107 | Free | Weekdays 10–4.

**White Buffalo Park.** In 1876, when J. Wright Moore killed one of the rare white buffalo in this area, he received so much attention from the press that he gained the means to start his own ranch. Now a fiberglass replica of the luckless beast marks the event and a sign provides the details of the hunt. After the requisite photo-op with the buffalo, picnic here among the mesquite trees. | North on 180, follow signs to the park | 915/573–3558 | Free | Daily.

**JUNE:** *Western Swing Festival.* For a long weekend in June, the over-50 RV crowd descends on Snyder to dance Western swing–style at the Scurry County Coliseum. Bands play from 11 AM to 11 PM. Arts and crafts booths provide diversions from the music, and food vendors keep your energy up. | 900 E. Coliseum Dr. | 915/573–3558.

**SEPT.:** *Scurry County Fair.* Arts and crafts, kids' activities, games, livestock show, live music, exhibits. | 915/573–3558 or 915/574–8585.

## Dining

**Shack.** Steak. This is a casual family-style restaurant charmingly decorated with a large collection of license plates from every state. Especially known for their steak; Mexican food, seafood, hamburgers and sandwiches are also served. Salad bar. | 1005 25th St. | 915/573–4921 | No supper Sun. | $7–$15 | AE, D, DC, MC, V.

**Spanish Inn.** Mexican. Festive flowerpots and mirrors from south of the border brighten up this comfortable restaurant. It's most popular dishes are Papachon's Deluxe and the Spanish Inn Spread (platters with a variety of Mexican favorites, such as tacos, chalupas, and enchiladas). If you haven't had enough Texas steaks, however, the restaurant also offers tasty T-Bones and, of course, chicken-fried steak. | 2212 College Ave. | 915/573–2355 | Closed Mon. | $5–$10 | AE, MC, V.

## Lodging

**Beacon Lodge and RV Campground.** A complete renovation in 1999 restored the Beacon to its original 1950s state, without sacrificing modern innovations. Old Coca-Cola memorabilia adorns the lobby and Elvis posters dress up some bedrooms. The hotel, on 6 acres of land, has grills available for all guests. Picnic area, complimentary Continental breakfast, some microwaves, some refrigerators, cable TV, laundry facilities, pets allowed. | 1900 E. U.S. 180 | 915/573–8526 | fax 915/573–4731 | 36 rooms | $38–$52 | AE, MC, V.

**Purple Sage.** A purple sage bush is just outside the front door of this family-owned friendly inn. Furnished in a traditional style, it is within walking distance of Snyder Coliseum, and Western Texas College is 5 mi away. Picnic area, complimentary Continental breakfast, refrigerators, cable TV, pool, playground, business services, pets allowed. | 1501 E. Coliseum Dr. | 915/573–5491 or 800/545–5792 | fax 915/573–9027 | 45 rooms | $34–$53 | AE, D, DC, MC, V.

# SONORA

MAP 8, F5

*(Nearby towns also listed: Ozona, San Angelo)*

This wool and mohair center is best known by travelers because of its convenient location on I–10, an easy stop on the drive to or from El Paso. Sonora is home to the most formation-rich caverns in the state.

**Information:** **Sonora Chamber of Commerce** | Box 1172, Sonora, TX 76950 | 915/387–2880 | soncoc@sonoratx.net.

## Attractions

**Caverns of Sonora.** Often cited as the most beautiful caverns in Texas, these caves feature a large variety of formations. Guided tours are available. | FM 1989 Carvens of Sonora Rd., Sonora, TX. 76950 | 915/387–3105 | $9–$17 for tours | Daily 8–6.

**Historic Walking Tour.** Pick up a brochure and map at the chamber of commerce for this self-guided walking tour which will lead you to historic homes, the former jailhouse, and the Old Santa Fe Depot. | 707 N. Crockett St. | 915/387–2248 | Free | Daily.

SONORA

INTRO
ATTRACTIONS
DINING
LODGING

**AUG.:** *Sutton County Days and Outlaw Pro Rodeo.* This event includes a parade, a rodeo, and live entertainment. | 915/387–2880.

**NOV.:** *Sutton County Game Dinner.* Every second Sunday in November, the Sutton County Game Association hosts a dinner at the Civic Center for some 1,500 hungry hunters and game fans. You can choose your meal among local white-tail deer, wild turkey, and wild boar. Call the chamber of commerce for details. | 915/387–3880.

## Dining

**La Mexicana Restaurant.** Mexican. Flour tortillas are made fresh daily at this colorful restaurant, and the meat is carefully char-grilled. For dessert, the flan and the ice cream sundaes win kudos, but it's the creamy Trés Léches Cake that will keep you coming back for more. | 308A U.S. 277N | 915/387–3401 | Breakfast also available | $4–$15 | AE, D, DC, MC, V.

## Lodging

**Best Western Sonora Inn.** This hotel welcomed its first guests in May 2000 and is in pristine condition. It is within walking distance of several restaurants and less than a mile from the center of town. Complimentary Continental breakfast, some refrigerators, some microwaves, cable TV, pool, laundry facilities, pets allowed (fee). | 270 U.S. 277N | 915/387–9111 | 48 rooms | $56–$73 | AE, D, DC, MC, V.

**Days Inn Devil's River.** Sonora Caverns are 15 mi from this two-story motel. Restaurant, cable TV, pool, laundry facilities, business services, some pets allowed (fee). | 1312 N. Service Rd. | 915/387–3516 | fax 915/387–2854 | 99 rooms | $39–$58 | AE, D, DC, MC, V.

# SOUTH PADRE ISLAND

MAP 8, I9

*(Nearby towns also listed: Brownsville, Harlingen, McAllen, Mission, Padre Island, Port Isabel)*

All too often, this southern island is mistaken for her sister, Padre Island. Originally, the two were one single island. In 1964 South Padre Island became a separate entity with the completion of the Port Mansfield Gulf Channel. Today South Padre is the capital of tourism in this tropical tip of Texas.

South Padre stretches for 34 mi, hugging the Texas coastline as a protective barrier against Gulf storms. At its widest point, the island is only a half mile across, providing every one of the 5,000 hotel rooms with an unbeatable view. Miles of toasted sand invite travelers to enjoy horseback riding, sailboarding, surfing, sandcastle building, or just wave hopping in the surf.

Fishing is also a popular activity, in both bay and Gulf waters. Sailboarding and surfing keep restless travelers occupied at a site called "the Flats" on the north side of town.

South Padre Island is also a gateway to two other popular South Texas sights. A short drive from the island, Laguna Atascosa National Wildlife Refuge is a must-see for birders. The refuge has recorded more species than any other wildlife refuge in the nation. South of the island, shopping in Matamoros, Mexico, 25 minutes from the island, is a popular day trip for many travelers.

**Information: South Padre Island Convention and Visitors Bureau** | 600 Padre Blvd., South Padre Island, TX 78597 | 956/761–6433 or 800/SO–PADRE | info@sopadre.com | www.sopadre.com.

## Attractions

**Sea Turtle, Inc.** This is the home of the "Turtle Lady," Ila Loetscher. Her conservation efforts focused the attention of the world on Kemp's Ridley sea turtles. Today volunteers run shows on Tuesday and Saturday at 10 AM. | 5805 Gulf Blvd. | 956/761–2544 | $2 | Tues. and Sat., 10 AM.

**University of Texas Pan American Coastal Studies Laboratory.** Just south of town, the University of Texas Coastal Studies Laboratory offers another chance to learn more about Gulf marine life. Here research focuses on coastal ecosystems, including a study of the sea turtles and dolphins that live in the area. You can stop by the lab Sunday through Friday for a look at aquariums filled with marine life. | Isla Blanca Park at south end of island | 956/761–2644 | Free | Sun.–Fri. 1:30–4:30.

### ON THE CALENDAR

**MAR.: *Spring Break.*** Month-long celebration with students from around the country and Canada. Concerts, athletic events, parties. | 956/761–6433 or 800/SO–PADRE.
**MAY: *South Padre Island Windsurfing Blowout.*** This windsurfing tournament features competitors from around the country. | 956/761–6433 or 800/SO–PADRE.
**JULY: *Bob Marley Festival.*** Reggae performances, dances, poetry readings, arts and crafts, and traditional Caribbean and African foods can be found on the Convention Center lawn. | 713/688–3900 or 956/761–6433.
**SEPT.: *Fireworks Over the Bay.*** Fireworks can be seen on the bay side of the island. 956/761–6433

## Dining

**Amberjacks.** Seafood. This colorful low-key restaurant is known for its tropical Caribbean flavor and fanciful fish decorations. Try the rasta shrimp, snapper Rockefeller and sautéed Amberjack. Entertainment weekends. Kids' menu. | 209 W. Amberjack St. | 956/761–6500 | Closed Mon. | $19–$28 | AE, D, DC, MC, V.

**Blackbeard's.** Seafood. A 12-ft alligator and other large fish mounted on the walls add to the nautical theme at this casual family restaurant with two levels of seating. Try the fried shrimp plate or the flounder sandwich with onion rings amidst photographs of fish from the fifties. | 103 E. Saturn St. | 956/761–2962 | $16–$23 | AE, D, DC, MC, V.

**Great Wall.** Chinese. Try General Tso's chicken or chin pi beef. Salad bar. Kids' menu. Beer and wine only. | 5800 Padre Blvd. | 956/761–9378 | $13–$19 | MC, V.

**Grill Room.** Continental. Elegant white tablecloths set the tone for this rather old-fashioned restaurant with beautiful landscapes on the walls. Try the filet mignon, lump crab

TX

SOUTH PADRE
ISLAND

INTRO
ATTRACTIONS
DINING
LODGING

## KODAK'S TIPS FOR USING LIGHTING

**Daylight**
· Use the changing color of daylight to establish mood
· Use light direction to enhance subjects' properties
· Match light quality to specific subjects

**Dramatic Lighting**
· Anticipate dramatic lighting events
· Explore before and after storms

**Sunrise, Sunset, and Afterglow**
· Include a simple foreground
· Exclude the sun when setting your exposure
· After sunset, wait for the afterglow to color the sky

From *Kodak Guide to Shooting Great Travel Pictures* © 2000 by Fodor's Travel Publications

St. Charles, baked shrimp Buba, or the red snapper. | 708 Padre Blvd. | 956/761–9331 | Closed Mon. and 2 weeks in Dec. No lunch | $13–$27 | AE, DC, MC, V.

**Jesse's.** Tex-Mex. This restaurant celebrates the great outdoors with its deer and fish ornaments. The fajitas, enchiladas and combination plates are the draw here. | 2700 Padre Blvd. | 956/761–4500 | $6–$15 | AE, D, DC, MC, V.

**La Jaiba Oyster Bar.** Seafood. Antiques, pictures, seashells and fish are on display at this one family-owned restaurant in the downtown tourist area. Kids' menu. | 2001 Padre Blvd. | 956/761–9878 | Closed Mon. | $5–$20 | AE, D, MC, V.

**Lantern Grill.** Contemporary. This upscale restaurant takes its name from the gas lanterns that adorn the entrance way. The chef pairs seafood and meat with inventive sauces, and gives each dish a little southwestern kick. The grilled beef tenderloin comes with potato flautas and a portobello mushroom glaze; the sautéed red snapper is served with saffron rice and a shrimp-Chardonnay sauce. | 3109 Padre Blvd. | 956/761–4460 | fax 956/761–4460 | Closed Mon. No lunch | $15–$26 | AE, D, DC, MC, V.

**Scampi's.** Seafood. This casual, family-friendly restaurant on the waterfront is one of South Padre's busiest; expect crowds on peak nights. Homemade pasta. Open-air dining overlooking the bay. | 206 W. Aries St. | 956/761–1755 | Closed Dec. 12–25. No lunch | $19–$23 | AE, D, MC, V.

## Lodging

**Bahia Mar.** The Bahia Mar is in a subtropical area where guestrooms overlook the gulf or the Laguna Madre Bay. Restaurant, bar, picnic area, cable TV, pool, hot tub, beach. | 6300 Padre Blvd. | 956/761–1343 or 800/997–2373 | fax 956/761–6287 | www.bahiamar.com | 236 rooms; 26 cottages | $85–$145, $270–$310 | AE, DC, MC, V.

**Best Western Fiesta Isles.** A horseshoe-shape hotel on a channel of Laguna Madre Bay. There is a kite shop, T-shirt vendor, and other tourist shopping opportunities nearby. Many kitchenettes, cable TV, pool, hot tub, pets allowed. | 5701 Padre Blvd. | 956/761–4913 | fax 956/761–2719 | www.bestwestern.com | 58 rooms | $69–$79 | AE, D, DC, MC, V.

**Days Inn.** This chain hotel offers an inexpensive way to be close to the gulf beach area, bars, and restaurants. Refrigerators, cable TV, pool, hot tub, laundry facilities, pets allowed (fee). | 3913 Padre Blvd. | 956/761–7831 | fax 956/761–2033 | 57 rooms | $55–$75 | AE, D, DC, MC, V.

**Holiday Inn Sun Spree.** This Holiday Inn is an ideal home base for a family who wants access to the beach and bay, or to sun themselves around the pool. Restaurant, bar, in-room data ports, room service, cable TV, 2 pools, wading pool, hot tub, exercise equipment, children's programs, playground, laundry facilities, business services, free parking. | 100 Padre Blvd. | 956/761–5401 or 800/531–7405 (outside TX), 800/292–7506 (TX) | fax 956/761–1560 | www.holidayinn.com | 227 rooms | $119–$129 | AE, D, DC, MC, V.

**Howard Johnson's.** Opened in 2000, this sparkling hotel is half a block from the beach in both directions. Bayside rooms on upper floors have a view of the water, and, from certain balconies, you can see South Padre Island's weekly fireworks display. Start the night out with a cocktail at the pool-side lounge where you can also enjoy live music on weekends. Bar, complimentary Continental breakfast, microwaves, refrigerators, cable TV, pool, outdoor hot tub, gym, laundry facilities, pets allowed (fee). | 1709 Padre Blvd. | 956/761–5658 | fax 956/761–5520 | 89 rooms | $99–$156 | AE, D, DC, MC, V.

**Radisson.** This tropical paradise has 10-acres of beach front property with water sports on the premises. It's 2 minutes from golf, horseback riding as well as close to Mexico for shopping. Bar (with entertainment), snack bar, refrigerators (in condos), room service, cable TV, 2 pools, hot tubs, beach, boating, fishing, bicycles, children's programs, business services. | 500 Padre Blvd. | 956/761–6511 | fax 956/761–1602 | www.radissonspi.com | 182 rooms, 54 apartments | $155–$285, $195–$235 | AE, D, DC, MC, V.

**Ramada Limited.** This bright hotel, opened in 1997, is just a block from the beach. Complimentary Continental breakfast, microwaves, refrigerators, cable TV, pool, outdoor hot tub, laundry facilities, no pets. | 4109 Padre Blvd. | 956/761–4097 | fax 956/761–4097 | 48 rooms | $95–135 | AE, D, DC, MC, V.

**Sheraton Fiesta.** This hotel is 30 minutes from Mexico and has wonderful views of the Gulf. The convention center is 4 mi away. Restaurants, bar (with entertainment), in-room data ports, some kitchenettes, refrigerators, cable TV, pool, wading pool, hot tub, tennis, exercise equipment, beach, laundry facilities, business services. | 310 Padre Blvd. | 956/761–6551 | fax 956/761–6570 | www.sheraton.com | 248 rooms | $99–$260 | AE, D, DC, MC, V.

**Super 8.** The beach is 2 blocks away from this Super 8, and Blackbeard's restaurant is directly across the street. Be sure to request a room with a view of the bay. Complimentary Continental breakfast, refrigerators, microwaves, cable TV, pool, outdoor hot tub, gym, laundry facilities, no pets. | 4205 Padre Blvd. | 956/761–6300 | fax 956/761–6300 | 65 rooms | $79–$200 | AE, D, DC, MC, V.

# STEPHENVILLE

MAP 8, H3

STEPHENVILLE

INTRO
ATTRACTIONS
DINING
LODGING

*(Nearby towns also listed: Comanche, Dublin, Glen Rose, Granbury, Hico)*

This North Texas community was started by the Stephens brothers in the mid-1800s. Today the area is an agricultural center with a large dairy business. The town is a good stop on the way to Fort Worth or to Glen Rose. It is also the home of Tarleton State University.

**Information: Stephenville Chamber of Commerce** | 187 W. Washington, Stephenville, TX 76401 | 254/965–5313 | chamber@our-town.com | www.our-town.com/~chamber/.

## Attractions

**Cowboy Capital Walk of Fame.** Bronze plaques line the Stephenville streets to commemorate the accomplishments of particularly proficient cowboys and cowgirls. On the plaques, you'll see listed the names and rodeo championships of each member of the Walk of Fame. New plaques are added each May with a festive induction ceremony, parade, and official luncheon. Contact the Stephenville Chamber of Commerce for more information. | Downtown Plaza | 254/965–2443 | Free | Daily.

**Cross Timbers Country Opry.** Live family entertainment of country music performances with a different show each week just 1 mi east of 281. | On U.S. 377 | 254/965–4132 | www.countryopry.com | $7 | Sat. 7:30 PM–10 PM.

**Dinosaur Valley State Park.** This park, 5 mi west of Glen Rose, showcases several dinosaur tracks in the riverbed of the Paluxy River. | U.S. 67 to Rte. 205 | 254/897–4588 | fax 254/897–3409 | www.tpwd.state.tx.us | $5 | Daily 8 AM–10 PM.

**Historical House Museum Complex.** These 19th-century structures are furnished with period items and artifacts, each an example of homes during the early days of Stephenville. | 525 E. Washington St. | 254/965–5880 | Free | Fri.–Sun. 2–5.

### ON THE CALENDAR

**MAY:** *Cowboy Capital of the World Pro Rodeo.* Bull riding, calf roping, and steer wrestling, are among the events at this annual five-day rodeo, officially sponsored by the Professional Rodeo Cowboys Association. It concludes with the Cowboy Capital Walk of Fame Induction Ceremony. | 254/965–5313 | www.stephenvilleprca.com.

## Dining

**Cotton Patch.** American. Cheerful red tablecloths and lucky horseshoes lend a Western mood to this informal family restaurant, just across the street from the Holiday Inn. Try a good old Texan favorite, the fried catfish, or opt for the decadent KC's Grilled Chicken (a chicken breast loaded with barbecue sauce, bacon and two kinds of cheese). Plenty of vegetarian options are also available. | 2860 W. Washington | 254/965–5255 | $6–$14 | AE, D, DC, MC, V.

**Jose's.** Mexican. Enjoy casual dining accompanied by dim lighting and soft Spanish music. The fajitas, enchiladas and the all-you-can-eat buffet are very popular choices. | 1044 W. Washington St. | 254/965–7400 | $15–$18 | AE, D, MC, V.

**Montana's Restaurant.** American. Settle into a cozy booth at this friendly local hangout for a plate of chicken tenders or chicken-fried steak. Black and white photographs, portraying Stephenville's past, adorn the walls. | 1376 W. Washington | 254/968–5707 | $3–$11 | AE, D, DC, MC, V.

## Lodging

**Best Western Cross Timbers.** This motel is less than a mile west of downtown Stephenville. A 24-hour restaurant serving breakfast, sandwiches, and burgers, is on the same lot, and a 24-hour Walmart is a few blocks away. Complimentary Continental breakfast, microwaves, refrigerators, cable TV, pool, laundry facilities, some pets allowed. | 1625 S. Loop | 254/968–2114 | fax 254/968–2299 | 50 rooms | $53–$69 | AE, D, DC, MC, V.

**Days Inn.** Two restaurants are across the street, and a neighborhood park is 2 blocks away from this motel. In-room data ports, cable TV, pool, business services, some pets allowed (fee). | 701 S. Loop | 254/968–3392 | fax 254/968–3527 | 60 rooms | $45–$75 | AE, D, DC, MC, V.

**Holiday Inn.** A movie theater is across the street and a bowling alley is 4 mi away. Restaurant, in-room data ports, room service, cable TV, pool, business services, pets allowed. | 2865 W. Washington St. | 254/968–5256 | fax 254/968–4255 | www.holidayinn.com | 100 rooms | $64–$69 | AE, D, DC, MC, V.

**Hummingbird.** You can angle for catfish in the man-made pond behind this hotel. Picnic area, complimentary breakfast, some refrigerators, hot tub, no kids allowed, business services. | Rte. 403, Walnut Springs | 254/897–2787 | fax 254/897–3459 | hbird@eace.net | 6 rooms (1 with shower only) | $85–$115 | AE, MC, V.

**Inn of Stephenville.** This motel, built in 1997, is a mile and a half west of Tarleton State University. It is also across the street from the Bosque River Shopping Center. Complimentary Continental breakfast, microwaves, refrigerators, some in-room hot tubs, cable TV, pool, outdoor hot tub, some pets allowed. | 2925 W. Washington | 254/965–7162 | fax 254/965–7913 | 51 rooms | $64 | AE, D, DC, MC, V.

**Texan Motor Inn.** Truck parking is available at the one-story motel. Restaurants are next door and a shopping center is within walking distance. Complimentary Continental breakfast, cable TV, business services, some pets allowed (fee). | 3030 W. Washington St. | 254/968–5003 | fax 817/968–5060 | 30 rooms | $45–$65 | AE, D, MC, V.

# SULPHUR SPRINGS

MAP 8, J2

*(Nearby towns also listed: Greenville, Paris)*

This North Texas town is one of the top dairy producers in the country. The city of about 15,000 residents is the gateway to a state park with two units on Cooper Lake.

Information: **Hopkins County Chamber of Commerce** | 1200 Houston St., Sulphur Springs, TX 75482 | 903/885–6515 | tourss@coyote.com.

## Attractions

**Cooper Lake State Park.** This park offers boating, camping, hiking, a playground, a beach, and picnic facilities. The park also includes two units located on Cooper Lake, both with complete facilities. | 1664 FM 1529S, Cooper | 903/395–3100 or 945–5256 | $2 | Daily.

**Music Box Gallery.** This gallery, within a library, includes an extensive collection of music boxes. | 201 N. Davis St. | 903/885–4926 | Free | Weekdays 9–6, Sat. 9–noon.

**Southwest Dairy Center.** Exhibits on history and processes of the dairy industry are on display in this dairy barn complete with silo. Visitors can also stop at an old-fashioned soda fountain for malts and frozen dairy treats. | 1210 Houston St. | 903/439–MILK | Free | Mon.–Sat. 9–4.

### ON THE CALENDAR

**MAY: Hopkins County Folk Festival.** Travel back in time at this day-long festival celebrating 19th-century arts and crafts. Costumed pioneers re-create the daily life of a frontier village at the Hopkins County Museum and Heritage Park, with candle-dipping, butter-churning, and broom-making demonstrations. You can also observe blacksmiths, soap-makers and corn-grinders at work, or listen to musical entertainment. | 903/885–2387.

**SEPT.: Hopkins County Fall Festival.** This festival at the Hopkins County Regional Civic Center features cook-offs, games, food, and arts and crafts. | 903/985–8071 or 903/885–2811.

**NOV.: UPRA Finals Rodeo.** Rodeo riding, roping, and entertainment round out this event's activities at the Civic Center. | 903/885–8071.

## Dining

**San Remo Italiano Restaurante and Pizzeria.** Italian. With its homemade pastas and pizzas, you'll find this restaurant is a little slice of Italy in the heart of Texas. Try the popular Russian Shrimp (fettucine with jumbo shrimp, sautéed spinach and a vodka sauce) or the Rigatoni Paesano (with broccoli, chicken and shaved Parmesan in white wine and olive oil). The gnocchi and the baked polenta with gorgonzola are also sure to please. Live piano music from September to April. | 1316 S. Broadway | 903/438–1243 | $7–$13 | AE, MC, V.

## Lodging

**Best Western Trail Dust Inn.** The sulphur springs themselves may be all dried up in this town, but the hospitality flows freely at the local Best Western. The personnel on hand encourage you to brush off the trail dust and enjoy their affordable accommodations. Complimentary Continental breakfast, some refrigerators, cable TV, pool, playground, laundry facilities, business services. | 1521 Shannon St. | 903/885–7515 | fax 903/885–7515 | www.best-western.com | 102 rooms | $49–$69 | AE, D, DC, MC, V.

**Comfort Suites Inn.** At this three-story, all-suites hotel, just off of I–30 East, several room configurations are "available." You can have a king-size bed or two queens for your bedroom, and the convertible sofa in your sitting room folds out to sleep additional guests. Two televisions in each suite. Complimentary Continental breakfast, microwaves, refrigerators, cable TV, pool, gym, laundry facilities, some pets allowed. | 1521 Industrial Dr. E | 903/438–0918 | fax 903/438–0329 | 60 suites | $74 | AE, D, DC, MC, V.

**Holiday Inn.** This newly remodeled hotel is just five minutes from Cooper Lake and Lake Fort. The dairy museum is less than 10 minutes away, and the Heritage Center is nearby. Restaurant, bar, in-room data ports, some refrigerators, room service, cable TV, pool, laundry facilities, free parking, some pets allowed. | 1495 E. Industrial Ave. | 903/885–0562 | fax 903/885–0562 | www.holidayinn.com | 98 rooms | $54–$64 | AE, D, DC, MC, V.

# SWEETWATER

MAP 8, F3

*(Nearby towns also listed: Abilene, Snyder)*

Listed in the National Register of Historic Places, this downtown boasts many long-standing buildings. Sweetwater became the training ground for the Women's Airforce Service Pilots (WASPS) in World War II. Today the community is home to Texas State Technical College.

Information: **Sweetwater Chamber of Commerce** | 810 E. Broadway, Sweetwater, TX 79556 | 915/235–5488.

## Attractions

**Pioneer City-County Museum.** Local history exhibits on early pioneers and Native Americans are found at this museum. | 610 E. 3rd St. | 915/235–8547 | Free | Tues.–Sat. 1–5.

**WASP Monument and Walk of Honor.** This monument is dedicated to the Women's Airforce Service Pilots and honors the brave women who flew 60 million miles during World War II, ferrying aircraft for the military. You can read the names of the more than one thousand women on the monument at their former training ground, now Texas State Technical College. | 300 College Dr. | 915/235–5488 | Free | Daily.

### ON THE CALENDAR

**MAR.: *Rattlesnake Roundup.*** This event held at the Nolan County Coliseum includes rattlesnake displays, performances with live rattlesnakes, and food offerings. | 915/235–5488.

**JUNE: *Texas Midwest Soapbox Derby.*** On one Saturday in June, kids in two different age groups careen down Crane Street Hill in homemade soapbox cars (now assembled from kits). The daring winners of the competition qualify to go to the national finals in Akron, Ohio. The Derby takes place just west of Sweetwater High School. | Crane St. Hill | 915/235–5488.

**JULY: *American Junior Rodeo National Finals.*** Rodeo riding, precision riding, roping, entertainment come to the Nolan County Coliseum. | 915/235–5488.

## Dining

**Miss Allen's Family Style Meals.** American. For close to 50 years, Miss Allen's has been serving family-style meals in the same location. Just grab a seat at any table in this beloved Sweetwater institution and load up your plate with crispy fried chicken, squash, beet salad, and okra gumbo. Miss Allen's grandson runs the restaurant now, just as his grandmother once did; he always makes sure there is plenty of peach cobbler to go around. | 1301 E. Broadway | 915/235–2060 | Closed Mon. No dinner | $7 | AE, MC, V.

## Lodging

**Holiday Inn.** Across the expressway from this Holiday Inn you can enjoy steaks and barbecued food at Bucks. Sweetwater Lake is less than 10 mi away. Restaurant, some refrigerators, room service, cable TV, pool, playground, laundry facilities, business services, pets allowed. | 500 N.W. Georgia St. | 915/236–6887 | fax 915/236–6887 | www.holidayinn.com | 110 rooms | $59–$99 | AE, D, DC, MC, V.

**Motel 6.** If you're looking to pull off the highway and get a good night's rest without spending a fortune, look no further. Truck parking available. Cable TV, pool, laundry facilities, pets allowed. | 510 N.W. Georgia St. | 915/235–4387 | fax 915/235–8725 | 79 rooms | $30–$43 | AE, D, DC, MC, V.

**Ramada Inn.** This chain hotel is within easy access of I–20. You'll find hearty American food at the hotel restaurant, and drinks and entertainment at the Sunday House lounge. You are welcome to act out your country-star dreams at the Sunday House's lively weekly karaoke night. Restaurant, bar, room service, cable TV, pool, pets allowed. | 701 S.W. Georgia | 915/235–4853 | fax 915/235–8935 | 131 rooms | $51 | AE, D, DC, MC, V.

# TEMPLE

*(Nearby towns also listed: Killeen, Salado, Waco)*

With 45,000 residents, this city is the medical center for central Texas and an important industrial producer. Temple was established by the Gulf, Colorado and Santa Fe Railroad and named for its chief construction engineer. Railroads still play a big role in the city's economy.

Information: **Temple Convention and Visitors Bureau** | Box 231, Temple, TX 76503 | 254/773–2105. **Visitor Center** | 2 N. Main St. 76501 | 254/770–5720 | www.temple-tx.org.

## Attractions

**Bell County Museum.** Local history is the focus of this museum. It also contains the Miriam A. Ferguson Collection, which features materials regarding the life of Texas's first female governor. | 201 N. Main St., Belton | 254/933–5243 | Free | Tues.–Sat. 1–5.

**Belton Lake.** This lake offers 13 public parks with camping and picnicking. | Off of FM 2271 and FM 2305 | 254/939–1829 | Free | Daily dusk to dawn.

**Czech Heritage Museum.** Czechs played an important role in settling central Texas, and their contribution is remembered in this museum housed in the SPJST (Slovanska Podporujici Jednota Statu Texas, or Slavonic Benevolent Order State of Texas) Insurance Company. The museum contains Czech costumes, a circa AD 1530 Bible, quilts, a handmade dulcimer, and household items. | 520 N. Main St. | 254/773–1575 | Free | Weekdays 8–5.

**Railroad and Pioneer Museum.** The old railroad depot once located in nearby Moody was transported here—boards, floor, and all. It's now a museum and library. | 315 W. Ave. B | 254/298–5172 | fax 254/298–5171 | $4 | Tue.–Sat. 10–4, Sun. noon–4.

**Summer Fun USA.** This waterpark includes a sandy beach, an inner-tube ride, and horseshoe pits. | 1410 Wado Rd., Belton | 254/939–0366 | $13 | Tues.–Sun. 11–7.

### ON THE CALENDAR
**JULY:** *Independence Day Celebration and Belton PRCA Rodeo.* Live entertainment, barrel racing, precision riding, and trick roping take place in nearby Belton. | 817/939–3551.
**DEC.:** *Annual Christmas Parade.* The oldest, lighted Christmas parade in the area, with more than 100 entries each year ranging from floats and fancy cars to marching bands, takes over downtown Temple on every first Mon. in Dec. Prizes are awarded to the top 10 floats and the best visiting high school band. | 254/773–2105.

## Dining
**Las Casas Restaurant and Patio.** Tex-Mex. At this retro-style restaurant, go for the trademark "white wings": chicken breasts stuffed with jalapeño pepper and monterey jack cheese, wrapped in bacon, and char-grilled. For dessert, try the homemade pecan pralines or the superlative fried ice cream—the crust is made of cinnamon, sugar, and rice krispies. The enclosed patio is good for dining in all weather. | 2907 S. General Bruce St. | 254/774–7496 | fax 254/774–7481 | $7–$10 | AE, D, DC, MC, V.

**Olive Garden.** Italian. A stand-by favored by families, the Olive Garden chain offers familiar specialty pastas in addition to other choices. Try fettuccine chicken florentine, linguine alla marinara, or seafood Alfredo. Kids' menu. | 1902 S.W. H.K. Dodgen Loop | 254/778–4492 | No lunch | $13–$17 | AE, D, DC, MC, V.

## Lodging

**Holiday Inn Express.** About half a mile north from the center of town, this hotel can be easily reached from I–35. You'll find many fast food and restaurant chains nearby. Complimentary Continental breakfast, microwaves, refrigerators, cable TV, pool, gym, laundry facilities, some pets allowed. | 1610 W. Nugent Ave. | 254/770–1100 or 877/732–3320 | fax 254/770–1500 | 61 rooms | $72–$199 | AE, D, DC, MC, V.

**Inn at Scott and White.** This motel is part of Scott and White hospital and is near Belton Lake and several restaurants. It's also just 10 mi from a popular shopping mall. Restaurant, some refrigerators, room service, cable TV, pool, business services, free parking, some pets allowed. | 2625 S. 31st St., Belton | 254/778–5511 | fax 254/773–3161 | 129 rooms | $56–$74 | AE, D, DC, MC, V.

**La Quinta.** Temple High School is across the street from this traditionally decorated chain hotel. You'll find friendly service and great accommodations here. A family restaurant is directly behind. The more adventurous can drive a few miles to Stampede, a dance club. Continental breakfast, cable TV, pool, business services, some pets allowed. | 1604 W. Barton Ave. | 254/771–2980 | fax 254/778–7565 | 106 rooms | $69–$90 | AE, D, DC, MC, V.

**Luxury Inn.** This modernized hotel has a quiet and relaxing atmosphere. It's so comfortable that many locals stay here as well. There is entertainment every night except Sunday in Drake's Lounge. Restaurant, bar, picnic area, in-room data ports, cable TV, pool, exercise room, laundry facilities, business services, free parking, some pets allowed. | 802 N. General Bruce Dr., | 254/778–4411 | fax 254/778–8086 | 132 rooms | $48–$62 | AE, D, DC, MC, V.

**Travel Lodge.** Just off I–35 (exit 302), this large, two-story motel is near many area restaurants. Complimentary Continental breakfast, microwaves, refrigerators, cable TV, pool, gym, laundry facilities, some pets allowed. | 802 N. Bruce St. | 254/778–4411 | fax 254/778–8086 | 132 rooms | $48–$58 | AE, D, DC, MC, V.

# TERLINGUA

MAP 8, D6

*(Nearby town also listed: Big Bend National Park)*

During its boom days, quicksilver mines helped the population reach nearly 2,000. When the price of mercury dropped in the 1940s, Terlingua became a ghost town. Thanks in part to tourism generated by adjacent Big Bend Ranch State Park and Big Bend National Park, the area's economy is improving.

Each November, Terlingua swells when thousands descend upon the town for its famous chili cook-off.

Information: **Terlingua Chamber of Commerce** | Rte. 118 and Rte. 170, Terlingua, TX 79852 | 915/371–2320.

## Attractions

**Barton Warnock Environmental Education Center.** The center serves as one of two entrances to the Big Bend Ranch State Park. The two-acre Desert Garden, which exhibits plants native to the Chihuahuan Desert, surrounds the center. | Rte. 170, Lajitas | 915/424–3327 | $3 | Daily 8–4:30.

**Lajitas Stables.** Guided horseback rides are available across the land where the Chihuahuan Desert meets the Southwest Rocky Mountains. Tours can last from one hour to five days. | Rte. 170, Lajitas | 915/424–3238 or 888/508–7667 | www.lajitasstables.com | $25–$100 daily, $140–$160 multiday | Daily 9–5.

**Terlingua Trading Company.** You'll find jewelry, books, gourmet foods, and an extensive selection of Mexican imports in the former headquarters of the Chisos Mining Company. | 100 Ivy St. | 915/371–2234 | Free | Daily 9–9.

ON THE CALENDAR
**NOV.: *International Chili Cook-off.*** First started in 1967, this cook-off takes place the first Saturday in November. | Rancho Casi de los Chisos, Rte. 170 | 806/352–8783.

## Dining
**Big Bend Cafe.** Mexican. This informal café is within a mile of two hotels in Study Butte. Chicken-fried steak and hot steak sandwiches with gravy are among the popular dishes. | Rtes. 118 and 170, Study Butte | 915/371–2483 | Breakfast also available | $2–$10 | AE, D, MC, V.

**La Kiva.** American. Mexican. The surroundings are cozy (rock walls, natural wood furnishings) and the food basic. Try barbecue, steak, and coleslaw. | Hwy. 70 | 915/371–2250 | $8–$18 | No credit cards.

## Lodging
**Big Bend Motor Inn.** This lodging complex includes a one-story motel, four duplexes with kitchens, and a cottage. Special rates are available during Terlingua's chili cook-off weekend. Restaurant. Satellite TV. Pool, laundry facilities. | Rtes. 118 and 170, Study Butte | 915/371–2218 or 800/848–2363 | 37 rooms | $65–$130 | AE, D, MC, V.

**Lajitas on the Rio Grande.** This resort complex has a variety of accommodations. It's surrounded on the east by Big Bend National Park, and on the West by Big Bend State Park. 9-hole golf course, tennis. | Rte. 170 | 915/424–3471 | www.lajitas.com | 81 rooms | $60–$195 | D, MC, V.

**Mission Lodge.** This one-story motel is across the street from a restaurant. There is a river-rafting outfitter on the property that leads rafting trips on the Rio Grande. Satellite TV. Pool. | Rte. 118 at Rte. 170, Study Butte | 915/371–2555 or 800/848–2363 | 49 rooms | $55–$60 | D, MC, V.

# TEXARKANA

MAP 8, K2

*(Nearby towns also listed: Jefferson, Mount Pleasant, Paris)*

This community is located on the state line between Texas and Arkansas and visitors often get their photo taken standing in both states. Texarkana has been home to two famous residents: musician Scott Joplin and entrepreneur and politician Ross Perot. The city is home to the Texarkana Community College and Texas A&M–Texarkana.

**Information: Texarkana Chamber of Commerce** | Box 1468, Texarkana, TX 75504 | 903/792–7191 | chamber@tkx.com | www.texarkanachamber.com.

## Attractions
**Perot Theatre.** Honoring Texarkana's most famous resident, Ross Perot, this theater hosts a variety of performances. | 219 Main St. | 903/792–4992 | Prices vary with shows | Mon.–Fri. 9–5.

**Scott Joplin Mural.** This mural recalls the life and career of ragtime's Scott Joplin, one of the best known residents of Texarkana. | 311 Main St. | No phone | Free | Daily.

**Texarkana Historical Museum.** Housed in the oldest brick building in Texarkana, this home features period furnishings in a Victorian parlor, kitchen, and more. It includes an

1890s farmstead model and local history exhibits including many Caddo Indian artifacts. | 219 State Line Ave. | 903/793–4831 | fax 903/793–7108 | $2 | Tues.–Sat. 10–4.

**Wright Patman Dam and Lake.** On the Sulphur River, this expansive lake offers watersports, camping, hiking, and fishing. There are also picnic sites. | Off Rte. 2148. | 903/838–8636 or 903/796–2419 | Marina, ramps | $1 | Daily.

### ON THE CALENDAR

**AUG.–SEPT.: *Labor Day Bluegrass Festival.*** This live bluegrass music festival at Strange Family Bluegrass Park also features food booths. There are camping facilities, as well. | 903/792–2481 or 903/791–0342.

**SEPT.: *Four States Fair and Rodeo.*** This event held on the Fairgrounds features competitors from Texas, Louisiana, Arkansas, and Oklahoma, and is filled with rodeo fun: calf roping, bronc busting, bull riding, barrel racing, and more. | 800/776–1836.

**SEPT.: *Quadrangle Festival.*** Events such as the Quadrangle Run (a running race downtown), the Regional Cheerleading Competition, and the Saturday Evening Street Dance liven up this weekend festival sponsored by the Texarkana Museum System. Go to the outdoor market to see or buy arts and crafts, antiques, and collectibles; all-day live country and rock music shows; or, for younger audiences, story-telling and puppet shows. All proceeds benefit Texarkana museums. | 903/793–4831.

## Dining

**Bryce's Cafeteria.** American. In business since 1931, this cafeteria is undoubtedly the most popular spot in town. Bryce's accommodates 300 diners, all lining up for Southern fare, such as baked chicken pie, spare ribs, candied yams, and black-eyed peas. Close to 50 different desserts are made on the premises, but in peach season, Texarkansans clamor for Bryce's homemade fresh peach pie. Drive-through service is also available. | 2021 Mall Dr. | 903/792–1611 | $3–$7 | AE, D, DC, MC, V.

**Outback Steakhouse.** Steak. From the busy bar (where diners watch sporting events) to the informal booths, Outback Steakhouse is known for top of the line beef served in a friendly, family style atmosphere. Try the 14-oz Rockhampton rib-eye or the 14-oz New York strip. Kids' menu. | 3209 Mall Dr., Central Mall | 903/831–4252 | Lunch Sun. | $18–$32 | AE, D, DC, MC, V.

**Park Place Restaurant.** Seafood. You'll find the elegant Park Place is as delightful for its romantic candlelight and white tablecloths as for its gourmet cuisine. You may have trouble ordering, though: the marinated crab claws and the oysters Rockefeller are equally delicious appetizers, and both the prime rib and the lobster tail are specialties of the house. | 2905 Arkansas Blvd. | 870/772–2201 | Closed Sun. No lunch | $10–$25 | AE, MC, V.

## Lodging

**Four Points Sheraton Hotel.** This hotel is 15 minutes from the airport and 15 minutes from downtown. Complimentary donuts and coffee are served during the week. There is a restaurant, the Garden Room, in the hotel, and your room key gains you entry to the club adjacent to the hotel, where you can hear live music most nights of the week. Restaurant, bar, room service, in-room data ports, cable TV, pool, indoor hot tub, gym, laundry service, business services, airport shuttle, pets allowed (fee). | 5301 N. Stateline Ave. | 903/792–3222 | fax 903/793–3930 | 147 rooms | $80 | AE, D, DC, MC, V.

**Holiday Inn Express.** This chain has been modernized and it is near the expressway and 2 mi from shopping (many antiques stores) and Discovery Place, a science museum. Complimentary Continental breakfast, in-room data ports, some microwaves, refrigerators, cable TV, pool, hot tub, laundry facilities, business services, airport shuttle. | 5401 N. State Line Ave. | 903/792–3366 | fax 903/792–5649 | www.holidayinn.com | 112 rooms | $72–$79 | AE, D, DC, MC, V.

**Holiday Inn Texarkana.** This Holiday Inn near downtown Texarkana is filled with Early American furniture. It is just 2 mi from the Fairgrounds. Restaurant, in-room data ports, room service, cable TV, pool, hot tub, exercise equipment, game room, laundry facilities, business services. | 5100 N. State Line Ave. | 870/774–3521 | fax 870/772–3068 | www.holidayinn.com | 210 rooms | $7–$89 | AE, D, DC, MC, V.

**La Quinta.** This La Quinta is on the Arkansas border and is big on a country-style relaxing atmosphere, but if you're eating at the nearby Denny's or at the Waffle House, you're in Texas. Complimentary Continental breakfast, in-room data ports, cable TV, pool, airport shuttle, pets allowed. | 5201 State Line Ave. | 903/794–1900 | fax 903/792–5506 | 130 rooms | $57–$67 | AE, D, DC, MC, V.

**Mansion on Main.** Built in 1895, this Victorian mansion has bed chambers that are furnished with antiques and has Victorian bedclothes. The hotel is romantic, cozy and comfortable. It is close to shopping malls, The Pearl Theatre and good area restaurants. It is 20 mi from Arkansas and 70 mi from Louisiana. | 5 rooms (2 with shower only), 1 suite. Breakfast, in-room data ports, cable TV, business services. | 802 Main St., | 903/792–1835 | fax 903/793–0878 | www.bbonline.com/tx/mansion/ | $65–$75, $109 suite | AE, MC, V.

**Ramada Inn.** Just off I-30, this hotel is easy to find and it has much to offer: the restaurant serves a bountiful Southern buffet at lunchtime, you can sing karaoke at the bar two nights a week, and you can exercise for free at a nearby health club. Antiques decorate this Ramada Inn's unusual lobby. Restaurant, bar, room service, in-room data ports, cable TV, pool, pets allowed (fee). | 2005 Mall Dr. | 903/794–3131 | fax 903/793–0606 | 98 rooms | $51 | AE, D, DC, MC, V.

# TEXAS CITY

MAP 8, K6

*(Nearby towns also listed: Galveston, Houston, La Porte)*

Along with its sister city, La Marque, Texas City is an important port city located between Houston and Galveston. Along with its petrochemical industries, the city is home to many watersport activities including fishing and sailing. Outlet shopping also draws many day trippers from Houston.

**Information: Texas City-LaMarque Chamber of Commerce** | 8419 Emmett F. Lowry Expressway, Texas City 77592 | 409/935–1408 | www.texascitychamber.org.

## Attractions

**Bay Street Park.** This 50-acre park is the site of the first U.S. Aerosquadron from 1913 to 1915, and home to several commemorative installations: the Wings of Heritage, a display of life-size airplanes; the Thomas S. Mackey Nature Center, a wildlife habitat dedicated to Eagle Boy Scouts and Golden Girl Scouts; and the Challenger Seven Memorial, in memory of the astronauts who died in the 1986 space shuttle tragedy. There are picnic areas, playground equipment, and birding observation decks throughout the park. | 9th Ave. and Bay St. | 409/643–5990 | Free | Daily 9–9.

**Mainland Museum of Texas City.** This museum features the history of Texas City, industries of the region, a railroad depot, an old schoolhouse, and a general store. | 409 6th St. N | 409/948–9570 | $3 | Tues., Thurs.–Sun. 1–4.

### ON THE CALENDAR

**JUNE: *Funfest*.** This festival kicks off summer Texas-style with a barbecue cook-off, amusement rides, a children's parade, and live music. Watch the local tennis and golf competitions, and the rollerblading and BMX bicycle demonstrations, scattered throughout the city. Most events are held on Texas City's historic Sixth St. | 409/935–1408.

**AUG.:** *Shrimp Boil.* The "harvest" of the Texas Gulf is celebrated at this shrimp boil, with hundreds of pounds of boiled shrimp and vegetables as well as live entertainment. If you are hungry, show up at the Rotary Pavilion in Nessler Park. | 409/935–1408.

## Dining

**Gringo's.** Mexican. Gringo's is the place to be on Friday nights when the locals flock here for the seafood specials and tropical drinks. Try the Veracruz combo special: grilled brochettes of huge gulf shrimp wrapped in bacon and stuffed with monterey jack cheese, served alongside fajitas; or try the cheese enchiladas, served with shrimp and crawfish tails.| 10200 E.F. Lowry | 409/986–6864 | $5–$8 | AE, D, DC, MC, V.

**Olive Garden.** Italian. Always a popular choice with families, this restaurant chain presents specialties which include pastas and seafood. Try fettuccine chicken florentine, shrimp primavera, and Mediterranean garlic shrimp. Kids' menu. | 10212 Emmett F. Lowry Expressway | 409/986–7471 | No lunch | $8–$20 | AE, D, DC, MC, V.

## Lodging

**La Quinta.** The NASA Space Center is 15 mi from this chain hotel, but if you want to fish off the world's largest fishing pier, you need only drive 5 minutes into town. This chain hotel's great service and comfortable accommodations are well known. Complimentary Continental breakfast, cable TV, pool, laundry facilities, business services, pets allowed. | 1121 Rte. 146N | 800/687–6667 | fax 409/945–4412 | 121 rooms | $49–$89 | AE, D, DC, MC, V.

**Ramada Inn.** With the Mall of the Mainland across the street, and the Gulf Greyhound racing park nearby, this hotel is a good choice for outlet shoppers and dog-race gamblers alike. There's live music in the hotel bar on weekends. Restaurant, bar, cable TV, pool, outdoor hot tub, laundry service, pets allowed (fee). | 5201 Gulf Fwy | 409/986–9777 | fax 409/ 986–5295 | 150 rooms | $59–$99 | AE, D, DC, MC, V.

# THREE RIVERS

MAP 8, H7

*(Nearby town also listed: Goliad)*

Three rivers—the Frio, Atascosa, and Nueces—give this South Texas community its name. The city is the center for the area's ranches and farms but is best known by travelers as the gateway to Choke Canyon, a 26,000-acre reservoir on the Frio River.

Information: **Three Rivers Chamber of Commerce** | Box 1648, Three Rivers, TX 78071 | 361/786–4330 | www.threerivers.com.

## Attractions

**Choke Canyon State Park.** Located on Choke Canyon Reservoir, 4 mi off 72W, this park offers camping, fishing, and boating. There are also areas for picnicking. | Rte. 72 | 361/786–3538 | $3 | Daily.

### ON THE CALENDAR

**APR.:** *Three Rivers Salsa Festival.* A 12-piece salsa band takes the stage while aspiring salsa chefs, competing in three categories, try to impress the judges with their homemade entries. For 50¢, you too can taste the offerings—chunky, sweet, or fire-engine hot—and place your vote for the people's choice award. Call the Chamber of Commerce for more information on this one-day festival, or to enter your own salsa recipe. | 361/ 786–4330.

## Dining

**Nolan Ryan's Waterfront Steakhouse.** Steak. Every now and then you can spy pitching star Nolan Ryan overseeing the action at his laid-back restaurant and bar, 7½ mi west of Three Rivers. If he's not in you can still buy merchandise he has personally autographed. The restaurant operates the only bar in two counties to serve hard alcohol so it draws quite a thirsty crowd. Drive out on a Thursday night when the steakhouse packs them in for all-you-can-eat grilled quail, or on a Wednesday when catfish and hush puppies are the specials of the day. | U.S. 72W | 361/786–4938 | $4–$18 | AE, D, DC, MC, V.

## Lodging

**Best Western.** Sparkling interiors reflect a southwestern influence in this Best Western, opened in 1998. There's a laundromat next door and a Mexican restaurant a block away. Complimentary Continental breakfast, some microwaves, some refrigerators, cable TV, pool, pets allowed (fee). | 900 N. Harbor Ave. | 361/786–2000 | fax 361/786–1022 | 38 rooms | $60 | AE, D, DC, MC, V.

# TYLER

MAP 8, J3

*(Nearby towns also listed: Athens, Jacksonville, Jefferson, Kilgore, Longview, Marshall, Palestine)*

This community is a popular getaway from Dallas, just 90 mi west, and is noted for its spectacular roses, which it celebrates in its annual Texas Rose Festival. Tyler is also a popular destination in fall months for its autumnal colors. The city is home to the University of Texas at Tyler, Tyler Junior College, and Texas College.

**Information: Tyler Area Convention and Visitors Bureau** | 315 N. Broadway, Tyler, TX 75710 | 903/592–1661 or 800/235–5712 | www.tylertexas.com.

## Attractions

**Brookshire's World of Wildlife Museum and Country Store.** Besides a 1928 country store, animal dioramas and an antique fire truck are on view here. There are also areas for picnicking. | 1600 W. Southwest Loop 323 | 903/534–2169 | Free | Tues.–Sat. 9–noon, 1–5.

**Caldwell Zoo.** Exotic species, as well as a native Texas animal display, are the focus of this zoo, which sprawls across 35 acres. | 2203 Martin Luther King Blvd. | 903/593–0121 | Free | Apr.–Sept., daily 9:30–6; Oct.–Mar., daily 9:30–4:30.

**Goodman-LeGrand Home.** This 1859 mansion is now home to the local history museum. On display are exhibits on the city's founding and early days. | 624 N. Broadway | 903/531–1286 | Free | Mar.–Oct., Wed.–Sun. 1–5; Nov.–Feb., weekdays 1–5.

**Hudnall Planetarium.** One of the largest planetariums in the state, this site on the Tyler Junior College campus also features replicas of exploratory space vehicles. | 1200 S. Mahon | 903/510–2312 | $2 | Sept.–mid-May, Wed. 1 PM–2 PM, Sun. 2 PM–3 PM.

**Municipal Rose Garden and Museum.** With more than 38,000 bushes, this is the largest rose garden in the nation. The peak time for blooms is May through November. The museum contains exhibits on the city's rose industry as well as memorabilia from the Rose Festival. | 420 S. Rose Park Dr. | 903/531–1212 or 903/597–3130 | fax 903/531–1211 | Free | Mon.–Fri. 8–5, Sun. 9–5.

**Smith County Historical Museum.** Dioramas, original flags, military paraphernalia, and other historical items depict the history of Native Americans, the Republic era, early settlement, the Civil War, Reconstruction, the Gilded Age, and the 20th century. There is special emphasis on the Caddo Indians, who once lived in East and Northeast Texas, and on the Civil War arms produced by the Confederate Army Works, the old artillery factory in Tyler. The museum is in a 1904 Carnegie Library building. | 125 S. College Ave. | 903/592–5993 | Free | Tues.–Sat. 10–4, closed Sun.–Mon.

**Tyler Museum of Art.** You can see this collection of 19th- and 20th-century art and temporary special exhibitions displayed in four galleries on the east side of the Tyler Junior College campus. Special shows are, for example, a solo artist's work or a thematic show on artists of the American West. | 1300 S. Mahon Ave. | 903/595–1001 | Free | Tues.–Sat. 10–5, Sun. 1–5, closed Mon.

**Tyler State Park.** Available here in the East Texas woods are camping, a nature trail, fishing, swimming, and boating. There are also areas for picnicking. | 789 Park Rd. 16 | 903/597–5338 | fax 903/533–0818 | www.tpwd.state.tx.us | $3 | Daily.

### ON THE CALENDAR

**MAR.–APR.: *Azalea Trail.*** Self-guided look at spring blossoms along 7-mi trail. Guided tours of historic homes. Carriage rides. | 903/592–1661 or 800/235–5712.

**SEPT.: *East Texas State Fair.*** Live entertainment, arts and crafts, exhibits, and livestock shows. | 903/597–2501.

**SEPT.: *The Festival on the Square.*** This upscale arts fair, held in downtown Tyler on the first Saturday after Labor Day, is billed as the "ultimate block party"—besides the display and sale of artwork, there is live entertainment by bluegrass and reggae bands, and games and face-painting for the kids. | 903/593–6905.

**OCT.: *Texas Rose Festival.*** Rose Museum show, Palette of Roses Art Show, Rose Queen coronation, arts and crafts show, and parade. | 903/597–3130.

## Dining

**Bernard's Mediterranean Restaurant.** Mediterranean. At this French- and Italian-influenced restaurant, paintings adorn the walls, candles illuminate the tables, and a vaulted ceiling arches over a well-stocked wine cellar. Bernard's seafood is particularly flavorful—the yellowfin tuna is made with a teriyaki and ginger sauce—as is the popular rack of lamb, prepared with rosemary and tarragon. | 212 Grande Blvd. | 903/534–0265 | Closed Sun. No lunch Mon. and Sat. | $14–$19 | AE, D, DC, MC, V.

**Cace's Seafood.** Seafood. It's Mardi Gras every day at this New Orleans–style seafood restaurant in central Tyler. Amidst pictures of Mississippi riverboats, hanging from green and burgundy walls, you can dine on the Big Easy favorite, shrimp creole, or the fresh catch of the day, from flounder to snapper, prepared as you like it. A decadent white-chocolate bread pudding tops off your festive meal. | 7011 S. Broadway | 903/581–0744 | Closed Mon. | $6–$16 | AE, D, DC, MC, V.

**Liang's.** Chinese. Oriental decor with wooden sculptures of dragons and tigers adds to the festive family atmosphere. Try the chicken Liang, Hunan beef, or the salt and pepper shrimp. Kids' menu. No smoking. | 1828 E. SE Loop 323 | 903/593–7883 | $7–$15 | AE, D, DC, MC, V.

**Olive Garden.** Italian. A favorite with families, offering pastas, grilled items, and seafood. Try chicken scampi or the shrimp primavera. Kids' menu. | 5520 S. Broadway Ave. | 903/509–3363 | $8–$16 | AE, D, DC, MC, V.

**Potpourri House.** American. This is a traditional family-style restaurant. Try the chicken crispy Caesar salad. Salad bar. No smoking. | 2320 Troup Highway Blvd. 300 | 903/592–4171 | Closed Sun. | $7–$18 | AE, D, MC, V.

## Lodging

**Charnwood Hill Inn.** This grand, historical inn, inspired by Greek Revival architecture, has served many functions, from a hospital to a women's seminary, and was also previously owned by oil billionaire H. L. Hunt. Large, deluxe bedrooms and meticulously tended grounds will transport you to an era of luxury and glamor. In the morning, a full, gourmet breakfast awaits you in the formal dining room. Complimentary breakfast, no TV in some rooms, TV in common area, no pets, no kids under 13, no smoking. | 223 E. Charnwood St. | 903/597–3980 or 877/597–3980 | fax 903/597–7432 | info@charnwoodhillinn.com | www.charnwoodhillinn.com | 6 rooms | $95–$175 | AE, D, MC, V.

**Days Inn.** This two-story motel is ½ mi from a zoo and next door to a restaurant. Restaurant, complimentary Continental breakfast, some refrigerators, room service, cable TV, pool, barbershop, beauty salon, exercise equipment, laundry facilities, business services, free parking, pets allowed. | 3300 Mineola | 903/595–2451 | fax 903/595–2261 | 139 rooms | $45–$60 | AE, D, DC, MC, V.

**Holiday Inn–Southeast Crossing.** You will find contemporary architecture inside and outside of this Holiday Inn, on the southeast side of town around the corner from a bowling alley and near many shopping centers. Don't forget to save time to admire the landscaping. It's 10 minutes from Lake Tyler and within walking distance of area restaurants. Restaurant, in-room data ports, room service, cable TV, pool, laundry facilities, business services, airport shuttle, free parking, pets allowed. | 3310 Troup Hwy. | 903/593–3600 | fax 903/533–9571 | www.holidayinn.com | 160 rooms | $69–$78 | AE, D, DC, MC, V.

**La Quinta.** This modernized hotel is close to downtown Tyler, a selection of steakhouses and fast-food restaurants, and bargain shopping outlets. Complimentary Continental breakfast, in-room data ports, cable TV, pool, airport shuttle, free parking, some pets allowed. | 1601 W. Southwest Loop 323 | 903/561–2223 | fax 903/581–5708 | www.laquinta.com | 130 rooms | $69–$79 | AE, D, DC, MC, V.

**Radisson.** Completely modernized, the rooms are traditionally decorated. The more expensive restaurants and shopping opportunities are 10 mi south on the loop, but there is fast food and a movie theater close to this Radisson. It's also close to the Caldwell Zoo and the downtown square. Restaurant, complimentary Continental breakfast, refrigerators, microwaves, in-room safes, in-room data ports, cable TV, pool, business services, airport shuttle, some pets allowed. | 2843 N.W. Loop 323 | 903/597–1301 | fax 903/597–9437 | 139 rooms | $69–$79 | AE, D, DC, MC, V.

**Residence Inn by Marriott.** This updated Marriott offers upscale accommodations for visitors intending to spend more than a night or two in the area. It is across the road from restaurants. Picnic area, complimentary Continental breakfast, in-room data ports, cable TV, pool, hot tub, laundry facilities, business services, airport shuttle, free parking, pets allowed (fee). | 3303 Troup Hwy. | 903/595–5188 | fax 903/595–5719 | 128 kitchen suites | Kitchen suites $86–$125; weekend rates available | AE, D, DC, MC, V.

**Rosevine Inn.** A Georgian-style inn, built in 1986 on a hill in the Historic Brick Street District of Tyler, the Rosevine combines the conveniences of a modern structure with the charm of a much older house. Outside, the inn is surrounded by mature pecan and oak trees; inside it is furnished with comfortable, French-country antiques. The separate brick cottage (dating from 1934), with privacy and room to roam, is good for families, as is the Lodge Game Room, stocked with billiards, Ping-Pong, and an assortment of other games, in the red barn. In the winter, warm up by any of the blazing fireplaces—there are several both inside and outside the inn. Complimentary breakfast, TV in common area, outdoor hot tub, no pets, no smoking. | 415 S. Vine Ave. | 903/592–2221 | fax 903/593–9500 | www.rosevine.com | 5 rooms, 1 cottage | $85–$150 | AE, D, DC, MC, V.

**Sheraton.** Modern and clean, this hotel is on the main strip in Tyler, surrounded by places to eat and shop. It is within 10 min of the Caldwell Zoo and the Rose Garden. Restaurant (with entertainment), in-room data ports, some refrigerators, cable TV, pool, wading pool, hot tub, business services, airport shuttle. | 5701 S. Broadway | 903/561–5800 | fax 903/561–9916 | 185 rooms | $69–$89 | AE, D, DC, MC, V.

**Travel Inn.** This chain hotel is perfect for tourists on a budget or business travelers looking for no-frills accommodations. Cable TV, pool, business services, pets allowed (fee). | 3209 W. Gentry Pkwy. | 903/593–0103 | fax 903/593–0103 | 50 rooms | $35–$39 | AE, D, DC, MC, V.

**Woldert-Spence Manor.** This bed-and-breakfast is in a majestic, 19th-century building, but its comfort and warmth will make you feel at home. Many rooms include private covered balconies or screened porches, and several bathrooms are equipped with restored claw-foot tubs. Start your day with a bountiful breakfast served family-style on antique china. Later, soak in the outdoor hot tub under a wooden gazebo, or relax by the decorative koi pool in the shade of pecan and magnolia trees. Complimentary breakfast, no room phones, TV in common area, outdoor hot tub, no pets, no kids under 10, no smoking. | 611 W. Woldert St. | 903/533–9057 or 800/965–3378 | fax 903/531–0293 | www.woldert-spence.com | 7 rooms | $80–$125 | AE, D, DC, MC, V.

# UVALDE

MAP 8, G6

*(Nearby towns also listed: Castroville, Del Rio)*

Uvalde is located on the Leona River in the last outreaches of the Hill Country, an area first settled by the Spanish who attempted to convert the Lipan-Apache. Uvalde's most famous citizen was John Nance Garner who was vice president during Franklin D. Roosevelt's first and second presidential terms. The political leader is remembered at a downtown museum.

Information: **Uvalde Convention and Visitors Bureau** | 300 E. Main Ave., Uvalde, TX 78801 | 830/278–4115. | uaco@admin.hillconet.com | www.uvalde.org.

## Attractions

**The Briscoe Art and Antique Collection at the First State Bank of Uvalde.** Former Texas Governor Dolph Briscoe and his wife amassed this impressive collection of painting, sculpture, and decorative arts and had it installed in this turn-of-the-20th-century working bank. The focus is on Western art, including several Remington bronzes, but you will also find works by Rembrandt, Gainsborough, and Reynolds scattered throughout the bank. Over 100 Oriental rugs carpet the bank's floor. Guided tours are available; call for scheduling. | 200 E. Nopal St. | 830/278–6231 | Free | Weekdays 9–3, closed weekends.

**Garner Memorial Museum.** This was once the home of Uvalde's most famous citizen: John Nance Garner, vice president of the United States during Franklin D. Roosevelt's first and second presidential terms. The museum is filled with reminders of Garner's political career. | 333 N. Park St. | 830/278–5018 | Free | Mon.–Sat. 9–5.

**Garner State Park.** Named for John Nance Garner, this beautiful state park, 30 mi north of Uvalde, is on the chilly, spring-fed waters of the Frio River (*frio* means "cold" in Spanish). There are campsites, screened shelters, cabins with double beds, an 18-hole miniature golf course, and a 1-mi hiking trail built by the Civilian Conservation Corps during the 1930s. The highlight of the park is the river, filled with swimmers, inner-tubers, and paddleboats during the warmer months. | U.S. 83 to Rte. 29 to Park Rd. 29 | 830/232–6132 | www.tpwd.state.tx.us | $5 | Daily.

**Uvalde Grand Opera House.** This 1891 opera house has been restored and now hosts various performances. | 104 W. North St. | 830/278–4184 | Prices vary with shows | Mon.–Fri. 9–5.

## ON THE CALENDAR

**JULY:** *Sahawe Indian Dancers Summer Ceremonials.* This annual event showcases traditional Native American dances as well as foods. The event is held at Memorial Park's Sahawe Outdoor Theater. | 830/278–4115.

**NOV.** *Hunters' Roundup.* This dinner is held in appreciation of the hundreds of hunters who come to the Uvalde area for its deer, quail, and feral hog. Complimentary wild game is served to any hunter with a valid hunter's license. Camping and hunting gear is raffled off, and awards are bestowed on the oldest and youngest hunters present. A country-western dance concludes the festivities. | 300 E. Main St. | 830/278–4115 or 800/588–2533.

## Dining

**Cactus Jack Cafe and Tortilla Factory.** Tex-Mex. A casual restaurant with tasty chicken con queso, as well as tacos, fajitas, pizza, and steaks. | 2217 E. Main St. | 830/278–4422 | $9–$19 | No credit cards.

**Evett's Barbecue.** Barbecue. Rustic restaurant in the downtown area with picnic table seating and good down-home cooking. Known for the chicken plates, brisket, ribs, and sausage. | 301 E. Main St. | 830/278–6204 | Closed Sun.–Mon. | $5 | No credit cards.

**Town House Restaurant.** Southern. This casual locally popular family restaurant offers comfort food in comfortable surroundings. Known for enchiladas, seafood, steaks, and chicken-fried steak. | 2105 E. Main St. | 830/278–2428 | Breakfast also available | $11–$18 | AE, D, MC, V.

## Lodging

**Best Western Continental Inn.** This motel is on U.S. 90, within walking distance of downtown. You can cook any fish you catch in one of Uvalde's famous clear-running rivers in the barbecue pit located behind the motel. Truck parking is available. Picnic area, cable TV, pool, pets allowed. | 701 E. Main St. | 830/278–5671 | fax 830/278–6351 | 87 rooms | $58 | AE, D, DC, MC, V.

**Holiday Inn.** Near Garner State Park, you will find clean and modern rooms at this hotel. There's a jukebox in this hotel's lounge, The Corral Club, or you can drive a mile east to the six-screen Forum Theater. Restaurant, bar, room service, cable TV, pool, laundry facilities, free parking, some pets allowed. | 920 E. Main St. | 830/278–4511 | fax 830/591–0413 | www.holidayinn.com | 150 rooms | $59–$65 | AE, D, DC, MC, V.

# VAN HORN

*(Nearby town also listed: Marfa)*

Situated in West Texas, this community is a popular stop for I–10 travelers. The town has a long history of mining. Today visitors often make a stop here on their way to Marfa or Alpine.

**Information: Van Horn Convention and Visitors Bureau** | Box 488 79855 | 915/283–2682. **Visitor Center** | 1801 W. Broadway Suite 101, Van Horn, TX 79855 | 915/283–2682.

## Attractions

**Culberson County Historical Museum.** The local history exhibits here in the Clark Hotel include Native American artifacts and frontier memorabilia. | 110 W. Business Loop 10 | 915/283–8028 | Free | Daily.

**Smokehouse Auto Museum.** This classic car museum at the Smokehouse Restaurant boasts a large collection of restored autos. Also on view are memorabilia related to the auto. | 905 W. Business Loop 10 | Free | Mon.–Sat. 6 AM–10:30 PM.

### ON THE CALENDAR
**JUNE: *Frontier Days and Rodeo Celebration.*** This event includes rodeo performances and live entertainment. | 915/283–2682.
**AUG.: *Old Car Festival.*** Over 100 antique automobiles make the trip to Van Horn for this annual show. A cruise parade through town on Friday kicks off the festivities. That night, join the vintage car enthusiasts for a 1950s sockhop held at the local Dairy Queen. On Sat-

urday the cars are displayed at the Convention Center, and, at the end of the festival, there is an awards ceremony for the best entries in a number of categories. | 915/283–2682.

**SEPT.: *Culberson County Fair.*** This fair includes a carnival, games, entertainment, and children's activities. | 915/283–2682.

## Dining

**Chuy's Restaurant.** Mexican. You may have heard about Chuy's from sports announcer John Madden, the unofficial celebrity sponsor of the restaurant. Enchiladas and fajitas are popular choices on the menu, as is Chuy's seafood and steak. Or follow Madden's lead with the steak picado chicken: cubed chicken breast fried on the grill with pepper, onions, and tomatoes, topped with a cheese sauce and served with rice, beans, and a tortilla on the side. | 1200 W. Broadway | 903/283–2066 | $3–$13 | AE, D, DC, MC, V.

**Smokehouse.** Barbecue. The restaurant has tables and booths and several rooms with different moods and themes—from sports and aviation memorabilia to antiques. In addition to their specialty of smoked meats, the restaurant also has steaks, sandwiches, and Mexican food. Kids' menu. | 905 Broadway | 915/283–2453 | Breakfast also available | $16–$24 | AE, D, DC, MC, V.

## Lodging

**Best Western Inn of Van Horn.** At this Western style hotel you will have privileges at a nearby golf course and the world's largest telescope is a little over an hour away. Restaurant, complimentary Continental breakfast, cable TV, pool, business services, some pets allowed. | 1705 Broadway, | 915/283–2410 | fax 915/283–2143 | www.bestwestern.com | 60 rooms | $55–$60 | AE, D, DC, MC, V.

**Days Inn of Van Horn.** This motel has the unusual benefit of a peaceful setting—in back, you'll find a shady wooded area with a picnic table. A quarter mile off of I–10, the motel is within walking distance of several Van Horn eateries. Picnic area, complimentary Continental breakfast, some microwaves, some refrigerators, cable TV, pool, pets allowed (fee). | 600 E. Broadway | 915/283–1007 | fax 915/283–1189 | 58 rooms | $45–$55 | AE, D, DC, MC, V.

**Ramada Inn.** Stay at this Ramada by night and take day trips to the caverns up north or to Big Bend National Park 100 mi south. This is 78 mi from Marfa "ghost lights." Pool, wading pool, laundry facilities, business services, some pets allowed. | 200 Golf Course Dr. | 915/283–2780 | fax 915/283–2804 | 98 rooms | $38–$58 | AE, D, DC, MC, V.

# VERNON

MAP 8, G1

*(Nearby towns also listed: Quanah, Wichita Falls)*

This North Texas community, named for George Washington's Mount Vernon home, is the center for the surrounding farm and ranch land. Although there are few attractions in the small community, it makes a nice stop on an area drive.

Information: **Vernon Chamber of Commerce** | Box 1538, Vernon, TX 76385 | 940/552–2564 or 800/687–3137 | chamber@vernontx.com | www.vernontx.com.

## Attractions

**Historic Doan's Adobe House.** The oldest building in Wilbarger County, this house was constructed in 1881 for Mr. and Mrs. Corwin Doan and family. It is on the Western Trail's cattle crossing over the Red River, where thousands of cattle passed annually on the way north to the Kansas cattle markets. The one-room house is furnished as it might have been in the heyday of the cattle drives. | Follow signs on U.S. 283 N | 940/552–2564 or 800/687–3137 | Free | Call for hours.

**Red River Valley Museum.** This museum displays exhibits on ranching, as well as local artwork and Native American artifacts. | 4600 College Dr. | 940/553–1848 | Free | Tues.–Sun. 1–5.

ON THE CALENDAR
**MAY: _Santa Rosa Roundup._** This four-day rodeo held the 3rd week in May includes precision riding by the Santa Rosa Palomino Club, who have performed across the U.S. and Canada, a downtown parade, and live music. The event is considered one of the best rodeos for its size in the country. | 800/687–3137.
**AUG.: _Summer's Last Blast._** Car show with procession of cars downtown and a block-party atmosphere. | 800/687–3137.

## Dining
**Brown Cow.** American. Come to the Brown Cow for down-home cooking in a rustic dining room decorated with iron work. Everything served in the Brown Cow is made from scratch: the chicken-fried steak, always a hit, is hand-breaded, as are the fried okra and fried squash. Hamburgers are made from quality aged steak and are always a hit with the local diners and through traffic that keeps the Brown Cow bustling. Come hungry on Sundays for an all-you-can-eat-buffet. | 3205 U.S. 287S | 940/553–3322 | $5–$15 | AE, D, DC, MC, V.

## Lodging
**Best Western Village Inn.** This motor lodge is near the many restaurants along U.S. 287. Also, the restaurant on the premises, Norman's Catfish, will deliver to your room. Restaurant, bar, complimentary Continental breakfast, room service, cable TV, pool, laundry service, some pets allowed. | 1615 U.S. 287 | 940/552–5417 or 800/600–5417 | rogers@chipshot.net | www.bestwestern.com/villageinnvernon | 46 rooms | $53 | AE, D, DC, MC, V.

**Days Inn.** On the highway (with truck parking available) and a few restaurants in the area. This is 5 minutes from downtown and 2 mi from the museum. Cable TV, pool, business services, pets allowed. | 3110 Frontage Rd. | 940/552–9982 | fax 940/552–7851 | 50 rooms | $47–$53 | AE, D, DC, MC, V.

**Green Tree Inn.** This is a privately owned, recently modernized and updated motel less than 5 minutes from Vernon Regional Junior College (visit their museum on the history of Vernon). Complimentary Continental breakfast, in-room data ports, cable TV, pool, pets allowed. | 3029 Morton St. | 940/552–5421 or 800/600–5421 | fax 940/552–5421 | 30 rooms | $39–$45 | AE, D, DC, MC, V.

# VICTORIA

MAP 8, 16

*(Nearby towns also listed: Goliad, Port Lavaca)*

Named for the first president of Mexico, this community dates back to 1824. The town was one of the first incorporated by the Republic of Texas and today has many historic structures. Victoria is a popular stop for travelers headed to the Gulf but also draws visitors to its unique Texas Zoo.

**Information: Victoria Convention and Visitors Bureau** | Box 2465, Victoria, TX 77902 | 361/573–5277 or 800/926–5774. **Visitor Center** | 700 Main Center, Suite 101, Victoria, TX 77902 | 512/573–5277 | viccvb@icsi.net | www.visitvictoria.org.

## Attractions
**Coleto Creek Reservoir.** This angling and water recreation area was originally a cooling pond for the power and light company. Camping, picnicking, boating, fishing are available. | 365 Coleto Park Rd., Fannin | 361/575–6366 | www.coletocreekpark.com | $6 | Daily.

**Memorial Square.** This city park features a wind-powered grist mill with grindstones from Germany, used by early settlers in the Victoria area. It's also home to the steam locomotive, Southern Pacific Old No. 771, a gift from the Southern Pacific railroad. The locomotive was built in 1913 by Baltimore Locomotive Works. Memorial Square is also the city's oldest public burial ground. | Commercial and Wheeler Sts. | No phone | Free | Daily.

**Riverside Park.** Situated on the Guadalupe River, this park offers picnicking areas and playgrounds. | Red River and Memorial Sts. | No phone | Free | Daily.

Also within the park, the **Texas Zoo** is filled with Texas species only. All are housed in animal-friendly habitats without bars or cages. | 110 Memorial Dr. | 361/573-7681 | www.viptx.net.texaszoo | $3 | Daily 9-5.

**Victoria County Courthouse.** A Romanesque structure built in 1892, this granite and limestone building served as the county courthouse for three quarters of a century. The second-floor district courtroom has been fully restored to its earlier grandeur, and the old courthouse clock still reliably marks the passing hours. Group tours are available. | Bridge St. at Constitution St. | 361/573-5277 or 800/926-5774 | Free | Call for hours.

## ON THE CALENDAR
**FEB.: *PRCA Rodeo.*** Rodeo riding and entertainment are held at the Victoria Community Center. | 361/573-5277 or 800/926-5774.

**MAR.: *Livestock Show and Parade.*** Livestock show, parade and livestock events are on display at the Livestock Center. | 361/576-4300.

**AUG.: *Victoria Bach Festival.*** Since 1976, this annual festival has drawn music lovers from all over the country for a week of orchestral music, choral works, and chamber concerts by baroque, classical, romantic, and contemporary composers. Concerts are held outdoors and at historic sites throughout the city. Exciting performances by both acclaimed and emerging artists have prompted National Public Radio to deem the festival "the best-kept little secret in Texas." Concerts cost $15 a night or you can buy season tickets for $40. There are discounts for senior citizens and students, and a variety of free programming. | 361/570-5788 | www.victoriabachfestival.org.

## Dining
**Maggie's Meat Market.** Steak. Originally a meat market purveying all cuts of beef, Maggie's now serves steak, chicken, and seafood at a restaurant adjacent to the marketplace. A subtle bovine theme runs through this relaxed restaurant: black and white tablecloths evoke cowhides. Couples can opt for the top sirloin for two, or you might try other best-sellers such as the fried shrimp or the chicken salad plate. Finish up your meal with Maggie's well-loved banana pudding. | 2001 John Stockbauer | 361/573-0428 | $8-$30 | D, MC, V.

**Olde Victoria.** Continental. This restaurant is housed in a Victorian home with traditional decor and is decorated with historic pictures. Try the beef tenderloin, linguine with shrimp, duck with raspberry sauce, or the broiled salmon. Sample them all on the covered patio with a view of the garden. Kids' menu. | 207 N. Navarro St. | 361/572-8840 | No lunch Sat. | $8-$21 | AE, D, MC, V.

**Tejas Cafe.** Continental. This restaurant has a full stop bar for smoking and non-smoking and caters to large parties. Try the ribs, chicken-fried steak, and fajitas. Kids' menu. | 2902 Navarro St. | 361/572-9433 | $7-$15 | AE, D, DC, MC, V.

**Vera Cruz.** Mexican. This Spanish-theme family restaurant can be found in the heart of the city. The fajitas, grilled shrimp, enchiladas, and combination plates are all popular choices. | 3110 Navarro St. | 512/576-6015 | Closed Sun. | $6-$20 | AE, D, MC, V.

## Lodging
**Fairfield Inn.** At the intersection of Loop 463 and U.S. 77, this three-story hotel, built in 1995, could not be more convenient. Complimentary Continental breakfast, cable TV, pool, indoor

hot tub, laundry services, no pets. | 7502 N. Navarro St. | 361/582–0660 | fax 361/582–0660 | 64 rooms | $65 | AE, D, DC, MC, V.

**Friendly Oaks Bed and Breakfast.** The Friendly Oaks house, built in 1916, and the 600-year-old live oaks that surround it, have been lovingly preserved. Each of the inn's four guest rooms is decorated with period furniture according to a theme: the intimate Boudoir Room, for example, is ideal for newlyweds, and the rugged Ranch Room follows a Southwestern motif. Enjoy a full gourmet breakfast, including exotic fruit in season, in the dining room or, weather permitting, out on the veranda under the oaks. Complimentary breakfast, no TV in some rooms, no pets, no smoking. | 210 E. Juan Linn | 361/575–0000 | www.bbhost.com/friendlyoaks | 4 rooms | $55–$80 | AE, D, MC, V.

**Hampton Inn.** This privately owned hotel is modern and comfortable. It is just 5 minutes from shopping, restaurants, and museums in the historical downtown area. Complimentary Continental breakfast, in-room data ports, cable TV, pool, business services, airport shuttle, free parking, pets allowed. | 3112 Houston Hwy. | 361/578–2030 | fax 361/573–1238 | 102 rooms | $63–$83 | AE, D, DC, MC, V.

**Holiday Inn.** A mainly corporate hotel that gives business travelers access to Union Carbide, BP Chemical, Dupont, and other plants in the area. It is near such historical sites as Riverside Park and the Texas Zoo, and is 12 mi from the Rose Garden, golfing, and playground area. Restaurant, bar, in-room data ports, room service, cable TV, pool, hot tub, exercise equipment, game room, video games, laundry facilities, business services, airport shuttle, free parking, pets allowed. | 2705 E. Houston Hwy., | 361/575–0251 | fax 361/575–8362 | www.holidayinn.com | 226 rooms | $70 | AE, D, DC, MC, V.

**La Quinta.** A strong Southwestern feeling greets you at this La Quinta which is close to several restaurants, the Victoria Mall, and movie theaters. Complimentary Continental breakfast, in-room data ports, cable TV, pool, business services, pets allowed. | 7603 N. Navarro Hwy. | 361/572–3585 | fax 361/576–4617 | 130 rooms | $49–$89 | AE, D, DC, MC, V.

**Ramada Inn.** This is a typical Ramada offering Texas hospitality to business travelers. Century Lanes Bowling is near the hotel, and guests can go dancing at the West Key Lounge or Cactus Canyon further down "the strip." It's not far from the OK Corral for more dancing and music. Restaurant, bar, in-room data ports, room service, cable TV, pool, hot tub, sauna, business services, airport shuttles, pets allowed. | 3901 Houston Hwy. | 361/578–2723 | fax 361/578–2723 | 126 rooms | $49–$59 | AE, D, DC, MC, V.

# WACO

MAP 8, I4

*(Nearby towns also listed: Hillsboro, Temple)*

This central Texas town at the confluence of the Brazos and Bosque Rivers was named for the Hueco (pronounced Way-co) Indians who were drawn to the area's rich, fertile land. Although Spanish explorers named this site "Waco Village" in 1542, more than 300 years elapsed before permanent settlement began.

In the 1870s Waco became a center of trade with the completion of a 474-ft suspension bridge across the Brazos River. The bridge was designed by the same engineers who later constructed New York's Brooklyn Bridge and it still spans the river, which slices through the city. Along the riverbanks are miles of shoreline parks, shady walks, and downtown camping areas.

**Information: Waco Convention and Visitors Bureau** | 100 Washington Ave., Waco, TX 76702 | 254/750–5810 or 800/321–9226 | www.wacocvb.com.

## Attractions

**The Art Center.** This exhibit hall and teaching center is located in the Mediterranean-style home of the late lumber magnate William Waldo Cameron. Exhibits here focus on Texas artists in all media. | 1300 College Dr. | 254/752–4371 | Free | Tues.–Sat. 10–5, Sun. 1–5.

**Baylor University.** This Baptist liberal arts college enrolls 11,000 students. Within the campus are several worthwhile sights. | 500 Speight St. | 254/710–1011.

The works of Elizabeth Barrett Browning and husband Robert Browning fill the two-story **Armstrong Browning Library.** The building also boasts the world's largest collection of secular stained-glass windows, which illustrate the works of both writers (including Robert Browning's *The Pied Piper of Hamlin*). A guided tour offers a look at the upstairs rooms furnished with the couple's belongings. | 700 Speight St. | 254/710–3566 | www.baylor.edu | Free | Weekdays 9–5, Sat. 9–noon.

**The Strecker Museum.** This is the oldest continually operating museum in Texas. The natural history collection includes displays on the rocks, fossils, and wildlife of Texas. | Sid Richardson Science Building | 254/710–1110 | Free | Mon.–Fri. 9–5, Sat. 10–4.

The **Gov. Bill and Vara Daniel Historic Village.** A 19th-century riverboat town is re-created here. It includes a schoolhouse, a mercantile store, and, of course, a Wild West saloon. The buildings, once the property of Governor Daniel, were moved to this site from a plantation community in Liberty County, Texas, and restored by Baylor University. | 218 S. University Parks Dr. | 254/710–1160 | $3 | Mon.–Sat. 10–4.

**Dr Pepper Museum and Free Enterprise Institute.** The Dr Pepper soft drink was invented by pharmacist Dr. Charles Alderton at the Old Corner Drug Store in Waco. Today the drugstore is gone, but the original bottling plant remains open as a museum. Interesting exhibits and films offer a look at some early promotional materials as well as the manufacturing process of the unusual soft drink. Upstairs, much of the second floor is devoted to promotional materials tracing the drink's history. After a look through the museum, most travelers make their last stop at the re-creation of the Old Corner Drug Store fountain for an ice cream soda or (what else?) a Dr Pepper. | 300 S. 5th St. | 254/757–2433 | www.drpeppermuseum.com | $4 | Mon.–Sat. 10–5, Sun. noon–5.

**Fort Fisher Park.** Set right on the banks of the Brazos River, Fort Fisher Park is a favorite stop for travelers on I–35; the City of Waco operates a visitors center here. | 100 Texas Ranger Trail | 254/750–8630 | Free | Daily | www.texasranger.org.

Within the park lies the **Texas Ranger Hall of Fame and Museum.** Here visitors can see guns of every description used by the Rangers, who had the reputation of lone lawmen who always got their man. Dioramas in the Hall of Fame recount the early days of the Rangers, including their founding by Stephen F. Austin. A 20-minute slide show recalls the history of the Rangers.

**Lake Waco.** On the Bosque River. Boating, beaches, swimming, marinas, and fishing are all on hand at Lake Waco. | On Rte. 1637 (N. 19th St.) | 254/756–5379 | Free | Daily.

**Suspension Bridge and River Walk.** Designed by the New York firm of engineers that later oversaw the construction of the Brooklyn Bridge, this is one of the earliest suspension bridges in America, and for a time was the longest single-span suspension bridge west of the Mississippi. Completed in 1870 with a span of 470 feet, it supplied the cowboys and cattle, following the Chisholm Trail, with the only means of crossing the Brazos River with wagons. Now closed to traffic, the bridge offers splendid views of the scenic Brazos River. Ramps and steps from the bridge lead to the landscaped River Walk, the Waco Tourist Information Center, and the Texas Hall of Fame and Museum at Fort Fisher. | Washington Ave. and University Parks Dr. | 254/750–5810 or 800/321–9226 | Free | Daily.

**Texas Sports Hall of Fame.** Honoring Texan athletes—baseball players, tennis players, high school footballers, and high school basketball players—the Texas Sports Hall of Fame displays trophies, jerseys, and sports equipment linked to accomplished Texan athletes. The Tom Landry Theater shows films of college and professional sports highlights. Interactive exhibits are scattered throughout the museum; kids can compare their shoe size to NBA players. | 1108 S. University Parks Dr. | 254/756–1633 | www.hallofame.org | $4 | Mon.–Sat. 10–6, Sun. 12–6.

## ON THE CALENDAR

**MAR.–SEPT.:** *Heart o' Texas Speedway.* This speedway features auto racing on select weekends. | 254/829–2294.

**APR.:** *Brazos River Festival and Pilgrimage.* This festival at Fort Fisher Park features music, food, and activities for kids. | 800/922–6386.

**OCT.:** *Heart o' Texas Fair and Rodeo.* Bull riding, barebacking riding, rodeo clowns, live entertainment, steer scrambles, and more fill this event at the Coliseum and Fairgrounds. | 800/922–6386.

**DEC.:** *Holidays on the Brazos.* The holiday season is celebrated with traditional carols, holiday foods, candlelight home tours, tree lightings, and more. | 800/922–6386.

## Dining

**Brazos Belle.** Continental. Board this stationary, floating riverboat in the Brazos River for upscale dining or drinks before shimmering river views and a cinematic sunset. Enjoy such sophisticated entrées as prime rib, gulf prawns, or mesquite-grilled duckling, and rich desserts such as the amaretto tiramisu or the Brazos Belle Mudpie. On Thursdays, Fridays, and Saturdays, a live band completes the setting for your romantic riverfront dinner. | 33 I–35 | 254/714–2933 | No lunch | $8–$19 | AE, D, MC, V.

**Elite Cafe.** American. This restaurant is a historic landmark with a '50s theme and signs pointing to where Elvis actually sat when he dined here. Try the chicken-fried steak, chicken tenders, ribs, and the good bite-chicken breast with mushrooms and onions topped with cheese. Kids' menu. | 2132 S. Valley Mills Dr. | 254/754–4941 | $9–$15 | AE, D, DC, MC, V.

**Franklin's.** Seafood. A 50-ft mural of the ocean, and mounted artificial fish and nets, set the scene for a seafood extravaganza at this downtown restaurant. If you can't decide between the tempting offerings on the menu, order the mixed seafood grill, a shish kebab with scallops, shrimp, and pieces of tuna and salmon cooked over a wood-burning grill. From Wednesday through Saturday, linger over a nightcap at the bar; its scenic outdoor balcony overlooks the center of town. | 215 S. Second St. | 254/754–3474 | $7–$15 | AE, D, DC, MC, V.

**Ninfa's.** Mexican. Join the fun at this hopping hangout, patronized by college kids and older locals alike. In a renovated warehouse building, with exposed brick and expansive windows, Ninfa's prepares tacos and other Mexican standbys according to well-guarded recipes. The fajitas stand out in particular. Don't miss Ninfa's much-loved variation on the classic margarita, the Ninfarita. | 220 S. 3rd St. | 254/757–2050 | $7–$17 | AE, D, DC, MC, V.

## Lodging

**Best Western Old Main Lodge.** This motel is filled with Western furnishings. It is near Baylor University, the Texas Sports Hall of Fame, and the Dr Pepper Museum. The Brazos River and other tourist attractions are close by. Some microwaves, cable TV, pool, business services, free parking, some pets allowed. | I–35 at 4th St. | 254/753–0316 | fax 254/753–3811 | www.bestwestern.com | 84 rooms | $64–$83 | AE, D, DC, MC, V.

**Brazos House Bed and Breakfast.** In a 19th-century brick house on the Brazos River, this luxurious bed-and-breakfast's four bedrooms—two in the main house and two in private cottages—are distinguished by individual decorating schemes. The cowhide rugs in one cottage room lend it a Western character, while the mahogany canopy bed in another bedroom will make you feel like royalty. Two of the private baths have old-fashioned claw-foot tubs. Antique gas chandeliers hang from the 12-ft ceilings in the common rooms. The generous breakfasts vary from day to day. Complimentary breakfast, cable TV, no pets, no smoking. | 1316 Washington Ave. | 254/754–3565 or 800/729–7313 | fax 254/754–3568 | 4 rooms | $75–$120 | AE, D, MC, V.

**Clarion.** This is an upscale, full-service hotel, close to the airport and ideal for business travelers. Restaurant, bar, complimentary Continental breakfast, in-room data ports, room service, cable TV, indoor pool, hot tub, exercise equipment, game room, laundry facilities, business services, airport shuttle, free parking. | 801 S. 4th St. | 254/757–2000 | fax 254/757–1110 | 148 rooms | $79–$125 | AE, D, DC, MC, V.

**Comfort Inn.** This motel is 2 mi from downtown Waco and the Cameron Park Zoo. Complimentary Continental breakfast, in-room data ports, cable TV, pool, business services. | 1430 I–35S, | 254/752–1991 | fax 254/752–2084 | comfortinnwaco@juno.com | 53 rooms | $56–$89 | AE, D, DC, MC, V.

**Courtyard by Marriott.** Rooms in this three-story hotel look out onto the scenic Brazos River, or open out onto courtyard balconies or patios. The hotel is in Waco's historic downtown area and is only a block and a half from the Warehouse District, a lively area filled with renovated shops and restaurants. Restaurant (breakfast only), bar, in-room data ports, some refrigerators, some microwaves, cable TV, pool, outdoor hot tub, gym, laundry facilities, laundry service, airport shuttle, free parking, no pets. | 101 Washington Ave. | 254/752–8686 | fax 254/752–1011 | wacocy@aol.com | www.courtyard.com/wcocy | 153 rooms | AE, D, DC, MC, V.

**Hilton Inn.** Set on the Brazos River, this hotel has been modernized and is next to the convention center and Indian Spring Park. It is also near the Texas Ranger Hall of Fame and Texas Sports Hall of Fame, and is within walking distance of the playhouse and several restaurants. Restaurant, bar, cable TV, pool, hot tub, tennis, airport shuttle. | 113 S. University Parks Dr., | 254/754–8484 | fax 254/752–2214 | 199 rooms | $79–$89 | AE, D, DC, MC, V.

**Holiday Inn.** This four-story hotel, built in the 70s, is half a mile south of Baylor University and the Texas Sports Hall of Fame. Restaurant, lounge, room service, cable TV, outdoor pool, gym, laundry facilities, airport shuttle, pets allowed (fee). | 1001 Martin Luther King, Jr. Blvd. | 254/753–0261 | fax 254/753–0227 | 171 rooms | $82–$92 | AE, D, DC, MC, V.

**La Quinta Motor Inn.** This contemporary chain motel is near Baylor University. It is within blocks of the Texas Ranger Hall of Fame, the Texas Sports Hall of Fame, and area restaurants. Complimentary Continental breakfast, in-room data ports, cable TV, pool, business services, free parking, some pets allowed. | 1110 S. 9th St., | 254/752–9741 | fax 254/757–1600 | 102 rooms | $72–$79 | AE, D, DC, MC, V.

**Lexington Inn.** Watch them make Dr Pepper soda at the nearby Dr Pepper Museum, or take a walk down crime-fighting memory lane at the Texas Ranger Hall of Fame. It is also close to downtown Waco and the suspension bridge. Complimentary Continental breakfast, in-room data ports, some microwaves, refrigerators, cable TV, pool, hot tub, laundry facilities, business services, airport shuttle, free parking. | 115 Jack Kultgen Fwy. | 254/754–1266 or 800/92–SUITE | fax 254/755–8612 | 114 rooms | $49–$62 | AE, D, DC, MC, V.

# WAXAHACHIE

MAP 8, T3

*(Nearby towns also listed: Arlington-Grand Prairie, Dallas, Ennis)*

Waxahachie is home to numerous restored picture-book homes from the turn of the 20th century. Its name derives from the Indian word for either cow or buffalo creek. Films like *Tender Mercies* and *Places in the Heart* were filmed here.

**Information: Chamber of Commerce** | 102 YMCA Dr., Waxahachie, TX 75165 | 972/937–2390.

## Attractions

**Ellis County Museum.** Local history is recounted through artifacts, photos, and furnishings in this museum located in a restored 19th-century building on the town square. | 201 South College | 972/937–0681 | Donations accepted | Tues.–Sat. 10–5, Sun. 1–5.

**Ellis County Courthouse.** Built in 1895 for the then-outrageous price of $150,000, this is one of the most impressive courthouses in Texas. Italian artisans were hired to complete the exterior's elaborate stone carvings. | 1201 N. Hwy. 77 | 972/923–5000 | Free | Mon.–Fri. 8–5.

## Dining

**Brooklyn's Best Pizza.** Pizza. The name tells all for this pizza joint. Open late on weekends. | 1102 Ferris Ave. | 972/937–2601 | $3–$8 | MC, V.

**Catfish Plantation.** Southern. In a converted 1895 house, this restaurant has a reputation for being haunted. In fact, the owners keep a detailed log of their patrons' supernatural experiences. Try the chicken fried steak, blackened chicken, blackened catfish, crawfish, and fried pickles. Kids' menu. No smoking. | 814 Water St. | 972/937–9468 | Closed Mon.–Wed. No lunch Thurs., Fri. | $13–$25 | AE, D, DC, MC, V.

**Chantilly Place Tea Room.** American. Specialty sandwiches, soups, and salads fill the menu at this lunchtime spot. | 311½ S. Rogers | 972/923–0770 | Closed Sun. | $5–$6 | No credit cards.

## Lodging

**Bonny Nook Inn.** This Queen Anne Victorian house is furnished with period antiques. It is within walking distance of local restaurants, although private, candle-lit dinners can be arranged ahead of time. No smoking. Restaurant, picnic area, complimentary breakfast, some in-room hot tubs, massage, business services. | 414 W. Main, Waxahachie | 972/938–7207 or 800/486–5936 | fax 972/937–7700 | 5 rooms | $65–$115 | AE, D, DC, MC, V.

**Chaska House Bed and Breakfast.** Built ca. 1900, this Victorian home is listed on the National Register of Historic Places and contains an extensive collection of period antiques. Two guest cottages modeled after Ernest Hemingway's home in Key West, FL, are on the property. Dining room, complimentary breakfast. Library, hot tub. | 716 W. Main | 972/937–3390 or 800/931–3390 | www.chaskabb.com | 4 rooms | $100–$110 | A, MC, V.

**Ramada Limited.** This mid-size hotel is close to town and a public golf course is just 8 miles away. Restaurant, complimentary Continental breakfast, cable TV, pool, hot tub, golf, laundry facilities. | 795 S. I–35E | 972/937–4982 | 95 rooms | $49–$69 | AE, D, MC, V.

WEATHERFORD

INTRO
ATTRACTIONS
DINING
LODGING

# WEATHERFORD

MAP 8, H3

*(Nearby towns also listed: Fort Worth, Granbury, Mineral Wells)*

This North Texas community began as a wagon stop. Today Weatherford is known for its historic structures, many dating back to the late 19th century. The city is also home to Weatherford Junior College, the Southwest's oldest two-year college.

Information: **Weatherford Chamber of Commerce** | 401 Fort Worth Hwy., Weatherford, TX 76086 | 817/596–3801 | wchamb310@aol.com.

## Attractions

**Holland Lake Park.** This park is home to a nature trail, as well as historic cabins. There are also a playground and areas for picnicking. | Exit Santa Fe from I–20 on Holland Lake Rd. | 817/598–4131 | Free | Daily.

**Lake Weatherford.** This Trinity River lake offers fishing in several areas. | I–20 to Old Highway 180 | Free | Daily.

**Peter Pan Statue.** Weatherford's best known citizen was Broadway star Mary Martin, who played the role of Peter Pan, as well as many others. This bronze statue stands at the library. Inside are displays on the famous native. | 1214 Charles St. | No phone | Free | Daily.

### ON THE CALENDAR

**JULY: *Peach Festival.*** The peach harvest is celebrated with games, peach-y foods, and live entertainment. | 817/594–3801.

**SEPT.: *Weatherford's Annual Civil War Weekend.***During a long weekend in September, over 2,000 Civil War re-enactors descend on Weatherford to set up an authentic Civil War army camp, and a civilian encampment for women and children. The re-enactors live there in conditions similar to those of the war. You can observe soldiers participating in activities common to life in an army bivouac: Watch civilians make soap or play 19th-century games, or cheer on infantry, artillery, and cavalry on the field. Re-enactors show you how to prepare dinner in a Dutch oven, demonstrate lace and rope making crafts, and serenade you with period songs. Call the Chamber of Commerce for more details. | 817/594–3801 or 888/594–3801.

## Dining

**Out to Lunch.** American. Walk two blocks from the town square for tasty, light fare at this cheerful, country restaurant. The chef uses fresh ingredients, often from the Farmer's Market across the street, to prepare sandwiches, salads, and quiches for lunch, and pastas, seafood, chicken, and steak for dinner. The Florentine quiche with chicken, spinach and mushrooms sells fast, as does the Italian cream cake, a yellow cake with pecans, coconut, and a cream cheese icing. | 104 S. Walnut St. | 817/599–5271 | No supper Mon.–Wed. Closed weekends | $5–$15 | AE, D, MC, V.

## Lodging

**Best Western Santa Fe Inn.** This hotel, off of I–20 at exit 409, is designed in Spanish-style architecture, with Spanish tiles that continue the motif indoors. A restaurant on the premises serves Mexican and American food, but you won't find alcohol in this dry county. Restaurant, some refrigerators, some microwaves, cable TV, outdoor pool, laundry facilities, pets allowed (fee). | 1927 Santa Fe Dr. | 817/594–7401 | fax 817/594–5542 | 45 rooms | $59 | AE, D, DC, MC, V.

# WHITNEY

MAP 8, I3

*(Nearby town also listed: Cleburne)*

This town is nestled along Lake Whitney, a 1,280-acre lake that offers a variety of watersports, including scuba diving and fishing. Mountain biking is also popular in Lake Whitney State Park, which blooms with 40 species of wildflowers during the spring months.

**Information: Whitney Chamber of Commerce** | 112 W. Washington Ave., Whitney, TX 76692 | 254/694–2540.

## Attractions

**Lake Whitney State Park.** Located on the banks of Lake Whitney near the ruins of an early Texas settlement named Towash, with camping, screened shelters, boating, picnicking, swimming, and fishing. | FM 1244 | 254/694–3793 | fax 254/694–4915 | www.tpwd.state.tx.us | $2 | Fri., Sat. 8–10, Sun.–Thurs. 8–5.

**Lake Whitney.** An extremely popular recreation area, one of the busiest in the nation, with fishing, camping, and marinas. | 285 Corps Rd. #3602, Laguna Park | 254/694–3189 | fax 254/622–3243 | $2 | Daily 6 AM–10 PM.

**ON THE CALENDAR**
**OCT.: *Fall Festival.*** For over twenty years, Whitney has hosted this annual festival of arts, crafts, entertainment, and food vendors, on the first weekend of October. A parade winds through town, and the main stage showcases area talent, while a street dance guarantees fun for all. Watch for an unusual variety of festival programs, including a karate demonstration and a dog show starring locally trained guard dogs. | 254/694–2540.

## Dining
**VZJ Grill and Cafe.** American. You will find the usual home-cooked specialties at this ultra-casual eatery: the chicken-fried steak is made fresh every day; and the Charburger, a favorite among Whitney regulars, is char-broiled over an open flame. For dessert, rhapsodize over the fresh strawberry pie in season. Arrive early for dinner because the restaurant keeps limited evening hours. | 1317 N. Brazos; (Rte. 933N.) | 254/694–2265 | Breakfast also available. Closed weekends | $6–$10 | AE, D, MC, V.

## Lodging
**Cedar Creek Lodge.** If you want to spend some time on the shores of Lake Whitney, the Cedar Creek lodge can accommodate you and your family on two wooded acres, in a cabin, trailer, or mobile home. You will be within easy access of the lake, with its sandy beaches, gentle inclines, and white limestone cliffs. After a day of boating, fishing, or watersports, you can amble back to the lodge to cook your catch, play a game of horseshoes, and watch the sun set over the lake. The lodge can accommodate large parties and can also arrange for boat rental. Stay for a week and your seventh night is free. Picnic area, kitchenettes, microwaves, refrigerators, no room phones, basketball. | 329 Juniper Cove Rd. | 254/694–3514 | fax 254/694–3874 | www.cedarcreeklodge.com | 11 cabins, 4 mobile homes, 2 travel trailers | $59 | AE, D, MC, V.

# WICHITA FALLS

MAP 8, H2

*(Nearby towns also listed: Childress, Gainesville, Graham, Vernon)*

Named for the Wichita Indians, this community was first an agricultural hub but boomed at the turn of the 20th century with the discovery of oil. Today the community is still active in the petroleum business as well as the military world. Wichita Falls is home to Sheppard Air Force Base, which hosts the world's only NATO pilot training program. The city is also home to Midwestern State University.

Information: **Wichita Falls Convention and Visitors Bureau** | 1000 Fifth St., Wichita Falls, TX 76301 | 940/716–5500 | www.wichitafalls.org.

## Attractions
**Diversion Lake.** Located on a tributary of the Red River, this lake is used for watersports and fishing. | U.S. 82 to Rte. 258 | Free | Daily.

**Kell House.** This historic home is outfitted with 19th-century furnishings. Guided tours are available. | 900 Bluff St. | 940/723–2712 | $3 | Tues.–Wed. 2–4, Sun. 2–4.

**Lake Arrowhead State Park.** Watersports, fishing, swimming, and camping are available at this state park 18 mi southeast of Witchita Falls. | FM 1954 | 817/528–2211 | www.tpwd.state.tx.us | $2 | Daily.

**Lake Kickapoo.** Watersports, fishing, swimming, boating, and camping are all options here. There are also areas for picnicking. | HC 51 Box 148C, Holliday | 940/525–4431 | Free | Daily.

**Lake Wichita.** Swimming, picnicking, and fishing are available at this small lake. | Off Fairway Blvd. | Free | Daily.

**Wichita Falls Museum and Art Center.** This museum includes a planetarium with laser shows. There are also numerous scientific exhibits on view. | 2 Eureka Circle | 940/692–0923 | $4 | Tues.–Fri. 9:30–4:30.

**Wichita Theatre and Opera House.** This theater features country-and-western shows aimed at a family audience. | 924 Indiana St. | 940/723–9037 or 888/879–SHOW | $5–$10 | Fri.–Sat. 7:30 or by appointment.

### ON THE CALENDAR

**MAR.: *Arts and Crafts Festival.*** Artists from around the state display and sell wares at the MPEC Exhibit Hall. There are also crafts demonstrations. | 940/263–7690.
**AUG.: *Hotter 'n Hell 100 Bicycle Ride.*** Largest bike association–approved bicycle race in the United States. | 940/716–5500.
**AUG.: *Texas Ranch Roundup.*** Twelve working ranches enter a competition with riding, roping, and ranch tasks at the Wichita County Mounted Patrol Arena. | 940/322–0771.
**DEC.: *Fantasy of Lights.*** Light display on Midwestern State University campus, 2 mi southwest of Wichita Falls. | 940/716–5500.

## Dining

**Casa Mañana.** Mexican. This bustling restaurant opened its doors in 1947 and hasn't had a quiet moment since. Customers both young and old pile into '50s-style booths amid sombreros and other Mexican souvenirs for tasty Mexican specialties. The restaurant is perhaps best known for its signature soft red tacos, served with salad and an onion ring. | 609 8th St. | 940/723–5661 | Closed Sun. | $4–$9 | No credit cards.

**El Chico.** Tex-Mex. Traditional Tex-Mex is the order of the day here; look for plenty of chips and salsa as well as entrées such as tacos and enchiladas. Kids' menu. | 1028 Central Fwy. | 940/322–1455 | $11–$22 | AE, D, MC, V.

**McBride's Land and Cattle.** Steak. A Wichita Falls institution since 1973, McBride's serves mesquite-grilled steaks in addition to chicken, shrimp, and quail entrées. Dig into a perfectly cooked rib-eye steak, served with a baked potato, salad, garlic toast, and an onion ring, or stop by on Friday nights for McBride's celebrated prime rib. | 501 Scott | 940/322–2516 | No lunch weekends | $9–$15 | AE, D, DC, MC, V.

**McBride's Steak and Seafood.** Seafood. While McBride's sister restaurant serves steak and some seafood, McBride's Steak and Seafood serves seafood and some steak. Confused? Don't worry, you can find succulent steak and tasty seafood at both McBride's. This one, on Seymour Highway, is a bit more upscale, with low lighting, tablecloths, and comfy booths. Repeat customers love the lobster tail, crab legs, and mesquite-broiled shrimp, as well as the filet mignon and KC Sirloin. Larger groups are easily accommodated at the 10-seat Captain's Table. | 5400 Seymour Hwy. | 940/692–2462 | No lunch Sun. | $6–$26 | AE, D, DC, MC, V.

**Olive Garden.** Italian. The Olive Garden chain is popular with families. Try chicken scampi or lasagna classico. Kids' menu. | 33916 Kemp Blvd. | 940/692–4714 | No lunch | $16–$23 | AE, D, DC, MC, V.

# Lodging

**Econo Lodge.** This hotel has been modernized and is traditionally decorated. There is a man-made waterfall about 30 ft from the hotel and a park within walking distance. Complimentary Continental breakfast, cable TV, pool, business services. | 1700 Fifth St. | 940/761–1889 | fax 940/761–1505 | 115 rooms | $40–$100 | AE, D, DC, MC, V.

**Holiday Inn.** There isn't much to do in the immediate area, but if you drive 10 minutes from this chain hotel you'll find nightclubs such as Grahm's Central Station. It is also a 5-minute drive to Midwestern University. Restaurant, bar, refrigerators (in suites), room service, cable TV, 2 pools (1 indoor), wading pool, hot tub, sauna, putting green, game room, laundry facilities, business services. | 401 Broad St. | 940/766–6000 | fax 940/766–5942 | www.holidayinn.com | 241 rooms | $75 | AE, D, DC, MC, V.

**Kings Inn.** This inexpensive and centrally located motel has many corporate clients and is within walking distance of Denny's, Long John Silver, El Chico, and China Star. Cable TV, pool, playground. | 1211 Central Fwy. | 940/723–5541 | fax 940/723–6342 | 101 rooms | $35–$53 | AE, D, DC, MC, V.

**La Quinta.** The Wichita Falls Arts and Science Museum and Midwestern University are close to this renovated La Quinta. Area restaurants are a pleasant walk away. Complimentary Continental breakfast, in-room data ports, cable TV, pool, laundry facilities, business services, free parking, pets allowed. | 1128 Central Fwy. N | 940/322–6971 | fax 940/723–2573 | 139 rooms | $49–$65 | AE, D, DC, MC, V.

**Motel 6.** There is a mall beside this modern chain motel called the Skies Center which also has a multiplex. It is 1 mi from The Falls where you can enjoy the park and man-made waterfall. It's also 2 mi from Sheppard Airforce Base. Restaurant, cable TV, pets allowed. | 1812 Maurine St. | 940/322–8817 | fax 940/322–5944 | 82 rooms | $43–$47 | AE, D, DC, MC, V.

**Oaks at Floral Heights.** Luxuriate in the special spa treatments at this well-appointed bed-and-breakfast. Each suite includes a private bathroom and sitting room, which can also be equipped for business meetings. The prairie-style house was built in 1919 in this designated historic area, and it retains many of the features of the period such as narrow-board oak floors, detailed moldings, and hand-carved mantelpiece. Complimentary breakfast, in-room data ports, refrigerators, cable TV, no pets, no smoking. | 2014 11th St. | 940/322–2299 | 2 suites | $100–$200 | AE, D, DC, MC, V.

**Radisson.** The Wichita Falls Red River runs right beside this totally redone hotel, and the MPEC (Multi-Purpose Events Center) features arts and crafts, guns and knives, and other shows across the expressway. It is within walking distance of Lucy Park and the Waterfall. Restaurant, bar (with entertainment), in-room data ports, refrigerators (in suites), room service, cable TV, pool, hot tub, game room, business services, airport shuttle. | 100 Central Fwy., | 940/761–6000 | fax 940/766–1488 | 167 rooms | $99–$199 | AE, D, DC, MC, V.

**Ramada Limited.** This two-story hotel is 2 mi north of downtown and the airport, and is close to many area restaurants. Complimentary breakfast, some refrigerators, some microwaves, cable TV, pool, laundry facilities, laundry service, free parking, pets allowed (fee). | 3209 NW U.S. 287 | 940/855–0085 | fax 940/855–0040 | www.ramadawichitafalls.com | 59 rooms | $45–$64 | AE, D, DC, MC, V.

**Super 8.** This motel is close to Lucy Park. The rooms are spacious and comfortable. Cable TV. | 1307 Kenley Ave. | 800/800–8000 | fax 940/766–1488 or 940/322–8880 | 104 rooms | $47–$58 | AE, D, DC, MC, V.

**Trade Winds Motor Hotel.** This motor lodge focuses primarily on extended-stay clientele. No matter the length of your visit, however, you will surely appreciate the large swimming pool and the hotel's proximity to the convention center and antique district. A bar on the premises, the Windjammer Lodge, once functioned as a private club and is now open to the public. Complimentary Continental breakfast, some refrigerators, some microwaves, cable TV, pool, laundry facilities, free parking, pets allowed (fee). | 1212 Broad St. | 940/723–8008 | fax 940/723–5160 | msallis@wf.net | www.bcscenter.com/tradewinds | 150 rooms | $35–$50 | AE, D, MC, V.

# WIMBERLEY

MAP 8, H5

*(Nearby towns also listed: New Braunfels, San Antonio, San Marco, Sequin)*

Founded in 1848, today Wimberley has a reputation as a charming town, picturesque resort area, and thriving retirement community. In recent years, its popularity has grown, due to nearby Austinites wishing to escape city life.

**Information: Wimberley Chamber of Commerce** | 14100 Ranch Rd. 12, Wimberley, TX 78676. 512/847–2201 | www.visitwimberley.com.

## Attractions

**Blue Hole Recreation Club and Campground.** An old-fashioned swimming hole and campground sit on the clear-running Cypress Creek. There's a two-night minimum for camping on weekends, and a three-night minimum on holidays. | Off of Old Kyle Rd. | 512/847–9127 | www.bluehole.net | $5 day use, $30–$35 per night (includes membership and based on 5-person occupancy) | Daily.

**Wimberley Glass Works.** You can watch artisans create glass treasures before your eyes, then shop and put the store's motto "we blow glass, not your budget" to the test. | 201 W. Spoke Hill Dr. | 512/847–9348 | www.wgw.com | Free | Daily 10–5.

**Rancho Deluxe.** One of the town square's surprisingly eclectic boutiques, this place is carefully packed with Mexican imports and unique home furnishings. | 14010 Ranch Road 12 | 512/847–9570 | Free | Sun.–Fri. 10–6, Sat. 10–7.

## Dining

**Cypress Creek Cafe.** American. Italian quesadillas and southern-fried catfish are popular at this restaurant on the square. Live music is performed every Friday and Saturday night. | 302 Wimberley Sq | 512/847–2515 | Closed Mon. | $5–$15 | AE, D, MC, V.

**La Casa Loma Cocina y Cantina.** Tex-Mex. Touted as serving some of Wimberley's best Tex-Mex, this restaurant has a casual, family-friendly setting. Live music is performed occasionally. | 100 Cypress Creek Ln | 512/842–1361 | Closed Mon. and late Dec. | $6–$9 | AE, D, MC, V.

**Wimberley Pie Company.** Housed in a former gas station ¼ mi south of town square, this place is scheduled to move to a larger and finer building. It's known for its decadent pies and cakes, and ships its delicacies all over the country. | 13619 Ranch Road 12 | 512/847–9462 | www.wimberleypie.com | Breakfast also available, excluding Sun. No supper | $9–$20 | MC, V.

## Lodging

**Homestead Cottages.** Sixteen fully equipped cottages, ranging from 500–1,000 square ft, rest on 7 acres near Cypress Creek. Complimentary Continental breakfast. Cable TV. Hot tub. | 105 Scudder Ln. | 512/847–8788 or 800/918–8788 | www.homestead-tx.com | 16 cottages | $89–$99 | D, MC, V.

**Singing Cypress Gardens.** Nestled among ancient cypress trees along the banks of Cypress Creek, this three-acre private estate is within walking distance of the town square. | 400 Mill Race Ln | 512/847–9344 or 800/827–1913 | www.scgardens.com | 6 rooms | $65–$150.

**Southwind Bed and Breakfast and Cabins.** This complex is 3 mi from town on a wooded hilltop. The main building has three rooms with private baths, and two secluded cabins have fireplaces. Complimentary full breakfast, some kitchenettes, hot tub, outdoor hot tub. | 2701 Rte. 3237 | 512/847–5277 or 800/508–5277 | 3 rooms, 3 cabins | $80–$90 rooms, $105 cabins | AE, D, MC, V.

# Index

# Notes

# Notes

# Notes

# Notes

# Notes

# Notes

# Notes

# TALK TO US

Fill out this quick survey and receive a free *Fodor's How to Pack*
(while supplies last)

1  Which Road Guide did you purchase?
(Check all that apply.)

- ❏ AL/AR/LA/MS/TN
- ❏ AZ/CO/NM
- ❏ CA
- ❏ CT/MA/RI
- ❏ DE/DC/MD/PA/VA
- ❏ FL
- ❏ GA/NC/SC
- ❏ ID/MT/NV/UT/WY
- ❏ IL/IA/MO/WI
- ❏ IN/KY/MI/OH/WV
- ❏ KS/OK/TX
- ❏ ME/NH/VT
- ❏ MN/NE/ND/SD
- ❏ NJ/NY
- ❏ OR/WA

2  How did you learn about the Road Guides?

- ❏ TV ad
- ❏ Radio ad
- ❏ Newspaper or magazine ad
- ❏ Newspaper or magazine article
- ❏ TV or radio feature
- ❏ Bookstore display/clerk recommendation
- ❏ Recommended by family/friend
- ❏ Other:_____

3  Did you use other guides for your trip?

- ❏ AAA
- ❏ Compass American Guide
- ❏ Fodor's
- ❏ Frommer's
- ❏ Insiders' Guide
- ❏ Mobil
- ❏ Moon Handbook
- ❏ Other:_____

4  Did you use any of the following for planning?
❏ Tourism offices   ❏ Internet   ❏ Travel agent

5  Did you buy a Road Guide for (check one):

- ❏ Leisure trip
- ❏ Business trip
- ❏ Mix of business and leisure

6  Where did you buy your Road Guide?

- ❏ Bookstore
- ❏ Other store
- ❏ On-line
- ❏ Borrowed from a friend
- ❏ Borrowed from a library
- ❏ Other:_____

7  Why did you buy a Road Guide? (Check all that apply.)

- ❏ Number of cities/towns listed
- ❏ Comprehensive coverage
- ❏ Number of lodgings   ❏ Driving tours
- ❏ Number of restaurants ❏ Maps
- ❏ Number of attractions ❏ Fodor's brand name
- ❏ Other:_____

8  Did you use this guide primarily:
❏ For pretrip planning      ❏ While traveling
❏ For planning and while traveling

9  What was the duration of your trip?

- ❏ 2-3 days
- ❏ 4-6 days
- ❏ 7-10 days
- ❏ 11 or more days
- ❏ Taking more than 1 trip

10  Did you use the guide to select
❏ Hotels          ❏ Restaurants

11  Did you stay primarily in a

- ❏ Hotel
- ❏ Motel
- ❏ Resort
- ❏ Bed-and-breakfast
- ❏ RV/camper
- ❏ Hostel
- ❏ Campground
- ❏ Dude ranch
- ❏ With family or friends
- ❏ Other:_____

12  What sights and activities did you most enjoy?

- ❏ Historical sights
- ❏ Sports
- ❏ National parks
- ❏ State parks
- ❏ Shopping
- ❏ Theaters
- ❏ Museums
- ❏ Major cities
- ❏ Attractions off the beaten path

13  How much did you spend per adult for this trip?

- ❏ Less than $500
- ❏ $501-$750
- ❏ $751-$1,000
- ❏ More than $1,000

14  How many traveled in your party?
___ Adults      ___ Children      ___ Pets

15  Did you

- ❏ Fly to destination
- ❏ Drive your own vehicle
- ❏ Rent a car
- ❏ Rent a van or RV
- ❏ Take a train
- ❏ Take a bus

16  How many miles did you travel round-trip?

- ❏ Less than 100
- ❏ 101-300
- ❏ 301-500
- ❏ 501-750
- ❏ 751-1,000
- ❏ More than 1,000

17  What items did you take on your vacation?

- ❏ Traveler's checks
- ❏ Credit card
- ❏ Gasoline card
- ❏ Phone card
- ❏ Camera
- ❏ Digital camera
- ❏ Cell phone
- ❏ Computer
- ❏ PDA
- ❏ Other

18  Would you use Fodor's Road Guides again?
❏ Yes          ❏ No

19  How would you like to see Road Guides changed?

❑ More  ❑ Less  Dining
❑ More  ❑ Less  Lodging
❑ More  ❑ Less  Sports
❑ More  ❑ Less  Activities
❑ More  ❑ Less  Attractions
❑ More  ❑ Less  Shopping
❑ More  ❑ Less  Driving tours
❑ More  ❑ Less  Maps
❑ More  ❑ Less  Historical information
❑ Other:_____

20  Tell us about yourself.

❑ Male        ❑ Female

Age:
❑ 18-24     ❑ 35-44     ❑ 55-64
❑ 25-34     ❑ 45-54     ❑ Over 65

Income:
❑ Less than $25,000      ❑ $50,001-$75,000
❑ $25,001-$50,000        ❑ More than $75,000

Name:_____  E-mail: _____

Address:_____  City: _____  State: _____  Zip: _____

Fodor's Travel Publications
Attn: Road Guide Survey
280 Park Avenue
New York, NY 10017

The information herein will be treated in confidence. Names and addresses will not be
released to mailing-list houses or other organizations.

# Atlas

TANA

NORTH DAKOTA

MINNESOTA

YOMING

SOUTH DAKOTA

W

COLORADO

NEBRASKA

IOWA

KANSAS

MISS

NEW MEXICO

OKLAHOMA

ARKA

TEXAS

LO

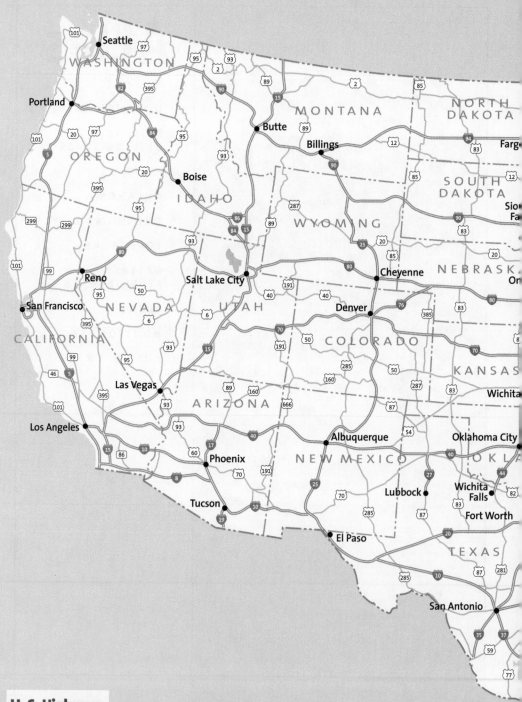

## U. S. Highways

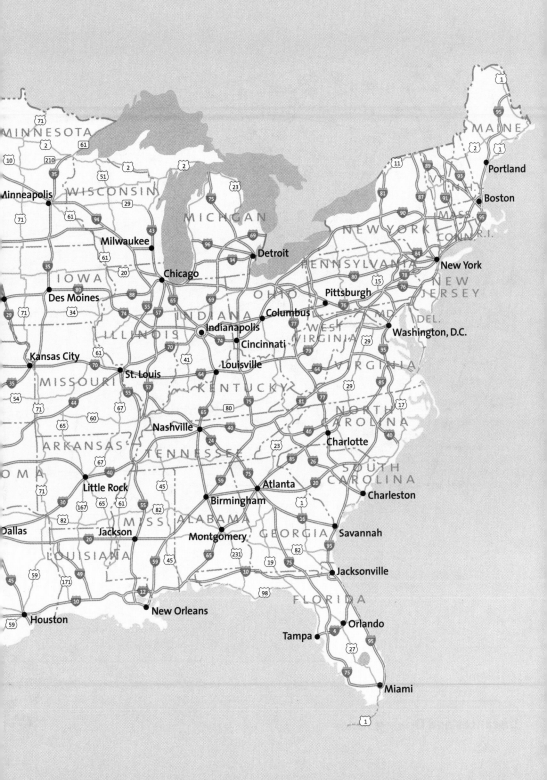

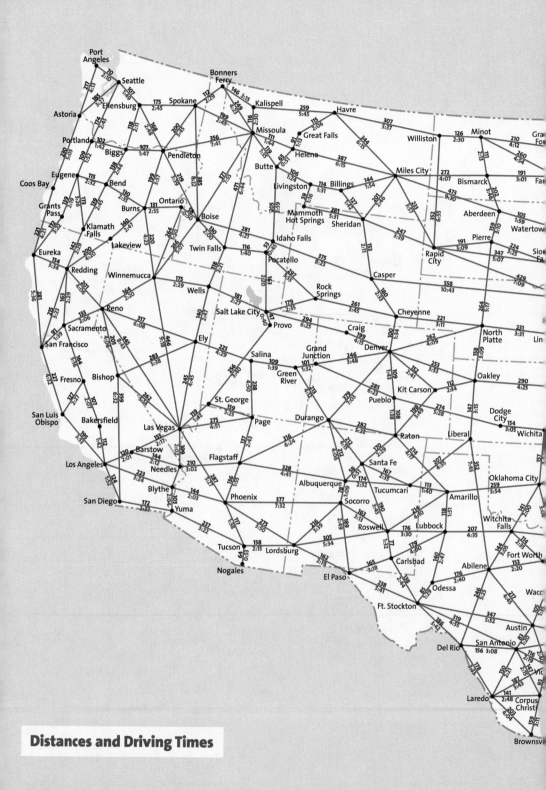

# Distances and Driving Times

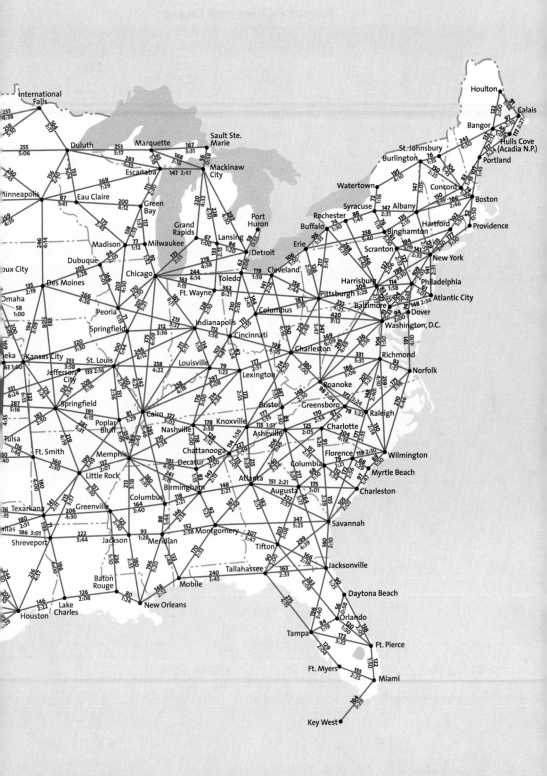

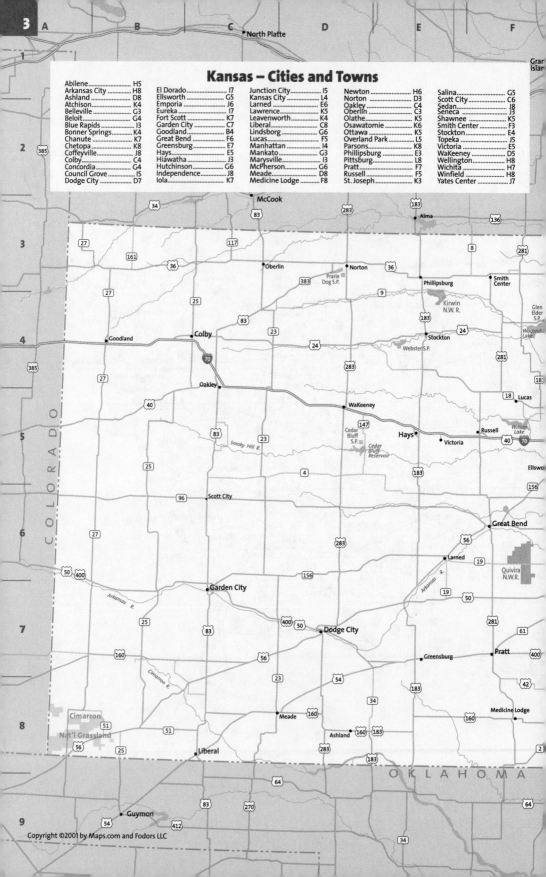

# Kansas – Cities and Towns

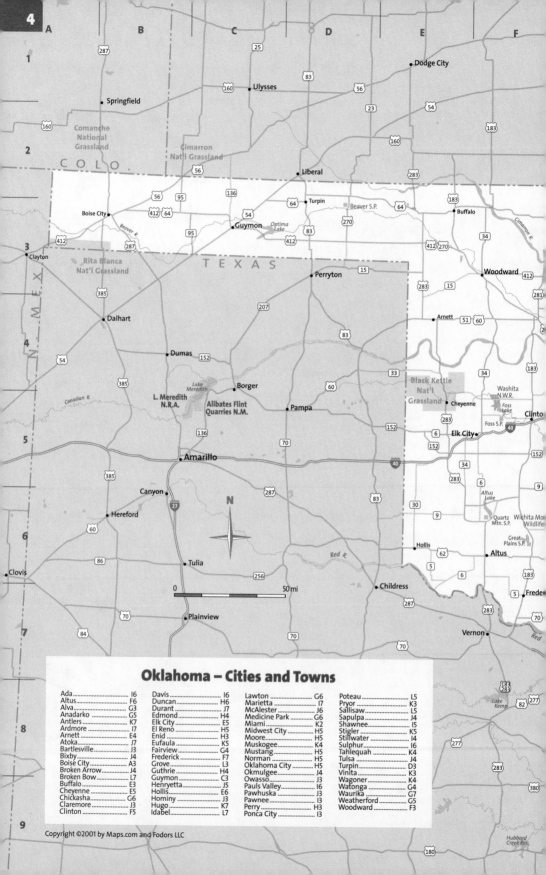

## Oklahoma – Cities and Towns

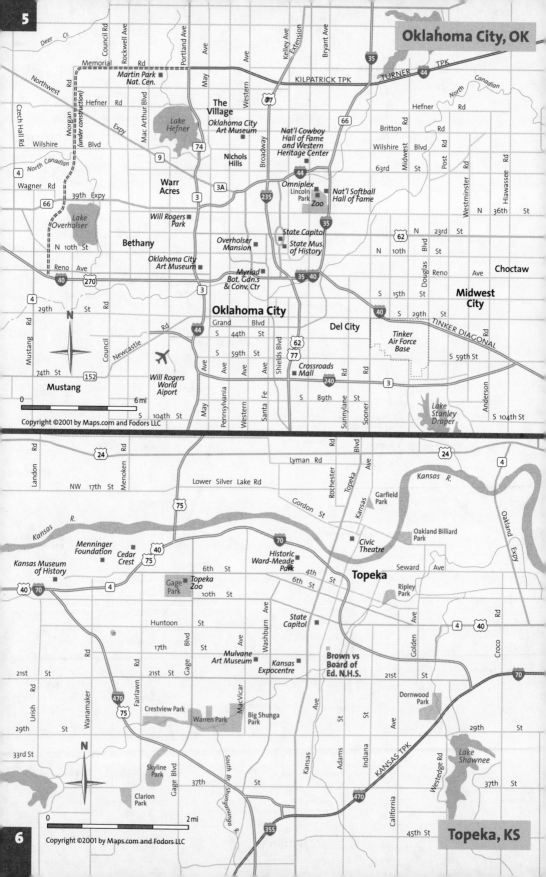

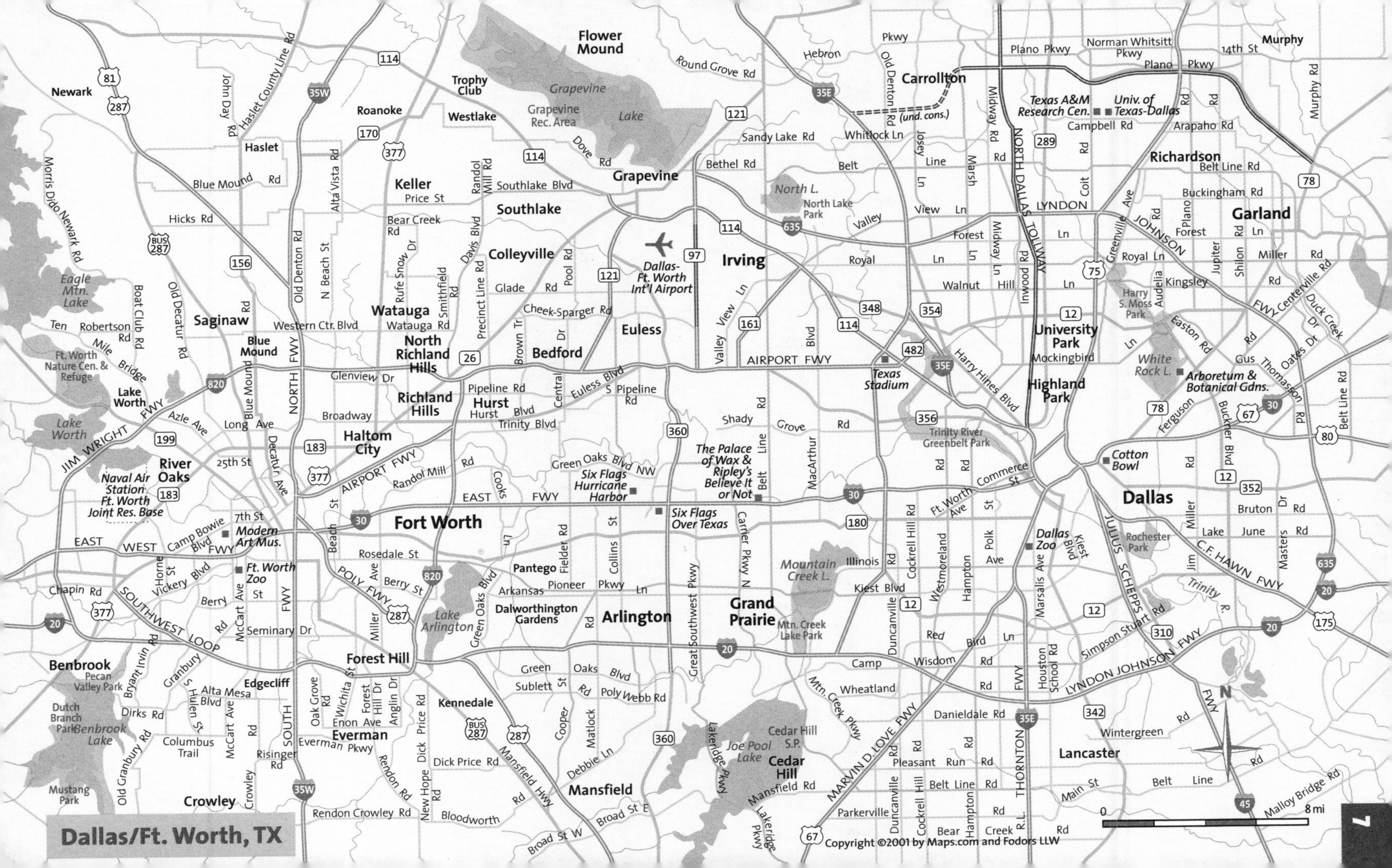

Dallas/Ft. Worth, TX
7
Dallas
Fort Worth
Arlington
Irving
Grand Prairie
Garland
Richardson
Carrollton
Grapevine
Flower Mound
Trophy Club
Westlake
Roanoke
Keller
Southlake
Colleyville
Haslet
Newark
Saginaw
Blue Mound
Watauga
North Richland Hills
Richland Hills
Bedford
Euless
Hurst
Haltom City
River Oaks
Lake Worth
Benbrook
Edgecliff
Forest Hill
Everman
Kennedale
Crowley
Mansfield
Cedar Hill
Lancaster
Pantego
Dalworthington Gardens
University Park
Highland Park
Murphy
Dallas-Ft. Worth Int'l Airport
Texas Stadium
Cotton Bowl
Dallas Zoo
Arboretum & Botanical Gdns.
Texas A&M Research Cen.
Univ. of Texas-Dallas
Six Flags Over Texas
Six Flags Hurricane Harbor
The Palace of Wax & Ripley's Believe It or Not
Modern Art Mus.
Ft. Worth Zoo
Naval Air Station Ft. Worth Joint Res. Base
Ft. Worth Nature Cen. & Refuge
Grapevine Lake
Grapevine Rec. Area
North L.
North Lake Park
White Rock L.
Harry S. Moss Park
Mountain Creek L.
Mtn. Creek Lake Park
Joe Pool Lake
Cedar Hill S.P.
Lake Arlington
Lake Worth
Eagle Mtn. Lake
Benbrook Lake
Pecan Valley Park
Dutch Branch Park
Mustang Park
Rochester Park
Trinity River Greenbelt Park
Trinity R.
NORTH DALLAS TOLLWAY
LYNDON JOHNSON FWY
C.F. HAWN FWY
JULIUS SCHEPPS FWY
MARVIN D. LOVE FWY
R.L. THORNTON FWY
AIRPORT FWY
NORTH FWY
SOUTH FWY
EAST FWY
WEST FWY
JIM WRIGHT FWY
SOUTHWEST LOOP
POLY FWY
Harry Hines Blvd
Great Southwest Pkwy
Carrier Pkwy N
Lakeridge Pkwy
Mansfield Hwy
Old Denton Rd
Western Ctr. Blvd
Precinct Line Rd
Pipeline Rd
Green Oaks Blvd
Rufe Snow Dr
Round Grove Rd
Sandy Lake Rd
Belt Line Rd
Midway Rd
Plano Pkwy
Norman Whitsitt Pkwy
Copyright ©2001 by Maps.com and Fodors LLW
0
8 mi
N

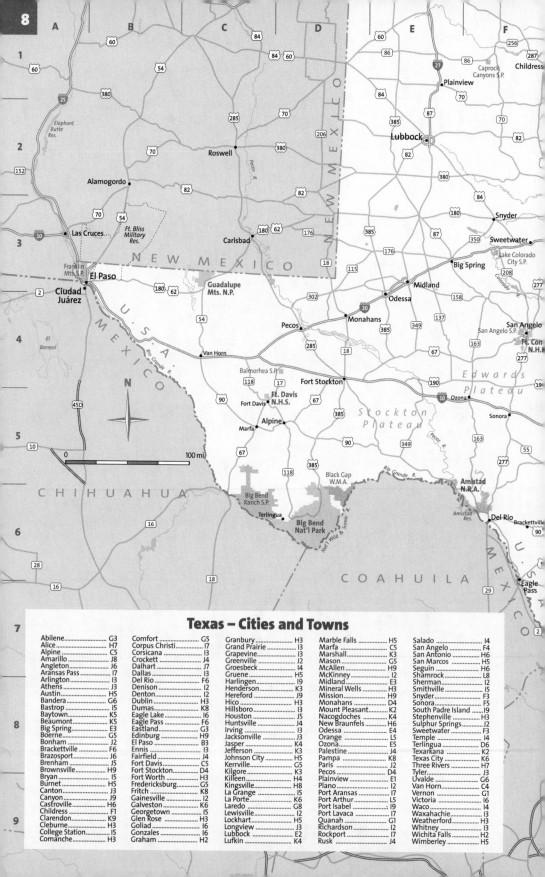

# Texas – Cities and Towns

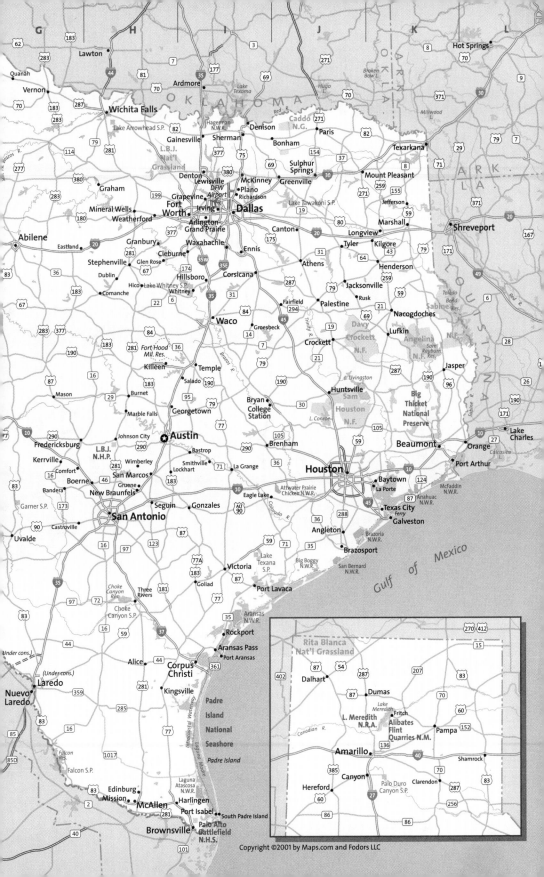

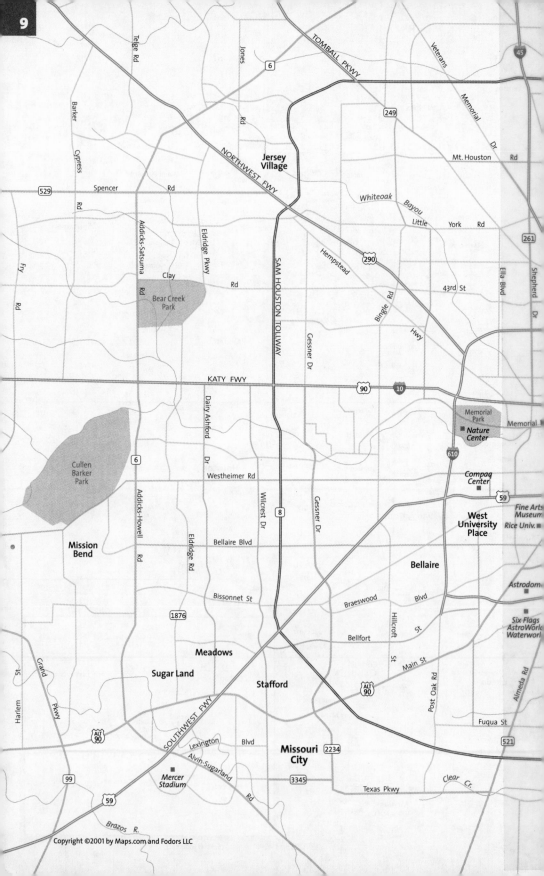

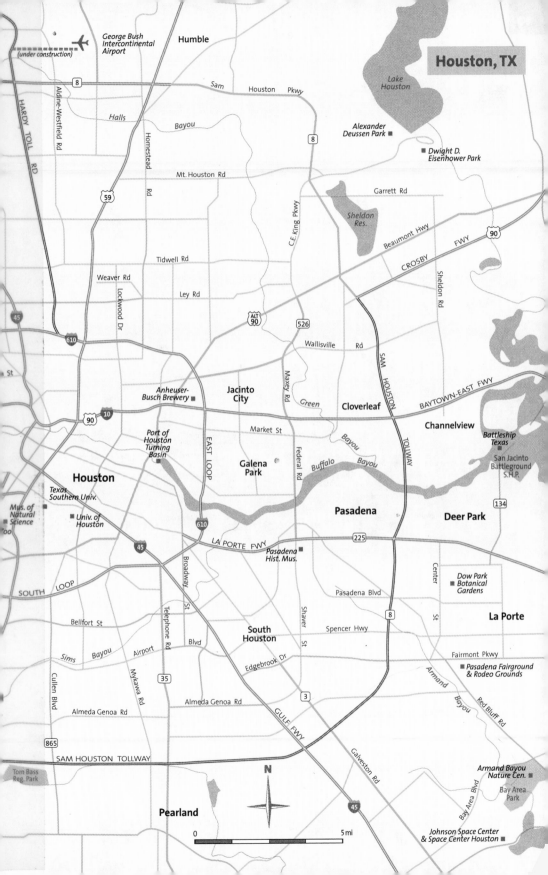

# Austin, TX

2222

360

City Park Rd

Lake Austin Metro. Park

Colorado R.

Lake Austin

Spicewood Springs Rd

Spicewood Springs Rd

Jollyville Rd

183

1

Braker Ln

Walnut Creek Metro. Park

Yager Ln

275

Walnut Creek

1325

Kramer Ln

Braker Ln

Research Blvd

Burnet Rd

Rutland Dr

Parkfield Dr

Lamar Blvd

Dessau Rd

Greystone Dr

Far West Blvd

Mesa Dr

Spicewood Springs Rd

Burnet Rd

Shoal Creek Blvd

183

Anderson Ln

Peyton Gin Rd

Rundburg Ln

35

Ferguson Ln

Bull Creek Rd

Northland Dr

Burnet Rd

Koenig Ln

Lamar Blvd

Airport Blvd

Cameron Rd

290

Westlake Dr

Toro Canyon Rd

Red Bud Tr

Mt. Bonnell Rd

Balcones Dr

Bull Creek Rd

Hancock Dr

N. Loop Blvd

51st St

45th St

41st

38th St

Guadalupe St

Duval St

Ney Museum

Robert Mueller Municipal Airport

51st St

Berkman Dr

Manor Rd

Springdale Rd

969

Lake Austin

Austin Museum of Art

1

Winsor Rd

Enfield Rd

Exposition Blvd

Lake Austin Blvd

MO-PAC EXPY

University of Texas - Austin

L.B.J. Presidential Library & Museum

Manor Rd

Martin Luther King Jr. Blvd

Webberville Rd

Bluestein Blvd

183

West Lake Hills

360

Westlake Dr

2244

Austin Nature & Science Center

Rollingwood

Austin

15th St

12th St

Oak Springs Dr

Carver Museum

Springdale Rd

111

Colorado River

Ed Bluestein

Barton Springs

Zilker Park

Barton Cr.

343

Bluebonnet Ln

Mary St

Oltorf

Blvd

6th St

Cesar Chavez St

7th St

Town L.

Pleasant Valley Rd

Hergotz Ln

Edwin Ln

1

290

71

Sunset Valley

Brodie Ln

Lamar

Manchaca Rd

S. 1st St

Congress Av

Av

Woodward St

35

290

Riverside Dr

Montopolis Dr

183

71

Austin-Bergstrom International Airport

Westgate Blvd

Stassney Ln

275

290

71

William Cannon

Manchaca Rd

Dittmar Rd

Cannon Dr

Av

St. Elmo Rd

Teri Rd

Burleson Rd

McKinney Falls State Park

N

2304

S. 1st St

Congress

35

William Cannon Dr

0          2 mi